Lecture Notes in Artificial Intelligence 9403

Subseries of Lecture Notes in Computer Science

LNAI Series Editors

Randy Goebel
University of Alberta, Edmonton, Canada
Yuzuru Tanaka
Hokkaido University, Sapporo, Japan
Wolfgang Wahlster
DFKI and Saarland University, Saarbrücken, Germany

LNAI Founding Series Editor

Jörg Siekmann
DFKI and Saarland University, Saarbrücken, Germany

More information about this series at http://www.springer.com/series/1244

Songmao Zhang · Martin Wirsing
Zili Zhang (Eds.)

Knowledge Science, Engineering and Management

8th International Conference, KSEM 2015
Chongqing, China, October 28–30, 2015
Proceedings

Springer

Editors
Songmao Zhang
Chinese Academy of Sciences
Beijing
China

Zili Zhang
Southwest University
Chongqing
China

Martin Wirsing
Ludwig-Maximilians-Universität München
Munich
Germany

ISSN 0302-9743   ISSN 1611-3349 (electronic)
Lecture Notes in Artificial Intelligence
ISBN 978-3-319-25158-5   ISBN 978-3-319-25159-2 (eBook)
DOI 10.1007/978-3-319-25159-2

Library of Congress Control Number: 2015950047

LNCS Sublibrary: SL7 – Artificial Intelligence

Springer International Publishing AG Switzerland is part of Springer Science+Business Media
(www.springer.com)

Preface

The 8th International Conference on Knowledge Science, Engineering and Management 2015 (KSEM 2015) was the latest of the KSEM series, building on the success of seven previous events held, respectively, in Guilin, China (KSEM 2006); Melbourne, Australia (KSEM 2007); Vienna, Austria (KSEM 2009); Belfast, UK (KSEM 2010); Irvine, USA (KSEM 2011); Dalian, China (KSEM 2013), and Sibiu, Romania (KSEM 2014). The series was initiated in 2006 by Prof. Ruqian Lu from the Chinese Academy of Sciences, with the aim of providing a forum for researchers in the broad areas of knowledge science, knowledge engineering, and knowledge management to exchange ideas and to report state-of-the-art research results.

KSEM 2015 was held in Chongqing, a major city in Southwest China and the largest of China's four direct-controlled municipalities by administration the other three being Beijing, Shanghai, and Tianjin. The conference was hosted by Southwest University, which was officially established in July 2005 with a history that can be traced back to the foundation of East Sichuan Teachers College in 1906. The main theme of KSEM 2015 was on how knowledge science, engineering, and management contribute to big data analytics. This yielded a larger part of the presentations and discussions on machine learning, classification and clustering, knowledge discovery and recognition, and text mining and analysis. Knowledge and data processing techniques in various types of domains were tackled, including mobile data analytics, bioinformatics, and recommendation systems. Theoretical studies in formal reasoning and ontologies, detection, evidence theory, and conceptual analysis dealt with the fundamental issues in knowledge representation, management, and acquisition.

KSEM 2015 consisted of the main conference and three special sessions. It attracted a total of 247 submissions from 17 countries all over the world, including 58 papers submitted to the special sessions. The Program Committee members together with external reviewers contributed 546 reviews. As a result, a combination of 57 full papers and 22 short papers were selected to be included in the proceedings with a very competitive full paper acceptance rate of 23% and overall acceptance rate of 32%. Moreover, we were honored to have five prestigious scholars giving keynote speeches at the conference, Dr. Dean Allemang (Working Ontologist LLC, USA), Dr. Sheng-Chuan Wu (Franz Inc., USA), Prof. Aoying Zhou (East China Normal University, China), Prof. Mark Reynolds (University of Western Australia, Australia), and Prof. Lorna Uden (Staffordshire University, UK). The abstracts of their talks are included in this volume.

KSEM 2015 would not have been possible without the contributions and efforts of a large scientific community. We thank our authors for being willing to submit their work to KSEM. We sincerely appreciate the large amount of valuable and timely reviews from the members of the Program Committee, the members of three special session committees, and helpful external reviewers. Moreover, we would like to express our gratitude to the conference honorary general chair, Prof. Hojjat Adeli (The Ohio State

University, USA), the conference general co-chair, Prof. Dimitris Karagiannis (University of Vienna, Austria), and the co-chairs of the special sessions, Prof. Li Liu (National University of Singapore, Singapore), Prof. Li Li (Southwest University, China), Prof. Le Zhang (Southwest University, China), and Prof. Yong Deng (Southwest University, China). The organization committee from Southwest University in Chongqing provided extensive support for the conference, and we especially thank Prof. Guoqiang Xiao and Associate Prof. Guoxian Yu. We are also grateful to the team at Springer led by Alfred Hofmann for publication of this volume.

Many thanks go to Franz Inc. for sponsoring the best paper award of KSEM 2015. The conference management system EasyChair was used to handle the submissions, conduct the electronic Program Committee meetings, and assist with the assembly of the proceedings.

August 2015

Songmao Zhang
Martin Wirsing
Zili Zhang

Organization

KSEM 2015 was hosted and organized by the Faculty of Computer and Information Science of Southwest University, China. The conference was held during October 28–30, 2015, in Chongqing, China.

Organizing Committee

Honorary General Chair

Hojjat Adeli   The Ohio State University, USA

General Co-chairs

Zili Zhang   Southwest University, China
Dimitris Karagiannis   University of Vienna, Austria

Program Committee Co-chairs

Songmao Zhang   Chinese Academy of Sciences, China
Martin Wirsing   Ludwig-Maximilians-Universität München, Germany

Local Organizing Chair

Guoqiang Xiao   Southwest University, China

Publication Chair

Yong Deng   Southwest University, China

Publicity Co-chairs

Li Tao   Southwest University, China
Guoxian Yu   Southwest University, China
Shiping Chen   CSIRO, Australia

Special Session Chair

Li Li   Southwest University, China

Webmasters

Guodong Wang   Southwest University, China
Yuxin Liu   Southwest University, China

Steering Committee

Ruqian Lu (Honorary Chair)   Chinese Academy of Sciences, China
Chengqi Zhang (Past Chair)   University of Technology, Sydney, Australia

Hui Xiong (Chair)	The State University of New Jersey, Rutgers, USA
Dimitris Karagiannis (Deputy Chair)	University of Vienna, Austria
David Bell	Queen's University, Belfast, UK
Yaxin Bi	Ulster University, Belfast, UK
Cungen Cao	Chinese Academy of Sciences, China
Zhi Jin	Peking University, China
Claudiu Kifor	Sibiu University, Romania
Jérome Lang	University Paul Sabatier, France
Yoshiteru Nakamori	JAIST, Japan
Jörg Siekmann	DFKI and Saarland University, Saarbrücken, Germany
Eric Tsui	The Hong Kong Polytechnic University, Hong Kong, SAR China
Zongtuo Wang	Dalian Science and Technology University, China
Kwok Kee Wei	City University of Hong Kong, Hong Kong, SAR China
Mingsheng Ying	Tsinghua University, China
Zili Zhang	Southwest University, China

Program Committee

Andreas Albrecht	Middlesex University, UK
Klaus-Dieter Althoff	DFKI/University of Hildesheim, Germany
Nathalie Aussenac-Gilles	IRIT CNRS, France
Serge Autexier	DFKI, Germany
Costin Badica	University of Craiova, Romania
Salem Benferhat	Université d'Artois, France
Philippe Besnard	IRIT CNRS, France
Remus Brad	Lucian Blaga University of Sibiu, Romania
Krysia Broda	Imperial College, UK
Robert Andrei Buchmann	University of Vienna, Austria
Cungen Cao	Chinese Academy of Sciences, China
Melisachew Chekol	University of Mannheim, Germany
Enhong Chen	University of Science and Technology of China, China
Paolo Ciancarini	University of Bologna, Italy
Ireneusz Czarnowski	Gdynia Maritime University, Poland
Richard Dapoigny	LISTIC/Polytech'Savoie, France
Juan Manuel Dodero	Universidad de Cádiz, Spain
Josep Domenech	Universitat Politècnica de València, Spain
Josep Domingo-Ferrer	Universitat Rovira i Virgili, Spain
Dieter Fensel	University of Innsbruck, Austria
Hans-Georg Fill	University of Vienna, Austria
Adina Magda Florea	University Politehnica of Bucharest, Romania
Fausto Guinchiglia	University of Trento, Italy
Yoshinori Hara	Kyoto University, Japan

Qingtian Zeng	Shandong University of Science and Technology, China
Chunxia Zhang	Beijing Institute of Technology, China
Shuigeng Zhou	Fudan University, China

Special Session Organizing Committees

Special Session on Mobile Data Analytics and Knowledge Management

Co-chairs

| Li Liu | National University of Singapore, Singapore |
| Li Li | Southwest University, China |

Program Committee

Shiping Chen	CSIRO, Australia
Rong Xie	Wuhan University, China
Huawen Liu	Zhejiang Normal University, China
Lifei Chen	Fujian Normal University, China
Xianchuan Yu	Beijing Normal University, China
Yufang Zhang	Chongqing University, China
Ying Xia	Chongqing University of Posts and Telecommunications, China
Jason Teutsch	National University of Singapore, Singapore
Guoxin Su	National University of Singapore, Singapore
Xianyue Li	Lanzhou University, China
Yonggang Lu	Lanzhou University, China
Zigang Huang	Arizona State University, USA

Special Session on Bioinformatics and Computational Biology

Chair

| Le Zhang | Southwest University, China |

Program Committee

Badong Chen	Xi'an Jiaotong University, China
Ge Gao	Peking University, China
Jianxin Wang	Central South University, China
Linqiang Pan	Huazhong University of Science and Technology, China
Yan Qiang	Taiyuan University of Technology, China

Special Session on Evidence Theory and Its Application

Chair

Yong Deng   Southwest University, China

Program Committee

Sankaran Mahadevan   Vanderbilt University, USA
Rehan Sadiq   University of British Columbia, Canada
Deqiang Han   Xi'an Jiaotong University, China
Zhunga Liu   Northwestern Polytechnical University, China
Jean Dezert   The French Aerospace Lab (ONERA), France
Yan Qiang   Taiyuan University of Technology, China

Additional Reviewers

Acar, Erman
Akbar, Zaenal
Alebrahim, Azadeh
Ayzenshtadt, Viktor
Becheru, Alex
Belzner, Lenz
Bouraoui, Zied
Bouzar, Lydia
Breazu, Macarie
Calvino, Aida
Chen, Badong
Chen, Lifei
Chen, Weihua
Chen, Xiaohong
Colhon, Mihaela
de Lima, Tiago
de Oliveira Melo, Andre
Dranidis, Dimitris
Dutta, Arnab
Efendioglu, Nesat
Everaere, Patricia
Falcioni, Damiano
Fensel, Anna
Furtmueller, Elfi
Ghiran, Ana-Maria
He, Gang
Heap, Bradford
Huang, Jie
Huang, Zi-Gang
Jin, Xiaolong

Jurek, Anna
Kröger, Peer
Kärle, Elias
Li, Xiaoyu
Lila, Meziani
Liu, Huawen
Liu, Lin
Lu, Yonggang
Maier, Edith
Mailly, Jean-Guy
Mandel, Christian
Mao, Wenji
Martinez, Sergio
Mcconville, Ryan
Meilicke, Christian
Meis, Rene
Moca, Mircea
Mocanu, Andrei
Moldovan, Darie
Morariu, Daniel
Pan, Linqiang
Papasalouros, Andreas
Patroumpas, Kostas
Petrusel, Razvan
Przybylinski, Thomas
Qian, Wei
Qiang, Yan
Rajaratnam, David
Ren, Xuguang
Reuss, Pascal

Ritze, Dominique
Sabaté Pla, Albert
Salas, Julián
Santen, Thomas
Santipantakis, Georgios
Schwind, Nicolas
Sitar-Taut, Dan-Andrei
Slavkovik, Marija
Soria-Comas, Jordi
Spahiu, Blerina
Stan, Alexandru-Ioan
Su, Guoxin
Thiel, Christian
Toma, Ioan
Ulfat-Bunyadi, Nelufar
Ullrich, Carsten
Varzinczak, Ivan
Wang, Zhe
Wilke, Gwendolin
Xie, Rong
Yu, Jian
Zhang, Hong
Zhang, Yufang
Zhao, Hong
Zheng, Shuai
Zhuang, Zhiqiang
Zied, Bouraoui
Zirn, Caecilia

Sponsors

Southwest University, China

Franz Inc., USA

Keynotes

Industrial Big Data - When Big Data Meets Big Business

Dean Allemang

Working Ontologist, LLC
Oakland, CA, USA
dallemang@workingontologist.com

Abstract. It is no secret that the world is drowning in data. Technologies for collecting and storing data have resulted in a data glut that has given rise to the rather general, catch-all topic of "Big Data".

In many circles, Big Data has taken on a very specific meaning of searching through large amounts of end-user data for a web site, to project their behavior and tune the site to some optimal performance. In this sense, Big Data is closely associated with SEO. It is natural that this sort of application of Big Data would come first; the data is collected by and belongs to a single organization, and the value from correct analysis of that data goes back to that same organization.

In this talk, I want to introduce a trend in Big Data that has much more potential for having a lasting impact on the world. It is something that I call Industrial Big Data. Like Big Data within an enterprise, Industrial Big Data involves large amounts of interconnected data, over which we wish to perform a wide variety of complex queries. But in addition to these features of Big Data, Industrial Big Data involves data from multiple sources, with multiple owner-ship, where the data has to be linked not just on an enterprise scale, but an industrial scale. In short, industrial Big Data requires Semantic Web technology as well as large-scale data technology.

Several industries (including Pharmaceuticals, Oil and Gas, and Finance) are facing and addressing Industrial Big Data challenges today. In order to gain real insights into production and consumption, industries need to connect data across the supply chain, from tiny produces through international traders all the way to retail customers. These insights provide value far beyond improved sales figures for some quarter; these insights are being used to improve transparency of financial data, improve accountability of these industries, and to streamline utilization of scarce resources.

For all of these industries, the stakes are high. In this talk, I will summarize how these industries are approaching these challenges, and lessons we can learn from them.

Separating the Reality from the Hypes of Big Data

Sheng-Chuan Wu

Franz Inc.
Oakland, CA, USA
scw@franz.com

Abstract. The world is drowning in data. Modern technologies and digital devices have made it very easy to generate, collect and store mammoth data that gives rise to the term, Big Data. Everyone wants to collect, analyze, invest in and make money from Big Data. Market research firms predict exciting business opportunity of US$50 billions for Big Data tools by 2017. Industrial experts promise Big Data to solve virtually any problem we encounter. Is Big Data really what all the market hypes allege to be? There is no doubt that, by combining the enormous modern and inexpensive computing power and sophisticated Data Mining programs, we are able to process the zettabytes of digital data produced every minute. However, several challenges besides the sheer data size make it difficult to extract the essential value from big data, namely heterogeneous data sources, convolute data relations and complex queries inherent to predictive analytics. A new analytic architecture has been developed, combining the popular big data Hadoop framework, semantic index and distributed query to extract actionable business insight from big data in nearly real-time. A couple of real-world examples in Customer Relation Management (CRM) and Healthcare are discussed to show the power of this new architecture.

Big Data Knowledge Engineering: Essence and Applications

Aoying Zhou

Institute for Data Science and Engineering
Software Engineering Institute
East China Normal University
Shanghai, China
ayzhou@sei.ecnu.edu.cn

Abstract. Knowledge Engineering has been evolved for almost four decades. Since it was proposed by Edward Feigenbaum in 1977, a lot of significant progress has been made in this area, not only in theoretical aspects but also in practice. The emergence of Internet has been changing the world, knowledge engineering is no exception. In the era of big data, knowledge engineering faces fundamental challenges induced by fragmented knowledge from heterogeneous, autonomous sources with complex and uncertain relationships, which are generally called User Generated Content. It means that knowledge creation is not proprietary to experts, everyone who are Internet service consumers could be knowledge creators to some extent. Therefore, knowledge engineering and the associated issues which were studied profoundly should be reexamined in the new context.

In this talk, in addition to the retrospect of the glorious history of knowledge engineering, the essential issues of big data knowledge engineering will be discussed, which distinguished it from the conventional one. It is anticipated that the advance in big data knowledge engineering will bring dramatic impact on knowledge infrastructure construction and knowledge services and even lead to paradigm shift in the field of knowledge engineering.

Representing Knowledge About Continuous Time

Mark Reynolds

The University of Western Australia
Perth, Australia
mark.reynolds@uwa.edu.au

Abstract. Temporal logic is a widely used formalism for specification and reasoning about the correctness of hardware and software systems. For many applications there are good reasons to use a formalisms based on some sort of dense or continuous model of time rather than the traditional discrete model. Examples include multi-agent systems, AI planning, concurrency and refinement.

In contrast to the solid understanding of the reasoning tasks for discrete time temporal languages, the development of techniques for working with more general linear flows of time have been rather patchy. We discuss some recent developments in this direction.

Big Data in Knowledge Management for Innovation

Lorna Uden

School of Computing, FCES
Staffordshire University
Stafford, UK
L.uden@staffs.ac.uk

Abstract. Big Data is the bridge to the next wave of innovation and growth. By combining data from multiple channels and sources and discovering patterns of interest, a business can realize operational efficiency and find new ways of growing the business. Data by itself is useless, especially for improved decision making, unless it can be turned into knowledge. Knowledge is the true destination in the pursuit of data. When the enterprise turns its data into knowledge, it has the potential to gain competitive advantage, and even build entirely new business models.

Knowledge is the most valuable asset of all organizations. Knowledge creation is the process that produces new knowledge and innovation. Effective knowledge management involves (a) identifying knowledge (b) creation of new knowledge (c) building competence (d) effective management of innovation.

A goal of knowledge management is the ability to integrate information from multiple perspectives to provide the insights required for valid decision-making. Knowledge Management today has the opportunity and capability to synthesize data from diverse sources and arrive at new knowledge.

These data can be used to improve the design, operation, maintenance, and repair of assets or to enhance how an activity is carried out. Converting data and analysis collected through the Internet of Things generates better information and analysis, which can significantly enhance decision making. The real time data also enables rapid, real-time sensing of unpredictable conditions and instantaneous responses guided by automated systems.

Combining real-time events with historic patterns allows predictive and prescriptive analytics to emerge. Such evolutionary analytics allows of knowledge management applications to solve issues and prescribe solutions in real-time. A smarter approach to the challenge of Big Data can be achieved through better knowledge management. This talk discusses the importance of effective knowledge management from big data to create value for innovation.

Contents

Knowledge Management and Concept Analysis

Knowledge Discovery and Recognition Methods

Recommendation Algorithms and Systems

Machine Learning Algorithms

Detection Methods and Analysis

Classification and Clustering

Mobile Data Analytics and Knowledge Management

Bioinformatics and Computational Biology

Evidence Theory and Its Application

Formal Reasoning and Ontologies

Subset Spaces Modeling Knowledge-Competitive Agents

Bernhard Heinemann$^{(\boxtimes)}$

Faculty of Mathematics and Computer Science,
University of Hagen, 58084 Hagen, Germany
`bernhard.heinemann@fernuni-hagen.de`

Abstract. The bi-modal logic of subset spaces, LSS, was originally designed for revealing the intrinsic relationship between knowledge and topology. In recent years, it has been developed in several directions, not least towards a comprehensive knowledge-theoretic formalism. As to that, subset spaces have been shown to be smoothly combinable with various epistemic concepts, at least as long as attention is restricted to the single-agent case. Adjusting LSS to general multi-agent scenarios, however, has brought about few results only, presumably due to reasons inherent in the system. This is why one is led to consider more special cases. In the present paper, LSS is extended to a particular two-agent setting, where the peculiarity is given by the case that the agents are competitive in a sense; in fact, it is assumed here that one agent is always able to go ahead of another one regarding knowledge (or, the other one is possibly lagging behind in this respect), and vice versa. It turns out that such circumstances can be modeled in corresponding logical terms to a considerable extent.

Keywords: Reasoning about knowledge · Epistemic logic · Subset space semantics · Knowledge-competitive agents · Completeness · Decidability

1 Introduction

Our topic in this paper is *reasoning about knowledge.* This important foundational issue has been given a solid logical basis right from the beginning of the research into theoretical aspects of artificial intelligence, as can be seen, e.g., from the classic textbook [5]. According to this, a binary *accessibility relation* R_A connecting *possible worlds* or *conceivable states of the world,* is associated with every instance A of a given finite group G of agents. The *knowledge of A* is then defined through the set of all *valid formulas,* where validity is understood with regard to every state the agent considers possible at the actual one. This widespread and well-established view of knowledge is complemented by Moss and Parikh's bi-modal *logic of subset spaces,* LSS (see [11], [4], or Ch. 6 of [1]), of which the basic idea is reported in the following.

The *epistemic state* of an agent in question, i.e., the set of all those states that cannot be distinguished by what the agent topically knows, can be viewed

© Springer International Publishing Switzerland 2015
S. Zhang et al. (Eds.): KSEM 2015, LNAI 9403, pp. 3–14, 2015.
DOI: 10.1007/978-3-319-25159-2_1

as a *neighborhood U* of the actual state x of the world. Formulas are now interpreted with respect to the resulting pairs x, U called *neighborhood situations*. Thus, both the set of all states and the set of all epistemic states constitute the relevant semantic domains as particular subset structures. The two modalities involved, K and □, quantify over all elements of U and 'downward' over all neighborhoods contained in U, respectively. This means that K captures the notion of knowledge as usual (see [5] again), and □ reflects a kind of *effort to acquire knowledge* since gaining knowledge goes hand in hand with a shrinkage of the epistemic state. In fact, knowledge acquisition is this way reminiscent of a *topological procedure*. Thus, it was natural to ask for the appropriate logic of 'real' topological spaces, which could be determined by Georgatos shortly afterwards; see [6]. The subsequent research into subset and topological spaces, respectively, is quoted in the handbook [1], whereas more recent developments include, among others, the papers [2] and [12].

Despite the fact that most treatises on LSS deal with the single-agent case, a corresponding multi-agent version was proposed in the paper [7]. The key idea behind that approach is to incorporate the agents in terms of additional modalities. This clearly leads to an essential modification of the logic, while the original semantics basically remains unchanged. However, avoiding such substantial add-ons to the logic in case of multiple agents, if at all possible, calls for restricting to special cases. It is the purpose of this paper to consider one of these.

The scenarios we are interested in here are (first and foremost) constituted by *two agents* which are *competitive* in the following sense. One of these can always surpass the other one with regard to knowledge.[1] Here, 'always' means formally: at every neighborhood situation referring to the latter. And what's good for the goose is good for the gander: a knowledge state of the first agent can always be beaten by one of the second. (Note, however, that such a notion of 'being better than' is assumed to be not necessarily strict everywhere, since otherwise it could be 'not converging' in some sense.) These ideas will be made precise below, with some new technical peculiarities coming along, opening up interesting new lines of research into logics of subset spaces.

Clearly, settings like this have a strong temporal flavor. Thus, it should be possible to model them by means of the common logic of knowledge with incorporated time as well (cf. [5], Sect. 4.3.), which is justified whenever one is obliged to focus on the chronological order most notably. But sometimes it is unnecessary or even undesirable to make time explicit. For example, with regard to certain teacher-student relationships, the *effort* of teaching and, respectively, learning in order to catch up with or even overtake the conveyer of knowledge might be rated as more important than just the amount of time it costs or the exact point of time it meets with success. We shall, therefore, introduce two-agent subset spaces in such a way that this kind of mutual consecutiveness of the agents is reflected. Our main concern is then dealing with the arising two-agent subset space logic.

---

[1] Thus, the use of the term 'competitive' is here different from the one that is nowadays common in the multi-agent systems community.

The rest of the paper is organized as follows. In the next section, we recapitulate the language and the logic of subset spaces for single agents. In Section 3, the scenarios of two knowledge-competitive agents, as sketched above, are formalized. In Section 4, the completeness of the resulting logic is proved. The subsequent Section 5 is devoted to the corresponding decidability problem. Finally, we summarize and make some additional remarks. – All relevant facts from modal logic not explicitly introduced here can be found in the standard textbook [3].

2   The Language and the Logic of Subset Spaces Revisited

The purpose of this section is threefold: to clarify the starting point of our investigation on a technical level, to set up some concepts and results to be introduced and, respectively, proved later on, and to enable a posterior validation of the thesis that the common single-agent case and the novel two-agent framework follow a closely related idea of knowledge; as to the latter, see the comments on Definition 4 below.

First in this section, the language for (single-agent) subset spaces, $\mathcal{L}$, is defined precisely. Then, the semantics of $\mathcal{L}$ is linked with the common relational semantics of modal logic. Finally, the ensuing relationship is utilized after the most important facts on the logic of subset spaces have been recalled.

To begin with, we define the syntax of $\mathcal{L}$. Let $\mathsf{Prop} = \{p, q, \dots\}$ be a denumerably infinite set of symbols called *proposition variables* (which shall represent the basic facts about the states of the world). Then, the set SF of all *subset formulas* over Prop is defined by the rule $\alpha \ ::= \ \top \mid p \mid \neg\alpha \mid \alpha \wedge \alpha \mid \mathsf{K}\alpha \mid \Box\alpha$. The missing boolean connectives are treated as abbreviations, as needed. The operators which are dual to K and $\Box$ are denoted by L and $\Diamond$, respectively. In view of our remarks in the previous section, K is called the *knowledge operator* and $\Box$ the *effort operator*.

Second, we fix the semantics of $\mathcal{L}$. For a start, we single out the relevant domains. We let $\mathcal{P}(X)$ designate the powerset of a given set X.

Definition 1 (Semantic Domains).

1. *Let X be a non-empty set (of states) and $\mathcal{O} \subseteq \mathcal{P}(X)$ a set of subsets of X. Then, the pair $\mathcal{S} = (X, \mathcal{O})$ is called a subset frame.*
2. *Let $\mathcal{S} = (X, \mathcal{O})$ be a subset frame. The set $\mathcal{N}_{\mathcal{S}} := \{(x, U) \mid x \in U \text{ and } U \in \mathcal{O}\}$ is then called the set of neighborhood situations of $\mathcal{S}$.*
3. *Let $\mathcal{S} = (X, \mathcal{O})$ be a subset frame. Under an $\mathcal{S}$-valuation we understand a mapping $V : \mathsf{Prop} \to \mathcal{P}(X)$.*
4. *Let $\mathcal{S} = (X, \mathcal{O})$ be a subset frame and V an $\mathcal{S}$-valuation. Then, $\mathcal{M} := (X, \mathcal{O}, V)$ is called a subset space (based on $\mathcal{S}$).*

Note that neighborhood situations denominate the semantic atoms of the bimodal language $\mathcal{L}$. The first component of such a situation indicates the actual state of the world, while the second reflects the uncertainty of the agent in question about it. Furthermore, Definition 1 shows that values of proposition variables depend on states only. This is in accordance with the common practice in epistemic logic; see [5] once more.

For a given subset space $\mathcal{M}$, we now define the relation of *satisfaction*, $\models_\mathcal{M}$, between neighborhood situations of the underlying frame and formulas from SF. Based on that, we define the notion of *validity* of formulas in subset spaces. In the following, neighborhood situations are often written without parentheses.

Definition 2 (Satisfaction and Validity). *Let $\mathcal{S} = (X, \mathcal{O})$ be a subset frame.*

1. *Let $\mathcal{M} = (X, \mathcal{O}, V)$ be a subset space based on $\mathcal{S}$, and let $x, U \in \mathcal{N}_\mathcal{S}$ be a neighborhood situation of $\mathcal{S}$. Then*

$$
\begin{array}{lll}
x, U \models_\mathcal{M} \top & & \text{is always true} \\
x, U \models_\mathcal{M} p & : \Longleftrightarrow x \in V(p) \\
x, U \models_\mathcal{M} \neg\alpha & : \Longleftrightarrow x, U \not\models_\mathcal{M} \alpha \\
x, U \models_\mathcal{M} \alpha \wedge \beta & : \Longleftrightarrow x, U \models_\mathcal{M} \alpha \text{ and } x, U \models_\mathcal{M} \beta \\
x, U \models_\mathcal{M} \mathsf{K}\alpha & : \Longleftrightarrow \forall y \in U : y, U \models_\mathcal{M} \alpha \\
x, U \models_\mathcal{M} \Box\alpha & : \Longleftrightarrow \forall U' \in \mathcal{O} : [x \in U' \subseteq U \Rightarrow x, U' \models_\mathcal{M} \alpha],
\end{array}
$$

where $p \in$ Prop and $\alpha, \beta \in$ SF. In case $x, U \models_\mathcal{M} \alpha$ is true we say that α holds in $\mathcal{M}$ at the neighborhood situation x, U.

2. *Let $\mathcal{M} = (X, \mathcal{O}, V)$ be a subset space based on $\mathcal{S}$. A subset formula α is called* valid *in $\mathcal{M}$ iff it holds in $\mathcal{M}$ at every neighborhood situation of $\mathcal{S}$.*

Note that the idea of knowledge and effort described in the introduction is made precise by Item 1 of this definition. In particular, knowledge is here, too, defined as validity at all states that are indistinguishable to the agent.

Subset frames and subset spaces can be considered from a different perspective, as is known since [4] and reviewed in the following, for the reader's convenience. Let a subset frame $\mathcal{S} = (X, \mathcal{O})$ and a subset space $\mathcal{M} = (X, \mathcal{O}, V)$ based on it be given. Take $X_\mathcal{S} := \mathcal{N}_\mathcal{S}$ as a set of worlds, and define two accessibility relations $R_\mathcal{S}^\mathsf{K}$ and $R_\mathcal{S}^\Box$ on $X_\mathcal{S}$ by

$$
\begin{array}{l}
(x, U)\, R_\mathcal{S}^\mathsf{K}\, (x', U') : \Longleftrightarrow U = U' \text{ and} \\
(x, U)\, R_\mathcal{S}^\Box\, (x', U') : \Longleftrightarrow (x = x' \text{ and } U' \subseteq U),
\end{array}
$$

for all $(x, U), (x', U') \in X_\mathcal{S}$. Moreover, let a valuation be defined by $V_\mathcal{M}(p) := \{(x, U) \in X_\mathcal{S} \mid x \in V(p)\}$, for all $p \in$ Prop. Then, bi-modal Kripke structures $S_\mathcal{S} := (X_\mathcal{S}, \{R_\mathcal{S}^\mathsf{K}, R_\mathcal{S}^\Box\})$ and $M_\mathcal{M} := (X_\mathcal{S}, \{R_\mathcal{S}^\mathsf{K}, R_\mathcal{S}^\Box\}, V_\mathcal{M})$ result in such a way that $M_\mathcal{M}$ is equivalent to $\mathcal{M}$ in the following sense.

Proposition 1. *For all $\alpha \in$ SF and $(x, U) \in X_\mathcal{S}$, we have that $x, U \models_\mathcal{M} \alpha$ iff $M_\mathcal{M}, (x, U) \models \alpha$.*

Here (and later on as well), the non-indexed symbol '$\models$' denotes the usual satisfaction relation of modal logic. – The proposition can easily be proved by structural induction on α. We call $S_\mathcal{S}$ and $M_\mathcal{M}$ the Kripke structures *induced* by the subset structures $\mathcal{S}$ and $\mathcal{M}$, respectively.

We now turn to the *logic* of subset spaces, LSS. The subsequent axiomatization from [4] was proved to be sound and complete in Sect. 1.2 and, respectively, Sect. 2.2 there.

1. All instances of propositional tautologies
2. $K(\alpha \to \beta) \to (K\alpha \to K\beta)$
3. $K\alpha \to (\alpha \land KK\alpha)$
4. $L\alpha \to KL\alpha$
5. $(p \to \Box p) \land (\Diamond p \to p)$
6. $\Box(\alpha \to \beta) \to (\Box\alpha \to \Box\beta)$
7. $\Box\alpha \to (\alpha \land \Box\Box\alpha)$
8. $K\Box\alpha \to \Box K\alpha$,

where $p \in \mathsf{Prop}$ and $\alpha, \beta \in \mathsf{SF}$. – The last schema is by far the most interesting one, as it displays the interrelation between knowledge and effort. The members of this schema are called the *Cross Axioms* since [11]. Note that the schema involving only proposition variables is in accordance with the remark on Definition 1 above. (In other words, it is expressed by the latter schema that $\mathcal{L}$ 'only' speaks about the ongoing modification of *knowledge*.)

As the next step, let us take a brief look at the effect of the axioms from the above list within the framework of common modal logic. To this end, we consider bi-modal Kripke models $M = (W, R, R', V)$ satisfying the following four properties:

- the accessibility relation R of M belonging to the knowledge operator K is an equivalence,
- the accessibility relation R' of M belonging to the effort operator $\Box$ is reflexive and transitive,
- the composite relation $R' \circ R$ is contained in $R \circ R'$ (this is usually called the *cross property*), and
- the valuation V of M is constant along every R'-path, for all proposition variables.

Such a model M is called a *cross axiom model* (and the frame underlying M a *cross axiom frame*). Now, it can be verified without difficulty that LSS is sound with respect to the class of all cross axiom models. And it is also easy to see that every induced Kripke model is a cross axiom model (and every induced Kripke frame a cross axiom frame). Thus, the completeness of LSS for cross axiom models follows from that of LSS for subset spaces (which is Theorem 2.4 in [4]) by means of Proposition 1. This inferred completeness result can be used for proving the decidability of LSS; see [4], Sect. 2.3. We shall proceed in a similar way below, in Section 5.

3   Knowledge-Competitive Agents

The formalisms from the previous section will now be extended to the case of two knowledge-competitive agents. We again start with the logical language, which comprises two $\Box$-operators as of now. (This may appear a little surprising at first glance.) Thus, the set 2SF of all *2-subset formulas* over Prop is defined by the rule $\alpha ::= \top \mid p \mid \neg\alpha \mid \alpha \wedge \alpha \mid \mathsf{K}\alpha \mid \Box_1\alpha \mid \Box_2\alpha$. The above syntactic conventions apply correspondingly here. Concerning semantics, the crucial modifications follow right now.

Definition 3 (Two-Agent Subset Structures).

1. *Let X be a non-empty set and $\mathcal{O}_1, \mathcal{O}_2 \subseteq \mathcal{P}(X)$ two sets of subsets of X satisfying*
   (a) for all $U_1 \in \mathcal{O}_1$ and every $x \in U_1$, there exists some $U_2 \in \mathcal{O}_2$ such that $x \in U_2 \subseteq U_1$, and
   (b) for all $U_2 \in \mathcal{O}_2$ and every $x \in U_2$, there exists some $U_1 \in \mathcal{O}_1$ such that $x \in U_1 \subseteq U_2$.
   Then, the triple $\mathcal{S} = (X, \mathcal{O}_1, \mathcal{O}_2)$ is called a two-agent subset frame.
2. *Let $\mathcal{S} = (X, \mathcal{O}_1, \mathcal{O}_2)$ be a two-agent subset frame. The set $\mathcal{N}_{\mathcal{S}} := \{(x, U) \mid x \in U \text{ and } U \in \mathcal{O}_1 \cup \mathcal{O}_2 \cup \{X\}\}$ is then called the set of neighborhood situations of $\mathcal{S}$.*
3. *The notions of $\mathcal{S}$-valuation and* two-agent subset space *are completely analogous to those introduced in Definition 1.*

Some comments on this definition seem to be appropriate. First, the just introduced structures obviously do not correspond to the most general two-agent scenarios, but have already been adjusted to those indicated above. In fact, given that $\mathcal{O}_i$ is associated with agent i for $i \in \{1, 2\}$, condition 1.(a) says that the set of knowledge states of the first agent is 'filtered' by certain knowledge states of the second with respect to the inclusion relation; in this sense, the second agent can always increase her knowledge so that she is (at least temporarily) on par with or superior to the first. And the same applies the other way round. Thus – to say it with the example from the introduction –, the agents mutually assume the student's and the teacher's role, respectively. (This is not typical of teacher and learner in the classical understanding, but should, e.g., be kind of normal for professors and their best students.) We shall obtain simple logical counterparts to the requirements 1.(a) and 1.(b), capturing their intended meaning as just described; see below. Second, the set of all neighborhood situations of a two-agent subset frame not only is constituted of $\mathcal{O}_1$ and $\mathcal{O}_2$ but makes use of X as well. This will be advantageous for the proof of Theorem 1 below. The very fact that $\{X\}$ is written separately in Definition 3 means that the set of all states, X, is considered *indefinite*, i.e., it cannot be allocated to a particular agent.

With regard to satisfaction and validity, we need not completely present the analogue of Definition 2 here, but may confine ourselves to the clauses for the new operators.

Definition 4 (Satisfaction). *Let $\mathcal{S} = (X, \mathcal{O}_1, \mathcal{O}_2)$ be a two-agent subset frame, $\mathcal{M} = (X, \mathcal{O}_1, \mathcal{O}_2, V)$ a two-agent subset space based on $\mathcal{S}$, and $x, U \in \mathcal{N}_{\mathcal{S}}$ a neighborhood situation of $\mathcal{S}$ (i.e., $U \in \mathcal{O}_1 \cup \mathcal{O}_2 \cup \{X\}$). Then, for every $\alpha \in$ 2SF,*

$$x, U \models_{\mathcal{M}} \Box_1\alpha : \Longleftrightarrow \forall U_1 \in \mathcal{O}_1 : [x \in U_1 \subseteq U \Rightarrow x, U_1 \models_{\mathcal{M}} \alpha]$$
$$x, U \models_{\mathcal{M}} \Box_2\alpha : \Longleftrightarrow \forall U_2 \in \mathcal{O}_2 : [x \in U_2 \subseteq U \Rightarrow x, U_2 \models_{\mathcal{M}} \alpha].$$

Now, the knowledge of the two involved agents can be defined through the validity of knowledge formulas at the *respective* neighborhood situations; in other words, *agent 1 knows* α *at* x, U by definition, iff $x, U \models_\mathcal{M} \mathsf{K}\alpha$ *and* $U \in \mathcal{O}_1$, and *agent 2 knows* α *at* x, U, iff $x, U \models_\mathcal{M} \mathsf{K}\alpha$ *and* $U \in \mathcal{O}_2$.

These fixings clearly require justification. To this end, note that the knowledge operator K can no longer be assigned to a particular agent unambiguously. This instead happens 'externally', i.e., by means of an additional semantic condition having no direct counterpart in the object language, namely the requirement that the subset component U of the actual neighborhood situation be contained in the set of all knowledge states of the agent in question; i.e., U must have been 'enabled' for the usage of K by a preceding application of the corresponding $\Box$. The modality $\Box_i$ might therefore be called the *knowledge-enabling operator of agent i*, whereas $\mathsf{K}\alpha$ expresses that knowledge of α by agent i is actually present ($i = 1, 2$). Relating to this, it should be mentioned that all the knowledge of agents we talk about in this paper is an 'ascribed' one (cf. [5], p. 8), in fact, by the system designer utilizing epistemic logic as a formal tool for specifying multi-agent scenarios. This gives us a kind of freedom regarding the choice of the relevant system properties, which is only limited by the suitability of the approach for the intended applications. Here, the expressive power of formulas has to be restricted to some extent, on the other hand, the appearing relaxation makes it possible to describe the competitive knowledge development of the two agents under discussion; see below for some examples.

The final semantic issue to be mentioned is that *induced* Kripke structures are formed in the same way as in Section 2 here so that the two-agent analogue of Proposition 1 is obviously valid.

The *subset space logic of two knowledge-competitive agents*, 2LSS, is given by the following list of axioms, where $i, j \in \{1, 2\}$, $p \in$ Prop, and $\alpha, \beta \in$ 2SF.

1. All instances of propositional tautologies
2. $\mathsf{K}(\alpha \rightarrow \beta) \rightarrow (\mathsf{K}\alpha \rightarrow \mathsf{K}\beta)$
3. $\mathsf{K}\alpha \rightarrow (\alpha \wedge \mathsf{KK}\alpha)$
4. $\mathsf{L}\alpha \rightarrow \mathsf{KL}\alpha$
5. $(p \rightarrow \Box_i p) \wedge (\Diamond_i p \rightarrow p)$
6. $\Box_i (\alpha \rightarrow \beta) \rightarrow (\Box_i \alpha \rightarrow \Box_i \beta)$
7. $\Box_i \alpha \rightarrow \Box_j \Box_i \alpha$
8. $\mathsf{K}\Box_i \alpha \rightarrow \Box_i \mathsf{K}\alpha$
9. $\Box_i \alpha \rightarrow \Diamond_i \alpha$

At first glance, this list is like a doubling of that for LSS; cf. Section 2. Differences arise, in particular, in the seventh schema. The original one obviously consists of two parts, $\Box\alpha \rightarrow \alpha$ and $\Box\alpha \rightarrow \Box\Box\alpha$, by means of which, regarding the relational semantics, the reflexivity and the transitivity, respectively, of the associated accessibility relation are expressed. Now, the reflexivity axiom has been separated off and weakened to *seriality* with respect to both agents; this yields the new schema 9.[2] This schema is responsible for the above mentioned

---

[2] A binary relation R is called *serial* iff $\forall x \exists y\, xRy$; see [5], p. 57.

filtering of $\mathcal{O}_1$ by $\mathcal{O}_2$ and vice versa (which may, therefore, be also called the *interleaving* of $\mathcal{O}_1$ and $\mathcal{O}_2$). Thus, this is the point where, compared to LSS, one of the crucial changes appears: that weakening of $\square$ allows for interpreting the $\square_i$'s in knowledge-competitive scenarios as described above; and Theorem 1 below can, in fact, be proved with this.

On the other hand, the new schema 7 comprises, in particular, two-agent transitivity, by letting $i = j$. In case $i \neq j$, however, additional new axioms appear, mirroring the fact that the interleaving of $\mathcal{O}_1$ and $\mathcal{O}_2$ is compatible with the subset space structure of the respective collections of knowledge states; see the proof of Proposition 2 (and also the comments on Definition 5) below.

As to examples of derived 2LSS-sentences, let us call a formula α *i-stable* in a two-agent subset space, iff $\mathsf{K}\square_i\alpha$ is valid there. Since $\mathsf{K}\square_i\alpha$ implies $\square_i\mathsf{K}\alpha$, i-stability means, in particular, that agent i knows α with a kind of future certainty. Moreover, it can be asserted that i-stable formulas will in actual fact be known, because $\diamondsuit_i\mathsf{K}\alpha$ can be deduced from $\mathsf{K}\square_i\alpha$. Going beyond that, it can easily be shown that i-stability itself is stable knowledge of each of the two agents, or, to put it another way, $\mathsf{K}\square_i\alpha \rightarrow \mathsf{K}\square_j\mathsf{K}\square_i\alpha$ belongs to 2LSS for $i, j \in \{1, 2\}$. All this can easily be obtained with the aid of the above axioms.

Concluding our discussion on the arising logic, we would like to draw the reader's attention to the multi-method logics of subset spaces examined in [8], Sect. 4. Despite all the differences in details, those are formally more similar to the present approach than the multi-agent version of LSS quoted in the introduction.

Finally in this section, it is proved that the logic 2LSS is *sound* with respect to the class of all two-agent subset spaces.

Proposition 2. *Let* $\mathcal{M} = (X, \mathcal{O}_1, \mathcal{O}_2, V)$ *be a two-agent subset space. Then, every axiom from the above list is valid in* $\mathcal{M}$.

Proof. We confine ourselves to the instance $\square_1\alpha \rightarrow \square_2\square_1\alpha$ of the seventh schema. Let $x, U \models_{\mathcal{M}} \square_1\alpha$ be satisfied. This means that, for all $U_1 \in \mathcal{O}_1$ such that $x \in U_1 \subseteq U$, we have $x, U_1 \models_{\mathcal{M}} \alpha$. Now, let $U_2 \in \mathcal{O}_2$ be any subset of U containing x. Furthermore, let $U' \in \mathcal{O}_1$ be an arbitrary element satisfying $x \in U' \subseteq U_2$. Then, in particular, $U' \subseteq U$. Thus, $x, U' \models_{\mathcal{M}} \alpha$. It follows that $x, U_2 \models_{\mathcal{M}} \square_1\alpha$. Consequently, $x, U \models_{\mathcal{M}} \square_2\square_1\alpha$, since U_2 was chosen arbitrarily as well. This proves (the particular case of) the proposition.

As the transitivity of the subset relation is crucially used for the preceding proof, one may call the just treated schemata the *quasi-transitivity axioms*.

4   Completeness

In this section, we primarily present the new concepts required for proving the semantic completeness of 2LSS on the class of all two-agent subset spaces. As it is mostly the case with subset space logics, the overall structure of such a proof consists of an infinite step-by-step model construction.[3] Utilizing a procedure of that kind seems to be necessary, since subset spaces in a sense do not harmonize with the main modal means supporting completeness, viz *canonical models*.

The canonical model of 2LSS will come into play nevertheless. So let us fix some notations concerning that model first. Let $\mathcal{C}$ be the set of all maximal 2LSS-consistent sets of formulas. Furthermore, let $\xrightarrow{\mathsf{K}}$ and $\xrightarrow{\Box_i}$ be the accessibility relations induced on $\mathcal{C}$ by the modalities K and $\Box_i$, respectively, where $i \in \{1,2\}$. And finally, let $\alpha \in 2\mathsf{SF}$ be a formula which is *not* contained in 2LSS. Then, we have to find a model for $\neg\alpha$.

This model is constructed stepwise and incrementally in such a way that better and better intermediary structures are obtained (which means that more and more existential formulas are realized). In order to ensure that the finally resulting limit structure behaves as desired, several requirements on those approximations have to be met at every stage. This makes up the technical core of the proof, of which only the outset is specified in detail below. With this aim in view, we need a definition.

Definition 5 (Almost Partially Ordered Sets). *Let P be a non-empty set.*

1. *A binary relation $\sqsubset$ on P is called* weakly trichotomous *iff, for all $\pi, \rho \in P$, at most one out of $(\pi \sqsubset \rho, \rho \sqsubset \pi, \pi = \rho)$ is true. Now, $(P, \sqsubset)$ is called an* almost partially ordered (apo) *set and $\sqsubset$ an* almost partial order *on P, iff $\sqsubset$ is transitive and weakly trichotomous.*

2. *Let $\sqsubset_1, \sqsubset_2$ be almost partial orders on P. Then, $(P, \sqsubset_1, \sqsubset_2)$ is called a* twofold almost partially ordered (2apo) *set iff, for all $\pi, \rho, \sigma \in P$ and $i, j \in \{1,2\}$, it ensues from $\pi \sqsubset_i \rho \sqsubset_j \sigma$ that $\pi \sqsubset_j \sigma$.*

We comment on 5 first. Compared against partial orders, reflexivity is obviously missing, whereas antisymmetry ensues from weak trichotomy. – Concerning 5, it should be remarked that not only are 2apo-sets those equipped with two almost partial orders, but these satisfy an additional requirement corresponding, among other things, to the fact that the interleaving of the two distinguished sets of subsets of a two-agent subset frame is 'good-natured' with respect to inclusion. Actually, this condition is the semantic equivalent of the quasi-transitivity axioms in case $i \neq j$, hence itself is called *quasi-transitivity (of $(\sqsubset_1, \sqsubset_2)$).*

We now describe the ingredients of the above mentioned approximation structures. Their possible worlds are successively taken from a denumerably infinite set of points, Y, chosen in advance. Also, another denumerably infinite set, Q, is chosen such that $Y \cap Q = \emptyset$. The latter set shall gradually contribute to a 2apo-set representing the subset space structure of the desired limit model. Finally, we fix particular 'starting elements' $x_0 \in Y$, $\bot \in Q$, and $\Gamma \in \mathcal{C}$ containing the formula $\neg\alpha$ from above. Then, a sequence of quadruples (X_m, P_m, j_m, t_m) has to be defined inductively such that, for all $m \in \mathbb{N}$,

---

[3] See [4], Sect. 2.2, for a fully completed proof regarding LSS, and [9], Sect. 5, for an outline of a particular variation.

- X_m is a finite subset of Y containing x_0,
- P_m is a finite subset of Q containing $\perp$ and carrying two almost partial orders $\sqsubseteq_1, \sqsubseteq_2$ such that
  - $(P_m, \sqsubseteq_1, \sqsubseteq_2)$ is a 2apo-set and
  - $\perp$ is the *least element* in P_m (i.e., $\perp \sqsubseteq_1 \pi$ or $\perp \sqsubseteq_2 \pi$ for all $\pi \in P_m$),
- $j_m : P_m \to \mathcal{P}(X_m)$ is a function satisfying ($\pi \sqsubseteq_i \rho \iff j_m(\pi) \supset j_m(\rho)$), for all $\pi, \rho \in P_m$ and $i \in \{1, 2\}$, and
- $t_m : X_m \times P_m \to \mathcal{C}$ is a *partial* function such that, for all $x, y \in X_m$ and $\pi, \rho \in P_m$,
  - $t_m(x, \pi)$ is defined iff $x \in j_m(\pi)$; in this case it holds that
    * if $y \in j_m(\pi)$, then $t_m(x, \pi) \xrightarrow{\mathsf{K}} t_m(y, \pi)$,
    * if $\pi \sqsubseteq_i \rho$, then $t_m(x, \pi) \xrightarrow{\square_i} t_m(x, \rho)$, where $i \in \{1, 2\}$,
  - $t_m(x_0, \perp) = \Gamma$.

By the way, the intermediary sets $\mathcal{O}_1^m$ and $\mathcal{O}_2^m$ of subsets of X_m are obtained from that as follows: $\mathcal{O}_i^m := \{j_m(\pi) \mid \pi \in P_m$ and π has a $\sqsubseteq_i$ -predecessor$\}$, for $i = 1, 2$.

During the construction indicated above, the sets X_m and P_m must be enlarged with new elements and the mappings j_m and t_m correspondingly be extended in each step. It turns out that this plan can indeed be followed faithfully. All this finally yields the subsequent theorem.

Theorem 1 (Completeness). *Let $\alpha \in$ 2SF be a formula which is valid in all two-agent subset spaces. Then α belongs to the logic 2LSS.*

5   Decidability

The standard method for proving the decidability of a given modal logic is *filtration*, which restricts inspection of the relevant models to the finite ones among them and enables a decision procedure thus. However, just as subset spaces do not harmonize with canonical models, they are incompatible with filtration. Thus, a detour is required, which takes us back into the relational semantics. In the following, we shall single out a class of tri-modal Kripke structures for which 2LSS is as well sound and complete, and which is closed under filtration in a suitable manner. This will give us the desired decidability result. Subsequently, K is supposed to correspond to R, and $\square_i$ to R_i' for $i = 1, 2$.

Definition 6 (Two-Agent Model). *Let $M := (W, R, R_1', R_2', V)$ be a tri-modal Kripke model, where $R, R_1', R_2' \subseteq W \times W$ are binary relations and V is a valuation. Then M is called a two-agent model, iff the following conditions are satisfied.*

1. *R is an equivalence relation,*
2. *both R_1' and R_2' are serial and transitive,*
3. *both pairs (R_1', R_2') and (R_2', R_1') satisfy the quasi-transitivity condition,*
4. *both pairs (R, R_1') and (R, R_2') satisfy the cross property, and*

5. *the valuation V of M is constant along every R'_i-path, for $i \in \{1,2\}$ and all proposition variables.*

The class of all Kripke models induced by a two-agent subset space is contained in the class of all two-agent models, as can be seen easily. It follows that 2LSS is (sound and) complete with respect to the latter class; see the final part of Section 2 above. Therefore, it remains to be proved that this class is closed under filtration.

For this purpose, let a 2LSS-consistent formula $\alpha \in$ 2SF be given. Then, a *filter set* of formulas, involving the set sf(α) of all subformulas of α, is defined as follows. We start off with $\Sigma_0 := \text{sf}(\alpha) \cup \{\neg\beta \mid \beta \in \text{sf}(\alpha)\}$. In the next step, we take the closure of Σ_0 under finite conjunctions of pairwise distinct elements of Σ_0. After that, we close under single applications of the operator L. And finally, we join the sets of subformulas of all the elements of the set obtained last. (This final step is necessary because L was introduced as an abbreviation.) The resulting set of formulas, denoted by Σ, is the one that meets the current requirements. Note that Σ is *finite*.

Now, the canonical model of 2LSS is filtered through Σ. As a filtration of the corresponding accessibility relations, we take the *smallest* one in each of the three cases. Let $M := (W, R, S_1, S_2, V)$ be the resulting model, where the valuation V shall be in accordance with Definition 6 for the proposition variables outside of Σ. Then, the following lemma is crucial.

Lemma 1. *The structure M is a finite two-agent model. Furthermore, the size of M can be computed from the length of α.*

Proof. The finiteness of W follows from that of Σ, and we must now show that the five conditions from Definition 6 are satisfied. According to the way the filter set Σ was formed, the verification of 1 and 4 is not difficult. Next, both the validity of 5 for the proposition variables occurring in Σ and the seriality of the R'_is can easily be concluded from the fact that M is the result of a filtration. Moreover, establishing the transitivity of the R'_is is covered by the proof of Lemma 2.10 from [4]. Thus only the verification of the third condition requires a separate argument. Fortunately, it turns out that one can proceed for it in a way similar to the one taken for transitivity (but this is the most sophisticated portion of the whole proof). In this manner, the lemma is proved.

The desired decidability result is now an immediate consequence of Lemma 1 and the facts stated above.

Theorem 2 (Decidability). *The logic 2LSS is a decidable set of formulas.*

6   Conclusion

In this paper, a subset space logic of two knowledge-competitive agents, denoted by 2LSS, has been introduced. A corresponding axiomatization was proposed, which turned out to be *sound and complete* with respect to the intended class of models. This constitutes the first of our main results. The second assures the *decidability* of the new logic.

It is to be expected that the *complexity* of 2LSS can be determined not until solving this problem for the usual logic of subset spaces. As to that, only partial results are known; see [2].

Generalizing our approach to the case of *more than two agents* does not pose difficulties on the formal side. However, the interpretation of some of the competitively relevant formulas is different then; for example, seriality in the more general context means that all agents different from a particular one can do better than the latter. Finally, the question for *other interesting agent interrelationships* and the effects of them on knowledge comes up and should be answered by future research; concerning this, the paper [10] may serve as a starting point.

References

1. Aiello, M., Pratt-Hartmann, I.E., van Benthem, J.F.A.K.: Handbook of Spatial Logics. Springer, Dordrecht (2007)
2. Balbiani, P., van Ditmarsch, H., Kudinov, A.: Subset space logic with arbitrary announcements. In: Lodaya, K. (ed.) Logic and Its Applications. LNCS, vol. 7750, pp. 233–244. Springer, Heidelberg (2013)
3. Blackburn, P., de Rijke, M., Venema, Y.: Modal Logic, Cambridge Tracts in Theoretical Computer Science, vol. 53. Cambridge University Press, Cambridge (2001)
4. Dabrowski, A., Moss, L.S., Parikh, R.: Topological reasoning and the logic of knowledge. Annals of Pure and Applied Logic **78**, 73–110 (1996)
5. Fagin, R., Halpern, J.Y., Moses, Y., Vardi, M.Y.: Reasoning about Knowledge. MIT Press, Cambridge (1995)
6. Georgatos, K.: Knowledge theoretic properties of topological spaces. In: Masuch, M., Polos, L. (eds.) Logic at Work 1992. LNCS, vol. 808, pp. 147–159. Springer, Heidelberg (1994)
7. Heinemann, B.: Topology and knowledge of multiple agents. In: Geffner, H., Prada, R., Machado Alexandre, I., David, N. (eds.) IBERAMIA 2008. LNCS (LNAI), vol. 5290, pp. 1–10. Springer, Heidelberg (2008)
8. Heinemann, B.: Logics for multi-subset spaces. Journal of Applied Non-Classical Logics **20**(3), 219–240 (2010)
9. Heinemann, B.: Coming upon the classic notion of implicit knowledge again. In: Buchmann, R., Kifor, C.V., Yu, J. (eds.) KSEM 2014. LNCS, vol. 8793, pp. 1–12. Springer, Heidelberg (2014)
10. Lomuscio, A., Ryan, M.: Ideal agents sharing (some!) knowledge. In: Prade, H. (ed.) 13th European Conference on Artificial Intelligence, ECAI 1998, pp. 557–561. John Wiley & Sons Ltd, Chichester (1998)
11. Moss, L.S., Parikh, R.: Topological reasoning and the logic of knowledge. In: Moses, Y. (ed.) Theoretical Aspects of Reasoning about Knowledge (TARK 1992), pp. 95–105. Morgan Kaufmann, Los Altos (1992)
12. Wáng, Y.N., Ågotnes, T.: Subset space public announcement logic. In: Lodaya, K. (ed.) Logic and Its Applications. LNCS, vol. 7750, pp. 245–257. Springer, Heidelberg (2013)

A Distance-Based Paraconsistent Semantics for DL-Lite

Xiaowang Zhang[1]([✉]), Kewen Wang[2], Zhe Wang[2], Yue Ma[3], and Guilin Qi[4]

[1] School of Computer Science and Technology, Tianjin University, Tianjin, China
xiaowangzhang@tju.edu.cn
[2] School of Information and Communication Technology, Griffith University, Brisbane, Australia
[3] Laboratoire de Recherche En Informatique, University Paris Sud, Paris, France
[4] School of Computer Science and Engineering, Southeast University, Nanjing, China

Abstract. DL-Lite is an important family of description logics. Recently, there is an increasing interest in handling inconsistency in DL-Lite as the constraint imposed by a TBox can be easily violated by assertions in ABox in DL-Lite. In this paper, we present a distance-based paraconsistent semantics based on the notion of feature in DL-Lite, which provides a novel way to rationally draw meaningful conclusions even from an inconsistent knowledge base. Finally, we investigate several important logical properties of this entailment relation based on the new semantics and show its promising advantages in non-monotonic reasoning for DL-Lite.

1 Introduction

The DL-Lite [2] is a family of lightweight description logics (DLs), the logical foundation of OWL 2.0 QL, one of the three profiles of OWL 2.0 for Web ontology language recommended by W3C [4]. In description logics, an ontology is expressed as a knowledge base (KB). Inconsistency is not rare in ontology applications and can be caused by several reasons, such as errors in modeling, migration from other formalisms, ontology merging, and ontology evolution. In the age of big data, it is becoming impossible to avoid inconsistency of larger scale of KBs. Therefore, handling inconsistency is always considered as an important problem in DLs and ontology management communities [18]. However, DL-Lite reasoning mechanism based on classical DL semantics faces a problem when inconsistency occurs, which is referred to as the triviality problem. That is, any conclusions, that are possibly irrelevant or even contradicting, will be entailed from an inconsistent DL-Lite ontology under the classical semantics.

In many practical ontology applications, there is a strong need for inferring (only) useful information from inconsistent ontologies. For instance, consider a simple DL-Lite KB $\mathcal{K} = (\mathcal{T}, \mathcal{A})$ where $\mathcal{T} = \{Penguin \sqsubseteq Bird, Swallow \sqsubseteq Bird,$

X. Zhang—Supported by the project-sponsored by School of Computer Science and Technology in Tianjin University.

S. Zhang et al. (Eds.): KSEM 2015, LNAI 9403, pp. 15–27, 2015.
DOI: 10.1007/978-3-319-25159-2_2

$Bird \sqsubseteq Fly\}$ and $\mathcal{A} = \{Penguin(tweety),\ \neg Fly(tweety),\ Swallow(fred)\}$. That KB tells us that penguins are birds; swallows are birds; birds can fly; *tweety* is a penguin; *tweety* cannot fly; and *fred* is a swallow. Under the classical DL semantics, anything can be inferred from $\mathcal{K}$ since $\mathcal{K}$ is not consistent (i.e., it has no any model.). Intuitively, one might wish to still infer $Bird(fred)$ and $Fly(fred)$, while it is useless to derive both $Fly(tweety)$ and $\neg Fly(tweety)$ from $\mathcal{K}$.

There exist several proposals for reasoning with inconsistent DL-Lite KBs in the literature. These approaches usually fall into one of two fundamentally different streams. The first one is based on the assumption that inconsistencies are caused by erroneous data and thus, they should be removed in order to obtain a consistent KB [9,16,5,6]. In most approaches in this stream, the task of repairing inconsistent ontologies is actually reduced to finding a maximum consistent subset of the original KB. A shortcoming of these approaches is similar to the so-called *multi-extension problem* in Reiter's default logic. That is, in many cases, an inconsistent KB may have several different sub-KBs that are maximum consistent. The other stream, based on the idea of living with inconsistency, is to introduce a form of paraconsistent reasoning or inconsistency-tolerant reasoning by employing non-standard reasoning methods (e.g., non-standard inference and non-classical semantics). There are some strategies to select consistent subsets from an inconsistent KB as substitutes of the original KB in reasoning [19,8,13,10,7,21]. The Belnap's four-valued semantics has been successfully extended into DL-Lite [14] where two additional logical values besides "true" and "false" are introduced to indicate contradictory conclusions. Inference power of the four-valued semantics is further enhanced by a new quasi-classical semantics for DLs proposed by Zhang et al. [23], which is a generalization of Hunter's quasi-classical semantics for propositional logic. However, the reasoning capability of such paraconsistent methods is not strong enough for many practical applications. For instance, a conclusion ϕ, that can inferred from a consistent KB $\mathcal{K}$ under the classical semantics, may become not derivable under their paraconsistent semantics. We argue that approaches in these two streams are mostly *coarse-grained* in the sense that they fail to fully utilize semantic information in the given inconsistent KB. For instance, when two interpretations make a concept unsatisfiable, one interpretation may be more reasonable than the other. But existing approaches to paraconsistent semantics in DLs do not take this into account usually.

Recently a distance-based semantics presented by Arieli [1] has been proposed to deal with inconsistent KBs in propositional logic, which is inspired from distance-based merging procedures in propositional logic [11]. However, it is not straightforward to generalize this approach to DLs because it directly works on models (it is feasible in propositional logic since a propositional KB has a finite number of finite models) while, in DLs, a KB might have infinite number of models and a model might also be infinite [3]. Additionally, it is also a challenge in adopting distance-based semantics for complex constructors in DLs.

To overcome these difficulties, in this paper we first use the notion of *features* [20] and then introduce a distance-based semantics for paraconsistent reasoning with DL-Lite. Features in DL-Lite are Herbrand interpretations extended with limited structure, which provide a novel semantic characterization for DL-Lite.

In addition, features also generalize the notion of *types* for TBoxes [12] to general KBs. Each KB in DL-Lite has a finite number of features and each feature is finite. This makes it possible to cast Arieli's distance-based semantics to DL-Lite.

The main innovations and contributions of this paper can be summarized as follows. We introduce distance functions on *types* of DL-Lite$_{bool}^{\mathcal{N}}$ KBs, which avoids the problem of domain infiniteness and model infiniteness in defining the distance function in terms of models of KBs. We choose DL-Lite$_{bool}^{\mathcal{N}}$ [2], one of the most expressive members of the DL-Lite family, and define distance-based semantics for DL-Lite$_{bool}^{\mathcal{N}}$ in a way analogous to the model-based approaches in propositional logic. Although our approach is based on DL-Lite$_{bool}^{\mathcal{N}}$, we argue that our technique can easily be adapted to other DLs. Based on the new distance function on types, we develop a way of measuring types that are closest to a TBox and the notion of *minimal model types* is introduced. This notion is also extended to *minimal model features* for KBs. We propose a distance-based semantics for DL-Lite$_{bool}^{\mathcal{N}}$ so that useful information can still be inferred when a KB is inconsistent. This is accomplished by introducing a novel entailment relation (i.e. distance-based entailment) between a KB and an axiom in terms of minimal model features. Our results show that the distance-based entailment is paraconsistent, non-monotonic, cautious as the paraconsistent based on multi-valued semantics. We also show that the distance-based entailment is not over-skeptical in the sense that for a classically consistent KB, the distance-based entailment coincides with the classical entailment, which is missing in most existing paraconsistent semantics for DLs. Due to the space limitation, all proofs are omitted but they are available in an extended technical report in [22].

2   The DL-Lite Family and Features

DL-Lite $_{bool}^{\mathcal{N}}$. A *signature* is a finite set $\Sigma = \Sigma_A \cup \Sigma_R \cup \Sigma_I \cup \Sigma_N$ where Σ_A is the set of atomic concepts, Σ_R the set of atomic roles, Σ_I the set of individual names (or, objects) and Σ_N the set of natural numbers in Σ. We use capital letters A, B, C (with subscripts C_1, C_2) to denote concept names, P, R, S (with subscripts P_1, P_2) to denote role names, lowercase letters a, b, c to denote individual names and assume 1 is always in Σ_N. $\top$ and $\bot$ will not be considered as concept names or role names.

Formally, given a signature Σ, the DL-Lite$_{bool}^{\mathcal{N}}$ language is inductively constructed by syntax rules: (1) $R \leftarrow P \mid P^-$; (2) $B \leftarrow \top \mid A \mid \geq nR$; and (3) $C \leftarrow B \mid \neg C \mid C_1 \sqcap C_2$. We say B a *basic concept* and C a *general concept*. Other standard concept constructs such as $\bot$, $\exists R$, $\leq nR$ and $C_1 \sqcup C_2$ can be introduced as abbreviations: $\bot$ for $\neg\top$, $\exists R$ for $\geq 1R$, $\leq nR$ for $\neg(\geq (n+1)R)$ and $C_1 \sqcup C_2$ for $\neg(\neg C_1 \sqcap \neg C_2)$. For any $P \in \Sigma_R$, $P^{--} = P$.

A TBox $\mathcal{T}$ is a finite set of *(concept) inclusions* of the form $C_1 \sqsubseteq C_2$ where C_1 and C_2 are general concepts. An ABox $\mathcal{A}$ is a finite set of concept assertions $C(a)$ and role assertions $R(a, b)$. Concept inclusions, concept assertions and role assertions are axioms. A KB is composed of a TBox and an ABox, written by $\mathcal{K} = (\mathcal{T}, \mathcal{A})$. $Sig(\mathcal{K})$ denotes the signature of $\mathcal{K}$.

An interpretation $\mathcal{I}$ is a pair $\langle \Delta^{\mathcal{I}}, \cdot^{\mathcal{I}} \rangle$, where $\Delta^{\mathcal{I}}$ is a non-empty set called the *domain* and $\cdot^{\mathcal{I}}$ is an interpretation function such that $a^{\mathcal{I}} \in \Delta^{\mathcal{I}}$, $A^{\mathcal{I}} \subseteq \Delta^{\mathcal{I}}$ and $P^{\mathcal{I}} \subseteq \Delta^{\mathcal{I}} \times \Delta^{\mathcal{I}}$. General concepts are interpreted as usual. The definition of interpretation is based on the *unique name assumption* (UNA), i.e., $a^{\mathcal{I}} \neq b^{\mathcal{I}}$ for two different individual names a and b.

An interpretation $\mathcal{I}$ is a *model* of a concept inclusion $C_1 \sqsubseteq C_2$ (a concept assertion $C(a)$, or a role assertion $R(a,b)$) if $C_1^{\mathcal{I}} \subseteq C_2^{\mathcal{I}}$ ($a^{\mathcal{I}} \in C^{\mathcal{I}}$, or $(a^{\mathcal{I}}, b^{\mathcal{I}}) \in R^{\mathcal{I}}$); and $\mathcal{I}$ is called a *model* of a TBox $\mathcal{T}$ (an ABox $\mathcal{A}$) if $\mathcal{I}$ is a model of each inclusion of $\mathcal{T}$ (each assertion of $\mathcal{A}$). $\mathcal{I}$ is called a *model* of a KB $(\mathcal{T}, \mathcal{A})$ if $\mathcal{I}$ is a model of both $\mathcal{T}$ and $\mathcal{A}$. We use $Mod(\mathcal{K})$ to denote the set of models of $\mathcal{K}$. A KB $\mathcal{K}$ *entails* an axiom ϕ, if $Mod(\mathcal{K}) \subseteq Mod(\{\phi\})$. Two KBs $\mathcal{K}_1$ and $\mathcal{K}_2$ are *equivalent* if $Mod(\mathcal{K}_1) = Mod(\mathcal{K}_2)$, denoted by $\mathcal{K}_1 \equiv \mathcal{K}_2$. A KB $\mathcal{K}$ is *consistent* if it has at least one model, *inconsistent* otherwise.

Features. Let Σ be a signature. A Σ-*type* (or simply a *type*) is a set of basic concepts over Σ, s.t., $\top \in \tau$, and for any $m, n \in \Sigma_N$ with $m < n$, $R \in \Sigma_R \cup \{P^- \mid P \in \Sigma_R\}$, $\geq nR \in \tau$ implies $\geq mR \in \tau$. As $\top \in \tau$ for any type τ, we omit it in examples for simplicity. T_Σ denotes the set of all Σ-types. Note that if $\exists P$ (or $\exists P^-$) occurs in a general concept C then $\exists P^-$ (or $\exists P$) should be also considered as a new concept independent of $\exists P$ (or $\exists P^-$) in computing types of C respectively. In the rest of the paper, we will use Ξ to denote a set of types $\{\tau_1, \ldots, \tau_m\}$ (called a *type set*) and use Π to denote a set of type sets $\{\Xi_1, \ldots, \Xi_n\}$ (called a *type group*). Then we denote $\cup \Xi = \tau_1 \cup \cdots \cup \tau_m$ and $\cap \Pi = \Xi_1 \cap \ldots \cap \Xi_n$.

A type τ *satisfies* a basic concept B if $B \in \tau$, τ satisfies $\neg C$ if τ does not satisfy C, and τ satisfies $C_1 \sqcap C_2$ if τ satisfies both C_1 and C_2. $T_\Sigma(C)$ denotes a collection of all Σ-types of C. In this way, each general concept C over Σ corresponds to a set $T_\Sigma(C)$ of all Σ-types satisfying C. A type τ *satisfies* a concept inclusion $C \sqsubseteq D$ if $\tau \in T_\Sigma(\neg C \sqcup D)$. And a type τ is a *model type* of a TBox $\mathcal{T}$ iff it satisfies each inclusion in $\mathcal{T}$. *Model type sets* and *model type groups* are analogously defined. If Ξ is a model type set of a TBox $\mathcal{T}$ then $\exists P \in \cup \Xi$ iff $\exists P^- \in \cup \Xi$. This property is called *role coherence* which can be used to check whether a type set is the model type set of some TBox. $\Pi_\Sigma(\mathcal{T})$ denotes the model type group $\{T_\Sigma(\neg C_1 \sqcup D_1), \ldots, T_\Sigma(\neg C_n \sqcup D_n)\}$ of $\mathcal{T}$ where $\mathcal{T} = \{C_1 \sqsubseteq D_1, \ldots, C_n \sqsubseteq D_n\}$ is a TBox over Σ. It appears that $\cap \Pi_\Sigma(\mathcal{T})$ is the collection of model Σ-types of $\mathcal{T}$.

A Σ-*Herbrand set* (or simply *Herbrand set*) $\mathcal{H}$ is a finite set of member assertions satisfying: (1) for each $a \in \Sigma_I$, if $B_1(a), \ldots, B_k(a)$, where $\{B_1, \ldots, B_k\} \subseteq \Sigma_B$ are all the concept assertions about a in $\mathcal{H}$, then the set $\{B_1, \ldots, B_k\}$ is a Σ-type; (2) for each $P \in \Sigma_R$, if $P(a, b_i)(1 \leq i \leq n)$ are all the role assertions about a in $\mathcal{H}$, then for any $m \in \Sigma_N$ with $m \leq n$, $(\geq mP)(a)$ is in $\mathcal{H}$; (3) for each $P \in \Sigma_R$, if $P(b_i, a)(1 \leq i \leq n)$ are all the role assertions in $\mathcal{H}$, then for any $m \in \Sigma_N$ with $m \leq n$, $(\geq mP^-)(a)$ is in $\mathcal{H}$.

We simply write $\tau(a) = \{B_1(a), \ldots, B_k(a)\}$ where $\tau = \{B_1, \ldots, B_k\}$. Moreover, given a set of types $\Xi = \{\tau_1, \ldots, \tau_m\}$, $\Xi(a)$ denotes $\{\tau_1(a), \ldots, \tau_m(a)\}$ without confusion. In this case, we say $\tau(a)$ is in $\mathcal{H}$ if $\{B_1(a), \ldots, B_k(a)\} \subseteq \mathcal{H}$.

A Herbrand set $\mathcal{H}$ *satisfies* a concept assertion $C(a)$ (a role assertion $P(a,b)$ or $P^-(b,a)$) if $\tau(a)$ is in $\mathcal{H}$ and $\tau \in T_\Sigma(C)$ ($P(a,b) \in \mathcal{H}$ or $P^-(b,a) \in \mathcal{H}$). A Herbrand set $\mathcal{H}$ *satisfies* an ABox $\mathcal{A}$ if $\mathcal{H}$ satisfies all assertions in $\mathcal{A}$.

A Σ-*feature* (or simply a *feature*) $\mathcal{F}$ is a pair $\langle \Xi, \mathcal{H} \rangle$, where Ξ is a non-empty set of Σ-types and $\mathcal{H}$ a Σ-Herbrand set, if $\mathcal{F}$ satisfies: (1) for each $P \in \Sigma_R$, $\exists P \in \bigcup \Xi$ iff $\exists P^- \in \bigcup \Xi$ (i.e., Ξ holds role coherence); and (2) for each $a \in \Sigma_I$ and $\tau(a)$ in $\mathcal{H}$, s.t., τ is a Σ-type, $\tau \in \Xi$. A feature $\mathcal{F}$ *satisfies* an inclusion $C_1 \sqsubseteq C_2$ over Σ, if $\Xi \subseteq T_\Sigma(\neg C_1 \sqcup C_2)$; $\mathcal{F}$ *satisfies* a concept assertion $C(a)$ over Σ, if $\tau(a) \in \mathcal{H}$ and $\tau \in T_\Sigma(C)$; and $\mathcal{F}$ *satisfies* a role assertion $P(a,b)$ (resp., $P^-(b,a)$) over Σ, if $P(a,b) \in \mathcal{H}$. A feature $\mathcal{F}$ is a *model feature* of KB $\mathcal{K}$ if $\mathcal{F}$ satisfies each inclusion and each assertion in $\mathcal{K}$. $Mod^F(\mathcal{K})$ denotes the set of all model features of $\mathcal{K}$. It easily concludes that $\mathcal{K}$ is consistent iff $Mod^F(\mathcal{K}) \neq \emptyset$. Given two KBs $\mathcal{K}_1$ and $\mathcal{K}_2$, let $\Sigma = Sig(\mathcal{K}_1 \cup \mathcal{K}_2)$, $\mathcal{K}_1$ F-entails $\mathcal{K}_2$ if $Mod^F(\mathcal{K}_1) \subseteq Mod^F(\mathcal{K}_2)$, written by $\mathcal{K} \models^F \mathcal{K}_2$; and $\mathcal{K}_1$ is F-equivalent $\mathcal{K}_2$ if $Mod^F(\mathcal{K}_1) = Mod^F(\mathcal{K}_2)$, written by $\mathcal{K} \equiv^F \mathcal{K}_2$. In [20], we conclude that: *(1)* $\mathcal{K}_1 \models \mathcal{K}_2$ iff $\mathcal{K}_1 \models^F \mathcal{K}_2$; *(2)* $\mathcal{K}_1 \equiv \mathcal{K}_2$ iff $\mathcal{K}_1 \equiv^F \mathcal{K}_2$.

3   Distance-Based Semantics for TBoxes

To measure the closeness of two types, we first define a distance function between two types in terms of the symmetric difference for sets.

Definition 1. *Let Σ be a signature, a total function $d : T_\Sigma \times T_\Sigma \to \mathbb{R}^+ \cup \{0\}$ is a pseudo-distance function (for short, distance function) on T_Σ if it satisfies: (1) $\forall \tau_1, \tau_2 \in T_\Sigma, d(\tau_1, \tau_2) = 0$ iff $\tau_1 = \tau_2$; and (2) $\forall \tau_1, \tau_2 \in T_\Sigma, d(\tau_1, \tau_2) = d(\tau_2, \tau_1)$.*

Given a type $\tau \in T_\Sigma$ and a type set $\Xi \subseteq T_\Sigma$, the distance function between τ and Ξ is defined as $d(\tau, \Xi) = min\{d(\tau, \tau') \mid \tau' \in \Xi\}$.

If $\Xi = \emptyset$, then we set $d(\tau, \Xi) = \mathbf{d}$ where $\mathbf{d}$ is a default value of distance function greater than any value the to considered. This setting is used to exclude all contradictions (e.g., $\top \sqsubseteq \bot$) under our candidate semantics since a contradiction can bring less useful information.

There are two representative distance functions on types, namely, *Hamming distance function* where $d^H(\tau_1, \tau_2) = |(\tau_1 - \tau_2) \cup (\tau_2 - \tau_1)|$ and *drastic distance function* where $d^D(\tau_1, \tau_2) = 0$ if $\tau_1 = \tau_2$ and $d^D(\tau_1, \tau_2) = 1$ otherwise.

An *aggregation function* f is a total function that accepts a multi-set of real numbers and returns a real number, satisfying: (1) f is non-decreasing in the values of its argument; (2) $f(\{x_1, \ldots, x_n\}) = 0$ iff $x_1 = \ldots = x_n = 0$; and (3) $\forall x \in \mathbb{R}^+ \cup \{0\}, f(\{x\}) = x$. There exist some popular aggregation functions [15]:

- The *summation* function: $f^s(x_1, \ldots, x_n) = \sum_{1 \leq i \leq n} x_i$;
- The *maximum* function: $f^m(x_1, \ldots, x_n) = max_{1 \leq i \leq n} x_i$;
- The κ-*voting* function $(0 < \kappa < 1)$: $f^\kappa(x_1, \ldots, x_n) = 0$ if $Zero(\{x_1, \ldots, x_n\}) = n$; $f^\kappa(x_1, \ldots, x_n) = \frac{1}{2}$ if $\lceil \kappa \cdot n \rceil \leq Zero(\{x_1, \ldots, x_n\}) < n$ and $f^\kappa(x_1, \ldots, x_n) = 1$ otherwise, where $Zero(\{x_1, \ldots, x_m\})$ is the number of zeros in $\{x_1, \ldots, x_n\}$.

Definition 2. *Let Σ be a signature, τ a type and $\Pi = \{\Xi_1, \ldots, \Xi_n\}$ a type group. Given a distance function d and an aggregation function f, $\lambda_{d,f}$ between τ and Π is defined as $\lambda_{d,f}(\tau, \Pi) = f(\{d(\tau, \Xi_1), \ldots, d(\tau, \Xi_n)\})$. Furthermore, τ is called df-minimal (for short, minimal) w.r.t. Π if for any type $\tau' \in T_\Sigma$, $\lambda_{d,f}(\tau, \Pi) \leq \lambda_{d,f}(\tau', \Pi)$.*

We use $\Lambda_{d,f}(\Pi, \Xi)$ to denote a set of all df-minimal types w.r.t. Π in Ξ.

Proposition 1. *Let Σ be a finite signature and $\Pi = \{\Xi_1, \ldots, \Xi_n\}$ $(n \geq 1)$ a type group over Σ. If Ξ_i For any distance function d and any aggregation function f, we have (1) $\Lambda_{d,f}(\Pi, T_\Sigma) \neq \emptyset$ and (2) If $\cap \Pi \neq \emptyset$ then $\Lambda_{d,f}(\Pi, T_\Sigma) = \cap \Pi$.*

The first statement guarantees that every type group has always at least minimal type if this type group contains a non-empty type set and the second shows that each type belong to all members of a type group is exactly a minimal type.

Let Σ be a signature and $\mathcal{T} = \{\psi_1, \ldots, \psi_n\}$ a TBox over Σ. Each axiom ψ_i is of the form $C_i \sqsubseteq D_i$ $(1 \leq i \leq n)$ where C_i, D_i $(1 \leq i \leq n)$ are concepts. We simply write $\Pi_\Sigma(\mathcal{T})$ as $\Pi(\mathcal{T})$ if $\Sigma = Sig(\mathcal{T})$.

Corollary 1. *Let Σ be a finite signature and $\mathcal{T}$ a TBox over Σ. For any distance function d and any aggregation function f, we have (1) $\Lambda_{d,f}(\Pi_\Sigma(\mathcal{T}), T_\Sigma) \neq \emptyset$; and (2) If $\mathcal{T}$ is consistent then $\Lambda_{d,f}(\Pi_\Sigma(\mathcal{T}), T_\Sigma) = \cap \Pi_\Sigma(\mathcal{T})$.*

The above second item is no longer true if a TBox $\mathcal{T}$ is not consistent.

Example 1. Let $\mathcal{T} = \{\top \sqsubseteq A, A \sqsubseteq \exists P, \exists P \sqsubseteq \bot\}$ and $\Sigma = Sig(\mathcal{T})$. So $\Sigma = \{A, P\}$ and $\mathcal{T}$ is inconsistent. $\mathcal{T}$ has eight possible types: $\tau_{11} = \{\}$, $\tau_{12} = \{\exists P^-\}$, $\tau_{21} = \{\exists P\}$, $\tau_{22} = \{\exists P, \exists P^-\}$, $\tau_{31} = \{A\}$, $\tau_{32} = \{A, \exists P^-\}$, $\tau_{41} = \{A, \exists P\}$ and $\tau_{41} = \{A, \exists P, \exists P^-\}$. Thus, we have $\Lambda_{d^H, f^s}(\Pi(\mathcal{T}), T_\Sigma) = \{\tau_{11}, \tau_{12}, \tau_{31}, \tau_{32}, \tau_{41}, \tau_{42}\}$ while $\cap \Pi(\mathcal{T}) = \emptyset$.

Unfortunately, $\Lambda_{d,f}(\Pi(\mathcal{T}), T_\Sigma)$ does not always satisfy the role coherence as the following example shows.

Example 2. Let $\mathcal{T} = \{\top \sqsubseteq A \sqcap \exists P, \exists P^- \sqsubseteq \bot\}$ and $\Sigma = Sig(\mathcal{T})$. If d is the Hamming distance function and f is the summation function, then $\Lambda_{d^H, f^s}(\Pi(\mathcal{T}), T_\Sigma) = \{\{A, \exists P\}\}$. Note that $\exists P^- \notin \cup \Lambda_{d^H, f^s}(\Pi(\mathcal{T}), T_\Sigma)$.

The reason that the role coherence might be absent in $\Lambda_{d,f}(\Pi(\mathcal{T}), T_\Sigma)$ is that $\exists P$ and $\exists P^-$ are taken as two independent concepts so that the relation of satisfiability between $\exists P$ and $\exists P^-$ cannot be captured when minimal types are computed [24]. To construct a model type set from a random type set Ξ, we introduce an iterative operator $\mu_{d,f}(\Xi)$ and its fixpoint.

Given an arbitrary type set Ξ, if it is not a model type set of any TBox, there are two possible options to recovery the role coherence: removing and adding. For instance, if $\tau \in \Xi$ such that $\exists R \in \tau$ and $\exists R^- \notin \cup \Xi$ for some role R, then we can either remove τ from Ξ or add a new type τ such that $\exists R^- \in \tau$ in to

Ξ. In Example 2, if we remove the type $\{A, \exists P\}$, then $\Lambda_{d^H, f^s}(\Pi(\mathcal{T}), \mathcal{T}_\Sigma)$ will be empty, which is not desirable. In other words, the removing approach could cause the empty type set where the reasoning becomes trivial. So we will extend the type violating the role coherence. Consider Example 2 again, there are three possible types $\tau_1 = \{\exists P^-\}, \tau_2 = \{A, \exists P^-\}$ and $\tau_3 = \{A, \exists P, \exists P^-\}$ such that $\exists P^- \in \tau_i$ $(i = 1, 2, 3)$ where $\lambda_{d^H, f^s}(\tau_1, \Pi(\mathcal{T})) = 3$, $\lambda_{d^H, f^s}(\tau_2, \Pi(\mathcal{T})) = 2$ and $\lambda_{d^H, f^s}(\tau_3, \Pi(\mathcal{T})) = 1$. So we can pick τ_3 as the desired minimal type. Furthermore, this extension is an iterative process since newly added types possibly contains new role names and role incoherence is not yet satisfied at every step. To construct a model type set from a random type set Ξ, we introduce an iterative operator $\mu_{d,f}(\Xi)$ and its fixpoint.

Formally, let Σ be a finite signature and Π a type group over Σ. Given a type set Ξ over Σ, let $\mu_{d,f}(\Xi) = \Xi \cup \Xi'$, where $\Xi' \subseteq \mathcal{T}_\Sigma$ and $\Xi' = \{\tau \mid$ for some role R, $\exists R \in \cup \Xi$ and $\exists R^- \notin \cup \Xi$, $\exists R^- \in \tau$ and for any type $\tau' \in \mathcal{T}_\Sigma$, $\exists R^- \in \tau'$ implies $\lambda_{d,f}(\tau, \Pi) \leq \lambda_{d,f}(\tau', \Pi)\}$. We use Ξ^+ to denote the *fixpoint* of $\mu_{d,f}$, i.e., $\Xi^+ = FP(\mu_{d,f})(\Xi)$. For any distance function d, any aggregation function f, and any type set Ξ, we can conclude that Ξ^+ always exists since $\mu_{d,f}$ is inflationary (i.e., $\Xi \subseteq \mu_{d,f}(\Xi)$) and Σ is finite.

Given a signature Σ and a TBox $\mathcal{T}$ over Σ, we say $\Lambda_{d,f}^+(\Pi(\mathcal{T}), \mathcal{T}_\Sigma)$ is the *minimal model type set* of $\mathcal{T}$. Intuitively, a minimal model type set is a set of minimal types with maintaining role coherence. In Example 2, $\Lambda_{d^H, f^s}^+(\Pi(\mathcal{T}), \mathcal{T}_\Sigma)$ $= \Lambda_{d^H, f^s}(\Pi(\mathcal{T}), \mathcal{T}_\Sigma) \cup \{\tau_3\} = \{\{A, \exists P\}, \{A, \exists P, \exists P^-\}\}$.

We show that minimal model type sets meet our motivation.

Proposition 2. *Let Σ be a signature and $\mathcal{T}$ a TBox over Σ. For any distance function d and aggregation function f, we have*

- $\Lambda_{d,f}^+(\Pi_\Sigma(\mathcal{T}), \mathcal{T}_\Sigma) \neq \emptyset$;
- $\Lambda_{d,f}^+(\Pi_\Sigma(\mathcal{T}), \mathcal{T}_\Sigma) = \cap \Pi_\Sigma(\mathcal{T})$, *if $\mathcal{T}$ is coherent;*
- $\exists P \in \cup \Lambda_{d,f}^+(\Pi_\Sigma(\mathcal{T}), \mathcal{T}_\Sigma)$ *iff* $\exists P^- \in \cup \Lambda_{d,f}^+(\Pi_\Sigma(\mathcal{T}), \mathcal{T}_\Sigma)$ *for any $P \in \Sigma_R$.*

In Proposition 2, the first item states that there always exist minimal model types for any non-empty TBox; the second shows that when a TBox is consistent, each minimal model type is exactly a model type; and the third ensures that minimal model type sets always satisfy the role coherence.

Definition 3. *Let Σ be a signature, $\mathcal{T}$ a TBox, and, ϕ an inclusion over Σ. Given a distance function d and an aggregation function f, $\mathcal{T}$ distance-based entails (d-entails) ϕ, denoted by $\mathcal{T} \models_{d,f} \psi$, if $\Lambda_{d,f}^+(\Pi_\Sigma(\mathcal{T}), \mathcal{T}_\Sigma) \subseteq Mod^T(\{\phi\})$.*

In Example 2, $\mathcal{T} \models_{d^H, f^s} \top \sqsubseteq A$.

4   Distance-Based Semantics for Knowledge Bases

Compared with inconsistency of TBoxes, inconsistency occurring in KBs is much more complex. For instance,

Example 3. Let $\mathcal{K} = (\{\exists P^- \sqsubseteq \bot\}, \{\exists P(a)\})$ be a KB and $\Sigma = \{P, a, 1\}$. $\mathcal{K}$ is inconsistent and thus has no model feature.

We first introduce *concept profiles* and then use type distance function to describe how far apart features are. Let Σ be a signature and $\mathcal{A}$ an ABox over Σ. Assume that N_A is a set of all named individuals in $\mathcal{A}$. Let $\mathcal{A}_R = \{P(a, b) \mid P(a, b) \text{ or } P^-(b, a) \in \mathcal{A}\}$. A *concept profile* of a in $\mathcal{A}$, denoted by $\Sigma_C(a)$, is defined as follows:

$$\Sigma_C(a) = \bigcup_{D(a) \in \mathcal{A}} \{D\} \cup \bigcup_{P(a, b_1), \ldots, P(a, b_n) \in \mathcal{A}_R} \{\geq m\, P \mid m \in \Sigma_N, m \leq n\}$$

$$\cup \bigcup_{P(b_1, a), \ldots, P(b_n, a) \in \mathcal{A}_R} \{\geq m\, P^- \mid m \in \Sigma_N, m \leq n\}.$$

Intuitively, a set of concept profiles is a partition of concepts that are realized in that ABox w.r.t. individuals. For instance, let $\Sigma = \{C, D, P, a, b_1, b_2, 1, 2\}$ and $\mathcal{A} = \{C \sqcap D(a), P(a, b_1), P(a, b_2), D(b_1)\}$. Thus $\Sigma_C(a) = \{C \sqcap D, \exists P, \geq 2P\}$, $\Sigma_C(b_1) = \{D, \exists P^-\}$, and $\Sigma_C(b_2) = \{\exists P^-\}$.

Let $\mathcal{K} = (\mathcal{T}, \mathcal{A})$ be a KB. We extend the signature $Sig(K)$ of $\mathcal{K}$ as $Sig^*(\mathcal{K}) = Sig(\mathcal{T}) \cup Sig(\Sigma_C(\mathcal{A}))$ where $\Sigma_C(\mathcal{A}) = \bigcup_{a \in N_A} \Sigma_C(a)$. Indeed, $Sig^*(\mathcal{K})$ is obtained from $Sig(\mathcal{K})$ by adding all possible natural numbers occurring in all concept profiles but not occurring in $\mathcal{K}$. In other words, $Sig^*(\mathcal{K})$ and $Sig(\mathcal{K})$ are no different except Σ_N. In the above example, $Sig(\mathcal{A}) = \{C, D, P, a, b_1, b_2\}$ while $Sig^*(\mathcal{A}) = \{C, D, P, a, b_1, b_2, 1, 2\}$.

Next, we will define the notion of minimal model features.

Definition 4. *Let Σ be a signature and $\mathcal{K} = (\mathcal{T}, \mathcal{A})$ a KB over Σ. Denote $\Pi_\Sigma(a) = \{T_\Sigma(D) \mid D \in \Sigma_C(a)\}$. Given a distance function d and an aggregation function f, a df-minimal model feature of $\mathcal{K}$ is a feature $\mathcal{F} = \langle \Xi, \mathcal{H} \rangle$ satisfying the following four conditions:*

- $\Xi \subseteq \Lambda^+_{d,f}(\Pi_\Sigma(\mathcal{T}), T_\Sigma)$;
- *for each $P \in \Sigma_R$, $\exists P \in \cup\Xi$ iff $\exists P^- \in \cup\Xi$;*
- $\tau \in \Lambda^+_{d,f}(\Pi_\Sigma(a), \Lambda^+_{d,f}(\Pi_\Sigma(\mathcal{T}), T_\Sigma)) \cap \Xi$ *for each $a \in \Sigma_I$ and $\tau(a) \in \mathcal{H}$;*
- *for any role assertion $P(a, b) \in \mathcal{A}_R - \mathcal{H}$, either $\geq n+1\, P(a) \notin \mathcal{H}$ and $P(a, b_1)$, $\ldots, P(a, b_n) \in \mathcal{H}$, or $\geq n+1\, P^-(b) \notin \mathcal{H}$ and $P(a_1, b), \ldots, P(a_n, b) \in \mathcal{H}$.*

Let $Mod^F_{d,f}(\mathcal{K})$ denote the set of df-minimal model features of $\mathcal{K}$.

In Definition 4, a minimal model feature is a feature $\mathcal{F}$ which contains two parts, namely, a type set Ξ and a Herbrand set $\mathcal{H}$. The first condition requires that all types of Ξ are minimal; the second says that Ξ should be a model type set, i.e., it satisfies the property of role coherence; the third guarantees that each type of Ξ satisfying each concept assertion in $\mathcal{H}$ has the minimal distance function to its corresponding concept profile, that is, if a concept assertion $D(a)$ is satisfied by $\mathcal{H}$ then types satisfying D are minimal w.r.t. type group $\Pi_\Sigma(a)$ of concept profile $\Sigma_C(a)$; and the last ensures that $\mathcal{F}$ is consistent by those role assertions conflicting with concept assertions.

Example 4. In *Penguin* KB, we abbreviate *Penguin* to P, *Swallow* to S, *Bird* to B, *Fly* to F, *tweety* to t and *fred* to r. Let $\Sigma = \{P, S, B, F, t, r\}$, $\Sigma_C(t) = \{P, \neg F\}$ and $\Sigma_C(r) = \{S\}$. We have $\Lambda^+_{d^H, f^s}(\Pi_\Sigma(T), T_\Sigma) = \{\tau_1, \tau_2, \tau_4, \tau_8, \tau_{12}, \tau_{16}\}$. Here $\tau_1 = \{\}$, $\tau_2 = \{F\}$, $\tau_4 = \{B, F\}, \tau_8 = \{S, B, F\}$, $\tau_{12} = \{P, B, F\}$, and $\tau_{16} = \{P, S, B, F\}$. All of whose distance is 0. We have $\Lambda^+_{d^H, f^s}(\Pi_\Sigma(t), \Lambda^+_{d^H, f^s}(\Pi_\Sigma(T), T_\Sigma)) = \{\tau_1, \tau_{12}, \tau_{16}\}$ and $\Lambda^+_{d^H, f^s}(\Pi_\Sigma(r), \Lambda^+_{d^H, f^s}(\Pi_\Sigma(T), T_\Sigma)) = \{\tau_8, \tau_{16}\}$. All types in $\Lambda^+_{d^H, f^s}(\Pi_\Sigma(t), T_\Sigma)$ have distance equal to 1 while all types in $\Lambda^+_{d^H, f^s}(\Pi_\Sigma(r), T_\Sigma)$ have distance equal to 0. Thus, $Mod^F_{d, f}(\mathcal{K}) = \{\langle \Xi, \tau(t) \cup \tau'(r)\rangle \mid \tau \in \{\tau_1, \tau_{12}, \tau_{16}\}$, $\tau' \in \{\tau_8, \tau_{16}\}, \{\tau, \tau'\} \subseteq \Xi$ and $\Xi \subseteq \{\tau_1, \tau_8, \tau_{12}, \tau_{16}\}\}$.

We find that minimal model features can reach our aim.

Proposition 3. *Let Σ be a signature and $\mathcal{K}$ a KB over Σ. For any distance function d and any aggregation function f, we have*

- *$Mod^F_{d, f}(\mathcal{K}) \neq \emptyset$;*
- *$Mod^F_{d, f}(\mathcal{K}) = Mod^F(\mathcal{K})$, if $\mathcal{K}$ is consistent.*

An expected result is that the second statement of Proposition 3 does not necessarily hold if $\mathcal{K}$ is inconsistent. For instance, in Example 3, $Mod^F_{d, f}(\mathcal{K}) = \{\mathcal{F}_1, \mathcal{F}_2\}$ where $\mathcal{F}_1 = \langle \{\exists P\}, \{\exists P(a)\}\rangle$ and $\mathcal{F}_2 = \langle \{\exists P, \exists P^-\}, \{\exists P(a), \exists P^-(a)\}\rangle$ while $Mod^F(\mathcal{K}) = \emptyset$.

Now, based on minimal model features, we are ready to define the *distance-based entailment* for KBs, written $\models_{d, f}$, under which meaningful information can be entailed from an inconsistent KB.

Definition 5. *Let Σ be a signature, $\mathcal{K}$ a KB, and, ϕ an axiom over Σ. Given a distance function d and an aggregation function f, $\mathcal{K}$ distance-based entails (d-entails) ϕ, still denoted by $\mathcal{K} \models_{d, f} \phi$, if $Mod^F_{d, f}(\mathcal{K}) \subseteq Mod^F(\{\phi\})$.*

Distance-based entailment brings a new semantics (called *distance-based semantics*) for inconsistent KBs by weakening classical entailment. It is not hard to see that no contradiction can be entailed in this semantics. For instance, in *Penguin* KB, $\neg Fly \sqcap Fly(tweety)$ cannot be entailed but $\neg Fly \sqcup Fly(tweety)$ can under our new semantics.

In the rest of this section, we exemplify that the distance-based semantics is suitable for reasoning with inconsistent KBs.

Consequences are intuitive and reasonable under the distance-based semantics. In *Penguin* KB, $\mathcal{K} \models_{d^H, f^s} Fly(fred)$ while $\mathcal{K} \not\models_{d^H, f^s} Penguin(tweety)$ and $\mathcal{K} \not\models_{d^H, f^s} Fly(tweety)$. We further analyze those conclusions under distance-based semantics. The inconsistency of $\mathcal{K}$ is caused by statement about *tweety*. On the one hand, *tweety* is a penguin which cannot fly, i.e., $\neg Fly(tweety)$. On the other hand, a penguin is a bird which can fly, i.e., $Fly(tweety)$. Moreover, there exists no more argument for either $Penguin(tweety)$ or $Fly(tweety)$. In this sense, neither $Penguin(tweety)$ nor $Fly(tweety)$ can be entailed under distance-based semantics. However, the statement about *fred* in $\mathcal{K}$ contains no conflict. Thus $Fly(fred)$ can be entailed under distance-based semantics. Additionally, let us consider a simple example: let $\mathcal{A} = \{A(a), \neg A(a), B(b)\}$. We can conclude that $\mathcal{A} \models_{d^H, f^s} B(b)$ while neither $\mathcal{A} \not\models_{d^H, f^s} A(a)$ nor $\mathcal{A} \not\models_{d^H, f^s} \neg A(a)$.

In general, different result for a KB would be brought by selecting different distance function and different aggregation.

Example 5. Let $\mathcal{A} = \{A(a), \neg A \sqcap \exists P(a), \neg\exists P(a)\}$ be an inconsistent ABox and $\Sigma = \{A, P, a\}$. Thus $\mathcal{A} \models_{d^H, f^m} \neg A \sqcup \exists P(a)$ while $\mathcal{A} \not\models_{d^D, f^m} \neg A \sqcup \exists P(a)$.

For instance, in Example 3, $\mathcal{A} \models_{d^H, f^{\frac{1}{2}}} A(a)$ while $\mathcal{A} \not\models_{d^H, f^s} A(a)$.

5   Properties of Distance-Based Semantics

In this section, we present some useful properties of the distance-based semantics.

If $\mathcal{K}$ is inconsistent and there exists an axiom ϕ such that $\mathcal{K} \not\models_p \phi$ where $\models_p$ is an entailment relation, then we say $\models_p$ is *paraconsistent*. It is well known that the classical entailment $\models$ is not paraconsistent. We reconsider Example 3 and we have $\mathcal{K} \models_{d^H, f^s} \exists P^- \sqsubseteq \bot$ while $\mathcal{K} \not\models_{d^H, f^s} \exists P(a)$.

The following result shows that the distance-based entailment is paraconsistent.

Proposition 4. *For any distance function d and any aggregation function f, $\models_{d,f}$ is paraconsistent.*

Most existing semantics for paraconsistent reasoning in DLs are much weaker than the classical semantics in this sense that there exists a consistent KB $\mathcal{K}$ and an axiom ϕ such that $\mathcal{K} \models \phi$ (also called *consistency preservation*) but ϕ is not entailed by $\mathcal{K}$ under the paraconsistent semantics. The following result shows that the distance-based semantics does not have such shortcoming.

We can conclude a result directly following Proposition 3.

Proposition 5. *Let Σ be a signature, $\mathcal{K}$ a KB, and, ϕ an axiom over Σ. For any distance function d and any aggregation function f, if $\mathcal{K}$ is consistent then we can conclude that $\mathcal{K} \models_{d,f} \phi$ iff $\mathcal{K} \models \phi$.*

Under the classical semantics, a property that $\mathcal{K} \models \psi$ iff $\mathcal{T} \models \psi$ for any inclusion ψ is called *TBox-preservation* where the problem of subsumption checking is irrelevant to ABoxes. Our distance-based semantics satisfies such a property.

Proposition 6. *Let Σ be a signature, $\mathcal{K} = (\mathcal{T}, \mathcal{A})$ a KB, and, ψ an inclusion over Σ. For any distance function d and any aggregation function f, $\mathcal{K} \models_{d,f} \psi$ iff $\mathcal{T} \models_{d,f} \psi$.*

By Proposition 6, TBox preservation property means that if the TBox by itself is consistent, then it will be entailed (and hence preference is given to preserving TBox statements over ABox statements), such as the same treatment in [13]. This is different from some other approaches to inconsistency-handling in DLs, where the TBox and ABox are equally treated, or the ABox is given preference such as [15,21,23].

The closure w.r.t. $\models_{d,f}$ of an arbitrary KB is always consistent.

Proposition 7. *Let Σ be a signature and $\mathcal{K} = (\mathcal{T}, \mathcal{A})$ a KB over Σ. For any distance function d and any aggregation function f, let $Cn_{d,f}(\mathcal{T}) = \{\psi$ is an inclusion $\mid \mathcal{T} \models_{d,f} \psi\}$ and $Cn_{d,f}^{\mathcal{T}}(\mathcal{A}) = \{\varphi$ is an assertion $\mid (\mathcal{T}, \mathcal{A}) \models_{d,f} \varphi\}$. We conclude that both $Cn_{d,f}(\mathcal{T})$ and $Cn_{d,f}^{\mathcal{T}}(\mathcal{A})$ are consistent.*

Proposition 7 provides a theoretical foundation of applying our approach to *inconsistency-tolerant conjunctive query answering* [3].

Let Σ be a signature. A distance function d is Σ-*unbiased*, if for any Σ-concept C and any two Σ-types τ_1, τ_2, $B \in \tau_1$ iff $B \in \tau_2$ for any basic concept B occurring in C implies $d(\tau_1, T_\Sigma(C)) = d(\tau_2, T_\Sigma(C))$. The Hamming distance function and the drastic distance function are unbiased.

Let us consider a distance function $d^\cup$ defined as follows: for any two sets S_1, S_2, $d^\cup(S_1, S_2) = 0$ if $S_1 = S_2$; and $d^\cup(S_1, S_2) = 1 + |S_1 \cup S_2|$. It clearly concludes that $d^\cup(S_1, S_2) = 0$ iff $S_1 = S_2$ and $d^\cup(S_1, S_2) = d^\cup(S_2, S_1)$. Thus $d^\cup$ is a distance function. Let $\Sigma = \{A_1, A_2, A_3, A_4\}$ and $C = A_1 \sqcap A_2$. For each type $\tau \in T_\Sigma(C)$, $\{A_1, A_2\} \subseteq \tau$. Let $\tau_1 = \{A_1, A_2\}$ and $\tau_2 = \{A_1, A_2, A_3, A_4\}$. Thus $d(\tau_1, T_\Sigma(C)) = 5$ and $d(\tau_2, T_\Sigma(C)) = 7$. Then $d^\cup$ is not unbiased.

Unbiasedness will bring a good property of relevance in reasoning since the unbiased distance is not sensitive to those irrelevant basic concepts.

Proposition 8. *Let Σ be a signature, $\mathcal{K}$ a KB, and, ϕ a non-tautology over Σ. If d is an unbiased distance function and $Sig(\mathcal{K}) \cap Sig(\{\phi\}) = \emptyset$ then for any aggregation function f, $\mathcal{K} \not\models_{d,f} \phi$.*

An entailment relation $\models_m$ is *monotonic* if $\mathcal{K}' \models_m \phi$ implies $\mathcal{K} \models_m \phi$ for any KB $\mathcal{K}' \subseteq \mathcal{K}$; and *nonmonotonic* otherwise. Another characteristic property of $\models_{d,f}$ is its non-monotonic nature.

Proposition 9. *For any distance function d and any aggregation function f, $\models_{d,f}$ is non-monotonic.*

A relation $\mid\approx$ is *cautious* if it satisfies:

- (*cautious reflexivity*) If $\mathcal{K} = \mathcal{K}' \oplus \mathcal{K}''$ and $\mathcal{K}'$ is consistent, then $\mathcal{K}\mid\approx\varphi$ for all axiom $\varphi \in \mathcal{K}'$;
- (*cautious monotonicity*) If $\mathcal{K}\mid\approx\varphi$ and $\mathcal{K}\mid\approx\psi$, then $\mathcal{K} \cup \{\varphi\}\mid\approx\psi$;
- (*cautious cut*) If $\mathcal{K}\mid\approx\varphi$ and $\mathcal{K} \cup \{\varphi\}\mid\approx\psi$ then $\mathcal{K}\mid\approx\psi$.

Proposition 10. *For any distance function d and any monotonic hereditary aggregation function f, $\models_{d,f}$ is cautious.*

Example 6. Consider an ABox $\mathcal{A} = \{HasWife(Mike, Rose), HasWife(Mike, Mary), \neg(\geq 2\,HasWife)(Mike)\}$. Let $\Sigma = \{HasWife, Mike, Mary, Rose, 1, 2\}$. The first statement claims that *Mike* has at most one wife. Moreover, we are informed that *Mike* has two wives *Rose* and *Mary*. We conclude that $\mathcal{A}$ is inconsistent and $\mathcal{A} \models_{d^H, f^s} \geq 1\,HasWife(Mike)$. Moreover, we can also conclude that $\mathcal{A} \not\models_{d^H, f^s} HasWife(Mike, Rose)$, and $\mathcal{A} \not\models_{d^H, f^s} HasWife(Mike, Mary)$. Intuitively, *Mike* has a wife while we don't know whether his wife is *Rose* or *Mary* under our distance-based semantics.

6   Discussions

Existing model-centered approaches for inconsistency handling are usually based on various forms of inconsistency-tolerant semantics, such as four-valued description logics [14,15], quasi-classical description logics [23], the argumentation-based semantics for description logics [10,21], and the MKNF-based semantics for description logics [7]. Compared to them, our distance-based semantics works on classical interpretations but still can draw more useful and reasonable logical consequences. Different from [7] which introduces a weak negation **not** to tolerate inconsistency, our approach does not change the syntax of DLs. Different from syntax-based paraconsistent approaches taking some consistent subsets as substitutes of KBs in reasoning [19,8,9,16,6,18], our approach can satisfy the closure consistency.

There are some model-based approaches presented in [17,13]. Compared with it directly working on models, our approach works on types and features which take advantage of finiteness. Moreover, we construct those models which are closer to a KB according to some distance functions and aggregation functions when there exists no model in an inconsistent KB. A distance-based approach is proposed to measure inconsistency of TBoxes [15]. However, this approach might be difficult to do so because of infinite number of models of DL KBs since it is based on the distance between models. As a future work, we employ our distance-based technique to measure inconsistency of KBs. A simpler semantic characterisation called type semantics has been developed for DL-Lite in [24]. We plan to study the issue of handling DL paraconsistency using the type semantics.

Acknowledgments. This work was supported by the program of the National High-tech R&D Program of China (863 Program) under 2013AA013204 and the National Natural Science Foundation of China (NSFC) under 61502336, 61373035.

References

1. Arieli, O.: Distance-based paraconsistent logics. Int. J. Approx. Reasoning **48**(3), 766–783 (2008)
2. Artale, A., Calvanese, D., Kontchakov, R., Zakharyschev, M.: The DL-Lite family and relations. J. of Artif. Intell. Research **36**, 1–69 (2009)
3. Bienvenum, M., Rosati, R.: Tractable approximations of consistent query answering for robust ontology-based data access. In: Proc. of IJCAI (2013)
4. Cuenca Grau, B., Horrocks, I., Motik, B., Parsia, B., Patel-Schneider, P.F., Sattler, U.: OWL 2: The next step for OWL. J. Web Sem. **6**(4), 309–322 (2008)
5. Dolby, J., et al.: Scalable cleanup of information extraction data using ontologies. In: Aberer, K., et al. (eds.) ASWC 2007 and ISWC 2007. LNCS, vol. 4825, pp. 100–113. Springer, Heidelberg (2007)
6. Du, J., Sheng, Y.: Computing minimum cost diagnoses to repair populated DL-based ontologies. In: Proc. of WWW, pp. 565–574 (2008)
7. Huang, S., Li, Q., Hitzler, P.: Reasoning with inconsistencies in hybrid MKNF knowledge bases. Logic Journal of the IGPL **21**(2), 263–290 (2013)

8. Huang, Z., van Harmelen, F., ten Teije, A.: Reasoning with inconsistent ontologies. In: Proc. of IJCAI, pp. 454–459 (2005)

9. Kalyanpur, A., Parsia, B., Sirin, E., Cuenca-Grau, B.: Repairing unsatisfiable concepts in OWL ontologies. In: Sure, Y., Domingue, J. (eds.) ESWC 2006. LNCS, vol. 4011, pp. 170–184. Springer, Heidelberg (2006)

10. Kamide, N.: Embedding-based approaches to paraconsistent and temporal description logics. J. Log. Comput. **22**(5), 1097–1124 (2012)

11. Konieczny, S., Pino-Pérez, R.: On the logic of merging. In: Proc. of KR, pp. 488–498 (1998)

12. Kontchakov, R., Wolter, F., Zakharyaschev, M.: Can you tell the difference between DL-Lite ontologies? In: Proc. of KR, pp. 285–295 (2008)

13. Lembo, D., Lenzerini, M., Rosati, R., Ruzzi, M., Savo, D.F.: Inconsistency-tolerant semantics for description logics. In: Hitzler, P., Lukasiewicz, T. (eds.) Web Reasoning and Rule Systems. LNCS, vol. 6333, pp. 103–117. Springer, Heidelberg (2010)

14. Ma, Y., Hitzler, P.: Paraconsistent reasoning for OWL 2. In: Polleres, A., Swift, T. (eds.) Web Reasoning and Rule Systems. LNCS, pp. 197–211. Springer, Heidelberg (2009)

15. Ma, Y., Hitzler, P.: Distance-based measures of inconsistency and incoherency for description logics. In: Proc. of DL (2010)

16. Meyer, T.A., Lee, K., Booth, R., Pan, J.Z.: Finding maximally satisfiable terminologies for the description logic ALC. In: Proc. of AAAI, pp. 269–274 (2006)

17. Qi, G., Du, J.: Model-based revision operators for terminologies in description logics. In: Proc. of IJCAI, pp. 891–897 (2009)

18. Rosati, R., Ruzzi, M., Graziosi, M., Masotti, G.: Evaluation of techniques for inconsistency handling in OWL 2 QL ontologies. In: Cudré-Mauroux, P., et al. (eds.) The Semantic Web – ISWC 2012. LNCS, vol. 7650, pp. 337–349. Springer, Heidelberg (2012)

19. Schlobach, S., Cornet, R.: Non-standard reasoning services for the debugging of description logic terminologies. In: Proc.of IJCAI, pp. 355–362 (2003)

20. Wang, Z., Wang, K., Topor, R.W.: A new approach to knowledge base revision in DL-Lite. In: Proc. of AAAI, pp. 369–374 (2010)

21. Zhang, X., Lin, Z.: An argumentation framework for description logic ontology reasoning and management. J. Intell. Inf. Syst. **40**(3), 375–403 (2013)

22. Zhang, X., Wang, K., Wang, Z., Ma, Y., Qi, G., A Distance-based paraconsistent semantics for DL-Lite (2013). CoRR abs/1301.2137

23. Zhang, X., Xiao, G., Lin, Z., Van den Bussche, J.: Inconsistency-tolerant reasoning with OWL DL. Int. J. Approx. Reasoning **55**(2), 557–584 (2014)

24. Zhuang, Z., Wang, Z., Wang, K., Qi, G.: Contraction and revision over DL-Lite TBoxes. In: Proc. of AAAI, pp. 1149–1156 (2014)

Tractable Computation of Representative ABox Repairs in Description Logic Ontologies

Jianfeng Du[1]([✉]) and Guilin Qi[2]

[1] Guangdong University of Foreign Studies, Guangzhou 510006, China
jfdu@gdufs.edu.cn
[2] Southeast University, Nanjing 211189, China

Abstract. Computing all ABox repairs is a key to cautious or brave reasoning over inconsistent description logic (DL) ontologies. However, the number of ABox repairs can be exponential in the number of assertions in the ABox even for very lightweight DLs. Hence we propose to compute a minimal representative set of ABox repairs. A set of ABox repairs is representative, if every assertion occurring in at least one ABox repair also occurs in at least one element of this set, while every assertion occurring in all ABox repairs occurs in all elements of this set. Cautious or brave reasoning then can be approximated by standard reasoning over a minimal representative set other than the complete set of ABox repairs. However, computing a minimal representative set of ABox repairs is still intractable in general. To guarantee the tractability in data complexity for computing a minimal representative set, we focus on a class of DL ontologies called the first-order rewritable class. We propose a tractable method for computing a minimal representative set of ABox repairs in an inconsistent first-order rewritable ontology. Experimental results demonstrate the high efficiency and scalability of the proposed method.

1 Introduction

Description logics (DLs) [1] are popular knowledge representation languages underpinning the Web Ontology Language (OWL). A DL ontology consists of a TBox and an ABox, where the TBox describes relations between concepts and roles, and the ABox describes instances of concepts and roles. The semantics of DLs is inherited from the first-order logic, thus inconsistency can incur in a DL ontology. Standard reasoning over an inconsistent DL ontology results in anything and is meaningless. In some popular applications such as data integration, the TBox of an inconsistent ontology is consistent and the inconsistency is caused by logical conflicts in the ABox w.r.t. the TBox. To deal with this situation, two general approaches called *cautious reasoning* and *brave reasoning* can often be employed. Both of them have widely been used in the context of logic programming [7] and can be adapted to DLs to define meaningful consequences in an inconsistent DL ontology. Cautious reasoning defines a meaningful consequence of an inconsistent DL ontology as a formula entailed by the union of the TBox and every ABox repair of the ontology, where an *ABox repair* is a maximal

© Springer International Publishing Switzerland 2015
S. Zhang et al. (Eds.): KSEM 2015, LNAI 9403, pp. 28–39, 2015.
DOI: 10.1007/978-3-319-25159-2_3

subset of the ABox that is consistent with the TBox. This approach is said to be *cautious* since a meaningful consequence is required to hold in all ABox repairs. Brave reasoning defines a meaningful consequence of an inconsistent DL ontology as a formula entailed by the union of the TBox and some ABox repair of the ontology. This approach is said to be *brave* since a meaningful consequence is only required to hold in at least one ABox repair.

Computing all ABox repairs is a key to cautious or brave reasoning in a DL ontology because a meaningful consequence is defined by the complete set of ABox repairs. However, this computation is often infeasible since the number of ABox repairs can be exponential in the number of assertions in the ABox even for DL-Lite$_{core}$, the least expressive DL in the lightweight DL-Lite family [4], as shown in the following example. Let $\mathcal{O}$ be a DL-Lite$_{core}$ ontology with the TBox {Man $\sqsubseteq$ ¬Woman} and the ABox {Man(a_i), Woman(a_i) | $1 \le i \le n$}, where a_i is an individual and $n \ge 1$. Then there are 2^n ABox repairs of $\mathcal{O}$, each of which is of the form {$A_i(a_i)$ | $1 \le i \le n$} where A_i is Man or Woman. Moreover, unless P=NP, it is impossible to perform cautious or brave reasoning in PTIME even in terms of *data complexity*, the complexity measured in the size of the ABox only. This is due to the following complexity results. First, cautious or brave reasoning in a datalog program with constraints is already NP-hard [7]. Second, cautious reasoning is coNP-complete in data complexity even for DL-Lite$_{core}$ [11].

The above results suggest that both cautious reasoning and brave reasoning need to be approximated for practical use. A natural idea for the approximation is to consider some but not all ABox repairs. In this line the notion of minimal representative set of explanations [14] can be adapted. A minimal representative set of ABox repairs can be defined as a minimal set of ABox repairs, such that every assertion occurring in at least one ABox repair also occurs in at least one element of this set, and that every assertion occurring in all ABox repairs also occurs in all elements of this set. It can be seen from [14] that the cardinality of an arbitrary minimal representative set of ABox repairs is not larger than the number of assertions in the ABox. Moreover, it can be shown that the replacement of the set of ABox repairs with a minimal representative set of ABox repairs in either cautious or brave reasoning does not impact the result for determining whether an assertion in the ABox is a meaningful consequence.

Based on the above properties, it is reasonable to approximate cautious or brave reasoning by a minimal representative set of ABox repairs. However, it can be seen from [14] that computing a minimal representative set of ABox repairs is NP-hard even when the TBox contains only axioms that are translated to constraints. Fortunately, this NP-hardness result does not tell that there is no tractable (i.e. PTIME) method for certain DLs in data complexity. To develop a tractable method, we focus on a class of DL ontologies, called *first-order rewritable* class [6], which guarantees that the number of minimal subsets of the ABox that are inconsistent with the TBox (called *minimal inconsistent ABox subsets* or simply *MIASes*) is at most polynomial in the number of assertions in the ABox. This class is rather expressive, sufficient for many real-life applications such as the ontology-based data access (OBDA) systems. We develop an efficient PTIME algorithm for computing a minimal representative set of ABox repairs from the set of MIASes. By combining it with a PTIME (data complexity) algorithm for computing all MIASes in first-order rewritable ontologies [6], we obtain a tractable method for computing a minimal representative set of ABox repairs in an inconsistent first-order rewritable ontology.

We conduct experiments on large inconsistent first-order rewritable ontologies that have up to tens of millions of assertions. Experimental results show that the proposed method is highly efficient and scalable. Moreover, every minimal representative set of ABox repairs computed in our experiments has a rather small cardinality (at most 115), implying that the proposed method can provide a rather efficient approximation of cautious or brave reasoning over inconsistent first-order rewritable ontologies. All proofs are available at http://www. dataminingcenter.net/jfdu/KSEM15-full.pdf.

2   Related Work

ABox repairs have been widely used in reasoning over inconsistent DL ontologies. In [12] the authors study a variant of cautious reasoning defined by preferred ABox repairs, where the preference is given by priority levels of assertions. They propose a method for computing a disjunctive DL knowledge base (DKB) from a given DL ontology so that cautious reasoning can be performed over the DKB. In [11] the authors propose the AR semantics and the IAR semantics for reasoning under inconsistency. The AR semantics coincides with the semantics of cautious reasoning. The IAR semantics defines a meaningful consequence as a formula entailed by the TBox and the intersection of all ABox repairs. The authors also study the complexity of these two semantics in DL-Lite$_{\mathcal{A}}$ ontologies. In [5] a variant of cautious reasoning defined by weighted-sum-maximal ABox repairs is studied; accordingly, a practical method is proposed for this variant of cautious reasoning, based on calling off-the-shelf SAT solvers. In [2] the authors extend the main results of [11] by studying the complexity of several variants of cautious reasoning defined by preferred ABox repairs in DL-Lite$_{\mathcal{R}}$ ontologies, where the preference can be given by cardinalities, weights or priority levels. They get a negative result that all the considering variants of cautious reasoning cannot be performed in PTIME in data complexity. In contrast, our proposed method for computing a minimal representative set of ABox repairs provides a PTIME (data complexity) variant of cautious or brave reasoning for DL-Lite$_X$ or DL-Lite$_{X,\sqcap}$ ontologies, where $X \in \{\mathcal{F}, \mathcal{R}, \mathcal{A}\}$. Moreover, the output of our method can be directly used in the IAR semantics according to Definition 1.

3   Preliminaries

We only present necessary background for DLs and refer the reader to the DL handbook [1] for more details. A DL ontology consists of a TBox and an ABox, where the TBox is a finite set of axioms on relations between concepts and roles, and the ABox is a finite set of axioms (also called *assertions*) declaring instances of concepts and roles. We treat a DL ontology (a TBox or an ABox) as a set of axioms. In this work we only consider *normalized* ABoxes that have only *basic assertions*, namely concept assertions of the form $A(a)$ and role assertions of the form $r(a, b)$, where A is a concept name and r is a role name. Other concept assertions and role assertions can be normalized to basic ones in a standard way.

The semantics of DLs is inherited from the classical first-order semantics. A DL ontology $\mathcal{O}$ is said to be *consistent* if it has at least one model, otherwise *inconsistent*. A set S of axioms is said to be *consistent with* another set S' of axioms if $S \cup S'$ is consistent. An assertion α is said to be *entailed by* a DL ontology $\mathcal{O}$, denoted by $\mathcal{O} \models \alpha$, if α is satisfied by all models of $\mathcal{O}$.

Given a DL ontology $\mathcal{O}$ with TBox $\mathcal{T}$ and ABox $\mathcal{A}$, where $\mathcal{T}$ is consistent, we call a subset R of $\mathcal{A}$ an *ABox repair* of $\mathcal{O}$ if $\mathcal{T} \cup R$ is consistent and $\mathcal{T} \cup R'$ is inconsistent for all subsets R' of $\mathcal{O}$ such that $R \subset R'$; we call a subset S of $\mathcal{A}$ a *minimal inconsistent ABox subset (MIAS)* of $\mathcal{O}$ if $\mathcal{T} \cup S$ is inconsistent and $\mathcal{T} \cup S'$ is consistent for all proper subsets S' of S. By $\mathsf{AR}(\mathcal{O})$ we denote the set of ABox repairs of $\mathcal{O}$ and by $\mathsf{MIAS}(\mathcal{O})$, the set of MIASes of $\mathcal{O}$. Cautious reasoning defines an assertion α as a meaningful consequence of an inconsistent DL ontology $\mathcal{O}$, denoted by $\mathcal{O} \models_c \alpha$, if $\mathcal{T} \cup R \models \alpha$ for all ABox repairs $R \in \mathsf{AR}(\mathcal{O})$. Correspondingly, brave reasoning defines α as a meaningful consequence of $\mathcal{O}$, denoted by $\mathcal{O} \models_b \alpha$, if $\mathcal{T} \cup R \models \alpha$ for at least one ABox repair $R \in \mathsf{AR}(\mathcal{O})$.

Since our proposed method is based on the rewriting of Boolean conjunctive queries (BCQs), in the following we also introduce BCQs and the datalog$^\pm$ [3] language which supports query rewriting.

A *BCQ* $Q(\boldsymbol{x})$ is a formula of the form $\exists \boldsymbol{x}\, \phi(\boldsymbol{x})$, where $\phi(\boldsymbol{x})$ is a conjunction of atoms over concept names, role names, the inequality predicate, and the existentially quantified variables $\boldsymbol{x}$. In this paper a BCQ is written and treated as a set of atoms. For example, the BCQ $\exists x\, A(x) \wedge B(x)$ is written as $\{A(x), B(x)\}$. By $|S|$ we denote the cardinality of a set S. A *substitution* for a first-order entity (such as atom, formula, etc.) E is a mapping from variables in E to individuals or variables; it is *ground* if it maps variables in E to individuals only. A *disjunction* of BCQs is a formula of the form $Q_1 \vee \ldots \vee Q_n$ where $n \geq 1$ and $Q_1, \ldots, Q_n$ are BCQs. We say a disjunction of BCQs Q_D is *entailed by* $\mathcal{O}$, denoted by $\mathcal{O} \models Q_D$, if Q_D is satisfied by all models of $\mathcal{O}$.

Datalog$^\pm$ [3] extends datalog with *existential rules* R of the form $\forall \boldsymbol{x} \forall \boldsymbol{y}\, \phi(\boldsymbol{x}, \boldsymbol{y}) \rightarrow \exists \boldsymbol{z}\, \varphi(\boldsymbol{x}, \boldsymbol{z})$, where $\phi(\boldsymbol{x}, \boldsymbol{y})$ and $\varphi(\boldsymbol{x}, \boldsymbol{z})$ are conjunctions of atoms and $\boldsymbol{x}$, $\boldsymbol{y}$ and $\boldsymbol{z}$ are pairwise disjoint sets of variables. The part of R at left-hand side of $\rightarrow$ is the *body* of R, whereas the part of R at right-hand side of $\rightarrow$ is the *head* of R. An existential rule is called an *equality generating dependency (EGD)* if its head is of the form $x_1 = x_2$ where x_1 and x_2 are different variables appearing in the body of it; called a *constraint* if its head is empty; otherwise, called a *tuple generating dependency (TGD)*. A TGD is said to be *linear* if its body contains a single atom; *multi-linear* if all atoms in its body have the same variables. A linear TGD is also a multi-linear TGD. A datalog$^\pm$ *program* is a finite set of existential rules. Since both datalog$^\pm$ and DLs are fragments of first-order logic, a DL ontology may be translatable to the union of a datalog$^\pm$

program and a normalized ABox. We call such an ontology *datalog$^\pm$-translatable*. Since datalog$^\pm$ works with the *unique name assumption*, this assumption is also adopted in a considering datalog$^\pm$-translatable ontology, which means that all individuals appearing in the ontology are interpreted as different in any model of the ontology.

A set $\mathcal{S}_T$ of TGDs is said to be *first-order rewritable* if for every BCQ Q, there is a finite disjunction of BCQs Q_D such that $\mathcal{S}_T \cup \mathcal{A} \models Q$ if and only if $\mathcal{A} \models Q_D$ for all ABoxes $\mathcal{A}$. It has been shown [3] that a set $\mathcal{S}_T$ of TGDs is first-order rewritable if all TGDs in $\mathcal{S}_T$ are multi-linear. A set $\mathcal{S}_E$ of EGDs is said to be *separable* from a set $\mathcal{S}_T$ of TGDs if the following holds for every ABox $\mathcal{A}$ [3]: if there exists an EGD $\forall \boldsymbol{x}\, \phi(\boldsymbol{x}) \rightarrow x_1 = x_2$ in $\mathcal{S}_E$ and a ground substitution σ for $\boldsymbol{x}$ such that $\mathcal{S}_T \cup \mathcal{A} \models \phi(\boldsymbol{x}\sigma)$ and $x_1\sigma \neq x_2\sigma$, then there is a ground substitution θ for $\boldsymbol{x}$ such that $\mathcal{A} \models \phi(\boldsymbol{x}\theta)$ and $x_1\theta \neq x_2\theta$; otherwise, $\mathcal{S}_T \cup \mathcal{S}_E \cup \mathcal{A} \models Q$ if and only if $\mathcal{S}_T \cup \mathcal{A} \models Q$ for all BCQs Q.

4   Minimal Representative Set of ABox Repairs

As mentioned in Section 1, computing all ABox repairs is a key to cautious or brave reasoning over an inconsistent DL ontology. However, since cautious or brave reasoning is intractable and the number of ABox repairs can be exponential in data complexity, we need to approximate cautious or brave reasoning by considering some but not all ABox repairs. The notion of minimal representative set of explanations, proposed in the context of constraint-based systems [14], sheds light on a promising approximate approach. In [14] an *explanation* is defined as a pair made up of a *relaxation* and its complement set of facts, where a relaxation is a maximal set of facts consistent with the set of constraints. A set of explanations is said to be *representative*, if every fact occurring in at least one relaxation also occurs in at least one element of this set, while every fact occurring in all relaxations also occurs in all elements of this set. By treating ABox repairs as relaxations, we have the corresponding notion on ABox repairs.

Definition 1. *Let $\mathcal{O}$ be an inconsistent DL ontology with TBox $\mathcal{T}$ and ABox $\mathcal{A}$, where $\mathcal{T}$ is consistent. A* representative set $\mathcal{S}$ of ABox repairs *of $\mathcal{O}$ is a subset of $\mathsf{AR}(\mathcal{O})$ such that $\bigcup \mathcal{S} = \bigcup \mathsf{AR}(\mathcal{O})$ and $\bigcap \mathcal{S} = \bigcap \mathsf{AR}(\mathcal{O})$; it is said to be* minimal *if there is no representative set $\mathcal{S}'$ of ABox repairs of $\mathcal{O}$ such that $\mathcal{S}' \subset \mathcal{S}$.*

In the above definition, $\bigcup \mathcal{S} = \bigcup \mathsf{AR}(\mathcal{O})$ amounts to that every assertion occurring in at least one ABox repair of $\mathcal{O}$ also occurs in at least one ABox repair in $\mathcal{S}$, while $\bigcap \mathcal{S} = \bigcap \mathsf{AR}(\mathcal{O})$ amounts to that every assertion occurring in all ABox repairs of $\mathcal{O}$ also occurs in all ABox repairs in $\mathcal{S}$. The following example shows that a minimal representative set of ABox repairs can have a small cardinality even when there are exponentially many ABox repairs in terms of data complexity.

Example 1. Let $\mathcal{O}$ be a DL ontology with TBox $\mathcal{T} = \{A \sqsubseteq B,\ B \sqsubseteq \neg C\}$ and ABox $\mathcal{A} = \{A(a_i), C(a_i) \mid 1 \leq i \leq n\}$ where $n \geq 1$. It is not hard to see that $\mathcal{O}$ is inconsistent, $\mathcal{T}$ is consistent, and $\mathsf{AR}(\mathcal{O})$ consists of 2^n ABox repairs of the form $\{P_i(a_i) \mid 1 \le i \le n\}$ where P_i is either A or C. Consider a set of ABox repairs $\mathcal{S} = \{R_1, R_2\}$, where $R_1 = \{A(a_i) \mid 1 \le i \le n\}$ and $R_2 = \{C(a_i) \mid 1 \le i \le n\}$. We can see that $\bigcup \mathcal{S} = \bigcup \mathsf{AR}(\mathcal{O})$ and $\bigcap \mathcal{S} = \bigcap \mathsf{AR}(\mathcal{O})$, hence $\mathcal{S}$ is a minimal representative set of ABox repairs. Note that $|\mathcal{S}| = 2$ even though $|\mathsf{AR}(\mathcal{O})| = 2^n$, i.e., $|\mathsf{AR}(\mathcal{O})|$ is exponential in $|\mathcal{A}|$.

In what follows, by $\mathcal{O}$ we denote an inconsistent DL ontology with TBox $\mathcal{T}$ and ABox $\mathcal{A}$ where $\mathcal{T}$ is consistent. It can be seen from [14] that an arbitrary minimal representative set of ABox repairs of $\mathcal{O}$ contains at most $|\mathcal{A}|$ ABox repairs. Moreover, cautious or brave reasoning about assertions in the ABox remains sound and complete over an arbitrary minimal representative set of ABox repairs, as shown in the following proposition.

Proposition 1. *Let $\mathcal{S}$ be a minimal representative set of ABox repairs of $\mathcal{O}$. Then, for every assertion $\alpha \in \mathcal{A}$, we have (1) $\mathcal{O} \models_c \alpha$ if and only if $\alpha \in \bigcap \mathcal{S}$, and (2) $\mathcal{O} \models_b \alpha$ if and only if $\alpha \in \bigcup \mathcal{S}$.*

The above results show that it is reasonable to use a minimal representative set of ABox repairs to approximate cautious or brave reasoning. However, the computation of a minimal representative set of ABox repairs is generally hard. According to the NP-hardness result for computing a minimal representative set of explanations [14], we know that computing a minimal representative set of ABox repairs is also NP-hard in *combined complexity*, the complexity measured in both the size of the TBox and the size of the ABox. Surprisingly, we find that, after the set of MIASes is computed, we can compute a minimal representative set of ABox repairs in time polynomial in the size of the set of MIASes. This finding is based on an observation that the complement sets of ABox repairs and MIASes are mutually minimal hitting sets, as shown in the following proposition, where a set H of assertions is called a *hitting set* for a set $\mathcal{S}$ of sets of assertions if $H \cap S \ne \emptyset$ for all $S \in \mathcal{S}$, and H is further said to be *minimal* if none of the proper subsets of H is a hitting set for $\mathcal{S}$.

Proposition 2. $\{\mathcal{A} \setminus R \mid R \in \mathsf{AR}(\mathcal{O})\}$ *is the set of minimal hitting sets for* $\mathsf{MIAS}(\mathcal{O})$. $\mathsf{MIAS}(\mathcal{O})$ *is the set of minimal hitting sets for* $\{\mathcal{A} \setminus R \mid R \in \mathsf{AR}(\mathcal{O})\}$.

By the above proposition, we immediately have the following corollary, which shows a method for computing $\bigcap \mathsf{AR}(\mathcal{O})$ from $\mathsf{MIAS}(\mathcal{O})$.

Corollary 1. $\bigcap \mathsf{AR}(\mathcal{O}) = \mathcal{A} \setminus \bigcup \mathsf{MIAS}(\mathcal{O})$.

The dual relation between $\mathsf{AR}(\mathcal{O})$ and $\mathsf{MIAS}(\mathcal{O})$ also enables a method for computing $\bigcup \mathsf{AR}(\mathcal{O})$ from $\mathsf{MIAS}(\mathcal{O})$, as shown in the following proposition.

Proposition 3. $\bigcup \mathsf{AR}(\mathcal{O}) = \mathcal{A} \setminus \bigcup \{M \in \mathsf{MIAS}(\mathcal{O}) \mid |M| = 1\}$.

By Corollary 1 and Proposition 3, we develop an algorithm (see Algorithm 1) for computing a minimal representative set of ABox repairs of $\mathcal{O}$ from $\mathsf{MIAS}(\mathcal{O})$, where $\mathcal{A}_1$ is the intersection of all complement sets of ABox repairs of $\mathcal{O}$.

Algorithm 1. Computing a minimal representative set of ABox repairs

---

Input: An inconsistent DL ontology $\mathcal{O}$ where MIAS($\mathcal{O}$) has been computed.
Output: A minimal representative set of ABox repairs of $\mathcal{O}$.
1: Let $\mathcal{A}$ be the ABox of $\mathcal{O}$ and $\mathcal{A}_1$ be $\bigcup\{M \in \text{MIAS}(\mathcal{O}) \mid |M| = 1\}$
2: $\mathcal{S}' \leftarrow \emptyset$
3: **for all** $\alpha \in \bigcup \text{MIAS}(\mathcal{O})$ **do**
4:     **if** $\alpha \notin \bigcup_{R \in \mathcal{S}'}(\mathcal{A} \setminus R)$ **then**
5:         Select an element M in MIAS($\mathcal{O}$) such that $\alpha \in M$
6:         $H \leftarrow$ ComputeMinHittingSet($\{M' \setminus M \mid M' \in \text{MIAS}(\mathcal{O}), \alpha \notin M'\}$)
7:         $\mathcal{S}' \leftarrow \mathcal{S}' \cup \{\mathcal{A} \setminus (H \cup \{\alpha\})\}$
8:     **end if**
9: **end for**
10: **for all** $\alpha \in \bigcup \text{MIAS}(\mathcal{O}) \setminus \mathcal{A}_1$ **do**
11:     **if** $\alpha \in \bigcap_{R \in \mathcal{S}'}(\mathcal{A} \setminus R)$ **then**
12:         $H \leftarrow$ ComputeMinHittingSet($\{M \setminus \{\alpha\} \mid M \in \text{MIAS}(\mathcal{O})\}$)
13:         $\mathcal{S}' \leftarrow \mathcal{S}' \cup \{\mathcal{A} \setminus H\}$
14:     **end if**
15: **end for**
16: **repeat**
17:     $\mathcal{S} \leftarrow \mathcal{S}'$
18:     **for all** $R \in \mathcal{S}'$ **do**
19:         **if** $\bigcup_{R' \in \mathcal{S}' \setminus \{R\}}(\mathcal{A} \setminus R') = \bigcup \text{MIAS}(\mathcal{O})$ and $\bigcap_{R' \in \mathcal{S}' \setminus \{R\}}(\mathcal{A} \setminus R') = \mathcal{A}_1$ **then**
20:             $\mathcal{S}' \leftarrow \mathcal{S}' \setminus \{R\}$
21:         **end if**
22:     **end for**
23: **until** $\mathcal{S} = \mathcal{S}'$
24: **return** $\mathcal{S}$

Function ComputeMinHittingSet($\mathcal{M}$)
Input: A collection $\mathcal{M}$ of sets.
Output: A minimal hitting set for $\mathcal{M}$.
1: $H \leftarrow \emptyset$
2: **for all** $M \in \mathcal{M}$ such that $H \cap M = \emptyset$ **do**
3:     Select an element α in M
4:     $H \leftarrow H \cup \{\alpha\}$
5: **end for**
6: **return** ComputeMinHittingSubset($\mathcal{M}, H$)

Function ComputeMinHittingSubset($\mathcal{M}, H$)
Input: A collection $\mathcal{M}$ of sets and a hitting set H for $\mathcal{M}$.
Output: A minimal hitting set for $\mathcal{M}$ that is also a subset of H.
1: **repeat**
2:     $H' \leftarrow H$
3:     **for all** $\alpha \in H$ **do**
4:         **if** $(H \setminus \{\alpha\}) \cap M \neq \emptyset$ for all $M \in \mathcal{M}$ **then**
5:             $H \leftarrow H \setminus \{\alpha\}$
6:         **end if**
7:     **end for**
8: **until** $H = H'$
9: **return** H

The immediate goal of Algorithm 1 is to compute a minimal set S of ABox repairs of $\mathcal{O}$ such that $\bigcup_{R \in S}(\mathcal{A} \setminus R) = \bigcup \mathsf{MIAS}(\mathcal{O})$ and $\bigcap_{R \in S}(\mathcal{A} \setminus R) = \bigcup \{M \in \mathsf{MIAS}(\mathcal{O}) \mid |M| = 1\}$. By Corollary 1 we have $\bigcap S = \mathcal{A} \setminus \bigcup_{R \in S}(\mathcal{A} \setminus R) = \mathcal{A} \setminus \bigcup \mathsf{MIAS}(\mathcal{O}) = \bigcap \mathsf{AR}(\mathcal{O})$. By Proposition 3 we have $\bigcup S = \mathcal{A} \setminus \bigcap_{R \in S}(\mathcal{A} \setminus R) = \mathcal{A} \setminus \bigcup \{M \in \mathsf{MIAS}(\mathcal{O}) \mid |M| = 1\} = \bigcup \mathsf{AR}(\mathcal{O})$. Hence S is a minimal representative set of ABox repairs of $\mathcal{O}$. There are three main steps for computing S. The first step (lines 2–9) computes a set S' of ABox repairs of $\mathcal{O}$ such that $\bigcup_{R \in S'}(\mathcal{A} \setminus R) = \bigcup \mathsf{MIAS}(\mathcal{O})$. For every assertion $\alpha \in \bigcup \mathsf{MIAS}(\mathcal{O})$ such that $\alpha \notin \bigcup_{R \in S'}(\mathcal{A} \setminus R)$, this step adds to S' the complement set of a minimal hitting set H for $\mathsf{MIAS}(\mathcal{O})$ such that $\alpha \in H$, making $\alpha \in \bigcup_{R \in S'}(\mathcal{A} \setminus R)$. The second step (lines 10–15) computes a superset S'' (also written as S' in the algorithm) of S' such that $\bigcap_{R \in S''}(\mathcal{A} \setminus R) = \bigcup \{M \in \mathsf{MIAS}(\mathcal{O}) \mid |M| = 1\}$. For every assertion $\alpha \in \bigcup \mathsf{MIAS}(\mathcal{O}) \setminus \bigcup \{M \in \mathsf{MIAS}(\mathcal{O}) \mid |M| = 1\}$ such that $\alpha \in \bigcap_{R \in S''}(\mathcal{A} \setminus R)$, this step adds to S'' the complement set of a minimal hitting set H for $\mathsf{MIAS}(\mathcal{O})$ such that $\alpha \notin H$, making $\alpha \notin \bigcap_{R \in S''}(\mathcal{A} \setminus R)$. Since $S' \subseteq S'' \subseteq \mathsf{AR}(\mathcal{O})$ and $\bigcup_{R \in \mathsf{AR}(\mathcal{O})}(\mathcal{A} \setminus R) = \bigcup \mathsf{MIAS}(\mathcal{O})$, we also have $\bigcup_{R \in S''}(\mathcal{A} \setminus R) = \bigcup \mathsf{MIAS}(\mathcal{O})$. The last step (lines 16–23) computes a minimal subset S of S'' such that $\bigcup_{R \in S}(\mathcal{A} \setminus R) = \bigcup \mathsf{MIAS}(\mathcal{O})$ and $\bigcap_{R \in S}(\mathcal{A} \setminus R) = \bigcup \{M \in \mathsf{MIAS}(\mathcal{O}) \mid |M| = 1\}$ by removing redundant ABox repairs from S'' one by one. The following theorem shows the correctness and the complexity of Algorithm 1.

Theorem 1. *After* $\mathsf{MIAS}(\mathcal{O})$ *is computed, Algorithm 1 computes a minimal representative set* S *of ABox repairs of* $\mathcal{O}$ *such that* $|S| \leq 2|\bigcup \mathsf{MIAS}(\mathcal{O})|$, *with the time complexity* $O(|\bigcup \mathsf{MIAS}(\mathcal{O})||\mathsf{MIAS}(\mathcal{O})|^3 + |\bigcup \mathsf{MIAS}(\mathcal{O})|^3)$.

Example 2. This example illustrates how Algorithm 1 works. Let $\mathcal{O}$ be the ontology given in Example 1. It is not hard to see that $\mathsf{MIAS}(\mathcal{O})$ consists of n MIASes of the form $\{A(a_i), C(a_i)\}$ for $1 \leq i \leq n$. We can compute that $\bigcup \mathsf{MIAS}(\mathcal{O}) = \mathcal{A}$ and $\mathcal{A}_1 = \bigcup \{M \in \mathsf{MIAS}(\mathcal{O}) \mid |M| = 1\} = \emptyset$. Consider the first step (lines 2–9) in Algorithm 1. In the first iteration, we select $A(a_1)$ from $\bigcup \mathsf{MIAS}(\mathcal{O})$, select $M = \{A(a_1), C(a_1)\}$ from $\mathsf{MIAS}(\mathcal{O})$, and compute a minimal hitting set H for $\{M' \setminus M \mid M' \in \mathsf{MIAS}(\mathcal{O}), A(a_1) \notin M'\}$. Suppose H is $\{C(a_i) \mid 2 \leq i \leq n\}$, then we add $R_1 = \mathcal{A} \setminus (H \cup \{A(a_1)\}) = \{C(a_1)\} \cup \{A(a_i) \mid 2 \leq i \leq n\}$ to S'. In the second iteration, we select $C(a_1)$ from $\bigcup \mathsf{MIAS}(\mathcal{O}) \setminus \bigcup_{R \in S'}(\mathcal{A} \setminus R) = \bigcap S'$, select $M = \{A(a_1), C(a_1)\}$ from $\mathsf{MIAS}(\mathcal{O})$, and compute a minimal hitting set H for $\{M' \setminus M \mid M' \in \mathsf{MIAS}(\mathcal{O}), C(a_1) \notin M'\}$. Suppose H is $\{C(a_i) \mid 2 \leq i \leq n\}$, then we add $R_2 = \mathcal{A} \setminus (H \cup \{C(a_1)\}) = \{A(a_i) \mid 1 \leq i \leq n\}$ to S'. In the third iteration, we select $A(a_2)$ from $\bigcup \mathsf{MIAS}(\mathcal{O}) \setminus \bigcup_{R \in S'}(\mathcal{A} \setminus R) = \bigcap S'$, select $M = \{A(a_2), C(a_2)\}$ from $\mathsf{MIAS}(\mathcal{O})$, and compute a minimal hitting set H for $\{M' \setminus M \mid M' \in \mathsf{MIAS}(\mathcal{O}), A(a_2) \notin M'\}$. Suppose H is $\{A(a_1)\} \cup \{A(a_i) \mid 3 \leq i \leq n\}$, then we add $R_3 = \mathcal{A} \setminus (H \cup \{A(a_2)\}) = \{C(a_i) \mid 1 \leq i \leq n\}$ to S'. By now $\bigcup \mathsf{MIAS}(\mathcal{O}) = \bigcup S'$, thus the first step ends. Consider the second step (lines 10–15) in Algorithm 1. Since $(\bigcup \mathsf{MIAS}(\mathcal{O}) \setminus \mathcal{A}_1) \cap (\bigcap_{R \in S'}(\mathcal{A} \setminus R)) = \emptyset$, this step does nothing. Consider the last step (lines 16–23) in Algorithm 1. Since $\bigcup_{R' \in S' \setminus \{R_1\}}(\mathcal{A} \setminus R') = \bigcup \mathsf{MIAS}(\mathcal{O})$ and $\bigcap_{R' \in S' \setminus \{R_1\}}(\mathcal{A} \setminus R') = \mathcal{A}_1$, we remove R_1 from S', yielding $S = \{R_2, R_3\}$. Since $\bigcup_{R' \in S \setminus \{R\}}(\mathcal{A} \setminus R') \subset \bigcup \mathsf{MIAS}(\mathcal{O})$ and

$\mathcal{A}_1 \subset \bigcap_{R' \in \mathcal{S} \setminus \{R\}} (\mathcal{A} \setminus R')$ for $R = R_2$ or $R = R_3$, the last step ends. We finally get $\mathcal{S} = \{R_2, R_3\}$, which is a minimal representative set of ABox repairs of $\mathcal{O}$.

To achieve a tractable method for computing a minimal representative set of ABox repairs of $\mathcal{O}$, the remaining problem lies in how to compute $\mathsf{MIAS}(\mathcal{O})$ in PTIME and ensure both $|\mathsf{MIAS}(\mathcal{O})|$ and $|\bigcup \mathsf{MIAS}(\mathcal{O})|$ to be polynomial in data complexity. This problem is currently open for arbitrary DLs, but for a class of DL ontologies called the *first-order rewritable* class, a PTIME (data complexity) algorithm has been proposed in [6]. A *first-order rewritable ontology* $\mathcal{O}$ with TBox $\mathcal{T}$ can be defined as a datalog$^\pm$-translatable ontology (see Section 3) such that the set $\mathcal{S}_T$ of TGDs translated from $\mathcal{T}$ is first-order rewritable and the set $\mathcal{S}_E$ of EGDs translated from $\mathcal{T}$ is separable from $\mathcal{S}_T$.

To show an algorithm for computing $\mathsf{MIAS}(\mathcal{O})$ for an inconsistent first-order rewritable ontology $\mathcal{O}$ with TBox $\mathcal{T}$ and ABox $\mathcal{A}$, some notations need to be introduced. For an existential rule R, by $\rho(R)$ we denote the BCQ $\exists \boldsymbol{x}\, \phi(\boldsymbol{x})$ if R is a constraint $\forall \boldsymbol{x}\, \phi(\boldsymbol{x}) \rightarrow$, or the BCQ $\exists \boldsymbol{x}\, \phi(\boldsymbol{x}) \wedge x_1 \neq x_2$ if R is an EGD $\forall \boldsymbol{x}\, \phi(\boldsymbol{x}) \rightarrow x_1 = x_2$. For a first-order rewritable set $\mathcal{S}_T$ of TGDs and a BCQ Q, by $\gamma(Q, \mathcal{S}_T)$ we denote a set $\mathcal{S}_Q$ of BCQs such that $\mathcal{S}_T \cup \mathcal{A}' \models Q$ if and only if $\mathcal{A}' \models \bigvee \mathcal{S}_Q$ for all ABoxes $\mathcal{A}'$, where $\mathcal{S}_Q$ can be computed by an existing query rewriting method such as Requiem [15]. For a set S of assertions that possibly contain inequality assertions of the form $a \neq b$, we write $S \subseteq \mathcal{A}$ if all inequality assertions in S are not of the form $a \neq a$ and other assertions in S occur in $\mathcal{A}$.

$\mathsf{MIAS}(\mathcal{O})$ is computed by the following steps [6]: we first translate $\mathcal{T}$ to the union of a set $\mathcal{S}_T$ of TGDs, a set $\mathcal{S}_C$ of constraints and a set $\mathcal{S}_E$ of EGDs, then compute $\Lambda(\mathcal{O}) = \{Q\theta \mid Q \in \bigcup\{\gamma(\rho(R), \mathcal{S}_T) \mid R \in \mathcal{S}_C\} \cup \{\rho(R) \mid R \in \mathcal{S}_E\}, \theta$ is a ground substitution for Q such that $Q\theta \subseteq \mathcal{A}\}$, and finally remove non-minimal elements from $\Lambda(\mathcal{O})$. It has been shown [6] that $\mathsf{MIAS}(\mathcal{O}) = \{M \in \Lambda(\mathcal{O}) \mid \nexists M' \in \Lambda(\mathcal{O}) : M' \subset M\}$ can be computed in PTIME in data complexity; moreover, both $|\mathsf{MIAS}(\mathcal{O})|$ and $|\bigcup \mathsf{MIAS}(\mathcal{O})|$ are polynomial in $|\mathcal{A}|$.

It immediately follows from Theorem 1 that we can compute a minimal representative set of ABox repairs of an inconsistent first-order rewritable ontology $\mathcal{O}$ in PTIME in data complexity. The proposed method first computes $\mathsf{MIAS}(\mathcal{O})$ by calling the algorithm described above, then computes a minimal representative set of ABox repairs of $\mathcal{O}$ from $\mathsf{MIAS}(\mathcal{O})$ by calling Algorithm 1. Although the method works for first-order rewritable ontologies only, it can still be used in many applications such as the OBDA systems that are based on an ontology expressed in a certain DL in the DL-Lite family [4]. This is because most DLs in the DL-Lite family such as DL-Lite$_X$ and DL-Lite$_{X,\sqcap}$ for $X \in \{\mathcal{F}, \mathcal{R}, \mathcal{A}\}$ belong to the first-order rewritable class [3].

5   Experimental Evaluation

We implemented the proposed method (named RepAR) in Java, using the Requiem [15] API for query rewriting and the MySQL engine to store and access ABoxes. We compared RepAR with a state-of-the-art method for computing a

Table 1. The average cardinality and the maximum cardinality of the minimal representative set of ABox repairs of LUBMn_{+m} computed by RepAR

n	1	1	1	1	1	5	10	10	10	10	10	50	100
m	0	100	200	300	400	400	0	100	200	300	400	400	400
average cardinality	1	29	43	63	79	111	1	28	47	65	88	70	59
maximum cardinality	1	31	45	67	82	115	1	30	50	66	91	72	62

single ABox repair (named SinAR), which applies the divide-and-conquer strategy [10] to perform a sequence of consistency checks. More precisely, SinAR calls $f(\mathcal{T}, \mathcal{A})$ to compute an ABox repair of $\mathcal{O}$. Given two sets of axioms S and S', $f(S, S')$ returns a maximal subset of S' that is consistent with S. It is recursively defined as $\Delta \cup f(S \cup \Delta, S'_2)$ with $\Delta = f(S, S'_1)$ if $|S'| > 1$, or as S' if $|S'| \leq 1$ and $S \cup S'$ is consistent, or as $\emptyset$ otherwise, where S'_1 and S'_2 are two subsets of S' such that $S'_1 \cup S'_2 = S'$, $S'_1 \cap S'_2 = \emptyset$ and $-1 \leq |S'_1| - |S'_2| \leq 1$. The implementation of SinAR uses the KAON2 [9] API to perform consistency checks. This comparison can also reveal whether RepAR is significantly more efficient than the general method for computing a representative set of relaxations [14], which repeatedly calls a subroutine for computing a single relaxation, where the subroutine also performs a sequence of consistency checks.

We compared RepAR with SinAR on LUBMn ontologies from the Lehigh University Benchmark [8], where $n = 1, 5, 10, 50, 100$ is the number of universities. The implementation of SinAR is efficient in reasoning over LUBMn ontologies since the core reasoner KAON2 has been shown to be so in [13]. Since Requiem cannot handle transitivity axioms and domain declarations on datatype properties, we removed these axioms from LUBMn. The resulting LUBMn is consistent and cannot directly be used to compare RepAR with SinAR, thus we added to LUBMn disjointness axioms for every two sibling concept names in the concept hierarchy of the LUBM TBox whenever these two concept names have no common instances in any LUBMn. In addition, we used the `Injector` tool provided by [5] to insert conflicts to LUBMn. By $\mathcal{O}_{+m}$ we denote the ontology obtained from $\mathcal{O}$ by inserting m conflicts. We generated LUBM1_{+m} and LUBM10_{+m} ($m = 0, 100, 200, 300, 400$) to evaluate the methods against an increasing number of conflicts, and generated LUBMn_{+400} ($n = 1, 5, 10, 50, 100$) to evaluate the methods against an increasing number of universities. All resulting test ontologies have 43 concept names, 32 role names, 158 TBox axioms, 17,174 (LUBM1_{+0}) to 2,179,956 (LUBM100_{+400}) individuals, and 100,543 (LUBM1_{+0}) to 13,825,027 (LUBM100_{+400}) ABox assertions.

The output of RepAR depends on the selection steps in Algorithm 1, hence we adopted the random selection strategy in the implementation of RepAR and evaluated RepAR ten times for each test ontology. We set a time limit of 10,000 seconds for both RepAR and SinAR to handle a test ontology. All experiments were conducted on a laptop with Intel Dual-Core 2.60GHz CPU and 8GB RAM, running Windows 7 with the maximum Java heap size set to 8GB.

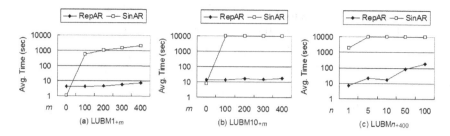

Fig. 1. The average execution time for computing a minimal representative set of ABox repairs by RepAR and the execution time for computing a single ABox repair by SinAR

Figure 1 reports the average execution time for computing a minimal representative set of ABox repairs by RepAR and the execution time for computing a single ABox repair by SinAR, where the latter is approximated as 10,000 seconds in every timeout case. The execution time of RepAR includes the time for loading the test ontology and computing the set of MIASes. The execution time of SinAR excludes the time for loading the test ontology. When the test ontology $\mathcal{O}$ is LUBM1$_{+0}$ or LUBM10$_{+0}$, $\mathcal{O}$ is consistent and MIAS($\mathcal{O}$) is empty. In this case, RepAR directly returns $\{\mathcal{O}\}$ as the unique minimal representative set of ABox repairs after computing MIAS($\mathcal{O}$), while SinAR computes the unique ABox repair $\mathcal{O}$ by a single consistency check. Except for this case, RepAR is significantly faster than SinAR; especially, this gap widens when the number of conflicts increases. In addition, SinAR cannot finish within the time limit for LUBM10$_{+m}$ ($m \geq 100$) and LUBMn_{+400} ($n \geq 5$). In contrast, RepAR works efficiently for all test cases. As expected, the largest ontology LUBM100$_{+400}$ costs the most time for RepAR, but RepAR still finishes in three minutes. Moreover, RepAR scales well to hundreds of conflicts and tens of millions of assertions.

Table 1 reports the average cardinality and the maximum cardinality of the minimal representative set of ABox repairs computed in ten runs for each test ontology. It can be seen that the cardinality of a computed minimal representative set of ABox repairs is rather small (at most 115). This implies that the minimal representative set of ABox repairs computed by RepAR provides a rather efficient approximation of cautious or brave reasoning over inconsistent first-order rewritable ontologies, where the approximate reasoning can often be done by standard reasoning over tens of ABox repairs in turn.

6   Conclusions and Future Work

In this paper we have presented a solution to make cautious or brave reasoning practical over inconsistent DL ontologies. We made the following main contributions. Firstly, we introduced the notion of minimal representative set of ABox repairs to approximate cautious or brave reasoning. Secondly, we proposed a PTIME (data complexity) method for computing a minimal representative set of ABox repairs in an inconsistent first-order rewritable ontology. The method combines an algorithm for computing all MIASes [6] and a novel algorithm for computing a minimal representative set of ABox repairs from the set of MIASes. Finally, our experimental results showed that the proposed method is efficient and scalable while the cardinality of a computed minimal representative set is rather small. For future work, we plan to identify more classes of DLs beyond the first-order rewritable class, which guarantee that the number of MIASes is polynomial and the set of MIASes is computable in PTIME in data complexity.

Acknowledgments. This work is partly supported by NSFC grants (61375056 and 61272378) and Guangdong Natural Science Foundation (S2013010012928).

References

1. Baader, F., Calvanese, D., McGuinness, D.L., Nardi, D., Patel-Schneider, P.F. (eds.): The Description Logic Handbook: Theory, Implementation, and Applications. Cambridge University Press (2003)
2. Bienvenu, M., Bourgaux, C., Goasdoué, F.: Querying inconsistent description logic knowledge bases under preferred repair semantics. In: AAAI, pp. 996–1002 (2014)
3. Calì, A., Gottlob, G., Lukasiewicz, T.: A general datalog-based framework for tractable query answering over ontologies. J. Web Sem. **14**, 57–83 (2012)
4. Calvanese, D., Giacomo, G., Lembo, D., Lenzerini, M., Rosati, R.: Tractable reasoning and efficient query answering in description logics: The DL-Lite family. J. Autom. Reasoning **39**(3), 385–429 (2007)
5. Du, J., Qi, G., Shen, Y.: Weight-based consistent query answering over inconsistent $\mathcal{SHIQ}$ knowledge bases. Knowl. Inf. Syst. **34**(2), 335–371 (2013)
6. Du, J., Wang, K., Shen, Y.: Towards tractable and practical ABox abduction over inconsistent description logic ontologies. In: AAAI, pp. 1489–1495 (2015)
7. Eiter, T., Faber, W., Fink, M., Pfeifer, G., Woltran, S.: Complexity of model checking and bounded predicate arities for non-ground answer set programming. In: KR, pp. 377–387 (2004)
8. Guo, Y., Pan, Z., Heflin, J.: LUBM: A benchmark for OWL knowledge base systems. J. Web Sem. **3**(2–3), 158–182 (2005)
9. Hustadt, U., Motik, B., Sattler, U.: Reasoning in description logics by a reduction to disjunctive datalog. J. Autom. Reasoning **39**(3), 351–384 (2007)
10. Junker, U.: QUICKXPLAIN: Preferred explanations and relaxations for over-constrained problems. In: AAAI, pp. 167–172 (2004)
11. Lembo, D., Lenzerini, M., Rosati, R., Ruzzi, M., Savo, D.F.: Inconsistency-tolerant semantics for description logics. In: Hitzler, P., Lukasiewicz, T. (eds.) RR 2010. LNCS, vol. 6333, pp. 103–117. Springer, Heidelberg (2010)
12. Meyer, T., Lee, K., Booth, R.: Knowledge integration for description logics. In: Veloso, M., Kambhampati, S. (eds.) AAAI, pp. 645–650 (2005)
13. Motik, B., Sattler, U.: A comparison of reasoning techniques for querying large description logic aboxes. In: Hermann, M., Voronkov, A. (eds.) LPAR 2006. LNCS (LNAI), vol. 4246, pp. 227–241. Springer, Heidelberg (2006)
14. O'Sullivan, B., Papadopoulos, A., Faltings, B., Pu, P.: Representative explanations for over-constrained problems. In: AAAI, pp. 323–328 (2007)
15. Pérez-Urbina, H., Motik, B., Horrocks, I.: Tractable query answering and rewriting under description logic constraints. J. Applied Logic **8**(2), 186–209 (2010)

Restricted Four-Valued Logic for Default Reasoning

Chen Chen and Zuoquan Lin[✉]

School of Mathematical Sciences, Peking University, Beijing 100871, China
skydark2@gmail.com, linzuoquan@pku.edu.cn

Abstract. In Reiter's default logic, it is possible that no useful information can be brought from inconsistent knowledge or no extension of incoherent default theories exists. In this paper, based on Belnap's four-valued logic, we propose a new variant of default logic called the restricted four-valued default logic to tolerate inconsistency and incoherency of knowledge in default reasoning. Our proposal can maintain both the expressive power of full default logic and the ability of default reasoning. Moreover, we present a transformation-based approach to compute the restricted four-valued extensions.

1 Introduction

Reiter's default logic [20] is a widely studied nonmonotonic logic. Despite that, default logic has its own shortcomings. Some default theories have only one trivial extension, which contains everything as its conclusion. Even the existence of extensions is not always guaranteed. Such incoherences may happen when contradictions occur in defaults or between defaults and facts.

To deal with incoherences, some variants of default logic were introduced. Some researchers treat incoherences as illegal. With this viewpoint, they focus on finding characterizations of default theories which have extensions, such as normal default theories [20] and ordered default theories [18] among others. These fragments of default logic are strictly weak and, as a result, lost full expressive power of default logic.

Another approach to handle incoherences is to modify the definition of extensions. For instances, the justified default extensions [16], the constrained default extensions [21] and the cumulative default extensions [12] are all guaranteed to exist for every default theory. However, these extensions have different semantics from Reiter's, even when Reiter's default extensions exist and are consistent.

To deal with inconsistencies, an approach is to transform inconsistent default theories into consistent ones, but still hold some useful conclusions. In [10], the authors handle inconsistencies by default logic itself. Another approach takes advantage of paraconsistent logics, which do not infer everything from contradictions, such as the question marked logic [1], the four-valued default logic [23],

---

This work is partially supported by the Advance Programs Fund of Ministry of Education of China and Natural Science Foundation of China.

S. Zhang et al. (Eds.): KSEM 2015, LNAI 9403, pp. 40–52, 2015.
DOI: 10.1007/978-3-319-25159-2_4

the bi-default logic [14], the fault-tolerant default logic [15], and the annotated default logic [22]. However, some of these attempts cannot handle all inconsistent and incoherent problems, or have different semantics from Reiter's.

In this paper we introduce a novel extension of default logic named the restricted four-valued default logic, based on Belnap's four-valued logic [3,8, 9], which is a multi-valued paraconsistent logic, to handle both inconsistencies and incoherences. Not like in [23], which is also based on Belnap's four-valued logic, we ensure that every default theory has at least one nontrivial extension. Moreover, we keep our extensions as similar as Reiter's original ones. Finally, we proved that Reiter's default logic is a special case of our logic on consistent and coherent default theories. Interestingly but not too surprisingly, we also show that our default logic is indeed an expansion of the preferred four-valued logic.

The paper is structured as follows. First we review preliminaries in section 2. Our main contributions are presented in sections 3 and 4, in which we describe our restricted four-valued default logic from underlying logic to extensions, together with comparison with default logic and four-valued logic. To calculate the restricted four-valued extensions, we present an approach of the formula transformation in section 5. We compare our results with related works in section 6, and summarize in section 7 as conclusion.

2   Preliminaries

In the rest of this paper we denote $\mathcal{L}$ as a propositional language, $\mathcal{A}$ as the set of all atoms, $\models_2$ as the classical propositional consequence relation and Th as the consequence operator. The propositional constants t and f are interpreted as true and false in all interpretations respectively.

2.1   Default Logic

A *default* d is an inference rule of form $d = \frac{\alpha : \beta_1, \ldots, \beta_n}{\gamma}$, where $\alpha, \beta_1, \ldots, \beta_n, \gamma$ are all propositional formulas. We define $Pre(d) = \alpha$ as *prerequisite* of d, $Just(d) = \{\beta_1, \ldots, \beta_n\}$ as *justification* of d, and $Con(d) = \gamma$ as *consequence* of d. For a set of defaults D, define $Pre(D) = \{Pre(d)|d \in D\}$, $Just(D) = \bigcup\{Just(d)|d \in D\}$, and $Con(D) = \{Con(d)|d \in D\}$.

A *default theory* is a pair $T = (D, W)$, where D is a set of defaults and W is a set of formulas. For convenience, neither t nor f is permitted to be presented in D or W.

An *extension* of a default theory is defined as follows.

Definition 1 ([20]). *Let* $T = (D, W)$ *be a default theory. For any set of formulas* E, *let* $\Gamma(E)$ *be the smallest set of formulas such that:*

1. $W \subseteq \Gamma(E)$;
2. $Th(\Gamma(E)) = \Gamma(E)$;
3. *For any* $d \in D$, *if* $\Gamma(E) \models_2 Pre(d)$ *and* $\neg\beta \notin E$ *for all* $\beta \in Just(d)$, *then* $\Gamma(E) \models_2 Con(d)$.

A set of formulas E is an (default) extension *of T iff $\Gamma(E) = E$, i.e. E is a fixed point of the operator Γ.*

We say T skeptically entails a formula set F, if all extensions of T entail F.

A default theory may have none, one or many extensions. Sometimes the extension may be trivial, which means it contains all propositional formulas.

Example 1. Let $T_i = (D_i, W_i)(i = 1, 2, 3, 4)$ be a default theory, where

1. $D_1 = \{\frac{:p}{q}\}$, $W_1 = \{\neg p, r, \neg r\}$;
2. $D_2 = \{\frac{:p}{\neg p}\}$, $W_2 = \{q\}$;
3. $D_3 = \{\frac{:p}{q}, \frac{:p}{\neg q}\}$, $W_3 = \emptyset$;
4. $D_4 = \{\frac{:q}{\neg r}, \frac{:r}{\neg p}, \frac{:p}{\neg q}\}$, $W_4 = \emptyset$.

T_1 has a trivial extension, while, none of T_2, T_3, T_4 has any extension.

2.2   Four-Valued Logic

To deal with inconsistent and incomplete knowledge, Belnap's four-valued logic [3,8,9] is constructed on the bilattice structure $FOUR = \{t, f, \top, \bot\}$. The elements of $FOUR$ can also be represented by pairs of two-valued truth values: $t = (1,0)$, $f = (0,1)$, $\top = (1,1)$, $\bot = (0,0)$. Intuitively, the truth values $\top$ and $\bot$ represent inconsistencies and lacking of information respectively.

The *set of designated elements* is chosen as $\mathcal{D} = \{t, \top\}$. A *four-valued valuation* is a function that assigns a truth value from $FOUR$ to each atomic formula. The truth operators on $\langle FOUR \rangle$ are defined as follows: $\neg(x, y) = (y, x)$, $(x_1, y_1) \wedge (x_2, y_2) = (x_1 \wedge x_2, y_1 \vee y_2)$, $(x_1, y_1) \vee (x_2, y_2) = (x_1 \vee x_2, y_1 \wedge y_2)$ and $(x_1, y_1) \supset (x_2, y_2) = (\neg x_1 \vee x_2, x_1 \wedge y_2)$. For constants, let $v(\mathbf{t}) = t$ and $v(\mathbf{f}) = f$.

A valuation v *satisfies* a formula ϕ if $v(\phi) \in \mathcal{D}$. We say v is a *model* of a formula set S if v satisfies every formula in S. We use $\langle FOUR \rangle$ to denote the structure $FOUR$ together with $\mathcal{D}$. The consequence relation on $\langle FOUR \rangle$ are defined in the following.

Definition 2 ([3]). *Suppose that Γ and Δ are two sets of formulae. $\Gamma \models_4 \Delta$ if every model of Γ in $\langle FOUR \rangle$ is a model of some formula of Δ.*

Definition 3 ([3]). *Let u, v be four-valued valuations. u is more classical than v if $v(p) \in \{\top, \bot\}$ whenever $u(p) \in \{\top, \bot\}$.*

Suppose that Γ and Δ are two sets of formulas. $\Gamma \models_{cl}^4 \Delta$ if every most classical model of Γ is a model of some formula of Δ.

As a nonmonotonic and paraconsistent consequence relation, $\models_{cl}^4$ is equivalent to classical logic on consistent theories. For more details, see [3].

3   Restricted Four-Valued Default Logic

3.1   Restricted Four-Valued Logic

In this section, we present a *restricted four-valued logic* as the underlying logic of our default logic. In our restricted four-valued logic, we focus on those valuations whose nonclassical values only occur in a given set of atoms. The idea of restricting paraconsistent atoms in a fixed subset can be inspired from Vasil'év's imaginary logic [7].

Definition 4. *Let S be a set of atoms. A four-valued valuation v is* restricted by S, *if $\{a \in \mathcal{A} | v(a) \notin \{t, f\}\} \subseteq S$.*

Definition 5. *Let S be a set of atoms, Γ, Σ be sets of formulas. A four-valued valuation v is a* four-valued model of Γ restricted by S *if v is a four-valued model of Γ and restricted by S.*

$\Gamma \models_S \Sigma$ if every four-valued model of Γ restricted by S is a four-valued model of Σ.

Denote $Th_S(\Gamma)$ as the consequence operator restricted by S: $Th_S(\Gamma) = \{\alpha | \Gamma \models_S \alpha\}$.

The motivation for restricting nonclassical values is a trade-off between classical reasoning power and paraconsistent properties. Obviously, classical logic and four-valued logic can be treated as two extreme cases of our restricted four-valued logic.

Proposition 1. *Let S be a set of atoms, Γ a set of formulas and ϕ a formula. $\Gamma \models_\emptyset \phi$ iff $\Gamma \models_2 \phi$, and $\Gamma \models_\mathcal{A} \phi$ iff $\Gamma \models_4 \phi$.*

In fact, our restricted four-valued logic can be expressed in four-valued logic.

Theorem 1. *Let S be a set of atoms, Γ a set of formulas and ϕ a formula. $\Gamma \models_S \phi$ iff $\Gamma \cup f_\mathcal{A}(S) \models_4 \phi$, where $f_\mathcal{A}(S) = \bigcup_{a \in \mathcal{A} \setminus S}\{a \vee \neg a, (a \wedge \neg a) \supset f\}$.* [1]

Proof. For any four-valued valuation v and atom a, v satisfies $a \vee \neg a$ iff $v(a) \neq \bot$ and v satisfies $(a \wedge \neg a) \supset f$ iff $v(a) \neq \top$. As a result, v satisfies $f_\mathcal{A}(S)$ iff $v(a) \in \{t, f\}$ for all $a \notin S$, i.e. v is restricted by S.

Therefore, the four-valued models of $\Gamma \cup f_\mathcal{A}(S)$ are exactly the four-valued models of Γ restricted by S.   □

By Theorem 1, many properties of restricted four-valued logic can be proved by transforming them to four-valued logic, such as monotonicity.

Proposition 2 (Monotonicity). *Let Γ, Σ be sets of formulas, S a set of atoms and ϕ a formula. If $\Gamma \subseteq \Sigma$ and $\Gamma \models_S \phi$, then $\Sigma \models_S \phi$.*

Proof. $\Gamma \models_S \phi$ infers that $\Gamma \cup f_\mathcal{A}(S) \models_4 \phi$, where f is defined in Theorem 1. As four-valued logic is monotonic([3]) and $\Gamma \subseteq \Sigma$, we know that $\Sigma \cup f_\mathcal{A}(S) \models_4 \phi$, which is equivalent to $\Sigma \models_S \phi$ according to Theorem 1.   □

---

[1]   It may be argued that $f_\mathcal{A}(S)$ can cause infiniteness if $\mathcal{A}$ is not finite. In fact, $\mathcal{A}$ can be replaced by any atom set which contains all atoms occur in Γ and ϕ.

3.2   Restricted Four-Valued Extension

In this subsection, we introduce the restricted four-valued extensions based on the restricted four-valued logic. We include a restricting set as a part of an extension.

In Reiter's default logic, a justification is satisfiable in a formula set E if its negation is not in E. The corresponding concept in restricted four-valued extension has a subtle distinction since a formula may coexist with its negation in the same formula set but not be trivial in restricted four-valued logic. We use formula $\beta \supset \mathbf{f}$ as a stronger negation of β, since $\{\beta, \beta \supset \mathbf{f}\}$ is always unsatisfiable in restricted four-valued logic. We also need to ensure that restricted four-valued extension is satisfiable, since we should better enlarge the restricting set rather than accept it as an extension if it is not satisfiable. We define the restricted four-valued extension as follows.

Definition 6 (Restricted Four-Valued Extension). *Let $T = (D, W)$ be a default theory and S a set of atoms. For any set of formulas E, let $\Gamma_S(E)$ be the smallest set satisfying the following properties:*

1. *$\Gamma_S(E) \not\models_S \mathbf{f}$;*
2. *$W \subseteq \Gamma_S(E)$;*
3. *$Th_S(\Gamma_S(E)) = \Gamma_S(E)$;*
4. *For any $d \in D$, if $\Gamma_S(E) \models_S Pre(d)$ and $\beta_i \supset \mathbf{f} \notin E$ for any $\beta_i \in Just(d)$, then $\Gamma_S(E) \models_S Con(d)$.*

For any set of formulas E and set of atoms S, $\langle E, S \rangle$ is a restricted four-valued extension iff $\Gamma_S(E) = E$, i.e. E is a fixed point of the operator Γ_S. We denote S as the restricting set of $\langle E, S \rangle$ and say that $\langle E, S \rangle$ is restricted by S.

We review Example 1 to show that the restricted four-valued extensions follow our intuition and recover several useful conclusions which are lost in Reiter's.

Example 2. (Continuation of Example 1) Consider default theories in Example 1 which are all trouble in Reiter's default logic. In contrast, all these default theories have restricted four-valued extensions which are nontrivial and intuitive.

1. One restricted four-valued extension of T_1 is $\langle Th_{S_1}(W_1), S_1 \rangle$, where $S_1 = \{r\}$. This extension keeps all information of W_1 but is not trivial. For instance, it rejects q as its conclusion.
2. One restricted four-valued extension of T_2 is $\langle Th_{S_2}(\{\neg p, q\}), S_2 \rangle$, where $S_2 = \{p\}$. It means that we allow $\neg p$ in this extension, but leave p with suspicion in S_2. This extension has no doubt on formula q since it is independent of p.
3. One restricted four-valued extension of T_3 is $\langle Th_{S_3}(\{q, \neg q\}), S_3 \rangle$, where $S_3 = \{q\}$. We keep two conflict default consequences q and $\neg q$ together with no explosion. Also $\neg p$ is not derivable, since we still treat p as a classical atom.

4. Three restricted four-valued extensions of T_4 are: $\langle Th_{S_4^1}(\{\neg p, \neg q\}), S_4^1 \rangle$, $\langle Th_{S_4^2}(\{\neg q, \neg r\}), S_4^2 \rangle$, and $\langle Th_{S_4^3}(\{\neg r, \neg p\}), S_4^3 \rangle$, where $S_4^1 = \{p\}$, $S_4^2 = \{q\}$, $S_4^3 = \{r\}$. All these extensions entail two of $\{\neg p, \neg q, \neg r\}$, but none of them entail all these three formulas. Our intuition is that the three rules in D_4 cannot be executed together unless considering one of their justifications as troubled.

Restricted four-valued extensions inherit many properties of Reiter's extensions due to the monotonic property. Although most variants of default logic hold these properties naturally, it is not the same as paraconsistent ones, especially those whose underlying logic is nonmonotonic. For example, the following propositions hold and can be proved by the same way of Reiter's original proofs.

Proposition 3. *Let $T = (D, W)$ be a default theory, and let S be a set of atoms. For any set of formulas E, $\langle E, S \rangle$ is a restricted four-valued extension iff $E \not\models_S \mathbf{f}$ and $E = \bigcup_{i=0}^{\infty} E_i$, where:*

1. $E_0 = W$;
2. *For all $i \geq 0$, $E_{i+1} = Th_S(E_i) \cup \{\gamma \in Con(d) | d \in D, where Pre(d) \in E_i and \beta \supset \mathbf{f} \notin E for all \beta \in Just(d)\}$.*

Proposition 4. *Let $T = (D, W)$ be a default theory. Suppose $\langle E, S \rangle$ is a restricted four-valued extension of T, then $E = Th_S(W \cup Con(GD(E, T)))$, where $GD(E, T) = \{d \in D | Pre(d) \in E, \beta \supset \mathbf{f} \notin E for any \beta \in Just(d)\}$.*

Our restricted four-valued default logic can ensure that the extensions of any default theory always exist.

Theorem 2. *Every default theory has restricted four-valued extensions.*

Proof. Let $T = (D, W)$ be a default theory and S the set of all atoms occurs in T. Let $E = \bigcup_{i=0}^{\infty} E_i$, where:

1. $E_0 = W$;
2. For all $i \geq 0$, $E_{i+1} = Th_S(E_i) \cup \{\gamma \in Con(d) | d \in D, Pre(d) \in E_i\}$.

Let v be the valuation with $v(a) = \top$ for all $a \in \mathcal{A}$. v is a four-valued model of E while only classical connectives occurs in E([3]). Because $v(\mathbf{f}) = \mathbf{f}$ which is not a designated value, $E \not\models_S \mathbf{f}$. For any $\beta \in Just(D)$, $v(\beta) = \top$ implies $v(\beta \supset \mathbf{f}) = \mathbf{f}$, so $E \not\models_S \beta \supset \mathbf{f}$. Compare with Proposition 3, we have proved that $\langle E, S \rangle$ is a restricted four-valued extension of T. ☐

3.3 Preferred Restricted Four-Valued Extension

Although we guarantee that every default theory has at least one restricted four-valued extension, it is still too tolerant to permit all of them.

Example 3. (Continuation of Example 2) Considering default theory T_1 in Example 2, all restricted four-valued extensions of T_1 are:

1. $E_1 = \langle Th_{S_1^1}(W_1), S_1^1 \rangle$, where $S_1^1 = \{r\}$. This is our intuitive extension.
2. $E_2 = \langle Th_{S_1^2}(W_1 \cup \{q\}), S_1^2 \rangle$, where $S_1^2 = \{r, p\}$. The unnecessary atom p in restricting set causes $\neg p$ not enough to prevent applying of the only default rule and causes q be included as a counter-intuitive conclusion.
3. $E_3 = \langle Th_{S_1^3}(W_1), S_1^3 \rangle$, where $S_1^3 = \{r, q\}$. The unnecessary atom q in restricting set weakens reasoning power. For example, E_1 entails $\neg q \rightarrow s$, which does not hold in E_3.
4. $E_4 = \langle Th_{S_1^4}(W_1 \cup \{q\}), S_1^4 \rangle$, where $S_1^4 = \{r, p, q\}$. This is an even worse extension since it merges both shortcomings of E_2 and E_3.
5. We have more extensions if we add other atoms which are not present in our language to any restricting sets above.

As we can see in the above example, adding redundant atoms to restricting set would cause unwanted or/and weaker conclusions. We prefer to extensions which have only necessary atoms in their restricting sets.

Definition 7 (Preferred Restricted Four-Valued Extension). *Let T be a default theory. A restricted four-valued extension $\langle E, S \rangle$ of T is a preferred restricted four-valued extension of T, if there is no restricted four-valued extension of T restricted by R and $R \subsetneq S$.*

Example 4. The restricted four-valued extensions mentioned in Example 2 are whole preferred restricted four-valued extensions of their corresponding default theories respectively. As explained before, they are all conform to our intuition.

Similarly, we also ensure the existence of preferred extensions.

Theorem 3. *Every default theory has at least one preferred restricted four-valued extension.*

Proof. Let T be a default theory. T has a restricted four-valued extension $\langle E, S \rangle$ by Theorem 2. Since the atom set S is finite, there is a minimal atom set R which restricts a restricted four-valued extension $\langle E', R \rangle$ of T and is a subset of S. $\langle E', R \rangle$ is also a preferred restricted four-valued extension. □

4   Discussions

4.1   Connection with Reiter's Default Logic

Restricted four-valued default logic enhances the flexibility of default logic. On the other hand, if default extensions are consistent, we should not make any of them invalid. It is even better if we do not accept any out of them either.

Fortunately, the restricted four-valued extensions have the classical property, which can be formalized by the following theorem.

Theorem 4. *Let T be a default theory. E is a consistent default extension of T iff $\langle E, \emptyset \rangle$ is a restricted four-valued extension of T.*

Proof. According to the difference between default extension and restricted four-valued extension, we need to prove:

1. E is consistent iff $E \not\models_\emptyset \mathbf{f}$;
2. $Th_\emptyset(E) = Th(E)$;
3. for any formula α and formula set Σ, $\Sigma \models_2 \alpha$ iff $\Sigma \models_\emptyset \alpha$; and
4. for any formula β and formula set Σ, $E \not\models_2 \neg\beta$ iff $E \not\models_\emptyset \beta \supset \mathbf{f}$.

which are all corollaries of Proposition 1.   □

Now we can see why the preferred restricted four-valued extensions are intuitive: the classical extensions are always preferred, and the only preferred.

Corollary 1. *Let T be a default theory which has a consistent default extension. E is a default extension of T iff $\langle E, \emptyset \rangle$ is a preferred restricted four-valued extension of T.*

Proof. Combine Theorem 4 and the following fact:
    if $\langle E, \emptyset \rangle$ is a restricted four-valued extension of T, then all preferred restricted four-valued extension of T are restricted by $\emptyset$.   □

Theorem 4 and Corollary 1 show that (preferred) restricted four-valued default logic is an expansion to Reiter's default logic. In fact, Reiter's default extensions are only distinguishable with preferred restricted four-valued default extensions when there is no nontrivial default extension. So we can safely replace Reiter's default extensions with preferred restricted four-valued extensions.

4.2   Connection with Preferred Four-Valued Logic

Restricted four-valued default logic is not only a default logic, but also four-valued. The following theorem reveals that the four-valued consequence relation $\models_{cl}^4$ can be treated as a special case of restricted four-valued skeptical entailment.

Theorem 5. $W \models_{cl}^4 \phi$ *iff all preferred restricted four-valued extensions of default theory $T = (W, \emptyset)$ entail ϕ.*

Proof. Denote M as the model set of all minimal four-valued model of W.
    For any model $m \in M$, let $S(m) = \{a \in \mathcal{A} | m(a) \notin \{\mathbf{t}, \mathbf{f}\}\}$, i.e. m is exactly restricted by $S(m)$. We denote $M'(m) = \{n \in M | S(n) = S(m)\}$ as the set of minimal models which share the same restricted set as m. Since $m \in M'(m)$, we know that $M = \bigcup_{m \in M} M'(m)$. As a result, $W \models_{cl}^4 \phi$ iff $M'(m) \models \phi$ for all $m \in M$.
    Note that m is already one four-valued model of W and restricted by $S(m)$, we know that $W \not\models_{S(m)} \mathbf{f}$. According to the definition of restricted four-valued extension, $\langle W, S(m) \rangle$ is a restricted four-valued extension of T. We call this extension be generated by m and denote it as $E(m)$.

In fact, all models of W restricted by $S(m)$ are minimal models. Otherwise, there would be a minimal model n restricted by R and $R \subsetneq S(m)$, which contradicts with m is minimal. So $M'(m) = \{n|n\,is\,a\,model\,of\,W\,restricted\,by\,S(m)\}$. As a result, $E(m) \models \phi$ iff $M'(m) \models \phi$.

Now we want to show the equivalent relation between preferred restricted four-valued extensions and generated extensions. We prove it in two directions:

1. $E(m)$ is preferred for any $m \in M$. If $E(m)$ is not preferred, then there is a restricted four-valued extension $\langle E, R\rangle$ of default theory T and $R \subsetneq S(m)$. Since $E \not\models_R \mathbf{f}$, E has a four-valued model m' restricted by R. Because $R \subsetneq S(m)$, m' is a four-valued model of W and is more consistent than m, which contradicts with m is minimal.

2. Every preferred restricted four-valued extension $\langle E, S\rangle$ is generated by some $m \in M$. Since $E \not\models_S \mathbf{f}$, there is a four-valued model n of E restricted by S. If $n \in M$, let m be n itself. Otherwise, there is a minimal model $m \in M$ which is more consistent than n. In both case m is restricted by S. So $S(m) \subseteq S$. Because both $\langle E, S\rangle$ and $E(m) = \langle W, S(m)\rangle$ are preferred restricted four-valued extensions, we also know that $S(m) \not\subseteq S$. Therefore, $S = S(m)$.

Altogether, we show that $W \models_{cl}^4 \phi$ iff $M'(m) \models \phi$ for all $m \in M$, iff $E(m) \models \phi$ for all $m \in M$, iff all preferred restricted four-valued extensions entail ϕ. □

5 Calculate Restricted Four-Valued Extensions

To compute the restricted four-valued extensions, we introduce the formula transformation proposed in [4]. The main purpose of this approach is to simulate four-valued reasoning by classical reasoning, which can be achieved by separating the truth relation of a formula and its negation. The technique details have been explained in [2,4,5].

Definition 8. *For any atom $p \in \Sigma$ and formula $\phi, \psi \in L$, define inductively:*

- $\overline{\mathbf{t}}^+ = \mathbf{t}, \overline{\mathbf{t}}^- = \mathbf{f}, \overline{\mathbf{f}}^+ = \mathbf{f}, \overline{\mathbf{f}}^- = \mathbf{t};$
- $\overline{p}^+ = p^+, \overline{p}^- = p^-;$
- $\overline{\neg\phi}^+ = \overline{\phi}^-, \overline{\neg\phi}^- = \overline{\phi}^+;$
- $\overline{\phi \vee \psi}^+ = \overline{\phi}^+ \vee \overline{\psi}^+, \overline{\phi \vee \psi}^- = \overline{\phi}^- \wedge \overline{\psi}^-;$
- $\overline{\phi \wedge \psi}^+ = \overline{\phi}^+ \wedge \overline{\psi}^+, \overline{\phi \wedge \psi}^- = \overline{\phi}^- \vee \overline{\psi}^-;$
- $\overline{\phi \supset \psi}^+ = \neg\overline{\phi}^+ \vee \overline{\psi}^+, \overline{\phi \supset \psi}^- = \overline{\phi}^+ \wedge \overline{\psi}^-;$

Theorem 6 ([4]). $\Sigma \models_4 \phi$ *iff* $\overline{\Sigma}^+ \models \overline{\phi}^+$.

The following theorem is a restricted four-valued version of Theorem 6.

Theorem 7. *For any formula set E and formula ϕ, let $\overline{E}_S^+ = \{\overline{\phi}^+ | \phi \in E\} \cup \{p^+ \leftrightarrow \neg p^- | p \notin S\}$). $E \models_S \phi$ iff $\overline{E}_S^+ \models \overline{\phi}^+$.*

Proof. According to Theorem 1 and 6, we have

$$E \models_S \phi \text{ iff } E \cup \bigcup_{p \notin S}\{p \vee \neg p, (p \wedge \neg p) \supset \mathbf{f}\} \models_4 \phi, \text{ iff } \overline{E}^+ \bigcup_{p \notin S}\{\overline{p}^+ \vee \overline{p}^-, \neg \overline{p}^+ \vee \neg \overline{p}^-\} \models \overline{\phi}^+, \text{ iff } \overline{E}_S^+ \models \overline{\phi}^+. \qquad \square$$

In [11], they construct their paraconsistent logic by transforming proposition theories to default theories after applying signed transformation. In contrast, we want to apply our signed transformation on default theories.

Definition 9. *For any default rule $d = \frac{\alpha:\beta_1,...,\beta_n}{\gamma}$, let $\overline{d}^+ = \frac{\overline{\alpha}^+ : \overline{\beta_1}^+, ..., \overline{\beta_n}^+}{\overline{\gamma}^+}$.*

Let $T = (D, W)$ be a default theory. The transformed default theory $\overline{T}_S^+$ of T restricted by S, is defined as $\overline{T}_S^+ = (\overline{D}^+, \overline{W}_S^+)$, where $\overline{D}^+ = \{\overline{d}^+ | d \in D\}$.

Theorem 8. *Let $T = (D, W)$ be a default theory. E is a restricted four-valued extension of T restricted by S, iff $\overline{E}_S^+$ is a consistent extension of $\overline{T}^+$.*

Proof. According to Theorem 7 and the definition of restricted four-valued extension, we only need to prove that $E \not\models_S \beta \supset \mathbf{f}$ iff $\overline{E}_S^+ \not\models \neg\overline{\beta}^+$, which is also proved by Theorem 7. $\qquad \square$

Theorem 8 represents a feasible approach to convert a restricted four-valued default logic problem to the corresponding default logic problem.

6 Related Works

As an important nonmonotonic logic, Reiter's default logic has been widely used in knowledge representation. In [11], their signed system is paraconsistent by using default logic to restore information from inconsistent theories. In [6], they also use default logic to process inconsistent knowledge. Conversely, we introduce paraconsistency to default logic. In [17], they develop a novel framework to deal with default reasoning with fuzzy and uncertain information. In this paper, we focus on handling inconsistent and incoherent information.

Reiter's default logic has many variants presented by different researchers. In justified default extensions [16], constrained default extensions [21] and cumulative default extensions [12], they modify the definition of extensions to ensure their existences. However, they have different semantics from default logic and still cannot deal with inconsistencies.

To take advantage of tolerance on inconsistencies, paraconsistent variants of default logic are represented by several researchers. Among these, question marked logic [1] is a generalization of the inconsistent default logic [19] which is based on Da Costa's paraconsistent logic [13]. The basic idea is annotating formulas with a hierarchy of meta-levels by question marks, and preventing trivialization by paraconsistent logic. Also, its semantics is different from Reiter's.

The bi-default logic [14] is based on a signed system and proposed for handling inconsistencies by splitting default theories to two consistent parts. The four-valued default logic [23] is based on Belnap's four-valued logic and can be treated as an expansion of four-valued logic in k-minimally reasoning. However, these approaches focus on eliminating inconsistencies but not on preventing incoherences. Also, our preferred extensions can infer stronger consequences than the k-minimal models. For example, the law of excluded middle can be infered from the only preferred restricted four-valued extension of default theory $(\emptyset, \emptyset)$, but cannot be concluded in its k-minimal models.

The fault-tolerant default logic [15] is constructed on its own paraconsistent reasoning relation $\vdash_{mc}$, and succeeds in handling inconsistencies and incoherences simultaneously. Unfortunately, it still needs to be clarified that how to compute its extensions. In contrast, we have provided a transformation from our logic to classical default logic.

By using a nonmonotonic underlying logic based on a 16-valued lattice, the annotated default logic [22] also guarantees the existence of nontrivial extensions and characterizes Reiter's default extensions in its extensions. By contrast, our default logic does not only take these advantages, but also keeps our underlying logic monotonic. As a result, our default logic holds some useful properties such like Proposition 4, which do not hold if the underlying logic is nonmonotonic.

An approach to the trivial extension problem by transforming default theories with minimally unsatisfiable subformulas is also presented in [10]. The transformed default theories still hold some information from original ones. Despite that, this approach does not handle incoherences, and some propositions only hold on normal default theories but not general ones. Even more, some information may be lost in transformation. As a comparison, our extensions are based on general default theories. We also ensure that the facts W of a default theory $T = (D, W)$ always hold in every restricted four-valued extensions.

7   Conclusion

In this paper we present our restricted four-valued default logic based on the monotonic restricted four-valued logic. In our default logic, we guarantee the existence of nontrivial extensions of default theories with inconsistent or incoherent knowledge. We also have showed that our default logic is an expansion of both default logic and preferred four-valued logic. To compute restricted four-valued extensions, a signed formula transformation is also presented.

In future, we would consider other features of restricted four-valued default logic and try to extend our work in first-order logic.

References

1. van den Akker, J., Tan, Y.H.: QML: A Paraconsistent Default Logic. Logique Et Analyse **143**(143–144), 311–328 (1993)
2. Arieli, O.: Paraconsistent preferential reasoning by signed quantified boolean formulae. In: Proceedings of the 16th Eureopean Conference on Artificial Intelligence, ECAI 2004, including Prestigious Applicants of Intelligent Systems, PAIS 2004, Valencia, Spain, August 22–27, pp. 773–777 (2004)

3. Arieli, O., Avron, A.: The value of the four values. Artificial Intelligence **102**(1), 97–141 (1998)
4. Arieli, O., Denecker, M.: Modeling paraconsistent reasoning by classical logic. In: Eiter, T., Schewe, K.-D. (eds.) FoIKS 2002. LNCS, vol. 2284, p. 1. Springer, Heidelberg (2002)
5. Arieli, O., Denecker, M.: Reducing preferential paraconsistent reasoning to classical entailment. Journal of Logic and Computation **13**(4), 557–580 (2003)
6. Arioua, A., Tamani, N., Croitoru, M., Fortin, J., Buche, P.: Investigating the mapping between default logic and inconsistency-tolerant semantics. In: Rutkowski, L., Korytkowski, M., Scherer, R., Tadeusiewicz, R., Zadeh, L.A., Zurada, J.M. (eds.) Artificial Intelligence and Soft Computing. LNCS, vol. 9120, pp. 554–564. Springer, Heidelberg (2015)
7. Arruda, A.I.: Non-classical logics, model theory, and computability on the imaginary logic of n. a. vasil'év. Studies in Logic and the Foundations of Mathematics **89**, 3–24 (1977)
8. Belnap, N.: How a computer should think. In: Ryle, G. (ed.) Contemporary Aspects of Philosophy. Oriel Press Ltd. (1977)
9. Belnap Jr., N.D.: A useful four-valued logic. In: Modern uses of multiple-valued logic, pp. 5–37. Springer (1977)
10. Besnard, P., Grégoire, É., Ramon, S.: A default logic patch for default logic. In: Sossai, C., Chemello, G. (eds.) ECSQARU 2009. LNCS, vol. 5590, pp. 578–589. Springer, Heidelberg (2009)
11. Besnard, P., Schaub, T.: A simple signed system for paraconsistent reasoning. In: Orłowska, E., Alferes, J.J., Moniz Pereira, L. (eds.) JELIA 1996. LNCS, vol. 1126, pp. 404–416. Springer, Heidelberg (1996)
12. Brewka, G.: Cumulative default logic: in defense of nonmonotonic inference rules. Artificial Intelligence **50**(2), 183–205 (1991)
13. Costa, N.C.A.D.: On the Theory of Inconsistent Formal Systems. Notre Dame Journal of Formal Logic **15**(4), 497–510 (1974)
14. Han, Q., Lin, Z.: Paraconsistent default reasoning. In: Proceedings of the 10th International Workshop on Non-Monotonic Reasoning (NMR 2004), Whistler, Canada, June 6–8, pp. 197–203 (2004)
15. Lin, Z., Ma, Y., Lin, Z.Q.: A fault-tolerant default logic. In: Fisher, M., van der Hoek, W., Konev, B., Lisitsa, A. (eds.) JELIA 2006. LNCS (LNAI), vol. 4160, pp. 253–265. Springer, Heidelberg (2006)
16. Łukaszewicz, W.: Considerations on default logic: an alternative approach. Computational intelligence **4**(1), 1–16 (1988)
17. Luo, X., Zhang, C., Jennings, N.R.: A hybrid model for sharing information between fuzzy, uncertain and default reasoning models in multi-agent systems. International Journal of Uncertainty, Fuzziness and Knowledge-Based Systems **10**(04), 401–450 (2002)
18. Papadimitriou, C.H., Sideri, M.: Default theories that always have extensions. Artificial Intelligence **69**(1), 347–357 (1994)
19. Pequeno, T.H.C., Buchsbaum, A.: The logic of epistemic inconsistency. In: Proceedings of the 2nd International Conference on Principles of Knowledge Representation and Reasoning (KR 1991), Cambridge, MA, USA, April 22–25, pp. 453–460 (1991)
20. Reiter, R.: A logic for default reasoning. Artificial intelligence **13**(1), 81–132 (1980)

21. Schaub, T.: On constrained default theories. In: Proceedings of the 10th European Conference on Artificial Intelligence (ECAI 1992), pp. 304–308. John Wiley & Sons Inc, New York (1992)
22. Yue, A., Lin, Z.: A coherent and paraconsistent variant of the default logic. In: AAAI Spring Symposium: Logical Formalizations of Commonsense Reasoning, pp. 162–162 (2007)
23. Yue, A., Ma, Y., Lin, Z.Q.: Four-valued semantics for default logic. In: Lamontagne, L., Marchand, M. (eds.) Canadian AI 2006. LNCS (LNAI), vol. 4013, pp. 195–205. Springer, Heidelberg (2006)

A Divergence Measure between Mass Functions

Jianbing Ma[1,2]([⊠])

[1] Faculty of Science and Technology, Bournemouth University,
Bournemouth BH12 5BB, UK
ac1023@coventry.ac.uk
[2] Department of Computing, Coventry University, Coventry CV1 2BS, UK

Abstract. Evidence theory is widely used in data mining, machine learning, clustering and database systems. In these applications, often combination of mass functions is performed without checking the degree of consistency between the mass functions, which may lead to counterintuitive results. In this paper, we aim to measure the divergences among mass functions which can hence prevent highly inconsistent mass functions from been combined. To this end, we propose a divergence measure between two mass functions. In addition, incompleteness measures and similarity measures are also provided based on divergence measures.

1 Introduction

The Dempster-Shafer theory of evidence [7,25] is a well known framework to model and reason with incomplete information in intelligent systems. In knowledge discovery community, this theory is widely used in data mining [1,2], machine learning [11,33], clustering [24,29], bus surveillance [17,20,21], belief revision [16], gender profiling [18,19] and database systems [10,22], etc. In these applications, generally Dempster's combination rule is applied to mass functions from multiple sources to obtain an aggregated result. However, this rule for combining two sources of conflicting beliefs is criticized by many authors, e.g., [6,15,32], as it may lead to some counterintuitive results such as an almost impossible choice (with a very small degree of belief) by both sources becomes the unique and certain choice after combination.

To remedy this weakness, a set of alternative combination rules are proposed, e.g., [9,12,26–28,30,31], etc. These studies are mainly focused on investigating the conditions by which these alternatives can be used to resolve the conflict. However, a fundamental question that what does *conflict* mean between two sources of beliefs was almost ignored in a long time. These papers by default follow the perspective of Dempster's rule that the conflict can be measured by the so-called *conflicting* mass, i.e., the mass of the combined belief assigned to the empty set before normalization. In [15], this issue is observed and examined in details. Liu argued that the conflicting mass itself cannot be an adequate measurement for conflict between two sources of beliefs, but it needs to be grouped with another dimension of conflict measure, i.e., the distance between betting commitments of beliefs, to form a safe measure of conflict. More precisely, only

© Springer International Publishing Switzerland 2015
S. Zhang et al. (Eds.): KSEM 2015, LNAI 9403, pp. 53–65, 2015.
DOI: 10.1007/978-3-319-25159-2_5

when the two components of Liu's measure both give high values, it is safe to declare that the two sources of beliefs are in conflict.

However, in these two components of Liu's measure, the conflict brought by the incompleteness (or ignorance) nature of the beliefs is neglected. For instance, these two components might both give 0 when the two beliefs are not the same, e.g., when one belief is represented as a vacuous belief and the other is represented by an evenly distributed mass function. In that situation, the inconsistency, or more precisely divergence (or difference), of the two beliefs due to the incompleteness of the former is not present in the two components of Liu's measure. Similarly it is neithter considered in other measures of conflict, e.g. [5,23]. Hence, it is interesting to investigate the divergence of beliefs on the base of incompleteness. In this paper, we therefore propose a *divergence* measure to compare two sources of beliefs considering both uncertainty and incompleteness. Based on the divergence measure, the incompleteness measure is also provided.

Similarity measures between two bbas are widely used in clustering [24,29]. However, typically such measures are not well justified. In this paper, we also propose a similarity measure based on divergence measure and hence with good properties. In addition, in [8], a set of six properties for similarity measure between two focal elements are proposed, here we verify that the similarity measure defined on divergence measure for two focal elements does satisfy half of the properties proposed in [8], obeys stronger versions for two remaining ones and the last property is not reasonable in some sense.

The rest of the paper is organized as follows. In Section 2, we recall some basic concepts of evidence theory. In Section 3, 4, and 5, we propose the divergence measure, incompleteness measure and similarity measure, respectively. Finally, in Section 6, we conclude the paper.

2   Preliminaries

By abuse of notation, when A is a set, $|A|$ denotes its cardinality, when a is a real value, $|a|$ denotes the absolute value of a. The semantics of $||$ will be made clear by the context.

For reader's convenience, we recall some basic concepts of Dempster-Shafer's theory of evidence.

Let Ω be a finite set called the frame of discernment. In this paper, we denote $\Omega = \{\omega_1, \ldots, \omega_n\}$.

Definition 1. *A basic belief assignment (bba for short) is a mapping* $m : 2^\Omega \to [0,1]$ *such that* $\sum_{A \subseteq \Omega} m(A) = 1$.

A bba m is also called a mass function when $m(\emptyset) = 0$ is required. In this paper, all the bbas we consider are mass functions.

From a bba m, two associated functions: belief function Bel and plausibility function Pl, can be defined as follows:

$$Bel(A) = \sum_{B \subseteq A} m(B),$$

$$Pl(A) = 1 - Bel(\Omega \setminus A).$$

$Bel(A)$ depicts the amount of belief that directly supports that A is true while $Pl(A)$ denotes the amount of belief that does not contradict A.

If $m(A) > 0$, then A is called a focal element of m. Let $\mathscr{F}_m$ be the set of focal elements in m and $\mathscr{C}_m = \bigcup_{A \in \mathscr{F}_m} A$ be the union of all focal elements of m. A bba m is called *categorical* if and only if m has only one focal element.

Two bbas m_1 and m_2 are called *orthogonal* iff there exists $A_1 \in \mathscr{F}_{m_1}, A_2 \in \mathscr{F}_{m_2}$ such that $Bel_1(A_1) = Bel_2(A_2) = 1$ and $A_1 \cap A_2 = \emptyset$. They are called *orthogonal categorical* when m_1 and m_2 are both categorical bbas and they are orthogonal.

A bba m is called *Bayesian* iff all of its focal elements are singletons. In this situation, m is in fact a probability function. A bba m is called *partitioned* iff its focal elements $A_1, \cdots, A_k$ satisfy

$$A_1 \cup \cdots \cup A_k = \Omega, \quad and \quad A_i \cap A_j = \emptyset \ for \ i \neq j.$$

The famous Dempster's rule of combination on two bbas m_1 and m_2 from two distinct sources is defined as

$$m_{12}(C) = \frac{\sum_{A \cap B = C} m_1(A) m_2(B)}{1 - \sum_{A \cap B = \emptyset} m_1(A) m_2(B)}, \forall C \neq \emptyset.$$

$$m_{12}(\emptyset) = 0.$$

Here m_{12} denotes the bba after applying Dempster's combination rule. We also use $m^{12}(\emptyset)$ to denote the conflicting mass such that $m^{12}(\emptyset) = \sum_{A \cap B = \emptyset} m_1(A) m_2(B)$. Note that Dempster's rule only applies when $m^{12}(\emptyset) < 1$.

Definition 2. *Let m be a bba over Ω. Its associated pignistic probability function $BetP_m : \Omega \to [0,1]$ is defined as:*

$$BetP_m(w) = \sum_{A \subseteq \Omega, w \in A} \frac{1}{|A|} \frac{m(A)}{1 - m(\emptyset)}, m(\emptyset) < 1.$$

where $|A|$ is the cardinality of A.

Usually, $BetP_m(A)$ is called the *betting commitment* to A, and $BetP_m$ is the *probability expectation function* of m [12]. Note that the transformation from m to $BetP_m$ eliminates the influence of incompleteness.

In [15], the *distance between betting commitments of beliefs* is defined as follows.

Definition 3. *Let m_1, m_2 be two bbas over Ω, and their corresponding pignistic probability function be $BetP_{m_1}$ and $BetP_{m_2}$ respectively, then the distance between betting commitments of m_1 and m_2 is defined as: $difBetP_{m_1}^{m_2} = max_{A \subseteq \Omega}(|BetP_{m_1}(A) - BetP_{m_2}(A)|)$.*

According to [15], $difBetP_{m_1}^{m_2}$ gives the maximum extent of the differences between betting commitments to all the subsets. Hereafter we will simply write $difBetP$ instead of $difBetP_{m_1}^{m_2}$ if there is no confusion as which two bbas are being compared.

$difBetP$ does not consider any incompleteness information, as illustrated by the following result [4,5].

Proposition 1. $difBetP = \frac{\sum_{w \in \Omega} |BetP^{m_1}(w) - BetP^{m_2}(w)|}{2}$.

This result shows that $difBetP$ totally depends on values of singletons, which does not involve incompleteness.

3   Divergence Between Two Basic Belief Assignments

Although the conflict mass $m^{12}(\emptyset)$ and the difference between betting commitment $difBetP$ present a good measure as to whether two bbas are in high conflict, they cannot distinguish two bbas which are different but in harmony. Thus they are neither good enough for classification of small conflicts nor conflictness/non-conflictness. More precisely, there could be two different bbas such that the corresponding $m^{12}(\emptyset)$ and $difBetP$ both are zero.

Example 1. *Let* m_1, m_2 *be two bbas from two distinct sources on frame* $\Omega = \{\omega_1, \omega_2, \omega_3, \omega_4, \omega_5\}$ *be:*

$$m_1(\{\omega_1\}) = m_1(\{\omega_2\}) = m_1(\{\omega_3\}) = m_1(\{\omega_4\}) = m_1(\{\omega_5\}) = 0.2,$$

$$m_2(\{\omega_1, \omega_2, \omega_3, \omega_4, \omega_5\}) = 1.$$

Obviously, m_1 *and* m_2 *are different, but we have* $m^{12}(\emptyset) = 0$ *and* $difBetP = 0$. *This example shows difference between conflict and divergence.*

From the above example, it is obvious that the conflict mass and the difference between betting commitment could not fully reflect the difference between two bbas. It might be argued that in some sense, m_1 and m_2 in the above example are *coherent*. However, in many applications, e.g., in classification problems [3], m_1 has a clear meaning that one item is classified as ω_1 (resp. $\omega_2, \omega_3, \omega_4, \omega_5$) with a degree of certainty 0.2, whilst m_2 just tells that the item cannot be classified. That is, m_2 contains much more incompleteness (which is in full ignorance) than m_1 (which has no ignorance). Therefore, we need a kind of measure that can distinguish these two bbas. Intuitively, the measure is required to have the following constraints. Formally, let $div(m_1, m_2)$ denote a measure of divergence of two bbas m_1 and m_2, we should have:

Non-negativeness $div(m_1, m_2) \geq 0$, and $div(m_1, m_2) = 0$ iff $m_1 = m_2$.
   Explanation: Any two different bbas could be distinguished by this measure.

Orthogonality $div(m_1, m_2) \leq 1$, and $div(m_1, m_2) = 1$ iff m_1 and m_2 are orthogonal categorical.

Explanation: Intuitively and semantically, orthogonal categorical bbas are in total conflict. Therefore, this measure gives a greatest value 1 to indicate this *total conflict* whilst for other occasions, this measure should give a value less than 1.

Obviously, $m^{12}(\emptyset)$ and $difBetP$, does not satisfy the above two conditions.

Now we start to define a *divergence* measure to describe the difference between two bbas satisfying the above conditions. This definition takes several steps. First, we define the divergence between two focal elements of two bbas, respectively.

Definition 4. *Let m_1, m_2 be two bbas over Ω, and A_1, A_2 be two arbitrary focal elements of m_1 and m_2, respectively, we define the divergence of A_1 and A_2 w.r.t m_1 and m_2 as* $div_{m_2}^{m_1}(A_1, A_2) = \frac{1}{2}(m_1(A_1)\frac{|A_1-A_2|}{|A_1|} + m_2(A_2)\frac{|A_2-A_1|}{|A_2|} + |m_1(A_1)\frac{|A_1 \cap A_2|}{|A_1|} - m_2(A_2)\frac{|A_1 \cap A_2|}{|A_2|}|).$

Here $m_1(A_1)\frac{|A_1-A_2|}{|A_1|}$ indicates the part that A_1 differs from A_2, $m_2(A_2)\frac{|A_2-A_1|}{|A_2|}$ indicates the part that A_2 differs from A_1, and $|m_1(A_1)\frac{|A_1 \cap A_2|}{|A_1|} - m_2(A_2)\frac{|A_1 \cap A_2|}{|A_2|}|$ indicates the difference of the intersected part.

In particular, if $A_1 \cap A_2 = \emptyset$, then $div_{m_2}^{m_1}(A_1, A_2) = \frac{1}{2}(m_1(A_1) + m_2(A_2))$. If $A_1 = A_2 = A$, then $div_{m_2}^{m_1}(A_1, A_2) = \frac{1}{2}(|m_1(A) - m_2(A)|)$. $div_{m_2}^{m_1}(A_1, A_2)$ can be seen as the degree that A_1 can be adapted to A_2.

We find that $div_{m_2}^{m_1}(A_1, A_2)$ has some good properties, i.e., it is a super-distance in the following sense.

Proposition 2. *Let m_1, m_2 be two bbas over Ω, and A_1, A_2 be two arbitrary focal elements of m_1 and m_2, respectively, then we have:*

F-Super-Nonnegativeness $div_{m_2}^{m_1}(A_1, A_2) \geq 0$, *and* $div_{m_2}^{m_1}(A_1, A_2) = 0$ *iff* $A_1 = A_2$ *and* $m_1(A_1) = m_2(A_2)$.
F-Symmetry $div_{m_2}^{m_1}(A_1, A_2) = div_{m_1}^{m_2}(A_2, A_1)$.
F-Triangle Inequity *Let A_3 be a focal element of a bba m_3 over Ω, then we have* $div_{m_2}^{m_1}(A_1, A_2) + div_{m_3}^{m_2}(A_2, A_3) \geq div_{m_1}^{m_3}(A_3, A_1)$.
F-Orthogonality $div_{m_2}^{m_1}(A_1, A_2) = 1$ *iff* $A_1 \cap A_2 = \emptyset$ *and* $m_1(A_1) = m_2(A_2) = 1$.

Here $F-$ indicates that these properties are for divergence between focal elements.

We then define the divergence between a focal element A_1 of m_1 to m_2, i.e., $div^{m_1}(A_1, m_2)$ as follows.

Definition 5. *Let m_1, m_2 be two bbas over Ω, and A_1 be an arbitrary focal element of m_1, then we define the divergence of A_1 to m_2 as*

$$div^{m_1}(A_1, m_2) = min_{A_2 \in \mathscr{F}_{m_2}} div_{m_2}^{m_1}(A_1, A_2).$$

By convention the divergence of A_1 to m_2 is the minimal divergence of A_1 to any focal element of m_2. $div^{m_1}(A_1, m_2)$ can be viewed as the minimal degree that A_1 can be adapted to some focal element(s) of m_2.

Based on $div^{m_1}(A_1, m_2)$, we can define the divergence of one bba m_1 to another bba m_2, i.e., $div^{m_1}(m_2)$, as follows.

Definition 6. *Let m_1, m_2 be two bbas over Ω, then we define the divergence of m_1 to m_2 as $div^{m_1}(m_2) = max_{A_1 \in \mathscr{F}_{m_1}} div^{m_1}(A_1, m_2)$.*

Here the reason why we use max instead of using min is that if m_1 and m_2 are partly consistent, using min will make the divergence equivalent to zero.

Example 2. *Let m_1, m_2 be two bbas from two distinct sources on frame $\Omega = \{\omega_1, \omega_2, \omega_3, \omega_4, \omega_5\}$ be:*

$$m_1(\{\omega_1\}) = 0.1, m_1(\{\omega_2\}) = m_1(\{\omega_3\}) = 0.45,$$

$$m_2(\{\omega_1\}) = 0.1, m_2(\{\omega_4\}) = m_2(\{\omega_5\}) = 0.45.$$

If we use min in Def. 6, then as m_1 and m_2 are partly consistent on $\{\omega_1\}$, we get $div^{m_1}(m_2) = 0$ which is against our assumption.

The reason why we use max instead of using $+$ is to avoid multiple uses of one focal element, as illustrated by the following example.

Example 3. *(Example 2 Continued) Let m_1, m_2 be two bbas as indicated in Example 2. Note that from Definition 5 we have $div^{m_1}(\{\omega_1\}, m_2) = div^{m_1}(\{\omega_1\}, \{\omega_1\})$, $div^{m_1}(\{\omega_2\}, m_2) = div^{m_1}(\{\omega_2\}, \{\omega_1\})$, and $div^{m_1}(\{\omega_3\}, m_2) = div^{m_1}(\{\omega_3\}, \{\omega_1\})$. Hence if we use $+$ instead of max in Def. 6, then $\{\omega_1\}$ in m_2 will be added by three times in summation (since we assume to use $+$) which is not reasonable.*

If we consider $div^{m_1}(A, m_2)$ as the degree of minimal change that A can be adapted to a focal element in m_2, then $div^{m_1}(m_2)$ can be regarded as the upper bound of degree of minimal change that (any) focal element of m_1 can be adapted to a focal element of m_2.

For divergence of one bba to another, we can prove that it satisfies the proposed two conditions. Namely, we have:

Proposition 3. *Let m_1, m_2 be two bbas over Ω, then $div^{m_1}(m_2)$ satisfies the NonNegativeness and Orthogonality properties.*

It is not very surprising that $div^{m_1}(m_2) \neq div^{m_2}(m_1)$. Since although $div^{m_1}(m_2)$ is distance alike, it is not a distance measure. $div^{m_1}(m_2)$ gives the maximal degree of all the focal elements of m_1 in *adaption* to m_2, whilst $div^{m_2}(m_1)$ is for focal elements of m_2 in *adaption* to m_1. But the adaption itself is not symmetrical. That is, if $div^{m_1}(A_1, m_2) = div^{m_1}(A_1, A_2)$, then it is not necessary that $div^{m_2}(A_2, m_1) = div^{m_2}(A_2, A_1)$.

Of course, we can define symmetric divergence measures between two bbas based on $div^{m_1}(m_2)$.

Definition 7. *Let m_1, m_2 be two bbas over Ω, then we define the divergence between m_1 and m_2 as $div(m_1, m_2) = max\big(div^{m_1}(m_2), div^{m_2}(m_1)\big)$.*

$div(m_1, m_2)$ gives the minimal degree of changes that any focal element of m_1 could be adapted to a focal element of m_2, and vice versa.

It is obvious that $div(m_1, m_2)$ also satisfies the proposed two conditions.

Proposition 4. *Let m_1, m_2 be two bbas over Ω, then $div(m_1, m_2)$ satisfies the NonNegativeness and Orthogonality properties.*

Nonnegativeness $div(m_1, m_2) \geq 0$, and $div(m_1, m_2) = 0$ iff $m_1 = m_2$.
Orthogonality $div(m_1, m_2) \leq 1$ and $div(m_1, m_2) = 1$ iff m_1, m_2 are orthogonal categorical.

4   An Incompleteness Measure of a Single BBA

It is well known that probability measures are used to represent uncertainty and bbas are used to represent both uncertainty and incompleteness. However, there are no measures on bbas to detect in what degree it is incomplete. We think this fundamental problem should be considered. Therefore, in this section, we propose a measure on the incompleteness of a bba. This incompleteness measure is based on the divergence measure $div(m_1, m_2)$. To illustrate the problem clearer, we first look at the following examples.

Example 4. *Let m_1, m_2, m_3 be three bbas from three distinct sources on the same frame be:*

$$m_1(\omega_1) = m_1(\omega_2) = m_1(\omega_3) = m_1(\omega_4) = m_1(\omega_5) = 0.2,$$

$$m_2(\{\omega_1, \omega_2\}) = 0.4, m_2(\{\omega_3, \omega_4, \omega_5\}) = 0.6, m_3(\{\omega_1, \omega_2, \omega_3, \omega_4, \omega_5\}) = 1.$$

For m_1 and m_2, we get $m^{12}(\emptyset) = 0.48$, $difBetP^{m_1}_{m_2} = 0$, and $div(m_1, m_2) = 0.2$.
For m_1 and m_3, we get $m^{13}(\emptyset) = 0$, $difBetP^{m_1}_{m_3} = 0$, but $div(m_1, m_3) = 0.4$.

It is not surprising to see that $div(m_1, m_3)$ is greater than $div(m_1, m_2)$. Compared with m_2, although the corresponding pignistic functions of m_2 and m_3 are the same, m_3 increases the incompleteness of belief. For the conflict mass $m^{12}(\emptyset)$ and $m^{13}(\emptyset)$, it is somehow counterintuitive that increasing incompleteness actually reduces conflict. For $difBetP$, it simply cannot measure the change of incompleteness in this occasion. In fact, as $difBetP$ is based on pignistic transformation which completely removes the incompleteness (Prop. 1), this is not astonishing. In contrast, $div(m_1, m_2)$ can nicely reflect the change of incompleteness. In this sense, $div(m_1, m_2)$ can be seen as depicting the conflict brought by incompleteness.

Now we define the incompleteness of a bba.

Definition 8. *Let m be a bba over Ω, then we define the incompleteness of m as*

$$icmp(m) = div(m, BetP_m)$$

where $BetP_m$ be the pignistic probability function of m.

Intuitively, as $BetP_m$ is the corresponding pignistic probability function of m, in some sense, it can be seen as measuring the uncertainty part of m, hence a divergence measure between m and $BetP_m$ can intuitively *remove* the influence of uncertainty in m, and reveal the incompleteness of m only.

Example 5. *Let m be a bba over $\Omega = \{\omega_1, \omega_2, \omega_3\}$ such that $m_1(\{\omega_1, \omega_2\}) = 0.7$, $m_1(\{\omega_3\}) = 0.3$, then we have $icmp(m) = 0.35$.*

Naturally, if m is already a Bayesian bba, then it is not incomplete. In fact, we actually have the following result.

Proposition 5. *Let m be a Bayesian bba over Ω, then we have $icmp(m) = 0$.*

A direct and clear illustration of incompleteness is the partitioned bbas.

Example 6. *Let m_1, m_2 be two bbas over $\Omega = \{\omega_1, \omega_2, \omega_3, \omega_4, \omega_5\}$ such that $m_1(\{\omega_1, \omega_2, \omega_3\}) = 0.6, m_1(\{\omega_4, \omega_5\}) = 0.4$, and $m_2(\{\omega_1\}) = 0.2, m_2(\{\omega_2, \omega_3\}) = 0.4, m_2(\{\omega_4\}) = 0.2, m_2(\{\omega_5\}) = 0.2$.*
Obviously, m_1 is more incomplete than m_2. In fact, we do have $icmp(m_1) = 0.4 > 0.2 = icmp(m_2)$.

It could be generalized to the following result. But first we need to introduce a concept. For two partitioned bbas m_1 and m_2, m_2 is called *finer* than m_1 iff any focal element of m_2 is a subset of a focal element of m_1, i.e., $\forall A_2 \in \mathscr{F}_{m_2}$, $\exists A_1 \in \mathscr{F}_{m_1}$, s.t., $A_2 \subseteq A_1$.

Proposition 6. *Let m_1, m_2 be two partitioned bbas and m_2 be finer than m_1. If $BetP_{m_1} = BetP_{m_2}$, then we have $icmp(m_1) \geq icmp(m_2)$.*

5   Similarity Measures

In [29], similarity measures based on bbas are used for clustering as follows.
Let $\mathscr{M} = \bigcup_{A \in \mathscr{F}_m} A$ be the union of all focal elements in a bba m, usually called the *core* of m.
The similarity measure from [29] is $sim(m_1, m_2) = min(\sum_{A \subseteq \mathscr{M}_2} m_1(A), \sum_{B \subseteq \mathscr{M}_1} m_2(B))$.
In [24], entropy based similarity measures are used for clustering. In both papers, the proposed similarity measures are not well justified.
It is obvious that divergence measures and similarity measures are two sides of one coin. Namely, we can define our similarity measure based on divergence measures.

Definition 9. *Let m_1, m_2 be two bbas over Ω, then a similarity measure is defined as*

$$sim'(m_1, m_2) = 1 - div(m_1, m_2),$$

where $div(m_1, m_2)$ is the divergence measure between m_1 and m_2 defined in Definition 7.

Properties of the similarity measure sim' can be easily induced from those of the divergence measure.

In [8], a set of conditions for similarity measures between focal elements are proposed as follows (Let S be a similarity measure between two focal elements A, B):

S1 Normalization: $S(A, B) \in [0, 1]$
S2 Symmetry: $S(A, B) = S(B, A)$
S3 Both increasing on $|A \cap B|$ and decreasing on $|A - B|$ and $|B - A|$
S4 $S(A, B) = 1$ if and only if $A = B$
S5 Exclusiveness: $S(A, B) = 0$ if and only if $A \cap B = \emptyset$
S6 Decreasing on R where $R = \frac{|A \cup B|}{|\Omega|}$

Since the similarity measure used in the above conditions consider focal elements, we have to use $S(A_1, A_2) = 1 - div_{m_2}^{m_1}(A_1, A_2)$ as a similarity measure defined between two focal elements A_1, A_2 of m_1, m_2, respectively.

It is easy to verify that $S(A_1, A_2)$ satisfies S1-3, and impose stronger constraints compared to S4 and S5 (see Proposition 2). S6 is indeed debatable since the possible world can be viewed with different granularity (and hence the size of the subsets changes) but the similarity should not change according to the different views since the events actually do not change. For example, suppose $\Omega = \{w_1, \cdots, w_{10}\}$, $A = \{w_1, \cdots, w_6\}$ and $B = \{w_4, \cdots, w_9\}$, then we can see that $|A - B| = |B - A| = |A \cap B| = 3$, and $R = 0.9$. However, if we view $A - B$, $B - A$ and $A \cap B$ as subsets that contain only a single big possible world, that is, let $\{w_1'\} = \{w_1, w_2, w_3\}$, $\{w_2'\} = \{w_4, w_5, w_6\}$, and $\{w_3'\} = \{w_7, w_8, w_9\}$[1] be three coarsened possible worlds, then we have $\Omega' = \{w_1', w_2', w_3', w_{10}\}$, $A' = \{w_1', w_2'\}$, $B' = \{w_1', w_3'\}$, and now we have $R = 0.75$. However, the only change in this example is that the granularity of possible worlds instead of the events, so the similarity value in this case have a good reason to remain the same.

6 Conclusion and Future Work

In this paper, we investigated how to measure the difference between two bbas and the incompleteness information contained by a bba. We hence proposed

---

[1] This can happen when we want to coarsen our frame of discernment. For instance, a subset containing two possible worlds *red and long sock* and *red and short sock* can be coarsened as a big possible world *red sock* if the granularity of possible worlds becomes coarser.

divergence measures for bbas indicating the degree to which one bba can adapt to another. Based on the divergence measure, incompleteness and similarity measures were also provided. In addition, properties of the proposed measures were studied.

The idea of divergence measure does not come from the distance between two bbas. However, from the properties it seem that the measure has a close relationship to distance measures. So it will be an interesting issue to explore the relationships between the divergence measure and the distance measures [13,14] in the future.

In addition, we want to study the sufficient and necessary conditions when $div_{m_2}^{m_1} = div_{m_1}^{m_2}$. We will also try to explore characteristics of other measures such as if we define the divergence between two bbas m_1 and m_2 as follows:

$$div_{m_2}^{m_1}(A_1, A_2) =$$

$$\frac{1}{2}(m_1(A_1)\frac{|A_1 - A_2|}{|A_1|} + m_2(A_2)\frac{|A_2 - A_1|}{|A_2|} + |m_1(A_1) - m_2(A_2)|(\frac{|A_1 \cap A_2|}{|A_1|} + \frac{|A_1 \cap A_2|}{|A_2|}))$$

Here we can see that only the intersection part in the divergence measure is modified to reflect the difference between m_1 and m_2 on both their mass values and sizes of the focal elements. Other min, max based alternatives also deserve exploration.

Furthermore, as a verification, we aim to use the measures in real applications like clustering and data mining.

Acknowledgement. The author thanks to Dr. Milan Daniel for his comments and great help.

References

1. Anand, S., Bell, D., Hughes, J.: Edm: A general framework for data mining based on evidence theory. Data & Knowledge Engineering **18**(3), 189–223 (1996)
2. Aslandogan, Y., Mahajani, G., Taylor, S.: Inter. Conf. on Information Technology: Coding and Computing. Chapter Evidence Combination in Medical Data Mining, vol. 2 (2004)
3. Bi, Y., Guan, J., Bell, D.: The combination of multiple classifiers using an evidential reasoning approach. Artif. Intell. **172**(15), 1731–1751 (2008)
4. Daniel, M.: Belief functions: a revision of plausibility conflict and pignistic conflict. In: Subrahmanian, V.S., Liu, W., Wijsen, J. (eds.) SUM 2013. LNCS(LNCS), vol. 8078, pp. 190–203. Springer, Heidelberg (2013)
5. Daniel, M.: Properties of plausibility conflict of belief functions. In: Rutkowski, L., Korytkowski, M., Scherer, R., Tadeusiewicz, R., Zadeh, L.A., Zurada, J.M. (eds.) ICAISC 2013, Part I. LNCS(LNAI), vol. 7894, pp. 235–246. Springer, Heidelberg (2013)
6. Daniel, M., Ma, J.: Conflicts of belief functions: continuity and frame resizement. In: Calì, A., Straccia, U. (eds.) SUM 2014. LNCS, vol. 8720, pp. 106–119. Springer, Heidelberg (2014)

7. Dempster, A.P.: Upper and lower probabilities induced by a multivalued mapping. The Annals of Statistics **28**, 325–339 (1967)

8. Diaz, J., Rifqi, M., Bouchon-Meunier, B.: A similarity measure between basic belief assignments. In: Proceedings of the 9th International Conference on Information Fusion, pp. 1–6, July 2006

9. Dubois, D., Prade, H.: Representation and combination of uncertainty with belief functions and possibility measures. Comput. Intel. **4**, 244–264 (1988)

10. He, D., Göker, A., Harper, D.: Combining evidence for automatic web session identification. Information Processing & Management **38**(5), 727–742 (2002)

11. Hegarat-Mascle, S., Bloch, I., Vidal-Madjar, D.: Application of dempster-shafer evidence theory to unsupervised classification in multisource remote sensing. IEEE transactions on geoscience and remote sensing **35**(4), 795–979 (1997)

12. Josang, A.: The consensus operator for combining beliefs. Artificial Intelligence **141**(1–2), 157–170 (2002)

13. Jousselme, A., Grenier, D., Bosse, E.: A new distance between two bodies of evidence. Information Fusion **2**(2), 91–101 (2001)

14. Jousselme, A., Maupin, P.: Distances in evidence theory: Comprehensive survey and generalizations. International Journal of Approximate Reasoning **53**(2), 118–145 (2012)

15. Liu, W.: Analyzing the degree of conflict among belief functions. Artificial Intelligence **170**, 909–924 (2006)

16. Ma, J., Liu, W., Dubois, D., Prade, H.: Bridging jeffery's rule, agm revision, and dempster conditioning in the theory of evidence. International Journal of Artificial Intelligence Tools **20**(4), 691–720 (2011)

17. Ma, J., Liu, W., Miller, P.: Event modelling and reasoning with uncertain information for distributed sensor networks. In: Deshpande, A., Hunter, A. (eds.) SUM 2010. LNCS, vol. 6379, pp. 236–249. Springer, Heidelberg (2010)

18. Ma, J., Liu, W., Miller, P.: Evidential fusion for gender profiling. In: Link, S., Fober, T., Seeger, B., Hüllermeier, E. (eds.) SUM 2012. LNCS, vol. 7520, pp. 514–524. Springer, Heidelberg (2012)

19. Ma, J., Liu, W., Miller, P.: An evidential improvement for gender profiling. In: Denoeux, T., Masson, M.-H. (eds.) Belief Functions: Theory and Applications. AISC, pp. 29–36. Springer, Heidelberg (2012)

20. Ma, J., Liu, W., Miller, P., Yan, W.: Event composition with imperfect information for bus surveillance. In: Proc. of AVSS 2009, pp. 382–387 (2009)

21. Ma, W., Liu, W., Ma, J., Miller, P.: An extended event reasoning framework for decision support under uncertainty. In: Bouchon-Meunier, B., Yager, R.R., Laurent, A., Strauss, O. (eds.) IPMU 2014, Part III. CCIS, vol. 444, pp. 335–344. Springer, Heidelberg (2014)

22. McClean, S., Scotney, B.: Using evidence theory for the integration of distributed databases. International Journal of Intelligent Systems **12**(10), 763–776 (1998)

23. Daniel, M.: Conflict between belief functions: a new measure based on their non-conflicting parts. In: Cuzzolin, F. (ed.) BELIEF 2014. LNCS(LNAI), vol. 8764, pp. 321–330. Springer, Heidelberg (2014)

24. Perry, W., Stephanou, H.: Proc. of IEEE Inter. Symp. on Intelligent Control. Chapter Belief Function Divergence as a Classifier, pp. 280–285 (1991)

25. Shafer, G.: A Mathematical Theory of Evidence. Princeton University Press (1976)

26. Smarandache, F., Dezert, J.: An introduction to the dsm theory for the combination of paradoxical, uncertain, and imprecise sources of information. http://arxiv.org/abs/cs/0608002

27. Smets, P.: Data fusion in the transferable belief model. In: Proceedings of International Conference on Information Fusion, Paris, July 2000
28. Smets, P., Kennes, R.: The transferable belief model. Artificial Intelligence **66**(2), 191–234 (1994)
29. Xie, Y., Phoha, V.: Procs. of 1st inter. conf. on knowledge capture, K-cap 2001, pp. 202–208. ACM (2001)
30. Yager, R.: On the relationships of methods of aggregation of evidence in expert systems. Cybernetics and Systems **16**, 1–21 (1985)
31. Yager, R.: On the dempster-shafer framework and new combination rules. Inform. Sci. **41**, 93–138 (1987)
32. Zadeh, L.: A simple view of the dempster-shafer theory of evidence and its implication for the rule of combination. AI Magazine **7**, 85–90 (1986)
33. Zeng, D., Xu, J., Xu, G.: Data fusion for traffic incident detection using d-s evidence theory with probabilistic svms. Journal of Computers **3**(10), 36–43 (2008)

Appendix

We only give the proof of Proposition 2. Other proofs are omitted due to their straightforwardness.

Proof of Proposition 2: The F-symmetry property is straightforward.

For F-Super-NonNegativeness, we get $div_{m_2}^{m_1}(A_1, A_2) = 0$ if and only if we have $m_1(A_1)\frac{|A_1-A_2|}{|A_1|} = m_2(A_2)\frac{|A_2-A_1|}{|A_2|} = |m_1(A_1)\frac{|A_1 \cap A_2|}{|A_1|} - m_2(A_2)\frac{|A_1 \cap A_2|}{|A_2|}| = 0$, as A_1, A_2 are focal elements, from $m_1(A_1)\frac{|A_1-A_2|}{|A_1|} = m_2(A_2)\frac{|A_2-A_1|}{|A_2|} = 0$, we get $|A_1 - A_2| = |A_2 - A_1| = 0$, namely $A_1 = A_2$, hence from $|m_1(A_1)\frac{|A_1 \cap A_2|}{|A_1|} - m_2(A_2)\frac{|A_1 \cap A_2|}{|A_2|}| = 0$, we get $m_1(A_1) = m_2(A_2)$.

For F-Triangle Inequity, let $x_1 = \frac{m_1(A_1)}{2*|A_1|}$, $x_2 = \frac{m_2(A_2)}{2*|A_2|}$ and $x_3 = \frac{m_3(A_3)}{2*|A_3|}$, notice that $|A - A'| = |A| - |A \cap A'|$, we only need to show for any $0 < x_1, x_2, x_3$, $x_1(|A_1| - |A_1 \cap A_3|) + x_2(|A_2| - |A_2 \cap A_3|) + x_3(|A_3| - |A_1 \cap A_3|) + x_3(|A_3| - |A_2 \cap A_3|) + |(x_1 - x_3)|A_1 \cap A_3| + |(x_2 - x_3)|A_2 \cap A_3| \geq x_1(|A_1| - |A_1 \cap A_2|) + x_2(|A_2| - |A_2 \cap A_1|) + |(x_1 - x_2)|A_1 \cap A_2|$.

For simplicity, denote $L(X,Y,Z) = X(|A_1| - |A_1 \cap A_3|) + Y(|A_2| - |A_2 \cap A_3|) + Z(|A_3| - |A_1 \cap A_3|) + Z(|A_3| - |A_2 \cap A_3|) + |(X - Z)|A_1 \cap A_3| + |(Y - Z)|A_2 \cap A_3|$ and $R(X,Y) = X(|A_1| - |A_1 \cap A_2|) + Y(|A_2| - |A_2 \cap A_1|) + |(X - Y)|A_1 \cap A_2|$, we need to show $L(x_1, x_2, x_3) \geq R(x_1, x_2)$. We consider the following three cases.

Case 1: If $x_1 \leq x_2 \leq x_3$, let $\delta_x = x_3 - x_2 \geq 0$, we get $L(x_1, x_3, x_3) = L(x_1, x_2, x_3) + \delta_x(|A_2| - |A_2 \cap A_3|) - \delta_x|A_2 \cap A_3|$ and $R(x_1, x_3) = R(x_1, x_2) + \delta_x(|A_2| - |A_1 \cap A_2|) + \delta_x|A_1 \cap A_2| = R(x_1, x_2) + \delta_x|A_2|$. Hence we only need to $L(x_1, x_3, x_3) - \delta_x(|A_2| - |A_2 \cap A_3|) + \delta_x|A_2 \cap A_3| \geq R(x_1, x_3) - \delta_x|A_2|$ or $L(x_1, x_3, x_3) + 2 * \delta_x|A_2 \cap A_3| \geq R(x_1, x_3)$. As $2 * \delta_x|A_2 \cap A_3| \geq 0$, it is sufficient to show $L(x_1, x_3, x_3) \geq R(x_1, x_3)$. Let $\lambda_x = x_3 - x_1 \geq 0$, we get $L(x_1, x_3, x_3) = L(x_1, x_1, x_1) + \lambda_x(|A_2| - |A_2 \cap A_3|) + \lambda_x(|A_3| - |A_1 \cap A_3|) + \lambda_x(|A_3| - |A_2 \cap A_3|) + \lambda_x|A_1 \cap A_3|$ and $R(x_1, x_3) = R(x_1, x_1) + \lambda_x(|A_2| - |A_2 \cap A_1|) + \lambda_x|A_1 \cap A_2|$. So we remain to show $L(x_1, x_1, x_1) + \lambda_x(|A_2| - |A_2 \cap A_3|) + \lambda_x(|A_3| - |A_1 \cap A_3|) +$

$\lambda_x(|A_3| - |A_2 \cap A_3|) + \lambda_x |A_1 \cap A_3| \geq R(x_1, x_1) + \lambda_x(|A_2| - |A_2 \cap A_1|) + \lambda_x |A_1 \cap A_2|$
which can be simplified to $L(x_1, x_1, x_1) + 2 * \lambda_x(|A_3| - |A_2 \cap A_3|) \geq R(x_1, x_1)$.
As $2 * \lambda_x(|A_3| - |A_2 \cap A_3|) \geq 0$, it is sufficient to show $L(x_1, x_1, x_1) \geq R(x_1, x_1)$
which can be written as $x_1(|A_1| - |A_1 \cap A_3|) + x_1(|A_2| - |A_2 \cap A_3|) + x_1(|A_3| - |A_1 \cap A_3|) + x_1(|A_3| - |A_2 \cap A_3|) \geq x_1(|A_1| - |A_1 \cap A_2|) + x_1(|A_2| - |A_2 \cap A_1|)$
and simplified to $|A_3| + |A_1 \cap A_2| \geq |A_1 \cap A_3| + |A_2 \cap A_3|$, let $|A_1 \cap A_3| = a$,
$|A_2 \cap A_3| = b$, and $|A_1 \cap A_2 \cap A_3| = c$, we have $|A_3| \geq a + b - c$ and $|A_1 \cap A_2| \geq c$,
therefore, $|A_3| + |A_1 \cap A_2| \geq a + b = |A_1 \cap A_3| + |A_2 \cap A_3|$. So finally we proved
$L(x_1, x_2, x_3) \geq R(x_1, x_2)$ when $x_1 \leq x_2 \leq x_3$. Similar proofs can be made for
the case $x_2 \leq x_1 \leq x_3$.

Case 2: If $x_3 \leq x_1 \leq x_2$, then if $|A_3| - |A_1 \cap A_3| - |A_2 \cap A_3| \geq 0$, we get
$L(x_1, x_2, x_3) = L(x_1, x_2, 0) + x_3(|A_3| - |A_1 \cap A_3|) + x_3(|A_3| - |A_2 \cap A_3|) - x_3|A_1 \cap A_3| - x_3|A_2 \cap A_3| = L(x_1, x_2, 0) + 2 * x_3(|A_3| - |A_1 \cap A_3| - |A_2 \cap A_3|) \geq L(x_1, x_2, 0) = x_1(|A_1| - |A_1 \cap A_3|) + x_2(|A_2| - |A_2 \cap A_3|) + x_1|A_1 \cap A_3| + x_2|A_2 \cap A_3| = x_1|A_1| + x_2|A_2| \geq x_1|A_1| + x_2|A_2| - (x_1|A_1 \cap A_2| + x_2|A_2 \cap A_1| - |x_1|A_1 \cap A_2| - x_2|A_1 \cap A_2||) = R(x_1, x_2)$. If $|A_3| - |A_1 \cap A_3| - |A_2 \cap A_3| < 0$, let $\delta_x = x_1 - x_3 \geq 0$, we have
$L(x_1, x_2, x_1) = L(x_1, x_2, x_3) + \delta_x(|A_3| - |A_1 \cap A_3|) + \delta_x(|A_3| - |A_2 \cap A_3|) - \delta_x|A_1 \cap A_3| - \delta_x|A_2 \cap A_3| = L(x_1, x_2, x_3) + 2 * \delta_x(|A_3| - |A_1 \cap A_3| - |A_2 \cap A_3|) \leq L(x_1, x_2, x_3)$,
so we only need to show $L(x_1, x_2, x_1) \geq R(x_1, x_2)$ which can be written as
$x_1(|A_1| - |A_1 \cap A_3|) + x_2(|A_2| - |A_2 \cap A_3|) + x_1(|A_3| - |A_1 \cap A_3|) + x_1(|A_3| - |A_2 \cap A_3|) + (x_2 - x_1)|A_2 \cap A_3| \geq x_1(|A_1| - |A_1 \cap A_2|) + x_2(|A_2| - |A_2 \cap A_1|) + (x_2 - x_1)|A_1 \cap A_2|$ and simplified to $|A_3| + |A_1 \cap A_2| \geq |A_1 \cap A_3| + |A_2 \cap A_3|$
which is already proved in Case 1. So we now have $L(x_1, x_2, x_3) \geq R(x_1, x_2)$
when $x_3 \leq x_1 \leq x_2$. Similar proofs can be made for the case $x_3 \leq x_2 \leq x_1$.

Case 3: If $x_1 \leq x_3 \leq x_2$, let $\delta_x = x_3 - x_1$, then we have $L(x_1, x_2, x_3) = L(x_1, x_2, x_1) + \delta_x(2 * |A_3| - |A_1 \cap A_3| - |A_2 \cap A_3|) + \delta_x|A_1 \cap A_3| + \delta_x|A_2 \cap A_3| = L(x_1, x_2, x_1) + 2 * \delta_x|A_3| \geq L(x_1, x_2, x_1)$, and in Case 2, we already showed
that $L(x_1, x_2, x_1) \geq R(x_1, x_2)$. So we now have $L(x_1, x_2, x_3) \geq R(x_1, x_2)$ when
$x_1 \leq x_3 \leq x_2$. Similar proofs can be made for the case $x_2 \leq x_3 \leq x_1$. Q. E. D.

Fusion of Static and Temporal Information for Threat Evaluation in Sensor Networks

Wenjun Ma[1]([⊠]), Weiru Liu[2], and Jun Hong[2]

[1] Department of Philosophy, East China Normal University, Shanghai, China
phoenixam@sina.com
[2] EEECS, Queen's University Belfast, Belfast, UK

Abstract. In many CCTV and sensor network based intelligent surveillance systems, a number of attributes or criteria are used to individually evaluate the degree of potential threat of a suspect. The outcomes for these attributes are in general from analytical algorithms where data are often pervaded with uncertainty and incompleteness. As a result, such individual threat evaluations are often inconsistent, and individual evaluations can change as time elapses. Therefore, integrating heterogeneous threat evaluations with temporal influence to obtain a better overall evaluation is a challenging issue. So far, this issue has rarely be considered by existing event reasoning frameworks under uncertainty in sensor network based surveillance. In this paper, we first propose a weighted aggregation operator based on a set of principles that constraints the fusion of individual threat evaluations. Then, we propose a method to integrate the temporal influence on threat evaluation changes. Finally, we demonstrate the usefulness of our system with a decision support event modeling framework using an airport security surveillance scenario.

1 Introduction

CCTV and sensor network-based intelligent surveillance systems are increasingly critical for public security and infrastructure protection due to the growing threat of terrorist attack, anti-social and criminal behaviors. Since events in surveillance systems are detected from different intelligent sensor technologies including audio, video and infrared, RFID, logs, or other sensory devices, how to combine events detected from multiple sources relating to the same suspect (hereafter, we refer it as *subject*) to obtain an overall estimation of its potential threat is a challenging problem. For example, a scenario can be of that from a camera in a security domain a male is detected (with a higher degree of threat) while from the personnel authentication identification system it indicates the person is a new member of staff (with a lower degree of threat). A straightforward method to handle this problem is to apply a number of independent criteria (e.g., gender, age, ID, behavior) to individually assess the potential threat of a subject, and then to combine these individual evaluations to produce an overall assessment. Since these individual evaluations cannot always be in complete agreement and the priorities of these criteria are different, adequate fusion operators (e.g., weighted aggregation operators) are necessary to obtain the overall

© Springer International Publishing Switzerland 2015
S. Zhang et al. (Eds.): KSEM 2015, LNAI 9403, pp. 66–77, 2015.
DOI: 10.1007/978-3-319-25159-2_6

estimation of potential threat for each subject and resolve the inconsistent or conflicting information.

At the same time, there may be multiple subjects with potential threats occurring simultaneously. Either due to the limited security resources, or due to the degree of potential threat is not significant enough to trigger an action, sometimes a security force will not take actions to prevent a potential threat immediately. In this case, the temporal influence on the threat degree, i.e., how the threat degree changes with time without external intervention, or how the threat degree changes with time when new evidence is collected, are both important to consider in an intelligence surveillance system.

In the literature, although there have been several event modeling and reasoning systems proposed [2,3,5,6,8], however, none of the models has properly addressed these two issues (detailed discussions will be in the related work section). In order to address these problems, in this paper, we first analyze general principles that should be obeyed by a fusion process that combines individual threat evaluations. Then, we introduce a weighted aggregation operator to obtain the overall degree of potential threat for each subject after considering all related criteria, from which we can set the priority for each subject. After that, we propose a method to revise the potential threat degree based on elaping time to take into account the temporal influence of that criteria of each subject. Finally, we will illustrate our method with an airport security surveillance scenario.

This paper advances the state of the art on information fusion for decision support for intelligent surveillance systems in the following aspects. (i) We analyze general principles for an appropriate aggregation operator in the surveillance system. It gives a cornerstone to build up a generic axiomatic framework for the integration of heterogeneous threat evaluation. (ii) We introduce a weighted aggregation operator to combine the degrees of potential threats of each criterion and give an overall estimation to each subject. (iii) We propose a method to deal with two types of temporal influence for the potential threats.

The rest of this paper is organized as follows. Section 2 recaps some basic concepts in Dempster-Shafer theory. Section 3 discusses some principles govern threat evaluation fusion processes. Section 4 introduces an aggregation operator that obeys the principles to fuse degrees of potential threats. Sections 5 provides a case study to illustrate the usefulness of our model. Finally, Section 6 discusses the related work and concludes the paper with future work.

2 Preliminaries

Definition 1. *[10] Let Θ be a set of exhaustive and mutually exclusive elements, called a frame of discernment (or simple a frame). Function $m : 2^\Theta \to [0,1]$ is a mass function if $m(\emptyset) = 0$ and $\sum_{A \subseteq \Theta} m(A) = 1$. And a function $Pl : 2^\Theta \to [0,1]$, defined as follows, is called a plausibility function over Θ:*

$$Pl(A) = \sum_{B \cap A \neq \phi} m(B). \tag{1}$$

One advantage of D-S theory is that it provides a method to accumulate and combine evidence from multiple sources by using *Dempster combination rule.*

Definition 2 (Dempster combination rule). *Let m_1 and m_2 be two mass functions over a frame of discernment Θ. Then Dempster combination function $m_{12} = m_1 \oplus m_2$ is given by:*

$$m_{12}(X) = \begin{cases} 0 & \text{if } X = \emptyset \\ \dfrac{\sum\limits_{A \cap B = X} m_1(A)m_2(B)}{1 - \sum\limits_{A \cap B = \emptyset} m_1(A)m_2(B)} & \text{if } X \neq \emptyset \end{cases} \tag{2}$$

When a new piece of evidence, which is collected after fusion, Jeffrey-Dempster revision rule [7] can be applied to update the current evidence. This rule is useful for considering the temporal influence for the DPTC (Degree of Potential Threat for a subject w.r.t a given Criterion).

Definition 3 (Jeffrey-Dempster revision rule). *Let m and m_I be two mass functions over a frame of discernment Θ. The Jeffrey-Dempster revision function of m by m_I, denoted as $m \circ_{JD} m_I$, is defined by:*

$$(m \circ_{JD} m_I)(C) = \sum_{A \cap B = C} \sigma_m(A,\ B)m_I(B), \quad for\ any\ C \neq \emptyset, \tag{3}$$

$$where\ \sigma_m(A,\ B) = \begin{cases} \frac{m(A)}{Pl(B)} & for\ Pl(B) > 0, \\ 0 & for\ Pl(B) = 0\ and\ A \neq B, \\ 1 & for\ Pl(B) = 0\ and\ A = B. \end{cases}$$

3   Principles of Threat Evaluation Aggregation

In order to hold commonalities for the aggregation process in different specific surveillance situations and develop adequate weighted aggregation operators for specific applications, in this section, we propose some basic principles for threat evaluation aggregation. These principles aim for revealing commonalities for general aggregation processes, that specific, appropriate weighted aggregation operators should satisfy.

(i) **Conclusion Modification:** Consider one more threat evaluation for a given subject w.r.t a new criterion can modify the current evaluation to either increase, decrease, or unchange.

(ii) **Evaluation Consistency:** The overall potential threat evaluation for a given subject should increase when the point valued degree of potential threat for such subject w.r.t each related criterion increase.

(iii) **Evaluation Commensurability:** A system shall provide an overall evaluation for each subject after the aggregation process, and the overall evaluations for different subjects are comparable (on a commensurable scale).

(iv) **Irrelevance of Evidence Ordering:** The result of an aggregation should not be affected by the ordering of aggregation.

(v) **Importance Dependency:** The effect of the DPTC for the overall evaluation is dependent on the importance (reflected as a weight) of this criterion.

The *first* principle translates the DPTC into three types of influence for
the overall evaluation. (i) Positive evidence: the degree of threat will increase
after considering a DPTC. For example, the fact that a person holding a knife
will enhance our belief that this person is dangerous. (ii) Negative evidence:
the degree of threat will decrease after considering a DPTC. For instance, age-
information with an age value as *old* will weaken our belief that this person is
dangerous. And (iii) neutral evidence, the degree of threat is not affected after
considering a DPTC. for example, the evidence that a person has been waiting
for friends has no influence on our beliefs about his degree of threat.

The *second* principle captures the monotonicity of the aggregation operation:
the higher value a DPTC will be, the higher value the overall degree of threat for
the subject is, *ceteris paribus*. Also, the second principle guarantees the property
of strict transitivity for the ranking order about potential threat for the subjects
in a surveillance environment. That is, suppose $a \succ b$ means subject a is more
dangerous than subject b, if for subjects a, b, c, we have $a \succ b$ and $b \succ c$, then
$a \succ c$. The violation of the strict transitivity axiom implies that an intelligence
surveillance system will be unable to determine the most dangerous subject.

The *third* principle means that a surveillance system can give a complete
ranking order for subjects in a given situation based on their overall potential
threat evaluations. Hence, the requirement of overall commensurability among
the subjects of different situations suggests that all the outcomes of overall evaluations need to be in a unified bounded range.

The *forth* principle guarantees that the overall potential threat evaluation
shall not be influenced by the order of fusing the individual DPTCs. Thus, it
reveals two properties in the surveillance system (let $R(x_i, x_j)$ be the aggregation of evaluations about x_i and x_j.). (i) Associativity: $R(R(x_1, x_2), x_3) =
R(x_1, R(x_2, x_3))$. (ii) Symmetry: $R(x_1, x_2) = R(x_2, x_1)$

The *fifth* principle reveals the essential meaning of weights: (i) when a DPTC
increases, the weighted DPTC should also increase; (ii) after considering the
effect of weight in our aggregation operator, the first principle to the forth principle should be remained.

4   A Weighted Aggregation Operator

The basic principles for the weighted aggregation operator in surveillance systems, proposed in the previous section, is a set of constraints of information
fusion frameworks. It can be instantiated in different ways. We discuss one
weighted aggregation operator in this section that satisfies these principles
(below, without losing general, we assume the individual DPTC is a point-value
in [0,1]).

Since a DPTC is a point value in a range, the distinction of three types of
evidence (positive, neutral, negative) to some extent suggests the setting of an

Table 1. The terms in weighted aggregation operators

Terms	Interpretation
$\nu_i(x)$	DPTC of subject x for criterion i
w_i	the weight for criterion w_i
$g(w_i, \nu_i(x))$	weighted DPTC
$R(g(w_i, \nu_i(x)), g(w_j, \nu_j(x)))$	aggregated assessment of $g(w_i, \nu_i(x))$ and $g(w_j, \nu_j(x))$
$e \in (0, 1)$	the threshold to distinguish different types of evidence

expectation threshold for the degrees of potential threats w.r.t each criterion. Thus, when a DPTC exceeds the threshold, it is positive evidence; when equals to the threshold, neutral evidence; and when below the threshold, negative evidence. Table 1 summarizes a list of terms (and notations) used in a weighted aggregation operator.

Now, we can introduce a weighted aggregation operator for the overall degree of potential threat for any two criteria 1 and 2 as follow:

$$R(g(w_1, \nu_1(x)), g(w_2, \nu_2(x)))$$
$$= \frac{(1-e)g(w_1, \nu_1(x))g(w_2, \nu_2(x))}{(1-e)g(w_1, \nu_1(x))g(w_2, \nu_2(x)) + e(1-g(w_1, \nu_1(x)))(1-g(w_2, \nu_2(x)))}, \quad (4)$$
$$where$$
$$g(w_i, \nu_i(x)) = w_i \nu_i(x) + (1 - w_i)e. \quad (5)$$

Here, e is the threshold value to distinguish different types of evidence. Moreover, in Equation (5), we combine a uninorm aggregation operator $R(x, y) = \frac{(1-e)xy}{(1-e)xy + e(1-x)(1-y)}$ as shown in [4] with a weighting function $g(w_i, \nu_i(x)) = w_i \nu_i(x) + (1 - w_i)e$ in [11]. Finally, with the proof in [11], the weighting function $g(w_i, \nu_i(x)) = w_i \nu_i(x) + (1 - w_i)e$ satisfies the following four conditions:

- Monotonicity in value: if $\nu_i(x) > \nu_i(y)$, then $g(w_i, \nu_i(x)) > g(w_i, \nu_i(y))$. It means that as the degree of potential threat with respect to a given criterion i for subject x increases, the weighted value should also increase.
- Normality of importance of one: $g(1, \nu_i(x)) = \nu_i(x)$. Thus, when the weight is set to 1, the weighted value does not change.
- No effect for zero importance elements: $g(0, \nu_i(x)) = e$, where e is a threshold in our operator $R(\nu_1(x), \nu_2(x))$.
- Consistency of effect on w_i: for $a \geq b$, $g(a, \nu_i(x)) \geq g(b, \nu_i(x))$ if $\nu_i(x) \geq e$; for $a \geq b$, $g(a, \nu_i(x)) \leq g(b, \nu_i(x))$ if $\nu_i(x) \leq e$. Here consistency means that after considering the effect of weight in our aggregation operator, the property of the uninorm aggregation operator as shown in the following Equations (6)-(8) will be remained.

The aggregation operator introduced is a weighted uninorm aggregation operator [11] that satisfies: (i) Monotonicity: $x_1 \geq y_1 \wedge x_2 \geq y_2 \Rightarrow R(x_1, x_2) \geq R(y_1, y_2)$. (ii) Boundary conditions: $R(0, 0) = 0$; $R(1, 1) = 1$. (iii) Associativity: $R(R(x_1, x_2), x_3) = R(x_1, R(x_2, x_3))$. (iv) Symmetry: $R(x_1, x_2) = R(x_2, x_1)$. (v) Neutral element: $\exists e \in (0, 1), \forall x \in [0, 1], R(e, x) = x$.

Finally, we introduce the preference ordering to rank the potential threat of subjects according to their overall evaluations with the following definition.

Definition 4. *For two subjects x and y, the strict preference ordering $\succ$ is defined as follows:*

$$x \succ y \Leftrightarrow R(g(w_i, \nu_i(x)), \ldots, g(w_n, \nu_n(x))) > R(g(w_j, \nu_j(y)), \ldots, g(w_m, \nu_m(y)))$$

This ordering states that the potential threat of x is higher than that of y, if the overall evaluation of x is greater than that of y. Thus, with the equivalence relation $\sim$ (i.e., $x \sim y$ if $x \not\succ y$ and $y \not\succ x$), we can compare any two subjects as shown in the following theorem.

Theorem 1. *For a set of subjects X, the strict preference ordering $\succ$ in Definition 4 satisfies:*

- **Completeness.** *For any subjects x and y in X, we have $x \succ y$ or $x \prec y$ or $x \sim y$.*
- **Strict Transitivity.** *For any subjects x, y and z in X, if $x \succ y$ and $y \succ z$, then $x \succ z$.*

Proof. (i) By Definition 4, we have

$$x \succ y \Leftrightarrow R(g(w_i, \nu_i(x)), \ldots, g(w_n, \nu_n(x))) > R(g(w_j, \nu_j(y)), \ldots, g(w_m, \nu_m(y))),$$

which means that $y \not\succ x$. That is, the preference order $\succ$ satisfies asymmetry: if x is strictly preferred to y, then y is not strictly preferred to x. Also $x \sim y$ iff $x \not\succ y$ and $y \not\succ x$. As a result, the preference order $\succ$ satisfies the completeness that follows from the definition of $\sim$ and the fact that $\succ$ is asymmetric. So, property (i) holds.

(ii) Suppose $x \succ y$ and $y \succ z$. By Definition 4, $x \succ y$ and $y \succ z$ imply that $R(g(w_i, \nu_i(x)), \ldots, g(w_n, \nu_n(x))) > R(g(w_j, \nu_j(y)), \ldots, g(w_m, \nu_m(y)))$ and $R(g(w_j, \nu_j(y)), \ldots, g(w_m, \nu_m(y))) > R(g(w_k, \nu_k(z)), \ldots, g(w_o, \nu_o(z)))$, respectively. As a result, $R(g(w_i, \nu_i(x)), \ldots, g(w_n, \nu_n(x))) > R(g(w_k, \nu_k(z)), \ldots, g(w_o, \nu_o(z)))$. Thus $x \succ z$. So, propertyp (ii) holds. $\square$

Now, we show that such a weighted aggregation operator satisfies the principles that we proposed in the previous section.

For the *first* principle about Conclusion Modification, it is equivalent to prove that our operator satisfies the following Theorem:

Theorem 2. *Let $\nu_c(x)$ be the point valued degree of potential threat for subject x with respect to criterion c, w_c be the weight of criterion c, $e \in (0,1)$ be the threshold to distinguish different types of evidence, $D(x)$ be the degree of overall potential threat for all related criteria except criterion c for subject x, and $R(A, B)$ be the combined assessment of degrees of two potential threat A and B. Then we have*

(i) *Effect of positive evidence:* if $\nu_c(x) > e$, then $R(D(x), g(w_c, \nu_c(x)) \geq D(x)$.
(ii) *Effect of negative evidence:* if $\nu_c(x) < e$, then $R(D(x), g(w_c, \nu_c(x)) \leq D(x)$.
(iii) *Effect of neutral evidence:* if $\nu_c(x) = e$, then $R(D(x), g(w_c, \nu_c(x)) = D(x)$.

Proof. By Equation (5), we have

$$g(w_c, \nu_c(x)) - e = w_c \nu_c(x) + (1 - w_c)e - e = w_c(\nu_c(x) - e)$$

Thus, if $\nu_c(x) > e$, $g(w_c, \nu_c(x)) > e$ and if $\nu_c(x) < e$, $g(w_c, \nu_c(x)) < e$. So, since $D(x) = R(D(x), e)$, by Monotonicity, items (i) and (ii) holds. Moreover, by the property of Neutral element for our aggregation operator, we have $R(D(x), e) = D(x)$. Then item (iii) holds. □

For the *second* principle of Evaluation Consistency, the monotonicity of the aggregation operator is proved in [11] and the strict transitivity for the ranking order is shown by the second item of Theorem 1.

For the *third* principle of Evaluation Commensurability, the completeness of the ranking order over potential threats for the subjects is shown by the first item of Theorem 1. With monotonicity, the property of boundary conditions says that the aggregated assessment value is in the interval $[0, 1]$. Thus, our operator gives a unified range for the value of overall evaluation as well.

For the *forth* principle of Irrelevance of Evidence Ordering, the properties of associativity and commutativity together show that we can combine the weighted DPTCs in any order. Thus, our operator satisfies the forth principle.

For the *fifth* principle, it is guaranteed by the four conditions about the weighting function $g(w_i, \nu_i(x)) = w_i \nu_i(x) + (1 - w_i)e$ in our operator.

Finally, our aggregation operator also satisfies the properties in [11] that:

$$\forall x, y \in (e, 1), R(x, y) \geq \max\{x, y\} \tag{6}$$
$$\forall x, y \in (0, e), R(x, y) \leq \min\{x, y\} \tag{7}$$
$$\forall x \in (0, e), y \in (e, 1), x \leq R(x, y) \leq y \tag{8}$$

These three equations (Equations (6)-(8)) not only point out the different aggregation results of our operator, but also reveal a desirable property in our operator: if all the degrees of potential threats exceed a threshold, the operator should produce a higher degree of threat, hence, the corresponding subject is of higher priority to deal with. If all of the degrees are below a threshold, the operator produces a lower level degree of threat and hence no immediate actions taken. For example, suppose a young man holds a knife and intrudes into a secured area. All criteria: age, gender, intentions show that the person is dangerous, then the surveillance system (after aggregating all the evidence) should produce a strong alert indicator for taking actions. On the other hand, in the case that an old lady holds a walking stick and passes the security door, since all criteria show that the person is harmless, the surveillance system will not raise any alert unless other strong evidence has emerged showing that the woman is dangerous. In terms of fusion, it has an reinforcement effect: when all the evidence are strongly suggesting a subject is dangerous, the overall degree of threat of the subject is increased above any individual degrees.

5   Temporal Influence for Point Valued Potential Threats

Now, we consider the temporal influence issue in surveillance systems. Generally speaking, a temporal influence of a given criterion on the assessment of the degree of threat of a subject can be divided into two categories: the temporal influence without external intervention and the temporal influence with new evidence observed.

To investigate the first category of temporal influence, let us consider the following scenario. A person is loitering near the ticket counter at 9:10 pm. The security team for the area cannot take any action due to limited security resources. Twenty minutes later, one security team returned. Now, the security manager should pay more attention to this person since it is unusual for a person to loiter near the ticket counter for such a long time, even without any new evidence about the subject w.r.t this criterion.

Intuitively, there should be three types of temporal influences without external intervention for the point valued degree of potential threat with respect to different criteria: increase, neutral, and decrease. For example, for age or gender, their threat degrees will not change with time; for leaving objects (e.g., a bag) alone, the threat degree should change over time; but for some emotions, such as anger, their threat degrees should decrease with time (a person will fight with others when he is very angry. However, after a while, his potential threat for engaging into a fight will decrease). Based on this intuition, we can obtain the following equation.

$$v_c(x) = v_c(x)^{\gamma^{\lfloor \frac{t-t_0}{n} \rfloor}} \tag{9}$$

where

$$\begin{cases} \gamma < 1 \text{ increasing DPTC with time change;} \\ \gamma = 1 \text{ neutral DPTC with time change;} \\ \gamma > 1 \text{ decreasing DPTC with time change.} \end{cases} \tag{10}$$

Here, $v_c(x)$ is the point valued degree of potential threat for subject x w.r.t. criterion c that is calculated at point of time t_o (here t_o is the latest time-point for the $occT$'s of all related events to generate $v_c(x)$), t is the current time-point, n ($n > 0$) is the time interval between two key time points for updating, and γ ($\gamma \in (0, +\infty)$) is the influence rate. Moreover, in real-life applications, surveillance systems will update evidence regularly, we introduce the time interval n, and $\lfloor \frac{t-t_0}{n} \rfloor$ means that we will take integers downwards in function $\frac{t-t_0}{n}$. Hence, in real-life applications, always the change of the DPTC is limited: a positive evidence will never turn out to be a negative evidence no matter how much time elapse. For example, for the emotion of anger, it will be positive evidence that will increase the potential threat, even after a moment of calming down, it will not become negative evidence, which will decrease the potential threat of a given subject. Similarly, most negative evidence will not become positive evidence, even though it might be natural. However, some negative evidence may become positive evidence, such as a member of staff staying overly long in a security field. Based on Equation (9), it is possible to obtain the following definition for the degree of potential threats updated by temporal influences without external intervention.

Definition 5. *Consider the condition that the temporal influences without external intervention, let $\nu_c(x)$ be the degree of potential threat with respect to criterion c for subject x generated at point of time t_o (here t_o is the latest time point for the occTs of all related events to generate $\nu_c(x)$), t be the current time, n (n > 0) be the time interval between two key time points for updating, γ be the degree of influence rate that $\gamma \in (0, +\infty)$, and $e \in (0, 1)$ be the threshold to distinguish different types of evidence, then the degrees of potential threats w.r.t. criterion c for subject x for temporal influence, denote as $a_c(x)$ is*

$$a_c(x) = h^{-1}(\nu_c(x)^{\gamma^{\lfloor \frac{t-t_0}{n} \rfloor}}) \tag{11}$$

where

$$\begin{cases} h(x) = \frac{1}{e}x & \text{if } \gamma < 1, \text{ negative evidence will not become positive,} \\ & \text{and } \nu_c(x) < e; \\ h(x) = \frac{1}{1-e}(x - e) & \text{if } \gamma > 1, \text{ positive evidence will not become negative,} \\ & \text{and } \nu_c(x) > e \text{ ;} \\ h(x) = x & \text{otherwise.} \end{cases} \tag{12}$$

The first condition means that the updated degree of potential threat will not be greater than the threshold e when evidence is negative, i.e., $a_c(x) \in [0, e]$ when $\nu_c(x) < e$. Hence, if $\gamma \geq 1$, it is clear that $a_c(x) \in [0, e]$ if $\nu_c(x) < e$. Similarly, the updated degree of potential threat will not be less than the threshold e when $\nu_c(x) > e$, i.e., $a_c(x) \in [e, 1]$ when $\nu_c(x) > e$. This is the exact meaning of the function $h(x)$.

Moreover, when $\gamma \neq 1$, the value of γ is determined by the real-time duration of observing a given criterion or the termination of observing the criterion. For example, consider the criterion of *person leaving an item*, after detecting a person abandoning an items, it can be set as that 15-minutes is the maximum time duration for taking a further action. Suppose the time interval between two key time points for updating evidence is 1 minute, the significant figure is 0.001, and the potential threat higher than 0.9 means a very dangerous situation that the security team has to take further action, then for any $\nu_{PL}(x) > e$, we should have $\nu_{PL}(x)^{\gamma^{15}} \geq 0.9$ by Definition 5. Hence, we can obtain that $\gamma = \sqrt[15]{\log_{e+0.001} 0.9}$. Similarly, consider the criterion of emotion, after detecting the person is angry, 10-minutes can be the maximum time period for angry emotion to disappear. As a result, suppose the time interval between two key time points for updating evidence is 1 minute, the significant figure is 0.001, and the potential threat lower than $e+0.01$ means the effect can be ignored, consider that such positive evidence will not become a negative one, by Definition 5, we have $(1 - e)(\nu_c(x)^{\gamma^{10}}) + e = e + 0.01$. Then, we have $\gamma = \sqrt[10]{\log_{0.999} \frac{0.01}{1-e}}$.

Now, we consider the second category of time influence: the temporal influence with new evidence occurs. For example, in the case of a person loitering

near the ticket counter at 9:10 p.m., if there is new information in 9:10 p.m. to
9:30 p.m., which points out that the person had met a friend and left in the
passed 20 minutes. Then, in this case, we should consider the effect of new evidence for the threat degree of this person. In fact, since the effect of new event
is to update the belief for the possible outcomes related to a given criterion for
a given subject. Hence, since the new evidence reveals the more recent situation
for the subject, i.e., the new evidence is more reliable than the pervious one, it
should be retained whilst the prior belief of the system should be changed.

As a result, first, we will use the Dempster combination rule (Equation (2))
to obtain the overall mass function for all new evidence of a given criterion.
Then, we apply the Jeffrey-Dempster revision rule (Equation (3)) to update the
mass function for the possible outcome of a given criterion. After considering all
evidence that are related to the belief about the possible outcomes w.r.t a given
criterion, we can apply the model in [8] to obtain the degree of potential threat
with time influence in this condition directly. Finally, our weighted aggregation
operator can be applied to obtain the overall degree of a potential threat for
each subject.

6   Case Study

Let us consider a scenario in an airport, which covers the following two areas:
Shopping Area (SA) and Control Center (CC).

- In the Shopping Area (SA), a person (id: 13) loiters near a Foreign Currency
  Exchange office (FCE) for a long time. Also, camera 42 catches its back image
  at the entrance of the shopping area at 9:01 pm and camera 45 catches its
  side face image at FCE from 9:03 pm to 9:15 pm;
- In airport terminal 1 a person (id: 21) leaved a bag and disappeared. That
  is, camera 49 captures its side face and that it brings a bag at 9:01 pm,
  camera 44 captures its back at 9:02 pm and camera 43 captures the bag on
  the ground without a person around from 9:03 pm to 9:15 pm.

Now, suppose the only one security team was at another area to prevent
threat and returned at 9:30 pm. And during this time period, camera 45 captured
the person (id:13) leaving the shopping area and walking towards east. Suppose
there are no other emergency happening during this time interval, then what
will the surveillance system suggest to do?

As the security team does not eliminate these two potential threats (id:13 and
id:21) immediately, the surveillance system has to consider the new evidence and
the temporal influence for the point valued degrees of potential threats for each
criterion of these two subject at 9:30 pm. Moreover, with the event modeling in
[8], for the person (id: 13) in FCEC, we have a piece of new evidence about the
movement criterion: e_5^m=(FCEC, 9:03-9:15 p.m, 45, 0.9, 0.6, movement, 0.8, 13,
FCEC, $m_2^m(\{toward\,east\}) = 1$). Thus, by the degree of reliability of sensor 42,
$m_3^m(\{walk\,east\})$=0.9, $m_3^m(\{walk\,east,\ldots,run\,east,\ldots,stay,\,loiter\})$=0.1.

Hence, considering the temporal influence with new evidence occurs by Jeffrey-Dempster revision rule (Equation (3)), we have $m_{123}^m(\{walk\,east\})=0.9$, $m_{123}^m(\{walk \quad east, \quad loiter\}) \quad = \quad 0.0137, \quad m_{123}^m(\{loiter\}) \quad = \quad 0.081,$ $m_{123}^m(\{walk\,east, \ldots, run\,east, \ldots, stay, loiter\}) = 0.0053$. As a result, since the mass value $m_{123}^m(\{loiter\}) = 0.081$ and we suppose the condition of the only one inference rule about the movement is defined as $m_i^m(\{loiter\}) >$ $0.5 \wedge e.location = FCEC \wedge t_n - t_0 > 10\,min$, we will omit the criterion of movement for the reason that we cannot confirm the intention of the subject based on the already known evidence about behaviors.

Now, we consider the time influence for the criteria without external intervention for two potential threats (id:13 and id:21) by Definition 5. Clearly, the degrees of potential threats for the criteria of *age* and *gender* should not change with time ($\gamma = 1$) and the degrees of potential threats for the criteria of *PL (Intention of Person loitering)* and *PLI (Intention of Person Leaving an Item)* should increase with time. Moreover, for the criterion of *PL*, since there exists new evidence about it, we do not need to consider the temporal influence for the degree of potential threat with respect to the criterion of *PL*. Now, suppose the degree of influence rate for the criteria of *PLI* is ($\gamma = 0.8$). Then, by Definition 5 and $\nu_a(21) > e$ ($e = 0.5$), we have $a_a(13) = \nu_a(13) = 0.56$, $a_g(13) = 0.547$; $a_a(21) = 0.565$, $a_g(21) = 0.582$, $a_{PLI}(21) = (0.672)^{0.8^{\lfloor \frac{9:30-9:15}{1} \rfloor}} = 0.986$.

Moreover, by the weighted aggregation operator, we have

$$R(g(0.3, \nu_a(13)), g(0.3, \nu_g(13))) = 0.518 * 0.514 = 0.532$$
$$R(g(0.3, \nu_a(21)), g(0.3, \nu_g(21)), g(0.8, \nu_{IPLI}(21))) = 0.906$$

Finally, by Definition 4, we have $id\,21 \succ id\,13$. So the surveillance system will suggest the security team to intervene $id\,21$. That is, to find out what is contained in the abandoned bag and arrest the person (id:21) if it is necessary.

7   Related Work and Summary

In the literature, there are plenty of event modeling and reasoning systems, such as Finite State Machines [3], Bayesian Networks [2], and event composition with imperfect information [5,6], event modeling with decision support[8], etc. In general, these systems consider two branches to address the integration of heterogeneous information: most of them consider all information in a scenario as a whole, and with rules or fusion algorithms for each specific scenario. So, if we add a new criterion into a scenario, all of these systems must modify the knowledge base and other related aspects with the new criterion. Therefore, these systems are somehow not flexible and effective for dynamic surveillance environment with a huge volume of surveillance data from different sensors. Another line of research [8] applies aggregation process we suggested in this paper. However, the operator proposed in [8] does not satisfy all the basic principles for an adequate aggregation operator. Moreover, the aggregation process in surveillance systems have also been discussed in the literature. Albusac *et al.* in [1] analyzed different aggregation operators and proposed a new aggregation method based on the Sugeno integral for multiple criteria in the domain of intelligent surveillance. Also, Rudas et al. in [9] offered a comprehensive study of information aggregation in intelligence systems from different application fields such as robotics, vision, knowledge based systems and data mining, etc. However, to the best of our knowledge, there is no research suggesting a set of basic principles to define an adequate operator for the aggregation process or considering the temporal influence in surveillance systems.

In this paper, we introduced the basic principles to handle the integration of heterogeneous threat evaluation in surveillance systems and proposed a weighted aggregation operator to instantiate such principle. We also discussed the temporal influence in the aggregation process. Our next step of work is to build up a general axiom framework for the aggregation process and test such framework with surveillance data.

Acknowledgement. This work has been partially funded by EPSRC PACES project (Ref: EP/J012149/1).

References

1. Albusac, J., Vallejo, D., Jimenez, L., Castro-Schez, J.J., Glez-Morcillo, C.: Combining degrees of normality analysis in intelligent surveillance systems. In: FUSION 2012, pp. 2436–2443 (2012)
2. Cheng, H.Y., Weng, C.C., Chen, Y.Y.: Vehicle detection in aerial surveillance using dynamic Bayesian networks. IEEE Transactions on Image Processing **21**(4), 2152–2159 (2012)
3. Fernández-Caballero, A., Castillo, J.C., Rodríguez-Sánchez, J.M.: Human activity monitoring by local and global finite state machines. Expert Systems with Applications **39**(8), 6982–6993 (2012)
4. Luo, X., Jennings, N.R.: A spectrum of compromise aggregation operators for multi-attribute decision making. Artificial Intelligence **171**, 161–184 (2007)
5. Ma, J., Liu, W., Miller, P., Yan, W.: Event composition with imperfect information for bus surveillance. In: AVSS 2009, pp. 382–387 (2009)
6. Ma, J., Liu, W., Miller, P.: Event modelling and reasoning with uncertain information for distributed sensor networks. In: SUM 2010, pp. 236–249 (2010)
7. Ma, J., Liu, W., Dubois, D., Prade, H.: Bridging Jeffrey's Rule, AGM Revision and Dempster Conditioning in the Theory of Evidence. International Journal on Artificial Intelligence Tools **20**(04), 691–720 (2011)
8. Ma, W., Liu, W., Ma, J., Miller, P.: An extended event reasoning framework for decision support under uncertainty. In: Bouchon-Meunier, B., Yager, R.R., Laurent, A., Strauss, O. (eds.) IPMU 2014, Part III. CCIS, vol. 444, pp. 335–344. Springer, Heidelberg (2014)
9. Rudas, I.J., Pap, E., Fodor, J.: Information aggregation in intelligent systems: An application oriented approach. Knowledge-Based Systems **38**, 3–13 (2013)
10. Shafer, G.: A Mathematical Theory of Evidence. Princeton University Press, Princeton (1976)
11. Yager, R., Rybalov, A.: Uninorm aggregation operators. Fuzzy Sets and Systems **80**, 111–120 (1996)

Towards Extracting Ontology Excerpts

Jieying Chen[1], Michel Ludwig[2], Yue Ma[3], and Dirk Walther[2(✉)]

[1] College of Computer Science and Technology, Jilin University, Changchun, China
chenjy12@mails.jlu.edu.cn
[2] Theoretical Computer Science, TU Dresden, Dresden, Germany
{michel,dirk}@tcs.inf.tu-dresden.de
[3] Laboratoire de Recherche en Informatique, Université Paris-Sud, Orsay, France
yue.ma@lri.fr

Abstract. In the presence of an ever growing amount of information, organizations and human users need to be able to focus on certain key pieces of information and to intentionally ignore all other possibly relevant parts. Knowledge about complex systems that is represented in ontologies yields collections of axioms that are too large for human users to browse, let alone to comprehend or reason about it. We introduce the notion of an ontology excerpt as being a fixed-size subset of an ontology, consisting of the most relevant axioms for a given set of terms. These axioms preserve as much as possible the knowledge about the considered terms described in the ontology. We consider different extraction techniques for ontology excerpts based on methods from the area of information retrieval. To evaluate these techniques, we propose to measure the degree of incompleteness of the resulting excerpts using the notion of logical difference.

1 Introduction

Ontologies based on Description Logics (DL) [2] have become a well-established paradigm used in the Web Ontology Language OWL [11] and by several biomedical ontologies like CPO, FMA, GALEN, SNOMED CT, etc. An increasing number of ontologies of large sizes have been developed and made available in repositories such as the NCBO Bioportal.[1] Ensuring efficient access to the knowledge contained in such ontologies has become an import concern.

The sheer size of some real-world ontologies is too large for human users to browse, let alone to comprehend or reason about it. Also, for automated reasoning systems these tasks could be challenging to accomplish within certain resource bounds. To facilitate the reuse of the knowledge contained in ontologies, module extraction [4] and approximate reasoning techniques [10], among others, have been suggested.

A module $\mathcal{M}$ of an ontology $\mathcal{O}$ for a signature Σ, i.e. a set of concept and role names, is a subset of $\mathcal{O}$ that preserves the knowledge of the terms in Σ. The idea

---

Partially supported by German Research Foundation (DFG) within the Cluster of Excellence 'cfAED'.

[1] http://bioportal.bioontology.org/

S. Zhang et al. (Eds.): KSEM 2015, LNAI 9403, pp. 78–89, 2015.
DOI: 10.1007/978-3-319-25159-2_7

is that $\mathcal{M}$ can serve as a substitute for $\mathcal{O}$ regarding the terms in Σ. The smaller the module compared to the size of the ontology, the better it can be understood by a human user, and the more efficiently it can be distributed and reasoned with. Typically, entailment-based modularity notions are considered [4]. The meaning of the terms in Σ is preserved when $\mathcal{M}$ and $\mathcal{O}$ give the same answers to queries about the Σ-terms. However, this module notion allows for little *control* over the number of axioms that are included in a module. Even minimal modules can be as large as the entire ontology. To influence the size of a module, our only option is to adapt the signature for which the module is extracted and the query language underlying the module notion. Generally, we have that the smaller the signature and the weaker the expressivity of the query language, the smaller the modules of an ontology are. But no strict upper bound on the module size can be guaranteed this way.

In this paper, we introduce the notion of an *ontology excerpt* as a fixed-size subset of an ontology that captures as much as possible of the "meaning" of the terms in a given signature. Ontology excerpts facilitate comprehension by human users by aiding them to focus on a relatively small part of an ontology that is relevant for a considered signature.

To evaluate the quality of ontology excerpts, we define a semantics-based measure *Gain*, using Logical Difference [5], to quantify how much semantic meaning is preserved in an excerpt w.r.t. the original ontology. The logical difference is taken to be the set of queries relevant to an application domain that produce different answers when evaluated over ontologies that are to be compared. In this paper we are only interested in concept subsumption queries.

Using an exhaustive search to find the excerpts of an ontology that best preserve the semantic information w.r.t. the ontology is futile as it involves computing all (i.e. exponentially many) subsets of the ontology. We therefore want to investigate the feasibility of using, among others, excerpt extraction techniques stemming from the area of information retrieval (IR) [9], i.e. a research area which is generally concerned with developing techniques to extract the "most relevant" documents for a query from large data sources.

2   Preliminaries

We briefly recall basic notions related to the description logic $\mathcal{ELH}$ [1], modularity of ontologies [4,6] and the logical difference between ontologies [5,7].

2.1   The Description Logic $\mathcal{ELH}$

Let N_C and N_R be mutually disjoint and countably infinite sets of concept names and role names. In the following we use A, B, X, Y, Z to denote concept names, and r, s stand for role names. The set of $\mathcal{EL}$-*concepts* C and the sets of $\mathcal{ELH}$-*inclusions* α are built according to the following grammar rules:

$$C ::= \top \mid A \mid C \sqcap C \mid \exists r.C$$
$$\alpha ::= C \sqsubseteq C \mid C \equiv C \mid r \sqsubseteq s$$

where $A \in \mathsf{N_C}$ and $r, s \in \mathsf{N_R}$. $\mathcal{ELH}$-inclusions that are not of the form $r \sqsubseteq s$ are called $\mathcal{EL}$-concept inclusions. An $\mathcal{ELH}$-ontology $\mathcal{O}$ is a finite set of $\mathcal{ELH}$-inclusions, which are also referred to as axioms.

The semantics is defined using interpretations $\mathcal{I} = (\Delta^{\mathcal{I}}, \cdot^{\mathcal{I}})$, where the domain $\Delta^{\mathcal{I}}$ is a non-empty set, and $\cdot^{\mathcal{I}}$ is a function mapping each concept name A to a subset $A^{\mathcal{I}}$ of $\Delta^{\mathcal{I}}$ and every role name r to a binary relation $r^{\mathcal{I}}$ over $\Delta^{\mathcal{I}}$. The extension $C^{\mathcal{I}}$ of a possibly complex concept C is defined inductively as: $(\top)^{\mathcal{I}} := \Delta^{\mathcal{I}}$, $(C \sqcap D)^{\mathcal{I}} := C^{\mathcal{I}} \cap D^{\mathcal{I}}$, and $(\exists r.C)^{\mathcal{I}} := \{x \in \Delta^{\mathcal{I}} \mid \exists y \in C^{\mathcal{I}} : (x, y) \in r^{\mathcal{I}}\}$.

An interpretation $\mathcal{I}$ satisfies a concept C, an axiom $C \sqsubseteq D$, $C \equiv D$, or $r \sqsubseteq s$ if $C^{\mathcal{I}} \neq \emptyset$, $C^{\mathcal{I}} \subseteq D^{\mathcal{I}}$, $C^{\mathcal{I}} = D^{\mathcal{I}}$, or $r^{\mathcal{I}} \subseteq s^{\mathcal{I}}$, respectively. We write $\mathcal{I} \models \alpha$ if $\mathcal{I}$ satisfies the axiom α. Note that every $\mathcal{EL}$-concept is satisfiable. An interpretation $\mathcal{I}$ is a model of $\mathcal{O}$ iff $\mathcal{I}$ satisfies all axioms in $\mathcal{O}$. An axiom α follows from an ontology $\mathcal{O}$, written $\mathcal{O} \models \alpha$, iff for all models $\mathcal{I}$ of $\mathcal{O}$, we have that $\mathcal{I} \models \alpha$.

An $\mathcal{ELH}$-terminology $\mathcal{O}$ is an $\mathcal{ELH}$-ontology consisting of axioms α of the form $A \sqsubseteq C$, $A \equiv C$, or $r \sqsubseteq s$, where A is a concept name, C an $\mathcal{EL}$-concept and no concept name A occurs more than once on the left-hand side of an axiom. A terminology is said to be acyclic iff it can be unfolded (i.e., the process of substituting concept names by the right-hand sides of their defining axioms terminates).

We denote the number of axioms in an ontology $\mathcal{O}$ with $|\mathcal{O}|$. A signature Σ is a finite subset of $\mathsf{N_C} \cup \mathsf{N_R}$. For a syntactic object X, the signature $\mathsf{sig}(X)$ is the set of concept and role names occurring in X.

2.2   Logical Concept Difference

We now recall basic notions related to the logical difference [5,7] between two $\mathcal{EL}$-ontologies for $\mathcal{EL}$-inclusions as query language.

Definition 1 (Concept Inclusion Difference). *Let $\mathcal{O}_1$ and $\mathcal{O}_2$ be two $\mathcal{ELH}$-ontologies, and let Σ be a signature. The $\mathcal{EL}$-concept inclusion difference between $\mathcal{O}_1$ and $\mathcal{O}_2$ w.r.t. Σ is the set $\mathsf{Diff}_{\Sigma}(\mathcal{O}_1, \mathcal{O}_2)$ of all $\mathcal{EL}$-inclusions α of the form $C \sqsubseteq D$ for $\mathcal{EL}$-concepts C and D such that $\mathsf{sig}(\alpha) \subseteq \Sigma$, $\mathcal{O}_1 \models \alpha$, and $\mathcal{O}_2 \not\models \alpha$.*

In case two ontologies are logically different, the set $\mathsf{Diff}_{\Sigma}(\mathcal{O}_1, \mathcal{O}_2)$ consists of infinitely many concept inclusions. The *primitive witnesses theorems* from [5] allow us to consider only certain inclusions of a simpler syntactic form.

Theorem 1. *Let $\mathcal{O}_1$ and $\mathcal{O}_2$ be $\mathcal{ELH}$-terminologies and let Σ be a signature. If $\alpha \in \mathsf{Diff}_{\Sigma}(\mathcal{O}_1, \mathcal{O}_2)$, then either $A \sqsubseteq C$ or $D \sqsubseteq A$ is a member of $\mathsf{Diff}_{\Sigma}(\mathcal{O}_1, \mathcal{O}_2)$, where $A \in \mathsf{sig}(\alpha)$ is a concept name, and C, D are $\mathcal{EL}$-concepts occurring in α.*

Definition 2 (Primitive Witnesses). *Let $\mathcal{O}_1$ and $\mathcal{O}_2$ be $\mathcal{ELH}$-terminologies and let Σ be a signature. We say that $\mathcal{EL}$-concept inclusion difference witnesses in Σ w.r.t. $\mathcal{O}_1$ and $\mathcal{O}_2$ are concept names contained in Σ that occur on the left-hand side of inclusions of the form $A \sqsubseteq C$ in $\mathsf{Diff}_\Sigma(\mathcal{O}_1, \mathcal{O}_2)$ or on the right-hand side of inclusions of the form $D \sqsubseteq A$ in $\mathsf{Diff}_\Sigma(\mathcal{O}_1, \mathcal{O}_2)$. The set of all such witnesses will be denoted by $\mathsf{Wtn}_\Sigma(\mathcal{O}_1, \mathcal{O}_2)$.*

Observe that the set $\mathsf{Wtn}_\Sigma(\mathcal{O}_1, \mathcal{O}_2)$ is finite as Σ is finite. Consequently, it can be seen as a succinct representation of the set $\mathsf{Diff}_\Sigma(\mathcal{O}_1, \mathcal{O}_2)$ in the sense that: $\mathsf{Diff}_\Sigma(\mathcal{O}_1, \mathcal{O}_2) = \emptyset$ iff $\mathsf{Wtn}_\Sigma(\mathcal{O}_1, \mathcal{O}_2) = \emptyset$ [5]. In the remainder of this paper, we use the size of the set $\mathsf{Wtn}_\Sigma(\mathcal{O}_1, \mathcal{O}_2)$ as a measure for the concept inclusion difference between $\mathcal{O}_1$ and $\mathcal{O}_2$ w.r.t. Σ. We leave investigating alternative measures which allow for a possibly more faithful representation of the logical difference for future work.

Example 1. Let $\mathcal{O}$ consist of the following four axioms:

$$\alpha_1 : A \sqsubseteq B \sqcap \exists r.X \qquad \alpha_2 : B \sqsubseteq A$$
$$\alpha_3 : X \equiv A \sqcap B \qquad \alpha_4 : Y \equiv B \sqcap \exists r.(X \sqcap \exists s.A)$$

For $\Sigma = \{A, B\}$, it holds that $\mathsf{Wtn}_\Sigma(\mathcal{O}, \{\alpha_1, \alpha_2\}) = \mathsf{Diff}_\Sigma(\mathcal{O}, \{\alpha_1, \alpha_2\}) = \emptyset$ and $\mathsf{Wtn}_\Sigma(\mathcal{O}, \emptyset) = \Sigma$ as $A \sqsubseteq B, B \sqsubseteq A \in \mathsf{Diff}_\Sigma(\mathcal{O}, \emptyset)$. If $\Sigma = \{A, r\}$, we have that $\mathsf{Wtn}_\Sigma(\mathcal{O}, \mathcal{O} \setminus \{\alpha_1\}) = \{A\}$ as $A \sqsubseteq \exists r.\top \in \mathsf{Diff}_\Sigma(\mathcal{O}, \mathcal{O} \setminus \{\alpha_1\})$.

Algorithms for computing the witness sets, and hence for deciding whether a logical difference w.r.t. a signature exists, have been implemented in the CEX2.5 tool.[2] Given two acyclic $\mathcal{EL}$-terminologies and a signature Σ as input, CEX2.5 can compute and output the set $\mathsf{Wtn}(\mathcal{O}_1, \mathcal{O}_2)$ in a fully automatic way.

We still note that a new approach for computing logical differences that can also handle large cyclic terminologies has recently been introduced [3,8].

3   Ontology Excerpts

Ontologies appear to exhibit a strong dependency between the size of a signature Σ and the size of a module for the symbols in Σ. This dependency is a natural consequence of the structure of the ontology. We are interested in gaining more control over the size of a module in order to be able to reuse the knowledge contained in an ontology in a scenario where resources are restricted in terms of cognitive ability in human users, and time and space available in technical systems.

Definition 3 (Ontology Excerpt). *Let $\mathcal{O}$ be an ontology and let $k > 0$ be a natural number. A k-excerpt of $\mathcal{O}$ is a subset $\mathcal{E} \subseteq \mathcal{O}$ consisting of k axioms, i.e. $|\mathcal{E}| = k$.*

---

[2] The tool is available under an open-source license from http://lat.inf.tu-dresden.de/~michel/software/cex2/

An ontology excerpt is a subset of the ontology of a certain size. However, we are interested in those excerpts that preserve (as much as possible) the meaning of the symbols in a signature of interest. To quantify the meaning of an excerpt, we need some metric μ. We assume that the lower the value of μ for an excerpt is, the more meaning is preserved by the excerpt. This is made precise as follows.

Definition 4 (Incompleteness Measure). *Let $\mathcal{O}$ be an ontology. An incompleteness measure μ is a function that maps every triple $(\mathcal{O}, \Sigma, \mathcal{E})$ consisting of an ontology $\mathcal{O}$, a signature Σ, and an excerpt $\mathcal{E} \subseteq \mathcal{O}$ to a non-negative natural number.*

In this paper we use as incompleteness measure μ the number $\mathsf{Idiff}(\mathcal{O}, \Sigma, \mathcal{E})$ of $\mathcal{EL}$-concept inclusion difference witnesses in Σ w.r.t. $\mathcal{O}$ and $\mathcal{E}$, which is formally defined as $\mathsf{Idiff}(\mathcal{O}, \Sigma, \mathcal{E}) = |\mathsf{Wtn}_\Sigma(\mathcal{O}, \mathcal{E})|$. In the remainder of this paper we only consider this incompleteness measure. We leave investigating and comparing alternative notions of incompleteness measures for future work.

Definition 5 (Best k-Excerpt). *Let $\mathcal{O}$ be an ontology, let Σ be a signature, and let $k > 0$ be a natural number. Additionally, let μ be an incompleteness measure. A best k-excerpt of $\mathcal{O}$ w.r.t. Σ under μ is a k-excerpt $\mathcal{E}$ of $\mathcal{O}$ such that*

$$\mu(\mathcal{O}, \Sigma, \mathcal{E}) = \min\{ \mu(\mathcal{O}, \Sigma, \mathcal{E}') \mid \mathcal{E}' \text{ is a } k\text{-excerpt of } \mathcal{O} \}.$$

Example 2 (Ex. 1 contd.). The values $\mathsf{Idiff}(\mathcal{O}, \Sigma, \mathcal{E})$ for all 2-excerpts $\mathcal{E}$ of $\mathcal{O}$ are given in the second row of the table below.

$\{\alpha_1, \alpha_2\}$	$\{\alpha_1, \alpha_3\}$	$\{\alpha_1, \alpha_4\}$	$\{\alpha_2, \alpha_3\}$	$\{\alpha_2, \alpha_4\}$	$\{\alpha_3, \alpha_4\}$
0	2	2	2	2	2

One can thus see that $\{\alpha_1, \alpha_2\}$ is the best 2-excerpt of $\mathcal{O}$ w.r.t. Σ under Idiff.

To preserve the largest possible amount of semantic information in a k-excerpt, it would be preferable to extract k-excerpts that have the lowest Idiff-value among all the subsets of size k. However, it is difficult in general to compute all such excerpts in an exhaustive way as all the $\binom{|\mathcal{O}|}{k}$ subsets of size k would have to be enumerated. In the next section, we give introduce two excerpt extraction techniques and evaluate them subsequently.

4   Extraction Techniques

In this section, we introduce two different k-excerpt extraction approaches. One is based on the simple intuition that axioms comprising more elements from Σ should be preferred to be included in an excerpt for Σ. The other approach is inspired by ideas from the area of information retrieval [9]: we view each axiom in $\mathcal{O}$ as a document, and the input signature Σ as the set of keywords from a query. The top-k retrieved documents for the given keywords then correspond to a k-excerpt. These two approaches share a common methodology in the sense that they define a "similarity" between each axiom w.r.t. a given signature such that selecting the k axioms closest to the given signature results in a k-excerpt. We make this idea more precise in the following definition.

Definition 6. *Let $\mathcal{O}$ be an ontology and let $\Sigma \subseteq \mathsf{sig}(\mathcal{O})$. Additionally, let s be a function that maps every pair (α, Σ) consisting of an $\mathcal{EL}$-axiom α and of a signature to a real number. We can then define a ranking of axioms w.r.t. Σ that is induced by s as follows: $\alpha \rhd \beta$ if and only if $s(\alpha, \Sigma) > s(\beta, \Sigma)$. Given an integer k, we define a k-excerpt of an ontology $\mathcal{O}$ for a signature Σ under s as the set $\{\, \alpha \in \mathcal{O} \mid |\{ \beta \in \mathcal{O} \mid s(\beta, \Sigma) > s(\alpha, \Sigma) \}| \le k \,\}$, named a* similarity based excerpt.

A k-excerpt consists of those axioms α in $\mathcal{O}$ for which there are at most $k-1$ axioms β in $\mathcal{O}$ that precede α w.r.t. $\rhd$. Note that such a definition leaves the possibility that such k-excerpts of $\mathcal{O}$ for Σ under s can contain more than k axioms due to an equivalent distance of several axioms w.r.t. Σ. In real-world applications there would exist different remedies to such a situation. Since we aim to compare different excerpt extraction techniques in this paper, we choose to apply a random cut whenever there are more than k axioms contained in a k-excerpt.

4.1   Common Signature Based k-Excerpts

A naïve extraction method for k-excerpts w.r.t. a signature Σ simply consists in a random selection of k axioms from the considered ontology. As a first improvement of the random selection, it is possible to guide the selection of the axioms by considering the number of concept and role names shared by an axiom and Σ, defined formally as follows:

Definition 7. *Given an axiom α and a signature Σ, the* COM-similarity *between α and Σ is defined as $s_{com}(\alpha, \Sigma) = |\mathsf{sig}(\alpha) \cap \mathsf{sig}(\Sigma)|$.*

Example 3 (Ex. 2 contd.). Let $\alpha_1, \alpha_2, \alpha_3, \alpha_4$ be four axioms defined as in Example 1 and let $\Sigma = \{A, B, r\}$. Then we have $s_{com}(\alpha_1, \Sigma) = 3$, $s_{com}(\alpha_2, \Sigma) = 2$, $s_{com}(\alpha_3, \Sigma) = 2$, and $s_{com}(\alpha_4, \Sigma) = 3$. Therefore, the ranking of the axioms will be: $\alpha_1, \alpha_4 \rhd \alpha_2, \alpha_3$. The first and the last axiom are ranked higher than the other two, but no preference between α_1 and α_4 (or between α_2 and α_3) exists.

4.2   Information Retrieval Based k-Excerpts

In IR vector representations of documents and queries are a fundamental tool to model problems, based on which different retrieval strategies can be applied. We first define the vector representation for axioms and signatures.

In the remainder, we assume that every ontology $\mathcal{O}$ is associated with a strict total order $\prec$ on the elements of $\mathsf{sig}(\mathcal{O})$. Whenever we want to access the i-th signature element of $\mathcal{O}$ we refer to the i-element w.r.t. the assumed order $\prec$, starting from the smallest element. For a signature $\Sigma \subseteq \mathsf{sig}(\mathcal{O})$ or axiom $\alpha \in \mathcal{O}$, we can define the signature vector of Σ and the axiom vector of α as follows:

Definition 8 (Signature and Axiom Vector). *For a signature $\Sigma \subseteq \mathsf{sig}(\mathcal{O})$, the signature vector of Σ, written $\overrightarrow{\Sigma} = [v_1, v_2, \cdots]$, is a vector of length $|\mathsf{sig}(\mathcal{O})|$ such that $v_i = 1$ if the i-th element of $\mathsf{sig}(\mathcal{O})$ appears in Σ, otherwise $v_i = 0$. Similarly, for an axiom $\alpha \in \mathcal{O}$ we define $\overrightarrow{\alpha} = \overrightarrow{\mathsf{sig}(\alpha)}$.*

Example 4 (Ex. 2 contd.). Let $\mathcal{O}$ be the ontology defined as in Example 1, and let $\Sigma = \{A, B, r\}$. We assume the strict total order $\prec \subseteq \mathsf{sig}(\mathcal{O}) \times \mathsf{sig}(\mathcal{O})$ given by $A \prec B \prec X \prec Y \prec r \prec s$. Then we obtain the following signature vector for Σ and axiom vectors for each axiom of $\mathcal{O}$:

$$\overrightarrow{\Sigma} = [1,1,0,0,1,0] \ \overrightarrow{\alpha_1} = [1,1,1,0,1,0] \ \overrightarrow{\alpha_2} = [1,1,0,0,0,0]$$
$$\overrightarrow{\alpha_3} = [1,1,1,0,0,0] \ \overrightarrow{\alpha_4} = [1,1,1,1,1,1]$$

Then we can define the distance of an axiom and a set of signature by the distances measures between the axiom and signature vectors. A first measure is the cosine value, resulting in the COS-k-module.

Definition 9 (COS-Distance between Axiom and Signature). *Given an axiom α and a signature set Σ, the COS-distance between α and Σ is defined as follows:*

$$d_{cos}(\alpha, \Sigma) = \cos(\overrightarrow{\alpha}, \overrightarrow{\Sigma}) = \frac{\sum_{i=1}^{n} x_i y_i}{\sqrt{\sum_{i=1}^{n} x_i^2} \sqrt{\sum_{i=1}^{n} y_i^2}},$$

where $\overrightarrow{\alpha} = [x_1, x_2, ..., x_n]$ and $\overrightarrow{\Sigma} = [y_1, y_2, ..., y_n]$.

Example 5 (Ex. 4 contd.). Let $\mathcal{O}$ be the ontology defined as in Example 1, let $\prec$ be the total order on $\mathsf{sig}(\mathcal{O})$ as defined in Example 4, and let $\Sigma = \{A, B, r\}$. Then we have that:

$$d_{cos}(\alpha_1, \Sigma) = 3/(\sqrt{4}\sqrt{3}) \approx 0.8660 \ d_{cos}(\alpha_2, \Sigma) = 2/(\sqrt{2}\sqrt{3}) \approx 0.8164$$
$$d_{cos}(\alpha_3, \Sigma) = 2/(\sqrt{3}\sqrt{3}) \approx 0.6667 \ d_{cos}(\alpha_4, \Sigma) = 3/(\sqrt{6}\sqrt{3}) \approx 0.707$$

Therefore, the ranking of the axioms will be $\alpha_1 \triangleright \alpha_2 \triangleright \alpha_4 \triangleright \alpha_3$.

5 Evaluation

In this section, we present a first evaluation of the proposed excerpt extraction techniques. To this end, we implemented the previously introduced excerpt extraction methods, and we compared them on the following real-world biomedical ontologies with the help of a normalized evaluation metric based on Idiff.

We consider four prominent biomedical ontologies: SNOMED CT (SM) from IHTSDO[3] (first release of 2012), MESH[4], NCBI[5] and NCI[6] (version 10.02d). Table 1 presents the metrics of these ontologies, including the number of logical axioms as well as the number of concept names and role names.

---

[3] http://www.ihtsdo.org/snomed-ct/
[4] http://bioportal.bioontology.org/ontologies/MESH
[5] http://bioportal.bioontology.org/ontologies/NCBITAXON
[6] http://evs.nci.nih.gov/ftp1/NCI_Thesaurus/

Table 1. Metrics of the Considered Ontologies

	SM	MESH	NCBI	NCI	SM-f	MESH-f	NCBI-f
Nr. of logical axioms	291156	403210	847755	75239	50034	49991	51879
Nr. of concepts	291145	286380	847760	76708	50520	50888	82778
Nr. of roles	62	0	0	124	62	0	0

5.1 Experimental Setup

In our experiments, for the four considered biomedical ontologies SNOMED CT, MESH, NCBI, and NCI, we first removed non-$\mathcal{EL}$ axioms from them to be able to use the CEX2.5 tool to compute ldiff values. Note that, however, the proposed extraction techniques can operate on ontologies formulated in any DL. To speed up the experiments, we then selected fragments of SM, MESH, and NCBI, which will be denoted using a '-f' suffix as given in Table 1.

As baseline, we use a *random choice* strategy which randomly selects k axioms from an input ontology to extract a k-excerpt. To estimate the quality of excerpts $\mathcal{E}$, we made use of the following metric, named Gain (G), which is based on the ldiff measure:

$$G_{\mathcal{O}}(\mathcal{E}, \Sigma) = 1 - \frac{\mathsf{ldiff}(\mathcal{O}, \Sigma, \mathcal{E})}{|\Sigma \cap \mathsf{sig}(\mathcal{O}) \cap \mathsf{N_C}|}.$$

That is, Gain is inverse to ldiff normalized by the total number of possible witness concept names. Intuitively, the higher the Gain value of an excerpt $\mathcal{E}$ for a signature Σ is, the more semantic information is preserved by $\mathcal{E}$.

5.2 Results

The four charts in Figure 1 report on the results for the different excerpt extraction techniques on the considered ontologies. The values along the x-axis in each chart represent the parameter k, i.e. the excerpt size, whereas the Gain value of the corresponding k-excerpts is shown along the y-axis. The excerpts were generated for each ontology w.r.t. one randomly generated signature, containing 100 concept names and 30–50 role names in the case of SM and NCI, and 1 000 concept names and no role names for the remaining two ontologies. The vertical line in each chart represents the size of the locality-based module for the signatures.

From the charts 1(a)–1(d) one can see that the Gain values for IR-based excerpts are higher than or equal to the values for other excerpt extraction strategies. In the case of the NCBI and MESH ontologies, one can observe that the ComSig- and IR-based excerpts result in the same Gain values. Indeed, these two strategies yield the same axiom ranking if the signature of all the axioms contains the same number of signature elements, which is the case for NCBI and

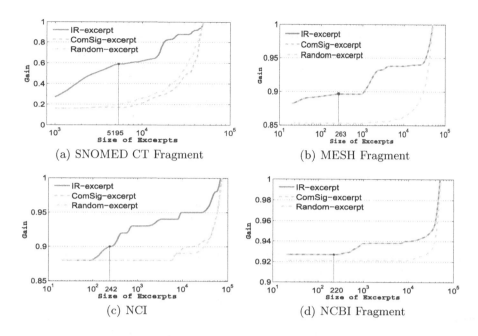

Fig. 1. Gain-Measure for k-Excerpts of Various Ontologies

MESH (each axiom is of the form $A \sqsubseteq B$ for concept names A and B). In all, we can conclude that the excerpts produced by the IR-technique consistently have higher Gain values than excerpts obtain by using the other two methods on the tested ontologies and signatures.

To better understand the distribution of Gain values that we have observed for the ontology MESH (cf. Chart 1(c)), we performed an experiment in which we randomly extracted excerpts and computed their ldiff-value w.r.t. a considered signature containing 5 000 concept names and no role names such that the corresponding locality-based module contained 1610 axioms. To limit the search space, we selected a subset of MESH containing 2 491 axioms, from which we randomly extracted 93 170 many k-excerpts, for $k = 100$. Indeed, for an

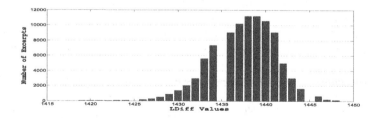

Fig. 2. Distribution of 93170 Random Excerpts over Respective ldiff-Values

Table 2. Percentage of k-Excerpts Falling into Various ldiff-Value Intervals

Nr. of Excerpts	ldiff-Value Intervals					
	$[1\,419, 1\,420]$	$[1\,421, 1\,425]$	$[1\,426, 1\,430]$	$[1\,431, 1\,435]$	$[1\,436, 1\,440]$	$[1\,441, 1\,448]$
6.2×10^{180}	2.14×10^{-5}	0.16	3.45	19.26	56.03	21.10

ontology of that size and a k-value of 100, there exist around 6.2×10^{180} k-excerpts, which renders an exhaustive search through all the excerpts impossible. The results that we obtained are summarized in Table 2. The total number of possible k-excerpts is given in the first column, and the ldiff-values that we observed, except for the value $1\,416$, were regrouped into several intervals that are shown in the 6 right-most columns of the table. The percentage of k-excerpts whose ldiff-value fell into the respective intervals is shown in the second row of these columns.

Figure 2 shows the distribution of the Gain value over the $93\,170$ excerpts of the MESH fragment, i.e. each bar in the chart shows the number of excerpts that have the ldiff-value shown on the x-axis that is associated with the bar (no excerpts having an ldiff-value of 1435 or 1445 were found). We note that the excerpt extracted using the IR-technique had a Gain value (lowest ldiff-value of $1\,416$) that was higher than the values of all the random excerpts we extracted.

Judging from the experimental results that we obtained so far, one could draw the conclusion that excerpts produced by the IR-technique appear to result in high Gain values (i.e. low ldiff-values) in general. To test this hypothesis, we conducted another experiment in which we limited the size of the ontology in such a way that an exhaustive enumeration of all its excerpts is feasible.

We performed an exhaustive computation of all the k-excerpts, with $1 \leq k \leq 19$, together with the ldiff-values of a fragment $\mathcal{O}_f$ of SNOMED CT that contains 19 axioms, using $\Sigma = \text{sig}(\mathcal{O}_f)$ as signature. For every $1 \leq k \leq 19$ we also computed the excerpt returned by the IR method for Σ. The results that we obtained are shown in Table 3. The first column indicates the value of k and the total number of possible k-excerpts is given in the second column. The 24 ldiff-values that we observed were then regrouped into 8 intervals of three elements, and the percentage of k-excerpts whose ldiff-value fell into the respective intervals is shown in the last 8 columns. The interval that contained the ldiff-value for the excerpt computed by the IR-method is indicated using a background coloured in gray. One can see that in none of the cases for $k < 19$, the k-excerpt obtained using the IR-based technique had the lowest ldiff-value. In other words, the IR-based technique fails to extract the best excerpt for $k < 19$.

The previous experiment has thus established that our hypothesis was wrong, i.e. the IR-based technique cannot guarantee to find the best excerpts in every case. Moreover, we can derive an ever stronger conclusion using the following example.

Table 3. Percentage of k-Excerpts Falling into Various ldiff-Value Intervals

k	Nr. of Excerpts	ldiff-Value Intervals							
		$[0, 2]$	$[3, 5]$	$[6, 8]$	$[9, 11]$	$[12, 14]$	$[15, 17]$	$[18, 20]$	$[21, 23]$
1	19	0.00	0.00	0.00	0.00	0.00	0.00	0.00	100.00
2	171	0.00	0.00	0.00	0.00	0.00	0.00	0.00	100.00
3	969	0.00	0.00	0.00	0.00	0.00	0.00	0.10	99.90
4	3876	0.00	0.00	0.00	0.00	0.00	0.00	0.52	99.48
5	11628	0.00	0.00	0.00	0.00	0.00	0.02	1.52	98.46
6	27132	0.00	0.00	0.00	0.00	0.00	0.10	3.46	96.44
7	50388	0.00	0.00	0.00	0.00	0.03	0.34	6.67	92.97
8	75582	0.00	0.00	0.00	0.00	0.10	0.87	11.45	87.58
9	92378	0.00	0.00	0.00	0.00	0.31	1.94	17.89	79.87
10	92378	0.00	0.00	0.00	0.00	0.78	3.96	25.58	69.68
11	75582	0.00	0.00	0.00	0.00	1.78	7.63	33.31	57.28
12	50388	0.00	0.00	0.00	0.05	3.83	13.79	38.80	43.52
13	27132	0.00	0.00	0.00	0.35	8.10	22.56	39.18	29.81
14	11628	0.00	0.00	0.01	1.94	16.10	31.49	32.68	17.78
15	3876	0.00	0.00	0.70	7.22	27.73	34.73	20.92	8.69
16	969	0.00	0.00	4.75	19.09	37.36	26.73	8.98	3.10
17	171	0.00	2.34	18.71	34.50	31.58	10.53	1.75	0.58
18	19	0.00	36.84	31.58	26.32	5.26	0.00	0.00	0.00
19	1	100.00	0.00	0.00	0.00	0.00	0.00	0.00	0.00

Example 6. Let $\mathcal{O}$ consist of the following three axioms:

$$\alpha_1 : A_1 \sqsubseteq B_1 \sqcap \exists r.X, \qquad \alpha_2 : A_3 \sqsubseteq A_2 \sqcap B_3, \qquad \alpha_3 : A_2 \sqsubseteq B_2$$

Let $\Sigma = \mathrm{sig}(\mathcal{O})$. Then the ldiff-values for all 1- and 2-excerpts of $\mathcal{O}$ are respectively shown in the left- and right-hand side of the table below.

	$\{\alpha_1\}$	$\{\alpha_2\}$	$\{\alpha_3\}$	$\{\alpha_1, \alpha_2\}$	$\{\alpha_1, \alpha_3\}$	$\{\alpha_2, \alpha_3\}$
ldiff	4	5	6	3	4	2

The COS-distance between each of the three axioms α_i and Σ is as follows (using an implicit order on the signature elements): $d_{cos}(\alpha_1, \Sigma) \approx 0.707$, $d_{cos}(\alpha_2, \Sigma) \approx 0.612$, $d_{cos}(\alpha_3, \Sigma) = 0.5$. Thus, we obtain the following IR-ranking for the axioms: $\alpha_1 \vartriangleright \alpha_2 \vartriangleright \alpha_3$. Although the best 1-excerpt is $\{\alpha_1\}$, the best 2-excerpt is given by $\{\alpha_2, \alpha_3\}$ without having the highest ranked axiom α_1.

As the example shows, an extraction technique that is based on assigning a unique and static (i.e. independent of the excerpt size k) ranking to all the axioms contained in the input ontology cannot be used to extract the best k-excerpts for every value of k. We conjecture that the size parameter k has to be an input parameter to any algorithm that aims at extracting best excerpts for a given signature.

6   Conclusion

We have introduced the notion of ontology excerpts as a fixed-size subset of an input ontology w.r.t. a signature of interest. We have presented several strategies for excerpt extraction and we evaluated them based on how well the resulting excerpts capture the knowledge about the input signature. The extraction strategy based on IR-techniques clearly outperformed the others in our experiments involving large ontologies. However, this work is a first application of IR-techniques to excerpt extraction. A more extensive evaluation is needed to investigate the advantages of IR-techniques.

We also showed, however, that a static axiom ranking technique (assigning unique rankings) cannot be used in general to obtain best excerpts for every excerpt size. We leave finding an algorithm for computing best excerpts as future work, for which we want to investigate the use of simulation-based techniques that are capable of identifying logical differences [3,8].

References

1. Baader, F., Brandt, S., Lutz, C.: Pushing the $\mathcal{EL}$ envelope. In Proceedings of IJCAI 2005. Morgan-Kaufmann Publishers (2005)
2. Baader, F., Calvanese, D., McGuinness, D.L., Nardi, D., Patel-Schneider, P.F. (eds.): The description logic handbook: theory, implementation, and applications. Cambridge University Press, New York (2007)
3. Ecke, A., Ludwig, M., Walther, D.: The concept difference for $\mathcal{EL}$-terminologies using hypergraphs. In: Proceedings of DChanges 2013. CEUR-WS.org (2013)
4. Grau, B.C., Horrocks, I., Kazakov, Y., Sattler, U.: Modular reuse of ontologies: theory and practice. JAIR **31**, 273–318 (2008)
5. Konev, B., Ludwig, M., Walther, D., Wolter, F.: The logical difference for the lightweight description logic $\mathcal{EL}$. JAIR **44**, 633–708 (2012)
6. Konev, B., Lutz, C., Walther, D., Wolter, F.: Semantic modularity and module extraction in description logics. In: Proceedings of ECAI 2008. Frontiers in Artificial Intelligence and Applications, vol. 178, pp. 55–59. IOS Press (2008)
7. Konev, B., Walther, D., Wolter, F.: The logical difference problem for description logic terminologies. In: Armando, A., Baumgartner, P., Dowek, G. (eds.) IJCAR 2008. LNCS (LNAI), vol. 5195, pp. 259–274. Springer, Heidelberg (2008)
8. Ludwig, M., Walther, D.: The logical difference for $\mathcal{ELH}^{\nabla}$-terminologies using hypergraphs. In: Proceedings of ECAI 2014. Frontiers in Artificial Intelligence and Applications, vol. 263, pp. 555–560. IOS Press (2014)
9. Manning, C.D., Raghavan, P., Schütze, H.: Introduction to Information Retrieval. Cambridge University Press, New York (2008)
10. Rudolph, S., Tserendorj, T., Hitzler, P.: What is approximate reasoning? In: Lausen, G., Calvanese, D. (eds.) RR 2008. LNCS, vol. 5341, pp. 150–164. Springer, Heidelberg (2008)
11. W3C OWL Working Group. OWL 2 Web Ontology Language: Document Overview (2009). http://www.w3.org/TR/owl2-overview/

Toward a Type-Theoretical Approach for an Ontologically-Based Detection of Underground Networks

Meriem Hafsi[✉], Richard Dapoigny, and Philippe Bolon

LISTIC/Polytech'Annecy-Chambéry, University Savoie Mont-Blanc, Po. Box 80439,
74944 Annecy-le-Vieux Cedex, France
{Meriem.Hafsi,richard.dapoigny,philippe.bolon}@univ-smb.fr
http://www.polytech.univ-smb.fr/index.php?id=listic-accueil&L=1

Abstract. In this article, we present a new approach for the purpose of providing a Knowledge-based system able to solve the problem of reliable detection of underground networks by optimization of the existing methods. The method must be able to provide an accurate geo-detection of underground networks regardless of their material, their purpose or even the composition of the soil in which they are buried. We investigate an approach based on knowledge reasoning using ontologies. We show that OWL-DL/SWRL suffers from a lack of expressiveness and that to overcome their limitations regarding the representation and reasoning, we propose a new approach using the proof system Coq for the formalization of knowledge and reasoning. We show on a case study the strengths and limitations of this proposal.

Keywords: Knowledge representation · Ontology · Knowledge reasoning · Underground networks detection · Type theory · Proof search

1 Introduction

In this article, we focus on the prevention of accidents that occurs during public works near underground networks or buried pipelines. These accidents have consequences that can be catastrophic such as significant financial losses or damage. Four methods are planned to identify these pipelines but they have limits and depend on many factors. Our investigation aims to solve the problem of reliable detection of underground networks by aggregation of the existing methods and reasoning at different abstraction levels. For that purpose, we must be able to provide an accurate geo-detection of underground networks regardless of their material, their function or the soil. The information collected in the field or soil by these detection methods will be merged in order to achieve and obtain an accurate and reliable single result of geo-detection.

The long-term goal is to check independently these distinct methods and then to aggregate the information/data they provide. Besides, the first step will consists of the representation of this information into symbolic knowledge.

© Springer International Publishing Switzerland 2015
S. Zhang et al. (Eds.): KSEM 2015, LNAI 9403, pp. 90–101, 2015.
DOI: 10.1007/978-3-319-25159-2_8

The second step is to overcome the limitations of current methods to provide a reliable and expressive reasoning system. The new approach stems from previous works which have demonstrated their effectiveness [4,5,7]. Knowledge representation [13] is a field of artificial intelligence that provides a set of tools and methods for representing and organizing human knowledge for reuse and able to share them. More complex tools allow to formalize the knowledge in a formal language allowing them to be understood and reused by computers. Formal ontology appears as one of the most promising tool used in knowledge representation.

A formal ontology, in the scope of computing systems, can be broadly seen as a set of concepts and their properties interconnected by different kinds of relationships. Formal ontologies include at least foundational ontologies which deal with formal aspects of entities irrespective of their particular nature and domain ontologies (e.g., the DOLCE ontology [12]). Foundational ontologies are basically directed towards formal structures and relations in reality. They are necessary for the organization of the world into well-defined categories which are required for enforcing consistency of the domain ontology content. For that purpose, they should rely on formal foundations [9] and should include an expressive logic. Alternatively, domain ontologies are rather based on expert knowledge within a given domain.

Assuming the view of an ontology as a representation of a conceptual system through a logical theory, we will consider that the whole system is constructively arranged as a core ontology, i.e., DOLCE on which rely all domain ontologies. In the context of the funded ENGIE project, the representation of the information provided by the detection methods (Gas Tracker, electromagnetic and RFID) will be described in domain ontologies and will be further used as a support for the spatio-temporal reasoning on GPR images.

A preliminary study centered on OWL-DL and SWRL will highlight some drawbacks that hamper the expected expressiveness of the reasoning process. Therefore, we turn to a more expressive and reliable language, i.e., the Coq proof assistant based on dependent type theory. Using a dependent type theory based on (higher-order) constructive logic we are able to propose a very expressive specification of concepts and relations that is both ontologically well-founded and logically certified. Using Coq as a core language, a small example using a fragment of a domain ontology will demonstrate the strength of the ideas.

2   Related Works

Ontologies have been investigated in some works in the domain of image processing. They were used to upgrade expressiveness for image annotation [6] and also to formalize a domain knowledge in remote sensing [18] or even as a guide for image segmentation [10]. Other applications of ontologies are prospected e.g., in the area of heart electrophysiology [8] or for reasoning about satellite images [1]. They are an effective tool to represent a priori knowledge (expert knowledge) and can improve or guide treatments in many domains.

3   Domain Ontologies

Our contribution will focus on the representation of the geo-detection domain and a priori knowledge (obtained with Gas Tracker, electromagnetic and RFID) that will ultimately be used to reason about radargrams (images obtained with the GPR). The following domain ontologies will help to divide the whole application in modular domains and aggregate them using DOLCE as a unifying core.

- **The domain ontology of underground networks and pipelines :** describes the different types of networks (distribution, transmission), their types (steel, cast iron, HDPE, concrete,etc), their characteristics or properties (operator, owner, depth, diameter), components (fittings, pipes, cables, etc.) and products carried (natural gas, oil, electricity, drinking water, etc).
- **The domain ontology of soil and its components :** represents different soils (clay soil, topsoil, fill, sand, tar, etc.) where the networks are buried, their components (sand, stones, organic matter, etc.) and their physical properties (moisture, conductivity, etc.).
- **The domain ontology the GPR :** describes the domain which contains the physical and magnetic properties used by the GPR, the waves sent and their interactions with the field and potential targets (pipelines or others).
- **The task ontology of radargram analysis :** describes the complete process and the different tasks to analyze and interpret the GPR image. After that, extract the different profiles which can represent buried pipelines.
- **The domain ontology of the electromagnetic technology :** describes the operating tools of the electromagnetic technology and their interactions with the soil and the buried metallic targets.
- **The domain ontology of the Gas Tracker :** describes the Gas Tracker and the technical process for detect plastics pipes transporting gas.
- **The domain ontology of the detection using RFID :** describes the RFID technical and the knowledge contained in the RFID Chips integrated in the pipelines.
- **The application ontology of Geo-detection :** An application ontology which will be linked to the seven previous ontologies and describe the application that will do the aggregation of knowledge acquired on the field.

In this article, we limit the scope to the creation of the first domain ontology of underground networks and pipelines. In this framework, the rule-based process is at the heart of reasoning.

4   Domain Ontology for Underground Networks

Using HCOME [20], the development process for the ontology boils down to the following steps. First, it is mandatory to prepare a formal document describing the requirements in which we detail the domain to represent. The second step turns out to conceptualize, i.e., to define all the concepts and properties.

Each concept is defined by its attributes and relationships with other concepts. The most widely studied types of relations are the subsumption relation and the part-whole relation. The subsumption relation (*is-a*) is a hierarchical relationship that orders the concepts in a taxonomy. If a class A is subclass of class B, then every instance of A is also an instance of B and values of properties of B are inherited by instances of A. In Description Logics (DL), the underlying support for OWL, subsumption is restricted to *is-a* relations. The *Part-of* relationship links parts to their whole and is at the heart of most mereological theories. Part-whole theories such as mereology postulates an extensional view by considering that part-whole relations hold between particulars (and not universals). The major interest of these relations is their set of mathematical properties that can be formally checked to guarantee well-formed ontologies. Other semantic relations link the concepts of a given domain by giving them an additional semantics.

4.1 Conceptualization

In this step we create the dictionary of concepts that describes all the concepts of the modeled domain, the glossary of binary relations and the glossary of attributes. This step is done in collaboration with industrial and experts where each concept is well analyzed. The concepts of the ontology are primarily organized into a hierarchy using the subsumption relationship.

4.2 Formalization and Implementation of the Conceptual Ontology

Usually, most approaches express the conceptual knowledge in a formal knowledge representation language which enables them to be understood by computers. The ontology is expressed in DL [2] by creating the TBox and ABox. Some definition examples using some concepts in a TBox are given below:

```
Network ⊑ ∀ Made_of.Material ⊓ Carry=1Product_carried ⊓
∃ Has_part.(Link ⊓ Node) ⊓ Proprietor=1String ⊓ Owner=1String
⊓ Function_network=1String

Naturalgas_System ⊑ Network ⊓ ∀ Has_part.(Pipeline ⊓ Node) ⊓
Carry="Natural gas"

Power_grid ⊑ Network ⊓ ∀ Has_part.(Cable ⊓ Node) ⊓
Carry="Electricity"
```

The formal ontology has been implemented with OWL in Protegé 4.3. Three steps are required: (i) description of concepts, their properties and relationships, (ii) then, individuals (or instances), their properties and relationships are inserted and (iii) the consistency of the ontology is checked to ensure its correct formalization. The OWL-DL ontology can be downloaded : Here

5   Reasoning on the Ontology in SWRL

The reasoning in OWL-DL is done at two levels, the level of the TBox and the level of the ABox. Several research groups have identified missing capabilities of OWL-DL described in [19]. Thereby, the logical descriptions have a limited expressiveness and they are not able to do more advanced reasoning. To this aim, we need to use a rules language to express the knowledge which is not expressible in OWL-DL. Several rules languages have been proposed. Among them SWRL (Semantic Web Rule Language) which is based on descriptions logic and Horn rules. The expressiveness of OWL is therefore extended by adding SWRL.

5.1 Creating SWRL Rules

SWRL rules[1] are structured into `Antecedent→Consequent` which means that if `Antecedent` is true then `Consequent` is also true. These items are conjunctions of atoms where each atom is structured as one of the atom families proposed:

- **Class atoms:** consist of a description and either an individual name or a variable name e.g., `Network(?x)`, `Network(GasNetwork64)`
- **Property atoms:** consist of a property name and two elements that can be individual names, variable names or data values. e.g., `Carry(?x,?y)`, `YearInstallation(GasNetwork64,1998)`
- **DifferentIndividual atom:** e.g., `DifferentFrom(Client1,Client2)`
- **SameIndividual atom:** it asserts equality between sets of individual and variable names: `SameAs(Client1,Meter215)`
- **Datarange atoms:** they consist of a data range and either a literal or a variable name e.g., `[1,2,3](?x)`
- **Built'in atoms:** they provide an interface to the built-ins and add some functionalities e.g., `GreatherThan(YearInstallation(?x),1995)`

The underlying logic involve terms that belong to the domain of underground networks and interconnection components. As defined in the ontology, a buried network is a set of nodes (accessories or end nodes) interconnected by links (pipes or cables). Each link has a diameter, a depth and exactly two end parts through which is attached to two nodes. A node has only one end part if it is an end node (client, source or cut) and at least two end parts otherwise (two in the case of a reducer and three for T connection, etc). Two nodes are connected together if there is a link to which they are both attached. This knowledge is expressed by the following SWRL rule:

    `Node(?a) , Node(?c) , DifferentFrom(?a,?c) , Link(?b) ,`
    `Attached(?a,?b) , Attached(?c,?b) → Connected(?a,?c) ... (1)`

The OWL axiom `"InverseOf"` defines two inverse relationships. The attachments between a node and a link make use of the two inverse relations `Attached(Node,Link)` and `Attached(Link,Node)`. Having only the knowledge `Attached(Node,Link)`, the inverse information can be deduced through the OWL axiom. This axiom will satisfy the rule (1) in all scenarios. The rule allows to reconstruct an underground network whose elements are previously unknown. Once all these nodes are interconnected, it is necessary to associate them to the

---

[1] Semantic Web Rule Language: http://www.w3.org/Submission/SWRL/

network they form. If we know that a node or pipeline is part of a given network, then all nodes or links to which it is connected or attached are part of the same network. For this, the following rules have been added:

```
Network(?a), Link(?b), Part_of(?b,?a), Node(?c),
Attached(?b,?c) → Part_of(?c,?a) ... (2)
```

```
Network(?a), Node(?b), Node(?c), Connected(?b,?c),
Part_of(?b,?a) → Part_of(?c, ?a) ... (3)
```

The pipeline system and all its components carry the same product or fluid. If the fluid transported by the network is unknown, we must identify it through at least one of its components. That is, if a pipe is carrying a given fluid, then the network to which it belongs and all its components carry the same fluid:

```
Link(?a), Product_carried(?b), Carry(?a,?b), Network(?c),
Part_of(?a,?c) → Carry(?c,?b) ... (4)
```

```
Network(?a), Product_carried(?b), Carry(?a,?b), Part_of(?c,?a)
→ Carry(?c,?b) ... (5)
```

Other rules can be introduced for the specialization of networks. The following rule represents the fact: any gas network carries only natural gas.

```
Naturalgas_network(?x) → Carry(?x, Natural_gas) ... (6)
```

5.2 Using SWRL Rules

Figure 1 shows a distribution network of natural gas (GasNetwork64) that carries the gas from a source (SourceAB) to two customers (ClientA and ClientB) through six pipes and four accessories (2 elbows, 1 T connection and 1 reducer). We provide very little information about the network topology to test the defined rules. The ABox initially contains 28 assertions including the instantiation of the network, its pipes and accessories. We attach each pipe to its nodes using the relationship Attached(Link,Node) and define the relations Part-of(Channel_5,GasNetwork64) and Carry(Channel_1A,Natural_gas).

After running the rules, the ABox gain new knowledge. It jumps from 28 to 103 statements which enhance the knowledge about the underground network and all its components. For example, the instance of the T connection called T_AB which initially contains no specific knowledge, has been connected to other components. After having run the rules, the added knowledge looks like: T_AB is part of the GasNetwork64 network and carries natural gas. It is attached to three pipes: Channel_1B, Channel_2AB and Channel_3 and connected to ClientA, ElbowA and ReducerB.

5.3 Limits of the SWRL Rules

After having re-built the network and deduced the transported product, we wish to explore new ways of reasoning. We also have the requirement for numerical values. We need to infer the existence of a network component if all the necessary knowledge is met. For example, if we have the following knowledge: *"two nodes*

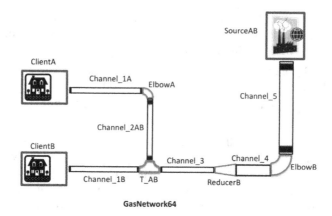

Fig. 1. A fragment of Underground Distribution Network (UDM).

in the same network are connected implies that a link exists between them". We cannot express such rules using SWRL because they involve the deduction of the existence of a new instance that is not present in the ABox.

Despite the benefits of SWRL rules, the expressiveness they allow is not sufficient to ensure a high-level reasoning [11,14]. Indeed, SWRL rules can bring new knowledge only about individuals that already exist in the ABox, but do not allow the creation of new instances. In addition, SWRL rules may apply if the type of all these instances is known. The identity of these instances must also be known and present in the ontology to be treated with the SWRL rules. The fact that OWL and SWRL are two distinct systems also yields some problems such as the fact that new assertions by rules may violate existing restrictions in ontology. Alternatively, there are well-known drawbacks of SWRL e.g., (i) arbitrary OWL expressions, such as restrictions, can appear in the head or body of a rule and (ii) it adds significant expressive power to OWL, but causes undecidability. Furthermore, higher order reasoning is neither available whereas it could be interesting for reasoning about meta-properties.

6   Using the Coq Proof System

6.1   A Short Introduction to the Coq Theorem Prover

The Coq language is a tool for developing mathematical specifications and proofs. As a specification language, Coq is both a higher order logic (quantifiers may be applied on natural numbers, on functions of arbitrary types, on propositions, predicates, types, etc.) and a typed lambda-calculus enriched with an extension of primitive recursion (further details are given in [3]). The underlying logic of the Coq system is an intuitionist logic. This means that the proposition $A \vee \neg A$ is not taken for granted and, if it is needed, the user has to assume it explicitly. This allows to clarify the distinction between classical and constructive proofs. Its building blocks are terms and the basic relation is the typing relation. Coq is designed such that it ensures decidability of type checking. All logical judgments are typing judgments. The type-checker checks the correctness of proofs, that is, it checks that a data structure complies to its specification. The language of the Coq theorem prover consists in a sequence of declarations and definitions. A declaration associates a name with a qualification which can be either a logical propositions which resides in the universe *Prop* or an abstract type which belongs to the universe *Type* (the universe Type is stratified but this aspect is not relevant here). Conversion rules such as β-reduction allow for term reductions. Standard equality in Coq is the Leibniz equality where propositionally equal terms are meant to be equivalent with respect to all their properties. Coq mixes types and expressions to produce code that is proven to be correct with respect to its expected behavior. The proof engine also provides an interactive proof assistant to build proofs using specific programs called tactics. Tactics are the cornerstone of proof-search in the process of theorem proving.

6.2   Formalizing the Domain Ontology in Coq

Assuming that any concept or relation is described with types, we present an excerpt of the domain ontology and define some rules which are not easily expressible in OWL-DL and SWRL. While the notion of type is central in all major conceptual modeling languages e.g., Object-Oriented classes and OWL concepts, its expressiveness in Coq goes far beyond their simple use. Unlike FOL-based ontologies, it describes in a natural and simple way the relation between universals and individuals without the need to introduce specialized ad'hoc constructs like in [15]. Using the DOLCE taxonomy for root concepts, we extend it with a fragment of the ontology of underground networks. We assume that:

- Atomic concepts are represented by well-formed types.
- An individual is represented by any proof object (instance) that holds for a well-formed type.
- The hierarchy of concepts is ordered by coercions which formalize subsumption in type theory.

The first reasoning mode concerns type checking which is decidable in Coq. It results that all declared concepts are well-typed otherwise an error is detected. Using types instead of unary predicates for the ontological categories (i) gives the possibility to find an unintended application of n-ary predicates during the type checking (e.g., for non well-typed types) and (ii) offers a rich structural knowledge representation by means of partially ordered types. The following fragment illustrates how the DOLCE taxonomy is represented with **kind**, the root concept.

```
Class PT : Type.
Parameter D1 : PT → kind. Coercion D1 : PT ↣ kind.
Class PD : Type.
Parameter D2 : PD → PT. Coercion D2 : PD ↣ PT.
```

Class **ED** : Type.
Parameter *D3* : **ED** → **PT**. Coercion *D3* : **ED** ↣ **PT**.
Class **AB** : Type.
Parameter *D4* : **AB** → **PT**. Coercion *D4* : **AB** ↣ **PT**.
Class **Q** : Type.
Parameter *D5* : **Q** → **PT**. Coercion *D5* : **Q** ↣ **PT**.

In the same way, the domain ontology extends the above fragment as follows:

Class **Network** : Type.
Parameter *D29* : **Network** → **NAPO**. Coercion *D29* : **Network** ↣ **NAPO**.
Class **DistributionNetwork** : Type.
Parameter *D30* : **DistributionNetwork** → **Network**.
Coercion *D30* : **DistributionNetwork** ↣ **Network**.
Class **UndergroundDistributionNetwork** : Type.
Parameter *D31* : **UndergroundDistributionNetwork** → **DistributionNetwork**.
Coercion *D31* : **UndergroundDistributionNetwork** ↣ **DistributionNetwork**.
Class **UDNNode** : Type.
Parameter *c1* : **UDNNode** → **NAPO**.
Coercion *c1* : *UDNNode* ↣ **NAPO**.
Class **UDNLink** : Type.
Parameter *c2* : **UDNLink** → **NAPO**.
Coercion *c2* : **UDNLink** ↣ **NAPO**.

Class **C_UndergroundDistributionNetwork** (*x1*:**UDNNode**)(*x2*:**UDNLink**)
        (*x*:**UndergroundDistributionNetwork**) :=
        CUndergroundDistributionNetwork :> *x1* $\sqsubseteq$ *x* $\wedge$ *x2* $\sqsubseteq$ *x*.

Class **UDNEndNode** : Type.
Parameter *D32* : **UDNEndNode** → **UDNNode**.
Coercion*D32* : **UDNEndNode** ↣ **UDNNode**.
Class **UDNInterconnectionNode** : Type.
Parameter*D33* : **UDNInterconnectionNode** → **UDNNode**.
Coercion*D33* : **UDNInterconnectionNode** ↣ **UDNNode**.
Class **UDNReducer** : Type.
Parameter *D34* : **UDNReducer** → **UDNInterconnectionNode**.
Coercion *D34* : **UDNReducer** ↣ **UDNInterconnectionNode**.
Class **UDNTConnection** : Type.
Parameter *D35* : **UDNTConnection** → **UDNInterconnectionNode**.
Coercion *D35* : **UDNTConnection** ↣ **UDNInterconnectionNode**.
Class **UDNElbow** : Type.
Parameter *D36* : **UDNElbow** → **UDNInterconnectionNode**.

The second mode in automated reasoning relies on Type Classes (TC) in Coq which are a recent appealing structure [16,17] having many interesting properties. TCs are just dependent inductive types with one constructor and some fields which are eliminators corresponding to each constructor argument. Coq allows us to specify the rules inside TCs. Dependent types give new power to TCs while types and values are unified. TCs allow parametric arguments, multiple inheritance and multiple fields [17]. Coq's TCs are first class, i.e., classes and their instances are designed as record types and registered as constants of these types. If parameters are marked as implicit (i.e., using curly brackets) then Coq will try to infer them (instance resolution) automatically using type inference. Canonical names for reusable components are achieved with single-field TCs containing a single component each, also referred to as *operational type classes* [17]. Part-whole relations are specified using dependent operational TCs labeled C_XX. In the above fragment, the TC **CUndergroundDistributionNetwork** describes a property of these networks: it is a whole composed of two parts, a node and a link transmitted as explicit arguments. In such a way, complete partwhole hierarchies can be described in which all part instances are automatically created from a unique whole instance (see e.g., [7] for more details).

The third mode addresses the pure reasoning style. Axioms (domain rules) are listed in the fragment above.

Definition Attached_to (a:**UDNLink**)(a':**UDNNode**) := Association a a'.
Definition Connected_to (a a':**UDNNode**) := Association a a'.

Axiom r_of_part_of : **Reflexive** Part_of.
Axiom a_of_part_of : **Asymmetric** Part_of.
Axiom t_of_part_of : **Transitive** Part_of.
Axiom t_of_has_part : **Transitive** has_part.
Axiom s_of_connected_to : **Symmetric** Connected_to.
Axiom t_of_connected_to : **Transitive** Connected_to.

The term *Association* refers to a relation type and terms having this type are concrete relations. All following axioms correspond to meta-rules in usual first-order languages.

Axiom NDist_Part_Attached_to : $\forall$ ($l1$:**UDNLink**)($n1$:**UDNNode**)($udn1$:**Underground
   DistributionNetwork**), Attached_to $l1$ $n1$ $\wedge$ $n1$ $\sqsubseteq$ $udn1$ $\rightarrow$ $l1$ $\sqsubseteq$ $udn1$.
Axiom LDist_Part_Attached_to : $\forall$ ($l1$:**UDNLink**)($n1$:**UDNNode**)($udn1$:**Underground
   DistributionNetwork**), Attached_to $l1$ $n1$ $\wedge$ $l1$ $\sqsubseteq$ $udn1$ $\rightarrow$ $n1$ $\sqsubseteq$ $udn1$.
Axiom intro_of_connected_to : $\forall$ ($n1$ $n2$:**UDNNode**)($l1$:**UDNLink**),
   Attached_to $l1$ $n1$ $\wedge$ Attached_to $l1$ $n2$ $\rightarrow$ Connected_to $n1$ $n2$.
Axiom elim_of_connected_to : $\forall$ ($n1$ $n2$:**UDNNode**), Connected_to $n1$ $n2$ $\rightarrow$
   $\exists$ $l1$:**UDNLink**, Attached_to $l1$ $n1$ $\wedge$ Attached_to $l1$ $n2$.

Once the above axioms have been described, they can be used to derive some lemmas at the type level. Let us consider the following lemma which states that if two nodes are connected and if one of them is a part of a given UDN, then the other node is also part of the UDN. It is derivable from other axioms using appropriate tactics.

Lemma Dist_Part_Connected_to : $\forall$ ($n1$ $n2$:**UDNNode**)($udn1$:**Underground
   DistributionNetwork**), Connected_to $n1$ $n2$ $\wedge$ $n1$ $\sqsubseteq$ $udn1$ $\rightarrow$ $n2$ $\sqsubseteq$ $udn1$.
Proof.
```
        intros n1 n2 net1 H1.
        destruct H1 as [H1 H2].
        apply elim_of_connected_to in H1.
        elim H1; intros l1 H3;clear H1.
        destruct H3 as [H3 H4].
        assert (H5:Attached_to l1 n1 ∧ n1 ⊑ net1).
        split;assumption.
        apply NDist_Part_Attached_to in H5.
        assert (H6:Attached_to l1 n2 ∧ l1 ⊑ net1).
        split;assumption.
```

`apply` LDist_Part_Attached_to in H6;`assumption`.
`Qed.`

Such lemmas can be reused in other theorems. A last mode of reasoning consists in collecting axioms and variables into *HintDb* databases. Then requests provided by the user (similar to databases queries), constitute initial goals over which automatic searches (e.g., the **eauto** tactic) using a depth-first search algorithm (100 is the default depth) are achieved. Notice that apart from reasoning, Coq is able to work on numerical values and perform computations. Furthermore, the deduction of the existence of a new instance that was not present in the ABox is solved in Type theory with Coq because if the premises of a rule (described by a dependent type) are proved, then the conclusion is proved as well.

7   Conclusion

In this article, we introduced a novel approach to reason about concrete knowledge resulting from domain ontologies in the gas distribution environment. This study has investigated two alternative approaches, i.e., the OWL-DL/SWRL machinery and the Coq proof assistant. Coq is able to provide reasoning in many aspects, i.e., type-checking, automatic instance creation, partial automated reasoning with tactics and automated reasoning with instance databases. In such a way, Coq offers encouraging capabilities to overcome many limitations of OWL-DL and SWRL. While tactic-based reasoning is only partial, the meta-language *Ltac* will seriously reduce this limitation. Of course, the size limitation of the search algorithm yields another limitation. This article has presented a preliminary work and future investigations will concern an interface for the translation between user queries and the Coq system.

Acknowledgments. This research is supported by the G4M project founded by an FUI.

References

1. Andres, S., Arvor, D., Pierkot, C.: Towards an ontological approach for classifying remote sensing images. In: Eighth International Conference on Signal Image Technology and Internet Based Systems, SITIS 2012, 25–29 November 2012, Sorrento, Naples, Italy, pp. 825–832 (2012)
2. Baader, F., Horrocks, I., Sattler, U.: Description logics as ontology languages for the semantic web. In: Hutter, D., Stephan, W. (eds.) Mechanizing Mathematical Reasoning. LNCS (LNAI), vol. 2605, pp. 228–248. Springer, Heidelberg (2005)
3. Bertot, Y., Castéran, P.: Interactive Theorem Proving and Program Development: Coq'Art: The Calculus of Inductive Constructions. Texts in Theoretical Computer Science, An EATCS series. Springer Verlag, Heidelberg (2004)
4. Dapoigny, R., Barlatier, P.: Towards Ontological Correctness of Part-whole Relations with Dependent Types. FOIS **45–58**, 2010 (2010)

5. Dapoigny, R., Barlatier, P.: Modeling Ontological Structures with Type Classes in Coq. ICCS **135–152**, 2013 (2013)
6. Kurtz, C., Beaulieu, C.F., Napel, S., Rubin, D.L.: A hierarchical knowledge-based approach for retrieving similar medical images described with semantic annotations. Journal of Biomedical Informatics **49**, 227–244 (2014)
7. Dapoigny, R., Barlatier, P.: Specifying Well-Formed Part-Whole Relations in Coq. ICCS **2014**, 159–173 (2014)
8. Gonçalves, B., Zamborlini, V., Guizzardi, G., Filho, J.G.P.: An ontology-based application in heart electrophysiology: representation, reasoning and visualization on the web. In: Proceedings of the 2009 ACM Symposium on Applied Computing (SAC), 9–12 March 2009, Honolulu, Hawaii, USA, pp. 816–820 (2009)
9. Guarino, N., Welty, C.A.: A formal ontology of properties. In: Dieng, R., Corby, O. (eds.) EKAW 2000. LNCS (LNAI), vol. 1937, pp. 97–112. Springer, Heidelberg (2000)
10. Palombi, O., Bousquet, G., Jospin, D., Hassan, S., Revéret, L., Faure, F., My corporis fabrica: a unified ontological, geometrical and mechanical view of human anatomy. In: Procs of Modelling the Physiological Human, 3D Physiological Human Workshop, 3DPH 2009, pp. 209–219, Zermatt, Switzerland (2009)
11. Hirankitti, V., Xuan, T.M.: A meta-reasoning approach for reasoning with SWRL ontologies. In: Procs. of IMECS 2011, vol. 1, Hong-Kong (2011)
12. Masolo, C., Borgo, S., Gangemi, A., Guarino, N., Oltramari, A.: Ontology Library (D18), Laboratory for Applied Ontology-ISTC-CNR (2003)
13. Pomponio, L., Le Goc, M.: Reducing the gap between experts' knowledge and data: The TOM4D methodology. Data & Knowledge Engineering **94**(Part A), 1–37 (2014)
14. Şensoy, M., Vasconcelos, W.W., Norman, T.J.: Combining semantic web and logic programming for agent reasoning. In: Dechesne, F., Hattori, H., Dignum, F., Such, J.M., Weyns, D., ter Mors, A. (eds.) AAMAS 2011 Workshops. LNCS, vol. 7068, pp. 428–441. Springer, Heidelberg (2012)
15. Smith, B., Rosse, C.: The role of foundational relations in the alignment of biomedical ontologies. In: Procs. of MEDINFO 2004, pp. 444–449 (2004)
16. Sozeau, M., Oury, N.: First-class type classes. In: Mohamed, O.A., Tahar, S., Muñoz, C. (eds.) TPHOLs 2008. LNCS, vol. 5170, pp. 278–293. Springer, Heidelberg (2008)
17. Spitters, B., van der Weegen, E.: Type classes for mathematics in type theory. Mathematical Structures in Computer Science **21**(4), 795–825 (2011)
18. Durand, N., Derivaux, S., Forestier, G., Wemmert, C., Gançarski, P., Boussaid, O., Puissant, A.: Ontology-based object recognition for remote sensing image interpretation. In: 19th IEEE International Conference on Tools with Artificial Intelligence (ICTAI 2007), 29–31 October 2007, Patras, Greece, vol. 1, pp. 472–479 (2007)
19. Taylor, D.: Increasing the expressiveness of OWL through procedural attachments. In: InterSymp-2009: Focus Symposium Preconference Proceedings, Baden-Baden, Germany (2009)
20. Kotis, K., Vouros, G.A.: Human-centered ontology engineering: The HCOME methodology. Knowl. Inf. Syst. 109–131 (2006)

RETRACTED CHAPTER: A Situation-Aware Method Based on Ontology Analysis of the Semantic Social Network

Wenbin Hu[(✉)] and Huan Wang

School of Computer, Wuhan University, Wuhan, Hubei Province, China
hwb@whu.edu.cn, 694789758@qq.com

Abstract. Situation awareness relies on the situation context, classifying context and inferring further situation about context. However, the relevant applications have to deal with the inherent imperfection of situation recognition for decision making. The current researches of situation-aware focused on situation recognition based on modeling, classifying and apperceiving of context information, which were insufficiency in the researches and utilization in situation relevance. To overcome this deficiency, this paper fully analyzes the situation relevance (including the trigger and dependency among situations) based on situation ontology, and puts forward a situation-aware method based on ontology analysis of the semantic social network (SR-SSNOA). The main research includes that: (1) SR-SSNOA converts the situation ontology into different figures, and introduces semantic social network to analyze situation ontology. (2) SR-SSNOA realizes the recognition and recommendation of situation by synthetically considering the situation quality, the situation relevance and the community impact. Extensive experiments are carried out, which reveals the performance of SR-SSNOA at different parameter values. A questionnaire is conducted to evaluate the results, which further proves our method's accuracy and correctness.

Keywords: Situation-aware · Community · Semantic social network · Ontology analysis · Situation recommendation

1 Introduction

Context awareness has emerged as a promising way to build the intelligent and dynamic system to overall computer science areas, which contributes to the location-based services, user web recommendation and so on. The main researches of context-aware computing include environment information perceiving and obtaining, context information classifying and reasoning. Situation-aware is an extension of the context-aware. The typical researches are trying to exploit the concept of the situation for representing computing environments beyond the context, and focus on situation recognition based on modeling, classifying and apperceiving of context information. However, there are two difficulties in situation-aware computing from the recent researches.

(1)The situation is difficult to define clearly and there are ambiguities of differentiating situation from different context. The description of situation should include the

The correction to this chapter is available at https://doi.org/10.1007/978-3-319-25159-2_80

© Springer International Publishing Switzerland 2015
S. Zhang et al. (Eds.): KSEM 2015, LNAI 9403, pp. 102–114, 2015.
DOI: 10.1007/978-3-319-25159-2_9

situation Goals, action history, environment (time, object, location and so on), triggering operation, and relations among situations.

(2) How to use the situation relevance (including the trigger and dependency among situations)? The situation-aware is mainly through the rules and reasoning to achieve the identification of the situation. Because of lacking utilization of the relationship among situations and the complexity of situation itself, it is difficult to effectively define rules to convey a specific situation.

The motivation of this work is to overcome the above difficulties. Situation modeling directly decides the quality of situation reasoning. Ontological knowledge analysis is the most effective method to model and describe complex information for semantically and conceptually oriented techniques [1], and social relations and semantic information of situation are two crucial factors to help prepare the ground for the development of situation-aware application. Based on these analyses, this paper proposes a situation-aware method based on ontology analysis of the semantic social network (SR-SSNOA), which is based on situation ontology (hierarchical model), and uses semantic social network to analyze situation ontology. SR-SSNOA synthetically takes into account the situation quality, the situation relevance and the community impact to realize the situation recognition and recommendation. Our contributions in this paper can be summarized as:

(1) The situation ontology is extended to deal with diverse task situations that may occur in the real application.

(2) Algorithm CommunityRank is proposed to measure community influence of situation by using the trigger and dependency among situations to construct the situation relationship and detect the situation community. Algorithm GoalRank is proposed to evaluate quality of situation and algorithm GoalTIDF is proposed to measure the relevance of situation by mapping the situation ontology into Word Wide Web.

(3) SR-SSNOA method is combined with algorithms CommunityRank, GoalRank and GoalTIDF to realize situation recognition and recommendation by synthetically considering the situation quality, the situation relevance and the community impact.

The rest part of this paper are organized as follows. Section 2 introduces the related works. Section 3 describes the extension technology of situation ontology. Section 4 presents the method of SR-SSNOA. Section 5 presents the performance of the proposed method. Section 6 draws a conclusion and the perspectives.

Related Works

Significant research efforts about situation aware have been devoted on context information obtaining, classifying and modeling of situation and situation reasoning.

The typical situation modeling methods are as follows: 1) The Graphical Unified Modeling Language (UML) is suitable to implement and describe the complex modeling process [8], but it need know the relationship of situation. 2) Object orient model, which can extend and encapsulate the situation.3) Modeling based on logic, which describes the system behavior by the conditions and resultant rules. 4) Modeling based on ontology, which contains the situation concepts and the relevance of properties and combines the advantages of the above three methods. Ontological knowledge has become a main vehicle for situation modeling and applications such as word sense disambiguation, searching, classifying, question answering, entity resolution, and context/situation-aware reasoning for personalized services [1]. Weißenberg [2] adopted ontology technology, users' personal information and other service information to realize situation identification on the basis of an intelligent personal service platform. He built the ontology library by ontology layering and classifying, including time, place, weather, service and so on. He also mapped ontology library into the users' personal information and achieved the final situation recommendation service by semantic matching of situation ontology and ontology reasoning. But the instance scale of his ontology library is little, and needs too much reasoning rules to identify the situation. The situation relevance should be fully used. Stan [3] built users' profile mode based on ontology, and the ontology data source is from the study of the users' behavior. The model used clustering algorithm to classify context information, and the pattern mining algorithm is used to situation recognition. By matching the real-time monitoring users' information with the situation ontology, the model identified the users' current situation. Chen [4] extended COBRA ontology, and proposed COBRA-ONT ontology method. COBRA-ONT included location, agents, events and other main concepts, which is used for modeling the smart environment. The situation recommendation is implemented by OWL reasoning engine. The methods of Stan [3] and Chen [4] needed to rely on a large number of rules, and were lacking of the use of situation relevance. Kim [5] extended the standard definition of situation-aware computing, and analyzed the situation classification, situation flow and situation composition. Jung [1] adopted natural language processing techniques to obtain a highly refined situation ontology, which could help to detect the current situation of a user in a daily life and suggest a solution suitable for the problem a hand if any. In the process of analyzing the situation ontology, he took into account the complex of situation relevance. But Kim and Jung did not specify how to implement the associated utilization of the situation.

The current ontology reasoning is conducted mainly by rules and ontology reasoning machine. Because the situation is complicated, rules are hard to comprehensively describe the situation. Semantic social network was put forward by Downes [6] at 2004. The current researches of semantic social network are mainly about the network topology relationship among the ontology. Wang [7] put forward unstructured P2P autonomous semantic model of the community based on the evaluation of trust mechanism. Meanwhile, he provided the independent node, the independent semantic social network model. But the ontology constructing and the data source were limited. Davoodi [8] presented a framework to build a hybrid expert recommendation system that integrated the characteristics of content-based recommendation algorithms into a social network-based collaborative filtering system. The proposed method aimed at improving the accuracy of recommendation prediction by considering the social aspect of experts' behaviors. The above researches all adopted semantic social network, but they mainly studied the relevance of ontology, not focused on ontology analysis by semantic social network. Hoser [9] clearly put forward a semNA method based on ontology analysis of semantic social network. The method analyzed the basis structural characteristics of ontology, without the further research and exploration about community detection.

Based on the above related works, this paper proposed SR-SSNOA method, which realizes the recognition and recommendation of situation by synthetically considering the situation quality, the situation relevance and the community impact. The situation ontology extends the work of Jung [1], and the ontology data source comes from Website wikiHow and eHow, which contain an enormous amount of how-to instructions (e.g., "How to drive a car").

3   Extension Situation Ontology

We adopt nature language processing to construct situation ontology based on wiki-How and eHow. The situation ontology included six classes and six object attributes. This section introduces the extension of this situation ontology, and adopts semantic social network to analyze the extended situation ontology.

3.1   The Extension of Ontology Attributes

The relevance among Goal instances does not express in the situation ontology of Jung [1]. So we extend the situation ontology of Jung, the main works include: (1) The connecting extension of the situation ontology attributes; (2) The connecting building of the situation ontology attribute. The connecting extension of the situation ontology attributes is shown in Table 1. *hasNextGoal* and *communityOf* are the supplement of relevance among Goals. *hasNextGoal* expresses the order relevance among the Goals, which exits transitive nature as *hasNextGoal*. *communityOf* expresses affiliation among Goals. *mapWith* expresses the mapping relation among action and Goal instances, which exits symmetric nature.

The extended situation ontology model is shown in Figure 1. The Goal layer clearly reflects the relevance among Goals, and the relevance of hasAction and mapWith exits in action and Goal layer.

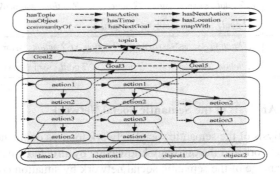

Fig. 1. The extended situation ontology model

Table 1. The connecting extension of the situation ontology attributes

Object property	characteristics	domains	ranges	annotations
hasNextGoal	Transitive	Goal	Goal	The next Goal
mapWith	Symmetric	action	Goal	The mapping of action and Goal
communityOf		Goal	Goal	The community members of Goal

3.2   The Relevance Building of Goals

The relevance of actions relies on hasAction and hasNextAction. This paper establishes the relevance of Goals according to the relevance of actions.

(1) The mapping between Goals and actions
Each action is the simplification of steps in Goal, and remains the core action of the Goal steps. The string similarity matching is used in the mapping between Goals and actions as (a) of Figure 2. The semantic relevance matching based on the WordNet is used in the mapping between Goals and actions as (b) of Figure 2.

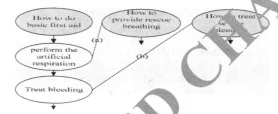

Fig. 2. The mapping between Goals and action

(2) Goal relevance
After the mapWith relevance is built, the order and dependence relevance are built according to the mapWith relevance by Jena rules reasoning. The rules are detailed in Table 2.

Table 2. Rules of the extended ontology

Rule name	Rule content
Order relevance	(? $goal_2$ <sr:hasAction> ? $action_1$),(? $action_1$ <sr:mapWith> ? $goal_1$)-> (? $goal_2$ <sr:communityOf> ? $goal_1$)
Dependence relevance	(? $action_1$ <sr:hasNextAction> ? $action_2$),(? $action_1$ <sr:mapWith> ? $goal_1$),(? $action_2$ <sr:mapWith> ? $goal_2$) -> (? $goal_1$ <sr:hasNextGoal> ? $goal_2$);

3.3   Ontology Analysis of the Semantic Social Network

The ontology analysis of the semantic social network focuses on the network structure in the ontology network and the ontology knowledge by structure analysis. This paper mainly takes advantage of the semantic social network by situation community detection and the mapping between the World Wide Web pages and the community.

(1) Graphic converting of ontology

The semantic social network is based on graphic, so the ontology should be converted into a graphic. The ontology graphic is a digraph of c-d mode. The extended situation ontology has six classes and nine attributors. So the situation ontology is converted into a digraph with six-nine modes.

(2) Community detecting of Goals

In the Goal layer, we convert its node into one-two model, the node is Goal, and the node connection includes hasNextGoal and communityOf. The Goal and the connection Goals by communityOf are union by connection with hasNextGoal and communityOf. There is connection of communityOf between the Goal of How to drive a car safely and the Goal of How to take action after a car accident in Figure 2.

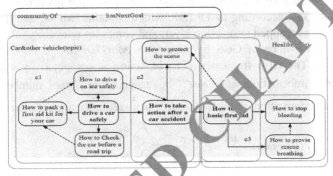

Fig. 3. Community of situation ontology

4   SR-SSNOA

The processes of SR-SSNOA are detailed in Algorithm SR-SSNOA.

Algorithm SR-SSNOA
1: Building a situation ontology.
2: Ontology analysis by semantic social network.
3: Computing the rank of situation quality by Algorithm GoalRank. (detail in section 4.1).
4: Getting the context information.
5: Computing relevance value of Goal by Algorithm goalTIDF. (detail in section 4.2).
6: Computing community influence value of Goal by Algorithm communityRank. (detail in section 4.3).
7: Computing final rank of Goal. (detail in section 4.4).
8 Recommend the situation according the final rank.

4.1   Algorithm GoalRank

The situation quality is calculated by equation (1). Where $goalRank_i$ is ith iteration result of situation quality. A is matrix of Goals. λ is dynamic factor and usually set as 0.2 or smaller. N is the number of Goals, and I is the unit vector of N.

$$goalRank_i = (1 - \lambda) A * goalRank_{i-1} + \frac{\lambda}{N} * I \tag{1}$$

The initial value of situation quality is calculated by equation (2). Where $goalRank_0$ is the initial value of Goal.

$$goalRank_0 = (\frac{1}{N}, \frac{1}{N}, \ldots, \frac{1}{N})^T \tag{2}$$

4.2   Algorithm Goal TIDF

Method of term frequency–inverse document frequency (TF-IDF) is typical statistical approach in relevance of Webpages. We establish *Algorithm goalTIDF* to compute relevance value Goal according to TF-IDF, which contains two steps: (1) Reasoning backward, which is mapped into action layer, and computes relevance value of action. (2) Computing relevance of Goal by *Algorithm goalTIDF* based on the relevance value of action. The term frequency (TF) of action is computed by equation (3), where q is input information; $\inf erCount_q^{action}$ is reasoning backward number of action under this input information; $ingredientsCount^{action}$ is ingredient number of action.

$$tf(q, action) = \frac{\inf erCount_q^{action}}{ingredientsCount^{action}} \tag{3}$$

$$idf(action) = \lg(\frac{N}{nDegree^{action}}) \tag{4}$$

Based on equation (3) and (4), we can compute the relevance value of action $actionTIDF$ by equation (5), where $actionTIDF(q, action)$ is the relevance value of action under the input information q; k is the input keyword number.

$$actionTIDF(q, action) = \sum_{i=1}^{k} tf(q_i, action) \times idf(action) \tag{5}$$

The relevance of Goal relies on the relevance of action, which expresses as follows: (1) The relevance of action with the input information of Goal; (2) The relevance of action with connection *mapWith* of Goal. Based on the above considerations, we can compute the relevance of Goal by equation (6), where $goalTIDF(q, Goal)$ is the relevance value of Goal under the input information q; β is adjustment factor; m is the number of action with connection *mapWith* of Goal.

$$goalTIDF(q, Goal) =$$
$$\beta * \frac{\sum_{j=1}^{m} actionTIDF(q, action_j)}{m} + (1 - \beta) * actionTIDF(q, action) \tag{6}$$

4.3   Algorithm Community Rank

We establish *Algorithm communityRank* to compute community influence value of Goal, which contains two steps: (1) Goal is recommended as community representatives of other Goals. (2) Goal is recommended as the next Goal of other Goals.

(1) When the Goal is recommended as community representatives of other Goals, it needs to consider the quality of recommenders, number of recommenders and the length of input information. The quality of recommenders is expressed by value of *goalRank*. The number of recommenders is the reasoning backward number of Goal. The community influence value of Goal can be computed by equation (7). Where $goalCommunity(q, Goal)$ is the community influence value of Goal under input information q, when the Goal is recommended as community representatives of other Goals. $Goal_{communityof}$ is the recommenders of Goal. $size(q)$ is the length of input information q.

$$goalCommunity(q, Goal) = \frac{\sum goalRank(Goal_{communityof})}{size(q)} \tag{7}$$

(2) When Goal is recommended as the next Goal of the other Goals, it also needs to consider the quality of recommenders, number of recommenders and the length of input information. The community influence value of Goal can be computed by equation (8). Where $goalNext(q, Goal)$ is the community influence value of Goal under input information q, when Goal is recommended as the next Goal of the other Goals. $Goal_{hasNextGoal}$ is the Goals with *hasNextGoal* connection of the Goal.

$$goalNext(q, Goal) = \frac{\sum goalRank(Goal_{hasNextGoal})}{size(q)} \tag{8}$$

(3) Based on the above computations, we can compute the total community influence value by equation (9). Where $communityRank(q, Goal)$ is the total community influence value of Goal under input information q. ∂ is a coordination factor of community.

$$communityRank(q, Goal) = \partial * goalCommunity(q, Goal) + (1 - \partial) * goalNext(q, Goal) \tag{9}$$

4.4   Goal Final Rank Computing

The situation recommendation considers three factors: community influence value of Goal, quality value of Goal and relevance value of Goal. So the final rank of Goal can be computed as equation (10). Where $goalFinalRank(q, Goal)$ is the final rank value of Goal under input information q.

$$goalFinalRank(q, Goal) = goalRank(Goal) * goalTIDF(q, Goal) + communityRank(q, Goal) \tag{10}$$

5   Experiment and Application

5.1   Experiment Setup

The data of situation ontology comes from Website of wikiHow and eHow [10]. The parameters setting are shown in Table 3. The situation instance of experiment is shown in Table 4. There are many Goals in Website of wikiHow under the situation instance of Table 4. Our experiments only focus the top ten Goals, which is shown in Table 5.

Table 3. Parameter setting

Parameter	Parameter description	value	Adjustment
$Goalcount$	The number of Goal in situation ontology	31780	N
$actioncount$	The number of action in situation ontology	31725	N
$objectcount$	The number of object in situation ontology	89432	N
$timecount$	The number of time in situation ontology	372	N
$locationcount$	The number of location in situation ontology	63372	N
R^t	relevance computing threshold of action and Goal	0.4	Y
∂	coordination factor of community in Algorithm communityRank	0.5	Y
ζ	converging factor in iteration of Algorithm Goal-Rank	0.01	N
λ	dynamic factor in Algorithm GoalRank	0.2	Y
β	adjustment factor in Algorithm goalTIDF	0.3	Y

Table 4. Description of situation instance

Situation description	You are driving a car on the ice road, suddenly a crash happens, and someone is hurt.
Time	Winter
Location	road
Object	Car accident first aid

Table 5. The top ten Goals in Website wikiHow under the situation instance of Table 4

NO.	List Of Goals
1	How to take action after a car accident
2	How to do basic first aid
3	How to react when you witness a crash
4	How to survive a car accident
5	How to stop bleeding
6	How to provide rescue breathing
7	How to protect the scene after a car accident
8	How to pack a first aid kit for your car
9	How to Assemble an Emergency Roadside Kit for Winter
10	How to drive a car safely

5.2   Experiment Comparison

This section is devoted to evaluate the method SR-SSRNOA and its algorithms *Goal-Rank*, *goalTIDF* and *communityRank*. We convert the situation instance into key words: car, accident and first aid, and use method SR-SSNOA to compute the rank of Goals, which is listed in Table 7. Compared with the results of Table 7 with Table 5, we can make the following conclusion.

(1) The results (Table 7) of Goal rank listing by SR-SSNOA are better than the wikiHow results (Table 5) in the situation instance of Table 4. The Goals in Table 7 are close to the situation instance, which all contain traffic accident treatment, emergency treatment and so on. So the situation recommended by method SR-SSNOA is better than wikiHow.

(2) Based on the results of Table 7, some Goals (NO2, NO10) are not consistent with the situation instance. The reason is that the key words miss the environment information, such as winter, road. So we convert the situation instance into key words: winter, road, car, accident, first aid, and use method SR-SSNOA to compute the rank of Goal again, the new results is listed in Table 8. The results of Table 8 are better than the results of Table 8 and Table 5.

Table 6. Information description of the main action

NO.	actions	Goals (#has.....tion)	Goals (#mapWith)	In Degree
1	take action after a car accident	G9	G1	4
2	do basic first aid	G1	G2	20
3	react when you witness a crash	none	G3	10
4	survive a car accident	G1	G4	11
5	stop bleeding	G2	G5	28
6	provide rescue breathing	G2	G6	35
7	protect the scene after a car accident	G1	G7	3
8	pack a first aid kit for your car	G10	G8	7
9	drive on ice safely	G10	G9	9
10	drive a car safely	None	None	2

Table 7. Goals rank listing by SR-SSNOA (car, accident and first aid)

NO.	List Of Goals
1	How to pack a first aid kit for your car
2	How to react when you witness a crash
3	How to know what you need in your car's first aid kit
4	How to do basic first aid
5	How to survive a car accident
6	How to provide first aid for a broken Bone
7	How to assemble an emergency roadside kit for winter
8	How to provide rescue breathing for an infant during first aid
9	How to make a car emergency kit

Table 8. Goals rank listing by SR-SSNOA (winter, road, car, accident, first aid)

NO.	List Of Goals
1	How to assemble an emergency roadside kit for winter
2	How to overcome a driving phobia
3	How to drive on Black Ice
4	How to survive a car accident
5	How to take a road trip
6	How to do basic first aid
7	How to make a car emergency kit
8	How to prepare for a long car trip
9	How to drive tactically
10	How to drive a car safely

5.3   Evaluation

This section designs a questionnaire to evaluate the results of SR-SSNOA. We built a program by tomcat+JSP+Jena, and invite 20 postgraduate students as evaluators. They recognize and select each situation of Table 9.

Table 9. Evaluation situation instances

Situation		
Location	Content ingredients	Most frequently selected situation
(1)You've arrived at Wuhan TianHe Airport while on a business trip	Ticket, departure board	Make airport Check-in fast and safe
(2)You are driving a car on a highway. Suddenly one tire is blown out	Spare tire, trunk	Change a flat tire
(3)You are on a business trip to Beijing. You are now arriving at the Beijing Railroad Station	Ticket, luggage	Book train travel
(4)You are enjoying your vacation on SanYa Beach. You have sunburn while tanning	Swim-suit, sun block	Enjoy vacation at beach
(5)You are driving a car on an ice road, suddenly a crash happens, and someone is injured	Car accident first aid	Take action after a car accident

After the questionnaire, we make a statistic of the results, which is shown in Figure 4. On the basis of these results of Figure 4, we can draw the following conclusions.

The results of the left figure do not use the method SR-SSNOA. 13% is irrelevant. 48.32% is new and relevant, and the evaluators are unexpected. The results of the right figure use the method SR-SSNOA. Only 3% is irrelevant, which is only in situation 5 of Table 10. 55% is relevant.

Compared with the results of the right and left, SR-SSNOA can effectively decrease the irrelevant, and increase the relevant and new recommendation.

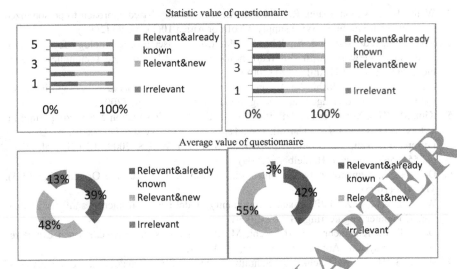

Fig. 4. Statistic of recommended results comparison

6   Conclusions

This paper proposes a situation recommendation method SR-SSNOA, which is based on ontology analysis of semantic social network. Compared with other state-of-the-art situation recommendation methods, method SR-SSNOA can make full use of the situation relevance and not only rely on inference rules. What's more, it converts ontology into graphic and analyzes the ontology by semantic social network, and realizes the recognition and recommendation of situation by synthetically considering the situation quality, the situation relevance and the community impact.

Extensive experiments and a questionnaire are conducted to prove the proposed method's accuracy and correctness. Some conclusions can draw from the experiments:

(1) Method SR-SSNOA provides accurate recommendation situation to users by synthetically considering the situation quality, the situation relevance and the community impact. The questionnaire shows that the relevance of situation recommended by SR-SSNOA is 97%, which upgrade 11.5% than the relevance of situation not recommended by SR-SSNOA. This is a very meaningful and inspiring result.

(2) The key words of situation are very important in SR-SSNOA, which determine the effectiveness of method SR-SSNOA.

References

1. Jung, Y., Ryu, J., Kim, K.M., Myaeng, S.H.: Automatic construction of a large-scale situation ontology by mining how-to instructions from the web. Web Semantics: Science, Services and Agents on the World Wide Web **8**(2), 110–124 (2010)

2. Weißenberg, N., Gartmann, R., Voisard, A.: An ontology-based approach to personalized situation-aware mobile service supply. GeoInformatica **10**(1), 55–90 (2006)
3. Stan, J., Egyed-Zsigmond, E., Joly, A., Maret, P.: A user profile ontology for situation-aware social networking. In: 3rd Workshop on Artificial Intelligence Techniques for Ambient Intelligence (AITAmI 2008) (2008)
4. Chen, H., Finin, T., Joshi, A.: An ontology for context-aware pervasive computing environments. The Knowledge Engineering Review **18**(03), 197–207 (2003)
5. Kim, M., Kim, M.: A formal definition of situation towards situation-aware computing. In: Lytras, M.D., Damiani, E., Carroll, J.M., Tennyson, R.D., Avison, D., Naeve, A., Dale, A., Lefrere, P., Tan, F., Sipior, J., Vossen, G. (eds.) WSKS 2009. LNCS, vol. 5736, pp. 553–563. Springer, Heidelberg (2009)
6. Downes, S.: Semantic networks and social networks. The Learning Organization **12**(5), 411–417 (2005)
7. Wang, L., Hu, G.X.: P2P semantic community model based on interest and trust evaluation. Computer Engineering **13**, 007 (2009)
8. Davoodi, E., Kianmehr, K., Afsharchi, M.: A semantic social network-based expert recommender system. Applied Intelligence, 1–13 (2013)
9. Hoser, B., Hotho, A., Jäschke, R., Schmitz, C., Stumme, G.: Semantic network analysis of ontologies. In: Sure, Y., Domingue, J. (eds.) ESWC 2006. LNCS, vol. 4011, pp. 514–529. Springer, Heidelberg (2006)
10. wikiHow. http://www.wikihow.com/Main-Page (accessed May 1, 2013)

Fm-QCA: A Novel Approach to Multi-value Qualitative Comparative Analysis

Ke Wu[1], Shiping Tang[2], Geguang Pu[1]([✉]), Min Wu[1], and Ting Su[1]

[1] Shanghai Key Laboratory of Trustworthy Computing, East China Normal University, Shanghai, China
bukawu@126.com, {ggpu,mwu}@sei.ecnu.edu.cn, tsuletgo@gmail.com
[2] Center for Complex Decision Analysis (CCDA), Fudan University, Shanghai, China
twukong@gmail.com

Abstract. Qualitative comparative analysis (QCA) is a technique originally developed by Charles Ragin in the field of political science. It accepts data sets from the problem of interest, and applies the rules of logical inference to determine the relations between combinations of variables and outcomes, which helps researchers validate hypotheses or discover new implications. However, existing QCA approaches or tools have limited capacities in handling multivalued explanatory and outcome variables, as well as in outputting compact results for human analysis. In this paper, we propose a novel QCA approach, which can deal with multivalued variables and support more complicated analysis. Our approach enables 1) multi-value reduction of candidate rules; and 2) effective counterfactual analysis associated with expert knowledge. We also implemented a new tool called fully functional multi-value QCA (fm-QCA). Through the evaluation, our tool outperforms existing state-of-the-art QCA tools in producing more compact analysis results as well as discovering more inferences.

Keywords: QCA · Case-based Reasoning · Multi-value Logic

1 Introduction

Qualitative comparative analysis (QCA) is a technique introduced by Ragin [18–20] to analyze small to medium data sets. By counting all combinations of explanatory variables (*i.e.*, configurations) instead of single variable, QCA can discover the relations between combinations of explanatory variables and outcomes. This technique has already demonstrated its usefulness in many fields, *e.g.*, political science, social science [1,5,8,17,23], economics [3], business [7,11], and environmental sciences [2,9]. Take foreign affairs as example, several potential variables, *e.g.*, GDP per capita (GDP), military infrastructure (MI), laws and regulations (LR), could affect the diplomatic status of a country. QCA can analyze the configurations of these variables to discover the potential configuration, *e.g.*, *GDP*MI*, which indicates GDP and MI can affect the diplomatic status. In general, QCA can produce three different solutions (*i.e.*, sets of rules):

© Springer International Publishing Switzerland 2015
S. Zhang et al. (Eds.): KSEM 2015, LNAI 9403, pp. 115–127, 2015.
DOI: 10.1007/978-3-319-25159-2_10

complex, parsimonious and *intermediate* solutions. Complex and parsimonious solutions are directly generated from the data set, while intermediate solution is produced by combining the previous two solutions and expert knowledge. Therefore, the intermediate solution is the most meaningful and effective solution.

However, the state-of-the-art multi-value approaches still suffer from the following limitations: 1) inadequate filtering of candidate rules and multi-value reduction for multivalued outcomes, which results in redundant inference rules [4,22]; and 2) inadequate counterfactual analysis with expert knowledge, which may lose meaningful inference rules [4].

To this end, we propose a novel approach to tackle these issues. Moreover, we implement a new tool called fully functional multi-value **QCA** (fm-QCA[1]) to perform efficient analysis. The main contributions of this paper are summarized as follows:

- We propose a novel approach to handle multivalued reasoning, which includes efficient multi-value reduction algorithm and a new counterfactual analysis.
- We implement a new tool called fm-QCA and compare it with the state-of-the-art QCA tools. The results show that our approach outperforms the other tools.

The remainder of this paper is organized as follows. Section 2 discusses related work in QCA. Section 3 introduces some background knowledge. Section 4 details the techniques used in our approach. Section 5 presents the evaluation results and outlines the comparison between the existing QCA tools. Section 6 makes a conclusion.

2   Related Work

Ragin [18] first proposes a crisp QCA approach to tackle dichotomous data and develops it into a systematic methodology. Later, some generalizations [19,20] are made on QCA to tackle fuzzy data (tool: fs/QCA). Mendel and Korjani [12,14–16] propose a theoretical summarization of fuzzy QCA and present an approach to accelerate its analysis performance. But all of these approaches can only deal with dichotomous and fuzzy data.

In recent years, Cronqvist [4] proposes a multi-value approach to process multivalued data sets (tool: Tosmana). Thiem and Dusa [22] propose another superior multi-value approach (tool: R-QCA). For tool Tosmana, the variables being processed can be multivalued and the complex, parsimonious solutions can be obtained automatically. However, it cannot generate intermediate solution due to the lack of counterfactual analysis. R-QCA makes some improvements on this point and can provide a better solution.

---

[1] https://github.com/buka632/Fm-QCA

3   Notion and Problem Formulation

The main objective for QCA is to discover connections between variables and outcomes through logic inferences. For example, A, B, C are three-valued explanatory variables, R is a desired outcome and the set $\{\{0, 0, 1 \rightarrow 1\}, \{0, 2, 1 \rightarrow 1\}, \{0, 1, 1 \rightarrow 1\}, \{1, 1, 0 \rightarrow 1\}, \{2, 1, 0 \rightarrow 0\}\}$ contains five cases, which is used to discover inference rules in the form of $\{A, B, C \rightarrow R\}$. QCA generates the truth table which contains all the possible rules of A, B, C, $e.g.$, $A\{0\}B\{1\}C\{1\}$, $A\{2\}B\{0\}C\{1\}$, and then derives new inference rules. The final result is a set of rules which are possible paths lead to the outcome R, such as $A\{0\}C\{1\} \rightarrow R$, $A\{1\}B\{1\}C\{0\} \rightarrow R$. Typically, QCA generates three different solutions, $i.e.$, $complex$ solution, $parsimonious$ solution and $intermediate$ solution. The difference among them is whether to include $remainders$ ($i.e.$, rules that appear in truth table but not in the dataset) for logic reduction. Expert knowledge will be used in intermediate solution to produce more meaningful results. In the following, we give the formal definitions of three kinds of solutions that QCA could handle.

Let V be the set of variables, T be the truth table of V, E be the set of cases, O be the outcome, K be the expert knowledge, $\boldsymbol{mvQM}$ be the multi-value logic reduction function, $\boldsymbol{mvCA}$ be the counterfactual analysis function, $N_c(r_i)$ be the coverage filter function for candidate rule r_i, $C_c(r_i)$ be the consistency filter function for candidate rule r_i, λ be the coverage threshold specified by user, μ be the consistency threshold specified by user ($\boldsymbol{mvQM}$, $\boldsymbol{mvCA}$, $N_c(r_i)$ and $C_c(r_i)$ will be discussed in the following sections), Assume that $V = \{v_i | i = 1, ..., k\}$ where each $v_i \in V$ is an N-valued (mark N as $Len(v_i)$) variable.

Remainders. For V, there are totally $T = \prod_{i=1}^{k} Len(v_i)$ rules in the truth table. Define that remainders $R = \{r_i | r_i \in T \wedge N_c(r_i) < \lambda\}$.

Complex Solution. For $T = \prod_{i=1}^{k} Len(v_i)$ rules in the truth table, define that complex solution $R_{cps} = \boldsymbol{mvQM}(\mathrm{C})$ where $C = \{r_i | r_i \in T \wedge N_c(r_i) \geq \lambda \wedge C_c(r_i) \geq \mu\}$.

Parsimonious Solution. For $T = \prod_{i=1}^{k} Len(v_i)$ rules in the truth table, define that parsimonious solution $R_{pms} = \boldsymbol{mvQM}(\mathrm{P})$ where $P = \{r_i | r_i \in T \wedge N_c(r_i) \geq \lambda \wedge C_c(r_i) \geq \mu\} \bigcup R$.

Intermediate Solution. For $T = \prod_{i=1}^{k} Len(v_i)$ rules in the truth table, define that intermediate solution $R_{ims} = \boldsymbol{mvQM}(\mathrm{I})$ where $I = \{r_i | r_i \in T \wedge N_c(r_i) \geq \lambda \wedge C_c(r_i) \geq \mu\} \bigcup \boldsymbol{mvCA}(R, K)$.

The intermediate solution is based on complex solution and parsimonious solution, and is the most valuable one compared to the other two since the expert knowledge has been taken into consideration.

4   Our Approach

The framework of our approach, as illustrated in Figure 1, consists of four main components: 1) generating candidate rules, 2) filtering candidate rules,

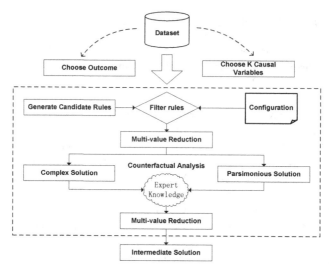

Fig. 1. Framework of fm-QCA

3) computing complex and parsimonious solutions by logical inference, and 4) performing counterfactual analysis to derive intermediate solution. In this framework, multi-value reduction of candidate rules and counterfactual analysis are the most important components, which will be discussed in detail in the sequel.

4.1   Filtering of Candidate Rules and Multi-value Reduction

The major parts in QCA contain filtering of candidate rules and performing multi-value simplification algorithm. Fm-QCA generates all the possible rules in the truth table and takes them as candidate rules. It is crucial to properly filter the candidate rules, since the selection of these rules determines the final analysis. However, for tool Tosmana [4], the filtering of candidate rules is inaccurate. More than two cases that share the same variable value but different outcomes will lead to **contradiction** (C) and these rules will be dropped. For example, there are two cases, $\{0, 0, 1 \rightarrow 1\}$ and $\{0, 0, 1 \rightarrow 0\}$, they both have the same variable value $\{0, 0, 1\}$ but different outcomes, so rule $A\{0\}B\{0\}C\{1\}$ will be dropped. In fact, if there are 100 cases that are $\{0, 0, 1 \rightarrow 1\}$ and only one case is $\{0, 0, 1 \rightarrow 0\}$, the impact of the latter rule can be ignored in spite of its contradiction. In fm-QCA, two parameters **consistency** and **coverage** are introduced to raise the accuracy.

We define two functions $A_R^E(e_j, r_i)$ and $A_O^E(e_j, m)$ to determine whether one rule r_j appears in case e_j and whether the outcome of case e_j is the desired value m. $e_j\{v_i\}$ means the value of variable v_i in case e_j, $r_i\{v_i\}$ means the value of variable v_i in rule r_i and $e_j\{O\}$ means the value of outcome in case e_j, e.g., if $e_j = \{0, 0, 1 \rightarrow 1\}$ and $r_i = A\{0\}B\{1\}C\{2\}$, then $e_j\{B\} = 0$, $r_i\{B\} = 1$ and $e_j\{O\} = 1$. For $\prod_{i=1}^{k} Len(v_i)$ candidate rules, $N_c(r_i)$ can show their coverage of cases and only these rules that $N_c(r_i)$ is no less than λ (specified by user) will be kept, others will be marked as **remainders** (cannot be found in real cases).

$$A_R^E(e_j, r_i) = \begin{cases} 1 & \sum_{i=1}^{|V|} |e_j\{v_i\} - r_i\{v_i\}| = 0 \\ 0 & \sum_{i=1}^{|V|} |e_j\{v_i\} - r_i\{v_i\}| \neq 0 \end{cases} \tag{1}$$

$$A_O^E(e_j, m) = \begin{cases} 1 & e_j\{O\} = m \\ 0 & e_j\{O\} \neq m \end{cases} \tag{2}$$

$$N_c(r_i) = \sum_{j=1}^{|E|} A_R^E(e_j, r_i) \tag{3}$$

Another essential parameter is $C_c(r_i)$ which represents the consistency of one rule. It will consider the number of cases other than single contradiction and it can be obtained by Formula 4.

$$C_c(r_i) = \frac{\sum_{j=1}^{|E|} min\{A_R^E(e_j, r_i), A_O^E(e_j, m)\}}{\sum_{j=1}^{|E|} A_R^E(e_j, r_i)} \tag{4}$$

For multivalued outcome and outcome combinations, we redesigned this parameter as $C_c'(r_i)$. It can be obtained by Formula 5 where m is the desired outcome and $m_1, m_2, \ldots, m_n$ are possible supplements.

$$C_c'(r_i) = \frac{\sum_{j=1}^{|E|} min\{A_R^E(e_j, r_i), max\{A_O^E(e_j, m), A_O^E(e_j, m_1), \ldots, A_O^E(e_j, m_n)\}\}}{\sum_{j=1}^{|E|} A_R^E(e_j, r_i)} \tag{5}$$

With these properly filtered candidate rules, fm-QCA can discover potential rules by logical inferences. For example, if rules $A\{0\}B\{0\}C\{0\} \to R$, $A\{0\}B\{1\}C\{0\} \to R$ and $A\{0\}B\{2\}C\{0\} \to R$ are true, then it can be inferred that $A\{0\}C\{0\} \to R$ is true where variable B is logically omitted.

Both Tosmana and R-QCA propose some new techniques for multi-value reduction. However, the results obtained still contain redundant rules in many occasions. Several algorithms including Quine-McCluskey [13], DeMorgan's law, Karnaugh Map [10] and *etc.*, can be applied for Boolean reduction, but not for multi-value occasion. Gao *et al.* [6] develop MVSIS which aims at multi-value logic synthesis, but we find it not suitable for QCA because many useful potential rules are lost. So, we extend Quine-McCluskey approach to multi-value level as described in Algorithm 1.

The basic idea is to expand rules and find rules that are *near* (*i.e.*, only one variable is different while the others are the same, *e.g.*, $AB\{0, 1\}$ and $AB\{2\}$ are near) and combine them as a new rule iteratively. For Boolean logic, many laws can be used to simplify rules directly, *e.g.*, $A + \sim A * B = A + B$. But when it refers to multi-value occasion, the situation becomes very complex. In our approach, we firstly expand the rule A as $A* \sim B + A * B$, then, we can achieve the simplification based on these expansion rules (line 9). In each iteration, new rules will be generated based on near rules (lines 20-21) and this procedure will iterate until no new rules can be found. To speed it up, we use a hash bucket to record all the rules and store them separately according to the number of

Algorithm 1. Multi-value Reduction ($mvQM$)

Input: Rule set R,
Output: Simplified rule set R_s
 1: set R_s=empty set
 2: set S=empty Stack
 3: set B=empty HashBucket
 4: **for** each $r_i \in R$ **do**
 5:    S.push(r_i)
 6: **end for**
 7: **while** !S.empty **do**
 8:    r_t=S.pop()
 9:    New rule set R_t=expand(r_t) //Expand one rule into several rules
10:    **for** each $r_j \in R_t$ **do**
11:      //The condition can be the number of iterations
12:      **if** r_j matches the required condition **then**
13:        B.add(r_j)
14:      **else**
15:        S.push(r_j)
16:      **end if**
17:    **end for**
18: **end while**
19: **while** Find Near Rules in B **do**
20:    New rule r_n=CombineNearRules() //Combine near rules as a new rule
21:    B.add(r_n)
22: **end while**
23: return **Petrick**(B) //Use Petrick algorithm to choose final results

---

variables they contain. At last, the final simplified results can be derived through this hash bucket (line 23). The experiments show that, this multi-value reduction algorithm in QCA can achieve more simplified and effective results.

4.2 Counterfactual Analysis

Counterfactual analysis can take the expert knowledge into consideration and combine the complex and parsimonious solutions as intermediate solution. For complex solution, no remainders will be included for multi-value reduction. For parsimonious solution, all possible remainders will be included, while for intermediate solution, only partial of remainders will be included. The key point in counterfactual analysis is choosing those *remainders* for reduction. Recall that remainders do not appear in the given data set but impact the final result, the basic idea is to judge whether one remainder is **easy** or **difficult** ([18]) to happen in reality according to the expert knowledge. For example, if rule $A\{0\}B\{0\}C\{1\}$ is a candidate rule but the experts do not think $A\{0\}$ has positive correlation on outcome, then remainders $A\{1\}B\{0\}C\{1\}$ and $A\{2\}B\{0\}C\{1\}$ will be considered as **easy** to happen because these three rules together can omit variable $A\{0\}$ as rule $B\{0\}C\{1\}$. It is essential in QCA, but Tosmana cannot perform counterfac-

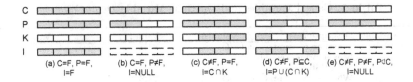

Fig. 2. Counterfactual Analysis in Multi-value situation

tual analysis. In the sequel, we present a new technique on counterfactual analysis for multivalued outcome with a mechanism to compute intermediate terms.

From the perspective of logic reduction, this can be seen as taking each term from complex solution constrained to each term in parsimonious solution, *e.g.*, complex term is $v_1\{0\}v_2\{0,1\}v_3\{1,2\}$, parsimonious term is $v_2\{1\}$ (v_1, v_2, v_3 are three-valued), then, the intermediate term should keep term $v_2\{1\}$, and can be $v_1\{0\}v_2\{1\}v_3\{1,2\}$, $v_2\{1\}v_3\{1\}$, $v_2\{0,1\}v_3\{1,2\}$ and *etc.* If the experts believe that $v_1\{0\}$, $v_2\{1\}$ and $v_3\{2\}$ all have positive effect on outcome while $v_2\{0\}$, $v_3\{1\}$ not, the intermediate term will be $v_1\{0\}v_2\{1\}v_3\{2\}$.

We summarize all the situations for generating intermediate terms in Figure 2 where C represents complex term, P represents parsimonious term, K represents the expert knowledge, I represents intermediate term and F represents the full state of one term. Take (d) for example, if the complex term is $A\{0,1,3\}$ (A is four-valued), the parsimonious term is $A\{1,3\}$ and the expert knowledge is $A\{0,2\}$, then, the intermediate term will be $A\{1,3\} \cup (A\{0,1,3\} \cap A\{0,2\}) = A\{0,1,3\}$.

5   Experiments and Validations

In this section, we evaluate our approach to demonstrate its advantage and effectiveness over other state-of-the-art multi-value QCA tools, *i.e.*, *Tosmana* and *R-QCA*. We implement a new tool called fm-QCA based on our approach and readers can access it online[2]. In addition, we outline a comparison with existing multi-value QCA tools.

5.1   Dataset

The dataset *the democracy robustness of former socialist countries* in the evaluation is provided by an international political research group from Fudan University. This dataset consists of 26 countries and is used to reveal the way toward democracy of a country. There are totally 13 different variables and 3 outcomes. In this evaluation, we choose 10 different variable groups and compare each result with other two state-of-the-art tools. One sample variable group is shown in Table 1. The marker ∗ indicates the expert knowledge is supplied. It means that the experts consider these values have positive correlation

---

[2] https://github.com/buka632/Fm-QCA

Table 1. Causal Variables and Outcome Variable *DemoConmv*

Causal Variables	Description	Value{0}	Value{1}	Value{2}
USSRRep	Whether a country had been a former republic of the USSR.	NO *	YES	-
DemExp	Whether a country had experience of democracy before 1990.	NO	YES *	-
Statehood	Whether a country had experience of statehood before 1990.	NO	YES *	-
Incomemv	A country's average GDP per capita in 1990 in constant US\$ 1990.	< 2000	2000 ∼ 4000 *	> 4000*
EImv	A country's economic inefficiency at 1990 (the higher the score, the more inefficient of an economy).	< 2.0	2.0 ∼ 4.0 *	> 4.0*
DemoConmv	The average POLITY IV scores of a country, 2000-2010.	< 5	5, 6, 7	≥ 8

on the outcome. Readers can refer to [21] for details on the dataset, which is also available online[3].

5.2 Experimental Setup

Step 1. Import datasets into fm-QCA, Tosmana and R-QCA. Choose one variable group, *e.g.*, *USSRRep, DemExp, Statehood, Incomemv* and *EImv* as the explanatory variables, *DemoConmv{2}* as the outcome.

Step 2. Set $\lambda = 1$ and $\mu = 0.85$ (0.95, 1.0) as the threshold. Initialize the expert knowledge on variables, *i.e.*, marked by * in Table 1.

Step 3. Run QCA and obtain complex, parsimonious solutions in fm-QCA, Tosmana, R-QCA. We can obtain intermediate solutions from fm-QCA and R-QCA (Note Tosmana cannot derive intermediate solution).

5.3 Experimental Results

Advantage. The advantages of fm-QCA include: (1) it can discover more potential rules in parsimonious solution and provide more useful analyses, (2) with more potential rules in parsimonious solution, the final result (intermediate solution) becomes more compact, (3) it can process multivalued outcome.

The experimental results of 10 groups are shown in Table 2. It contains 30 experiments. It can be seen that fm-QCA can find more potential rules in parsimonious solution and finally derive a more compact solution (intermediate solution) with the same coverage.

---

[3] https://github.com/buka632/Fm-QCA

Table 2. Experimental results of different datasets. "-" means it cannot support such calculation.

Evaluation		Configuration			Experimental Results			
Dataset	Tool	Num of variables	λ for $N_c(r_i)$	μ for $C_c(r_i)$	Complex	Parsimonious	Intermediate	Coverage
Dataset1								
	fm-QCA	5	1	0.85	6	3	4	0.93
	Tosmana	5	1	0.85	9	2	-	0.93
	R-QCA	5	1	0.85	9	2	5	0.93
Dataset2								
	fm-QCA	5	1	0.85	4	3	3	0.67
	Tosmana	5	1	0.85	5	3	-	0.67
	R-QCA	5	1	0.85	5	3	4	0.67
Dataset3								
	fm-QCA	5	1	0.85	9	1	5	0.93
	Tosmana	5	1	0.85	7	1	-	0.93
	R-QCA	5	1	0.85	7	1	5	0.93
Dataset4								
	fm-QCA	5	1	0.85	5	1	2	0.73
	Tosmana	5	1	0.85	5	1	-	0.73
	R-QCA	5	1	0.85	5	1	3	0.73
Dataset5								
	fm-QCA	5	1	0.95	5	1	1	0.93
	Tosmana	5	1	0.95	4	1	-	0.93
	R-QCA	5	1	0.95	4	1	4	0.93
Dataset6								
	fm-QCA	5	1	0.95	7	6	7	0.80
	Tosmana	5	1	0.95	7	4	-	0.80
	R-QCA	5	1	0.95	7	4	5	0.80
Dataset7								
	fm-QCA	6	1	0.95	8	6	5	0.87
	Tosmana	6	1	0.95	8	3	-	0.87
	R-QCA	6	1	0.95	8	3	5	0.87
Dataset8								
	fm-QCA	6	1	0.95	8	4	4	0.93
	Tosmana	6	1	0.95	10	2	-	0.93
	R-QCA	6	1	0.95	10	2	5	0.93
Dataset9								
	fm-QCA	7	1	1.0	8	1	3	0.93
	Tosmana	7	1	1.0	8	1	-	0.93
	R-QCA	7	1	1.0	8	1	3	0.93
Dataset10								
	fm-QCA	7	1	1.0	9	5	7	0.93
	Tosmana	7	1	1.0	10	2	-	0.93
	R-QCA	7	1	1.0	9	2	8	0.93

Take the variables in Table 1 as example. The intermediate solution in R-QCA is as shown in Table 4. It is evident that rules 4, 5 in R-QCA are contained in rule 2 in fm-QCA (Table 3), rule 2 in R-QCA is contained in rule 3 in fm-QCA, rule 3 in R-QCA is contained in rule 4 in fm-QCA. This can show that, with the novel counterfactual analysis and multi-value reduction, our tool can discover more simplified and meaningful solutions.

For multivalued outcome and outcome combination, only fm-QCA can perform this analysis. One sample result is shown in Table 5.

Table 3. Intermediate Solution Obtained by fm-QCA for DemoConmv{2}

Rules	Unique Coverage
1. ~USSRRep*Statehood	0.33333334
2. ~USSRRep*Incomemv{1,2}*EImv{1,2}	0.2
3. Statehood*Incomemv{1,2}*EImv{1}	0.2
4. ~USSRRep*DemExp*Incomemv{1,2}	0.06666667
Solution coverage(14/15): 0.93333334	
Not covered: 16	

Table 4. Intermediate Solution Obtained by R-QCA for DemoConcs2

1. ~USSRRep*Statehood
2. Statehood*Incomemv{1}*EImv{1}
3. ~USSRRep*DemExp*Incomemv{1}
4. ~USSRRep*Incomemv{1}*EImv{2}
5. ~USSRRep*Incomemv{2}*EImv{2}

Table 5. Intermediate Solution Obtained by fm-QCA for DemoConmv{0} Combined with {1}

1. USSRRep*~DemExp*~Statehood*Incomemv{0}*EImv{0,1}
Solution coverage(7/7): 1.0
Not covered: NULL

Effectiveness. We compare the solutions from fm-QCA and fs/QCA to demonstrate the effectiveness of our approach. As shown in Table 3, the combination of $\sim USSRRep*$ $Statehood$ has the highest unique coverage (0.33). The combination of $\sim USSRRep*$ $Incomemv\{1,2\}$*EImv$\{1,2\}$ and the combination of $Statehood*Incomemv\{1,2\}$*EImv$\{1\}$ both have the second highest unique coverage at 0.2. The last combination of $\sim USSRRep*$ $DemExp*Incomemv\{1,2\}$ has a value of unique coverage of 0.067. Together, these four combinations have the coverage ratio of 0.9333, which is exactly the same coverage ratio obtained by the best solution generated by fs/QCA (Table 5 in [21]).

The overall solution and the combinations are highly consistent with the solution generated by fs/QCA (Table 5 in [21]). These results together testify that fm-QCA does produce results that are consistent with the results produced by fs/QCA. Notably, with multivalued dataset rather than dichotomous dataset, rule $incomecs1*statehood*demexp$ can be logically omitted and the solution generated by fm-QCA is even more parsimonious (Table 4 and table 5 in [21]). This result indicates that fm-QCA outperforms fs/QCA in dealing with multivalued data and generating more effective solutions.

Table 6. Comparison of Existing QCA Tools

Function	fs/QCA	Tosmana	R-QCA	fm-QCA
Crisp				
complex				
parsimonious				
intermediate				
Fuzzy				
complex				
parsimonious				
intermediate				
Multi-value				
complex				
parsimonious				
intermediate				
compact multi-value reduction				
multivalued outcome				
outcome combination				
Easy GUI				
Cross-platform				

5.4 Comparison of Existing QCA Tools

The major existing QCA tools now include *fs/QCA* [19,20], *Tosmana* [4], *R-QCA* [22] and *fm-QCA*. The comparison of these QCA tools is shown in Table 6 where represents *fully supported*, represents *partially supported* and represents *not supported*.

Table 6 shows that fm-QCA can provide more functions for multi-value qualitative comparative analysis due to the new algorithmic contributions proposed in this paper.

6 Conclusions

In this paper, we propose a novel approach to multi-value QCA and implement a new tool called fm-QCA based on our approach. The major contribution in this paper lies in the novel QCA approach which includes properly filtering of candidate rules, efficient multi-value logic reduction and new counterfactual analysis. The experiments justified the advantage and effectiveness of fm-QCA compared with other state-of-the-art QCA tools.

References

1. Amenta, E., Caren, N., Olasky, S.J.: Age for leisure? political mediation and the impact of the pension movement on us old-age policy. American Sociological Review **70**(3), 516–538 (2005)
2. Basurto, X.: Linking multi-level governance to local common-pool resource theory using fuzzy-set qualitative comparative analysis: insights from twenty years of biodiversity conservation in costa rica. Global Environmental Change **23**(3), 573–587 (2013)

3. Cartwright, N.: Hunting causes and using them: approaches in philosophy and economics. Cambridge University Press (2007)

4. Cronqvist, L.: Tosmana, version 1.3. 2.0 [computer program], p. 88. University of Trier, Trier (2011)

5. Dixon, M., Roscigno, V.J., Hodson, R.: Unions, solidarity, and striking. Social Forces **83**(1), 3–33 (2004)

6. Gao, M., Jiang, J.H., Jiang, Y., Li, Y., Sinha, S., Brayton, R.: Mvsis. In: Proc. of the Intl. Workshop on Logic Synthesis (2001)

7. Greckhamer, T., Misangyi, V.F., Elms, H., Lacey, R.: Using qualitative comparative analysis in strategic management research: An examination of combinations of industry, corporate, and business-unit effects. Organizational Research Methods (2007)

8. Hagan, J., Hansford-Bowles, S.: From resistance to activis m: The emergence and persistence of activism among american vietnam war resisters in canada. Social Movement Studies **4**(3), 231–259 (2005)

9. Hellström, E., Seura, S.M.: Conflict cultures: qualitative comparative analysis of environmental conflicts in forestry, vol. 2. Finnish Society of Forest Science [and] Finnish Forest Research Institute (2001)

10. Karnaugh, M.: The map method for synthesis of combinational logic circuits. Trans. AIEE. Pt. I **72**(9), 593–599 (1953)

11. Kask, J., Linton, G.: Business mating: when start-ups get it right. Journal of Small Business & Entrepreneurship **26**(5), 511–536 (2013)

12. Korjani, M.M., Mendel, J.M.: Fuzzy set qualitative comparative analysis (fsqca): Challenges and applications. In: 2012 Annual Meeting of the North American Fuzzy Information Processing Society (NAFIPS), pp. 1–6. IEEE (2012)

13. McCluskey, E.J.: Minimization of boolean functions*. Bell System Technical Journal **35**(6), 1417–1444 (1956)

14. Mendel, J.M., Korjani, M.: Fast fuzzy set qualitative comparative analysis (fast fsqca). Submitted for Presentation at NAFIPS (2012)

15. Mendel, J.M., Korjani, M.M.: Charles ragin's fuzzy set qualitative comparative analysis (fsqca) used for linguistic summarizations. Information Sciences **202**, 1–23 (2012)

16. Mendel, J.M., Korjani, M.M.: Theoretical aspects of fuzzy set qualitative comparative analysis (fsqca). Information Sciences **237**, 137–161 (2013)

17. Osa, M., Corduneanu-Huci, C.: Running uphill: political opportunity in non-democracies. Comparative Sociology **2**, 605–630 (2003)

18. Ragin, C.C.: The Comparative Method: Moving Beyond Qualitative and Quantitative Strategies. Univ. of California Press (1989)

19. Ragin, C.C.: Fuzzy-set social science. University of Chicago Press (2000)
20. Ragin, C.C.: Redesigning social inquiry: Fuzzy sets and beyond. Wiley Online Library (2008)
21. Tang, R., Tang, S.: The historical heritage and the former soviet union and east european countries democratic transition. World Economics and Politics **2**, 39–57 (2013)
22. Thiem, A., Dusa, A.: Qca: A package for qualitative comparative analysis. The R Journal **5**(1), 87–97 (2013)
23. Wickham-Crowley, T.P.: A qualitative comparative approach to latin american revolutions. International Journal of Comparative Sociology **32**(1), 82–109 (1991)

Rational Partial Choice Functions and Their Application to Belief Revision

Jianbing Ma[1,2]([⊠]), Weiru Liu[3], and Didier Dubois[3,4]

[1] Faculty of Science and Technology, Bournemouth University,
Bournemouth BH12 5BB, UK
ac1023@coventry.ac.uk
[2] Department of Computing, Coventry University, Coventry CV1 2BS, UK
[3] School of Electronics, Electrical Engineering and Computer Science,
Queen's University Belfast, Belfast BT7 1NN, UK
w.liu@qub.ac.uk
[4] IRIT, University Paul Sabatier, Toulouse Cedex 9, France
dubois@irit.fr

Abstract. Necessary and sufficient conditions for choice functions to be rational have been intensively studied in the past. However, in these attempts, a choice function is completely specified. That is, given any subset of options, called an issue, the best option over that issue is always known, whilst in real-world scenarios, it is very often that only a few choices are known instead of all. In this paper, we study partial choice functions and investigate necessary and sufficient rationality conditions for situations where only a few choices are known. We prove that our necessary and sufficient condition for partial choice functions boils down to the necessary and sufficient conditions for complete choice functions proposed in the literature. Choice functions have been instrumental in belief revision theory. That is, in most approaches to belief revision, the problem studied can simply be described as the choice of possible worlds compatible with the input information, given an agent's prior belief state. The main effort has been to devise strategies in order to infer the agents revised belief state. Our study considers the converse problem: given a collection of input information items and their corresponding revision results (as provided by an agent), does there exist a rational revision operation used by the agent and a consistent belief state that may explain the observed results?

1 Introduction

Choice functions are commonly used in economic and social sciences to describe the process following which, faced with a ranking problem, an individual makes choices by selecting a few outcomes in each subset of possible outcomes (such a subset is called an *issue*); the selected outcomes are those to which no other outcomes can be strictly more preferred according to its preference. These observable choices testify of a non-directly observable preference relation. There has been a

© Springer International Publishing Switzerland 2015
S. Zhang et al. (Eds.): KSEM 2015, LNAI 9403, pp. 128–140, 2015.
DOI: 10.1007/978-3-319-25159-2_11

considerable amount of study about the definition of optimal choices under different types of preference relations (e.g., [2]). Equally interesting is the converse problem described as: given a choice function, that is, an abstract mapping that selects some *desirable* outcomes for each issue [23], does there exist an underlying *rational* preference relation from which this choice function can be derived? Several solutions to this problem exist for a long time, for instance [7,23,25]. However, in these attempts, the choice functions are full-fledged mappings that provide *every* issue with a set of mapped outcomes. In real-world scenarios, it is very often that choices of only a few issues are known, instead of choices over all the issues. Actually it is natural that given the whole set of issues, only a subset of them may have been exposed to the agent and hence the agent can only provide a limited response to the issues. Therefore, it is interesting to study conditions ensuring the existence of a rational preference that can reflect these choices. In this paper, we define the concept of partial choice functions and investigate their necessary and sufficient conditions for scenarios where only a few choices are known. We also examine the relationships between partial and (complete) choice functions and between their necessary and sufficient conditions.

Interestingly, our study and investigation result can be applied to study the converse belief revision problem. Belief revision [1,8,11,13,16–22] performs belief change on an agent's beliefs when new evidence is received. In classical belief revision, it is a default assumption that there is a clear and consistent belief structure (e.g., a total pre-order over possible worlds, the most plausible possible worlds of which generate the belief set) embedded in an agent's mind, based on which this agent performs revision upon receiving new information. Here, we consider the converse of this problem. That is, if there are several *revision scenarios*, each of which consisting of a piece of new information and its corresponding revision result (represented as pairs (μ_i, ϕ_i) subsequently), then does there exist a *rational* belief structure from which these revision scenarios proceed. In other words, for each input μ_i, does the agent exhibit the existence of a belief structure where ϕ_i is exactly the revision result based on μ_i in scenario (μ_i, ϕ_i)? Figures 1 and 2 provide intuitive illustration of the difference between classic belief revision and its converse problem. That is, in classic belief revision, given an agent's a priori belief state and a newly received piece of information, appropriate revision strategies (operators) are designed to revise the agent's belief set and derive a new one. Whilst the converse problem is: given a set of revision scenarios (pairs of evidence and revision result), does the agent exhibit the existence of a consistent prior epistemic state justifying these revision results? Here by epistemic state, we mean the ranking of possible worlds, hence the corresponding prior belief set.

Belief revision[1] always respects the *Success* postulate such that the revision result (ϕ_i) should respect the new information (μ_i). Semantically, the models of the revision result should be a subset of the models of the formula representing the new information (i.e., $Mod(\phi_i) \subseteq Mod(\mu_i)$). Therefore, the converse belief revision problem reduces to what we have discussed above on inducing a preference

---

[1] Here we do not consider non-prioritized belief revision which can be seen as belief merging.

relation for choices. Actually, belief revision theory has borrowed material from choice function theory via axioms 7 and 8 of the AGM framework (see Section 4 for details). This does not come as a surprise. An extensive discussion of the relationships between choice function axioms and properties of non-monotonic consequences, a topic closely related to belief revision, can be found in [14,15,24]. These papers also include an extensive bibliography on that topic. The last two AGM axioms are in fact not characteristic of the revision problem and one may argue that, by means of the two axioms, the AGM approach chooses as much an uncertainty framework that is not probabilistic by means of such two axioms as it provides core axioms for belief revision (the first six).

Fig. 1. Classic (a) and Inversed (b) Belief Revision

Note that the converse belief revision problem discussed here is different from the converse problem of iterated belief revision addressed in [6] and the converse belief revision in multi-agent systems [4]. Here, the multiple revision scenarios do not correspond to a sequence of revision actions, where the iteration may cause successive changes of an agent's belief structure. Instead, here we assume a given agent's belief structure, to which every new piece of information is applied separately so as to derive a different new belief state. This is in line with the view of *belief revision as defeasible inference* discussed in [10,12], one of the three kinds of belief revision perspectives.

Below, we first provide some preliminaries in Section 2. In Section 3, we define the notion of partial choice function and propose a necessary and sufficient condition for a partial choice function to be rational. We then compare our solution with related works in Section 4, showing that our condition can recover the conditions proposed in the literature. In Section 5, we show how this condition can be used to solve the converse belief revision problem. Finally, in Section 6, we conclude the paper.

2   Preliminaries

Logic: We consider a propositional language $\mathcal{L}$ defined in a usual sense. We use $Mod(\phi)$ to denote the set of models for ϕ. We write $\phi \models \mu$ iff $Mod(\phi) \subseteq Mod(\mu)$.

For a set A of models, $form(A)$ denotes a formula whose set of models is A. That is, $Mod(form(A)) = A$.

Choice Functions: Let X denote the finite set of all conceivable outcomes, and $\mathcal{P}(X)$ represent the family of all non-empty subsets of X. Each $A \in \mathcal{P}(X)$ is called an issue (or agenda) and let R denote a complete and reflexive binary relation defined on X. R is a *total pre-order* if it is transitive, i.e., xRy, yRz implies xRz for any $x, y, z \in X$.

Let $M(A, R)$ denote the set of maximal elements (choices) in A such that (so here xRy means $x \geq y$): $M(A, R) = \{x | x \in A \text{ and } xRy, \forall y \in A\}$. A choice function is a mapping $\mathcal{F} : \mathcal{P}(X) \to \mathcal{P}(X)$ satisfying: $\forall A \in \mathcal{P}(X), \mathcal{F}(A) \subseteq A$. A choice function $\mathcal{F}$ is said to be *rational*, if there is a total preorder R such that for all $A \in \mathcal{P}(X), \mathcal{F}(A) = M(A, R)$.

Elements x and y are called *indifferent* in terms of R, denoted $x \sim_R y$, if both xRy and yRx hold.

3   Rational Partial Choice Functions

If $\mathcal{F}$ is a mapping from $\mathcal{P}(X) \to \mathcal{P}(X)$, then for any issue $A \subseteq X$, we know the choice $\mathcal{F}(A)$ over A. But in real-world applications, usually we only know choices over a few issues. For instance, if we view a country as the set of its cities, then for a familiar country, we can tell our choices on preferred cities, while for unfamiliar countries, we cannot. Formally, we define the notion of a *partial choice function*.

Definition 1. *Let Ω be a subset of $\mathcal{P}(X)$, a partial choice function $\mathcal{F}$ over Ω is a mapping: $\Omega \to \mathcal{P}(X)$ satisfying: $\forall A \in \Omega, \mathcal{F}(A) \subseteq A$.*

Here Ω denotes the set of issues whose maximal elements are known. Note that in [5], although it is not explicitly defined, the choice frame proposed does contain a partial choice function.

Let $\bigcup \Omega = \bigcup_{A \in \Omega} A$ denote the union of all sets in Ω. Similarly, we denote a partial choice function $\mathcal{F}$ over Ω as *rational*[2] if there is a total pre-order R over $\bigcup \Omega$ such that for all $A \in \Omega, \mathcal{F}(A) = M(A, R)$. Obviously, if $\Omega = \mathcal{P}(X)$, then our definition reduces to the standard definition.

Note that a total pre-order R over $\bigcup \Omega$ can be easily extended to X such that: for any $w, w' \notin \bigcup \Omega, w \sim_R w'$; and for $w \in \bigcup \Omega, w' \notin \bigcup \Omega, wRw'$ but not $w'Rw$ (this is a matter of convention, considering that options outside $\bigcup \Omega$ are less relevant here). With this extension, $A \in \Omega, \mathcal{F}(A) = M(A, R)$ still holds for any $A \in \Omega$.

Now we provide a necessary and sufficient condition ensuring the rationality of a partial choice function: Let $(A_1, \cdots, A_i, \cdots, A_k)$ be a sequence of issues and the circular permutation $\sigma(i) = i + 1, i = 1, \ldots, k - 1$ and $\sigma(k) = 1$.

---

[2] An alternative definition would be to say a partial choice function $\mathcal{F}$ is rational if and only if it can be extended to a rational choice function over $\mathcal{P}(X)$ (i.e., there is a rational choice function over $\mathcal{P}(X)$ that agrees with $\mathcal{F}$ on Ω). These two definitions are equivalent.

Circular Consistency

$$\text{If } A_{\sigma(i)} \cap \mathcal{F}(A_i) \neq \emptyset, 1 \leq i \leq k,$$

$$\text{then } A_{\sigma(i)} \cap \mathcal{F}(A_i) = A_i \cap \mathcal{F}(A_{\sigma(i)}), 1 \leq i \leq k.$$

This Circular Consistency condition shows that if an issue and the outcomes of the next issue are *correlated* circularly for k issues, then this correlation establishes equivalent relations between issues and outcomes circularly.

We have the following result on two successive issues.

Lemma 1. *Let $\Omega = \{A, A'\}$, if the Circular Consistency condition holds, and $A' \cap \mathcal{F}(A) = A \cap \mathcal{F}(A')$, then $A' \cap \mathcal{F}(A) = \mathcal{F}(A) \cap \mathcal{F}(A')$.*

Fig. 2 illustrates Lemma 1. The two circles represent A_i and A_{i+1}, respectively. The intersections of the rectangle with the two circles represent $\mathcal{F}(A_i)$ and $\mathcal{F}(A_{i+1})$, respectively, and the crossed section represents $\mathcal{F}(A_i) \cap \mathcal{F}(A_{i+1})$. Now we give the following representation theorem which shows that the above

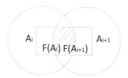

Fig. 2. Illustration of the two issue case

condition is necessary and sufficient to ensure the partial choice function being rational.

Theorem 1. *Let $\mathcal{F}$ be a partial choice function over Ω, then $\mathcal{F}$ is rational if and only if $\mathcal{F}$ satisfies the Circular Consistency condition.*

Proof: The *only if* part is simple and we omit it here due to lack of space.

For the *if* part, assume that $\mathcal{F}$ satisfies the Circular Consistency condition.

We use graph theory to prove the existence of a total pre-order R. We view each issue $A \in \Omega$ as a point. If $\mathcal{F}(A_i) \cap \mathcal{F}(A_j) \neq \emptyset$, then we connect points A_i and A_j with an edge (no direction). Let G denote the formed graph. Graph G has several ($\leq n$) connected components[3], each of which contains a set of points (issues).

---

[3] In graph theory [3], a *connected component* of an undirected graph is a subgraph in which any two vertices are connected to each other by paths, and which (the subgraph) is connected to no additional vertices. A *directed connected component* of a directed graph is a subgraph in which any two vertices are connected to each other by a direct path, and which is connected to no additional vertices.

Graph G has n connected components only when all A_is are pairwise disjoint. In all other cases, G has less than n connected components. Here notice that the connected components, when viewed as a set of A_is (its points), are a partition of Ω.

A simple fact that should be mentioned here is that for any two points A_i, A_j in the same connected component, we could find a set of points $\{A_{t_1}, \cdots, A_{t_m}\}$ such that $A_{t_1} = A_i, A_{t_m} = A_j$ and for any t_s, t_{s+1}, $\mathcal{F}(A_{t_s}) \cap \mathcal{F}(A_{t_{s+1}}) \neq \emptyset$. That is, there is a path between points A_i and A_j, which is ensured by the connectiveness of the connected component.

Now we view each connected component as a node. For two points A_i, A_j in different nodes X, Y, respectively, if $\mathcal{F}(A_i) \cap A_j \neq \emptyset$, then we create a **directed** edge from X to Y. If there are multiple directed edges from X to Y, we compress them as one edge. This forms a new graph G'.

Here we should point out an important fact: G' has no directed cycles. Otherwise suppose G' has a cycle $X_1 \to X_2 \to \cdots \to X_k \to X_1$. Without loss of generality, let points A_{i_1}, A_{i_2} be contained in X_i $(1 \leq i \leq k)$ and $\mathcal{F}(A_{(i-1)_2} \cap A_{i_1} \neq \emptyset$, $\mathcal{F}(A_{i_2}) \cap A_{(i+1)_1} \neq \emptyset$ hold (when $i = k$, $i + 1$ is changed to 1; when $i = 1$, $i - 1$ is changed to k). As mentioned earlier, points i_1 and i_2 in connected component X_i can also be connected by a path $\{A_{t_1} = A_{i_1}, \cdots, A_{t_{m_i}} = A_{i_2}\}$ such that $\mathcal{F}(A_{t_s}) \cap A_{t_{s+1}} \neq \emptyset$ (Actually it is $\mathcal{F}(A_{t_s}) \cap \mathcal{F}(A_{t_{s+1}}) \neq \emptyset$. However, clearly $\mathcal{F}(A_{t_s}) \cap \mathcal{F}(A_{t_{s+1}}) \neq \emptyset$ implies $\mathcal{F}(A_{t_s}) \cap A_{t_{s+1}} \neq \emptyset)$, $1 \leq s < m_i$. Hence finally we get a cycle $\{A_{i_1}, \cdots, A_{i_2}, A_{(i+1)_1}, \cdots, A_{(i+1)_2}, \cdots, A_{(i-1)_2}, A_{i_1}\}$. For any two adjacent points $A_l, A_{l'}$ in that cycle, we always have $\mathcal{F}(A_l) \cap A_{l'} \neq \emptyset$. By the Circular Consistency condition and Lemma 1, we get $\mathcal{F}(A_{(i-1)_2}) \cap \mathcal{F}(A_{i_1}) = \mathcal{F}(A_{(i-1)_2}) \cap A_{i_1} \neq \emptyset$. That is, points $A_{(i-1)_2}$ and A_{i_1} should be in the same node, which creates a contradiction since they are in different nodes X_{i-1} and X_i, respectively.

Since G' has no directed cycles, each of its directed connected component is a connected directed acyclic graph (DAG). For each of such DAG H with nodes $Y_1, \cdots, Y_k \in H$, we establish a mapping f_H associating each node of H with a natural number. To do this, first we associate each node with a number indicating its maximal level.

- Any node with 0 in-degree[4] is assigned level 0.
- Iteratively, a node is assigned with level k if each of its parent nodes is assigned with a level value such that the maximal value among these is $k - 1$[5].

With the concept of level of node, we define f_H as follows.

- Any node with 0 in-degree (level 0) is assigned 1.
- Iteratively (by increasing the level value by 1 each time), for any node Z with s in-degree and hence has s directed in-edges, $Z_1 \to Z, \cdots, Z_s \to Z$, $f_H(Z) = \sum_{i=1}^{s} f_H(Z_i) + s$.

This construction ensures that if a directed edge $Z' \to Z$ exists, then $f_H(Z') < f_H(Z)$.

---

[4] The number of directed edges pointing to a node is called the in-degree of the node.
[5] Here we can prove that the level of a node is the maximal length of any path from some 0 in-degree node to this node. However, this result is not essential in our proof so we omit it here.

Now we establish a mapping $f : G \to N$ such that for any point A_i in tree H (in fact in a node Y_t of H), $f(A_i) = f_H(Y_t)$. Obviously we can see that any two points in the same sub-graph of G (hence in the same node) have the same f value.

Finally we establish a mapping $g : \bigcup \Omega \to N \cup \{0\}$ as follows.

If $w \in \mathcal{F}(A_i)$, then $g(w) = f(A_i)$. If $w \notin \bigcup_{A_i \in \Omega} \mathcal{F}(A_i)$, then $g(w) = 0$.

Here we need to clarify that g is a valid mapping. That is, we must show if $w \in \mathcal{F}(A_i) \cap \mathcal{F}(A_j)$, then $f(A_i) = f(A_j)$. In fact, if $\mathcal{F}(A_i) \cap \mathcal{F}(A_j) \neq \emptyset$, then points A_i and A_j are in the same connected component of G, and hence $f(A_i) = f(A_j)$.

We define R as: wRw' if and only if $g(w) \geq g(w')$. It remains to show $\forall i$, $\mathcal{F}(A_i) = M(A_i, R)$.

By the definition of g, we know that if $w, w' \in \mathcal{F}(A_i)$, then $g(w) = g(w')$. Now it is sufficient to show that if $w \in \mathcal{F}(A_i)$ and $w' \in A_i \setminus \mathcal{F}(A_i)$, then $g(w) > g(w')$.

If $w' \notin \bigcup_{A_i \in \Omega} \mathcal{F}(A_i)$, then $g(w) \geq 1 > 0 = g(w')$.

Else suppose w' is in some $\mathcal{F}(A_j)$ (hence $w' \in A_i \cap \mathcal{F}(A_j)$), then $\mathcal{F}(A_j) \cap A_i \neq \emptyset$. If $\mathcal{F}(A_j) \cap \mathcal{F}(A_i) \neq \emptyset$, then according to Lemma 1, we have $\mathcal{F}(A_j) \cap \mathcal{F}(A_i) = \mathcal{F}(A_j) \cap A_i$, hence $w' \in \mathcal{F}(A_i) \cap \mathcal{F}(A_j)$ which contradicts with $w' \notin \mathcal{F}(A_i)$.

Therefore, we should have $\mathcal{F}(A_j) \cap \mathcal{F}(A_i) = \emptyset$, which implies that points A_j and A_i are not in the same connected component of G, otherwise $\mathcal{F}(A_j) \cap \mathcal{F}(A_i) = \mathcal{F}(A_j) \cap A_i \neq \emptyset$. Now we can conclude that in graph G', there is a directed edge from the node containing point A_j to the node containing point A_i. Therefore, by the definition of f_H and f, we know $f(A_i) > f(A_j)$. Hence $g(w) = f(A_i) > f(A_j) = g(w')$. This completes the proof. $\square$

Note that this proof also shows how to construct such a pre-order R by which $\mathcal{F}$ is rationalized.

Fig. 3 illustrates the above theorem where each solid circle represents an A_i. The intersection of a solid circle (representing A_i) with the dashed red ring in the center represents $\mathcal{F}(A_i)$. Note that Fig. 3 just shows a sequence of issues

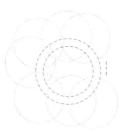

Fig. 3. Illustration of the k Issue Case

that satisfy the Circular Consistency condition. However, there could be multiple sequences (not necessarily disjoint), each of which satisfies the Circular Consistency condition. So Fig. 3 is not necessarily a complete view for all sets $A_1, \cdots, A_n$.

From Fig. 3, we can also see that $\forall x \in \mathcal{F}(A_i), y \in \mathcal{F}(A_j), 1 \leq i, j \leq k$, we have $x \sim_R y$ (as elements in the dashed red ring have the same plausibility). Note that for $z \in \mathcal{F}(A_m), m > k$, we do not necessarily have $x \sim_R z$.

4   Related Work

Classical works proved that a choice function $\mathcal{F}$ is rational if and only if it satisfies the following condition [23, 25]:

Sen for all $B \in \mathcal{P}(X)$ and all $a \in B$, $a \in \mathcal{F}(B)$ if and only if $\forall b \in B, a \in \mathcal{F}(\{a, b\})$.

As a corollary, when a partial choice function turns into a choice function, our Circular Consistency condition implies condition Sen.

Corollary 1. *Let $\mathcal{F}$ be a choice function, then if it satisfies Circular Consistency, it satisfies Sen.*

Also, in [7], Chernoff introduced a necessary condition for a choice function to be rational:

Chernoff for all $B, B' \in \mathcal{P}(X)$, if $B \subseteq B'$, then $\mathcal{F}(B') \cap B \subseteq \mathcal{F}(B)$.

Again, when a partial choice function turns into a choice function, our Circular Consistency condition also induces condition Chernoff.

Corollary 2. *Let $\mathcal{F}$ be a choice function, then if it satisfies Circular Consistency, it satisfies Chernoff.*

A lot of choice function conditions are reviewed in [14, 15, 24] relating choice function theory to AGM theory and nonmonotonic reasoning. It can be shown that most of these conditions are derivable from our Circular Consistency condition. Since most of these conditions are straightforward to understand and also due to space limitation, here we omit most of them and only present the well-known Chernoff and Sen conditions. Interested readers can refer to [15] for details.

Now we first explore relationships between our approach to the well-known AGM framework. Let K be a consistent belief set representing the agent's initial beliefs. K is represented as a set of formulas. Let B_K be a mapping from K to any subset of formulas. The AGM axioms are listed as follows:

AGM1 $B_K(\phi) = [B_K(\phi)]^{PL}$ where for any set of formulas S, $[S]^{PL}$ is defined as the PL-deductive closure of S in the usual way.

AGM2 $\phi \in B_K(\phi)$.

AGM3 $B_K(\phi) \subseteq [K \cup \{\phi\}]^{PL}$.

AGM4 If $\neg\phi \notin K$, then $[K \cup \{\phi\}]^{PL} \subseteq B_K(\phi)$.

AGM5 $B_K(\phi) = \Phi_0$ if and only if ϕ is a contradictory, where Φ_0 is the set of formulas of the propositional language.

AGM6 If $\phi \leftrightarrow \psi$ is a tautology, then $B_K(\phi) = B_K(\psi)$.

AGM7 $B_K(\phi \wedge \psi) \subseteq [B_K(\phi) \cup \{\phi\}]^{PL}$.

AGM8 If $\neg\psi \notin B_K(\phi)$, then $[B_K(\phi) \cup \{\phi\}]^{PL} \subseteq B_K(\phi \wedge \psi)$.

Note that the Chernoff condition is very similar to the above AGM7 and AGM8 axioms[6]. It is easy to see that B_K is a choice function at the semantic level. That is, $Mod(B_K(\phi)) \subseteq Mod(\phi)$ for any ϕ. For simplicity, by abuse of notation, we write $B_K(Mod(\phi)) \subseteq Mod(\phi)$ (here notation B_K is taken as a mapping from a set of models to another set of models). Now, let $B = Mod(\psi \wedge \phi), B' = Mod(\phi)$ and $F = B_K$, then $B \subseteq B'$, and hence we obtain $B_K(B') \cap B \subseteq B_K(B)$ which is equivalent to $B_K(\phi) \wedge \psi \models B_K(\psi \wedge \phi)$.

A general condition called Arrow's condition [2] that generalizes both Sen and Chernoff says: if $B \subseteq B'$, and $\mathcal{F}(B') \cap B \neq \emptyset$, then $\mathcal{F}(B) = \mathcal{F}(B') \cap B$. Indeed, if some of the best in B', belong to its subset B, none of the other elements in B can be a best element in B (they are dominated inside B'). This is closely connected to Axiom 8 in the AGM framework.

In [5], the correspondence between AGM revision and rational choice functions is studied. It shows that a choice frame[7] is rational if and only if it is *AGM-consistent*, where AGM-consistent is defined as: for every interpretation[8] of the choice frame, the associated partial belief revision function can be extended to a full-domain belief revision function that satisfies the AGM-postulates.

Let $FORM(A) = \{\phi : Mod(\phi) \in A\}$ be a set of formulas whose set of models are subsets of A. Note that $FORM(A)$ is different from $form(A)$. With this notation, for a partial choice function, the associated partial belief revision function is defined as follows.

Definition 2. *Let $\mathcal{F}$ be a partial choice function such that $\mathcal{F} : \Omega \rightarrow \mathcal{P}(X)$, the associated belief revision function $B_{\mathcal{F}}$ is a mapping $B_{\mathcal{F}} : FORM(\Omega) \rightarrow FORM(\mathcal{P}(X))$ such that $B_{\mathcal{F}}(\phi) = \mathcal{F}(Mod(\phi))$.*

A full-domain belief revision function $B : FORM(\mathcal{P}(X)) \rightarrow FORM(\mathcal{P}(X))$ is called an *extension* of a partial belief revision function $B_{\mathcal{F}}$ if for any $\phi \in FORM(\Omega)$, $B(\phi) = B_{\mathcal{F}}(\phi)$.

We can also define a partial choice function is *AGM-consistent* if its associated partial belief revision function can be extended to a full-domain belief revision function that satisfies the AGM-postulates.

Now we have the following corollary.

Corollary 3. *Let $\mathcal{F}$ be a partial choice function, then it satisfies Circular Consistency if and only if it is AGM-consistent.*

---

[6] The similarity between Chernoff and AGM7, AGM8 axioms can be shown more clearly if we define $B'_K(\phi) = \bigwedge_{\psi \in B_K(\phi)} \psi$, and hence AGM7 and AGM8 axioms are translated as:

AGM7' $B'_K(\phi) \wedge \psi \models B'_K(\psi \wedge \phi)$.
AGM8' If $B'_K(\phi) \not\models \neg\psi$, then $B'_K(\psi \wedge \phi) \models B'_K(\phi) \wedge \psi$.

[7] In [5], a choice frame consists of a set of alternatives X, a collection Ω of subsets of X, and a partial choice function $\mathcal{F} : \Omega \rightarrow \mathcal{P}(X)$.

[8] In [5], an interpretation of a choice frame is obtained by adding a valuation V that assigns to every atom p the subset of X at which p is true, and it is extended to formulas in the usual way. This is a standard definition of an interpretation.

This Corollary suggests that there is an unearthed relationship between the Circular Consistency condition and the AGM postulates. We will leave this topic in future work.

Remarks: Although condition Chernoff looks similar to a Monotonicity property, Monotonicity does not hold for rational partial choice functions in general.

Mon If $A_1 \subseteq A_2$, then $\mathcal{F}(A_1) \subseteq \mathcal{F}(A_2)$.

Example 1. *Let $A_1 = \{w_1, w_2\}$, $A_2 = \{w_1, w_2, w_3\}$, $\mathcal{F}(A_1) = \{w_1, w_2\}$, and $\mathcal{F}(A_2) = \{w_3\}$. We could see that $\mathcal{F}$ is a partial choice function over $\Omega = \{A_1, A_2\}$ and it is rational in terms of a pre-order $\preceq$ such that $w_3 \prec w_1 \simeq w_2$, i.e., we indeed have $\mathcal{F}(A_1) = M(A_1, \preceq)$ and $\mathcal{F}(A_2) = M(A_2, \preceq)$. But it does not satisfy the Monotonicity property. That is, we have $A_1 \subset A_2$, but we do not have $\mathcal{F}(A_1) \subseteq \mathcal{F}(A_2)$.*

5 Converse Belief Revision Problem

As mentioned in Introduction, our result can be applied to the converse belief revision problem. Here we provide two necessary and sufficient conditions such that if a set of revision scenarios satisfy these two conditions, then there must be a consistent belief structure in the agent's mind, and vice versa.

To proceed, first, let us formalize the definition of a revision scenario.

Definition 3. *(Revision scenario) A revision scenario, denoted as $rs = (\mu, \phi)$, is a pair of formulae μ and ϕ, where μ represents a new piece of evidence and ϕ represents the revision result upon receiving μ.*

Below, we simply call a revision scenario *a scenario*.

Now we propose two conditions, i.e., *Success* and *Circular Consistency* conditions. Let $rs_i = (\mu_i, \phi_i), 1 \leq i \leq n$ be n distinct revision scenarios.

Success. For any $rs_i = (\mu_i, \phi_i)$, $\phi_i \models \mu_i$, $1 \leq i \leq n$.
   Explanation: This is a variant of the well-known success postulate in the AGM framework. The revision result should respect the evidence.
Circular Consistency. Let $\{(\mu^1, \phi^1), \cdots, (\mu^k, \phi^k)\}$ be any set of revision scenarios (i.e., a subset of the set of all rs_is) such that $k \leq n$, and let σ be a circular permutation such that $\sigma(i) = i + 1, i = 1 \ldots k, \sigma(k) = 1$. Then

$$\text{If } \mu^{\sigma(i)} \wedge \phi^i \not\models \bot, 1 \leq i \leq k,$$

$$\text{Then } \mu^{\sigma(i)} \wedge \phi^i \equiv \mu^i \wedge \phi^{\sigma(i)}, 1 \leq i \leq k.$$

As a corollary of Theorem 1, the following representation theorem shows that the above two conditions are necessary and sufficient to ensure that an agent has a consistent belief structure.

Corollary 4. *Let $\mathcal{RS}$ be a set of scenarios, then there exists a belief structure, represented by a total pre-order $\preceq$ over W, s.t., $\forall rs = (\mu, \phi) \in \mathcal{RS}$, $\phi = min(Mod(\mu), \preceq)$ if and only if scenarios in $\mathcal{RS}$ satisfy Success and Circular Consistency.*

Example 2. *Suppose a hacking action was discovered originating from one of the PCs in an office. The log file shows that the action was conducted between 4pm to 5pm. A suspect Y declared that he left the office between 4pm and 5pm and he did not log on to any computer before he left. A witness suggested that Y was seen doing something with that particular computer at that time. Now if suspect Y explains:*

Viewing web pages: *Y was viewing web pages, OR*
Cleaning the monitor: *Y was cleaning the equipment.*

Does Y have a consistent belief structure with each one of these two explanations? The answer to the above question is important. Certainly, we cannot say Y is innocent if Y does have a consistent belief structure, as it only shows that Y's statements are coherent. However, Y should be considered highly suspiciously if he fails to demonstrate consistency in its response to questions/evidence.

Here suppose a system security engineer has two pieces of evidence: there was a hacking action during 4pm to 5pm *and* Y was seen using the PC at the time. *Y's reactions to the two pieces of evidence may allow the security engineer spotting an inconsistency between the statements, or equivalently, establishing whether Y is applying a consistent belief structure when responding to the two inputs.*

Let μ_1 be 'a hacking action was discovered from 4pm to 5pm', ψ_1 be 'Y did not log on to any computer in the office'. Then $\phi_1 = \mu_1 \wedge \psi_1$ is Y's revision result upon receiving μ_1, meaning that "although there was a hacking action, it is not me (i.e., Y) since I did not log on to any computer". Let μ_2 be 'Y was seen doing something with the PC at that time'. To consider possible revision results for the two situations described above, let ϕ_2 be 'Y was viewing web pages', and ϕ_2' be 'Y was cleaning the monitor'. *Here we should note that $\phi_1 \wedge \phi_2 \equiv \perp$ since if Y was viewing web pages, then Y must have logged on to the PC, conflicting with Y's claim not logging on to any computers in the office. In this situation, as we only focus on two possibilities:* 'Y was viewing web pages' *and* 'Y was cleaning the monitor', *for simplicity we can assume that these two are exclusive and exhaustive. Hence it is easy to see that* 'Y was cleaning the monitor' *indicates* 'Y did not log on to the PC' *and* 'Y was viewing web pages' *indicates* 'Y had logged on to the PC', *therefore we have $\phi_2 = \mu_2 \wedge \neg\psi_1$ and $\phi_2' = \mu_2 \wedge \psi_1$.*

Now to justify whether Y has a consistent belief structure, we check the two postulates.

Success. *Obviously we have $\phi_1 \models \mu_1$, $\phi_2 \models \mu_2$, and $\phi_2' \models \mu_2$.*
Circular Consistency. *For the two revision results ϕ_2 and ϕ_2',*
  – *we have $\mu_1 \wedge \phi_2 \not\models \perp$ and $\mu_2 \wedge \phi_1 \not\models \perp$, but we do not have $\mu_1 \wedge \phi_2 \equiv \mu_2 \wedge \phi_1$,*

– we have $\mu_1 \wedge \phi_2' \not\models \bot$ and $\mu_2 \wedge \phi_1 \not\models \bot$, and we have $\mu_1 \wedge \phi_2' \equiv \mu_2 \wedge \phi_1$.

Therefore, by Corollary 4, we obtain the following conclusions:

- *If the revision result by Y is 'Y was viewing web pages', then Y does not have a consistent belief structure, and hence Y is highly suspect.*
- *If the revision result by Y (his explanation) is 'Y was cleaning the monitor, then Y has a consistent belief structure, and hence Y might be innocent.*

These conclusions are in line with our intuition. In the second case, a belief structure for Y is: $\preceq: \{\mu_1 \wedge \psi_1 \prec \mu_1 \wedge \neg\psi_1 \simeq \mu_2 \wedge \psi_1 \prec \mu_2 \wedge \neg\psi_1\}$. Here note that there are both models for ψ_1 and models for $\neg\psi_1$ appearing in Y's belief structure. This is because it is an inferred belief structure from the current information. Y's actual belief structure could be more elaborated, but should be consistent with the inferred belief structure.

6 Conclusion

In this paper, we proved a necessary and sufficient condition, i.e., Circular Consistency, for a partial choice function to be rational. Also, we have demonstrated that this solution can be used to construct a consistent belief structure for an agent from a set of revision scenarios. In addition, by comparing with related works, we proved that when a partial choice function turns into a choice function, our Circular Consistency condition can recover the necessary and sufficient conditions proposed before.

In terms of belief revision, our study hinted why lying could be a hard thing to do: one always needs to keep a track of what had been said to maintain consistency between different scenarios. This commonsense is widely acknowledged, and it is again partially proved in this paper in the belief revision scenario. Our study also provided some insights about belief revision in general.

As future work, one attempt is to investigate whether there are simpler conditions that can be used to replace the Circular Consistency condition, especially on whether the Circular Consistency condition can be *decomposed* into some AGM-like or Sen, Chernoff-like conditions. In addition, there is a notion called *sub-rationality* introduced by Deb [9] such that a choice function F is sub-rational if for some order R, $M(A, R) \subseteq \mathcal{F}(A)$ holds for all $A \in \mathcal{P}(X)$. It is interesting to study the necessary and sufficient conditions for sub-rational partial choice functions.

Acknowledgement. This work has been partially funded by EPSRC PACES project (Ref: EP/J012149/1).

References

1. Alchourrón, C.E., Gärdenfors, P., Makinson, D.: On the logic of theory change: Partial meet functions for contraction and revision. J. Sym. Log. **50**, 510–530 (1985)

2. Arrow, K.: Uncertainty and the welfare economics of medical care. American Economic Review **53**(5), 941–973 (1963)
3. Biggs, N., Lloyd, E., Wilson, R.: Graph Theory. Oxford University Press (1986)
4. Biskup, J., Tadros, C.: Revising belief without revealing secrets. In: Sali, A., Lukasiewicz, T. (eds.) FoIKS 2012. LNCS, vol. 7153, pp. 51–70. Springer, Heidelberg (2012)
5. Bonanno, G.: Rational choice and agm belief revision. Artificial Intelligence **173**(12–13), 1194–1203 (2009)
6. Booth, R., Nittka, A.: Reconstructing an agent's epistemic state from observations. In: Procs. of IJCAI, pp. 394–399 (2005)
7. Chernoff, H.: Rational selection of decision functions. Econometrica **22**(4), 422–443 (1954)
8. Darwiche, A., Pearl, J.: On the logic of iterated belief revision. Artificial Intelligence **89**, 1–29 (1997)
9. Deb, R.: Binariness and rational choice. Mathematical Social Sciences **5**, 97–106 (1983)
10. Delgrande, J., Dubois, D., Lang, J.: Iterated revision as prioritized merging. In: Proceedings of Knowledge Representation and Reasoning, (KR 2006), pp. 210–220 (2006)
11. Delgrande, J., Jin, Y.: Parallel belief revision: Revising by sets of formulas. Artificial Intelligence **176**(1), 2223–2245 (2012)
12. Dubois, D.: Three scenarios for the revision of epistemic states. Journal of Logic and Computation **18**(5), 721–738 (2008)
13. Katsuno, H., Mendelzon, A.O.: Propositional knowledge base revision and minimal change. Artificial Intelligence **52**, 263–294 (1991)
14. Lehmann, D.: Nonmonotonic logics and semantics. Journal of Logic and Computation **11**(2), 229–256 (2001)
15. Lindström, S.: A semantic approach to nonmonotonic reasoning: inference operations and choice (1994)
16. Ma, J., Benferhat, S., Liu, W.: A belief revision framework for revising epistemic states with partial epistemic states. International Journal of Approximate Reasoning **59**, 20–40 (2015)
17. Ma, J., Liu, W.: A general model for epistemic state revision using plausibility measures. In: Procs. of ECAI, pp. 356–360 (2008)
18. Ma, J., Liu, W.: Modeling belief change on epistemic states. In: Procs. of FLAIRS, pp. 553–558 (2009)
19. Ma, J., Liu, W.: A framework for managing uncertain inputs: an axiomization of rewarding. International Journal of Approximate Reasoning **52**(7), 917–934 (2011)
20. Ma, J., Liu, W., Benferhat, S.: A belief revision framework for revising epistemic states with partial epistemic states. In: Procs. of AAAI, pp. 333–338 (2010)
21. Ma, J., Liu, W., Dubois, D., Prade, H.: Bridging jeffery's rule, agm revision, and dempster conditioning in the theory of evidence. International Journal of Artificial Intelligence Tools **20**(4), 691–720 (2011)
22. Ma, J., Liu, W., Hunter, A.: Modeling and reasoning with qualitative comparative clinical knowledge. International Journal of Intelligent Systems **26**(1), 25–46 (2011)
23. Moulin, H.: Choice functions over a finite set: A summary. Social Choice and Welfare **2**(2), 147–160 (1985)
24. Rott, H.: Change, choice and inference. Clarendon Press, Oxford (2001)
25. Sen, A.K.: Internal consistency of choice. Econometrica **61**(3), 495–521 (1993)

The Double-Level Default Description Logic $\mathcal{D}3\mathcal{L}$

Liangjun Zang[1]($^{\boxtimes}$), Weimin Wang[3], Bo Chen[2], and Cungen Cao[2]

[1] State Key Laboratory of Computer Science,
Institute of Software, Chinese Academy of Sciences, No. 4, South 4th Street,
Zhongguancun, Haidian District, Beijing 100190, China
zhxlyh@sina.com

[2] Key Laboratory of Intelligent Information Processing,
Institute of Computing Technology, Chinese Academy of Sciences, No. 6 Kexueyuan
South Road, Haidian District, Beijing 100190, China
cgcao@ict.ac.cn

[3] School of Computer Science and Engineering, Jiangsu University of Science and
Technology, No. 2 Mengxi Road, Zhenjiang 212003, Jiangsu, China

Abstract. We propose the default description logic $\mathcal{D}2\mathcal{L}$ and the double-level default description logic $\mathcal{D}3\mathcal{L}$. $\mathcal{D}2\mathcal{L}$ embeds normal defaults inside the basic description logic $\mathcal{ALC}$, and $\mathcal{D}3\mathcal{L}$ augments $\mathcal{D}2\mathcal{L}$ with normal double-level defaults. Double-level defaults are defaults of defaults and can be used to represent default inheritance of default properties of concepts in ontologies. A $\mathcal{D}3\mathcal{L}$ knowledge base ($\mathcal{D}3\mathcal{L}$-KB) can be divided into two levels of knowledge bases, and correspondingly its extensions can be computed in two steps. $\mathcal{D}3\mathcal{L}$ is more expressive than $\mathcal{D}2\mathcal{L}$ since there is a $\mathcal{D}3\mathcal{L}$-KB that cannot reduce to any $\mathcal{D}2\mathcal{L}$-KB. Specifically, there is a $\mathcal{D}3\mathcal{L}$-KB such that the set of all its extensions cannot be exactly generated by any $\mathcal{D}2\mathcal{L}$-KB.

Keywords: Description logics · Double-level defaults · Irreducibility

1 Introduction

Description logics (DLs) are a family of knowledge representation languages with wide applications in ontology modeling, especially as the underpinnings of the Ontology Web Language (OWL) in the context of the Semantic Web. An important limitation of DLs is that they do not allow for expressing defeasible knowledge, so several non-monotonic extensions of DLs have been proposed. These work extend DLs with default logic[1,8], with circumscription [2], with epistemic operator[4], with rational closure[3], and with typicality operator[5].

In this paper we focus on the approaches to extending DLs with default logic by Reiter[7], which we call *default description logics*. The work[1] augments a DL

The work is supported by NSFC grants (No. 91224006, No. 61173063, and No. 61203284) and a MOST grant (No. 201303107).

© Springer International Publishing Switzerland 2015
S. Zhang et al. (Eds.): KSEM 2015, LNAI 9403, pp. 141–146, 2015.
DOI: 10.1007/978-3-319-25159-2_12

knowledge base (TBox and ABox) with a finite set of default rules whose prerequisites, justifications, and consequents are concepts. However, its treatment of open defaults via Skolemization may lead to an undecidable default consequence relation. In order to retain the decidability, open default rules are only applied to explicit individuals in the ABox. The work [8] proposes a new semantics for open defaults, where open defaults can be applied to unnamed individuals and reasoning under the semantics is decidable.

One limitation of the above default description logics is that they fail to represent default inheritance of default properties of concepts. Such knowledge should be represented as default rules of default rules, which we call *double-level defaults* to distinguish it from the default proposed by Reiter. For example, the rule 'any sub-concept of birds can inherit the default property *flying* of birds by default'can be represented as the following double-level default

$$\frac{X \sqsubseteq Bird, Bird \sqsubseteq_d Flier : X \sqsubseteq_d Flier}{X \sqsubseteq_d Flier} \tag{1}$$

where X is a concept variable that can be assigned with any concept. For typical birds like 'sparrows', we can infer '*Sparrow* $\sqsubseteq_d$ *Flier*'from '*Bird* $\sqsubseteq_d$ *Flier*'and '*Sparrow* $\sqsubseteq$ *Bird*'directly. For untypical birds 'penguins', the conclusion '*Penguin* $\sqsubseteq_d$ *Flier*'should be blocked if we know '*Penguin* $\sqsubseteq_d$ ¬*Flier*'.

In this paper we propose the default description logic $\mathcal{D}2\mathcal{L}$, which enriches the description logic $\mathcal{ALC}$ with normal defaults of the form $C \sqsubseteq_d D$, and the double-level default description logic $\mathcal{D}3\mathcal{L}$, which enriches $\mathcal{D}2\mathcal{L}$ with double-level defaults. Let $\mathcal{A}$ be an ABox and $\mathcal{T}$ a TBox of $\mathcal{ALC}$, $\mathcal{D}$ a set of defaults and the negation of defaults, and $\mathcal{D}^2$ a set of double-level defaults. Thus, $(\mathcal{A}, \mathcal{T}, \mathcal{D})$ constitute a $\mathcal{D}2\mathcal{L}$ knowledge base, and $(\mathcal{A}, \mathcal{T}, \mathcal{D}, \mathcal{D}^2)$ constitute a $\mathcal{D}3\mathcal{L}$ knowledge base. A $\mathcal{D}3\mathcal{L}$ knowledge base can be divided into two levels and correspondingly its extensions are computed in two steps. We will prove that $\mathcal{D}3\mathcal{L}$ is more expressive than $\mathcal{D}2\mathcal{L}$. More specifically, there exists a $\mathcal{D}3\mathcal{L}$-KB such that the set of its extensions cannot be exactly generated by any $\mathcal{D}2\mathcal{L}$-KB.

Similar to our work, preferential description logics can reason about prototypical properties and inheritance with exceptions. $\mathcal{ALC}$-$\mathbf{T}$ [6] use $\mathbf{T}(C) \sqsubseteq D$ to represent 'typical members of C are instances of concept D', where $\mathbf{T}$ is a typicality operator and its semantics can be specified by enriching standard $\mathcal{ALC}$ models with a preference relation $<$ over them. $\mathcal{ALC}$-$\mathbf{T}_{min}$ [5] extends the monotonic logic $\mathcal{ALC}$-$\mathbf{T}$ with a 'minimal model'semantics that allows to perform useful non-monotonic inferences. By contrast, our framework does not introduce any modal operator and can be easily applied to any default DL.

Our contributions include: (1) propose the default description logic $\mathcal{D}3\mathcal{L}$, (2) define the extensions of $\mathcal{D}3\mathcal{L}$-KBs and analyze their properties, and (3) prove that there exist some $\mathcal{D}3\mathcal{L}$-KB that cannot reduce to any $\mathcal{D}2\mathcal{L}$-KB.

2   Double-Level Default Description Logic

The language of $\mathcal{D}3\mathcal{L}$ contains the following symbols: individual constants: $c_0, c_1, ...$; individual variables: $x_0, x_1, ...$; atomic concepts: $A_0, A_1, ...$; concept constructors:

$\neg, \sqcap, \sqcup, \forall, \exists$; concept variables: $X_0, X_1, ...$; roles: $R_0, R_1, ...$; inclusion relation: $\sqsubseteq$; default inclusion relation: $\sqsubseteq_d$; logical connectives: $\neg$.

A term t is any expression of the form $c \mid x$ where c is an individual constant and x is an individual variable. A concept C is any expression of the form

$$A \mid X \mid \neg D \mid D \sqcap E \mid D \sqcup E \mid \forall R.D \mid \exists R.D$$

where A is an atomic concept, X is a concept variable, R is a role name, and D, E are concepts. A formula ϕ is any expression of the form

$$C(t) \mid R(t, t') \mid C \sqsubseteq D \mid C \sqsubseteq_d D \mid \neg\psi$$

where C, D are concepts, R is a role name, t, t' are terms, and ψ is a formula. A formula ϕ is *closed* if ϕ contains neither concept variable nor individual variable; else ϕ is *open*.

Before defining double-level defaults, we first discuss the negation of default subsumption of concepts. For example, $Bird \not\sqsubseteq_d Swim$ means 'abnormally birds can swim'. Notice that it is different from $Bird \sqsubseteq_d \neg Swim$, which means or 'normally birds cannot swim'. Intuitively, $Bird \sqsubseteq_d \neg Swim$ entails $Bird \not\sqsubseteq_d Swim$, but $Bird \not\sqsubseteq_d Swim$ does NOT entail $Bird \sqsubseteq_d \neg Swim$. The relations between concept subsumption, default concept subsumption, and the negation of them can be summarized as follows: (1) if $C \sqsubseteq D$ then $C \sqsubseteq_d D$; (2) if $C \not\sqsubseteq_d D$ then $C \not\sqsubseteq D$; (3) if $C \sqsubseteq_d \neg D$ and $C \not\sqsubseteq \bot$ then $C \not\sqsubseteq_d D$.

Definition 1. *(Double-level Default) A double-level default θ is any expression of the form*

$$\frac{\phi_1, ..., \phi_n : \phi}{\phi}$$

where $\phi_1, ..., \phi_n$ are formulas of the form $C \sqsubseteq D$ or $C \sqsubseteq_d D$, and ϕ is a formula of the form $C \sqsubseteq_d D$ or $C \not\sqsubseteq_d D$. If each of $\phi_1, ..., \phi_n$ is of the form $C \sqsubseteq_d D$ then θ is a pure *double-level default; else θ is a* hybrid *double-level default. If θ contains no variable, then θ is a* closed *double-level default; else θ is an* open *double-level default.*

Intuitively the double-level default θ can be interpreted as follows: if $\phi_1, ..., \phi_n$ hold, and if it is consistent to assume ϕ, then conclude ϕ.

An ABox $\mathcal{A}$ is a set of closed formulas of the form $C(c)$ or $R(c, d)$. A TBox $\mathcal{T}$ is a set of closed formulas of the form $C \sqsubseteq D$ or $C \not\sqsubseteq D$. A DBox $\mathcal{D}$ is a set of closed formulas of the form $C \sqsubseteq_d D$ or $C \not\sqsubseteq_d D$. A DDBox $\mathcal{D}^2$ is a set of double-level defaults.

A $\mathcal{D}2\mathcal{L}$ *Knowledge Base* $\mathcal{K} = (\mathcal{A}, \mathcal{T}, \mathcal{D})$ comprises an ABox, a TBox, and a DBox.

A $\mathcal{D}3\mathcal{L}$ *Knowledge Base* $\mathcal{K} = (\mathcal{A}, \mathcal{T}, \mathcal{D}, \mathcal{D}^2)$ comprises an ABox, a TBox, a DBox, and a DDBox.

So far we have defined $\mathcal{D}3\mathcal{L}$ knowledge base. Intuitively we can describe the procedure of computing all extensions of a $\mathcal{D}3\mathcal{L}$ knowledge base $(\mathcal{A}, \mathcal{T}, \mathcal{D}, \mathcal{D}^2)$ as follows. First, we apply the double-level defaults to the formulas of TBox and DBox, and produce new formulas in DBox. That is, $(\mathcal{T}, \mathcal{D}, \mathcal{D}^2)$ constitute a knowledge base and we compute its extensions $\{E_d\}$. We call them *concept-level knowledge base* and *D-extensions* because they contain neither individual constant nor individual variable. Second, we view the default formulas of a concept-level extension as default rules, and apply them to the formulas of ABox, producing new formulas in ABox. That is, $(\mathcal{A}, \mathcal{T}, E_d)$ constitute a knowledge base and we compute its extensions $\{E_a\}$. We call them *individual-level knowledge base* and *A-extensions*.

To define the extension of concept-level and individual-level knowledge bases, we define the operator $\Lambda_\mathcal{K}$ and $\Gamma_\mathcal{K}$ respectively. We use **ABox** to denote the set of all closed formulas of the form $C(c)$ or $R(c, d)$, **TBox** the set of all closed formulas of the form $C \sqsubseteq D$ or $C \not\sqsubseteq D$, **DBox** the set of all closed formulas of the form $C \sqsubseteq_d D$ or $C \not\sqsubseteq_d D$.

Definition 2. *($\Lambda_\mathcal{K}$ Operator) Let $\mathcal{K} = (\mathcal{T}, \mathcal{D}, \mathcal{D}^2)$ be a concept-level knowledge base and $S \subseteq$ **TBox** $\cup$ **DBox**. $\Lambda_\mathcal{K}(S)$ is the $\subseteq$-minimal set that satisfies:*

$\Lambda_\mathcal{K}1 : \mathcal{T} \cup \mathcal{D} \subseteq \Lambda_\mathcal{K}(S)$;
$\Lambda_\mathcal{K}2 : Th(\Lambda_\mathcal{K}(S)) = \Lambda_\mathcal{K}(S)$;
$\Lambda_\mathcal{K}3 : For\ all\ \frac{\phi_1,\ldots,\phi_n : \phi}{\phi} \in \mathcal{D}^2,\ \phi \in \Lambda_\mathcal{K}(S)\ if\ \phi_1,\ldots,\phi_n \in \Lambda_\mathcal{K}(S)\ and\ \neg\phi \notin S.$

Definition 3. *(Concept-level Extension and D-extension) Let $\mathcal{K} = (\mathcal{A}, \mathcal{T}, \mathcal{D}, \mathcal{D}^2)$ be a $\mathcal{D}3\mathcal{L}$ knowledge base and $E \subseteq$ **TBox** $\cup$ **DBox**. E is a concept-level extension of $\mathcal{K}$ if $E = \Lambda_{(\mathcal{T}, \mathcal{D}, \mathcal{D}^2)}(E)$. $E \cap$ **DBox** is a D-extension of $\mathcal{K}$ if E is a concept-level extension of $\mathcal{K}$.*

Definition 4. *($\Gamma_\mathcal{K}$ Operator) Let $\mathcal{K} = (\mathcal{A}, \mathcal{T}, \mathcal{D})$ and $S \subseteq$ **ABox** $\cup$ **TBox**. $\Gamma_\mathcal{K}(S)$ is the $\subseteq$-minimal set satisfying the following conditions:*

$\Gamma_\mathcal{K}1 : \mathcal{A} \cup \mathcal{T} \subseteq \Gamma_\mathcal{K}(S)$;
$\Gamma_\mathcal{K}2 : Th(\Gamma_\mathcal{K}(S)) = \Gamma_\mathcal{K}(S)$;
$\Gamma_\mathcal{K}3 : For\ all\ C \sqsubseteq_d D \in \mathcal{D}\ and\ for\ all\ individual\ constant\ a,\ if\ C(a) \in \Gamma_\mathcal{K}(S)$
$\quad\quad and\ \neg D(a) \notin S,\ then\ D(a) \in \Gamma_\mathcal{K}(S).$

Definition 5. *(Individual-level Extension and A-extension) Let $\mathcal{K} = (\mathcal{A}, \mathcal{T}, \mathcal{D}, \mathcal{D}^2)$ be a $\mathcal{D}3\mathcal{L}$ knowledge base, E_d a D-extension of $\mathcal{K}$, and $E \subseteq$ **ABox** $\cup$ **TBox**. E is an individual-level extension of $\mathcal{K}$ if $E = \Gamma_{(\mathcal{A}, \mathcal{T}, E_d)}(E)$. $E \cap$ **ABox** is an A-extension of $\mathcal{K}$ if E is an individual-level extension of $\mathcal{K}$.*

Below we present the properties for D-extensions and A-extensions respectively. Since the concept-level knowledge of a $\mathcal{D}3\mathcal{L}$-KB can be viewed as a normal default theory in default logic, the D-extensions of $\mathcal{D}3\mathcal{L}$-KBs have all properties of extensions of Reiter's normal default theories.

Proposition 1. *(Properties of D-extension)*
Existence: A $\mathcal{D}3\mathcal{L}$ knowledge base always has a D-extension.
Consistency: Let $\mathcal{K} = (\mathcal{A}, \mathcal{T}, \mathcal{D}, \mathcal{D}^2)$ be a $\mathcal{D}3\mathcal{L}$-KB and E_d a D-extension of $\mathcal{K}$. If $\mathcal{T} \cup \mathcal{D}$ is consistent, then E_d is consistent.

Minimality: Let $\mathcal{K} = (\mathcal{A}, \mathcal{T}, \mathcal{D}, \mathcal{D}^2)$ be a $\mathcal{D}3\mathcal{L}$ knowledge base and E_d, E'_d D-extensions of $\mathcal{K}$. If $E_d \subseteq E'_d$, then $E_d = E'_d$.

Semi-monotonicity: Let $\mathcal{K}_1 = (\mathcal{A}, \mathcal{T}, \mathcal{D}, \mathcal{D}_1^2)$ and $\mathcal{K}_2 = (\mathcal{A}, \mathcal{T}, \mathcal{D}, \mathcal{D}_2^2)$ be $\mathcal{D}3\mathcal{L}$ knowledge bases and $\mathcal{D}_1^2 \subseteq \mathcal{D}_2^2$. If E_1 is a D-extension of $\mathcal{K}_1$, then there is a D-extension E_2 of $\mathcal{K}_2$ such that $E_1 \subseteq E_2$.

Orthogonality: Let $\mathcal{K}$ be a $\mathcal{D}3\mathcal{L}$-KB. If E_d and E'_d are two D-extensions of $\mathcal{K}$, then E_d is inconsistent with E'_d.

The A-extensions of $\mathcal{D}3\mathcal{L}$-KBs do **NOT** satisfy *minimality* and *orthogonality*, which are proved by creating a $\mathcal{D}3\mathcal{L}$-KB that has two *strictly inclusive* and *consistent* extensions. See the example of the *irreducibility* theorem in the next section.

Proposition 2. *(Properties of A-extension)*

Existence: A $\mathcal{D}3\mathcal{L}$-KB always has an A-extension.

Consistency: Let $\mathcal{K} = (\mathcal{A}, \mathcal{T}, \mathcal{D}, \mathcal{D}^2)$ be a $\mathcal{D}3\mathcal{L}$ knowledge base and E_a an A-extension of $\mathcal{K}$. If $\mathcal{A} \cup \mathcal{T}$ is consistent, then E_a is consistent.

Non-minimality: There is a $\mathcal{D}3\mathcal{L}$ knowledge base such that it has two extensions E_a and E'_a such that $E_a \subset E'_a$.

Semi-monotonicity: Let $\mathcal{K}_1 = (\mathcal{A}, \mathcal{T}, \mathcal{D}, \mathcal{D}_1^2)$ and $\mathcal{K}_2 = (\mathcal{A}, \mathcal{T}, \mathcal{D}, \mathcal{D}_2^2)$ be $\mathcal{D}3\mathcal{L}$ knowledge bases and $\mathcal{D}_1^2 \subseteq \mathcal{D}_2^2$. If E_1 is an A-extension of $\mathcal{K}_1$, then there is an A-extension E_2 of $\mathcal{K}_2$ such that $E_1 \subseteq E_2$.

Non-orthogonality: There is a $\mathcal{D}3\mathcal{L}$ knowledge base such that it has two A-extensions E_a and E'_a such that E_a is consistent with E'_a.

3 Irreducibility of $\mathcal{D}3\mathcal{L}$-KBs

The following theorem states that there exists a $\mathcal{D}3\mathcal{L}$ knowledge base whose extensions cannot be exactly generated by any single default description logic.

Theorem 1. *(Irreducibility) There is a $\mathcal{D}3\mathcal{L}$ knowledge base $\mathcal{K}$ such that there exists no $\mathcal{D}2\mathcal{L}$ knowledge base $\mathcal{K}'$ such that, for any set E of formulas, E is an A-extension of $\mathcal{K}$ iff E is an A-extension of $\mathcal{K}'$.*

Proof. onstruct a $\mathcal{D}3\mathcal{L}$ knowledge base $\mathcal{K}$ such that (1) $\mathcal{K}$ has 3 D-extensions E_1, E_2, E_3; (2) $\mathcal{K}$ has 7 A-extensions $E_{11}, E_{12}, E_{21}, E_{22}, E_{31}, E_{32}, E_{33}$; (3) E_{11} is consistent with E_{21}.

Let $\mathcal{K} = (\mathcal{A}, \mathcal{T}, \mathcal{D}, \mathcal{D}^2)$ is a $\mathcal{D}3\mathcal{L}$ knowledge base where $\mathcal{A} = \{A(x)\}, \mathcal{T} = \{\}$,

$\mathcal{D} = \{B \sqsubseteq_d F,\ F \sqsubseteq_d \neg T,\ A \sqsubseteq_d T,\ D \sqsubseteq_d T,\ T \sqsubseteq_d \neg F,\ A \sqsubseteq_d F\}$,

$$\mathcal{D}^2 = \left\{ \frac{: A \sqsubseteq_d B}{A \sqsubseteq_d B},\ \frac{A \sqsubseteq_d B : A \not\sqsubseteq_d D}{A \not\sqsubseteq_d D},\ \frac{: A \sqsubseteq_d D}{A \sqsubseteq_d D},\ \frac{A \sqsubseteq_d D : A \not\sqsubseteq_d B}{A \not\sqsubseteq_d B} \right\}.$$

Here A denotes 'Archaeopteryx', B 'Bird', D 'Dinosaur', F 'Feather', and T 'Teeth'. $\mathcal{K}$ generates 3 D-extensions:

$$E_1 = \mathcal{D} \cup \{A \sqsubseteq_d B, A \not\sqsubseteq_d D\},$$
$$E_2 = \mathcal{D} \cup \{A \sqsubseteq_d D, A \not\sqsubseteq_d B\},$$
$$E_3 = \mathcal{D} \cup \{A \sqsubseteq_d B, A \sqsubseteq_d D\};$$

and $\mathcal{K}$ has 7 A-extensions:

$$E_{11} = Th(\{A(x), B(x), F(x), T(x)\}),$$
$$E_{12} = Th(\{A(x), B(x), F(x), \neg T(x)\});$$
$$E_{21} = Th(\{A(x), D(x), F(x), T(x)\}),$$
$$E_{22} = Th(\{A(x), D(x), \neg F(x), T(x)\});$$
$$E_{31} = Th(\{A(x), B(x), D(x), F(x), T(x)\}),$$
$$E_{32} = Th(\{A(x), B(x), D(x), \neg F(x), T(x)\}),$$
$$E_{33} = Th(\{A(x), B(x), D(x), F(x), \neg T(x)\}).$$

We can see that E_{11}, E_{21}; E_{11}, E_{31}; E_{21}, E_{31}; E_{12}, E_{33}; and E_{22}, E_{32} are all consistent. According to the orthogonality property of extensions of $\mathcal{D}2\mathcal{L}$-KBs, there is no $\mathcal{D}2\mathcal{L}$-KB $\mathcal{K}'$ such that both E_{11} and E_{21} are A-extensions of $\mathcal{K}'$. $\square$

4   Conclusion

In an attempt to represent the default inheritance of default properties of concepts in ontological modeling, we introduced double-level defaults and double-level default knowledge bases as a hierarchical variant of classical defaults and default knowledge bases. We propose double-level default description logic ($\mathcal{D}3\mathcal{L}$) and present the properties of extensions of $\mathcal{D}3\mathcal{L}$ knowledge bases. In addition, we prove that there is a $\mathcal{D}3\mathcal{L}$ knowledge base that cannot reduce to any $\mathcal{D}2\mathcal{L}$ knowledge base. In future work, we would like to investigate the semantics for $\mathcal{D}3\mathcal{L}$ and implement a reasoning system.

References

1. Baader, F., Hollunder, B.: Embedding defaults into terminological knowledge representation formalisms. Journal of Automated Reasoning **14**(1), 149–180 (1995)
2. Bonatti, P.A., Lutz, C., Wolter, F.: The complexity of circumscription in dls. Journal of Artificial Intelligence Research, 717–773 (2009)
3. Casini, G., Straccia, U.: Defeasible inheritance-based description logics. Journal of Artificial Intelligence Research, 415–473 (2013)
4. Donini, F.M., Nardi, D., Rosati, R.: Description logics of minimal knowledge and negation as failure. ACM Transactions on Computational Logic (TOCL) **3**(2), 177–225 (2002)
5. Giordano, L., Gliozzi, V., Olivetti, N., Pozzato, G.L.: A non-monotonic description logic for reasoning about typicality. Artificial Intelligence **195**, 165–202 (2013)
6. Giordano, L., Olivetti, N., Gliozzic, V., Pozzato, G.L.: Alc+ t: a preferential extension of description logics. Fundamenta Informaticae **96**(3), 341 (2009)
7. Reiter, R.: A logic for default reasoning. Artificial Intelligence **13**(1–2), 81–132 (1980)
8. Sengupta, K., Hitzler, P., Janowicz, K.: Revisiting default description logics – and their role in aligning ontologies. In: Supnithi, T., Yamaguchi, T., Pan, J.Z., Wuwongse, V., Buranarach, M. (eds.) JIST 2014. LNCS, vol. 8943, pp. 3–18. Springer, Heidelberg (2015)

Discovering Classes of Strongly Equivalent Logic Programs with Negation as Failure in the Head

Jianmin Ji[✉]

School of Computer Science and Technology,
University of Science and Technology of China, Hefei, China
jianmin@ustc.edu.cn

Abstract. In this paper, we apply Fangzhen Lin's methodology of computer aided theorem discovery to discover classes of strongly equivalent logic programs with negation as failure in the head. Specifically, with the help of computers, we discover exact conditions that capture the strong equivalence between small sets of rules, which have potential applications in the theory and practice of logic programming. In the experiment, we extend the previous approach to semi-automatically generate plausible conjectures. We also show that it is possible to divide the original problem in simpler cases and combine their solutions in order to obtain the solution of the original problem.

1 Introduction

Fangzhen Lin introduced a methodology, called computer-aided theorem discovery [2], to discover some theorems using computers in a given theory. The methodology has been successfully applied to discover classes of strongly equivalent logic programs in the theory of logic programming [3].

In this paper, we report on another successful experiment of the methodology for logic programs with negation as failure in the head [1] and make three contributions. First, we extend Lin and Chen's approach [3] to semi-automatically generate candidates of theorems that need to be discovered in the experiment. Second, we show that when the methodology cannot be directly applied, since it would be computationally unfeasible, it is possible to divide the original problem in simpler cases and combine their solutions in order to obtain the solution of the original problem. Third, we discover the new and non-trivial conditions that capture certain classes of strongly equivalent logic programs, which contribute to the theory and practice of logic programming.

2 Logic Programs with Negation as Failure in the Head

Logic programming with answer set semantics has been considered as one of the most popular nonmonotonic rule-based formalisms [1]. In this paper, we consider only fully grounded finite logic programs.

Let L be a propositional language, *i.e.*, a set of atoms. An *extended logic program* (ELP) is a finite set of (*extended*) *rules* of the form

$$a_1 \vee \cdots \vee a_k \vee not\, a_{k+1} \vee \cdots \vee not\, a_h \leftarrow a_{h+1}, \ldots, a_m, not\, a_{m+1}, \ldots, not\, a_n, \quad (1)$$

© Springer International Publishing Switzerland 2015
S. Zhang et al. (Eds.): KSEM 2015, LNAI 9403, pp. 147–153, 2015.
DOI: 10.1007/978-3-319-25159-2_13

where $n \geq m \geq h \geq k \geq 0$, $n \geq 1$ and $a_1, \ldots, a_n$ are atoms in L. If $h = k$, it is a *disjunctive rule*; if $h = k$ and $m = n$, it is a *positive rule*. In particular, a *disjunctive logic program* (DLP) is a finite set of disjunctive rules and a positive program is a finite set of positive rules. An ELP is also called a *logic program with negation as failure in the head* [1]. Note that, generally it is impossible to translate an ELP to a DLP without adding new atoms.

We will also write rule r of form (1) as $head(r) \leftarrow body(r)$, where $head(r) = head^+(r) \vee head^-(r)$, $body(r) = body^+(r) \wedge body^-(r)$, $head^+(r)$ is $a_1 \vee \cdots \vee a_k$, $head^-(r)$ is $\neg a_{k+1} \vee \cdots \vee \neg a_h$, $body^+(r)$ is $a_{h+1} \wedge \cdots \wedge a_m$, and $body^-(r)$ is $\neg a_{m+1} \wedge \cdots \wedge \neg a_n$. In the following, we identify $head^+(r)$, $head^-(r)$, $body^+(r)$, $body^-(r)$ with their corresponding sets of atoms.

Two ELPs P_1 and P_2 are *strongly equivalent*, if for any ELP P', programs $P_1 \cup P'$ and $P_2 \cup P'$ have the same set of answer sets. In general, checking if two ELPs or DLPs are strongly equivalent is coNP-complete. There is a mapping from logic programs to propositional theories and showed that two logic programs are strongly equivalent iff their corresponding theories in propositional logic are equivalent. This result provides the basis for applying Lin's computer-aided theory discovery.

3   Discovering Classes of Strongly Equivalent ELPs

In this paper, we extend Lin and Chen's approach to discovering classes of strongly equivalent ELPs. We focus on discovering necessary and sufficient conditions for answering the k-m-n problem for ELPs, *i.e.*, is an ELP $\{r_1, \ldots, r_k, u_1, \ldots, u_m\}$ strongly equivalent to an ELP $\{r_1, \ldots, r_k, v_1, \ldots, v_n\}$?

Following Lin's computer-aided theory discovery, we first construct a first-order language F_L based on the propositional language L of ELPs. In specific, F_L has equality, two unary predicates H_1 and H_2, and four unary predicates PH_r, NH_r, PB_r, and NB_r for each rule r in L. An *intended model* of F_l is one whose domain is L, and for each rule $r \in L$, the unary predicates PH_r, NH_r, PB_r, and NB_r are interpreted by the sets of atoms $head^+(r)$, $head^-(r)$, $body^+(r)$, and $body^-(r)$, respectively.

Theorem 1. *P_1 and P_2 are strongly equivalent in L iff the following sentence*

$$\forall x (H_1(x) \supset H_2(x)) \supset \left(\bigwedge_{r \in P_1} \gamma(r) \equiv \bigwedge_{r \in P_2} \gamma(r) \right) \tag{2}$$

is true in all intended models of F_L, where $\gamma(r)$ is the conjunction of the following two sentences:

$[\forall x (PB_r(x) \supset H_1(x)) \wedge \forall x (NB_r(x) \supset \neg H_2(x))] \supset [\exists x (PH_r(x) \wedge H_1(x)) \vee \exists x (NB_r(x) \wedge \neg H_2(x))]$,

$[\forall x (PB_r(x) \supset H_2(x)) \wedge \forall x (NB_r(x) \supset \neg H_2(x))] \supset [\exists x (PH_r(x) \wedge H_2(x)) \vee \exists x (NB_r(x) \wedge \neg H_2(x))]$.

Given a k-m-n problem, *i.e.*, $P_1 = \{r_1, \ldots, r_k, u_1, \ldots, u_m\}$ and $P_2 = \{r_1, \ldots, r_k, v_1, \ldots, v_n\}$, if a conjecture for answering the k-m-n problem is represented by the formula $\exists \boldsymbol{x} \forall \boldsymbol{y}\, \Phi$ in F_L, then verifying the conjecture is equivalent to verifying the formula $\exists \boldsymbol{x} \forall \boldsymbol{y}\, \Phi \supset$ (2). Now we have the following theorem.

Theorem 2. *Given ELPs $P_1 = \{r_1, \ldots, r_k, u_1, \ldots, u_m\}$ and $P_2 = \{r_1, \ldots, r_k, v_1, \ldots, v_n\}$ in the propositional language L, if $\exists \boldsymbol{x} \forall \boldsymbol{y}\, \Phi$ is a property about P_1 and P_2 in F_L, where $\boldsymbol{x}$ is a tuple of w variables, and Φ a quantifier-free, function-free, and constant-free formula, then the following two assertions are equivalent:*

1. *If $\exists \boldsymbol{x} \forall \boldsymbol{y}\, \Phi$ is true in F_L, then P_1 is strongly equivalent to P_2.*
2. *For any ELPs P_1 and P_2 with at most $w + 2(k + \max\{m, n\})$ atoms when $\min\{m, n\} > 0$ and $\max\{w + 2k, 1\}$ atoms when $\min\{m, n\} = 0$, if $\exists \boldsymbol{x} \forall \boldsymbol{y}\, \Phi$ is true in an intended model of F_L, then P_1 is strongly equivalent to P_2.*

Then the correctness of the conjecture for the k-m-n problem can be verified by considering corresponding ELPs with a small size of atoms.

4   The Theorems

4.1   The 0-1-0 Problem

This problem asks if a rule can always be deleted from any program. With the help of computers[1], we get the following experimental result:

Lemma 1. *If a rule r mentions three distinct atoms, then $\{r\}$ is strongly equivalent to $\emptyset$ iff $(head^+(r) \cup body^-(r)) \cap body^+(r) \neq \emptyset$ or $head^-(r) \cap body^-(r) \neq \emptyset$.*

Lemma 2. *If there is a rule r such that $\{r\}$ and $\emptyset$ are strongly equivalent, but the condition in Lemma 1 does not hold, then there is a such rule that mention at most three atoms.*

Theorem 3 (The 0-1-0 Problem). *Lemma 1 holds in the general case, without any restriction on the number of atoms in r.*

4.2   The 1-1-0 and the 0-1-1 Problems

With the help of computers, we get the following result for the 1-1-0 problem:

Lemma 3. *For any two rules r_1 and r_2 that mention four atoms, $\{r_1, r_2\}$ and $\{r_1\}$ are strongly equivalent iff one of the following three conditions is true:*

1. *$\{r_2\}$ is strongly equivalent to $\emptyset$.*
2. *$head^+(r_1) \subseteq head^+(r_2) \cup body^-(r_2)$, $head^-(r_1) \subseteq head^-(r_2) \cup body^+(r_2)$, $body^+(r_1) \subseteq body^+(r_2)$, and $body^-(r_1) \subseteq body^-(r_2)$.*

---

[1] Source codes of computer programs for verifying conjectures can be downloaded from http://staff.ustc.edu.cn/%7ejianmin/discover/code.zip.

3. $head^+(r_1) \subseteq body^-(r_2)$, $head^-(r_1) \subseteq head^-(r_2) \cup body^+(r_2)$, $body^+(r_1) \subseteq head^-(r_2) \cup body^+(r_2)$, and $body^-(r_1) \subseteq body^-(r_2)$.

Lemma 4. *If there are two rules r_1 and r_2 such that $\{r_1, r_2\}$ and $\{r_1\}$ are strongly equivalent, but none of the three conditions in Lemma 3 hold, then there are two such rules that mention at most four atoms.*

Theorem 4 (The 1-1-0 Problem). *Lemma 3 holds in the general case, without any restriction on the number of atoms in r_1 and r_2.*

Theorem 5 (The 0-1-1 Problem). *For any two rules r_1 and r_2, $\{r_1\}$ and $\{r_2\}$ are strongly equivalent iff one of the following three conditions is true:*

1. *$\{r_1\}$ and $\{r_2\}$ are both strongly equivalent to $\emptyset$.*
2. *$body^+(r_1) = body^+(r_2)$, $body^-(r_1) = body^-(r_2)$, $head^-(r_1) \cup body^+(r_1) = head^-(r_2) \cup body^+(r_2)$, and $head^+(r_1) \cup body^-(r_1) = head^+(r_2) \cup body^-(r_2)$.*
3. *$head^+(r_1) \subseteq body^-(r_1)$, $head^+(r_2) \subseteq body^-(r_2)$, $body^-(r_1) = body^-(r_2)$, and $head^-(r_1) \cup body^+(r_1) = head^-(r_2) \cup body^+(r_2)$.*

4.3   The 2-1-0, 0-2-1, and 0-2-2 Problems

As the 2-1-0 problem is too hard to be solved directly, we need to first divide the problem into simpler cases.

Property 1. For any rules r_i and r_3, $\{r_i, r_3\}$ and $\{r_i\}$ are not strongly equivalent iff $\{r_3\}$ is not strongly equivalent to $\emptyset$ and one of the five conditions is true:

1. There is an atom p such that: $p \in body^-(r_i)$ and $p \notin body^-(r_3)$.
2. There is an atom p such that: $p \in head^-(r_i)$ and $p \notin head^-(r_3) \cup body^+(r_3)$.
3. There is an atom p such that: $p \in body^+(r_i)$ and $p \notin head^-(r_3) \cup body^+(r_3)$.
4. There is an atom p such that: $p \in head^+(r_i)$ and $p \notin head^+(r_3) \cup body^-(r_3)$.
5. There are two atoms p, q such that: $p \in body^+(r_i)$, $p \notin body^+(r_3)$, $p \in head^-(r_3)$, $q \in head^+(r_i)$, $q \notin body^-(r_3)$ and $q \in head^+(r_3)$.

Property 2. For any rules r_1, r_2 and r_3, one of the four conditions is true:

1. $\{r_3\}$ is strongly equivalent to $\emptyset$.
2. $\{r_i, r_3\}$ is strongly equivalent to $\{r_i\}$, for $i = 1, 2$.
3. $\{r_3\}$ is not strongly equivalent to $\emptyset$, one of the conditions from (1) - (4) of Property 1 is true, and the condition (5) of Property 1 is not true, where $i = 1$ or 2.
4. $\{r_3\}$ is not strongly equivalent to $\emptyset$, $\{r_1, r_3\}$ is not strongly equivalent to $\{r_1\}$, $\{r_2, r_3\}$ is not strongly equivalent to $\{r_2\}$, and the condition (5) of Property 1 is true, where $i = 1$ or 2.

Lemma 5. *For any three rules r_1, r_2 and r_3 that make the condition (3) of Property 2 true and mention at most five atoms, $\{r_1, r_2, r_3\}$ and $\{r_1, r_2\}$ are strongly equivalent if there is an atom p such that:*

1. $p \in (head^-(r_1) \cup body^+(r_1)) \cap (body^-(r_2) \cup head^+(r_2))$,
2. $\{r_i^*, r_3\}$ is strongly equivalent to $\{r_i^*\}$, for $i = 1, 2$,
3. If $p \in body^+(r_1) \cap body^-(r_2)$, then $head^+(r_1) \subseteq body^-(r_3)$,
4. If $p \in body^+(r_1) \cap head^+(r_2)$, then $head^+(r_1) \subseteq body^-(r_3)$ or $body^+(r_2) \subseteq body^+(r_3)$,

where r_1^* is a new rule obtained from r_1 by deleting p from $head^-(r_1)$ and $body^+(r_1)$, and r_2^* is obtained from r_2 by deleting p from $body^-(r_2)$ and $head^+(r_2)$.

Lemma 6. *For any three rules r_1, r_2 and r_3 that make the condition (3) of Property 2 true and mention at most five atoms, $\{r_1, r_2, r_3\}$ and $\{r_1, r_2\}$ are strongly equivalent if there is an atom p such that:*

1. $p \in (body^-(r_1) \cup head^+(r_1)) \cap (head^-(r_2) \cup body^+(r_2))$,
2. $\{r_i^*, r_3\}$ is strongly equivalent to $\{r_i^*\}$, for $i = 1, 2$,
3. If $p \in body^-(r_1) \cap body^+(r_2)$, then $head^+(r_2) \subseteq body^-(r_3)$,
4. If $p \in head^+(r_1) \cap body^+(r_2)$, then $head^+(r_2) \subseteq body^-(r_3)$ or $body^+(r_1) \subseteq body^+(r_3)$,

where r_1^* is a new rule obtained from r_1 by deleting p from $body^-(r_1)$ and $head^+(r_1)$, and r_2^* is obtained from r_2 by deleting p from $head^-(r_2)$ and $body^+(r_2)$.

Lemma 7. *For any three rules r_1, r_2 and r_3 that make the condition (3) of Property 2 true and mention at most five atoms, $\{r_1, r_2, r_3\}$ and $\{r_1, r_2\}$ are strongly equivalent iff the condition in Lemma 5 or Lemma 6 is true.*

Lemma 8. *If there are three rules r_1, r_2 and r_3 such that the condition (3) of Property 2 is true, $\{r_1, r_2, r_3\}$ and $\{r_1, r_2\}$ are strongly equivalent, but the condition in Lemma 7 does not hold, then there are three such rules that mention at most five atoms.*

Theorem 6. *Lemma 7 holds in the general case, without any restriction on the number of atoms in r_1, r_2 and r_3.*

Lemma 9. *For any three rules r_1, r_2 and r_3 that make the condition (4) of Property 2 true and mention at most six atoms, $\{r_1, r_2, r_3\}$ and $\{r_1, r_2\}$ are strongly equivalent if there are two atoms p and q such that:*

1. $p \in head^-(r_1) \cap head^+(r_2) \cap head^+(r_3)$, $p \notin body^+(r_1)$ and $p \notin body^-(r_2)$,
2. $q \in head^+(r_1)$ and $q \in body^+(r_2)$,
3. $\{r_i^*, r_3\}$ is strongly equivalent to $\{r_i^*\}$, for $i = 1, 2$,
4. $body^+(r_2) \setminus \{q\} \subseteq body^+(r_3)$, and $body^+(r_1) \subseteq body^+(r_3)$,

where r_1^* is a new rule obtained from r_1 by deleting p from $head^-(r_1)$ and deleting q from $head^+(r_1)$, and r_2^* is obtained from r_2 by deleting p from $head^+(r_2)$.

Lemma 10. *For any three rules r_1, r_2 and r_3 that make the condition (4) of Property 2 true and mention at most six atoms, $\{r_1, r_2, r_3\}$ and $\{r_1, r_2\}$ are strongly equivalent if there are two atoms p and q such that:*

1. $p \in head^+(r_1) \cap head^-(r_2) \cap head^+(r_3)$, $p \notin body^-(r_1)$ and $p \notin body^+(r_2)$,
2. $q \in body^+(r_1)$ and $q \in head^+(r_2)$,
3. $\{r_i^*, r_3\}$ is strongly equivalent to $\{r_i^*\}$, for $i = 1, 2$,
4. $body^+(r_1) \setminus \{q\} \subseteq body^+(r_3)$, and $body^+(r_2) \subseteq body^+(r_3)$,

where r_1^* is a new rule obtained from r_1 by deleting p from $head^+(r_1)$, and r_2^* is obtained from r_2 by deleting p from $head^-(r_2)$ and deleting q from $head^+(r_2)$.

Lemma 11. *For any three rules r_1, r_2 and r_3 that make the condition (4) of Property 2 true and mention at most six atoms, $\{r_1, r_2, r_3\}$ and $\{r_1, r_2\}$ are strongly equivalent iff the condition in Lemma 7, Lemma 9 or Lemma 10 is true.*

Lemma 12. *If there are three rules r_1, r_2 and r_3 such that the condition (4) of Property 2 is true, $\{r_1, r_2, r_3\}$ and $\{r_1, r_2\}$ are strongly equivalent, but the condition in Lemma 11 does not hold, then there are three such rules that mention at most six atoms.*

Theorem 7. *Lemma 11 holds in the general case, without any restriction on the number of atoms in r_1, r_2 and r_3.*

Theorem 8. *For any three rules r_1, r_2 and r_3, $\{r_1, r_2, r_3\}$ and $\{r_1, r_2\}$ are strongly equivalent iff one of the following three conditions is true:*

1. *$\{r_3\}$ is strongly equivalent to $\emptyset$.*
2. *$\{r_i, r_3\}$ is strongly equivalent to $\{r_i\}$, where $i = 1$ or 2.*
3. *the condition in Lemma 5, 6, 6, or 10 is true.*

Theorem 9 (The 0-2-1 Problem). *For any three rules r_1, r_2 and r_3, $\{r_1, r_2\}$ and $\{r_3\}$ are strongly equivalent iff the following two conditions are true:*

1. *$\{r_1, r_2, r_3\}$ and $\{r_1, r_2\}$ are strongly equivalent, and*
2. *$\{r_i, r_3\}$ and $\{r_3\}$ are strongly equivalent, for $i = 1, 2$.*

Theorem 10 (The 0-2-2 Problem). *For any rules r_1, r_2, r_3 and r_4, $\{r_1, r_2\}$ and $\{r_3, r_4\}$ are strongly equivalent iff the following two conditions are true:*

1. *$\{r_1, r_2, r_i\}$ and $\{r_1, r_2\}$ are strongly equivalent, for $i = 3, 4$, and*
2. *$\{r_3, r_4, r_i\}$ and $\{r_3, r_4\}$ are strongly equivalent, for $i = 1, 2$.*

5 Conclusion

In this paper, we report on another successful experiment of Lin's computer-aided theory discovery for discovering classes of strongly equivalent extended logic programs. The paper makes three contributions. First, we extend Lin and Chen's approach to semi-automatically generate plausible conjectures. Second, we show that when the methodology cannot be directly applied, since it would be computationally unfeasible, it is possible to divide the original problem in simpler cases and combine their solutions in order to obtain the solution of the original problem. Third, we discover the new and non-trivial conditions that capture certain classes of strongly equivalent extended logic programs, which contribute to the theory and practice of logic programming.

Acknowledgments. We thank Xiaoping Chen for helpful discussions. The work was supported by NSFC under grant 61175057, NSFC for the Youth under grant 61403359, as well as the USTC Key Direction Project and the USTC 985 Project.

References

1. Inoue, K., Sakama, C.: Negation as failure in the head. The Journal of Logic Programming **35**(1), 39–78 (1998)
2. Lin, F.: Finitely-verifiable classes of sentences. In: Proceedings of the 8th International Symposium on Logical Formalizations of Commonsense Reasoning (Commonsense 2007), pp. 89–94 (2007)
3. Lin, F., Chen, Y.: Discovering classes of strongly equivalent logic programs. In: Proceedings of the 19th International Joint Conference on Artificial Intelligence (IJCAI-2005), pp. 516–521 (2005)

Knowledge Management
and Concept Analysis

Mining Conceptual Knowledge from Network Traffic Data for Traffic Measurement Optimization

Petko Valtchev[✉], Omar Mounaouar, Omar Cherkaoui,
and Alexandar Dimitrov

Déptartment Informatique, UQÀM, CP 8888, Succ. CV, Montreal H3C 3P8, Canada
{valtchev.petko,cherkaoui.omar}@uqam.ca

Abstract. Formal concept analysis (FCA) is a knowledge discovery approach aimed at extracting conceptual hierarchies from data. Due to the exhaustiveness of its output, a typical FCA-based solution would filter large parts thereof using an ad-hoc quality criterion. In this paper, we present an FCA-based solution to an optimization problem from network traffic control that is akin to information retrieval (queries set up to measure specific traffic, i.e., packet flows). The goal is to minimize the number of counters used to answer a given query set. Our solution explores a contextual substructure of the (flows x flow descriptors) lattice, that we called the projection subsemilattice: The optimal set of counters is shown to correspond to a class of concepts from the semilattice. We present an effective computing method and provide empirical evidence of its performances on realistic network settings.

1 Introduction

Formal concept analysis (FCA) is a mathematically-founded approach towards the elicitation of conceptual knowledge from data [1]. It extracts conceptual abstractions, called (formal) *concepts*, from (object x attributes) cross-tables, a.k.a. (formal) *contexts*, which are pairs (objects, attributes) of mutually corresponding and maximal sets. The concepts are ordered w.r.t. a generality relation which induces a complete lattice. FCA has been widely used as a framework for extracting domain knowledge from concrete observations –as well as further representing and maintaining such knowledge– within a variety of concrete situation and in application domains ranging from software engineering to information retrieval to social network analysis. Our own study pertains to work on FCA for information retrieval [2] and for pattern and association rule mining [3].

Here, we present an FCA-based solution to an optimization problem from traffic measurement in modern networks (e.g., implementing the OpenFlow protocol). Network traffic management recognizes *flows*, i.e., sets of packets sharing routing information (as expressed in their header fields), and assigns them dedicated processing rules. Traffic measurement, in turn, amounts to gathering a variety of statistics about packets of specific profiles which are also expressed

© Springer International Publishing Switzerland 2015
S. Zhang et al. (Eds.): KSEM 2015, LNAI 9403, pp. 157–169, 2015.
DOI: 10.1007/978-3-319-25159-2_14

as filters on packet headers, called *queries*. Measurement relies on counters that are updated by each passage of a packet. It is an essential activity that allows network managers to get the visibility required for daily operations. Hence tools to observe traffic must scale with a wide spectrum of applications, flows and queries while maintaining the performance of the network devices and achieving accurate measurements [4]. Current flow-aware solutions, e.g., Cisco's NetFlow, sample traffic and send per-flow statistics to a remote server, which amounts to a one-counter-per-flow assignment schema. This ensures all potential queries can be answered at the price of inaccurate statistics and intensive resource usage. On the other extreme, recent approaches [5,6] to application-aware traffic measurement use prior knowledge of the set of queries to achieve adaptive measurements: Counters are assigned to sub-queries that are output by a query decomposition method. However, as the decomposition ignores existing flows, sub-queries are not guaranteed to match real packets.

As a trade-off solution, we examined an approach that takes into account both the existing flows and the known queries, by exploiting their combinatorial interplay induced by the respective matchfields. Indeed, from information processing point of view, the problem is akin to information retrieval as queries set up against packets actually also match the flows describing those packets. However, instead of retrieving the flows corresponding to each query, here the goal is to assign (a minimal number of) hardware counters to (sets of) flows in order to answer a given set of queries in a precise manner.

Our solution explores a contextual substructure of the (flows x matchfields) lattice: The optimal set of counters is shown to correspond to a class of concepts, called the ground ones, from what we defined as the projection subsemilattice of the query set. We also describe an efficient algorithm for computing the ground set that avoids multiple traversals of the lattice structure. Empirical evidence for the practicality of our solution in realistic network settings is also provided.

In what follows, we provide background on traffic measurement and on FCA, and state the traffic measurement problem (section 2). The mathematical foundations of our solution and its algorithmic components are presented in sections 3 and 4, respectively. Section 5 provides initial evidence about the practicality of our solution. We discuss related work in section 6 and conclude in section 7.

2   Background and Problem Statement

We provide some context for the traffic measurement problem and state it in terms of FCA.

2.1   Network Traffic Measurement

In modern networks, packet processing, is based on flows, i.e., groups of packets that are processed in the same way by a network switch. Flows are two-fold: 1) a filter part states conditions on packet headers (a set of fields such as source and destination IP, ports, protocols, etc.), and 2) a rule part that describe the

actions to perform on packets matching the filter. For instance, assume a flow of the following composition:
f = ([Ingress Port = 1], [IPv4 src =10/8], [IPv4 dst = 132.208.130.1]) Beside the exact values in the 1st and the 3rd field, the flow comprises an expression, aka matchfield, that admits a (wide) range of possible exact values for the *IPv4 src* field. Moreover, the fields not mentioned explicitly remain unconstrained.

Traffic measurement allows network managers to monitor activities, in particular, packet processing, and plan for network maintenance and evolution[1]. It materializes in the form of queries, which, like flows, constrain specific header fields of the packets. However, rather than being composed of all matching packets, query answers consist actually of some quantities representing basic statistics about those packets, esp. their number. Answers are computed from the values of packet counters, hardware-based mechanisms that account for each passing packet, and sent to user applications upon request. For instance, a possible query might be: q = ([Ingress Port = 1])

Counters can be attached to a particular flow or set of flows, if available, or implemented independently from packet processing. Existing flow-based measurement methods typically assign a counter to each flow. Moreover, they compute statistics continuously, regardless of user application needs, as applications are in charge of pulling the desired counters. This results in a large number of transactions and generates excessive bandwidth usage that may adversely affect packet processing. For example, in a Cisco Netflow-capable switch, flow statistics are tracked continuously at a specific sampling rate and sent to a Netflow Data Collector that serves applications. The resulting transactions and bandwidth usage are proportional to the number of flows (typically in the 1000s).

Now, observe that both flows and queries may be thought of as sets of matchfields whose exact semantics is immaterial here. What matters however, is the capacity of comparing these matchfields for generality and hence checking whether a flow matches a query. Hereafter, we shall assume such mechanism is available. This allows us to further assume a collection of flows $\mathcal{F}$, e.g., all flows installed in a given switch, and of queries Q with a common set of matchfields $\mathcal{H} = \{h_1, h_2, \ldots, l_m\}$. A flow $f \in \mathcal{F}$ is assumed to be fully determined by its set of matchfields $\{h_{i_1}, h_{i_2}, .., h_{i_k}\}$ from $\mathcal{H}$ (deterministic packet sorting bars identical flows). Similarly, a query $q \in Q$ is determined by its set of matchfields from $\mathcal{H}$. The grounding idea of our study is to leverage the interplay between members of $\mathcal{F}$ and of Q in optimizing the number of counters to answer each q in Q.

2.2   Formal Concept Analysis

Hereafter we recall the basics of FCA, whereas the details can be found in [1].

First, FCA introduces data as a (formal) *context* $K(G, M, I)$, where G is a set of *objects*, M a set of *attributes*, and $I \subseteq G \times M$ an *incidence* relation where a pair (g, m) from I means the object g has the attribute m. For consiseness

---

[1] For an in-depth coverage of the field readers are referred to [5].

Table 1. Input data: the flow context $\mathcal{K}(\mathcal{F}, \mathcal{H}, \mathcal{M})$ and the query set Q.

	h_1	h_2	h_3	h_4	h_5	h_6	h_7	h_8	h_9	h_{10}
f_0	x			x		x		x		
f_1	x			x	x	x				x
f_2		x			x		x			
f_3		x			x		x			x
f_4	x					x		x		
f_5	x			x		x				x
f_6			x			x		x		x
f_7			x			x	x		x	x
q_1										x
q_2		x				x		x		
q_3	x									
q_4	x			x		x				
q_3						x				

h_1 - Ingress Port = 1
h_2 - Ingress Port = 2
h_3 - Ingress Port = 3
h_4 - MAC src = MAC$_1$
h_5 - MAC dst = MAC$_{12}$
h_6 - IPv4 src = 132.208.130/32
h_7 - IPv4 src =10/8
h_8 - IPv4 dst = 10/8
h_9 - IPv4 dst = 132.208.130.1
h_{10} - Layer 4 dst port = 21

reasons we swith to our own measurement-oriented notations where the context is $\mathcal{K}(\mathcal{F}, \mathcal{H}, \mathcal{M})$ in which, beside the set of flows and matchfields, the incidence $\mathcal{M}$ is based on packet matching: (f, h) is in it whenever all the packets selected by f satisfy h. Our running example shown in Table 1 is organized as a formal context made of eight flows and ten matchfields. Five queries are provided yet do not formally belong to the context. FCA defines a two-fold derivation operator $'$ that maps sets of flows to all shared matchfields and vice-versa:

- $' : \wp(\mathcal{F}) \to \wp(\mathcal{H})$, $F' = \{h \in \mathcal{H} \mid \forall f \in F, (f, h) \in M\}$,
- $' : \wp(\mathcal{H}) \to \wp(\mathcal{F})$, $H' = \{f \in \mathcal{F} \mid \forall h \in H, (f, h) \in M\}$.

A (formal) *concept* of $\mathcal{K}$ is a pair $(F, H) \in \wp(\mathcal{F}) \times \wp(\mathcal{H})$ where $F = H'$ and $H = F'$. Moreover, the set F is termed the *extent* whereas H is the *intent*. For instance, in our example, $(\{f_3, f_6, f_7\}, \{h_6, h_{10}\})$ is a concept, while $(\{f_3, f_6\}, \{h_6, h_{10}\})$ is not. The set of all concepts in $\mathcal{K}$, denoted $\mathcal{C}_\mathcal{K}$, forms a complete lattice with respect to the extent-inclusion order: $(F_1, H_1) \leq_\mathcal{K} (F_2, H_2) \Leftrightarrow F_1 \subseteq F_2$.

Figure 1 shows the Hasse diagram of the lattice $\mathcal{L}_\mathcal{K} = \langle \mathcal{C}_\mathcal{K}, \leq_\mathcal{K} \rangle$ of our example. Here, concepts are identified by integer indexes and provided with their intents/extents (tagged I and E). Both are reduced as deducible information is not shown, e.g., c_{13}, although seemingly empty, is in fact $(\{f_3, f_6, f_7\}, \{h_6, h_{10}\})$.

2.3   Problem Statement

Now, the traffic measurement optimization problem consists in, given a set of flows $\mathcal{F}$ to monitor and a set of users queries Q, finding the minimal number of hardware counters that need to be maintained in order for all queries to get an exact answer. As a reasonable constraint that helps keep the maintenance overhead low, we assume that each flow reports to at most one counter. This means that the set of counters describes a partition of $\mathcal{F}$ and that we are after a partition of a minimal size.

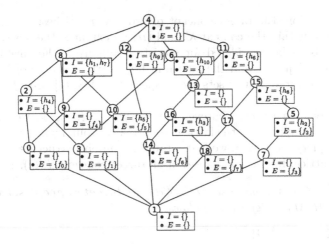

Fig. 1. Concept lattice of the input context $\mathcal{K}(\mathcal{F}, \mathcal{H}, \mathcal{M})$.

3   Mapping Flows to Queries Over the Concept Lattice

We define a straightforward mapping of queries into concepts and show that it induces a subsemilattice of the flow-to-matchfield lattice. We then show that concepts from the subsemilattice that are minimal for at least one flow define a minimal partition for the set of flows.

3.1   Overview of the Approach

Our approach relies on the recognition of three subsets of $\mathcal{C}_\mathcal{K}$, the set of all concepts of $\mathcal{K}(\mathcal{F}, \mathcal{H}, \mathcal{M})$. T is the set of *target* concepts: for a query q its target is $\gamma(q) = (q', q'')$, i.e., the concept whose intent q'' is the smallest comprising q (a.k.a. the closure of q). Next, P is the set of *projections*, i.e., the lattice meets of all non-empty subset of T: $P = \{\bigwedge T_p - T_p \in \wp(T)\}$. Finally, G is the set of *ground* projections: for a flow f its ground is $\mu(f) = \min(\{(F, H) \in P | f \in F\})$, the minimal projection concept whose extent comprises f. In the following paragraphs, we formally define these and provide some further results that enable their efficient computation, as presented in the next section.

3.2   Query Concepts and their Semi-lattice

A first observation is that each q may be mapped to a unique concept of the lattice, called hereafter its *target concept*, that is identified by the closure q'':

Definition 1. *Given a query $q \subseteq \mathcal{H}$, its **target** concept within the context $\mathcal{K}(\mathcal{F}, \mathcal{H}, M)$ is defined as follows:*

- $\gamma : \wp(\mathcal{H}) \to \mathcal{C}_\mathcal{K}$ *with* $\gamma(q) = (\{q\}', \{q\}'')$,

By its definition, the target concept of a query q satisfies: (i) its intent is the closure of q within the context $\mathcal{K}$, and (ii) its extent is the answer flow set of q that needs to be considered for statistics computing. For instance, with our sample set of queries and the lattice in Fig. 1, $\gamma(q_2) = c_5$, $\gamma(q_3) = c_8$, and $\gamma(q_5) = c_8$. The three answer sets are, respectively, $\{f_2, f_3\}$ are $\{f_0, f_1, f_4, f_5\}$ (twice).

It is readily shown that, whatever the query $q \subseteq \mathcal{H}$, the answer flow set of such q necessarily appears in the lattice. To formally ground our reasoning about statistics for query answering, we first establish a support structure for Q within the concept lattice. Its basis is the set of all target concepts $T(Q)$.

Definition 2. *Given a query set $Q \subseteq \wp(\mathcal{H})$, its **target concept set** within the context $\mathcal{K}(\mathcal{F}, \mathcal{H}, M)$ is defined as follows:*

- $T(Q) = \{\gamma(q) \mid q \in Q\}$,

In the running example, $T(Q) = \{c_2, c_5, c_6, c_8\}$. Hereafter, whenever Q is clear from the context, we shall simply write T instead of $T(Q)$.

A straightforward solution would now be to keep one counter per $c \in T(Q)$ thus making statistics directly available (no summing). Yet this is unrealistic since whenever a flow appears in two or more target concepts (e.g., f_5 is in both c_6 and c_8), it should contribute to as many counters, which is a breach of the above single-counter constraint. Further to that, a more purposeful solution would focus on the intersections of target concept extents so that each flow is assigned a unique smallest subset whose counter it should increment. *Query statistics* can then be computed by *summing up the counters* corresponding to the relevant subsets of its extent flowset.

We thus shift our focus to a wider family of flowsets made of target extents and *all* intersections thereof. Indeed, it is easily seen that the above reasoning could be inductively applied to pair-wise intersections, then to second-level ones, and so forth, until all possible intersections are proven to require consideration for counter assignment. As a matter of fact, such intersections correspond to extents of concepts from $\mathcal{C}_{\mathcal{K}}$ (actually, arbitrary meets of concepts from T). Consider the lattice sub-structure induced by $T(Q)$ through arbitrary meets:

Definition 3. *Given a query set $Q \subseteq \wp(\mathcal{H})$, its **projection** concept set within the context $\mathcal{K}(\mathcal{F}, \mathcal{H}, M)$ is defined as follows:*

- $P(Q) = \{\bigwedge X \mid X \subseteq T(Q); \ X \neq \emptyset\}$,

Again, P will be used for $P(Q)$ whenever confusion is impossible. In our example, $P(Q) = \{c_1, c_2, c_3, c_5, c_6, c_7, c_8, c_{10}\}$. Moreover, $P(Q)$ forms a meet semi-lattice w.r.t. the order in the concept lattice, denoted $\mathcal{L}_{|Q} = \langle P(Q), \leq_{\mathcal{K}|P(Q)} \rangle$. Observe that $\mathcal{L}_{|Q}$ is a meet sub-semi-lattice of $\mathcal{L}_{\mathcal{K}}$ henceforth referred to as the *projection semi-lattice*.

Next, consider the mapping of flows to projection concepts: For a flow f covered by least one q, there is always a unique minimal concept in $P(Q)$.

Table 2. Flow-to-ground concept mapping

Flow	Ground	Flow	Ground	Flow	Ground	Flow	Ground
f_0	c_2	f_1	c_3	f_2	c_5	f_3	c_7
f_4	c_8	f_5	c_{10}	f_6	c_6	f_7	c_6

Property 1. Given a context $\mathcal{K}(\mathcal{F}, \mathcal{H}, \mathcal{M})$, a query set $Q \subseteq \wp(\mathcal{H})$ and a flow $f \in \mathcal{F}$ s.t. at least one q covers f, the concept $\bigwedge \{(F, H) \mid (F, H) \in P(Q); \ f \in F\}$ is the minimal projection concept comprising f.

We thereby define a map from a flow f to the minimal projection comprising it. For completeness, if no query covers f, it is mapped to the lattice top $\top$.

Definition 4. *The map* $\mu : \mathcal{F} \to P(Q) \cup \{\top\}$ *maps a flow f into the minimal projection called its* **ground** *one:*

$$\mu(f) = \bigwedge \{(F, H) \mid (F, H) \in P(Q); \ f \in F\}.$$

Table 2 illustrates μ. Then, the set of ground projections is defined as follows:

Definition 5. *Given a query set $Q \subseteq \wp(\mathcal{H})$, its* **ground projection** *concept set within the context $\mathcal{K}(\mathcal{F}, \mathcal{H}, M)$ is:*

– $G(Q) = \{\mu(f) \mid f \in \mathcal{F}\} - \top,$

In our example, $G(Q) = \{c_2, c_3, c_5, c_6, c_7, c_8, c_{10}\}$.

3.3   Counter Assignment and Minimality Results

Counter assignment exploits $G(Q)$ and $T(Q)$: Each ground projection is assigned a counter, i.e., a particular flow f is uniquely "wired" to the counter of $\mu(f)$ (if $\mu(f) \neq \top$). Thus, the exact statistics of a concept $c_t \in T(Q)$ is the sum of all counters in sub-concepts of c_t plus, possibly, its own counter if $c_t \in G(Q)$. For instance, for the target concept of q_2, i.e., c_5, the sum comprises the counter of the ground concept c_7 (of f_3) and its own counter as c_5 id the ground for f_2. Similarly, the sum of c_6 comprises the counters of concepts: c_3, c_6, c_7 and c_{10}.

We prove that our ground concept-based counter assignment is: (1) correct, and (2) of minimal cardinality. Recall that each ground $c_g \in G$ is assigned a counter whose support is the set of grounded flows denoted $g(c_g) = \{f \mid \mu(f) = c_g\}$. This is a unique counter assignment (uniqueness of $\mu(f)$) and w.l.o.g. we assume that each flow is grounded. Furthermore, for each $q \in Q$ the set of relevant counters compose to a sum and let the underlying total set of flows be $S(q)$. As a counter enters a query sum iff its ground is below the corresponding target, we have $\forall f \in \mathcal{F}, q \in Q, \ f \in S(q)$ iff $\mu(f) \leq \gamma(q)$.

Correctness means a $S(q)$ is the set of flows satisfying q:

Theorem 1. $\forall q \in Q, f \in \mathcal{F}, \ q \subseteq f'$ *iff* $\mu(f) \leq \gamma(q)$.

Minimalness means no unique counter assignment among a smaller set of counters could answer all q in Q. We focus on the underlying partition of $\mathcal{F}$:

Theorem 2. *Let cpt : $\mathcal{F} \to \wp(\mathcal{F})$ with $cpt(f) = F$ iff $f \in F$ and assume $|\mathsf{ran}(cpt)| < |G|$. Then $\exists q \in Q$ s.t. $S(q)$ is not decomposable into the union of some sets from $\mathsf{ran}(cpt)$.*

4   Effective Partitioning of the Set of Flows

While the first step in the partition of $\mathcal{F}$ is to construct the concept lattice $\mathcal{L}_{\mathcal{K}}$, we skip this well-known problem here to focus on the computation of T, P and G. While given Q, detecting T within $\mathcal{C}_{\mathcal{K}}$ is straightforward, spotting all lattice meets of T might prove too costly. However, as shown in [7], meets may be computed by label propagation along a lattice traversal: The labels to propagate are the IDs of concepts from the base that lay *above* a given concept. The procedure ensures meets are identified through a mere comparison of resulting labels between a concept and its immediate successors.

In what follows, given a concept c, we shall use the following non standard notations: I_c and E_c for its intent and extent, respectively; $\hat{c}$ for its immediate successors; $t(c)$ and $g(c)$ for the sets of queries targeted to c and for the set of flows grounded to c, respectively; $v(c)$ for the query vector identifying the query whose target concepts are greater or equal to c.

Now, given the concept set $\mathcal{C}_{\mathcal{K}}$ and the query set Q, Algorithm 1 parses $\mathcal{C}_{\mathcal{K}}$ to identify T, P and G. Projection computation is supported by a bitvector whose value for $c = (F, H)$ reflects the queries satisfied by flows in F. Formally, the query vector $v(c)$ is an N-bit string indicating which q_i are matched by H:

$$v((F, H))[i] = \begin{cases} 1, & \text{if } q_i \subseteq H \\ 0, & \text{otherwise} \end{cases} \quad 1 \leq i \leq N$$

First, the concepts list $\mathcal{C}_{\mathcal{K}}$ is sorted in decreasing order of extent sizes (line 1), to ensure the first concept whose intent matches a $q \in Q$ is its target (line 4). Matched q are removed from the list (line 6). In our example, the algorithm outputs the targets c_6, c_5, c_8, c_2 and c_8, for q_i ($i = 1..5$), respectively. Then, the value of $v(c)$ is finalized (line 7): the local part (targeted queries, line 5) is merged with the inherited parent values (see results in Table 3). Projections are concepts whose query vectors have more 1s than any of their respective parent ones (line 8). For instance, c_{10} has three 1s, more than its parents c_8 (one) and c_6 (two), hence it is a projection (as meet of the targets c_6 and c_8). Finally, the ground concept of a $f \in \mathcal{F}$ is the projection with the same query vector as the flow concept (f'', f) (lines 10-13).

Algorithm 1 detects the sets P, T and G along the lattice traversal. Observe $\gamma(q)$ is the maximal $(F, H) \in \mathcal{C}_{\mathcal{K}}$ s.t. $q \subseteq H$ while F is the set of all flows f satisfying q ($q \subseteq f'$). Moreover, $\mu(f)$ is well defined: it is the meet of the targets of queries satisfied by f ($\mu(f) = \bigwedge\{\gamma(q)|q \in Q; \ q \subseteq f'\}$).

The main tasks in Algorithm 1 are detecting all $\gamma(q)$ (the highest concept (F, H) with $q \subseteq H$) and propagating the targeted q downwards in the lattice.

Table 3. Query vectors values

Query vector	Concepts	Query vector	Concepts
00000	$c_4, c_{11}, c_{12}, c_{15}$	00111	$c_0, \mathbf{c_2}$
10000	$\mathbf{c_6}, c_{13}, c_{14}, c_{16}, c_{17}, c_{18}$	10101	c_{10}
01000	$\mathbf{c_5}$	11000	$\mathbf{c_7}$
10111	$\mathbf{c_3}$	00101	$\mathbf{c_8}, c_9$
11111	$\mathbf{c_1}$		

Algorithm 1. Flowset partition identification algorithm

---

input : The list of all concepts $\mathcal{C}_\mathcal{K}$;   A set of queries $Q = (q_1, .., q_i, .., q_n)$
output: Target, projection and ground sets (T, P, G)

1   $Sort(\mathcal{C}_\mathcal{K})$;
2   **foreach** c in $\mathcal{C}_\mathcal{K}$ **do**
3   **for** q_i in Q **do**
4   **if** $q_i \subseteq I_c$ **then**
5          $v(c)[i] \leftarrow 1$;
6          $T \leftarrow T \cup \{c\}$; $Q \leftarrow Q - \{q_i\}$;

7      $v(c) \leftarrow v(c) \cup \bigcup_{\bar{c} \in c^\frown} v(\bar{c})$;
8   **if** $|v(c)| > \max_{\bar{c} \in c^\frown} (|v(\bar{c})|)$ **then**
9        $P \leftarrow P \cup \{c\}$;

10   **if** $|I_c| = 1$ **then**
11   **for** $p \in P$ **do**
12   **if** $v(p) = v(c)$ **then**
13          $G \leftarrow G \cup \{p\}$; $break()$;

These q are stored in the bitvectors $v()$ for further projection tests. Now, a projection c is exactly the meet of the targets of queries in $v(c)$:

Property 2. $c \in P$ iff $c = \bigwedge \{\gamma(q_i) \mid v(c)[i] = 1\}$.

As a corollary, the projection extent is the intersection of the target ones ($F = \bigcap \{E_{\gamma(q_i)} | v(c)[i] = 1\}$). Then, c is maximal for $v(c)$ and thus can be recognized by comparing its bitvector to those of parent concepts:

Property 3. $c \in P$ iff $\forall \bar{c} \in c^\frown, v(\bar{c}) \neq v(c)$.

As it is readily shown that as a function $v()$ is monotonously non increasing w.r.t. $\leq_\mathcal{F}$, the property may be recast in terms of cardinalities: $|v(c)| > \max_{\bar{c} \in c^\frown}(|v(\bar{c})|)$.
Finally, G is tested by comparing $v(c)$ to bitvectors of flow concepts:

Property 4. For a $c = (F, H)$, $c \in G$ iff $\exists f \in F$ s.t. for $\bar{c} = (f'', f')$, $v(\bar{c}) = v(c)$.

Moreover, as in our specific case, no flow has a subset of another flow's match-fields, $\forall f \in \mathcal{F}$, $f'' = f$. Hence flow concepts are those with singleton extents.

5   Implementation and Practical Evaluation

FlowME is an implementation of our approach over an OpenFlow switch that adapts algorithms from the Galicia FCA tool [8]. It was experimentally compared to a base line that simulates per-flow traffic measurement, i.e., maintenance of a dedicated counter for each flow. Thus, the counter number N_c for the per-flow measurement approach equals $|\mathcal{F}|$. Since our own solution relies on shared counters, we measure its utility in the decrease of counter usage. We therefore observed the average N_c value reached by FlowME under various scenarios, in particular its evolution w.r.t. to $|\mathcal{F}|$, over stable sets of user queries Q.

Our testbed comprises a switch with per-flow counter support, a flow generator, a collector and user applications generating queries. The collector gets the set of flows $\mathcal{F}$ installed in the switch's flow table. It calls upon the lattice algorithms to calculate the optimal flow partition and places counters accordingly. Next, packets matching $\mathcal{F}$ are passed and increment the counters. The collector reads counter values, computes query answers and sends them to user applications.

Our flow benchmark exploits on Flexible Rule Generator [9], a user controlled benchmarking tool for evaluating packet forwarding algorithms that generate sets of OpenFlow flow entries based on predefined matchfield distributions. We extract matchfield distributions from packet traces provided by *packetlife.net*. As a result, a total of 12 standard OpenFlow matchfields are used in the benchmark. Application queries were filled with two types of values: a wildcard value that matches all possible expressions in a matchfield versus a concrete expression that may (and typically will) mismatch part of flow values. Queries were generated with the same distributions of matchfield value as in flow entries, while inserting a specific percentage of wildcards. That percentage varied in order to cover a wide range of scenarios, i.e., from strong predominance of wildcards to almost absence thereof.

For instance, the curbs in Figure 2 depict evolution of N_c upon increasing $\mathcal{F}$ for three different Q, of sizes 100, 500 and 1000, respectively, all of them having a 50% rate of wildcards. Quite to our satisfaction, while rather steep in the beginning, each curb quickly reaches a plateau, as opposed to the linear increase of the counter number (the diagonal in the diagram). Moreover, that trend was observed regardless of the exact proportion of the wildcards. Thus, in the 1000-query cases, FlowME reached reduction ratios of 1/10 (least wildcards) to 1/3 (most wildcards) over 10000 flows (hence 10000 per-flow counters). Further details about our performance study, skipped here for space limitation reasons, may be found in [10].

6   Related Work

The closest approach to the ours is ProgME [5], a traffic measurement tool, which expresses application requirements in a rich query language where ∩, ∪ and \ are used to compose queries from simpler ones. To answer a set of queries, ProgME

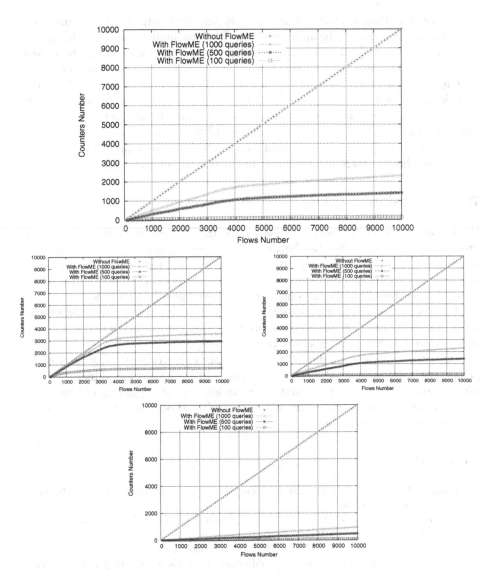

Fig. 2. Number of managed counters for varying query set sizes.

decomposes them into a set of disjoints subqueries, and assigns a counter to each one. In that, it does not rely on predefined flows. While our query answering seemingly only admits conjunctive queries, the very way ground sets of flows emerge from the lattice enables set-theoretic difference to be simulated. Moreover, ProgME's disentangling algorithm has not been proven optimal.

AutoFocus [11] is a tool for offline hierarchical traffic analysis. Like ProgME, it doesn't use predefined flows but rather discovers them. To that end, it mines hierarchies of frequent generalized values for each matchfield and combines them into a global multidimensional structure that pinpoints both the most significant and some deviant flows. The approach boils down to mining frequent generalized patterns on multiple dimensions. In comparison, our lattice contains the *closed* patterns of matchfield values from $\mathcal{F}$ which is a strict subset of all patterns.

Current flow-based monitoring and collection systems like Cisco Netflow, FlowScan [12] and sFlow [13] track all flow statistics continuously at a specific sampling rate. This generates a large number of transactions and a management bandwidth usage proportional to the number of flows, regardless of real application needs. The comparison of FlowME to a flow-based measurement technique (section 5) shows a large improvement in the number of managed flows.

7   Conclusion

We presented an FCA-based solution to the traffic measurement optimization problem which looks after the hardware counters required in order to answer a given set of measurement queries. The underlying mathematical approach amounts to finding a minimal partition of the set flows currently installed in a switch and then assigning a counter to each set from the ppartition.

The main benefits of our approach have been experimentally confirmed within a realistic situation: The results show both a significant reduction in the number of hardware counters and excellent performances.

Our current focus is on dynamic maintenance of the ordered structures composing the solution, i.e., the concept lattice and its projection subsemilattice. We consider various realistic evolution scenarios, e.g., the injection of new flows and/or queries, and examine the adaptation of methods for what is known as incremental lattice construction [14].

References

1. Ganter, B., Wille, R.: Formal Concept Analysis: Mathematical Foundations. Springer-Verlag (1999)
2. Godin, R., Saunders, E., Gecsei, J.: Lattice model of browsable data spaces. Information Sciences **40**(2), 89–116 (1986)
3. Valtchev, P., Missaoui, R., Godin, R.: Formal concept analysis for knowledge discovery and data mining: the new challenges. In: Eklund, P. (ed.) ICFCA 2004. LNCS (LNAI), vol. 2961, pp. 352–371. Springer, Heidelberg (2004)
4. Estan, C., Varghese, G.: New directions in traffic measurement and accounting. SIGCOMM Comput. Commun. Rev. **32**(4), 323–336 (2002)
5. Yuan, L., Chuah, C.-N., Mohapatra, P.: Progme: towards programmable network measurement. IEEE/ACM Trans. Netw. **19**(1), 115–128 (2011)
6. Ghannadian, F., Fang, L., Quinn, M.J.: Adaptive, flow-based network traffic measurement and monitoring system. U.S. Patent US 7639613, 29 December 2009
7. Valtchev, P.: An algorithm for minimal insertion in a type lattice. Computational Intelligence **15**(1), 63–78 (1999)
8. Valtchev, P., Grosser, D., Roume, C. Rouane-Hacene, M.: Galicia: an open platform for lattices. In: Using Conceptual Structures: Contrib. to 11th Intl. Conf. on Conceptual Structures (ICCS 2003), pp. 241–254. Shaker Verlag (2003)

9. Ganegedara, T., Jiang, W., Prasanna, V.: Frug: a benchmark for packet forwarding in future networks. In: Proc. of the 29th IEEE Intl. Perform. Comp. & Comm. Conf. (IPCCC 2010), pp. 231–238, December 2010

10. Mounaouar, O.: Étude stratégique de déploiement de compteurs d'un noeud de communication basée sur des approches de treillis. Master's thesis, Université du Québec à Montréal (2013)

11. Estan, C., Savage, S., Varghese, G.: Automatically inferring patterns of resource consumption in network traffic. In: Proc. of the 2003 Conf. on Appl., Technol., Architect., and Protocols for Comp. Comm. (SIGCOMM 2003), pp. 137–148. ACM, New York (2003)

12. Plonka, D.: Flowscan: a network traffic flow reporting and visualization tool. In: Proc. of the 14th USENIX Conf. on System administration, LISA 2000, pp. 305–318. USENIX Assoc., Berkeley (2000)

13. Phaal, P., Panchen, S., McKee, N.: Inmon corporation's sflow: a method for monitoring traffic in switched and routed networks. In: RFC 3176, Internet Engineering Task Force, September 2001. http://www.ietf.org/rfc/rfc3176.txt

14. Valtchev, P., Rouane-Hacene, M., Missaoui, R.: A generic scheme for the design of efficient on-line algorithms for lattices. In: Lex, W., de Moor, A., Ganter, B. (eds.) ICCS 2003. LNCS, vol. 2746. Springer, Heidelberg (2003)

Research on Fair Use of Digital Content in Social Network

Yingyu Huo[✉], Li Ma, and Yong Zhong

Electronic and Information Engineering School, Foshan University, Foshan, China
fosuhyy@163.com, zhongyong@fosu.edu.cn

Abstract. The convenience of sharing of digital contents in social network makes protection of copyrighted digital content a concerned problem. So many strict methods such as DRM technology are used to protect digital content, which makes enforcement of properly copyright laws difficult in social network such as *fair use*, a general concept denoting the legally protected right of people to use content based on exceptions and limitations of copyright laws. The paper firstly discusses the problem of *fair use* in social network from point of view of laws, rights holders and users of digital content. Then a *fair use* mechanism based on MRuleSN model, a multi-party authorization model for social networks proposed by the author. Finally, an example demonstrates the effects and flexibility of the methods.

Keywords: *Fair use* · Social network · Digital content · Copyright

1   Introduction

The convenience of sharing of digital contents in social network makes protection of copyrighted digital content a concerned problem. So many strict methods such as DRM technology are used to protect digital content. Digital Rights Management (DRM) technology has been promoted as the solution to protecting copyright of digital media. However, current DRM technologies do well in limiting usage of a work, but are basically not good in enforcing properly copyright laws. In most countries, copyright law allows for a number of exceptions that allow users to make use of a work that would otherwise be a violation of copyright. These exceptions are known as *copyright exceptions* in Europe and *fair use* in the USA [1].

Fair use is a difficult problem to implement on a computer. Felten [2] argues that complexity of evaluating *fair use* is a *"AI-hard problems"*. Timothy [3] sums up a number of thoughtful suggestions concerning how best to implement copyright exceptions. And Cheun *et al.* [4] propose a two-part approach that can allow both users to assert new rights contributed to *fair use* and the copyright owners to track the source of possible copyright infringement. We [5] propose a *fair use* mechanism whose

This paper is supported by the National Natural Science Foundation of China under Grant No. 61373015 and 11326123, Science and Technology Foundations of Foshan under Grant No. 2012AA100251, Science Research Project of Foshan University.

S. Zhang et al. (Eds.): KSEM 2015, LNAI 9403, pp. 170–176, 2015.
DOI: 10.1007/978-3-319-25159-2_15

features include rights assertion without limitation, audit logging and misuses trigger, which brings a *fair use* mechanism nearer to offline world.

The paper present a *fair use* mechanism based on MRuleSN model, a multi-party authorization model for social networks proposed by the author, which demonstrates the effects and flexibility of the methods. The methods can get an excellent balance among social network system, right holders and users under copyrights laws.

2   MRuleSN Model

MRuleSN is a multi-party authorization model for social networks, which processes the problem of ownership by single ownership and multi-party shareholders. The model adopts extended w-Datalog rules to express authorization, which owns more powerful flexibility, fine-grained access control and authorization expressiveness.

MRuleSN divides the subjects of a social networks into three parts: users, user groups and system group, which forms a hierarchy as follows.

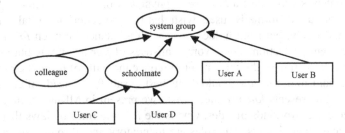

Fig. 1. Hierarchy of users in social network.

In the hierarchy, users can join a user group to become the group member, and all user groups belong to the system group. We stipulate a user group can't belong to another group and all users belong to the system group by default.

Definition 1 (Subject Hierarchy). A subject hierarchy is a 3-tuple $(U, UG \cup SG, \leq)$. Where U is a set of user-ids and G is a set of identifiers of user groups, SG is the set of identifiers of system group. $\leq$ is a partial ordering having following rules:

(1) $\forall u \in U, g \in UG \cup SG, u \leq g \Rightarrow u$ is a member of g.
(2) $\forall u \in U, sg \in SG \Rightarrow u \leq g$.
(3) $\#SG = 1$

The rule 1 shows if u is a member of g then $u \leq g$. The rule 2 shows that all users are members of system group by default. The last rule shows there is only one system group in the system.

[6] proposes a rule-based access control model in terms of the relationship type, depth and trust level existing among users in the network. Our rules adopt extended w-Datalog rules to express authorization as following rule:

$$w_0{:}P \leftarrow w_1{:}L_1, \cdots, w_k{:}L_k, [w_{k+1}{:}L_{k+1}], \cdots, [w_m{:}L_m], L_{m+1}, \cdots, L_n \qquad (1)$$

where p is an atom and $L_i(1 \leq i \leq n)$ is a literal, $w_i(0 \leq i \leq m)$ is a weight which is a real number greater than zero. [] means the literal is optional.

A w-Datalog rule is an extended Datalog rule that adds weights to head and some literals of Datalog rules. We need $\sum_{i=1}^{k} w_i + [\sum_{i=k+1}^{m} w_i] \geq w_0$ when evaluates a w-Datalog rule except the evaluation of a normal Datalog rule. If the literals in [] aren't true which can't influence if the rule is true like standard datalog rule. But if the literals in [] are true they contribute their weights to the evaluation of rules.

3   Fair Use in MRuleSN Model

Fair use indicates the exceptions that allow the rights to use a copyrighted work without a license. We consider there are three aspects to apply the *fair use*. From point of laws, some situations for *fair use* can be necessary and mandatory for right holders such as criticism, comment, news reporting, and teaching. From point of users, the digital content should have a *fair use* as physical world such as lending to a friend or some private uses. Normally, users wish that the protection of digital content is more loosely and freely, but right holders may wish a balance between *fair use* rights and digital content protection. They worry   misuses of *fair use* rights but also worry too restrictive protection of digital content to reduce the wills of using their products, So a good mechanism of *fair use* should do its best to satisfy the needs of all three parties.

Figure 2 represents *fair use* mechanism we present in MRuleSN model. In system level, there are two kinds of rules. One is the *fair use* rules by laws that are the parts of clear and unambiguous. The rules are mandatory and all other *fair use* rules must obey the rules if there are conflicts among them. So we set the rules for system group that has a global effect in the system. Except the rules by law, the system maybe has some specific *fair use* rules that are negotiated by system、 right holders and users to balance their relations, which consider the balance of rights protection and ease of use.

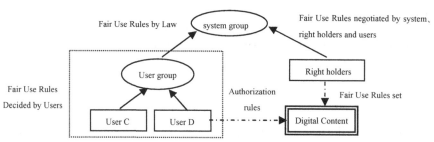

Fig. 2. Hierarchy of users in social network

To right holders, they maybe have some more restrictions on *fair use* of the content so they can set some special rules on the content. To users or user groups, they maybe have some their own judgments about their *fair use* rights so they can set the *fair use* rules themselves. And the right holders and users all are inclined to expand their rights so the system must have some mechanisms to adjust their tendency so that a reasonable authorization can be achieved.

So a good *fair use* authorization rule is similar to some voting mechanisms, the *fair use* rules by law have the mandatory preemptive rights, the *fair use* rules in system level are negotiated by system, right holders and users, which also decide the voting mechanism and authorization decision. *Fair use* rules decided by users means users can assert their *fair use* rights without limitation. To prevent misusing the rights, an audit logging and warning mechanism must be included in the mechanism. As shown in figure 3, the authorization rule should be a rule similar to the following rule:

$$cando(s,\ o,\ p) \leftarrow AuthbyLaw(s,\ o,\ p) \tag{2}$$

$$cando(s, o, p) \leftarrow l: Authbyuser(s, o, p), [m: Authbyuser(s, o, p)], [n\ Authbyowner(s, o, p)] \tag{3}$$

The rule (2) says the users can do their jobs authorized by laws. The rule (3) specifies authorization by system is necessary and also some authorizations from right holders or uses themselves may be needed to acquire enough weights to do their jobs.

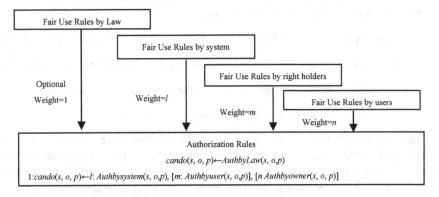

Fig. 3. Authorization Mechanism in Social Network for *fair use*.

4   Implementation and Example

In our previous research, we have realized the evaluation of w-Datalog rules and implementation of MRuleSN Model. Here we only show how to implement the *fair use* mechanism. We assumes there are two user groups in our social network. One is the education group consisted of the students and teachers in a non-profitable school. Another is the training group which is a profitable business training group. David is the teacher of the education group and also a part-time teacher of training group. "*Physical World*" is a digital content David has buy from content provider.

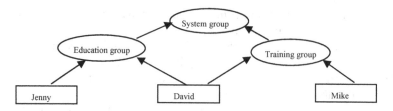

Fig. 4. Authorization Mechanism in Social Network for *fair use*.

Firstly, we have the following rules by laws:

$$AuthbyLaw(s_1,s_2, o, p) \leftarrow own(s_1,o), purpose(s_1,s_2, o, p, \text{"teaching"}) \quad (4)$$

$$AuthbyLaw (s_1,s_2, o, excerpt) \leftarrow own(s_1, o), purpose(s_1,s_2, o, excerpt, \text{"news reporting"}) \quad (5)$$

The rule (4) explains that if s_1 owns a digital content and for the purpose of teaching, s_1 can give the right to s_2. The rule (5) shows that if s_1 owns a digital content and for the purpose of news reporting, s_1 can grant s_2 to excerpt the content.

Secondly, *fair use* rules by system as follows:

$$purpose(s_1,s_2, o, p, \text{"teaching"}) \leftarrow member(s_1,g), member(s_2,g), type(g, \text{"education"}) \quad (6)$$

$$purpose(s_1,s_2, o, p, \text{"training"}) \leftarrow member(s_1,g), member(s_2,g), type(g, \text{"training"}) \quad (7)$$

$$AuthbySystem(s_1,s_2, o, p) \leftarrow own(s_1,o), purpose(s_1, s_2, o, p, \text{"training"}) \quad (8)$$

$$AuthbySystem(s_1,s_2, o, copy) \leftarrow friend(s_1, s_2) \quad (9)$$

The rule (6) explains concretely what is the purpose of teaching in the system, which is if s_1 and s_2 belong to the same group and the type of the group is *"education"*. The same method the rule (7) explains concretely what is the purpose of training. The rule (8) shows that if the purpose is train the system also allow s_1 gives the right to s_2. The rule (9) shows if s_1 has a direct friend relation with s_2 then s_1 can give a copy to s_2.

Thirdly, we has the following rules set by right holder of *"Physical World"*

$$Authbyowner(s_1, s_2, \text{"physical world"}, excerpt) \leftarrow own(s_1, \text{"physical world"}), AuthbyLaw$$
$$(s_1, s_2, o, excerpt), sendmessage(\text{SYSTEM}, s_2, \text{"physical world"}, \text{"excerpt"}) \quad (10)$$

$$Authbyowner(s_1, s_2, \text{"physical world"}, copy) \leftarrow AuthbySystem(s_1, s_2, \text{"physical world"}, copy),$$
$$DeleteObject(s_1, \text{"physical world"}) \quad (11)$$

The rule (10) shows the right holder of *"Physical World"* wish a message can be sent to system if someone wants to excerpt the content. The rule (11) shows if s_1 sends a copy of *"physical world"* to s_2 and the authorization comes from system then the copy of s_1 must be deleted. That is, only one copy of the digital content can be existed among s_1 and his friends.

Fourthly, the authorization rules are as follows:

$$cando(s_2, o, p) \leftarrow AuthbyLaw(s_1,s_2, o, p) \quad (12)$$

$$1{:}cando(s, o, p) \leftarrow 0.5{:}\ Authbysystem(s, o,p),\ [0.4{:}\ Authbyuser(s, o,p)],\ [0.6\ Authbyowner(s, o, p)] \tag{13}$$

$$cando(s, o, excerpt) \leftarrow Assert(s, o, excerpt),\ sendmessage(\text{SYSTEM},\ s, o,\ \text{"}excerpt\text{"}) \tag{14}$$

The rule (12) shows if permmitted by laws, the authorization is permmitted. The rule (13) shows the weight proportion of three parties in deciding the authorization, which means if permitted by sytem and right holders or by users and right holders or by three parties together, the authorization is true. And authorization by system is necessary, the others are optional. The rule (14) shows if the users assert his *excerpt* right, then he can get the authorization with a message sent to system.

Lastly, we consider how David executes his *fair use* rights. David has the following methods to execute their *fair use* rights:

(1) Rights given by laws. For example, if David want to copy his "*Physical World*" digital book to Jenny for a class, then Jenny needs an authorization *cando(jenny,* "*Physical World*", *copy)*, which can be acquired from rule (12), (4) and (6).

(2) Rights negotiated among system, right holders and users. For example, if David want to copy his "*Physical World*" digital book to Mike, then Mike needs an authorization *cando(Mike,* "*Physical World*", *copy)*. From rule (13) we know Mike needs an accumulation of weight greater and equal 1. Then from rule (8) we know Mike can acquires system authorization with a weight 0.5, and from rule (11) we know Mike can acquire authorization of right holders with a weight 0.6, which make Mike acquire his authorization with the cost from rule (11) that David loses his authorization on "*Physical World*".

(3) Rights asserted by the users. If David want to excerpt his "*Physical World*" for some purposes of comments. He thinks it is his *fair use* right, but he can't acquire authorization from existing rules. From rule (14), he can simply assert the right and executes it by his own way, and the tradeoff is the assertion and some of information of his will be sent to system.

In our *fair use* mechanism, the social network system play an important third party role, which is in the neutral position of deciding authorization of *fair use* of copyrighted works and may be a government-operated licensing authority according to Timothy [3]. In the example of David asserting his *excerpt* rights, the right holders can't limit the *fair use* rights assertion of users directly, but they can set some notices from the third party authority if the users have some misuses matching the rules.

5   Conclusions

Fair use allows "unauthorized but not illegal" actions, which brings a difficult problem to implement on a computer. In this paper we have proposed a *fair use* mechanism in social network which combines social network system, right holders and users under copyrights laws. The methods can get an excellent balance among the three parties.

References

1. Arnab, A., Hutchison, A.: Fairer usage contracts for DRM. In: Proc. of the Fifth ACM Workshop on Digital Rights Management, Alexandria, VA, pp. 1–7 (2005)
2. Felten, E.: Skeptical view of DRM and Fair Use. Communications of the ACM **46**(4), 57–59 (2003)
3. Timothy, K.A.: Digital Rights Management and the Process of Fair Use. Harvard Journal of Law & Technology **20**(1), 49–122 (2006)
4. Chong, C.N., Etalle, D.S., et al.: Approximating fair use in licensescript. In: 6th Int. Conf. of Asian Digital Libraries, Kuala Lumpur, Malaysia, pp. 432–443 (2003)
5. Zhong, Y., Zhen, Z., Lin, D.-m., Qin, X.-L.: A method of fair use in digital rights management. In: Goh, D.H.-L., Cao, T.H., Sølvberg, I.T., Rasmussen, E. (eds.) ICADL 2007. LNCS, vol. 4822, pp. 160–164. Springer, Heidelberg (2007)
6. Carminati, B., Ferrari, E., Perego, A.: Rule-based access control for social networks. In: Meersman, R., Tari, Z., Herrero, P. (eds.) OTM 2006 Workshops. LNCS, vol. 4278, pp. 1734–1744. Springer, Heidelberg (2006)

Preserving Multi-view Consistency
in Diagrammatic Knowledge Representation

Dominik Bork[1(✉)], Robert Buchmann[2], and Dimitris Karagiannis[1]

[1] Faculty of Computer Science, University of Vienna, Vienna, Austria
dominik.bork@univie.ac.at, dk@dke.univie.ac.at
[2] Faculty of Economic Sciences and Business Administration,
Babes Bolyai University, Cluj-Napoca, Romania
robert.buchmann@econ.ubbcluj.ro

Abstract. Multi-view conceptual modeling provides means for representing, with diagrammatic means, the knowledge describing a "system under study" whose complexity cannot be captured in a single comprehensible representation. Typical examples are available in the field of enterprise modeling, where models are inherently layered or partitioned, a feature that must be enabled at meta-modeling level by means of abstraction and decomposition. Multi-view modeling must provide means for coping with the complexity of enterprise knowledge representations through consistency preservation techniques across multiple, interrelated views. The paper at hand formulates the conceptual functions fulfilled by multi-view modeling and provides a demonstrative implementation in the context of the Semantic Object Model enterprise modeling method.

Keywords: Multi-view modeling · Diagrammatic knowledge representation · Metamodeling

1   Introduction

Diagrammatic conceptual models *as means of knowledge representation* emerged at the intersection of *knowledge management* (seen as a specialization of intangible asset management) and *knowledge engineering* (seen as a specialization of artificial intelligence). They can be involved in the typical scenarios and stages addressed by the knowledge science, as identified by [1] (e.g., process mining/discovery, reasoning, organizational knowledge creation). One particular concern that distinguishes diagrammatic modeling from non-visual knowledge representation is a decomposition requirement, and a particular answer to this is **multi-view modeling**, where different types of models represent different facets of the same system. Their **consistency** must be preserved due to existing structural or semantic dependencies. Depending on the application domain, various meanings for the "view" and "multi-view modeling" notions are implied (cf. [2] for an overview). In the following, **multi-view modeling methods** are considered a specialized instantiation of the generic modeling method definition introduced by Karagiannis and Kühn [3]. **Conceptual viewpoints** may be conceived by defining metamodel partitions with different conceptual coverage,

S. Zhang et al. (Eds.): KSEM 2015, LNAI 9403, pp. 177–182, 2015.
DOI: 10.1007/978-3-319-25159-2_16

having structural or semantic dependencies between their concepts. We hereby reduce their consistency preservation strategies to two techniques defined on an conceptual level - **state translation** and **transition translation** – then we illustrate the two techniques by implementing them for the **Semantic Object Model (SOM)** enterprise modeling method [4]. The proof-of-concept modeling tool is hosted by the Open Model Initiative Laboratory[1] (OMiLAB) [5].

The remainder of the paper is structured as follows: Section 2 states the research challenges and discusses related works. In Section 3, the two proposed techniques are formulated as abstract patterns on a metamodeling level. These are instantiated in a modelling tool [6] implemented for an illustrative project-based case in Section 4. Conclusions are drawn in Section 5.

2   Research Challenges and Related Works

The work started its investigation from trying to understand the rationale for which views are necessary in enterprise modeling (addressed by Section 1). Further on, we faced the following challenges when engineering new modeling methods and developing modeling tools for concrete cases: *RC1. What techniques are necessary on metamodeling level to preserve consistency in multi-view diagrammatic knowledge representation? RC2. How can these techniques be instantiated for concrete cases of enterprise view representation?*

While the multi-view concept is not an innovation in itself, in the existing literature it has been employed as means of facilitating separation of concerns in the contexts of enterprise architecture frameworks or software engineering. Standards such as ISO/IEC/IEEE 42010:2011 prescribe software architecture design methodologies that acknowledge the need for viewpoint specifications. Software engineering typically deals with a three-layered schema (physical, conceptual, external according to ANSI/X3/SPARC [7]) or a four-view schema (development, process, physical, logical, according to the 4+1 model [8]).

[9] investigates four domain-specific modeling language tools supporting view-based modeling from an industrial background and builds a taxonomy for view-based domain-specific modeling. However, the authors focus on the specification of the views and not on the consistent utilization of multi-view modeling. [10] developed multi-view modeling principles for the SOM method, contrasting diagram-oriented and system-oriented approaches. Recently, [11] characterized a set of multi-view modeling approaches in the context of embedded and cyber-physical systems. The work of [12] provides a multi-view method without considering consistency preservation strategies at metamodeling level, while [13] integrates views weakly by means of annotative semantic relations.

None of the identified approaches discusses multi-view modeling on a generic level taking into account not only the origin of the viewpoints – the decomposition requirement – but also the processing of the multiple views by means of modeling operations and the inconsistencies raised by their execution.

---

[1] OMiLAB SOM project page, http://www.omilab.org/web/som, last checked: 23.07.15

3   Preserving Consistency in Multi-view Models

Knowledge representation traditionally deals with rule processing, either in the form of **domain-specific heuristics** or in the form of **deductive/production rules**. The aim is to generate explicit representations of implicit knowledge or to check consistency of integrated representations. We transfer this desideratum to diagrammatic conceptual modeling and distinguish two consistency preservation techniques. Thus we also narrow down the generic multi-view modeling framework of [14] into:

- The viewpoint **(VP$_j$, VP$_k$)** is the metamodel part covered by a type of model. It contains only those concepts from the holistic enterprise metamodel which are relevant to the viewpoint according to the decomposition requirement;
- the view **(v$_1$, v$_2$, ...)** is the model, thus an instance of a viewpoint;
- the instance function **(μ(Viewpoint, state))** relates a state of the system under study to a view, also considering the viewpoint as a schema, hence delimiting the modeling constructs based on the viewpoint specification and the knowledge base describing the state to be modeled;
- the operation **Op()** alters the content of a model (v), shifting it in another state (v`);
- the consistency preserving function **T()**, which can be instantiated to **state translation (T$_S$)** and **transition translation (T$_T$)**.

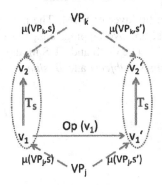

Fig. 1. T$_S$ for *Views-by-generation*

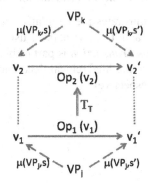

Fig. 2. T$_T$ for *Views-by-design*

In the **views-by-generation** approach, **state translations (T$_S$)** specify the transformation of a complete view v$_1$ (reflecting a system state from viewpoint VP$_j$) into a new view v$_2$ (reflecting the same system state from a different viewpoint VP$_k$). At the time the transformation terminates, consistency must be ensured by the translation specification. Whenever the view v$_1$ is altered by applying some editing operation Op(), the state translation must be executed again on the output (v$_1$') to generate a new consistent view (v$_2$'). Hence, consistency preservation is decoupled from the editing operation Op(). On the metamodeling level, state translations typically have an algorithmic or formal rule-based implementation, triggered manually by the modeler.

In the **views-by-design** approach, **transition translations (T_T)** specify the transformation of the effects of a modeling operation Op_1, applied to v_1, into a semantically equivalent operation Op_2 that needs to be applied to v_2. Thus, transition translations integrate the multiple views in a dynamic manner.

4   Preserving Consistency in the SOM Modeling Method

The SOM method [4] enables integrated modeling of enterprises by combining three layers. Each layer is further decomposed into multiple viewpoints. On the first layer, the **enterprise plan layer** is specified using the viewpoints **object system** and **target system**; hereby taking an external perspective on the enterprise. At the central layer, the **business process layer**, business processes (bp) are described from an internal perspective composing four viewpoints: **Interaction Schema (IAS)**, **Task-Event Schema (TES)**, **Object Decomposition Schema (ODS)**, and **Transaction Decomposition Schema (TDS)**. The **business application system layer** specifies the resources from an internal perspective composing the viewpoints: **Schema of Task Classes (TAS)** and **Schema of Conceptual Classes (COS)**. On each layer different multi-view modeling approaches are utilized as discussed in the following.

4.1   Transition Translations for SOM Views-by-Design Modeling

Fig. 3 illustrates the integrated metamodel of the bp layer of SOM. The metamodels of IAS and TES, visualized using dashed boxes, are overlapping, e.g., the concept *Business Transaction* is part of both, IAS and TES. The ODS and TDS models solely visualize the hierarchical decompositions of *Business Objects* and *Business Transactions*, respectively.

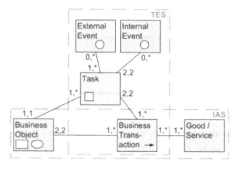

Fig. 3. Views-by-design in SOM modeling [4]

SOM also specifies the initial business process model the modeler interacts with simultaneously, following the views-by-design approach. SOM defines modeling operations a modeler applies in order to refine the initial model. These rules are specified formally [15] using the modeling constructs of the integrated metamodel. The effects of applying a modeling operation to one view are immediately transformed into semantically equivalent changes to all other affected views (i.e., transition translations). Changing the name of a business transaction in e.g., the TDS would immediately cause corresponding changes of the names of the dependent business transactions in the IAS and TES viewpoints.

4.2   State Translations for SOM Views-by-Generation Modeling

SOM utilizes a top down approach. Hence, modelers should start with the enterprise plan, then define the bp models, and finally specify the business application systems. Considering adjoining layers, state translations are utilized for views-by-generation modeling. Initial TAS and COS are generated using state translations, realized using metamodel-based model transformations. Whenever TAS and COS are generated, consistent is given. Changes to the derived TAS and COS are not considered in the business process layer, i.e., no transition translations are specified.

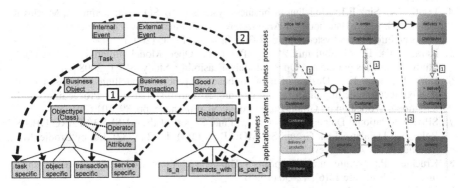

Fig. 4. Views-by-generation in in SOM modeling

Fig. 4 illustrates the specification for the state translations (on the left side) and exemplarily their application (on the right side) in the implemented SOM tool [6]. Generally, the transformations are based on a comprehensive SOM bp model consisting of four views. Due to limited space, the state translation between bp views and the COS view is exemplified. *Business Transactions* of the bp are transformed into *transaction-specific Objecttypes* in the COS (rule 1). Rule 2 transforms *internal events* into corresponding *interacts_with* relationships, connecting the transformed *transaction-specific Objecttypes* in order to preserve the process behaviour.

5   Conclusions and Future Work

The paper at hand introduced two consistency preservation techniques for multi-view knowledge representation through diagrammatic models – state translation and transition translation. The techniques were *evaluated through instantiation* in the SOM modeling tool which is regularly used for experimentation and didactic purposes at three universities. Future work focuses on a) the further application of the hereby introduced techniques for implementing an extensive corpus of established enterprise modeling methods; b) the integration of the presented techniques into MUVIEMOT, a conceptual modeling method for multi-view modeling tools [16]; c) the identification of multi-view requirements that cannot be supported with the presented techniques.

References

1. Nakamori, Y.: A perspective of knowledge science. In: Xiong, H., Lee, W.B. (eds.) KSEM 2011. LNCS, vol. 7091, pp. 171–182. Springer, Heidelberg (2011)
2. Kheir, A., Naja, H., Oussalah, M.C., Tout, K.: Overview of an approach describing multi-views/multi-abstraction levels software architecture. In: Maciaszek, L., Filipe, J. (eds.) Evaluation of Novel Approaches to Software Engineering, pp. 140–148 (2013)
3. Karagiannis, D., Kühn, H.: Metamodelling platforms. In: Bauknecht, K., Tjoa, A.M., Quirchmayr, G. (eds.) EC-Web 2002. LNCS, vol. 2455, p. 182. Springer, Heidelberg (2002)
4. Ferstl O.K., Sinz E.J.: Modeling of business systems using SOM. In: Bernus P., Mertins K., Schmidt G. (eds.) Handbook on Architectures of Information Systems. International Handbooks on Information Systems, pp. 347–367. Springer, Berlin (2005)
5. Karagiannis, D., Grossmann, W., Hoefferer, P.: Open Model Initiative: A Feasilbility Study. http://files.omilab.org/Open_Models_Feasibility_Study_SEPT_2008.pdf
6. Bork, D., Sinz, E.J.: Design of a SOM business process modelling tool based on the ADOxx meta-modelling platform. In: de Lara, J., Varro, D. (eds.) Pre-Proceedings 4th International Workshop on Graph-Based Tools, NL-Enschede, pp. 89–101 (2010)
7. SPARC Relational Database Task Group: Final Report of the ANSI/X3/SPARC DBS-SG Relational Database Task Group. SIGMOD Rec. **12**(4), 1–62 (1982). Ed. by Brodie, M.L., Schmidt, J.W.: ACM, New York
8. Kruchten, P.: Architectural Blueprints - The "4 + 1" View Model of Software Architecture. IEEE Software **12**(6), 42–50 (1995)
9. Goldschmidt, T., Becker, S., Burger, E.: Towards a tool-oriented taxonomy of view-based modelling. In: Proceedings Modellierung 2012, Bamberg, pp. 59–74 (2012)
10. Bork, D., Sinz, E.J.: Bridging the Gap from a Multi-View Modelling Method to the Design of a Multi-View Modelling Tool. Enterprise Modelling and Information Systems Architectures **8**(2), 25–41 (2013)
11. Persson, M., Törngren, M., Qamar, A., Westman, J., Biehl, M., Tripakis, S., Vangheluwe, H., Denil, J.: A characterization of integrated multi-view modeling in the context of embedded and cyber-physical systems. In: Proceedings of the International Conference on Embedded Software, pp. 1–10 (2013)
12. Masuda, H., Utz, W., Hara, Y.: Development of an evaluation approach for customer service interaction models. In: Buchmann, R., Kifor, C.V., Yu, J. (eds.) KSEM 2014. LNCS, vol. 8793, pp. 150–161. Springer, Heidelberg (2014)
13. Fill, H.-G.: On the social network based semantic annotation of conceptual models. In: Buchmann, R., Kifor, C.V., Yu, J. (eds.) KSEM 2014. LNCS, vol. 8793, pp. 138–149. Springer, Heidelberg (2014)
14. Bork, D., Karagiannis, D.: Model-driven development of multi-view modelling methods: the MuVieMoT approach. In: Holzinger, Cardoso, Cordeiro, van Sinderen, Mellor (eds.) International Conference on Software Paradigm Trends, pp. 11–23 (2014)
15. Bork, D., Fill, H.-G.: Formal aspects of enterprise modeling methods: a comparison framework. In: Hawaii International Conference on System Sciences, pp. 3400–3409 (2014)
16. Bork, D.: Using conceptual modeling for designing multi-view modeling tools. In: 21st Americas Conference on Information Systems (AMCIS) (2015)

The Impact of Big Data and Knowledge Management on R&D Projects from Automotive Industry

Horaţiu Constantin Palade[1,2(✉)], Sergiu Ştefan Nicolaescu[1,2(✉)], and Claudiu Vasile Kifor[1]

[1] "Lucian Blaga" University of Sibiu, Sibiu, Romania
claudiu.kifor@ulbsibiu.ro
[2] Continental Automotive Systems S.R.L., Sibiu, Romania
Horatiu.2.palade@continental-corporation.com,
sergiu.nicolaescu@ulbsibiu.ro

Abstract. The automotive industry is becoming increasingly innovative, generating data of massive dimensions during development. The paper analyzes the impact of Big Data on the automotive industry and presents a detailed study on the current and future contribution that Big Data has on the performance of organizations. As an original solution, the paper analyses the mapping of Knowledge Management and Big Data in R&D projects from Automotive Industry.

Main contributions of the research are the creation and study of a model comprising the activities that should be performed inside an automotive organization for Big Data projects. The paper presents an applicative mathematical paradigm for pilot projects in order to have a positive ROI (Return of Interest) and enhance their success rate. The methodologies used during research were bibliographic research, mathematical modeling, interviews and an observational study in a top-tier automotive organization.

Keywords: Big data model · Knowledge management · Automotive industry · Pilot projects

1 Introduction

Information, data and knowledge are all gathered to produce wisdom, this being the main objective in organizations of all kind; by having more data inputs, storage, and computing resources than ever [1], Big Data becomes a defining feature of the world around us. The key characteristic of BD *("BIG DATA" will be referred on this paper as simply BD)* is the exponential grow of created data that must be collected, structured and stored. Because currently 90% of existing data was created in the last years [2] and it is continuously growing, it is harder and harder for people to extract the relevant information's for their work or personal activities.

The growth rate of information in the world is reaching new heights in every domain: in 2013, according to the EMC/IDC Digital Universe Studies there were about 4 zettabytes (a zettabyte is 10 power 21 bytes or a billion terabytes) of stored information in the whole world and this amount is doubling every two years [3].

© Springer International Publishing Switzerland 2015
S. Zhang et al. (Eds.): KSEM 2015, LNAI 9403, pp. 183–189, 2015.
DOI: 10.1007/978-3-319-25159-2_17

By 2016, global Internet traffic is expected to reach a massive increase by 1.3 zetta-bytes annually (according to a report by Cisco [4]), approximately the equivalent of 10.000 DVDs per second. The size of data, its variety and the generating rate are increasing in other fields as well: astronomers expect to be delivering up to an exabyte (a exabyte is 10 power 18 bytes or a million terabytes) a day of raw data [5] (that is 2.800 DVDs per second) from the Square Kilometer Array (SKA). Biology adds value and veracity to the needed attributes when decoding the human genome and trying to replicate the DNA storing capacity [6]; scientist estimate that one gram of DNA can (theoretically) hold 455 exabytes (that is 3500 DVD pers second !).

The result of this paper is intended to provide an overview regarding the impact and risk that Big Data is having on the business and activities of organisations and can be used by management or workers in the R&D centers of automotive industry.

2   Big Data and KM Research - Interest and Results

Google was one of the firsts to realize the potential of Big Data and apply it in real world situation for identifying flu outbreaks based on USA citizen search terms regarding flu symptoms. Initially the reports showed an accurate presumption rate (better than that of the CDC- Centers for Disease Control and Prevention) but later this attempt on Big Data mining subject led to the controversial *Google Flu Trends* failure: "large errors in flu prediction were largely avoidable, which offers lessons for the use of big data"[7].

Nevertheless there are also recent appraisal stories concerning big data impact, as this one involving Twitter and pooling on American Elections, where the model proved to be a success and of a real use in future prediction on USA Presidency winners based on number of tweeted messages concerning them [8].

It has been observed a clear fall of interest (scholar one alike) in the field of Knowledge Management, after its popularity spike started in the 90', mostly because of setbacks in practical implementation inside companies; but there were also other reasons accounted for

Fig. 1. Interest over Big Data vs. Knowledge Management

that, like : lack of performance indicators, inadequate management support, problems with organizational culture improper budgeting [9], these are to be considered key points for assuring the success of implementing Big Data initiatives and evading the down road of previous endeavors.

Google Trends analyzes a percentage of Google web searches to determine how many searches have been done for the terms you've entered compared to the total number of Google searches done during that time. Figure 1 is a graphical representation of the relative popularity of "knowledge management" and "big data" as a search term from 2004 to present by Google Trends™ [10], and not intended as an academic impact survey.

Following a recent IDG Enterprise survey [11] of 1,139 IT decision makers, the *interest in BD inside organizations continues its steady rise.* More than half (53%) of respondents are currently implementing or intend to implement Big Data-driven projects within their organizations in the next year (this being a 6% increase from 2014) and a further 8% of companies are considering starting their own programs in the near future.

3   An Approach on Handling BD and KM in Automotive Industry

Big data is one of the key points and opportunities for automotive industry (OEMs suppliers, automakers and aftermarkets sellers alike) regarding information technology solutions, according to a new Center for Automotive Research study released recently [12]. In the automotive industry, that ranges from your vehicle's driving data to analyzing how efficient an assembly line worker's movements are when assembling a vehicle.

For a BD project to become a success, a steady flow of revenue has to be considered from the start, proving the usefulness of the concept and acquiring *Management support.* Furthermore, *IT collaboration* is needed on every step in order to fulfill the continuous integration of the current project inside the organization workflow.

A suggested *flow in automotive industry to implement Big Data programs* is presented here. Data, from Big Data as itself, can become a new revenue streams for 3rd parties and partners based on monetizing

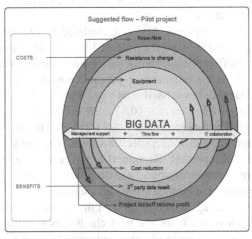

Fig. 2. Flow for Big Data projects in automotive industry

the analysis of vehicle data, with respecting all the concerns regarding privacy and the ethics altogether, and giving value to *Knowledge Management.* When referring of the sensors that are in the car cockpit or the infotainment system, these could track what genre of music or cigarettes a driver use and then suggest real-time targeted ads for the band newest album or such.

The model proposed describes the life-cycle of an automotive project, with a normal duration of 3-5 years and introduces a new KPI for acquiring *Management support*: ROI,

Return of Interest metric, a mathematic estimation of the time when a Big Data Initiative will turn profitable and prove its utility, taking in consideration the factors described below. The proposed model can be modularized and particularized by adding another layer and thus extending it. The circles represent the time flow until project kickoff and a proven successful investment, with the identified modeled costs and benefits:

$$Costs(t) = \frac{KH*[E(t)+RC(t)]}{CR(t)}, t \in (0,7)$$ (1)

$$Benefits(t) = DR(t) + PK(t), t \in (0,7)$$ (2)

$$\boldsymbol{ROI(t) = f\big(B(t) + C(t)\big)}$$ (3)

Where t is time of the project, a normal medium-based automotive project with BD technology applied can take up to 3-4 years. In this model a larger limit was set in order to apply the function to specific customer projects: short carry-overs or complex long term.

- KH is Know-How (*Knowledge Management*) needed to start the project modeled as $KC = -K$; a constant that will become a descending line variable ($y = a * x + b$) on future projects that slowly approaches 0 as the technology is fully grasped; KH directly influences the other two costs, being the most important aspect, and the one that will be carried over to the future projects, influencing both the personal and material factor.
- E is Equipment/ Material, modeled as a linear amortization $E(t) = \varepsilon * t - Pd$ (proportional set with the product lifecycle immobilization) with ε the amortization factor for different equipments, defined in catalogues and Pd the estimated Project Duration.
- RC is the organization/people Resistance to Change; expressed as $RC(t) = IR * \sin(t * FF - \pi), t \in (0,6)$ $IR \in (1,10)$ – initial resistance and $FF \in (1,2)$ – flexibility factor, organization specific values. The sinus model represent the natural initial resistance, until some profit/benefit is discovered, slowly passing the neutral stance and starting to be-

come an agent of change until the current project is finish and then slowly descending again below 0 for the next challenges (similar trajectory as the normal seven years market life cycle of a new automobile, until a change is needed to preserve customer interest). Its top point is attained when the real benefits appear, at the end of the project, at 4.4 years in our plotted example. Plot[3 * Sin[1.1 * x- π], {x,0,5}].
- CR is Cost Reduction applied to all previous costs, modeled as a compressing factor as $CR(t) = \frac{Pd}{Pd-Rc}, Pd > Rc$ and can be considered the "*continuous improvement factor*"; where Rc is the reduced costs and is always lower than the current Pd value; for example in the third year there can't be more than two reduced costs, with the goal for Rc to approach Pd as much as possible, and making all the costs 0 at the limit of Rc.

Detailed *costs* expression: $C(t) = -ct \, \frac{[\varepsilon * t - Pd + IR * \sin(t * FF - \pi)]}{Pd/(Pd - Rc)}, t \in (0,7)$ (4)

- *DR* is Data Resell to other organizations, modeled as $DR(t) = \text{Max}\left(t - \frac{Pd}{PCt}, t \in \right.$

$\left(\frac{Pd}{PCt}, Pd\right); 0, \ t < \frac{Pd}{PCt} \ or \ t > Pd\right)$ and represented by an increasing slope only after the
project has proven concept (ex: after a quarter
duration has passed) and finishing soon after the
project ended; legal limitations to selling data to
3rd party after the project ended are implied here
as well. PCt- project specific constant, defines

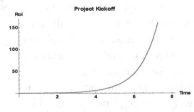

the time from which structured BD starts to prove useful to other organizations. 3rd
party data revenue stream inflexion point generally coincides with RC inflexion point
on the time scale, because when a stream of benefits starts, the personal perception
towards the project shifts on an optimistic side. On future projects when the Know
How constant will become a variable, it will also influence the DR starting point to
generate revenue, moving it earlier.

- *PK* is the final Project Kickoff, delivery, mass production and sale inflow start to
roll up, modeled as $PK(t) = e^{(t - \frac{Pd}{De})}$ where Pd is project duration, $De \in (0, Pd)$ normal delay factor, calculated considering all the time buffers taken through various
stages of the project in order to obtain the KPI of "No delay to final customer".
Plot$[e^{-2.2 + t}, \{t, 0, 8\}]$.

Transforming the detailed *Benefits* expression:

$$B(t) = e^{(t - \frac{Pd}{De})} + Max\left(t - \frac{Pd}{PCt}, t \in \left(\frac{Pd}{PCt}, Pd\right); 0, t < \frac{Pd}{PCt} \ or \ t > Pd\right), t \in (0,7) \quad (5)$$

The Return of Interest (ROI) is a time based function which will be represented as
the benefits minus the costs and taking into consideration the unknown risks and external technological factors. ROI will become slowly positive after *P*, inflexion point
(defined at t=0), but the main stream of revenue will be seen at the end of the pilot
project due to the exponential model of the main benefit; in this way, one project will
fund and accompany the next one. $ROI(t) = \left(B(t) + C(t) - \frac{R}{Rm}\right) * \tau$ (6)

- *R*, unexpected factor - risks in development stage; *Rm* - needed Risk Management
effort.
- τ is the outside, external, technological advance (considering the start of the project
as a milestone) that can disrupt the projected expected margin; a value of 1 meaning
that other organizations haven't accomplished any breakthroughs since the start of the
pilot project.

Now, by replacing -4- and -5- into -3- we obtain the *final complex* ROI function.

$$\mathbf{ROI(t)} = \left(e^{(t - \frac{Pd}{De})} + t - \frac{Pd}{PCt} - K \, \frac{[\varepsilon * t - Pd + IR * \sin(t * FF - \pi)]}{\frac{Pd}{Pd - Rc}} - \frac{R}{Rm}\right) * \tau \quad (7)$$

Example: A standard expected ROI for a 5 year projects with the factors as follow:
De=2.27, Pct=2, ε=3, K=5, IR=2, FF=1.5, Rc=4, R=14, Rm=4, τ=1; Result plotted

with *Wolfram Mathematica*™ Plot[$e^{-2.2+x} - 2*x - 1 - 2*\text{Sin}[1.5*x - \pi]$] $\{x, 0,6\}$].

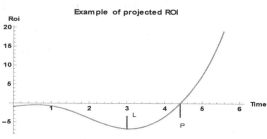

Example of projected ROI

The L point on the graph represents the lower bound of the ROI; from there, all cost elements (personal, material and knowledge) start to decrease until the calculated P inflexion point, where the project is already turning profitable. The project is generating positive ROI after 4.4 years from a total of 5, whereas traditional models generally accomplish this only after the final stages of development, when the project has successfully ended and the sales operation begins.

The mathematical model can be future improved by changing it to an integrative, economic approach using $\int f(ROI) dt$ for better refining the final outcome as the sum of all the previous ROI stages; from point based to continuous calculation.

It's important to start thinking about data as an asset, rather than as a cost, organizations would have to spend some initial money to develop on the long term, and this is always the fearsome part without solid ROI projection at the beginning. We consider that pilot projects, following a solid proof of concept for the high-end managers, will help create a clear road map for any Big Data initiative and weigh heavily on its success by adding real business value.

4   Conclusion and Further Applicable Work

The result of the research is a model that can be deployed into R&D centers of automotive organizations, especially on BD pilot project that enhance the success rate. The return of investment is calculated, being proved that will be a positive one, through a metric that can be simulated and presented to higher management for a starting decision.

For further research it is intended to implement the model into a R&D BD project and also to analyze the BD approach for another important field from automotive industry, the interconnected cars. The old Renaissance desideratum where "one can gather all the knowledge" might come in our grasp sooner than expected thanks to the exponential growth and expenditure of Big Data.

References

1. Kosciejew, M.: The Era of Big Data. Feliciter **59**(4), 52–55 (2013)
2. SINTEF ScienceDaily: Big Data, for better or worse: 90% of world's data generated over last two years, May 22, 2013. http://www.sciencedaily.com/releases/2013/05.htm (accessed May 17, 2015)

3. Frické, M.: Big data and its epistemology. Journal of the Association for Information Science & Technology **66**(4), 651–661 (2015). doi:10.1002/asi.23212

4. Cisco Visual Networking Index (VNI): Annual Cisco VNI Forecast Expects Worldwide Devices & Connections to Grow to Almost 19 Billion (2014). http://www.cisco.com (accessed May 11, 2015)

5. Computerworld: SKA telescope to generate more data than entire Internet in 2020, IDG Communications, July 7, 2011. http://www.computerworld.com.au/article/392735/ (accessed May 14, 2015)

6. Grass, R.N., Heckel, R., et al.: Robust Chemical Preservation of Digital Information on DNA in Silica with Error-Correcting Codes. Angewandte Chemie International Edition **54**(8), 2552–2555 (2015)

7. Lazer, D., Kennedy, R., King, G., Vespignani, A.: The Parable of Google Flu: Traps In Big Data Analysis. Science **343**, 1203–1205 (2014)

8. Beauchamp, N.: Predicting and interpolating state-level polling using Twitter textual data. In: New Directions in Analyzing Text as Data Workshop, September 10–16, 2013

9. Alan Frost M.Sc: A Synthesis of Knowledge Management Failure Factors. http://www.knowledge-management-tools.net (accessed April 15, 2015, retrieved January 5, 2014)

10. Data Source: Google Trends http://www.google.com/trends, Google and the Google logo are registered trademarks of Google Inc., used with permission (accessed April 24, 2015)

11. Exclusive Research from IDG Enterprise: 2015 Big Data and Analytics Survey (2015). http://www.idgenterprise.com/report/2015-big-data-and-analytics-survey (accessed March 19, 2015)

12. Greg Schroeder: Advanced Information Technology Solutions: An Engine of Innovation, Center for Automotive Research, 10–15, March 25, 2014

Attractors in Web Based Educational Systems a Conceptual Knowledge Processing Grounded Approach

Sanda Dragoş$^{(\boxtimes)}$, Diana Haliţă, and Christian Săcărea

Department of Computer Science, Babeş-Bolyai University, Cluj-Napoca, Romania
{sanda.dragos,diana.halita}@ubbcluj.ro, csacarea@math.ubbcluj.ro

Abstract. Users behavioral patterns are one of the main research directions in web usage mining. Web based educational systems are particularly interesting since behavioral patterns are closely related to educational performance. In this paper we focus on attractors in web based educational systems, i.e., qualitative specific behavioral patterns to which users adhere over time. The research has been conducted on a locally developed e-learning platform called PULSE. Data gathered from weblogs have been preprocessed and conceptual landscapes of knowledge have been built using Formal Concept Analysis. Users behavioral patterns have been detected herefrom, or by moving ahead a triadic view. Triadic concepts enabled us to detect unstructured attractors, while conceptual hierarchies and triadic concept sets made possible to investigate the educational attractors and to derive valuable knowledge about bundle of users and their behavior related to their educational performance.

Keywords: Web usage mining · Behavioral patterns · Formal concept analysis · Triadic formal concept analysis

1 Introduction

Web analytics provide a rough insight about the usage of a website. Even if they are mainly used on e-commerce site they are not precise enough for educational content [1]. Web usage mining [2] constitutes an important feedback for website optimization, personalization [3] and predictions [4]. Survey [5] present educational data mining work on recent educational data mining advances. It is found in [4] that offline information such as classroom attendance, participation and attention were suggested to increase the efficiency of such algorithms.

In this paper we focus on detecting users behavioral patterns in web based systems which might give interesting clues related to user interaction with the

This paper is a result of a doctoral research made possible by the financial support of the Sectoral Operational Programme for Human Resources Development 2007-2013, co-financed by the European Social Fund, under the project POSDRU/187/1.5/S/155383- Quality, excellence, transnational mobility in doctoral research.

S. Zhang et al. (Eds.): KSEM 2015, LNAI 9403, pp. 190–195, 2015.
DOI: 10.1007/978-3-319-25159-2_18

web system. The study of users behavioral patterns might give valuable knowledge on how the system works from the users point of view or valuable insights on how the system itself can be improved. This research is a direct continuation of [6], where we have studied users behavioral patterns using Triadic Formal Concept Analysis (3FCA). In this paper, we focus on *attractors*, behavioral patterns to which users *adhere* while using the web based educational system: *educational attractors*, suggested or desired either by the educator or by the structure of the e-platform; or *unstructured attractors*, i.e., frequent user behavioral patterns independent of the imposed navigational structure of the e-platform. Every attractor defines a bundle of users having a certain behavioral pattern after adhering to it. One can investigate how these behavioral patterns are related to the educational performance or check some temporal related aspects. We have grounded this research on the Conceptual Knowledge Processing paradigm, since knowledge inference and acquisition stays in the foreground of this approach. By this, we have filtered knowledge structures using Formal Concept Analysis (FCA). Herefrom, behavioral patterns are detected and attractors are highlighted. We would like to emphasize that even if we have focused this research on a locally developed e-learning instrument called PULSE [7], the study of attractors and of the knowledge derived from behavioral patterns can be easily extended to any platform which can be freely accessed and is open to navigation [4].

The PULSE platform, which is personalized for every user that enters it, was mainly designed to be used for presenting theoretical support for the studied subjects and automatically setting assignments and recording evaluations for individual work and tests. The system was progressively built and enhanced according to its users needs. This gave us the necessary access to improve not only the educational content on PULSE but also to its design, since we wanted to have an informed learning management system that continually *educates* itself about the requirements of its users as a result of the feedback offered by various pattern mining tools and thus to evaluate the effectiveness of PULSE.

2 Investigating Behavioral Patterns Using Conceptual Landscapes

Web usage behavior and user dynamics are captured in logs, which were cleaned from accesses of robots and spider crawlers. We clustered our data corresponding to actual student groups, academic week time intervals and classes of access files. Conceptual landscapes of knowledge have been built using the conceptual knowledge management system ToscanaJ [8]. When appropriate, we switch to a triadic view, using a locally developed extension Toscana2TRIAS which allows the selection of triadic data starting from a given set of scales, even if the underlying dataset does not have an inherently triadic structure. In [6], we have detected mainly quantitative behavioral patterns (e.g., *relaxed*, *normal* and *intense*). In this paper, we make a step forward towards the study of more qualitative behavioral patterns, by combining them with *attractors*.

Conceptual landscapes are a metaphor introduced by R. Wille [9], where various tasks of knowledge processing like exploring, analyzing, investigating, improving and restructuring are described within the framework of FCA. The major advantage of using FCA w.r.t. other methods rely on the effectiveness of its algorithms and on the graphical expressiveness of conceptual hierarchies, used for further communication and processing, knowledge acquisition and inference.

3   Attractors in Web Based Educational Systems

Behavioral patterns of user visits of an e-platform are characterized by some parameters (visited pages, frequency, time on page). These are either individual patterns or (sub)group patterns and their study gives a valuable insight on how users are navigating and behaving in such a web based platform. On the other hand, one would like that users adhere to some specific patterns and then evaluate the efficiency and the compliance of this adhesion to the scopes of the platform, but also one might be interested in types of behavioral patterns which are to some degree unintended or independent to the design and the content of the web platform. These are called *attractors*, behavioral patterns to which users adhere while using the educational system, and are distilled from frequently visited chain of pages where some deviation from the visit habit is allowed. Finding these attractors is particularly valuable since they offer a more qualitative perspective of users behavior. Moreover, the entire design and scopes of some web based platform can be defined and modeled in terms of attractors: state what should users do and then evaluate if they adhered to these views or have found their own ways to use the system. For web based educational systems, we focus on three main types of attractors: *educational, popular* and *critical* attractors.

3.1   Educational Attractors

Educational attractors should reflect the educational purpose of the instructor and convince or persuade users to adhere to them. The browsing behavior was captured in so-called page chains (i.e., sequences of visited pages where the accessed page becomes the referrer for the next one). When the referrer is not the same as the last page accessed it means that the user opened a new browser tab or window, and we called that part of our page chain a new *branch*. We are interested in specific subchains which reflect the structure of the educational attractor, allowing one or two pages deviation from that. Conceptual landscapes have been used in order to investigate how students adhere over time to the educational requirements of the web platform, respectively to correlate their performance with these attractors. Figure 1 displays the results of this investigation for the 9th week of the semester. There were considered sessions of all enrolled students on the subpages related to that particularly laboratory. The 88,07% represents the number of total visits on all other laboratories. The educational attractor contains visits of the material provided for a laboratory, the related lecture, the test paper given during the lecture and their corresponding explanations Figure 1(b) highlights one of the main advantages of FCA,

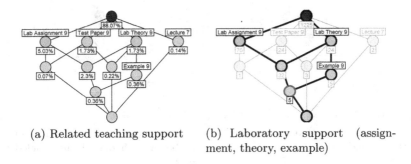

(a) Related teaching support   (b) Laboratory support (assignment, theory, example)

Fig. 1. Educational attractors for the 9th Laboratory

showing the interdependencies between the related pages (i.e., Lab Assignment, Theory and Example) and the number of visits users made on exact these pages together within the same visit. Thus, on average a student with higher performance was more active, having more visits. However there are students from all these categories in our points of interest as marked in Figure 1(b).

Then, using a triadic approach, we investigated our data, we have built triadic data sets and we have computed triconcepts. These triconcepts express maximal clusters of students, their pattern of handing the lab assignment, behavior and performance at the practical exam, laboratory activity and final exam.

Investigating the triconcepts, we have noticed that there are students that do not respect imposed deadlines or have an inconsistent behavior. As a consequence, they have small grades, even if sometimes they have an *intense* usage behavior. Students that have a normal or intense behavior and hand their assignments in time receive good and very good final grades.

3.2   Popular Attractors: Branches

Popular attractors are those to which users adhere without being explicitly intended by the design or the content of the portal. This type of attractor might give important clues to what users consider to be interesting or the way they would like the website to be designed. For instance, "branch-ing" behavior proved to be a popular attractor. Students quite often open new tabs or browser windows within the same session/visit. In order to understand this type of attractor, we investigated what these separate branches contain. We discovered that more than half of these visits contain branches with lab related content as shown in Figure 2(a). Figure 2(b) depicts that only a fraction out of these visits have consecutive branches that end and begin with such pages, which would suggest the need of placing that content on the same page in PULSE. Similar happens with lecture content pages.

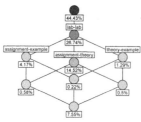
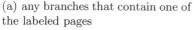
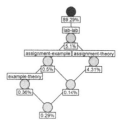

(a) any branches that contain one of the labeled pages

(b) consecutive branches that end and begin with one of the labeled pages

Fig. 2. Sessions containing branches with laboratory related content

3.3 Critical Attractors

Critical attractors are behavioral patterns to which users adhere in stressful situations (deadlines, results posting). Critical attractors are a subclass of popular attractors, but we emphasized them since they reflect different habits. From a quantitative perspective, the number of visits increases in such periods of time. It was interesting to detect that critical attractors are sometimes related to accesses that are made on pages that contain either marks or results on which students wait or some content which they copy and paste. The main pattern for this type of attractor is a flash-like visit: students stay only a few seconds and/or they refresh allot to see new content. Once this type of attractor has been detected, we were interested in what are the students looking for in the period of examinations, when this attractor is mostly active. The conceptual hierarchy of Figure 3(a) shows that out of all pages which are flash-like visited, the students visit the most the educational content. And within the educational content the accesses are quite balanced as depicted in Figure 3(b).

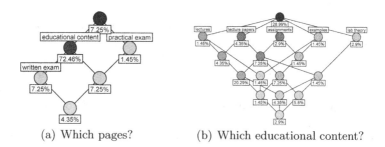

(a) Which pages?

(b) Which educational content?

Fig. 3. Qualitative Behavior: What are students visiting while preparing for exams?

4   Conclusions and Future Work

This research was devoted to the study of a series of subclasses of behavioral patterns in web based educational systems. While a general approach to web usage behaviors has been conducted in [6], we identified in this paper specific behavioral patterns which we called *attractors* which have been investigated using conceptual landscapes (and by this, FCA and 3FCA). Nevertheless it would be interesting to investigate the evolution over time of one user or that of bundles of users adhering to a specific attractor using Temporal Concept Analysis as well as to detect so-called *trend-setters*, i.e., users which firstly adhere to an attractor and then generate a bundle of users following them.

These results also offer us a more detailed view on how students are using PULSE. They also show us very precisely how this portal can and should be changed to better serve students needs as content (eg., better deadline notification) and as presentation (eg., more related content presented on the same page to avoid the "branch-ing" behaviour).

References

1. Macfadyen, L.P., Dawson, S.: Numbers are not enough. why e-learning analytics failed to inform an institutional strategic plan. Educational Technology & Society **15**(3), 149–163 (2012)
2. Spiliopoulou, M., Faulstich, L.C.: WUM: a tool for web utilization analysis. In: Mecca, G., Mendelzon, A.O., Atzeni, P. (eds.) WebDB 1998. LNCS, vol. 1590, pp. 184–203. Springer, Heidelberg (1999)
3. Romero, C., Ventura, S., Zafra, A., De Bra, P.: Applying web usage mining for personalizing hyperlinks in web-based adaptive educational systems. Computers & Education **53**(3), 828–840 (2009)
4. Romero, C., Espejo, P.G., Zafra, A., Romero, J.R., Ventura, S.: Web usage mining for predicting final marks of students that use moodle courses. Computer Applications in Engineering Education **21**(1), 135–146 (2013)
5. Romero, C., Ventura, S.: Data mining in education. Wiley Interdisciplinary Reviews: Data Mining and Knowledge Discovery **3**(1), 12–27 (2013)
6. Dragoş, S., Haliţă, D., Săcărea, C., Troancă, D.: Applying Triadic FCA in studying web usage behaviors. In: Kifor, C.V., Yu, J., Buchmann, R. (eds.) KSEM 2014. LNCS, vol. 8793, pp. 73–80. Springer, Heidelberg (2014)
7. Dragos, S.: PULSE Extended. In: 4th International Conference Internet and Web Applications and Services. IEEE Computer Society, pp. 510–515 (2009)
8. Becker, P., Correia, J.H.: The ToscanaJ suite for implementing conceptual information systems. In: Ganter, B., Stumme, G., Wille, R. (eds.) Formal Concept Analysis. LNCS (LNAI), vol. 3626, pp. 324–348. Springer, Heidelberg (2005)
9. Wille, R.: Conceptual landscapes of knowledge: a pragmatic paradigm for knowledge processing. In: Proceedings of the International Symposium on Knowledge Representation, Use, and Storage Efficiency, pp. 2–13 (1997)

Knowledge Discovery and Recognition Methods

Recognizing the Operating Hand
from Touchscreen Traces on Smartphones

Hansong Guo[1], He Huang[2]([✉]), Zehao Sun[1], Liusheng Huang[1], Zhenyu Zhu[1],
Shaowei Wang[1], Pengzhan Wang[1], Hongli Xu[1], and Hengchang Liu[1]

[1] University of Science and Technology of China, Hefei, China
[2] Soochow University, Suzhou, China
huangh@suda.edu.cn

Abstract. As the size of smartphone touchscreens becomes larger and
larger in recent years, operability with single hand is getting worse especially for female users. We envision that user experience can be significantly improved if smartphones are able to detect the current operating
hand and adjust the UI subsequently. In this paper, we propose a novel
scheme that leverages user-generated touchscreen traces to recognize current operating hand accurately, with the help of a supervised classifier
constructed from twelve different kinds of touchscreen trace features. As
opposed to existing solutions that all require users to select the current
operating hand or dominant hand manually, our scheme follows a more
convenient and practical manner, and allows users to change operating
hand frequently without any harm to user experience. We conduct a
series of real-world experiments on Samsung Galaxy S4 smartphones,
and evaluation results demonstrate that our proposed approach achieves
94.1% accuracy when deciding with a single trace only, and the false
positive rate is as low as 2.6%.

Keywords: Operating hand recognition · Smartphone touchscreen ·
User interface adjustment · Supervised classification

1 Introduction

As technology advances, smartphones with abundant built-in sensors are becoming more and more ubiquitous in our daily lives, which stimulates the blooming
of smartphone sensing researches, such as healthcare, localization, human computer interaction and makes our lives more efficient, more intelligent and more
enjoyable. In this paper, we also focus on this field. Although left-handed people
account for a significant proportion in the total population, nowadays most of
smartphone designs are only considered for right-handed people, especially the
UI. In addition, some users change operating hands frequently. The result of
our investigation about the dominant hand when operating smartphones participated by 500 randomly selected USTC students shows that 34% of them usually
operate the smartphones with left hand, 50% usually with right hand, and almost

© Springer International Publishing Switzerland 2015
S. Zhang et al. (Eds.): KSEM 2015, LNAI 9403, pp. 199–211, 2015.
DOI: 10.1007/978-3-319-25159-2_19

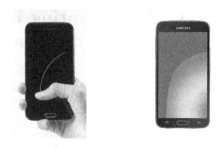

Fig. 1. Limited touching range of thumb on Samsung Galaxy S5.

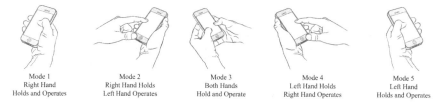

Mode 1	Mode 2	Mode 3	Mode 4	Mode 5
Right Hand	Right Hand Holds	Both Hands	Left Hand Holds	Left Hand
Holds and Operates	Left Hand Operates	Hold and Operate	Right Hand Operates	Holds and Operates

Fig. 2. Five smartphone operation modes.

16% operate the smartphones utilizing the right or left hand with the same frequency. This problem was not that severe previously since the sizes of smartphone screens were small. However, things are worse as the sizes become larger in recent years. For example, the screen size of iPhone 6 has already reached 4.7 inches [2], while the screen size of iPhone 4 is only 3.5 inches [2], and the screen sizes of Nokia Lumia 930 and Samsung Galaxy S5 have already reached 5.0 and 5.1 inches respectively [3,4]. Users' visual experiences are improved with the continuous increase of smartphone screens sizes, meanwhile, single hand operability of smartphones is significantly getting worse, as depicted in Fig. 1, especially for female users.

To address this challenge, we propose, to the best of our knowledge, the first scheme for detecting current operating hand from touchscreen traces **only** and the accuracy is 94.1% when deciding with a single trace only. We divide smartphone operation modes into five main categories based on numerous observations of users' daily lives, as shown in Fig. 2. User interfaces of large-screen smartphones can be adjusted for each particular mode, especially for mode one and mode five, whose touching ranges are limited.

1.1 Motivations

Following are some common scenarios in smartphone(with large screen) users' daily lives.

- People are operating smartphones with right(or left) hand, but the buttons they want to press are on top left(or right) corner. Since smartphone screens are large, they have to try their best to reach these buttons. They will be forced to use both hands if these buttons are too far away, because almost all of user interfaces today are fixed, which is inconvenient when the other hand is busy doing other things, such as eating, carrying heavy loads, holding the handle of metro and driving a car.

- People frequently use the input method or dialing keyboard to interact with smartphones and these two approaches usually occupy the entire width of smartphone screen nowadays. So they have to use both hands to input if the smartphone screens are large. User experience will be greatly improved if the smartphone can dynamically detect current operating hand and then shrink the area of input method or dialing keyboard proportionally and automatically let them gather on the side of this hand. Because users can complete the whole input process with single hand even the smartphone screens are very large.

- There are numerous kinds of buttons on smartphone UI and some of them are sensitive or even destructive. For example, Send button of SMS, Dislike button of social software such as facebook, and Delete button of photo album. A series of serious consequences may be caused if user accidentally touches these buttons and is completely unaware of that. So these buttons should be placed on specific position(red area in Fig. 1) of the smartphone UI which is closely related to current operating hand. Then users need to make some efforts to reach these buttons if they really want to, so casual touching event will never happen.

- There are three buttons at the bottom of most Android based smartphones today, which are Back button, Home button and Menu button respectively. The use of Back button is more frequent than Menu button for almost all users in our investigation. But as far as we know the positions of these three buttons on Android based smartphone UI are all fixed nowadays. One more reasonable approach is putting Back button on the position which is easier to be touched among three positions according to current operating hand.

1.2   Challenges

We face three major challenges in this paper.

- The first challenge is to choose effective features that can be utilized to recognize current operating hand. This challenge is mainly reflected in two aspects. First, in previous papers, researchers often design a series of complicated touchscreen traces in advance, then pick out several kinds of traces with optimal degree of distinction after comprehensive evaluation and comparison. But in this paper, features are extracted from traces generated during user's daily and totally indeliberate smartphone operation process. So these traces could have all kinds of shapes and totally have no obvious regularity. Second, in previous papers, touchscreen traces are used for authentication purpose so traces need to be distinguished are generated by different persons(legitimate user and imposters). But in this paper, all traces are generated by the same person so biometric behaviors are much more similar compared with traces generated by different persons.

- The second challenge is to construct efficient classifier which can recognize current operating hand through features extracted from touchscreen traces generated by a given user and result in high accuracy. For a particular feature, there may be diverse degree of distinction for different users. For example, length of traces may provide ideal degree of distinction for female users but not work well on male users.
- The third challenge is to preprocess coordinate data. Raw coordinate data collected through smartphone touchscreen can't be used for feature vector computation directly. There are two main reasons. First, user's finger may provisionally leave smartphone touchscreen surface occasionally during sliding process which generates traces with only a few of sampling points. Second, there will be some sampling points with the same coordinate data but different sampling time at the beginning and ending of every trace. These two reasons will lead to errors during feature vector computation so we preprocess coordinate data at the beginning.

2   System Overview

In this section, we provide a system overview of our operation mode recognition scheme.

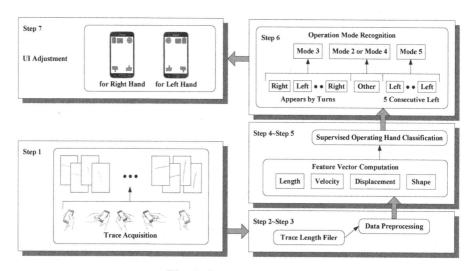

Fig. 3. System overview.

The first step is the acquisition of touchscreen trace data from smartphone touchscreen which are organized in the form of a series of coordinate data with corresponding timestamp at every sampling point. There is a length filter in the second step. Traces are delivered to this filter where the length of every trace will be compared with a certain threshold. Then our scheme discards traces whose length are below this threshold because these traces are too short to carry enough useful information and features extracted from these traces provide poor degree of distinction. Our scheme preprocesses coordinate data of touchscreen traces in the third step in order to improve the accuracy of feature vector computation. In the fourth step(presented in Section 3), our scheme computes a feature vector consisting of features that can be utilized to recognize current operating hand. Then our scheme constructs a supervised classifier(presented in Section 4) called Random Forest, which outputs recognition result $Left, Right, Other$ for current operating hand(finger) using features extracted in the fourth step. In the sixth step, our scheme recognizes current operation mode(as shown in Fig. 2) according to the continuous sequence of supervised operation hand classification results within a previous period of time. Our scheme recognizes user's current operation mode as mode five or mode one when the results sequence contains at least n consecutive $Left$ or n consecutive $Right$ respectively. n is a predefined variate which represents the tradeoff between the response time of our scheme and recognition accuracy, and its value is 5 in this paper. Otherwise, if $Left$ and $Right$ appear by turns in results sequence, then user's current operation mode will be judged as mode three by our scheme. Our scheme believes that user is operating the smartphone with mode two or mode four when the operation hand classification result is $Other$. In the last step, there are a lot of things smartphone can do according to the operation mode recognition result, and the most relevant one is adjusting UI to user if the recognition result is mode one or mode five.

3 Feature Vector Computation

In this section, we introduce features which are selected to distinguish current operating hand, as shown in TABLE. 1.

- **Length Features:**
  Total Length.
- **Velocity Features:**
  Maximum & Average Velocity.
  Standard Deviation of Velocity. The changing process of velocity on a trace contains two phases: acceleration and deceleration. The durations

Table 1. Feature set.

Length Features	
1	Total Length
Velocity Features	
3	Maximum & Average Velocity, Standard Deviation of Velocity
Displacement Features	
4	Total & Maximum X-Displacement, Total & Maximum Y-Displacement
Shape Features	
4	Root Mean Squared Error, Maximum & Average Curvature, Curve Convex Orientation

of acceleration processes are different between traces generated by index fingers and thumbs because of the different lengths of traces. The deceleration processes of traces generated by index fingers are shorter because these traces often slide out of the touchscreens directly without deceleration. Therefore, the velocity features of traces generated by index fingers and thumbs are different. Fig. 4 plots the change of velocity magnitude with displacement on traces performed by different fingers of the same participant. The directions of traces are left in Fig. 4(a) and up in Fig. 4(b). We can observe that, for this participant, velocity features can be utilized to distinguish traces generated by different fingers.

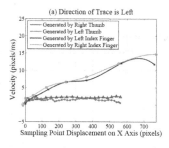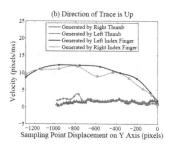

Fig. 4. Velocity magnitude of each sampling point.

- **Displacement Features:**
  Total & Maximum X-Displacement.
  Total & Maximum Y-Displacement.
- **Shape Features:** In order to describe the shape features of traces quantitatively and accurately, we carry on curve fitting on discrete sampling points of every trace using quartic polynomial, which is a tradeoff among fitting precision, computational complexity and degree of distinction on traces generated by different fingers.

Root Mean Squared Error. This feature measures the smooth degree of traces. Index fingers are more flexible and have larger touching ranges than thumbs. When operating smartphones, index fingers exert less pressure on touchscreens and receive less friction resistance, so traces generated by index fingers are always smoother than those generated by thumbs. The RMSE of trace S_i is calculated as:

$$RMSE_i = \sqrt{\frac{1}{n_i} \sum_{j=1}^{n_i} (y_{ij} - \hat{y}_{ij})^2}$$

where y_{ij} indicates the true y coordinate value of the jth discrete sampling point on the trace S_i and $\hat{y}_{ij}$ indicates the predicted y coordinate value of the jth discrete sampling point calculated by carrying out curve fitting on the trace S_i. n_i indicates the number of sampling points on the trace S_i. Fig. 5 plots the distribution of RMSE from 200 traces generated by right thumb(as shown in Fig. 5(a)) and right index finger(as shown in Fig. 5(b)) respectively of the same participant. The number of each kind of traces is 100 and all directions of traces are right. We can observe that, for this participant, the values of RMSE feature are different among traces generated by different fingers.

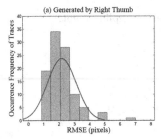 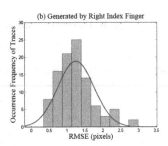

Fig. 5. RMSE of 200 touchscreen traces.

Maximum & Average Curvature. These two features measure the curvature degree of traces. Users slide on touchscreens exploiting the most effortless approach unconsciously. When users operate smartphones with thumbs, restricted to the limited touching ranges, most of traces generated are curves whose centers are on the same side as the operating hand. The touching ranges of index fingers are significantly larger, which produces straighter traces. The curvature at the jth sampling point of trace S_i is calculated as:

$$Curvature_{ij} = \frac{f_i''(x_{ij})}{(1 + f_i'(x_{ij})^2)^{3/2}}$$

where $f_i(x)$ indicates the fitting curve function of trace S_i and $f_i'(x)$, $f_i''(x)$ indicates the first order derivative and the second order derivative of $f_i(x)$ respectively. x_{ij} indicates the x coordinate value of the jth discrete sampling point on the trace S_i. Fig. 6 plots the curvature magnitude at every sampling point on traces performed by different fingers of the same participant. The directions of traces are left in Fig. 6(a) and up in Fig. 6(b). We can observe that, for this participant, curvature features can be utilized to distinguish traces generated by different fingers.

Curve Convex Orientation. This feature measures the curve's convex orientation which can be very useful in distinguishing traces generated by left thumb and right thumb. To calculate the CCO of trace S_i, first we randomly choose a sampling point which is close to the middle of the trace. Second we construct two vectors which are from this sampling point to the first and the last sampling point respectively. Then we calculate the cross

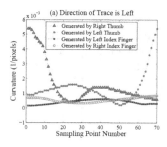 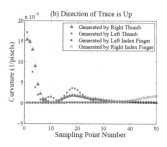

Fig. 6. Curvature magnitude of each sampling point.

product between these two vectors.

$$z_i = det \begin{vmatrix} x & y & z \\ x_{i1} - x_{ik} & y_{i1} - y_{ik} & 0 \\ x_{in_i} - x_{ik} & y_{in_i} - y_{ik} & 0 \end{vmatrix}$$

where (x_{i1}, y_{i1}) and (x_{in_i}, y_{in_i}) indicates the coordinates of the first and the last sampling point of trace S_i respectively. (x_{ik}, y_{ik}) indicates the coordinates of the randomly chosen sampling point. Finally, the CCO of trace S_i is calculated as:

$$CCO_i = sgn \left\{ (y_{in_i} - y_{i1}) z_i \cdot z \right\}$$

where sgn is the sign function.

4   Evaluation

In this section, we present the results of our experiments. This section consists of three parts. In the first part, we compare the differences in classification performance among five common classifiers. Then in the following part, we study the impact of the number of training samples on classification performance. Finally, we report the real world evaluation results of our scheme.

According to the direction(displacement characteristics), we divide all touch-screen traces into four categories: right, left, up and down. We ask every participant to generate traces in each direction with the right thumb, left thumb, right index finger and left index finger successively in the procedure of data collection. But in the actual use of our scheme, user could only generate traces in a subset of four directions if traces with directions in the complementary set don't appear frequently in her daily smartphone operation. That is to say, user can make a tradeoff between the convenience of training traces acquisition process and response time, because our scheme will not respond to traces the directions of which are not in the subset above. In this paper, we request all participants to generate traces in all directions in order to adequately test the classification performance of our scheme on multifarious traces. So there will be 16 trace subsets in total.

4.1   Classification Performance of Different Classifiers

In this paper, we use precision, recall, F1, false positive rate and AUC to measure classification performance and AUC is the area under the receiver operating characteristic(ROC) curve.

In this part, we construct five different classifiers [14], [9], which are Decision Tree, Random Forest, Naive Bayes, Multi Layer Perceptron, k-Nearest Neighbors and compare their classification performance on our touchscreen traces data. The number of traces in each training subset and test subset is 40 and 10 respectively in this part, so the total number of traces in training set and test set is 640 and 160. TABLE 2 shows the classification performance and Fig. 7 shows the total time(training time+test time) and false positive rate of these five classifiers.

Table 2. Classification performance of different classifiers.

	Precision	Recall	F1	AUC
DT	92.2%	91.8%	91.8%	0.975
RF	95.6%	95.6%	95.6%	0.990
NB	82.4%	71.5%	72.8%	0.919
MLP	96.9%	96.8%	96.8%	0.999
kNN	88.1%	88.2%	88.2%	0.951

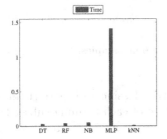
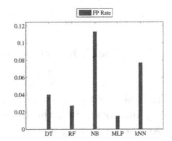

Fig. 7. Total time and FP rate of different classifiers.

We can make two observations here. First, on the one hand, Multi Layer Perceptron gives the best classification performance which achieves 96.9% precision and 1.5% false positive rate and Random Forest gives the second best classification performance which achieves 95.6% precision and 2.7% false positive rate. On the other hand, Naive Bayes achieves the worst classification performance and k-Nearest Neighbors is also not good enough. Second, as shown in Fig. 7, the total time of Multi Layer Perceptron is 1.41s but the total time of Random Forest is only 0.04s. The former is 35 times as long as the latter. After considering all factors above, we finally choose Random Forest as our classifier in this paper, which is extremely effective for data sets containing a lot of redundant features.

4.2   Impact of the Number of Training Samples

In this part, we indicate the impact of the number of training samples on the classification performance. The number of training samples is a significant parameter in the construction process of a classification model. On the one hand, if the number of training samples is too large, the workloads of training traces acquisition will become onerous for users. Moreover, although the training error of classification model is low, the generalization error may be high sometimes, because the classification model is over fitting, which will lead to poor classification performance eventually. On the other hand, if the number of training samples is too small, the classification model will be under fitting, which also leads to inaccurate classification results. The number of traces in each test subset is 5 so the total number of traces in test set is 80 in this part. Fig. 8 shows the change of classification performance with the increase in the number of traces in each training subset.

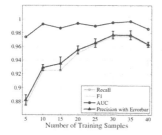 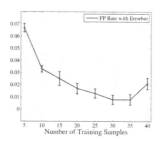

Fig. 8. Impact of the number of training samples.

We can make two observations here. First, the classification performance is significantly improved with the increase in the size of each training subset from 5 to 10. As shown in Fig. 8, the precision increases from 88.2% to 92.9% and the false positive rate drops from 6.7% to 3.3%. This is because the number of traces in training set is larger than test set for the first time. Second, the Random Forest achieves the optimal classification performance when there are 30 traces in each training subset. Fig. 8 shows that the precision can be as high as 97.7% and the false positive rate achieves 0.8% accordingly.

4.3   Real World Evaluation

In this part, we evaluate our scheme on two sets of 14 participants(7 male and 7 female participants) in real world. We ask every participant to generate traces in four directions with right thumb, left thumb, right index finger and left index finger respectively, among which left(or right) traces are generated by some operations such as navigating among main screen pages or viewing images and up(or down) traces are generated by reading documents or browsing webpages.

The number of traces in each subset is 25. Then we conduct a 5-fold cross-validation experiment on these traces. The average precision, false positive rate of left thumb and false positive rate of right thumb over all 14 participants turned out to be 94.1%, 2.7%, 2.4% respectively when deciding with a single trace only. Fig. 9(a) and Fig. 9(b) show bar plots of real world evaluation results of 14 participants.

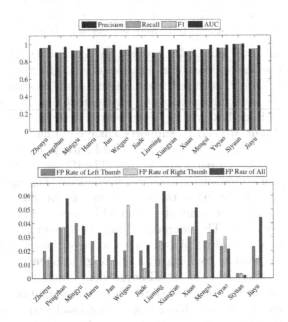

Fig. 9. Real world evaluation results of 14 participants.

5   Related Work

In this section, we describe two areas of related work.

Touch Behavioral Biometrics Based Authentication: In recent years there are some smartphone-based biometric authentication work. Sae-Bae et al. [10] presented an authentication mechanism using multi-touch traces and then they defined a comprehensive five-finger touchscreen trace set which makes use of biometric information such as hand size and finger length. Shahzad et al. [12] defined 10 kinds of specific touchscreen traces in their paper and proposed an authentication scheme for the secure unlocking of touchscreen devices using these touchscreen traces. There are some other touch features based identification-related work, e.g., [6], [11], [13]. Recently, some identification-related researches focus on using not only touchscreen but also smartphone equipped sensors such as accelerometer, gyroscope to enrich features can be used when identifying. The GripSense [8] recognizes four kinds of hand postures leveraging both smartphone touchscreens and inertial sensors(gyroscopes, accelerometers) and achieves 84.3% accuracy. Frank et al. [7] proposed an authentication scheme using 30 features, including touch features and inertial sensors features. But the overfitting problem becomes more severe when too many features are used, which is called the curse of dimensionality. In their work, the EER was approximately 13% when deciding with a single stroke. There may be some challenges to be addressed when using inertial sensors, such as high energy consumption, cumulative errors, interference signals from concurrent activities and inexistence in some smartphones today. In this paper, we use touchscreen only and achieve a high accuracy.

Smartphone User Interface Adjustment: Several latest large screen smartphones and applications support the function of UI adjustment in order to improve user experience. The smartphone Smartisan [5] lets user select dominant hand when the smartphone boots up for the first time and allows user to set the positions of Back button and Menu button according to her operation habit. The Baidu Input Method [1] supports single hand mode. User can make the interactive interface shrink proportionally and gather on the side of current operating hand by clicking a particular button. The iPhone 6 [2] user can make the whole smartphone interactive interface descend by tapping Home button twice, so the buttons on the top of the smartphone screen can be reached. But this approach also makes the same operation which needs only one click originally now need three clicks. The interactive interface of Samsung Note 3 [4] can be shrunk in proportion and be placed on a corner of the smartphone screen, but apparently, this practice conflicts with the original intention of using large screen smartphone. These state-of-art UI adjustment functions all require user's intervention such as one step or many steps of selecting operation, so these functions are impractical when user changes operating hand frequently. According to our research, all functions mentioned above can be achieved automatically or improved.

6   Conclusion

User experience can be significantly improved if smartphones are able to detect the current operating hand and adjust the UI subsequently. In this paper, we present a mechanism for current operating hand recognition using the touchscreen traces performed by users. Our scheme utilizes a supervised classifier constructed from twelve different kinds of touchscreen trace features. We implemented our scheme on Android based smartphones and conducted a series of experiments. Real world evaluation results demonstrate that our scheme can identify current operating hand accurately for different users. To the best of our knowledge, this is the first paper which proposed the idea of smartphone UI automatic adjustment and gave a complete technical solution using touchscreen traces only.

Acknowledgement. This paper was supported by National Science and Technology Major Project under Grant No. 2012ZX03005009, National Science Foundation of China under Grant No. U1301256, 61170058, 61272133, BJ2260080039 and GG2260080042, Special Project on IoT of China NDRC(2012-2766), USTC Innovation funding DG2260010011, and Research Fund for the Doctoral Program of Higher Education of China No. 2010340211 0041.

References

1. Baidu Input Method. http://srf.baidu.com
2. iPhone. https://www.apple.com
3. Nokia. http://www.microsoftstore.com
4. Samsung. http://www.samsung.com
5. Smartisan. http://www.smartisan.com
6. De Luca, A., Hang, A., Brudy, F., Lindner, C., Hussmann, H.: Touch me once and i know it's you!: implicit authentication based on touch screen patterns. In: CHI, pp. 987–996. ACM (2012)
7. Frank, M., Biedert, R., Ma, E., Martinovic, I., Song, D.: Touchalytics: On the applicability of touchscreen input as a behavioral biometric for continuous authentication. IEEE Transactions on Information Forensics and Security 8(1), 136–148 (2013)
8. Goel, M., Wobbrock, J., Patel, S.: Gripsense: using built-in sensors to detect hand posture and pressure on commodity mobile phones. In: UIST, pp. 545–554. ACM (2012)
9. Gu, B., Sheng, V.S., Wang, Z., Ho, D., Osman, S., Li, S.: Incremental learning for ν-support vector regression. Neural Networks **67**, 140–150 (2015)
10. Sae-Bae, N., Ahmed, K., Isbister, K., Memon, N.: Biometric-rich gestures: a novel approach to authentication on multi-touch devices. In: CHI, pp. 977–986. ACM (2012)
11. Seo, H., Kim, E., Kim, H.K.: A novel biometric identification based on a users input pattern analysis for intelligent mobile devices. International Journal of Advanced Robotic Systems 9 (2012)
12. Shahzad, M., Liu, A.X., Samuel, A.: Secure unlocking of mobile touch screen devices by simple gestures: you can see it but you can not do it. In: MobiCom, pp. 39–50. ACM (2013)
13. Vu, T., Baid, A., Gao, S., Gruteser, M., Howard, R., Lindqvist, J., Spasojevic, P., Walling, J.: Distinguishing users with capacitive touch communication. In: Mobicom, pp. 197–208. ACM (2012)
14. Zheng, Y., Jeon, B., Xu, D., Wu, Q.J., Zhang, H.: Image segmentation by generalized hierarchical fuzzy c-means algorithm. Journal of Intelligent and Fuzzy Systems

iCHUM: An Efficient Algorithm for High Utility Mining in Incremental Databases

Hai-Tao Zheng[(⊠)] and Zhuo Li

Tsinghua-Southampton Web Science Laboratory, Graduate School at Shenzhen,
Tsinghua University, Shenzhen, China
zheng.haitao@sz.tsinghua.edu.cn, lizhuo13@mails.tsinghua.edu.cn

Abstract. High utility mining is a fundamental topic in association rule mining, which aims to discover all itemsets with high utility from transaction database. The previous studies are mainly based on fixed databases, which are not applicable for incremental databases. Although incremental high utility pattern (IHUP) mining has been proposed, its tree structure IHUP-Tree is redundant and thus IHUP algorithm has relative low efficiency. To address this issue, we propose an incremental compressed high utility mining algorithm called iCHUM. The iCHUM algorithm utilizes items of high transaction weighted utilization (TWU) to construct its tree structure, namely iCHUM-Tree. The iCHUM algorithm updates iCHUM-Tree when new database is appended to the original database. The information of high utility itemsets is maintained in the iCHUM-Tree such that candidate itemsets can be generated through mining procedure. Performance analysis shows that our algorithm is more efficient than baseline approaches in incremental databases.

Keywords: Data mining · Association rule · High utility mining · Incremental mining

1 Introduction

Mining association rule is a fundamental topic in the data mining applications, especially in market analysis. In association rule mining, frequent pattern mining was firstly proposed to find all itemsets which frequently appear together in the transaction database. The initial solution is based on downward closure property [1,2], which is a level-wise approach. However, it requires multiple database scans and generates a large number of candidate itemsets to search and identity. Extensive studies have been proposed to address the issues by introducing a frequent pattern (FP) tree structure and corresponding FP-growth algorithm [5,6], which is a pattern-growth approach. The main difference between both approaches is whether the database is compressed into other data structure.

However, FP mining is prone to generate many frequent but low profitable itemsets. The reason is that FP mining treats all items with the same weight,

© Springer International Publishing Switzerland 2015
S. Zhang et al. (Eds.): KSEM 2015, LNAI 9403, pp. 212–223, 2015.
DOI: 10.1007/978-3-319-25159-2_20

and each item appears in binary format. In fact, weight and quantity are significant for addressing the decision problems in the real world where sellers require maximizing profit from transaction records [8,9,18,19].

A high utility mining model [13,14] is defined to discover all high utility patterns from the transaction databases. The significance of itemsets is measured by the concept of utility. An itemset is called a high utility itemset if its utility is no less than a user-specified minimum utility threshold represented by min_util. Moreover, most previous studies [4,11,13,15,16] are based on a fixed transaction database and have not taken dynamic increase in database size into consideration. In practice, the real markets add their transaction records dynamically, where utility mining for incremental databases is required to be solved.

Studies [3,10,12,17] have been conducted based on incremental databases. IUM and FIUM algorithm [17] are proposed to mine high temporal utility itemsets, which are temporary and may be not high utility itemsets in the whole database. FUP algorithm [10,12] is a level-wise approach, and its efficiency becomes worse due to multiple scans of the whole database. IHUP [3] is a pattern-growth solution for high utility mining in incremental databases. It compresses databases into the IHUP-Tree and avoids multiple scans. IHUP could update its IHUP-Tree when new transaction records are inserted. However, it becomes inefficient when the number of items in the database is relatively large. IHUP maintains its redundant IHUP-Tree, which takes excess time to process items that are unpromising to be high utility itemsets. In fact, not all items need be maintained in tree structure according to transaction weighted downward closure (TWDC) property [13,14].

Most existing methods for fixed databases are not applicable for incremental databases. The approaches for incremental databases spend much time on maintaining redundant information, which causes a relatively low performance. The situations get worse when the size of database becomes large. To address the issues, we propose an incremental compressed high utility mining (iCHUM) algorithm for high utility mining in incremental databases. In this paper, we have three main contributions as below.

1. We propose the iCHUM algorithm for high utility mining in incremental databases. The algorithm performs efficiently to obtain all high utility itemsets as transaction records increase dynamically.

2. The iCHUM algorithm constructs and updates iCHUM-Tree incrementally, which maintains high utility itemsets information of the transaction database. The iCHUM algorithm avoids rebuilding the tree structure entirely and reduces construction and update runtime.

3. We conduct a series of experiments on both real and synthetic datasets. We compare the performance between ours and baseline methods. The results show that our algorithm is more efficient in incremental databases.

The rest of this paper is organized as follows. In Section 2, we introduce the related work. In Section 3, we propose iCHUM algorithm in details following the problem definition. The experimental results and evaluations are shown in Section 4 and the conclusion and future work are given in Section 5.

2   Related Work

The definition of utility mining problem is given in [13,14], which is similar to what we adopt. In their work, they propose the Two-Phase algorithm and introduced the concept of transaction weighted utilization (TWU), which satisfies the downward closure property. The Two-Phase algorithm adopts a level-wise generation-and-test approach. It firstly finds all one-element high TWU itemsets and then generates two-element candidate itemsets to test whether there exist two-element high TWU itemsets or not. If there exist any high TWU candidate itemsets, Two-Phase algorithm generates candidate itemsets by adding one more element. Otherwise, it stops generation process and then identifies utility of all candidate itemsets. It finds all high TWU itemsets level by level, and it needs to scan the whole transaction for each generation-and-test iteration. Therefor, Two-Phase algorithm suffers from the multiple scans of database and huge candidates.

Studies [3,4,11,15] are proposed together with their corresponding tree structure as pattern-growth approaches. The main difference between them is how to construct their tree structure. These approaches scan the database to build their corresponding tree structure separately at first. They compress the entire transaction records into their corresponding tree structure. The mining process utilizes property of prefix-tree and introduces conditional pattern base [6]. Thus the high TWU itemsets are generated by mining the compressed tree structure instead of the whole transaction database. The pattern-growth approaches largely reduce the amount of scans and that of candidates. They perform better in the relatively dense or long pattern databases. However, most pattern-growth methods above are designed for the fixed databases. Their tree structures need to be reconstructed once the database is updated.

There exist some researches based on high utility itemset mining for incremental database [3,10,12,17]. Yeh et al. [17] proposed two methods: incremental utility mining (IUM) algorithm and fast incremental utility mining (FIUM) algorithm. However, these algorithms find high temporal utility itemsets, which are high utility itemsets in the part of the database. When parts joint into the whole, some of high temporal utility itemsets may not be high utility ones. Lin et al. [10,12] proposed an incremental updated HUP maintenance algorithm. The algorithm divides the incremental databases into four cases when new transactions are appended to an original database. However, their algorithm suffers from multiple scans and excessive candidates. Ahmed [3] proposed their incremental mining method IHUP based on the IHUP-Tree. The IHUP-Tree maintains all of the items, and it inserts new transaction records without rebuilding the whole tree. All it needs is to maintain the order of the items by TWU and it is convenient for mining procedure. Limited to the property of their tree structure, the efficiency of the algorithm is not satisfactory when the number of items is large or number of high TWU items is small. On those conditions, IHUP should maintain unnecessary inserting or reordering operation for those low utility items.

Our proposed iCHUM algorithm aims to improve time efficiency by maintaining promising items which may be elements of high utility itemsets.

When transaction database grows incrementally, we recall such high TWU items in new database, whose TWU is low in original database. Then we insert high TWU items of both original and new databases to update the iCHUM-Tree without rebuilding the tree structure entirely. It is efficient to mine the updated iCHUM-Tree to obtain high utility itemsets compared with baseline methods.

3   iCHUM Algorithm

3.1   Problem Definition

Let $I = \{i_1, i_2, \ldots, i_m\}$ be a finite item set. Each item has its profit $p(i_j)$ where $1 \leq j \leq m$. A transaction database consists of a finite set of transaction records $D = \{T_1, T_2, \ldots, T_n\}$ and item profit table. Each transaction $T_s = \{i_{s1}, i_{s2}, \ldots, i_{st}\} \subseteq I$ where $1 \leq s \leq n, 1 \leq t \leq m$. In each T_s, each item has its quantity $q(i_j, T_s)$ where $1 \leq j \leq m, 1 \leq s \leq n$. Let Table 1 be an example of transaction database and Table 2 be a profit table.

Set $X = \{i_{j1}, i_{j2}, \ldots, i_{jl}\} \subseteq I$ is an itemset, where $1 \leq l \leq m$, and l is the length of itemset X. $\forall i_j \in X$, if $i_j \in T_s$, then the itemset $X \subseteq T_s$, which means that T_s contains X.

Table 1. Transaction database

	Tid	Transaction	TU
D0	T_1	(A,5) (B,2)	9
	T_2	(A,2) (B,1) (D,1)	6
	T_3	(E,1) (F,2)	7
	T_4	(C,3) (D,2)	13
	T_5	(A,2) (B,2) (C,1) (D,2)	11
D1	T_6	(A,3) (B,1) (E,2)	15
	T_7	(B,1) (D,1) (E,1) (F,1)	10
	T_8	(A,2)	2

Table 2. Profit table

Item	Profit
A	1
B	2
C	3
D	2
E	5
F	1

Table 3. TWU table

Item	TWU	
	D0	D0 + D1
A	26	43
B	26	51
C	24	24
D	30	40
E	7	32
F	7	17

Definition 1. *The utility of an itemset X is denoted as $U(X)$. An itemset X is a* **high utility itemset** *if $U(X) \geq min\_util$.* **High utility mining** *is to find the set of all itemsets* $\mathbf{X} = \{X_1, X_2, \ldots, X_m\}$ *satisfies the condition that $\forall X_i \in \mathbf{X}, U(X_i) \geq min\_util$.*

$$U(X) = \sum_{X \subseteq T_d \in D} \sum_{i_j \in X} p(i_j) \times q(i_j, T_d) \qquad (1)$$

After we define utility mining problem, we introduce TWU [13] which helps build up iCHUM-Tree.

Definition 2. *The transaction weighted utility (TWU) of an itemset X denoted as $TWU(X)$ is the sum of the transaction utilities (TU) of all transaction records*

*containing X, shown in Table 3. An itemset X is a **high TWU itemset** if*
$TWU(X) \geq min\_util.$

$$TWU(X) = \sum_{X \subseteq T_d \in D} TU(T_d) = \sum_{X \subseteq T_d \in D} \sum_{i_j \in T_d} p(i_j) \times q(i_j, T_d) \qquad (2)$$

Noted that $U(X) \leq TWU(X)$ for $\forall X$, if $TWU(X) < min\_util$, then
$U(X) < min\_util$. If X is not a high TWU itemset, then X is not a high utility
itemset. Moreover, $TWU(X)$ satisfies downward closure property [13,14] while
$U(X)$ does not. Therefore, high utility mining problem is divided into high TWU
itemsets mining and corresponding utility identification, which constitutes the
framework of our algorithm.

Definition 3. *An item $i \in I$ is a promising item if $TWU(i) \geq min\_util$. Otherwise, the item is an unpromising item.*

If an item i_u is unpromising, all itemsets containing i_u should not be high
TWU itemsets, which are not high utility itemsets accordingly.

3.2 iCHUM Algorithm Framework

The framework of iCHUM algorithm includes four procedures: iCHUM-Tree construction, iCHUM-Tree update, mining procedure and candidates identifying,
which are shown in Fig. 1. The overall inputs consist of the transaction database
and a user-specified minimum utility threshold called min_util. Actually, for the
incremental databases, we have two parts of the transaction database, an original database $D0$ and a new database $D1$. The final output is the collection of
high utility itemsets in both database $D0$ and database $D0 + D1$.

According to the flow of the iCHUM framework, we firstly construct an initial
iCHUM-Tree from the original database $D0$. Through mining procedure of the
iCHUM-Tree, we get the collection of high TWU itemsets in $D0$. We obtain the
collection of high utility itemsets in $D0$ following identifying procedure. Then
when a new database $D1$ is appended to $D0$ as an incremental database, the
iCHUM-Tree is to be updated instead of being rebuilt. The iCHUM-Tree update
procedure is to update the iCHUM-Tree according to transaction records in
database $D1$. The updated iCHUM-Tree is then the input of mining procedure,
which produces the candidate itemsets with high TWU value. The final step
of identifying is to pick up real high utility itemsets from the candidates. After
that, we obtain all high utility itemsets in the whole transaction database namely
$D0 + D1$, which consists of $D0$ and $D1$.

3.3 iCHUM-Tree Construction and Update

The iCHUM-Tree consists of tree structure and its headtable H for traversal,
shown in Fig. 2. In the iCHUM-Tree, the nodes includes its name, TWU value,
count, a parent node, a brother node and a collection of child nodes, expressed as

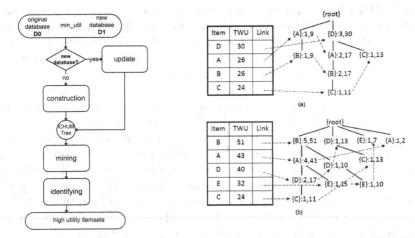

Fig. 1. Framework of iCHUM

Fig. 2. Construction and update of iCHUM-Tree (a) after inserting T_5, (b) after inserting T_8

$\{name\} : (count, TWU)$. In the headtable, each entry consists of the item name, TWU value and a link pointed to nodes with the same name in the iCHUM-Tree.

The **iCHUM-Tree construction** is to build iCHUM-Tree from the original database $D0$, shown in Algorithm 1. According to the TWDC property, the items with low TWU value cannot appear in high utility itemsets. Therefore, the headtable of iCHUM-Tree exclusively maintains the promising items whose $TWU \geq min\_util$. Before each transaction record is inserted to iCHUM-Tree, we arrange the items in TWU descending order. It is efficient for mining procedure when traversing branches from bottom to top orderly. When mining process enters entry of higher TWU items, it would not check those low TWU items. If an item has been existed during insertion operation, we add its count by one and its TWU by the TU of current transaction record inserted. Otherwise, we create a node of the item and set its count as one and its TWU as TU value of the current record. The space complexity to construct iCHUM-Tree is $O(m_p^2)$, where m_p represents number of promising items.

Algorithm 1. iCHUM-Tree Construction

Input: original database $D0$, minimum utility threshold min_util
Output: item TWU table $TWU[1..m]$, iCHUM-Tree and its headtable H of $D0$
    Scan $D0$ to update $TWU[1..m]$
    Create H for each i satisfying $TWU[i] \geq min\_util$ in TWU descending order
    /* **Scan** and **Insert** process is as below */
    for each T_d in $D0$ do
        Sort T_d to T_d' in TWU descending order
        Insert i to iCHUM-Tree for each i $\in H$ in T_d'
    end for

The **iCHUM-Tree update** is performed when a new transaction database $D1$ comes to be appended based on original database $D0$, shown in Algorithm 2. In new database, there would exist such items whose TWU value is high in new database but low in original database. Among such items, **recalled items** are ones whose TWU value is greater than min_util in the whole transaction database $D0 + D1$, such as item E in Fig. 2b. In this case, the iCHUM algorithm needs to find the recalled items from $D0$, and insert them to headtable H as well as iCHUM-Tree. Moreover, the iCHUM-Tree should be maintained in TWU descending order after recalled items are appended. We adopt bubble sort operation [7] to reorder the nodes in the iCHUM-Tree and its headtable. The operation exchanges adjacent items to meet the order. If an item X is adjacent to an item Y in headtable and X is Y's parent node in iCHUM-Tree, the bubble sort operation is performed when Y's TWU becomes greater than that of X. The time complexity of update is $O(nm_p^2)$, where n represents number of transaction records. In worst case, it needs to bubble sort n times for m_p entries.

Algorithm 2. iCHUM-Tree Update

Input: $D0$, new database $D1$, min_util , $TWU[1..m]$, iCHUM-Tree and its H of $D0$
Output: updated iCHUM-Tree and its headtable H of $D0 + D1$
  Scan $D1$ to update $TWU[1..m]$ and **Find** collection of recalled items I'
  if $I' \neq \emptyset$ **then**
    Add all i$'$ $\in$ I' to H
    Scan $D0$ and **Insert** i$'$ to iCHUM-Tree
  end if
  Scan $D1$ and **Insert** i $\in$ H to iCHUM-Tree
  Reorder H and iCHUM-Tree by bubble sort operation

Let us give an example of the construction and update procedure. Considering $D0$ in Table 1, we set the min_util 40% of the sum of all TU, which is 18.4. The headtable H is created with items whose TWU $\geq$ 18.4. The items of H are "D A B C" in TWU descending order. We insert these items in each transaction by the order and formulate iCHUM-Tree in Fig. 2a. When $D1$ comes, TWU of items changes and min_util is 29.2, shown in Table 3. We insert E to the headtable and iCHUM-tree following the previous order. Here, we keep the unpromising item C because it had once been high TWU items. It is likely that it becomes high TWU item again in incremental databases. We rearrange the iCHUM-Tree and its headtable in the "B A D E C" order by bubble sort operation. Not only items in headtable should be sorted in this order, but also the corresponding nodes in the iCHUM-Tree do the same as well. After all items have been sorted, the iCHUM-Tree is updated as shown in Fig. 2b.

3.4   Mining and Identifying Procedures

Mining procedure discovers the collection of high TWU candidate itemsets represented by *cand* from iCHUM-Tree. The mining procedure is a pattern-growth approach, which is shown in Algorithm 3. It is based on the FP-growth mining algorithm [6]. We firstly construct conditional tree CT_α for each entry α in H. We follow the link in α's entry to obtain all transaction records containing item α. For each α node in iCHUM-Tree, we find its prefix nodes and calculate TWU of its prefix nodes based on TWU of α. If prefix node β's TWU $\geq min\_util$ in CT_α, then we add β to CT_α and add $\{\alpha\beta\}$ to $cand$. The time complexity to mine iCHUM-Tree is $O(hm_p^2)$, where h is the height of iCHUM-Tree and m_p represents number of promising items. The mining recursion complexity is determined by the height and node number of iCHUM-Tree.

For example, we construct B's conditional tree CT_B from iCHUM-Tree in Fig. 2a. For node {B}:(1,7), we obtain its prefix node A as {A}:(1,9). In terms of node {B}:(2,17), we add A's count and TWU by 2 and 17 respectively. Besides, we obtain B's another prefix node D as {D}:(2,17). The prefix nodes of B is now that {A}:(3,26) and {D}:(2,17). Considering min_util is 18.4, B's conditional tree consists of node A and discards node D. We add itemset {AB} into set $cand$. For {AB}'s prefix nodes, we can obtain that {D}:(2,17), which is less than min_util. Mining procedure for B is finished and then iCHUM continues to process item A. After iCHUM processes each entry in headtable H, we can obtain the set $cand$ containing {C},{CD},{B},{AB},{A},{D} in original database $D0$.

Algorithm 3. Mining procedure

Input: min_util , iCHUM-Tree, headtable H
Output: collection of high TWU itemsets $cand$
    for each entry α in H **do**
        Add $\{\alpha\}$ to $cand$
        Call Mining(CT_α, H_α, α)
    end for
    proc Mining(CT_α,H_α, α)
        Create α's conditional tree CT_α from iCHUM-Tree
        Create headtable H_α for CT_α
        for each entry β in H_α
            Add $\{\beta\} \cup \{\alpha\}$ to $cand$
            Call Mining($CT_{\alpha\beta}$, $H_{\alpha\beta}$, $\alpha\beta$)
        end for

Identifying procedure is to calculate the utility of these itemsets in the collection of high TWU candidate itemsets $cand$ according to Definition 1. The iCHUM algorithm needs to rescan the transaction database to obtain utility of all itemsets in $cand$. For those recalled items and their corresponding itemsets, we need to rescan the original database as well as the new database. We calculate their utility in each transaction records and sum them up. For other items, we have had calculated their utility in the identifying process of $D0$. We only rescan the new database for those itemsets and add to their utility.

In the above example, we calculate the utility of each itemset in $cand$ according to Table 1. $U(\{C\}), U(\{B\}), U(\{A\}), U(\{D\})$ is 12, 10, 9, 10 respectively.

The utilities of items in headtable H are less than min_util. For two-element itemsets, $U(\{CD\})$ is 20 and $U(\{AB\})$ is 19, which are high utility itemsets for transaction database $D0$. After a new database $D1$ is inserted, the updated iCHUM-Tree is as shown in Fig. 2b. Following mining procedure, we obtain the $cand$ of the database $D0 + D1$, which includes $\{E\},\{D\},\{A\},\{AB\},\{B\}$. For $\{E\}$, we rescan the whole transaction database and obtain its utility as 20. For the rest, we add their utility in $D1$ and obtain their final utility as 12, 14, 24, 14. Because the utility of each candidate itemset is less than min_util 29.2, there is no high utility itemset for transaction database $D0 + D1$ when min_util is set as 40% of total transaction utilities.

4   Experiment

In this section, we evaluate the performance of iCHUM algorithm written in C++. The experiment were conducted on Ubuntu server with a dual-2.4GHz CPU processor and 4G memory. Both real and synthetic dataset could be obtained from NU-MineBench [1]. Real dataset, named *Chainstore*, is a sparse and large database. It contains 1,112,949 transaction records and total 46,086 kinds of items. We split the database into $D0$ of 700,000 and $D1$ of 412,949. Synthetic dataset, named T10I6D100, contains 100 items and 93,058 transaction records whose average length is 10, where $|D0|$ is 60,000 and $|D1|$ is 33,058.

As a comparison, we implement the IHUP algorithm [3] and an iCHUM without update (iCHUMxU) algorithm in C++ as baseline methods. The iCHUMxU algorithm mines iCHUM-Tree twice without update procedure regarding the $D0$ and $D0 + D1$ as original database input respectively. The iCHUMxU is a high utility mining algorithm for fixed database and we compare its mining efficiency with iCHUM's in incremental databases.

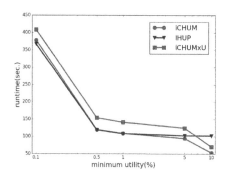

Fig. 3. Runtime on T10I6D100

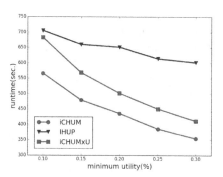

Fig. 4. Runtime on Chainstore

Fig. 3 shows the execution runtime on T10I6D100. With a logarithmical X axis, the runtime at different minimum utility thresholds is easy to view.

---

[1] http://cucis.ece.northwestern.edu/projects/DMS/MineBench.html

For larger min_util or minimum utility, runtime of iCHUM is less than that of IHUP. When min_util is 10%, the total runtime of iCHUM is 52.99 seconds, compared with 101.65 seconds of IHUP and 70.17 seconds of iCHUMxU. It is because that the items in iCHUM-Tree is a small part of the total items. It takes less time on update and does not need to reconstruct the whole iCHUM-Tree. However, the performance of iCHUM algorithm becomes worse when min_util gets smaller compared with IHUP. When min_util is 0.1%, the total runtime of iCHUM is 378.43 seconds, which is larger than 366.97 seconds of IHUP. It is because that the number of items with high TWU value reaches close to the total items number. In time complexity, m_p is approximated with number of items m. The cost of maintaining headtable is almost the same. Besides, the iCHUM algorithm should spend more time on finding back recalled items. That happens in such a dataset, where there are less items and transaction length is longer.

The iCHUM algorithm has an advantage over IHUP on sparse and large database, shown in Fig. 4. In Chainstore dataset, each item accounts for small proportion of whole transaction $(m_p \ll m)$, where maintaining headtable with high TWU items is efficient. When min_util is 0.2%, total runtime of iCHUM is 435.86 seconds, which is less than 651.61 seconds of IHUP. IHUP should maintain entire items and takes overhead time, which is larger than 501.41 seconds of iCHUMxU. The reason is that valuable items in a large transaction database is rare, and thus it is efficient to maintain these promising items instead of entire items. From runtime distribution in Table 4, runtime is largely reduced in construction and update procedures, which the iCHUM algorithm focuses on. The fewer items save the execution time on construction and update of the iCHUM-Tree. Besides, the iCHUMxU is a time-consuming method in both datasets. It is more efficient to update iCHUM-Tree than to rebuild the tree structure entirely since we reuse the previous tree structure and mining results.

Table 4. Runtime Distribution (sec.) of iCHUM and IHUP

Dataset	Algorithm	D0			D1			Time
		construction	mining	identify	update	mining	identify	
T10I6D100	IHUP	33.89	0.27	0.07	67.40	0.42	0.22	102.27
0.5%	iCHUM	**30.60**	0.26	0.07	**62.64**	0.41	0.22	**94.20**
Chainstore	IHUP	209.14	1.45	46.09	318.78	2.29	73.86	651.61
0.2%	iCHUM	**113.98**	1.33	46.00	**199.74**	2.18	72.63	**435.86**

To verify whether the iCHUM algorithm obtains all high utility itemsets, we keep records of mining results from both iCHUM and IHUP. Moreover, we compare the results on different datasets with that of Two-Phase algorithm provided by NU-MineBench [13,14]. Table 5 shows that the number of high utility itemsets at different minimum utility threshold on T10I6D100 dataset. Table 6 shows the mining results on Chainstore dataset.

Table 5. Number of High Utility Itemsets on T10I6D100

Database	Minimum Utility Threshold				
	10%	5%	1%	0.5%	0.1%
D0	0	2	292	1643	46471
D0 + D1	0	2	292	1644	45614

Table 6. Number of High Utility Itemsets on Chainstore

Database	Minimum Utility Threshold				
	0.30%	0.25%	0.20%	0.15%	0.10%
D0	15	18	29	48	86
D0 + D1	15	17	26	50	80

5 Conclusion and Future Work

In this paper, we propose an efficient iCHUM algorithm for mining high utility itemsets in incremental databases. The iCHUM algorithm compresses transaction database into a compact tree structure called iCHUM-Tree. The update of iCHUM-Tree maintains the tree structure with all promising items which guarantees all high utility itemsets to be found. Experimental analysis shows that iCHUM performs better than other baselines in incremental databases, especially in terms of those with large number of transaction records or items. We believe that iCHUM algorithm will play an important role for high utility mining in incremental databases in practice.

We notice that the performance of the iCHUM algorithm degrades as the amount of the recalled items increases. In the future, we will explore a knowledge-based method to improve the promising item discovering. In addition, we will study the idea of B+ tree to improve our data structure and algorithm in construction and mining procedures.

Acknowledgments. This research is supported by the 863 project of China (2013AA013300), National Natural Science Foundation of China (Grant No. 61375054 and 61402045), Tsinghua University Initiative Scientific Research Program (Grant No.20131089256), and Cross fund of Graduate School at Shenzhen, Tsinghua University (Grant No. JC20140001).

References

1. Agrawal, R., Imieliński, T., Swami, A.: Mining association rules between sets of items in large databases. ACM SIGMOD Record **22**(2), 207–216 (1993)
2. Agrawal, R., Srikant, R.: Fast algorithms for mining association rules. In: Proceedings of the 20th International Conference on Very Large Data Bases, pp. 487–499 (1994)
3. Ahmed, C.F., Tanbeer, S.K., Jeong, B.S., Lee, Y.K.: Efficient tree structures for high utility pattern mining in incremental databases. IEEE Transactions on Knowledge and Data Engineering **21**(12), 1708–1721 (2009)

4. Erwin, A., Gopalan, R.P., Achuthan, N.: Ctu-mine: an efficient high utility itemset mining algorithm using the pattern growth approach. In: 2007 7th IEEE International Conference on Computer and Information Technology, pp. 71–76 (2007)
5. Grahne, G., Zhu, J.: Fast algorithms for frequent itemset mining using fp-trees. IEEE Transactions on Knowledge and Data Engineering 17(10), 1347–1362 (2005)
6. Han, J., Pei, J., Yin, Y.: Mining frequent patterns without candidate generation. ACM SIGMOD Record 29(2), 1–12 (2000)
7. Koh, J.-L., Shieh, S.-F.: An efficient approach for maintaining association rules based on adjusting fp-tree structures. In: Lee, Y.J., Whang, K.-Y., Li, J., Lee, D. (eds.) DASFAA 2004. LNCS, vol. 2973, pp. 417–424. Springer, Heidelberg (2004)
8. Li, Y.C., Yeh, J.S., Chang, C.C.: Efficient algorithms for mining share-frequent itemsets. In: Proceedings of the 11th International Fuzzy Systems Association World Congress, pp. 534–539 (2005)
9. Li, Y.C., Yeh, J.S., Chang, C.C.: Isolated items discarding strategy for discovering high utility itemsets. Data & Knowledge Engineering 64(1), 198–217 (2008)
10. Lin, C.W., Hong, T.P., Lu, W.H.: Maintaining high utility pattern trees in dynamic databases. In: 2010 2nd International Conference on Computer Engineering and Applications, pp. 304–308 (2010)
11. Lin, C.W., Hong, T.P., Lu, W.H.: An effective tree structure for mining high utility itemsets. Expert Systems with Applications 38(6), 7419–7424 (2011)
12. Lin, C.W., Lan, G.C., Hong, T.P.: An incremental mining algorithm for high utility itemsets. Expert Systems with Applications 39(8), 7173–7180 (2012)
13. Liu, Y., Liao, W.K., Choudhary, A.: A fast high utility itemsets mining algorithm. In: Proceedings of the 1st International Workshop on Utility-based Data Mining, pp. 90–99 (2005)
14. Liu, Y., Liao, W., Choudhary, A.K.: A two-phase algorithm for fast discovery of high utility itemsets. In: Cheung, D., Ho, T.-B., Liu, H. (eds.) PAKDD 2005. LNCS (LNAI), vol. 3518, pp. 689–695. Springer, Heidelberg (2005)
15. Tseng, V.S., Wu, C.W., Shie, B.E., Yu, P.S.: Up-growth: an efficient algorithm for high utility itemset mining. In: Proceedings of the 16th ACM SIGKDD International Conference on Knowledge Discovery and Data Mining, pp. 253–262 (2010)
16. Wu, C.W., Shie, B.E., Tseng, V.S., Yu, P.S.: Mining top-k high utility itemsets. In: Proceedings of the 18th ACM SIGKDD International Conference on Knowledge Discovery and Data Mining, pp. 78–86 (2012)
17. Yeh, J.S., Chang, C.Y., Wang, Y.T.: Efficient algorithms for incremental utility mining. In: Proceedings of the 2nd International Conference on Ubiquitous Information Management and Communication, pp. 212–217 (2008)
18. Yun, U.: Efficient mining of weighted interesting patterns with a strong weight and/or support affinity. Information Sciences 177(17), 3477–3499 (2007)
19. Yun, U., Leggett, J.J.: Wfim: weighted frequent itemset mining with a weight range and a minimum weight. In: Proceedings of the 2005 SIAM International Conference on Data Mining, pp. 636–640 (2005)

Interval-Index: A Scalable and Fast Approach for Reachability Queries in Large Graphs

Fangxu Li, Pingpeng Yuan$^{(\boxtimes)}$, and Hai Jin

Services Computing Technology and System Lab, Cluster and Grid Computing Lab,
Huazhong University of Science and Technology, Wuhan 430074, China
{ppyuan,hjin}@mail.hust.edu.cn

Abstract. Now more and more large graphs are available. One interesting problem is how to effectively find reachability between any vertex pairs in a very large graph. Multiple approaches have been proposed to answer reachability queries. However, most approaches only perform well on small graphs. Processing reachability queries on large graphs requires much storage and computation and still remains challenges. In this paper, we propose a scalable and fast indexing approach called Interval-Index, based on traversal tree-based partitioning and relabeling scheme. Our approach has several unique features: first, the traversal tree-based partitioning ensures access locality and parallelism in computation; second, continuous relabeling ensures fast querying and saves search space; third, we convert the entire graph database into a traversal tree graph on a smaller scale, to reach a compact storage structure. Finally, we run extensive experiments on synthetic graphs and real graphs with different sizes, and show that Interval-Index approach outperforms the state-of-the-art Feline in both storage size and the performance of query execution.

1 Introduction

Highly connected data sets have increased exponentially over the past several years. For example, Facebook had more than 800 million users by the end of 2011 [2]. With the continued growth of graph-structured data, a common graph application is to query whether there exist paths between two vertices in a graph, namely reachability queries. In most cases of reachability queries, users always lack exact knowledge of the graph. They can only provide a rough query description. Thus, it is difficult to describe reachability queries using SQL-style (SPARQL, etc.) languages due to their uncertain patterns.

Diverse approaches have been proposed to answer reachability queries. However, most approaches only perform well on relatively small graphs, with hundreds of thousands of vertices and edges at most [3]. But for processing larger graphs, they are either too costly in storage or slow in query time. For example, Path-tree [11] has the restriction on scalability, as its index size on large dense graphs may be very large. So many approaches, e.g., PWAH [12], GRAIL [4], SCARAB [3], TF-Label [6] and Feline [7] are proposed to process large graphs recently. However, the approaches are still crucial for performance limits.

© Springer International Publishing Switzerland 2015
S. Zhang et al. (Eds.): KSEM 2015, LNAI 9403, pp. 224–235, 2015.
DOI: 10.1007/978-3-319-25159-2_21

For example, PWAH requires large memory to hold index in order to ensure efficiency. So it is not scalable for large graphs. For GRAIL, the inclusion relation between labels is necessary to indicate reachability, but not a sufficient one. So GRAIL can only answer un-reachability between two vertices, otherwise GRAIL requires to traverse the graph using DFS. Feline needs to keep the primitive graph in memory, since it cannot answer reachability merely by the index. So it requires long time to load data, and large memory. Like GRAIL, partial order-based scheme in Feline is not a sufficient condition for reachability. So DFS is also required to exclude those un-reachable vertex pairs in the worst case.

In this paper, we present a scalable and fast indexing approach for very large graphs, named as Interval-Index. Our approach is motivated by our observation that processing reachability queries need traverse graphs. But traversal through large graphs will bring immeasurable time and space consumption. Therefore, we first partition a large graph into tree-based partitions to improve access locality and reduce search space. In order to build interval indexes on partitions easily, we further assign vertices of each partition continuous IDs in parallel. By this means, we further maximize sequential access and minimize random access on storage media. Third, since vertex IDs of each partition are continuous, we build an interval index which helps to determine the reachability in each tree-partition. Our approach can prune search space greatly during answering reachability queries. The main contributions of our research are as follows.

- A traversal tree-based partitioning approach is proposed to search each partition in parallel. Partitioning a graph into multiple smaller trees does not break the relationships of graph. Furthermore, it ensures access locality and reduces the storage space.
- An efficient and scalable graph indexing technique - Interval-Index is proposed to help quickly determine which trees a vertex is in. In order to facilitate building interval index, vertices of each partition are assigned continuous IDs so that vertex IDs of each partition will not overlap. The relabeling scheme ensures high efficiency in pruning of search space during answering reachability queries.

2 Preliminary

Since undirected graphs can be converted into directed connected graphs and disconnected graphs can be split into connected subgraphs, thus, we will mainly discuss directed connected graph in the following.

Definition 1 (Graph). *A graph $G = (V, E)$ is defined by a finite set V of vertices, $\{v_i | v_i \in V\}$ ($0 \leq i < |V|$), and a set E of directed edges which connect certain pairs of vertices, and $E = \{e = (u, v) \in E | u, v \in V\}$.*

The in-degree of vertex u is denoted as $deg^-(u) = |\{v | (v, u) \in G\}|$. Its out-degree $deg^+(u) = |\{v | (u, v) \in G\}|$, and $d(u) = deg^-(u) + deg^+(u)$.

Definition 2 (Traversal Tree). *A traversal tree $T = (V_T, E_T)$ of $G = (V, E)$ is defined as follows: 1) $E_T \subseteq E$; (2) $\exists v_r \in V_T$, $\forall u \in V_T$,$(u, v_r) \notin E_T$. v_r is the root of T; (3) $\forall u \in V_T$, u satisfies the following conditions: (i) $\exists v \in V$, u is v or u is a dummy copy of v; (ii) $\exists v \in V_T$ and v is a child of u s.t. $(u, v) \in E_T$; (iii) if u is a leaf of T, u is a dummy vertex or $deg^+(u) = 0$. if u is a non-leaf of T, u has at most $deg^+(u)$ children.*

Definition 3 (Rooted Traversal Tree). *An Rooted Traversal Tree (RT-Tree) $R = (V_T, E_T)$ of $G = (V, E)$ is a traversal tree starting from a vertex $v \in V$ whose $deg^-(v)=0$.*

For instance, the tree indicated by the dotted line in Fig. 1(a) is an RT-Tree. G may have multiple RT-Trees. The number of RT-Trees of G depends on the number of vertices with zero in-degree. The intersection of two RT-Trees may be not empty. Here, we define the intersection of two RT-Trees as pivotal tree because two or more RT-Trees share it.

Definition 4 (Pivotal Tree). *Given a directed graph $G = (V, E)$, assume $R_m, R_n(m \neq n)$ are RT-Trees of G. The pivotal tree P_T of R_m and R_n is defined as follows: (i) $P_T = R_m \bigcap R_n$; (ii) $\exists < v_0, v_1, ..., v_k >$, such that $v_0 = v_{rt}(R_i)(i = m, n), v_k = v_{rt}(P_T), \forall j \in [0, k-1] : (v_j, v_{j+1}) \in R_i$. The root of pivotal tree is named as pivotal vertex.*

Achieving high performance in processing a large scale graph requires partitioning of the graph. Here, we partition a graph into multiple non-overlaping traversal trees. In the following, traversal trees indicate non-overlapping traversal trees if we do not state explicitly.

Definition 5 (k-way Partition). *Let $P_1, P_2, \ldots, P_k$ denote a set of traversal trees of $G = (V, E)$, where (1) $P_i = (V_{P_i}, E_{P_i})$, $V_{P_1} \cup V_{P_2} \cup \ldots \cup V_{P_k} = V$, $V_{P_i} \cap V_{P_j} = \emptyset(i \neq j)$; (2) $\forall(u, v) \in E, u \in V_{P_i}$, $v \in V_{P_i} \Rightarrow (u, v) \in E_{P_i}$. $P_1, P_2, \ldots, P_k$ ($1 \leq k \leq |V|$) are named as k partitions of G.*

Definition 6 (Graph of Traversal Trees). *Given a directed graph $G = (V, E)$, and $\mathcal{T}$ is the set of non-overlapping traversal trees, which is a partition of G. $|\mathcal{T}| \geq 1$. The graph of traversal trees $G_T = (V_{G_T}, E_{G_T})$ of G is defined as follows: (i) The function $f : \mathcal{T} \leftrightarrow V_{G_T}$ is bijective. Namely, each traversal tree in $\mathcal{T}$ is mapping into a vertex of V_{G_T}; (ii)$\forall T_i, T_j \in \mathcal{T}(i \neq j)$, if the root of T_j is reachable from the root of T_i, $(f(T_i), f(T_j)) \in E_{G_T}$.*

3   The Interval-Index Approach

In our approach, we first traverse a graph and construct its RT-Trees, and then split these RT-Trees into multiple non-overlapping traversal trees based partitions. So parallelism and locality of the computation can be improved. The vertices in the same partition will be assigned continuous IDs in order to build a compact index easier. So we can quickly determine which partition or RT-Trees a vertex is in by comparing vertex id with the ranges of partitions. Thus, the reachability between two vertices can be determined by the relationship between two IDs. In the following, we will first introduce how to search pivotal vertex, partitioning a graph into traversal trees, relabeling. Finally, we will build interval index and store it in an efficient manner.

3.1   Searching Pivotal Vertices

Traversal of large graphs will cause huge cost. Consider the case to answer reachability queries, we always have to frequently access the neighborhood of the recent visited vertices, or the paths where the recent visited vertices are. Therefore, to improve access locality and reduce search space, we need place those neighboring vertices in paths into a same partition. Each partition can be an RT-Tree. However, there may exist overlapping subgraphs, namely pivotal trees among RT-Trees of a graph. These pivotal trees may also overlap with each other. Since the intersection of traversal trees is not empty, it is difficult to index traversal trees and answer reachability. So we need to further partition RT-Trees into disjoint traversal trees.

Algorithm 1. Searching Pivotal Vertex

Require: Graph G, root set $\mathcal{S}$
1: Pivotal vertex set $\mathcal{P} \leftarrow \emptyset$;
2: **for** each $root \in \mathcal{S}$ **do**
3:    **if** $root$ is unvisited **then**
4:       $enqueue(root)$;
5:    **while** $queue$ is not empty **do**
6:       $j = dequeue()$;
7:       **if** j is unvisited **then**
8:          $label(j) \leftarrow root$;
9:          **for** each direct successor u of j **do**
10:             $enqueue(u), deg^-(u) \leftarrow deg^-(u) - 1$;
11:          **else if** $label(j) \neq root$ and $deg^-(u) == 0$ **then**
12:             $\mathcal{P} \leftarrow \mathcal{P} \cup \{j\}$;

To partition RT-Trees further into disjoint parts, we first find out pivotal vertices using BFS. The traversal starts from the root of each RT-Tree. Each time when a vertex is visited, the in-degrees of its direct successors should be reduced by one. Assume we visit vertex j, there are three situations depending on whether vertex j was visited before (Algorithm 1). Consider the situation in which vertex j has not been visited yet, we label it with the vertex ID of the current tree's root. If j has been visited before and its label is not equal to the current root ID, j belongs to a pivotal tree. If the in-degree of j is zero, j is a pivotal vertex. If j has been visited yet, and its label is equal to current root ID, it indicates that the RT-Tree has cross edges (e.g., edge: $v_{27} \rightarrow v_{98}$). For example, in Fig. 1(a), all the pivotal vertices are v_7, v_9.

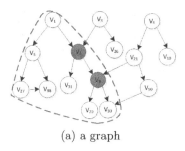

(a) a graph

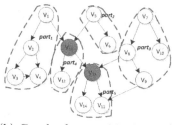

(b) Graph after partitioning and relabeling

Fig. 1. Tree-based partitioning and relabeling

3.2   Traversal Tree-Based Partitioning

After finding all the pivotal vertices, we then partition the graph using traversal tree-based partitioning (Algorithm 2). If we can reach a vertex u (e.g. v_{30} in Fig. 1(a)) via pivotal vertex s_1 (e.g. v_9 in Fig.1(a)), or a vertex s_2 (e.g.,v_{99} in Fig.1(a)), the topological traversal process will assign u to the partition s_1 resides due to its in-degree restriction on visiting order. However, DFS or BFS can not do it correctly. For instance, in BFS, if the traverse from s_2 to u is earlier than from s_1 to u, u will be assigned to the partition s_2 resides, otherwise, the partition s_1 resides. Actually, since u is a successor of a pivotal vertex, it should be as a part of the pivotal tree to be partitioned.

When we reach an unvisited vertex u (not a pivotal vertex) from a root, we assign it to the partition where this root is, and delete u and its direct out-edges from the graph. Otherwise, if u is a pivotal vertex, the RT-Trees where u appears will be recorded in a data structure (e.g. Table 1). Thus, we can easily find the RT-Trees where a pivotal vertex appears. When we finish the topological traversal from one root, we can get a partition. The above steps are performed for each root of RT-Trees repeatedly until all vertices are assigned.

Consider the graph in Fig. 1(a) again, initially, partition $part_1 = \{V_1, E_1\}$, $V_1 = E_1 = \emptyset$. The traversal begins at root vertex v_1 and v_1 is inserted into the queue. Now, $V_1 = V_1 \cup \{v_1\} = \{v_1\}$. If $queue$ is not empty, execute $dequeue$ (v_1) and delete its out-edges $(v_1, v_5), (v_1, v_7)$ from the graph. Among v_1's direct successors $\{v_5, v_7\}$, v_5 is unvisited and not a pivotal vertex, and its current $deg^-(v_5)$ is zero. So we visit v_5, $enqueue(v_5)$ and $V_1 = \{v_1\} \cup \{v_5\} = \{v_1, v_5\}$. Then, we reach v_7. Since v_7 is a pivotal vertex, we just record (v_1, v_7) and (v_3, v_7), where v_1,v_3 are the roots of RT-Trees where v_7 resides. Now $queue = \{v_5\}$. The above steps will be executed until the queue is empty. Finally, we can get three partitions $part_1$, $part_2$, and $part_3$.

After traversing all RT-Trees, we perform the same steps as the above repeatedly to get pivotal trees from pivotal vertices. The partitioning result is indicated using dotted lines in Fig. 1(b) (IDs in Fig. 1(b) are assigned using Algorithm 2).

Algorithm 2. Tree-Based Partitioning

Require: Graph G=(V,E), root set $\mathcal{S}$, pivotal vertex set $\mathcal{P}$
1: $i \leftarrow 1, \mathcal{D} = (\emptyset, \emptyset)$;
2: **for** each unvisited vertex $root \in \mathcal{S}$ **do**
3:    $enqueue(root)$;
4:    $part_i = (V_i, E_i), E_i \leftarrow \emptyset, V_i \leftarrow \{root\}$;
5:    **while** $queue$ is not empty **do**
6:       $j = dequeue()$;
7:       **for** each successor u of j **do**
8:          $deg^-(u) \leftarrow deg^-(u) - 1$;
9:          **if** $u \in \mathcal{P}$ **then**
10:             **for** each $t \in Root(u)$ **do**
11:                $\mathcal{D} \leftarrow \mathcal{D} \cup (t, u)$;
12:          **else**
13:             **if** u is unvisited and $deg^-(u) == 0$ **then**
14:                $enqueue(u); V_i \leftarrow V_i \cup \{u\}$; set u as visited;
15:    **for** each edge $(u, v) \in E$ and $u, v \in V_i$ **do**
16:       $E_i \leftarrow E_i \cup (u, v)$;
17:    $i \leftarrow i + 1$;
18: **for** each vertex $j \in \mathcal{P}$ **do**
19:    execute step 3-17;

Our traversal tree-based partitioning scheme has three salient advantages. First, since neighboring vertices and paths are in same partitions, it can improve memory and disk access locality. Second, it prunes unnecessary search space, and ensure a quick index lookup. Third, smaller tree-partitions facilitate parallel processing.

3.3   Relabeling Trees

Each vertex of a graph has an ID. Since the initial vertex IDs are randomly assigned and the vertices are distributed over the graph, it is difficult to build the index on vertices. To improve locality for search and facilitate index construction, vertices belonging to the same partition are assigned with continuous IDs. So each partition can be indicated by a range (interval). We can efficiently determine which partitions a vertex is in merely using intervals, and further determine the corresponding RT-Trees it resides. Then, the reachability of two vertices can be partially determined by checking whether their IDs fall in a range.

Algorithm 3 shows the relabeling process using DFS. Global variable *idcount* indicate the starting ID assigned to every partition. In each partition, atomic *__sync_fetch_and_add* operation is used to seize the interval of IDs first. Then vertices in each partition are assigned ids according to theirs visiting order. For example, $V_1 = \{v_1, v_5, v_{27}, v_{98}\}$ of $part_1$ is relabeled as $\{v_1, v_2, v_3, v_4\}$ (Fig. 1(b)).

Distribution of pivotal vertices has been recorded during partitioning. So we can easily search for their corresponding RT-Trees to merge partitions. For example, Table 1 records distribution of pivotal vertices in Fig. 1, $part_4$ with old

---

Algorithm 3. Relabeling Traversal Trees

Require: Partition set $\mathcal{P}$, vertex size set $\mathcal{C}$ of partitions, global variable $idcount$
1: **parfor** each $part_i = (V_i,\ E_i) \in \mathcal{P}$ **do**
2:    $new\_id \leftarrow \_sync\_fetch\_and\_add(\&idcount,\ \mathcal{C}_i)$;
3:    **for** each vertex $v \in V_i$ in DFS order **do**
4:      $old\_id(v) \leftarrow new\_id$;
5:      $new\_id \leftarrow new\_id+1$;

---

root v_7 resides in two RT-Trees with old root v_1 and v_3 (v_1 and v_5 are their new root IDs). So $part_4$ should be merged into these two RT-Trees. Table 2 is the collection of partitions described by intervals for each RT-Tree (after relabeling). For example, $[5, 6], [11, 12]$ and $[13, 15]$ compose a RT-Tree with new root v_5.

Table 1. Distribution of pivotal vertices

old root ID	pivotal vertex
v_1	v_7
v_3	v_7
v_1	v_9
v_3	v_9
v_4	v_9

Table 2. Partition-based RT-Tree

new root ID	partition
v_1	[1, 4], [11, 12], [13, 15]
v_5	[5, 6], [11, 12], [13, 15]
v_7	[7, 10], [13, 15]

3.4   Interval-Index Construction

After partitioning a large graph into a set of tree-partitions, we may get a large number of tree partitions. It is important to lookup a tree in order to answer reachability. Since vertices of each partition are assigned the continuous IDs, each partition can be indicated by a minimal id and a maximal id. The minimal id of a partition is a root of traversal tree. Thus, we can quickly locate a traversal trees where a vertex is. It greatly reduces the search space. We will construct the graph of traversal tree. Specifically, we consider the partition with continuous IDs as a vertex in the graph of traversal trees. If two partitions are in the same RT-Tree, we add an edge between them into the graph of traversal trees. The traversal tree graph of Fig. 1(b) is shown in Fig. 2. Now, only direct edges between two vertices should be taken into consideration. That is, there exists no transitive relation in a traversal tree graph. Vertices v_3, v_5 reside in different RT-Trees, even though the two partitions denoted by interval [1, 4] and [5, 6] are indirectly connected by partition [11, 12].

We build an adjacency list index for the graph of traversal trees. Table 3 shows the adjacency list index of Fig. 2. Because it indicates a range, we call it interval index. We can determine the reachability of vertex pairs by checking the adjacency list index. The reachability of any two vertices can be determined using the interval index. Concretely, we first search the partition where the first vertex resides and locate the corresponding row in the adjacency list. All the neighboring partitions of this partition can be found in the list. Second, we check whether the second vertex resides in the neighboring partitions. By this way, we can quickly answer the reachability of vertex pairs.

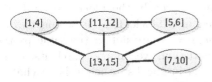

Fig. 2. The graph of traversal trees

Table 3. Adjacency list index

vertex	list of edges
[1, 4]	[11, 12],[13, 15]
[5, 6]	[11, 12], [13, 15]
[7, 10]	[13, 15]
[11, 12]	[1, 4], [5, 6],[13 15]
[13, 15]	[1, 4],[5, 6], [7, 10],[11, 12]

With interval index, the reachability of vertex pairs can be determined quickly. It requires two binary searches. First, we search *offset_index* for the offset address of the partition where the first vertex resides and locate the corresponding row in the adjacency list. And all the neighboring partitions of this partition can be found in the list. Second, we search whether the second vertex resides in these neighboring partitions to answer the reachability.

3.5   Delta Compression and Integer Encoding

Relabeling scheme makes differences among IDs residing in the same partition smaller to further improves locality. We store the interval-based adjacency list using byte-level delta compression scheme [8], in which the minimum number of bytes are used to label the delta value between IDs. The relabeling scheme makes the difference between IDs or intervals smaller. For one row of the adjacency list like $[id_1, id_2] : [s_1, e_1], [s_2, e_2]...$, we store it as $id_1, id_2 - id_1, s_1, e_1 - s_1, s_2 - e_1, e_2 - s_2, ...$ We then append the first interval $[id_1, id_2]$ and the offset of its corresponding row into a file named *offset_index* in order to efficiently locate its row in subsequent query processing.

The ID (including the delta value) is an integer. The size for storing an integer is typically 4 bytes. Not all integers require the whole word space to store them. For example, in small graphs like *linkedmdb*, the number of vertices is about 1 million. The storage for each id is at most 3 bytes. So it is wasteful to store them with a larger number of bytes when a smaller number of bytes are sufficient. However, for bigger graph, 4 bytes may be not enough to store an ID. Thus, we use the flexible approach - variable integer encoding [8].

3.6   Complexity Analysis

Index construction involves four steps: we need search pivotal vertices first, then partition the graph using traversal trees and relabel vertices. Finally, we build interval index. The complexity of Algorithm 1 is $O(|E|)$, because both of them enumerate all vertices once. The complexity of Algorithm 2 is $O(|V| + |E|)$, because each vertex is visited when every edge is visited. The index construction can be executed when the relabeling process finishes (Algorithm 3). The complexity of the last two steps is $O(|V|)$. Thus, its final complexity is $O(|V| + |E|)$.

Assume vertex pairs (u, v), our approach first locate the partition where u appears. The way is to perform binary search in the storage block in which u's partition is stored. Thus, the complexity depends on the average number of partitions in a storage block. In our approach, the block size is 4KB. Thus, there are not many partitions stored in a block. If u, v belong to the same partition, then v is reachable from u. If u, v are not in the same partition, after determining the location of a partition, we binary search its adjacent list to check whether v appears. If v is in the list, then v is reachable from u. Otherwise, they are not reachable. Thus, our approach takes time $O(log(\text{block\_size}) + log(average\_len))$, where $average\_len$ is the average length of adjacent lists of partitions. $average\_len$ is less than the average depth of rooted traversal trees.

4   Experimental Evaluation

Since Veloso et al. [7] showed that Feline outperforms the recently systems, such as GRAIL [4], we choose Feline as the competitor. Both Feline and our method are complied using g++. We run all experiments on a server with an Intel 2.13GHz CPU, 48GB memory, and CentOS 6.5 (2.6.32 kernel).

4.1   Performance on Real Graphs

Real Data Sets. We use six real-world data sets from a wide spectrum of domains: *linkedmdb*[1], *de wiktionary*[2], *dblp*[3], *pagelinks_en*[4], *yago*[3] and *wikidata*[2]. These real graphs vary both in size and in average degree (i.e., d_{avg}). The characteristics of the data sets are shown in Table 4.

Table 4. Characteristics of real data sets

Data sets	linkedmdb	de wiktionary	dblp	pagelinks_en	yago	wikidata
vertices	1,404,454	3,499,638	30,812,730	18,268,992	101,722,334	164,223,339
edges	3,087,311	8,518,892	67,840,417	136,591,822	205,638,803	377,173,710
d_{avg}	2.20	2.43	2.20	7.48	2.02	2.30

Storage. Table 5 reports the results. Interval-Index approach requires less storage than Feline does. The reason is that Interval-Index approach is based on

---

[1] http://queens.db.toronto.edu/~oktie/linkedmdb/

[2] http://www.rdfhdt.org/datasets

[3] http://datahub.io/zh_CN/dataset

[4] http://data.dws.informatik.uni-mannheim.de/dbpedia

local partitioning and byte-level delta compression. Moreover, relabeling makes the IDs residing in the same partition continuous, significantly improving compactness of the index.

Table 5. Storage for real data sets (in MB)

Data sets	linkedmdb	de wiktionary	dblp	pagelinks_en	yago	wikidata
Interval-Index	108.6	108.0	308.0	2798.2	3133.5	10250.2
Feline	153.3	182.3	524.6	4831.0	4690.0	13230.0
Reduction	40.8%	41.3%	42.1%	33.2%	22.5%	44.3%

Query Answering Time. We randomly select 1,000k pairs of vertices for each data set. Table 6 reports the total time taken to run queries in real graphs. The experimental results are the average values of 5 runs. Since Feline uses a memory-based access mechanism, its query time includes the loading time of the graph and the time for processing 1,000k pairs of vertices. On the contrary, Interval-Index's access mechanism is based on external memory operation, implemented by *mmap virtual storage* technique. So it only needs to load the required data into memory. More importantly, its local partitioning holds neighbors together, so the search space is well pruned. Continuous IDs in each partition further reduce query time. The results clearly show that Interval-Index outperforms Feline in all data sets.

Table 6. Query time for real data sets (in second)

Data sets	linkedmdb	de wiktionary	dblp	pagelinks_en	yago	wikidata
Interval-Index	139.43	69.65	532.87	132.32	926.73	22037.29
Feline	181.82	86.73	685.91	438.25	1267.26	32159.30

4.2 Scalability

We also perform experiments on six synthetic random graphs with different size generated using LUBM data generator [1]. So we can evaluate the scalability of our approach. The characteristics of six data sets are shown in Table 7.

Table 7. Characteristics of synthetic data sets

Data sets	LUBM10M	LUBM50M	LUBM100M	LUBM200M	LUBM300M	LUBM500M
vertices	3,303,724	16,349,317	32,905,170	65,764,621	98,640,459	164,416,780
edges	13,409,395	66,751,196	133,613,894	267,027,610	400,512,826	667,592,614

Fig. 3 reports the results on synthetic data sets. The storage of Interval-Index increases more slowly than Feline does as the graph sizes grow. Since Feline needs to keep the primitive graph in memory, thus larger storage restricts its scalability. The right part of Fig. 3 shows that our approach is again faster than Feline. As the number of edges increases, the query time of Interval-Index increases slowly, while the time of Feline increases more quickly. The reason is that Interval-Index's partition-based index sharply reduces search space to ensure efficient query performance. Its external memory-based access mechanism further ensures robust performance against the growth in graph size. Since it only needs to load the required data into memory, the graph size does not have much effect on IO and memory read/write. However, Feline requires much time to load all data into memory for computation. Thus, the performance of Feline is not better than our approach.

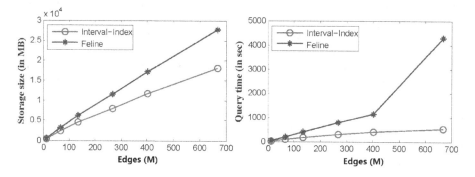

Fig. 3. Performance on varying edges ($M = 10^6$)

5   Related Work

Reachability querying is a fundamental graph operation with numerous applications both in research and in industry. Due to the emergence of large graph-structured data sets, reachaility queries have attracted enormous attention currently. Although many efforts have been devoted to it, it is still a challenge whether we can do faster and more scalable to answer reachability queries over even larger graphs with minimum cost (time and/or space).

Wei et al. [10] classifies existing approaches into two categories: Label-Only and Label+G. The label-only methods only utilize the labels to answer reachability queries, e.g., 3-Hop [9] and TF-Label [6]. Some of these methods [9] compress TC (transitive closure) to reduce index size. But majority of them are still space-consuming, and thus they are not so promising with regard to scalability on large graphs. SCARAB [3] is recently proposed as a general framework to represent a reachability backbone. It is used to further improve the scalability of existing methods. Since the backbone is much smaller than the graph itself, querying can generally be faster. However, if the size of backbone remains too large, these methods probably do not work [3,6]. TF-Label [6] is constructed based on a topological folding structure that recursively folds a target graph into half to restrict the size of label. The Label+G methods will answer reachability queries only by label if possible, otherwise DFS will be required. GRAIL [4], Ferrari [5] and Feline [7] are classified to this category. GRAIL is a reachability index formed by multiple intervals obtained by the traditional min-post strategy. Randomized interval labeling is applied to it. Ferrari employs a selective interval set compression and a topological ordering to prune search space.

6 Conclusions

In this paper, we propose a scalable and fast graph indexing scheme, Interval-Index to answer reachability queries in large graphs. The Interval-Index approach, converts a large graph into a collection of fewer tree-partitions. The reachability of any two vertices can be determined effectively and accurately using the interval index. With extensive experiments, we demonstrate that Interval-Index outperforms Feline, one of the recent best systems in storage and query answering. Furthermore, Interval-Index is scalable proven to be not only efficient, but also robust against the increase in graph size.

Acknowledgments. The research is supported by National High Technology Research and Development Program of China (863 Program) under grant No.2012AA011003.

References

1. LUBM. http://swat.cse.lehigh.edu/projects/lubm/
2. http://www.facebook.com/press/info.php?statistcs
3. Jin, R., Ruan, N., Dey, S., Yu, J.X.: SCARAB: scaling reachability computation on large graphs. In: Proc. of SIGMOD 2012, pp. 169–180 (2012)
4. Yildirim, H., Chaoji, V., Zaki, M.J.: GRAIL: Scalable reachability index for large graphs. PVLDB **3**(1), 276–284 (2010)
5. Seufert, S., Anand, A., Bedathur, S.J., Weikum, G.: FERRARI: flexible and efficient reachability range assignment for graph indexing. In: Proc. of ICDE 2013, pp. 1009–1020 (2013)
6. Cheng, J., Huang, S.L., Wu, H.H., Fu, A.W.-C.: TF-label: a topological-folding labeling scheme for reachability querying in a large graph. In: Proc. of SIGMOD 2013, pp. 193–204 (2013)
7. Veloso, R., Cerf, L., Junior, W., Zaki, M.: Reachability queries in very large graphs: a fast refined online search approach. In: Proc. of EDBT 2014, pp. 511–522 (2014)
8. Yuan, P., Liu, P., Wu, B., Liu, L., Jin, H., Zhang, W.: TripleBit: a fast and compact system for large scale RDF data. PVLDB **6**(7), 517–528 (2013)
9. Jin, R., Xiang, Y., Ruan, N., Fuhry, D.: 3-HOP: a high-compression indexing scheme for reachability query. In: Proc. of SIGMOD 1999, pp. 813–826 (2009)
10. Wei, H., Yu, J.X., Lu, C., Jin, R.M.: Reachability querying: An independent permutation labeling approach. PVLDB **7**(12), 1191–1202 (2014)
11. Jin, R., Ruan, N., Xiang, Y., Wang, H.: Path-tree: An efficient reachability indexing scheme for large directed graphs. TODS **36**(1), 7 (2011)
12. Schaik, S.J., Moor, O.D.: A memory efficient reachability data structure through bit vector compression. In: Proc. of SIGMOD 2011, pp. 913–924 (2011)

Accuracy-Preserving and Scalable Column-Based Low-Rank Matrix Approximation

Jiangang Wu and Shizhong Liao [(✉)]

School of Computer Science and Technology, Tianjin University,
Tianjin 300072, China
szliao@tju.edu.cn

Abstract. Column-based low-rank matrix approximation is a useful method to analyze and interpret data in machine learning and data mining. However existing methods will face some accuracy and scalability problems when dealing with large-scale data. In this paper we propose a new parallel framework for column-based low-rank matrix approximation based on divide-and-conquer strategy. It consists of three stages: (1) Dividing the original matrix into several small submatrices. (2) Performing column-based low-rank matrix approximation to select columns on each submatrix in parallel. (3) Combining these columns into the final result. We prove that the new parallel framework has $(1+\epsilon)$ relative-error upper bound. We also show that it is more scalable than existing work. The results of comparison experiments and application in kernel methods demonstrate the effectiveness and efficiency of our method on both synthetic and real world datasets.

Keywords: Low-rank matrix approximation · Divide-and-conquer · Scalability · Machine learning

1 Introduction

Matrices are widely used in machine learning and data mining to model the real world data, such as kernel methods [19,23], social computing [20] and media computing [8]. Typically a matrix $\mathbf{M} \in \mathbb{R}^{m \times n}$ can represent n instances each with m features. Some examples of such instance-feature data include people and face images in face recognition [12], user and rating in recommendation system [3] and so on. In practical applications, the huge amount of data brings some challenges in computing the data matrix. Faced with there problems, we need to seek new ways to construct compressed representation and effective approximation of matrices.

The most classical and common approach to approximation of matrix is the truncated singular value decomposition (SVD) that obtains a low-rank approximation of the matrix. For a rank $k \leq \min\{m, n\}$, this method can give the best rank-k approximation to $\mathbf{M}$. Although the SVD method is widely used, it is not interpretable from the resulting singular vectors in terms of the underlying data, as the singular vectors are the combination of columns of the matrix, they are not informative in many cases.

© Springer International Publishing Switzerland 2015
S. Zhang et al. (Eds.): KSEM 2015, LNAI 9403, pp. 236–247, 2015.
DOI: 10.1007/978-3-319-25159-2_22

Column-based matrix approximation methods [10] represent a matrix using a small number of actual columns and/or rows of the matrix, therefor it has an advantage over SVD when analysing data [7,9,22].

The core issue in column-based matrix approximation is how to choose proper columns to improve the approximation accuracy. Many algorithms have been proposed to address this problem [1,2,5,14]. Some algorithms can achieve $(1 + \epsilon)$ relative-error bound and [14] gives a detailed summary of these algorithms. However most algorithms are not practical when dealing with large-scale data due to their high time complexity.

In order to improve the scalability of column-based matrix approximation algorithms, some work focuses on speeding up the SVD which is involved in most algorithms. They studied the underlying numerical iterations [13], randomized algorithms [15] and approximation algorithms [6] of SVD respectively.

Except these work aiming at speeding up the SVD, [18] proposed a parallel framework for column-based low-rank matrix approximation to handle the scalability problem. It is based on the divide-and-combine strategy which is inspired by [17] in which the strategy is used to improve the scalability of both matrix completion and robust principal component analysis. They select a small submatrix from the original matrix using matrix factorization in parallel, and then perform the column-based matrix approximation on the submatrix. Their parallel framework has relative-error upper bound and reduces the size of matrices from $m \times n$ to $m \times \sqrt{kn}$, where k is a low rank parameter.

In this paper, we propose a new parallel framework for column-based low-rank matrix approximation based on the divide-and-conquer strategy. We divide the original matrix into several small submatrices, perform column-based low-rank matrix approximation algorithms in parallel, then combine the results into the desired columns. The new parallel framework has the same relative-error bound as the base column-based matrix approximation algorithm, and the original matrix can be divided into extremely small submatrices as long as the the number of parallel nodes is large enough. Compared with existing work, our new parallel framework has better theoretical upper bound and is more scalable.

The rest of this paper is organized as follows: We introduce the notation and some preliminary algorithms in next section. Section 3 gives a detailed description and theoretical analysis about our method. Then we conduct experiments in Section 4 to illustrate the advantages of our method. Finally we conclude in Section 5.

2   Preliminaries

In this section, we will introduce some notational conventions and base algorithms which will be involved in our parallel framework and experiments.

2.1   Notation

We let $\| \cdot \|_2$ and $\| \cdot \|_F$ denote the spectral norm and Frobenius norm respectively and $\| \cdot \|_\xi$ denotes either $\| \cdot \|_2$ or $\| \cdot \|_F$. For a matrix $\mathbf{M} \in \mathbb{R}^{m \times n}$, we let

$r = \text{rank}(\mathbf{M})$ denote its rank. We write the compact singular value decomposition of $\mathbf{M}$ as $\mathbf{U}_M \boldsymbol{\Sigma}_M \mathbf{V}_M^{\mathrm{T}}$. $\boldsymbol{\Sigma}_M$ is a diagonal matrix containing r non-zero singular values of $\mathbf{M}$ in decreasing order, denoted as $\sigma_1(\mathbf{M}) \geq \sigma_2(\mathbf{M}) \geq \cdots \geq \sigma_r(\mathbf{M}) > 0$. $\mathbf{U}_M \in \mathbb{R}^{m \times r}$ and $\mathbf{V}_M \in \mathbb{R}^{n \times r}$ are the corresponding left and right singular vectors of $\mathbf{M}$ and we let $\mathbf{u}_i(\mathbf{M})$ and $\mathbf{v}_i(\mathbf{M})$ denote the i-th left and right singular vector. $\mathbf{M}^+ = \mathbf{U}_M \boldsymbol{\Sigma}_M^{-1} \mathbf{V}_M^{\mathrm{T}}$ denotes the Moore-Penrose pseudoinverse of $\mathbf{M}$ and $\mathbf{P}_M = \mathbf{M}\mathbf{M}^+$ represents the orthogonal projection onto the column space of $\mathbf{M}$.

2.2 Best Rank-k Approximation

For a matrix $\mathbf{M} \in \mathbb{R}^{m \times n}$ and $k \leq \min\{m, n\}$, we let $\mathbf{M}_k$ denote its best rank-k approximation which is defined in the following way:

$$\mathbf{M}_k = \sum_{i=1}^{k} \sigma_i(\mathbf{M})\mathbf{u}_i(\mathbf{M})\mathbf{v}_i(\mathbf{M})^{\mathrm{T}},$$

which satisfies $\|\mathbf{M} - \mathbf{M}_k\|_\xi = \min_{\text{rank}(\mathbf{A}) \leq k} \|\mathbf{M} - \mathbf{A}\|_\xi$. The most straightforward way to get $\mathbf{M}_k$ is to truncate the full SVD and remain the top k singular values and singular vectors, thus the running time is $O(mn\min\{m, n\})$ for this method. There is also $O(mnk)$ time complexity algorithm to calculate $\mathbf{M}_k$ [13].

2.3 Column-Based Matrix Approximation

In some application areas such as machine learning, data mining and statistical data analysis, the best rank-k approximation might be undesirable since the singular vector representation is not suitable to make inferences about the actual underlying data, because they are generally combinations of the columns of $\mathbf{M}$.

In contrast to the SVD approach, column-based matrix approximation constructs low-rank matrix approximations that are explicitly expressed in terms of a small number of columns and/or rows of the input matrix. Its formal definition [11] is as follows:

Definition 1. *Let* $\mathbf{M}$ *be an* $m \times n$ *matrix. For any given* $\mathbf{C}$, *an* $m \times l$ *matrix whose columns consist of* l *columns of the matrix* $\mathbf{M}$, *the* $m \times n$ *matrix* $\mathbf{CX}$ *is a column-based matrix approximation to* $\mathbf{M}$, *or* CX *matrix decomposition, for any* $l \times n$ *matrix* $\mathbf{X}$.

In general case we have $l \ll n$, thus we can treat l as a constant. From the above definition we can see that CX matrix decomposition expresses each of the columns of $\mathbf{M}$ in terms of a linear combination of $\mathbf{C}$, which are actual columns of $\mathbf{M}$. When $\mathbf{C}$ is given, we can set $\mathbf{X} = \mathbf{C}^+\mathbf{M}$, then obtain the low-rank approximation $\mathbf{CC}^+\mathbf{M}$. Indeed, this is the best approximation we can get because $\|\mathbf{M} - \mathbf{CC}^+\mathbf{M}\|_F = \min_{\mathbf{X} \in \mathbb{R}^{l \times n}} \|\mathbf{M} - \mathbf{CX}\|_F$.

Many CX algorithms, both deterministic and randomized, can give a relative-error upper bound, that is $\|\mathbf{M} - \mathbf{CC}^+\mathbf{M}\|_\xi \leq \Delta_{\mathrm{CX}}\|\mathbf{M} - \mathbf{M}_k\|_\xi$ with $\Delta_{\mathrm{CX}} \geq 1$. In this paper we mainly consider the relative-error bound in Frobenius norm. Some algorithms with $(1 + \epsilon)$ relative-error bound have been summarized in [14], from which we can see that these algorithms are not scalable dealing with large-scale data because of the high time complexity, therefor we need a parallel method to handle this problem.

3   New Parallel Framework

In this section, we will describe, analyse and discuss our parallel framework for column-based low-rank matrix approximation in detail.

3.1   Divide-and-Conquer Strategy

Given a matrix $\mathbf{M} \in \mathbb{R}^{m \times n}$, $r = \text{rank}(\mathbf{M})$. We want to select l columns of $\mathbf{M}$, denoted as $\mathbf{C}$, in order to make $\|\mathbf{M} - \mathbf{CC}^{+}\mathbf{M}\|_F$ close to $\|\mathbf{M} - \mathbf{M}_k\|_F$ for a given number k, where $k \leq r$ and $k \leq l \leq n$. Our parallel framework consists of the following three stages:

Divide matrix into submatrices: Let t be the number of parallel nodes, we divide $\mathbf{M}$ into t submatrices in the following way $\mathbf{M} = [\mathbf{M}^{(1)}, \dots, \mathbf{M}^{(t)}]$, where $\mathbf{M}^{(i)}$ contains n/t columns[1], $i = 1, 2, \dots, t$.

Perform CX algorithm in parallel: We perform CX algorithm on $\{\mathbf{M}^{(1)}, \dots, \mathbf{M}^{(t)}\}$ in parallel, then from each submatrix we can obtain l/t columns[2]. It yields t results $\{\mathbf{C}^{(1)}, \dots, \mathbf{C}^{(t)}\}$.

Merge selected columns: We merge the selected columns in last stage to form the final output $\mathbf{C} = [\mathbf{C}^{(1)}, \dots, \mathbf{C}^{(t)}] \in \mathbb{R}^{m \times l}$.

We summarize the above stages into Algorithm 1. Note that we do not specify the CX algorithm, thus any CX algorithm can be applied to our framework. Furthermore, we make no assumption about the matrix and no randomization is needed from beginning to end, which means our method can be totally deterministic as long as the base CX algorithm is deterministic.

Next we analyse the time complexity of Algorithm 1. Let $\text{T}_{\text{CX}}(m, n)$ denote the running time of the base CX algorithm on an $m \times n$ matrix. As the running time of Step 1 and Step 5 is trivial, the bottleneck of Algorithm 1 is Step 3, thus the time complexity of Algorithm 1 is $\text{T}_{\text{CX}}(m, n/t)$.

3.2   Theoretical Analysis of Accuracy-Preserving Property

Our parallel framework is accuracy-preserving, that is it has exactly the same relative-error bound as that of the base CX algorithm we used. The main theorem is as follow.

---

[1]   We assume $n \bmod t = 0$ for simplicity, then each submatrix contains n/t columns. In a general case we can also partition $\mathbf{M}$ into t submatrices and each contains $\lfloor n/t \rfloor$ or $\lceil n/t \rceil$ columns.

[2]   Here we also assume $l \bmod t = 0$ for simplicity. In a general case we can select $\lfloor l/t \rfloor$ or $\lceil l/t \rceil$ columns from each submatrix in order to insure that the number of entire selected columns is l.

Algorithm 1. Divide-and-Conquer Parallel Framework

Input: a matrix $\mathbf{M} \in \mathbb{R}^{m \times n}$, number of parallel nodes t, number of selected
    columns l
Output: selected columns $\mathbf{C} \in \mathbb{R}^{m \times l}$
1: divide matrix $\mathbf{M} = [\mathbf{M}^{(1)}, \ldots, \mathbf{M}^{(t)}]$
2: **do in parallel**
3:    $\mathbf{C}^{(i)}$=CX-Algorithm$(\mathbf{M}^{(i)})$
4: **end do**
5: $\mathbf{C} = [\mathbf{C}^{(1)}, \ldots, \mathbf{C}^{(t)}]$
6: **return** $\mathbf{C}$

Theorem 1. *Given a matrix* $\mathbf{M} \in \mathbb{R}^{m \times n}$, $r = \text{rank}(\mathbf{M})$ *and* $\mathbf{M}_k$ *is the best rank-k approximation to* $\mathbf{M}$, *where* $k \leq r$. *Given constants* t *and* l, *where* $k \leq l \leq n$. *If the base CX algorithm yields*

$$\|\mathbf{M}^{(i)} - \mathbf{C}^{(i)}\mathbf{C}^{(i)+}\mathbf{M}^{(i)}\|_F \leq \Delta_{\text{CX}}\|\mathbf{M}^{(i)} - \mathbf{M}_k^{(i)}\|_F$$

for $\Delta_{\text{CX}} \geq 1$ *by choosing* l/t *columns* $\mathbf{C}^{(i)}$ *from* $\mathbf{M}^{(i)}$. *Then perform Algorithm 1 on* $\mathbf{M}$ *we can get*

$$\|\mathbf{M} - \mathbf{C}\mathbf{C}^+\mathbf{M}\|_F \leq \Delta_{\text{CX}}\|\mathbf{M} - \mathbf{M}_k\|_F.$$

Proof.

$$\|\mathbf{M} - \mathbf{C}\mathbf{C}^+\mathbf{M}\|_F^2 = \sum_{i=1}^{t} \|\mathbf{M}^{(i)} - \mathbf{C}\mathbf{C}^+\mathbf{M}^{(i)}\|_F^2$$

$$\overset{(a)}{\leq} \sum_{i=1}^{t} \|\mathbf{M}^{(i)} - \mathbf{C}^{(i)}\mathbf{C}^{(i)+}\mathbf{M}^{(i)}\|_F^2$$

$$\leq \sum_{i=1}^{t} \Delta_{\text{CX}}^2 \|\mathbf{M}^{(i)} - \mathbf{M}_k^{(i)}\|_F^2$$

$$= \Delta_{\text{CX}}^2 \sum_{i=1}^{t} \|\mathbf{M}^{(i)} - \mathbf{M}_k^{(i)}\|_F^2.$$

(a) follows from the fact that the column space of $\mathbf{C}^{(i)}$ is the subspace of that of $\mathbf{C}$, therefor projecting $\mathbf{M}^{(i)}$ onto the column space of $\mathbf{C}^{(i)}$ instead of the column space of $\mathbf{C}$ will increase the deviation between $\mathbf{M}^{(i)}$. Divide $\mathbf{M}_k = [\mathbf{N}^{(1)}, \ldots, \mathbf{N}^{(t)}]$ according to $\mathbf{M} = [\mathbf{M}^{(1)}, \ldots, \mathbf{M}^{(t)}]$. Then

$$\sum_{i=1}^{t} \|\mathbf{M}^{(i)} - \mathbf{M}_k^{(i)}\|_F^2 \overset{(b)}{\leq} \sum_{i=1}^{t} \|\mathbf{M}^{(i)} - \mathbf{N}^{(i)}\|_F^2$$

$$= \|\mathbf{M} - \mathbf{M}_k\|_F^2.$$

(b) follows from $\text{rank}(\mathbf{N}^{(i)}) \leq \text{rank}(\mathbf{M}_k) = k = \text{rank}(\mathbf{M}_k^{(i)})$. Thus we have

$$\|\mathbf{M} - \mathbf{C}\mathbf{C}^+\mathbf{M}\|_F^2 \leq \Delta_{\mathrm{CX}}^2 \|\mathbf{M} - \mathbf{M}_k\|_F^2,$$

and therefor

$$\|\mathbf{M} - \mathbf{C}\mathbf{C}^+\mathbf{M}\|_F \leq \Delta_{\mathrm{CX}} \|\mathbf{M} - \mathbf{M}_k\|_F.$$

3.3 Discussion

Above we have analysed our framework with deterministic CX algorithms, it is easy to get the same result for randomized CX algorithms just by adding the expectation. From Theorem 1 we can see that our framework has $(1 + \epsilon)$ relative-error bound as long as the base CX algorithm gives $(1 + \epsilon)$ relative-error bound. Note that in Algorithm 1 we can divide the matrix into more than t submatrices to speed up the computation with the same bound in Theorem 1. Generally more submatrices may result in worse performance, thus the choice of the number of submatrices is balance of performance and speed.

Another benefit of our parallel framework is the settlement of data storage. Our parallel framework only distributes an $m \times n/t$ matrix to each parallel node which can be much smaller than the original matrix when t is large enough.

It is notable that [18] proposed a parallel framework for column-based matrix approximation based on divide-and-combine strategy. Compared with their method, the advantages of ours are reflected on the following aspects:

(1) Simpler: They first select an ensemble matrix using low-rank matrix approximation and matrix factorization algorithm in parallel and then perform CX algorithm on the ensemble matrix serially. Our method don't need the selection stage and perform CX algorithm in parallel directly, which does not involve other algorithms and is easier to implement.

(2) Faster: Their method involves three algorithms: rank-k approximation and interpolative decomposition in parallel and CX algorithm in serial. Our method only need to perform CX algorithm in parallel, thus is more time-saving when t getting larger.

(3) More scalable: Their divide-and-combine framework consists of parallel parts and serial parts, therefor they need to set the number of parallel nodes $t = \lceil \sqrt{n/k} \rceil$ in order to achieve the best running time, and the increase or decrease of t will both result in worse running time. However our method makes no constraint on t, and the bigger t is the faster our method will be.

(4) More accurate: Their method has relative-error bound, and our method has a tighter $(1 + \epsilon)$ relative-error bound.

It is worth mentioning that the method of [18] gives a relative-error bound proportional to $\sqrt{kn/t}$. In order to improve the relative-error bound, they propose a optional adaptive sampling stage which comes from [7]. By sampling additional $O(k\sqrt{kn/t}\epsilon^{-1})$ columns they can get $(1 + \epsilon)$ relative-error bound in theory. However, as this process is time-consuming and impractical they do not include it in their experiments.

4   Empirical Evaluation

Our experiments consist of two parts: we first compare the approximation accuracy and scalability of our parallel framework with existing methods, and then compare their performance when applied to kernel methods.

4.1   General Settings

We compare three different methods: (1) Performing CX algorithm directly. (2) Divide-and-combine parallel framework proposed by [18]. (3) Our divide-and-conquer parallel framework. For the base CX algorithm we follow the choices of [18], in which two CX algorithms are used: (1) A deterministic CX algorithm with $O(mnk + nlk^2)$ time complexity proposed by [1], denoted as Det. (2) A randomized CX algorithm with $O(mnk)$ time complexity proposed by [11], denoted as Rand. All the algorithms are implemented in R with package parallel. The rank parameter k is set to be 15. For fairness, we set $t = \lceil \sqrt{n/k} \rceil$ for $m \times n$ matrix as default because it is the most proper setting for [18]. We run all algorithms 20 times and report the average results.

4.2   Approximation Accuracy and Scalability

We use the reconstruction error ratio to measure the approximation accuracy of each method, which is defined as follows: $\|M - CC^+M\|_F / \|M - M_k\|_F$. we carry out experiments on two datasets, artificial dataset and real dataset.

The artificial dataset used in our experiments are two kinds of random $n \times n$ matrices [5]: (1) Log: Random matrix with singular values equally spaced between 1 and $10^{-\log n}$. (2) Scaled Random: Random matrix created by assigning each entry a number between -1 and 1 from uniform distribution, and then scaling the ith row of that matrix by $(20\epsilon^{i/n})$ where ϵ is the machine precision, for example 2.22×10^{-16} in our machine.

For real dataset we use the Extended Yale Face Database B [12,16]. There are totally 2414 human face images with 192×168 pixels. Thus we can obtain a 32256×2414 matrix with each column representing a face image.

We first evaluate the approximation accuracy of each method along with the increase of number of selected columns. For artificial data, we set $n = 5000$. The performance results are shown in Figure 1. For Face dataset, the results are shown in Figure 2. We can see that the reconstruction error ratio of our method is nearly the same with that of the direct method, which is in accordance with the accuracy-preserving property of our method. The divide-and-combine parallel framework has a higher reconstruction error ratio due to a looser relative-error bound.

For comparing the scalability of each method, we first evaluate how running time changes along with the increase of the data's scale. We carry out experiments on artificial dataset with $n = 1000, 3000, 5000, 7000$ and $l = 50$. The results are summarized in Table 1, which show our method is more efficient

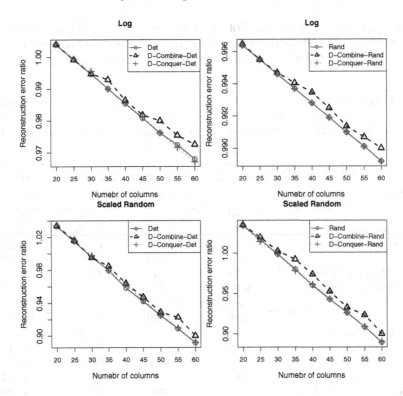

Fig. 1. Reconstruction error ratio of each method on Log and Scaled Random. The legend represents direct method, divide-and-combine parallel framework and our divide-and-conquer parallel framework respectively. Size of matrix $n = 5000$, rank parameter $k = 15$ and the number of parallel nodes $t = \lceil \sqrt{n/k} \rceil = 19$.

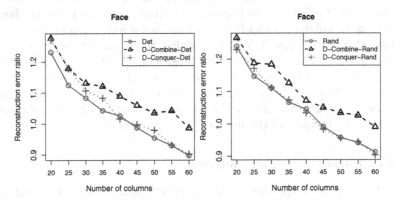

Fig. 2. Reconstruction error ratio of each method on Face dataset. rank parameter $k = 15$ and the number of parallel nodes $t = \lceil \sqrt{n/k} \rceil = 13$.

and has super-linear speed-up. Note that we set $t = \lceil \sqrt{n/k} \rceil$ in this experiment, which makes the divide-and-combine parallel framework achieve the best running time, however it is not the best setting for our method.

Table 1. Running time (in seconds) of each method on Log and Scaled Random, where size of matrix $n = 1000, 3000, 5000, 7000$ and the number of parallel nodes $t = \lceil \sqrt{n/k} \rceil = 9, 15, 19, 22$. The number of selected columns $l = 50$ and rank parameter $k = 15$.

Method \ Size of matrix	1000 × 1000	3000 × 3000	5000 × 5000	7000 × 7000
Log				
Det	3.04	253.11	809.43	1817.36
D-Combine Det	0.83	8.24	26.75	56.95
D-Conquer Det	0.74	7.46	16.14	37.36
Rand	2.82	240.24	796.91	1710.22
D-Combine Rand	0.72	8.04	24.82	53.76
D-Conquer Rand	0.70	7.31	15.72	35.56
Scaled Random				
Det	1.96	107.00	409.18	1101.17
D-Combine Det	0.77	7.51	20.00	50.85
D-Conquer Det	0.66	6.70	14.97	35.12
Rand	1.65	109.00	406.18	1044.17
D-Combine Rand	0.61	7.80	19.51	49.34
D-Conquer Rand	0.56	6.38	14.30	32.90

Next we evaluate how running time changes along with the increase of the number of parallel nodes. We carry out experiment on Face dataset to select $l = 50$ columns with $t = 5, 6, \ldots, 30$ (we omit the cases that t are too small because the divide-and-combine parallel framework cannot select enough columns). The results are shown in Figure 3. We can see that the running time of divide-and-combine parallel framework achieves the best value when $t = \lceil \sqrt{n/k} \rceil$, then it increases with t getting larger. We have mentioned this limitation in Section 3.3. However our method does not have this problem and the larger t is the more efficient our method will be. The results show our method is more scalable dealing with the increase of the number of parallel nodes.

4.3 Application in Kernel Methods

Column-based matrix approximation algorithms can be used to select informative columns to speed up machine learning and data mining tasks. Next we carry out experiments to speed up two kernel-based learning algorithms: least squares support vector machine (LSSVM) [21] and kernel ridge regression (KRR) [19]. We use 6 datasets from LIBSVM [4] which are summarized in Table 2. Each dataset is randomly divided into two halves, one for training set

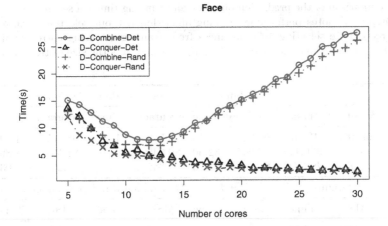

Fig. 3. The evolution of running time of Det and Rand algorithm under divide-and-combine parallel framework and our divide-and-conquer parallel framework on Face dataset. The number of parallel nodes $t = 5, 6, \ldots, 30$, the number of selected columns $l = 50$ and rank parameter $k = 15$.

and another for test set. We use LSSVM for classification tasks and report classification accuracy. We use KRR for regression tasks and report mean square errors (MSE). The kernel function used in our experiment is Gaussian kernel $K(\boldsymbol{x}_i, \boldsymbol{x}_j) = \exp(-\gamma\|\boldsymbol{x}_i - \boldsymbol{x}_j\|_2^2)$ with $\gamma = 2^{-3}$. The regularization parameter μ of LSSVM and KRR is searched in the range $\{2^{-15}, 2^{-14}, \ldots, 2^0\}$ using 5-fold cross validation. We select 10% instances of each dataset's training set and then compare the prediction outcomes using the selecting instances. The results are in Table 3 (for brevity we only present the results of Rand). It shows that our parallel framework can tremendously reduce the running time and preserve good prediction results.

Table 2. Information of datasets used in experiment.

Dataset	Instance	Feature	Type
mushrooms	8124	112	classification
a7a	16100	123	classification
w6a	17188	300	classification
space-ga	3107	6	regression
abalone	4177	8	regression
cpusmall	8192	12	regression

Table 3. Comparison of the prediction outcome and running time (in seconds) of each method. Original denotes performing learning algorithm without selection step, and the last three denote selecting 10% instances from training set using corresponding method. The number of parallel nodes $t = \lceil \sqrt{n/k} \rceil$, where n is the size of training set and $k = 15$.

Dataset	Original		Rand		D-Combine-Rand		D-Conquer-Rand	
	Accuracy	Time	Accuracy	Time	Accuracy	Time	Accuracy	Time
mushrooms	99.16%	139.68	98.85%	12.15	98.52%	1.28	98.80%	1.09
a7a	83.77%	330.113	82.94%	32.50	80.34%	2.49	81.53%	1.89
w6a	96.97%	492.787	96.85%	42.30	95.34%	3.67	96.23%	2.03

Dataset	Original		Rand		D-Combine-Rand		D-Conquer-Rand	
	MSE	Time	MSE	Time	MSE	Time	MSE	Time
space-ga	0.024	25.43	0.026	3.21	0.034	0.89	0.027	0.82
abalone	5.35	47.32	5.81	7.32	6.23	0.94	5.88	0.91
cpusmall	85.36	113.53	89.39	11.53	93.53	1.17	92.96	1.02

5   Conclusion

As existing column-based low-rank matrix approximation algorithms suffer from the issues of approximation accuracy and scalability, we propose a new parallel framework for column-based low-rank matrix approximation based on the divide-and-conquer strategy. The new parallel framework gives the same relative-error bound as the base algorithm, which leads to a $(1+\epsilon)$ relative-error bound, and is scalable dealing with large-scale data and has super-linear speed-up. Empirical results illustrate the advantages of our method on approximation accuracy and scalability.

Acknowledgments. This work was supported in part by Natural Science Foundation of China under Grant No. 61170019.

References

1. Boutsidis, C., Drineas, P., Magdon-Ismail, M.: Near optimal column-based matrix reconstruction. In: Proceedings of the IEEE 52nd Annual Symposium on Foundations of Computer Science (FOCS), pp. 305–314 (2011)
2. Boutsidis, C., Mahoney, M.W., Drineas, P.: An improved approximation algorithm for the column subset selection problem. In: Proceedings of the Twentieth Annual ACM-SIAM Symposium on Discrete Algorithms, pp. 968–977 (2009)
3. Breese, J.S., Heckerman, D., Kadie, C.: Empirical analysis of predictive algorithms for collaborative filtering. In: Proceedings of the Fourteenth Conference on Uncertainty in Artificial Intelligence, pp. 43–52 (1998)
4. Chang, C.C., Lin, C.J.: LIBSVM: A library for support vector machines. ACM Transactions on Intelligent Systems and Technology **2**, 27:1–27:27 (2011)

5. Civril, A., Magdon-Ismail, M.: Column subset selection via sparse approximation of svd. Theoretical Computer Science **421**, 1–14 (2012)

6. Clarkson, K.L., Woodruff, D.P.: Low rank approximation and regression in input sparsity time. In: Proceedings of the Forty-Fifth Annual ACM Symposium on Theory of Computing, pp. 81–90 (2013)

7. Deshpande, A., Rademacher, L., Vempala, S., Wang, G.: Matrix approximation and projective clustering via volume sampling. Theory of Computing **2**, 225–247 (2006)

8. Dorai, C., Venkatesh, S.: Media computing: computational media aesthetics, vol. 4. Springer Science & Business Media (2002)

9. Drineas, P., Kannan, R.: Pass efficient algorithms for approximating large matrices. In: Proceedings of the 14th Annual ACM-SIAM Symposium on Discrete Algorithms, pp. 223–232 (2003)

10. Drineas, P., Mahoney, M.W., Muthukrishnan, S.M.: Subspace Sampling and Relative-Error Matrix Approximation: Column-Based Methods. In: Zwick, U., Díaz, J., Jansen, K., Rolim, J.D.P. (eds.) APPROX 2006 and RANDOM 2006. LNCS, vol. 4110, pp. 316–326. Springer, Heidelberg (2006)

11. Drineas, P., Mahoney, M.W., Muthukrishnan, S.: Relative-error CUR matrix decompositions. SIAM Journal on Matrix Analysis and Applications **30**(2), 844–881 (2008)

12. Georghiades, A.S., Belhumeur, P.N., Kriegman, D.: From few to many: Illumination cone models for face recognition under variable lighting and pose. IEEE Transactions on Pattern Analysis and Machine Intelligence **23**(6), 643–660 (2001)

13. Golub, G., Van Loan, C.: Matrix Computations. Johns Hopkins University Press, Baltimore (1996)

14. Guruswami, V., Sinop, A.K.: Optimal column-based low-rank matrix reconstruction. In: Proceedings of the Twenty-Third Annual ACM-SIAM Symposium on Discrete Algorithms, pp. 1207–1214 (2012)

15. Halko, N., Martinsson, P.G., Tropp, J.A.: Finding structure with randomness: Probabilistic algorithms for constructing approximate matrix decompositions. SIAM Review **53**(2), 217–288 (2011)

16. Lee, K.C., Ho, J., Kriegman, D.: Acquiring linear subspaces for face recognition under variable lighting. IEEE Transactions on Pattern Analysis and Machine Intelligence **27**(5), 684–698 (2005)

17. Mackey, L.W., Jordan, M.I., Talwalkar, A.: Divide-and-conquer matrix factorization. In: Advances in Neural Information Processing Systems, pp. 1134–1142 (2011)

18. Pi, Y., Peng, H., Zhou, S., Zhang, Z.: A scalable approach to column-based low-rank matrix approximation. In: Proceedings of the 23rd International Joint Conference on Artificial Intelligence (IJCAI 2013), pp. 1600–1606 (2013)

19. Saunders, C., Gammerman, A., Vovk, V.: Ridge regression learning algorithm in dual variables. In: Proceedings of the 15th International Conference on Machine Learning, pp. 515–521 (1998)

20. Schuler, D.: Social computing. Communications of the ACM **37**(1), 28–29 (1994)

21. Suykens, J., Vandewalle, J.: Least squares support vector machine classifiers. Neural Processing Letters **9**(3), 293–300 (1999)

22. Tyrtyshnikov, E.: Incomplete cross approximation in the mosaic-skeleton method. Computing **64**(4), 367–380 (2000)

23. Vapnik, V.N.: Statistical Learning Theory. John Wiley & Sons, New York (1998)

Segment-Based Depth Estimation in Light Field Using Graph Cut

Wenjie Shao[1]([✉]), Hao Sheng[1,2], and Chao Li[1,2]

[1] State Key Laboratory of Software Development Environment, School of Computer Science and Engineering, Beihang University, Beijing 100191, People's Republic of China
wenjie668@qq.com

[2] Shenzhen Key Laboratory of Data Vitalization, Research Institute in Shenzhen, Beihang University, Shenzhen 518057, People's Republic of China

Abstract. In this paper, we present a depth-extracting method on the scenes of 4D light fields. The method is based on image segmentation and epipolar plane images. We extract disparity map and reliability map from the original image of 4D light fields. Then this information is applied to image segmentation, in which a large number of planes are produced, so that the disparity map which is consist of pixels can be transferred to the disparity map which is consist of planes. In the resulting optimization problem, graph-cut technique is used to assign a corresponding disparity plane to each segment. Our method is tested on a number of synthetic and real-world examples captured with a light field camera, and compared to ground truth where available. Furthermore, an approach to optimize the method to reduce the running time is also proposed.

Keywords: Light fields · Depth estimation · Graph cuts · Imgae segmentation

1 Introduction

The 4D light field has been established as a promising paradigm to describe the visual appearance of a scene. Compared to a traditional 2D image, it contains not only the accumulated information at each image point, but also separate information for each ray direction. With such additional information, a wide range of applications in a light field have been developed. They achieved some functions which can't be applied in ordinary camera. Digital zooming, also called refocusing, is an important use [7]. It can invert a defocused image to highly accurate focused image and reduce the difficulty of auto focusing. Super-resolution reconstruction is another active research in 4D light field.

More importantly, reconstruction from 4D light fields requires getting an accurate disparity map, which is still a challenging in computer vision. There are many mature methods in depth estimation, such as stereo matching [16]. They can be divided into two major classes, local algorithms and global algorithms. Both of them have some disadvantages. Local algorithms only uses the pixel

S. Zhang et al. (Eds.): KSEM 2015, LNAI 9403, pp. 248–259, 2015.
DOI: 10.1007/978-3-319-25159-2_23

which is in a finite neighboring window so that it has low accuracy. Global algorithms make explicit smoothness assumptions of the disparity map and they require a lot of time in the minimization techniques [9]. As is commonly known, the real scene structure could be approximated by a set of planes in disparity space. After image segmentation, every region could be fitted to a plane formula using pixel locations and local depth estimates. However, a common scene could be divided into thousands of regions after Mean shift algorithm and it will cost a lot of time to give every region a fitting plane, and more importantly, a large number of the planes are inaccurate [13]. In our method, several measures are used to choose the accurate planes. For example, a precise plane must be big enough which means it has a lot of points and the points with high reliability must occupy most of all points in this plane [2]. After plane fitting, the problem is converted into assigning labels to planes which can be easily formulated as an energy minimization problem in the segment domain.

To solve the energy minimization problem, graph cuts technique and Markov random fields is used. Li Hong and George Chen proposed a graph cuts method in stereo matching based on separated pixels [6]. In general, the number of segments is much less than pixels, which leads to a simple graph structure and fast computation. But because of our over-segmentation, the runtime tends to exceeded our expectation. We apply an optimism method to reduce the number of regions. We combine those regions whose plane equation is similar to a large region. According to our experiments, this approach will reduce the runtime by thirty percent .

This paper proposes a region-based global algorithm to obtain the disparity map in 4D light fields. It makes full use of image information and produced much better results than stereo matching [4]. More importantly, it greatly reduces the running time which is a big problem for global algorithms, especially in 4D light fields. It combines the traditional image segmentation with light fields.

The rest of the paper is organized as follows: First we introduce the related work on image segmentation in Section 2. Then we present how to obtain disparity map in the 3D light field (Section 3) and how to give every region produced by Meanshift a plane label (Section 4). In Section 5 we apply graph cuts to solve the energy minimization problem which assign the corresponding disparity plane to each segment. We provide experimental results in Section 6. Finally, we conclude our paper and discuss related advantages and disadvantages of our approach in Section 7.

2   Related Work

The concept of light fields mainly came from computer graphics. One of the first approaches using *EPIs* to analyze the scene geometry was by Bolled et al. [10]. To reconstruct the 3D structure, they detect edges, peaks and troughs with a subsequent line fitting in the *EPI*. Another approach is presented by Criminisi et al. [2], who use an iterative extraction procedure for collections of EPI-lines of the same depth, which they call an *EPI*-tube. They also proposed procedure to remove specular highlights from already extracted *EPI*-tubes.

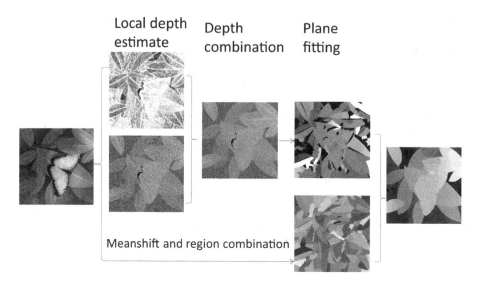

Fig. 1. The whole process of our method, from the original picture to the final depth image.We extract disparity map and reliability map from the original image of 4D light fields. Then we apply these information on image segmentation, in which we get accurate segments in a large number of planes, so that we can get transfer the disparity map which is consist of pixels to the disparity map which is consist of planes.

Sven Wanner and Bastian Golduecke introduced a novel local data term for depth estimation [13], which is tailored to the structure of light field data. They use the coherence of the structure tensor as the reliability measure and the direction of the local level lines to obtain the depth estimated.

Image segmentation is an active research area, especially in stereo matching. Andreas Klaus, Mario Sormann and Konrad Karner proposed segment-based stereo matching using belief propagation and a self-adapting dissimilarity measure [3]. They apply Mean Shift color segmentation to image segmentation which is first used in Comaniciu and Meer. The main advantage of the mean-shift approach is the fact that edge information is incorporated as well.

Christoph Straehle and Sven Wanner gave an assignment of globally consistent multi-labels on the 4D light fields [15]. They provided an optimal data structure for label optimization by implicitly providing scene geometry information. It is thus possible to consistently optimize label assignments over all views simultaneously.

In Matousek et al. [6], a cost function is formulated to minimize a weighted path length between points in the first and the last row of an EPI, which prefers constant intensity in a small neighborhood of each EPI-line. However, their method only works in the absence of occlusions. Berent et al. [8] deal with the simultaneous segmentation of EPI-tubes by a region competition method using active contours, imposing geometric properties to enforce correct occlusion ordering.

Multi view object co-segmentation is similar to light field image segmentation. Adrsh Kowdle and Sudipta N.Sinha proposed an algorithm formulated using an energy minimization framework that combines stereo and appearance cues, where for each surface; an appearance model is learnt using an unsupervised approach [1]. Dorit S.Hochbaum proposed an efficient algorithm for Co-segmentation on object which is in two images with arbitrary background [14]. To solve the difficult optimization problem of Markov Random Field (MRF), they designed a new algorithm which can solve for optimal in polynomial time using a maximum flow procedure on an appropriately constructed graph [11].

3   Local Depth Estimate in 3D Light Field

As mentioned before, *EPI*, which can be viewed as 2D slices of constant angular and spatial directions could be obtained through the Lumigraph from 3D light field. There are several ways to represent light fields. In this paper, we adopt the two-plane parametrization. It can be treated as a map

$$L : \Omega \times \Pi \to \mathbb{R}, \qquad (x, y, s, t) \mapsto L(x, y, s, t) \tag{1}$$

It can be viewed as an assignment of an intensity value to the ray $(R_{x,y,s,t})$ passing through $(x, y) \in \Omega$ and $(s, t) \in \Pi$. Fix a horizontal line of constant (y) in the image plane and a constant camera coordinate (t), and restrict the light field to an (x,s) slice Σ_{y^*,t^*}. The *EPI* could be described as.

$$S_{y^*,t_*} : \Sigma_{y^*,t^*} \to \mathbb{R},$$
$$(x, s) \mapsto S_{y^*,t^*}(x, s) := L(x, y*, s, t^*) \tag{2}$$

The next step is to get the depth of every pixel. In the *EPI*, a pixel is a slant. According to its depth in the scene, the slant slope is different. The farther the object, more inclined the line is. There is a very simple formula to calculate its slope.

$$l = -f \frac{\Delta s}{\Delta x} \tag{3}$$

However there are several problems in this formula. The first is some of the lines which are corresponding to a fixed pixel whose texture is not clear enough is very hard to be distinguished from many lines. So the depth could be wrong. Another problem is the *EPI* will contain some lines which are not long enough, which means there are some obstructions blocking the pixel. It could be solved by only using part of the line to calculate despite that it will reduce the accuracy.

Fortunately there is a measure of accuracy. Using the coherence of the structure tensor to calculate reliability is advisable. It can effectively reflect the accuracy of the depth estimate of every pixel.

$$r_{y^*,t^*} := \frac{(J_{xx} - J_{yy})^2 + 4J_{xy}{}^2}{(J_{yy} + J_{xx})^2} \tag{4}$$

Using the local depth estimates for all the *EPIs* in horizontal and vertical directions, respectively, different view points could produce different disparity maps and reliability maps. For example, for the original picture from a light field camera which produces 9×9 photos, using the local depth estimates we can get 9×9 *EPIs*, it is necessary to choose how to combine such information into one disparity map. Paper [5] used an algorithm which is similar to stereo matching. It is very complex and for some scenes which have little texture, its performance is not good enough. So our method only apply a very simple method. It gives up some information and only uses two *EPIs*. Obviously both of them are obtained from the same view point. A simple method is to combine them with a comparison of whose reliability is larger.

Fig. 2. Combination of two disparity maps in different directions. The left is the horizontal disparity map. The middle is vertical disparity map. The right is the result.

As indicated in Fig. 2, the horizontal *EPI* is sensitive to horizontal edges because the corresponding reliability is bigger in horizontal direction. The vertical is similar. After combining them, both directions seem clear.

4   Plane Segmentation and Fitting

In the above steps, texture is used to get rough depth information. The next step is to combine these pixels into several regions. Color is a good feature for segmentation. Our method uses Mean Shift to split the original picture, which is corresponding to the center image in light field, into small regions. Because of the view point of the center image is the same as the disparity map and the reliability map, the deviation could be reduced from parallax maximally. In this part, an over-segmented image is preferred and these tiny regions will be combined at last. It may cost extra time for the merging step. But if some region boundaries are not boundaries in the segmented image, nothing can be done to correct this error. The mean-shift analysis approach is essentially defined as a gradient ascent search for maxima in a density function defined over a high dimensional feature space. To get the over-segmentation image, the spatial radiation and color radiation of Mean Shift need to be a small value, especially the color radiation, when the image is almost a same color.

After plane segmentation, thousands of, maybe more, regions are produced. The next step is to specify a fitting plane to each region with the disparity and reliability from last part. Every plane can be describe as

$$ax + by + cz + 1 = 0 \tag{5}$$

Where x and y are the coordinates of a pixel, z is the disparity of the pixel. A plane is been calculated for each region using least square. It is easy to realize and efficient to solve the plane fitting problem. If the disparity of each pixel is not all accurate, it will affect the result of least square remarkably. Fortunately there is reliability to exclude those impurities with threshold. Note that the large number of regions will cost a very long time to calculate the fitting plane of each region and in fact there is no need to divide a scene into thousands of planes. We use a method to eliminate the regions with small reliability and only calculate those high reliable planes. The method comprises several thresholds:

$$\begin{cases} |N_1| > T_1 \ N_1 = \{p|r_p > r_c \& p \in R\} \\ |N_2| > T_2 \ N_2 = \{p|p \in R\} \\ \frac{|N_1|}{|N_2|} > T_3 \\ |N_3| > T_4 \ N_3 = \{p|p \text{ is on edge } \& p \in R\} \end{cases} \tag{6}$$

1) $|N_1|$ is the number of reliable pixel is larger than T1, where T1 is a fixed amount; 2)$|N_2|$ is the number of all pixels is larger than T2, where T2 is a fixed amount; 3) the percentage of reliable pixels in all pixels is larger than T3, where T3 is a fixed amount; 4)$|N_3|$ is the reliable pixels which is on the edge is larger than T4, where T4 is a fixed amount. The above T1, T2, T3, T4 need to be set before plane fitting to insure that the number of plane, after elimination, is at a proper size. In some cases, the number of regions generated by Mean shift is not so many, maybe a hundred, then we can only use the principle 1) to assure the reliability of plane.

After this step, there are several planes. These planes are all extracted from the scene. It means the scene could be rebuilt by these planes. This will be described in the next part.

5   Disparity Plane Assignment

In this section, a final global optimum for the disparity plane assignment is searched. In general, a global optimization function could be divided into two parts, the local cost and the global cost. It is necessary to find a solution to make the sum of both costs to be the minimum.

5.1   Plane Assignment

In our method, the local costs could be treated as the deviation when we assign a plane to a region. It means that the smaller the difference between the disparity which is calculated with the plane formula and the original disparity, the smaller the local cost is. On the other hand, the global cost is behalf of the deviation between adjacent regions. When two planes are assigned respectively to two adjacent regions, it is preferred to assign similar planes to similar regions. Similar regions in here mean both regions have similar disparity in average and in boundary. Similar planes mean both planes have similar parameters, it can be formulated as

$$S = (\frac{a_1}{a_2} - \frac{a_2}{a_1})^2 + (\frac{b_1}{b_2} - \frac{b_2}{b_1})^2 + (\frac{c_1}{c_2} - \frac{c_2}{c_1})^2 \tag{7}$$

where a, b, c are the parameters of plane formula. S is the similarity of both planes. In the above steps, a lot of regions which is divided from the image and several planes come out. Next is to assign a corresponding plane to every region. Therefore, the problem is formulated as an energy minimization problem. The energy for an assignment is given by:

$$E = E_{DATA} + E_{SMOOTH} \tag{8}$$

where the local cost could be calculated as

$$E_{DATA} = \sum |d_p - d_o| e^{1 - \frac{s}{n}} \tag{9}$$

and the global cost could be calculated as

$$E_{SMOOTH} = \sum^{Pairs} (\frac{1}{n} \sum d_p^1 - \frac{1}{m} \sum d_p^2) \tag{10}$$

where d_p is the disparity of the pixel when set the region with a fixed plane, d_o is the original disparity of the pixel, s is the number of fitting pixels of a fixed plane, which means the pixel is near from the plane, n is the number of pixels in the region. *Pairs* is the amount of adjacent region. Before these variables are calculated, we eliminate those unreliable pixels for each region. The same process is carried out in plane fitting. This is necessary in our method because it is sensitive for the small errors. So making full use of reliability map to reduce the deviation is important. Note that there is a little difference in eliminating process. In plane fitting, a threshold is set to determine reliability of each pixel and delete the pixels with small reliability. However, in this part, we statistic amount of pixels for each disparity in one region and choose the major, depends on the sum of pixels to choose the top three or four, to calculate the cost. This is because the reliability is calculated pixel by pixel and represents changes in small area. In the optimizing process, it is necessary to take the whole region into account. The pixels whose amount is in major to represent the region are chosen; and in our experiment it provided better results than simply using a threshold.

5.2   Region Merging

Several algorithms based on graph cuts have been developed recently to efficiently solve the problem of energy minimization. Here we use the Markov

Fig. 3. Threshold in region merging. Regions in red rectangle need to be combined. The left is small region in a huge region. The middle is thin and long region between two regions. The right is small region surrounded by several regions.

random vector field algorithm in graph cuts to solve this problem. Its time-requirement is in proportion to the nodes and segments number. To make this process faster, a region merging process is applied before energy minimization, as the term suggests, those tiny regions are combined with low confidence into a larger, more reliable region. Our method uses fifteen thresholds, some of which are like the threshold in plane fitting, to find the adjacent regions that could be combined. As shown in Fig. 3: 1) if a region is small enough, and only has one neighbor which means this region is surrounded by a large region, it could be combine with the surrounding region; 2) if a region is thin and long and has only two neighbors which in general means it is an edge of over-segmentation, the similarity is calculated respectively between the region and its two neighbors, then we choose the similar one to combine into; 3) if a region is surrounded by several regions whose number of pixels is much larger than itself and these regions has similar disparity, assuming all of these regions comprise a big region. Furthermore, if several similar regions could be connected to a closed area, it is possible to assume it a bigger region. To use this principle, its necessary to strict the definition of similarity .

6   Experiments

In this section, we discuss our experiments for evaluating the performance of our method qualitatively and relative to earlier approaches. Besides, we precede our experimentation to assume the running time. The dataset and groundtruth are from HCI light field archive, which have 9×9 images at resolution 768×768 (picture horse is 1024×576 resolution) per picture.

With our experiments we show that our methods provide better results in some part of image with comparable computational effort. In the first step, we compared the consistency between our result and groundtruth. In the second step, we compared the running time and accuracy between our method and HCI's local method. Then, the influence of the amount of merging terms on run time and average error is measured. Finally, we compared the running time between method without region merging and methods with merging.

Consistency with Groundtruth. Fig 4 shows the result image of our method. One could see the boundary of our result is smooth and in some large plane we could find clearly that there is gradual change in gray level, which means depth estimate changes smooth in those planes. It is more real in a 3D scene. Besides, in the textureless region, such as the light in MonasRoom, our results has good performance. It means our global method provide cracking result in depth recovery. For comparing local depth estimate and global estimate, we could find the result almost eliminate all noise produced by occlusion or textureless. But when some regions, such as the background which is surrounded by leaves in Papillon, is occluded in all pictures, it will get wrong depth label in global method. That's because it's local cost is large for all plane label, the smooth cost must be set small for minimization, the region will be given a label similar with surrounding. To solve this problem, the local depth estimate must be improved. This is what we will do in future.

Comparison with Other. Table 1 shows the quality and running time between our method and other global methods in plane segmentation. To highlight the various, the experiments are implemented on the same platform, which is on an ATI Radeon HD 4300 hosted on two Intel Core E7500 CPUs.

While testing the running time, we run these method three times. Note that the process only use one CPU core. HCI method means the local depth estimate method in Paper [12]. The global method of them is very time consuming hence is not on the same order of magnitude with the local method, even running on GPU. So we did not show its running time in Table 1. It can be seen that although there are many inputs in our method and global method is used for final smoothing, we use the same time, some of them even to be short, to process our experiment. It shows that our method is efficient and can deal with large 4D light fields quickly.

Table 1. Comparison of our method and HCI method. In these experiments, HCI global method is applied on single view. Our method is applied on two views. All of these method are implemented on an ATI Radeon HD 4300 hosted on two Intel Core E7500 CPUs.

images	Ave-running time(s)				Ave-error(%)			
	local depth	global	global without merging	HCI	local depth	global without merging	global	HCI
Papillon	5.6	28.7	243.2	26.0	12.4	4.8	4.8	5.6
MonasRoom	10.4	31.4	291.4	29.8	25.1	1.8	3.1	2.1
Horse	3.7	38.8	223.4	47.6	16.1	1.7	3.8	1.8
Buddha	4.7	34.2	173.9	40.1	10.6	2.0	4.3	1.9

While testing accuracy, we static the number of pixels, which has more than two error gray level from groundtruth. Before the comparison, gray order reset is processed to keep the result and groundtruth in the same depth level. Obviously the error reduces a lot after global optimization. While compared with HCI local depth estimation, our method has better accuracy and is less time consuming.

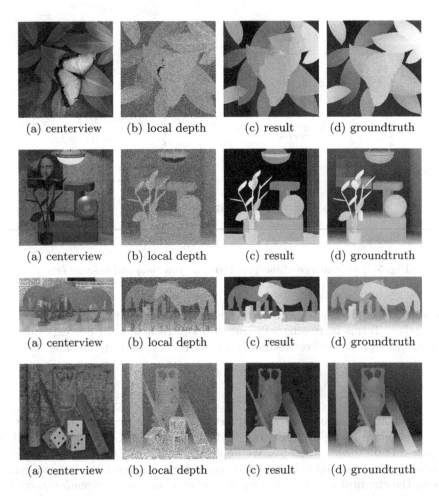

Fig. 4. Experiment result. (a) is the center view image in 4D light filed. (b) is local depth estimate after merging. (c) is the result of our method. (d) is ground truth

Influence of Merging Terms. In this part, we tried to change the number of merging terms and find out how the terms influence run time and average error. Fig. 5 shows the change curve of picture MonasRoom. As the chart indicates that the run time and average error decrease while the terms' amount increasing, but both of them will increase after the trough. Note that the trough differs from each other and in some cases it will emerge twice. It all depends on the selection of thresholds.

Comparison with Methods without Region Merging. We test our global method without region merging. As Table 1 shows, it costs decuple times more than the method which is proceeded after region merging. Note that in some cases, too many terms for merging will increase the run time. Because every

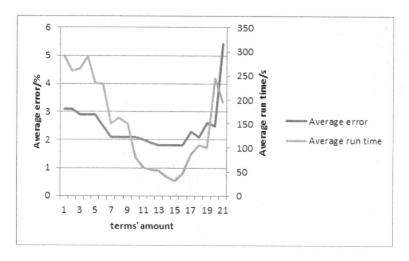

Fig. 5. The influence of merging terms on run time and average error.

merging procedure needs to proceed separately to reduce the influence between each other. Terms increasing will lead to more recursion. In our experiments, fifteen terms produced best results and required the shortest run time.

7 Conclusion

We demonstrated a depth-extracting method on the scene of 4D light fields. It has good performance in processing 4D light field images, especially those that do not contain obvious texture. We applied a highly efficient method of stereo matching on a dense 4D light field and changed some means to make the method fitting the circumstance well. Owing to the large amount information provided by the 4D light field, the deviation could be smaller than the traditional stereo match method. Compared with those existing global algorithm, our method provide a less time consuming and highly efficient way to distract the depth.

Apart from those advantages, the current version of our algorithm will not be able to handle the situation comprised with too many small objects rich in texture. It will cost a very long time and reach a bad result eventually. In future research, we plane to use more information in the 4D light fields to obtain a high efficient method in depth-extracting.

Acknowledgments. This study was partially supported by the National Natural Science Foundation of China (No. 61370122), the National High Technology Research and Development Program of China (No. 2013AA01A603) and the National Aerospace Science Foundation of China (No.2013ZC51). Supported by the Programme of Introducing Talents of Discipline to Universities and the Open Fund of the State Key Laboratory of Software Development Environment under grant #SKLSDE-2015ZX-21.

References

1. Chambolle, A., Pock, T.: A first-order primal-dual algorithm for convex problems with applications to imaging. J. Math. Imaging Vis **40**(1), 120–145 (2011)
2. Criminisi, A., Kang, S., Swaminathan, R., Szeliski, R., Anandan, P.: Extracting layers and analyzing their specular properties using epipolar-plane-image analysis. Computer vision and image understanding **97**(1), 51–85 (2005)
3. Goldluecke, B., Wanner, S.: The variational structure of disparity and regularization of 4d light fields. In: International Conference on Computer Vision and Pattern Recognition (2013)
4. Strekalovskiy, E., Cremers, D.: Generalized ordering constraints for multilabel optimization. In: International Conference on Computer Vision (2011)
5. He, K., Sun, J., Tang, X.: Single image haze removal using dark channel prior. In: Computer Vision and Pattern Recognition (2009)
6. Berent, J., Dragotti, P.: Segmentation of epipolar-plane image volumes with occlusion and disocclusion competition. In: IEEE 8th Workshop on Multimedia Signal Processing, pp. 182–185 (2006)
7. Bleyer, M., Rother, C., Kohli, P., Scharstein, D., Sinha, S.: Object stereo - joint stereo matching and object segmentation. In: Computer Vision and Pattern Recognition (2011)
8. Matousek, M., Werner, T., Hlavac, V.: Accurate correspondences from epipolar plane images. Computer Vision Winter Workshop, pp. 181–189 (2001)
9. Campbell, N., Vogiatzis, G., Hernandez, C., Cipolla, R.: Automatic object segmentation from calibrated images. In: Conference for Visual Media Production (2011)
10. Bolles, R., Baker, H., Marimont, D.: Epipolar-plane image analysis: An approach to determining structure from motion. International Journal of Computer Vision **1**(1), 7–55 (1987)
11. Vicente, S., Kolmogorov, V., Rother, C.: Joint optimization of segmentation and appearance models. In: International Conference on Computer Vision and Pattern Recognition (2009)
12. Wanner, S., Goldluecke, B.: Globally consistent depth labeling of 4d light fields. In: Computer Vision and Pattern Recognition, pp. 41–48 (2012)
13. Wanner, S., Fehr, J., Jähne, B.: Generating EPI Representations of 4D Light Fields with a Single Lens Focused Plenoptic Camera. In: Boyle, R., Parvin, B., Koracin, D., Wang, S., Kyungnam, K., Benes, B., Moreland, K., Borst, C., Di Verdi, S., Yi-Jen, C., Ming, J., Bebis, G. (eds.) ISVC 2011, Part I. LNCS, vol. 6938, pp. 90–101. Springer, Heidelberg (2011)
14. Bishop, T.E., Favaro, P.: Full-Resolution depth map estimation from an aliased plenoptic light field. In: Sugimoto, A., Klette, R., Kimmel, R. (eds.) ACCV 2010, Part II. LNCS, vol. 6493, pp. 186–200. Springer, Heidelberg (2011)
15. Pock, T., Cremers, D., Bischof, H., Chambolle, A.: Global solutions of variational models with convex regularization. SIAM Journal on Imaging Sciences (2010)
16. Lee, W., Wontack, W., Boyer, E.: Silhouette segmentation in multiple views. Transactions on Pattern Analysis and Machine Intelligence (2010)

String Similarity Join with Different Thresholds

Chuitian Rong[1]([✉]) and Xiangling Zhang[2,3]

[1] School of Computer Science and Software Engineering,
Tianjin Polytechnic University, Tianjin, China
chuitian@tjpu.edu.cn
[2] Key Labs of Data Engineering and Knowledge Engineering, MOE, Beijing, China
zhangxiangling@ruc.edu.cn
[3] School of Information, Renmin University of China, Beijing, China

Abstract. String similarity join is an essential operation of many applications that need to find all similar string pairs from given two collections. The existing approaches are using the uniform and predefined similarity thresholds. While in real applications, regarding that the longer string pairs typically tolerate many more typos, it is necessary to apply variable thresholds to different strings instead of a constant one. Therefore, we proposed a solution for string similarity joins with different similarity thresholds in one procedure. In order to support different similarity thresholds, we devised the similarity aware index and index probing technique. To our best knowledge, it is the first work to address the problem. Experimental results on real-world datasets show that our solution can tackle with different similarity thresholds efficiently.

1 Introduction

String is a fundamental data type and widely used in a variety of applications, such as recording product and customer names in marketing, producing publications in academic research, publishing contents in websites. Frequently, different strings in different sources may refer to the same real-world entity due to various reasons. In order to combine heterogenous data from different sources and provide a unified view of entities, the string similarity join is proposed to find all pairs of strings in a given string collection, based on a string similarity function and a user specified threshold. The existing similarity functions fall into two categories: set-based similarity functions (e.g., Jaccard [9]) and character-based similarity functions (e.g., Edit distance). For the set-based similarity functions, the implementations tokenize each string into a set of tokens and extract its signatures, and then index the signatures using inverted index [2,12]. A pair of strings that share a certain number of signatures are regarded as a candidate pair. Our solution in this paper falls into this category.

To identify all similar string pairs in given two collections of strings, the methods follow a filter and refine process. In the filter step, they generated a set of candidate pairs who share a common token. In the verification step, they verified the candidate pairs to generate the final answers. However, if the strings contain popular tokens the qualified candidate pairs will grow exponentially. To address

© Springer International Publishing Switzerland 2015
S. Zhang et al. (Eds.): KSEM 2015, LNAI 9403, pp. 260–271, 2015.
DOI: 10.1007/978-3-319-25159-2_24

Table 1. Data Sets

	ID	String
	r_1	Topk set similarity joins
$\mathcal{R}$	r_2	Efficient exact set-similarity joins
	r_3	Efficient parallel set similarity joins using MapReduce
	s_1	Top-k set similarity joins
$\mathcal{S}$	s_2	Efficient exact set similarity joins
	s_3	Efficient parallel set-similarity joins using MapReduce

Table 2. Prefix Tokens Using Different Thresholds

θ	ID	String
	s_1	**Top-k** similarity set joins
0.8	s_2	**similarity** set joins exact Efficient
	s_3	**using set-similarity** MapReduce parallel joins Efficient
	s_1	**Top-k similarity** set joins
0.6	s_2	**similarity set** joins exact Efficient
	s_3	**using set-similarity MapReduce** parallel joins Efficient

this problem, the prefix filtering [1] method has been proposed. According to the prefix filtering, all the strings in the collections are sorted based on a global ordering and the first T tokens are selected as their prefix. The number of T is determined by $|s|$ (the number of words in s), the similarity function sim, and the user specified similarity threshold θ. Take Jaccard similarity function as an example, $T = |s| - \lceil |s| * \theta \rceil + 1$. It shows that for any other string r, the necessary condition of $sim(s, r) \geq \theta$ is that the prefix of s and r must have at least one token in common [1,2,17]. Let us consider the Example 1 and apply a prefix filtering technique to generate its candidate pairs, based on the Jaccard similarity function.

Example 1. Table 1 lists two string collections of publication titles from different data sources. We sorted words of each string in $\mathcal{R}$ and $\mathcal{S}$ based on alphabetical order and selected the first $(|s| - \lceil |s| * \theta \rceil + 1)$ words (prefixes) as their prefix. Then, we construct two inverted indices for prefix tokens of each string in $\mathcal{S}$ using $\theta = 0.8$ and $\theta = 0.6$, respectively. The prefix tokens of strings in $\mathcal{R}$ are given in Table 2. The inverted indices for prefix tokens of strings in $\mathcal{S}$ are shown in Figure 1.

When performing similarity joins, we derive candidate string pairs by probing inverted index using the prefix tokens of each string in $\mathcal{R}$ based on the same global ordering. When $\theta = 0.8$, the candidate pair set is $\{<r_2, s_3>, <r_3, s_3>\}$. After verification, we can get the result $<r_3, s_3>$. When $\theta = 0.6$, the candidate pair set is $\{<r_1, s_1>, <r_1, s_3>, <r_2, s_1>, <r_2, s_3>, <r_3, s_3>, <r_3, s_3>, <r_3, s_2>\}$. The final results is $<r_1, s_1>$ and $<r_3, s_3>$. In fact, all the pairs $<r_i, s_i>$(i=1,2,3) refer to the same publications, respectively.

However, all the existing works are applying the predefined and uniform similarity threshold like above. From the above example, we can find that we will lose some results when using a uniform similarity threshold for all string pairs. It is due to that one spelling difference between r_i and s_i can make remarkable different in $sim(r_i, s_i)$(i=1,2,3). So, we prefer a solution that applying different thresholds to different strings. In this paper, we mainly focus on the solutions to support different similarity thresholds, and leave the problem of designating suitable similarity thresholds to strings as a future work.

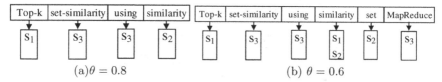

(a)$\theta = 0.8$ (b) $\theta = 0.6$

Fig. 1. Inverted Index For Prefix Tokens

Applying a predefined and uniform threshold as all existing works do, it is easy for implementation and optimization. When applying different similarity thresholds, there are three challenges need to be addressed:(1)As there are a variety of different thresholds, the widely used prefix filtering method can not be applied in inverted index construction;(2)As we can not predict the thresholds of that will perform joins, we should devise a similarity aware index mechanism;(3)We should explore new index probing techniques to avoid iterative accessing and improve the performance.

In summary, we make the following contributions.

- We proposed a solution for string similarity join with different similarity thresholds. This is the first work to explore similarity join that using diverse thresholds in one procedure.
- We devised the similarity aware index technique to support different similarity thresholds when performing similarity joins.
- We provided new index probing technique and filtering mechanism to improve the join performance.

The rest of the paper is organized as follows. The related works are given in Section 2. Section 3 presents the problem definitions and preliminaries. Section 4 describes the implementation of similarity aware index. Section 5 presents how to perform similarity joins by employing new index probing technique. Experimental evaluations are given in Section 6. Section 7 concludes the paper.

2   Related Work

String similarity join is a primitive operation in many applications such as merge-purge [6], record linkage [15], object matching [13] and reference reconciliation[3]. In order to avoid verifying every pair of strings in the dataset and improve performance, string similarity join typically follows a filtering and refine process [4,10]. In the filtering step, the signature assignment process or blocking process is invoked to group the candidates into groups by using either an approximate or exact approach, depending on whether some amount of error could be tolerated or not. In past two decades, there are more ten different algorithms proposed to solve this problem [7]. In [7], they evaluated existing algorithms under the same experimental framework and reported comprehensive findings. Since we aim to provide exact answers, we will focus on the exact approaches. Recent works that provide exact answers are typically built on top of some traditional indexing methods, such as tree based or inverted index based.

Table 3. Symbols and Definitions

Symbols	Definition
$\mathcal{R}, \mathcal{S}$	collections of strings
$|\cdot|$	the element number of a set
t	a token of s
T_r	set of tokens for string r
V_r	T_r presents in Vector Space Model
T_r^p	the first p tokens of string r
θ	pre-assigned threshold
$Sim(r_i, s_j)$	similarity between r_i and s_j
$\mathcal{O}$	global ordering
$T_r^p(\mathcal{O})$	T_r^p under $\mathcal{O}$

Table 4. Similarity Functions

SimilarityFunction	Definition	Prefix Length
$sim_{dice}(r_i, s_j)$	$\dfrac{2 \times |T_{r_i} \cap T_{s_j}|}{|T_{r_i}| + |T_{s_j}|}$	$|T_s| - \lceil |T_s| * \theta \rceil + 1$
$sim_{jaccard}(r_i, s_j)$	$\dfrac{|T_{r_i} \cap T_{s_j}|}{|T_{r_i} \cup T_{s_j}|}$	$|T_s| - \lceil |T_s| * \theta \rceil + 1$
$sim_{cosine}(r_i, s_j)$	$\dfrac{V_{r_i} \cdot V_{s_j}}{\sqrt{|V_{r_i}| \times |V_{s_j}|}}$	$|T_s| - \lceil |T_s| * \theta^2 \rceil + 1$

The methods making use of the inverted index are based on the fact that similar strings share common parts and consequently they transform the similarity constraints into set overlap constraints. Based on the property of set overlap [2], the prefix filtering was proposed to prune false positives [1,2,5]. In these methods, the partial result of the filtering step is a superset of the final result. The *AllPairs* method proposed in [1] builds the inverted index for prefix tokens and each string pair in the same inverted list are considered as candidates. This method can reduce the false positives significantly compared to the method that indexes all tokens of each strings [12]. In order to prune false positives more aggressively, the *PPJoin* method applies the position information of the prefix tokens of the string. Based on the *PPJoin*, the *PPJoin+* uses the position information of suffix tokens to prune false positives further [17]. In [14], they observed that prefix lengths have significant effect on pruning false positives and the join performance. They proposed the *AdaptJoin* method by utilizing different prefix lengths. [11] proposed the *MGJoin* method that based on multiple prefix filters, each of which is based on a different global ordering. [8] studied the problem with synonyms by utilizing a novel index that combines different filtering strategies.

All the aforementioned works applied a predefined and uniform threshold when performing joins. Further, the index that used to accelerate the join process is constructed for one time use.

3   Preliminary

3.1   Problem Definition

In this paper, we consider string as set of tokens, each of which can be a word or n-gram. For example, the tokens set of r_2 in $\mathcal{R}$(Table 1) is {*Efficient, exact, set, similarity, joins*}. The string similarity join is defined as follow.

Definition 1. *String Similarity Join.* *Given two string collections $\mathcal{R}$ and $\mathcal{S}$, a similarity function Sim and each $r \in \mathcal{R}$ has its own join threshold $r.\theta$, string similarity join finds all string pairs (r, s), such that $Sim(r, s) \geq r.\theta$.*

3.2   Similarity Measures

A similarity function measures how similar two strings are. There are two main types of similarity functions for strings, set-based similarity functions and character-based similarity functions. In this paper, we utilize three widely used set-based similarity functions, namely Jaccard [9], Dice and Cosine [16], whose computation problem can be reduced to set overlap problem [1]. They are based on the fact that similar strings share common components. Their definitions are summarized in Table 4, in which T_r denotes the tokens set of r ,the V_r denotes the vector transformed from T_r and $|\cdot|$ denotes the size of set. Unless otherwise specified, we use Jaccard as the default function, i.e., $sim(r, s) = sim_{jaccard}(r, s)$. For example, $sim_{jaccard}(r_2, s_2) = \frac{3}{6}$.

4   Index Technique to Support Different Similarity Thresholds

All the existing works on similarity joins are using the predefined and uniform thresholds for all objects in collections, we say that they are applying the same similarity threshold. Applying the same threshold, it is easy to implement and optimize the algorithms. However, the objects in collections that to perform joins are different to each other, e.g, length, typographies, abbreviation. If applying the same threshold to all the objects, we will lose some promising results. Further more, in order to satisfy the diverse and personalized requirements of data analysis the string similarity joins to support different similarity thresholds are indeed. The prefix filtering technique is widely used in existing works due to its effective pruning power. The prefix filtering is based on a necessary condition for similar pairs of strings, which is that they must share at least one prefix token when sorted by the same global order. The prefix tokens of two strings are determined by their length and the uniform threshold. When applying different thresholds for objects in collection that to perform joins, there is a big challenge. When constructing the inverted index for prefix tokens of each string $s \in \mathcal{S}$, we can not predict the threshold of $r \in \mathcal{R}$ that will to perform join with s. The problem is that we can not certify the number of prefix tokens of $s \in \mathcal{S}$. In this section, we propose the index techniques that can support different similarity thresholds.

4.1   Straightforward Approach

As above analyzed we can not predict the threshold of $r \in \mathcal{R}$, we can not certify the number of prefix tokens of $s \in \mathcal{S}$ and can not construct the inverted index. The straightforward approach is to map all tokens of $s \in \mathcal{S}$ to inverted lists. When performing joins, we enumerate each string $r \in \mathcal{R}$ and get its prefix tokens. Then, we can get the candidate pairs by merging the corresponding inverted lists. Obviously, this approach will map unnecessary tokens into inverted lists and increase the index size. As the results, there are many unnecessary cost when probing the inverted lists and the similarity join performance is low.

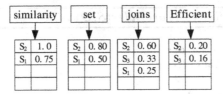

Fig. 2. Similarity Aware Inverted Index

4.2 Similarity Aware Index

The partition-based inverted index can decrease the unnecessary probing cost to some extent, while there is much space to improve. In order to improve the performance further, we proposed a **Similarity Aware Index** by exploiting the relationship of token position and similarity threshold, denoted as $\mathcal{SAI}$.

Definition 2. *Threshold Upper Bound.* *For one string $r \in \mathcal{R}$ or($s \in \mathcal{S}$), it is tokenized into token set T_r and sorted by global ordering $\mathcal{O}$. The tokens that determined as prefix tokens are related with the value of threshold. The maximum threshold for a token to be prefix token is defined as threshold upper bound, denoted as **TUB**.*

Theorem 1. *Let token $t \in T_r$ be located at the position n when T_r is sorted by global ordering $\mathcal{O}$. If t is a prefix token, $TUB(n) = \frac{|T_r|-n+1}{|T_r|}$.*

Proof. For the token set T_r, its prefix tokens size $|T_r^p|$ is determined by the below formula.

$$|T_r^p| = |T_r| - \lceil |T_r| * \theta \rceil + 1$$

Let $|T_r^p| = n$, that is to say the last prefix token is located at the position n. Then, we can get

$$|T_r| - n < |T_r| * \theta \leq |T_r| - n + 1$$

We can get $\theta \leq \frac{|T_r|-n+1}{|T_r|}$. So,

$$TUB(n) = \frac{|T_r|-n+1}{|T_r|}.$$

Based on above analysis, we can get that the token $t \in T_r$ to be selected as prefix token is related to its position n and $TUB(n)$ when $|T_r|$ is sorted by a global ordering. So, we can map the token t and $TUB(n)$ to the inverted index when constructing inverted index for collection $\mathcal{S}$. When probing the inverted index, it can support any threshold of $r \in \mathcal{R}$. Unlike the partition-based inverted that sorted the inverted lists by the length of the string, we sorted the inverted list by the value of $TUB(n)$. The Figure 2 shows a partial lists of similarity aware inverted index for collection $\mathcal{S}$ in Table 1.

The pseudo-code of similarity aware index construction algorithm is shown in Algorithm 1. For each string $s \in \mathcal{S}$, it generates a sorted token list by applying *Tokenize* function. Then, for each token in *TokenList*, it computes the $TUB(n)$ based on the token's position n and the size of *TokenList*. Finally, it maps the pair $<t, TUB(n)>$ into $\mathcal{SAI}[t]$. Noting that, each inverted list is sorted by the value of TUB.

Algorithm 1. *SimilarityAwareIndex*($\mathcal{S}, \mathcal{O}$)

Input :
    $\mathcal{S}$: the collection of string
    $\mathcal{O}$: one global ordering
Output:
    SAI: similarity aware index

1 **foreach** $s \in \mathcal{S}$ **do**
2     $TokenList(s) \leftarrow$ Tokenize($s,\mathcal{O}$);
3     $\mathcal{N} \leftarrow$ TokenList.$size$;
4   **for** $n = 0 \to N$ **do**
5        $TUB(n) \leftarrow \frac{\mathcal{N}-n+1}{\mathcal{N}}$;
6        $t \leftarrow$ TokenList[n];
7   Map $<t, TUB(n)>$ into $SAI[t]$;

5   String Similarity Join Processing

In this section, we perform the similarity joins using the proposed index mechanism. We present the details about how to handle different thresholds in one join procedure.

In general, the similarity join methods employing inverted index follows a filtering and refine framework and consists of three phases, including index construction, candidate pairs generation and verification .

In order to support different similarity thresholds in string similarity joins, the straightforward approach is to extend the *PPJoin+* [17] using the index as described in section 4.1. As it mapped all tokens into inverted lists, the join procedure will probe the index with much unnecessary cost.

5.1   Similarity Join on SAI

In $\mathcal{SAI}$, the inverted lists are sorted to the ascending order of $\mathcal{TUB}$ values of tokens. In order to avoid probing the inverted lists iteratively and improve the efficiency, the string collection $\mathcal{R}$ is sorted to the ascending order of the threshold of strings. By doing that, we can utilize the $\mathcal{TUB}$ filter when probing inverted lists.

Definition 3. $\mathcal{TUB}$ **Filter.** *For a string $r \in \mathcal{R}$, its threshold is $r.\theta$ and prefix tokens set is T_r^p. If $\exists s \in \mathcal{S} \wedge sim(r, s) \geq r.\theta$, then $\exists t' \in s \wedge \exists t \in T_r^p \wedge t' = t \wedge TUB(t') \geq r.\theta$.*

The $\mathcal{TUB}$ filter is a necessary condition for two strings being similar. It can be used to decrease the cost of probing inverted lists. By applying this filter during performing joins, we can just probe the first part of the corresponding inverted lists to get the results. The pseudo-code of similarity join on $\mathcal{SAI}$ is shown in Algorithm 2.

Algorithm 2. $SimJoinOnSAI(\mathcal{R}, \mathcal{S})$

Input :
> $\mathcal{R}$: the string collection $\mathcal{R}$
> $\mathcal{S}$: the string collection $\mathcal{S}$

Output:
> $< r, s >$: similar pairs

1   **foreach** $r \in \mathcal{R}$ **do**
2     $TokenList(\text{r}) \leftarrow \text{Tokenize}(r, \mathcal{O})$;
3     $T_r^p \leftarrow \text{getPrefixToken}(\text{TokenList(r)}, r.\theta)$;
4   **foreach** $t \in T_r^p$ **do**
5   **while** $i + + < I[t].size$ **do**
6   **if** $r.\theta > I[t].tub$ **then**
7   break;
8   **if** $r.length > \mathcal{S}[I[t].rid].length * \theta \parallel r.length < \mathcal{S}[I[t].rid].length/\theta$ **then**
9   continue;
10         $\mathcal{C}.push(\mathcal{S}[I[t].rid])$;
11   Verification($\mathcal{C}$);

For each string $r \in \mathcal{R}$, it is tokenized by the same global ordering $\mathcal{O}$, which applied to $\mathcal{S}$. Its prefix tokens T_r^p can be acquired based on the number of tokens and its own threshold $r.\theta$(Lines 2-3). Then, the inverted lists of tokens in T_r^p will be probed and merged. During the processing, two filters are applied. The first is to probe the inverted list until $r.\theta$ greater than the token's $\mathcal{TUB}$ value. This filter assures only the first short part of inverted lists to probe(Line 6). The second is length filter. If two strings are similar their length must satisfy a length constraints. If r is similar with one string $s \in \mathcal{S}$, the length of r must be in $(s.length * \theta, s.length/\theta)$(Line 8). Only the strings that passed the two filters are considered as candidates and to be verified.

6   Experimental Evaluation

6.1   Experiments Setup

We selected two publicly available real data sets of bibliography records from two different data sources in the experiment. They cover a wide range of data distributions and are widely used in previous studies. In order to evaluate the efficiency of our techniques in supporting different similarity thresholds, we generated three sets of thresholds for each dataset. The thresholds sets conform to three distributions, *Uniform*, *Poisson* and *Normal*.

- **DBLP** is a snapshot of the bibliography records downloaded from DBLP website[1]. It contains 1,021,062 records, each of which is the concatenation

---

[1] http://www.informatik.uni-trier.de/~ley/db

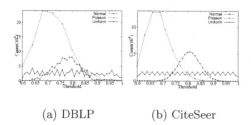

(a) DBLP   (b) CiteSeer

Fig. 3. Threshold Distribution Statistic

Table 5. Data Sets Information

Data Set	Size	Distribution	Mean	Std
CiteSeer	69.7M	Normal	0.8078	0.0420
		Poisson	0.6865	0.0481
		Uniform	0.8000	0.1156
DBLP	218M	Normal	0.7774	0.0531
		Poisson	0.7227	0.0676
		Uniform	0.7923	0.1122

of author name(s) and the title of a publication. The minimum, maximum, average length (number of tokens) of records are 2, 207 and 13, respectively.

- **CiteSeer** is also a snapshot of bibliography records downloaded from the CiteSeer website[2]. It contains 568,237 records. Each record is a concatenation of author names and the title of a publication. The minimum, maximum, average length of records are 1, 84 and 7, respectively.

The Figure 3 and Table 5 show the distribution of threshold θ and the size of two data sets. All experiments were carried out on a single machine with AMD 15x4 cores 1GHz and 60GB main memory. The operating system is CentOS with installed GCC 4.3. The algorithms were implemented in C++ and compiled using GCC 4.3 with -O3 flag.

The *PPJoin+*[17] is the well known method for set-based string similarity join. However, it requires predefined and uniform threshold. Due to its disadvantages, *PPJoin+* can not support similarity joins with different similarity thresholds directly. In this work, we extended the *PPJoin+* to support similarity joins with different thresholds as the baseline and denoted it as *ExtendJoin*. We denoted our proposed methods as *SAIJoin*.

6.2   Comparison on Different Indices

In this section, we evaluate the efficiency of two join methods. We conducted three experiments on two data sets *CiteSeer* and *DBLP* with three threshold distributions as shown in Figure 3. We conducted one RS-Join, *CiteSeer* ⋈ *DBLP*, and two Self-Joins, *DBLP* ⋈ *DBLP* and *CiteSeer* ⋈ *CiteSeer*, using *Jaccard* similarity measure. We plotted the running time cost of two methods in Figure 4. From the three figures in Figure 4, we can see that *SAIJoin* outperforms *ExtendJoin* remarkably, regardless of the join types and threshold distributions.

It is because of that the index probing technique applied in *PPJoin+*[17] is not suitable when applying different thresholds. After sorted by their length, the strings that located near to each other may own different thresholds. So, the length constraint is not effective yet. In order to get all possible candidates, *ExtendJoin* must probe large range of inverted lists iteratively. Noted that, in order to utilize the $\mathcal{SAI}$ index and $\mathcal{TUB}$ filter in an efficient way, the string

---

[2] http://citeseerx.ist.psu.edu

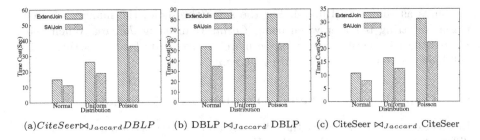

Fig. 4. Comparison On Different Indices

collections are sorted by their thresholds and the inverted lists are sorted by the $\mathcal{TUB}$ values of tokens. By doing that, the promising results are gathered to the head of inverted lists. For each string $r \in \mathcal{R}$, we can get its threshold $r.\theta$ and prefix tokens set T_r^p. When performing joins, we just probe lists $I[t]$ of $t \in T_r^p$ and stop when $r.\theta > t.tup$. This makes $SAIJoin$ just probe a small head part of related lists and has a better performance.

6.3 Comparison on Different Similarity Measures

In order to evaluate the scalability and robustness of our proposed method, we conducted experiments using another widely used similarity measure, *Cosine*. We used the same datasets as in above experiments. We carried out three types of joins, one RS-Join and two Self-Joins. The experiment results are plotted in Figure 5.

From the experiment results, we can observe that the $SAIJoin$ is over one time faster than $ExtendJoin$ under different experiment conditions. This is because $ExtendJoin$ applies the framework and filters of $PPJoin+$, which based on pre-defined and uniform threshold. The filters are not efficient when the data own different similarity thresholds, especially when using *Cosine*.

Compared with the results of using *Jaccard* similarity measure, the $SAIJoin$ performs better than $ExtendJoin$ when using *Cosine* similarity measure, as shown in Figure 4 and Figure 5. This can be explained by their definition of similarity

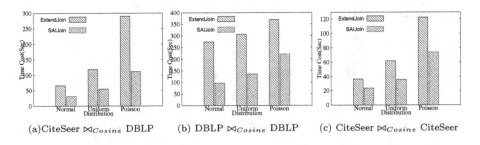

Fig. 5. Comparison On Cosine Similarity Measure

measures as shown in Table 4. For the same threshold, the number of prefix tokens of string is larger when using *Cosine* than using *Jaccard*. When using *Cosine* the join methods must probe more inverted lists for each string and it will incur more time cost than using *Jaccard*.

6.4   Comparison on Different Distributions of Threshold

In this experiment, we verify the efficiency and robustness of our methods with different distributions of thresholds. We conducted experiment on two data sets and performed three different join operations using *Jaccard*. The results are shown in Figure 6. In this figure, *R* represents *CiteSeer* and *S* represents *DBLP* for simplicity, and *X* denotes the join operation.

From the Figure 6, we can observe that the *SAIJoin* outperforms *ExtendJoin* by a wide margin on different kinds of distributions. Before performing joins, *ExtendJoin* sorted the string collections by the string length to utilize the length constraints. However, the strings that located as neighbors with different thresholds own different length constraints. So, *ExtendJoin* must probe a range of inverted lists to get exact results. While, *SAIJoin* using $\mathcal{SAI}$ index and $\mathcal{TUB}$ filter just probe a little part of the inverted lists. So, it can get high performance under different threshold distributions.

For the two methods, they performs best when the threshold distribution is *Normal*, followed by *Uniform* and *Poisson*. This can be observed in Figure 4, Figure 5 and Figure 6. For the DBLP dataset, when the threshold distribution is *Normal*, the average of threshold is 0.8078 and *std* is 0.0420. It is to say the value of thresholds are distributed intensively and the average of threshold is higher than other two distributions. The higher threshold lead to the smaller number of prefix tokens and less time cost on probing inverted list. So, the two methods spend less time on *Normal* distribution than other two distributions. When the distribution is *Uniform*, the value of threshold is distributed uniformly. The average of thresholds is 0.8000, while the *std* is 0.1156. It is to say the threshold values varied obviously. For the *Poisson* distribution, the average of thresholds is 0.6865. The thresholds are distributed intensively and most of them is small. As the smaller value of threshold lead to the larger number of prefix tokens, the

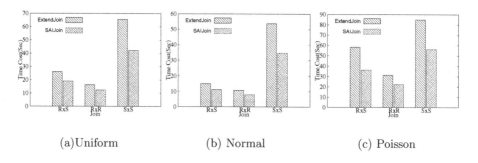

(a)Uniform   (b) Normal   (c) Poisson

Fig. 6. Comparison On Different Threshold Distribution

join operations must probe more inverted lists. So, the two join methods spent the most time on the data set when threshold distribution is *Poisson*.

7 Conclusions

In this paper, we have studied the problem of similarity join with different similarity thresholds. We devised similarity aware index and new filtering technique. The experimental results on real-world datasets show that our proposed method can support different similarity thresholds efficiently. For the future work, we plan to find a solution to assign suitable similarity thresholds to different strings.

Acknowledgments. This work was supported by the National Natural Science Foundation of China under grant No.61402329.

References

1. Bayardo, R., Ma, Y., Srikant, R.: Scaling up all pairs similarity search. In: WWW, pp. 131–140. ACM (2007)
2. Chaudhuri, S., Ganti, V., Kaushik, R.: A primitive operator for similarity joins in data cleaning. In: ICDE, pp. 61–72. IEEE (2006)
3. Dong, X., Halevy, A., Madhavan, J.: Reference reconciliation in complex information spaces. In: SIGMOD, pp. 85–96. ACM (2005)
4. Elmagarmid, A., Ipeirotis, P., Verykios, V.: Duplicate record detection: A survey. TKDE **19**(1), 1–16 (2007)
5. Gravano, L., Ipeirotis, P., Jagadish, H., Koudas, e.: Approximate string joins in a database (almost) for free. In: VLDB, pp. 491–500. ACM (2001)
6. Hernández, M., Stolfo, S.: The merge/purge problem for large databases. In: SIGMOD, pp. 127–138. ACM (1995)
7. Jiang, Y., Li, G., Feng, J., Li, W.S.: String similarity joins: an experimental evaluation. In: PVLDB, pp. 625–636. ACM (2014)
8. Lu, J., Lin, C., Wang, W., Li, C., Wang, H.: String similarity measures and joins with synonyms. In: SIGMOD, pp. 373–384. ACM (2013)
9. Monge, A., Elkan, C.: The field matching problem: algorithms and applications. In: SIGKDD, pp. 267–270. ACM (1996)
10. Naumann, F., Herschel, M.: An Introduction to Duplicate Detection. Synthesis Lectures on Data Management **2**(1), 1–87 (2010)
11. Rong, C., Lu, W., Wang, X., Du, X., Chen, Y., Tung, A.K.: Efficient and scalable processing of string similarity join. TKDE **25**(10), 2217–2230 (2013)
12. Sarawagi, S., Kirpal, A.: Efficient set joins on similarity predicates. In: SIGMOD, pp. 743–754. ACM (2004)
13. Sivic, J., Zisserman, A.: Video google: a text retrieval approach to object matching in videos. In: Computer Vision, pp. 1470–1477. IEEE (2003)
14. Wang, J., Li, G., Feng, J.: Can we beat the prefix filtering? an adaptive framework for similarity join and search. In: SIGMOD, pp. 85–96. ACM (2012)
15. Winkler, W.: The state of record linkage and current research problems. In: Statistical Research Division (1999)
16. Witten, I.H., Moffat, A., Bell, T.C.: Managing Gigabytes: Compressing and Indexing Documents and Images, 2nd edn. Morgan Kaufmann (1999)
17. Xiao, C., Wang, W., Lin, X., Yu, J.: Efficient similarity joins for near duplicate detection. In: WWW, pp. 131–140. ACM (2008)

Text Mining and Analysis

A Chinese Framework of Semantic Taxonomy and Description: Preliminary Experimental Evaluation Using Web Information Extraction

Liangjun Zang[1]([✉]), Weimin Wang[3], Ya Wang[2], Fang Fang[2], Cong Cao[2],
Xiaolong Wu[2], Qi Zhou[3], Ye Lu[3], Tingyu Li[3], and Cungen Cao[2]

[1] State Key Laboratory of Computer Science, Institute of Software,
Chinese Academy of Sciences, No. 4, South 4th Street, Zhongguancun,
Haidian District, Beijing 100190, China
zhxlyh@sina.com
[2] Key Laboratory of Intelligent Information Processing,
Institute of Computing Technology, Chinese Academy of Sciences,
No. 6 Kexueyuan South Road, Hai Dian Distinct, Beijing 100190, China
cgcao@ict.ac.cn
[3] School of Computer Science and Engineering,
Jiangsu University of Science and Technology, No. 2 Mengxi Road,
Zhenjiang 212003, Jiangsu, China

Abstract. The Chinese Framework of Semantic Taxonomy and Description (FSTD) is a linguistic resource that stores lexical and predicate-argument semantics about events or states in Chinese text, developed with the application of knowledge acquisition from Chinese text in mind. In this paper we build a web information extraction system, called NkiExtractor, to evaluate FSTD experimentally. We use two metrics: *grammar coverage* measures whether there is a semantic category of FSTD that corresponds to an event description in text, and *extraction precision* measures whether the correct predicate-argument structure can be extracted from text. Experimental results show that FSTD is a fairly comprehensive and effective resource for knowledge acquisition. We also discuss future work for expanding FSTD and improving extraction precision of NkiExtractor.

Keywords: Chinese linguistic resource · Event taxonomy · Web information extraction

1 Introduction

The explosive growth of the Web brings tremendous text to humans that far exceeds the ability of humans to read it. To extract high quality knowledge form massive text on the Web, several projects have been conducted to build

---

The work is supported by NSFC grants (No. 91224006, No. 61173063, and No. 61203284) and a MOST grant (No. 201303107).

S. Zhang et al. (Eds.): KSEM 2015, LNAI 9403, pp. 275–286, 2015.
DOI: 10.1007/978-3-319-25159-2_25

web information extraction (Web IE) systems, notably including the *open information extraction* systems [6,8,10,13,14] of the KNOWITALL project [4] at the University of Washington, the NELL system [7,12] of the research project *Read the Web* [3] at CMU. The state-of-art Web IE systems have repeatedly shown that using a parser can bring gains on extraction quality and quantity. For example, OLLIE [13] use features from dependency parse trees and SRLIE [8] depends on semantic role labeling system, both achieving higher precision and more yields than those without using parsers. There is no such thing as a free lunch, however, such parsers heavily depend on training corpus such as Penn Treebank, Propbank, and FrameNet.

The *Framework of Semantic Taxonomy and Description* (FSTD) is developed by a thorough analysis of semantic phenomena concerning states and events in Chinese text, with the application of knowledge acquisition from text in mind. In FSTD, events and states are grouped and abstracted into a collection of semantic categories, and all semantic categories form a taxonomy by *isa* relation. All semantic categories are represented as *frames*. Each frame contains a list of words or phrases, called *predicates*, that evoke the frame when occur in text, and a set of event participants, called *arguments*, labeled with a set of *roles*. Each frame also includes a set of rules that describe typical linguistic expressions of events as well as a set of knowledge extraction patterns corresponding to the rules. So far FSTD has included 5120 frames, 31100 predicates, and 10278 rules. It is time to use it to acquire knowledge from the Web and test its comprehensiveness and effectiveness.

In this paper we present a preliminary implementation of a Web IE system based on FSTD, called *NkiExtractor*. Our system output parse trees and knowledge tuples for Chinese sentences. It contains two core components: a parser and an extractor. The parser matches a given sentence with FSTD rules to derive all possible parse trees, and outputs the parse trees with top-k highest scores. The extractor produces knowledge tuples from a parse tree, using the extraction templates corresponding to the rules used in the tree.

We evaluate FSTD with two metrics: *grammar coverage* and *extraction precision*. Grammar coverage measures whether there is a semantic category of FSTD that corresponds to an event expression in text. Extraction precision measures whether the correct predicate-argument structure can be extracted from text. Experimental results show that FSTD is a fairly comprehensive and effective resource to extract knowledge from Chinese text. Fair comprehensiveness means that, for an event description in a sentence, FSTD usually contains the corresponding predicate and semantic category but often misses the rule to parse them. Fair effectiveness means that, for an event description in a sentence, NkiExtractor often fail to identify the correct frame structure but it can constrain the frame structure candidates to a very small set. Based on the experimental results, we analyze the problems of FSTD and NkiExtractor and give some promising directions to improve them.

Our contribution includes: (1) preliminary implementation of a Web IE system based on FSTD, (2) preliminary experimental evaluation on FSTD.

The outline of the paper is as follows. First, we provide background on Web IE and semantic resource construction. Section 3 describes the Framework of Semantic Taxonomy and Description. Section 4 presents the overall architecture of our Web IE system NkiExtractor and describes its core components briefly. Section 5 evaluates the performance of FSTD and NkiExtractor and analyze experimental results. Finally we conclude our work and discuss future work.

2   Related Work

There are some famous projects that aim to extract knowledge tuples form text on the Web, such as the open information extraction systems (TEXTRUNNER[6], WOE[14], REVERB[10], SRLIE[8], OLLIE[13]) of KnowItAll project[4] in UW, NELL system[12][7] of research project 'Read the Web'[3] in CMU. All of them deal with English text. Our work has similar objective but deal with Chinese text. A important difference is that they usually use automatically learned extraction templates but our system depend on manually designed grammar and extraction templates (automatical extension of grammar is a future work).

FrameNet[2,5,11] is a semantic resource in various languages. So far Chinese FrameNet[1] has created 323frames, 3947 lexical units, 20000 annotated sentences and 200 annotated discourses. Similar to FSTD, FrameNet contains a collection of frames as well as various relations (e.g. isa relation) between frames, where a frame contains a set of evoking words or phrases and a set of arguments with role labels. In contrast to FrameNet, FSTD add rules that characterize typical linguistic expressions in Chinese text as well as knowledge templates that correspond to each rule. So FSTD can be used to extract knowledge from text.

Given the limited size of FrameNet corpus, frame semantic parsing [9] aims to produce frame-semantic structures with high precision and high coverage.

3   Framework of Semantic Taxonomy and Description

The Framework of Semantic Taxonomy and Description (FSTD) is developed by conducting a thorough analysis of semantic phenomena concerning states and events in Chinese text, with the application of knowledge acquisition from text in mind.

3.1   A Taxonomy of Semantic Categories

A key concept of FSTD is *semantic category*. A semantic category abstracts and characterizes a group of similar events or states with the same predicate-argument structure, which contains (1) a collection of words or phrases, called *predicates*, that evoke the semantic category if they are found in text, (2) a set of *arguments* that can be viewed as event participants with *role* labels (e.g. agent or patient) w.r.t. the predicate.

All semantic categories are organized into a taxonomy by *isa* relation, more higher more abstract. There are only two semantic categories, i.e. *event* and *state*, at the first level. At the second level, event and state are further divided into 33 semantic categories, each of which is divided to several subcategories further. Besides isa relation there are several other relations between semantic categories, including *synonym, antonym, cause, partOf*, and *temporal* relations (i.e. before, starts, finishes, meets, equal, overlaps, during).

So far we have 5120 semantic categories with 31100 predicates and 5886 example sentences.

3.2   Representation

A semantic category is represented as a frame with slots as follows:

- **Definition:** interpretation in natural language.
- **Predicate:** words or phrases that may evoke the semantic category.
- **Rule:** production rules that characterize typical linguistic expressions of events, used to match text.
- **Template:** knowledge templates used to extract knowledge from matching results of rules.
- **Example:** illustrative sentences.
- **Precondition:** something required in advance before an event happens.
- **Effect:** something that follows and is caused by an event.
- **Axiom:** axioms that describe relations among different semantic categories.

Figure 1 illustrates a frame of a semantic category called *EquipPropertySemanticCategory*. This frame describes that an object is equipped with something (e.g. components or technology) that characterize the object as a property with some value. It contains a set of predicates and three arguments with labels *Essive, Property*, and *PropertyValue*. It also contains a rule used to parse sentences and two knowledge templates corresponding to the rule. The next subsection will describe the rule in detail.

3.3   Rule Description

A semantic category may be described in various ways in text. Each kind of typical expressions may be represented by a rule for the semantic category. The left-hand-side of a rule is a *nonterminal* representing the semantic category. The right-hand-side of a rule is a sequence of *units*, which may be a *keyword* or a *constant* or a *variable* or a *nonterminal*, and the optional forms of units, which denotes the unit is optional. These symbols are interpreted as follows:

- A keyword is simply a string. The successful match of a keyword against a string to parse means that it successfully matches the beginning of the string to parse.
- A constant is a set of keywords, with a exclamatory mark at head. For example, the constant ⟨*!AuxiliaryToVerb*⟩ contains three auxiliary words 'zhe', 'le', and 'guo'.

Fig. 1. Semantic Category Example

- A variable can match any string. The matched string must satisfy some constraint if there is a constraint in the variable symbol. Frequently used constraints include punctuation mark exclusion and string length limits.
- A nonterminal may be either a syntactic symbol or a semantic symbol. Take ⟨*Property : Component*|*Technology*⟩ as an example. The first item *Property* shows that the nonterminal is a semantic symbol. It describes the sematic role relation between the predicate *equip* and the matched argument *processor*. The second item *Component*|*Technology* indicates that the matched argument is usually a component or some technology.
- The optional form of a unit means that the unit can be skipped successfully if it cannot match the beginning of the string to parse. The optional nonterminal *[⟨Head-Modifier⟩]* is a good example.

4   NkiExtractor

Figure 2 illustrates the architecture for NkiExtractor. It outputs all knowledge tuples for a given sentence, with top-k best parse trees as by-products.

First, the sentence is segmented and POS tagged in the preprocessing. Second, the *GrammarFilter* excludes the rules that are impossible to match the given sentence successfully, producing a small size subset of all rules. Third, the *Parser* use the remaining rules to parse the sentence, deriving top-k best parse trees. Finally, the *Extractor* use knowledge templates to match the parse trees, yielding all knowledge tuples. The remainder of this section will describe these components in detail, using the sentence in figure 1 as a running example.

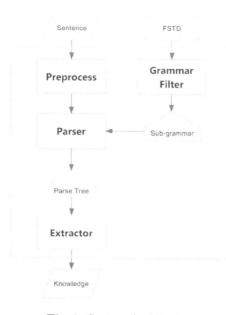

Fig. 2. System Architecture

4.1   GrammarFilter

Suppose $\mathcal{R}$ be set of all rules of FSTC. This component tries to reduce $\mathcal{R}$ to a subset $\mathcal{R}'$ of $\mathcal{R}$ that contains every *potentially matching rule* for the given sentence.

Definition 1 (Potentially Matching Rule). *A rule r potentially matches a sentence s if every unit (i.e. a keyword or a constant or a variable or a nonterminal or their optional forms) in the right hand side of r potentially matches s, where*

- *a keyword k potentially matches s if k match the beginning of s,*
- *a constant c potentially matches s if there is a keyword of c that potentially matches s,*
- *any variable potentially matches s,*
- *a nonterminal n potentially matches a sentence s if there exists a rule r that take n as its left hand side and potentially match s,*
- *any optional form potentially matches s.*

According to the above definitions, we implemented an algorithm that determines the set of rules that potentially match a given sentence. The experimental results show that we can reduce tens of thousands of rules to hundreds of rules before parsing.

4.2 Parser

The parser uses the rules of FSTD to parse a sentence, outputting top-k best parse trees. The correct parse tree corresponding to figure 1 is as follows. The node ⟨EquipPropertySentence⟩ corresponds to the EquipPropertySemanticCategory, each child node of which corresponds to a unit in the body of the rule for the semantic category.

```
⟨EventSentence⟩
|—⟨EventSimpleSentence⟩
|—|—⟨PropertySentence⟩
|—|—|—⟨EquipPropertySentence⟩
|—|—|—|—[⟨HeadModifier⟩]
|—|—|—|—⟨Essive:Object⟩
|—|—|—|—|—⟨NounPhrase⟩
|—|—|—|—|—|—⟨Noun⟩
|—|—|—|—|—|—|—MI (MI)
|—|—|—|—|—|—⟨SimpleNounPhrase⟩
|—|—|—|—|—|—|—⟨Noun⟩
|—|—|—|—|—|—|—|—Note (Note)
|—|—|—|—[⟨InternalModifier⟩]
|—|—|—|—⟨!EquipPredicate⟩
|—|—|—|—|—搭载 (is equipped with)
|—|—|—|—⟨PropertyValue:Thing⟩
|—|—|—|—|—⟨#PropertyValue$Nopunctuation⟩
|—|—|—|—|—|—高通蛟龙801四核 (Qualcomm Dragon 801 quad-core)
|—|—|—|—[⟨!AuxiliaryDE⟩]
|—|—|—|—⟨Property:Material|Component⟩
|—|—|—|—|—⟨NounPhrase⟩
|—|—|—|—|—|—⟨SimpleNounPhrase⟩
|—|—|—|—|—|—|—⟨Noun⟩
|—|—|—|—|—|—|—|—处理器 (processor)
```

Fig. 3. Parse Tree Example

The parsing techniques used in our parser could be characterized by three properties: *Top-down*, *Directional*, and *depth-first search* (also called *backtracking*). Top-down means that the parse tree is reconstructed from the top (i.e. the start symbol of the grammar) downwards. Directional means that process the input symbol by symbol, from left to right. Depth-first search technique is used to guide the non-deterministic parsing through all its possibilities to find all successful parse trees.

However, this requires in principle exponential time since any of the predictions may turn out to be wrong and may have to be corrected by trying other rules of the same head (i.e. the left hand side of rule). We use top-down dynamic programming technique, also called *memoization*, to reduce parsing time.

Note the matching process of variable nodes. What a variable matches depends on the matching result of the node directly following the variable node. For example, the right bound of ⟨#PropertyValue$Nopunctuation⟩ can be identified only after the node ⟨Property:Material|Component⟩ successfully matches string 'processor'. Once we get the value of a variable node, it needs to check the value if there is a constraint in the variable node. In our example there must not be any punctuation mark in the value of the variable.

4.3 Extractor

We now describe how knowledge templates of semantic categories are used to extract knowledge tuples from parse trees.

We first search a parse tree for the nodes that correspond to semantic categories. In our example it is the node ⟨EquipPropertySentence⟩. We then get the rule used in the parse tree and find all knowledge templates corresponding to the rule. We finally fill each knowledge template with the strings matched by tree nodes, yielding all knowledge tuples. Figure 4 lists the extraction templates used in our running example and corresponding extractions.

Template 1:	⟨Property⟩ (⟨Essive⟩, ⟨PropertyValue⟩)
Extraction:	processor (MI Note, Qualcomm Dragon 801 quad core)
Template 2:	hasPart (⟨Essive⟩, ⟨PropertyValue⟩ ⟨Property⟩)
Extraction:	hasPart (MI Note, Qualcomm Dragon 801 quad core processor)

Fig. 4. Extraction Template Example

5 Experiments

In this section we first define the metrics that we use to measure and present motivation of introducing it. We then present the settings of our experiment, including grammar statistics and data sets. Finally we present and analyze experimental results and suggest some possible solutions.

5.1 Experimental Setup

FSTC data. Table 1 lists the statistics of FSTC data, which presents the numbers of different items in FSTC.

Web corpus. Table 2 lists the statistics of web corpus. The first column is the domain, the second column is the number of sentences in each corpus, and the third column is the data sources from which these corpus are extracted.

We sample 100 sentences from the three web corpus respectively, generating a test corpus of 300 sentences. We refer to this corpus as *hybrid test corpus* and use it in the remainder of this section.

Table 1. FSTD statistics

Item	Number
frame	5120
predicate	31100
rule	10278
template	2637

Table 2. Web Corpus

Domain	Size	Source
cars	745,908	autohome
IT products	585,334	pcpop
news	55,817	sina news

Metrics. We can extract a knowledge tuple correctly only if we can identify the corresponding frame structure correctly. The correct identification of frame structure can be divided into two sub-problems: (1) there is a frame structure of FSTD that can be used to extract the knowledge tuple, and (2) the frame structure can be identified correctly. According to the two sub-problems, we propose two metrics for FSTD:

- *Grammar coverage*: how often is there a semantic category of FSTD that corresponds to a given event expression?
- *Extraction precision*: how often is the correct frame structure identified by NkiExtractor?

The first metric measures the comprehensiveness of FSTD directly, and the second metric measures the effectiveness of FSTD on knowledge acquisition indirectly. More effective FSTD helps build a more accurate NkiExtractor.

5.2 Grammar Coverage

There is a corresponding frame structure in FSTD for a given event expression if (1) FSTD has the evoking word/phrase of the event expression as a predicate, (2) FSTD has the correct sense of the predicate as a frame (i.e. semantic category), and (3) FSTD has a rule of the frame that match the event expression successfully. So this metric can be further divided into three metrics as follows.

Let $\mathcal{P}, \mathcal{F}, \mathcal{R}$ be sets of predicates, frames, rules of FSTD respectively, and $\mathcal{P}_C, \mathcal{F}_C, \mathcal{R}_C$ sets of predicates, frames, rules presenting event expressions in the web corpus respectively.

- **Predicate coverage**: How many expected predicates for the web corpus are included in FSTD? $Coverage_p = \dfrac{|\{p : p \in \mathcal{P}_C \wedge p \in \mathcal{P}\}|}{|\{p : p \in \mathcal{P}_C\}|}$
- **Frame coverage**: How many expected frames for the web corpus are included in FSTD? $Coverage_f = \dfrac{|\{f : f \in \mathcal{F}_C \wedge f \in \mathcal{F}\}|}{|\{f : f \in \mathcal{F}_C\}|}$
- **Rule coverage**: How many expected rules for the web corpus are included in FSTD? $Coverage_r = \dfrac{|\{r : r \in \mathcal{R}_C \wedge r \in \mathcal{R}\}|}{|\{r : r \in \mathcal{R}_C\}|}$

One knowledge engineer is required to label each event expression in the *hybrid test corpus* with correct predicate, frame name, and rule. Table 3 presents the values of the above metrics. We can see that FSTD has most corresponding predicates and frames for the test corpus, because new predicates and frames are easy to discovered by knowledge engineers with support of NkiExtractor. However, FSTD misses many rules to match event expressions. The reason may be that they only present rules for typical event expressions.

Table 3. FSTD Coverage

hit	miss		
	predicate	frame	rule
52%	5%	9%	34%

5.3   Extraction Precision

The extraction precision measures the precision of identifying the correct frame structure from all possible frame structures for an event description, provided that there is a corresponding frame for the event description.

Top-1 Precision. Let $f_{i,j}^*, f_{i,j}$ be the correct frame structure and the predicted one for the j-th event description in the i-th sentence respectively. Let $\mathcal{F}$ be the sequence of all predicted frame structures in the hybrid test corpus. The precision is defined as follows.

$$Precision = \frac{\mid \{f_{i,j} : f_{i,j} \in \mathcal{F} \land f_{i,j} = f_{i,j}^*\} \mid}{\mid \{f_{i,j} : f_{i,j} \in \mathcal{F}\} \mid}$$

Table 4 list the reasons of failure of identifying the correct frame structure, including (1) fail to identify noun phrases (NP) due to wrong word segment or POS tagging or named entity recognition, (2) fail to assign the correct frame to the invoking predicate, (3) fail to identify the correct boundaries of arguments or provide arguments with wrong labels, (4) other (e.g. special characters or wrongly written words lead to mismatch).

Table 4. Top-1 Precision

true	false			
	seg/pos/ner	frame	argument	other
46%	19%	10%	18%	7%

Top-K Precision. Let $f^*_{i,j}$ be the correct frame structure and the predicted one for the j-th event description in the i-th sentence, $s^k_{i,j}$ the set of k predicted frame structures for the j-th event description in the i-th sentence. Let $\mathcal{F}^k$ be the sequence of sets of k predicted frame structures in the hybrid test corpus. The precision of top-k frame structures then is defined by

$$Precision(k) = \frac{\mid \{s^k_{i,j} : s^k_{i,j} \in \mathcal{F}^k \wedge f^*_{i,j} \in s^k_{i,j}\} \mid}{\mid \{s^k_{i,j} : s^k_{i,j} \in \mathcal{F}^k\} \mid}$$

While our system often fail to derive the correct frame structure directly, we observe that the correct frame structure is often included in the top-k trees with highest scores. Table 5 shows the small number k indicates that we have constrained the space of frame structures into a very small size.

Table 5. Top-k Precision

top-k	1	3	5	10
precision	46%	57%	67%	72%

6   Conclusion and Discuss

In this paper we implement a preliminary Web IE system, called NkiExtractor, to evaluate a Framework of Semantic Taxonomy and Description. We found that FSTD is fairly comprehensive and fairly effective when used to extract knowledge from a test web corpus. First, for most event descriptions in the corpus, FSTD includes the corresponding predicates and frames but often miss rules to math them. Second, we can constrain the extraction candidates of an event description to a set of very small size by only matching FSTD rules against text, without using any statistical model of semantic role labeling.

One of future work is to improve the coverage of FSTD. We are doing automatic grammar learning to learn more rules for parsing, which enables our web IE system to successfully parse more event expressions and thus yield more knowledge tuples. Another important task is to improve extraction precision by: (1) Add component of *named entity recognition* (NER). We find that most of wrong word segment and POS tagging are due to named entities (e.g. product names), so NER can be done before parsing a sentence. (2) Add component of argument validation, which help identify the correct argument by excluding wrong argument candidates. (3) Add component of reranking extractions by redundancy. An extraction acquired from many sentences in many times should be given more confidence than another extracted by few times, so the extractions with low redundancy may be abandoned.

References

1. Chinese framenet. http://sccfn.sxu.edu.cn/portal-en/home.aspx
2. Framenet. https://framenet.icsi.berkeley.edu/fndrupal/home
3. Read the web project. http://rtw.ml.cmu.edu/rtw/
4. KnowItAll project. http://openie.allenai.org/
5. Baker, C.F., Fillmore, C.J., Lowe, J.B.: The berkeley framenet project. In: Proceedings of the 17th International Conference on Computational Linguistics, vol. 1, pp. 86–90. Association for Computational Linguistics (1998)
6. Banko, M., Cafarella, M.J., Soderland, S., Broadhead, M., Etzioni, O.: Open information extraction for the web. IJCAI **7**, 2670–2676 (2007)
7. Carlson, A., Betteridge, J., Kisiel, B., Settles, B., Jr., E.R.H., Mitchell, T.M.: Toward an architecture for never-ending language learning. In: Proceedings of the Twenty-Fourth Conference on Artificial Intelligence (AAAI 2010) (2010)
8. Christensen, J., Soderland, S., Etzioni, O., et al.: An analysis of open information extraction based on semantic role labeling. In: Proceedings of the Sixth International Conference on Knowledge Capture, pp. 113–120. ACM (2011)
9. Das, D., Chen, D., Martins, A.F., Schneider, N., Smith, N.A.: Frame-semantic parsing. Computational Linguistics **40**(1), 9–56 (2014)
10. Fader, A., Soderland, S., Etzioni, O.: Identifying relations for open information extraction. In: Proceedings of the Conference on Empirical Methods in Natural Language Processing, pp. 1535–1545. Association for Computational Linguistics (2011)
11. Fillmore, C.J., Johnson, C.R., Petruck, M.R.: Background to framenet. International Journal of Lexicography **16**(3), 235–250 (2003)
12. Mitchell, T., Cohen, W., Hruschka, E., Talukdar, P., Betteridge, J., Carlson, A., Dalvi, B., Gardner, M., Kisiel, B., Krishnamurthy, J., Lao, N., Mazaitis, K., Mohamed, T., Nakashole, N., Platanios, E., Ritter, A., Samadi, M., Settles, B., Wang, R., Wijaya, D., Gupta, A., Chen, X., Saparov, A., Greaves, M., Welling, J.: Never-ending learning. In: Proceedings of the Twenty-Ninth AAAI Conference on Artificial Intelligence (AAAI 2015) (2015)
13. Schmitz, M., Bart, R., Soderland, S., Etzioni, O., et al.: Open language learning for information extraction. In: Proceedings of the 2012 Joint Conference on Empirical Methods in Natural Language Processing and Computational Natural Language Learning, pp. 523–534. Association for Computational Linguistics (2012)
14. Wu, F., Weld, D.S.: Open information extraction using wikipedia. In: Proceedings of the 48th Annual Meeting of the Association for Computational Linguistics, pp. 118–127. Association for Computational Linguistics (2010)

Tree Based Shape Similarity Measurement for Chinese Characters

Yanan Cao[1], Shi Wang[2(✉)], and Cungen Cao[2]

[1] Institute of Information Engineering, Chinese Academy of Science, Beijing, China
caoyanan@iie.ac.cn
[2] Institute of Computer Science, Chinese Academy of Science, Beijing, China
{wangshi,cgcao}@ict.ac.cn

Abstract. In Chinese, there are many characters which are similar in shape, and this phenomenon usually induces writing errors. As one important issue in spelling automatic correction, shape similarity measurement is still a challenging problem. To address this issue, we propose a component-tree based method in this paper, which is based on the hypothesis "characters are similar if their construction and components are both similar". Firstly, we decompose each character to a tree recursively, in which the root node is the character and the leaf nodes are atomic parts, called strokes. Then, we align any pair of trees using their minimal super-tree and calculate their similarity from bottom to up based on weighted edit distance. Finally, the cognitive prominence is used to adjust the similarity scores. In text proofreading experiments, our method achieved 97% precision and 95.6% recall, which can be applied in practical systems.

Keywords: Shape similarities · Chinese characters components · Cognitive similarity · Automatic text proofreading

1   Introduction

There are lots of shape similar characters in many languages, which is the main cause for people to write incorrect characters. Especially in Chinese, characters such as "戈/弋/戋", "两/丙/俩", "鬃/鬟/髦", etc., are very easy to confuse. How to measure the shape similarity between different characters is an important issue in spelling automatic correction.

Shape similarity between characters is ill defined. Given two characters, from dif-ferent points of view, their similarity may be different. Taking "戈/弋/戋" for exam-ple, in an optical character recognition (OCR) system, '戈' is more likely to be recog-nized as '戋' because they are more similar in lattice data, but people tend to miswrite '戈' to '弋' because they are more familiar with '弋'.

Most related works focus on evaluating shape similarities for OCR system and have achieved a good performance in Chinese [1][2] and other Oriental languages [3]. In this paper, we aim to measure shape similarity in Chinese from the perspective of handwriting, and propose a novel approach which combines character component analysis and cognitive prominence measurement.

© Springer International Publishing Switzerland 2015
S. Zhang et al. (Eds.): KSEM 2015, LNAI 9403, pp. 287–298, 2015.
DOI: 10.1007/978-3-319-25159-2_26

Chinese characters are made up of atom components in various constructions. Briefly speaking, if two characters contain similar construction and components, they are likely to be similar. Based on this hypothesis, we firstly decompose each character to a component tree recursively, in which the root node is the character and the leaf nodes are strokes. Component tree embodies the character structure (such as "left-right", "top-down"), atom components (such as '⺧', '曰') and strokes (such as '一', ' | '). Then, we align any pair of trees using their minimal super-tree and calculate their similarity from bottom to up based on weighted edit distance. Finally, we con-sider the impact of cognitive prominence on miswriting behaviors, and utilize an asymmetric hypothesis that "Given two similar characters, the one which is more uncommon is likely to be miswritten" to adjust similarities scores. In the text proof-reading experiment, the top1 precision and recall rate reached 97% and 95.6% respectively.

The main contributions of this paper are as follows.

1. We certified fine-grained strokes in terms of their similarity, avoiding the confusion of similar components.
2. We propose a new automatic method to decompose a character into components and compute their similarity.
3. Cognitive prominence is introduced in shape similarity measurement, and obtains good effectiveness.

2   Related Works

For shape similarity calculation, previous methods can roughly be categorized as lattice-based method and stroke-based method. The former is commonly used in OCR systems, and the latter is mainly applied in handwriting recognition. Here, we just focus on stroke-based methods.

In stroke-based character similarity measurement, one key problem is splitting a character to components and strokes, which demands on a basic dictionary. In this respect, Chinese Character Information Dictionary [4] divides characters into single-component and multi-component ones, and provides fundamental strokes. According to different composition structures, characters are categorized into five groups including left-right, top-bottom, containing, be-contained, and nesting. Based on [4], the standard database of Chinese characters components [5] lists 560 components and gives all decomposing information for 20,902 Chinese characters. Among these characters, single-component characters account for only 4.96%, while the rest are compound ones. The Character Description Language (CDL) proposed by [6] is designed to describe and display characters precisely. CDL describes how characters are decomposed into components and strokes. Up until now, CDL has described more than 40,000 Chinese characters with about 50 stroke classes.

Based on pre-defined stroke dictionaries, previous works proposed grammar based or other expression based methods to decompose characters. [7] adopts context-free grammars to describe characters in tree-like expressions, and points out that components serve as bridges connecting a dozen or more stokes with huge amounts of characters. [8] converts Chinese characters into mathematical expressions in which operation data are 505 atom components and operators are 6 components structures. Based on these expressions, they defined a group of operating theorems and calculating formulas which can be effectively used in character generation, displaying, and analysis.

Among researches which measure shape similarity based on character database and character description, the ones combining component analysis and structure analysis perform better. Such approach proposed by [1] has achieved desirable results in both manual and OCR correction experiments. Compared with manual tests, these algorithms generated a matching rate up to 94%. They proposed that guaranteeing coincident granularity of components is one of challenges in shape similarity measurement. Besides, [1] proposes that the uncertainty of structure decomposition of Chinese characters would affect the similarity measurement. This work calculated the similarity between single-component characters manually, which may be affected by subjective cognition of critics. It pointed out that the similarity of single-component characters is the basis of the similarity of multi-component characters, which may affect the measurement of similarity of multi-component characters. In addition, only the difference in the number of strokes is used when considering the effect of strokes on the similarity. For example, '无' and '日' are of the same number of strokes, but they differ much from each other.

Using "Cangjie", [9] and [10] calculate shape similarities of traditional Chinese characters by combining their structure information. They used plane decomposition rather than recursive decomposition method which reduced their results. On the basis of stroke-segment net description, [2] measures character shape similarity using position and attribute of lattice data for stroke-segments as well as the difference between stroke-segments and have achieved significant results.

To our best knowledge, most of previous works used character components and structure to measure shape similarity, but they seldom consider the effect of cognitive prominence. In this paper, we are inspired by [11] which simulates the character shape cognitive process according to cognitive psychology. Using several features consisting of the structure, components, shape, position, etc., they constructed a neutral network model of human cerebral cognition for characters. The trained model was able to cluster characters according to shape similarity simulating human cognition.

3   Method

In this paper, we firstly measure character similarity based on component analysis, and then introduced cognitive prominence of characters. Four key issues are addressed, including component tree generation, component tree alignment, component similarity measurement, and cognitive prominence adjustment.

3.1   Stroke Set of Characters

A well pre-defined stroke set is the foundation of this work. Traditional dictionaries divide all strokes into dot (' ヽ '), horizontal ('一'), vertical (' | '), left-falling (' ノ '), right-falling ('ヽ'), and turning ('¬', '乙', 'L', etc.), which are too rough to get precise description of characters. For instance, '马' and '乡 ' consist of identical strokes "turning+turning+horizontal". To avoid such confusion, we further define a fine-grained stroke set with 36 elements. Taking turning for an example, we subdivided it into "horizontal right-falling hook (□)", "vertical horizontal hook (L)" and so on. We don't list all stokes in this paper due to the limit space.

3.2   Component Tree Generation

The aim of components analysis is to decompose a character into components hierarchically, and finally generate a component tree. Then, the shape similarity of two characters can be measured by calculating the similarity of their component trees. Formally, given a character c with stroke sequence $B = b_1 b_2 \ldots b_n$, its component tree is a multi-way tree, in which the root is c, intermediate nodes are continuous sub-sequences of B, and leaf nodes are the smallest (or atom) components. Compared with traditional ways which use just stroke sequences to represent characters, component tree is more preferable for its synthesis of composition structure and strokes.

Given a character, how to generate its component tree is still a challenge. [1] pointed out that, it is very difficult to set a uniform decomposing standard and components granularity. Besides, a character should be decomposed in different ways when it is compared with different characters in order to gain high similarity score. Taking '寞' for an example, it is decomposed into "((宀艹)(曰大))" when compared with '宽', while it is decomposed into "(宀(艹曰大))" when compared with '莫'. We can see that, multiple candidate trees may be generated for one character according to the structure of its comparative target.

However, in existing databases, only one decomposing tree is available for one character. So, we designed an automatic method to decompose each character into at least one atom component. All generated trees were stored as a resource for relative applications. The automatic character component analysis process is divided into two phases: atom-component sequence generation and component tree construction.

Firstly, we decompose characters into linear atom components based on backward maximum matching. Each character is converted into a stroke sequence based on predefined 36 strokes, and then atom components are extracted by backward maximum matching. The basis 560 atom components were proposed by [5]. Unknown components are considered illegal ones, that is to say, if the primary establishment of a certain atom component lead to the failure of recombining the rest strokes, this decomposing process will be broken. Moreover, the ambiguity of decomposing, such as "立十", "亠丷干" of '辛', are all reserved.

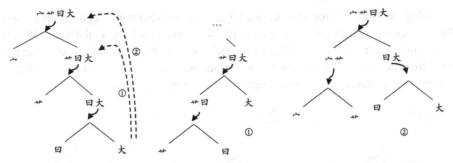

Fig. 1. Recursive component analysis process for '寞'. Component '宀' is set as the first direct child node of the root, the rest sequence '莫' is its brothers, '寞' is firstly decomposed into "((宀) (莫))" and the two parts are then be decomposed recursively.

In the second phase, we construct component trees for a character by constituting its atom components recursively. In this process, we prune illegal intermediate nodes with low integrity eigenvalue. The integrity eigenvalue of a multi-component part involves two important features, one is the co-occurrence frequency of components, and the other is the number of strokes. Intuitively, if the combination of several components occur in many characters, this combination is more likely to be valid. From another aspect, if only frequency is considered, the more atom components are combined, the lower their co-occurrence frequency is. So, we also take the number of strokes into account. Formally, given a character c and its atom component sequence $B = b_1 b_2 \ldots b_n$, the integrity eigenvalue of a component $B_{ij} = b_i b_{i+1} \ldots b_j$ is computed as follows,

$$I_{B_{ij}} = g(B_{ij})h(B_{ij}) ,\tag{1}$$

where $g(B_{ij})$ is the frequency of B_{ij} in the character set, $h(B_{ij}) = j - i + 1$ is the number of strokes of B_{ij}. After experimenting with 6763 characters in [5], we pruned nodes with integrity eigenvalue lower than 100, which was set as a threshold.

According to above method, we automatically generated multiple component analysis trees for each character. Consequently, we manually check each tree for correctness and construct a database of character component trees for other relative applications.

3.3　Component Trees Alignment

Given two component trees t_1 and t_2, if they are of different structures, we should align them to unify levels and bifurcations before calculating their similarity. The basic way is to build a minimal super-tree $st_{1,2}$ of which t_1 and t_2 are both sub-trees and there is no tree with less nodes that is also a super-tree of t_1 and t_2 [14]. Deriving the minimal super-tree is a restricted case of the smallest tree edit distance between two trees. Then, we get two isomorphic trees by embedding t_1 and t_2 into $st_{1,2}$ respectively, while the empty nodes are virtual ones.

Taking '寞' and '寥' for an example, Fig.2 (a), (b) gives their component trees, and Fig.2 (c) shows their minimal super-tree. If '寥' is embedded into c, the node O5 will be the filled visual node. The other tree is embedded in the same way to generate the filled tree. In Fig.2, O7-O10 will be the virtual nodes after '寞' is embedded. When two trees are identical in structure, alignment has been completed.

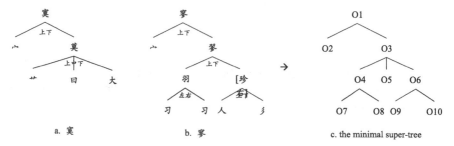

Fig. 2. The minimal super tree of '寞' and '寥'

3.4   Component Trees Similarity Measurement

After two component trees are aligned, we use a bottom-up approach to calculate the similarity between them, which depends on both the similarity between their compositional structures and atom components. Note that any node in the component tree is the character or its part, and similarity between two nodes can be calculated by the structure of their component trees and their direct child nodes. Apparently, this process is recursive which ends if all leaf nodes are visited. Given two nodes n_1 and n_2, their basic similarity is measured as follows.

$$BasicSim(n_1, n_2) = StructSim(n_1, n_2) \sum_{cn_1 \in CN_1, cn_2 \in CN_2} BasicSim(cn_1, cn_2) \text{ ,(2)}$$

where CN_i denotes all direct child nodes of n_i. In this formula, the first operator $StructSim(n_1, n_2)$ denotes the compositional structure similarity between n_1 and n_2, which can be looked up from Table 1. Structure labels are annotated automatically during the component analysis procedure, including half-encircled, single, top-left-right, encircled, top-down, top-middle-down, left-right, left-middle-right and alignment. The children similarity between n_1 and n_2 is measured by accumulating the similarity of all their corresponding child nodes. This similarity is calculated directly if n_1 and n_2 are left nodes.

In character component trees, each leaf node is an atom component which can be seen as a sequence of strokes. We use weighted edit distance to measure the similarity between atom components. As we all know, edit distance measures similarities between two sequences by quantifying the complexity of transforming one sequence into the other through adding, deleting, and replacing operations [12]. It is suitable to quantify the difference between characters caused by writing incorrect strokes.

Table 1. Similarity weights between character structures

ID	StruSim	1	2	3	4	5	6	7	8	9
1	half-encircled	1.0	0.6	0.0	0.6	0.0	0.0	0.0	0.0	0.8
2	single	0.6	1.0	0.0	0.5	0.8	0.7	0.8	0.7	0.8
3	top-left-right	0.0	0.6	1.0	0.0	0.3	0.0	0.0	0.0	0.8
4	encircled	0.6	0.5	0.0	1.0	0.0	0.0	0.0	0.0	0.8
5	top-down	0.0	0.8	0.3	0.0	1.0	0.9	0.0	0.0	0.8
6	top-middle-down	0.0	0.7	0.0	0.0	0.9	1.0	0.0	0.0	0.8
7	left-right	0.0	0.8	0.0	0.0	0.0	0.0	1.0	0.9	0.8
8	left-middle-right	0.0	0.7	0.0	0.0	0.0	0.0	0.9	1.0	0.8
9	alignment	0.8	0.8	0.8	0.8	0.8	0.8	0.8	0.8	0.5

As different strokes affect the character shape from different extent, we should set specific weight for each stroke to reflect how important it is. The adding weight and deleting weight of a stroke are determined by its sophistication and location. In terms of sophistication, the distinction caused by a more sophisticated stroke will lead to less similarity between two characters. For example, 'horizontal vertical' is of higher weight than just 'horizontal'. In terms of location, the first stroke and the last one are of higher weight than others, for they are likely to be easier for people to remember. The revising weight of two strokes is decided by their shape similarity. For example, the similar strokes 'horizontal' and 'horizontal left-falling' are of lower revising weight, while 'horizontal' and 'vertical' are of higher one. Take stroke location into consideration, the first and last stroke are of higher revising weight than others.

Based on weighted edit distances between strokes, similarity between two atom components p_1 and p_2 is evaluated as follows.

$$BasicSim(p_1, p_2) = \frac{1 - WED(p_1, p_2)}{\max\left(WED(p_1, \text{NULL}), WED(p_2, \text{NULL})\right)}, \qquad (3)$$

where $WED(p_1, p_2)$ is the weighted edit distance of components p_1 and p_2, $WED(p_1, \text{NULL})$ is the edit distance between p_1 and a virtual component with no strokes at all, representing adding or deleting a component.

Given two characters c_1 and c_2, we denote their decomposing trees as $T_1 = \{t_{11}, t_{12}, ..., t_{1n}\}$ $(n \in N)$ and $T_2 = \{t_{21}, t_{22}, ..., t_{2n}\}$ $(m \in N)$ respectively. We calculate pairwise similarity between t_{1i} and t_{2j} and choose the maximum one as similarity score between c_1 and c_2.

3.5 Cognitive Prominence in Character Shape

The basic similarity between two characters is measured based on composition structure and components, which represents main features of character images. However, people's cognitive similarity also impacts their mis-writing behaviours to some extent, so we further leverage the cognitive prominence in shape similarity measurement.

Recently, cognitive scientists have found that people tend to regard the objects of lower cognitive prominence as similar with the ones of higher cognitive prominence but not the converse [13]. Here, we use cognitive prominence to represent how familiar we are with a certain character. That is to say, common characters are easier to be misused as uncommon ones, but not the converse. For example, '徉' is easily to be written as '徜', but we seldom miswrite '徜' as '徉'. To better explain this asymmetrical relation between two characters, we primarily give a formal definition of cognitive similarity.

Definition 1. Given a character set C, $C \times C' \rightarrow [0,1]$ is a function describing the cognitive similarity between characters. For two different characters $c_1 \in C$, $c_2 \in C$, $\lambda(c_1, c_2)$ is the cognitive similarity between c_1 and c_2, which represents the probability of c_1 is miswritten as c_2.

Cognitive similarity is asymmetrical: for two characters c_1 and c_2 ($c_1 \neq c_2$), in general, $\lambda(c_1, c_2) \neq \lambda(c_2, c_1)$; if c_1 is of higher cognitive prominence than c_2, then $\lambda(c_1, c_2) < \lambda(c_2, c_1)$; otherwise $\lambda(c_1, c_2) \geq \lambda(c_2, c_1)$. We briefly use the probability $p(c)$ to represent the cognitive prominence of a character c, and we conclude that $p(c_2)/p(c_1) \propto \lambda(c_1, c_2)$. This relation will be further discussed in the Experiments Session. Fusing the character cognitive similarity with the basic shape similarity measurement, we produce the following formula,

$$ShapeSim(c_1, c_2) = BasicSim(c_1, c_2) \times \lambda(c_1, c_2) \tag{4}$$

Cognitive similarity can be calculated by simulating people's miswriting behaviors which is of high complexity and time-consuming. Here, we make use of the relation between cognitive prominences of two characters to approximate their cognitive similarity in the shape similarity measurement.

$$ShapeSim(c_1, c_2) = BasicSim(c_1, c_2) \times \frac{1 - e^{p(c_2)/p(c_1)}}{1 + e^{p(c_2)/p(c_1)}} \tag{5}$$

In this formula, we use a transformed sigmoid function to map $p(c_2)/p(c_1)$ to the interval $(0,1)$. $p(c_2)/p(c_1)$ is estimated by MLE method based on the occurrence frequency of c_1 and c_2 in a large scale corpus. Particularly, if $c_1 = c_2$, $ShapeSim(c_1, c_2) = 1$.

4   Experiments

4.1   Data Setting

Since there has been no benchmark for miswritten characters, we manually extracted 611 mis-written sentences from 10,000 short messages generated by stroke input in mobile phones. In these sentences, there is at least one incorrect characters caused by cognitive shape confusion. We manually annotated each incorrect character and gave its corresponding right one, which constitute word pairs "wrong words → right words". For instance, in the sentence "此号码是什么时侯激活的? (Eng. When the phone number was activated?)", we annotated "时侯→时候".

4.2   Effectiveness of Cognitive Prominence

In this session, we designed an experiment to argue for the proportional relation between cognitive prominence and cognitive similarity. We select several pairs of similar characters as experimental objects. Three factors are considered in choosing characters, including shape sophistication, shape similarities and commonness.

For each character pair c_1 and c_2, we calculate their cognitive similarity and cognitive prominence respectively, which is based on the occurrence frequency of c_1 and c_2 in a large-scale corpus. In this paper, we use the web corpus for its availability and sufficiency as well as its plenty of man-make mistakes on characters deriving from cognitive confusion. Frequency of a query item is returned by the Google engine. Some examples of experimental characters and their frequency are shown in Table 2.

Table 2. Characters and their frequencies in web corpus returned by Google

id	c_1	c_2	id	c_1	c_2
1	戈(4910)	弋(427)	6	戊(913)	戍(261)
2	盲(1660)	肓(70.3)	7	盲(1660)	育(6920)
3	栗(1900)	粟(803)	8	栗(1900)	票(28300)
4	裁(2040)	裁(2080)	9	裁(2040)	载(33000)
5	徙(266)	陡(578)	10	徙(266)	徒(555)

The ratio of cognitive prominence $p(c_2)/p(c_1)$ can be easily derived from $f(c_2)/f(c_1)$. However, we don't know whether a separate character is miswritten. If the character is embedded in a word, we can automatically judge its validity based on a word dictionary. For example, from the word "弋壁" we can easily see '弋' was miswritten as '戈'. We firstly got all words containing c_1, which is denoted by $W(c_1) = \{w_1, w_2, ... w_n\}$. Then we generate a negative word set $W(c_1 \rightarrow c_2)$, by replacing c_1 with c_2. We can estimate the cognitive similarity about miswritting c_1 as c_2 according to the following formula,

$$\lambda(c_1, c_2) = \frac{\sum_{w' \in W(c_1 \rightarrow c_2)} f(w')}{\sum_{w \in W(c_1)} f(w) + \sum_{w' \in W(c_1 \rightarrow c_2)} f(w')}, \tag{6}$$

where f(w) denotes the occurrence frequency of w. Then we undertake the same process but switch the right character and incorrect character to see whether $\lambda(c_1, c_2)$ equals $\lambda(c_2, c_1)$.

Table 3. Experiment results for asymmetrical cognitive similarity

id	$\lambda(c_1,c_2)$	$\lambda(c_2,c_1)$	id	$\lambda(c_1,c_2)$	$\lambda(c_2,c_1)$
1	0.038	0.621	6	0.004	0.000
2	0.089	0.126	7	0.003	0.001
3	0.000	2.114	8	0.007	0.005
4	0.000	0.000	9	0.031	0.002
5	0.193	0.053	10	0.008	0.011

Table 3 shows results for the effect of cognitive similarity. We can see that the cognitive similarity between characters is asymmetric, and $p(c_2)/p(c_1) \propto \lambda(c_1, c_2)$. Besides, combining character frequency information, we conclude that if two characters are both commonly (or uncommonly) used, such as "裁/载" and "徙/徒", their cognitive similarity is low, i.e., people generally don't confuse them.

4.3   Effectiveness of Shape Similarity Measurement

In order to test the effectiveness of our similarity measurement, we designed an automatic method to correct characters in the test dataset. For each sentence, we firstly computed the shape similarity between the wrong character and the others in a dictionary. Characters with top n similarities are selected to replace the wrong character, which are considered correct if the generated sentence is available.

For example, in the sentence "此号码是什么(时侯→时候)激活的", the incorrect character is '侯'. The top 7 similar characters with their similarity score in brackets are $W=\{$堠(0.938), 候(0.900), 缑(0.867), 糇(0.763), 喉(0.733), 猴(0.733), 俟 (0.652)$\}$. We replace '侯' with all candidates one by one and check whether the new word "时*" is contained in the dictionary. If it is, this character is likely to be the correct one.

We take precision, recall and F-score of using top N candidate characters to correct all sentences to evaluate our method. If any character in these N candidates is correct, we consider this sentence is corrected. In this way, p denotes the rate of how many modified sentences are correct, while r denotes the rate of how many sentences are corrected. Two options are given in this experiment, including using *BasicSim* or *ShapeSim* to compute the shape similarity.

Table 4. Results for shape similarity measurement

	Cognitive similarity un-considered			Cognitive similarity considered		
	top1	top2	top3	top1	top2	top3
p	0.970	1.000	1.000	0.970	1.000	1.000
r	0.941	0.971	0.971	0.956	0.985	0.985
$F1$	0.955	0.985	0.985	0.963	0.993	0.993

Table 4 shows the results for shape similarity measurement. We can see that cognitive prominence in shape similarity promotes the recall of character correction. Taking character '(涕)泠' for example, its basic similarity with the corresponding incorrect character '冷' is BasicSim(泠,冷)=0.900. Considering the effect of cognitive prominence, λ(泠,冷)$\approx$1. That is to say, people usually misuse '冷' as '泠'. For '(金)券/卷', '(不)详/祥', '(地)理/里', top1 correction failed when only basic similarity is taken into account.

Further analysis suggested that our approach performs well in decomposing characters. Taking "辛/幸" as an example, '辛' was decomposed into "立十" as well as "亠丷干", while '幸' was decomposed into "土丷干". The second decomposing way of '辛' made it more similar with '幸' (the similarity score is 0.877), while the first one made '辛' dissimilar with '幸' (the similarity score is 0.220). This example indicates that people always decompose characters at their subject wills when they write incorrect character. Generating all decomposition trees makes it possible to find the best way to compare characters.

Some typical mistakes are listed as follows.

1. If the same main component has different location in two characters, our approach will give them low similarity. For example, "副/辐", "敲/搞", "珊/删" are easy to confuse but missed by our method.
2. Some characters similar in lattice-data, such as "卅/州", "升/什", were not identified by our approach.
3. Lack of consideration in how strokes are connected leads to some mistakes in similarity measurement of single-component characters, such as "丁/寸", "上/口", "下/土", "不/卅". These mistakes may induce more errors in similarity measurement between multi-components characters containing them.

5   Conclusion and Future Work

This paper proposes an approach to measure cognitive shape similarities between Chinese characters combining component analysis and cognitive prominence measurement. We designed a new tree based method for automatic component decomposition and similarity calculation. Besides, cognitive prominence is introduced in shape similarity measurement, and obtains good effectiveness. Our future work will focus on combining lattice-based similarity and stroke-based one, which is likely to work better.

Acknowledgement. This work was supported by the National Natural Science Foundation of China grants (NO. 61403369, NO. 61203284, No. 91224006, No.61173063, and No.61203284), the Strategic Leading Science and Technology Projects of Chinese Academy of Sciences (No. XDA06030200), and a MOST grant (No. 201303107).

References

1. Rou, S., Min, L., Shili, G.: Similarity Calculation of Chinese Character Glyph and its Application in Computer Aided Proofreading System. Journal of Chinese Computer Systems **29** (2008)
2. Lin, M., Song, R.: A Stroke-Segment-Mesh (SSM) Glyph Description Method of Chinese Characters. Journal of Computer Research and Development **47**(2) (2010)
3. Nagata, M.: Japanese OCR error correction using character shape similarity and statistical language model. In: Proceedings of the 17th International Conference on Computational Linguistics (1998)
4. Chinese Character Coding Group: Shanghai Jiaotong University: Chinese Character Information Dictionary. Science Press, Beijing (1988)
5. National Languate Committee: GF3001-1997 Chinese Character Component Standard of GB 13000.1 Character Set for Information Processing. Language & Culture Press, Beijing (1997)
6. Bishop, T., Cook, R.: A Specification for CDL (Character Description Language). http://www.wenlin.com/cdl/cdl_spec_2003_10_32.pdf
7. ZhiWei, F.: Description of Chinese Character Structure by Context Free Grammar. Lingustic Sciences **5**(3), 14–23 (2006)
8. Xingming, S., Jianping, Y., Huowang, C.: On Mathematical Expression of a Chinese Character. Journal of Computer Research and Development **39**(6), 707–711 (2002)
9. ChuBong-Foo: Handbook of the Fifth Generation of the Cangjie Input Method (2008). http://www.cbflabs.com/book/ocj5/ocj5/index.html
10. Liu, C.L., Lin, J.H.: Using structural information for identifying similar Chinese characters. In: Proceedings of the 46th Annual Meeting of the Association for Computational Linguistics on Human Language Technologies (2008)
11. Jing, C., Zhichun, M., Youqian, S.: Computer simulation of the cognition of Chinese characters. Transactions on Intelligent Systems **3** (2008)
12. Marzal, A., Vidal, E.: Computation of normalized edit distance and applications. IEEE Transactions on Pattern Analysis and Machine Intelligence **15** (1993). Ph.D. Dissertation Submitted to UC Berkeley, Department of Linguistics (2003)
13. Tversky, A.: Preference, Brlief, and Similarity. MIT Press (2003)
14. Jiang, T., Wang, L., Zhang, K.: Alignment of trees: an alternative to tree edit. Theoretical Computer Science **143**(1), 137–148 (1995)

A Hierarchical Pachinko Allocation Model for Social Sentiment Mining

Li Liu[1,2(✉)], Zigang Huang[3], Yuxin Peng[4], and Ming Liu[5]

[1] School of Software Engineering, Chongqing University, Chongqing 400044, China
dcsliuli@cqu.edu.cn
[2] School of Computing, National University of Singapore,
Singapore 117417, Singapore
[3] School of Electrical, Computer and Energy Engineering,
Arizona State University, Tempe 85287, USA
[4] School of Biomedical Engineering, National University of Singapore,
Singapore 117575, Singapore
[5] Faculty of Computer and Information Science, Southwest University,
Chongqing 400715, China

Abstract. Existing topic models for mining sentiments from articles often ignores the fact that intra-topic correlations are common and useful to uncover a large number of fine-grained and tightly-coherent topics. This paper is concerned with the problem of social sentiment mining by modeling topic correlations. We aim to not only discover the connections between sentiments and topics, but also reveal the deeper relationship among topics where some topics may co-occur more frequently than others in articles. More specifically, we join sentiment mining with *hierarchical pachinko allocation model* to represent topic correlations by a hierarchy. In our model, the hierarchical pachinko allocation is employed to generate the latent hierarchical topic variables and sentiment variables. Experimental results on a collected news corpus show that our model can effectively identify latent topics in a hierarchical structure, and outperforms competing sentiment-topic models such as Latent Dirichlet Allocation based model in sentiment prediction.

1 Introduction

A rapid growth of online users inspires numerous news websites and portals to allow users to share their feelings or emotions after reading news articles. These user-generate social sentiments such as like, shock, sadness, angry and enlightenment can reveal the delicate human feelings and emotions found in texts. Knowing what social users think and feel is necessary for general people, marketers, public relations officials, politicians and managers to make decisions for the purposes like product recommendation, advertising and customer evaluation.

Probabilistic topic models have been successfully used to analyze large amounts of such social sentiment articles. Topic models are a suite of algorithms to uncover the hidden thematic structure of a collection of articles [4]. Latent Dirichlet Allocation (LDA) [5] is a widely-used topic model applied to textual

© Springer International Publishing Switzerland 2015
S. Zhang et al. (Eds.): KSEM 2015, LNAI 9403, pp. 299–311, 2015.
DOI: 10.1007/978-3-319-25159-2_27

data. In LDA model, each article is represented as a mixture of topics, where each topic is a multinomial distribution over words. Bao et al. [2,3] presented an emotion-topic model to discover the connections between articles and user-generated social emotions by augmenting LDA with an intermediate layer for emotion modeling, where each emotion is a multinomial distribution over topics. To generate an emotional article, the model first samples a per-article multinomial distribution over emotions. Then it repeatedly samples a topic from the emotion, and samples a word from the topic. Rao et al. [10,11] also presented similar algorithms of constructing a sentiment-topic model for social sentiment mining.

The sentiment-topic models extending from LDA capture correlations between sentiments and topics and correlations between topics and words, but they do not explicitly model correlations among topics. However, topic correlations are common in practical articles. Consequently, these LDA-based sentiment-topic models have difficulty modeling data in which some topics co-occur more frequently than others. Ignoring topic correlations limits LDA-based sentiment-topic models to uncover a large number of fine-grained and tightly-coherent topics [8]. Such limitation may propagate to hamper the discover of correlations between topics and sentiments.

In this paper, we exploit the *hierarchical pachinko allocation model* to represent topic correlations by a hierarchy. The hierarchical pachinko allocation model is also a topic model. It improves LDA by modeling correlations between topics in addition to the word correlations that constitute topics. In hierarchical pachinko allocation model, words and topics are connected with an hierarchical directed acyclic graph, where topic nodes occupy the interior levels and the leaves are words. Our sentiment-topic model augments the hierarchical pachinko allocation with a layer for sentiment modeling, in which each sentiment node links to the root topic node. The hierarchical pachinko allocation sentiment-topic model can provide more flexibility and greater expressive power than LDA-based sentiment-topic model.

In what follows we first provide the background by formalizing sentiment-word and LDA-based sentiment-topic models for social sentiment mining in section 2. Section 3 describes our hierarchical pachinko allocation sentiment-topic model, and illustrates our Gibbs sampling method for parameter estimation and inference. Section 4 presents the experimental results. Finally, we conclude this paper in section 5.

2   Background

A news article d is associated with a vocabulary of words $\mathbf{W} = \{w_1, \ldots, w_V\}$ and a set of social sentiments $\mathbf{E} = \{e_1, \ldots, e_K\}$. The number of words in the article d is denoted as $\mid d \mid$. The sentiment ratings of the article d over $\mathbf{E}$ is denoted by $\mathbf{r} = \{r_1, r_2, \ldots, r_K\}$, where r_j is the percentage of votes on sentiment e_j, and $\sum_{j=1}^{K} r_j = 1$. A corpus of D sentimental articles is defined by $\mathcal{D} = \bigcup\{(d, r_d)\}$.

2.1   Sentiment-Word Model

In sentiment-word model, words and sentiments are straightforwardly associated using Naïve Bayes method by assuming words are independent with each other. For any article d,

$$r_k = P(e_k \mid d) = \frac{P(d \mid e_k)P(e_k)}{P(d)} \propto P(d \mid e_k)P(e_k) = P(e_k) \prod_{w \in \mathbf{W}} P(w \mid e_k)^{n_{d,w}}$$

(1)

where $n_{d,w}$ is the frequency count of word w in article d.

$P(w \mid e_k)$ indicates the conditional probability of w given a sentiment e_k, which can be estimated according to the percentage of the co-occurrence between w and e_k in corpus $\mathcal{D}$, that is, $P(w \mid e_k) = \frac{P(w,e_k)}{P(e_k)} = \frac{|(w,e_k)|}{\sum_{w' \in \mathbf{W}} |(w',e_k)|} \cdot |(w,e_k)|$ can be derived from the word frequency count and the sentiment rating as a weight on it, i.e. $|(w,e_k)| = \sum_{d \in D} n_{d,w} \cdot r_k + \epsilon$, where ϵ is a very small smoothing value to avoid the situation of division by zero. $P(e_k)$ is the priori probability of sentiment e_k that can be estimated by the entire corpus, e.g. $P(e_k) = \sum_{w' \in V} |(w',e_k)|$.

Also, $P(w \mid e_k)$ and $P(e_k)$ can be estimated using Bayesian probability besides frequency probability. For instance, we can assume that $P(w \mid e_k)$ follows the multinomial distribution, i.e. $w \mid e_k \sim Multinomial(\theta)$. The parameter θ can be calculated by maximum likelihood estimation from the entire collection.

2.2   Sentiment-Topic Model

Topic models are used for discovering the main themes from massive collections of articles. The topic model assumes that to generate an article, topics are generated at first and then words are chosen according to the topics. Each topic is a probability distribution over words. Latent Dirichlet Allocation (LDA) is an independent topic model. LDA uses generative process to model the generation of a corpus. First, for each article, a distribution over topics is sampled from a Dirichlet distribution. Second, for each word in the article, a single topic is chosen according to the distribution. Finally, each word is sampled from a multinomial distribution over words specific to the sampled topic.

Let $\mathcal{T}$ be the set of T latent topics associated with articles. In sentiment-topic model, there are three steps to describe the conditional probability of topics given a sentiment. First, if topics are assumed to be independent with each other, the model is similar to the model in E.q.(1), i.e. $P(d \mid e_k) = \prod_{t \in \mathcal{T}} P(t \mid e_k)$. Second, if the probabilities of topic distribution on an article d is known, $P(d \mid e_k) = P(\theta_1, \theta_2, \ldots, \theta_T \mid e_k)$, where θ_i represents the probability the article contains topic t_i and $\sum_{i=1}^{T} \theta_i = 1$ $(1 \le \theta \le T)$. We can define $\theta_1, \theta_2, \ldots, \theta_T$ follow Dirichlet distribution. The parameter of the Dirichlet distribution can be calculated by maximum likelihood estimation from the entire collection. Last, a generative method is to assume each word needs to be assigned to a topic, $P(n_1, n_2, \ldots, n_T \mid e_k)$ can be describe as a multinomial probability distribution

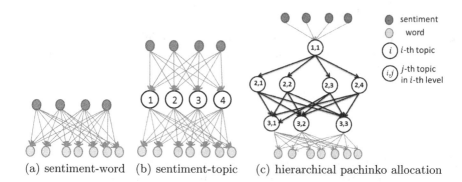

(a) sentiment-word   (b) sentiment-topic   (c) hierarchical pachinko allocation

Fig. 1. Model structures for three social sentiment mining models (a) Sentiment-word model: For each sentiment, a multinomial distribution over words is estimated directly from a corpus. (b) Sentiment-topic model: This model samples a multinomial over topics for each sentiment, and then generates words from the topics. (c) Hierarchical pachinko allocation model: A multilevel hierarchy consisting of a root and a set of topics. Each topic is sampled by a multinomial distribution over its parent topics.

conditioned on sentiment e_k, and here n_i indicates the number of words that have been assigned to topic t_i.

The graphical structures of the sentiment-word model and LDA-based sentiment-topic model are shown in Figures 1(a) and 1(b), respectively.

3   Hierarchical Pachinko Allocation Sentiment-Topic Model

In this section, we present the hierarchical pachinko allocation sentiment-topic model for mining social sentiments from corpus. The hierarchical pachinko allocation sentiment-topic model consists of a set of sentiments, a set of topics and a word vocabulary. The topics are organized in a hierarchy (tree) starting from a root topic. The graphical structure of the model is shown in Figure 1(c). In what follows we elaborate on the model, its parameter estimation and a variety of inference tasks based on the model.

3.1   The Model

Suppose an article d contains a set of topics organized with an ℓ-level hierarchy, i.e. $\mathcal{T} = \{t_{(1,1)}, \ldots, t_{(1,M_1)}, \ldots, t_{(\ell,1)}, \ldots, t_{(\ell,M_\ell)}\}$, where $t_{(i,j)}$ is the j-th topic of the i-level, and M_i is the number of topics in the i-level. The set of topics in the i-level is $\{t_{(i,1)}, t_{(i,2)}, \ldots, t_{(i,M_i)}\}$. The total number of topics is $M_1 + M_2 + \ldots + M_\ell$. Each topic $t_{(i,j)}$ in the i-level is represented as a multinomial distribution *Multinomial*$(\theta_{i,j})$ over the $(i+1)$-level topics. Each topic $t_{(\ell,j)}$ of the last level is represented as a multinomial distribution *Multinomial*$(\theta_{\ell,j})$ over words. For each multinomial distribution $Multinomial(\theta_{i,j})$ $(1 \le i \le \ell, 1 \le j \le M_i)$, $\theta_{i,j}$ is associated with a Dirichlet distribution $Dir(\alpha_{i,j})$ over a parameter $\alpha_{i,j}$, where $\alpha_{i,j}$ is a vector of dimension M_{i+1} (notice that $M_{\ell+1} = V$ when $i = \ell$). Now we define

Table 1. Notation of variables and probability distributions.

Parameter	Description
α	the set of hyperparameters for the topic mixtures θ, $\alpha_{i,j,k}$ is the Dirichlet prior for the distribution of topic $t_{(i+1,k)}$ conditioned on $t_{(i,j)}$
β	the set of hyperparameters for the sentiment mixtures φ, $\beta_{j,k}$ is the Dirichlet prior for the distribution of topic $t_{(1,k)}$ conditioned on e_j

Variable	Description
r	the set of sentiment rating, r_j is the sentiment rating over e_j for article d
w	the set of words, $\mathbf{w}(n)$ is the n-th word in article d
e	the set of sentiment assignment, $\mathbf{e}(n)$ is the sentiment assignment for $\mathbf{w}(n)$
z	the set of topic assignment, $\mathbf{z}_i(n)$ is the i-level topic assignment for $\mathbf{w}(n)$

Probability Distribution	Description
$\varphi_j \sim Dir(\beta_j)$	the mixture over β_j
$\theta_{i,j} \sim Dir(\alpha_{i,j})$	the mixture over $\alpha_{i,j}$
$e \sim Multinomial(\mathbf{r})$	the distribution of sentiment over $\mathbf{r}$
$\mathbf{z}_1 \mid e_j \sim Multinomial(\varphi_j)$	the distribution of the first-level topics conditioned on the sentiment e_j
$\mathbf{z}_{i+1} \mid t_{(i,j)} \sim Multinomial(\theta_{i,j})$	the distribution of the $(i+1)$-level topics conditioned on the j-th topic in the i-level
$\mathbf{w} \mid t_{(\ell,j)} \sim Multinomial(\theta_{\ell,j})$	the distribution of words conditioned on the j-th topic of the last level

the association between sentiment and news article. Each sentiment $e_j \in E$ is represented as a multinomial distribution $Multinomial(\varphi_j)$ over the first-level topics, and φ_j is associated with a Dirichlet distribution $Dir(\beta_j)$, where β_j is a M_1-dimensional vector. Sentiment e_j is associated with a multinomial distribution $Multinomial(\mathbf{r})$. The notation of variables and probability distributions is summarized in Tab.1.

Given the parameters of the number of topic levels ℓ, a set of ℓ topic numbers M, a set of topic hyperparameters α and a set of sentiment hyperparameters β, our model assumes the generative process depicted in Algorithm 1 for each article d with a sentiment rating r.

Algorithm 1. Generative process of our sentiment-topic model.

Choose every φ_j from $Dir(\beta_j)$ $(1 \le j \le K)$; similarly, choose every $\theta_{i,j}$ from $Dir(\alpha_{i,j})$;
for each word $\mathbf{w}(n)$ in d **do**
  Choose a sentiment $\mathbf{e}(n)$ from $Multinomial(\mathbf{r})$;
  Choose a first-level topic $\mathbf{z}_1(n)$ from $Multinomial(\varphi_j)$ conditioned on $\mathbf{e}(n)$, where $\mathbf{e}(n) = e_j$;
  for each level i from 1 to $\ell - 1$ **do**
    Choose a $(i + 1)$-level topic $\mathbf{z}_{i+1}(n)$ from $Multinomial(\theta_{i,j})$ conditioned on $\mathbf{z}_i(n)$, where $\mathbf{z}_i(n) = t_{(i,j)}$;
  end for
  Choose a word $\mathbf{w}(n)$ from $Multinomial(\theta_{\ell,j})$ conditioned on $\mathbf{z}_\ell(n)$, where $\mathbf{z}_\ell(n) = t_{(\ell,j)}$;
end for

According to this process, for a single news article d, the joint distribution of a set of K sentiment rating $\mathbf{r}$, a set of $\mid d \mid$ words $\mathbf{w}$, a set of $\mid d \mid$ sentiments $\mathbf{e}$, and a set of $\mid d \mid$ topics $\mathbf{z}$ is given by:

$$P(\mathbf{r}, \mathbf{e}, \mathbf{z}, \mathbf{w}; \ell, M, \alpha, \beta) = \prod_{n=1}^{|d|} \Big(P(\mathbf{e}(n); \mathbf{r}) P(\mathbf{z}_1(n) \mid \mathbf{e}(n); \beta)$$

$$\prod_{i=1}^{\ell-1} P(\mathbf{z}_{i+1}(n) \mid \mathbf{z}_i(n); \alpha) P(\mathbf{w}(n) \mid \mathbf{z}_\ell(n); \alpha) \Big)$$

where $\mathbf{w}(n)$ is the n-th word in d, $\mathbf{e}(n)$ is the sentiment assignment for word $\mathbf{w}(n)$, and $\mathbf{z}_j(n)$ is the j-level topic assignment for word $\mathbf{w}(n)$.

Since φ and θ are mixtures of α and β, we can obtain the following distributions by integrating over them to:

$$P(\mathbf{z}_1(n) \mid \mathbf{e}(n); \beta) = \int_{\varphi_j} P(\mathbf{z}_1(n) \mid \varphi_j) P(\varphi_j \mid \beta_j) d\varphi_j$$

$$where \quad \mathbf{e}(n) = e_j.$$

For each topic level j $(1 \leq j \leq \ell - 1)$,

$$P(\mathbf{z}_{i+1}(n) \mid \mathbf{z}_i(n); \alpha) = \int_{\theta_{i,j}} P(\mathbf{z}_{i+1}(n) \mid \theta_{i,j}) P(\theta_{i,j} \mid \alpha_{i,j}) d\theta_{i,j}$$

$$where \quad \mathbf{z}_i(n) = t_{(i,j)}.$$

$$P(\mathbf{w}(n) \mid \mathbf{z}_\ell(n); \alpha) = \int_{\theta_{\ell,j}} P(\mathbf{w}(n) \mid \theta_{\ell,j}) P(\theta_{\ell,j} \mid \alpha_{\ell,j}) d\theta_{\ell,j}$$

$$where \quad \mathbf{z}_\ell(n) = t_{(\ell,j)}.$$

3.2   Parameter Estimation

Given a training corpus D with sentiment ratings $\mathbf{r}$, we obtain its probability by taking the product of the marginal probability of single articles:

$$P(D, \mathbf{r}; \ell, M, \alpha, \beta) = \prod_{d \in D} P(\mathbf{r}_{(d)}, \mathbf{e}_{(d)}, \mathbf{z}_{(d)}, \mathbf{w}_{(d)}; \ell, M, \alpha, \beta)$$

where $\mathbf{r}_{(d)}$, $\mathbf{e}_{(d)}$, $\mathbf{z}_{(d)}$ and $\mathbf{w}_{(d)}$ are variables for news article d. Hence, for a news corpus D, the variables are $\mathbf{r} = \bigcup_{d \in D} \mathbf{r}_{(d)}$, $\mathbf{e} = \bigcup_{d \in D} \mathbf{e}_{(d)}$, $\mathbf{z} = \bigcup_{d \in D} \mathbf{z}_{(d)}$ and $\mathbf{w} = \bigcup_{d \in D} \mathbf{w}_{(d)}$.

Estimating Conditional Probability Distributions. We develop an approximate method based on Gibbs sampling to perform inference. Gibbs sampling can generate a set of samples that approximately obey the hierarchical sentiment-topic joint distribution. We have the conditional probability distributions on $\mathbf{e}$ and $\mathbf{z}$ as follows:

$$P(\mathbf{e}(p) = e_\xi \mid \mathbf{r}, \mathbf{e}_{-p}, \mathbf{z}, \mathbf{w}; \ell, M, \alpha, \beta) \propto \frac{r_{\xi(d)}}{nr_{\xi(d)}^{-p} + 1} \times \frac{ne_{\xi, \mathbf{z}_1(p)}^{-p} + \beta_{\xi, \mathbf{z}_1(p)}}{\sum_{j=1}^{M_1} (ne_{\xi, j}^{-p} + \beta_{\xi, j})}$$

$$P(\mathbf{z}_1(p) = t_{(1,\xi)} \mid \mathbf{r}, \mathbf{e}, \mathbf{z}_{-1p}, \mathbf{w}; \ell, M, \alpha, \beta)$$
$$= \frac{ne_{\mathbf{e}(p), \xi}^{-p} + \beta_{\mathbf{e}(p), \xi}}{\sum_{j=1}^{M_1} (ne_{\mathbf{e}(p), j}^{-p} + \beta_{\mathbf{e}(p), j})} \times \frac{nz_{1, \xi, \mathbf{z}_2(p)}^{-p} + \alpha_{1, \xi, \mathbf{z}_2(p)}}{\sum_{j=1}^{M_2} (nz_{1, \xi, j}^{-p} + \alpha_{1, \xi, j})}$$

For the $(i+1)$-level topic assignment $(2 \leq i+1 \leq \ell - 1)$,

$$P(\mathbf{z}_{i+1}(p) = t_{(i+1,\xi)} \mid \mathbf{r}, \mathbf{e}, \mathbf{z}_{-(i+1)p}, \mathbf{w}; \ell, M, \alpha, \beta)$$
$$= \frac{nz_{i, \mathbf{z}_i(p), \xi}^{-p} + \alpha_{i, \mathbf{z}_i(p), \xi}}{\sum_{j=1}^{M_{i+1}} (nz_{i, \mathbf{z}_i(p), j}^{-p} + \alpha_{i, \mathbf{z}_i(p), j})} \times \frac{nz_{i+1, \xi, \mathbf{z}_{i+2}(p)}^{-p} + \alpha_{i+1, \xi, \mathbf{z}_{i+2}(p)}}{\sum_{j=1}^{M_{i+2}} (nz_{i+1, \xi, j}^{-p} + \alpha_{i+1, \xi, j})}$$

and

$$P(\mathbf{z}_\ell(p) = t_{(\ell,\xi)} \mid \mathbf{r}, \mathbf{e}, \mathbf{z}_{-\ell p}, \mathbf{w}; \ell, M, \alpha, \beta)$$
$$= \frac{nz_{\ell-1, \mathbf{z}_{\ell-1}(p), \xi}^{-p} + \alpha_{\ell-1, \mathbf{z}_{\ell-1}(p), \xi}}{\sum_{j=1}^{M_\ell} (nz_{\ell-1, \mathbf{z}_{\ell-1}(p), j}^{-p} + \alpha_{\ell-1, \mathbf{z}_{\ell-1}(p), j})} \times \frac{nw_{\xi, \mathbf{w}(p)}^{-p} + \alpha_{\ell, \xi, \mathbf{w}(p)}}{\sum_{j=1}^{V} (nw_{\xi, j}^{-p} + \alpha_{\ell, \xi, j})}$$

where, p represents the n-th word of article d, and $r_{\xi(d)}$ is the rating over sentiment e_ξ for d. $nr_{\xi(d)}$ is the number of times the sentiment e_ξ has been assigned for the words in d. $\mathbf{e}(p)$ and $\mathbf{z}_i(p)$ are the sentiment assignment and the i-level topic assignment for the word $\mathbf{w}(p)$, respectively. $\mathbf{e}_{-p}$ means all sentiment variables other than the current assignment of sentiment for word $\mathbf{w}(p)$, and $\mathbf{z}_{-ip}$ means all topic variables other than the current assignment of the i-level topic for word $\mathbf{w}(p)$. $ne_{i,j}$ is the number of times the first-level topic $t_{(1,j)}$ has been assigned to the sentiment e_i. $nz_{i,k,j}$ is the number of times the $(i+1)$-level topic $t_{(i+1,j)}$ has been assigned to the i-level topic $t_{(i,k)}$. $nw_{i,j}$ is the number of times the word w_j has been assigned to the ℓ-level topic $t_{(\ell,i)}$. The superfix $-p$ of nr, ne, nz and nw means that the count does not include the current assignment of sentiment and topics for word $\mathbf{w}(p)$. Due to the page limitation, we will skip technical details of the derivations here, and provide the full derivations in a journal version.

After Gibbs sampling, we can obtain N samples of the variables $\mathbf{e}$, $\mathbf{z}$, and $\mathbf{w}$. The mean values $\overline{ne}_{j,k}$, $\overline{nz}_{i,j,k}$ and $\overline{nw}_{j,k}$ of the N samples approximately obey the joint distribution of $P(D; \mathbf{r}, \ell, M, \alpha, \beta)$, where $\overline{ne}_{j,k} = \frac{1}{N} \times \sum_{s=1}^{N} ne_{j,k}^{(s)}$, $\overline{nz}_{i,j,k} = \frac{1}{N} \times \sum_{s=1}^{N} nz_{i,j,k}^{(s)}$ and $\overline{nw}_{j,k} = \frac{1}{N} \times \sum_{s=1}^{N} nw_{j,k}^{(s)}$. s indicates the s-th sample generated by Gibbs sampling. Hence, we can estimate the following probabilities:

$$P(t_{(1,k)} \mid e_j) = \frac{\overline{ne}_{j,k} + \beta_{j,k}}{\sum_{k'=1}^{M_1}(\overline{ne}_{j,k'} + \beta_{j,k'})}$$

$$P(t_{(i+1,k)} \mid t_{(i,j)}) = \frac{\overline{nz}_{i,j,k} + \alpha_{i,j,k}}{\sum_{k'=1}^{M_{i+1}}(\overline{nz}_{i,j,k'} + \alpha_{i,j,k'})}, \text{ where } 1 \le i \le \ell - 1$$

$$P(w_k \mid t_{(\ell,j)}) = \frac{\overline{nw}_{j,k} + \alpha_{\ell,j,k}}{\sum_{k'=1}^{V}(\overline{nw}_{j,k'} + \alpha_{\ell,j,k'})}$$

Since $P(t_{(1,k)} \mid e_j)P(e_j) = P(e_j \mid t_{(1,k)})P(t_{(1,k)})$, and $P(t_{(1,k)}) = \frac{\overline{nz}_{1,k}}{\sum_d |d|}$ and $P(e_j) = \frac{\overline{ne}_j}{\sum_d |d|}$, where $\overline{nz}_{1,k}$ and $\overline{ne}_j$ means the mean times of N samples that $t_{(1,k)}$ and e_j has been assigned to words, respectively, i.e., $\overline{nz}_{1,k} = \sum_{k'=1}^{M_2} \overline{nz}_{1,k,k'}$ and $\overline{ne}_j = \sum_{k'=1}^{M_1} \overline{ne}_{j,k'}$, we have

$$P(e_j \mid t_{(1,k)}) = \frac{\overline{ne}_{j,k} + \beta_{j,k}}{\sum_{k'=1}^{M_1}(\overline{ne}_{j,k'} + \beta_{j,k'})} \times \frac{\overline{ne}_j}{\overline{nz}_{1,k}}$$

$$P(t_{(i,j)} \mid t_{(i+1,k)}) = \frac{\overline{nz}_{i,j,k} + \alpha_{i,j,k}}{\sum_{k'=1}^{M_{i+1}}(\overline{nz}_{i,j,k'} + \alpha_{i,j,k'})} \times \frac{\overline{nz}_{i,j}}{\overline{nz}_{i+1,k}}, \text{ where } 1 \le i \le \ell - 1$$

$$P(t_{(\ell,j)} \mid w_k) = \frac{\overline{nw}_{j,k} + \alpha_{\ell,j,k}}{\sum_{k'=1}^{V}(\overline{nw}_{j,k'} + \alpha_{\ell,j,k'})} \times \frac{\overline{nz}_{\ell,j}}{\overline{nw}_k}$$

Estimating Hyperparameters α and β. The hyperparameters α and β have to be defined before the start of Gibbs sampling, but they are generally unknown upfront. Normally, in topic model, parameters either in α or in β are predefined equivalently to each other. For instance, the α and β are set to symmetric Dirichlet priors with values of 0.1 and $50/M_1$, respectively [2,3,6,10,11]. The hyperparameter can also be automatically learned using a gradient descent method. Zhu and Xing [12] use a generic grid search based on cross-validation to select the hyper-parameters. Avetisyan and Fox [1] estimate the Dirichlet prior parameters from the marginal maximum likelihood are the values for the parameters that maximize the marginal log-likelihood function. Heinrich [7] introduces an analytical expression of the marginal log-likelihood of the Dirichlet parameters to facilitate the computation of marginal maximum likelihood estimates. Several approaches to learn Dirichlet parameter vectors from data are known, but unfortunately no exact closed-form solution exists, nor is there a conjugate prior distribution for straight-forward Bayesian inference. The most exact approaches are iterative approximations.

In our hierarchical sentiment-topic model, the total number of prior parameters needed in α and β are $\sum_{i=1}^{\ell} M_i M_{i+1}$ and KM_1, respectively. It is hard to handcraft each parameter accurately, and therefore we have to learn each prior parameters in different levels to produce reasonable results. As we use Gibbs sampling in our distribution estimation, we give a general framework for tuning α and β in Gibbs sampling process as follows:

Algorithm 2. Hyperparameter Tuning Algorithm.

Input: the training corpus D with sentiment rating **r**;
Output: the parameter values of α and β;
   Initialize α and β;
  repeat
     Generate a set of samples by Gibbs Sampling;
     Update $\alpha' = f(\alpha)$, $\beta' = g(\beta)$;
  until condition is satisfied
  return α, β;

In the algorithm, the sentiment assignments and topic assignments are available as a sample after each iteration. One of the most exact approaches to learn Dirichlet parameters is iterative approximation of maximum likelihood estimation by using counts of sentiment and topic assignments of samples. We use a convergent method [9] to update the parameters α and β as follows:

$$\alpha'_{i,j,k} = f(\alpha) = \alpha_{i,j,k} \frac{\sum_s \Psi(nz^{(s)}_{i,j,k} + \alpha_{i,j,k}) - \Psi(\alpha_{i,j,k})}{\sum_s \Psi(\sum_k (nz^{(s)}_{i,j,k} + \alpha_{i,j,k})) - \Psi(\sum_k \alpha_{i,j,k})}$$

$$\beta'_{j,k} = g(\beta) = \beta_{j,k} \frac{\sum_s \Psi(ne^{(s)}_{j,k} + \beta_{j,k}) - \Psi(\beta_{j,k})}{\sum_s \Psi(\sum_k (ne^{(s)}_{j,k} + \beta_{j,k})) - \Psi(\sum_k \beta_{j,k})}$$

where Ψ is digamma function.

3.3 Inference

With all the conditional probabilities derived above, we can estimate the probability of sentiment e_j on a word w_k by summing over $z_1, z_2, \ldots, z_\ell$:

$$P(e_j \mid w_k) = \sum_{z_1} \sum_{z_2} \cdots \sum_{z_\ell} P(e_j \mid z_1) P(z_2 \mid z_1) \ldots P(z_\ell \mid w_k) \qquad (2)$$

We can also estimate the probability of word w_k given a sentiment e_j, the probabilities of a topic in any level given a sentiment or a word, and the probabilities of a sentiment or a word given a topic. To predict the sentiment e_d of a new article d, we can use the posterior probability of the training corpus D as follows:

$$e_d = \arg\max_{1 \leq j \leq K} r_j = \arg\max_{1 \leq j \leq K} P(e_j \mid d; D) = \arg\max_{1 \leq j \leq K} \prod_{w \in d} P(e_j \mid w) \qquad (3)$$

4 Experiments

This section reports the experimental results on hierarchical pachinko allocation (HPA for short) sentiment-topic model.

4.1   Dataset

We collected 13, 280 news articles between July 2014 and January 2015 from the society channel of AsiaOne.com (http://www.asiaone.com/), which is the leading news portal in southern Asia. The online users can vote these news articles for one of the eight social sentiments, i.e. amused, like, shocked, enlightened, angry, indifferent, disgusted and sad, as shown in Figure 2. The website only provides the percentages of sentiment votes, and therefore the sentiment ratings of articles are collected only. In the following experiment, we use a subset of 3, 766 articles,

Fig. 2. Users can vote for one of the eight sentiments after reading an article in AsiaOne.com.

in which each article has at least one vote. Table 2 summarizes the detailed statistics for each social sentiment.

Table 2. Statistics of the AsiaOne.com corpus.

Sentiment	♯ of articles	Average rating (%)	Sentiment	♯ of articles	Average rating (%)
Amused	551	12.19	Like	1021	23.31
Shocked	231	6.98	Enlightened	221	7.27
Angry	322	9.28	Indifferent	173	6.77
Disgusted	748	19.61	Sad	507	14.58

4.2   Results of HPA-Based Sentiment-Topic Model

We first use Stanford Log-linear Part-Of-Speech Tagger to extract words and their parts of speech from each article. The reason of extracting part-of-speech rather than merely word counting is that the same word may convey different sentiment in different parts of speech, e.g. *"fine"* describes something good as it is an adjective in a sentence, while it means a punishment as it acts as a noun. The second advantage of using part-of-speech is that we can remove the preposition (e.g. *in, of*), conjunction (e.g. *and, but*) and pronoun (e.g. *them, he*), which do not show strong sentiment.

After the extraction, we can use the HPA-based sentiment-topic model to discover the correlation between words and sentiments, as shown in Table 3. The results confirm that our model is effective in discovering words for each emotion.

Table 3. The top ranked words discovered by the hierarchical pachinko allocation sentiment-topic model with strong sentiments. Note that the character following colon for each word represents the part of speech, i.e. n-noun, v-verb, a-adjective, r-adverb. The value in brackets following each word is the probability of the corresponding sentiment of the word, calculated by Eq.(2).

Sentiment	Top Ten Words in Each Sentiment
Amused	relatively:r(0.92), heavily:r(0.88), indeed:n(0.88), mature:a(0.87), leap:n(0.87), transform:v(0.86), regret:n(0.86), county:n(0.85), graham:n(0.84), peninsular:n(0.84), reply:v(0.84)
Like	superintendent:n(0.93), incidence:n(0.91), wireless:a(0.91), fundamental:a(0.90), shield:v(0.90), Suk*:n(0.89), Bambang*:n(0.89), tale:n(0.88), boycott:n(0.87), tour:v(0.86)
Shocked	exemption:n(0.89), pin:n(0.89), sales:n(0.87), car:n(0.87), mixture:n(0.85), promote:v(0.85), research:v(0.84), priority:n(0.83), funds:n(0.82), dictatorship:n(0.81)
Enlightened	orphanage:n(0.89), matt:n(0.87), maintenance:n(0.87), words:n(0.85), vacant:a(0.84), better:r(0.84), isle:n(0.81), young:n(0.78), like:a(0.77), royal:n(0.72)
Angry	Zulkifli*:n(0.73), gruesome:a(0.72), raise:n(0.71), force:n(0.71), shape:v(0.70), integral:a(0.69), race:v(0.68), historically:r(0.67), plight:n(0.67), fighting:n(0.67)
Indifferent	execution:n(0.86), venture:n(0.85), reduction:n(0.85), humans:n(0.85), recorded:a(0.84), humanitarian:n(0.84), kneel:v(0.83), communal:a(0.83), cancelled:a(0.82), residents:a(0.81)
Disgusted	suffer:v(0.96), polling:n(0.96), bad:a(0.95), medium:n(0.95), blood:n(0.94), fade:v(0.94), trolley:n(0.94), catch:v(0.93), signal:n(0.93), justification:n(0.93)
Sad	penetrate:v(0.94), nervous:a(0.94), pregnant:a(0.90), respond:v(0.89), sensitive:a(0.89), notoriously:r(0.89), breeding:n(0.89), pump:n(0.87), action:n(0.87), deterrent:n(0.86)

* Suk Samran is a district of Ranong Province in southern Thailand; Bambang is a first class municipality in the province of Nueva Vizcaya in Philippines; Zulkifli Abdhir was a Malaysian who was one of the FBI Most Wanted Terrorists.

In Fig. 3, we can find that a four-level HPA-based sentiment-topic model is generated with a total number of 19 topics. In our experiment, all the topics share the same topic in lower level. As we can see, for example, *accident* is assigned with sentiment *sad* in a 3rd-level topic $(3, 2)$ which is closely associated with the sentiment *sad*. Its parent topic $(2, 3)$, which is highly correlated with topic $(3, 2)$, is closely associated with the word *passenger*. *Passenger* is more likely to be a *indifferent* word. We find that two topics at different levels with high correlations can be associated with different sentiments in our model. We also find that the sentiments of topics in upper level are more likely to be equally distributed. On average, our model can be more effective in revealing sentiment-dependent topics which have inherent correlations.

4.3 Sentiment Prediction Comparison

To evaluate our model, we compare the predicted probabilities (i.e. using Eq. (5)) with the actual distributions of sentiments. We use the metric $Accu@k$, which evaluates the accuracy at top k predicted sentiments. The metric is also used for evaluating the sentiment-word and sentiment-topic models in [3,10]. Given an article d, the top ranked predicted sentiment e'_d and the truth sentiment set $E_{topk@d}$ including the k top-ranked sentiments, $Accu@k$ is defined as

$$Accu_d@k = \begin{cases} 1 & \text{if } e'_d \in E_{topk@d} \\ 0 & \text{otherwise} \end{cases} \tag{4}$$

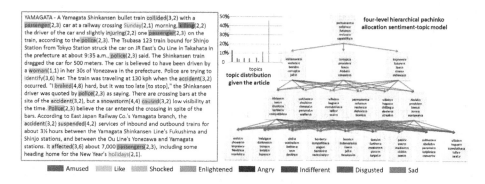

Fig. 3. Example of article generation with sentiments. The color indicates the word's sentiment, and the numbers in bracket indicates the topic assigned by our model. The chart shows the topic distribution given the article. The four-level HPA-based sentiment-topic model is learned from the collected corpus.

Thus, the $Accu@k$ for the entire corpus $\mathcal{D}$ is

$$Accu@k = \frac{\sum_{d \in \mathcal{D}} Accu_d@k}{|\mathcal{D}|} \tag{5}$$

Fig. 4 compares the sentiment prediction results on our collection corpus. Our HPA-based sentiment-topic model outperforms the baseline sentiment-word model and LDA-based sentiment-topic model. More specifically, our HPA-based sentiment-topic model significantly improves the prediction performance with an accuracy of 0.451 using $Accu@1$ as compared with the baseline accuracy of 0.278 and the accuracy of 0.329 using the LDA-based sentiment-topic model. Considering the complexity of social sentiments, the accuracy of 0.451 on predicting eight sentiments can be deemed to a relatively high score, as suggested by Bao et al. [3] and Rao et al. [11] who get similar accuracy for emotion prediction on their collected datasets.

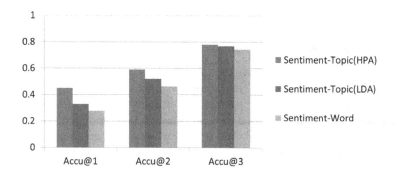

Fig. 4. Comparison of sentiment prediction accuracy on $Accu@1, 2, 3$

5   Conclusion

In this paper, we propose a hierarchical pachinko allocation sentiment-topic model for social sentiment mining. Rather than LDA-based sentiment-topic models that do not explicitly uncover correlations among topics, our model allows associating the intra-topic relationship which is organized in a hierarchy. Experimental results show that the model is not only effective in extracting the latent topics, but also improves the performance of social sentiment prediction compared with the baseline sentiment-word model and LDA-based sentiment-topic model. As for future work, we are planning to relax the parameter settings in pachinko allocation hierarchy, i.e. the depth of hierarchy, and the number of topics in each level. Generally, the hierarchy in our model is unknown in advance. Semi-parameter and non-parameter models need to be implemented for corpus whose latent topic structures are hard to manually predefine beforehand.

References

1. Avetisyan, M., Fox, J.P.: The dirichlet-multinomial model for multivariate randomized response data and small samples. Psicológica **33**(2) (2012)
2. Bao, S., Xu, S., Zhang, L., Yan, R., Su, Z., Han, D., Yu, Y.: Joint emotion-topic modeling for social affective text mining. In: Ninth IEEE International Conference on Data Mining, ICDM 2009, pp. 699–704. IEEE (2009)
3. Bao, S., Xu, S., Zhang, L., Yan, R., Su, Z., Han, D., Yu, Y.: Mining social emotions from affective text. IEEE Transactions on Knowledge and Data Engineering **24**(9), 1658–1670 (2012)
4. Blei, D.M.: Probabilistic topic models. Communications of the ACM **55**(4), 77–84 (2012)
5. Blei, D.M., Ng, A.Y., Jordan, M.I.: Latent dirichlet allocation. Journal of machine Learning research **3**, 993–1022 (2003)
6. Griffiths, T.L., Steyvers, M.: Finding scientific topics. Proceedings of the National academy of Sciences of the United States of America **101**(Suppl 1), 5228–5235 (2004)
7. Heinrich, G.: Parameter estimation for text analysis. Brigham Young University, Tech. rep. (2005)
8. Li, W., McCallum, A.: Pachinko allocation: dag-structured mixture models of topic correlations. In: Proceedings of the 23rd International Conference on Machine Learning. pp. 577–584. ACM (2006)
9. Minka, T.: Estimating a dirichlet distribution. Tech. rep, MIT (2000)
10. Rao, Y., Lei, J., Wenyin, L., Li, Q., Chen, M.: Building emotional dictionary for sentiment analysis of online news. World Wide Web, pp. 1–20 (2013)
11. Rao, Y., Li, Q., Mao, X., Wenyin, L.: Sentiment topic models for social emotion mining. Information Sciences (2014)
12. Zhu, J., Xing, E.P.: Sparse topical coding. arXiv preprint arXiv:1202.3778 (2012)

Subtopic-Level Sentiment Analysis
of Emergencies

Kunmei Wen[(✉)], Zhijiang Liu, Shuai Xu, Ruixuan Li, Yuhua Li,
Xiwu Gu, and Jie Zan

Huazhong University of Science and Technology, Wuhan, China
{kmwen,rxli,idcliyuhua,guxiwu}@hust.edu.cn,
{liuzhijiang_123,xushuaixu_shuai}@126.com, zanjie@outlook.com

Abstract. With the rapid development of microblog, millions of Internet users share their opinions on different aspects of daily life. By analyzing and monitoring sentiment information extracting from tweets related to an important event, we are able to gain insights into variation trends of users' sentiment. In this paper, we focus on extracting public sentiment of microblog emergencies. A subtopic-level opinion mining method is proposed based on two-phase optimization. Different subtopics of emergencies are extracted based on retweets. Opinion tweets are classified to different subtopics. The sentiment score of opinion holders is calculated. The above results are optimized based on users and endorsement interactions between users. Experimental results validate the effectiveness of the proposed method.

Keywords: Sina microblog · Opinion · Sentiment analysis

1 Introduction

More and more people post tweets by using microblog platforms such as Twitter[1] and Chinese Sina Weibo[2]. These opinion-based data which cover the most diverse topics enable the creation of valuable real-time applications that monitor public opinion and summarize the aggregated sentiment of online society. This problem can be addressed as Sentiment Analysis or Opining Mining. One method is based on opinion words in context by using an opinion dictionary to identify and determine sentiment orientation [1]. The other method applies machine learning techniques and treats sentiment analysis as a classification problem [2].

Recently, the existing methods of sentiment analysis are employed into the scenario of microblog. Davidov et al. [3] utilized Twitter characteristics and language conventions as features to train sentiment classifier. Silva et al. [4] proposed an augmentation train procedure. Tweets were classified into positive, negative and neutral according to the classifier. O'Connor et al. [5] found that

---

[1] http://www.twitter.com
[2] http://www.weibo.com

© Springer International Publishing Switzerland 2015
S. Zhang et al. (Eds.): KSEM 2015, LNAI 9403, pp. 312–317, 2015.
DOI: 10.1007/978-3-319-25159-2_28

surveys of consumer condence and political opinion correlate with sentiment word frequencies in tweets. Barbosa et al. [6] investigated a two-stage SVM classifier with two sets of features: meta-information about the words of tweets and the written style of tweets. Instead of learning textual models to predict content polarity, Guerra et al. [7] proposed a transfer-learning approach which utilized the user bias to analysis the sentiment orientation of tweets. However, it selected a few users named attractors who had clearly bias toward one or more sides of a discussion, based on prior knowledge.

In this paper, we propose a subtopic-level sentiment analysis method to extract microblog users' opinions toward different subtopics of an emergency. The proposed approach is different from the methods mentioned above. It is not necessary to select attractors for each discussion side. Instead of assuming one's opinion keeps stable in the whole discussion, we assume users' opinions only keep stable in the period of a time parameter.

2 The Proposed Method

2.1 Subtopic Extraction Based on Retweets

A subtopic is defined as a set of noun words or noun phrases that appear explicitly in tweets. The frequent noun words and phrases are extracted as candidate subtopics. A term-tweet matrix TW, as shown in Formula (1), is defined to represent the frequency of each candidate subtopic.

$$[TW]_{m \times n} = \begin{bmatrix} t_0 w_0 & t_0 w_1 & \cdots & t_0 w_{n-1} \\ t_1 w_0 & t_1 w_1 & \cdots & t_1 w_{n-1} \\ \vdots & \vdots & \ddots & \vdots \\ t_{m-1} w_0 & t_{m-1} w_1 & \cdots & t_{m-1} w_{n-1} \end{bmatrix} \tag{1}$$

Here, m is the number of candidate subtopics, n is the number of tweets. $t_i w_j$ is the frequency of keyword t_i which appears in tweet w_j. A matrix WW, as shown in Formula (2), is defined to represent the retweet relationship between tweets.

$$[WW]_{n \times n} = \begin{bmatrix} w_0 w_0 & w_0 w_1 & \cdots & w_0 w_{n-1} \\ w_1 w_0 & w_1 w_1 & \cdots & w_1 w_{n-1} \\ \vdots & \vdots & \ddots & \vdots \\ w_{n-1} w_0 & w_{n-1} w_1 & \cdots & w_{n-1} w_{n-1} \end{bmatrix} \tag{2}$$

Here, n is the number of tweets. $w_i w_j$ equals 1 if one of the following conditions is satisfied: 1) $i = j$; 2) tweet w_i is a retweet of tweet w_j; 3) tweet w_j is a retweet of tweet w_i. Otherwise, $w_i w_j$ equals 0. A multiplication is executed on the above two matrixes. A new term-tweet matrix $TW=TW \times WW$ is generated. By using the multiplication operation, the candidate subtopics appear in tweets and retweets can be reinforced mutually.

2.2 Two-Phase Sentiment Optimization

User-Based Optimization. A time decay function is designed to model tweets over time posted by the same user. The probability of tweets sharing the same sentiment is calculated. The time decay function is normally defined as Formula (3) based on time-stamps, which is a monotonic decreasing function.

$$f(x) = \frac{1}{1 + \alpha \times e^{(x/c_1 - c_2)}} \tag{3}$$

The value of the function is in the range $(0, 1)$ and will be reduced within a time interval. Where α is a parameter that adjusts the curve shape of the function. c_1 and c_2 are used to determine the time duration. x represents duration between tweets' time-stamp.

All tweets have been divided into positive or negative class according to their sentiment scores. We don't consider the neutral class which sentiment score is zero. A graph $G(V, E)$ is constructed as shown in Figure 1. V represents all tweets which have been divided into two classes(positive or negative). An edge in E connects two tweets which are posted by the same user toward a same sub-topic, as shown in Figure 1. A solid line rectangular is drawn around the tweets which posted by a same user, for example tweet (w_1, w_2, w_3, w_4) and (w_5, w_6, w_7, w_8). Inside this rectangular, tweets that surrounded by dot line rectangular and connected by solid line are the same sub-topic, such as (w_1, w_2, w_3, w_4), (w_5, w_7) and (w_6, w_8). The weight of each edge means the probability of tweets sharing the same sentiment measured by the time-decay function based on the duration between two tweets, as in Formula (4).

$$f(\Delta ts) = \begin{cases} 1 & if \quad \Delta ts = 0 \\ \frac{1}{1 + \alpha \times e^{(\Delta ts/c_1 - c_2)}} & otherwise \end{cases} \tag{4}$$

Where Δts is the duration between two tweets. We set the time-stamp unit as one day, for example, the weight of $E(w_1, w_2)$ is 1.0 means tweet w_1 and w_2 are posted by the same user about one sub-topic in one day, as show in Figure 1.

Definition 1. *Each class $C\{positive, negative\}$ has an attraction to each tweet w calculated by the probability of all the tweets which have connections with it in class C. It is defined as $attract\langle w, C\rangle$, as Formula (5).*

$$attract\langle w_i, C\rangle = \sum_{w_j \in C \cap E(w_i, w_j) \in E} f(\Delta ts_{ij}) \tag{5}$$

Retweet-Based Optimization. Retweet means users can repost a tweet and append some comments or do nothing. Through retweeting users just want to share the original tweet with more users. Therefore, it is difficult to mine the sentiment of these tweets if only considering the content of tweets. Retweets represent the endorsement interactions, through which a user explicitly agrees

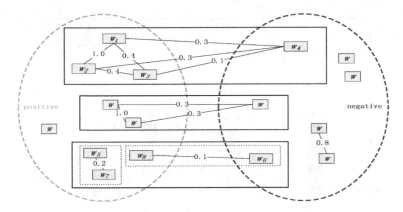

Fig. 1. An Example of User-Based Optimization Graph

with other users. A retweet-tree is completed for each subtopic. These trees can be called retweet-forest. As illustrated in Figure 2, it is an example of retweet-forest about a certain subtopic. A node indicates a tweet. In each retweet-tree, except the root node, any node is a retweet that repost its parents.

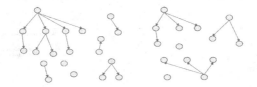

Fig. 2. An Example Retweet-Forest About A Certain Sub-Topic

If the sentiment score of a tweet is lower than the predefined threshold β, it will be optimized by the function as follow Formula (6).

$$op(w_c) = op(w_c) + (1 - \alpha) * op(w_p)$$

$$\alpha = \begin{cases} 0 & if \quad |OP(w_c)| \leq \beta \\ 1 & otherwise \end{cases} \tag{6}$$

Where w_p represents one tweet in the retweet-tree and w_c is the child node of w_p, β is the predefined threshold, α is 0 if the sentiment score of w_c is smaller than β, otherwise α is 1.

3   Experiment

3.1   Dataset Description

We obtained the dataset from *Sina Weibo* by searching keywords *"7.23bullet train collision"*. About 424,090 tweets were posted by 322,523 users.

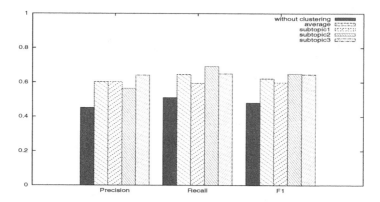

Fig. 3. Performance of Opinion Identifier with Retweet-based Optimization

Table 1. Subtopics of "7.23 bullet train collision"

Subtopic	keywords
subtopic1	Ministry of Railways, Shinkansen, real-name system, transport, EMU
subtopic2	victims, survivors, natural disasters, compensation
subtopic3	press conference, female reporter, spokesman, Central Propaganda Department

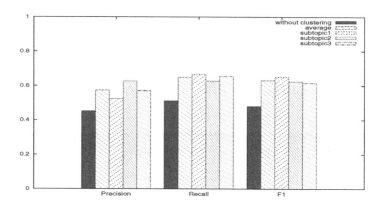

Fig. 4. Performance of Opinion Identifier with user-based optimization

3.2   Experimental Results and Evaluation

Based on the relationship between original tweets and retweets, we run *K-means* clustering algorithm. Table 1 indicates that the accident can be clustered into three subtopics: Ministry of Railways, passengers and reaction after the outbreak.

1000 tweets are randomly selected for each subtopic. These tweets are manually labeled by three annotators. The performance of subjective identifier, i.e., whether a tweet is opinionated, is evaluated. We use the standard evaluate measures: precision, recall and F-score. The proposed method is mainly compared with the one only based on lexicon without clustering subtopics. The results shown in Figure 3 indicate that the retweet-based method outperforms the baseline method. The average measure value is better than the one without cluttering subtopic, exceeding 11.5%, 11.4% and 18.4%, respectively. The results shown in Figure 4 indicate that the method with user-based optimization outperforms the baseline method. The average measure value is better than the one without cluttering subtopic, exceeding 12.3%, 13.8% and 21.2%, respectively.

Acknowledgments. This work is supported by National Natural Science Foundation of China under grants 61300222, 61433006, U1401258 and 61173170, Innovation Fund of Huazhong University of Science and Technology under grants 2015TS069 and 2015TS071, and Science and Technology Support Program of Hubei Province under grant 2014BCH270.

References

1. Hu, M., Liu, B.: Mining and summarizing customer reviews. In: 10th ACM SIGKDD International Conference on Knowledge Discovery and Data Mining, pp. 168–177. ACM Press, New York (2004)
2. Pang, B., Lee, L.: A sentimental education: sentiment analysis using subjectivity summarization based on minimum cuts. In: 42nd Annual Meeting of the Association for Computational Linguistics, pp. 271–278 (2004)
3. Davidov, D., Tsur, O., Rappoport, A.: Enhanced sentiment learning using twitter hashtags and smileys. In: 23rd International Conference on Computational Linguistics, pp. 241–249 (2010)
4. Silva, I.S., Gomide, J., Veloso, A., Meria, Jr., W., Ferreira, R.: Effective sentiment stream analysis with self-augmenting training and demand-driven projection. In: 34th Annual ACM SIGIR Conference, pp. 475–484 (2011)
5. OConnor, B., Balasubramanyan, R., Routledge, B.R., Smith, N.A.: From tweets to polls: linking text sentiment to public opinion time series. In: 24th International AAAI Conference on Weblogs and Social Media, pp. 122–129 (2010)
6. Barbosa, L., Feng, J.: Robust sentiment detection on twitter from biased and noisy data. In: 23rd International Conference on Computational Linguistics: Posters, pp. 3644 (2010)
7. Guerra, P.H.C., Veloso, A., Meira, Jr., W., Almeida, V.: From bias to opinion: a transfer-learning approach to real-time sentiment analysis. In: 17th ACM SIGKDD International Conference on Knowledge Discovery and Data Mining, pp. 150–158 (2011)

Summarizing Product Aspects from Massive Online Review with Word Representation

Kai Ye, Liangqiang Li, Mengzhuo Guo, Yu Qian, and Hua Yuan[✉]

School of Management and Economics, University of Electronic Science
and Technology of China, Chengdu 611731, China
{tingxueye,langmalee}@gmail.com, guomengzhuolovely@163.com,
{qiany,yuanhua}@uestc.edu.cn

Abstract. For the task of information retrieval from massive online reviews, people may be faced to some challenges in feature extraction, and then aspects summarization from these features. In this paper, by combining two methods of word vector representing and k-means clustering, an unsupervised method for product aspects summarizing is proposed. The experimental results with real data set verify the validity of the proposed method. Moreover, in comparison with the common LDA like methods, the proposed method shows better performance on both aspect mining and aspect features clustering.

Keywords: Aspect mining · Feature extraction · Word vector · Clustering

1 Introduction

The potential value of the online reviews is so important that the review contents related research, such as extracting aspects, topics and sentiments as well, become a hot topic in text mining [7,8]. A feature or aspect is an attribute or component of an entity, e.g., the screen of a cell phone. Therefore, aspect features extraction is the most important subtask for the work of mining from massive online textual contents (e.g., documents, blogs, reviews, tweets and short messages).

In literature, manual annotation [3] is a good method for accurate attribute classification, but it is not an efficient work [5,8,13]. Following the LDA (Latent Dirichlet Allocation) model proposed by Blei et al. [4], many scholars use topic model to mining aspect in online reviews. Lin and He [10] proposed a joint topic model to mining the aspect and sentiment in online reviews. Andrzejewski et al. [1] proposed DF-LDA. Zhai et al. [14] annotated several aspects manually, and proposed a so called SC-EM algorithm to address aspect classification. Kim et al. [9] proposed a hierarchical aspect and sentiment model. They used HLDA to extract aspect in review sentences that move the progress of online review mining. Researchers also want to use topic model to solve aspect extraction and classification at the same time, but the feature sparseness in short text and the noise caused by high frequency public word make topic model fails.

Y. Qian—Thank the support of the national Natural Science Foundation of China No.71572029

© Springer International Publishing Switzerland 2015
S. Zhang et al. (Eds.): KSEM 2015, LNAI 9403, pp. 318–323, 2015.
DOI: 10.1007/978-3-319-25159-2_29

In this paper, an unsupervised attribute classification method is proposed by combining two methods of word vector and k-means clustering. The rest of the paper is organized as follows: Section 2 proposes the framework and the methodology in detail. Section 3 presents the experimental results of the proposed method with a real data set and Section 4 concludes the work.

2   The Method

Figure 1 sketches out the research framework as a whole, in which, five parts are involved: review contents crawling and preprocessing, candidate words mining, word vector training and word clustering.

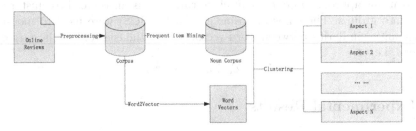

Fig. 1. The research framework.

2.1   Data Preprocessing

In the preprocessing stage, we truncate the review text by the punctuations in sentence. Sequentially, word segmentation is usually involving the tokenization of the input text into words for natural language processing task. For the word cleaning subtask, three types of following words are removed:

- General stop words;
- Meaning less word phases; and
- Words with very low frequency.

2.2   Frequent Features Word Mining

In general, frequent patterns are itemsets that appear in a data set with frequency no less than a user-specified threshold [6]. The objective of frequent pattern mining in this work is to mine some representative noun words as the candidates of the latent product features reviewed by users [7].

2.3   Word Vector Training

Word2vec, published by Google in 2013 [2], is a neural network implementation that learns distributed representations for words. Recently, Mikolov et al. [11] introduced the Skip-gram model, an efficient method for learning high-quality vector representations of words from large amounts of unstructured text data. Based on this genius work, Word2vec learns quickly relative to other models. In addition, Word2vec does not need labels in order to create meaningful representations. This is useful, since most data in the real world is unlabeled.

2.4 Word Clustering

Clustering is the task of grouping a set of objects in such a way that objects in the same group (called a cluster) are more similar to each other than to those in other groups.

Since the online review contents are represented with a set of vector after pre-processing, in accordance with the definition, it seems that the k-means method is suitable for the word clustering task. However, the k-means itself would have the problems of setting an appropriate value of k and converging to a local optimum value. To make the computation results more reliable, in this work, the bisecting k-means method, whose performance is better than that of the standard k-means approach in document clustering [12], is introduced to cluster the words into groups. The sums of cosine similarity (SCS) were used to measure the semantic similarity between word vector $\mathbf{w}$ and the centroid of the targeted cluster i, i.e., $\mathbf{c_i}$:

$$SCS = \Sigma_{\mathbf{c_i}} \Sigma_{\mathbf{w}} \cos(\mathbf{w}, \mathbf{c_i}).\tag{1}$$

3 Experimental Results

3.1 The Data

The reviews data were crawled from a shopping mall of Jingdong (jd.com, NAS-DAQ: JD), a famous B2C platform in China. Table 1 summarizes the characters of the experiment data set.

Table 1. Data set used in the experiments

Items	Statistical description
# of cell phones	2,877
# of reviews	1,120,196
Maximum length of review text	1265 words
Mode of the length of review text	24.8 words
Minimum length of review text	1 word
Average length of review text	24.8 words

There are a mass of reviewers, in contrast with the huge number of short length review text, which would results in the sparsity of the distribution of reviewing words. It will be a huge challenge for the normal classification algorithms to do a better feature extraction and then further to do a better feature categorization.

3.2 Candidate Words Mining, Word Vector Training and Word Clustering

In the stage of candidate words mining, we choose 60 as the threshold degree of support count in frequent pattern mining. An open source tool called

Table 2. The extracted aspects and their representative features (The number in the bracket refers to the frequency of the corresponding word).

外观(Appearance)		摄像头(Camera)		声音(Voice)	
屏幕(Screen)	30407	像素(pixels)	6428	声音(Voice)	16587
外观(Appearance)	13251	效果(effects)	4169	字体(Font)	4223
手感(Handle)	6485	分辨率(Resolution)	3819	通话(Call)	2982
后盖(Back Cover)	4324	音质(Sound Quality)	2799	铃声(Ringtones)	2800
习惯(Habit)	3244	通话质量(Call Quality)	1987	电话(Cell Phone)	2712
样子(Style)	3001	摄像头(Camera)	1854	按键(Key)	2110
大气	2635	照片(Photo)	838	音量(Voice Volume)	1523
想象(Imagination)	2399	续航(Battery Life)	746	太小(Volume)	1136
		色彩(Color)	659	听筒(Earphone)	968
		清晰度(Clearness)	571	音乐(Music)	713

系统(System)		电池(Battery)		京东(JingDong)	
系统(System)	13580	电池(Battery)	15337	京东(JingDong)	33036
信号(Signal)	6530	垃圾(Rubbish)	4154	评价(Comment)	10912
软件(Software)	6132	时间(Time)	2628	物流(Logistics)	9600
玩游戏(Gaming)	2433	耳机(Earphone)	2452	购物(Shopping)	7966
死机(Crash)	2297	缺点(Shortcomings)	2234	商品(Commodities)	5312
开机(Boot)	2209	待机(Standby)	2192	发货(Deliver Goods)	5091
自带(Built-in)	2053	电(Electricity)	1876	货(Goods)	4440
游戏(Game)	1629	长度(Length)	1387	客服(Customer Service)	2770
2g(2g)	1350	小时(Hour)	1368	下单(Place Order)	2439
视频(Video)	1329	情况(Situation)	1317	售后(Post Sale)	1972

品牌(Brand)		价格&质量(Price & Quality)		赠品&套装(Gift & Suite)	
华为(Huawei)	17475	东西(Goods)	22152	套装(Suite)	2903
国产(Domestic)	13078	质量(Quality)	19059	配件(Accessories)	2446
国货(Domestic Goods)	5702	价格(Price)	15191	原装(Original)	2081
诺基亚(Nokia)	5525	价钱(Price)	4024	评(Review)	2008
品牌(Brand)	5317	价格便宜(Cheap)	3973	赠品(Gift)	1172
信赖(Trust)	3894	值(Worth)	2640	手机套(Cell Phone Case)	352
酷派(Coolpad)	3635	宝贝(Treasure)	2331	皮套(Leather Case)	312
产品(Product)	3267	体验(Experience)	2262	宝(Treasure)	225
国产手机(Domestic Cell Phone)	2383	降价(Depreciate)	2109	礼品(Gift)	220
荣耀(Honor)	2324	实体店(Store)	1057	话费(Telephone Bill)	148

Word2Vector[1] developed by Google is used in word vector training, and the important parameter of dimension for the trained word vector is set as 100.

The bisecting k-means method is used to cluster the vectors: initially, all training data are in a only same cluster. In each iteration, using a similarity measurement and picking the cluster with largest Sum of Squared Error (SSE) to split by using bisecting algorithm, until the desired number of k clusters is reached. In the

---

[1] http://code.google.com/p/word2vec/

experiments, the clustering process stopped when the sum of cosine distance is 60, and the corresponding cluster number, k, is approximate to 15.

The top 9 of such clusters (aspects) and their associated representative features are show in Table 2 (words in the same cluster are ordered by its frequency), from which, people can see that the extracted features in the same cluster having more close semantic similarity than that from the different cluster. Moreover, the calculation of the semantic similarity is context based which may be better than that based only on the original semantics of each word statically. In another words, the clustering results in Table 2 is very comprehensible.

3.3   Comparison Experiments

We compare our method to three typical aspect mining methods of LDA, s-LDA [10] and HLDA [9].

The comparison results e of perplexity show that the proposed method in this paper has a better performance in aspect mining and feature clustering from online reviews 2.

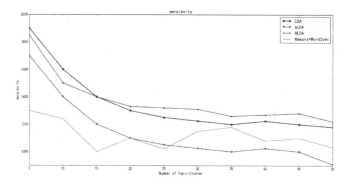

Fig. 2. The comparison of perplexity.

4   Conclusion

In this paper, an unsupervised attribute classification method is proposed by combining two methods of word vector and k-means clustering. To that end, the words used by the reviewers are extracted to form a training data set firstly. Then, all the words are trained and transformed into word vectors. At last, all the words are clustered into groups according to the similarity of word vector and sentence structure where the word appeared.

The experimental results with real data set verify the validity of the proposed method in this paper, and, in comparison with the common LDA like methods, the proposed method shows better performance on the metric of perplexity and the macro average accuracy as well.

Acknowledgments. The work was partly supported by the Foundation of the National Natural Science Foundation of China (71271044/U1233118/71102055).

References

1. Andrzejewski, D., Zhu, X., Craven, M.: Incorporating domain knowledge into topic modeling via dirichlet forest priors. In: ACM International Conference Proceeding Series, ICML, vol. 382, p. 4 (2009)
2. Bengio, Y., Ducharme, R., Vincent, P., Janvin, C.: A neural probabilistic language model. Journal of Machine Learning Research **3**, 1137–1155 (2003)
3. Blei, D.M., Jordan, M.I.: Modeling annotated data. In: Proceedings of the 26th Annual International ACM SIGIR Conference on Research and Development in Informaion Retrieval, SIGIR 2003, pp. 127–134 (2003)
4. Blei, D.M., Ng, A.Y., Jordan, M.I.: Latent dirichlet allocation. J. Mach. Learn. Res. **3**, 993–1022 (2003)
5. Brody, S., Elhadad, N.: An unsupervised aspect-sentiment model for online reviews. In: The 2010 Annual Conference of the North American Chapter of the Association for Computational Linguistics Human Language Technologies, HLT 2010, pp. 804–812 (2010)
6. Han, J., Cheng, H., Xin, D., Yan, X.: Frequent pattern mining: Current status and future directions. Data Min. Knowl. Discov. **15**(1), 55–86 (2007)
7. Hu, M., Liu, B.: Mining and summarizing customer reviews. In: Proceedings of the Tenth ACM SIGKDD International Conference on Knowledge Discovery and Data Mining, KDD 2004, pp. 168–177 (2004)
8. Jo, Y., Oh, A.H.: Aspect and sentiment unification model for online review analysis. In: Proceedings of the Fourth ACM International Conference on Web Search and Data Mining, WSDM 2011, Hongkong, China, pp. 815–824 (2011)
9. Kim, S., Zhang, J., Chen, Z., Oh, A.H., Liu, S.: A hierarchical aspect-sentiment model for online reviews. In: AAAI (2013)
10. Lin, C., He, Y.: Joint sentiment/topic model for sentiment analysis. In: Proceedings of the 18th ACM Conference on Information and Knowledge Management, pp. 375–384 (2009)
11. Mikolov, T., Sutskever, I., Chen, K., Corrado, G.S., Dean, J.: Distributed representations of words and phrases and their compositionality. Advances in Neural Information Processing Systems **26**, 3111–3119 (2013)
12. Steinbach, M., Karypis, G., Kumar, V.: A comparison of document clustering techniques. In: Workshop on Text Mining, KDD 2000 August 20, Boston, MA, pp. 109–111 (2000)
13. Titov, I., McDonald, R.: Modeling online reviews with multi-grain topic models. In: Proceedings of the 17th International Conference on World Wide Web, pp. 111–120 (2008)
14. Zhai, Z., Liu, B., Xu, H., Jia, P.: Grouping product features using semi-supervised learning with soft-constraints. In: Proceedings of the 23rd International Conference on Computational Linguistics, COLING 2010, pp. 1272–1280 (2010)

Building a High Performance End-to-End Explicit Discourse Parser for Practical Application

Jianxiang Wang[1] and Man Lan[1,2(✉)]

[1] Department of Computer Science and Technology, East China Normal University, Shanghai, People's Republic of China
51141201062@ecnu.cn, mlan@cs.ecnu.edu.cn
[2] Shanghai Key Laboratory of Multidimensional Information Processing, East China Normal University, Shanghai, People's Republic of China

Abstract. To build practical end-to-end discourse parser, labeling arguments to discourse is the bottleneck to improve performance of whole parser. In consideration of the difference between syntactic and discourse arguments of connectives and the difference between two arguments to discourse in SS and PS cases, we present a method to build two separate argument extractors for two arguments. To evaluate the performance of whole parser, we build an end-to-end explicit discourse parser on PDTB. Experimental results showed that our proposed discourse parser achieved the best performance on explicit discourse so far.

Keywords: End-to-end discourse parser · Arguments labeling · Discourse relation

1 Introduction

A discourse relation (or rhetorical relation) between two segments of textual units expresses how they are logically connected to one another (*cause* or *contrast*), which is considered a crucial step for the ability to properly interpret or produce discourse. It can be of great benefit to many downstream natural language processing (NLP) applications, such as question answering (QA) [1], information extraction (IE) [2], and machine translation (MT), etc. With the release of manually annotated corpus, such as Penn Discourse Treebank 2.0 (PDTB) [3], recent studies performed study of discourse relation recognition on natural (i.e., genuine) discourse data [4–9] with the use of linguistically informed features and machine learning algorithms.

A PDTB style end-to-end discourse parser is given free texts as input and returns discourse relations in a PDTB style, where a connective acts as a predicate that takes two text spans as its arguments. The overall performance of discourse parser depends upon two things: (1) discourse relation identification and (2) discourse arguments labeling. On one hand, discourse relation can sometimes be marked lexically by words and expressions (i.e., cue words) in the texts,

© Springer International Publishing Switzerland 2015
S. Zhang et al. (Eds.): KSEM 2015, LNAI 9403, pp. 324–335, 2015.
DOI: 10.1007/978-3-319-25159-2_30

such as *but* usually conveys a contrast relation or *because* always indicates a contingency relation in texts. Although there are two types of ambiguity of a word or phrase serving for discourse connective (i.e., the ambiguity between discourse and non-discourse usage and the ambiguity between two or more discourse relations if the word or phrase is used as a discourse connective), previous work [8] proved that using just the connectives in text, the accuracy of explicit discourse connective function and sense classification can reach 90% and 93%, respectively. On the other hand, discourse relations are assumed to hold between two and only two arguments, which are simply labelled Arg1 and Arg2. However, due to the mismatch between the syntactic and discourse arguments of connectives, simply taking the syntactic arguments of a connective to be its discourse arguments yields an incorrect semantic interpretation. Among the above two components, the second is the key to the performance of an end-to-end explicit discourse parser. For example, as the first PDTB-style end-to-end discourse parser [10] showed that, with full automation and error propagation, the performance of explicit sense classifier on Level 2 types is an F1 of 80.61%. However, the whole relation parser achieved only an F1 of 20.64% for exact match for both Explicit and Non-Explicit relations. One main reason for the poor performance results from the poor result of recognizing the span of discourse relations. Therefore, in this work, we focus on the improvement of arguments labeling for the purpose of improving the whole performance of an end-to-end explicit discourse parser.

To address this problem, unlike previous work which built a global model for Arg1 and Arg2, in this work we build two different extractors for Arg1 and Arg2 to perform explicit arguments span labeling, respectively. This is based on our consideration that the two arguments usually have different syntactic and discourse properties, thus two different models are expected to capture salient characteristics of observed regularities in two specific arguments. Besides, in order to build a real world-oriented discourse parser, we propose novel features to perform the disambiguation of discourse connectives.

We performed evaluation of the proposed approach and two baseline systems on PDTB 2.0 corpus. Experimental results showed that using separate discourse argument extractors for each argument can significantly improve the performance of arguments labeling. Moreover, the whole performance of our explicit discourse parser achieved the best known performance so far, which achieved an absolute average F1 improvement of 3% over a state of the art baseline system.

The organization of this work is as follows. Section 2 briefly introduces the related work. Section 3 first introduces the motivation of this work, then gives a detailed description of system architecture of our proposed parser. Section 4 reports the experimental results and analysis on benchmark dataset. Finally, Section 5 concludes this work.

2 Related Work

Since the release of Penn Discourse Treebank (PDTB) [3], much research has been carried out on PDTB to perform the subtasks of a full end-to-end parser, such as identifying discourse connectives, labeling arguments and classifying Explicit or Implicit relations. The discourse parser can be divided into Explicit discourse parser and Non-Explicit discourse parser. Explicit discourse parser is used to obtain the Explicit relations in the raw texts, whereas Non-Explicit discourse parser is to get Non-Explicit (i.e., Implicit, AltLex and EntRel) relations.

Explicit discourse parser consists of three parts: discourse connectives disambiguation, Explicit sense classification and arguments labeling. For the discourse connectives disambiguation, [8] extracted syntactic features of connectives from the constituent parses, and achieved the performance of 94.19% in F-measure using gold-standard parse trees. In addition to the syntactic features, [10] extracted features from the context and part-of-speech (POS) of the connectives, achieved 95.76% in F-measure on PDTB Section 23 using gold-standard parse trees. As for the Explicit sense classification, [8] used the syntactic features of connectives, and achieved the performance of 94.15% in accuracy on 4 level 1 classes. [10] achieved the performance of 86.77% in F-measure on classifying discourse relations into 16 level 2 types. For the arguments labeling of the Explicit relations, [4] regarded it as a token-level sequence labeling task using conditional random fields (CRFs). [10] proposed a tree subtraction algorithm to extract the arguments. Kong adopted a constituent-based approach to label arguments in [5] . However, the performance of the arguments labeling is still low, for example, [10] only achieved the performance of 53.85% in F-measure using gold-standard parse trees and connectives. While using the auto parser and in the error propagation, [10] only achieved the performance of 40.37% in F-measure.

As for the Non-Explicit discourse parser, the previous work mainly focus on the Implicit sense classification. [7], [6] and [9] performed the classification using several linguistically-informed features, such as verb classes, production rules and Brown cluster pair. [11] presented a multi-task learning framework with the use of the prediction of explicit discourse connective as auxiliary learning tasks to improve the performance. However, the performance of the Implicit sense classification is still low, and thus the Non-Explicit discourse parser is hard to be used in downstream NLP applications.

3   Our Proposed End-to-End Explicit Discourse Parser

3.1   Motivation

The idea of building two separate argument extractors for Arg1 and Arg2 span labeling is motivated by the observations and analysis that we have made on arguments to discourse connective.

On one hand, although two discourse arguments are assumed to be attached to an identified discourse relation, according to PDTB 2.0 Manual, there are a variety of cases in the attribution of the discourse relation or its arguments. For example, the relation and its arguments are attributed to the writer or someone other than the writer, as well as the relation and its arguments are attributed differently to different sources. Therefore, simply taking the syntactic arguments of connective to be its discourse arguments yields an incorrect semantic interpretation. Moreover, since the PDTB annotators followed the *minimality principle*, which states that the annotation should include in the argument the minimal span of text that is sufficient for the interpretation of the relation, small portions of text are deleted from or added to the spans in most cases. Thus recognizing the arguments spans within discourse relations is an important task for deriving the correct interpretation of the relations, which requires deep semantic analysis rather than syntactic alone.

On the other hand, in PDTB, discourse relations in text are realized in two types according to the existence of Explicit connectives. In the first type relations realized explicitly by Explicit connectives, the arguments of Explicit connectives are unconstrained in terms of their location, that is, arguments can be found anywhere in the text. Otherwise, the second type involves relations between two adjacent sentences in the absence of an Explicit connective. In all cases, discourse relations are assumed to hold between two and only two arguments and the two arguments to a connective are simply labelled Arg1 and Arg2. In the case of Explicit connectives, Arg2 is the argument to which the connective is syntactically bound, and Arg1 is the other argument. In the case of relations between adjacent sentences, Arg1 and Arg2 reflect the linear order of the arguments, with Arg1 before Arg2.

Note that in case of Explicit connective, a connective and its arguments can appear in any relative order, and an argument can be arbitrarily far away from its corresponding connective. Since Arg2 is defined as the argument with which the connective is syntactically associated, its position is relatively fixed once we locate the discourse connective C. However, the location of the Arg1 can be in any position, which is categorized into 4 types, as follows: (1) SS(same sentence): Arg1 in the same sentence as connective; (2) IPS (immediately previous sentence): Arg1 in previous, adjacent sentences; (3) NAPS (previous non-adjacent sentences): Arg1 in one or more previous, non adjacent sentences; (4) FS (following sentence): some sentences following the sentence containing the connective. To make a clear analysis, we count the distributions of the location of Arg1 in PDTB Explicit discourse relation and summarize in Table 1. We see that the SS

Table 1. Distribution of the location of Arg1 of Explicit connectives

	Count
Arg1 in same sentence as connective (SS)	11236
Arg1 in previous, adjacent sentence (IPS)	5549
Arg1 in previous, non adjacent sentence (NAPS)	1666
Arg1 in some sentence following the sentence containing the connective (FS)	8
total	18459

accounts for the largest proportion (60.9%), and PS (including IPS + NAPS, where Arg1 in previous sentences) accounts for 30.1%. Thus, we only consider the current sentence containing the connective and its immediately preceding sentence as the text span where Arg1 occurs, similar to what was done in [5,10].

[5] proposed a constituent-based approach and experiments showed that this method outperformed the tree subtraction algorithm by [10] for Explicit arguments labeling. [10] only focused on the SS case, and [5] treated the immediately preceding sentence as a special constituent for PS. That means, they just viewed the immediately preceding sentence as Arg1 and thus performed only Arg2 span extractor in PS case. Besides, they build a global model for both Arg1 and Arg2 extraction. Differ from their work, based on our observation and analysis mentioned above, we build two different extractors for Arg1 and Arg2 separately in both cases of SS and PS. Our consideration is that the two arguments have different syntactic and discourse properties and a unified model with the same feature set used for both cases may not have enough discriminating power.

3.2   System Overview

We design the Explicit discourse parser as a sequential pipeline, which consists of 7 components, shown in Figure 1.

Since the input of the parser is free text, the first step is to identify all connective occurrences in text, then we use the **connective classifier** to decide whether they function as discourse connectives or not. After that, the **arg1 position classifier** is to identify the relative position (i.e., SS or PS) for each discourse connective. Then in SS and PS cases, two argument extractors are built for Arg1 and Arg2 separately. Finally, we adopt **Explicit sense classifier** to identify the sense that the Explicit connective conveys.

3.3   Connective Classifier and Explicit Sense Classifier

The connective classifier identifies the discourse connectives from non-discourse ones. For each connective occurrence C in the text, we extract features from its context, part-of-speech (POS) and the parse tree of the connective's sentence. Note that $prev_1$ and $next_1$ indicate the first previous word and the first next

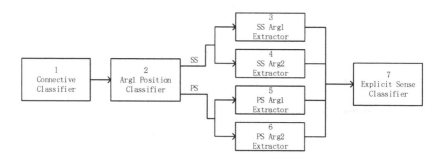

Fig. 1. System pipeline for the Explicit discourse parser

word of connective C respectively. For a node in the parse tree, we use the POS combinations of the node, its parent, its children to represent the *linked context*.

The features we used for connective classification consist of the following: (1) Pitler[8]'s: *C string* (case-sensitive), *self-category* (the highest node in the parse tree that covers only the connective words), *parent-category* (the parent of the *self-category*), *left-sibling-category* (the left sibling of the *self-category*), *right-sibling-category* (the right sibling of the *self-category*), C-Syn interaction (the pairwise interaction features between the connective C and each category feature (i.e., self-category, parent-category, left-sibling-category, right-sibling-category)) , Syn-Syn interaction (the interaction features between pairs of category features); (2) Lin[10]'s: C POS, $prev_1 + C$ string, $prev_1$ POS, $prev_1$ POS + C POS, C string + $next_1$, $next_1$ POS, C POS + $next_1$ POS, path of C's parent $\rightarrow$ root, compressed path of C's parent $\rightarrow$ root; (3) our newly proposed features: the POS tags of nodes from C's parent $\rightarrow$ root, *parent-category linked context*, *right-sibling-category linked context*. Our three new features are considered to capture more syntactic context information of the connective C for connective classification.

Since discourse connective has very close relationship with the sense of discourse relation, we extract features from its context, POS and the parse tree of its sentence to perform the Explicit sense classification, similar to the connective classifier. The features for this classifier consist of the following: (1) Lin's features: C string, C POS, $prev_1 + C$ (2) Pitler's features: *self-category*, *parent-category*, *left-sibling-category*, *right-sibling-category*, C-Syn interaction, Syn-Syn interaction. (3) our five newly proposed features: *parent-category linked context*, previous connective and its POS of *as* and previous connective and its POS of *when*. The first *parent-category linked context* feature is to provide more syntactic context information for the classification. The last four features are specially designed to disambiguate the relation senses of the connective *as* or *when*, since the two connectives often have ambiguity between Contingency.Cause.Reason and Temporal.Synchrony. As shown in Example 1, the previous connective of the discourse connective *as* is *But*, therefore the discourse connective *as* usually carries the Contingency.Cause.Reason sense rather than Temporal.Synchrony.

(1) *But the gains in Treasury bonds were pared* <u>as</u> **stocks staged a partial recovery.**   (Contingency.Cause.Reason – WSJ-1213)

3.4 Discourse Arguments Labeling

Based on our analysis in Section 3.1, we perform discourse arguments labeling in consideration of different cases in which discourse relation are realized.

3.5 Arg1 Position Classifier

The Arg1 position classifier is to decide the relative position of Arg1(i.e., SS or PS). We choose the following features: (1) Lin's: C string, C position (the position of connective C in the sentence: start, middle, or end), C POS, $prev_1$,

$prev_1$ POS, $prev_1$ + C, $prev_1$ POS + C POS, $prev_2$, $prev_2$ POS, $prev_2$ + C, $prev_2$ POS + C POS; (2) our newly proposed features: C POS + $next_1$ POS, $next_2$, path of $C \rightarrow$ root. Note that $prev_2$ and $next_2$ indicate the second previous word and the second next word of connective C, respectively.

3.6   In SS Case

In the case of SS, we follow Kong[5]'s constituent-based approach, which consists of three steps: (1) collecting argument candidates (i.e., constituents) from the parse tree of the sentence containing the connective C; (2) deciding each constituent whether it belongs to Arg1, Arg2 or NULL; (3) merging all the constituents for Arg1 and Arg2 to obtain the Arg1 and Arg2 text spans respectively.

In the first step, we use Kong's pruning algorithm to obtain all the argument candidates: starting from the target connective node, i.e. the lowest node dominating the connective. (1) First, collect all the siblings of the connective node as candidates; (2) then we move on to the parent of the connective node and collect its siblings; (3) repeat (1) and (2), until we reach the root of the parse tree. In addition, if the target connective node does not cover the connective exactly, the children of the target connective node are also collected.

However, in the second step, differ from Kong, we view it as a binary classification, that is, use the extractor to determine each constituent whether it belongs to the argument (Arg1 or Arg2). And in the third step, we merge the constituents for Arg1 and Arg2 from SS Arg1 Extractor and SS Arg2 Extractor to obtain the Arg1 and Arg2 text spans, respectively.

SS Arg1 Extractor: This extractor is only to extract Arg1 for SS. Note that NT indicates the constituent, and for a node in the parse tree, we use POS combination of the node, its parent, left sibling and right sibling to represent the *context*, and use *level distance* to represent the distance between the heights of two nodes in the parse tree.

The features for this classifier consist of the following: (1) the features chosen from Kong: lowercased C string, C category, C iRSib (number of right siblings of C), C iLSib (number of left siblings of C), NT *context*, the path from C's parent $\rightarrow NT$, C NT position (the position of NT relative to C: left or right), the path from C's parent $\rightarrow NT$ + whether iLSib greater than one (2) our newly proposed feature: C POS, *self-category*, *parent-category*, *left-sibling-category*, the path from C's parent $\rightarrow$ root, the POS tags of nodes from C's parent $\rightarrow$ root, C *context*, NT iLSib, NT *linked context*, the path from $NT \rightarrow$ root, the path of previous $NT \rightarrow$ current NT, the *level distance* between NT and C, whether pervious and current NT are in the same clause. The features we proposed are useful to capture more syntactic information of the connective C, the constituent NT, the relationship between C and NT and the relationship between previous NT and current NT.

SS Arg2 Extractor: Similar to the SS Arg2 Extractor, this extractor is used to extract Arg2 for SS, but the different features we adopt to build the classifier: (1) the features chosen from Kong: lowercased C string, C category, C iRSib,

C iLSib, NT *context*, the path from C's parent $\rightarrow NT$, C NT position; (2) our newly proposed feature: C POS, *self-category, parent-category, left-sibling-category*, the POS tags of nodes from C's parent $\rightarrow$ root, NT iLSib, NT *linked context*, the *linked context* of the parent node of NT, the path from NT $\rightarrow$ root, the path of previous NT $\rightarrow$ current NT, the *level distance* between NT and C.

3.7   In PS Case

For PS, we build two argument extractors for Arg1 and Arg2, respectively, as follows.

PS Arg1 Extractor: We consider the immediately previous sentence of connective C as the text span where Arg1 occurs and then build an extractor to label the Arg1 in it. Similar to Lin's Attribution span labeler, this extractor consists of two steps: splitting the sentence into clauses, and deciding, for each clause, whether it belongs to Arg1 or not. First we use nine punctuation symbols (...,.:;?!-~) to split the sentence into several parts and use the SBAR tag in its parse tree to split each part into clauses. Second, we build a classifier to decide each clause whether it belongs to Arg1 or not.

On the one hand, the attribution relation is annotated in PDTB, which expresses the "ownership" relationship between abstract objects and individuals or agents. And we want to extract the arguments without the attribution, therefore we borrow several attribution features from [10] in order to distinguish the attribution-related span from others. On the other hand, according to the *minimality principle* of PDTB, the argument annotation includes the minimal span of text that is sufficient for the interpretation of the relation. Since connectives have very close relationship with discourse relation, we consider to adopt connective-related features to capture text span for relation. We choose the following features: (1) attribution-related features from [10]: lemmatized verbs in *curr*, the first term of *curr*, the last term of *curr*, the last term of *prev* + the first term of *curr*, and (2) our proposed connective-related features: lowercased C string and C category (the syntactic category of the connective: subordinating, coordinating, or discourse adverbial), where *curr* and *prev* indicate the current and previous clause respectively and the corresponding category for the connective C is obtained from the list provided in [12].

PS Arg2 Extractor: The PS Arg2 Extractor is similar to the PS Arg1 Extractor. However, they differ as follows: (1) in the first step, we consider the sentence containing connective C as the text span where Arg2 occurs and besides the previous nine punctuation symbols, we also use the connective C to split the sentence; (2) we adopt different features to build the classifier: lowercased verbs in *curr*, lemmatized verbs in *curr*, the first term of *curr*, the last term of *curr*, the last term of *prev*, the first term of *next*, the last term of *prev* + the first term of *curr*, the last term of *curr* + the first term of *next*, production rules extracted from *curr*, *curr* position (i.e., the position of *curr* in the sentence: start, middle or end), C string, lowercased C string, C position, C category, path of C's parent $\rightarrow$ root, compressed path of C's parent $\rightarrow$ root.

4   Experiment

4.1   Experimental Settings

To implement the 7 components described above, we use the MaxEnt algorithm implemented in MALLET toolkit[1] to build classifiers.

Following previous work, we use PDTB Section 02-21 for training, Section 22 for development and Section 23 for testing. All the POS tags and parse tree we used in our parser are produced by the Berkeley parser[2].

Usually, an Explicit discourse relation is considered to be correct if and only if: (1) the discourse connective is correctly detected; (2) the sense of a discourse relation is correctly predicted; (3) the text spans of the two arguments as well as their labels (Arg1 and Arg2) are correctly predicted. To evaluate performance, F_1 score (harmonic mean of Precision and Recall) is adopted.

4.2   Baseline Systems

To make the performance comparison reasonable and reliable, we construct two baselines as follows.

The SS baseline is computed by labeling as Arg1 all tokens in the text span from the end of the previous sentence to the connective position and labeling as Arg2 the text span between the connective and the beginning of the next sentence. And the PS baseline is computed by labeling the previous sentence of the connective as Arg1, and the text span between the connective and the beginning of the next sentence as Arg2.

Moreover, in order to compare with the method we proposed, we also build another baseline for SS and PS, that is, using a global extractor to label Arg1 and Arg2. We adopt Kong's constituent-based approach to construct the global extractor for the SS case with the features they proposed. And for the global extractor of the PS case, we treat the immediately preceding sentence as a special constituent, as in [5], and then use the constituent-based approach to extract Arg1 and Arg2 with the same features used in the global extractor of SS case.

4.3   Results and Anlaysis

Table 2 reports the results of Explicit arguments extraction in SS and PS cases, with exact matching and without error propagation (EP). We see that the SS baseline system achieves 26.37% F_1 score in both arguments exactly matching which is shown in the third row, and the performance is improved by using a global extractor for SS. Furthermore, compared with the global argument extractor, our proposed two extractors for Arg1 and Arg2 separately are able to further improve the F_1 score of Arg1, Arg2 and both by more than 3%. And from Table 2, we find the similar observation in PS case. Compared with the

---

[1] mallet.cs.umass.edu

[2] code.google.com/p/berkeleyparser/

Table 2. Results of arguments extraction in SS and PS cases; no EP

	SS			PS		
	Arg1 F_1	Arg2 F_1	Both $F_1(\%)$	Arg1 F_1	Arg2 F_1	Both $F_1(\%)$
baseline	37.00	54.95	26.37	39.17	72.10	32.34
global extractor	63.24	85.29	58.09	39.17	76.75	33.23
two extractors	67.10	87.87	61.21	40.95	77.15	34.42

two baselines, the two different extractors for Arg1 and Arg2 again improve the performance of PS case.

Table 3 reports the overall results of Explicit arguments extraction, where "All" indicates the arguments extraction for all Explicit relations. Again using two separate extractors achieves much better performance than using a global extractor, which increases the F_1 of overall performance of arguments extraction by 2.39%.

Table 3. Results of overall arguments extraction on all Explicit relations; no EP

	Arg1 F_1 (%)	Arg2 F_1 (%)	Both F_1 (%)
All (baseline)	37.82	61.49	28.64
All (global extractor)	54.05	82.18	48.60
All (two extractors)	57.12	83.78	50.99

To examine the contributions of different components to overall performance of Explicit discourse parser, Table 4 reports the performance of other three components (i.e., Explicit connective classifier, Arg1 position classifier and Explicit sense classifier) in our proposed Explicit discourse parser. We see that these

Table 4. Results for Explicit connective classifier, Arg1 position classifier and Explicit sense classifier; no EP

other three components	P (%)	R (%)	F_1 (%)
Explicit connective classifier	94.83	93.49	94.16
Arg1 position classifier	97.70	97.15	97.41
Explicit sense classifier	86.98	86.98	86.98

three components have achieved a high performance, that is, they are not the main challenges in the Explicit discourse parser.

Table 5 gives the results for the arguments extraction and the overall performance of the Explicit discourse parser with error propagation. From the table, we see that the overall performance is increased along with the the performance of the arguments extraction. And using separate extractors increases the F_1 of the Explicit discourse by 2.81% compared with using a global extractor.

Table 5. Results for the arguments extraction and the overall performance of the Explicit discourse parser; EP

	Arg1 F_1 (%)	Arg2 F_1 (%)	Both F_1 (%)	overall performance F_1 (%)
baseline	35.44	57.51	26.82	22.67
global extractor	50.66	78.51	45.13	38.16
two extractors	53.45	81.32	48.03	40.97

Finally, we compare the performance with Lin and Kong, summarized in Table 6. Compared with Lin, we find that new features proposed in this work do help increase F_1 of Explicit connective classification by 0.54%, and our parser also achieves much better on the arguments extraction. We achieve the close performance to Kong on argument extraction. However, since Kong used good standard (GS) parse tree for training and the parse tree produced by Charniak parser for testing, whereas we use the parse tree along with the POS tags produced by Berkeley parser for training and testing, this may cause a slightly lower performance on argument extraction.

Table 6. Results for Lin's end-to-end parser, Kong's arguments extraction and our Explicit discourse parser; EP

	Lin F_1 (%)	Kong F_1 (%)	our parser F_1 (%)
Connective classifier	93.62	-	94.16
Arg1	47.68	56.04	53.45
Arg2	70.27	76.53	81.32
Both	40.37	48.89	48.03
Overall parser	-	-	40.97

In a nutshell, unlike most previous work focusing on only one or several components of discourse parser, the goal of our work is to build an end-to-end Explicit discourse parser for practical application. On one hand, this proposed system takes raw texts as input and outputs the discourse relations, which can be directly applied to downstream applications. On the other hand, compared with Lin's system, to the best of our knowledge, our Explicit discourse parser has achieved the best performance on PDTB so far.

5   Conclusion

In this work, we build a practical end-to-end discourse parser (i.e., Explicit discourse parser). We present a method to build two separate argument extractors for two arguments instead of using a global extractor. The evaluation on PDTB shows significant performance improvements of the arguments labeling. Experimental results showed that our proposed discourse parser achieved the best performance on explicit discourse so far.

Acknowledgments. This research is supported by grants from Science and Technology Commission of Shanghai Municipality under research grant no. (14DZ2260800 and 15ZR1410700) and Shanghai Collaborative Innovation Center of Trustworthy Software for Internet of Things (ZF1213).

References

1. Verberne, S., Boves, L., Oostdijk, N., Coppen, P.-A.: Evaluating discourse-based answer extraction for why-question answering. In: Proceedings of the 30th Annual International ACM SIGIR Conference on Research and Development in Information Retrieval, pp. 735–736. ACM (2007)
2. Cimiano, P., Reyle, U., Šarić, J.: Ontology-driven discourse analysis for information extraction. Data & Knowledge Engineering **55**(1), 59–83 (2005)
3. Prasad, R., Dinesh, N., Lee, A., Miltsakaki, E., Robaldo, L., Joshi, A.K., Webber, B.L.: The Penn Discourse TreeBank 2.0. In LREC. Citeseer (2008)
4. Ghosh, S., Johansson, R., Riccardi, G.,, Tonelli, S.: Shallow discourse parsing with conditional random fields. In: Proceedings of 5th International Joint Conference on Natural Language Processing, Chiang Mai, Thailand, pp. 1071–1079. Asian Federation of Natural Language Processing, November 2011
5. Kong, F., Ng, H.T., Zhou, G.: A constituent-based approach to argument labeling with joint inference in discourse parsing. In: Proceedings of the 2014 Conference on Empirical Methods in Natural Language Processing (EMNLP), Doha, Qatar, pp. 68–77. Association for Computational Linguistics, October 2014
6. Lin, Z., Kan, M.-Y., Ng, H.T.: Recognizing implicit discourse relations in the penn discourse Treebank. In: Proceedings of the 2009 Conference on Empirical Methods in Natural Language Processing, Singapore, pp. 343–351. Association for Computational Linguistics, August 2009
7. Pitler, E., Louis, A., Nenkova, A.: Automatic sense prediction for implicit discourse relations in text. In: Proceedings of the Joint Conference of the 47th Annual Meeting of the ACL and the 4th International Joint Conference on Natural Language Processing of the AFNLP, Suntec, Singapore, pp. 683–691. Association for Computational Linguistics, August 2009
8. Pitler, E., Nenkova, A.: Using syntax to disambiguate explicit discourse connectives in text. In: Proceedings of the ACL-IJCNLP 2009 Conference Short Papers, pp. 13–16. Association for Computational Linguistics (2009)
9. Rutherford, A.T., Xue, N.: Discovering implicit discourse relations through brown cluster pair representation and coreference patterns. In: EACL 2014, p. 645 (2014)
10. Lin, Z., Ng, H.T., Kan, M.-Y.: A PDTB-styled end-to-end discourse parser. Natural Language Engineering, 1–34 (2014)
11. Lan, M., Xu, Y., Niu, Z.-Y., et al.: Leveraging synthetic discourse data via multi-task learning for implicit discourse relation recognition. In: ACL, no. 1, pp. 476–485. Citeseer (2013)
12. Knott, A.: A data-driven methodology for motivating a set of coherence relations (1996)

Graph-Based Query-Focused Multi-document Summarization Using Improved Affinity Graph

Po Hu[1]([⊠]), Jiacong He[2], and Yong Zhang[1]

[1] School of Computer Science, Central China Normal University, Wuhan, China
{phu,ychang}@mail.ccnu.edu.cn
[2] Medallia Inc., Palo Alto, USA
hejiacongtheone@gmail.com

Abstract. Manifold ranking is one of the most competitive approaches for query-focused multi-document summarization. Despite its success for this task, it usually constructs a sentence affinity graph first based on inter-sentence content similarity, and then perform manifold ranking on the graph to score each sentence with the assumption that all the sentences live on a single manifold. Actually, for a document set to be summarized, the distribution of the sentences might form different, but related manifolds. This paper aims to generalize the basic manifold-ranking based approach to the more generic setting by introducing a novel affinity graph to estimate the similarity between sentences, which leverages both the local geometric structures and the contents of sentences jointly. Preliminary experimental results on the DUC datasets demonstrate the good effectiveness of the proposed approach.

Keywords: Query-focused multi-document summarization · Manifold ranking · Affinity graph construction

1 Introduction

With the explosive growth of the Internet, the volume of information keeps on expanding extremely fast, and we are overwhelmed by enormous amount of accessible information. To overcome this obstacle, new technologies that can alleviate the information overload crisis efficiently are in great need. The practical need for automatic summarization has become urgent.

As a particular summarization type, query-focused multi-document summarization aims to create from a document set a summary that preserves the most important information conveyed in the documents and meets the information need expressed in a given query. It can help readers quickly digest the desired information without having to read each individual document in detail, which is of great value to a variety of information services such as query-sensitive snippet generation for Web search engines, and personalized news recommendation, etc. Compared with generic multi-document summarization, the unique challenge for query-focused summarization is that the generated summary is not only required to remain the most salient information in the document set, but also is required to guarantee that the information is biased towards the given query.

© Springer International Publishing Switzerland 2015
S. Zhang et al. (Eds.): KSEM 2015, LNAI 9403, pp. 336–347, 2015.
DOI: 10.1007/978-3-319-25159-2_31

Recently, a number of graph-based ranking methods have been proposed, among which the manifold ranking method is a typical one which has achieved rather competitive performance [1]. However, this method and its subsequent extensions [2,22,23] usually come with the assumption that all the sentences live on a single manifold. Actually, in a given document set, it might have a number of subtopics, and the sentences from different subtopics might belong to different manifolds rather than reside on a single one. There are already some evidences showing that a semantically related set of words or phrases may reside on clusters with distributional semantics [28], so we assume that the sentences in a topical document set may actually be distributed in manifolds where similar sentences with similar semantics might be on the same manifold and dissimilar sentences might be on the different manifolds.

In this paper, we propose to construct a novel affinity graph to estimate the similarity between sentences in which both the local geometric structures and the contents of sentences are simultaneously investigated. Extensive experiments have been conducted on the standard summarization benchmark data sets, and the results demonstrate the effectiveness of the proposed approach.

2   Related Work

Traditional feature-based summarization approaches depend on a combination of statistical or linguistic features to compute the significance of each sentence [3]-[8]. In recent years, graph-based methods like LexRank and TextRank have been proposed to rank sentences [9]-[11], and these methods generally construct a graph firstly to represent the relationships between sentences, and then recursively calculate each sentences significance based on link structure analysis. For query-focused multi-document summarization, the significance of each sentence will be determined by a combination of two important factors: how relevant is that sentence to the given query and how important is the sentence in the context of the input documents in which it appears. Many existing approaches directly incorporated the query information into generic summarizers [12]-[14]. Supervised or semi-supervised learning methods, matrix factorization methods and topic models have also been used [15,16]. Wei et al. proposed a query-sensitive mutual reinforcement chain, which leverages various relationships among documents, sentences, and terms to rank sentences in a unified three-layer graph model [17]. Wan et al. propose a manifold-ranking based approach to make uniform use of sentence-to-sentence and sentence-to-query relationships [1], which has shown excellent performance and outperformed state-of-the-art approaches. Recently, the manifold-ranking algorithm has been further extended for learning from multiple modalities [2,18].

However, all the manifold ranking approaches consider that all the sentences in a document set live on a single manifold, without further analyzing the possible more complex cases mentioned above. Therefore, we argue that better summarization performance may be achieved by leveraging both the local geometric structures and the contents of sentences jointly. Our experimental results reveal that the summarization performance of manifold-ranking based approaches rely heavily on the constructed affinity graph, and the ranking process is able to work well when the pairwise sentences belonging to different manifolds have a relatively low similarity.

3 The Proposed Approach

3.1 Manifold-Ranking Approach

As one type of the representative approaches that has been successfully applied to query-focused multi-document summarization, the basic manifold-ranking approach [19] and its extensions usually assume that all the sentences in a document set are sampled from a single manifold. In these methods, a graph G will be constructed first by connecting any pair of sentences in the documents. The affinity matrix of G can be denoted by W with each element w_{ij} corresponding to the cosine similarity between sentences s_i and s_j. Then, the matrix W is symmetrically normalized into the matrix S by $S = D^{-1/2} \times W \times D^{-1/2}$, where D is the diagonal matrix with (i, i)-element equal to the sum of the i-th row of W. Lastly, the manifold-ranking process was employed on the matrix S via random walks to iteratively propagate the ranking scores of sentences to nearby sentences smoothly along the manifold structure. The final ranking score of a sentence indicates the query-biased informativeness of the sentence. Because the given query can be regarded as a pseudo-sentence, it can be processed in the same way as other sentences in the documents. In the basic manifold-ranking approaches for summarization, the construction of the affinity graph and its corresponding affinity matrix W are the key to guarantee the expected ranking performance of sentences.

3.2 Manifold Ranking Using Improved Affinity Graph

The basic manifold-ranking approaches discussed above make uniform use of the sentence relationships in a single manifold. However, there is no unique global manifold in many circumstances and the relationships between sentences may form different even mixture manifolds. It is noting that existing manifold-ranking approaches can not be directly applied to this setting, because the constructed affinity graph may make two sentences on different manifolds have a high similarity value. Even though each individual manifold obeys the ranking score smoothness assumption, nearby points on different manifolds may not satisfy this assumption. Straightforward application of existing manifold ranking algorithm may not achieve optimal performance, because it usually leads to diffuse ranking scores of sentences across the wrong manifolds.

Truly effective manifold-ranking approaches are expected to ensure that the ranking scores are propagated smoothly on each individual manifold while non-smoothly across different manifolds. Therefore, for the task of query-focused multi-document summarization, it would be more appropriate to generalize the basic manifold-ranking approach to the more complex case where all the sentences are assumed to be sampled from a mixture of manifolds. In this case, the sentence ranking function can be directly supported on the more complex structure.

Since the summarization performance of manifold-ranking approaches mainly relies on the affinity graph G, how to construct a more suitable affinity graph becomes critical.

New Affinity Graph Construction. Traditional affinity graph for summarization is usually constructed based on the Cosine similarity between sentences, which is not suitable for the case mentioned above since Cosine similarity based weights will mix up manifolds. To address the issue, we present a new method to construct a more suitable affinity graph by incorporating the geometry-related structural information as well as the content information of the sentences in a unified setting, which can encode the latent structures in the documents effectively.

Intuitively, if two sentences s_i and s_j have similar contents, then they should be regarded as similar. If two sentences belong to different manifolds, they should be considered dissimilar. The first intuition can be captured by the content similarity between two sentences and the second intuition can be captured by the structural similarity between them.

In the study, we compute the content similarity $Sim_C(s_i, s_j)$ between two sentences s_i and s_j by adopting the Cosine similarity measure like the existing studies.

$$Sim_C(s_i, s_j) = Sim_{Cosine}(s_i, s_j) \tag{1}$$

Where $Sim_{Cosine}(s_i, s_j)$ denotes the Cosine similarity between the corresponding term vectors of sentences s_i and s_j.

Besides, to estimate the structural similarity between two sentences, it is found that the local tangent space at each sentence provides a good approximation to the local geometric structure of the nonlinear manifold. If two sentences have similar local tangent spaces, then they are more likely to belong to the same manifold. For nearby sentences, if they have dissimilar local tangent spaces, then they are more likely to belong to different manifolds.

Suppose that the local tangent spaces at sentence s_i and s_j are θ_i and θ_j respectively, and the tangent space at each sentence can be constructed from the local neighborhood of it. Specifically, given a sentence s and its m closest neighbors N(s) in Euclidean space, the local geometric information around s can be captured by its local sample covariance matrix Σ_s, which can be defined as:

$$\Sigma_s = \frac{\sum_{s' \in N(s)} (s' - u_s)(s' - u_s)^T}{m} \tag{2}$$

Where $u_s = \frac{\sum_{s' \in N(s)} s'}{m}$ denotes the neighborhood mean of the sentence s. In our experiments, the number of the closest neighbors of each sentence m is fixed at 20 for simplicity.

Now, we can compute the structural similarity $Sim_S(s_i, s_j)$ between two sentences s_i and s_j based on the similarity of the local sample covariance matrices Σ_{s_i} and Σ_{s_j}. Considering that Hellinger distance is sensitive to local manifold structures, we use it to compute the distance between two local sample covariance matrices, which have encoded the local manifolds structural information. According to [20], the Hellinger distance $H(\Sigma_{s_i}, \Sigma_{s_j})$ between two covariance matrices Σ_{s_i} and Σ_{s_j} can be defined as follows, which is based on the extension of the traditional definition of Hellinger distance between two probability density functions.

$$H(\Sigma_{s_i}, \Sigma_{s_j}) \equiv H(N(s_i; 0, \Sigma_{s_i}), N(s_j; 0, \Sigma_{s_j})) = \sqrt{1 - 2^{d/2} \frac{|\Sigma_{s_i}|^{1/4} |\Sigma_{s_j}|^{1/4}}{|\Sigma_{s_i} + \Sigma_{s_j}|^{1/2}}}$$

(3)

Where $N(s_i; 0, \Sigma_{s_i})$ is a Gaussian for estimating the local structure of s_i with zero mean and covariance Σ_{s_i}, and $N(s_j; 0, \Sigma_{s_j})$ can be explained similarly. d is the dimensionality of the ambient feature space of sentences s_i and s_j, and $|\Sigma_{s_i}|$, $|\Sigma_{s_j}|$, and $|\Sigma_{s_i} + \Sigma_{s_j}|$ are the Frobenius norms of the corresponding matrices. It is noting that when the local geometry of two sentences s_i and s_j is similar, the Hellinger distance $H(\Sigma_{s_i}, \Sigma_{s_j})$ is small; When there is significant difference on the local geometry, the distance is large. Since the Hellinger distance is symmetric and in $[0, 1]$, we can naturally compute the structural similarity $Sim_S(s_i, s_j)$ between sentences s_i and s_j as follows.

$$Sim_S(s_i, s_j) = 1 - \lambda \times H(\Sigma_{s_i}, \Sigma_{s_j})$$

(4)

Where $\lambda(\lambda \in [0, 1])$ is the parameter used to adjust the influence of Hellinger distance.

From the high level point of view, the pairwise similarity based on Hellinger distance integrates the geometric information on two local sentence sets rather than two single sentences only, so it can be used to estimate the structural similarity between two sentences effectively.

Next, we will construct the new affinity graph by its corresponding matrix W' with each element w'_{ij} corresponding to the combination of both the content similarity $Sim_C(s_i, s_j)$ and the structural similarity $Sim_S(s_i, s_j)$. Finally, these two similarities are multiplied together to give an overall affinity value w'_{ij} as follows:

$$w'_{ij} = Sim_C(s_i, s_j) \times Sim_S(s_i, s_j) = Sim_{Cosine}(s_i, s_j) \times (1 - \lambda \times H(\Sigma_{s_i}, \Sigma_{s_j}))$$

(5)

It can be found that the new affinity graph combines both geometry and content of sentences: an element in the graph has larger affinity value when the corresponding two sentences have similar manifold structure and similar content. When two sentences are far from each other, the overall affinity value will tend to be zero due to the impact of the content similarity. While, when two sentences are close to the intersection of different manifolds, they will also have a relatively low overall affinity value due to the impact of the structural similarity.

Sentence Ranking Based on the New Affinity Graph. Once we have the affinity graph and its corresponding matrix, the basic manifold-ranking approach can be applied on it to rank sentences on the graph.

Given a set of sentences $S = \{s_0, s_1, ..., s_n\}$, the first sentence s_0 represents the given query and the rest n sentences represent all the sentences in the documents to be ranked. Let f denote a ranking function which assigns to each sentence s_i $(0 \leq i \leq n)$ a ranking score f_i. We can view f as a vector $f = [f_0, ..., f_n]^T$. We also define a prior vector $y = [y_0, ..., y_n]^T$, in which $y_0 = 1$ since s_0 is the given query and $y_i = 0 (1 \leq i \leq n)$ for all the sentences that we want to rank.

Next, the sentence ranking task can be formalized as follows via basic manifold ranking:

1. Compute the pair-wise similarity value between two different sentences by the overall affinity w'_{ij} according to the formula (5), and let $w'_{ii} = 0$;
2. Construct the affinity matrix W' to encode the latent manifold structure of the documents.
3. Symmetrically normalized W' by $S' = D'^{-1/2} W' D'^{-1/2}$ in which D' is the diagonal matrix with (i, i)-element equal to the sum of the i-th row of W'.
4. Iterate $f(t+1) = \alpha S' f(t) + (1-\alpha)y$ until convergence, where α is a parameter in (0,1).
5. Let f_i^* denote the limit of the sequence $\{f_i(t)\}$. Each sentence s_i obtains its ranking score.

In the approach, the parameter α specifies the relative contribution to the ranking score from neighbors and the initial ranking score. It is set to 0.6 in this study as in [2]. In the fourth step of the approach, all sentences including the given query spread their ranking scores to their neighbors via the corresponding affinity matrix, and the whole spreading process is repeated until a stable state is achieved. The theorem in [19] guarantees that the sequence $\{f_i(t)\}$ converges to $f_i^* = (1 - \alpha)(I - \alpha S')^{-1} y$.

After we obtain the ranking score of each sentence in the document set to be summarized, the same greedy algorithm in [1] is applied to remove redundancy between sentences and we choose a number of sentences with highest ranking scores into the summary.

4   Experiments

4.1   Experimental Setup and Metrics

Data Set. To evaluate the effectiveness of the proposed approach, we adopted the DUC 2005 and DUC 2007 datasets for evaluation. Table 1 provides a brief description of the datasets used in our experiments. Here each dataset consists of 45 or 50 topics with each topic consisting of a specified query and a number of relevant newswire documents. Multiple reference summaries have been created

Table 1. The description of DUC 2005 and DUC 2007 dataset

	DUC2005	DUC2007
Number of topics	50	45
Document number of each topic	25-50	25
Number of reference summaries of each topic	either 4 or 9	4
Document source	TREC	AQUAINT
Summary length limit	250 words	250 words

for each topic by different NIST professional assessors, which can be regarded as the golden standards for evaluation.

Evaluation Metric. In this study, we used the ROUGE toolkit for evaluation [21], which has long been officially adopted by DUC for automatic summarization evaluation. It measures summary quality by counting overlapping units between the automatically generated summary and the reference summary. A few recall-oriented ROUGE metrics have been employed such as ROUGE-1, ROUGE-2, and ROUGE-SU4, etc, among which ROUGE-1 has been shown to agree with human judgment most. Formally, ROUGE-N is an n-gram recall based measurement between a candidate summary and a set of reference summaries, which is computed as follows.

$$ROUGE - N = \frac{\Sigma_{s\in(refS)}\Sigma_{gram_n\in s}Count_{match}(gram_n)}{\Sigma_{s\in(refS)}\Sigma_{gram_n\in s}Count(gram_n)} \tag{6}$$

where n stands for the length of the n-gram, $gram_n$, and $Count_{match}(gram_n)$ is the maximum number of n-grams co-occurring in a candidate summary and a set of reference summaries $refS$.

Although we evaluated with all the metrics provided by ROUGE, in the following, we only report ROUGE-1 and ROUGE-2 at a confidence level of 95% and with significance tests conducted in the experiments (other metrics gives similar results).

4.2 Experimental Results

Overall Performance Comparison. As a preprocessing step, in the following experiments, queries and documents were segmented into sentences, stop-words were removed and the remaining words were stemmed using Porter Stemmer. The average recall scores of the above ROUGE metrics are demonstrated in the following experimental results.

For evaluation, we compared our proposed approach with several baselines including the basic manifold-ranking based approach and the participating systems in DUC 2005 and DUC 2007, which are described briefly as follows.

- NISTLead: The lead baseline is the official baseline system established by NIST, which takes the first 250 words of the most recent document for each topic, where documents in each topic are assumed to be ordered chronologically.

- DUC Average: It is the average ROUGE score of all the participating systems in DUC 2005/DUC 2007.
- DUC Best: It is the best performance of all the participating systems in DUC 2005/DUC 2007.
- DUC Worst: It is the worst performance of all the participating systems in DUC.
- SingleMR [1]: The SingleMR baseline is the basic manifold-ranking based approach, which makes uniform use of sentence-to-sentence and sentence-to-query relationships to rank sentences on a single manifold.

In our experiments, we use DUC 2006 dataset as the development set to decide the hyper parameter λ of our proposed approach, and use it to evaluate on both DUC 2005 and DUC 2007 datasets.

Table 2 and Table 3 show the overall ROUGE evaluation results of all the methods respectively.

In Table 2 and Table 3, the result of our approach is achieved when the parameter λ in the formula (5) for adjusting the influence of Hellinger distance is set as 0.5.

Seen from the tables, the proposed approach outperforms those of the baseline approaches in terms of ROUGE metrics consistently, which demonstrates that combining structural similarity and content similarity together is very important and effective for improving the performance of query-focused multi-document

Table 2. The overall evaluation results on DUC 2005

Method	ROUGE − 1	ROUGE − 2
OurApproach	**0.37123**	**0.06936**
SingleMR	0.36825	0.06801
DUC 2005 Average	0.33422	0.05785
DUC 2005 Best	0.37515	0.07251
DUC 2005 Worst	0.17935	0.02564
NISTLead	0.27523	0.04026

Table 3. The overall evaluation results on DUC 2007

Method	ROUGE − 1	ROUGE − 2
OurApproach	**0.41576**	**0.09837**
SingleMR	0.40598	0.09703
DUC 2007 Average	0.39728	0.09486
DUC 2007 Best	0.45258	0.12448
DUC 2007 Worst	0.24277	0.03813
NISTLead	0.31250	0.06039

summarization. It is worth noting the fact that the performance achieved by our proposed approach is very close to that of the best performing system in DUC 2005. However, our approach is not as good as the top participating systems in DUC 2007, it may owe to the fact that our approach neither use any supervised summarization models nor adopt any deep natural language processing techniques or external knowledge, such difference in ROUGE scores is reasonable because the top performing systems in DUC 2007 leverage supervised model with large training data or external knowledge bases like Freeebase or Wikipedia.

We also observe that our proposed approach performs better than the basic manifold-ranking approach, which demonstrates that modeling all the sentences in a document set by a possible mixture of manifolds rather than by a single manifold can benefit the summarization process significantly.

Besides, both the proposed approach and the manifold-ranking based approach can much outperform the NIST baseline. They also achieve much higher ROUGE scores than the average score of all the participating systems in DUC, which also demonstrates the superiority of using manifold ranking for query-focused multi-document summarization since it can take into account the inter-relationships between sentences to propagate query-biased ranking scores along the latent manifold structure of the documents.

We attribute the improvement of our proposed approach to its capability of incorporating manifold learning into the manifold ranking process, which can naturally rank sentences smoothly on each individual manifold while non-smoothly across different manifolds.

Influence of Parameter Tuning. In order to further investigate the influence of the parameter λ in the proposed approach, the value of it is varied from 0 to 1 with step length 0.1. Figure 1 and 2 demonstrate the ROUGE-1 score curves with different parameter values on the two datasets respectively.

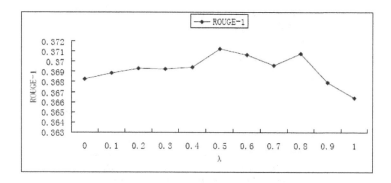

Fig. 1. ROUGE-1 scores vs. λ for our proposed approach on DUC 2005.

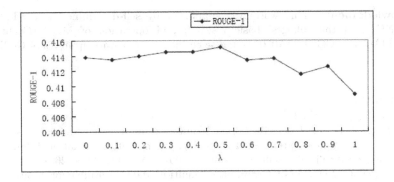

Fig. 2. ROUGE-1 scores vs. λ for our proposed approach on DUC 2007.

It can be seen from the figures that the experimental results convincingly show that the proposed similarity scores are useful, especially the joint use of the structural similarity can improve the performance at all interpolation points of λ. This also validated that incorporating appropriate structural similarity into the affinity graph is beneficial to the overall performance, but we can also find clearly from these figures that completely ignoring or making excessive emphasis on it may reduce the performance to a certain extent. Therefore, how to choose the most suitable parameter λ in an adaptive way remains a challenging task in our current approach, and we plan to handle it in our future work.

5   Conclusion and Future Work

In this study, we generalize the basic manifold-ranking based summarization approach to the more generic setting by introducing a novel affinity graph to estimate the similarity between sentences, which leverages both the local geometric structures and the contents of sentences in a unified framework. Extensive experimental results on the DUC benchmark datasets demonstrated the good effectiveness of the proposed approach, which achieved significantly better results than the basic manifold-ranking approach and other official baselines.

Since the major concern in the work is to validate the effectiveness of structural similarity on the performance of the existing manifold-ranking based summarization approaches, we did not yet take into account other possible methods to calculate the geodesic distances between sentences, such as ISOMAP [24], LLE [25], SNE [26], and t-SNE [27] etc. In future work, we will investigate them and try employing non-linear manifold learning with automatic parameter selection to further improve graph-based summarization performance. Besides, the cost of constructing the current affinity matrix is prohibitive for very large data set. Hence, we plan to reduce the time complexity of our approach by using effective anchor graph instead.

Acknowledgments. This work was supported by self-determined research funds of CCNU from the colleges' basic research and operation of MOE (Grant No. CCNU14A05015, CCNU14A05014) and scientific research start-up funds of CCNU.

References

1. Wan, X.J., Yang, J.W., Xiao, J.G.: Manifold-ranking based topic-focused multi-document summarization. In: Proceedings of the 20th International Joint Conference on Artificial Intelligence (IJCAI 2007), pp. 2903–2908 (2007)
2. Wan, X.J., Xiao, J.G.: Graph-based multi-modality learning for topic-focused multi-document summarization. In: Proceedings of the 21st International Joint Conference on Artificial Intelligence (IJCAI 2009), pp. 1586–1591 (2009)
3. Saggion, H., Bontcheva, K., Cunningham, H.: Robust generic and query-based summarization. In: Proceedings of the 10th Conference of the European Chapter of the Association for Computational Linguistics (EACL 2003), pp. 2903–2908 (2003)
4. Radev, D.R., Jing, H.Y., Stys, M., Tam, D.: Centroid-Based Summarization of Multiple Documents. Information Processing and Management **40**, 919–938 (2004)
5. Lin, C.Y., Hovy, E.: From single to multi-document summarization: a prototype system and its evaluation. In: Proceedings of the 40th Annual Meeting on Association for Computational Linguistics (ACL 2002), pp. 457–464 (2002)
6. Nenkova, A., Louis, A.: Can you summarize this? identifying correlates of input difficulty for generic multi-document summarization. In: Proceedings of the 46th Annual Meeting of the Association for Computational Linguistics: Human Language Technologies (ACL 2008), pp. 825–833 (2008)
7. Celikyilmaz, A., Hakkani-Tur, D.: A hybrid hierarchical model for multi-document summarization. In: Proceedings of the 48th Annual Meeting of the Association for Computational Linguistics (ACL 2010), pp. 815–824 (2010)
8. Gillick, D., Favre, B.: A scalable global model for summarization. In: Proceedings of the Workshop on Integer Linear Programming for Natural Language Processing (ILP 2009), pp. 10–18 (2009)
9. Erkan, G., Radev, D.R.: LexRank: Graph-Based Centrality as Salience in Text Summarization. Journal of Artificial Intelligence Research **22**, 457–479 (2004)
10. Mihalcea, R., Tarau, P.: TextRank-bringing order into text. In: Proceedings of the 2004 Conference on Empirical Methods in Natural Language Processing (EMNLP 2004), pp. 404–411 (2004)
11. Wan, X.J., Yang, J.W.: Multi-document summarization using cluster-based link analysis. In: Proceedings of the 31st Annual International ACM SIGIR Conference on Research and Development in Information Retrieval (SIGIR 2008), pp. 299–306 (2008)
12. Haveliwala, T.: Topic-Sensitive PageRank: A Context-Sensitive Ranking Algorithm for Web Search. IEEE Transactions on Knowledge and Data Engineering **15**, 784–796 (2003)
13. Zhao, L., Wu, L.D., Huang, X.J.: Query Expansion in Graph-Based Approach for Query-Focused Multi-Document Summarization. Information Processing and Management **45**, 35–41 (2009)

14. Carbonell, J., Goldstein, J.: The use of MMR, diversity-based reranking for reordering documents and producing summaries. In: Proceedings of the 21st Annual International ACM SIGIR Conference on Research and Development in Information Retrieval (SIGIR 1998), pp. 335–336 (1998)

15. Wang, D.D., Li, T., Zhu, S.H., Ding, C.: Multi-Document summarization via sentence-level semantic analysis and symmetric matrix factorization. In: Proceedings of the 31st Annual International ACM SIGIR Conference on Research and Development in Information Retrieval (SIGIR 2008), pp. 307–314 (2008)

16. Tang, J., Yao, L.M., Chen, D.W.: Multi-topic based query-oriented summarization. In: Proceedings of the 9th SIAM International Conference on Data Mining (SDM 2009), pp. 1147–1158 (2009)

17. Wei, F., Li, W., Lu, Q., He, Y.: A cluster-sensitive graph model for query-oriented multi-document summarization. In: Plachouras, V., Macdonald, C., Ounis, I., White, R.W., Ruthven, I. (eds.) ECIR 2008. LNCS, vol. 4956, pp. 446–453. Springer, Heidelberg (2008)

18. Tong, H.H., He, J.R., Li, M.J., Zhang, C.S., Ma, W.Y.: Graph based multi-modality learning. In: Proceedings of the 13th Annual ACM International Conference on Multimedia (MM 2005), pp. 862–871 (2005)

19. Zhou, D., Weston, J., Gretton, A., Bousquet, O., Scholkopf, B.: Ranking on Data Manifolds. Advances in Neural Information Processing Systems **16**, 169–176 (2004)

20. Goldberg, A.B., Zhu, X.J., Singh, A., Xu, Z., Nowak, R.: Multi-Manifold Semi-Supervised Learning. Journal of Machine Learning Research **5**, 169–176 (2009). Proceedings Track

21. Lin, C.Y., Hovy, E.: Automatic evaluation of summaries using N-gram cooccurrence statistics. In: Proceedings of the 2003 Conference of the North American Chapter of the Association for Computational Linguistics on Human Language Technology (NAACL 2003), pp. 71–78 (2003)

22. Cheng, X.Q., Du, P., Guo, J.F., Zhu, X.F., Chen, Y.X.: Ranking on Data Manifold with Sink Points. IEEE Transactions on Knowledge and Data Engineering **25**, 177–191 (2013)

23. Cai, X.Y., Li, W.J.: Mutually Reinforced Manifold-Ranking Based Relevance Propagation Model for Query-Focused Multi-Document Summarization. IEEE Transactions on Audio, Speech and Language Processing **20**, 1597–1607 (2012)

24. Tenenbaum, J.B., Silva, V., Langford, J.C.: A Global Geometric Framework for Nonlinear Dimensionality Reduction. Science **290**, 2319–2323 (2000)

25. Roweis, S., Saul, L.: Nonlinear Dimensionality Reduction by Locally Linear Embedding. Science **290**, 2323–2326 (2000)

26. Hinton, G., Roweis, S.: Stochastic Neighbor Embedding. Advances in Neural Information Processing Systems **15**, 833–840 (2003)

27. van der Maaten, L.J.P., Hinton, G.: Visualizing Data Using t-SNE. Journal of Machine Learning Research **9**, 2579–2605 (2008)

28. Georgia, A., Elias, I., Alexandros, P.: Low-dimensional manifold distributional semantic models. In: Proceedings of the 25th International Conference on Computational Linguistics (COLING 2014), pp. 731–740 (2014)

Hashtag Biased Ranking for Keyword Extraction from Microblog Posts

Lin Li[1], Chang Su[1], Yueqing Sun[1], Shengwu Xiong[1(✉)], and Guandong Xu[2]

[1] School of Computer Science & Technology, Wuhan University of Technology,
Wuhan, China
{cathylilin,suchang,yqsuan,xiongsw}@whut.edu.cn

[2] Advanced Analytics Institute, University of Technology, Sydney, Ultimo, Australia
Guandong.Xu@uts.edu.au

Abstract. Nowadays, a huge amount of text is being generated for social networking purpose on the Web. Keyword extraction from such text benefit many applications such as advertising, search, and content filtering. Recent studies show that graph based ranking is more effective than traditional term or document frequecy based approaches. However, most work in the literature constructs word to word graph within a document or a collection of documents before applying a kind of random walk. Such a graph does not consider the influence of document importance on keyword extraction. Moreover, social text like a microblog post usually has speical social features such as hashtag and so on, which can help us understand its topic. In this paper, we propose hashtag biased ranking for keyword extraction from a collection of microblog posts. We first build a word-post weighted graph by taking into account the posts themselves. Then, a hashtag biased random walk is applied on this graph, which guides our approach to extract keywords according to the hashtag topic. Last, the final ranking of a word is determined by the stationary probability after a number of interations. We evaluate our proposed method on a real Chinese microblog posts. Experiments show that our method is more effective than the traditional word to word graph based ranking in terms of precision.

1 Introduction

Recently, microblogs as a new social media have attracted researchers' interests [8]. Since there are usually thousands of posts in a miroblog platform, it is imporant for users to understand their content. For this purpose, various task have been studied, such as tag recommendation [23], keyword/keyphrase extraction [25,26], topic analysis [1,21], spammer detection [5], microblog retrieval [15,18]. However, current explorations are still in an early stage and our understanding of microblog post content still remains limited. Keyword extraction is a foundation work for the above tasks and targets to represent the core

This research was undertaken as part of Project 15BGL048, 2015AA015403, 2015BAA072 and 61303029 and supported by Hubei Key Laboratory of Transportation Internet of Things.

S. Zhang et al. (Eds.): KSEM 2015, LNAI 9403, pp. 348–359, 2015.
DOI: 10.1007/978-3-319-25159-2_32

content of a post or a collection of posts. Therefore, it becomes an important and emergent research topic.

There are many approaches for keyword extraction from long text documents, such as intuitive frequency based, cluster based [3,11], graph based [10,13,25] approaches. TextRank [13] is the first implemantation applying random walk on a word connnectivity graph. Those graph based ranking methods choose a word as one of topic keywowrds if the word frequently appears togehter with important words and show better than other approaches [10,13,25]. For graph based ranking, how to build graph is crucial. Previous methods mainly based on word to word relations weighted by statistical features such as term frequencies and co-occurences. For example, a link between two words are set up if the two words appear in at least a same document.

While it appears natural to use the graph based ranking to microblog posts, compared with traditonal long text collection, keyword extraction from microblog posts is more challenging in at least two aspects. The one is that microblog posts are short in length. Keyword extraction from traditional documents tries to filter less important words from a long text, but microblog posts themselve do not have enough good keywords. We obverse that users in microblogging like to publish posts related to a topic in a period of time. The accumulated number of topically related posts show the strength of the collective although a single post may not contain good enough keyword candidates. The traditional word to word graph in a single document does not model the relation between posts and thus is unable to use other posts to enhance keyword extraction. The other is that the social feature hashtag governs the main topic distribution of posts. The hashtag is a good topic indicator to build the topic relation among posts and then help us identify keywords from a collection of posts. How to use hashtag in keyword extraction is also another important problem. So far there is little work on keyword extraction from microblog posts [25,26] and they still follow the direction of building a word to word connectivity graph without considering the influences of post importance and social feature on keyword extraction.

In this paper, we propose a hashtag biased ranking for keyword extraction from a collection of microblog posts. We think that given a post, keywords should be topically related to hashtag words and other topic related posts may have good keywords as supplementary. Based on these, our work follows the standard three steps of graph based keyword extraction. We first build a word-post weighted graph. If a word appears in a post, a link between them is set up. In such graph, a word will be selected as a keyword if the word frequently appears in imporant posts and the importance of a post is naturally determined by the linked important words. Also, kinds of weights can be added such as term frequency, document frequency and so forth. Then, a hashtag biased random walk is applied on this graph, which is similar to topical PageRank method [4]. A hashtag embedded post explicitly tells us its topic trend, so keyword extraction should make use of this indicator for better keywords. Last, the final ranking of a word is determined by the stationary probability of the hashtag biased random walk on the proposed word-post graph.

Our method can find keywords from both of a single post and a collection of posts by adjusting a random jumping vector. As we discussed above, a microblog post is short and not so informative for users. For example, a user submits a query to a microblog retreival engine and reads the returned results post by post. In such way, user has to summarize the main topics of the whole results set for better understand, which tells us that the collection of short posts is more interesting than a single post. Therefore, in this work we do evaluation on finding keywords from a collection of posts and conduct experiments on a Chinese microblog texts. Experimental results show that our method is effective in terms of precision. Our key contribution is to argue for building word to post graph and hashtag biased ranking, which considers both of posts and hastag influences on keyword extraction.

2   Related Work

Our work is related to unsupervised graph based keyword extraction. TextRank proposed by Mihalcea and Tarau [13] is the first graph based ranking algorithm to extract keywords and sentences for a given text. Following it, Liu et al. [10] used a topic model to learn topics of a document and than build a Topical PageRank (TPR) on word graph to measure word importance with respect to different topics. Based on the study by Liu et al. [10], recent work [25] addressed how to extract keyphrases from Twitter by improving the graph edge through a topic sensitive weighting and giving a probabilistic model for keyphrase ranking. The above studies rely only on a given single text to derive important key units like words, phrases and sentences. We think that a single short microblog post is not informative engough, so we model a word to post graph which takes into accounts the importance of other related posts in improving the quality of keyword extraction.

Other studies make use of external knowledge sources to improve the performance of keyword extraction. Wang et al. [20] represented a document as a semantic graph with synset from WordNet and extracted keywords from a modified PageRank algorithm. Wang et al. [22] used Wikipedia to construct a two-level concept based graph, instead of word based graph and ran PageRank and HITS rank on the graph. Wan et al. [19] proposed to use a small number of nearest neighbor documents to provide more knowledge to improve single document keyphrase extraction. Without utilizing any external corpus, our work applies random walk biased by hashtag context, a intrinsic feature in microblog posts.

Supervised approaches of keyword extraction are studied [6,9,17,24]. Their experimental results show that supervised machine learning can obtain better results than traditional methods. Li et. al [9] investigated a set of features to measure the importance of keywords and select four supervised models for precision comparisons. Zhang et al. [24] utilized supervised randow walk for keyword extraction by combining multiple types of relations between words and automatically learning the weights of the edges between the words in the word graph of each document. Labelled training data is crucial to optimze supervised model parameters and largely affects the extraction precision. Our work is unsupervised and orthogonal to supervised approaches.

3   Hashtag Biased Graph Ranking

3.1   Our Problem

Microblogging is such an infomatioin propagation flatform where users like to discuss hot events or topics, share their opinions and spread messages through their social networks. A single short microblog post may not satisfy the information needs of users. A collection of related posts could give users better understanding on what is going on regarding a topic. This characteristics is quite different from the traditional long text which keyword extraction is based on the assumptation that a single long document itself contain enough imporant words. Therefore, we assume that there is a collection of related microblog posts. Our task is to extract keywords from this collection. We aruge that the collection of posts can give users a more overall vision than a single post. Moreover, by adjusting a random jumping vector, we can still generate keywords for a single post. The collections of microblog posts are common, such as a set of search reults of microblog posts, a topic discussion group and so forth.

3.2   Word to Post Bipartite Graph Construction

Now given a collection of microblog posts, the word-post relationship can be intuitively represented as a bipartite graph. A bipartite graph, also called a bigraph, is a special graph from which the set of vertices can be decomposed into two disjoint sets such that no two vertices within the same set are adjacent. In the mathematical definition, a simple undirected graph $G := (W \cup P, E)$ is called bipartite if W and P are disjoint sets, where W and P are the vertex set and E is the edge set of the graph. Let $n = |W \cup P|$. This graph is used as our original model where W is a set of words, the P is a set of microblog posts, as shown in Figure 1. An edge e connects a word w and a post p, if the word w is contained in the post p. In the context of KEYWORD EXTRACTION, we propose to rank words based on the inter-relationship of their corresponding posts. As a by-product, important posts could be mined as well by applying the proposed algorithm on the side of the posts with a relatively small modification.

3.3   Hashtag Biased Random Walk and Ranking

We rank word nodes in Figure 1 corresponding to the standing probability distribution (i.e. score) of a rankdom walker on the graph. Our hashtag biased random walk is defined as Equation 1, a modification of Tong et al. [16].

$$\vec{r} = \alpha \widetilde{Q} \vec{r} + (1 - \alpha)\vec{e_h} \tag{1}$$

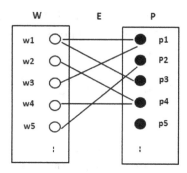

Fig. 1. Word-Post bipartite graph

$\overrightarrow{r}$ is $n \times 1$ rank vectors of nodes in the graph. $\widetilde{Q} = [q_{i,j}]$ is the weighted graph. In this paper, we investigate two popular weighting strategies, i.e., TF and TFIDF [12]. $\overrightarrow{e_h}$ is $n \times 1$ starting vector and h is the set of hashtag words with the constraint that $\sum_{j \in h} e(j) = 1$ and 0 for others. Our work directly uses the hashtag words to guide the jump probability of a random walk. Hashtag is generated by the author of a mircoblog post and explicitly reflect the topic of this post. Recent work [10,25] discovered the topic of a word by latent topic model analysis, which ignore the intrinsic feature of microblog posts. We tune up the walk behavior and the jump behavior by a mixing parameter α, $0 < \alpha < 1$. From this formula we determine the overall score of a target node by counting *both* the number of nodes linking to a target node *and* the relative quality of each pointing node.

After constructing the word to post graph and applying the random walk on it, we can sort the nodes by their ranks using Equation 1. The recursive running of Equation 1 gives the probability distribution that the walker is on nodes after t iterations. When t equals to 1, no heuristic is used. When t is large enough, r_i will gradually converge to a stationary distribution. Then, the distribution induced on the state transitions of all the nodes in the graph produces a final ranking of these nodes. The initial state is chosen uniformly at random because in general the initial value will not affect final values, just the rate of convergence [14].

3.4   Algorithm Description

Equation 1 defines a linear system problem, where $\overrightarrow{r}$ is determined by:

$$\begin{aligned} \overrightarrow{r} &= (1-\alpha)(I - \alpha\widetilde{Q})^{-1}\overrightarrow{e_h} \\ &= (1-\alpha)Q^{-1}\overrightarrow{e_h} \end{aligned} \tag{2}$$

As dicussed in [16], directly computing Q^{-1} is impractical when the dataset is larege, since it requires quadratic space and cubic pre-computation. Linear correlations exist in many real graph, which means that we can approaximate $\widetilde{Q}$ by low rank approximation and then compute Q^{-1} efficiently. In this paper, eigen-value decomposition is used after partition the whole graph into several commuties. We provide a sketch of our hashtag biased ranking procedure in the format of pseudo code in Table 1 and Table 2.

The input matrix $\widetilde{Q}$ is weighted by TF or TFIDF and normalized by graph Lapalician($\widetilde{Q}=D^{-1/2}Q'D^{-1/2}$) where Q' is the original weighting matrix [27]. The extraction of connected components from an undirected graph is calculated in Step 1 and 2. On the basic initialization of the disjoint-sets structure [2], each node in graph is in its own set. The connected components are calculated based on the edges, so update the disjoint-sets structure when each edge is added into the graph. Readers can refer to [2] for detail. The time complexity for calculating the connected components is only slightly larger than $O(n + |E|)$ where n, i.e., $|W \cup P|$ is the number of nodes and $|E|$ is number of edges in the graph.

Table 1. Hashtag biased graph ranking(Offline Part)

Input: The normalized weighted matrix $\widetilde{Q}$ and the starting vector $\overrightarrow{e_h}$.
Output: The ranking vector $\overrightarrow{r}$.
Offline: Graph Partition and Matrix Decomposition
1. Initializing disjoint-sets structure on word to post undirected graph [2];
2. The k connected components (partitions) are calculated based on the $O(n + |E|)$ edges in the graph.
3. Decompose $\widetilde{Q}$ into two matrices: $\widetilde{Q} = \widetilde{Q_x} + \widetilde{Q_y}$ $\qquad\qquad\qquad\qquad$ $O(|E|)$
4. Let $\widetilde{Q}_{x,i}$ be the ith partition.
5. Compute and store $Q_{x,i}^{-1}=(I - \alpha\widetilde{Q}_{x,i})^{-1}$ for each partition i according $O(2n^3 + 2n^2)$ to Equation 2;
6. Do eigen-value low rank approximation for $\widetilde{Q_y} = USV$ where each $O(2n^3)$ column of U is the eigen-vector of $\widetilde{Q_y}$ and S is a diagonal matrix whose diagonal elements are gigen values of $\widetilde{Q_y}$;
7. Let Q_x^{-1} is a block-diagonal matrix where each block is denoted as $Q_{x,i}^{-1}$;
8. Compute and store $\widetilde{\Lambda} = (S^{-1} - \alpha V Q_x^{-1} U)^{-1}$; $\qquad\qquad\qquad$ $O(6n^3 + 4n^2)$

Table 2. Hashtag biased graph ranking(Online Part)

Online: Iteration Computation
$\qquad$ Do Loop
9. $\overrightarrow{r}_0 \leftarrow Q_x^{-1}\overrightarrow{e_h}$, do random walk within the partition that contains the $O(2n^2)$ starting point $\overrightarrow{e_h}$;
10. $\overrightarrow{r} \leftarrow V\overrightarrow{r}_0$, jump from word-post space to latent space V; $\qquad\qquad$ $O(2n^2)$
11. $\overrightarrow{r} \leftarrow \widetilde{\Lambda}\overrightarrow{r}$, do random walk within the latent space $\widetilde{\Lambda}$; $\qquad\qquad$ $O(2n^2)$
12. $\overrightarrow{r} \leftarrow U\overrightarrow{r}$, jump back to word-post space U; $\qquad\qquad\qquad$ $O(2n^2)$
13. $\overrightarrow{r} \leftarrow Q_x^{-1}\overrightarrow{r}$, do random walk within each partition; $\qquad\qquad$ $O(2n^2)$
14. $\overrightarrow{r} \leftarrow (1 - \alpha)(\overrightarrow{r}_0 + \alpha\overrightarrow{r})$; $\qquad\qquad\qquad\qquad\qquad$ $O(3n + 1)$
$\qquad$ Until convergence
15. Quicksort the elements in $\overrightarrow{r}$ BY ASCENT; $\qquad\qquad\qquad$ $O(n\log n)$

Step 3 decomposes $\widetilde{Q}$ into two matrices: $\widetilde{Q} = \widetilde{Q_x} + \widetilde{Q_y}$ according to the connected components, where $\widetilde{Q_x}$ contains all within-paritition links and $\widetilde{Q_y}$ contains all cross-partition links. The time complexity of Step 3 is $O(|E|)$ depending on the number of edges in the graph [7]. Step 4 and 5 do matrix compuation for each partition in $\widetilde{Q_x}$ based on Equation 2. The time complexity of matrix muliplication and matrix substraction, i.e., $I - \alpha \widetilde{Q}_{x,i}$ is $O(2n^2)$ and its invert matrix computation needs $O(2n^3)$.

Step 6 and 7 do low rank approximation for $\widetilde{Q_y}$ for computation preparation of Q^{-1} in Equation 2. Step 8 is a key process to compute Q^{-1} by combing $\widetilde{Q_x}$ and $\widetilde{Q_y}$. As dicussed in [16], it is the most time-consuming step with the time complexity $O(6n^3 + 4n^2)$. The following proof gives computation details of Q^{-1}. According to Step 3, we have:

$$\widetilde{Q} = \widetilde{Q_x} + \widetilde{Q_y} = \widetilde{Q_x} + USV \tag{3}$$

Then the inverse matrix in Equation 2 is computed as:

$$
\begin{aligned}
Q^{-1} &= (I - \alpha \widetilde{Q})^{-1} \\
&= (I - \alpha \widetilde{Q_x} - \alpha USV)^{-1} \\
&= Q_x^{-1} + \alpha Q_x^{-1} U \widetilde{\Lambda} V Q_x^{-1}
\end{aligned} \tag{4}
$$

where

$$
\begin{aligned}
X &= (I - \alpha \widetilde{Q_x})^{-1} = Q_x^{-1} \\
(X - USV)^{-1} &= X^{-1} + X^{-1} U \widetilde{\Lambda} V X^{-1} \\
\widetilde{\Lambda} &= (S^{-1} - V X^{-1} U)^{-1}
\end{aligned}
$$

Based on Equation 2, Step 9 to 14 in online phase $\widetilde{r}$ is computed step by step, represented as:

$$\widetilde{r} = (1 - \alpha)(Q_x^{-1} \overrightarrow{e_h} + \alpha Q_x^{-1} U \widetilde{\Lambda} V Q_x^{-1} \overrightarrow{e_h}). \tag{5}$$

It can be seen that the approximation of our algorithm comes from the low rank decomposion for $\widetilde{Q_y}$. Our experiments show the online computation is very fast compared to the offline computation. In addition, users can select some words as the starting vector $\overrightarrow{e_h}$ to extract keywords related to it online. In this paper, we set the starting vector consisiting of hashtag words in microblog posts since hashtag intrinsically represents the key topics of a post. It will help us find good important keywords, which is verified by our experimental results.

4   Experiments

4.1   Dataset and Evaluation

The data used in our paper was crawled from Sina Weibo [1] from the end of March 2012 to the end of June 2012. There were 74662 microblog posts in total.

---

[1] http://www.weibo.com, one of most popular microblogging platform in China.

They were posted in 14 IT/technology related topics discussion groups. We segmented these mircoblog posts, filtered stop words, and finally got 13167 distinct words. After that, we computed TF and $TFIDF$ scores of those words and build different graphs for each discussion group. The precision score at the top K keywords of a discussion group is defined as:

$$Precision@K = \frac{\#important\ keywords}{K}. \tag{6}$$

The measure $Precision@K$ means how many good important keywords our algorithm gives at the top K list. We set K=5 and 10 in our evaluation. The average precision score of 14 topic discussion groups is reported.

We treat each topic group as a collection of posts where hashtags are topic related. Our target is to identify top K important keywords from each group. Whether a keyword is important or not in a group is judged by our three lab members. When we take the extracted top K representative keywords, the three lab memebers manually judge whether these keywords can be considered to accurately reflect the meaning of its post. The precision values of all 14 topics are computed and its average score by three members is reported in our experiments. In addition, for each word ranking list generated by different graphs, we remove the hashtag words from it. Since hashtag words are clearly important in these posts, we want to get other important keywords that should be more interesting to users.

4.2   Experimental Results and Discussions

We will compare the effectiveness of a set of ranking approaches with our approach according to three apsects, i.e., node types, jumping strategies and weighting strategies. The ranking approaches are listed as follow.

1. **WW-OC-A:** This approach builds **word to word** graph weighted by **co-occurences** and jumps to **any** nodes in the graph. It is widely used in recent works [10, 13, 25].
2. **WP-TF-A:** This is a **word to post** graph based ranking. The graph is weighted by **TF** and a random walker jumps to **any** nodes including word and post nodes. It is a variant and weighted verison proposed in [16].
3. **WP-TF-W:** This is a **word to post** graph based ranking. The graph is weighted by **TF** and a random walker jumps to any of **word** nodes. It is also a variant and weighted verison proposed in [16].
4. **WP-TF-H:** This is our proposed **word to post** graph based ranking. The graph is weighted by **TF** and a random walker jumps to any of **hashtag** word nodes.
5. **WP-TI-A:** This is a **word to post** graph based ranking. The graph is weighted by **TFIDF** and a random walker jumps to **any** nodes including word and post nodes.
6. **WP-TI-W:**This is a **word to post** graph based ranking. The graph is weighted by **TFIDF** and a random walker jumps to any of **word** nodes.

Table 3. The average precision scores of 14 discussion groups

	Precision@5	Precision@10
WW-OC-A	0.3857	0.3357
WP-TF-A	0.3429	0.4286
WP-TF-W	0.3571	0.4357
WP-TF-H	**0.6**	**0.5429**
WP-TI-A	0.4714	0.4571
WP-TI-W	0.4714	0.5143
WP-TI-H	**0.7571**	**0.6786**

7. **WP-TI-H:** This is our proposed **word to post graph** based ranking. The graph is weighted by **TFIDF** and a random walker jumps to any of **hashtag** word nodes.

Comparisons among Node Types. The overall experimental results are show in Table 3. The highest precison scores are achieved by our proposed hashtag biased ranking in both of Precision@5 and Precision@10. The nodes in the baseline WW-OC-A are only words and those in our proposed word to post graph are both of words and posts. We compare WW-OC-A with our proposed word to post graph (the last six rows in Table 3). In terms of Precision@10, our word to post graph based ranking shows higher scores than the word to word graph based ranking. The best one is our hashtag biased ranking by only jumping to hashtag words and its precision scores are **0.5429** using TF weighting and **0.6786** using TFIDF weighting. In terms of Precision@5, our word to post graphs win the word to word graph in most cases. Especially, our hash biased ranking shows much bettern results than the baseline, i.e., **0.6** VS. **0.3857**, **0.7571** VS. **0.3857**. These results tell us that the word to post graph takes into account the quality of posts in ranking, which can improve the quaity of keyword extraction. In other words, important keywords come from important posts with high probability.

Comparisons among Jumping Strategyies. Moreover, hashtag is natually existed in some posts and it highlights their topic. As defined in Equation 1, our proposed word to post graph with hashtag biased random walk produces keywords closely related to hashtag words, i.e., $\overrightarrow{e_h}$. We compare it with two other jumping strategies. One is jumping to any nodes in the word to post graph and the other is jumping to any word nodes. As shown in Figure 2, the last columns are produced by our hashtag biased jumping strategies, i.e., WP-TF-H and WP-TI-H. We can see that our hashtag biased jumping is much better than the two jumping strategies in both Precision@5 and Precision@10. Its improvements are **60.6%** and **48.46** compared with WP-TF-A and WP-TI-A which jump to any nodes in the word to post graph. Also its precision scores are higher than WP-TF-W and WP-TI-W which jump to any word nodes in the word to post graph. Users in a microblogging flatform publish posts and like to use hashtag to attract other users' attention. The user-generated hastag is a useful evidence

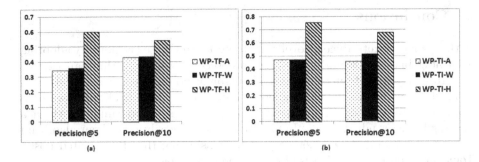

Fig. 2. Comparisons among different jumping strategies

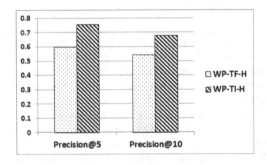

Fig. 3. Comparisons among different weighting strategies

to clearly tell us that those posts are topically related to it. Random walk in our word to post graph with hashtag biased jumping lets our ranking algorithm put more hashtag related keywords in the top ranking list.

Comparisons among Weighting Strategies. Last, our word to post graph can be weighted by TF or TFIDF which are commonly used in the field of Information Retrieval (IR). We investigate the influences of the two weighting stratgies on keyword extraction. To make it clear, we show the results of our hashtag biased random walk approaches, i.e., WP-TF-H and WP-TI-H, as shown in Figure 3. The left column is TFIDF wieghting and the right column is TF weighting at each precision measure. It is obvious that TFIDF weighting is much better than TF in both of Precision@5 and Precision@10. For example, using word to post graph with hashtag biased jumping, TFIDF produces **0.7571** and the score of TF is **0.6**. The improvement is **26.18%** in term of Precision@5 and it is **25%** in term of Precision@10. The results are consistent with the viewpoint of IR. TFIDF gives less weights on words with high document (post) frequency. In other words, the extracted keywords should be representative and infomative in a post, not commonly appeared in other posts.

5   Conclusions

In this paper, we introduce a novel word to post graph based ranking by adopting a hashtag biased random walk. The proposed ranking algorithm can extract important keywords from a collection of microblog posts. The experimental reults show that our algorithm has higher precision scores that traditional word to word graph based ranking and the word to post graph based ranking without a hashtag biased randwom walk. In the future, we can easily extend our algorithm to extract keywords from a single post by considering the other related posts. Topic space based weighting is also an interesting topic.

References

1. Bi, B., Tian, Y., Sismanis, Y., Balmin, A., Cho, J.: Scalable topic-specific influence analysis on microblogs. In: Proceedings of the 7th ACM International Conference on Web Search and Data Mining, WSDM 2014, pp. 513–522. ACM (2014)
2. Cormen, T.H., Leiserson, C.E., Rivest, R.L., Stein, C.: Introduction to Algorithms. McGraw-Hill (1990)
3. Grineva, M., Grinev, M., Lizorkin, D.: Extracting key terms from noisy and multi-theme documents. In: Proceedings of the 18th International Conference on World Wide Web, WWW 2009, pp. 661–670. ACM (2009)
4. Haveliwala, T.H.: Topic-sensitive pagerank: A context-sensitive ranking algorithm for web search. IEEE Trans. on Knowl. and Data Eng. **15**(4), 784–796 (2003)
5. Hu, X., Tang, J., Liu, H.: Leveraging knowledge across media for spammer detection in microblogging. In: Proceedings of the 37th International ACM SIGIR Conference on Research and Development in Information Retrieval, SIGIR 2014, pp. 547–556. ACM (2014)
6. Hulth, A.: Improved automatic keyword extraction given more linguistic knowledge. In: Proceedings of the 2003 Conference on Empirical Methods in Natural Language Processing, EMNLP 2003, pp. 216–223 (2003)
7. Karypis, G., Kumar, V.: Multilevel k-way partitioning scheme for irregular graphs. J. Parallel Distrib. Comput. **48**(1), 96–129 (1998)
8. Kwak, H., Lee, C., Park, H., Moon, S.: What is twitter, a social network or a news media? In: Proceedings of the 19th International Conference on World Wide Web, WWW 2010, pp. 591–600. ACM, New York (2010)
9. Li, Z., Zhou, D., Juan, Y.-F., Han, J.: Keyword extraction for social snippets. In: Proceedings of the 19th International Conference on World Wide Web, WWW 2010, pp. 1143–1144. ACM (2010)
10. Liu, Z., Huang, W., Zheng, Y., Sun, M.: Automatic keyphrase extraction via topic decomposition. In: Proceedings of the 2010 Conference on Empirical Methods in Natural Language Processing, EMNLP 2010, pp. 366–376. Association for Computational Linguistics, Stroudsburg (2010)
11. Liu, Z., Li, P., Zheng, Y., Sun, M.: Clustering to find exemplar terms for keyphrase extraction. In: Proceedings of the 2009 Conference on Empirical Methods in Natural Language Processing, EMNLP 2009, vol. 1, pp. 257–266. Association for Computational Linguistics (2009)
12. Manning, C.D., Raghavan, P., Schutze, H.: Introduction to information retrieval (2008)

13. Mihalcea, R., Tarau, P.: Textrank: bringing order into texts. In: Lin, D., Wu, D. (eds.), Proceedings of EMNLP 2004, pp. 404–411. Association for Computational Linguistics 2004

14. Page, L., Brin, S., Motwani, R., Winograd, T.: The pagerank citation ranking: Bringing order to the web. Technical report, Stanford Digital Library Technologies Project (1998)

15. Qiang, R., Liang, F., Yang, J.: Exploiting ranking factorization machines for microblog retrieval. In: Proceedings of the 22nd ACM international conference on Conference on Information and knowledge management, CIKM 2013, pp. 1783–1788. ACM (2013)

16. Tong, H., Faloutsos, C., Pan, J.-Y.: Fast random walk with restart and its applications. In Proceedings of the Sixth International Conference on Data Mining, ICDM 2006, pp. 613–622. IEEE Computer Society (2006)

17. Turney, P.D.: Learning algorithms for keyphrase extraction. Inf. Retr. **2**(4), 303–336 (2000)

18. Vosecky, J., Leung, K.W.-T., Ng, W.: Collaborative personalized twitter search with topic-language models. In: Proceedings of the 37th International ACM SIGIR Conference on Research and Development in Information Retrieval, SIGIR 2014, pp. 53–62. ACM (2014)

19. Wan, X., Xiao, J.: Single document keyphrase extraction using neighborhood knowledge. In: Proceedings of the 23rd National Conference on Artificial Intelligence, AAAI 2008, vol. 2, pp. 855–860. AAAI Press (2008)

20. Wang, J., Liu, J., Wang, C.: Keyword extraction based on pagerank. In: Li, H., Yang, Q., Zhou, Z.-H. (eds.) PAKDD 2007. LNCS (LNAI), vol. 4426, pp. 857–864. Springer, Heidelberg (2007)

21. Wang, W., Xu, H., Yang, W., Huang, X.: Constrained-hLDA for topic discovery in Chinese Microblogs. In: Ho, T.B., Zhou, Z.-H., Chen, A.L.P., Kao, H.-Y., Tseng, V.S. (eds.) PAKDD 2014, Part II. LNCS, vol. 8444, pp. 608–619. Springer, Heidelberg (2014)

22. Wang, X., Wang, L., Li, J., Li, S.: Exploring simultaneous keyword and key sentence extraction: Improve graph-based ranking using wikipedia. In: Proceedings of the 21st ACM International Conference on Information and Knowledge Management, CIKM 2012, pp. 2619–2622. ACM (2012)

23. Wu, W., Zhang, B., Ostendorf, M.: Automatic generation of personalized annotation tags for twitter users. In Human Language Technologies: The 2010 Annual Conference of the North American Chapter of the Association for Computational Linguistics, HLT 2010, pp. 689–692 (2010)

24. Zhang, W., Feng, W., Wang, J.: Integrating semantic relatedness and words' intrinsic features for keyword extraction. In: Proceedings of the Twenty-Third International Joint Conference on Artificial Intelligence, IJCAI 2013, pp. 2225–2231. AAAI Press (2013)

25. Zhao, W.X., Jiang, J., He, J., Song, Y., Achananuparp, P., Lim, E.-P., Li, X.: Topical keyphrase extraction from twitter. In: Proceedings of the 49th Annual Meeting of the Association for Computational Linguistics: Human Language Technologies, HLT 2011, vol.1, pp. 379–388 (2011)

26. Zhiyuan, L., Xinxiong, C., Maosong, S.: Mining the interests of chinese microbloggers via keyword extraction. Foundations and Trends in Information Retrieval **6**(1), 76–87 (2012)

27. Zhou, D., Bousquet, O., Lal, T.N., Weston, J., Schlkopf, B.: Learning with local and global consistency. In: Advances in Neural Information Processing Systems 16, pp. 321–328. MIT Press (2004)

Semi-supervised Microblog Clustering Method via Dual Constraints

Huifang Ma[1,2(✉)], Meihuizi Jia[1], Weizhong Zhao[3], and Xianghong Lin[1]

[1] College of Computer Science and Engineering, Northwest Normal University,
Lanzhou Gansu 730070, China
[2] Key Laboratory of Intelligent Information Processing of Chinese Academy of Sciences,
Institute of Computing Technology, Chinese Academy of Sciences, Beijing 10085, China
mahuifang@yeah.net
[3] College of Information Engineering, Xiangtan University, Xiangtan Hunan 411105, China

Abstract. In this paper, we present a semi-supervised clustering method for microblog in which both word-level and microblog (document)-level constraints are automatically generated totally based on statistical information rather than any kind of external knowledge. The key idea is first to explore term correlation data, which investigates both inter and intra correlation of words, and the initial similarity between words can therefore be deduced. And then an iterative method is established to calculate both word similarity and microblog similarity. The mechanism of incorporating dual constraints is presented based on word similarity and microblog similarity. We then formulate short text clustering problem as a non-negative matrix factorization based on dual constraints. Empirical study of two real-world dataset shows the superior performance of our framework in handling noisy and microblogs.

Keywords: Semi-supervised clustering · Microblogs · Term correlation matrix · Dual constraints · Nonnegative Matrix Factorization

1 Introduction

Nowadays, much more short texts appears in the internet, such as snippets in search results, tweets, status updates, comments, and reviews from various social platforms. These texts are in general much shorter, nosier, and sparser, therefore many traditional text clustering techniques cannot be directly applied to these short texts. The classical text representation vector space model[10] neither captures dependencies between related words, nor handles synonyms or polysemous words. Besides, as short text is a small piece of text that consists of only a few sentences, it will suffer from in sufficient word occurrences and severe sparsity.

Non-negative Matrix Factorization (NMF)[5]is a well-known clustering learning paradigm, which is later been extended for semi-supervised document clustering problems in which two different view for both word and document are available. However, experiments on short texts such as microblogs, Q&A documents and news titles, suggest unsatisfactory performance of NMF[12]. Most existing approaches for

© Springer International Publishing Switzerland 2015
S. Zhang et al. (Eds.): KSEM 2015, LNAI 9403, pp. 360–369, 2015.
DOI: 10.1007/978-3-319-25159-2_33

microblog clustering try to enrich the representation of a short text using additional semantics [2]. Besides, some researchers[1] introduce semi-supervised priors and explore the effects on accuracy of clustering.

Nevertheless, microblog always lack label information and it is time and labor consuming to label the huge amounts of messages. Therefore, it is useful to develop a mechanism to automatically get informative knowledge to improve the clustering performance. Ma et al.[7] take advantage of term correlation to enrich the semantics of microblog internally and incorporate word-level constraints into the NMF framework. In this paper, we have extended this work into a new semi-supervised clustering algorithm in which both word and document correlations are investigated. The inter and intra relationship of words are computed, and the initial similarity between words cantherefore be deduced. An iterative algorithm is presented to calculate both word similarity and microblog similarity. The prior knowledge in the word space can then be represented as word clusters while the microblog-level constraints is encoded as a set of pair-wise relations. NMF framework embedded with dual constraints is used to obtain the final clustering results. This extended NMF approach can enhance the clustering results for microblogs by introducing word and document correlations.

The contribution of this paper is non-trivial in that we put forward a solution of automatically investigating prior knowledge and present a systematic way to seamlessly integrate both word-level and document-level information for microblog semi-supervised clustering. This is the first time of establishing merely statistical information for short text clustering as far as we know.

The basic outline of this paper is as follows: Section 2 presents details of our approach. The experiments and results are given in Section 3. Lastly, we conclude our paper in Section 4.

2   Our Approach

In this section, we first introduce mechanism for term correlation computation, which provides an initial reflection of the inherent semantic association between terms and discuss how to iteratively compute word and microblog similarities. And then a mechanism for generation of both word-level and microblog-level constraints are established, by which these constraints are encoded into NMF framework. Finally, update rules are derived and the corresponding algorithm is illustrated. Figure 1 shows the general framework of our approach.

Phrase 1. Preprocessing of microblog messages. A microblog dictionary containing all the abbreviate forms of words is constructed to deal with some misspelled and informal expressions in microblogs. The informal words are detected and then corrected first. The conservative approach is then taken to word segmentation, splitting on whitespaces and punctuation mark. All terms that occur in the 'stop word list' are removed.

Phrase 2. Generation of Prior Knowledge. Two kinds of prior knowledge are provided. We have developed a new mechanism which utilizes internal word co-occurrence and context shared information of microblogs for generating the above prior knowledge.

Phrase 3. Construction for dual-constraints based on NMF. In order to fully integrate the prior knowledge into NMF framework, we have proposed a semi-supervised model based on dual constraints.

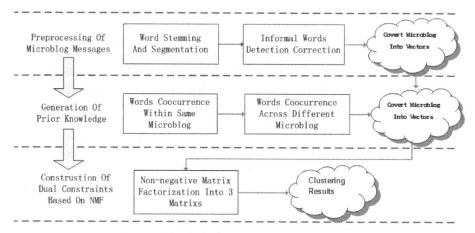

Fig. 1. The General Framework

2.1   Establishment of the Initial Similarity Between Words

Estimating the relation between terms takes advantage of co-occurrence information, which is based on the assumption that two terms are similar if they frequently co-occur in the same document. A term can then be represented by a term co-occurrence vector. We consider both the co-occurrence and dependency of terms to capture the underlying relationship between terms[3]. The co-occurrence of two terms is quantified by using positive point mutual information (PPMI) while the dependency of terms can be formalized by their interaction with all the link terms.

The weight of co-occurrence between two terms in a document can be defined as:

$$W_{ij} = PPMI(t_i, t_j) = \max(\log \frac{P(t_i, t_j)}{P(t_i)P(t_j)}, 0) \tag{1}$$

Probabilities $P(x)$ and $P(x,y)$ are estimated by counting the number of observations of x and co-occurrence of x and y in a corpus respectively, and normalizing by the size of the corpus,

$$P(t_i, t_j) = \frac{n(t_i, t_j)}{\sum_{kl} n(t_k, t_l)}, \; P(t_i) = \frac{\sum_j n(t_i, t_j)}{\sum_{kl} n(t_k, t_l)} \tag{2}$$

In order to define the direct dependency weight between ti and tj, which is referred as D-Dep(ti, tj), each term is represented by the a term co-occurrence vector, ti(wi1, wi2,.... win). We then apply the common vector-similarity measures, like cosine coefficient, to compute the $D\text{-}Dep(t_i, t_j)$ between any two terms as:

$$D-Dep(t_i, t_j) = Sim\ (t_i, t_j) \tag{3}$$

We then define the indirect dependency between two terms t_i and t_j by their interaction with the link term t_k as:

$$I - Dep(t_i, t_j | k) = min\ (D - Dep(t_i, t_k), D - Dep(t_j, t_k)) \tag{4}$$

The indirect dependency between two terms t_i and t_j is then defined by their interaction with all the link terms, formalized as:

$$I - Dep(t_i, t_j) = \sum_k Dep(t_i, t_j | t_k) \tag{5}$$

Given terms t_i and t_j in D, the initial similarity between t_i and t_j is defined as:

$$Sim(t_i, t_j) = \begin{cases} 1 & i = j \\ \alpha * D - Dep(t_i, t_j) + (1-\alpha) * I - Dep(t_i, t_j) & otherwise. \end{cases} \tag{6}$$

2.2   Iterative Calculation of Word Similarity and Microblog Similarity

The assumption underlying our approach is that the frequency (or weight) of each word, i.e., its relative importance to a certain document, is distributed among their synonyms. Therefore, the similarities between two microblog is not only determined by words, but also reinforced by its own representation. The reinforcement is of iterative nature, which means two texts should have a great probability to be similar, if it has strong correlations with similar words, and vice versa. An iterative method[6] is used to compute the similarity between microblogs and the similarity between words based on each other. The similarity between d1 and d2 is thus defined as:

$$sim(d_1, d_2) = \sum_{k=1}^{N} [(\sum_{j=1}^{N} tf_{1j} P_{jk})(\sum_{j=1}^{N} tf_{2j} P_{jk})] \tag{7}$$

where N is the number of terms, tf_{1j} and tf_{2j} denotes term frequency of different terms.

Likewise, based on the similarity between microblog snippets, the similarity between two words w_1 and w_2 can be re-defined as:

$$sim(w_1, w_2) = \sum_{k=1}^{M} [(\sum_{j=1}^{M} tf_{1j} T_{jk})(\sum_{j=1}^{M} tf_{2j} T_{jk})] \tag{8}$$

where $P_{jk} = \dfrac{sim(w_j, w_k)}{\sqrt{\sum_{l=1}^{N} sim(w_j, w_l)^2}}$ $T_{ik} = \dfrac{sim(d_i, d_k)}{\sqrt{\sum_{l=1}^{M} sim(d_i, d_l)^2}}$.

The weights are averaged by using the matrix before calculating the similarity by cosine measurement to make the vectors of the two microblog snippets share more non-zero elements. S_{jk} is derived from the similarity between words, whereas T_{ik} is derived from the similarity between documents. The similarity between text snippets and the similarity between words can then be calculated using the following iterative algorithm. The iterative functions are defined as follows:

$$sim^l(d_1,d_2) = (1-\beta)sim^{l-1}(d_1,d_2) + \beta\sum_{k=1}^{N}[(\sum_{j=1}^{N}tf_{1j}P_{jk})^{l-1}(\sum_{j=1}^{N}tf_{2j}P_{jk})^{l-1}] \tag{9}$$

$$sim^l(w_1,w_2) = (1-\beta)sim^l(w_1,w_2) + \beta\sum_{k=1}^{M}[(\sum_{j=1}^{M}tf_{1j}T_{jk})^{l-1}(\sum_{j=1}^{M}tf_{2j}T_{jk})^{l-1}] \tag{10}$$

Theoretically, the convergence of similarities using Eqs. (9) and (10) cannot be guaranteed. Thus, in order to guarantee convergence of the iterative algorithm, we decrease β by 20% after each iteration to accelerate the iterative procedure.

When $sim(d_i, d_j)$ is beyond a certain predefined threshold β_1, the two documents are considered to be in the same cluster. Likewise, when it below a predefined threshold β_2, they would be decided to be in two different clusters. Likewise, when $sim(w_i, w_j)$ is beyond a certain predefined threshold β_1, the two word are considered to be in the same cluster.

2.3   Incorporating Dual Constraints

The model treats the prior knowledge on the word side as categorization of words, represented by a complete specification F_0 for F. We make use of set A_{ml} to denote that *must-link* microblog pairs (d_{i1},d_{j1}) are similar and must be clustered into the same microblog cluster:

$$A_{ml} = \{(i_1;j_1)\,;...;(i_a;j_a)\}; a = |A_{ml}|. \tag{11}$$

Meanwhile, *cannot-link* document pairs are collected into another set:

$$B_{cl} = \{(i_1;j_1);...;(i_b;j_b)\}; b = |B_{cl}| \tag{12}$$

The *must-link* document pairs are then encoded as a symmetric matrix A whose diagonal entries all equal to one and the *cannot-link* pairs as another matrix B. The must-link and not link can be presented as

$$\max_{G} \sum_{(ij)\in A}(G^TG)_{ij} = \sum_{ij}A_{ij}(G^TG)_{ij} = TrGAG^T \tag{13}$$

$$\sum_{(ij)\in B}(G^TG)_{ij} = TrBG^TG = 0, \; or \; \min_{G} TrGBG^T \tag{14}$$

2.4   Algorithm Description

Combining the above constraints together, the objective function of our model is defined as follows[9]:

$$J = \min_{F \geq 0, S \geq 0, G \geq 0} \left\| X - FSG^T \right\|_F^2 + \eta \left\| F - F_0 \right\|_F^2 + Tr(-\gamma_1 GAG^T + \gamma_2 GBG^T) \qquad (15)$$

where X is the word-microblog matrix, G is the cluster indicator matrix for clustering of columns of X and F is the word cluster indicator matrix for clustering of rows of X.

Algorithm 1. The overall procedure of our approach

Input: Word-Microblog matrix X, number of word clusters k_1, number of microblog clusters k_2, word constraint matrix F_0, must-link document pairs A_{ml} and cannot-link document pairs B_{cl} .

Output: F, S, G.

Initialize F, S and G with non-negative values;
Construct *must-link* matrix A_{ml} and *cannot- link* matrix B_{cl};
Iterate for each k_1 and k_2 until convergence

$$F_{ik} = F_{ik} \sqrt{\frac{(XGS^T + \eta F_0)_{ik}}{(FF^T XGS^T + \eta FF^T F_0)_{ik}}}$$

$$S_{ik} = S_{ik} \sqrt{\frac{(F^T XG)_{ik}}{(F^T FSG^T G)_{ik}}}$$

$$G_{ik} = G_{ik} \sqrt{\frac{(S^T F^T X + \gamma_1 AG)_{ik}}{(G(SF^T FS^T + \lambda_2) + \gamma_2 BG)_{ik}}} \quad \textit{where } \lambda_2 \textit{ is Lagrangian multiplier.}$$

The correctness and convergence of our algorithm has already been proved [8].

3   Experiments and Results

In this section, we demonstrate the performance of the model for microblog clustering. The details of our experiments are demonstrated. Firstly, descriptions of data sets and the methodology and evaluation metrics are introduced. And then, experimental results are analyzed.

3.1   Dataset and Performance Metrics

Two large-scale real-world social media datasets (Twitter and Sina weibo) are constructed. For both of these two datasets, we construct a ground truth by selecting 15 topics and 10 topics from Google Trend respectively and retrieve the most relevant microblogs via its APIs. Based on selected trending topics, we obtain a collection of messages and then manually assign each messages into its predefined categories.

After filtering out non-ASCII microblog, some available microblog had been utilized as our data source. Further we partition messages into unigrams and remove the substring "RT @username:" We pre-process each microblog by tokenizing the text into bag-of-words. Then we apply stop-words removing and words stemming. The purpose of such processing is to eliminate terms which do not help in discriminating a cluster. In particular, words that occur in less than ten microblogs are removed.

The statistics of the datasets are presented in Table 1. The selected topics cover a variety of categories including sports, entertainment, music, movies, business, science, politics, education et al. In the experimental evaluations, the selected topics are treated as labels for the microblog messages. Both datasets contain very short texts; each text has, on average, less than 40 words.

Table 1. Statistics of the datasets

Dataset	Number of microblogs	Number of Classes	Vocabulary size	Average terms
Twitter	20312	15	15702	20.3
Sina weibo	15784	10	10310	28.5

3.2   Experimental Results

The experiments include two parts: 1) Comparison with that of 4 other algorithm utilizing a range of popular metrics; 2) The impact analysis on the parameter.

Comparison with that of 4 Other Algorithm

This experiment is designed to examine the overall clustering performance of our model and to compare it with some baseline methods on two datasets. Three popular measures for clustering: purity, Adjusted Rand Index (ARI) and normalized mutual information (NMI) are adopted as performance measures. Our method utilizing dual prior knowledge is denoted as TNMF-DuP (Tri-Factor Nonnegative Matrix Factorization Clustering with Dual Prior knowledge). To demonstrate the effectiveness of our proposed approach, we compare it against the following four state-of-the-art document clustering methods: Constrained-Kmeans[11], Information-Theoretic Co-clustering, which is referred to as IT-Co-clustering[4], TNMF-WP[6] (Tri-Factor Nonnegative Matrix Factorization Clustering with Word Prior knowledge) and TNMF-DP (Tri-Factor Nonnegative Matrix Factorization Clustering with Document Prior knowledge). We vary the parameters α, β_1 and β_2 in each experiment to investigate their impact on clustering performance and show each result with the best performance with the corresponding threshold. The following parameter settings is adopted: $\alpha = 0.6$, $\beta_1 = 0.45$, $\beta_2 = 0.4$ for Twitter and $\alpha = 0.7$, $\beta_1 = 0.52$, $\beta_2 = 0.3$ for SinaWeibo, respectively.

To give these algorithms some advantage, we set the number of clusters equal to the real number of all the document clusters. Figure 2 shows the experimental results on our dataset using purity, ARI and NMI as the performance measure. All the experimental results are obtained by averaging 20 runs.

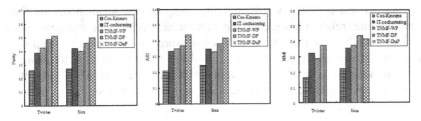

Fig. 2. Purity, ARI, and NMI results on our datasets

It is observed from figure 2 that our approach yields significant improved performance in terms of all evaluation metrics. This demonstrates the robustness of our method to noisy data. This observation also verifies the effectiveness of our method for microblog clustering. We can see that our method can greatly enhance the clustering results by benefitting from the dual prior knowledge. It achieves the highest performance for all evaluation criteria on the dataset. This means that our model is able to generate significantly better results by quickly learning from these constraints.

The Impact Analysis on the Parameter

Because the limitation of this paper, we only discuss parameters α, since it is the most important parameter in our method. It is used to balance the effects of internal and external term correlations. A larger α indicates that more information is preserved from direct co-occurrence while a smaller α means that the indirect co-occurrence within terms mined from external correlation play a dominant role in our model.

In figure 3, purity, ARI, and NMI scores are used to depict the performance of our proposed approach, varying along with the value of parameter α (from 0.1 to 0.9 with increment 0.1) for twitter dataset. We compare the initial word similarity mechanism with that of iterative calculation of word similarity.

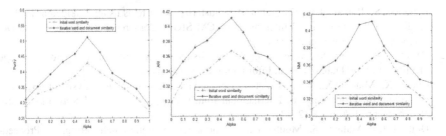

Fig. 3. Purity, ARI, and NMI results with different α for generation of word relations

Figure 3 reveals that the experimental results match favorably with our hypotheses and encourage us to further explore the reasons. First, the performance of our model is greater than that of either model in isolation, indicating that that an optimal performance comes from an appropriate combination of both the intra and inter relation among words. Second, the increase in all judging criteria is robust across a wide range of mixing proportions. Third, the iterative calculation mechanism shows superior performance to that of initial word similarity computation. All demonstrate that on one hand the inter-relation has great impact on the performance of microblog clustering, and on the other, the iterative calculation of word similarity reveals deep semantic information between words. Besides, we observe that the best performance with the different value of α on different evaluation metrics. Therefore, it's essential to optimize the setting of α when the application requires higher clustering accuracy.

4   Conclusions and Future Work

In this paper, we explore the performance of a term correlation based semi-supervised clustering approach for microblog posts. Given the short nature of the posts and no background knowledge source, both intra and inter relations among terms are investigated. And then an iterative calculation mechanism is established to further explore term similarity and document similarity. These semi-supervised priors are then introduced into NMF framework. Our evaluations demonstrated the effectiveness of the proposed method for clustering short texts. Nevertheless, microblogs (and possibly other short texts as well) offer several other priors that we have not yet discussed or explored. Future work aims at finding proper ways of adding different priors.

Acknowledgement. This work is supported by the National Natural Science Foundation of China (No.61363058, 61163039, 61165002), Youth Science and technology support program of Gansu Province(145RJZA232,145RJYA259) and the open fund of Key Laboratory of intelligent information processing Institute of computing technology of Chinese Academy of Sciences (IIP2014-4).

References

1. Banerjee, S., Ramanathan, K., Gupta, A.: Clustering short texts using Wikipedia. In: Proceedings of the 30th Annual International ACM SIGIR Conference on Research and Development in Information Retrieval, pp. 787–788. ACM (2007)
2. Carter, S., Tsagkias, M., Weerkamp, W.: Semi-supervised priors for microblog language identification. In: Dutch-Belgian Information Retrieval Workshop (2011)
3. Cheng, X., Miao, D.X., Wang, C., et al.: Coupled term-term relation analysis for document clustering. In: Proceedings of International Joint Conference on Neural Networks Neural Networks, pp. 1–8. IEEE (2013)
4. Dhillon, I.S., Mallela, S., Modha, D.S.: Information-theoretic co-clustering. In: Proceedings of the 9th ACM SIGKDD International Conference on Knowledge Discovery and Data Mining, pp. 89–98. ACM (2003)
5. Lee, D.D., Seung, H.S.: Algorithms for non-negative matrix factorization. In: Advances in Neural Information Processing Systems, pp. 556–562 (2001)
6. Liu, W.X., Quan, X.J., Feng, M., et al.: A short text modeling method combining semantic and statistical information. Information Sciences **180**(20), 4031–4041 (2010)
7. Ma, H., Jia, M., Shi, Y., Hao, Z.: Semi-supervised nonnegative matrix factorization for microblog clustering based on term correlation. In: Chen, L., Jia, Y., Sellis, T., Liu, G. (eds.) APWeb 2014. LNCS, vol. 8709, pp. 511–516. Springer, Heidelberg (2014)

8. Ma, H.F., Zhao, W.Z., Shi, Z.Z.: A nonnegative matrix factorization framework for semi-supervised document clustering with dual constraints. Knowledge and Information Systems **36**(3), 629–651 (2013)
9. Ma, H., Zhao, W., Tan, Q., Shi, Z.: Orthogonal nonnegative matrix tri-factorization for semi-supervised document co-clustering. In: Zaki, M.J., Yu, J.X., Ravindran, B., Pudi, V. (eds.) PAKDD 2010. LNCS, vol. 6119, pp. 189–200. Springer, Heidelberg (2010)
10. Salton, G., Wong, A., Yang, C.S.: A vector space model for automatic indexing. Communications of the ACM **18**(11), 613–620 (1975)
11. Wagstaff, K., Cardie, C., Rogers, S., et al.: Constrained k-means clustering with background knowledge. In: Proceedings of Eighteenth International Conference on Machine Learning. ICML, pp. 577–584 (2001)
12. Yan, X.H., Guo, J.F., Liu, S.H., et al.: Clustering short text using Ncut-weighted nonnegative matrix factorization. In: Proceedings of the 21st ACM International Conference on Information and Knowledge Management, pp. 2259–2262. ACM (2012)

Exploiting Capacity-Constrained K-Means Clustering for Aspect-Phrase Grouping

Shufeng Xiong[1,2] and Donghong Ji[1]([✉])

[1] School of Computer, Wuhan University, Wuhan, People's Republic of China
{xsf,dhji}@whu.edu.cn
[2] Pingdingshan University, Pingdingshan, People's Republic of China

Abstract. Aspect-phrase clustering is an important task for aspect finding in aspect-level sentiment analysis. Most of existing methods for this problem are based on a context model which aggregates related sentences that contains assigned aspect-phrase as context. In this paper, we explore a novel idea, *capacity limitation*, which states that the number of aggregated sentences in an aspect-phrase group has upper bound. And we propose a capacity constrained K-means algorithm to cluster aspect-phrases which encodes the capacity limitation as constraint. Empirical evaluation shows that the proposed method outperforms existing state-of-the-art methods.

Keywords: Constrained clustering · Aspect grouping · Sentiment analysis

1 Introduction

In recent years, social media (i.e., reviews, forum discussions, blogs and social networks) are playing an increasingly important role as information sources of public opinion, consumers are increasingly using these informations for their decision making. For consumers, it is very helpful to produce a meaningful summary of opinions based on product aspects (also called product feature in the literature). Under this background, aspect-level sentiment analysis has become a central task in sentiment analysis and attracted more and more attentions[3,6,13,14,18,24].

For aspect-level sentiment analysis, it is a necessary step to find aspects from the corpus. However, people can use different words/phrases referring to the same aspect in reviews. In order to understand it more clearly, we introduce two concepts, *aspect* and *aspect-phrase*. An aspect is the name of a feature of the product, while an aspect-phrase is a word or phrase that actually appears in a sentence to indicate the aspect. For example, "picture quality" could have some other expressions such as "photo", "image", "picture". All the aspect-phrases in a group indicate the same aspect. So grouping aspect-phrases is an important necessary work for aspect-level sentiment analysis. In this paper, we assume that

© Springer International Publishing Switzerland 2015
S. Zhang et al. (Eds.): KSEM 2015, LNAI 9403, pp. 370–381, 2015.
DOI: 10.1007/978-3-319-25159-2_34

all aspect-phrases have been identified by the existing extracting methods[6, 7, 9–11, 16], and we focus on grouping domain synonymous aspect-phrases[1].

Existing studies for this problem are mainly based on the assumption that different aspect-phrases of the same aspect should be in the similar context environment [5, 21–24]. The context environment is formed by aggregating related sentences which mention the same aspect-phrase. In addition to the conventional assumption, we address this problem from a new angle, which is based on **capacity limitation** assumption that the number of sentences which have mentioned the same aspect (we called it as aspect capacity) has upper bound. In other word, we argue that the capacity of each aspect should not exceed the upper bound when clustering aspect-phrases. The capacity of each aspect is the sum of all of its aspect-phrases.

---

1. *Glad to own.*
2. *I treat the **battery** well and it has lasted.*
3. *At my heaviest usage, I must recharge after 3 days.*
4. *The **volume** level of the phone is not all that good.*
5. *Some of the higher pitched **rings** are very easy to hear, but not easy to listen to.*
6. *The more subtle **tones** that were included with the phone are hard to hear at times.*
7. *The **vibration** is not top.*
8. *It is a teeny phone, so it is hard to put a big mechanism in.*
9. *Overall this has been my favorite **phone** that I have owned.*
10. *Great **battery life**, perfect **size**, but a tid bit quieter than I would like.*
11. *I do hope that they offer more faceplate options.*
12. *I am bored with the silver **look**.*

Fig. 1. An entire review written by a user. Bold words are the reviewed aspect in a sentence.

Take Fig. 1 as an example, it is an entire review written by a user. She writes twelve sentences (including four sentences which review implicit aspect). Since sentence 5 mentioned aspect-phrase "rings", sentence 6 mentioned aspect-phrase "tones" and sentence 7 mentioned aspect-phrase "vibration", all three aspect-phrases belong to aspect "rings". Therefore, there are three sentences mentioned "battery". Then, the upper bound of capacity for aspect "rings" is three in this review.

This assumption is also verified by our data. The statistics about capacity vs. aspect in *mp3 player dataset* is shown in Fig. 2. There are total twelve aspects that are expressed by Arabic numerals in X-axis. Aspect 3 has the maximum

---

[1] Another type of approach joint extracting and grouping aspect-phrase by using topic models which requests large scale domain corpus, we will discuss it in Section 4.

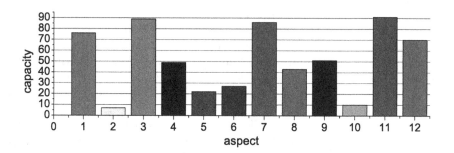

Fig. 2. Capacity statistics of reviews. The total number of sentences is 621. The capacity of the aspect is not more than 92.

capacity, its value is 92. The capacity vary widely, the maximum is 92 and the minimum is 7. Intuitively, those aspects which are concerned by the mainly consumers should be mentioned in more sentences.

Although the capacity has its upper and lower bound, we only consider the upper bound when clustering aspects. Because the cluster number k in algorithm is usually great than or equal to the real cluster number. A real cluster may be divided into two or more sub-clusters. So the capacity of a cluster may be smaller than the lower bound. Take aspect "rings" as an example in Fig. 1, its lower bound is 3. However, "rings" and "tones" may be grouped into cluster x while"vibration" is grouped into cluster y. This partition divide "rings" into two clusters x and y, the lower bound of cluster x and y are smaller than 3. At the same time, if the capacity of one aspect is bigger than its upper bound, that means there are some noise instances in the aspect group. Therefore, the maximum capacity can be used as a prior constraint which prevents noise instance to join a cluster.

In this paper, we propose a capacity constrained K-Means algorithm (called CC-Kmeans) to group aspect-phrases. Firstly, in our framework, we propose a constraint estimation approach which exploits the relationship between sentences and aspect-phrases. Secondly, we develop CC-Kmeans algorithm, which integrates the capacity prior constraint into clustering process, and it guarantees to satisfy capacity constraints in clustering process.

In summary, this paper makes three main contributions:

1. We study the problem of aspect-phrase grouping about integrating both context information and aspect capacity information.
2. We develop a capacity constrained K-Means method which encodes the number of sentences into constraint. This method ensures the purity of the cluster by preventing more noise instances into cluster.
3. Through experiments on four datasets, we demonstrate the effectiveness of our model on aspect-phrase grouping.

2   The Proposed Method

We now proceed with a discussion of our CC-Kmeans algorithm for the aspect-phrase grouping. In this work, we need to solve two problems: 1) To estimate the capacity prior which is used to prevent noise instance into cluster; 2) To provide a mechanism to adjust instances in a cluster when violating capacity constraint. We firstly discuss the estimation of capacity prior, then describe the capacity constrained k-means clustering algorithm.

2.1   Max Capacity Estimation

We have discussed *capacity limitation* in previous section with intuitive examples, in this section, we firstly give a formula description.

Give a reviews dataset R, it contains N reviews $\{r_i\}_{i=1}^{N}$, for each review r_i contains V sentences $\{s_l^i\}_{l=1}^{V}$. There are total T aspect $\{A_h\}_{h=1}^{T}$, an aspect A_h contains Z aspect-phrases $\{ap_j^h\}_{j=1}^{Z}$. In a review r_i, the user talk about U_i aspects. The task for aspect-phrase grouping is to cluster each aspect-phrase ap_j into its appropriate aspect A_h.

Intuitively, most users are interesting in a part of product aspects, and they usually write sentences to review their interested aspects. Take mobile phone reviews as an example, one who travels frequently may concern more about the battery life, the other one who is a music fans may concern more about sound quality. When they choose and review mobile phone, they will probably little or not mention other aspects that they are unconcerned. Based on this analysis, we have $1 < U_i \leq Z$. Suppose there are c_i^h sentences mentioned aspect A_h in review r_i. Because there is at least one sentence for an aspect, there are at least $U_i - 1$ sentences talk about other aspects in reviews r_i. The maximum limit of c_i^h is $s_l^i - U_i + 1$, namely, $c_i^h < s_l^i - U_i + 1$.

For aspect A_h, its capacity C^h in R satisfy the following equation:

$$
\begin{aligned}
C^h &= \sum_i c_i^h \\
&< \sum_i (s_l^i - U_i + 1) \\
&= \sum_i s_l^i - \sum_i U_i + n \\
&\propto \sum_i s_l^i - n * avg(U) + n
\end{aligned}
\tag{1}
$$

where $\sum_i s_l^i$ is the total number of sentences that explicitly mention an aspect in R and $avg(U)$ is the average number of aspects for each review.

For example, if there are total 100 sentences in 10 reviews, and each review mentions an average of 5 aspects, $C^h < 100 - 10 * 5 + n = 60$. Through the above discussion, we have demonstrated aspect capacity has upper bound. Actually, the upper bound will be lower than this estimation. In the following, we discuss how to lower the upper bound.

Since each aspect can be expressed with different aspect-phrases, the aspect capacity must be related with corresponding aspect-phrases. Aspect-phrases can be seen as a group of synonyms which is used to describe corresponding aspect. And yet, each aspect-phrase has different usage rate, the commonly used aspect-phrase may be mentioned more times than other aspect-phrase in reviews. We took *mp3 player reviews* as an example to carry on the statistical of the aspect-phrase capacity for each aspect. For example, the maximum capacity is 30 for aspect "sound" and 17 for aspect "appearance" etc.. In each aspect, the maximum capacity of the commonly used aspect-phrase is much bigger than others. Usually there is a most concerned aspect-phrase in each aspect, whose capacity is the maximum one, such as aspect-phrase "case" in aspect "appearance" whose capacity is 17. Therefore we use the maximum capacity in all aspect-phrases, denoted as M, to estimate the capacity constraint:

$$C = M * \alpha \tag{2}$$

where α is a scale coefficient. In our experiment we set it as 1.2.

2.2   The Capacity-Constrained K-Means Algorithm

Recent research has incorporated background knowledge, such as must-link and cannot-link constraints, into clustering algorithm. In addition, some work has considered balancing constraints, in which each cluster must have the same size. However, little work has been reported on using the capacity constraints for clustering. In our CC-Kmeans algorithm, the constraint is not the size of instances but the sum of capacities of all instances in each group. In other words, we constrain the total capacity in each cluster while balancing constrained algorithm constrains the number of instances.

In the problem of clustering with capacity constraint, it has given the maximum capacity of cluster as prior knowledge. And the preliminary partition result can be obtained by performing traditional K-means. Then the problem is formulated as follows.

Given a instance sets of n instances, for each instance p_i its capacity is C_i^p. Let $G = \{G_1, G_2, ..., G_k\}$ be a partition with k clusters, and G_j contains Z_j instances as $\{p_d^j\}_{d=1}^{Z_j}$. The capacity for cluster G_j denotes as C_j^G, then the capacity constraint is

$$C_j^G = \sum_{d=1}^{Z_j} C_d^p < C \tag{3}$$

For tackling the capacity constrained problem, we propose CC-Kmeans which is a modification to the standard k-means algorithm. CC-Kmeans provides a strategy to resolve conflict when not satisfying constraint. To be precise, there is a precondition that a cluster G_k has reached its capacity, and a new instance p_i is assigned to G_k by standard k-means. For this conflict, CC-Kmeans adjusts cluster-internal instances according to the distances between these instances and cluster center. Therefore the choice of the cluster center in CC-Kmeans is more sensitive than standard k-means.

In CC-Kmeans, we firstly randomly select the initial cluster center from the top $m\%$ instances according to its capacity. This step is under an assumption that the mostly frequent used aspect-phrases are usually coming from different aspects. Although the assumption is not always meet, it is still a well initialization approach and experimental results demonstrate its effectiveness. Secondly, we adjust some instances when occurring conflict like this: 1) Finding all instances whose distance to cluster center is larger than p_i; 2) If the capacity sum of these instances is smaller than C_i^p then move out enough instances and move p_i into cluster, otherwise group p_i to other cluster.

For example, in Fig.3, if grouping p_1 into cluster G_1, the cluster capacity violates constraint. So, it must move out some instances to satisfy the constraint. Since $d_1 < d_4 < d_3 < d_2$, the three instances d_4, d_3 and d_2 are undetermined instance in G_1. Then some undetermined instances will be moved out to free capacity. Because $C_2^p + C_3^p > C_1^p$, by removing p_2 and p_3, it will free enough capacity for populating p_1. Finally, p_1 is moved into cluster, G_1 and p_2 and p_3 are moved out.

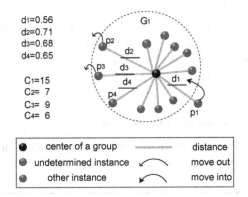

Fig. 3. A demo of Capacity-Constrained K-Means. p_1 is a new coming instance, d_i is the distance to cluster center and C_j is the capacity of each instance.

The algorithm is given in Fig. 1. Since our problem is unsupervised, the same as the existing method about this problem, we assume that the number of clusters k is specified by the user. The routine of our algorithm is similar to that of standard K-Means clustering. The input to CC-Kmeans consists of: the number of clusters k, the capacity constraint C, the factor m and the aspect-phrase instance list O. The output is k clusters. First, the algorithm initializes the center of k clusters from top $m\%$ instances (line 1). Then an iterative process is running for grouping instances until convergence (line 2-14). For each instance that has not assigned to any group, we cluster them under two conditions. If its closest cluster G_i has free capacity for it, then assign to G_i (line 5-7). If satisfying the specified condition, then move out some instance from G_i to free capacity and assign to G_i (line 8-11). Otherwise the distance to G_i is set as infinity (line 13). After those processing, the center of each cluster updates (line 14). Finally, the algorithm returns the clusters set $G = \{G_1, G_2, \cdots, G_k\}$.

Algorithm 1. Capacity-Constrained K-Means

Input:
k: the number of clusters
m: the factor for initial centers
O: the aspect-phrase instance list
C: the capacity constraint
Output: k clusters $G = \{G_1, G_2, \cdots, G_k\}$

1 Select $g_1, g_2, \cdots, g_k$ as the initial cluster centers from top $m\%$ instances;
2 **while** *not satisfy the convergence condition of K-Means* **do**
3   **for** $p_j \in O$ and $A_{p_j} = \emptyset$ **do** /* A_{p_j} denotes the assigned group for p_j */
4   finding the closest cluster G_i to p_j ;
5   **if** $C_i^G + C_j^p < C$ **then**
6   assign p_j to G_i;
7   break ;
8   **else if** *existing a minimize set* $G_i' = \{p_{i1}, p_{i2}, ..., p_{il}\}$ **and** *for each* $p_x \in G_i'$, $d_{p_x} < d_{o_i}$ and $C_i^{G'} > C_j^p$ **then**
9   for each $p_x \in G_i'$, set $A_{p_x} = \emptyset$;
10   assign p_j to G_i;
11   break ;
12   **else**
13   setting the distance of p_i to G_i as ∞ ;
14   For each cluster G_i, update its center by averaging all of the instances p_j that have been assigned to it;
15 **return** G

---

3   Experiments

In this section, we will evaluate our method and compare it with several baselines, and perform parameter tuning.

3.1   Data Preparation

Four product domains of customer reviews from *Customer Review Datasets* (CRD) [6]: digital camera (DC), DVD player, MP3 player (MP3) and cell phone (PHONE) are employed to evaluate our proposed approach. The aspect label of each aspect-phrase is annotated by human curators. The statistics are described in Table 1.

Table 1. Statistics of the review corpus. # donotes the size

Domain	#Sentences	#Aspect-phrases	#Aspect
DC	330	141	14
DVD	247	109	10
MP3	581	183	10
PHONE	231	102	12

3.2 Evaluation Measures

Since the problem of grouping aspect-phrase is a clustering task, four common measures for clustering algorithm are used to performance evaluation: *Purity, Entropy, Normalized Mutual Information and Rand Index.*

Purity: *Purity* is the percentage of correctly clustered point, i.e., a cluster contains only data point from one gold-standard partition.

Entropy: *Entropy* looks at how the various groups of data are distributed within each cluster.

NMI: The *Normalized Mutual Information(NMI)* is defined as the mutual information between the cluster assignments and the gold-standard normalized by the arithmetic mean of the maximum possible entropies of the empirical marginals.

RI: The *Rand Index(RI)* views a clustering of the data as a linkage decision for each pair of data points. A pair is considered correct if the proposed clustering agrees with the target clustering.

Table 2. Comparison of Purity and Entropy with baselines.

	Purity					Entropy				
	DC	DVD	MP3	PHONE	avg	DC	DVD	MP3	PHONE	avg
L-EM	0.392857	0.452528	0.286667	0.376471	0.37713075	2.377254	1.895629	2.603609	2.197380	2.26846800
Kmeans	0.419643	0.413793	0.260000	0.376471	0.36747675	2.049228	2.121276	2.599757	2.323000	2.27331525
CC-Kmeans	**0.461071**	**0.462759**	**0.316667**	**0.413529**	**0.4135065**	**1.913043**	**1.886443**	2.473213	2.062543	**2.0838105**

Table 3. Comparison of NMI and RI with baselines.

	NMI					RI				
	DC	DVD	MP3	PHONE	avg	DC	DVD	MP3	PHONE	avg
L-EM	0.333289	0.403164	0.210720	0.402587	0.33744000	0.730373	0.823518	0.714899	0.781793	0.76264575
Kmeans	0.381871	0.355836	0.193434	0.385966	0.32927675	0.832207	0.810211	0.771633	0.701961	0.77900300
CC-Kmeans	**0.419807**	**0.419813**	**0.233724**	**0.438543**	**0.37797175**	**0.845373**	**0.836140**	**0.791365**	**0.804902**	**0.81944500**

3.3   Baseline Methods and Settings

The proposed **CC-Kmeans** algorithm is compared with a number of existing methods, all of them are context-based models. We list these methods as follows.[2]

L-EM: This is a state-of-the-art unsupervised method for clustering aspect-phrases [22]. L-EM employed lexical knowledge to provide a better initialization for EM.

K-Means: It is the most popular clustering algorithm based on distributional similarity with *cosine* as the similarity measure and TF (Term Frequency) as the feature weight.

Since all methods based on Kmeans depend on the random initiation, we use the average results of 10 runs as the final result. For L-EM, we use the same parameter settings with the original paper.

3.4   Evaluation Results

Now, we present and compare the results of CC-Kmeans and the two baseline methods based on 4 domains. All the results are shown in Table 2, Table 3, **avg** represents the average result of the 4 domains. For *Entropy*, the smaller value is the better, but for *Purity, NMI and RI*, the larger the better. We can see that our approach outperforms baseline methods on the average result of all domains. In addition, we make the following observations:

- Without using any pro-existing knowledge, Kmeans performs poorly, which illustrates that only exploiting the distributional information of aspect-phrase is far from sufficient.
- L-EM gets the middle level results, where it exploits the unfiltered lexical knowledge to provide constraint which may suffer from noisy must-links. At the same time, it initializes group center by using lexical knowledge which improves the results.
- CC-Kmeans produces the optimal results among all models for clustering. It shows the advantages of our proposed capacity constrained method.

3.5   Influence of Parameter

We varied the factor m from 0 to 100 with an interval of 10 to see how it impacts on the performance of the proposed CC-Kmeans method. Take DVD data set as an example, we represent metric results using the percentage of growth compared with K-means, the results are given in Figure 4. When m is set to zero, it means that top k instances are selected. With the growth of m, the selection scope is more and more large, until $m = 100$ which means all of the instances may be selected as initial center (deduced to standard K-means initialization). As shown

---

[2] The topic-model-based method is another state-of-the-art method in which it need a large scale domain auxiliary corpus. Since our target corpus is small, it is unable to make a fair comparison with this kind of method.

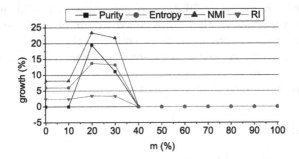

Fig. 4. Influence of the factor m in CC-Kmeans. The growth is based on the result of standard initialization in K-means, 0% means there is no increasement compare with standard initialization.

in Figure 4, the performance of the CC-Kmeans fluctuates up and down and peaks at $m = 20$. This phenomenon explains that assigning a small or large range to select initial center is not efficient, and the better way is to assign a proper range for initial center selection.

4   Related Work

Our work is related to two important research topics: aspect-level sentiment analysis and semi-supervised clustering.

For aspect-level sentiment analysis, there are many studies on clustering aspect-phrases. There are some topic-model-based approaches that works joint extract aspect-phrases and group them at the same time[2, 8, 12, 15, 17, 19, 23, 25]. Those methods tend to discover coarse-grained and grouped aspect-phrases but not specific opinionated aspect-phrase themselves. In addition, [22] showed that it does not perform well even considering pre-existing knowledge. And some other works focus on grouping aspect-phrases. [5] grouped aspect-phrases using multi-level LaSA method which exploited the virtual context documents and semantic structure of aspect-phrase. [21,23] used an EM-based semi-supervised learning method for clustering aspect-phrase in which the lexical knowledge is used to provide a better initialization for EM. [24] proposed a framework of Posterior Regularization to cluster aspect-phrases in which it formalizes sentiment distribution consistency as soft constraint. This method requests a special semi-structured customer reviews to estimate the sentiment distribution. Therefore, our method does not compared with it.

Our work is also related to semi-supervised clustering, which uses constraints in cluster process. First, there are two pair-wise constraints: must-link (ML) and cannot-link (CL). [20] incorporated ML and CL constraints into K-means proposed CopKmeans, in which the constraints are not allowed to violate during the clustering process. [1] exploited a small number of labelled samples to generate initial centroids for K-means. [4,26,27] were considered balanced clustering (can be seen as size constrained), they constrained the number of instance in each cluster with a fixed size. In our method, we constrain the capacity but not size of each cluster, in which the capacity can be seen as weight of an instance. Actually, capacity constraint can be regarded as a combination individual characteristic (weight) and group characteristic (capacity).

5   Conclusion

This paper studies the problem of product aspect-phrase grouping for aspect-level sentiment analysis. For this grouping task, this paper explores a novel concept, capacity limitation. We encode the number of sentences which has mentioned the same aspect as capacity, and then solve the capacity limitation clustering problem in our proposed CC-Kmeans algorithm. Experiments show that our approach is superior to state-of-the-art baselines.

Acknowledgments. This work is supported by the National Natural Science Foundation of China (No. 61173062, 61373108, 61133012), the major program of the National Social Science Foundation of China (No. 11&ZD189), the Youth Scientific researching Fund Projects of Pingdingshan University (No. 2012003) and the High Performance Computing Center of Computer School, Wuhan University.

References

1. Basu, S., Banerjee, A., Mooney, R.: Semi-supervised clustering by seeding. In: Proc. of ICML (2002)
2. Chen, Z., Mukherjee, A., Liu, B., Hsu, M., Castellanos, M., Ghosh, R.: Exploiting domain knowledge in aspect extraction. In: Proc. of EMNLP, pp. 1655–1667. ACL (2013)
3. Fang, L., Huang, M., Zhu, X.: Exploring weakly supervised latent sentiment explanations for aspect-level review analysis. In: Proc. of CIKM, pp. 1057–1066. ACM (2013)
4. Ghosh, A.B.J.: On scaling up balanced clustering algorithms, p. 333. Society for Industrial and Applied Mathematics (2002)
5. Guo, H., Zhu, H., Guo, Z., Zhang, X., Su, Z.: Product feature categorization with multilevel latent semantic association. In: Proc. of CIKM, pp. 1087–1096. ACM (2009)
6. Hu, M., Liu, B.: Mining and summarizing customer reviews. In: Proc. of KDD, pp. 168–177. ACM (2004)
7. Jin, W., Ho, H.H., Srihari, R.K.: Opinionminer: A novel machine learning system for web opinion mining and extraction. In: Proc. of KDD, pp. 1195–1204. ACM, New York (2009)
8. Jo, Y., Oh, A.H.: Aspect and sentiment unification model for online review analysis. In: Proc. of WSDM, pp. 815–824. ACM, New York (2011)

9. Kim, S.M., Hovy, E.: Extracting opinions, opinion holders, and topics expressed in online news media text. In: Proc. of ACL Workshop on Sentiment and Subjectivity in Text, pp. 1–8. Association for Computational Linguistics, Sydney (2006)
10. Kobayashi, N., Inui, K., Matsumoto, Y.: Extracting aspect-evaluation and aspect-of relations in opinion mining. In: Proc. of EMNLP-CoNLL, pp. 1065–1074. Association for Computational Linguistics, Prague (2007)
11. Ku, L.W., Liang, Y.T., Chen, H.H.: Opinion extraction, summarization and tracking in news and blog corpora. In: Proc. of AAAI-CAAW, vol. 100107 (2006)
12. Lin, C., He, Y.: Joint sentiment/topic model for sentiment analysis. In: Proc. of CIKM, pp. 375–384. ACM, Hong Kong (2009), 1646003
13. Liu, B.: Sentiment Analysis And Opinion Mining. Morgan Claypool Publishers (2012)
14. Liu, K., Xu, L., Zhao, J.: Extracting opinion targets and opinion words from online reviews with graph co-ranking. In: Proc. of ACL, pp. 314–324. Association for Computational Linguistics (2014)
15. Lu, B., Ott, M., Cardie, C., Tsou, B.K.: Multi-aspect sentiment analysis with topic models. In: Proc. of ICDMW, pp. 81–88. IEEE (2011)
16. Mei, Q., Ling, X., Wondra, M., Su, H., Zhai, C.: Topic sentiment mixture: Modeling facets and opinions in weblogs. In: Proc. of WWW, pp. 171–180. ACM, New York (2007)
17. Moghaddam, S., Ester, M.: On the design of lda models for aspect-based opinion mining. In: Proc. of CIKM, pp. 803–812. ACM (2012), 2396863
18. Pang, B., Lee, L.: Opinion mining and sentiment analysis. Foundations and Trends in Information Retrieval 2(1–2), 1–135 (2008)
19. Titov, I., Ryan, M.: Modeling online reviews with multi-grain topic models. In: Proc. of WWW, pp. 111–120 (2008)
20. Wagstaff, K., Cardie, C., Rogers, S., Schr O Dl, S.: Constrained k-means clustering with background knowledge. In: Proc. of ICML, pp. 577–584. Morgan Kaufmann Publishers Inc. (2001)
21. Zhai, Z., Liu, B., Xu, H., Jia, P.: Grouping product features using semi-supervised learning with soft-constraints. In: Proc. of COLING, pp. 1272–1280 (2010)
22. Zhai, Z., Liu, B., Xu, H., Jia, P.: Clustering product features for opinion mining. In: Proc. of WSDM, pp. 347–354. ACM (2011), 1935884
23. Zhai, Z., Liu, B., Xu, H., Jia, P.: Constrained lda for grouping product features in opinion mining. In: Proc. of PAKDD, pp. 448–459 (2011)
24. Zhao, L., Huang, M., Chen, H., Cheng, J., Zhu, X.: Clustering aspect-related phrases by leveraging sentiment distribution consistency. In: Proc. of EMNLP, pp. 1614–1623. Association for Computational Linguistics (2014)
25. Zhao, W.X., Jiang, J., Yan, H., Li, X.: Jointly modeling aspects and opinions with a maxent-lda hybrid. In: Proc. of EMNLP, pp. 56–65. Association for Computational Linguistics (2010), 1870664
26. Zhong, S., Ghosh, J.: A unified framework for model-based clustering. J. Mach. Learn. Res. 4, 1001–1037 (2003)
27. Zhu, S., Wang, D., Li, T.: Data clustering with size constraints. Knowledge-Based Systems 23(8), 883–889 (2010)

A Model for Discovering Unpopular Research Interests

Shanshan Feng$^{(\boxtimes)}$, Jian Cao, Yuwen Chen, and Jing Qi

Shanghai Jiao Tong University, Shanghai 200240, China
fswl6869@foxmail.com, cao-jian@sjtu.edu.cn, yuwen.chen@hotmail.com,
qijing9303@gmail.com

Abstract. Traditional topic models illustrate how documents can be modeled as mixtures of topic probability distributions, which provides a simple method for discovering author's research interests from a collection of documents. However, existing topic models such as the simplest author model [1] and the author-topic model (ATM) [2] mainly detect popular research topics and largely neglect unpopular ones. In these models, general topical words are grouped into the shared word distribution of each topic, but the words contained in each author-specific distribution that best describe the authors' research interests are not included. Thus, a novel author-topic model for discovering unpopular research interests (URI-ATM) is proposed, which incorporates a new control variable k that takes on different values when the words belong to different types of research topics. In the model, each topic is associated with two classes of word distributions: one is the popular class among all authors, and the other is the author-specific class from which the document comes. After the URI-ATM is explained, a variety of qualitative and quantitative evaluations are performed. The results demonstrate the advantage of our approach over comparative ones.

Keywords: Probabilistic topic model · Popular topics · Unpopular topics

1 Introduction

Research interests analysis is very useful in many applications such as finding a research partner or tracking hot topics. Fortunately, probabilistic topic models can be used in analyzing research interests, e.g. Multi-label text classification with a mixture model trained by EM (TCM) [1] and ATM. However, in these models, each topic is represented as a probability distribution over words for that topic, which is identical for all authors. Consequently, only popular research interests can be addressed and unpopular ones (e.g. topics researched by just one author) are neglected. This is undesirable in many real-world situations, where authors do not only share interests with others, but also have their special interests. Therefore, we propose a new author-topic model URI-ATM for discovering unpopular research interests, which combines ccMix (A cross-collection mixture

© Springer International Publishing Switzerland 2015
S. Zhang et al. (Eds.): KSEM 2015, LNAI 9403, pp. 382–393, 2015.
DOI: 10.1007/978-3-319-25159-2_35

model for comparative text mining) [3] with ATM. URI-ATM improves ccMix by replacing pLSI (probabilistic latent semantic indexing) [4] framework with ATM. Besides the advantages of ATM over pLSI such as the incorporation of Dirichlet priors, being a natural way to deal with new documents and better extracting authors' interests, our model also avoids the limitations of using a single user-defined parameter.

Unlike previous author models, in URI-ATM, each author is associated with two classes of words: one represents the popular topics, the other represents the unpopular ones. Therefore, URI-ATM not only can capture the common research interests of authors as ATM, but also discover the special research interests of authors, which can describe author preference better and cannot be discovered by all the previous author models. In addition, URI-ATM can be used to support a variety of interactive and exploratory queries on sets of documents and authors, including analysis of which word is unique and which word is shared for each topic and each author, who pays more attention on popular research interests, and who are experts in a special academic domain. In URI-ATM, the topic-word distributions which represent the common research interests and special research interests of authors are learned from data in an unsupervised manner using a Markov chain Monte Carlo algorithm.

The contributions of our work can be summarized as follows:

- We present a new author-topic model for better research interests extraction.
- We devise an inference scheme that can better generalize data and is less reliant on user-defined parameters.
- Experimental results demonstrate that the proposed model can extract important information on popular and unpopular research interests respectively. Additionally, it can achieve higher performance than TCM and ATM.

2   Related Work

Probabilistic topic models have been widely used in many academic domains [5,6], which can be applied to discover author's research interests.

The most basic generative model that assumes document topicality is the standard Naive Bayes model (NBM) [7]. But NBM is often too limited as it is a single-topic approach. A better assumption is that each document is a mixture of topics, probabilistic latent semantic indexing (pLSI) [4] is one of such models.

In pLSI, the probability of seeing the ith word w_i in a document d is:

$$p\left(w_i|d\right) = \sum_{z \in Z} p\left(w_i|z\right) p(z|d) \;, \tag{1}$$

where z denotes a single topic, Z is the set of topics. The main criticism to pLSI is that each document is represented as a variable d and it is not clear how to use it to assign probability to a previously unseen document. Blei et al. addressed this issue by proposing a more general Bayesian model called latent Dirichlet allocation (LDA) [8]. However, LDA has no explicit information about authors, and can not be used to discover the preferences of authors.

TCM is the primary probabilistic topic model, which can be used to detect author's interests. This Bayesian model simultaneously models document content and its authors' interests with a $1-1$ correspondence between topics and authors. However, TCM does not provide any information about document content that goes beyond the words that appear in the document and the authors of the document. Such problems can be resolved by ATM, in which each author is represented by a probability distribution over topics and each topic is represented as a probability distribution over words for that topic. Nevertheless, in ATM, each author is associated with one kind of topics. It doesn't distinguish between popular and unpopular ones for the interests of authors and only focus on the popular research interests, which is undesirable in many real-world situations. Because each author usually has his own research interests while sharing common ones with others. Furthermore, author-specific interest can best describe that authors' interests.

URI-ATM is also inspired by the success of the application of ccMix in information retrieval and text analysis domains. Under the ccMix model, the probability of generating a word in a document belonging to collection c is:

$$p(w) = (1 - \lambda_B) \sum_{z \in Z} p(z) (\lambda_C p(w|z) + (1 - \lambda_C) p(w|z, c)) + \lambda_B p(w|B) , \quad (2)$$

where λ_B is the probability of choosing a word from the background word distribution. λ_C is the probability of drawing a word from the collection-independent word distribution instead of the collection-specific distribution. In ccMix, both λ_B and λ_C are defined by users. The other parameters can be estimated using the Expectation-Maximization algorithm [9].

The proposed model, URI-ATM, drawing upon the strengths of the models described above. It can provide a more comprehensive extraction on research preferences by aditionally considering unpopular research interests. URI-ATM does not require a manually predefined parameter λ_C, which is learned automatically from the data. Furthermore, we allow the probability λ_C to depend on author and topic, which is a less restrictive assumption. Besides, an obvious structural difference between URI-ATM and ccMix is that ccMix has a special topic for background words, whereas we simply address this by removing stop words during preprocessing, which seems to give reasonable performance in this respect. Removing stop words significantly reduces the number of tokens in the data, which leads to shortening the time needed to estimate the model.

URI-ATM shares the same assumption with the LDA Collocation [10] and Topical N-Grams [11] models that each word can come from two different word distributions, one of which depends on another observable variable. The key difference here is that in these models, the alternative word distribution depends on the word preceding a token, while the one in URI-ATM depends on the document's author. The proposed model is also related to the hierarchical Pachinko allocation model (hPAM) [12]. One of the main differences here is that the discovered hierarchies in hPAM can be arbitrary, whereas the graphical structure of URI-ATM is pre-determined such that each topic has exactly one "sub-topic" representing each author. There are many other topic models which are used in computational linguistics, such as predicting response to political webposts [13], analyzing Enron and academic emails [14], analyzing voting records and corresponding text of resolutions from the U.S. Senate and the U.N. [15], as well as studying the history of ideas in various research fields [16,17]. In addition to this, Markov topic model (MTM) [18] can simultaneously learn the topic structure of a single collection while discovering correlated topics in other collections. However, all these existing approaches do not explicitly model the popular research interests and the unpopular research interests as we do in this research.

3   The Model for Discovering Unpopular Research Interests

In this section, we introduce an extension to the ATM for better exploring author's research interests, which is denoted as an author-topic model for discovering unpopular research interests (URI-ATM). URI-ATM belongs to the family of generative text models where words are viewed as discrete random variables, a document contains a fixed number of topics, and each word takes one value from a predefined vocabulary set. The model is similar to ATM, but with a key enhancement of categorizing words into two different kinds of research interests: popular research interests and unpopular ones.

3.1   An Overview of URI-ATM

In URI-ATM, each author is associated with a multinomial distribution over topics, represented by θ. Each topic is associated with two classes of word distributions: one is that shared among all authors, and the other is unique to the author from which the document comes, represented by ϕ and ϑ respectively. The multinomial distributions θ, ϕ and ϑ have corresponding Dirichlet priors with hyperparameters α, β and δ.

When generating a document under URI-ATM, an author a is firstly sampled uniformly from a_d (a_d is the set of authors), then a topic z is sampled from the multinomial distribution θ associated with author a, and a coin k is flipped to determine the word w whether to draw from the popular topic-word distribution ϕ or the topic's author-specific distribution ϑ. This sampling process is repeated N_d times to form document d. The probability of k being 1 or 0 comes from a Bernoulli distribution and depends on the author and the topic of current token.

The generative process is as following:

- Draw an author-independent multinomial word distribution ϕ_z from $Dirichlet(\beta)$ for each topic z.
- Draw an author-specific multinomial word distribution $\vartheta_{z,a}$ from $Dirichlet(\delta)$ for each topic z and each author a.
- Choose an author a and draw a multinomial topic distribution θ_a from $Dirichlet(\alpha)$ for each author a.

- Draw a Bernoulli distribution $\mu_{z,a}$ from $beta(\lambda_0, \lambda_1)$ for each topic z and each author a.
- For each document d, each word ω_i in d.
  - Sample a topic z_i from θ_a.
  - Sample k_i from $\mu_{z,a}$.
  - If $k_i = 0$, sample a popular word ω_i from ϕ_z;
    If $k_i = 1$, sample a unpopular word ω_i from $\vartheta_{z,a}$.

The graphical model corresponding to this process is shown in Fig.1.

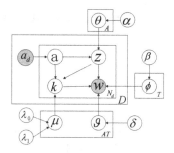

Fig. 1. Graphical representation of URI-ATM. A is the number of authors, T is the number of topics, D is the number of documents, a_d is the set of authors, and N_d is the length of each document d.

3.2   Inference and Parameter Estimation

A variety of algorithms have been used to estimate the parameters of topic models [7,19]. In this paper we utilize Gibbs sampling [19], a type of Markov chain Monte Carlo algorithm.

In some applications, topic models are very sensitive to hyper-parameters, and it is extremely important to set the right values for the hyper-parameters. However, for particular applications discussed in this paper, after trying out many different hyper-parameter settings, we find that the performance sensitivity in respect of hyper-parameter changes is not very strong. Thus, in all the experiments described in this paper we do not estimate the hyper-parameters α, β, δ, λ_0 and λ_1 – instead they are fixed to $50/T$, 0.01, 0.01, 1.0 and 1.0 respectively.

In a Gibbs sampler, one iteratively samples the new assignments of the variables by drawing from the distributions conditioned on the current assignments of all other variables in the model [20]. In each Gibbs sampling iteration we alternately sample new assignments of a, z, and k with the following equations:

$$p\left(a_i | \mathbf{a}_{-i}, \mathbf{z}, \alpha\right) \propto \frac{C_{a_i}^{z_i} + \alpha}{C_{a_i} + T\alpha} \tag{3}$$

$$p\left(z_i|k=0,\mathbf{z}_{-i},\mathbf{w},\mathbf{a},\alpha,\beta\right) \propto \frac{C_{z_i}^{w_i}+\beta}{C_{z_i}+W\beta} \times \frac{C_{a_i}^{z_i}+\alpha}{C_{a_i}+T\alpha} \tag{4}$$

$$p\left(z_i|k=1,\mathbf{z}_{-i},\mathbf{w},\mathbf{a},\alpha,\delta\right) \propto \frac{C_{z_i,a_i}^{w_i}+\delta}{C_{z_i,a_i}+W\delta} \times \frac{C_{a_i}^{z_i}+\alpha}{C_{a_i}+T\alpha} \tag{5}$$

$$p\left(k_i=0|\mathbf{k}_{-i},\mathbf{z},\mathbf{w},\mathbf{a},\lambda,\beta\right) \propto \frac{C_{z_i}^{w_i}+\beta}{C_{z_i}+W\beta} \times \frac{C_{z,a}^{k=0}+\lambda_0}{C_{z,a}+\lambda_0+\lambda_1} \tag{6}$$

$$p\left(k_i=1|\mathbf{k}_{-i},\mathbf{z},\mathbf{w},\mathbf{a},\lambda,\delta\right) \propto \frac{C_{z_i,a_i}^{w_i}+\delta}{C_{z_i,a_i}+W\delta} \times \frac{C_{z,a}^{k=1}+\lambda_1}{C_{z,a}+\lambda_0+\lambda_1} \tag{7}$$

where C_y^x denotes the number of times of topic x has been assigned to y, excluding the assignment of the current token i, C_y denotes the number of times of all topics have been assigned to y, W is the size of the vocabulary set. Because of the conjugacy of the *Beta/Dirichlet* and *binomial/multinomial* distributions, we can integrate out θ, ϕ, ϑ and μ to obtain these equations, a technique known as "collapsed" Gibbs sampling [21]. Meanwhile, k should be initialized as 0 for all tokens that is, we initially assume that everything comes from the popular word distributions, otherwise the author-specific word distributions will be formed independently.

4 Experiments

4.1 The Data

A real-world dataset was collected using Microsoft Academic Search (MAS) API, which includes 5320 authors, 5662 abstracts of documents. We preprocessed this dataset by removing stop words and words appearing less than five times, which yielded a vocabulary set containing 3273 distinct words. Besides, we partitioned the dataset into one subset of 4/5 of the data on which the models are learned and one evaluation set of the remaining 1/5 for all following experiments.

4.2 Learning Different Types of Author-Topics

In this experiment, we try to discover popular topics and unpopular topics by running our model on texts from the real-word dataset. We show some real examples of the experimental results in Table 1. From the table, we can know that **Topic 1** is the common topic which is popular among *Gunnar Ratsch, Pedro Domingos* and *Shie Mannor* etc. **Topic 2** is popular among *Sanda Harabagiu, Barry Smyth* and *Rina Dechter* etc. Meanwhile, all authors have their special research interests. For example, the words such as model, tree, task, depth etc. can describe the special research interest of *Rina Dechter*.

Table 1 demonstrates that URI-ATM does automatically discover meaningful research interests of authors with a satisfying accuracy. The words which are used to describe the popular topics and the unpopular topics are quite intuitive

Table 1. The popular topics and the unpopular topics discovered by URI-ATM

Topic 1: network detect logic error model learn domain algorithm measur stream			Topic 2: web source information knowledge methodology internet bayesian terabyte posterior mobile		
Gunnar Ratsch	*Pedro Domingos*	*Shie Mannor*	*Sanda Harabagiu*	*Barry Smyth*	*Rina Dechter*
classifier	relation	reinforcement	semantic	recommend	model
iteration	feature	empiric	extract	search	tree
linear	markov	weak	scenario	portal	task
boost	combine	consider	topic	feedback	depth
regress	origin	policy	textual	collaboration	algorithm
hypothesis	order	environment	summary	construct	graph
infinite	formula	term	information	preference	constraint
ensemble	uncertainty	achieve	answer	route	translation
margin	constant	repeat	technique	access	exploration
compound	decompose	support	approach	map	framework

and, indeed, quite precise in the sense of conveying the research interests. However, ATM can only detect the popular topics as it assumes that the distribution of words over topics − $p(w|z,a)$ is identical for each user. In contrast, we adopt an independent distribution of $p(w|z,a)$ for each author in URI-ATM, which seems to have reasonable performance in this respect. Because for the same topic **Topic** 1, different authors such as *Gunnar Ratsch* and *Pedro Domingos* who are researching different methods will have different distributions of $p(w|z,a)$.

4.3 Popular and Unpopular Topics for New Documents and Authors

In many applications, we would like to quickly obtain the topics assignments for new documents and authors not contained in the training dataset. Since our Monte Carlo algorithm requires significant processing time for many documents, it would be computationally inefficient to run the algorithm for every new document added to our dataset. Consequently, we impliment the Monte Carlo algorithm [19] that runs only on the word tokens in the new document, leading quickly to likely assignments of words to authors and topics. An example of this type of inference is shown in Fig.2. Five authors and their coauthored abstract. (In fact, this abstract is coauthored by nine authors, but MAS just display five authors).

Fig.2 shows the results after the model has classified each word according to these coauthors. Note that URI-ATM only sees a bag of words and is not aware of the word order that we see in the figure. Blue color (the italic words) shows the words classified by the model for the popular topics and green color (the underlined words) shows the words corresponding to the unpopular topics. The superscripts 1, 2, 3, 4, 5 indicate words classified by the model for *Sanda Harabagiu, Dan Moldovan, Rada Mihalcea, Vasile Rus,* and *Mihai Surdeanu* respectively.

This *paper*[1] *presents*[1] **an** *open*[2]*-domain*[1] textual[1] *Question*[1]*-Answering*[1] *system*[1] **that uses** *several*[1] *feedback*[1]_loops[3] **to** enhance[1] **its** *performance*[1]. **These** *feedback*[1] loops[3] *combine*[1] **in a new** *way*[1] *statistical*[1] *results*[3] **with** *syntactic*[1], semantic[1] **or** pragmatic[1] *information*[1] *derived*[1] **from** *texts*[1] **and** *lexical*[1] *databases*[2]. **The** *paper*[1] *represents*[1] **the** contribution[4] **of each** *feedback*[1] loop[5] **to** **the** overall[1] *performance*[1] **of 76%** *human*[2]*-assessed*[1] *precise*[1] *answers*[1]

Fig. 2. Automated labeling of an abstract from five authors by URI-ATM (Author1= *Sanda Harabagiu*; Author2= *Dan Moldovan*; Author3= *Rada Mihal-cea*; Author4= *Vasile Rus*; Author5= *Mihai Surdeanu*)

We can learn that all of the significant content words are classified correctly. The number of words in blue color is much more than that of the words in green.

4.4   Examples of Topic and Author Distributions

The proposed model can detect the contributions of different authors to partic-ular topics. Figures.3 ((a)-(d)) illustrate four examples of topics' distributions over different authors, which are obtained at the 200*th* iteration of a particular Gibbs sampler run using URI-ATM.

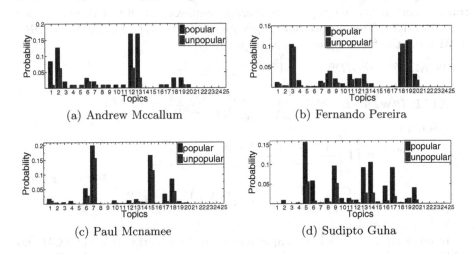

(a) Andrew Mccallum

(b) Fernando Pereira

(c) Paul Mcnamee

(d) Sudipto Guha

Fig. 3. Topics' distributions over different authors

In Fig.3, the blue color indicates the probability of popular words of each topic from the authors, the red color indicates the probability of unpopular words of each topic from the authors. Taking author *Fernando Pereira* and topic 1 as an example, we compute the probability p as:

$$p = \frac{the\ number\ of\ popular/unpopular\ words\ of\ topic1\ from\ Fernando\ Pereira}{the\ total\ number\ of\ popular/unpopular\ words\ of\ topic1}.$$

From the figures, we can learn that these four authors focus on distinct topics and their contributions to popular and unpopular topics are various. We can also find some other interesting differences. For example, the topic distributions corresponding to *Fernando Pereira*, *Sudipto Guha* and *Andrew Mccallum* are more extensive than the distribution corresponding to *Paul Mcnamee*, which shows they contributed on more topics than *Paul Mcnamee* did. Meanwhile, it is very obvious, *Paul Mcnamee* and *Fernando Pereira* are more closely related to unpopular words than *Andrew Mccallum* and *Sudipto Guha* relatively.

4.5   Evaluating the Prediction Power

Perplexity is a standard measure for estimating the performance of a probabilistic model, the lower the perplexity the better the performance of the model. We evaluated URI-ATM in terms of perplexity to demonstrate its ability to predict words on new unseen documents. The perplexity score of a new unseen document d that contains words $\mathbf{w}_d$, and is conditioned on the known authors $\mathbf{a}_d$ of the document, is defined as:

$$Perplexity(\mathbf{w}_d \mid \mathbf{a}_d, D^{train}) = exp\left(-\frac{\log p\left(\mathbf{w}_d \mid \mathbf{a}_d, D^{train}\right)}{N_d}\right) \qquad (8)$$

where N_d is the number of words in the test document, D^{train} is the set of training documents. We report the average perplexity of all test documents for all of the data. Therein, we obtain $p(\mathbf{w}_d|\mathbf{a}_d, D^{train})$ of TCM, ATM and URI-ATM using the following equations respectively:

TCM: $P(\mathbf{w}_d|\mathbf{a}_d, D^{train}) \approx \prod\limits_{i=1}^{N_d} \frac{1}{A_d} \sum\limits_{a \in \mathbf{a}_d} \frac{C_{a_i}^{w_i} + \beta}{C_{a_i} + W\beta}$

ATM: $P(\mathbf{w}_d|\mathbf{a}_d, D^{train}) \approx \prod\limits_{i=1}^{N_d} \frac{1}{A_d} \sum\limits_{a \in \mathbf{a}_d, z} \frac{C_{z_i,a_i}^{w_i} + \beta}{C_{z_i,a_i} + W\beta} \times \frac{C_{a_i}^{z_i} + \alpha}{C_{a_i} + T\alpha}$

URI-ATM:

$$P(\mathbf{w}_d|\mathbf{a}_d, D^{train}) \approx \prod\limits_{i=1}^{N_d} \left[\frac{1}{A_d} \sum\limits_{a \in \mathbf{a}_d, z} \left(\frac{C_{z_i}^{w_i} + \beta}{C_{z_i} + W\beta} \times \frac{C_{z,a}^{k=0} + \lambda_0}{C_{z,a} + \lambda_0 + \lambda_1} + \right. \right.$$
$$\left. \left. \frac{C_{z_i,a_i}^{w_i} + \delta}{C_{z_i,a_i} + W\delta} \times \frac{C_{z,a}^{k=1} + \lambda_1}{C_{z,a} + \lambda_0 + \lambda_1} \right) \times \frac{C_{a_i}^{z_i} + \alpha}{C_{a_i} + T\alpha} \right]$$

where A_d is the author number of document d.

In order to conduct a fair comparison, we test the performance of TCM and ATM by varying the number of topics, and set $T = 20$ for TCM, ATM and URI-ATM in the experiments since both TCM and ATM have their best performances in this case. Fig.4 shows the comparison of three models. Due to the much simpler model structure, TCM has much worse perplexity. We can also learn that all the lower perplexities obtained by URI-ATM with different numbers of topics are not achieved by ATM. It means that URI-ATM can predict words on new unseen documents well. It has significantly better predictive power than ATM over a large number of test documents. The main reason is as follows. In ATM, the distribution of words over topics $-$ $p(w|z,a)$ is uniform, there is no difference among different authors. However, $p(w|z,a)$ should be various for distinct authors in many real situations, because each user usually has his own research interests while sharing common ones with others. ATM can discover who are likely to have authored documents similar to an observed one, and who produces similar work. But it neglects the special aspects of a document or an author, some particular words may be assigned to common topics. In contrast, URI-ATM provides a more comprehensive solution: in addition to the distributions of the common topics, it also takes into consideration the distributions of the special topics. In URI-ATM, $p(w|z,a)$ has an independent distribution for each author. It can more precisely describe the documents' content by discovering both popular and unpopular topics. Therefore, it can be claimed that URI-ATM can yield more appropriate results than ATM in predicting words on new unseen documents, and better than the ATM in other performance metrics.

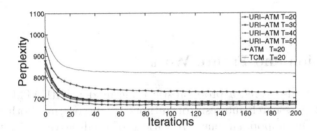

Fig. 4. Perplexity as a function of iterations of the Gibbs sampler

4.6   Document Classification

In this subsection, we describe an illustrative experiment to classify all the documents of the test set with the generative models. We give the comparative result of URI-ATM with TCM and ATM to evaluate the quality of our model. The result is shown in Table 2. For these models, classification of an unlabeled document d thus becomes the problem of choosing the author a that maximizes $p(a|d)$ as the following formulas respectively:

TCM: $p(a|d) \propto p(a) \prod_{w \in d} p(w|a)$

ATM: $p(a|d) \propto p(a) \prod_{w \in d} \sum_z p(z|w)p(w|z,a)$

URI-ATM:
$$p(a|d) \propto p(a) \prod_{w \in d} \sum_z p(z|w) \left[p(k=0|a,z)p(w|z,k=0) + \right.$$
$$\left. p(k=1|a,z)p(w|z,a,k=1) \right]$$

where $p(a) = S_N/D$, S_N is the number of documents coauthored by author a. All probabilities in these equations are obtained when the models are learned from the training set, except for $p(z|w)$, which depends on the new documents, we learn it through another sub-sampling procedure. The result of *recall@m* can effectively check if a model can successfully classify unlabeled documents by comparing the hit rate of the top m authors includes the real author. Hence, we evaluate *recall@m* over all comparative models, when $m = 10, 20, 30...100$. Obviously, as illustrated in Table 2, *recall@m* of URI-ATM are consistently larger than the other two models. Therefore, we can conclude that URI-ATM can better classify the unlabeled documents than TCM and ATM.

Table 2. The recall@ m of comparative models

Recall@ m	10	20	30	40	50	60	70	80	90	100
URI-ATM	0.414	0.484	0.512	0.530	0.566	0.590	0.616	0.638	0.648	0.662
ATM	0.324	0.370	0.404	0.434	0.456	0.490	0.510	0.538	0.560	0.570
TCM	0.262	0.294	0.306	0.328	0.330	0.334	0.340	0.348	0.356	0.360

5   Conclusion and Future Work

In this paper, we described a probabilistic topic model, URI-ATM, which can better extracting research interests of authors by discovering both the popular topics and the unpopular ones. A variety of qualitative and quantitative evaluations of URI-ATM are performed, including perplexity measurements and performance measurements of the model used as a generative classifier. Improvements over previous work are demonstrated. In the future, we may extend our model to be a time-varying one, since the interest of authors is always changing over time.

Acknowledgment. This work is partially supported by China National Science Foundation (Granted Number 61272438, 61472253), Research Funds of Science and Technology Commission of Shanghai Municipality (Granted Number 14511107702, 15411952502).

References

1. McCallum, A.: Multi-label text classification with a mixture model trained by em. In: AAAI 1999 Workshop on Text Learning, pp. 1–7 (1999)
2. Rosen-Zvi, M., Chemudugunta, C., Griffiths, T., Smyth, P., Steyvers, M.: Learning author-topic models from text corpora. ACM Transactions on Information Systems (TOIS) **28**(1), 4 (2010)

3. Zhai, C., Velivelli, A., Yu, B.: A cross-collection mixture model for comparative text mining. In: Proceedings of the Tenth ACM SIGKDD International Conference on Knowledge Discovery and Data Mining, pp. 743–748. ACM (2004)

4. Hofmann, T.: Probabilistic latent semantic indexing. In: Proceedings of the 22nd Annual International ACM SIGIR Conference on Research and Development in Information Retrieval, pp. 50–57. ACM (1999)

5. Grimmer, J.: A bayesian hierarchical topic model for political texts: Measuring expressed agendas in senate press releases. Political Analysis 18(1), 1–35 (2010)

6. Bao, Y., Zhang, H.F.J.: TopicMF: simultaneously exploiting ratings and reviews for recommendation (2014)

7. Mitchell, T.M.: Machine learning and data mining. Communications of the ACM 42(11), 30–36 (1999)

8. Blei, D.M., Ng, A.Y., Jordan, M.I.: Latent dirichlet allocation. The Journal of Machine Learning Research 3, 993–1022 (2003)

9. Dempster, A.P., Laird, N.M., Rubin, D.B.: Maximum likelihood from incomplete data via the EM algorithm. Journal of the Royal Statistical Society. Series B (Methodological), 1–38 (1977)

10. Griffiths, T.L., Steyvers, M., Tenenbaum, J.B.: Topics in semantic representation. Psychological Review 114(2), 211 (2007)

11. Wang, X., McCallum, A., Wei, X.: Topical n-grams: phrase and topic discovery, with an application to information retrieval. In: Seventh IEEE International Conference on Data Mining, ICDM 2007, pp. 697–702 (2007)

12. Mimno, D., Li, W., McCallum, A.: Mixtures of hierarchical topics with pachinko allocation. In: Proceedings of the 24th International Conference on Machine Learning, pp. 633–640. ACM (2007)

13. Yano, T., Cohen, W.W., Smith, N.A.: Predicting response to political blog posts with topic models. In: Proceedings of Human Language Technologies: The 2009 Annual Conference of the North American Chapter of the Association for Computational Linguistics, pp. 477–485. Association for Computational Linguistics (2009)

14. McCallum, A., Wang, X., Corrada-Emmanuel, A.: Topic and role discovery in social networks with experiments on enron and academic email. Journal of Artificial Intelligence Research, 249–272 (2007)

15. McCallum, A., Wang, X., Mohanty, N.: Joint group and topic discovery from relations and text. In: Airoldi, E.M., Xing, E.P., Blei, D.M., Goldenberg, A., Zheng, A.X., Fienberg, S.E. (eds.) ICML 2006. LNCS, vol. 4503, pp. 28–44. Springer, Heidelberg (2007)

16. Hall, D., Jurafsky, D., Manning, C.D.: Studying the history of ideas using topic models. In: Proceedings of the Conference on Empirical Methods in Natural Language Processing, pp. 363–371. Association for Computational Linguistics (2008)

17. Paul, M.J., Girju, R.: Topic modeling of research fields: an interdisciplinary perspective. In: RANLP, pp. 337–342 (2009)

18. Wang, C., Thiesson, B., Meek, C., Blei, D.M.: Markov topic models. In: International Conference on Artificial Intelligence and Statistics, pp. 583–590 (2009)

19. Griffiths, T.L., Steyvers, M.: Finding scientific topics. Proceedings of the National Academy of Sciences 101(suppl 1), 5228–5235 (2004)

20. Gilks, W.R., Richardson, S., Spiegelhalter, D.J.: Introducing markov chain monte carlo. In: Markov Chain Monte Carlo in Practice, vol. 1, p. 19 (1996)

21. Heinrich, G.: Parameter estimation for text analysis. Technical report (2005)

Improving Transfer Learning in Cross Lingual Opinion Analysis Through Negative Transfer Detection

Lin Gui[1], Qin Lu[2], Ruifeng Xu[1(✉)], Qikang Wei[1], and Yuhui Cao[1]

[1] Shenzhen Engineering Laboratory of Performance Robots at Digital Stage,
Harbin Institute of Technology Shenzhen Graduate School, Shenzhen, China
{Guilin.nlp,caoyuhuiszu}@gmail.com, xuruifeng@hitsz.edu.cn,
weiqikang@hotmail.com
[2] Department of Computing, The Hong Kong Polytechnic University, Hong Kong, China
csluqin@comp.polyu.edu.hk

Abstract. Transfer learning has been used as a machine learning method to make good use of available language resources for other resource-scarce languages. However, the cumulative class noise during iterations of transfer learning can lead to negative transfer which can adversely affect performance when more training data is used. In this paper, we propose a novel transfer learning method which can detect negative transfers. This approach detects high quality samples after certain iterations to identify class noise in new transferred training samples and remove them to reduce misclassifications. With the ability to detect bad training samples and remove them, our method can make full use of large unlabeled training data available in the target language. Furthermore, the most important contribution in this paper is the theory of class noise detection. Our new class noise detection method overcame the theoretic flaw of a previous method based on Gaussian distribution. We applied this transfer learning method with negative transfer detection to cross lingual opinion analysis. Evaluation on the NLP&CC 2013 cross-lingual opinion analysis dataset shows that the proposed approach outperforms the state-of-the-art systems.

Keywords: Negative transfer · Transfer learning · Class noise detection

1 Introduction

Transfer learning has been used as a machine learning method to make use of available language resources for other resource-scarce languages. One research area that makes use of transfer learning is cross-lingual opinion analysis (CLOA)(Arnold et al., 2007, Wang, 2009). Opinion analysis aims to identify positive and negative polarities of document in running text. Even though supervised learning is proven to be quite successful, it requires labeled samples, which are expensive and is the performance bottle-neck in opinion analysis especially for relatively resource scarce languages. To solve this problem, researchers use transfer leaning to make use of samples from a resource-rich source language to help the learning model of target language.

For languages like Chinese, there is a large quantity of opinion text available from Blogs, microblogs, online social networks and product reviews. Yet, labelling them

© Springer International Publishing Switzerland 2015
S. Zhang et al. (Eds.): KSEM 2015, LNAI 9403, pp. 394–406, 2015.
DOI: 10.1007/978-3-319-25159-2_36

for opinion analysis is still quite time consuming. With the availability of annotated resources in English, a natural question is whether we can make use of labeled data in English and unlabeled data in Chinese. This is exactly what transductive transfer learning (TTL). TTL algorithms try to select samples from unlabeled data in the target language with high probability. To obtain the probability of samples in the target language, researchers either use the conditional probability or the weighted conditional probability of samples in the source language. However, samples with large confidence scores can still have a probability of being misclassified. During training iterations,   misclassification probability will accumulate, causing gradual reduction of the quality of transferred samples and eventually triggering also called negative transfer (Pan et al., 2010) when the performance degradation when more training data are produced and used. A direct way to improve performance is to identify these noisy samples assigned with wrong labels and remove them from transferred training data.

The existing method in practice based on this idea, such as (Gui et. al 2014) and (Li and Zhou, 2011) both have theoretically flawed assumption. In their class noise detection method, they both use the kNN graph and Gaussian distribution. They use kNN graph to detect the concordance rate between a sample and its neighbors. It is obviously the low concordance rate of a sample and the neighbors indicate the sample have high probability to be a noisy sample. Such that a Gaussian distribution based hypothesis testing method is deployed to detect if the sample is a noisy sample. However, the further one requires small k to satisfy manifold assumption and the later on needs large k in kNN graph to cater for Center Limit Theorem. That is the theoretically flawing in their method.

In this paper, we propose a class noise reduction method, which use sum of Rademacher distribution instead of Gaussian distribution. The main contribution of our approach is to correct the theoretically flawing and achieves a better performance.

The rest of the paper is organized as follows. Section 2 introduces related works in transfer learning, cross lingual opinion analysis, and class noise detection technology. Section 3 presents our algorithm. Section 4 gives performance evaluation. Section 5 concludes this paper.

2   Related Work

For supervised learning, there are two basic methods for class noise detection: the classification based method (Brodley and Friedl, 1999; Zhu et al, 2003; Zhu 2004; Sluban et al., 2010) and the graph based method (Zighed et al, 2002; Muhlenbach et al, 2004; Jiang and Zhou, 2004). Class noise detection can also be applied in semi-supervised learning because noise will multiply in iterations too. Li employed Zighed's cut edge weight statistic method in self-training (Li and Zhou, 2005) and co-training (Li and Zhou, 2011). Chao used Li's kNN based method in tri-training (Chao et al, 2008). F. Fukumoto et al. used the support vectors to detect class noise in semi-supervised learning (Fukumoto et al, 2013). Y. Cheng has tried to use semi-supervised method (Jiang and Zhou, 2004) in transfer learning (Cheng and Li, 2009). His experiment shows that only when the source domain and the target domain share similar distributions, their approach will not work.

In TTL, noise detection methods developed for semi-supervised learning using classification based method cannot be used directly because semi-supervised learning assumes that the training and the testing samples have the same distribution. A preliminary attempt was made to use graph based method in TTL with negative transfer detection (Gui et. al., 2014). The detection method has proven effective, but the algorithm was designed based on the null hypothesis with two assumptions on the data: (1) the manifold assumption and (2) the central limit theorem. These assumptions are quite reasonable in general learning theory. But they are contradicting each other in class noise detection, thus the method has flaws limiting the performance.   How to identify the class noise in transfer learning during iterations and how to reduce negative transfer still remains a problem in transfer learning.

3   Our Approach

In this paper, we propose a new graph based method to detect class noise in transfer learning. The basic idea is to first select high quality transferred samples labeled by the learning algorithm after certain iterations to detect class noise. We then remove the class noises to obtain improved training data in the remainder of the training phase. This negative sample reduction process can be repeated several times during transfer learning.

Let ε_{t-1} be the error boundary estimated from samples in time step t-1 and ε_t be the error boundary estimated at the current time step t. Theoretically, if $\varepsilon_{t-1} > \varepsilon_t$, the quality of the transferred samples are better than its previous time step and thus the samples at t can serve as the guide to detect class noise in samples transferred up to time step t-1. In this process, we must address two main issues: the first is how to measure the quality of labeled samples from transfer learning; the second is how to utilize the high quality labeled samples to identify class noise in training data such that they can be removed.

3.1   Estimating Testing Error

To determine the quality of the samples from transfer learning, we cannot use the training error to estimate true error because the training data and the testing data may have different distributions in transfer learning. Hence we employ the Probably Approximately Correct (PAC) theory to estimate the error boundary (Angluin and Laird, 1988) similar the work by (Gui, et. Al., 2014). According to the PAC learning theory, the error rate boundary ε is determined by the size of training set m and the class noise rate η, defined by:

$$\varepsilon \propto \sqrt{1/(m(1-\eta)^2)} \qquad (1)$$

In TTL, m increases linearly and η is multiplied after each iteration. This means the significance of m to performance is higher at beginning of transfer learning and gradually slows down in later iterations. However, class noise accumulates in the whole transfer learning process. It is the reason why performance increases initially until negative transfer occurs when noise accumulation outperforms learned information.

From Formula (1) with an assumed fixed probability δ, the least error boundary ε is given by(Angluin and Laird, 1988):

$$\varepsilon = \sqrt{2\ln(2N/\delta)/(m(1-\eta)^2)} \tag{2}$$

Here, N is a constant decided by the hypothesis space.

In any iteration during TTL, the hypothesis space is the same and the probability δ is fixed. Thus, the error boundary is determined by the size of the transferred samples m and the class noise of transferred samples η. According to Formula (2), we apply a manifold assumption based method to estimate η. We set T as the number of iterations to serve as one period for quality estimate. Error boundary is measured over T. If the error boundary is reduced, it means that the transferred samples used in this period is improved, and the use of transferred samples can improve the performance of a classifier. Otherwise, transfer learning has fall into negative transfer and the learning process should be stopped.

3.2   Estimation Class Noise

To measure error boundary given in (2), we need to know the class noise rate η to calculate the error boundary. It is obvious that we cannot use the conditional probability from the source language to estimate the class noise rate of the transferred samples. Hence we propose to use the cut edge weight statistic method of the transferred samples to estimate the error rate of the labels in transfer learning (Blitzer et al, 2006).

In the first step, we build a kNN graph, which is sensitive to the class noise, on the transferred data using any similarity metric, for example, cosine similarity or the similarity exported by Euclidean distance. Then, for any two connected vertex (x_i, y_i) and (x_j, y_j) in the kNN graph, the edge weight is given by:

$$w_{ij} = sim(x_i, x_j) \tag{3}$$

Furthermore, a sign function I_{ij} for the two vertices (x_i, y_i) and (x_j, y_j), is defined as:

$$I_{ij} = \begin{cases} -1, if \ y_i = y_j \\ 1, if \ y_i \neq y_j \end{cases} \tag{4}$$

According to the manifold assumption, the conditional probability $P(y_i|x_i)$ can be approximated by the frequency of $P(y_i=y_j)$ which is equal to $P(I_{ij}=-1)$. However, in opinion annotations, the agreement of two annotators is often no larger than 0.8. This means that in the best case $P(I_{ij}=-1)=0.2$. Hence I_{ij} follows the Bernoulli distribution with $p=0.2$ in the best case in manual annotations.

Let $C_{ij}=\{(x_j, y_j)\}$ be the vertices adjacent to vertex i, the statistical magnitude S_i of vertex i can be defined as:

$$S_i = \sum_j w_{ij} \cdot I_{ij} \tag{5}$$

Where j refers to vertex j adjacent to vertex i.

Notice: Many researchers assume that S_i follows the normal distribution according to the Center Limit Theorem (Gui and Xu, 2014; Li and Zhou, 2011; Cheng and Li, 2009). But it requires the k in kNN graph is larger than 25, the distribution of S_i will approximate to normal distribution. Actually, in most cases, the degree of vertices in kNN graph is less than 10 making the Center Limit Theorem not suitable.

Hence we hereby propose to use the sum of Rademacher distribution to estimate the class noise. The sum of Rademacher distribution declares that for a series of random variates $\xi=\{\xi_1,\xi_2,...\xi_n\}$ where $P(\xi_i=1) = P(\xi_i=-1)$, the weighted sum S by a series of real positive numbers $x=\{x_1,x_2,...x_n\}$, $S=\sum\xi_i x_i$, for any $t>0$, the probability should follow the boundary:

$$P(S > t \cdot \|x\|_2) < e^{-\frac{t^2}{2}} \tag{6}$$

where, $\|x\|_2$ is the Euclidean norm of $\{x_1,x_2,...x_n\}$, that is l_2 space. Without loss of generality, we assume that S is positive here. According to S.J. Montgomery et al(Montgomery, Smith. S. J. ,1990), a more compact boundary is given by:

$$P(S > K_{1,2}(x,t)) \le e^{-\frac{t^2}{2}} \tag{7}$$

Where

$$K_{1,2}(x,t) = \inf\{\|x'\|_1 + t\|x''\|_2\} \tag{8}$$

Here, x',x'' $\in l_2$ space and x'+x''=x.

(Holmstedt, T. at 1970) has first given an approximation formula of $K_{1,2}(x,t)$ for n $\to \infty$ which is not directly applicable in our case. Hence we calculate $K_{1,2}(x,t)$ in the subspace of l_2 noted as $K'_{1,2}(x,t)$. It is obvious that $P(S>K'_{1,2}(x,t)) < \exp(-t^2/2)$. Let x'=αx and x''=βx, α, β are real number. It can be easily calculated as:

$$K'_{1,2}(x,t) = \sqrt{t\|x\|_1\|x\|_2} \tag{9}$$

Hence for any $x=\{x_1,x_2,...x_n\}$, $P(\xi_i=1) = P(\xi_i=-1)$. For $S=\sum \xi_i x_i$, $x_i>0$, Formula (7) is rewritten using (9) as:

$$P\left(S > \sqrt{t\|x\|_1\|x\|_2}\right) \le e^{-\frac{t^2}{2}} \tag{10}$$

Here $\|x\|_i$ is the l_i norm of x. Experiment shows that this boundary is more compact than Holmstedt's method when n is less than 10. Our target is to use Inequality (10) to estimate the probability of S_i. However, we cannot simply assume the probability $P(I_{ij}=-1)$ and $P(I_{ij}=1)$ equal to 1/2. Generally speaking, for a sub series $\{\xi_1,\xi_2,...\xi_i\}$, $P(\xi_i=1) =p/q$, where p and q are positive integers and $p<q$. Now, we need to find a transformation function to map the general p/q problem to the ½ problem. Let the number of -1 in the series as s_i and the number of 1 as t_i. We define a function $f_\xi(k)$ such that $f_\xi(k)=\xi_i$ if and only if $t_i(p-q)+s_i p>k>t_{i-1}(p-q)+s_{i-1}p$. By this definition, there exists a matrix M such that:

$$M = \left(\frac{\xi^T}{n}f_\xi(1), \frac{\xi^T}{n}f_\xi(2), ... \frac{\xi^T}{n}f_\xi(N)\right) \tag{11}$$

It can be proven that in the series $\xi'=\{\xi'_1,\xi'_2,...\xi'_N\}$ defined by $\xi'=\xi M$, $P(\xi'_i=1)=1/2$ if and only if $P(\xi'_i=1)=p/q$.

After this transformation, we can get a new series from I_{ij} noted as I'_{ij} and the corresponding $w=\{w'_{ij}\}$. Employ the (11) we can get:

$$P\left(\sum_j w'_{ij} \cdot I'_{ij} > \sqrt{t\|w\|_1\|w\|_2}\right) \le e^{-\frac{t^2}{2}} \tag{12}$$

We assume the S is positive at first, and the probability of $S > 0$ is 0.5 in sum of Rademacher distribution. This means the least class noise rate of samples (x_i, y_i) is:

$$\eta_i = 1 - 0.5 \times \exp\left(-\frac{\left(\sum_j w'_{ij} \cdot I'_{ij}\right)^4}{(2\|w\|_1\|w\|_2)^2}\right) \tag{13}$$

We take the general significant level of 0.05 to reject the null hypothesis. It means that if η_i of (x_i, y_i) is larger than 0.95, the sample will be considered as a noisy sample.

In experiment, the threshold calculated by our approach is more flexible and reasonable than the manual threshold in kNN and the original cut weight edge statistics based threshold.

Based on the equation (13), it can be easily calculate the error boundary of transferred samples after particular iteration is:

$$\varepsilon_{next} = \sqrt{\frac{2\ln(2N/\delta)\,|TS_l \cup TS_c|}{\left(|TS_l \cup TS_c| - \Sigma_i(1 - 0.5 \times \exp\left(-\frac{\left(\sum_j w'_{ij} \cdot I'_{ij}\right)^4}{(2\|w\|_1\|w\|_2)^2}\right))\right)^2}}$$

Here, TS_c is the candidate transfer set, TS_l is the labeled transfer set. $|\cdot|$ is the size of a set, ε_{next} is the error boundary of the classifier trained by the transfer samples in next iteration.

3.3   TTL with Class Noise Detection

Based on the class noise measures, we propose to introduce class noise detection into TTL to reduce cumulative noise and negative transfer.

Assume that there are n training samples from the source language distribution $S(x)$:

$$L = \{(x_i^S, y_i^S)|i.i.d. x_i^S \sim S(x), i = 1,2,...,n\},$$

here y_i^S is the label of x_i^S, and it comes from manual annotation so the class noise rate of this label is assumed to be 0. With similar definition, there are m unlabeled samples from the target language distribution $D(x)$:

$$U = \{x_i^T|i.i.d. x_i^T \sim D(x), i = 1,2,...,m\}$$

TTL uses labeled and unlabeled data from both L and U to solve the classification problem in the target language. Our algorithm periodically conducts class noise detection based on an algorithm parameter T, the quality estimate period(use fixed number of iterations), to estimate the class noise rate of transferred samples. Based on the average class noise, the error boundary is used as the indication of quality. If the added samples in the current T are of high quality, they can be used to detect class noise in transferred training data. Otherwise, transfer learning should terminate because there is no point to continue if the samples with the highest confidence still lead to negative transfer. Below is the pseudo code of our algorithm:

New Algorithm : Negative transfer detection and noise removal for transfer learning classifier C

Input: C, L, U, T, K

Variables: $TS_c = \emptyset$, /* candidate transfer set

$TS_l = \emptyset$, /* labeled transfer set

p,q, /* The number of positive and negative samples added in each iteration

$\varepsilon_{pre} = 1, \varepsilon_{next} = 1$, /*test error bounds of previous

/* period and current periods

G, /* kNN Graph

1. *Iter* = 1;   /* variable as iteration number

2. **While**(*Iter* < K) /* K is the maximum iterations

3.   Training classifier C on L;

4.   Use C to classify U, move p positive and q negative samples with highest confidence to TS_c with assigned labels;   /*transfer learning

5.   **If** i mod $T = 0$ **then** /* start the detection

6. $\forall x_i \in (TS_l \cup TS_c)$ built the kNN graph G;

7. $\forall x_i \in G$ calculate η_i by Equation (13);

8.   Estimate the test error bounds on $TS_l \cup TS_c$:

$$\varepsilon_{next} = \sqrt{\frac{2\ln(2N/\delta)\,|TS_l \cup TS_c|}{\left(|TS_l \cup TS_c| - \Sigma_i(1 - 0.5 \times \exp\left(-\frac{(\Sigma_j w'_{ij} \cdot I'_{ij})^4}{(2\|w\|_1\|w\|_2)^2}\right))\right)^2}}$$

9.   **If** $\varepsilon_{next} > \varepsilon_{pre}$ **then break**

10.   **Else**

11.   For $\forall x_i \in TS_l$, move x_i to U if $\eta_i > 0.95$;

12. $TS_l = TS_l \cup TS_c$ and $TS_c = \emptyset$;

13. $\varepsilon_{pre} = \varepsilon_{next}$;   **end**;

14.   **end**; /* end negative transfer detection

15. **end**;   /* end **while** statement

End   /* **Output:** Optimized classifier: C_*

It is well known the computational complexity of kNN is $O(n^2)$. Here, n is the size of training set of kNN graph. Such that for each round of negative transfer detection, the size of training set is $|TS_l \cup TS_c|$, such that the computational complexity of each round of negative transfer detection is $O(|TS_l \cup TS_c|^2)$.

4   Experiment

The proposed improved negative transfer detection method is evaluated on the NLP&CC 2013 dataset for cross-lingual opinion analysis (in short, NLP&CC)[1]. In the training set, there are 12,000 labeled English data, denoted by Train_ENG, from three categories of Amazon.com products reviews, namely DVD, BOOK, MUSIC. There are also 120 labeled Chinese product reviews, denoted by Train_CHN, and 94,651 unlabeled Chinese products reviews, denoted by Dev_CHN. The testing set, denoted by Test_CHN), has 12,000 Chinese product reviews with 4000 reviews for each category. Details of the dataset are given in Table 1.

Table 1. The NLP&CC 2013 CLOA dataset

	DVD	BOOK	MUSIC
Train_CHN	40	40	40
Train_ENG	4,000	4,000	4,000
Dev_CHN	17,814	47,071	29,677
Test_CHN	4,000	4,000	4,000

Due to the data is product reviews, the length of each review is limited. Usually each document contains one or two sentences. In the experiments, ICTCLAS is used as the Chinese word segmentation tool and Google Translator[2] is used as the translator. The monolingual opinion classifiers are based on SVMs (using SVM[light3]) while features are word unigram and word bigram.

4.1   Improved CLOA Experiment Result

In this paper, the basic transfer learning algorithm, used as the baseline system, is the co-training method widely used in cross-lingual domain and Support Vector Machines serves at the basic classifier. The first set of experiments given in Table 2 shows the performance of the baseline system using the same monolingual opinion classifier with three training datasets including Train_CHN, translated Train_ENG and their union, respectively. Table 2 shows that the classifier using Train_CHN are on avergage 20% worse than the English translated counter part. Using Train_CHN and translated Train_ENG, does not make much difference because if training data in the target language is too small, it has no impact to performance.

Table 2. Baseline performances

	DVD	BOOK	MUSIC	Average
Train_CHN	0.5515	0.5133	0.5000	0.5216
Train_ENG(trans)	0.7290	0.7328	0.7215	0.7278
Train_CHN+ Train_ENG(trans)	0.7373	0.7215	0.7423	0.7337

---

[1] http://tcci.ccf.org.cn/conference/2013/dldoc/evdata03.zip
[2] https://translate.google.com
[3] http://svmlight.joachims.org/

In the second set of the experiments, our algorithm(labeled as *New*) is compared to the official best in NLP&CC 2013 CLOA evaluation[4] (labeled as *HLT-HITSZ*) and the state-of-the-art system(labeled as *Gui*) by (Gui et. al., 2014), all of them take the co-training approach. Table 3 shows that our algorithm achieves the best performance, much better than HLT-HITSZ(3.53%increase), the system without using negative transfer detection.

Table 3. Performance compared to Top Systems (*p value is less than 0.01*)

Team	DVD	Music	Book	Accuracy
HLT-HITSZ	0.7773	0.7513	0.7850	0.7712
Gui	0.8155	0.7860	0.8005	0.8007
New	**0.8225**	**0.7973**	**0.8055**	**0.8084**

Our algorithm is similar to system Gui (Gui et. al, 2014) in that both are graph based and have class noise detection. That is why the performance gap is small. However, we differ in class noise detection methods used. The method in system Gui is based on theoretically flawed assumptions, and thus, its ability to detect noise class is more limited. This is reflected in the improved performance of our algorithm across the board. The p value of Wilcoxon Signed-Rank Test is less than 0.01 among 200 experiments, which means the improvement is significant.

The third set of experiment examines the effectiveness of negative transfer detection by comparing to co-training without negative transfer detection (labeled as *CO*) as well two other systems using negative transfer detection one is the classification based method (Labeled as *CB)* (Brodley and Friedl, 1999) and the graph based negative transfer method (labeled as GB) (Gui et. al, 2014). The union of Train_CHN and Train_ENG serve as labeled data and Dev_CHN as unlabeled data.

The evaluation on DVD and Book data corresponding to the four CLOA algorithms are shown in Fig. 1. The best performance, the average performance and the variance (denoted by *VA*) is given in Table 4. The black curves in Fig. 1 for *CO* are typical TTL curves. That is, accuracy increases quickly in the beginning of transfer learning. Due to the accumulation of noisy data in transferred samples, accuracy starts to decrease when negative transfer occurs. It should be pointed out that without the ability to detect when negative transfer occurs, there is no way CLOA algorithms can guarantee best result because they cannot pick the best termination point in the co-training algorithm. With negative transfer detection, our algorithm shows a very different behavior. In any case, our algorithm has ability to detect the negative transfer and terminate the algorithm such that the result of algorithm is guaranteed to be in the top range. By looking at the variance *VA* (in the scale of 10^{-5}), our algorithm also has the smallest value. This means that our algorithm is the most stable among all.

---

[4] http://tcci.ccf.org.cn/conference/2013/dldoc/evres03.pdf

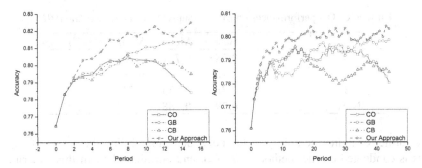

Fig. 1. Accuracy curves of CLOA for   DVD and Book

Table 4. CLOA performances on DVD and Book data(*p value is less than 0.01*)

	DVD			Book		
	Best	Mean	VA	Best	Mean	VA
CO	0.804	0.797	6.451	0.783	0.777	0.956
GB	0.816	0.805	3.281	0.786	0.78	0.395
CB	0.806	0.802	**0.622**	0.784	0.775	1.713
New	**0.823**	**0.814**	3.033	**0.805**	**0.799**	**0.377**

The accuracy curves for BOOK shown in the right diagram in Fig. 1 are similar to that of the DVD subset. An interesting note is that the curve of *CB* is worse than *CO* for quite some iterations. It means that a wrong strategy for negative transfer detection can overfit the bias of the basic classifier to get worse performance.

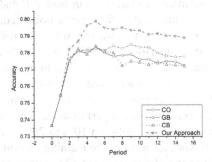

Fig. 2. Accuracy curves of CLOA approaches (MUSIC)

Fig. 2 shows the accuracy curves for the MUSIC dataset with corresponding best, average and variance data given in Table 5. The curve is comparatively different from DVD and BOOK data because there is no obviously negative transfer in this data set.

Table 5. CLOA performances on MUSIC subset (*p value is less than 0.01*)

	Best	Mean	Variance(10^{-5})
CO	0.783	0.777	0.956
GB	0.786	0.780	0.395
CB	0.784	0.775	1.713
New	**0.797**	**0.788**	**0.377**

To further examine the ability of the noise detection ability, the 4th set of experiments is conducted on the methods, *CB*, *CB*, and our algorithm. In this experiment, we take the labeled English and Chinese data in NLP&CC 2013 to train the three models 10%, 20%, and 30% levels of noise artificially injected with no transfer learning involved. Then, we conduct the negative transfer detection after training is completed to check the error rate, the lower the error is, the better the algorithm is.

Table 6. Training error with manually class noise

Language	Method	10% noise	20% noise	30% noise
	CB	0.173	0.201	**0.240**
ENG	GB	0.172	0.207	0.254
	New	**0.123**	**0.172**	0.258
	CB	0.162	0.178	**0.209**
CHN	GB	0.164	0.184	0.223
	New	**0.137**	**0.160**	0.210

Table 6 shows the evaluation results. Results show that our method has obvious advantage when noise level is in 10% and 20%. In fact, our noise detection method shows a much lower performance reduction than both *CB* and *GB* for both Chinese and English data. As we pointed out before, *GB*'s noise reduction ability is much limited due to the flaws in its design. However, when the noise level reaches 30%, classification based method outperforms graphic based methods although only by a small margin. This is because the advantage of *CB* is in its recall, not in its precision. When the class noise rate is low, *CB* will classify non-class noise data as class noise data and delete them. When noise rate increases, the mis-classification data are less, and the advantage of high recall makes the performance degrade slower. In practice, it is more reasonable to have noise rate between 10% to 20%. 30% noise rate for training data basically will not work for most of the learning algorithms in the first place.

To compare the performance of our proposed TTL with supervised learning, the 5th set of experiments is conducted. Here, we use 2/3 of Test_CHN with answers as training data and the rest as testing data. The performance of 3-fold cross validation is given in Table 7. The accuracy of our approach is only 0.4% lower than the supervised learning method using 2/3 of Test_CHN. In the BOOK dataset, our approach achieves even better result. The performance gap in different subsets shows positive correlation to the size of Dev_CHN. The more samples are given in Dev_CHN, a higher precision is achieved even though these samples are unlabeled. According to the PAC theory, we know that the accuracy of a classifier training from a large training set with confined class noise rate will approximate the accuracy of classifier training from a non-class noise training set. This experiment shows that our proposed negative transfer detection controls the class noise rate in a very limited boundary.

Table 7. Performance comparison with supervised learning

	DVD	BOOK	MUSIC	Average
Supervised	0.833	0.800	0.801	0.811
New	0.823	0.806	0.797	0.808

5   Conclusion

In this paper, we proposed a negative transfer detection approach for transductive transfer learning method in order to handle cumulative class noise and reduce the negative transfer in process of transfer learning. The basic idea is to utilize high quality samples after transfer learning to detect the class noise in transferred samples. Our new class noise detection method overcame the theoretic flaw of a previous method. Experiments using CLOA data show that our proposed approach obtains stable performance improvement by reducing negative transfer. The accuracy of our approach is better than the top system by 3.72% on NLP&CC 2013 CLOA evaluation dataset. It is also more stable and achieves a better performance than state-of-the-art system on this dataset. In future work, we plan to extend this method into other language/domain resources to identify more transferred samples.

Acknowledgements. This work was supported by National Natural Science Foundation of China (No. 61370165, 61203378), Natural Science Foundation of Guangdong Province S2013010014475, Shenzhen Development and Reform Commission Grant No.[2014]1507, Shenzhen Peacock Plan Research Grant KQCX20140521144507925, Baidu Collaborate Research Funding, and Hong Kong Polytechnic University Project Z0EP.

References

1. Angluin, D., Laird, P.: Learning from Noisy Examples. Machine Learning **2**(4), 343–370 (1988)
2. Arnold, A., Nallapati, R., Cohen, W.W.: A comparative study of methods for TTL. In: Proc. 7th IEEE ICDM Work-shops, pp. 77–82 (2007)
3. Blitzer, J., McDonald, R., Pereira, F.: Domain adaptation with structural correspondence learning. In: Proc. EMNLP, pp. 120–128 (2006)
4. Brodley, C.E., Friedl, M.A.: Identifying and Eliminating Mislabeled Training Instances. Journal of Artificial Intelligence Research **11**, 131–167 (1999)
5. Chao, D., Guo, M.Z., Liu, Y., Li, H.F.: Participatory learning based semi-supervised classification. In: Proc. of 4th ICNC, pp. 207–216 (2008)
6. Cheng, Y., Li, Q.Y.: Transfer learning with data edit. LNAI, pp. 427–434 (2009)

7. Fukumoto, F., Suzuki, Y., Matsuyoshi, S.: Text classification from positive and unlabeled data using misclassified data correction. In: Proc. of 51st ACL, pp. 474–478 (2013)
8. Holmstedt, T.: Interpolation of quasi-normed spaces. Math. Scand. **26**, 177–199 (1970)
9. Jiang, Y., Zhou, Z.-H.: Editing training data for kNN classifiers with neural network ensemble. In: Yin, F.-L., Wang, J., Guo, C. (eds.) ISNN 2004. LNCS, vol. 3173, pp. 356–361. Springer, Heidelberg (2004)
10. Li, M., Zhou, Z.-H.: SETRED: self-training with editing. In: Ho, T.-B., Cheung, D., Liu, H. (eds.) PAKDD 2005. LNCS (LNAI), vol. 3518, pp. 611–621. Springer, Heidelberg (2005)
11. Li, M., Zhou, Z.H.: COTRADE: Confident Co-Training With Data Editing. IEEE Transactions on Systems, Man, and Cybernetics—Part B Cybernetics **41**(6), 1612–1627 (2011)
12. Gui, L., Xu, R.F., Lu, Q. et. al.: Cross-lingual opinion analysis via negative transfer detection. In: Proc. of 52th ACL(2), pp. 860–865 (2014)
13. Montgomery-Smith, S.J.: The distribution of Rademacher sums. Proc. Amer. Math. Soc. **109**, 517–522 (1990)
14. Muhlenbach, F., Lallich, S., Zighed, D.A.: Identifying and Handling Mislabeled Instances. Journal of Intelligent Information System **22**(1), 89–109 (2004)
15. Pan, S.J., Yang, Q.: A Survey on Transfer Learning. IEEE Transactions on Knowledge and Data Engineering **22**(10), 1345–1360 (2010)
16. Sluban, B., Gamberger, D., Lavra, N.: Advances in class noise detection. In: Proc.19th ECAI, pp. 1105–1106 (2010)
17. Wan, X.: Co-training for cross-lingual sentiment classification. In: Proc. of the 47th Annual Meeting of the ACL and the 4th IJCNLP of the AFNLP, pp. 235–243 (2009)
18. Zhu, X.Q., Wu, X.D., Chen, Q.J.: Eliminating class noise in large datasets. In: Proc. of 12th ICML, pp. 920–927 (2003)
19. Zhu, X.Q.: Cost-guided class noise handling for effective cost-sensitive learning. In: Proc. of 4th IEEE ICDM, pp. 297–304 (2004)
20. Zighed, D.A., Lallich, S., Muhlenbach, F.: A statistical approach to class separability. Applied Stochastic Models in Business and Industry **21**(2), 187–197 (2005)

Mining User's Location Intention from Mobile Search Log

Yifan Sun[1], Xin Li[1], Lin Li[2], Qi Liu[1], Enhong Chen[1(✉)], and Haiping Ma[3]

[1] University of Science and Technology of China, Hefei, China
{sunyifan,leexin,}@mail.ustc.edu.cn, {qiliuql,cheneh}@ustc.edu.cn
[2] Wuhan University of Technology, Wuhan, China
cathylilin@whut.edu.cn
[3] IFLYTEK Co., Ltd, Hefei, China
mhp0814@mail.ustc.edu.cn

Abstract. Much attention has been paid to web search personalization and query optimization over the past decade. With the prevalence of smart phones, the mobile search results for the same query may vary in regard to the user's location. In order to provide more precise results for users, it's essential to take geographic location into account along with the user's input query. In this paper, we try to identify queries that have location intentions. For example, query "weather forecast" has a location intention of local city while "The Statue of Liberty" has a location intention of "New York city". To identify the location intention behind a query, we propose a novel method to extract a set of features and use neural network to classify queries. In the classification of queries without explicit location names, our experiment shows that our approach achieves 82.5% at F1 measure and outperforms baselines by 4.2%.

Keywords: Feature selection · Location intention · Query classification

1 Introduction

With the prevalence of smart phones and intelligent personal assistant such as Siri, the market share of mobile search has occupied half of the whole search market[1]. Thus, it becomes crucial to have an eye on the mobile search field. Conventional web search engines characterized by "one size fits all" provide the same results for the same keyword queries even though these queries from different users may contain different intentions. According to Welch's research [1], about 50% of web search queries with an intention of requesting local information, do not have explicit location names. If we can automatically identify queries that have a location intention, we can provide better user experience by saving user's time and reducing interaction times.

Here is a toy example. Some queries, such as "bus terminal" and "house price", have location intentions, but some other queries, such as "funny videos"

---

[1] http://ir.baidu.com/phoenix.zhtml?c=188488&p=irol-reportsAnnual

© Springer International Publishing Switzerland 2015
S. Zhang et al. (Eds.): KSEM 2015, LNAI 9403, pp. 407–420, 2015.
DOI: 10.1007/978-3-319-25159-2_37

and "jokes" do not. If a supplementary location name is added to the front ones, it might help the search engine to understand the user's intention and thus return more precise results. We term these two kinds of queries "location sensitive query" and "ordinary query" respectively in order to make consistency throughout this paper. Besides these two kinds of queries, there is also another scenario which is termed "fixed collocation query". When a user keys in "The Statue of Liberty", he most probably means the statue in New York city. This usually happens when users search for scenic spots, famous universities and other well-known places of interest.

In real life, if we can know a query is a "fixed collocation query" before searching, we can refine the query by adding a corresponding place name to it, if we can know the query is a "location sensitive query", we can utilize the locate function embbeded in cellphones and get location information to improve searching results. However, to classify queries according to its location intention is not a trivial problem. To achieve these goals, we face two challenges. Firstly, queries submitted to the search engine usually contain very short keywords. These keywords are insufficient to reveal user's real intention [2]. Secondly, in text classification, the demension of the feature space is very high. In this paper, we regard the problem of identifying the user's location intention as a classification problem, and we use our novel feature selection method and neural network classifier to achieve a high accuracy in the classification of "fixed collocation queries" and "location sensitive queries", which are two tasks we aim to address in this paper.

We conduct extensive experiments on a real-world dataset of mobile search log in comparison with five baseline methods. The results show the superiority of our method. In summary, we make the following contributions:

1) We propose a novel feature selection method in the classification of "location sensitive queries".

2) We devise a score function to measure the relevance between a word and a place name and this function is used to identify "fixed collocation queries".

3) The experiments on a real world dataset of mobile search log show that our approach outperforms the baseline methods.

The paper is organized as follows: Section 2 reviews some related works. Section 3 and Section 4 present our approaches to identify fixed collocation queries and location sensitive queries respectively. Section 5 describes our experiment results along with discussion. In the last section we conclude our work and point out possible directions for future work.

2   Related Work

In this section, we review the related work in personalized web search and user's intention recognition.

Personalized Web Search. Considerable work has been done in the field of personalized web search. Bennett et. al [3] investigated how short-term and long-term user behavior interact, and how they can be used to personalize search results. Matthijs and Randlinski [4] collected user's browsing history via a browser add-on and used the language model to analyze the captured pages for personalizing search results. Xiang et. al [5] analyzed the user's context and used those contextual features to rank the results of subsequent queries. Kharitonov and Serdyukov [6] used user's age and gender for re-ranking and personalizing search results. Teevan et. al [7] analyzed the re-visitation pattern of users and classified at least 15% of all clicks as personal navigation in which the user repeatedly searches for the same page. In the field of query refining or suggestion, Bhatia et. al [8] mined frequently occurring phrases and n-grams from text collections and deployed them for generating and ranking auto-completion candidates. Santos et. al [9] extracted queries that frequently co-appeared in the same sessions to generate query suggestions. Ozertem et. al [10] presented a learning-to-rank framework for ranking query suggestions. What differentiates our work from the previous ones is that we mine "the wisdom of the crowd" from the mobile search logs. It does not require a particular user's behavior data or contextual information to be collected. After the identification of fixed collocation queries and classification of location sensitive queries, the benefits can be enjoyed by all users even if we do not know any of a particular user's information.

User's Intention Recognition. Different classification schemes have been proposed to categorize user's intention behind his search. Lee et. al [11] presented a set of features to automatically classify user's intention as either navigational or informational. Yi [12] and Kamvar [13] categorized the mobile queries into a taxonomy with a total of 23 top-level predefined categories which covers most of the areas in the information space. Chuklin [14] proposed a way to model user's intention distribution and bias due to different document presentation types. Dhar [15] utilized semi-supervised learning and user's previous search log to classify query intentions.

Welch [1], Vadrevu [16] and Gravano [17] exploited classification techniques to categorize queries according to their geographic intentions, which are much related to our work. In Vadrevu's work [16], they relied on query term co-occurrence in query logs and built three classifiers to identify regional sensitive queries. However, their regional sensitive queries is coarse-grained, such as "U.S.A.", "Japan" and "India". In contrast, our location sensitive queries have a hierarchy of three levels: provinces, cities, and counties, which is more practical. Gravano [17] defined a categorization scheme for queries where they represented queries by features and used several classifiers to determine query's location intention. In Welch's work [1], a tagging technique and different features extracted from query logs are combined to classify queries. Several supervised classifiers were tested. Both of their experiments get a precision at 90% with a recall less than 50%. Ourdia [18] classified queries into three classes using Kurtosis and Kullback-Leibler Divergence measures, and their experiment on a dataset containing 200 queries achieved the F1 measure of 0.800. Different from their works, we propose our novel method to extract a set of features and use neural network to identify the location intention of a query and our experiments on a real world dataset which contains 1,000 queries get the F1 measure of 0.825. We also implement methods proposed by Welch [1] and Ourdia [18] as baselines and classification results show that our method outperforms theirs.

3   Identify Fixed Collocation Queries

Fixed collocation queries always occur with a corresponding place name. In this section, we will illustrate how to identify such kind of queries.

3.1   Data and Preprocess

The mobile search log containing 1,402,744 mobile search queries in Chinese character is provided by IFLYTEK company [2]. As Chinese characters do not have tense or any other form variation, there is no need of stemming or normalizing. When implementing word segmentation and stop words elimination, we adopt two open source packages, i.e., Lucene [3] and IKAnalyzer [4].

3.2   Fixed Collocation Queries Identification

We build a dictionary of 3,223 names of places in China, including all 34 province names, all 333 city names, and all 2,856 county names. We consider co-occurrence frequency and term frequency as factors and devise a score function to identify fixed collocation queries.

Here is an example to show how our approach works. We plot two figures in Fig. 1, where Fig. 1 (a) represents the co-occurrence frequency distribution of keyword "Tian'an men" over a set of province names and Fig. 1 (b) represents the co-occurrence frequency distribution of keyword "sight spot" over a set of province names as well.

From Fig. 1 (a), there are a total of 1,334 queries that "Tian'anmen" co-occurred with a province name, and within which 1,317 queries have the word "Beijing". From Fig. 1 (b), there are 712 times that "sight spot" co-occurred with a province name, and we can see that the distribution is much more uniform.

There are many metrics that can represent a distribution, such as variance and Kurtosis measure. We use co-occurrence frequency as criterion because in variance and Kurtosis measures, there is a precondition that the results have a center point. These two criterions are used to measure how much data is gathered to the center point or how far the numbers are spread out. They are more suitable for continuous number distribution. In this problem, there is no center point. Thus, we propose a function including term frequency and co-occurrence frequency to find out fixed collocation queries.

$$f(Term_i) = \max_{1 < j < N_i} \{ \frac{P_{ij}}{N_i} \}. \tag{1}$$

$$Score_i = (TF_i - \alpha) \times f(Term_i). \tag{2}$$

---

[2] http://iflytek.com/
[3] http://lucene.apache.org/
[4] https://code.google.com/p/ik-analyzer/

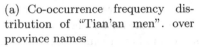
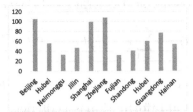

(a) Co-occurrence frequency distribution of "Tian'an men". over province names

(b) Co-occurrence frequency distribution of "sight spot". over province names

Fig. 1. Distribution of keywords "Tian'an men" and "sight spot".

To each word $Term_i$, TF_i is its occurrence times. N_i is the times $Term_i$ occurs with a place name. P_{ij} represents the times $Term_i$ occurs with a place name j. Function $f(Term_i)$ measures the max proportion of a term with a place name. To ensure accuracy, we empirically choose 0.9 as the threshold of $f(Term_i)$. We preserve those words whose $f(Term_i)$ is larger than 0.9 and judge whether its occurrence times is larger than a threshold α. Only when the both conditions are satisfied, we regard it as a fixed collocation query. In the experiment, we will futher discuss the effect of threshold α.

4   Classify Location Sensitive Queries

We adopt conventional classification techniques to classify location sensitive queries upon which we propose our feature selection method.

4.1   Feature Selection Methods

In text classification, there will be a large number of features in training and testing within which there is only a small proportion that is essential. Thus, how to select the best features becomes a key issue. We propose our novel feature selection method and use five baselines for comparison. These baselines are Document Frequency (*DF*), Information Gain (*IG*), Chi-Square Test (*CHI*), Expected Cross Entropy (*ECE*) and Mutual Information (*MI*).

Document Frequency is the number of documents in which a term occurs. The assumption is that rare terms are non-informative for category prediction and will not influence global performance. It is the simplest method and in our experiment, we select top K words as features in terms of the *DF* value.

Information Gain is frequently employed as a term goodness criterion in the field of machine learning [19,20]. It measures the number of bits of information obtained for category prediction by knowing the presence or absence of a term in a document. For term t and class c_i, M is the number of classes:

$$IG(t) = -\sum_{i=1}^{M} P(c_i)logP(c_i) + P(t)\sum_{i=1}^{M} P(t|c_i)logP(t|c_i) + P(\bar{t})\sum_{i=1}^{M} P(\bar{t}|c_i)logP(\bar{t}|c_i).$$

In our experiment, we select top K words in terms of the IG value.

Mutual Information is a criterion commonly used in statistical language modelling of word associations [21,22]. If we considers the two way contingency table of a term t and a category c, where A is the number of times t and c occur, B is the number of times t occurs without c, C is the number of times c occurs without t, and N is the total number of documents. Then the mutual information criterion between t and c is defined to be:

$$MI(t,c) = log\frac{P(t \wedge c)}{P(t) \times P(c)} \approx log\frac{A \times N}{(A+C) \times (A+B)}.$$

$MI(t,c)$ has a natural value of zero if t and c are independent. In our experiment, we select top K words in terms of the MI value.

λ^2 **Statistic** (*CHI*) measures the lack of independence between t and c and can be compared to the λ^2 distribution with one degree of freedom to judge extremeness. All the notations have the same definitions as before and D is the number of times both t and c do not occur. The λ^2 measure is defined as:

$$\lambda^2 = \frac{N \times (AD - CB)^2}{(A+C) \times (B+D) \times (A+B) \times (C+D)}.$$

The λ^2 statistic has a value of zero if t and c are independent. The weakness of the λ^2 statics is not to be reliable for low-frequency terms [23]. In our experiment, we select top K words in terms of the λ^2 value.

Expected Cross Entropy between two probability distributions over the same underlying set of events measures the average number of bits needed to identify an event drawn from the set [24]. In information theory, for term t and class c_i, the calculation is as follows:

$$ECE(t) = p(t)\sum_{i=1}^{M} p(t|c_i) \times log\frac{p(t|c_i)}{p(c_i)}.$$

In our experiment, we select top K words in terms of the ECE value.

In summary, apparently the DF measure is in favor of common terms over rare terms. It is not necessarily true in IG or CHI by definition. In theory, a common term can have a zero-valued IG or λ^2 score. It is proved by researches in past decades that the top three methods that get the best accuracy are λ^2 statistic, DF, and IG. However, they all have their own weaknesses.

4.2 Our Feature Selection Method

Our method is based on fuzzy set theory. Fuzzy sets are those whose elements have degrees of membership, which are introduced by Lotfi A. Zadeh [25] in 1965 as an extension of the classical notion of set. We mainly devise the membership function and the final score function.

Fuzzy Entropy. Information theory is concerned with quantification of information which is defined as the amount of information conveyed in an event and depends on the probability of the event. The definition is as follows:

$$I(A) = -logP(A).$$

The average information over all events is called the entropy. It is usually called Shannon entropy if it refers to the classical information entropy:

$$H(X) = -\sum_{k=1}^{n} P_k log P_k,$$

where X is a set of random variables and P_k is the set of all probabilities for the variables in X. $P_k = P[X = X_k]$, where $k = 1, 2, ..., n$.

The fuzzy entropy proposed by De Luca and Terminal [26] is shown in equation below. It is defined based on the concept of membership function where there are n membership functions (μ_i).

$$H_A = -K \sum_{i=1}^{n} \{\mu_i log(\mu_i) + (1 - \mu_i)log(1 - \mu_i)\}.$$

Membership Function Design. The design of membership function is the key point in calculation of fuzzy entropy. In short text classification, we consider two occasions as follows:

1) If one term occurs in one class frequently and seldom occurs in other classes, apparently it is a good feature.

2) In a given class, if one term spreads widely in many sentences or instances, it is a better feature than the one that only occurs in several instances.

The membership function is designed as follows:

$$\mu_{c_i}(t) = 4 \times (\frac{tf_{it}}{tf_t} - 0.5) \times (\frac{d_{it}}{C_i} - \frac{d_t}{N}), \tag{3}$$

where tf_{it} represents the number of times term t occurs in class c_i, tf_t represents the number of times t occurs in all classes, C_i is the total number of documents that belong to class c_i, d_t is the number of documents that contain t, d_{it} is the number of documents that contain t in class c_i and N is the total number of documents.

If a term follows the uniform distribution, the two parts in brackets both get a zero. From the definition, we can see $\frac{tf_{it}}{tf_t} \leq 0.5$, and $\frac{d_{it}}{C_i} - \frac{d_t}{N} \leq 0.5$. In order to make the maximum value equal to 1, we multiply them by 4.

Fuzzy Entropy Calculation. In regard to the definition of fuzzy entropy, we calculate our fuzzy entropy as:

$$FE(t) = -\frac{1}{m}\sum_{i=1}^{m}[\mu_{c_i}(t)log\mu_{c_i}(t) + (1 - \mu_{c_i}(t))log(1 - \mu_{c_i}(t))]. \quad (4)$$

$FE(t)$ means the fuzzy entropy of term t, $\mu_{c_i}(t)$ is the membership between term t and class c_i, and m is the number of classes.

Final Score Function. As we know, different feature selection methods have different emphases and drawbacks. *CHI* method does not take the term frequency into account and has a preference to low term frequency words. In order to overcome this weakness, we use tf_{it}/tf_t to represent the term frequency. In binary classification, tf_0 means the term frequency in negative class and tf_1 means the term frequency in positive class. tf_t is the sum of them. We use

$$ICHI(t) = Max\{tf_0/tf_t, tf_1/tf_t\} \times CHI(t), \quad (5)$$

as the improved *CHI* results. After calculation, we get the results sets of *ICHI(t)* and *FE(t)* and normalize each result set to [0, 1]. Then, we combine normalized *FE(t)* with *ICHI(t)* by a parameter β as the final score function:

$$FEICHI(t) = \beta \times Norm\{ICHI(t)\} + (1 - \beta) \times Norm\{FE(t)\}, \quad (6)$$

where $0 \leq \beta \leq 1$.

The description of our algorithm is shown in algorithm 1:

Algorithm 1. *FEICHI* feature selection method

Input: a) D={ $q_1, q_2, ..., q_N$ } be a set of N training set queries
b) Two predefined classes, C= {c_1, c_2 }
c) T= { $t_1, t_2, ..., t_n$ } is the set of n terms in the vocabulary
d) K is a threshold on the number of terms to be selected, $\beta \in [0,1]$
Output: A set of reduced terms TR

Steps:
1: TR $\leftarrow \emptyset$
2: **for** each $t_i \in T$ **do**
3:    Calculate $FEICHI(t_i)$ according to equation (6)
4: **end for**
5: Sort $FEICHI(t_i)$, $\forall$ $t_i \in$ T in descending order and the corresponding order of terms are $tr_1, tr_2, ..., tr_n$
6: **for** i $\leftarrow$ 1 to K **do**
7:    TR $\leftarrow$ TR $\cup$ tr_i
8: **end for**
9: **return** TR

4.3 Classification Schema

Many classifiers can be chosen such as naive bayes, linear regression, support vector machine, decision tree and neural network [27]. After feature selection, we test all these classifiers on various datasets and the results of neural network are more stable and reliable, so we choose neural network as our classifier.

5 Experiment Results

We evaluate the effectiveness of our feature selection method on a real world mobile search log provided by IFLYTEK [5]. Our experiments are five-fold.

1) The identification of fixed collocation queries is shown in *Exp. 1*.

2) We evaluate the performance of our novel feature selection method in comparison with five baseline methods, which will be analyzed in *Exp. 2*.

3) The performance of our method to identify location sensitive queries, along with the comparison to two state-of-the-art methods, is illustrated in *Exp. 3*

4) The influence of feature set size K is explored in *Exp. 4*.

5) We also analyze the effect of training set data size to the performance of our method, which is shown in *Exp. 5*.

5.1 Description of Dataset

Our dataset is approximately 950 MegaBytes and contains 1,402,744 mobile search queries which are in Chinese character, where 92,438 queries contain an explicit place name. In *Exp. 1*, we use these 92,438 queries as training set. In the next four experiments, we select 3,000 queries which contain an explicit place name as positive training set and adopt filter method to get negative training set. We build a dictionary that contains words related to location sensitive queries such as "where", "nearby" and "nearest". After filteration and selection, we ask 10 persons who are in master degree to examine the negative training set and pick out the false ones. Eventually we get a negative training set and a positive training set, each containing 3,000 queries. We randomly select 3,000 balanced queries as dataset 1 and split the remaining data into dataset 2 which contains 2,000 balanced queries and dataset 3 which contains 1,000 balanced queries. We public our datasets which can be downloaded from this link [6].

5.2 Evaluation Metrics

In order to evaluate the effectiveness of class assignments, we use the standard precision, recall and F1 measure. The definitions are as follows:

$$\text{precison} = \frac{\text{number of correct positive predictions}}{\text{number of positive predictions}}$$

---

[5] http://iflytek.com/
[6] http://pan.baidu.com/s/1mgmV3cs

$$recall = \frac{number\ of\ correct\ positive\ predictions}{number\ of\ positive\ examples}$$

$$F1\quad measure = \frac{2 \times recall \times precision}{recall + precision}$$

These scores are computed for the binary decisions on each individual class and then are aggregately averaged over all classes. A good algorithm should produce as high a recall value as possible without sacrificing precision. The closer the values of precision and recall are, the higher the F1 measure is. The value of F1 measure lies between 0 and 1 and a high value of F1 measure is desirable for good classification.

5.3   Exp. 1: Identify Fixed Collocation Queries

We use the 92,438 queries as the training data and function $Score_i$ proposed in section 3 as the criterion. As the value of threshold α changes, the number of fixed collocation queries as well as the classification accuracy, changes too, which is shown as Fig. 2.

When the term frequency is less than 5, we can see that there are many incorrect pairs. A word with a very low frequency happens to co-occur with a place name. As α increases, the reliability of the results increases as well. When α surpasses 80, accuracy begins to decline because more true fixed collocation queries are ignored than false ones. We manually check the results in terms of the accuracy and choose 80 as the threshold. Thus, we get an accuracy of 91%. We list several fixed collocation queries in Table 1.

Table 1. Queries and corresponding place names

Query	Place name
Guiyuan temple	Wuhan city
Yu Opera	Henan province
Lanzhou	Gansu province
Zhuizi	Henan province
Greeting Pine	Huangshan city
Panfu Road	Guangzhou city
The Classical Gardens	Suzhou city
Roast duck	Beijing city
The Captial	Beijing city
Chongqing University	Chongqing city
Guangzhou Daily	Guangzhou city
Bangzi	Hebei province
Daqing Oil Field	Daqing city

Fig. 2. The relation among threshold α, number of pairs left, and classification accuracy

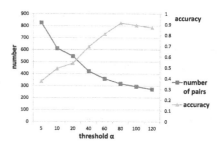

Table 2. Feature selection methods and classifiers of F1 measure with top 1,000 features

	NB [a]	Liblinear [b]	SVM	RBFNetwork	Tree
DF	0.692	**0.730**	0.544	0.704	0.695
IG	**0.498**	0.485	0.486	0.484	0.486
CHI	0.700	**0.753**	0.539	0.711	0.695
MI	0.537	0.572	0.486	**0.581**	0.494
ECE	**0.499**	0.485	0.480	0.484	0.486
FEICHI	0.703	**0.767**	0.54	0.757	0.696

[a] Naive Bayes Classifier
[b] Linear Regression Classifier

Table 3. Classification results of 1,000 queries

Method	Precision	Recall	F1
Ourdia et. al	0.805	0.797	0.783
Welch et. al	0.911	0.592	0.718
Our work	0.849	0.828	**0.825**

5.4 Exp. 2: Comparison of Feature Selection Methods

Dataset 1 is used in this experiment. Firstly, we tag the sentences in positive training set with 1 and negative training set with 0 as the class label. Secondly, we get the segmentation form of each sentence and remove the place names from each sentence. Thirdly, we utilize different feature selection methods to get top 1,000 features and then use multiple classifiers to get the results. We implement six feature selection methods and use classification tool Weka [7] to get the results. The value of β is set to 0.8 through cross validation. The results are shown in Table 2, in which the first column represents the feature selection methods and the first row represents the classifiers.

From Table 2, CHI method gets the best F1 score of 0.753 among baselines and DF method gets 0.73 at F1 score. When using CHI and DF methods, the linear regression and neural network classification methods outperform the others. Our method gets the highest score of 0.767 due to the reason that we take the weakness of CHI into account and combine fuzzy entropy method to help improve the performance. Both IG and ECE methods do not perform well, which indicate that these two methods are not suitable for short text classification.

By comparing the classifiers only, both SVM and $Tree$ models never get the best classification results. Linear regression model gets three best results, which follows our intuitions. Sentence is the linear combination of words, each making a different contribution to the sentence, so it is appropriate to use linear regression in text classification. On the contrary, SVM and $Tree$ models can not describe the characteristics or the structure of sentences, which leads to their poor F1 results in query classification.

5.5 Exp. 3: Comparison of Location Sensitive Queries Classification

In the detection of location sensitive queries, Ourdia [18] uses Kurtosis and Kullback-Leibler Divergence to measure the relevance between a query and a place names while utilizing SVM model for classification on a dataset containing

---

[7] http://www.cs.waikato.ac.nz/ml/weka/

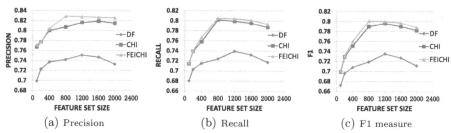

Fig. 3. Precison, Recall and F1 measure of three feature selection methods with different feature set size K.

200 queries. F1 score reported is 0.8. Welch [1] proposes "base queries" concept and utilizes clustering method to find base queries. Welch's experiment on 102 queries gets a precision of 0.94, however, the recall is 0.46. In summary, both of their F1 scores are less than 80%.

We evaluate our method along with their methods on dataset 3 with K set to 1,600. β is set to 0.5 through cross validation. The experiment results are shown in Table 3. We can see that our method achieves 82.5% at F1 score which outperforms the aforementioned two methods.

5.6   Exp. 4: Influence of Feature Set Size K

We vary feature set size from 50 to 2,000 and implement our method and two baseline methods on dataset 2. Results show that under any circumstances our method performs the best. We use neural network classifier on dataset 2 by setting β to 0.8 gained from *Exp. 2* and show the precision, recall and F1 value in Fig. 3.

As the feature set size K increases from 100 to 2,000, all of the curves first rise and then fall. It agrees with our expected results and priori knowledge. In the rising stage, more and more good features are selected for classification and in the falling stage, more and more irrelevant features are selected which make the classification result worse.

From Fig. 3, it is clearly shown that our method continuously outperforms the baselines. When the size of feature set is small, the improvement is not apparent. However, when K rises between 800 and 1,600, there is a significant improvement of 3% in precision.

5.7   Exp. 5: Influence of Training Set Proportion

To find the influence of the split percentage of training set and testing set, we evaluate our method and baseline methods on dataset 2. We still choose $\beta = 0.8$ and neural network as classifier, the results are shown in Fig. 4.

When the proportion of training set decreases, the precision, recall and F1 measure tend to decline. Our method still outperforms the others when the training set proportion varies from 0.9 to 0.5. In summary, our *FEICHI* feature selection method does have an improvement over baselines.

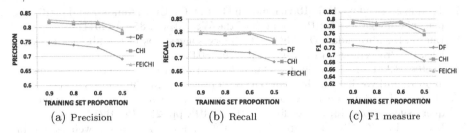

Fig. 4. Precison, Recall and F1 measure of three feature selection methods with different training set proportion.

6   Conclusion

In this paper, we propose an approach for identifying fixed collocation queries via "the wisdom of the crowd" and location sensitive queries via *FEICHI* and neural network. Specifically, we devise a score function to identify queries with a fixed corresponding place name. We propose our *FEICHI* feature selection method and get a better performance than the five baseline methods. We utilize neural network classifier and achieve 82.5% at F1 measure on the queries that have implicit location intentions. All the experiments are conducted on a real-world mobile search log. In future we plan to study how to identify the intentions of ambiguous search queries.

Acknowledgments. This research was partially supported by grants from the National High Technology Research and Development Program of China (Grant No. 2014AA015203), the Fundamental Research Funds for the Central Universities of China (Grant No. WK2350000001) and the Anhui Provincial Natural Science Foundation (Grant No. 1408085QF110).

References

1. Welch, M., Cho, J.: Automatically identifying localizable queries. In: Proceedings of the ACM SIGIR, pp. 1185–1186 (2008)
2. Kamvar, M., Baluja, S.: Deciphering trends in mobile search. Computer **40**(8), 58–62 (2007)
3. Bennett, N., Radlinski, F., White, R.W., Yilmaz, E.: Inferring and using location metadata to personalize web search. In: Proceedings of the SIGIR, pp. 135–144 (2011)
4. Matthijs, N., Radlinski, F.: Personalizing web search using long term browsing history. In: Proceedings of the WSDM, pp. 25–34 (2011)
5. Xiang, B., Jiang, D., Pei, J., Sun, X., Chen, E., Li, H.: Context-aware ranking in web search. In: Proceedings of the SIGIR, pp. 451–458 (2010)
6. Kharitonov, E., Serdyukov, P.: Demographic context in web search re-ranking. In: Proceedings of the CIKM, pp. 2555–2558 (2012)

7. Teevan, J., Liebling, D.J., Ravichandran Geetha, G.: Understanding and predicting personal navigation. In: Proceedings of the WSDM, pp. 85–94 (2011)
8. Bhatia, S., Majumdar, D., Mitra, P.: Query suggestions in the absence of query logs. In: Proceedings of the SIGIR, pp. 795–804 (2011)
9. Santos, R.L.T., Macdonald, C., Ounis, I.: Learning to rank query suggestions for adhoc and diversity search. Information Retrieval, 1–23 (2012)
10. Ozertem, U., et al.: Learning to suggest: a machine learning framework for ranking query suggestions. In: Proceedings of the SIGIR, pp. 25–34 (2012)
11. Lee, U., Liu, Z., Cho, J.: Automatic identification of user goals in web search. In: Proceedings of the WWW, pp. 391–400 (2005)
12. Yi, J., Maghoul, F., Pedersen, J.: Deciphering mobile search patterns: a study of Yahoo! mobile search queries, In: Proceedings of the WWW, pp. 257–266 (2008)
13. Kamvar, M., Baluja, S.: A large scale study of wireless search behavior: Google mobile search. In: Proceedings of the AIGCHI, pp. 701–109. ACM (2009)
14. Chuklin, A., Serdyukov, P., de Rijke, M.: Using intent information to model user behavior in diversified search. In: Braslavski, P., Kuznetsov, S.O., Kamps, J., Rüger, S., Agichtein, E., Segalovich, I., Yilmaz, E., Serdyukov, P. (eds.) ECIR 2013. LNCS, vol. 7814, pp. 1–13. Springer, Heidelberg (2013)
15. Dhar, S., Swain, S., Mishra, B.S.P.: Query intent classification using semi-supervised learning. In: Proceedings of the IJCA, pp. 40–43 (2014)
16. Vandrevu, S., Zhang, Y., Tseng, B., Sun, G., Li, X.: Identifying regional sensitive queries in web search. In: Proceedings of the WWW, pp. 507–514 (2008)
17. Gravano, L., Hatzivassiloglou, V., Lichtenstein, R.: Categorizing web queries according to geographical locality, In: Proceedings of the CIKM, pp. 325–323 (2003)
18. Bouidghaghen, O., et al.: Personalizing mobile web search for location sensitive queries. In: Mobile Data Management, pp. 110–118. IEEE (2011)
19. Mitchell, T.: Machine Learning, pp. 36–39. McCraw Hill (1996)
20. Quinlan, J.R.: Induction of decision trees. Machine Learning 1(1), 81–106 (1996)
21. Church, K.W., Hanks, P.: Word association norms, mutual information and lexicography. In: Proceedings of the ACL, pp. 76–83 (1989)
22. Wiener, E., Pedersen, J.O., Weigend, A.S.: A neural network approach to topic spotting. In: Proceedings of the DAIR, pp. 317–332 (1995)
23. Dunning, T.E.: Accurate methods for the statistics of surprise and coincidence. Computational Linguistics 19(1), 61–74 (1993)
24. De Boer, P.-T., et al.: A tutorial on the cross-entropy method. Annals of Operations Research 134(1), 19–67 (2005)
25. Zadeh, L.A.: Fuzzy sets. Information and Controls 8(3), 338–353 (1965)
26. Luca, A.D., Terminal, S.: A definition of non probabilistic entropy in the setting of the fuzzy set theory. Information and Control 20, 301–312 (1972)
27. Kotsiantis, S.B., et al.: Supervised machine learning: a review of classification techniques, pp. 3–24 (2007)

Course Similarity Calculation Using Efficient Manifold Ranking

Bingjie Zhao and Xueqing Li[✉]

School of Computer Science and Technology, Shandong University, Jinan, China
ZhaoBingJieBBST@163.com, xqli@sdu.edu.cn

Abstract. Course Similarity Calculation aims at quantitatively computing the cross degree of the knowledge points two courses contain. However, the polysemy and synonym of various knowledge points lead to the main challenge for calculation effectiveness. Existing course similarity calculation methods are mainly based on the traditional text mining approaches such as Latent Semantic Indexing (LSI) and Term Frequency-Inverse Document Frequency (TFIDF). However, these methods calculate the similarity between two courses simply by their absolute pairwise distance, which significantly limits the effectiveness of capturing the semantic relevance among all the courses. In this paper, we propose a novel course similarity calculation method using Efficient Manifold Ranking (EMR), which improves the traditional methods by measuring course similarities considering the underlying intrinsic manifold structure on the whole dataset. Experimental results on a real world course database demonstrate the outstanding performance of our proposed method. Furthermore, we extend the proposed method to major similarity calculation.

Keywords: Course similarity calculation · Text mining · EMR · Major similarity calculation

1 Introduction

Course Similarity of two courses refers to the cross degree of the knowledge points they contain. Course Similarity Calculation aims at calculating the similarity among different courses. In many cases, we have an urgent need to find out similarities among different majors. For example, when freshmen are faced with choosing majors, students pursue interdisciplinary studies, and graduates make sure of the fields of employment during hunting a job, all of them need a reference of the similarities among various majors. However, two majors with similar names may have completely different study contents (e.g., Geographic Sciences and Geographic Information Science). Therefore, we cannot identify the same or not of two majors simply by their names. A quantified measure need to be proposed to calculate the similarity of different majors. One basis is the curriculum of a major.

© Springer International Publishing Switzerland 2015
S. Zhang et al. (Eds.): KSEM 2015, LNAI 9403, pp. 421–432, 2015.
DOI: 10.1007/978-3-319-25159-2_38

While calculating the similarity of curriculums of two majors, we face a new vital issue: the similarity among different courses. Likewise, we need to quantitatively compute the cross degree of the knowledge points that two courses contain as the measure of their similarity. The challenge for course similarity calculation mainly exists in the polysemy and synonym of the extracted knowledge points. Thus, finding a method which can effectively narrow the semantic gap has a significant meaning for course similarity calculation.

Existing methods of calculating course similarity are mainly based on the traditional text similarity methods such as LSI [6,7] and TFIDF [3–6]. In these methods, a vector space model (VSM) [2] is constructed according to the knowledge points set each course contains, and the similarity between two courses is measured by the absolute pairwise distance of their feature vectors. However, these methods have a common drawback of neglecting the global intrinsic structure of the courses, leading to the inadequate mining of semantic relevance over the whole data set.

Methods that rank the relevant courses to a query based on the universal manifold structure of whole data set seem very promising to make up this defect. Actually, to a very large extent, the course similarity calculation problem is equivalent to a ranking problem that ranks a list of courses according to their relevance to a query. An efficient method should make sure that a course with higher relevance to the query has a higher ranking score. Therefore, in this paper, we propose a novel method based on EMR [16,17] to solve this problem.

Manifold Ranking (MR) [8] algorithm is a universal ranking algorithm, which ranks the data with respect to the intrinsic structure collectively revealed by the whole data set. By spreading the relevant ranking score via the global manifold structure, MR algorithm is superior to the traditional methods for its mining the semantic relevance among courses in the whole data set, thereby improving the overall accuracy performance of course similarity calculation.

Considering the computation efficiency on a large data set, in the proposed method, we use EMR to replace the original MR. The core idea of EMR is exactly the same as MR, except for the EMR algorithm altering the graph construction process of MR. According to Xu [16,17], EMR has a comparable performance but short computational time than the original MR algorithm.

In this paper, we propose a novel course similarity calculation method based on EMR. In the proposed method, we firstly use word segmentation component to extract the knowledge points from each course in the data set and get the whole knowledge points collection. Next we compute a TFIDF-weight feature vector of each course according to the knowledge points it contains, and feature vectors of all courses construct the VSM over the whole data set. Finally, EMR algorithm is used based on the VSM to calculate the similarity among different courses. In addition, in the end of the paper, we make a brief discussion about how to extend the proposed method to major similarity calculation. The main contributions of this paper are as follows:

1. We propose a novel course similarity calculation method using EMR, and experimental results demonstrate that the proposed method significantly outperforms the traditional text mining methods LSI and TFIDF.
2. We extend the proposed method to the calculation of major similarities, succeeding in providing a quantitative reference for those who are confused with the similarities among various majors.

The rest of the paper is organized as follows. Sect. 2 briefly discusses related work. The proposed method for course similarity calculation is described in detail in Sect. 3. Sect. 4 presents the experiment results on a real world course database. Finally we extend the proposed method in major similarity calculation in Sect. 5 and Sect. 6 concludes this paper.

2 Related Work

Text mining is an important part of natural language processing (NLP) with many potential applications, e.g., information retrieval, text categorization, text clustering, and text summarization. To the best of our knowledge, existing course similarity calculation methods are mainly based on the traditional text similarity calculation approaches. Gomaa et al. [1] make a survey of text similarity approaches. In text similarity calculation, VSM [2] is one of the mostly used models to represent the set of documents. Each document is identified by a set of terms that are collectively used to represent its contents: $D_j = \{d_{1,j}, d_{2,j}, \cdots, d_{t,j}\}$, where $d_{i,j}$ represent the weight of the i-th term in document j. TFIDF [3–6] is one of the most popular term weighting methods, which has an outstanding statistical quality that provides a good discriminative power of the index terms to identify the category of a document. However, a major drawback of TFIDF is the high dimensionality of the feature space, and most of the terms are redundant to the similarity calculation task. Then LSI [6,7] is proposed based on the need of reducing dimensions of the feature space without sacrificing similarity calculation performance, in which Singular Value Decomposition (SVD) is used to filter out some noise and get a low-dimensional reduced rank approximation of the original feature space. Zhang et al. [6] made a comparative study of TFIDF, LSI and multi-words for text classification, which demonstrates that LSI has both favorable semantic and statistical quality which come from good discriminative power. However, when reducing dimensions, LSI may lose a part of structural information, which deficiency can affect the calculation accuracy of partial data set. What's more, both the TFIDF and LSI calculate the similarity between two courses simply by their absolute pairwise distance, which ignore the underlying intrinsic global structure of the whole data set, thereby significantly limits the effectiveness of capturing the semantic relevance among all the courses.

Zhou et al. [8] propose MR algorithm for ranking problems in information retrieval. The core idea of MR method is to rank the data with respect to the intrinsic manifold structure collectively revealed by a great amount of data.

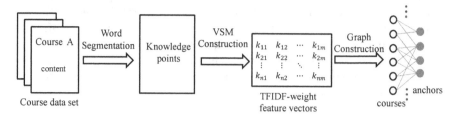

Fig. 1. The process of the proposed method. Note that we construct an anchor graph in process three, where the set of anchors is calculated using k-means algorithm based on VSM. Then EMR is applied based on the graph to calculate the similarities among different courses.

The MR's making full use of the underlying global structure advances capturing the semantic relevance among the whole data set. MR algorithm has been successfully applied in document similarity search [9] and many computer vision fields such as image retrieval [10–12], saliency detection [13] and person identification [14], and all achieve outstanding performance. Given the computational cost of MR is very expensive especially on large data sets, He et al. [15] propose the Fast Manifold Ranking(FMR) and Xu et al. [16,17] propose EMR to speed up the original MR algorithm. Experimental results demonstrate that EMR algorithm achieves better tradeoff between the accuracy and efficiency than FMR and MR. Zhou et al. [18] apply EMR in visual tracking and achieve excellent performance. Inspired by the above discussion, we propose a novel method based on EMR for course similarity calculation.

3 Overview of Method

In this section, we make a detailed description of how to calculate course similarity using EMR algorithm. Our proposed method mainly consists of the following three parts: Word Segmentation, VSM Construction, and Similarity Calculation Process Using EMR Algorithm. The process of the proposed method is described as Fig. 1.

3.1 Word Segmentation

Course Similarity Calculation aims at quantitatively computing the cross degree of the knowledge points that two courses contain. Thus above all, for each course, we need to extract the knowledge points from its course content, such as course description, catalog etc. In our experiment, we use JE-analysis word segmentation component to conduct word segmentation on the catalog of each course in the data set. After removing stop words and stemming process, we get the knowledge points collection T for all courses in the data set.

3.2 VSM Construction

Suppose the total course number in the dataset is n, the total number of the knowledge points in T we get in Sect. 3.1 is m. Then we construct the VSM as

$X = \{x_1, \ldots, x_n\}$, where x_i $(1 \le i \le n)$ represent the i-th course in the data set. In this model, each course x_i can be represented by a feature vector in m knowledge points dimensions, $x_i = [k_{i,1}k_{i,2}\cdots k_{i,m}]$, where $k_{i,j}$ $(1 \le i \le n, 1 \le j \le m)$ represent the weight of j-th knowledge point in i-th course. In our work, we use TFIDF measure to evaluate weight k. That is, $k_{i,j} = tf_{i,j} * idf_j$, where $tf_{i,j}$ represent the term frequency of knowledge point j in course i, idf_j represent the inverse document frequency of knowledge point j. Finally X is represented as Eq. 1.

$$X = \begin{bmatrix} k_{1,1} & k_{1,2} & \cdots & k_{1,m} \\ k_{2,1} & k_{2,2} & \cdots & k_{2,m} \\ \vdots & \vdots & \ddots & \vdots \\ k_{n,1} & k_{n,2} & \cdots & k_{n,m} \end{bmatrix} \tag{1}$$

3.3 Similarity Calculation Process Using EMR Algorithm

Considering the computation efficiency of MR, we use EMR rather than MR in our work. In this part, we make a detailed description of the calculation process using EMR.

In Sect. 3.2 we construct the VSM X as Eq. 1 with n courses and m knowledge points. To do the calculation using EMR algorithm, we need first use k-means algorithm to calculate d centers of X as a set of anchors sharing the same space with the data set, that is, $U = \{u_1, \cdots, u_d\} \subset R^m$. Suppose the q-th $(1 \le q \le n)$ course x_q is the query course and the rest are the courses that we want to rank according to their relevance to the query course x_q. Let $f : X \to R$ denote a ranking function which assigns to each course x_i $(1 \le i \le n)$ a ranking value f_i. Finally, we define the initial vector $y = [y_1, \cdots, y_n]^T$, in which $y_q = 1$ because course x_q is the query and all the other $y_i = 0$ $(1 \le i \le n$ and $i \ne q)$. Then the EMR algorithm goes as follows:

1. Calculate the weight matrix $Z \in R^{d*n}$, in which $z_{k,i}$ represent the weight between data point x_i and anchor u_k. e. g., calculate $z_{k,i}$ by the Nadaraya-Watson kernel regression (as Eq. 2) with the Epanechnikov quadratic kernel as Eq. 3.

$$z_{k,i} = \frac{K(\frac{|x_i - u_k|}{\lambda})}{\sum_{l=1}^{d} K(\frac{|x_i - u_l|}{\lambda})} \tag{2}$$

$$K_\lambda(t) = \begin{cases} \frac{3}{4}(1 - t^2) & if |t| \le 1 \\ 0 & otherwise. \end{cases} \tag{3}$$

where $\lambda(x_i) = |x_i - u_{[s]}|, u_{[s]}$ is the s-th closest anchor of x_i;

2. Build the anchor graph by connecting each data point to its s nearest anchors and then assign weights to each connection by Eq. 2 and Eq. 3;
3. Form the adjacency matrix W defined by $W = Z^T Z$, which means that if two data points x_i and x_j are correlative $(w_{i,j} > 0, 1 \le i, j \le n)$, they share at least one common anchor point, otherwise $w_{i,j} = 0$;

Algorithm 1. The EMR algorithm for course similarity calculation

---

Input: The VSM of the course data set X, the initial query vector $y = [y_1, \cdots, y_n]^T$;
Output: Ranking score f_i^* ;
1: Compute anchors set $U = \{u_1, \cdots, u_d\} \subset R^m$ using k-means algorithm;
2: Calculate the weight matrix $Z \in R^{d*n}$ by Eq. 2 and Eq. 3;
3: Form the adjacency matrix W by $W = Z^T Z$;
4: Symmetrically normalize W by $S = D^{-1/2} W D^{-1/2}$ and Eq. 4;
5: Iterate Eq. 5 until convergence and get the final ranking score f_i^*.

---

4. Symmetrically normalize W by $S = D^{-1/2} W D^{-1/2}$, in which D is the diagonal matrix with Eq. 4,

$$D_{i,i} = \sum_{j=1}^{n} w_{i,j} = \sum_{j=1}^{n} z_i^T z_j = z_i^T \nu \tag{4}$$

where z_i is the i-th column of Z and $\nu = \sum_{j=1}^{n} z_j$.
5. Iterate Eq. 5 until convergence, where α is a parameter in $[0, 1)$;

$$f(t+1) = \alpha S f(t) + (1 - \alpha) y \tag{5}$$

6. Let f_i^* denote the limit of the sequence $f_i(t)$. Rank each course x_i ($1 \leq i \leq n$) according to its ranking score f_i^* (largest points are ranked first).

A brief description of EMR algorithm for course similarity calculation is shown in Alg.1.

4   Experimental Results

4.1   Dataset

To perform the experiment, we choose from the available course database 3306 specialty courses about science and engineering as our dataset. After the word segmentation process to the catalog of each course, we finally get 8044 knowledge points in total.

As for the relevance rate among these courses, we classify each course in the data set into one or more correspondingly specific disciplines according to the knowledge points it contains. e. g. , course A "Advanced Computer Network" should be classified into "Computer Science and Technology- Computer Architecture- Computer Network"(first level discipline-second level discipline-third level discipline),whereas course B "Data Communication and Computer Network" should be classified into both "Computer Science and Technology-Computer Architecture- Computer Network" and "Electronics, Communications and Automatic Control Technology- Communications Technology" (first level discipline-second level discipline without third level discipline). Finally, all the courses in the dataset have been classified into eighteen first level disciplines

Table 1. The relevance rate between two courses

Graded Relevance	Score
Exactly same knowledge points	4
Common third level discipline	3
Common second level discipline	2
Common first level discipline	1
Different first level discipline	0

with their sub disciplines. Based on the most common discipline levels each two courses classified (e. g., we consider course A and course B above have common second level discipline "Computer Science and Technology- Computer Architecture"), we define the relevance rate between two courses as Tab. 1.

The definition of Tab. 1 indicates that, the two courses which gains score greater than zero are considered relevant. What's more, the higher score the two courses gain, the more similarity they have.

4.2   Evaluation Metric Discussion

In our work, we use Precision, Recall, F1-measure, Mean Average Precision (MAP) and NDCG [19] five evaluation metrics to evaluate the retrieval performance of our method.

For course similarity calculation, we consider these following two criteria are extremely important:

1. The more relevant courses existing in top k courses of the result list, the better performance the method gains.
2. The higher rank that the highly relevant course locates, the better performance the method gains.

Precision, Recall and F1-measure provide three evaluation metrics for the first criteria. MAP provides a single-value metric considering the order in which the retrieved items are presented. MAP for a set of queries is the mean of the Average Precision scores for each query. For a single query, Average Precision computes the average value of precision over every position in the ranked sequence of retrieved items:

$$AveP = \frac{\sum_{k=1}^{n}(P(k) \times rel(k))}{number\ of\ relevant\ items} \tag{6}$$

where k is the rank in the sequence of retrieved items, n is the number of retrieved items, $P(k)$ is the precision at cut-off k in the list, and $rel(k)$ is 0 if the relevance score of item ranking at k is 0 as we defined in Tab. 1, 1 otherwise. Finally, if the number of queries is Q, then

$$MAP = \frac{\sum_{q=1}^{Q} AveP(q)}{Q} \tag{7}$$

NDCG provides a different metric of ranking quality in the retrieved items. For each query, the NDCG at a particular rank position p is defined as:

$$NDCG_p = \frac{DCG_p}{IDCG_p} = \frac{1}{IDCG_p} \times \sum_{i=1}^{p} \frac{2^{rel_i} - 1}{\log_2(i+1)} \qquad (8)$$

where rel_i is the score of the result at position i as we defined in Tab. 1 according to its graded relevance to the query item. $IDCG_p$ is the maximum possible DCG_p so that the perfect ranking will produce an $NDCG$ of 1.0. Finally, the averaged $NDCG$ value for all queries is used for measuring the ranking performance of our methods.

4.3   Method Comparison

In order to show the good retrieval performance of the proposed method, we use several other methods in the experiments for comparison: the original MR, LSI, and TFIDF (baseline).Based on our selection of EMR only for its computation efficiency to the original MR, we focus our attention mainly on the comparison of manifold ranking methods (EMR and MR) to the traditional text mining methods (LSI and TFIDF).

In MR method, we construct a traditional k-nearest neighbor graph, rather than the altered anchor graph in the proposed method, based on the VSM matrix X we get in Sect. 3.2. The size of k-nearest neighbor and tradeoff parameter α in MR algorithm are 11 and 0.77 respectively.

In LSI method, SVD is used to decompose the original VSM matrix $X = U\sum V^T$,where $\sum$ is the singular values matrix, each column of U is the left singular vector of X, and each column of V is the right singular vector of X. In our work, we retain 5000 singular values in $\sum$ to produce the approximation matrix X' for similarity calculation.

TFIDF method is the baseline method in which we use the original VSM matrix X for similarity calculation.

Each course in the data set is chosen as a query respectively, and we calculate the average Precision, Recall, F1 score, NDCG and the MAP value over all the queries to compare the performance of different methods. The parameters in the proposed method are set as follows: $d = 450$, $\alpha = 0.3$ and $s = 5$.

Tab. 2 shows the average Precision, Recall (at 5 to 25) and MAP value of each method, and Fig. 2 prints the average F1 score (at 5 to 25) of each method. We find that comparing with the original MR method, although the proposed method loses little precision at top 5 to 25 (as Tab. 2 shows), when comprehensively considering Presicion and Recall performance (as F1 scores represented in Fig. 2), it gains overall higher F1 scores than the original MR method. What's more, the MAP values represented in Tab. 2 demonstrate that the the proposed method has an overall higher precision than MR. In any case, both the proposed method and MR method show better performance than the traditional text mining methods LSI and TFIDF.

Table 2. The average values of Precision, Recall on top 5 to 25, and MAP

	MR	EMR	LSI	TFIDF
P@5	0.9257	0.9177	0.9090	0.9087
P@10	0.8542	0.8513	0.8380	0.8429
P@15	0.8022	0.7994	0.7828	0.7932
P@20	0.7648	0.7647	0.7425	0.7469
P@25	0.7402	0.7360	0.7141	0.7151
R@5	0.0274	0.0272	0.0264	0.0263
R@10	0.0437	0.0447	0.0422	0.0416
R@15	0.0569	0.0572	0.0541	0.0538
R@20	0.0689	0.0691	0.0652	0.0647
R@25	0.0799	0.0802	0.0763	0.0753
MAP	0.4635	0.4664	0.4571	0.4603

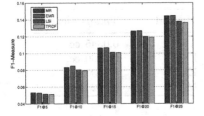

Fig. 2. The average F1 score at top 5 to 25 returned by MR (left),EMR,LSI and TFIDF (baseline)

Fig. 3. The average NDCG value at top 5 to 25 returned by EMR, MR, LSI and TFIDF (baseline) methods

Fig. 3 shows the average NDCG value (at 5 to 25) of each method. It is easy to find that the proposed method has the best ranking quality in the result list. Both manifold methods (EMR and MR) perform far better than LSI and the baseline algorithm TFIDF. Further, we give in Tab. 3 the statistics about average timing per similarity calculation among one course and others. We implemented our scheme in matlab language. Running our implementation on a laptop computer with an Intel Core(TM)2 Duo T6400 2.10GHz CPU and 2 GB memory.

The outstanding performance of the proposed method mainly benefits from that, rather than measuring the similarity between two courses simply by their absolute pairwise similarity, the manifold ranking algorithm makes full use of the inter-relationship of all the courses in the dataset, thereby effectively mining the semantic relevance among all the courses.

4.4   Parameter Tuning

When we use EMR algorithm to calculate the course similarity, parameter tuning plays an extremely important role in our work, for different parameter can significantly impact the performance of EMR algorithm. In order to make our method achieve the best performance, we conduct the following three experiments respectively to determine the optimal three parameters in EMR algorithm: d, α, and

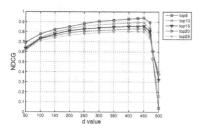

Fig. 4. The NDCG value of the proposed method versus different number of anchors d when $\alpha = 0.3$ and $s = 5$

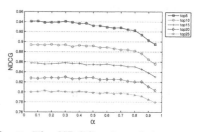

Fig. 5. The NDCG value of the proposed method versus different tradeoff parameter α when $d = 450$ and $s = 5$

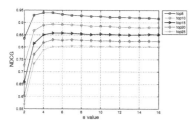

Fig. 6. The NDCG value of the proposed method versus different neighborhood size s when $d = 450$ and $\alpha = 0.3$

Table 3. The average timing per similarity calculation among one course and others

Method	Time/Calculation
TFIDF	0.0345sec.
LSI	0.0360sec.
EMR	0.3430sec.
MR	0.5623sec.

s, where d is the number of anchor points, α is the tradeoff parameter in EMR and MR, and parameter s is the neighborhood size in the anchor graph.

Fig. 4 demonstrates the performance of the proposed method ($NDCG_5$, $NDCG_{10}$, $NDCG_{15}$, $NDCG_{20}$ and $NDCG_{25}$) versus different number of anchors d in the whole data set when $\alpha = 0.3$ and $s = 5$. It is observed that the performance of the proposed method continuously increases until the number of anchors reaches 450, and after which number sharply declines. Therefore, we choose $d = 450$ in our method.

Fig. 5 demonstrates the performance of the proposed method ($NDCG_5$, $NDCG_{10}$, $NDCG_{15}$, $NDCG_{20}$ and $NDCG_{25}$) versus the tradeoff parameter α when $d = 450$ and $s = 5$. We can see that the performance of our method is not sensitive to α when α ranges from 0.05 to 0.7. When $\alpha > 0.7$, the performance shows decline trend. Finally, we choose the overall optimal value $\alpha = 0.3$ in our work.

Fig. 6 demonstrates the performance of the proposed method ($NDCG_5$, $NDCG_{10}$, $NDCG_{15}$, $NDCG_{20}$ and $NDCG_{25}$) versus the neighborhood size in the anchor graph s when $d = 450$ and $\alpha = 0.3$.

We find that the performance of our method changes little when the neighborhood size is larger than 4. In our work, we choose $s = 5$ for it provide the overall best performance. On the other side, small s is helpful to efficient computation.

5 Major Similarity Calculation Using The Proposed Method

In this section, we briefly discuss how to extend our proposed method to major similarity calculation. Suppose the curriculum of major A is $C_A = \{c_{a_1}, \cdots, c_{a_n}\}$, the curriculum of major B is $C_B = \{c_{b_1}, \cdots, c_{b_m}\}$, where c_{a_i} ($1 \leq i \leq n, 1 \leq a_i \leq N$) represent the a_i-th course in the data set, c_{b_j} ($1 \leq j \leq m, 1 \leq b_j \leq N$) represent the b_j-th course in the data set, N represent the total course number in the data set. Our goal is to firstly use our proposed course similarity calculation method to retrieve the top k(threshold) courses φ that are most relevant to the whole curriculum of major A. Next we compute the percentage of curriculum of major B in φ as Sim_{BA} to denote the relevance of major B to A. Then in the same way we compute the relevance of major A to B as Sim_{AB}. Finally, we use the mean value Sim to measure the similarity between major A and major B as:

$$Sim = \frac{Sim_{BA} + Sim_{AB}}{2} \tag{9}$$

The way of using our method to calculate the top k(threshold) courses φ that are most relevant to major A is as follows: for major A, each course c_{a_i} has a weight w_{a_i} ($1 \leq i \leq n, 1 \leq a_i \leq N$) which denotes the importance of c_{a_i} to major A. All the weights of the curriculum of major A need to satisfy the following conditions: $0 \leq w_{a_i} \leq 1$, and $\sum_{i=1}^{n} w_{a_i} = 1$ ($1 \leq i \leq n, 1 \leq a_i \leq N$).

Next we define the initial vector y in Alg.1 as $y_A = [y_1, \cdots, y_N]^T$, in which $y_{a_i} = w_{a_i}$ because the a_i-th course c_{a_i} is existing in major A and its weight w_{a_i} should be used as one of the combined retrieval conditions, and all the other $y_k = 0$ ($1 \leq k \leq N$ and $k \neq a_i$). Then y_A is used in EMR algorithm to get the ranking score list. Courses which gain top k ranking score make up φ.

6 Conclusion and Future Work

In this paper, we propose a novel method for course similarity calculation using EMR algorithm. The proposed method tries to improve the existing methods by calculating the relevance among different courses considering the global intrinsic manifold structure of the whole dataset. Experimental results demonstrate the outstanding performance of the proposed method.

In our future work, we will use machine learning methods to automatically select the optimal parameters in the proposed method. Furthermore, we will extend the proposed method to solve more problems associated to course similarity calculation, such as calculate the similarity among different cultivation schemes of different student types under a same major.

References

1. Gomaa, W.H., Fahmy, A.A.: A survey of text similarity approaches. International Journal of Computer Applications **68**(13), 13–18 (2013)

2. Salton, G., Lesk, M.E.: Computer evaluation of indexing and text processing. Journal of the ACM (JACM) **15**(1), 8–36 (1968)
3. Salton, G., Yu, C.T.: On the construction of effective vocabularies for information retrieval. ACM SIGPLAN Notices **10**(1), 48–60 (1973). ACM
4. Spärck Jones, K.: IDF term weighting and IR research lessons. Journal of Documentation **60**(5), 521–523 (2004)
5. Wu, H.C., Luk, R.W.P., Wong, K.F.: Interpreting tf-idf term weights as making relevance decisions. ACM Transactions on Information Systems (TOIS) **26**(3), 13 (2008)
6. Zhang, W., Yoshida, T., Tang, X.: A comparative study of TF* IDF, LSI and multi-words for text classification. Expert Systems with Applications **38**(3), 2758–2765 (2011)
7. Deerwester, S.C., Dumais, S.T., Landauer, T.K., Furnas, G.W., Harshman, R.A.: Indexing by latent semantic analysis. Journal of the American Society of Information Science **41**(6), 391–407 (1990)
8. Zhou, D., Weston, J., Gretton, A., Bousquet, O., Schölkopf, B.: Ranking on data manifolds. Advances in Neural Information Processing Systems **16**, 169–176 (2004)
9. Wan, X., Yang, J., Xiao, J.: Document similarity search based on manifold-ranking of texttiles. In: Ji, D., Kan, M.-Y., Ng, H.T., Leong, M.-K. (eds.) AIRS 2006. LNCS, vol. 4182, pp. 14–25. Springer, Heidelberg (2006)
10. He, J., Li, M., Zhang, H.J., Tong, H., Zhang, C.: Manifold-ranking based image retrieval. In: Proceedings of the 12th annual ACM international conference on Multimedia, pp. 9–16. ACM (2004)
11. Wan, X.: Content based image retrieval using manifold-ranking of blocks. In: 2007 IEEE International Conference on Multimedia and Expo, pp. 2182–2185. IEEE (2007)
12. Wang, F., Er, G., Dai, Q.: Inequivalent manifold ranking for content-based image retrieval. In: 15th IEEE International Conference on Image Processing, ICIP 2008, pp. 173–176. IEEE (2008)
13. Yang, C., Zhang, L., Lu, H., Ruan, X., Yang, M.H.: Saliency detection via graph-based manifold ranking. In: 2013 IEEE Conference on Computer Vision and Pattern Recognition (CVPR), pp. 3166–3173. IEEE (2013)
14. Loy, C.C., Liu, C., Gong, S.: Person re-identification by manifold ranking. ICIP **1**(4), 5 (2013)
15. He, R., Zhu, Y., Zhan, W.: Fast manifold-ranking for content-based image retrieval. In: ISECS International Colloquium on CCCM 2009, vol. 2, pp. 299–302. IEEE (2009)
16. Xu, B., Bu, J., Chen, C., Cai, D., He, X., Liu, W., Luo, J.: Efficient manifold ranking for image retrieval. In: Proceedings of the 34th international ACM SIGIR conference on Research and Development in Information Retrieval, pp. 525–534. ACM (2011)
17. Xu, B., Bu, J., Chen, C., Wang, C., Cai, D., He, X.: EMR: A Scalable Graph-Based Ranking Model for Content-Based Image Retrieval. IEEE Trans. Knowl. Data Eng. **27**(1), 102–114 (2015)
18. Zhou, T., He, X., Xie, K., Fu, K., Zhang, J., Yang, J.: Visual tracking via graph-based efficient manifold ranking with low-dimensional compressive features. In: 2014 IEEE International Conference on Multimedia and Expo (ICME), pp. 1–6. IEEE (2014)
19. Manning, C.D., Raghavan, P., Schütze, H.: Introduction to information retrieval. Cambridge University Press, Cambridge (2008)

Recommendation Algorithms
and Systems

Multi-faceted Distrust Aware Recommendation

Yaoyao Zheng[1,2], Yuanxin Ouyang[1,2]([✉]), Wenge Rong[2,3],
and Zhang Xiong[2,3]

[1] State Key Laboratory of Software Development Environment,
Beihang University, Beijing, China
[2] School of Computer Science and Engineering, Beihang University, Beijing, China
[3] Research Institute of Beihang University in Shenzhen, Shenzhen, China
{yy.zheng,oyyx,w.rong,xiongz}@buaa.edu.cn

Abstract. Currently the collaborative filtering based recommender system has become more and more indispensable due to its capability in providing users with personalised suggestions. Despite its advances in term of efficiency, easy implementation and robustness, traditional collaborative filtering techniques suffer from several challenges such as cold-start and data sparsity. To overcome these limitations, external information is expected to help improve the overall effectiveness. Among the diverse context information, trust relationships is a widely utilised mechanism. Meanwhile, researchers also found distrust relationships is unavoidable in social network and recommender systems can benefit from distrust information. However, most existed distrusted oriented methods do not take the property of multi-facets in distrust relationships into consideration. In this paper, we exploit distrust relationships in a multi-faceted perspective and proposed a matrix factorization based model with integration of different distrust relationship of quality user between different people. Experimental study on well-known dataset has shown promising result and it is expected that this work could provide insight for researchers in this domain to further discuss the distrust in recommender systems.

Keywords: Recommender system · Distrust · Multi-faceted · Matrix factorisation

1 Introduction

As an important branch of the research field of personalized service, the recommender systems have become increasingly indispensable since they can help users to deals with information overload and find interesting items (e.g., movies, books, music, news, Web pages, images, etc.) by excavating binary relation between users and items. Due to its potential commercial value and research challenges, recommender systems have drawn a lot of attention in many communities such as data mining [10], information retrieval [16] and machine learning [20].

One of the most important recommendation techniques is collaborative filtering (CF), which has developed for many years and achieved great success in both academic and industry aspects [13]. Though the advantages of collaborative filtering is well documented, there still exists some intrinsic challenges, such

© Springer International Publishing Switzerland 2015
S. Zhang et al. (Eds.): KSEM 2015, LNAI 9403, pp. 435–446, 2015.
DOI: 10.1007/978-3-319-25159-2_39

as cold-start and sparsity [21], because of the property that it only utilise users historical behaviour and user-item matrix for recommendation.

One of the possible solutions to overcome these limitations is to use external available information (e.g., time, location, mood, weather, and etc) to remedy the lack of information in rating matrix [28]. Currently, with the fast growth of online social network, researchers find that users choices and ideas are significantly influenced by their social context. Therefore, information accumulated in social network, such as user's preferences, item's general acceptance and social friends, would be rich side information to enhance recommender systems [6]. Among these potential external information, trust-based recommender systems, which utilise trust relationships among users, have been attached much attention and achieved appealing results [5,9,17,19].

While in the social networks, distrust relationships are also unavoidable besides trust relations [23]. Actually, if a user's review keeps offensive or out of fact persistently, he/she should be excluded in the recommendation process. Compared with trust-based recommender systems which have been greatly studied, recommender systems which utilise distrust relationships are less explored. Recently, researchers have corroborated that recommender systems can benefit from incorporating with distrust relationship properly [18,24,25]. Whilst most exist work which utilis distrust information just integrates this kind of relations singly and homogeneously, which means distrust relationships among users in these methods are all the same. However, just as trust relationships reported in [22], user's multi-faceted interests and expertise of different areas suggest that distrust relationships must be treated differently to different user.

In this paper, aiming at incorporating distrust relationships in multi-faceted way and making prediction more accurately, a recommendation model Multi-Faceted Distrust Aware Recommendation (MFDAR) is proposed. Its main intuition is that distrust relations among users do reflect the dissimilarity if the distrusted user is not a "bad" user. For instance, user u_j is distrusted by user u_i while he/she is trusted by others, we can consider that user u_i and user u_j may just have dissimilarity in some concrete facets. But if user u_k is distrusted by user u_i and he/she is also distrusted by many others, we could conclude that user u_k is not a high quality user and he/she should probably be ignored in predicting the recommendation. The main contributions in this paper is two folder: 1) we investigated the possibility to find out quality user whose information is reliable in distrust network and put the user in use to recommender system; and 2) we proposed a framework to treat distrust relationships between users in multi-facets perspective which means we place distrust information differently when meet different user. The promising experimental study on commonly used dataset has shown its potential for multi-faceted distrust aware recommendation.

The remainder of this paper is organised as follows. In Section 2, we put attention to the recommendation techniques and recent work on social recommender systems. Section 3 will focus on the proposed model with distrust relations. Section 4 will elaborate the experiment study and Section 5 will conclude this paper and point out some potential future work.

2   Related Work

Generally speaking, recommender systems can be classified into three categories [1], i.e., 1) content-based recommendation, which depends on the external information such user profile, item description to make prediction; 2) collaborative filtering recommendation, which relies on the user's historical behavior for recommendation; 3) hybrid method, which attempts to fusion content-based and collaborative filtering models [2]. Among these methods, collaborative filtering has been intensively studied due to its simpleness and robustness and has proven its success in real applications.

Traditional collaborative filtering can be further divided into memory-based and model-based methods. Memory-based methods, known as neighborhood-based methods, focus on calculating the similarity between users (user-oriented CF) [7], items (item-oriented CF) [13], or fusion of them together [16]. Though memory-based is effectiveness and gains a lot of success, it suffers form the problems of cold-start. As a result model-based method is proposed to overcome the limitation to some extent [15]. As an important model-based method, matrix factorisation has been attached much attention and there are two main approaches to apply matrix factorisation. The first one is optimisation based methods [3,11,14] and the another one is probabilistic based methods [20].

No matter how traditional collaborative filtering techniques developed, they are based on the hypothesis that users are independent and ignore the interrelationship among users. In fact, with the development of social network services, it is found that people's social context has significant influence in helping users make decision [6]. Accordingly a lot of approaches which use different social relationship among social networks have been proposed and among them trust-aware recommendation is becoming an promising direction [5,9,17,19]. Currently, recommendation from trust's perspective has been intensively studied. However, researchers also found that distrust also play an important role in social network [12,23,26]. Therefore it is argued that recommender systems could benefit from proper incorporation of distrust relationships [4,18,24,25].

Guha et al. first put forward to incorporate distrust in recommender system and demonstrates that recommendation benefit from this information [4]. Ma et al. further proposed an approach based on the assumption that latent feature between two user would be large if there exists distrust relationships between these two users [18]. Similarly, Victor et al. introduced a distrust-enhanced recommendation algorithm which employed distrust information to revise the user's trust propagation [25]. These above mentioned methods treat distrust relationships between users as homogeneous. However, as suggested in [22,27], trust is not single and homogeneous. As a social concept, trust should have many facets and indicate multiple and heterogeneous relationship between users, which means we should place trust differently to different people. As reported in [23], distrust relationships have many in common with trust relationship in recommendation. Since the multi-faceted trust relationships boost the accuracy of prediction in [22], it is also believed that multi-faceted distrust could also have positive effect on improvement of accuracy. As a result in this paper, we studied this intuition and proposed a Multi-Faceted Distrust-based Recommender framework.

3   Multi-faceted Distrust Aware Recommendation

In this paper, a recommendation model Multi-Faceted Distrust Aware Recommendation (MFDAR) is proposed, as shown in Fig. 1. In this model, a optimisation-based matrix factorization method is employed and distrust information is integrated in the process of making recommendation prediction.

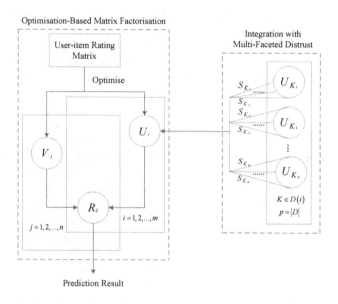

Fig. 1. Multi-faceted Distrust Aware Recommender Framework

3.1   Optimisation-Based Matrix Factorisation

Assume that we have a set of users $\mathcal{U} = \{u_1, \cdots, u_m\}$ and a set of items $\mathcal{I} = \{i_1, \cdots, i_n\}$, the rating information is represented in an $m \times n$ matrix $R \in \mathbb{R}^{m \times n}$, where m represent the numbers of users and n represent the number of items. We use i, j to specify user and item in the set respectively, where $1 \leq i \leq m$ and $1 \leq j \leq n$. The matrix factorisation methods is to factorises the user-item rating matrix R and employs a l-rank matrix $X = U^T V$ to fit it, where $U \in \mathbb{R}^{l \times m}$ and $V \in \mathbb{R}^{l \times n}$, thereby making further missing data prediction. In this paper, we use the optimisation based framework for matrix factorisation and then incorporate with distrust relations.

Let N^R be the indicator whether rating values have already been observed in user-item rating matrix R,

$$N^R_{i,j} = \begin{cases} 1 & \text{if } R_{i,j} \text{ is observed} \\ 0 & \text{if } R_{i,j} \text{ is not observed} \end{cases}$$

Hence, we can learn latent matrices U and V by solving the following optimisation problem[18]:

$$\min_{U,V} \mathcal{L}(U, V) = \frac{1}{2} \sum_{i=1}^{m} \sum_{j=1}^{n} N^R_{i,j} (R_{i,j} - g(U_i^T V_j))^2 + \frac{\lambda_U}{2} \|U\|_F^2 + \frac{\lambda_V}{2} \|V\|_F^2 \quad (1)$$

where $\| \bullet \|_F$ is the Frobenius norm of matrix, i.e, $\|U\|_F = \sqrt{\sum_{i=1}^{m} \sum_{j=1}^{n} |U_{i,j}|^2}$.

Same as many other traditional recommender systems, approach mentioned in Eq. 1 only utilises user-item rating matrix for recommendation. As discussed in previous section, utilising the distrust relationship among users could be promising as such we will integrated the distrust information into the matrix factorisation in multi-faceted perspective.

3.2   Integration with Multi-faceted Distrust

In this paper, the intuition of utilising distrust information is depicted as follow. Firstly, it is important to distinguish whether a user who is distrusted by other user is a "good" (reliable) user or not. If a user is not distrusted by most of other users, it is believed that his/her opinions are not offensive or with low quality and this user could be marked as reliable user. Imagine a scenario where user u_i finds that user u_j gives positive judgement of "Titanic" and "2012", while u_i cannot agree after watching these movies, he/she may place u_j in his/her distrust list. However, we cannot deem u_i's taste is totally different from u_j if u_j is a reliable user. Based on this assumption, we can use the distrust information to further improve the prediction in recommendation. Before doing this, some notations and concepts need to be explained.

Facet: Facet is proposed to represent a set of products which are similar to each other. Here we can define the probability that a user i's interest in facet k as follow:

$$f_i(k) = \frac{n_i(k)}{n_i} \quad (2)$$

where n_i is the total number of products that user u_i rated, and $n_i(k)$ is the number of products in facet k that user u_i rated.

Tensor Representation: Multi-faceted distrust relations between users can be represented as a quadruple $< user, user, facet, strength >$ which is beyond

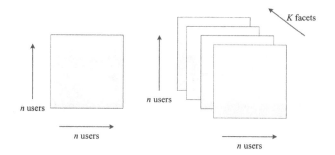

Fig. 2. Matrix Representation and Tensor Representation

the ability adjacency matrix can handle. *Matrix* must be extended to a *tensor* by adding extra dimension facet *facets*, which is demonstrated in Fig. 2.

In this paper, $\mathcal{A}(i, j, k) \in \mathbb{R}^{m \times m \times K}$ is used to represent the weight of distrust score, or distrust strength in other way between user u_i and u_j in facet K. The higher the value is, the more user u_i distrust u_j in facet K, as shown in Fig. 2.

Quality User: To utilise distrust relations properly, we must exclude users who are offensive or provide low quality ratings. In other words, we should find high quality users who are really useful in dissimilarity measure. We determine whether a user is high quality or not by calculating the proportion he/she is distrusted by others. More specifically, we can define the quality measurement as follow:

$$h(x) = \sum_i^m T(i) / (\sum_i^m T(i) + \sum_i^m D(i)) \tag{3}$$

where $T(i) = 1$ when user u_i trusts u_x, otherwise $T(i) = 0$. $D(i) = 1$ when user u_i distrusts u_x, otherwise $D(i) = 0$.

Based on the above interpretation, for all user in the user space, we can summarise the optimisation function as follow:

$$\max_U \frac{1}{2} \sum_i^m \sum_{d \in \mathcal{D}(i)} \sum_k^K h(d) \mathcal{A}(i, d, k) \| f_i(k) \cdot U_i - f_j(d) \cdot U_d \| \tag{4}$$

where $\mathcal{D}(i)$ is the set of users to whom user u_i distrusts. Based on Eqs. 1 and 4, the proposed recommendation model with integration of distrust relations can be defined as the follow optimisation function:

$$\min_{U,V} \mathfrak{L}_D(U, V) = \frac{1}{2} \sum_{i=1}^m \sum_{j=1}^n N_{i,j}^R (R_{i,j} - g(U_i^T V_j))^2 + \frac{\lambda_U}{2} \| U \|_F^2 + \frac{\lambda_V}{2} \| V \|_F^2$$

$$- \frac{\lambda_D}{2} \sum_i^m \sum_{d \in \mathcal{D}(i)} \sum_k^K h(d) \mathcal{A}(i, d, k) \| f_i(k) \cdot U_i - f_j(d) \cdot U_d \| \tag{5}$$

where $\mathcal{L}_D(U, V)$ is not jointly convex in both U and V, but it is convex in each of them. Therefore, local minimum solution can be found by standard gradient descent in U , V,

$$U_{x+1} \leftarrow U_x - \eta \nabla_U \mathcal{L}_D(U, V)|_{U=U_x, V=V_x}$$

$$V_{x+1} \leftarrow V_x - \eta \nabla_V \mathcal{L}_D(U, V)|_{U=U_x, V=V_x}$$

where η represents the step size, and ∇ represents the partial derivative.

3.3   Prediction

When latent feature U and V are learned, we can predict the rating for the users. The value predicted can be defined as follow:

$$\widehat{R}_{ij} = U_i^T V_j \tag{6}$$

4   Experimental Study

4.1   Dataset Description

In this paper Epinions[1] is used in our experimental study. Epinions is a popular e-commerce and consumer review website where consumer can browse reviews and make comments. It enables user to review products by adding text comments and making integer rating range from 1 to 5. These ratings and review will influence future user when they decide whether the certain products are worth buying or not. Furthermore, based on the quality of rating and reviews of other users, user can also explicitly specify other users as trust (to trust list) or distrust (to the block list) if the content is consistently valuable or useless for the user. Due to the explicit trust and distrust relations, Epinions is really appropriate to be studied in trust and distrust enhance recommender systems.

More specially, in this experimental study we adopt a dataset from Epinions available at [23], where the trust/distrust is indicated as bivalent value. Trust is labelled as 1 and distrust is labelled as −1. It consists of $n = 138106$ users who have rated at least one of the total $m = 200952$ different items that can be divide into different categories which we adopt as facets in our experiment in total number of 326978 users. The number of ratings observed is 703190. The density of the user-item matrix is 0.003%. As for user trust and distrust relations, total number of trust statement is 717667 and total number of distrust statement is 123705. The statistics of Epinions dataset is shown in Table 1.

---

[1] http://www.epinions.com

Table 1. Statistics of Dataset from Epinions

Statistics	Max	Min	Average
Trust per user	2070	0	2.195
Be trusted per user	3338	0	2.195
Distrust per user	1562	0	0.378
Be distrusted per user	540	0	0.378
Number of users		138106	
Number of items		200952	
Number of ratings		703190	
Number of trust relations		717667	
Number of distrust relations		123705	

4.2 Evaluation Metrics and Baselines

Two well-known evaluation criteria, the Mean Absolute Error (MAE) and the Root Mean Squared Error (RMSE), are employed to test the prediction quality of the proposed model [8].

MAE is defined as:

$$MAE = \frac{\sum_{i,j} |R_{i,j} - \widehat{R}_{i,j}|}{N} \tag{7}$$

where $R_{i,j}$ represents the rating user i gives to item j, $\widehat{R}_{i,j}$ denotes the rating user i gives to item j, and N is number of test dataset.

RMSE is defined as:

$$RMSE = \sqrt{\frac{\sum_{i,j} ((R_{i,j}) - \widehat{R}_{i,j})^2}{N}} \tag{8}$$

where $R_{i,j}$ represents the rating user i gives to item j, $\widehat{R}_{i,j}$ denotes the rating user i gives to item j, and N is number of test dataset.

To better evaluate the effect of the proposed model and overcome the impact of randomness, we have selected four training set amount, i.e., 60%, 70%, 80%, 90% respectively, where 60% means we randomly choose 60% rating record as training data and the rest 40% remaining as test data. In each setting, we randomly employ 5 pieces of the data source, then compare the average result to have a fair comparison. As for λ_U and λ_V, we set $\lambda_U = \lambda_V = 0.001$ to keep it consistent with methods we want to compare with.

In this paper we employ three methods to compare against the proposed method, i.e., traditional recommender techniques which only utilise user-item rating matrix, trust-aware recommender systems, recommender systems which only integrate distrust relations in single facet, as listed below:

1. **Probabilistic Matrix Factorization**, which is a basic matrix factorization proposed in [20], and uses only user-item rating matrix and does not take any social information into account.

2. **Recommendation With Trust (RWT)**, which is proposed in [18] and is a matrix factorisation based method by combining trust network though minimize the distance between the users' latent feature vectors.

3. **Recommendation With Distrust (RWD)**, which is proposed in [18] and is based on matrix factorisation and incorporates with distrust constraints though the maximum the distance between the user's feature vectors. RWD considers relationships of distrust in different users as single and homogeneous which means put the distrust relationships in one facet.

4.3   Results and Discussion

From Eq. 5 it can be seen that parameter λ_D is important since it controls the proportion of distrust information we will exploit in the proposed model. If the λ_D is extremely small, the model will degenerate into traditional optimization based matrix factorization which utilises rating matrix only. While on the other hand, if the λ_D is extremely large, the model will ignore the users preferences information in rating matrix. As to the parameter k, the number of latent features, it also plays an import role in factorisation process. As such it is essential to discuss the impact of value of λ_D and parameter k in the recommendation process.

In order to investigate the relationship between recommendation accuracy and λ_D and parameter k, we first plot the change of RMSE and MAE according to λ_D and parameter k, as shown in Fig. 3, where the training set is set to 90%. It is observed that no matter how the k varies, RMSE and MAE keep decreasing (which means the improvement of accuracy of prediction), along with the decrease of λ_D, while when λ_D reaches a certain value, they increase according to the increase of λ_D. According to the discussion above, we set $\lambda_D = 0.0004$ and the number of latent features $k = 25$ in rest of our experiment respect to the best performance of RMSE.

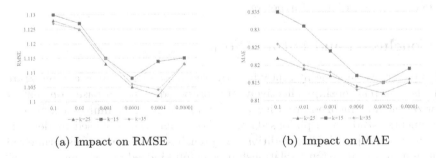

(a) Impact on RMSE   (b) Impact on MAE

Fig. 3. Impact of Parameter λ_D and k

The result of the experimental study is shown in Table. 2, where we set parameter $\lambda_D = 0.0004$ and the number of latent features $k = 25$. From the result it is concluded:

Table 2. Comparison Result against Baselines in Term of MAE and RMSE

Training Set	Measure	PMF	RWT	RWD	MFDAR
60%	MAE	0.938	0.881	0.910	0.893
	RMSE	1.500	1.261	1.342	1.267
70%	MAE	0.917	0.853	0.876	0.860
	RMSE	1.436	1.169	1.205	1.185
80%	MAE	0.902	0.826	0.847	0.824
	RMSE	1.292	1.146	1.194	1.137
90%	MAE	0.896	0.816	0.841	0.813
	RMSE	1.217	1.108	1.128	1.102

1. As expected, recommender systems incorporating with social relationships generate better accuracy than traditional matrix factorization indeed, typically when the training set is small, which demonstrates the advantage of social-enhanced recommendation.

2. The proposed model MFDAR performs better than traditional RWD in all settings, which demonstrates the advantage considering distrust in multi-faceted way.

3. The proposed model MFDAR is a little inferior compared to RWT when the training data set is not small. We think it is due to the huger number of trust relationships in our data set compared with distrust relationships. While when the training set increases, MFDAR shows better perform than RWT at a disadvantage lower average number per user, which led to believe that distrust relationship does play a role as important as trust relationships at least and should be investigated more carefully. Meanwhile, it reflects the differences in nature between trust and distrust relationships and demonstrates that distrust relationships require more further research.

5   Conclusion and Future Work

In this paper, we thoroughly study how the recommender systems can integrate with distrust relationships effectively and proposed a model based on matrix factorization and incorporate with distrust information in multi-faceted way. Experimental study on Epinions dataset shows that the proposed model performs better compared with traditional approaches. Furthermore, experimental result indicates that distrust relationships is helpful indeed in boosting the accuracy of recommendation and recommender systems integrate distrust information require deeper investigation.

Although we find a way to utilise distrust relationships in tradition recommender systems more effectively, there exists several challenges which deserve future research. Firstly, how to integrate trust and distrust information in same way and fuse them into one objective function and decrease the complexity simultaneously is a possible research direction in the future; Secondly, distrust relationship used in this paper is just binary and it is not enough to reflect the relations between users. Therefore, it is interesting to find a way to normalize the relationships between users and evaluate the strength of distrust. What's more, it is necessary to discuss the situation that all the set of items degenerate to one facet in later work.

Acknowledgments. This work was partially supported by the National Natural Science Foundation of China (No. 61472021), the National High Technology Research and Development Program of China (No. 2013AA01A601), and SKLSDE project under Grant No. SKLSDE-2015ZX-17. We are grateful to Shenzhen Key Laboratory of Data Vitalization (Smart City) for supporting this research.

References

1. Adomavicius, G., Tuzhilin, A.: Toward the next generation of recommender systems: A survey of the state-of-the-art and possible extensions. IEEE Transactions on Knowledge and Data Engineering **17**(6), 734–749 (2005)
2. Forsati, R., Doustdar, H.M., Shamsfard, M., Keikha, A., Meybodi, M.R.: A fuzzy co-clustering approach for hybrid recommender systems. International Journal of Hybrid Intelligent Systems **10**(2), 71–81 (2013)
3. Forsati, R., Mahdavi, M., Shamsfard, M., Sarwat, M.: Matrix factorization with explicit trust and distrust relationships. CoRR abs/1408.0325 (2014)
4. Guha, R.V., Kumar, R., Raghavan, P., Tomkins, A.: Propagation of trust and distrust. In: Proceedings of the 13th International Conference on World Wide Web, pp. 403–412 (2004)
5. Guo, G., Zhang, J., Thalmann, D., Basu, A., Yorke-Smith, N.: From ratings to trust: an empirical study of implicit trust in recommender systems. In: Proceedings of 29th ACM International Symposium on Applied Computing, pp. 248–253 (2014)
6. He, J., Chu, W.W.: A social network-based recommender system (SNRS). In: Data Mining for Social Network Data, pp. 47–74 (2010)
7. Herlocker, J.L., Konstan, J.A., Borchers, A., Riedl, J.: An algorithmic framework for performing collaborative filtering. In: Proceedings of the 22nd Annual International ACM SIGIR Conference on Research and Development in Information Retrieval, pp. 230–237 (1999)
8. Herlocker, J.L., Konstan, J.A., Terveen, L.G., Riedl, J.: Evaluating collaborative filtering recommender systems. ACM Trans. Inf. Syst. **22**(1), 5–53 (2004)
9. Jamali, M., Ester, M.: A transitivity aware matrix factorization model for recommendation in social networks. In: Proceedings of the 22nd International Joint Conference on Artificial Intelligence, pp. 2644–2649 (2011)
10. Koren, Y.: Factorization meets the neighborhood: a multifaceted collaborative filtering model. In: Proceedings of the 14th ACM SIGKDD International Conference on Knowledge Discovery and Data Mining, pp. 426–434 (2008)
11. Koren, Y., Bell, R.M., Volinsky, C.: Matrix factorization techniques for recommender systems. IEEE Computer **42**(8), 30–37 (2009)

12. Kunegis, J., Lommatzsch, A., Bauckhage, C.: The slashdot zoo: mining a social network with negative edges. In: Proceedings of the 18th International Conference on World Wide Web, pp. 741–750 (2009)

13. Linden, G., Smith, B., York, J.: Amazon.com recommendations: Item-to-item collaborative filtering. IEEE Internet Computing 7(1), 76–80 (2003)

14. Liu, J., Wu, C., Liu, W.: Bayesian probabilistic matrix factorization with social relations and item contents for recommendation. Decision Support Systems 55(3), 838–850 (2013)

15. Liu, N.N., Yang, Q.: Eigenrank: a ranking-oriented approach to collaborative filtering. In: Proceedings of the 31st Annual International ACM SIGIR Conference on Research and Development in Information Retrieval, pp. 83–90 (2008)

16. Ma, H., King, I., Lyu, M.R.: Effective missing data prediction for collaborative filtering. In: Proceedings of the 30th Annual International ACM SIGIR Conference on Research and Development in Information Retrieval, pp. 39–46 (2007)

17. Ma, H., King, I., Lyu, M.R.: Learning to recommend with social trust ensemble. In: Proceedings of the 32nd Annual International ACM SIGIR Conference on Research and Development in Information Retrieval, pp. 203–210 (2009)

18. Ma, H., Lyu, M.R., King, I.: Learning to recommend with trust and distrust relationships. In: Proceedings of the 2009 ACM Conference on Recommender Systems, pp. 189–196 (2009)

19. Massa, P., Avesani, P.: Trust-aware recommender systems. In: Proceedings of the 2007 ACM Conference on Recommender Systems, pp. 17–24 (2007)

20. Salakhutdinov, R., Mnih, A.: Probabilistic matrix factorization. In: Proceedings of the 21st Annual Conference on Neural Information Processing Systems, pp. 1257–1264 (2007)

21. Sarwar, B.M., Karypis, G., Konstan, J.A., Riedl, J.: Item-based collaborative filtering recommendation algorithms. In: Proceedings of the 10th International World Wide Web Conference, pp. 285–295 (2001)

22. Tang, J., Gao, H., Liu, H.: mTrust: discerning multi-faceted trust in a connected world. In: Proceedings of the 5th International Conference on Web Search and Web Data Mining, pp. 93–102 (2012)

23. Tang, J., Hu, X., Liu, H.: Is distrust the negation of trust?: the value of distrust in social media. In: Proceedings of 25th ACM Conference on Hypertext and Social Media, pp. 148–157 (2014)

24. Victor, P., Cornelis, C., Cock, M.D., Teredesai, A.: Trust- and distrust-based recommendations for controversial reviews. IEEE Intelligent Systems 26(1), 48–55 (2011)

25. Victor, P., Verbiest, N., Cornelis, C., Cock, M.D.: Enhancing the trust-based recommendation process with explicit distrust. ACM Transactions on the Web 7(2), 6 (2013)

26. Wei, W., Chan, K.T., King, I., Lee, J.H.: RATE: a review of reviewers in a manuscript review process. In: Proceedings of 2008 IEEE/WIC/ACM International Conference on Web Intelligence, pp. 204–207 (2008)

27. Wu, J., Chen, L., Yu, Q., Han, P., Wu, Z.: Trust-aware media recommendation in heterogeneous social networks. World Wide Web 18(1), 139–157 (2015)

28. Zhong, E., Fan, W., Yang, Q.: Contextual collaborative filtering via hierarchical matrix factorization. In: Proceedings of the 12th SIAM International Conference on Data Mining, pp. 744–755 (2012)

Distributed Recommendation Algorithm Based on Matrix Decomposition on MapReduce Framework

Sen Wu[✉], Dan Lu, Yannan Du, and Xiaodong Feng

Donlinks School of Economics and Management,
University of Science and Technology Beijing, Beijing 100083, People's Republic of China
wusen@manage.ustb.edu.cn, ludan_email@163.com,
285429073@qq.com, afengxd@aliyun.com

Abstract. This paper presents a recommendation algorithm based on matrix operations (RAMO), which integrates collaborative filtering algorithm with information network-based approach. RAMO exploits information from different objects to increase the recommendation accuracy. Furthermore, a distributed recommendation algorithm DRAMD is proposed based on matrix decomposition using the framework MapReduce. DRAMD can be run across multiple cluster nodes to reduce the computation time. Test results on MovieLens dataset show that the algorithms not only have better recommendation effectiveness but improve the efficiency of the computation.

Keywords: Recommender system · Matrix decomposition · Distributed computing · Mapreduce

1   Introduction

With the development of the Internet, the problem of information overload has become increasingly serious. Recommendation system is considered as an effective means to resolve the information overload problem. Many researchers have proposed lots of recommendation algorithms. Collaborative filtering [1] is a classical recommendation method which recommends items to users according to other users' ratings. However, the user-based collaborative filtering algorithm has large time complexity and space complexity when the number of users is large. Amazon proposes an item-based collaborative filtering [2], which computes the similarity between items with the historical track of the users' activities. There are also some researches on recommendation based on information networks such as bipartite graph [3] and heterogeneous information networks [4]. A path-constraint measure named HeteSim [5] can measure the relatedness of objects in heterogeneous networks. And based on HeteSim, a recommendation system called HeteRecom was designed [6]. However, these algorithms mainly focused on recommendation accuracy rather than computing time which are unsuitable when dealing with large datasets.

© Springer International Publishing Switzerland 2015
S. Zhang et al. (Eds.): KSEM 2015, LNAI 9403, pp. 447–457, 2015.
DOI: 10.1007/978-3-319-25159-2_40

Distributed computing is an effective way to reduce the computing time, and MapReduce [7] is a popular framework for distributed computing on Hadoop platform. Pessemier et al. proposed a content-based recommendation algorithm on MapReduce framework [8]. Jiang et al. designed an item-based collaborative filtering recommendation algorithm on MapReduce framework which shows that computing time of algorithm on MapReduce is obviously less than traditional algorithms with the increase of the size of dataset [9].

To improve the recommendation performance, RAMO proposed in this paper combines the collaborative filtering algorithm and information network-based approach based on matrix operation which is decomposable and can be run in distributed environment. Then a distributed recommendation algorithm DRAMD is designed on MapReduce framework on the basis of RAMO to improve the efficiency of the computation.

2   Recommendation Algorithm Based on Matrix Operations

In this section, we introduce a recommendation algorithm based on matrix operations. Since the need for response time in recommendation system is different, the Recommendation Algorithm based on Matrix Operations (RAMO) is designed as online algorithm and offline algorithm.

2.1   Problem Definition

Definition 1. Adjacency Matrix. In the recommendation system, an adjacency matrix is defined as a matrix which characterizes the relationship between nodes of networks. Given $G = (V, E)$ is a graph, where $V(G)$ is the set of vertices and $E(G)$ is the set of edges. G is usually a bipartite graph or a heterogeneous information network which can be split into multiple bipartite graphs, means $V(G)$ is composed of two kinds of entity types such as $U = \{u_1, u_2, ..., u_m\}$ and $I = \{i_1, i_2, ..., i_n\}$. The adjacency matrix A of graph G is defined as: $a_{pq} \in A$, $a_{pq} = \begin{cases} w_{pq}, & (u_p i_q \in E(G)) \\ 0, & (u_p i_q \notin E(G)) \end{cases}$, w_{pq} is the weight of $u_p i_q$, $u_p i_q \in E(G)$. Then the bipartite graph composed of entity U and entity I has an adjacency matrix A_{UI} which is $m \times n$ order matrix.

Definition 2. Self-adjacency Matrix. Given a recommendation system where $R = \{r_1, r_2, ..., r_m\}$ is an entity. The similarity between each two entity elements is defined as ω what can be calculated by algorithms such as collaborative filtering. Then the entity R has a self-adjacency matrix S which is defined as: $s_{ij} \in S, s_{ij} = \omega_{r_i r_j}$.

Through the above definition, we can deduce two corollaries:

Corollary 1. Self-adjacency matrix is symmetric.

Corollary 2. The diagonal elements of self-adjacency matrix are all 1.

Definition 3. Initial Matrix. A given recommendation system has an entity set $\Psi = \{R_1, R_2, ..., R_t\}$. For each pair related entities $< R_k, R_l >$, we can get three matrices through definition 1 and definition 2 which include self-adjacency matrices S_{R_k}, S_{R_l} and adjacency matrix $A_{R_k R_l}$. These self-adjacency matrices and adjacency matrix are initial matrices. $M_0 = \{S_{R_1}, S_{R_2}, ..., S_{R_t}, A_{R_1 R_2}, A_{R_1 R_3}, ..., A_{R_1 R_t}, A_{R_2 R_3}, ..., A_{R_{t-1} R_t}\}$ is the initial matrix set.

Definition 4. Target Matrix. A given recommendation system has an entity set $\Psi = \{R_1, R_2, ..., R_t\}$. Then there is a pair of entities $< R_k, R_l >$ meaning to recommend one element or multiple elements in entity R_l to an element in entity R_k. The target matrix M_{kl} is defined as: $m_{pq} \in M_{kl}, m_{pq} = \delta_{R_k R_l}$. $\delta_{R_k R_l}$ is the R_l's prediction score given by R_k which can be calculated by initial matrices' operation illustrated in detail in Algorithm 1.

Definition 5. Matrix Path. There are entity set $\Psi = \{R_1, R_2, ..., R_t\}$ and initial matrix set in a given recommendation system. Then we can find one matrix path or multiple matrix paths $P = R_k \circ R_{b_1} \circ R_{b_2} \circ ... \circ R_l$ which can get the target matrix $M_{kl} = A_{R_k R_{b_1}}(S_{R_k}) \times A_{R_{b_1} R_{b_2}}(S_{R_{b_1}}) \times ... \times A_{R_{l-1} R_l}(S_{R_l})$. Then the P is called matrix path. If there is only one kind of relationship between any two kinds of entities in matrix path, the matrix path can be represented by ordered entities such as $P = R_k R_{b_1} R_{b_2} ... R_l$.

Given two matrix paths $P_1 = R_k \circ R_{b_1} \circ R_{b_2} \circ ... \circ R_l$ and $P_2 = R_k' \circ R_{b_1}' \circ R_{b_2}' \circ ... \circ R_l'$, the two paths is joinable only when $R_l = R_k'$. The matrix path becomes $P = P_1 P_2 = R_k R_{b_1} R_{b_2} ... R_l R_k' R_{b_1}' R_{b_2}' ... R_l'$ after connected.

Example. In the collaborative filtering recommendation algorithm, U represents the user entity and I represents the item entity. U and I have the relationship of $U \xrightarrow{rating} I \xrightarrow{similar} I$, then the matrix path of this relationship is $P = UII$.

2.2 The Offline RAMO

The offline RAMO calculates the target matrix offline and saves the results in the backroom and returns the results to the users when needed. The overall algorithm process is depicted in Tab.1.

In a real recommendation system such as a movie recommendation system with users $U = \{u_1, u_2, ..., u_m\}$ and movies $I = \{i_1, i_2, ..., i_n\}$, the elements $a_{u_p i_q}$ of adjacency matrix A_{UI} is equal to the movie i_q's rating given by user u_p. The elements in self-adjacency matrix S_I represent the similarity between movies. The elements in self-adjacency matrix S_U represent the similarity between users. In this paper, the similarity between movies is given as:

$$sim(i_p, i_q) = \frac{\left|N(i_p) \cap N(i_q)\right|}{\sqrt{\left|N(i_p)\right|\left|N(i_q)\right|}} \tag{1}$$

$N(i_p)$ is the set of users which have made positive feedback to movie i_p and $N(i_q)$ is the set of users which have made positive feedback to movie i_q.

The similarity between users is given as:

$$sim(u_p, u_q) = \frac{\left|N(u_p) \cap N(u_q)\right|}{\sqrt{\left|N(u_p)\right|\left|N(u_q)\right|}} \tag{2}$$

$N(u_p)$ is the set of movies which the user u_p has made positive feedback to and $N(u_q)$ is the set of movies which the user u_q has made positive feedback to.

Table 1. The process of the offline RAMO

Algorithm 1. RAMO(offline)

Input: Matrix path P

Step 1: Initialize the target matrix with identity matrix $M_{kl} = I$ and the initial matrix set M_0

Step 2: Take two entities in matrix path $R_k, R_{b_1} \in P$ in turn from left.

Step 3: If $k = b_1$, $M_{kl}* = S_k$

Else $M_{kl} = A_{kb_1}$

$P = P - R_k$

Step 4: If R_{b_1} is the last entity in P, execute Output, else goto Step 2.

Output: Return target Matrix M_{kl}

The above algorithm can get the target matrix M_{kl}, which is the recommended entity's prediction score matrix given by the recommending entity. In the recommendation system, the i-th recommended element can get the recommend elements by sorting $M_{kl}[i]$ and taking the first k maximum elements.

2.3   The Online RAMO

The online RAMO calculates and returns the results when a user is visiting the system. The overall algorithm process is depicted in Tab.2.

Table 2. The process of the online RAMO

Algorithm 2. RAMO(online)

Input: Matrix path P and the index I of the recommended element

Step 1: Initialize the initial matrix set M_0 and take two entities in matrix path

$R_k, R_{b_1} \in P$ in turn from left.

Step 2: Initialize the target matrix M_{kl}

If $k = b_1$, $M_{kl}* = S_k[i]$

Else $M_{kl} = A_{kb_1}[i]$

$P = P - R_k$

Step 3: Take two entities in matrix path $R_{b_1}, R_{b_2} \in P$ in turn from left.

Step 4: If $b_1 = b_2$, $M_{kl}* = S_{b_1}$

Else $M_{kl}* = A_{b_1 b_2}$

Step 5: If R_{b_2} is the last entity in P, execute Output, else goto Step 3.

Output: Return target Matrix M_{kl}

2.4   The Algorithm Complexity Analysis

The offline RAMO will cost $O(n^2 m)$ to calculate the inner product while the online RAMO will only cost $O(nm)$. Thus it can be seen that the online algorithm reduces the operation time dramatically. However, in the recommendation system, it is still necessary to adopt the offline algorithm to cut down the computing workloads from the online computing request.

3   Distributed Recommendation Algorithm Based on Matrix Decomposition

Since the real recommendation system needs to handle massive amounts of data in a short time, this paper improves the RAMO and designs a distributed recommendation algorithm based on matrix decomposition (DRAMD) on MapReduce framework.

3.1   The Matrix Decomposition

The Matrix Decomposition is splitting matrix into sums or products of several matrices. The RAMO is based on matrix multiplication and matrix addition which can be decomposed and calculated on distributed framework.

Sun et al. proposed an approach to calculate the large matrix multiplication based on Hadoop [10]. The approach decomposes the left matrix by rows $A = (a_1^T, a_2^T, ..., a_m^T)$ where a_i^T is the i-th row in matrix A and decomposes the right matrix by columns $B = (b_1, b_2, ..., b_n)$ where b_j is the j-th column in matrix B. The computing process is shown as Fig.1.

This paper improved the approach in [10] to fit for computing sparse matrix by deleting the zeros in a_i^T and b_j. Then we can get $a_i^T \sim (e_{s_1}, e_{s_2}, ..., e_{s_k})$, e is the value of each element in a_i^T, $(s_1, s_2, ..., s_k)$ are the order of columns in a_i^T where is nonzero value. In a similar way, we can get $b_j \sim (e_{t_1}, e_{t_2}, ..., e_{t_l})$, where $(t_1, t_2, ..., t_l)$ are the order of columns in b_j where is nonzero value. Then the computing process is simplified into:

$$c_{ij} = \begin{cases} \sum_{x=1,y=1}^{x=k,y=l} e_{s_x} \times e_{t_y}, & s_x = t_y \\ 0, & s_x \neq t_y \end{cases} \tag{3}$$

Then, the algorithm reduces both time complexity and space complexity.

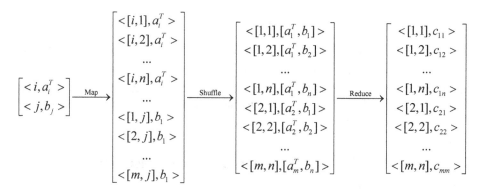

Fig. 1. The Computing Process of Matrix Multiplication

3.2   Algorithm

The DRAMD overall process is depicted in Tab.3.

Table 3. The process of DRAMD

Algorithm 3. DRAMD

Input: Matrix path P and initial matrix set M_0

Step 1: Initialize the target matrix with identity matrix $M_{kl} = I$

Step 2: Take two entities in matrix path $R_k, R_{b_i} \in P$ in turn from left.

Step 3: If $k = b_1$, Map: Change the format of matrix $M_{kl}(m \times n)$ and $S_k(n \times l)$ to key/value pairs $<[i, p], (M, j, a_{ij})>$ $(p = 1, 2, ...l$, a_{ij} is the element of $M_{kl}(m \times n))$ and $<[q, t], (S, j, b_{jt})>$ $(q = 1, 2, ..., m, b_{jt}$ is the element of $S_k(n \times l))$.

Else: Map: Change the format of matrix $M_{kl}(m \times n)$ and $A_{km}(n \times l)$ to key/value pairs $<[i, p], (M, j, a_{ij})>$ $(p = 1, 2, ...l, a_{ij}$ is the element of $M_{kl}(m \times n))$ and $<[q, t], (S, j, b_{jt})>$ $(q = 1, 2, ..., m, b_{jt}$ is the element of $A_{km}(n \times l))$.

Step 4: Reduce: Calculate the matrix multiplication according to (3) and get the key/value pairs $< i, (j, result) >$ of the matrix M_{kl}.

$P = P - R_k$

Step 5: If R_{b_i} is the last entity in P, execute Output, else goto Step 2.

Output: Arrange the key/value pairs of the matrix M_{kl} to final target matrix M_{kl} and return target Matrix M_{kl}

3.3 The Algorithm Complexity Analysis

Given two matrix $A(m \times k)$ and $B(k \times n)$ where the sparseness is $d(0 < d \ll 1)$ and N is the number of Hadoop clusters. The DRAMD will cost $O(n^2 md / N)$ to calculate the inner product and will store $(m + n)kd$ elements in memory. The degree of parallelism is $n \times m$.

4 Experimental Results

In this section, we conduct a number of experiments with the proposed algorithms to illustrate the effectiveness.

4.1 Experimental Environment

The single mode experiments are on a single Windows 7 personal computer. The computer has a 2.53GHz Inter Core i3 CPU, 2GB of memory, and 500G of disks.

The distribution experiments are on a cluster of 4 computers. Each computer has a 3.00GHz Inter Pentium 4 CPU, 1GB of memory, and 160G of disks. The experiments are on the VMware CentOS6.0 virtual machine, which has 512MB of memory. The master acts as NameNode and JobTracker while the slave1~slave3 act as DataNode and TaskTracker.

4.2   Data Preparation

The experimental dataset MovieLensconsists of 1682 movies and 943 users. And to test the recommendation algorithm, the dataset is randomly divided into two parts: The training set contains 75% of the data, and the remaining 25% of data constitutes the testing set.

4.3   Effective Experiments

To evaluate the proposed algorithms, this paper selects four evaluation parameters including precision, recall, coverage and computing time.

We adopt *precision* as accuracy index and *recall* as recall index. For a user in the recommendation system user set $u \in U$, $R(u)$ is the recommended item list obtained from the recommendation algorithm, and $T(u)$ is the real item list according to users' activities (In a movie recommendation system, it means users' rating to a movie is larger than threshold. The value is 2 in this paper). The *precision* and *recall* of the whole system is given as:

$$Precision = \frac{\sum_{u \in U} |R(u) \cap T(u)|}{\sum_{u \in U} |R(u)|} \tag{4}$$

$$Recall = \frac{\sum_{u \in U} |R(u) \cap T(u)|}{\sum_{u \in U} |T(u)|} \tag{5}$$

We adopt *coverage* to evaluate the ability of discovering the potential items. For a user in the recommendation system user set $u \in U$, I is the whole items in the recommendation system item set, and $R(u)$ is the recommended item list obtained from the recommendation algorithm. The *coverage* of the whole system is given as:

$$Coverage = \frac{|\bigcup_{u \in U} R(u)|}{|I|} \tag{6}$$

The results of the effective experiments with the matrix path UII are shown as Tab.4.

The results of the effective experiments with the matrix path UIUI are shown as Tab.5.

Table 4. The results of the effective experiments with UII

k	Precision	Recall	Coverage	Computing time(s)
5	0.475	0.058	0.115	4354
10	0.426	0.104	0.153	4371
20	0.358	0.175	0.206	4403
40	0.285	0.279	0.272	4468

Table 5. The results of the effective experiments with UIUI

k	Precision	Recall	Coverage	Computing time(s)
5	0.435	0.053	0.050	52
10	0.371	0.090	0.067	69
20	0.318	0.155	0.102	101
40	0.257	0.251	0.149	166

For precision, recall and coverage, the matrix path UII is better than UIUI. This is because the matrix path UII not only include the relationship between users and movies, but also include the relationship between movies, while the matrix path UIUI only include the relationship between users and movies. However, the computing time of UIUI is much less than UII. This is because calculating the adjacency matrix A_{UI} cost too much time. In the recommendation system, different matrix paths can be selected to balance the recommendation results and computing time.

The computing time of multiplying matrices is shown as Table 6 to compare offline RAMO and online RAMO.

Table 6. The computing time of multiplying matrices

The Matrix Path	The Offline RAMO	The Online RAMO
UII	1.422	0.005
UIUI	19.150	0.021

The computing time of once multiplying matrices cost by the offline algorithm is much less than by the online algorithm. And with the growth of the number of users and the times for multiplication, the gap is much wider.

4.4   Distributed Experiments

The distributed experiments are on the MovieLens100K dataset with 1682 movies and 943 users (1933KB) and the MovieLens1M dataset consisting of 3900 movies and 6040 users (24018KB). The speedup of the parallel computing time of multiplying matrices in Hadoop clusters is shown as Fig. 2.

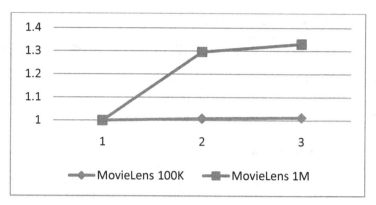

Fig. 2. The speedup of the parallel computing time of multiplying matrices in Hadoop clusters

The distributed experiments show that the speedup is more significant on large datasets. However, the speedup doesn't improve linearly because the cost of the communication between clusters offset the optimization. While in larger datasets, the speedup improves much rapidly.

5   Conclusions

In this paper, we fuse the classical recommendation algorithms and propose the Recommendation Algorithm based on Matrix Operations (RAMO) which is designed both offline and online. Then we present a distributed recommendation algorithm based on matrix decomposition (DRAMD) on MapReduce framework which can achieve the parallel computing to reduce the computing time. The experiments on MovieLens datasets show that the RAMO is effective and the DRAMD can enhance the computing efficiency.

Acknowledgments. This work is supported by National Natural Science Foundation of China (NSFC) under Grant No.71271027 and the Research Fund for the Doctoral Program of Higher Education under Grant No. 20120006110037.

References

1. Breese, J.S., Heckerman, D., Kadie, C.: Empirical analysis of predictive algorithms for collaborative filtering. In: Proceedings of the Fourteenth conference on Uncertainty in artificial intelligence, pp. 43–52 (1998)
2. Linden, G., Smith, B., York, J.: Amazon.com recommendations: Item-to-item collaborative filtering. IEEE Internet Computing 7(1), 76–80 (2003)
3. Zhou, T., Ren, J., Medo, M., Zhang, Y.C.: Bipartite network projection and personal recommendation. Physical Review E 76(4), 70–80 (2007)
4. Sun, Y., Han, J., Yan, X., Yu, P.S., Wu, T.: Pathsim: Meta path-based top-k similarity search in heterogeneous information networks. VLDB 4 (2011)

5. Shi, C., Kong, X., Yu, P.S., Xie, S., Wu, B.: Relevance search in heterogeneous networks. In: Proceedings of the 15th International Conference on Extending Database Technology, pp. 180–191. ACM (2012)
6. Shi, C., Zhou, C., Kong, X., Yu, P.S., Liu, G., Wang, B.: Heterecom: a semantic-based recommendation system in heterogeneous networks. In: Proceedings of the 18th ACM SIGKDD International Conference on Knowledge Discovery and Data Mining, pp. 1552–1555. ACM, August, 2012
7. Dean, J., Ghemawat, S.: MapReduce: simplified data processing on large clusters. Communications of the ACM **51**(1), 107–113 (2008)
8. De Pessemier, T., Vanhecke, K., Dooms, S., Martens, L.: Content-based recommendation algorithms on the hadoopmapreduce framework. In: 7th International Conference on Web Information Systems and Technologies (WEBIST 2011), pp. 237–240. Ghent University, Department of Information technology (2011)
9. Jiang, J., Lu, J., Zhang, G., Long, G.: Scaling-up item-based collaborative filtering recommendation algorithm based on hadoop. In: 2011 IEEE World Congress on Services (SERVICES), pp. 490–497. IEEE (2011)
10. Sun, Y., Chen, Y., Guan, X., Lin, C.: Approach of large matrix multiplication based on Hadoop. Journal of Computer Applications **33**(12), 3339–3344 (2013)

Crafting a Time-Aware Point-of-Interest Recommendation via Pairwise Interaction Tensor Factorization

Xinqiang Zhao[1], Xin Li[1(✉)], Lejian Liao[1], Dandan Song[1],
and William K. Cheung[2]

[1] Beijing Engineering Application Research Center of High Volume Language
Information Processing and Cloud Computing Applications, School of Computer
Science, Beijing Institute of Technology, Beijing 10081, China
{xinqiangzhao,xinli,liaolj,sdd}@bit.edu.cn
[2] Department of Computer Science, Hong Kong Baptist University,
Kowloon Tong, Hong Kong
william@comp.hkbu.edu.hk

Abstract. Location-based social networks have been increasingly used
to experience users new possibilities, including personalized point-of-
interest (POI) recommendation services which leverages on the overlapping of user trajectories to recommend POI collaboratively. POI recommendation is challenging as it does not just suffers from the problems
known for collaborative filtering such as data sparsity and cold-start, but
to a much greater extent. Most of the related works apply the conventional recommendation approaches to POI recommendation while over-
looking the personalized time-variant human behavioral tendency. In this
paper, we put forward a tensor factorization-based ranking methodology
to recommend users their interested locations by considering their time-
varying behavioral trends. We also propose to categorize the locations to
address data sparsity and cold-start issues, and accordingly new locations
the user have not been visited can thus be bubbled up during ranking
the location candidates. The tensor factorization is carefully studied to
prune the irrelevant factors to the ranking results to achieve efficient
POI recommendation. The experimental results validate the effectiveness of our proposed mechanism which outperforms the state-of-the-art
approaches by over 8% for precision.

Keywords: POI recommendation · Tensor · Markov chain

1 Introduction

Thanks to smart GPS-enabled phones and other GPS-enabled mobile devices,
the number of people who use location-based social networks (LBSNs) to share

The work of Xin Li is partially supported by National Program on Key Basic
Research Project under Grant No. 2013CB329605 and NSFC under Grant No.
61300178.

information is ever increasing [4]. Many LBSN systems, e.g., Foursquare and Gowalla have popped up to allow users to share their interests and obtain information anywhere and anytime. Its major difference from the conventional social networks lies in that what the users shared via the networks are now all related to locations.

In the literature, a bunch of location-aware data mining methods have been proposed which makes use of users' digital trajectories to predict the user behavior. For example, interesting locations and travel sequences can be detected from users' GPS trajectories [15]. However, LBSN data are different from GPS trajectories collected by system automatically. LBSN data contain only the spare information of check-in status which is posted to the network by the user voluntarily. Sometimes the users just do not update their status while they are on the spot, which intensifies the sparsity issue. Furthermore, the time gap between two successive check-in records can be long, which poses another challenge for POI recommendation. Fortunately, LBSN data also carry rich information related to the social structures (e.g. user's residence, friendship) like other information networks so that one can make best use of the contextual cues to address the challenges.

POI recommendation as a specialization of item recommendation [9,10] has attracted much attention of both academia and industry recently. Conventional recommendation methods such as collaborative filtering (CF)[7] and matrix factorization (MF)[2,6] have been adopted to solve this problem by considering new features, e.g., the relation of the two successive locations or the traveling restrictions (e.g. distance between two locations). Other machine learning approaches such as hidden Markov model(HMM) have also been adopted for location prediction[12]. FPMC-LR [3] considers successive POI recommendation by taking into account the temporal information and utilizes the distance limit to reduce the number of feasible locations. Although the authors claim that the temporal relation of locations is considered, the relations which are extracted via a Markov chain only captures the consecutive ordering relations instead of the behavior tendency over varying time explicitly. For example, most people prefer to go outside in the morning and go to nightClub at night. This trend can be observed clearly from Fig. 1.

LBSNs have some unique characteristics different from the other types of social networks or e-commerce websites. And we have considered these characteristics here to further boost the recommendation: (1) The visits of venues are highly related to varying time period as shown in Fig. 1. We can observe that the numbers of check-in different categories appear different patterns in one day; (2) The number of location candidates is large (there are thousands of POI per square kilometer) which makes the recommendation time-consuming and results in an inaccurate prediction; (3) The next type of visiting location is strongly correlated with the type of current location which is referred to as short-term preference in our paper. For example, people more likely check in a hotel after they step off a plane; (4) The visiting venues are also strongly affected by individuals' preference which is referred to as long-term preference. For example, people prefer those locations which they visit frequently; (5) In order to enhance user

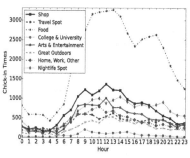   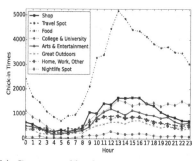

(a) Category Check-in Patterns of LA   (b) Category Check-in Patterns of NYC

Fig. 1. An illustration of the correlation between the time period and the number of check-in records over different location categories

experience and increase brand awareness of new venues, we need to recommend venues users have not visited yet.

The conventional item-based recommender systems recommend the items (music, movie, followship) which might of interest (listened, watched or accepted) to users at a later time which can be days, weeks, and even months. A good POI recommender system must have a real-time response, for example, it should be able to recommend the hotels instead of the nightspots or cinema if a user just gets off an airplane even though he enjoys nightlife and watches movies very often. And such a POI recommendation would soon be expired when she arrives at hotel. Then nightspots might be on top of the recommendation list during night.

Considering all these aforementioned characteristics, we propose a two-step personalized location recommendation methodology to enhance the recommendation performance. The system is supposed to recommend different places of interests to users with the change of time and current location. A a fourth rank tensor factorization is proposed to integrate user's short-term influence, long-term influence and time variant preference to effectively predict the category of next location, which can greatly alleviate the sparsity and cold-start issues for POI recommendation. Then the final location ranking list will be obtained based on the recommend action categories and our proposed metric on locations. We conducted extensive experiments to demonstrate the effectiveness of our proposed methodology. The prediction precision of category and location are 20% higher and 8% higher than that of the existing methods. The main contributions of this paper are as follows.

– We devise a two-step method to recommend user's most interested locations to users with higher accuracy efficiently. Firstly we predict user's preferred categories. Secondly we recommend the users most interested locations filtered with the distance restriction, given the preferred categories.

– We propose a fourth-rank tensor for modeling the category prediction which is capable of capturing user's personalized long-term preference, short-term preference, and the time-varying behaviors simultaneously.
– Category recommendation proposed in this paper allows the capturing of behavior pattern much easier. For example, traveling from Google's office to KFC and from Twitter's office to McDonalds should make not much a difference and grouping them as traveling from an office to a fast food restaurant can then be interpreted as a clear pattern that programmer likes going to a fast food restaurant after they get off work.
– The complexity has been sharply reduced due to the fact that the dimensionality of the problem has been reduced from the number of locations to the number of categories. Besides, category recommendation enables user to explore venues which they might be interested in but never visited before.

The rest of the paper is organized as follows. In Section 2, we review the related work to POI recommendation. The problem formulation and the proposed methodology are introduced in detail in Section 3. In Section 4 we evaluate the proposed method with comparative experiments on real LBSN data and analyze the performances. Finally, we conclude the paper in Section 5.

2   Related Work

POI recommendations based on LBSN data are much like trajectory-based location prediction or item recommendation but has its own characteristics.

In the literature, there are many works based on GPS trajectories mining for location prediction. A HITS (Hypertext Induced Topic Search)-based inference model[15] regards an individual's access to a location as a directed link from the user to the location for mining interesting locations and travel sequences from GPS trajectories. Compared with GPS data, the LBSN data are different as LBSN carries more social information, i.e., check-in tips, residence, and comments on the particular locations. However, with the rich information of LBSN social structure, LBSN data is still considered very sparse as the check-in data is updated by the user themselves unlike the GPS trajectory data which is collected by the system automatically. The physical distance between two successive check-in records is typically much larger than that of GPS data which makes the POI recommendation more challenging.

Collaborative Filtering(CF) is the most popular approach for item recommendation [7] and has been well studied for many years with real applications. CF-based models have also been adapted for POI recommendation. A collective matrix factorization method has been proposed to extract the interesting locations and activities [13]. In [14], the user related data are pulled together so as to apply collaborative filtering to find like-minded users and like-patterned activities at different locations. The idea behind the two approaches are to utilize the CF model to perceive the similarity between users or between locations, and then to recommend the user with the locations visited by their similar users.

However, the context-sensitive nature of POI recommendation cannot be well addressed by conventional collaborative filtering methods. For instance, the successive POI recommendation can be very different from the overall POI recommendation. A novel matrix factorization model named FPMC-LR has been proposed where a personalized Markov chain has been embedded to take into account user's movement restriction to predict user's next interested location.

All of the aforementioned models did not fully explore the characteristics of POI recommendation we have discussed in Section 1. In this paper, we develop our personalized time-aware FPMC (TA-FPMC) model which incorporate user's long-term preference, short-term preference and temporal information.

3   Problem Formulation

In this section, we introduce the details of our proposed methodology. We start with the notations and symbols used throughout the paper.

3.1   Notations and Symbols

Let u_i be the ith user and $\mathcal{U} = \{u_1, u_2, u_3, ..., u_{|U|}\}$ denote the set of the LBSN users. $\mathcal{L}$ denotes the set of the locations. $l_t \in \mathcal{L}$ denotes user's current location and $l_{t+1} \in \mathcal{L}$ the next location which is the output of related recommender system. $\mathcal{C}$ denotes the set of the location categories (e.g., school, restaurant, shopping mall and so on). We allow one location to possibly belong to multiple categories where $\mathcal{C}_t \subseteq \mathcal{C}$ denotes the set of user's current location categories and $\mathcal{C}_{t+1} \subseteq \mathcal{C}$ denote the set of next location categories. $T_i \in \mathcal{T} = \{T_1, T_2, T_3, T_4, T_5\}$ is the time intervals within a day where the user location is interested. In this paper, we divide a day into 5 time intervals according to the observation from Fig. 1 that there are roughly five different patterns in one day. And Δt indicates the time interval between the check-in time of the current location and that of the next location.

3.2   Time-Aware FPMC for POI Recommendation

In our time-aware FPMC (TA-FPMC), we consider only the transitions among the categories over time. Thus, the TA-FPMC yields a transition tensor $\chi \in [0, 1]^{|\mathcal{U}| \times |\mathcal{T}| \times |\mathcal{C}| \times |\mathcal{C}|}$ And we will show how the fourth-rank tensor is constructed by integrating the aforementioned characteristics step by step.

Category Information Incorporation. A first-order Markov chain model is used here to express the impact from the current categories to next categories. Compared with FPMC and FPMC-LR, our TA-FPMC can largely save the time cost due to the reduced dimensionality from the number of users to the number of categories. And the one-step transition probability is the probability of transiting from the current set of categories to the next set of categories.

$$p(c_{t+1}|C_t) = \frac{1}{|C_t|} \sum_{i=1}^{|C_t|} p(c_{t+1}|c_i \in C_t) \tag{1}$$

where the probability of transiting to one of the location categories in the next step c_{t+1} is independent of each other given the current category set C_t. Eq.(1) is a natural way to define the transition probability. However, for POI recommendation, the intensity of relation between the two successive check-in locations is assumed to be decaying with the time passing by. For example, if two successive check-in records span a year, we hardly expect much can be learned from the training data. Thus, we introduce an attenuation factor $D(\Delta t)$ to Eq.(1) to indicate the decay of the probability over time. With $D(\Delta t) = e^{-\alpha \Delta t}$ where $\alpha \in [0, 1]$, Eq.(1) can be rewritten as:

$$p(c_{t+1}|C_t) \propto \frac{1}{|C_t|} \sum_{i=1}^{|C_t|} D(\Delta t)p(c_{t+1}|c_i \in C_t) \propto \frac{1}{|C_t|} \sum_{i=1}^{|C_t|} e^{-\alpha \Delta t}p(c_{t+1}|c_i \in C_t) \tag{2}$$

Fig. 2(a) gives a graphic illustration of the transitions between the two successive location categories. The transition probability between two categories is labeled as "1" if we observe a transition between the two categories, and otherwise labeled as "?". Our objective is to somehow utilize Eq. (2) to train the model from the observed transitions and then estimate the transition probability between the unobserved category pair.

Temporal Information Incorporation. As shown from Fig. 1, we observed that the visiting trend of location categories shows different patterns over time. And we argue that the transition probability between the categories pair is also highly related to the specific time period. Thus we integrate the temporal information into the previous matrix to form a third-rank tensor. In our experiments, we divided the whole day into 5 different time periods to characterize the pattern. They are $T_1 = \{2, 3, 4, 5\}, T_2 = \{6, 7, 8, 9\}, T_3 = \{10, 11, 12, 13, 14\}, T_4 = \{15, 16, 17, 18\}, T_5 = \{19, 20, 21, 22, 23, 0, 1\}$ respectively. Fig. 2(b) shows our evolved third-rank tensor incorporating the temporal information.

Personalization. All user have their own preferences which lead to different patterns of daily activities. Thus we further extend the previous third-rank tensor by incorporating user preferences. Fig. 2(c) shows an example of our finally achieved fourth-rank tensor.

3.3   Partially Observed Fourth-Rank Tensor Recovery

There are many approximate approaches to recover a tensor with missing values e.g., Tucker Decomposition [11] and Parallel Factors [5], etc. Here we adopt a

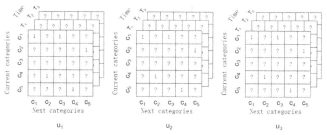

(a) A Matrix indicating the relation between current category and next category

(b) A Third-rank Time-aware Tensor

(c) A Fourth-rank Personalized Time-aware Tensor

Fig. 2. A fourth-rank Tensor Construction

special typed of Tucker Decomposition, PITF [10] to model the pairwise interaction between the four modes (i.e. user, time, the set of current categories and the set of next categories) for our proposed tensor:

$$
\hat{p}_{u,T,c_t,c_{t+1}} = u^T \cdot T^u + u^{c_t} \cdot c_t^{u} + u^{c_{t+1}} \cdot c_{t+1}^{u} + \\
T^{c_t} \cdot c_t^{T} + T^{c_{t+1}} \cdot c_{t+1}^{T} + c^{c_{t+1}} \cdot c_{t+1}^{c_t}
\tag{3}
$$

- For the interaction between user and time period: u^T modeling the user features and T^u for the time period.
- For the interaction between user and current location's categories: u^{c_t} modeling the user features and c_t^{u} for current location's categories.
- For the interaction between user and next location's categories: $u^{c_{t+1}}$ modeling the user features and c_{t+1}^{u} for next location's categories.
- For the interaction between time period and current location's categories: T^{c_t} modeling the time period features and c_t^{T} for next location's categories.
- For the interaction between time period and next location's categories: $T^{c_{t+1}}$ modeling the time period features and c_{t+1}^{T} for next location's categories.
- For the interaction between current location's categories and next location's categories: $c^{c_{t+1}}$ modeling the current location's categories features and $c_{t+1}^{c_t}$ for next location's categories.

Eq.(2) is further revised with the personalized preference and temporal information incorporated into the first-order Markov chain model. And we substitute

$p(c_{t+1}|c_i \in C_t)$ with Eq.(3):

$$\hat{p}_{u,T,C_t,c_{t+1}} = \frac{1}{|C_t|} \sum_{c_t \in C_t} e^{-\alpha \Delta t} \hat{p}_{u,T,c_t,c_{t+1}} = \frac{1}{|C_t|} \sum_{c_t \in C_t} e^{-\alpha \Delta t} (\boldsymbol{u}^T \cdot \boldsymbol{T}^u +$$
$$\boldsymbol{u}^{c_t} \cdot \boldsymbol{c_t}^u + \boldsymbol{u}^{c_{t+1}} \cdot \boldsymbol{c_{t+1}}^u + \boldsymbol{T}^{c_t} \cdot \boldsymbol{c_t}^T + \boldsymbol{T}^{c_{t+1}} \cdot \boldsymbol{c_{t+1}}^T + \boldsymbol{c_t}^{c_{t+1}} \cdot \boldsymbol{c_{t+1}}^{c_t}) \quad (4)$$

As the pairwise interactions of $\boldsymbol{u}^T \cdot \boldsymbol{T}^u$, $\boldsymbol{u}^{c_{t+1}} \cdot \boldsymbol{c_{t+1}}^u$ and $\boldsymbol{T}^{c_{t+1}} \cdot \boldsymbol{c_{t+1}}^T$ are independent of c_t, Eq.(4) can be rewritten as:

$$\hat{p}_{u,T,C_t,c_{t+1}} = \boldsymbol{u}^T \cdot \boldsymbol{T}^u + \boldsymbol{u}^{c_{t+1}} \cdot \boldsymbol{c_{t+1}}^u + \boldsymbol{T}^{c_{t+1}} \cdot \boldsymbol{c_{t+1}}^T +$$
$$\frac{1}{|C_t|} \sum_{c_t \in C_t} e^{-\alpha \Delta t} (\boldsymbol{u}^{c_t} \cdot \boldsymbol{c_t}^u + \boldsymbol{T}^{c_t} \cdot \boldsymbol{c_t}^T + \boldsymbol{c_t}^{c_{t+1}} \cdot \boldsymbol{c_{t+1}}^{c_t}) \quad (5)$$

BPR for TA-FPMC. Due to the sparsity of the dataset, we adopt a ranking approach as suggested in [8] to achieve the top-k list of categories that the user is most likely to visit. In dealing with the learning problem, here we adapt Bayesian Personalized Ranking (BPR) for ranking $>_{u,T,c_t}$ over all categories:

$$c_i >_{u,T,C_t} c_j \iff \hat{p}_{u,T,C_t,c_{t+1}=c_i} > \hat{p}_{u,T,C_t,c_{t+1}=c_j} \quad (6)$$

The problem of finding the best top-k ranking $>_{u,T,c_t}$ can be formalized as a problem maximizing the following posterior:

$$p(\Theta| >_{u,T,C_t}) \propto p(>_{u,T,C_t} |\Theta)p(\Theta) \quad (7)$$

where Θ are the model parameters. We also assume that the users's behaviors are independent which means that they have independent active time periods and independent preferred location categories. The likelihood $p(>_{u,T,c_t} |\Theta)$ is formalized by using the logistic function $\sigma(x) = \frac{1}{1+e^{-x}}$. By maximizing the posterior, we estimate the model parameters, given as:

$$\arg\max_{\Theta} \prod_{(u,T,C_t,c_i)\in D,(u,T,C_t,c_j)\notin D} p(>_{u,T,c_t} |\Theta)p(\Theta)$$
$$= \arg\max_{\Theta} \prod_{(u,T,C_t,c_i)\in D,(u,T,C_t,c_j)\notin D} p(\hat{p}_{u,T,C_t,c_{t+1}=c_i} - \hat{p}_{u,T,C_t,c_{t+1}=c_j} > 0|\Theta)p(\Theta)$$
$$= \arg\max_{\Theta} \prod_{(u,T,C_t,c_i)\in D,(u,T,C_t,c_j)\notin D} \sigma(\hat{p}_{u,T,C_t,c_{t+1}=c_i} - \hat{p}_{u,T,C_t,c_{t+1}=c_j})p(\Theta)$$
$$\quad (8)$$

where D denotes the training set. By assuming that the prior $p(\Theta)$ follows a Gaussian distribution, i.e., $\Theta \sim \mathcal{N}(0, \sigma_\theta I)$, an alternating maximum a posteriori estimation in logarithmic scale is given as:

$$\arg\max_{\Theta} \ln \prod_{(u,T,C_t,c_i)\in D,(u,T,C_t,c_j)\notin D} p(>_{u,T,c_t} |\Theta)p(\Theta)$$
$$= \arg\max_{\Theta} \sum_{(u,T,c_t,c_i)\in D,(u,T,C_t,c_j)\notin D} \ln \sigma(\hat{p}_{u,T,C_t,c_{t+1}=c_i} - \hat{p}_{u,T,C_t,c_{t+1}=c_j}) - \lambda_\theta ||\Theta||_F^2$$
$$\quad (9)$$

where λ_θ is the regularization constant corresponding to σ_θ. By replacing $\hat{p}_{u,T,c_t,c_{t+1}=c_i} - \hat{p}_{u,T,c_t,c_{t+1}=c_j}$ with Eq.(5), $\boldsymbol{u}^T \cdot \boldsymbol{T}^u$, $\boldsymbol{u}^{c_t} \cdot \boldsymbol{c_t}^u$ and $\boldsymbol{T}^{c_t} \cdot \boldsymbol{c_t}^T$ will vanish with no effect on the recommendation results. Then we update Eq.(5) as follows:

$$\hat{p}_{u,T,C_t,c_{t+1}} = \boldsymbol{u}^{c_{t+1}} \cdot \boldsymbol{c_{t+1}}^u + \boldsymbol{T}^{c_{t+1}} \cdot \boldsymbol{c_{t+1}}^T + \frac{1}{|C_t|} \sum_{c_t \in C_t} e^{-\alpha \Delta t} \boldsymbol{c_t}^{c_{t+1}} \cdot \boldsymbol{c_{t+1}}^{c_t}$$
(10)

By adapting stochastic gradient descent, the objective function is optimized. Algorithm 1 details how our time decaying FPMC(TAD-FPMC) is trained, the complexity of the algorithm is O($Num_{neg} \times Num_f$),where Num_{neg} is the number of neg-samples and Num_f is the number of features we used.

Algorithm 1. Learning Algorithm for TAD-FPMC

1: draw $\boldsymbol{u}^{c_{t+1}}, \boldsymbol{c_{t+1}}^u, \boldsymbol{T}^{c_{t+1}}, \boldsymbol{c_{t+1}}^T, \boldsymbol{c_t}^{c_{t+1}}, \boldsymbol{c_{t+1}}^{c_t}$ from $\mathcal{N}(0, \sigma_\theta I)$
2: **repeat**
3:    $\delta \leftarrow (1 - \sigma(\hat{p}_{u,T,c_t,c_{t+1}=c_i} - \hat{p}_{u,T,c_t,c_{t+1}=c_j}))$
4:    **for** $f = 1$ to the number of features **do**
5:      $u_f^{c_{t+1}} \leftarrow u_f^{c_{t+1}} + \alpha(\delta(c_{t+1,i,f}^u - c_{t+1,j,f}^u) - \lambda_\theta u_f^{c_{t+1}})$
6:      $T_f^{c_{t+1}} \leftarrow T_f^{c_{t+1}} + \alpha(\delta(c_{t+1,i,f}^T - c_{t+1,j,f}^T) - \lambda_\theta T_f^{c_{t+1}})$
7:      $c_{t+1,i,f}^u \leftarrow c_{t+1,i,f}^u + \alpha \delta u_f^{c_{t+1}} - \lambda_\theta c_{t+1,i,f}^u$
8:      $c_{t+1,i,f}^T \leftarrow c_{t+1,i,f}^T + \alpha \delta T_f^{c_{t+1}} - \lambda_\theta c_{t+1,i,f}^T$
9:      $c_{t+1,j,f}^u \leftarrow c_{t+1,j,f}^u + \alpha(-\delta u_f^{c_{t+1}} - c_{t+1,j,f}^u) - \lambda_\theta c_{t+1,j,f}^u$
10:     $c_{t+1,j,f}^T \leftarrow c_{t+1,j,f}^T + \alpha(-\delta T_f^{c_{t+1}} - c_{t+1,j,f}^T) - \lambda_\theta c_{t+1,j,f}^T$
11:     **for** $c \in C_t$ **do**
12:       $c_{t,f}^{c_{t+1}} \leftarrow c_{t,f}^{c_{t+1}} + \alpha(\delta \frac{1}{|C_t|} \sum_{c_t \in C_t} e^{-\alpha \Delta t}(c_{t+1,i,f}^{c_t} - c_{t+1,j,f}^{c_t}) - \lambda_\theta u_f^{c_{t+1}})$
13:       $c_{t+1,i,f}^{c_{t+1}} \leftarrow c_{t+1,i,f}^{c_{t+1}} + \alpha(\delta \frac{1}{|C_t|} \sum_{c_t \in C_t} e^{-\alpha \Delta t} c_{t+1,f}^{c_t} - \lambda_\theta c_{t+1,i,f}^{c_{t+1}})$
14:       $c_{t+1,j,f}^{c_{t+1}} \leftarrow c_{t+1,j,f}^{c_{t+1}} + \alpha(-\delta \frac{1}{|C_t|} \sum_{c_t \in C_t} e^{-\alpha \Delta t} c_{t+1,f}^{c_t} - \lambda_\theta c_{t+1,j,f}^{c_{t+1}})$
15:     **end for**
16:    **end for**
17: **until** convergence or reach the maximal number of iterations
18: **return** $\boldsymbol{u}^{c_{t+1}}, \boldsymbol{c_{t+1}}^u, \boldsymbol{T}^{c_{t+1}}, \boldsymbol{c_{t+1}}^T, \boldsymbol{c_t}^{c_{t+1}}, \boldsymbol{c_{t+1}}^{c_t}$

3.4 From Categories to Locations

In this section, we show how to achieve the top-k location list given the category recommendation results C_p. Based on the analyses of the spatial property versus the frequency of the visits, we can find that most of the successive check-ins are distributed within 5 kilometers. Here we propose a metric $score_{l,u}$ to evaluate the location ranks by considering the distance from the candidate of next locations to current location, the visiting frequency over the location candidate etc., with respective to user and location, given as:

$$score_{l,u} = \left(\sum_\tau H_u(\tau, l) \right) \left(\frac{\psi}{Dist(l_t, l)} \right)^{|C_l \cap C_p|^2}$$
(11)

where H_u is a $|\mathcal{T}| \times |\mathcal{L}|$ matrix, which describes the visiting history of user u. And $H(\tau, l)$ is the number of check-in records on location l during τ. $C_l \subset \mathcal{C}$ is the subset of categories which the location l belongs to. $Dist_{l_t, l_{t+1}}$ indicates the distance from l to the current location l_t. ψ is the threshold indicating the importance of the distance.

4 Experiments

In our evaluation, we investigate the operating efficiency and prediction quality of our proposed methodology. We take the matrix factorization algorithm, FPMC, FPMC-LR as baselines for the performance comparison.

4.1 Datasets

We evaluate our model on the data collected from Foursquare [1] during January, 2010 to June, 2011 for users living in Los Angels. The dataset contains 762 users, 144088 locations and 71880 checkins. The check-in data is very sparse (the average number of check-in is 5 for per user and only 75 percentage of the locations have the check-in status updated in Foursquare). So we filter out the inactive users. And we use the catalog Foursquare provided to infer the mapping from thousands of locations to 241 categories. 80% of the data are used as the training set and 20% of the data are used as the test set.

4.2 Category Prediction

Different from the conventional recommendation, our recommendation task only focus on the rightness of the next location(category) predication, which makes the upper-bound of the precision less than $1/|Recommendation\ Set|$. For instance, if we provide the recommendation list including 10 location(category) candidates for one user per round, the precision can either be 0.1 or 0 in conventional definition. Thus we propose the precision metric for our task to evaluate the accuracy as well as make a fair comparison with other approaches, given as:

$$P_u@N = \frac{\text{the number of locations(categories) which user } u \text{ visited in training set}}{\text{the number of recommendation rounds for user } u} \tag{12}$$

$$P@N = \frac{1}{|U|} \sum_{u \in U} P_u@N \tag{13}$$

The category predication experimental results are shown in Fig. 4(a). The compared approaches are Random Recommendation, FPMC, our proposed TA-FPMC without considering the time decaying influence, TA-FPMC with considering the time decaying influence(TAD-FPMC). It is obvious that both TA-FPMC and TAD-FPMC outperform FPMC and Random Recommendation by a large margin. It implies the incorporation of the time varying tendency is crucial for POI recommmendation. Furthermore, TAD-FPMC performs better than TA-FPMC, which verifies that the time decay function can further reduce noisy information and boost the performance.

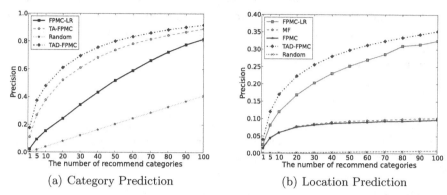

(a) Category Prediction   (b) Location Prediction

Fig. 3. Experimental Results Comparison for Category and Location Prediction

4.3 Location Prediction

Fig. 4(b) shows the experimental results of the location prediction. Similar to Fig. 4(a), the comparison are among the Random Recommendation, MF, FPMC, FPMC-LR, TAD-FPMC. The results are also consistent with the analysis we made in Sec. 4.2. It's obvious that TAD-FPMC outperform the other approaches by a large margin. When the size of the recommendation list is increasing, the performance curves of FPMC-LR and TAD-FPMC are approaching as they both provide a richer liable choices. However, our proposed TAD-FPMC outperforms FPMC-LR by a even larger margin given a shorter list of recommendation candidates. More specifically, TAD-FPMC improves FPMC-LR at least 8%. And the enhancement accounts to the effectiveness of the category prediction. And an effective short recommendation list conforms to the requirement of real recommender system.

We ran all our experiments on a machine with a Duel Xeon CPU 2.4GHz 16HT and the memory size of 24GB. Compared with the other models, TAD-FPMC is found to be the most efficient one. The running time of TAD-FPMC is around 1.3hr, while FPMC and FPMC-LR consumes over 35hrs. The efficiency benefits from the reduced dimensionality from the number of locations to the number of categories. More specifically, FPMC and FPMC-LR repeated its training process over $C_{|L|}^2$ pairs of the training data, while TAD-FPMC works towards $C_{|C|}^2$ pairs.

We observe that one location which belongs to multi categories has better chance to be next visiting location. For example, There is one test tips: $user : 1, Time : 5, categories : 207$ in our dataset. Our obtained candidate location list is l_{58797} and l_{11994}. l_{11994} belongs to two categories: 207 and 123, while l_{58797} only belongs to one category:207. The location l_{11994} is the observed target venue although l_{58797} is much nearer to the current location. This is reasonable as people intuitively tend to go to some centers providing high availability for multiple types of services and products just for convenience. The observation further validates the effectiveness of the category incorporation for POI recommendation.

5 Conclusion

In this paper, we take a two-step approach to tackle POI recommendation: (i) predicting the next location category set and (ii) recommending locations according to the predicted set of categories and a proposed metric. To recommend location categories, we propose a fourth-rank tensor model by considering the influence of the time-variant user preference, temporal information and the spanning time period between two successive check-in records. Then, we use the category prediction results together with some distance information to recommend locations as the potential POIs. Our experimental results obtained from the Foursquare dataset shows that a higher accuracy rate can be achieved and at the same time with a higher efficiency when compared with some existing methods.

References

1. Bao, J., Zheng, Y., Mokbel, M.F.: Location-based and preference-aware recommendation using sparse geo-social networking data. In: Gis, pp. 199–208 (2012)
2. Cheng, C., Yang, H., King, I., Lyu, M.R.: Fused matrix factorization with geographical and social influence in location-based social networks. In: Twenty-Sixth AAAI Conference on Artificial Intelligence (2012)
3. Cheng, C., Yang, H., Lyu, M.R., King, I.: Where you like to go next: successive point-of-interest recommendation. In: Proceedings of the Twenty-Third international joint conference on Artificial Intelligence, pp. 2605–2611. AAAI Press (2013)
4. Chow, C.Y., Bao, J., Mokbel, M.F.: Towards location-based social networking services. In: Proceedings of the 2nd ACM SIGSPATIAL International Workshop on Location Based Social Networks, pp. 31–38. ACM (2010)
5. Harshman, R.A., Lundy, M.E.: Parafac: Parallel factor analysis. Computational Statistics & Data Analysis 18(1), 39–72 (1994)
6. Koren, Y., Bell, R., Volinsky, C.: Matrix factorization techniques for recommender systems. In: IEEE COMPUTER (2009)
7. Linden, G., Smith, B., York, J.: Amazon. com recommendations: Item-to-item collaborative filtering. IEEE on Internet Computing 7(1), 76–80 (2003)
8. Rendle, S., Freudenthaler, C., Gantner, Z., Schmidt-Thieme, L.: Bpr: bayesian personalized ranking from implicit feedback. In: Proceedings of the Twenty-Fifth Conference on Uncertainty in Artificial Intelligence, pp. 452–461. AUAI Press (2009)
9. Rendle, S., Freudenthaler, C., Schmidt-Thieme, L.: Factorizing personalized markov chains for next-basket recommendation. In: Proceedings of the 19th international conference on World Wide Web, pp. 811–820. ACM (2010)
10. Rendle, S., Schmidt-Thieme, L.: Pairwise interaction tensor factorization for personalized tag recommendation. In: Proceedings of the third ACM international conference on Web Search and Data Mining, pp. 81–90. ACM (2010)

11. Tucker, L.R.: Some mathematical notes on three-mode factor analysis. Psychometrika **31**(3), 279–311 (1966)
12. Ye, J., Zhu, Z., Cheng, H.: Whats your next move: User activity prediction in location-based social networks. In: Proc. of SIAM International Conference on Data Mining (SDM) (2013)
13. Zheng, V.W., Zheng, Y., Xie, X., Yang, Q.: Collaborative location and activity recommendations with gps history data. In: Proceedings of the 19th international conference on World Wide Web, pp. 1029–1038. ACM (2010)
14. Zheng, V.W., Cao, B., Zheng, Y., Xie, X., Yang, Q.: Collaborativefiltering meets mobile recommendation: a user-centered approach. In: AAAI, vol. 10, pp. 236–241 (2010)
15. Zheng, Y., Zhang, L., Xie, X., Ma, W.Y.: Mining interesting locations and travel sequences from gps trajectories. In: Proceedings of the 18th international conference on World Wide Web, pp. 791–800. ACM (2009)

Novel Approaches for Shop Recommendation in Large Shopping Mall Scenario: From Matrix Factorization to Tensor Decomposition

Yue Ding[1]([✉]), Dong Wang[2], and Xin Xin[2]

[1] Department of Computer Science and Engineering,
Shanghai Jiaotong University, Shanghai, China
dingyue@cs.sjtu.edu.cn
[2] School of Software Engineering, Shanghai Jiaotong University, Shanghai, China
wangdong@cs.sjtu.edu.cn, xin.xsjtu@yahoo.com

Abstract. In this paper, we propose two novel approaches for recommendation in large shopping mall scenario. For matrix factorization approach, we construct a bias matrix utilizing graph computing which fuses user's long-term and short-term preferences. We exploit user trajectories to mine user's frequent paths and adopt to revamping rules to update ratings from the result of matrix factorization, thus solving the problem of re-predicting customer's preference to all shops in a new time window. For tensor decomposition approach, we add time dimension and construct a customer-shop-time three dimensional tensor, predict ratings are from the slice of the approximate tensor. We evaluate the result by top N recall and precision rate. Our data set is made on *JoyCity* which is a real shopping mall in Shanghai, the result is encouraging and it shows that our approach is applicative.

Keywords: Matrix factorization · RFID · Trajectories · Tensor decomposition

1 Introduction

Recommender systems have been successfully applied to help large websites such as Amazon.com to predict user's preference. Customers are more and more enjoying the process of online shopping. Compared with online websites, real shopping malls still have unique advantages that can never be replaced by online stores. Shopping malls provide real things instead of pictures of things, furthermore, a modern shopping mall is no longer a place for choosing goods, it has become a comprehensive large-scale shopping center integrating entertainment, leisure, shopping and dining functions. From another point of view, with the mature application in radio frequency identification devices (RFID), more and more large shopping malls have deployed RFID system, a customer's trajectory data can be captured by RFID readers, providing a new dimension to analyze a customer's preference. How to recommend shops that a customer may have interest

© Springer International Publishing Switzerland 2015
S. Zhang et al. (Eds.): KSEM 2015, LNAI 9403, pp. 471–482, 2015.
DOI: 10.1007/978-3-319-25159-2_42

and how to attract customers hanging out for more time? Solving these problems makes a great deal of sense.

Neighborhood-based collaborative filtering methods are basic algorithms in recommender systems. Neighborhood methods include user-based and item-based collaborative filtering. The essence of user-based and item-based approach is to find similar users and items for recommendation. Since the Netflix competition, latent factor model (LFM) has been a hot research topic in recommender system. The core concepts of LFM is to connect user and item by latent factors. On the other hand, graph-based models use bipartite graph to describe user's behavior. Recent years, researches on social networks for personalized recommendation prove to improve recommender system's performance [4]. The existing approaches are not applicable for shopping mall recommendation because we have to face the problem that how to re-predict a customer's preference to a shop if he has consumed in this shop. We define this as repetitive recommendation problem. Since a customer's preference is drifting and a shop's popularity is changing, the key point is to predict the customer's interest to all the shops in a new time window.

In this paper, we propose two approaches. The key point of matrix factorization approach is to construct the customer preference bias matrix fused customer's long-term and short-term preferences, we solve the repetitive recommendation problem by adding positive and negative factors. We exploit frequent paths mined from RFID trajectories as positive factors and revamp the ratings that the customer has consumed in a specific shop. The tensor decomposition approach is based on nonnegative Tucker decomposition, we predict the ratings by achieving the predict slice of the approximate tensor. Finally, evaluation is made on Top N recall and precision value. By top 10 recommendation, we achieve the best result of 23.56% recall rate and 9.62% precision rate by matrix factorization method and the result of 17.62% recall rate and 7.375% precision rate by tensor decomposition respectively.

The key contributions of the paper are:
(1) Matrix factorization combining bias matrix.
(2) Revising results utilizing positive and negative factors.
(3) Three dimensional tensor decomposition approach for rating prediction.

The rest of the paper is structured as follows. Section 2 presents related work. In Section 3, we describe the data set used in the paper. Section 4 expounds the algorithms and Section 5 is the experiment part. We make conclusion in Section 6.

2   Related Work

Collaborative Filtering (CF) includes user-based and item-based filtering. Latent factor model has been a popular approach these years and most successful applications are based on Matrix Factorization (MF). MF approaches construct two low-dimensional matrices $M \times D$ and $D \times N$ and approximate the observed matrix R under the given loss function, while R is $M \times N$ matrix. Koren [9] summarizes MF technology for recommender system and proposes improved MF models by adding biases and temporal dynamics to enhance accuracy. Based on basic MF, M. Andriy and S. Ruslan [13] present the Probabilistic Matrix Factorization (PMF) model and extend to include an adaptive prior on the model parameters. Josef [1] extends MF from normal distribution assumption to general probabilistic distributions. Liang Zhang [23] generalizes arbitrary regression models like LASSO, boosting, decision tree, etc. to incorporate features on factor estimates instead of linear regression.

Temporal dynamic is a challenging problem in recommender systems. Y. Ding [2] designs an algorithm that computes time weight for items by decreasing weight to old data. Koren [8] models the evolving behavior by adding time changing baseline predictors, capturing user biases and item biases and single day effect. Dawei [21] proposes a user-tag-specific temporal interests model to track users' interests in tagging systems. Approaches [14][16] to solve time-evolving models are built on graphic or tensor analysis. Instead of treating time as a universal dimension shared by all users, Liang [19] models user behavior fusing long term and short term preferences by dividing time into different sessions.

Personalized recommendation based on social networks has gradually been a hot topic these years. Researches on combining social factors including personal interest, interpersonal interest similarity and interpersonal influence show better performances than existing recommendation algorithms [12]. The emerging location-based and event-based social network services provide a new platform to understand users' preference [22]. Location and activity recommendations by mobile devices using history positioning data are increasingly popular [17][11]. Vincent [24] uses GPS history data and user comments to mine knowledge such as location features and activity-activity correlation and apply MF to discover interesting places and possible activities for recommendation. Yu [20] extends the probabilistic matrix factorization to apply explicit and implicit feedback data for IP-TV recommendation. Gideon [5] builds a session-based temporal dynamic model for Yahoo! Music recommendation with item taxonomy.

The tensor model can nicely represent high dimensional data without breaking its eigen structure. Decomposition of higher-order tensors(i.e.,N-way arrays with $N \geqslant 3$) have applications in data mining [15], graph analysis [7], computer vision [18], etc. CANDECOMP/PARAFAC(CP) [3] and Tucker decomposition [10] are two main approaches for tensor decomposition, based on that, there are many other approaches such as INDSCAL, PARAFAC2, CANDELING, DEDICOM, PARATUCK2 and nonnegative decomposition [6].

To the best of our knowledge, we have not seen any work focusing on shopping mall scenario recommendations. To formulize our task, given user set U, shop set I, user consumption set C and user RFID trajectory set F, we predict user ratings R_{ui} utilizing matrix factorization and tensor decomposition approaches. We evaluate the result by top N recall and precision rate.

3   Data Set Description

The test data set is made on *Joycity* RFID trajectories and purchasing history spanning 16 consecutive months. The tracking dataset has 150,858 disparate records. The total amount of consumption reaches 1,826,028 RMB. *Joycity* is a large-scale shopping center in downtown Shanghai, it has deployed RFID readers on different floors covering every indoor corner. *Joycity* issues membership cards to its registered members, once a member enters the shopping center, his tracking history will be recorded.

Table 1 describes the fields of RFID trajectories in database.

Table 1. Fields of RFID trajectories

Fields	Data type in Database	Description
TagID	Varchar	Member's ID
ReaderID	Int	The ID of RFID reader
RangeID	Int	RFID reader's Correspondent area
TimeStamp	Datetime	Sampling interval is 0.001 second

4   The Approaches

In this section, we present two recommendation approaches. The first approach is based on matrix factorization. We generate the original rating matrix converting from customer's consumption history, then we construct customer-shop bias matrix using session-based graph computing. We optimize the objective function implementing stochastic gradient descent and solve the repetitive recommendation by revising the rating value by adding positive and negative feedbacks. The second approach is based on Tucker nonnegative decomposition. We divide time dimension by months and construct a three dimensional tensor with 12 frontal training slices and one predict slice. We randomly set values to a small proportion of elements by using mean value and by values subject to Gaussian distribution. Prediction is made on the slice of approximate tensor.

4.1   Matrix Factorization Based Approach

Generate Rating Matrix. Let U and I be the customer and item set respectively. In our case, an item represents a specific store which may contain many kinds of products. Our purpose is to recommend stores that a customer may have interest. R is the rating matrix and $R \in (0,5)$ $|U| \times |I|$, $R_{ui} = 5$ indicates the highest preference and $R_{ui} = 0$ represents no preference on a given item.

In our dataset, a user's preference on a certain item is implicitly reflected by his sum of consumption. So we use a mapping function to convert all user's consumption to a rating matrix.

$$R_{ui} = F(S_{ui}) \tag{1}$$

$$S_{ui} = \sum_{t \in Time} A(ui), \quad A(ui) \text{is the amount that user } u \\ \text{consumes on item } i \text{ on time } t. u \in U \text{ and } i \in I. \tag{2}$$

$$F(x) = 10 \times \left(\left(\frac{1}{1 + exp(-\frac{1}{1000}x)} \right) - 0.5 \right) \tag{3}$$

The mapping function comes from the sigmoid function, since the sigmoid function can map any value x to value interval (0, 1), we revise the factors to convert all positive value x to value interval (0, 5)

Customer-item Interest Bias Matrix Fused Customer's Long-term and Short-term Preference. In recommender systems, a customer's interest may drift over time and an item's popularity may also changing. Koren[8] proposes different time sensitive predictors to capture user's preference over time, but the RMSE improvement is not obvious since linear baseline predictors are not accurate models.

Liang Xiang[19] proposes Session-based Temporal Graph(STG) model and Injected Preference Fusion(IPF) algorithm. This approach fuses user's long term and shot term preference over time. Inspired by this approach, we referred similar steps. Instead of making top N recommendation from graph computing, we use the result to construct user-item bias matrix for further computing. In STG, time is divided into bins and binds with corresponding users, so data is formed of $< user, item >$ and $< session, item >$ tuples. Here a *session* represents a period of time, we set 3 months as a *session*. STG is a directed bipartite graph $G(U, S, I, E, \omega)$, U denotes the set of user nodes, S denotes the set of session nodes, I denotes the set of item nodes, E is the edge and ω denotes a non-negative weight value for edges. A simple example of STG can be shown as the following figure:

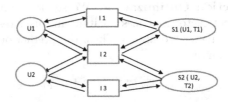

Fig. 1. A simple example of STG

The edge weights of G are defined as:

$$\omega(v, v') = \begin{cases} 1, & if \ \ v \in U \cup S, v' \in I \\ \eta_u, & if \ v \in I, v' \in U \\ \eta_s, & if \ v \in I, v' \in S \end{cases} \tag{4}$$

P represents paths from source node $v_0 \in \{v_u, v_{ut}\}$, $P = \{ v_0, v_1, \ldots v_n \}$. The final preference value propagated to v_n is defined as:

$$\Phi(P) = \prod_{\nu_k \in P, 0 \leq k < n} \Psi(v_k, v_{k+1}) \Upsilon(v_0) \tag{5}$$

$\Upsilon(v_0)$ is the value of injected preferences on the source node.

$$\Upsilon(v_0) = \begin{cases} \beta, & v_0 = v_u \\ 1 - \beta, & v_0 = v_{ut} \end{cases} \tag{6}$$

β is the parameter controls the ratio of injected preference. $\Psi(v_k, v_{k+1})$ is the the propagation function calculating the preference from node v_k to its succeed node v_{k+1}.

$$\Psi(v_k, v_{k+1}) = \begin{cases} \frac{1}{|out(v_k)|^\rho} & v_k \in U \cup S, v_{k+1} \in I \\ \left(\frac{\eta}{\eta|out(v_k) \cap U| + |out(v_k) \cap S|}\right)^\rho & v_k \in I, v_{k+1} \in U \\ \left(\frac{1}{\eta|out(v_k) \cap U| + |out(v_k) \cap S|}\right)^\rho & v_k \in I, v_{k+1} \in S \end{cases} \tag{7}$$

Where $out(v_k)$ denotes the out-degree of node v_k, it is clear that if node v_k has larger out-degree, then v_{k+1} will have lower incoming preference. Parameter ρ is the impact factor with the value in range of zero and one. Parameter $\eta = \eta_u$ / η_s, η_u and η_s are defined in Equation (4). In STG, only shortest paths from user or session nodes to unknown item nodes should be considered, the shortest paths can be obtained by Bread-First-Search. Finally, the estimated preference p_{ui} of users u on item i can be measured as Equation (8):

$$p_{ui} = \sum_{P \in \mathcal{P}(u, i)} \Phi(P) \tag{8}$$

Objective Function Optimization. We set low rank matrix q_i and p_u to represent the latent factor matrices for item and user respectively. We generate the bias matrix as presented above. Thus, the prediction of unknown item i by user u can be estimated by

$$r'_{ui} = \tau \cdot bias + q_i^T p_u \tag{9}$$

τ is the parameter to adjust bias's weight. The objective function is:

$$\Psi = \min_{q^*, p^*} \sum_{(u,i) \in k} (r_{ui} - \tau \cdot bias - q_i^T p_u)^2 \\ + \frac{\beta}{2} \left(||q_i||^2 + ||p_u||^2 \right) + \frac{\gamma}{2} \left(||bias||^2 \right) \tag{10}$$

The regularized constrains are $\frac{\beta}{2}\left(||q_i||^2 + ||p_u||^2\right) + \frac{\gamma}{2}\left(||bias||^2\right)$. We minimize the loss function by using a stochastic gradient descent algorithm.

$$\frac{\partial \Psi}{\partial q_i} = -2e_{ui} \cdot p_u + \beta \cdot q_i \tag{11}$$

$$\frac{\partial \Psi}{\partial p_u} = -2e_{ui} \cdot q_i + \beta \cdot p_u \tag{12}$$

Here e_{ui} represents error between real rating value r_{ui} and estimated rating value r'_{ui}. The update rules for q_i and p_u are:

$$q_i \leftarrow q_i + \alpha(2e_{ui} \cdot p_u - \beta \cdot q_i) \tag{13}$$

$$p_u \leftarrow p_u + \alpha(2e_{ui} \cdot q_i - \beta \cdot p_u) \tag{14}$$

α is the learning rate. If the value of α is too large, the algorithm may converge rapidly and miss possible local optimum. If α is too small, the speed of convergence will be slow.

Result Revamp Rules. To deal with the repetitive recommendation problem and accurately predict a customer's preference in a new time window, we design update rules to revamp the result from matrix factorization. The main idea is to add positive and negative feedbacks to analyze customer behavior more precisely. $\{r'\}$ is the revised rating set.

$$\{r'\} = \{I_{uj}R(r'_{uj})\} \cup \{I_{uk}\lambda r'_{uk}\} \cup \{r'_{ul}\}$$

I_{uj} and I_{uk} are the indicator function. r'_{uj} contains items that user u has consumed, $R(r'_{uj})$ revises ratings, δ and ξ are parameters controlling output result. μ is the average amount of customer consumption.

$$R(r'_{uj}) = r'_{uj} + \delta \cdot sign(\mu - r'_{uj}) \cdot |\mu - r'_{uj}|^\xi \tag{15}$$

r'_{uk} contains shops from customer's personal maximum frequent paths. We divide every customer's tracking data by different days, we mine maximum frequent paths by applying classic Apriori Algorithm. Once the algorithm is done, we obtain shops from customer's maximum frequent paths and accordingly increase ratings of these shops as positive factor. λ is the weight factor. r'_{ul} is the set containing elements that are not revised.

4.2 Nonnegative Tucker Decomposition Approach

Notation and Preliminaries. A tensor is a multidimensional array, the order of a tensor is the number of dimensions, or known as ways or modes. A first-order tensor is a vector, a second-order tensor is a matrix, a tensor with three or higher orders is a higher-order tensor. In this paper, vectors are denoted by boldface lowercase letters, e.g., $\boldsymbol{a}$. Matrices are denoted by boldface capital letters, e.g., A. Higher-order tensors are denoted by boldface Euler script letters, e.g., χ. A tensor's Slices are two-dimensional sections presented by two indices while fixing all the other indices. The horizontal and lateral and frontal slices of a three-dimensional tensor are normally denoted by $X_{i::}$, $X_{:j:}$ and $X_{::k}$, see figure 2.

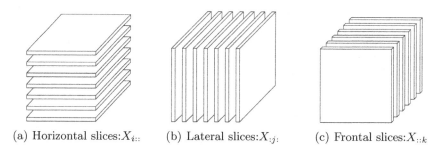

(a) Horizontal slices:$X_{i::}$ (b) Lateral slices:$X_{:j:}$ (c) Frontal slices:$X_{::k}$

Fig. 2. Slices of a three-dimensional tensor

Tuck Decomposition. Tensor n-mode product is a tensor multiplies a matrix or a vector in mode n. For example, a tensor $\chi \in \mathbb{R}^{I_1 \times I_2 \times \ldots \times I_N}$ multiplies a matrix $U \in \mathbb{R}^{J \times I_n}$ in mode n is denoted by $\chi \times_n U$. Tucker decomposition can be summarized as higher-order Principal Component Analysis(PCA). A tensor can be decomposed into a *core tensor* and matrices along each mode. For example, a three-dimensional tensor $\chi \in \mathbb{R}^{I \times J \times K}$ can be decomposed as

$$\chi \approx \varrho \times_1 A \times_2 B \times_3 C \tag{16}$$

Here, tensor $\varrho \in \mathbb{R}^{P \times Q \times R}$ is the *core tensor*, factor matrices $A \in \mathbb{R}^{I \times P}$ and $B \in \mathbb{R}^{J \times Q}$ and $C \in \mathbb{R}^{K \times R}$ are principal components in each mode and they are normally orthogonal. The HOOI(higher-order orthogonal iteration) algorithm is en efficient algorithm solving tucker decomposition based on ALS(alternating least square) [6].

Rating Prediction Calculating Procedure. Here are the steps we adopt for rating prediction:

Step 1. Divide the training set by months, thus construct 12 matrices or called "frontal slices" of a tensor.

Step 2. Assign some values for the initial predict matrix or called "predict slice". We adopt two ways of assigning values. One is to assign mean value got by training set to random elements of predict slice. Another way is to assign values subject to Gaussian distribution with expectation and standard deviation got from training set.

Step 3. Merge training slices and predict slice together and run nonnegative tucker decomposition.

Step 4. Utilize Equation(16) to calculate the approximate tensor and get the 13th slice as the predict matrix.

5   Experimental Evaluation

In this section, we present the experimental result we obtained. We separate data set into training set spanning 12 consecutive months and test set spanning 4 consecutive months respectively.

For Matrix Factorization Approach. The evaluation is formed of two parts. In the first part, we train parameters related to matrix factorization. The evaluation criterion is the root mean squared error (RMSE) between predicted ratings and true ones:

$$\mathbf{RMSE} = \sqrt{\frac{\sum_{(u,i)\in TEST}(r_{ui} - r'_{ui})^2}{|TEST|}}$$

In objective function Ψ, see formula (10), we test parameters τ, β and γ iteratively under feature number of 10, gradient descent factor α is equal to 0.002. Results are presented in table 2, table 3 and table 4. We achieve best RMSE value of 0.8358 when τ is equal to 3 and β is equal to 0.9 and γ is equal to 0.7.

Table 2. RMSE results when $\tau = 1$

	$\gamma = 0.1$	$\gamma = 0.2$	$\gamma = 0.3$	$\gamma = 0.4$	$\gamma = 0.5$	$\gamma = 0.6$	$\gamma = 0.7$	$\gamma = 0.8$	$\gamma = 0.9$
$\beta = 0.1$	1.2611	1.2611	1.2633	1.2566	1.2618	1.2602	1.2592	1.2640	1.2535
$\beta = 0.2$	1.2194	1.2249	1.2216	1.2247	1.2238	1.2254	1.2219	1.2248	1.2190
$\beta = 0.3$	1.1913	1.1990	1.1958	1.1918	1.2001	1.1911	1.1946	1.1919	1.1929
$\beta = 0.4$	1.1688	1.1647	1.1657	1.1623	1.1643	1.1712	1.1645	1.1722	1.1718
$\beta = 0.5$	1.1320	1.1268	1.1323	1.1291	1.1419	1.1380	1.1255	1.1319	1.1365
$\beta = 0.6$	1.0996	1.0971	1.1033	1.1019	1.1025	1.1038	1.1067	1.1022	1.0980
$\beta = 0.7$	1.0699	1.0706	1.0694	1.0694	1.0655	1.0650	1.0698	1.0671	1.0640
$\beta = 0.8$	1.0429	1.0415	1.0352	1.0421	1.0380	1.0402	1.0383	1.0396	1.0343
$\beta = 0.9$	1.0049	1.0022	1.0080	1.0097	1.0032	1.0048	1.0093	1.0067	1.0052

In the second part, evaluation is made on recall and precision rate(equation 17 and 18). We adopt top 10 recommendation. As approximate matrix is generated by production of latent factor matrices q_i^T and p_u under best value of parameters τ, β and γ as tested above, we use similar iterative steps to test parameters ξ, δ and λ. The best recall rate is 23.56% and best precision rate 9.962% both if ξ is equal to 0.3 and δ is equal to 0.5 and λ is equal to 1.2. Compared with non-revise output with best recall rate of 16.76% and best precision rate of 7.625%, the improvement is 40.6% and 30.6% respectively.

$$Precision = \frac{|\text{PredictionSet} \cap \text{ReferenceSet}|}{|\text{PredictionSet}|} \tag{17}$$

$$Recall = \frac{|\text{PredictionSet} \cap \text{ReferenceSet}|}{|\text{ReferenceSet}|} \tag{18}$$

Table 3. RMSE results when $\tau = 2$

	$\gamma = 0.1$	$\gamma = 0.2$	$\gamma = 0.3$	$\gamma = 0.4$	$\gamma = 0.5$	$\gamma = 0.6$	$\gamma = 0.7$	$\gamma = 0.8$	$\gamma = 0.9$
$\beta = 0.1$	1.1498	1.1480	1.1554	1.1576	1.1510	1.1530	1.1465	1.1490	1.1552
$\beta = 0.2$	1.1229	1.1192	1.1189	1.1143	1.1162	1.1172	1.1129	1.1198	1.1155
$\beta = 0.3$	1.0808	1.0846	1.0895	1.0904	1.0785	1.0819	1.0803	1.0807	1.0799
$\beta = 0.4$	1.0571	1.0551	1.0619	1.0571	1.0506	1.0554	1.0517	1.0611	1.0589
$\beta = 0.5$	1.0301	1.0221	1.0219	1.0260	1.0246	1.0218	1.0254	1.0196	1.0238
$\beta = 0.6$	0.9999	0.9896	0.9985	0.9950	0.9962	0.9938	0.9928	0.9971	0.9954
$\beta = 0.7$	0.9658	0.9648	0.9630	0.9668	0.9686	0.9682	0.9700	0.9657	0.9653
$\beta = 0.8$	0.9372	0.9354	0.9317	0.9356	0.9314	0.9349	0.9317	0.9329	0.9358
$\beta = 0.9$	0.9093	0.9104	0.9033	0.9068	0.9071	0.9046	0.9055	0.9047	0.9062

Table 4. RMSE results when $\tau = 3$

	$\gamma = 0.1$	$\gamma = 0.2$	$\gamma = 0.3$	$\gamma = 0.4$	$\gamma = 0.5$	$\gamma = 0.6$	$\gamma = 0.7$	$\gamma = 0.8$	$\gamma = 0.9$
$\beta = 0.1$	1.0710	1.0710	1.0766	1.0642	1.0750	1.0655	1.0678	1.0696	1.0628
$\beta = 0.2$	1.0314	1.0330	1.0391	1.0286	1.0286	1.0332	1.0357	1.0363	1.0396
$\beta = 0.3$	1.0007	1.0084	1.0096	1.0025	1.0013	0.9975	0.9971	1.0063	1.0039
$\beta = 0.4$	0.9841	0.9795	0.9762	0.9812	0.9800	0.9748	0.9749	0.9788	0.9861
$\beta = 0.5$	0.9487	0.9480	0.9468	0.9537	0.9528	0.9462	0.9486	0.9468	0.9515
$\beta = 0.6$	0.9173	0.9185	0.9176	0.9177	0.9270	0.9248	0.9196	0.9250	0.9178
$\beta = 0.7$	0.8921	0.8940	0.8994	0.8914	0.8899	0.8905	0.8932	0.8995	0.8953
$\beta = 0.8$	0.8693	0.8662	0.8630	0.8661	0.8627	0.8682	0.8589	0.8659	0.8615
$\beta = 0.9$	0.8367	0.8401	0.8364	0.8379	0.8397	0.8360	0.8358	0.8370	0.8358

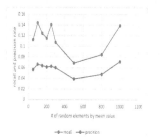 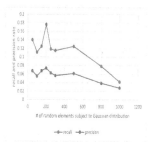

(a) Recall and precision rate by random elements with mean value

(b) Recall and precision rate by random elements subject to Gaussian distribution

Fig. 3. Recall and precision rate by random elements with mean value and elements subject to Gaussian distribution

For Nonnegative Tucker Decomposition. We adopt two different tactics to assign values on random position for the rating matrix that we need to predict. The number of assigned elements ranges from 50 to 1000. In figure 3, for elements assigned mean values got from training set, the result of tensor decomposition achieves best recall rate of 13.87% and precision rate of 7.125% if we use 1000 random elements. For assigned elements subject to Gaussian distribution with expectation and standard deviation got from training set, the best recall rate is 17.62% and precision rate is 7.375% when use 200 random elements.

6   Conclusion and Discussion

In this paper, we propose two approaches for shop recommendation in large shopping mall scenario. We construct the bias matrix based on graph computing and train the objective function by adding bias regularization. We solve the repetitive recommendation problem by revising results for adding positive and negative feedbacks. For tensor decomposition approach, we assign values to elements randomly and construct the initial predict matrix, after the nonnegative tucker decomposition, we do not revise any value and the result is still encouraging. Although the matrix factorization approach achieves better result, there is possible improvement can be made for tensor decomposition and future work may focus on it.

References

1. Bauer, J., Nanopoulos, A.: A framework for matrix factorization based on general distributions. In: RecSys 2014, pp. 249–256 (2014)
2. Ding, Y., Li, X.: Time weight collaborative filtering. In: CIKM 2005, pp. 485–492 (2005)
3. Dubroca, R., De Luigi, C., Moreau, E.: A parafac decomposition based algorithm for blind mimo source separation. In: 3rd IEEE International Workshop on Computational Advances in Multi-Sensor Adaptive Processing (CAMSAP), pp. 93–96 (2009)
4. Jamali, M., Ester, M.: A matrix factorization technique with trust propagation for recommendation in social networks. In: RecSys 2010, pp. 135–142 (2010)
5. Koenigstein, N., Dror, G., Koren, Y.: Yahoo! music recommendations: modeling music ratings with temporal dynamics and item taxonomy. In: RecSys 2011, pp. 165–172 (2011)
6. Kolda, T.G., Bader, B.W.: Tensor decompositions and applications. SIAM review **51**(3), 455–500 (2009)
7. Kolda, T., Bader, B., Kenny, J.: Higher-order web link analysis using multilinear algebra. In: Fifth IEEE International Conference on Data Mining (2005)
8. Koren, Y.: Collaborative filtering with temporal dynamics. Communications of the ACM **53**, 89–97 (2010)
9. Koren, Y., Bell, R., Volinsky, C.: Matrix factorization techniques for recommender systems. Computer **42**, 30–37 (2009)

10. Oseledets, I.V., Savostianov, D.V., Tyrtyshnikov, E.E.: Tucker dimensionality reduction of three-dimensional arrays in linear time. SIAM Journal on Matrix Analysis and Applications **30**(3), 939–956 (2008)
11. Park, M.-H., Hong, J.-H., Cho, S.-B.: Location-Based recommendation system using bayesian user's preference model in mobile devices. In: Cao, J., Ungerer, T., Ma, J., Yang, L.T., Indulska, J. (eds.) UIC 2007. LNCS, vol. 4611, pp. 1130–1139. Springer, Heidelberg (2007)
12. Qian, X., Feng, H., Zhao, G., Mei, T.: Personalized recommendation combining user interest and social circle. IEEE Trans. Knowl. Data Eng. **26**, 1763–1777 (2014)
13. Salakhutdinov, R., Mnih, A.: Probabilistic matrix factorization. In: NIPS (2011)
14. Sun, J., Faloutsos, C., Papadimitriou, S., Yu, P.S.: Graphscope: parameter-free mining of large time-evolving graphs. In: KDD 2007, pp. 687–696 (2007)
15. Sun, J., Papadimitriou, S., Yu, P.: Window-based tensor analysis on high-dimensional and multi-aspect streams. In: ICDM 2006, pp. 1076–1080 (2006)
16. Sun, J., Tao, D., Faloutsos, C.: Beyond streams and graphs: dynamic tensor analysis. In: KDD 2006, pp. 374–383 (2006)
17. Takeuchi, Y., Sugimoto, M.: Cityvoyager: An outdoor recommendation system based on user location history. In: Ubiquitous Intelligence and Computing, pp. 625–636 (2006)
18. Vasilescu, M., Terzopoulos, D.: Multilinear subspace analysis of image ensembles. In: IEEE Computer Society Conference on Computer Vision and Pattern Recognition, vol. 2, pp. II - 93–9 (2003)
19. Xiang, L., Yuan, Q., Zhao, S., Chen, L., Zhang, X., Yang, Q., Sun, J.: Temporal recommendation on graphs via long- and short-term preference fusion. In: KDD 2010, pp. 723–732 (2010)
20. Xin, Y., Steck, H.: Multi-value probabilistic matrix factorization for IP-TV recommendation. In: RecSys 2011, pp. 221–228 (2011)
21. Yin, D., Hong, L., Xue, Z., Davison, B.D.: Temporal dynamics of user interests in tagging systems. In: AAAI, pp. 1279–1285 (2011)
22. Yin, H., Sun, Y., Cui, B., Hu, Z., Chen, L.: Lcars: a location-content-aware recommender system. In: KDD 2013, pp. 221–229 (2013)
23. Zhang, L., Agarwal, D., Chen, B.C.: Generalizing matrix factorization through flexible regression priors. In: RecSys 2011, pp. 13–20 (2011)
24. Zheng, V.W., Zheng, Y., Xie, X., Yang, Q.: Collaborative location and activity recommendations with gps history data. In: WWW2010, pp. 1029–1038 (2010)

A Microblog Recommendation Algorithm
Based on Multi-tag Correlation

Huifang Ma[1,2(✉)], Meihuizi Jia[1], Meng Xie[1], and Xianghong Lin[1]

[1] College of Computer Science and Engineering, Northwest Normal University,
Lanzhou Gansu 730070, China
mahuifang@yeah.net
[2] Key Laboratory of Intelligent Information Processing of Chinese Academy of Sciences,
Institute of Computing Technology, Chinese Academy of Sciences, Beijing 10085, China

Abstract. In this paper, we present a microblog recommendation algorithm based on multi-tag correlation. Firstly, a tag retrieval strategy is designed to add tags for unlabeled users, the initial user-tag matrix is then constructed and user-tag weights are set. In order to represent user interests accurately, we fully investigate the associations between the tags. Both inner and outer correlation between tags are defined to conquer the problem of sparsity of user-tag matrix. The user interests can then be decided and microblogs can be recommended to users. Experimental results show that the algorithm is effective for microblog recommendation.

Keywords: Microblog recommendation · Tag retrieval · User-Tag weight · Tag correlation

1   Introduction

As a typical representative application of web 2.0, microblog has attracted a great number of users and rapidly developed in recent years. It is necessary to develop new algorithms to provide the personalized service for these users. And high quality information should be accurately pushed based on the user's interest[3].

In this paper, we present a microblog recommendation algorithm based on multi-tag correlation. First, a novel user tag retrieval strategy is developed to select the tags for unlabeled users and a user-tag matrix is created to represent the initial weight of users' tags. Second, we construct a correlation matrix of multi-tag by investigating inner and outer correlation between tags. Third, the original user-tag matrix is updated by correlation matrix of multi-tag to obtain the final weight.

The basic outline of this paper is as follows: Section 2 presents user method. The experiments and results are demonstrated in Section 3. Lastly, we conclude our paper in Section 4.

2   Our Approach

2.1   User Tag Retrieval and User-Tag Matrix Construction

If the tagging service is provided by microblog system, the built-in tags can be directly used. Otherwise, a tag retrieval method is adopted to acquire the personal tags from the microblog posted by that user.

S. Zhang et al. (Eds.): KSEM 2015, LNAI 9403, pp. 483–488, 2015.
DOI: 10.1007/978-3-319-25159-2_43

Table 1. Notions in tag retrieval

notion	definition
$U = \{u_1, u_2, \ldots, u_i, \ldots u_N\}$	The microblog user dataset
N	The number of users
$D_i = \{d_{i1}, d_{i2}, \ldots, d_{iM_i}\}$	The microblog collection for u_i
$M_i, \quad i=(1,2,\ldots,N)$	The number of microblog for u_i
$D = \bigcup_{i=1}^{N} D_i$	The microblog dataset of all users
$T_i = \{t_{i1}, t_{i2}, \ldots, t_{im_i}\}$	The terms set for microblog dataset D_i
$m_i, \quad m_i \ll M_i$	The number of terms
$L_i = \{l_{i1}, l_{i2}, \ldots, l_{in_i}\}$	The tag set for u_i
n_i	The number of tags for u_i
$L = \bigcup_{i=1}^{N} L_i$	The collection for all tags
n	The total number of tags in tag collection L

The most critical step for tag retrieval is to select most representative words from users previously posted microblog as query words. Ideally, the query words should be (i) well represent the main content of the microblog, and (ii) be topically indicative. The clarity score[1] is used to measure the topical-specificity of a certain term. Let the *j-th* term l_{ij} be a candidate word for selection, we use l_{ij} as a single-term query to retrieve its top-g_i most relevant microblogs, denoted by Q_{lij}. We use equation (1) to calculate the clarity score of term l_{ij}.

$$Clarity(l_{ij}) = \sum_{l_{ij} \in T_i} P(l_{ij} | Q_{l_{ij}}) \log \frac{P(l_{ij} | Q_{l_{ij}})}{P(l_{ij} | D_i)} \tag{1}$$

Then the score of the *j-th* word is computed as the equation below:

$$s_j = tf_j \times clarity(l_{ij}) \tag{2}$$

n_i words with the highest weight are chosen as user u_i's tags, and each tag is assigned a normalized weight:

$$normalized(s_j) = \frac{s_j}{\sum_{x=1}^{n_i} s_x} \tag{3}$$

The tag weight vector $V_i = (w_{i1}, w_{i2}, \ldots w_{in})$ is created for user u_i to represent the initial weights of tags[4]. If the tags are obtained from the above tag retrieval scheme, we use Eq. (3) to generate the initial weights for these tags. Otherwise, if the tags are provided by the tagging service, each tag is treated as of equal importance. Assuming that u_i has Z_i tags, the initial user's tag weight w_{ij} are defined as follows:

$$w_{ij} = \begin{cases} 1/Z_i, & \text{if tag } l_j \text{ assigned to } u_i, \\ normalized\left(s_j\right), & \text{tag retrieval,} \\ 0, & \text{otherwise,} \end{cases} \tag{4}$$

Based on users' weight vectors, we create a $N*n$ matrix M_{ul}, which is defined as:

$$M_{ul} = \begin{bmatrix} \overrightarrow{V_1} \\ \overrightarrow{V_2} \\ \cdots \\ \overrightarrow{V_N} \end{bmatrix} = \begin{bmatrix} w_{11} & w_{12} & \cdots & w_{1n} \\ w_{21} & w_{22} & \cdots & w_{2n} \\ \vdots & \vdots & \vdots & \vdots \\ w_{N1} & w_{N2} & \cdots & w_{Nn} \end{bmatrix} \tag{5}$$

Where N denotes the total number of users, n is the number of tags and w_{ij} is the weight of the j-th tag for the i-th user in matrix.

2.2   Multi-tag Correlation and the Recommendation Algorithm

Sun et al[2] have considered associations between terms for microblog hot topic detection, inspired by this, we investigate correlations between tags to update the original user-tag matrix.

If both tags are marked by one particular user, an **inner correlation** between two tags is established. Based on Jaccard similarity, the inner correlation between tags l_j and l_k can be quantified as:

$$LIR\left(l_j, l_k\right) = \frac{1}{|H|} * \sum_{y \in H} \frac{w_{ij} w_{ik}}{w_{ij} + w_{ik} - w_{ij} w_{ik}} \tag{6}$$

$|H|$ represents the number of elements in $H=\{y|(w_{ij}\neq 0)\&(w_{ik}\neq 0)\}$, We normalize $LIR(l_j,l_k)$ to [0,1], and the normalized inner correlation of tags l_j and l_k are defined as:

$$N-LIR\left(l_j, l_k\right) = \begin{cases} 1, & j = k \\ \dfrac{LIR\left(l_j, l_k\right)}{\displaystyle\sum_{j=1, j\neq k}^{n} LIR\left(l_j, l_k\right)}, & j \neq k \end{cases} \tag{7}$$

If two users u_1 and u_2 are simultaneously marked by the same tag, an **outer correlation** between two tags is established. Where tag l_q is a linked tag which links l_j and l_k. The outer correlation between two tags l_j and l_k linked by term l_q can be formalized as:

$$LOR\left(l_j, l_k | l_q\right) = \min\left(N-LIR\left(l_j, l_q\right), N-LIR\left(l_k, l_q\right)\right) \tag{8}$$

We then define the outer correlation between two tags l_j and l_k with all the linked terms and normalize the values to [0,1] as:

$$N-LOR\left(l_j,l_k\right)=\begin{cases}0, & j=k\\[2ex]\dfrac{\sum\limits_{\forall t_q\in E}LOR\left(l_j,l_k\mid l_q\right)}{|E|}, & j\neq k\end{cases} \tag{9}$$

Where $|E|$ denotes the number of link tags in $E=\{l_q|(N\text{-}LIR(l_j,l_q)\text{>}0)\&(N\text{-}LIR(l_k,l_q)\text{>}0)\}$.

Given a pair of tags l_j and l_k, the tag correlation between them can be defined as:

$$LR\left(l_j,l_k\right)=\begin{cases}1 & j=k\\\alpha*N-LOR\left(l_j,l_k\right)+(1-\alpha)*N-LIR\left(l_j,l_k\right) & otherwise\end{cases} \tag{10}$$

Where α ($\alpha\in[0,1]$) determines the importance of inner correlation and outer correlation between multi-tags. Then we create a $n\times n$ multi-tag relationship matrix M_{lr}, and $LR(l_j,l_k)$ are elements in this matrix, which not only includes inner correlation between tags but also consider outer correlations between multi-tags. The final user-tag matrix M_{re} can be defined:

$$M_{re}=M_{ul}\times M_{lr} \tag{11}$$

Given a microblog d_p, the ranking function $f(u_i,d_p)$ for a user u_i is defined as[4]:

$$f\left(u_i,d_p\right)=\mathop{E}_{P}\cdot\left(V_i^{'}\right)^{\mathrm{T}} \tag{12}$$

Which denotes the similarity between microblog d_p and user u_i. Each microblog d_p is represented as $\mathop{E}_{P}=\left(w_{p1},w_{p2},...,w_{pn}\right)$, if d_p contains tag l_j then $w_{pj}=1$, $w_{pj}=0$ otherwise. The vector $V_i^{'}=\left(w_{i1}^{'},w_{i2}^{'},...,w_{in}^{'}\right)$ is the updated tag weight vector for user u_i. We predefine a threshold γ_i, if $f(u_i,d_p)\text{>}\gamma_i$, then the microblog d_p will be recommended to the user u_i.

3   Experiments and Results

In this section, we show the experimental results on the dataset collected from Sina microblog platform. Our dataset includes 532 users who posted a large number of microblog from March 21th to March 25th, 2014. We preprocess a series of experimental data, and then the final experimental dataset is constructed. The dataset consists of 39,886 train and 9,100test datain14 categories, as shown in Table 2.

Table 2. Number of training/test data in the 14 categories

Category	#Train	#Test	Category	#Train	#Test
Sports	3481	800	Military	1880	300
Technology	2860	600	Parenting	2400	600
Estate	2650	600	Environmental protection	2880	600
Stock	2200	600	Health	2650	600
Emotion	3550	800	Travel	3260	800
Entertainment	4562	800	Medicine	2403	600
Political	1880	300	Commodity	3230	800

The experiments include two parts: 1) Comparison with that of 4 other algorithm on tag retrieval; 2) The impact analysis on the parameter to examine the overall recommending performance of our model.

Our method is denoted as *TF*Clarity* to demonstrate the effectiveness of our proposed approach, we compare it against the following four methods: *TF*, *TF*IDF*, *TF*Clarity*, *TF*IDF*Clarity*. For each scheme, we select top {1, 3, 5, 7, 9, 11} words with the highest scores as users' tags.

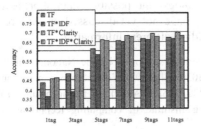

Fig. 1. Accuracy on F1 scores

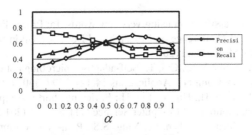

Fig. 2. Different α for our algorithm accuracy

From Figure 1 we can make the following observations. First, more tags (from 1 tag to7 tags) lead to better recommendation algorithm accuracy. When more than 7tags are chosen the improvement becomes minor. Second, among all tag selection methods, our method outperforms the others in most runs with three tags or more labels are marked by user. For one tag, *TF*IDF*Clarity* is the best scheme. However, if only one tag is obtained, the recommendation accuracy is very poor. Therefore, *TF * Clarity* is chosen as our method for tag retrieval.

Parameters α is the most important parameter in our method. It is used to balance the effects of inner and outer tag correlations. Figure 2 reveals that the experimental results match favorably with our hypotheses and encourage us to further explore the reasons. First, the performance of our algorithm is greater than that of either considering inner or outer correlation in isolation, indicating that that an optimal performance comes from an appropriate combination of both the inner and outer correlation among tags. Second, when parameter α is 0.5, our recommendation algorithm shows best performance, which means multi-tag inner correlation is as important as outer relationship. Third, when parameter α is 1, the performance of our algorithm is better than the value of parameter α is 0.

4   Conclusions and Future Work

In this paper, we explore the performance of a multi-tag correlation based approach for recommending microblog posts. Given the short nature of the posts and no background knowledge source, both inner and outer correlations among tags are investigated. Nevertheless, microblogs (and possibly other short texts as well) offer several other information that we have not yet discussed or explored. Future work aims at finding proper ways of adding different information.

Acknowledgement. This work is supported by the National Natural Science Foundation of China (No.61363058, 61163039,61165002), Youth Science and technology support program of Gansu Province (145RJZA232, 145RJYA259) and the open fund of Key Laboratory of intelligent information processing Institute of computing technology of Chinese Academy of Sciences (IIP2014-4).

References

1. Sun, A.: Short text classification using very few words. In: Proceedings of the 35th International ACM SIGIR Conference on Research and Development in Information Retrieval, pp. 1145–1146. ACM, Portland (2012)
2. Sun, Y.X., Ma, H.F., Shi, Y.K., Cui, T.: Self-adaptive microblog hot topic tracking method using term correlation. Computer Applications **34**(12), 3497–3501 (2014)
3. Tang, J., Wang, X., Gao, H., Hu, X., Liu, H.: Enriching short text representation in microblog for clustering. Frontiers of Computer Science **6**(1), 88–101 (2012)
4. Zhou, X., Wu, S., Chen, C., Chen, G., Ying, S.S.: Real-time recommendation for microblogs. Information Sciences **279**, 301–325 (2014)

Personalized Recommendation System Based on Support Vector Machine and Particle Swarm Optimization

Xibin Wang[1], Junhao Wen[1,2(✉)], Fengji Luo[3], Wei Zhou[1], and Haijun Ren[2]

[1] College of Computer Science, Chongqing University, Chongqing 400030, China
{binxiwang,wjhcqu,zhouwei}@cqu.edu.cn
[2] School of Software Engineering, Chongqing University, Chongqing 400030, China
{wjhcqu,jhren}@cqu.edu.cn
[3] Centre for Intelligent Electricity Networks, The University of Newcastle, Callaghan, Australia
fengji.luo@newcastle.edu.au

Abstract. Personalized recommendation system (PRS) is an effective tool to automatically extract meaningful information from the big data of the users. Collaborative filtering is one of the most widely used personalized recommendation techniques to recommend the personalized products for users. In this paper, a PRS model based on the support vector machine (SVM) is proposed. The proposed model not only considers the items' content information, but also the users' demographic and behavior information to fully capture the users' interests and preferences. Meanwhile, an improved particle swarm optimization (PSO) algorithm is applied to optimize the SVM's learning parameters. The efficiency of the proposed method is verified by multiple benchmark datasets.

Keywords: Personalized recommendation · Support Vector Machine · Particle Swarm Optimization · User's demographic information

1   Introduction

In recent years, with the advances in information technology, people have entered the "information overload" era, which imposes significant challenges on the provision of accurate and timely information to the users. PRS provides a promising solution for this problem. By analyzing the historical data, PRS automatically provides users with the suggestions based on their preferences. The core techniques used in the state-of-the-art PRSs can be classified as content-based recommendation (CBR) and collaborative filtering (CF). CBR selects the most relevant items to an active user by comparing the representations of the item's content and the user interest model [1]. The major limitation of CBR is that it is purely based on the item's textual information. Typically, a profile is formed for an individual user by analyzing the item's content in which they are interested, and the additional items can be inferred from this profile. However, in many cases, the contents of the items are difficult to analyze.

CF draws explicit or implicit rating from the users to recommend items to a specific user [2]. It can be further classified as memory-based and model-based techniques. The former methods firstly find neighbors of an active user, and then use the

© Springer International Publishing Switzerland 2015
S. Zhang et al. (Eds.): KSEM 2015, LNAI 9403, pp. 489–495, 2015.
DOI: 10.1007/978-3-319-25159-2_44

neighbors' preferences to predict the preferences of the active user. But it has some shortcomings, such as the inflexible similarity calculation, high computational complexity, etc. The latter methods firstly develop a model based on the historical data, and then use it to predict the preferences for an active user. Currently, many machine learning techniques have employed the model-based CF, such as backward propagation (BP) neural network [3], Adaptive learning [4], and Linear Classifier [5]. Meanwhile, CF algorithms have been applied in many real-applications, such as music recommendation, news recommendation, product recommendation, and so on.

Compared with other machine learning approaches, SVM has some advantages. For example, it can ensure the global optimality of the find solution. Since the forecasting accuracy of SVM is parameter sensitive, it is important to choose a good kernel function and tune the kernel parameters to achieve the optimal performance [6]. Currently, many heuristic methods have been used for the parameter optimization of SVM [7], such as grid search (GS), genetic algorithms (GA), and PSO. Among them, PSO has been proved to be easy to implement and have the strong global optimization capability [7]. But the standard PSO has some demerits, such as pre-matured into the local optimum and slow convergence. To overcome above defects, we proposed an improved PSO with the contraction factor and self-adaptively inertia weight (CF-IWA PSO). It is embedded with a self-adaptively parameter adjustment mechanism to enhance the algorithm's global search ability and convergence speed.

The major contribution of this paper is that we propose a PRS based on the SVM and CF-IWA PSO. There are two key features of the proposed model. Firstly, we propose the CF-IWA PSO to optimize parameters of SVM. In each iteration, the inertia weight of the CF-IWA PSO is self-adaptively updated based on the instant searching performance. This makes it have better performance than the standard PSO. Secondly, the proposed PRS overcomes the limitations of the traditional CF methods. Compared with the traditional CF methods which only use historical score data to calculate similarity, the proposed system not only utilizes the user's demographic information, but also their rating information. In addition, these two kinds of information can well reflect the user's preferences.

2 Introduction of the CF-IWA PSO Algorithm

2.1 Principles of the CF-IWA PSO Algorithm

PSO is a heuristic optimization algorithm proposed by Kennedy and Eberhart [8], and has been applied in many industrial applications [9, 10]. But the widely adopted linear weighting decreasing strategy has some disadvantages such as premature, decrease of the global search ability in later iterations, and slow convergence speed. These limitations affect the optimization performance of the algorithm. To improve the PSO's performance, we propose the self-adaptively update strategy for the inertia weight w. Specifically, in the algorithm's early iterations, w maintains a larger value to make the algorithm have strong global search ability and accelerate the convergence speed; in the later iterations, w maintains a smaller value, to improve the algorithm's local search ability and search accuracy. The update criterion is shown as below.

$$w(k) = \begin{cases} 2k^2\left(w_{end} - w_{start}\right)/T_{max}^2 + w_{start}, \ when \ k \le 1/2T_{max} \\ 2\left(k^2 - T_{max}^2\right)\left(w_{start} - w_{end}\right)/T_{max}^2 + w_{end}, \ when \ k > 1/2T_{max} \end{cases}. \tag{1}$$

where $w(k) \in [0.4, 0.9]$; k is the current iteration index.

To further improve the convergence speed of the PSO, this paper also introduces the contraction factor χ, and the velocity formula is converted into the following form:

$$v_{id}^{l+1} = \chi\left\{ w \times v_{id}^l + c_1 \times rd_1^l \times \left(p_{ij}^l - x_{ij}^l\right) + c_2 \times rd_2^l \times \left(p_{gi}^l - x_{ij}^l\right) \right\}. \tag{2}$$

where the expression of χ is shown as,

$$\chi = 1/\left|2 - \phi - \sqrt{\phi^2 - 4\phi}\right|, \phi = c_1 + c_2, \phi > 4. \tag{3}$$

We called this improved PSO algorithm with contraction factor adaptively dynamic inertia weight as CF-IWA PSO.

2.2   Principles of the SVM Based on CF-IWA PSO Algorithm

The procedures of the SVM classification model integrated with the CF-IWA PSO are shown in Table 1.

Table 1. The description of CF-IWA PSO–SVM

Step 1 : Read the sample data; prepare the training set and the testing set; pre-process the sample data.

Step 2 : PSO Population Initialization. Initialize the velocity and position vectors of each particle; set the values of the control parameters.

Step 3 : Set the values of P_i **and** P_g . Set the current optimal position of the particle i as $X_i = (x_{i1}, x_{i2}, \cdots, x_{id})$, that is $P_i = X_i (i = 1, \cdots, n)$ and the optimal individual in group as the current P_g .

Step 4 : Define and evaluate fitness function. Use the classification accuracy as the fitness function value, which is shown as the following formula. At the same time, the 5-fold cross validation is used to evaluate fitness.

$Acc = \dfrac{\text{The number of correctly classified samples}}{\text{The total number of samples}}$.

Step 5 : Update velocity and position of each particle. Search for the better c, σ and ε according to the velocity formal (2) and position formal $x_{id}^{l+1} = v_{id}^{l+1} + x_{id}^l$.

Step 6 : Update the number of iteration. Let $t = t+1$.

Step 7 : Judge the stop condition. If $t > T_{max}$ or $Acc_j > acc$, then stop the iteration and P_g is the optimal solution which represents the best parameters for SVM. Otherwise, go to step 4.

Step 8 : Decoding the obtained optimal solution, get the optimized parameters.

---

3   Experimental Results and Analysis

3.1   Verify the Validity of the CF-IWA PSO Algorithm

To test the efficiency of the proposed CF-IWA PSO algorithm, we adopt Wine data set [11]. For PSO and CF-IWA PSO, the parameter settings are: $c_1 = c_2 = 1.5$, $w_{start} = 0.9$, $w_{end} = 0.4$; the initial speed range of the particles is set to be $[-5, 5]$; population size is set to be 20; the maximum iteration number is set to be 100. In the SVM prediction model, we choose the Gaussian kernel.

Fig. 1 shows the fitness profiles (classification accuracies) of the two algorithms on the Wine data set. From Fig. 1, it can be seen the CF-IWA PSO has stronger global searching ability than PSO. The results show that the optimal parameter combinations under the CF-IWA PSO are more accurate than PSO. Specifically, after 20 iterations, the CF-IWA PSO adjusted search strategy, making the algorithm search the better parameter combinations.

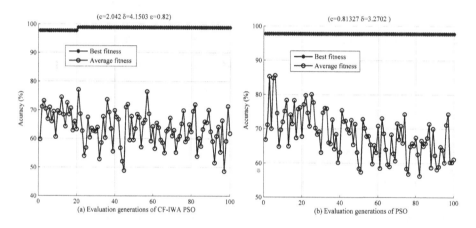

Fig. 1. The classification accuracy of CF-IWA PSO and PSO algorithm on Wine dataset

3.2   Personalized Recommendation Results and Analysis

We test the performance of the proposed PRS model in terms of the personalized movie recommendations. The MovieLens 1M data set was selected as the experimental data set [12], which includes usr.dat, movie.dat, and ratings.dat.

In this study, the personalized recommendation is converted into a binary classification problem. The item-based collaborative filtering (ItemCF), user-based collaborative filtering (UserCF), PSO-SVM, GA-SVM, GS-SVM, and the BP model are tested for the comparison purpose.

3.2.1   The PRS Model Based on CF-IWA PSO-SVM Model

We select 2,000 users' score data as the experimental data set. For each user, we randomly select 10 data as testing data, and add them to the test data set. The remaining data are used as the training set.

To some extent, taking into account the user's demographic information can alleviate the 'cold start' problem. Therefore, in our experiment, the user's demographic information, user's behavioral information ('ratings'), and movie's content information are used to construct a 'user-movie' correlation matrix. We then train the model based on the correlation matrix, and finally the movies are classified. According to the classification results, the PRS provides a list of recommended movies to users, instead of the similarity calculation of the traditional CF methods. Before establishing a classification model, the movies are divided into two categories based on the users' ratings: "like" (recommended) and "dislike" (not recommended). Let the "like" category correspond to the movies with 4 or 5 stars, and the "dislike" category correspond to the movies with 1, 2 or 3 stars.

3.2.2   Recommended Results and Analysis

A good recommendation system has not only high precision, but also high recall. The index F-Score can measure this performance. Besides, in many cases, users are more interested in several or dozens of items on top of the recommendation list. Therefore, in our study the accuracy analysis is restricted to the top 10 recommended movies.

Fig. 2 (a) illustrates the proposed PRS model based on CF-IWA PSO-SVM has higher classification accuracy than the other methods. When training samples reached 90% of the entire training set, the classification accuracy of the proposed model reached 74.9%, higher than the POS-SVM (73.7%), GA-SVM (72.2%), GS-SVM (74.5%), BP (70.1%), UserCF (68.6%), and ItemCF (68.9%). Fig. 2 (b) shows the evaluation results of the different methods in terms of the F-Score. The proposed method provides better results than the other six methods. Specifically, when the number of training samples up to 90% of the entire training set, its F-Score value reached the highest among all the seven methods. Fig. 2 (c) demonstrates that the Top-10 classification accuracy of the proposed method is significantly higher than other methods. When training samples reached 90% of the entire training set, the classification accuracy of CF-IWA PSO-SVM reached 79.6%, while POS-SVM obtained 73.5%, GA-SVM obtained 69.2%, GS-SVM obtained 75.5%, BP obtained 66.3%, UserCF obtained 51.7%, and ItemCF obtained 52.8%, respectively. These encouraging results prove that the well-designed machine learning method can significantly improve the prediction accuracy of the recommendation system.

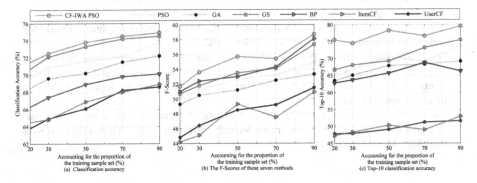

Fig. 2. The comparative results of seven methods

4   Conclusions

In this paper, to overcome the limitations of the traditional CF, a personalized recommendation model based on SVM is proposed. The proposed method not only uses the item's content information, but also uses the user's demographic information and behavior information to establish the "user-item" correlation matrix to capture the user's interests and preferences. To further improve the performance of the classification model, an improved PSO algorithm with contraction factor and dynamic adaptively inertia weight (CF-IWA PSO) is also proposed to optimize the parameters of the model. Experimental results on Wine data set show that the proposed CF-IWA PSO not only has stronger global search ability, but also has higher local search accuracy. Moreover, the MovieLens data set is also used to verify the effects of the proposed PRS. Experimental results indict that the proposed model can provide better recommendation results than other methods.

Acknowledgments. This work was supported by the National Science Foundations of China under Grant Nos. 61379158, and 71301177, and the Fundamental Research Funds for the Central Universities Project No. CDJZR12090004, and CDJZR1309551.

References

1. Pazzani, M., Billsus, D.: Learning and revising user profiles: the identification of interesting websites. Machine Learning **27**, 313–331 (1997)
2. Herlocker, J.L., Konstan, J.A., Borchers, A., Riedl, J.: An algorithmic framework for performing collaborative filtering. In: Proceedings of the 22nd Annual International ACM SIGIR Conference on Research and Development in Information Retrieval, pp. 230–237. ACM, New York (1999)
3. Billsus, D., Pazzani, M.J.: Learning collaborative information filters. In: Proceedings of the 15th International Conference on Machine Learning (ICML 1998), vol. 98, pp. 46–54. ACM, New York (1998)
4. Deng, W.Y., Zheng, Q.H., Lian, S., Chen, L.: Adaptive personalized recommendation based on adaptive learning. Neurocomputing **74**(11), 1848–1858 (2011)
5. Zhang, T., Iyengar, V.S.: Recommender systems using linear classifiers. Journal of Machine Learning Research **2**, 313–334 (2002)
6. Hong, W., Li, L., Li, T.: Product recommendation with temporal dynamics. Expert Systems with Applications **39**(16), 12398–12406 (2012)
7. Gu, J., Zhu, M., Jiang, L.: Housing price forecasting based on genetic algorithm and support vector machine. Expert Systems with Applications **38**(4), 3383–3386 (2011)
8. Kennedy, J., Eberhart, R.: Particle swarm optimization. In: Encyclopedia of Machine Learning, pp. 760–766 (2010)
9. Luo, F., Zhao, J., Qiu, J., Foster, J., Peng, Y., Dong, Z.: Assessing the transmission expansion cost with distributed generation: an Australia case study. IEEE Transactions on Smart Grid **5**(4), 1892–1904 (2014)

10. Zheng, Y., Dong, Z.Y., Luo, F.J., Meng, K., Qiu, J., Wong, K.P.: Optimal allocation of energy storage system for risk mitigation of DISCOs with high renewable penetrations. IEEE Transactions on Power Systems **29**(1), 212–220 (2014)
11. Witten, I.H., Frank, E.: Data mining: Practical machine learning tools and techniques. Morgan Kaufmann (2005). http://prdownloads.sourceforge.net/weka/datasets-UCI.jar
12. MovieLens Datasets. http://grouplens.org/datasets/movielens/

Machine Learning Algorithms

Transfer Learning in Large-Scale Short Text Analysis

Yan Chu[1(✉)], Zhengkui Wang[2], Man Chen[1], Linlin Xia[3], Fengmei Wei[1], and Mengnan Cai[1]

[1] College of Computer Science and Technology, Harbin Engineering University, Harbin, China
[2] Information Communications and Computing, Singapore Institute of Technology, Singapore, Singapore
[3] School of Automation Engineering, Northeast Dianli University, Chuanying, China
chuyan@hrbeu.edu.cn

Abstract. Transfer learning has emerged as a new learning technique facilitating an improved learning result of one task by integrating the well learnt knowledge from another related task. While much research has been devoted to develop the transfer learning algorithms in the field of long text analysis, the development of the transfer learning techniques over the short texts still remains challenging. The challenge of short text data analysis arises due to its sparse nature, noise words, syntactical structure and colloquial terminologies used. In this paper, we propose AutoTL(Automatic Transfer Learning), a transfer learning framework in short text analysis with automatic training data selection and no requirement of data priori probability distribution. In addition, AutoTL enables an accurate and effective learning by transferring the knowledge automatically learnt from the online information. Our experimental results confirm the effectiveness and efficiency of our proposed technique.

Keywords: Transfer learning · Long text analysis · Short text analysis · Latent semantic analysis

1 Introduction

Transfer learning is a new approach of improving the data learning result by utilizing the knowledge from different tasks and domains. The traditional machine learning or data mining approaches require the training and test data to be under the same feature space and the same distribution. Transfer learning, in contrast, allows the domains, tasks and distribution used in training and testing to be different. Specifically, when the training data in the target task are insufficient for a good data modeling, it transfers the useful knowledge from the related auxiliary data from another task to enrich the data features. In this case, more data characteristics are integrated into the data learning facilitating an improved learning results [1,2].

Much research has been devoted into the transfer learning in the domain of analyzing the long text data. To name a few, [3] proposed source free transfer

© Springer International Publishing Switzerland 2015
S. Zhang et al. (Eds.): KSEM 2015, LNAI 9403, pp. 499–511, 2015.
DOI: 10.1007/978-3-319-25159-2_45

learning to transfer knowledge from long texts to the long and [4] proposed latent dirichlet allocation to analyze two sets of topics on short and long texts. As the rapid development of Internet, more and more blog-sphere and social networking applications come into being, such as Microblog, Twitter, QQ news and online advertising. These applications exhibit two important features that differs themselves from traditional applications. First, data generated from these applications contain a lot of short texts, which contains rich useful information. Second, the text data vary dramatically every day, in terms of data size and data distribution. On one hand, these new features eventually challenge the traditional data mining and machine learning approaches, as the assumptions made do not hold in these new applications.On the other hand, the existing transfer learning algorithms tailored for long text analysis can not be directly applied in these application as well. The long text data analysis aims to analyze the long text data by utilizing the knowledge learnt from other long text datasets. The techniques are designed to handle the data that is well labeled, naturally compact and structured. However, the short text differs from the long text due to the sparse nature, noise words, syntactical structure and colloquial terminologies used, which result in unsatisfactory analysis results by directly using the transfer learning algorithms in the long text analysis domain.

In order to better utilize the short text data, it is essential to develop new transfer learning techniques in short text analysis. Given the fact that the result learnt from the long text analysis is enriched, one promising approach is to transfer the long text knowledge into the short text analysis. Several algorithms have been proposed under the similar methodology of utilizing the long text information to help the short text analysis. In their work, a major assumption is that source data are provided by the problem designers. This, however, would reduce the usability of these algorithms, as it requires the designers to have a well understanding of the source data. In addition, the prior probability distribution is required. In the big data era, it is significantly difficult to obtain such a data prior probability distribution. Therefore, this calls for the new algorithms that can release the dependency of specific source data and data prior probability distribution knowledge.

In this paper, we propose a novel framework, called AutoTL (Automatic Transfer Learning), which enables an automatic knowledge transferring. AutoTL differs itself by utilizing the informative online information to strengthen the short text analysis without the need of specifying the source training data, when the short text is not well labeled and without knowing the priori probability distribution. Specifically, using the latent semantic analysis techniques, it first extracts the semantic related keywords as the seed feature set between the online web (long text) data and the target data. This can be done by employing the online search engine via inputting the tags extracted from the target data to obtain the most relevant web data. It then builds one undirected graph for the online web data where the nodes represent the tags/labels. Within this graph, it further extracts one subgraph which is able to cover all the seed feature set. In addition, an improved Laplacian Eigenmaps is adopted to map the high-dimensional feature representation to a low-dimensional one. Finally, it classifies the target data through one constraint function of minimizing the mutual information between the instance and feature representation.

Our major contributions are summarized as follows:

- We propose AutoTL, an transfer learning algorithm of effective short text analysis. AutoTL is superior to other algorithms, as it automatically identifies the related source data from the rich online information and does not require the system to know the priori probability distribution of the data in advance.
- We provide the techniques to integrate the latent semantic analysis into the short text analysis which facilitates an effective learning.
- We conduct extensive experimental evaluations and experimental result indicate that our proposed technique is effective, efficient and practical.

The reminder of the paper is organized as follows. Section 2 introduces the automatic transfer learning algorithm. In Section3, we provide experimental evaluation. Section4 presents the existing work. In Section 5, we conclude the paper.

2 Automatic Transfer Learning Based on Latent Semantic Analysis

In this section, we introduce the proposed transfer learning framework for short text analysis. We will first define the short text analysis problem, then introduce the solution of constructing the feature representation for the target data based on the latent semantic analysis followed by the introduction of the classifier generation.

2.1 Problem Definition

The target domain or target data is referred to a large amount of short texts data $X = \{X_1, X_2, ..., X_n\}$, where X_i is one short text instance. Among the target domain, the known label space is referred to $L = \{l_1, l_2, ..., l_m\}$ related to X. In the short text analysis, the label space is normally very small and not sufficient to conduct an accurate classifying. In addition, no specific source data are given to the learning, in which case the traditional data mining and machine learning approaches are unable to be applied here. Furthermore, the data priori probability distribution is unknown as well. The problem that we study is given the target domain and limited labels, how to provide an accurate classification over the target domain.

To tackle this problem, in this paper, we propose AutoTL (automatic transfer learning) to increase the short text classification performance by automatically transferring the knowledge obtained from other online long text resources, also called source domain (e.g. the web information or social media). Intuitively, AutoTL adopts the latent semantic analysis approach to dig the semantics to both the target domain and source domain. Based on this semantic meaning, it formalizes the important features and make the connection between these two different type of data. It tries to find the best feature representation in order to keep the text semantics for a good classification. The key techniques are introduced in below.

2.2   Keyword Extraction

As the related source data are not provided, we have to figure out which online resources are most related to the target data first. In order to do so, a set of keywords are extracted from the target domain and are supplied to a search engine to search the related source data. For instance, a simple way is to utilize the top k related web pages as the source data. Therefore, the first step that AutoTL is to extract the representative keywords. It is insufficient to simply use the labels as the keywords, as this would lead the topic distillation. To overcome this, we adopt the mutual information to help for the source data selection. The mutual information captures the degree of mutual information between two objects which is defined as follows:

$$I(P; Q) = \sum_{x \in P} \sum_{y \in Q} p(x,y) log \frac{p(x|y)}{p(x)} = \sum_{x \in P} \sum_{y \in Q} p(x,y) log \frac{p(x,y)}{p(x)p(y)} \qquad (1)$$

A bigger mutual information indicates a higher correlation between two objects. Using the mutual information as the measure, the target domain is preprocessed to calculate the target feature seed sets which share the biggest mutual information with the target label space. Specifically, the mutual information is calculated as $I(x,c)$, where I is the feature seed and c is the label. When $I(x_i, c_j) > \epsilon$ where ϵ is the threshold, it indicates that the feature x_i is highly related to c_j. We can choose the x_i as the keywords.

2.3   Feature Weight Calculation

After selecting the source data, the next step is to identify the useful labels/features from the source data, which can be used to strengthen the target data classification. To do so, a naive approach is to calculate the similarity between different set of the features between the target domain and the source domain. According to the similarity among the words, the useful features can be selected. However, this approach treats each word as an individual, which ignores the relations between the text and the semantic relationship hidden in the context keywords. Hence, we utilize the latent semantic analysis approach instead [5]. Semantic analysis shows its superiority on this as it organizes the text into a space semantic structure that keeps the relation between the text and words.

Text matrix is used in the latent semantic analysis. It does not only capture the word frequency in the text and also the capability of distinguishing the texts. Typically, in latent semantic analysis, the feature weight is calculated as the multiplication between the local weight ($LW(i,j)$ indicating the weight of word i in text j) and the global weight ($GW(i)$ indicate the weight of word i in all the texts). Particularly, the feature weight can be calculated as follows:

$$W(i,j) = LW(i,j) * GW(i) = log(tf(i,j) + 1) * (1 - \sum_j \frac{p_{ij}log(P_{ij})}{logN}) \quad (2)$$

where $P_{ij} = \frac{lf(i,j)}{gf(i)}$, $lf(i,j)$ is the frequency of word i in text j, and $gf(i)$ is the frequency of word i in the all the texts.

This traditional method works well in the context where the target and source domains belong to the same type of data with the same data distribution. Unfortunately, the above method can not be directly applied to our context where the target and source data are completely different data types and most likely have different data distribution. The reason is the traditional method does not consider the difference between the source and target domains which may result in poor classification performance. Therefore, in this paper, we propose a new latent semantic analysis approach to enable an accurate classification by utilizing the word frequency and the entropy.

Word Frequency Weight. The word frequency weight is referred to the frequency of the feature appearing in different labels, which captures the capability of distinguishing the labels using the feature. In other words, if one feature appears frequently in one text, it indicates that this feature play an important role in this text. Meanwhile, if this feature has high frequency in other texts as well, we shall reduce its weight as it can not distinguish the texts much. Assume the labels we obtained from the source data represent the categories based on the keywords. So the word frequency weight can be calculated as below:

$$FW(C_i, j) = logcf(C_i, j) \times \frac{1}{log(\sum_{k \neq i}^{cf(C_k,j)})}$$

$$= log\frac{\sum_{j,t=1}^{m} tf(t,j)}{m} \times \frac{n(c-1)}{log(\sum_{k \neq i}^{c-1} \sum_{s=1}^{n} tf(s,j))} \quad (3)$$

where, $cf(C_i, j)$ is the frequency of feature j appearing in category C_i, $\sum_{k \neq i} cf(C_k, j)$ is frequency of feature j appearing in other categories, $\sum_{j,t=1}^{m} tf(t,j)$ is the frequency of feature j appearing in all the documents belonging to the category C_i, m is the number of documents in C_i and $c - 1$ is the number of labels of the documents.

Entropy Weight. In this paper, we use the entropy to represent the weight of the classification labels which is defined as $CW(c|i)$. The entropy weight represents degree of the importance of one feature to the classification labels. The entropy ($H(X)$) is the degree of the uncertainty to one signal X, which is calculated as:

$$H(X) = -\sum p(x_i)logp(x_i) \quad (4)$$

The conditional entropy ($H(X|Y)$) is the uncertainty degree of X when Y is confirmed, which is calculated as follows:

$$H(X|Y) = -\sum p(x_i|Y)logp(x_i|Y) = -\sum p(x_i,Y)log(x_i,Y) \tag{5}$$

Hence, the entropy weight can be calculated as the certainty degree of X when Y is confirmed, such as:

$$CW(C_i|j) = H(C_i) - H(C_i|j) \tag{6}$$

Normally, $H(C_i)$ is hard to calculate and satisfies the following condition: $H(C_i|j) \leq H(C_i) \leq log(c)$. So when the source documents contain similar length, $H(C_i)$ is close to $log(c)$. Thus, the entropy weight can be adjusted as follows:

$$CW(C_i|j) = H(C_i) - H(C_i|j) = log(c) + \sum p(t,j)log(t,j)$$
$$= log(c) + \sum \frac{tf(t,j)}{gf(j)} log(\frac{tf(t,j)}{gf(j)}) \tag{7}$$

To this end, the weight in our proposed approach is calculated as follows:

$$W(i) = FW(C_i,j) \times CW(C_i|j) \tag{8}$$

Different to the traditional latent semantic analysis that builds the feature-document weight matrix, AutoTL builds the feature-classification labels weight matrix. In the matrix, the weight w_{ij} in the ith row and j^{th} column represents the correlation between the feature and the classification labels. Assume the matrix obtained from the documents is M. After the SVD decomposition, we can get matrix M_k. In addition, via the feature similarity $M_k M_k^T$, we can obtain the features that are not labeled in the target domain, but highly related to the classification. So the best features are chosen as the feature seed set.

2.4   New Feature Space Construction

Consider that the features may contain many relations in a real life. In order to improve the classification quality, we try to capture the relations among these features. To do so, the approach we propose is to construct the source domain labels as one undirected graph, where the nodes capture the labels and the edges are their relations. To build the relation from the feature seed sets, we try to extract the subgraph that contains all feature seed sets from it. This eventually build the connections between the labels in the source domain and target domain.

Since the label graph is normally high-dimensional, we adopt the the Laplacian Eigenmaps algorithm [6] to map all the nodes in the sub-graph into one low-dimensional space. This effectively alleviates many problems (e.g. data over fitting, low efficiency and so on), which are caused by the high-dimension. The Laplacian Eigenmaps algorithm assumes that if the points are close in the high-dimensional space, the distances between them should be short when embedded into a low-dimensional space. As in the algorithm, it does not consider the category information of the samples when calculate the neighbor distance. No matter the point inside or outside the category, it gives the points same weight if the distances are the same. This, however, is not preferred for the target domain containing both labeled data and unlabeled data. In the paper, we improve the Laplacian Eigenmaps algorithm, using different methods to calculate the weight of labeled data and unlabeled data. Intuitively, we make point distance inside the category be less than the distance whose points are outside the category.

To construct a relative neighborhood graph, we use the unsupervised learning approach (e.g. Euclidean distance) to calculate the distance between the unlabeled data. Meanwhile, we use the supervised learning to calculate the distance between the labeled data, which is provided as follows:

$$D(x_i, x_j) = \begin{cases} \sqrt{1 - \exp(-d^2(x_i, x_j)/\beta} & c_i = c_j \\ \sqrt{\exp(d^2(x_i, x_j))/\beta} & c_i \neq c_j \end{cases} \tag{9}$$

where, c_i and c_j are categories of the samples x_i and x_j, $d(x_i, x_j)$ is the Euclidean distance between x_i and x_j. Parameter β can prevent $D(x_i, x_j)$ too large when $d(x_i, x_j)$ become larger which can effectively control the noises. If the distance between sample points x_i and x_j is smaller than the threshold ε, the two points are neighbor points.

Furthermore, the weight matrix W can be calculated, where if x_i and x_j are neighbor points, $W_{ij} = 1$, otherwise, $W_{ij} = 0$. The Laplacian generalized eigenvectors can be simply calculated by solving the following problem:

$$\begin{cases} \min \sum_{i,j} \|Y_i - Y_j\| w_{ij} \\ s.t. \quad Y^T D Y = I \end{cases} \tag{10}$$

where, D is a diagonal matrix. With the improved Laplacian Eigenmaps algorithm, we can map each high-dimensional node into a low-dimensional space. To this end, the data can get a new feature representation.

2.5   The Target Domain Classification

After getting the new feature representations of the target data, we can classify the target domain using the mutual information as what has been discussed in section 2.2. This can be done based on the existing classifier, such as SVM classifier. For the space limitation, we omit the details here. To better appreciate the framework, Figure 1 provides the main steps of the entire AutoTL framework.

3   Experiments

This section provides the experimental evaluation. All the experiments are conducted on a machine with Dual Core E5300 and 1.86GHz CPU and 16GB memory running in Windows 7. In order to evaluate the efficiency of the AutoTL, we

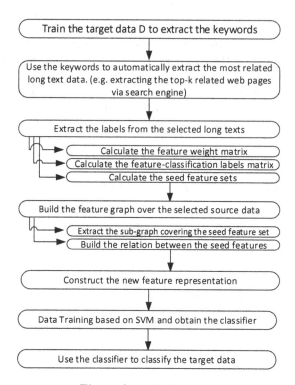

Fig. 1. AutoTL Framework.

use 20Newsgroups, SRAA (Simulated Real Auto Aviation) and Reuter-21578 as three main document classification tasks in the experiments. The 20Newsgroups includes 18774 news reports, which consists of 7 big categories, 20 small categories and 61188 vocabularies. SRAA includes more than 700,00 UseNet articles, which consists of 2 big categories and 4 small categories. Reuter-21578 includes 22 files, which consists of 5 categories. From these three tasks, we extract 7 different datasets/categories including: comp, sci, talk, rec, aviation, auto and topics. Meanwhile, we compare our framework with three classical algorithms: TrAdaboost[7], DATAT[8], TrSVM[9].

3.1   Analysis of Experimental Results

There are two important factors that would impact the algorithm performance: the mutual information threshold ϵ of determining whether two features are correlated and the number of web pages selected as the source data. Hence, we first run two sets of experiments to study how these two factors impact the performance and then figure out the right one as the default setting in the following experiments.

Impact of Mutual Information Threshold. First, we study how the mutual information threshold impacts the performance. This set of experiments is conducted using four different datasets: comp, talk, aviation and topics. Figure 2 presents the result of AutoTL when we vary the threshold from 0.2 to 0.8.

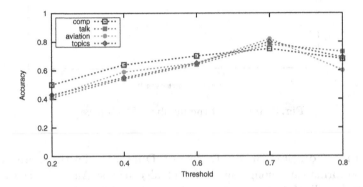

Fig. 2. Impact of the mutual information threshold.

From the result, we obtain two insights. First, selecting different mutual information threshold to determine whether two features are correlated impacts the performance. Second, AutoTL achieves a better performance when the threshold is set around 0.7. The performance decreases when the threshold is set too small or too large. For example, the performance of point 0.2 and 0.8 is worse than that of 0.7. This is within expectation, as a small or large threshold would either result in too many unrelated features or too less correlated features which all lead a worse learning result.

Impact of the Number of Web Pages. Next, we study how the number of web pages selected as the source data impacts the AutoTL performance. This set of experiments is conducted using four different datasets: sci, rec, auto and topics. Figure 3 provides the accuracy of AutoTL, when we vary the number of selected web pages as the source data from 5 to 20.

From the result, we observe that AutoTL performs better when the number is around 10. When the number of selected web pages is too small or too large, the performance decreases. This is reasonable. Since when the number of selected web pages is too small, the source data can not get enough feature information in the training which may decrease the performance. On the other hand, when the number of selected web pages is too large, the source data may involve more noises that may also decreases the performance. So according to the source data quality, choosing the right number of selected pages does impact the performance.

Based on these study, in the following experiments, we use 0.7 as the mutual information threshold and 10 web pages as the source data for AutoTL by default.

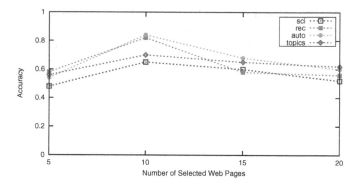

Fig. 3. Impact of the number of web pages.

Performance Comparison on Different Datasets. Furthermore, we compare the performance among four different algorithms: AutoTL, TrAdaBoost, DRDAT and TrSVM. The experiment is conducted based on seven datasets: comp, sci, talk, rec, aviation, auto and topics. Figure 4 shows the comparison results over different datasets. From the result, we can see that different algorithms perform different over different datasets. AutoTL outperforms other algorithms among the different datasets. This confirms the efficiency and effectiveness of AutoTL.

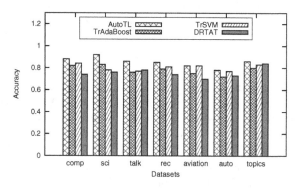

Fig. 4. Performance comparison over different datasets.

Performance Comparison Under Different Amount of Source Data. Finally, as an complete study, we also study the performance comparison among the four algorithms when we choose different number of web pages as the source data. Figure 5 (a) and (b) provides the comparison over comp and sci datasets while varying the number of selected web pages from 5 to 20 respectively. From the results, we can see that the number of selected web pages impact the algorithm performance. We can further obtain another two insights. The first one is all the algorithms follow the pattern that the algorithm performance would decrease when the number is too small or too large. The second one is when the number is set around 10, the algorithms achieve a better performance. The third one is that when in some of other settings, AutoTL may perform a little bit worse than other algorithms. For example, in Figure 5 (a), TrAdaBoost performs a little bit better than AutoTL. This could be because when the number is large, AutoTL affects by the noise more than TrAdaBoost.

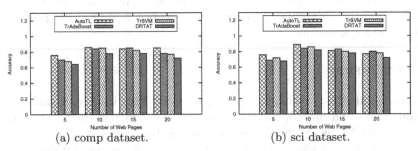

(a) comp dataset.   (b) sci dataset.

Fig. 5. Performance comparison over comp and sci datasets, when the number of web pages changes.

4 Related Work

Transfer learning has been widely used in long text analysis domain. To name a few, Dai et al. [7] proposed TrAdaboost, which improved the boosting technology in order to create an automatic weight adjustment mechanism. It filters out most of the data similar to the target areas from the source field so that it can enrich the training data to improve the accuracy of the classifier. Mei et al. [14] proposed WTLME which is based on maximum entropy model, using instance weighted technology. The algorithm transfers model parameters studied from the original field to the target domain and reduces the time of re-collection. Hong et al. [9] proposed TrSVM which requires weak similarity. All of these algorithms perform well when the source data and target data are in a very similar domain.

Dai et al. [10] proposed a CoCC algorithm, in which the co-occurrence of words in the source domain and the target domain were used as a bridge. The tag structures of the source field and the target domain were collaboratively clustering at the same time. By minimizing the mutual information between words and samples, it can achieve the goal that transfer the tag structure of the source domain to the target domain. Xue et al. [11] proposed a TPLSA algorithm which tried to bridge the relations between two related domains. Long et al. [12] proposed a GTL algorithm, which extracted the potential common themes between source and target domains and optimize maximum likelihood function to maintain the geometric structure of the documents. These algorithms are mainly used in the same language of the text files. Ling et al. [13] proposed an algorithm to handle the text analysis when they were in different languages by using the information bottleneck model. However, all these above mentioned algorithms are developed for analyzing the long text data.

Recently, some research has been conducted on the short text analysis by transferring the knowledge from the long texts. For example, Jin et al. [4] proposed a DLDA model, which extracts two sets of topics from the source and target domains and uses a binary switch variable to control the forming process of the documents. However, the algorithm requires the source data and the priori probability distribution to be known in advance. AutoTL differs itself from this algorithm by an automatic source data selection and no priori probability distribution requirement.

5   Conclusions

Transfer learning is a technique that finds useful knowledge and skills in the previous tasks and applies them to new tasks or domains. In this paper, we proposed AutoTL, an automatic transfer learning framework to analyze the short text data by utilizing the long text knowledge such as web data. AutoTL shows its superiority than other algorithms from different perspectives. First, it does not enforce the user to provide a specific source data for training, but conducts an automatic source data selection. Second, no priori probability distribution is required in advance. Third, AutoTL integrates the rich online information and latent semantic analysis in the short text learning task, which highly increases the learning accuracy. Extensive experimental evaluation indicates that AutoTL is practical, efficient and effective.

Acknowledgments. The work is funded by the Heilongjiang Scientific Research Foundation for Returned Scholars(Grant No.LC2015025), supported by Fundamental Research Funds for Central Universities(Grant No.HEUCFD1508 and HEUCF100602) and a special study of technological innovation fund of Harbin(Grant No.2013RFQXJ113 and 2013RFQXJ117). This work is also partially supported by China NSF(Grant No. 61402126, 61370083) and Postdoctoral Scientific Research Foundation of Heilongjiang Province.

References

1. Pan, S.J., Qiang, Y.: A Survey on Transfer Learning. IEEE Transactions on Knowledge and Data Engineering **22**(10), 1345–1359 (2010)
2. Yang, Q.: An introduction to transfer learning. In: Tang, C., Ling, C.X., Zhou, X., Cercone, N.J., Li, X. (eds.) ADMA 2008. LNCS (LNAI), vol. 5139, pp. 1–1. Springer, Heidelberg (2008)
3. Lu, Z., Zhu, Y., Pan, S.J., et al.: Source free transfer learning for text classification. In: Proceedings of the 28th AAAI Conference on Artificial Intelligence, pp. 122–128. AAAI Press, Québec (2014)

4. Jin, O., Liu, N.N., et al.: Transferring topical knowledge from auxiliary long texts for short text clustering. In: Proceedings of the 20th ACM Conference on Information and Knowledge Management, pp. 775–784. ACM Press, Glasgow (2011)

5. Dumais, S.T., Furnas, G.W., et al.: Using latent semantic analysis to improve information retrieval. In: Proceedings of the ACM Conference on Human Factors in Computing Systems, pp. 281–285. ACM Press, Washington D.C. (1988)

6. Belkin, M., Niyogi, P.: Laplacian eigenmaps for dimensionality reduction and data representation. Neural Computation **10**(5), 1373–1396 (2003)

7. Dai, W., Yang, Q., Xue, G., et al.: Boosting for transfer learning. In: Proceedings of The 24th Annual International Conference on Machine Learning, Corvallis, Oregon, USA, pp. 193–200 (2007)

8. Liu, W., Zhang, H.: Ensemble transfer learning algorithm based on dymaica dataset regroup. Computer Egineering and Applications **46**(12), 126–128 (2010)

9. Jiaming, H., Jian, Y., Yun, H., Yubao, Y., Jiahai, W.: TrSVM: A transfer learning method based on the similarity of domains. Computer Research and Development **48**(10), 1823–1830 (2011)

10. Dai, W., Xue, G.-R., et al.: Co-clustering based classification for out-of-domain documents. In: Proceedings of the Thirteenth ACM SIGKDD International Conference on Knowledge Discovery and Data Mining, San Jose, California, USA, pp. 210–219 (2007)

11. Xue, G., Dai, W., et al.: Topic-bridged PLSA for cross-domain text classification. In: Proceedings of the 31st Annual International ACM SIGIR Conference, pp. 627–634. ACM Press, Singapore (2008)

12. Long, M., Wang, J., Ding, G., Shen, D., Yang, Q.: Transfer learning with graph co-regularization. In: Proceedings of the 26th AAAI Conference on Artificial Intelligence. AAAI Press, Toronto, Ontario (2012)

13. Ling, X., Dai, W., et al.: Can Chinese web pages be classified with english data source. In: Proceedings of the 17th International Conference on World Wide Web 2008, Beijing, China, pp. 969–978 (2008)

14. Mei, C., Zhang, Y., Xuegang, H., Li, P.: Transfer learning algorithms based on maximum entropy model. Computer Research and Development **48**(9), 1722–1728 (2011)

Learning the Influence Probabilities Based on Multipolar Factors in Social Network

Weibo Wang, Zhaohui Peng$^{(\boxtimes)}$, Ziyan Liu, Tianchen Zhu, and Xiaoguang Hong

School of Computer Science and Technology, Shandong University, Jinan, China
wangweibo1001@gmail.com, {pzh,hxg}@sdu.edu.cn,
liuziyan1990@163.com, ztc1319@sina.cn

Abstract. How to model the influence propagation accurately in social network is a critical and challenge task. Although numerous attempts have been made for this topic, few of them consider the user's negative influence. Positive influence will encourage people to perform some action while the negative one will degrade the probability. Thus, it is meaningful to model the influence propagation by considering both the positive and negative influence. What's more, previous research is mostly based on the assumption that the influence probabilities between users are known, however, they are typically unknown in real-world social networks. To address these problems, a novel Multipolar Factors aware Independent Cascade model (MFIC) is proposed to outline the information diffusion in social network. Then, the user-to-user influence probability is learnt with the users' behavior logs based on the EM algorithm. We also apply the discovered influence probabilities to user behavior prediction. Experiments are conducted over real data sets, Flixster and Digg, validating the effectiveness of our methods.

Keywords: Social network · Multipolar influence · Influence probabilities

1 Introduction

The social networks such as Twitter, Digg and Flixster, providing platforms for people to share information and express their ideas, play an important role in information diffusion. Much attention has been paid to the research on social influence and influence-driven information diffusion in social network, which have been applied in many areas, such as viral marketing [1], product recommendation [2, 3] and user behavior prediction [4]. For example, in viral marketing application, if a seller wants to promote a new product under a limited budget, he will choose some users with high influence in the social network and give them free products to use, and then, by the cascade effects produced by word-of-mouth, more people will be driven to buy this product.

So far, a substantial research effort has been dedicated to develop more accurate propagation model [5,6] based on the Independent Cascade mode(IC) and Linear Thread model(LT) . However, these work only consider the positive influence between users. In addition to the positive influence, there is also negative influence

© Springer International Publishing Switzerland 2015
S. Zhang et al. (Eds.): KSEM 2015, LNAI 9403, pp. 512–524, 2015.
DOI: 10.1007/978-3-319-25159-2_46

between users. For example, in Flixster[1], the users will rate the movies they have seen, as shown in Fig.1. Given a movie i, the u_1' neighbors u_2, u_3, u_4 gave high scores (*4.5, 4.8, 4.7*), while the neighbors u_5, u_6, u_7 gave low scores (*2.5, 2.3, 1.5*). When u_1 makes a decision to see the movie or not, he may see the rating scores of his friends. It can be plausibly concluded that u_2, u_3, u_4 have a positive influence to u_1, because their high ratings tend to promote u_1 to see the movie and u_5, u_6, u_7 have a negative influence to u_1, because their low ratings tend to decrease the probability of u_1 seeing the movie. So it is important to model the influence propagation by considering both the positive and the negative factors.

Moreover, some conventional studies in social influence [1, 7, 8] arbitrarily assume the social network has edges labeled with the probability that a user's action will be influenced by his neighbor's behaviors. However, the influence probabilities are typically unknown in real-world social network. Despite previous work [9, 10] have studied how to estimate the influence probabilities in social network, a key limitation is their ignoring of negative influence aforementioned above.

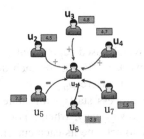

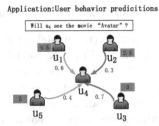

Fig. 1. An example of positive influence and negative influence

Fig. 2. An application of our work.

In this research, our goal is to address the issues above: we propose a novel model that modeling the information diffusion through analyzing the multipolar influence. And then, based on our proposed model, we learn the influence probabilities. We also introduce the application of user behavior prediction based on the learnt influence probability. For example, as depicted in Fig.2, in the time-step t, u_4's neighbors u_1, u_5 gave high rating scores on the movie "Avatar", while the neighbors u_2, u_3 gave low rating scores, and then we can predict whether u_4 will see the movie in the time-step $t+1$ based on the influence probabilities computed by our method. To summarize, this work contributes on the following aspects:

1. A novel Multipolar Factors aware Independent Cascade model (MFIC) is proposed to model the influence propagation in social network. In MFIC, we analyze the behaviors of users by considering both the neighbors' positive and negative influence on him.

---

[1] http://www.flixster.com/

2. We design a method based on the EM algorithm to learn the parameters in our model. In our method, we use the social relationship and the users' past behavior logs to learn the influence probabilities between users based our MFIC model. We also apply the discovered influence probabilities to user behavior prediction.
3. Experiments are conducted on two real data sets: Flixster and Digg. Experimental results show that the learnt influence probabilities based on our MFIC model can greatly improve the accuracy of user behavior prediction.

The rest of the paper are organized as follows: Section 2 formally formulates the foundations for our problem. Section 3 explains the proposed model MFIC and Section 4 introduces the method of parameter learning in detail. In Section 5, we introduce the application of user behavior prediction. In Section 6, we experimentally compare and evaluate our model with other models. Finally, Section 7 discusses the related work and Section 8 concludes the work.

2   Preliminaries

2.1   Independent Cascade (IC) Model

Independent Cascade (IC) model [1] is one of the widely used representative influence diffusion model. In the IC model, given a network G (V, E), for each directed link $e = (u, v) \in E$, we specify a value $p_{u,v}(0 < p_{u,v} < 1)$. Here $p_{u,v}$ is the influence propagation probability from u to v. The diffusion process starts with some initial active nodes (called "seeds") and proceeds in the following way: when a node u first becomes active at time-step t, it has only one chance to activate its each current inactive out-neighbor v and the attempt succeeds with the probability $p_{u,v}$. If the attempt succeeds, v becomes active at time $t+1$. The attempt is performed only at time-step t, whether or not u succeeds and u will not make any further attempts to activate v in the subsequent rounds. The process terminates until no more nodes can be activated.

2.2   Problem Formulation

Definition 1 (Social Network). A social network can be represented as $G = (V, E)$, where V denotes the set of users, E is the set of edges. A directed / undirected edge $(u,v) \in E$ represents a social link between user u and user v. In some social networks like Twitter and Digg the edge is directed which represents v has followed u and u will influence v while in Flixster and Facebook the edge is undirected which represents they are friends for each other and they will influence each other.

Definition 2 (User Behavior Log). The user behavior log Ω is a set of actions (*User, Item, Time*), which a tuple $(u, i, t_u) \in \Omega$ indicates that user u performs an action for item i at time t_u. We assume that no user performs the same action more than once. The projection of Ω on *User* is contained in the set of nodes V of the social network.

Definition 3 (Positive Neighbor and Negative Neighbor). For an edge $(u,v) \in E$, if u is active on item i at time t, we denote as $u_i^t = 1$, that is to say, u performs the action on item i at time t. If u has a positive opinion on the product, such as giving a high rating score to the movie, we think u is a positive user as well as a positive neighbor of v, $u \in N_v^{positive}$ and u will have a positive influence to v. Otherwise, if u has a negative opinion on the product, such as giving a low rating score to the movie, we think u is a negative user as well as a negative neighbor of v, $u \in N_v^{negative}$ and u will have a negative influnce to v.

3   MFIC: Multipolar Factors Aware Independent Cascade Model

In the proposed MFIC model, the working principle is similar to Independent Cascade model [1]. The diffusion process unfolds in discrete time-steps t and begins from a given initial active user set. When a user v observes a piece of information at time t, he makes his decision depending on his neighbor's status. If he adopts the information, his status becomes active at time $t+1$, otherwise inactive. For example, we can imagine the information is a movie in Flixster and user adopts a movie means he saw the movie. In time t, some of his neighbors saw the movie, which we think whether the user $(u_1$, as shown in Fig.1) will see the movie is influenced by both his positive neighbors(u_2, u_3, u_4) and negative neighbors(u_5, u_6, u_7). If u_1 sees the movie, we regard u_1 as influenced successfully by the positive neighbors or failure influenced by his negative neighbors and becoming active. Otherwise, if u_1 doesn't see the movie, we regard u_1 as influenced successfully by the negative neighbors or failure influenced by his positive neighbors and become inactive.

In each time-step $t+1$, the user v receives two kinds of influence, one is the positive influence effected by the positive neighbors $N_{positive,t}(v)$ in time-step t, and another is the negative influence effected by the negative neighbors $N_{negative,t}(v)$ in time-step t. We also assume that the probabilities of different neighbors influencing the user are independent, each neighbor has a probability to trigger the user to perform the action or not. In time-step $t+1$, the influence that user v receives from the positive neighbors denotes as $p_v^{positive}(t+1)$ and the influence that user v receives from the negative ones denotes as $p_v^{negative}(t+1)$. Their calculation formula are follows:

$$P_v^{positive}(t+1) = 1 - \prod_{u \in N_{positive,t}(v)} \left(1 - p_{u,v}\right) \tag{1}$$

$$P_v^{negative}(t+1) = 1 - \prod_{u \in N_{negative,t}(v)} \left(1 - p_{u,v}\right) \tag{2}$$

For example, in Flixster, if user u sees the movie i, we denote $s_i(u)=1$ and $r_i(u)$ represents the rating score that user u give to the movie i. We use $D_i(t)$ represent the users that saw the movie at time t. In reality, if the user very like the movie, he will give a high rating score to it, and if he dislike, he will give a low rating score. We use the avg(i) denotes the average score of the movie i. If u sees the movie i and the rating score $r_i(u) >$avg(i), we think u is a positive user at time t, $u \in D_{positive}(t)$, and u is a positive neighbor of v, i.e., $u \in N_{positive,t}(v)$. Otherwise, u gives a low rating score, i.e., $r_i(u) <$avg(i), we think u is a negative user at time t, $u \in D_{negative}(t)$, and u is a negative neighbor of v, $u \in N_{negative,t}(v)$.

In time-step $t+1$, user v will become active if the positive neighbors successfully influence v or the negative neighbors failure in influence v, and the probability that user v becomes active can be computed as follows.

$$\bar{p}_v^{active}(t+1) = P_v^{positive}(t+1) + \left(1 - P_v^{negative}(t+1)\right) - P_v^{positive}(t+1) * \left(1 - P_v^{negative}(t+1)\right)$$
$$= 1 - p_v^{negative}(t+1) + p_v^{positive}(t+1) * p_v^{negative}(t+1) \tag{3}$$

Equally, when the negative neighbors successfully influence v or the positive neighbors failure in influence v, user v will become inactive, and the probability of being inactive as following Eq.(4).

$$\bar{p}_v^{inactive}(t+1) = P_v^{negative}(t+1) + \left(1 - P_v^{positive}(t+1)\right) - P_v^{negative}(t+1) * \left(1 - P_v^{positive}(t+1)\right)$$
$$= 1 - p_v^{positive}(t+1) + p_v^{positive}(t+1) * p_v^{negative}(t+1) \tag{4}$$

To unified comparison, we normalize the $\bar{p}_v^{active}(t+1)$, $\bar{p}_v^{inactive}(t+1)$ as follows.

$$P_v^{active}(t+1) = \frac{\bar{p}_v^{active}(t+1)}{\bar{p}_v^{active}(t+1) + \bar{p}_v^{inactive}(t+1)}$$

The equation of $\bar{p}_v^{inactive}(t+1)$ is similar to $\bar{p}_v^{active}(t+1)$.

Following Saito $el\ al.$ [9], we also assume the input propagation have the same shape as they were generated by the MFIC model itself. This means that the propagation trace of an item i must be a sequence of sets of users $D_i(0),..., D_i(n)$, corresponding to the discrete time steps of the MFIC propagation. Moreover for each node $v \in D_i(t+1)$, there exists at least a neighbor u of v such that $u \in D_i(t)$. Next, let $B_i(t)$ denote a set of users having become active by time-step t, $B_i(t) = \cup_{t'<t} D_i(t')$. Let use $C(u)$ denotes the child nodes of $u:C(u)=\{v|(u,v) \in E\}$, $F(v)$ denotes the parent nodes of v: $F(v)=\{u|(u,v) \in E\}$. We use D_i denote the propagation trace of item i, for an propagation trace D_i we can define the following likelihood function as a joint probability of every observed user status on item i on every timestamps with respect to $\theta = \{p_{u,v}\}$ in Equation (5).

$$L(\theta, D_i) = \left(\prod_{t=0}^{T-1} \prod_{v \in D(t+1)} \left\{ P_v^{active}(t+1) \right\}\right) \left(\prod_{t=0}^{T-1} \prod_{u \in D(t)} \prod_{v \in C(u) \backslash B(t+1)} \left\{ P_v^{inactive}(t+1) \right\}\right) \tag{5}$$

There are many items propagation in the network, so we let $\{D_i : i = 1,...,I\}$ be a set of independent information diffusion episodes. Then we can define the following object function with respect to θ.

$$L(\theta) = \sum_{i=1}^{I} \log L(\theta, D_i)$$

$$= \sum_{i=1}^{I} \sum_{t=0}^{T-1} \left\{ \left(\sum_{v \in D_i(t+1)} \log P_v^{active,i}(t+1) \right) + \left(\sum_{u \in D_i(t)} \sum_{v \in C(u) \backslash B_i(t+1)} \log P_v^{inactive,i}(t+1) \right) \right\}$$

$$= \sum_{i=1}^{I} \sum_{t=0}^{T-1} \left[\left\{ \sum_{v \in D_i(t+1)} \left(\log[(1 - P_v^{negative,i}(t+1)) + P_v^{positive,i}(t+1) * P_v^{negative,i}(t+1)] \right) \right\} \right]$$

$$+ \sum_{i=1}^{I} \sum_{t=0}^{T-1} \left[\left\{ \sum_{u \in D_i(t)} \sum_{v \in C(u) \backslash B_i(t+1)} \left(\log[(1 - P_v^{positive,i}(t+1)) + P_v^{negative,i}(t+1) * P_v^{positive,i}(t+1)] \right) \right\} \right] \qquad (6)$$

where $P_v^{active,i}(t+1)$, $P_v^{inactive,i}(t+1)$ represent the probability of v become active or inactive about item i at time-step $t+1$. $P_v^{posotive,i}(t+1)$, $P_v^{negative,i}(t+1)$ stand for the probability that user v was affected by the positive influence or negative influence successfully at time-step $t+1$ about movie i, and their computational formulas as given in Eq.(1)-Eq.(4). Then our problem is to obtain the set of influence probabilities between users, $\theta = \{p_{u,v}\}$, which maximizes Eq.(6). In the next section we will illustrate how to obtain the parameters.

4   Learning the Parameters of MFIC

Directly maximizing Equation (6) is rather not tractable, so we apply the Expectation Maximization(EM) algorithm [13] to obtain the parameters $\theta = \{p_{u,v}\}$. In the rest of the paper, following the standard EM notation, $\hat{p}_{u,v}$ will represent the current estimate of the influence probability of user u to user v.

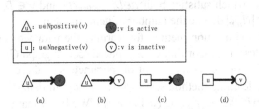

Fig. 3. The cases among link *(u, v)* for item *i*.

For a link *(u, v)* in the propagation trace D_i of item *i* where $u \in D_i(t)$, we know that the user u will attempt to influence v with the probability $\hat{p}_{u,v}$. There are four cases existing among link *(u, v)*, as shown in Fig. 3. For case (a), user u is a positive neighbor of user v, and user v became active at time step $t+1$, which means user v was successfully influenced by the positive influence or failure influenced by the negative influence, so the probability that user v was activated by user u is $\hat{p}_{u,v}/\hat{p}_v^{active,i}$ and v was activated not because of u with the probability $(1- \hat{p}_{u,v}/\hat{p}_v^{active,i})$, where $\hat{p}_v^{active,i}$ is calculated by using Eq.(3). On the   other hand, as is shown in case (b), user v is not   active at time step $t+1$, so we can be surely think the attempt that user u try to activate user v failed. Similar, for case (c), user u is a negative neighbor of user v and user v is active at time step $t+1$, and we can be surely think the attempt that user u try to make user v inactive failed. For case(d), user v is inactive at time step $t+1$, so the probability that user v was inactivated by user u is $\hat{p}_{u,v}/\hat{p}_v^{inactive,i}$ and v was inactivated not because of user v with the probability $(1- \hat{p}_{u,v}/\hat{p}_v^{inactive,i})$, where $\hat{p}_v^{inactive,i}$ is calculated by using Eq.(4). Considering these case, we have the following *Q-function* describe users' status for all propagation traces $D_i = \{i| i = 1,...,I\}$

$$Q(\theta|\hat{\theta}) = \sum_{i=1}^{I}\sum_{t=0}^{T-1}\sum_{u\in D_{i,positive}(t)}\left(\sum_{v\in C(u)\wedge v\in D_i(t+1)}\left\{\frac{\hat{p}_{u,v}}{p_v^{\wedge active,i}}\log p_{u,v} + \left(1-\frac{\hat{p}_{u,v}}{p_v^{\wedge active,i}}\right)\log(1-p_{u,v})\right\} + \sum_{v\in C(u)\backslash B_i(t+1)}\left\{\log(1-p_{u,v})\right\}\right)$$

$$+ \sum_{i=1}^{I}\sum_{t=0}^{T-1}\sum_{u\in D_{i,negative}(t)}\left(\sum_{v\in C(u)\backslash B_i(t+1)}\left\{\frac{\hat{p}_{u,v}}{p_v^{\wedge inactive,i}}\log p_{u,v} + \left(1-\frac{\hat{p}_{u,v}}{p_v^{\wedge inactive,i}}\right)\log(1-p_{u,v})\right\} + \sum_{v\in C(u)\wedge D_i(t+1)}\left\{\log(1-p_{u,v})\right\}\right) \quad (7)$$

Let $\partial Q/\partial p_{u,v} = 0$, obtaining the new estimate of $p_{u,v}$, the update equation is following:

$$p_{u,v} = \frac{1}{|P_{u,v}^+|+|P_{u,v}^-|+|N_{u,v}^+|+|N_{u,v}^-|}\left(\sum_{i\in P_{u,v}^+}\frac{\hat{p}_{u,v}}{p_v^{\wedge active,i}} + \sum_{i\in N_{u,v}^+}\frac{\hat{p}_{u,v}}{p_v^{\wedge inactive,i}}\right) \quad (8)$$

Here $P_{u,v}^+$ denotes the items that u successfully influence v by positive influence, which satisfies both $u\in D_{i,positive}(t)$ and $v \in D_i(t+1)$. $P_{u,v}^-$ denotes the items that u failure influence v by positive influence, which satisfies both $u\in D_{i,positive}(t)$ and $v \notin D_i(t+1)$. $N_{u,v}^+$ denotes the items that u successfully influence v by negative influence, which satisfies both $u\in D_{i,negative}(t)$ and $v\notin D_i(t+1)$. $N_{u,v}^-$ denotes the items that u failure influence v by negative influence, which satisfies both $u\in D_{i,negative}(t)$ and $v \in D_i(t+1)$. Moreover, $|P_{u,v}^+|$, $|P_{u,v}^-|$, $|N_{u,v}^+|$, $|N_{u,v}^-|$ denote the number of items in them .

Our Expectation-Maximization method for learning the parameters of MFIC is given in Algorithm 1. The learning algorithm takes input the social graph $G=(V,E)$ and a log of past propagations. The output is the set of all parameters θ: those are $p_{u,v}$ for all the edge $(u, v) \in E$. The learning method starts with a random initialization of the probabilities of all the edges with value $p_{u,v} \in (0\ 1)$ (line1). We know that the EM algorithm is related with the initial value, that is different initial parameters will bring different locally optimal solution, so we set various values in our experiments, and we find that the initial values set between 0.6 and 0.9 could get the best effects. Then for each edge $(u,v) \in E$ finding the items that u influenced v successfully by positive influence or negative influence, and we compute the probability of user v becomes active or inactive in these items (line3-line18), which equals the E-step in EM. And then, for each edge $(u,v) \in E,$ update the probability $p_{u,v}$ of user u influence user v using the Equations(8) (line19-line 21), which equals the M-step in EM. Finally, the process will end until the change of the probabilities between two times converge to a threshold. The EM is an iterative updating algorithm, which will update every parameter in every iteration. So when there are a lot of arguments, the running time will become longer.

Algorithm 1. EM method of learning the parameters of MFIC

Input: Social graph $G = (V, E)$, User behavior log Ω.
Output: The set of all parameters of MFIC θ, that is: $\forall (u, v) \in E$: $p_{u,v}$

1.   init $\{p_{u,v}\}$
2.   repeat
3.   **For** all the $(u,v) \in E$ **do**
4.   **For** every item i in Ω
5.   **If**$(u \in N_{positive,t}(v))$
6.   **If** (v is active)
7. $P_{u,v}^+ = P_{u,v}^+ \cup \{i\}$
8.   Compute $P_v^{active,i}(t+1)$
9.   **Else**
10. $P_{u,v}^- = P_{u,v}^- \cup \{i\}$
11.   **If**$(u \in N_{negative,t}(v))$
12.   **If** (v is active)
13. $N_{u,v}^- = N_{u,v}^- \cup \{i\}$
14.   **Else**
15. $N_{u,v}^+ = N_{u,v}^+ \cup \{i\}$
16.   Compute $P_v^{inactive,i}(t+1)$
17.   **End For**
18.   **End For**
19.   **For** every the $(u,v) \in E$ **do**
20. $p_{u,v} = \dfrac{1}{|P_{u,v}^+| + |P_{u,v}^-| + |N_{u,v}^+| + |N_{u,v}^-|} \left(\sum_{i \in P_{u,v}^+} \dfrac{\hat{p}_{u,v}}{\hat{P}_v^{active,i}} + \sum_{i \in N_{u,v}^+} \dfrac{\hat{p}_{u,v}}{\hat{P}_v^{inactive,i}} \right)$
21.   **End For**
22.   until convergence;

5   User Behavior Prediction

The learned influence probabilities among users can be used to help with many applications. Here we illustrate one application on user behavior prediction, i.e., how the learned influence can improve the performance of user behavior prediction.

Based on the MFIC model proposed in Section 3, we present the Algorithm 2 for predicting the user behavior. This algorithm focuses on the question of whether a user will perform a behavior at time-step $t+1$, given the behaviors of his neighbors at time-step t. For example, in Flixster, the behavior is defined as whether a user rates a movie and in Digg, the behavior is defined as whether a user digs a story. For a user u, if he performed the behavior, we think that user u is active. Otherwise, we think that u is inactive. For each item i and inactive user v in the testing dataset, we find his positive and negative neighbors in time-step t and calculate the user's the positive and negative influence receives from his positive and negative neighbors (line 3- line 6). Then we compute the probability that user be active and inactive (line 8-line 9). If the probability that user be active is larger than user be inactive, we think the user become active, otherwise, inactive (line 10- line 12).

Algorithm 2. User Behavior Prediction

Input: Social network $G=(V,E)$, User behavior log Ω, influence probabilities $\{P_{u,v}\}$
Output: The user's state for the item i in the testing dataset

1. **For** each item i in the testing dataset
2.   **For** each inactive   user v
3.   Find positive neighbors of v: $N_{positive}(v)$
4. $P_v^{positive} = $ 1- $\prod_{u \in N_{positive}(v)}(1 - p_{u,v})$
5.   Find   negative neighbors of v: $N_{negative}(v)$
6. $P_v^{negative} = $ 1- $\prod_{u \in N_{negative}(v)}(1 - p_{u,v})$
7.   **End   For**
8. $P_v^{active} = (1 - P_v^{negative}) + P_v^{positive} * P_v^{negative}$
9. $P_v^{inactive} = (1 - P_v^{positive}) + P_v^{positive} * P_v^{negative}$
10.   **If** $P_v^{active} \geq P_v^{inactive}$
11.   Then v is active;
12.   Else v is inactive;
13. **End For**

---

6   Experiments

In this section, we report our results on two real datasets and we compare our MFIC model to the state-of-the-art models. Our goal is to validate whether our proposed model can help to describe real-world influence cascade.

6.1   Datasets

The datasets in our experiments are Flixster[2] and Digg[3]. They are publicly available, both containing a social graph $G=(V,E)$ and a set of past propagation log $\Omega = \{(User, Item ,Time)\}$. Next we describe the data sets in the following:

Table 1. Details of the Flixster, Digg datasets

Statistics	Flixster		Digg	
	Training	Test	Training	Test
#Users	15,675	5,104	27,488	18,664
#Items	8,105	4613	3553	2786
#Actions	1,433,768	480,000	2,517,067	414,620
#Friendship	1,084,895	250,096	683,160	492,138

---

[2] http://www.cs.sfu.ca/~sja25/personal/datasets/
[3] http://www.isi.edu/~lerman/downloads/digg2009.html

Flixster. Flixster is one of the main players in the mobile and social movie rating business. In this context, the action is defined as user rate the movie, if user u gives a high score on the movie, we think a positive influence will happen between user u and user v. otherwise, we think a negative influence will happen between u and v.

Digg. Digg is a social network website, where users vote stories. In this context, if user u votes a story, we think u have a positive influence on v. If u didn't vote the story, but at least one of his neighbors did, we think u will impose negative influence on v.

We preformed some standard consistency cleaning on the two datasets. We remove those items that appear in the log Ω less than 20 times. We also remove those users that not appear in the log Ω and have no friends. Moreover, for the experiment we perform a chronological split of log Ω in both datasets into training (80%) and testing (20%). Details of datasets are shown in Table 1.

6.2   Experimental Setup

For different datasets, the life span of information is various, as shown in Fig. 4, in Digg (the left part), most behaviors occurred in the first 40 hours, so we set the time-step interval at 5, 10, 15, 20, 25, 30 hours respectively that divide the users in the dataset into different time-step. In Flixster (the right part), most behaviors occurred within the first 36 months, so we set the time-step interval at 4, 8, 12, 16, 20, 24 months.

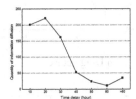 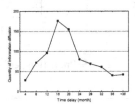

Fig. 4. The information diffusion quantity over time delay in Digg and Flixster.

We apply the learned influence probabilities for user behavior prediction as described in Section 5. We compare the following methods to our proposed PNIC model and evaluate its performance in terms of Precision, Recall and F1-Measure.

- PIC. The PNIC model which only consider the positive factor without the negative factor, the influence probabilities among users also are learnt.
- Static Model. Static model is the method proposed in [10], since we don't focus on the time-dependent influence propagation in this paper, so we only compare our method with the Static Model. The influence probability $p_{v,u}$ is computed by Equation (9), where $|I_{v,u}|$ is the number of actions that v has influenced u and $|I_v|$ is the number of actions performed by v.

$$p_{v,u} = \frac{|I_{v,u}|}{|I_v|} \tag{9}$$

- IC. The influence probability for each edge (u, v) is assigned as 0.01, which is widely adopted by previous studies with the IC model.

6.3   Prediction Performance Analysis

Fig. 5 and Fig. 6 show the prediction performances of all the tested approaches under different measurements at different time-step interval on Digg and Flixster dataset. We can see that the proposed PNIC model can consistently achieve better performance comparing with baseline methods, the IC model worst. Notably, both PNIC and PIC all perform better than Static Model (with an improvement 2-6%). Because in Static Model, the influence probability $p_{u,v}$ is computed only based the number of information diffusions from u to v. And in IC model, the influence probabilities among users are random assigned. Therefore, the predicting performances of Static Model and IC model are uncompetitive. In contrast, in PNIC and PIC model, the influence probabilities are learnt by the user behavior log and considering all the interacting users, so improve the performance significantly. The experiment results confirm that our model considering both positive and negative influence will better describe real-world.

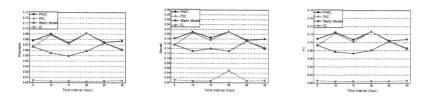

Fig. 5. Prediction performances on Digg dataset.

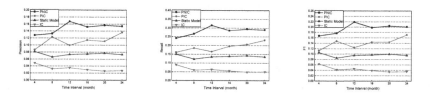

Fig. 6. Prediction performances on Flixster dataset.

Furthermore, we also can see the performance of our PNIC model outperforms the PIC in Flixster, significantly improvements (3-10%). While in Digg they perform similar, but still has an improvement 1.6% in some case. Our explanation is that in Flixster, when a user wants to see a movie, the opinion of his friends are very important. If the most friends gave a low rate, he may don't see the movie. So the negative influence plays an important role in user behavior. But in Digg, vote or not is a very easy action, so when he see his friends vote the story he may possible to vote it even though other friends didn't vote. We can conclusion that the importance of negative influence in Flixster is larger than in Digg. It is very useful when analyze the user behavior in different social network.

7   Related Work

The problem of influence propagation in social network has been widely studied [1, 7, 8]. While pervious works on influence maximization typically assume a social graph G with edges labeled with influence probabilities. Very few works focus on estimating the influence probabilities without the characteristic of items (such as the contents of Twitter). The most relevant works with us are [9, 10]. Satio *et al.* [9] focus on the IC model and defined the likelihood for multiple episodes. They present a method for predicting diffusion probabilities from a log of past propagations by using the EM algorithm. Bonchi *et al.* [10] devise various probabilistic models of influence and develop algorithms for learning the influence probabilities. However, none of them pay attention to the influence probabilities calculation by considering the negative influence.

To the best of our knowledge only few papers have analyzed social influence considering the negative factor [11, 12]. Li *et al.* [11] quantifies the influence and conformity of each individual in a network by utilizing the positive and negative relationships between individuals. However, they don't propose any propagation model, nor study the user-to-user influence probability. Chen *et al.*[12] discuss the influence diffusion considering the negative influence, but their focus is design efficient heuristic for influence maximization in social network rather than learning the influence probability.

8   Conclusion and Future Work

In this paper, a novel influence propagation model MFIC is proposed to model the information diffusion incorporating the positive and negative influence. We model the user's behavior consider the multipolar factors. Then, we design method to learn the influence probabilities based on the history behavior logs of users and we also apply the discovered influence probabilities to user behavior prediction. We conduct experiments to test the effectiveness of our model in real datasets. In future work, we will take advantage of the influence probabilities to design more accurate model to predict user's behaviors considering other factors, such as the user preference.

Acknowledgements. This work was supported by the National Natural Science Foundation of China (Grant No.61303005, No.61170052), the Natural Science Foundation of Shandong Province of China (Grant No.ZR2013FQ009), the Science and Technology Development Plan Project of Shandong Provience (Grant No.2014GGX101047, No.2014GGX101019).

References

1. Kempe, D., Kleinberg, J., Tardos, E.: Maximizing the spread of influence through a social network. In: KDD, pp. 57–66, August 2003
2. Huang, J., Cheng, X.Q., Shen, H.W., et al.: Exploring social influence via posterior effect of word-of-mouth recommendation. In: WSDM, pp. 573–582, February 2012
3. Ye, M., Liu, X., Lee, W.C.: Exploring social influence for recommendation: a generative model approach. In: SIGIR, pp. 671–680, August 2012
4. Tang, J., Sun, J., Wang, C., Yang, Z.: Social influence analysis in large-scale networks. In: KDD, pp. 807–816, June 2009
5. Barbieri, N., Bonchi, F., Manco, G.: Topic-aware social influence propagation models. In: ICDM, pp. 81–90 (2012)
6. Li, D., Xu, Z., Luo, Y., Li, S.: Modeling information diffusion over social networks for temporal dynamic prediction. In: CIKM, pp. 1477–1480, October 2013
7. Chen, W., Wang, C., Wang, Y.: Scalable influence maximization for prevalent viral marketing in large-scale social networks. In: KDD, pp. 1029–1038, July 2010
8. Chen, W., Wang, Y., Yang, S.: Efficient influence maximization in social networks. In: KDD, pp. 199–208, June 2009
9. Saito, K., Nakano, R., Kimura, M.: Prediction of information diffusion probabilities for independent cascade model. In: Lovrek, I., Howlett, R.J., Jain, L.C. (eds.) KES 2008, Part III. LNCS (LNAI), vol. 5179, pp. 67–75. Springer, Heidelberg (2008)
10. Goyal, A., Bonchi, F., Lakshmanan, L.: Learning influence probabilities in social networks. In: WSDM, pp. 241–250, February 2010
11. Li, H., Bhowmick, S.S., Casino, S.A.: Towards conformity-aware social influence analysis in online social networks. In: CIKM, pp. 1007–1012, August 2011
12. Chen, W., Collins, A., Cummings, R., et al.: Influence maximization in social networks when negative opinions may emerge and propagate. In: SDM, pp. 379–390, April 2011
13. Dempster, A.P., Laird, N.M., Rubin, D.B.: Maximum likelihood from incomplete data via the EM algorithm. Journal of the Royal Statistical Society **39**, 1–38 (1977)

Topic Network: Topic Model with Deep Learning for Image Classification

Zhiyong Pan[1,2], Yang Liu[1], Guojun Liu[1], Maozu Guo[1(✉)], and Yang Li[1]

[1] School of Computer Science and Technology, Harbin Institute of Technology, Harbin, China
{panzhiyong,yliu76,hitliu,maozuguo,liyang13}@hit.edu.cn
[2] College of Information Technology and Media, Beihua University, Jilin, China

Abstract. As a representative deep learning model, Convolutional Neural Networks (CNNs) can provide good features to represent the objects in image, and has made a great achievement in image classification and object detection. However, CNNs requires resizing the input images to a fixed size, which may affect the performance of the model due to information loss and distortion. To overcome the limitation, we replace the last pooling layer with topic model-LDA (Latent Dirichlet Allocation) to get a fixed-size output without resizing the input images, and we call it Topic Network. With Topic Network, the input images can be images of an arbitrary size and ratio without resizing, but the output is a k-dimension vector which represents the distribution of topics in image (k is the number of topics). Topic Network performs well in image classification task on Caltech101 and VOC2007 datasets.

Keywords: Deep learning · CNN · Topic model · LDA · Image classification

1 Introduction

Recently, deep learning makes a great progress in image classification [1-3] and object detection [2, 4]. Many approaches extended from deep learning achieve state-of-the-art classification task. Deep learning provides good representations of objects with multi-layers by forward and backward propagation algorithms. The representative deep learning algorithm is Convolutional Neural Networks (CNNs). However, the prevalent CNNs algorithms require all the images to be resized to a fixed input size (e.g., 224×224). To get fixed-size of images, cropping and warping are two important methods. Cropping always only contains the center of the image, which loses the information of the objects in the margin, and even some parts of the objects or small-scale objects. Wrapping makes the objects distorted, which will affect the representation of objects. These limitations of cropping and wrapping will reduce the accuracy of classification and detection dramatically.

According to [2], the fixed-size inputs are needed by fully-connected layer, but not by convolution layers. It means the inputs of convolution layers can be full images without wrapping and cropping, which will not lose any information of objects. Whereas the sizes of input images are different, the outputs of convolutional layers are

© Springer International Publishing Switzerland 2015
S. Zhang et al. (Eds.): KSEM 2015, LNAI 9403, pp. 525–534, 2015.
DOI: 10.1007/978-3-319-25159-2_47

different, which is unacceptable to fully-connected layers and classifiers. To resolve the problem, He et al. [2] replaces the last pooling layer with a spatial pyramid pooling layer, which converts the output with different sizes of the last convolutional layer to an input with fixed size of the fully-connected layer. The structures of CNNs and SPP_net are shown in Fig.1 (top and middle). No matter what the sizes of input images are, the outputs of SPP_net are kM-dimensional vectors (M is the total bin of spatial pyramid and k is the number of kernels in the last convolutional layer). [2] gets a good performance on classification and detection. However, SPP_net uses the maximum kernel to represent the regions of SPM and it may lose some other representative features. Meanwhile, the number of kernels of the last convolutional layer may affect the performance of SPP_net. In fact, there are some other algorithms to get a fixed dimension, such as Bag of Words (BOW) and topic model.

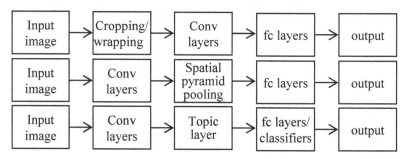

Fig. 1. Top: structure of CNNs. Middle: structure of SPP_net. Bottom: structure of Topic Network

Being inspired by [2], we replace the last pooling layer with topic model (LDA, Latent Dirichlet Allocation [5]) and we call it Topic Network. Fig.1 (bottom) shows the structure of Topic Network. The main contribution of Topic Network is that it is another effective method to overcome the limitations of resizing the input images of CNNs. Different from SPP_net [2], Topic Network learns visual words from the outputs of the last convolutional layer by means of clustering. All kernels are the element of vectors which represent visual words. Therefore, all kernels are considered rather than the maximum kernel and the number of kernels will not affect the outputs of Topic Network. Meanwhile, Topic Network shows the characteristic of images in the whole image set, which benefit from the co-occurrence of visual words. More importantly, both the distributions of topics in image and those in region can be computed and taken as the inputs of fully-connected layers and features of classifiers. In this paper, Topic Network performs well in image classification on Caltech101 [6] and Pascal VOC 2007 [7].

The rest of this paper is organized as follows. In Section 2, we introduce LDA briefly. Section 3 introduces Topic Network. Section 4 shows experimental results and related discussions. Finally, Section 5 summarizes the work.

2   Latent Dirichlet Allocation (LDA)

Latent Dirichlet Allocation (LDA) was proposed by Blei in 2003 [5] and has been widely used in natural language processing. A latent layer (topic layer) is the intermediate between words and documents. A topic is a cluster of words with different probabilities and a document is consisted of topics with different probabilities. Based on the co-occurrence of words in documents, the outputs of LDA are the distributions of topics in each document without considering the number of words in documents.

Fig. 2 shows the graphical model of LDA. The corpus is consisted of M documents and each document is made up of N words. α and β are Dirichlet prior in order to avoid over-fitting. θ and φ are the distributions of topics in one document and the distributions of words in each topic, respectively. The number of topics is K. Each word is assigned a topic in one document.

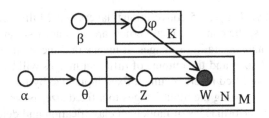

Fig. 2. Graphical model of LDA

The generative process of LDA is as follows:

(1) For a document, the distribution of topics, θ, is sampled from Dirichlet prior, $\theta \sim Dir(\alpha)$;

(2) For a topic, the distribution of words, φ, is sampled from Dirichlet prior, $\varphi \sim Dir(\beta)$;

(3) In a document, sampling a topic, $z_i \sim Multi(\theta)$;

(4) Sampling a word w_i from $p(w_i|\varphi_{z_i})$.

The distributions of topics in documents and the distributions of words in topics are multinomial distributions with Dirichlet prior. The parameters, θ and φ, can be computed via the number of each topic in one document and that of each word in one topic. Although the posterior, $p(z_i|w_i)$, is not inferred exactly, it is sampled by Gibbs sampling which integers out θ and φ [8].

$$p(z_i|Z_{\neg i}, W, \alpha, \beta) = \frac{p(W,Z)}{p(W_{\neg i}, Z_{\neg i})p(w_i)} \propto \frac{p(W,Z)}{p(W_{\neg i}, Z_{\neg i})} \propto \frac{n_{k,\neg i}^t + \beta_t}{\sum_{t=1}^V n_{k,\neg i}^t + \beta_t} \cdot \frac{n_{m,\neg i}^k + \alpha_k}{[\sum_{k=1}^K n_m^k + \alpha_k] - 1} \qquad (1)$$

where $Z_{\neg i}$ is the topics assigned to the words excluding the current topic z_i. $n_{k,\neg i}^t$ is the number of words in corpus to which topic k is assigned excluding the current word i. V is the size of the codebook. $n_{m,\neg i}^k$ is the number of topic k in the document excluding being assigned to the current word i. The distribution of topic k in document m ($\theta_{m,k}$) and that of word t in topic k ($\varphi_{k,t}$) can be computed by equation (2) and (3), respectively.

$$\theta_{m,k} = \frac{n_m^k + \alpha_k}{\sum_{k=1}^{K} n_m^k + \alpha_k} \qquad (2)$$

$$\varphi_{k,t} = \frac{n_k^t + \beta_t}{\sum_{t=1}^{V} n_k^t + \beta_t} \qquad (3)$$

The distributions of topics are effective features in document classification task. Similar to natural language processing, topic model also performs well in image processing by regarding local features (e.g. SIFT [9]) as visual words, images as documents and topics as parts of objects. LDA and its extended models perform well in image understanding [10-13].

3   Topic Network

The popular CNNs have 7 layers: 5 convolutional layers and 2 fully-connected layers. In convolutional layers, the convolutional kernels are similar to sliding windows and can slide in any size and any ratio of images. It means that the input images are not required to be a fixed size, and the outputs of different images will be different sizes. However, the fully-connected layers require a fixed input size by their definition. For this reason, it requires resizing the input images to a fixed size. Nevertheless, resized images will affect the performances of models in classification and detection. As previously described, the outputs of LDA are the fixed-size vectors with different size of input. Hence, we can replace the last pooling layer with LDA to get a fixed output size, and we call it Topic Network. Fig.3 shows the structure of Topic Network. For Topic Network, the inputs of are full images with any size and ratio and the outputs of Topic layer are fixed-size vectors (the distribution of topics) which are fit to be taken as the inputs of fully-connected layers or the effective features of classifiers.

In convolutional layers, Topic Network extracts the features of input images and the outputs of the last convolutional layer (e.g. conv5) are the nM-dimension vectors (n is the number of kernels in the last convolutional layer and M is the number of patches in the last convolutional layer). We cluster all the vectors to learn the codebook of visual words via k-means algorithm. Hence, as for the input of Topic layer, the vectors are represented by visual words via the nearest neighbor method. In LDA model, words are generated from topics. To get the assignment of topics, Gibbs sampling is used to infer the posterior $p(z_i|w_i)$. After a certain number of iterations, the posterior $p(z_i|w_i)$ will be stable, and each of visual word will be assigned one topic. Therefore, with the assignment of topics, the distributions of topics can be computed by equation (2).

The size of codebook and the number of topics play important roles in Topic Network and affect the performance of the model dramatically. Visual words reflect the attributes of objects. Too few visual words can't reflect and distinguish the characteristic of objects well, while too many visual words make many synonyms which make the influence on the assignments of topics. Topics are the cluster of visual words and represent the parts of objects. Too few topics will confuse the parts of different objects, while too many topics can't cluster visual words to meaningful parts. Hence, the size of codebook and number of topics determines the representation of the objects and the accuracy of image classification.

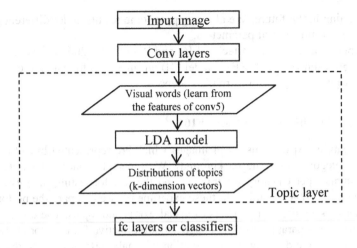

Fig. 3. Structure of Topic Network. Conv5 is the last convolutional layer.   k is the number of topics.

Just as the size of codebook determines the representation of objects, the number of visual words in one image affects the representation of the images. In one image, it can't reflect the attributes of the objects and the characteristics of the image with too few visual words, whereas it will increase the consumptions of resource and time with too many visual words. To avoid the problems, we resize the short side of the image to a fixed length (e.g., 224) and the images to a proper size with the original ratio.

The distributions of topics are the global parameter of the image. Besides them, the regional distributions of topics are also fit to be the inputs of fully-connected layers and the features of classifiers. Because topics are assigned to visual words, the regional distributions of topics are computed similar with SPM [14] to avoid losing the information of small parts of objects, and get a kM-dimensional feature (k is the number of topics and M is the total bin of spatial pyramid). However, it is different from SPP_net. In each scale of pyramid, SPP_net uses max-pooling to represent the regions by the maximal kernel. Topic Network computes the distributions of topics, which are similar to the histogram of topics and represent the regions by all topics.

There are also some other factors which affect the performance of LDA, such as the hyper-parameters and the numbers of visual words and topics. In this paper, we mainly discuss the feasibility of LDA on deep network to overcome the limitation of resizing input images, but we do not discuss how to get the optimal parameters.

4   Experiments

In this paper, we replace the last pooling layer by LDA to get a fixed-size vector for fully-connected layers or classifiers, and the experimental results in this section only show the performance of Topic Network with the cursory parameters of LDA and classifier. To improve the performance, more effective parameters for Topic Network need researching in the future. We also compare some results under different parameters to show the influences of parameters.

In all experiments, we use Caltech101 [6] and Pascal VOC2007 [7] as benchmarks, and use the pre-trained model (ZF-5 model [3]) on ImageNet to extract the features of the 5th convolutional layer and learn the codebook.

4.1   Image Classification on Caltech101

Caltech101 dataset [6] contains 9,144 images which are represented by102 categories (101 object categories and one background). We repeat 10 random splits (randomly sample 30 images per category for training and the rest for testing) and evaluate the performance by average accuracy. In these experiments, we compare the performances of Topic Network in different numbers of visual words and topics. The distributions of topics are the global parameter of the image and are effective features for classification task. However, to avoid losing the information of small parts of objects, the regional distributions of topics are computed by SPM [14], and get a kM-dimensional feature (k is the number of topics and M is the total bin of spatial pyramid).

In this paper, we train a linear SVM (liblinear [15]) and compare the affection of distributions of topics in image and in region with two different sizes of codebooks and six different numbers of topics. VW1000 and VW5000 indicate the codebooks which contain 1000 visual words and 5000 visual words, respectively. Theta and SPM indicate the distribution of topics in image and in region, respectively. A 3-level pyramid (1×1, 2×2, and 4×4) is used in SPM, which gets the distributions of topics in 21 regions. Fig.4 shows the results of comparisons. It shows VW5000 performs better

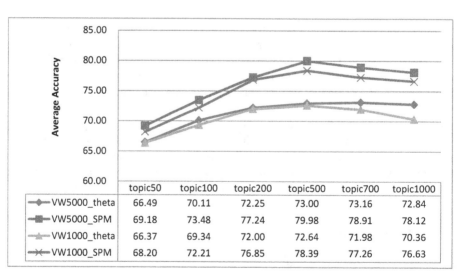

	topic50	topic100	topic200	topic500	topic700	topic1000
VW5000_theta	66.49	70.11	72.25	73.00	73.16	72.84
VW5000_SPM	69.18	73.48	77.24	79.98	78.91	78.12
VW1000_theta	66.37	69.34	72.00	72.64	71.98	70.36
VW1000_SPM	68.20	72.21	76.85	78.39	77.26	76.63

Fig. 4. Comparisons of different numbers of visual words and topics in Caltech101 (average accuracy)

than VW1000 and it performs best when the number of topics is 500. 5000 visual words can represent more attributes of the objects than 1000 visual words and 500 topics represent the shared parts of objects more effectively. To some extent, the accuracy of classification is influenced by the numbers of visual words and topics. Meanwhile, SPM performs better than theta due to the characteristic of the images. In Caltech101 dataset, one image mainly contains one object which occupies the center of the image. The same objects are always in the same direction and on similar scales. For these reasons, the features of SPM reflect more effective attribution of images and represent more accurate attributes of objects than those of theta.

4.2   Image Classification on VOC2007

VOC2007 [7] contains 9963 images which are mainly consisted of 20 object categories. There are 5011 images in train-val dataset to train the parameters of models, and 4952 images in test dataset to evaluate the performance of models. MAP (mean Average Precision) is used to evaluate the performance of the models.

With the same setting of the experiments in image classification on Caltech101, we also compare the performances of distributions of topics in image and in region with two different sizes of codebooks and six different numbers of topics. Fig.5 shows the results. As for the images of VOC2007, there are many objects in one image and the objects are at different positions with different scales and directions. Although SPM can get the regional attributes of images, the same region may reflect different attributes of images in VOC2007 dataset, and similar features of SPM may represent different object categories. Nevertheless, theta is the global feature of one image and isn't affected by the positions and the directions of objects. Hence, theta performs better than SPM when they are regarded as the features of classifier. Similar to Caltech101, enough number of visual words and topics can represent objects better and Topic Network performs best with 5000 visual words and 500 topics in these experiments.

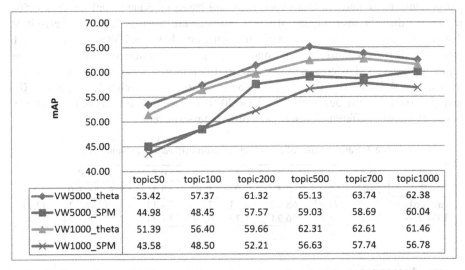

	topic50	topic100	topic200	topic500	topic700	topic1000
VW5000_theta	53.42	57.37	61.32	65.13	63.74	62.38
VW5000_SPM	44.98	48.45	57.57	59.03	58.69	60.04
VW1000_theta	51.39	56.40	59.66	62.31	62.61	61.46
VW1000_SPM	43.58	48.50	52.21	56.63	57.74	56.78

Fig. 5. Comparisons of different numbers of visual words and topics in VOC2007 (mAP)

Fig.4 and Fig.5 show Topic Network can performs well in image classification without resizing the input images. Although the results in this paper are not the best performances of Topic Network with the default parameters of LDA and linear SVM, they are better than some traditional algorithms, such as VQ [14], LCC [16], and FK [17] and are close to SPP_net [2]. Table 1 shows the comparisons of these models. In this table, the results of VQ [14], LCC [16], and FK [17] are reported by[18] and [2]. The results of SPP_net [2] are the accuracy of classification without the fully-connected layers. The level of pyramid also affects the accuracy. Deeper levels of pyramid can get more effective features. SPP_net uses 4-level pyramid (1×1, 2×2, 3×3, and 6×6), and our Topic Network uses 3-level pyramid (1×1, 2×2, and 4×4). With the same pyramid and without fully-connected layers, the mAP of SPP_net is 67.6 on VOC2007, which is close to that of Topic Network.

Table 1. Comparisons with other models

Models	Caltech101	VOC2007
VQ [14]	74.41	56.07
LCC [16]	76.95	57.66
FK[17]	77.78	61.69
SPP_net [2]	91.44	70.82
Ours	79.98	65.13

4.3   The Effect of Parameters of Topic Network

The parameters of Topic Network, such as the numbers of visual words and topics and the setting of hyper-parameters, affect the accuracy of classification dramatically. Fig.4 and Fig.5 show the influence of the numbers of visual words and topics. In this section, we compare the performances of Topic Network with different hyper-parameters (α and β). Our experiments are based on 5000 visual words and 500 topics and then the distributions of topics in image are taken as features of classifier. Table 2 shows the results of classification on Caltech101 and VOC2007. α and β affect the distributions of topics in one image and the distributions of words in one topic, respectively. Different settings lead to different performances. In these experiments, $\alpha = 0.5$ and $\beta = 0.01$, are the best results on Caltech101; while $\alpha = 0.1$ and $\beta = 0.01$ are the best results on VOC2007. Hence, on the basis of the characteristics of images, different datasets need different parameters.

Table 2. Some results of classification with different hyper-parameters

α	0.1	0.1	0.1	0.1	0.5	0.5	0.5	0.5	1
β	0.01	0.1	0.5	1.0	0.01	0.1	0.5	1.0	1
Caltech101	73.00	71.45	68.02	68.33	74.53	74.11	68.74	61.41	52.91
VOC2007	65.13	61.65	56.24	51.73	62.97	61.14	52.12	48.74	47.48

5   Conclusions

Replacing the last pooling layer with LDA, Topic Network is an effective algorithm to overcome the limitations of resizing the input images. The input images of Topic Network can be full images in any size and ratio without resizing. Topic Network uses LDA to convert the different sizes of outputs of the last convolutional layer into a fixed-size feature for fully-connected layers and classifiers. Regarding both the global and the regional distributions of topics as the features of classifier, Topic Network performs well in image classification. With effective algorithms of parameters learning, the accuracies of image classification will be improved and even get the state of the art in image classification.

Acknowledgement. Y. Liu is supported by Natural Science Foundation of China (61171185). M. Guo is supported by Natural Science Foundation of China (61271346). G. Liu is supported by Heilongjiang Province Science Foundation for Youths (QC2014C071).

References

1. Krizhevsky, A., Sutskever, I., Hinton, G.E.: Imagenet classification with deep convolutional neural networks. In: Advances in Neural Information Processing Systems, pp. 1097–1105 (2012)
2. He, K., Zhang, X., Ren, S., Sun, J.: Spatial pyramid pooling in deep convolutional networks for visual recognition. In: Fleet, D., Pajdla, T., Schiele, B., Tuytelaars, T. (eds.) ECCV 2014, Part III. LNCS, vol. 8691, pp. 346–361. Springer, Heidelberg (2014)
3. Zeiler, M.D., Fergus, R.: Visualizing and understanding convolutional networks. In: Fleet, D., Pajdla, T., Schiele, B., Tuytelaars, T. (eds.) ECCV 2014, Part I. LNCS, vol. 8689, pp. 818–833. Springer, Heidelberg (2014)
4. Girshick, R., Donahue, J., Darrell, T., Malik, J.: Rich feature hierarchies for accurate object detection and semantic segmentation. In: 2014 IEEE Conference on Computer Vision and Pattern Recognition (CVPR), pp. 580–587. IEEE (2014)
5. Blei, D.M., Ng, A.Y., Jordan, M.I.: Latent dirichlet allocation. The Journal of Machine Learning Research **3**, 993–1022 (2003)
6. Fei-Fei, L., Fergus, R., Perona, P.: Learning generative visual models from few training examples: An incremental bayesian approach tested on 101 object categories. Computer Vision and Image Understanding **106**, 59–70 (2007)
7. Everingham, M., Van Gool, L., Williams, C., Winn, J., Zisserman, A.: The PASCAL Visual Object Classes Challenge 2007 (VOC 2007)
8. Griffiths, T.L., Steyvers, M.: Finding scientific topics. Proceedings of the National academy of Sciences of the United States of America **101**, 5228–5235 (2004)
9. Lowe, D.G.: Distinctive image features from scale-invariant keypoints. International Journal of Computer Vision **60**, 91–110 (2004)
10. Fei-Fei, L., Perona, P.: A bayesian hierarchical model for learning natural scene categories. In: IEEE Computer Society Conference on Computer Vision and Pattern Recognition, CVPR 2005, pp. 524–531. IEEE (2005)
11. Li, L.-J., Socher, R., Fei-Fei, L.: Towards total scene understanding: classification, annotation and segmentation in an automatic framework. In: IEEE Conference on Computer Vision and Pattern Recognition, CVPR 2009, pp. 2036–2043. IEEE (2009)

12. Cao, L., Fei-Fei, L.: Spatially coherent latent topic model for concurrent segmentation and classification of objects and scenes. In: IEEE 11th International Conference on Computer Vision, ICCV 2007, pp. 1–8. IEEE (2007)
13. Zhao, B., Fei-Fei, L., Xing, E.P.: Image segmentation with topic random field. In: Daniilidis, K., Maragos, P., Paragios, N. (eds.) ECCV 2010, Part V. LNCS, vol. 6315, pp. 785–798. Springer, Heidelberg (2010)
14. Lazebnik, S., Schmid, C., Ponce, J.: Beyond bags of features: spatial pyramid matching for recognizing natural scene categories. In: 2006 IEEE Computer Society Conference on Computer Vision and Pattern Recognition, pp. 2169–2178. IEEE (2006)
15. Fan, R.-E., Chang, K.-W., Hsieh, C.-J., Wang, X.-R., Lin, C.-J.: LIBLINEAR: A library for large linear classification. The Journal of Machine Learning Research 9, 1871–1874 (2008)
16. Wang, J., Yang, J., Yu, K., Lv, F., Huang, T., Gong, Y.: Locality-constrained linear coding for image classification. In: 2010 IEEE Conference on Computer Vision and Pattern Recognition (CVPR), pp. 3360–3367. IEEE (2010)
17. Perronnin, F., Sánchez, J., Mensink, T.: Improving the fisher kernel for large-scale image classification. In: Daniilidis, K., Maragos, P., Paragios, N. (eds.) ECCV 2010, Part IV. LNCS, vol. 6314, pp. 143–156. Springer, Heidelberg (2010)
18. Chatfield, K., Lempitsky, V.S., Vedaldi, A., Zisserman, A.: The devil is in the details: an evaluation of recent feature encoding methods. In: BMVC, p. 8 (2011)

Fast Multi-label Learning via Hashing

Haifeng Hu[1], Yong Sun[1], and Jiansheng Wu[2,3(✉)]

[1] School of Telecommunication and Information Engineering,
Nanjing University of Posts and Telecommunications, Nanjing, China
[2] School of Geographic and Biological Information,
Nanjing University of Posts and Telecommunications, Nanjing, China
jansen@njupt.edu.cn
[3] Industrial Engineering, School of Computing, Informatics,
and Decision Systems Engineering, Arizona State University, Tempe, AZ, USA

Abstract. Multi-label learning (MLL) copes with the classification problems where each in-stance can be tagged with multiple labels simultaneously. During the last several years, many MLL algorithms were proposed and they achieved excellent performance in multiple applications. However, these approaches are usually time-consuming and cannot handle large-scale data. In this paper, we propose a fast multi-label learning algorithm HashMLL based on hashing schemes. The approach HashMLL takes advantage of a Locality Sensitive Hashing (LSH) to identify its neighboring instances for each unseen instance, and exploits label correlation by estimating the similarity of labels through a minwise independent permutations locality sensitive hashing (MinHash). After that, relied on statistical information attained from all related labels of the neighboring instances, maxi-mum a posteriori (MAP) principle is used to determine the label set for each unseen instance. Experiments show that the performance of HashMLL is highly competitive to state-of-the-art techniques, whereas its time cost is much less. Particularly, on the dataset NUS-WIDE with 269,648 instances and the dataset Flickr with 565,444 instances where none of existing methods can return results in 24 hours, HashMLL takes only 90 secs and 23266 secs respectively.

Keywords: Multi-label Learning · Fast · Hashing · Label dependency

1 Introduction

Traditional supervised learning algorithms work under the single-label scenario, i.e. one real-world object is associated with one label to show its property. However, in many real learning problems, each object is associated with multiple labels simulta-neously. For example, in text categorization tasks, a document may be owned by several themes, such as "government" and "health"; in bioinformatics, a gene can have multiple functions, such as "transcription" and "protein synthesis", and so on. In all these tasks, each instance in the training set is related with a set of labels, and the task is to output a label set whose size is unknown without a priori for each unseen instance.

© Springer International Publishing Switzerland 2015
S. Zhang et al. (Eds.): KSEM 2015, LNAI 9403, pp. 535–546, 2015.
DOI: 10.1007/978-3-319-25159-2_48

During the past decade, a number of MLL algorithms were proposed and applied in multiple applications. These approaches can be classified into two main groups: problem transformation methods and algorithm adaptation methods [1]. Program transformation methods are to transform a multi-label classification task into multiple single-label classification tasks or regression tasks [2,3,4,5,6]. Algorithm adaptation methods extend traditional single-label classification methods for handling multi-label classification problems directly [7,8,9,10,11]. These approaches achieved great performances and promoted the superiority of Multi-label learning framework in many applications. However, along with the improvement of expressive power, the hypothesis space of MLL expands exponentially, leading to the high complexity and low efficiency of existing approaches. Thus, these approaches are usually time-consuming, and are hard to handle large-scale data, resulting in a strong limitation of the application of multi-label learning.

In this paper, we propose a novel approach HashMLL to learn on multi-label data fast. As its name implied, through hashing schemes are employed for efficiency, HashMLL offers an effective approximation solution of the original MLL tasks. Specifically, for each unseen instance, a LSH scheme is adopted to identify its neighboring instances. Moreover, to utilize the relations among multiple labels, it is exploited by estimating the similarity between labels through a MinHash scheme.   After that, MAP principle is used to determine the label set for each unseen instance based on the statistical information which derives from all related label sets of its neighboring instances.

Experiments indicate that the performance of HashMLL is highly competitive to state-of-the-art methods, whereas its time cost is much less. Particularly, on the dataset NUS-WIDE with 269,648 instances and the dataset Flickr with 565,444 instances where none of existing methods can return results in 24 hours, HashMLL takes only 90 secs and 23266 secs. Experimental results demon-state that the time complexity of our model present approximately linear correlation with the sample size.

The rest of the paper is organized as follows. We propose the HashMLL approach in Section 2, and then present the experiments in Section 3. Section 4 concludes this work along with future work discussion.

2   The HashMLL Approach

The multi-label learning problem can be formulated as follows. Let $\mathcal{X} \in \mathbb{R}^d$ denotes the d-dimensional instance space and $\mathcal{Y} = \{1,2,\dots,Q\}$ denotes the label space with Q labels. Given a multi-label training set $D = \{(x_1, Y_1), \dots, (x_m, Y_m)\}$ of m training examples, where $x_i \in \mathcal{X}$ is a d-dimensional feature vector and $Y_i \in \mathcal{Y}$ is the set of labels associated with x_i, the goal of multi-label learning is to output a multi-label classifier $h: \mathcal{X} \to 2^{\mathcal{Y}}$ from the multi-label training set D. In most cases, the learning system will produce a ranking real-valued function $f: \mathcal{X} \times \mathcal{Y} \to \mathbb{R}$ with the interpretation that, where $f(x,y)$ can be regarded as the confidence of $y \in \mathcal{Y}$ being the proper label of x. Given an instance x_i and its associated label set Y_i, then a successful multi-label classifier will tend to rank labels in Y_i higher than those not in Y_i, i.e. $f(x_1, y_1) > f(x_2, y_2)$ for any $y_1 \in Y_i$ and $y_2 \notin Y_i$. The corresponding multi-label classifier $h(\cdot)$ can be conveniently derived from the ranking function $f(\cdot, \cdot)$ via:

$$h(x) = \{y | f(x, y) > t(x),\ y \in \mathcal{Y}\} \tag{1}$$

where $t(\cdot)$ is the threshold function.

In multi-label learning problem, instances with similar feature spaces usually tend to share common labels with a greater probability. That is to say, similar instances would be more likely to have the same labels. Therefore, the basic idea of this algorithm is to adapt k-nearest neighbor techniques to deal with multi-label data, where MAP rule is utilized to make prediction by reasoning with the labeling information embodied in the neighbors [8]. It can be formulated as follows: given the multi-label training set $D = \{(x_1, Y_1), \ldots, (x_m, Y_m)\}$, for each label, let H_j^1 be the event that the instance x has label j and H_j^0 be the event that the instance x does not have label j, based on the above notations, the label vector $y_x(j)$ of the instance x is determined using the following MAP principle:

$$y_x(j) = arg\ \max_{b \in \{0,1\}} P(H_j^b | x), j \in \mathcal{Y} \tag{2}$$

where $P(H_j^b | x)$ is the posterior probability of H_j^b conditioned on x. Using the Bayesian rule and adopting the assumption of label conditional independence among features as classic Naive Bayes classifiers do, Eq. (2) can be rewritten as:

$$y_x(j) = arg\ \max_{b \in \{0,1\}} \frac{P(H_j^b) P(x | H_j^b)}{P(x)} = arg\ \max_{b \in \{0,1\}} P(H_j^b) P(x | H_j^b) \tag{3}$$

where $P(H_j^b)$ is the prior probability of H_j^b, $P(x | H_j^b)$ is the conditional probability of x conditioned on H_j^b and $P(x)$ is the prior probability of x. The probability $P(H_j^b)$ and $P(x | H_j^b)$ can be estimated from the given data. Bayesian theorem is useful in that it provides a way of calculating the posterior probability.

Since the computational power required for finding the k-nearest neighbors using linear search approach is prohibitively large, in this work we use the LSH [12,13,14] approach to accelerate find the k-nearest neighbors of the instance. For each instance x in the dataset, let $N(x)$ denote the index set of the k-nearest neighbors of x identified in the training set using LSH approach. Thus, based on the label sets of these neighbors, a membership counting vector can be defined as:

$$C_x(j) = \sum_{a \in N(x)} y_a(j) \tag{4}$$

where $C_x(j)$ counts how many neighbors of x belong to the label j. Therefore, $P(H_j^b|x)$ and $P(x|H_j^b)$ can be rewritten as $P(H_j^b|C_x(j))$ and $P(C_x(j)|H_j^b)$. Thus,

$$y_x(j) = arg \max_{b\in\{0,1\}} P(H_j^b)P(C_x(j)|H_j^b) \tag{5}$$

Many real-world applications involve multi-label classification, in which the labels can have strong inter dependencies. Recently, a number of label relationship learning schemes have been proposed. However, most of them usually are time-consuming. To alleviate this problem, the MinHash [15] is used to capture label dependencies without increasing computational burden. MinHash is a technique for quickly estimating set similarities by Jaccard similarity. Here, for each label j, the label vector y_j is formulated as an m-dimensional vector:

$$y_j = \begin{cases} 1, & if\ x_i\ belongs\ to\ label\ j \\ 0, & if\ x_i\ not\ belongs\ to\ label\ j \end{cases}, i = 1,2,...,m \tag{6}$$

Suppose $h_{min}(y_j)$ is a k-dimensional integer vector of the label j which is obtained by using the MinHash scheme on the label vector y_j. Let R_j^i as the similarity coefficient which represents the dependence level between each pair of labels in the given multi-label data set. The larger the value of R_j^i, the most dependency between label j and label i. R_j^i can be calculated as follows:

$$R_j^i = Jaccrad(y_j,y_i) = \frac{h_{min}(y_j)\cap h_{min}(y_i)}{h_{min}(y_j)\cup h_{min}(y_i)} \tag{7}$$

In this paper, we exploit label dependency by using the k-nearest neighbors of label j instead of all labels when predicting the label vector of the instance. Let $N(y_j)$ denote the index set of the k-nearest neighbors of label j identified in the training set. Then, the classifiers function can be rewritten as:

$$y_x(j) = arg \max_{b\in\{0,1\}} \sum_{i\in N(y_j)} R_j^i P(H_j^b)P(C_x(j)|H_j^b) \tag{8}$$

Fig.1 shows the pseudo code of the HashMLL algorithm. The input arguments D is dataset, t is test instance, k_α is the number of nearest neighbors of t, k_β is the number of nearest neighbors of each label, and the output argument y_t is the predict label vector of t. While the input argument s is a smoothing parameter. Throughout the experiments, the Laplace smoothing is used which means that s is set to 1. K and L are the width parameter of the hash functions and the number of hash tables of LSH respectively. r_t is a real valued vector calculated for ranking labels in $\mathcal{Y}$.

$$[y_t, r_t] = HashMLL(D, t, k_\alpha, k_\beta, s, K, L)$$

% computing the prior probabilities

(1) $for\ q = 1 \dots Q$

(2) $P(H_q^1) = (s + \sum_{i=1}^m y_{x_i}(q))/(s \times 2 + m)$

(3) $P(H_q^0) = 1 - P(H_q^1)$

(4)   computing the label vector y_q by Eq.(6);

(5)   computing $h_{min}(y_q)$ of label y_q by Minhash scheme;

% computing the similarity coefficient matrix R_q^v and $N(y_q)$

(6) $for\ q = 1 \dots Q$

(7) $for\ v = 1 \dots Q$

(8)   computing R_q^v by Eq.(7);

(9)   identify $N(y_q)$ contains k_β labels by sorting R_q^v;

% computing the conditional probabilities

(10) identify $N(x_i), i = 1 \dots m$ using LSH scheme with the parameter K and L;

(11) $for\ q = 1 \dots Q$

(12) $for\ j = 1 \dots k_\alpha$

(13) $c[q][j] = 0; c'[q][j] = 0;$

(14) $for\ i = 1 \dots m$

(15) $\delta = C_{x_i}(q) = \sum_{a \in N(x_i)} y_a(q)$

(16) $if\ y_{x_i}(q) == 1\ then\ c[q][j] = c[q][j] + 1$

(17) $else\ c'[q][j] =$
$c'[q][j] + 1$

(18) $for\ j = 1 \dots k_\alpha$

(19) $P(C_q^j|H_q^1) = (s + c[q][j])/(s \times (k_\alpha + 1) + \sum_{p=0}^{k_\alpha} c[q][p])$

(20) $P(C_q^j|H_q^0) = (s + c[q][j])/(s \times (k_\alpha + 1) + \sum_{p=0}^{k_\alpha} c'[q][p])$

% computing y_t and r_t

(21)   Identify $N(t)$ using LSH scheme;

(22) $for\ q = 1 \dots Q$

(23) $C_t(q) = \sum_{a \in N(t)} y_a(q)$

(24) $y_t(q) = arg \max_{b \in \{0,1\}} \sum_{v \in N(y_q)} R_q^v P(H_a^b) P(C_x(v)|H_q^b)$

(25) $r_t(q) = \dfrac{\sum_{v \in N(y_q)} R_q^v P(H_a^1) P(C_x(v)|H_q^1)}{\sum_{v \in N(y_q)} R_q^v P(H_a^1) P(C_x(v)|H_q^1) + \sum_{v \in N(y_q)} R_q^v P(H_a^0) P(C_x(v)|H_q^0)}$

Fig. 1. Pseudo code of HashMLL

3   Experiments Results and Discussions

3.1   Experimental Configuration

We perform the experiments on 2 moderate-sized data sets and 3 large data sets which are commonly used in existing MLL works. Yeast [9] is gene functional data which consists of 2417 genes and is associated with 14 possible labels. Corel5K [16] contains 5000 segmented images and 374 labels, and each image is represented by 9 instances on average. The 3 large data sets are Mediamill, NUS-WIDE and Flickr. Mediamill [17] is a multimedia database recordings at the 2005 TRECVID corpus which consists of 43907 videos and 101 semantic concepts. NUS-WIDE [18] is a web image dataset created by Lab for Media Search in National University of Singapore which is comprising over 269,648 images and ground-truth of 81 concepts for the entire dataset. Flickr [19] is a network data set crawled from Flickr which consists of 565,444 instances and 1000 labels. Both the contact network and selected group membership information are included. The detailed characteristics of these data sets are summarized in Table 1.

The performances of the compared approaches are evaluated with five commonly used MLL criteria: Hamming loss (Hloss), OneError, Coverage, Ranking loss (Rloss) and Average Precision (AP). For AP, a larger value implies a better performance, while for the other four criteria, the smaller, the better. The definition of these criteria can be found in [23]. All experiments are conducted on a DELL workstation equipped with Intel eight-core CPU (frequency: 1.8 GHz) and 64G bytes physical memory.

Table 1. Characteristics of the Data Sets

name	domain	instances	nominal	numeric	labels	cardinality
Yeast	biology	2417	0	103	14	2.402
Corel5k	images	5000	499	0	374	3.522
Mediamill	video	43907	0	120	101	4.376
NUS-WIDE	images	269648	0	128	81	1.869
Flick	network	565444	0	297	1000	10.35

3.2   Performances of Models

We compare the HashMLL algorithms with five state-of-the-art MLL algorithms, i.e., RAkEL [3], ECC [6], MLkNN [8], IBLR-ML [20], and MetaLabeler (ML) [21]. The codes of compared MLL algorithms are shared by their authors in the Mulan package, and these algorithms are set to the best parameters reported in the papers. Mulan [22] is an open-source Java library for learning from multi-label datasets which is written in Java and is built on top of Weka. For our proposed algorithm HashMLL, the following hyper-parameters settings were used: (a) for the sake of fairness, we use the same neighborhood size of MLkNN and IBLR-ML, in conjunction with the kNN kernel, i.e. $k_\alpha = 10$; (b) the two main parameters of LSH, we set K=6 and L=45; (c) the third parameter is the number of nearest neighbors of labels, which is set to 4, i.e. $k_{label} = k_\beta = 4$.

We repeat three-fold cross validation for 10 times on the first four datasets and 1 times on the Flickr dataset. The mean ±std. performances are recorded for the proposed and compared methods. Table 2 - Table 6 summarize the experimental results of each compared algorithm on five datasets. For each evaluation criterion, "↓" indicates "the smaller the better" while "↑" indicates "the bigger the better". N/A indicates that no result is obtained in 24 hours. The experimental results show that the performance of HashMLL is highly competitive to state-of-the-art techniques, whereas its time cost is much less (Table 2 - Table 6). Particularly, on the dataset NUS-WIDE with 269,648 instances and 81 labels (Table 5), and the dataset Flickr with 565,444 instances and 1000 labels (Table 6) where none of existing methods can return results in 24 hours, HashMLL takes only 94 secs and 23266 secs respectively.

Table 2. Comparison Results (mean ± std.) with five baseline MLL Methods on Yeast

Yeast	Training time /s	Testing time /s	Hloss↓	OneError↓	Coverage↓	Rloss↓	AP↑
RAKEL	19.77	0.06	0.2500± 0.0085	0.2694± 0.0216	9.5983± 0.2523	0.3397± 0.0129	0.6381± 0.0126
IBLR-ML	5.07	0.56	0.1932± 0.0075	0.2296± 0.0225	6.1982± 0.2188	0.1638± 0.0104	0.7684± 0.0131
ML	8.8	0.02	0.2731± 0.0096	0.3868± 0.0470	9.4105± 0.2859	0.3219± 0.0144	0.6181± 0.0136
ECC	29.25	0.04	0.2075± 0.0070	0.2553± 0.0302	6.6212± 0.2670	0.1852± 0.0152	0.7439± 0.0173
MLkNN	5.05	0.72	0.1926± 0.0075	0.2276± 0.0198	6.2032± 0.2317	0.1644± 0.0108	0.7675± 0.0122
HashMLL	13.9	1.21	0.2246± 0.0058	0.2487± 0.0245	6.6417± 0.2396	0.1883± 0.0125	0.7338± 0.0154

Table 3. Comparison Results (mean ± std.) with five baseline MLL Methods on Core5k

Core5k	Training time /s	Testing time /s	Hloss↓	OneError↓	Coverage↓	Rloss↓	AP↑
RAKEL	N/A	N/A	N/A	N/A	N/A	N/A	N/A
IBLR-ML	764.21	24.98	0.0228± 0.0010	0.9356± 0.0116	239.8414± 25.7953	0.3414± 0.0559	0.1084± 0.0136
ML	1230.20	26.39	0.0164± 0.0004	0.7576± 0.0179	178.0430± 11.9325	0.2201± 0.0229	0.1984± 0.0159
ECC	5917.62	21.52	0.0096± 0.0003	0.7594± 0.0214	173.2818± 10.3356	0.2128± 0.0209	0.1974± 0.0184
MLkNN	100.17	39.70	0.0095± 0.0002	0.7804± 0.0322	173.0076± 12.7277	0.2160± 0.0236	0.1932± 0.0209
HashMLL	39.70	19.01	0.0094± 0.0002	0.8000± 0.0140	184.1848± 15.2215	0.2447± 0.0257	0.1764± 0.0108

Table 4. Comparison Results (mean ± std.) with five baseline MLL Methods on Mediamill

Mediamill	Training time /s	Testing time /s	Hloss↓	OneError↓	Coverage↓	Rloss↓	AP↑
RAKEL	N/A	N/A	N/A	N/A	N/A	N/A	N/A
IBLR-ML	959.58	194.22	0.0314± 0.0012	0.1743± 0.0057	18.0373± 0.3333	0.0504± 0.0007	0.7072± 0.0009
ML	2381.61	313.71	0.0441± 0.0028	0.4706± 0.0053	55.2502± 0.7985	0.1964± 0.0029	0.5203± 0.0023
ECC	13239.88	411.14	0.0305± 0.0009	0.1631± 0.0064	19.5700± 0.5440	0.0548± 0.0012	0.7098± 0.0029
MLkNN	275.35	146.82	0.0311± 0.0010	0.1749± 0.0059	18.6808± 0.3068	0.0526± 0.0008	0.7028± 0.0011
HashMLL	323.22	246.33	0.0343± 0.0014	0.2311± 0.0197	22.6811± 0.8423	0.0714± 0.0033	0.6425± 0.0097

Table 5. Comparison Results (mean ± std.) with five baseline MLL Methods on NUS-WIDE

NUS-WIDE	Training time /s	Testing time /s	Hloss↓	OneError↓	Coverage↓	Rloss↓	AP↑
RAKEL	N/A	N/A	N/A	N/A	N/A	N/A	N/A
IBLR-ML	N/A	N/A	N/A	N/A	N/A	N/A	N/A
ML	N/A	N/A	N/A	N/A	N/A	N/A	N/A
ECC	N/A	N/A	N/A	N/A	N/A	N/A	N/A
MLkNN	N/A	N/A	N/A	N/A	N/A	N/A	N/A
HashMLL	53.95	39.25	0.0228± 0.0002	0.7075± 0.0088	21.0761± 1.5469	0.1209± 0.0078	0.3741± 0.0044

Table 6. Comparison Results   with five baseline MLL Methods on Flickr

Flickr	Training time /s	Testing time /s	Hloss↓	OneError↓	Coverage↓	Rloss↓	AP↑
RAKEL	N/A	N/A	N/A	N/A	N/A	N/A	N/A
IBLR-ML	N/A	N/A	N/A	N/A	N/A	N/A	N/A
ML	N/A	N/A	N/A	N/A	N/A	N/A	N/A
ECC	N/A	N/A	N/A	N/A	N/A	N/A	N/A
MLkNN	N/A	N/A	N/A	N/A	N/A	N/A	N/A
HashMLL	10060	13206	0.0114	0.8922	905.2195	0.3798	0.0713

3.3   Efficiency Comparison

In Table 2 - Table 6, it can be seen that HashMLL outperforms the five baseline algorithms in terms of time either in the training or in the testing, except the smallest data set Yeast. On the other hand, the three algorithms IBLR-ML, ML and ECC which exploit label dependency takes more time than the two algorithms without using label dependency, RAkEL and MLkNN, both in training and in testing. Our proposed algorithm HashMLL costs the least time despite exploiting label dependency.

We did two extra experiment to validate the complexity HashMLL with the number of nearest neighbors of labels. The results are recorded in from Figure 2 to Figure 4. The 3 algorithms RAKEL, IBLR-ML and ECC didn't work on the Flickr dataset when the number of instances is more than 5000, so Figure 4 only show the other 3 algorithms, MLkNN, ML and HashMLL. It can be seen that HashMLL runs about dozen times faster both in training and in testing than the baseline algorithms for both Nus-wide and Flick data sets. Furthermore, HashMLL increases slowest than the baseline algorithms with the rising of the number of the instances. Another results are recorded in from Figure 5, it can be seen that the training time of HashMLL is almost unchanged with the rising of the number k_{label} and the testing time of HashMLL grows linearly with the rising of the number k_{label} .

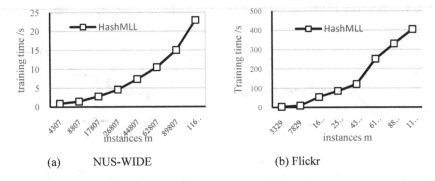

(a)   NUS-WIDE   (b) Flickr

Fig. 2. Training time of HashMLL on the NUS-WIDE and Flickr dataset with varying instances

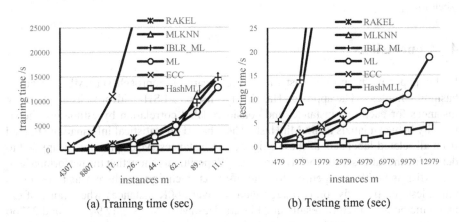

(a) Training time (sec)   (b) Testing time (sec)

Fig. 3. Comparison of Training and Testing time with five baseline MLL Methods on the NUS-WIDE dataset with varying instances

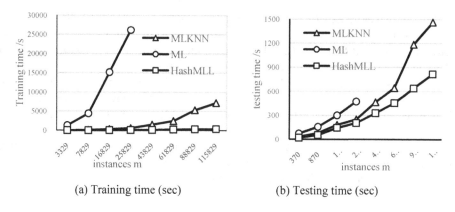

(a) Training time (sec)   (b) Testing time (sec)

Fig. 4. Comparison of training and testing time on the Flickr dataset with varying instances

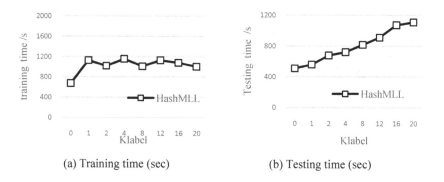

(a) Training time (sec)   (b) Testing time (sec)

Fig. 5. Training and testing time of HashMLL on the Flickr dataset with varying neighbor size of labels k_{label}

4   Conclusions

In this paper we propose a Fast Multi-label Learning approach HashMLL based on hashing schemes. The approach HashMLL relies on a LSH to identify its neighboring instances for each test instance, and considers label correlation by estimating the similarity between labels using MinHash. Then, based on statistical information attained from all related label sets of these neighboring instances, MAP principle is applied to determine the label set for each test instance. Experiments show that the performance of HashMLL is highly competitive to state-of-the-art techniques, whereas its time cost is much less. Particularly, on two large data set over 200K instances where none of existing methods can return results in 24 hours, HashMLL takes only 94 secs and 23266 secs. In the future, we will try to study larger scale problems and automatically learn and exploit multi-label correlations.

Acknowledgments. This research was supported by the National Science Foundation of China (61203289, 61071092, and 61205057), China Postdoctoral Science Foundation (20110490129, 2013T60523), Natural Science Foundation of the Higher Education Institutions of Jiangsu Province, China (12KJB520010), Huawei Company Innovation Research Program (YB2014010003) and the Key University Science Research Project of Jiangsu Province under Grant (14KJA510003). The authors want to thank Prof. Rong Jin of Michigan State University and Miao Xu of LAMDA group of Nanjing University for sharing their dataset and helpful comments.

References

1. Tsoumakas, G., Katakis, I.: Multi-label classification: An overview. International Journal of Data Warehousing and Mining (IJDWM) **3**, 1–13 (2007)
2. Boutell, M.R., Luo, J., Shen, X., Brown, C.M.: Learning multi-label scene classification. Pattern recognition **37**, 1757–1771 (2004)
3. Tsoumakas, G., Vlahavas, I.P.: Random k-labelsets: an ensemble method for multilabel classification. In: Kok, J.N., Koronacki, J., Lopez de Mantaras, R., Matwin, S., Mladenič, D., Skowron, A. (eds.) ECML 2007. LNCS (LNAI), vol. 4701, pp. 406–417. Springer, Heidelberg (2007)
4. Read, J.: A pruned problem transformation method for multi-label classification. In: Proc. 2008 New Zealand Computer Science Research Student Conference (NZCSRS), pp. 143–150 (2008)
5. Fürnkranz, J., Hüllermeier, E., Mencía, E.L., Brinker, K.: Multilabel classification via calibrated label ranking. Machine Learning **73**, 133–153 (2008)
6. Read, J., Pfahringer, B., Holmes, G., Frank, E.: Classifier chains for multi-label classification. Machine Learning **85**, 333–359 (2011)
7. Vens, C., Struyf, J., Schietgat, E., Blockeel, H.: Decision trees for hierarchical multi-label classification. Machine Learning **73**, 185–214 (2008)
8. Zhang, M.-L., Zhou, Z.-H.: ML-KNN: A lazy learning approach to multi-label learning. Pattern Recognition **40**, 2038–2048 (2007)
9. Elisseeff, A., Weston, J.: A Kernel Method for Multi-Labelled Classification. Advances in Neural Information Processing Systems **14**, 681–687 (2001)
10. Zhang, M.-L., Zhang, K.: Multi-label learning by exploiting label dependency. In: Proceedings of the 16th ACM SIGKDD International Conference on Knowledge Discovery and Data Mining, pp. 999–1008 (2010)
11. Guo, Y., Gu, S.: Multi-label classification using conditional dependency networks. In: IJCAI Proceedings-International Joint Conference on Artificial Intelligence, p. 1300 (2011)
12. Datar, M., Immorlica, N., Indyk, P., Mirrokni, V.S.: Locality-sensitive hashing scheme based on p-stable distributions. In: Proceedings of the Twentieth Annual Symposium on Computational Geometry, pp. 253–262 (2004)
13. Indyk, P., Motwani, R.: Approximate nearest neighbors: towards removing the curse of dimensionality. In: STOC 1998, Dallas, TX, vol. 52, pp. 604–613 (1998)
14. Gionis, A., Indyk, P., Motwani, R.: Similarity search in high dimensions via hashing. In: Proceedings of the 25th International Conference on Very Large Databases, pp. 518–529 (2000)
15. Broder, A.: On the resemblance and containment of documents. In: Compression & Complexity of Sequences Proceedings, pp. 21–29 (1997)

16. Duygulu, P., Barnard, K., de Freitas, J.F.G., Forsyth, D.: Object recognition as machine translation: learning a Lexicon for a fixed image vocabulary. In: Heyden, A., Sparr, G., Nielsen, M., Johansen, P. (eds.) ECCV 2002, Part IV. LNCS, vol. 2353, pp. 97–112. Springer, Heidelberg (2002)

17. Snoek, C.G.M., Worring, M., Gemert, J.C.V., Geusebroek, J.M., Smeulders, A.W.M.: The challenge problem for automated detection of 101 semantic concepts in multimedia. In: Proceedings of the ACM International Conference on Multimedia, pp. 421–430 (2006)

18. Chua, T.S., Tang, J., Hong, R., Li, H., Luo, Z., Zheng, Y.: NUS-WIDE: a real-world web image database from national university of Singapore. In: CIVR (2009)

19. Tang, L., Liu, H.: Relational learning via latent social dimensions. In: KDD Proceedings of ACM SIGKDD International Conference on Knowledge Discovery & Data, pp. 817–826 (2009)

20. Cheng, W., Hüllermeier, E.: Combining instance-based learning and logistic regression for multilabel classification. Machine Learning 76, 211–225 (2009)

21. Tang, L., Rajan, S., Narayanan, V.K.: Large scale multi-label classification via metalabeler. In: Proceedings of the 18th International Conference on World Wide Web, pp. 211–220 (2009)

22. Tsoumakas, G., Spyromitros-Xioufis, E., Vilcek, J., Vlahavas, I.: Mulan: A java library for multi-label learning. The Journal of Machine Learning Research 12, 2411–2414 (2011)

23. Zhang, M.L., Zhou, Z.H.: A Review on Multi-Label Learning Algorithms. IEEE Transactions on Knowledge & Data Engineering 26, 1 (2014)

Building Program Vector Representations for Deep Learning

Hao Peng, Lili Mou, Ge Li[✉], Yuxuan Liu, Lu Zhang, and Zhi Jin

Software Institute, School of EECS, Peking University Beijing, Beijing 100871,
People's Republic of China
{penghao.pku,doublepower.mou,liuyuxuan}@gmail.com,
{lige,zhanglu,zhijin}@sei.pku.edu.cn

Abstract. Deep learning has made significant breakthroughs in various
fields of artificial intelligence. However, it is still virtually impossible to
use deep learning to analyze programs since deep architectures cannot be
trained effectively with pure back propagation. In this pioneering paper,
we propose the "coding criterion" to build program vector representations, which are the premise of deep learning for program analysis. We
evaluate the learned vector representations both qualitatively and quantitatively. We conclude, based on the experiments, the coding criterion is
successful in building program representations. To evaluate whether deep
learning is beneficial for program analysis, we feed the representations to
deep neural networks, and achieve higher accuracy in the program classification task than "shallow" methods. This result confirms the feasibility
of deep learning to analyze programs.

1 Introduction

Machine learning-based program analysis has been studied long in the literature
[14,3]. Hindle et al. compare programming languages to natural languages and
conclude that programs have rich statistical properties [10]. These properties are
difficult for human to capture, but they justify using learning-based approaches
to analyze programs.

The deep neural network has become one of the prevailing machine learning
approaches since 2006 [11]. It has made significant breakthroughs in a variety of
fields, such as natural language processing [6,19], image processing [12,4], speech
recognition [7,15], etc. Such striking results raise the interest of its applications
in the field of program analysis. Using deep learning to automatically capture
program features is an interesting and prospective research area.

Unfortunately, it has been practically infeasible for deep learning to analyze
programs up till now. Since no proper "pretraining" method is proposed for
programs, deep neural networks cannot be trained effectively with pure back
propagation [2,8].

H. Peng and L. Mou—Equal contribution.

© Springer International Publishing Switzerland 2015
S. Zhang et al. (Eds.): KSEM 2015, LNAI 9403, pp. 547–553, 2015.
DOI: 10.1007/978-3-319-25159-2_49

In this paper, we propose novel "coding criterion" to build program vector representations based on abstract syntax trees (ASTs). In such vector representations, each node in ASTs (e.g. ID, Constant) is mapped to a real-valued vector. They can emerge high-level abstract features, and thus benefit ultimate tasks. We analyze the learned representations both qualitatively and quantitatively. We conclude from the experiments that the coding criterion is successful in building program vector representations.

In the rest of this paper, we first we explain our approach in detail in Section 2. Then we give experimental results in Section 3. Last, we draw our conclusion in Section 4.

2   Coding Criterion for Program Representation Learning

In this section, we first discuss the granularities of program representation. We settle for the granularity of nodes in abstract syntax trees (ASTs). In Subsection 2.2, we formalize our approach and give the learning objective. In Subsection 2.3, we present the stochastic gradient descent algorithm for training.

2.1   The Granularity

Vector representations map a symbol to a real-valued vector. Possible granularities of the symbol include character-level, token-level, etc.

- **Character-level.** Treating each character as a symol. Although some research explore character-level modeling for NLP [20], it is improper for programming languages. For example, the token double in a C code refers to a data type. But if one writes doubles, it is an identifier (e.g., a function name).
- **Token-level.** Learning the representations of all tokens, including types and identifiers etc. Since programmers can declare their own identifiers in their source codes, e.g., func1, func2, many of the identifiers may appear only a few times, resulting in the undesired data sparseness. Hence, it is improper for representation learning at this level.
- **Nodes in ASTs.** Learning the representations for nodes in ASTs, e.g., FuncDef, ID, Constant. The AST is more compressed compared with token-level representation. Furthermore, there are only finite many types of nodes in ASTs. The tree structural nature of ASTs also provides opportunities to capture structural information of programs. This level is also used in traditional program analysis like code clone detection [1,13], vulnerability extrapolation [21], etc.
- **Statement-level, function-level or higher.** Theoretically, a statement, a function or even a program can also be mapped to a real-valued vector. However, such representations cannot be trained directly. A possible approach of modeling such complex stuff is by composition. Such researches in NLP is often referred to as *compositional semantics* [18]. It is very hard to capture the precise semantics; the "semantic barrier" is still not overcome.

2.2   Formalization

The basic criterion of representation learning is that similar symbols should have similar representations. Further, symbols that are similar in some aspects should have similar values in corresponding feature dimensions.

In our scenario, similarity is defined based on the following intuition: similar symbols have similar usages: both ID and Constant can be an operand of a binary operator; both For and While are a block of codes, etc.

We denote the vector of node x as $\text{vec}(x)$. $\text{vec}(\cdot) \in \mathbb{R}^{N_f}$, where N_f is the dimension of features. For each non-leaf node p in ASTs and its direct children $c_1, \cdots, c_n$, their representations are $\text{vec}(p), \text{vec}(c_1), \cdots, \text{vec}(c_n)$. The primary objective is that

$$\text{vec}(p) \approx \tanh\left(\sum_{i=1}^{n} l_i W_i \cdot \text{vec}(c_i) + \boldsymbol{b}\right) \tag{1}$$

where $W_i \in \mathbb{R}^{N_f \times N_f}$ is the weight matrix for node c_i; $\boldsymbol{b} \in \mathbb{R}^{N_f}$ is the bias term. The weights (W_i's) are weighted by the number of leaves under c_i and the coefficients are

$$l_i = \frac{\#\text{leaves under } c_i}{\#\text{leaves under } p} \tag{2}$$

Since different nodes in ASTs may have different numbers of children, the number of W_i's is hard to determine. To solve this problem, we propose continuous binary tree, where there are two weight matrices as parameters, namely W_l and W_r. Any weight W_i is a linear combination of the two matrices. That is, regardless the number of children, we treat it as a "binary" tree. Formally, if p has n ($n \geq 2$) children, then for child c_i,

$$W_i = \frac{n-i}{n-1} W_l + \frac{i-1}{n-1} W_r \tag{3}$$

Now that we are able to calculate the weight W_i for each node, we measure closeness by the square of Euclidean distance, as below:

$$d = \left\| \text{vec}(p) - \tanh\left(\sum_{i=1}^{n} l_i W_i \cdot \text{vec}(c_i) + \boldsymbol{b}\right) \right\|_2^2 \tag{4}$$

We applied negative sampling [5,18,17]: for each data sample x, a new negative sample x_c is generated. We randomly select a symbol in each training sample and substitute it with a different random symbol. The objective is that d_c should be at least as large as $d + \Delta$, where Δ is the margin and often set to 1. The error function of training sample $x^{(i)}$ and its negative sample $x_c^{(i)}$ is then

$$J(d^{(i)}, d_c^{(i)}) = \max\left\{0, \Delta + d^{(i)} - d_c^{(i)}\right\} \tag{5}$$

To prevent our model from over-fitting, we can add ℓ_2 regularization to weights (W_l and W_r). The overall training objective is then

$$\underset{W_l, W_r, b}{\text{minimize}} \; \frac{1}{2N} \sum_{i=1}^{N} J(d^{(i)}, d_c^{(i)}) + \frac{\lambda}{2M} \left(\| W_l \|_F^2 + \| W_r \|_F^2 \right) \qquad (6)$$

where N is the number of training samples; $M = 2N_f^2$ denotes the number of weights; $\| \cdot \|_F$ refers to Frobenius norm; λ is the hyperparameter that strikes the balance between coding error and ℓ_2 penalty.

2.3 Training

The numerical optimization algorithm we use is stochastic gradient descent with momentum. The model parameters $\Theta = \left(\text{vec}(\cdot), W_l, W_r, b \right)$ are first initialized randomly. Then, for each data sample $x^{(i)}$ and its negative sample $x_c^{(i)}$, we compute the cost function according to Formula 6. Back propagation algorithm is then applied to compute the partial derivatives and the parameters are updated accordingly. This process is looped until convergence. The coding criterion of vector representation learning—as a pretraining phase for neural program analysis—is "shallow," through which error can back propagate. Thus, useful features are learned for AST nodes.

To speed up training, we adopt the momentum method, where the partial derivatives of the last iteration is added to the current ones with decay ϵ.

3   Experiments

We first evaluate our learned representations by k-means clustering. We then perform supervised learning in the program classification task. The experimental results show that meaningful representations, as a means of pretraining, make the network much easier to train in deep architectures. We also achieve higher accuracy with the deep, tree-based convolutional neural network compared with baseline methods.

3.1   Qualitative Evaluation: k-means Clustering

As we have stated, similar nodes in ASTs (like ID, Constant) should have similar representations. To evaluate whether our coding criterion has accomplished this goal, we perform k-means clustering, where k is set to 3. The result is shown in Table 1. As we see, almost all the symbols in Cluster 1 are related to data reference/manipulating. Cluster 2 is mainly about declarations. Cluster 3 contains more symbols, the majority of which are related to control flow. This result confirms our conjecture that similar symbols can be clustered into groups with the distributed vector representations that are learned by our approach.

Table 1. The result of k-means clustering. k is set to 3.

Cluster	Sybmols
1	UnaryOp, FuncCall, Assignment, ExprList, StructRef, BinaryOp, ID, Constant, ArrayRef
2	FuncDef, TypeDecl, FuncDecl, Compound, ArrayDecl, PtrDecl, Decl, Root
3	Typedef, Struct, For, Union, CompoundLiteral, TernaryOp, Label, InitList, IdentifierType, Return, Enum, Break, DoWhile, Case, DeclList, Default, While, Continue, ParamList, Enumerator, Typename, Goto, Cast, Switch, EmptyStatement, EnumeratorList, If

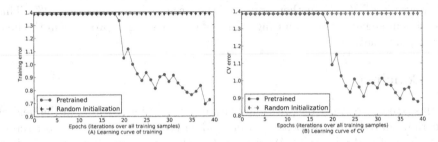

Fig. 1. Learning curves of training (A) and CV (B). The learned program vector representations improve supervised learning in terms of both generalization and optimization.

3.2   Quantitative Evaluation: Improvement for Supervised Learning

We now evaluate whether building program vector representations is beneficial for real-world tasks, i.e., whether they will improve optimization and/or generalization for supervised learning of interest.

The dataset comes from an online Open Judge system[1], which contains a large number of programming problems for students. We select four problems for our program classification task. Source codes (in C programming language) of the four problems are downloaded along with their labels (problem IDs). We split the dataset by $3 : 1 : 1$ for training, cross-validating (CV) and testing.

Since no effective program representation existed before, the TBCNN [16] model is not trained efficiently, as the blue curve demonstrates in Part A of Figure 1.

If the vector representations and the coding parameters, namely vec($\cdot$), W_l, W_r and b, are initialized as are learned by our coding criterion, the training and CV errors decrease drastically (the red and magenta curves) after a plateaux of about 15 epochs, which leads to the high performance of TBCNN.

To evaluate whether deep learning may be helpful for program analysis, we compare TBCNN to baseline methods in the program classification task. In these baseline methods, we adopt the bag-of-words model, which is a widely-used approach in text classification [9]. As shown in Table 2, logistic regression, as a

---

[1] http://programming.grids.cn/

Table 2. Accuracy of Program Classification.

Method	Accuracy
Random guess	25.00%
Logistic regression	81.16%
SVM with RBF kernel	91.14%
TBCNN (a deep learning approach)	**95.33%**

linear classifier, achieves 81.16% accuracy. The support vector machine (SVM) with radial basis function (RBF) kernel explores non-linearity, and improves the result by 10%. By automatically exploring the underlying features and patterns of programs, TBCNN further improves the accuracy by more than 4%. This experiment suggests the promising future of deep leaning approaches in the field of program analysis.

4   Conclusion

In this paper, we study deep learning and representation learning in the field of program analysis. We propose a novel "coding criterion" to build vector representations of nodes in ASTs. We also feed the learned representations to a deep neural network to classify programs. The experimental results show that our representations successfully capture the similarity and relationships among different nodes in ASTs. We conclude that the coding criterion is successful in building program vector representations. The experiments also confirm the feasibility of deep learning to analyze programs.

Acknowledgments. This research is supported by the National Basic Research Program of China (the 973 Program) under Grant No. 2015CB352201 and the National Natural Science Foundation of China under Grant No. 61232015.

References

1. Baxter, I., Yahin, A., Moura, L., Sant'Anna, M., Bier, L.: Clone detection using abstract syntax trees. In: Proceedings of the International Conference on Software Maintenance (1998)
2. Bengio, Y., Lamblin, P., Popovici, D., Larochelle, H.: Greedy layer-wise training of deep networks. In: Advances in Neural Information Processing Systems (2007)
3. Canavera, K., Esfahani, N., Malek, S.: Mining the execution history of a software system to infer the best time for its adaptation. In: Proceedings of the ACM SIG-SOFT 20th International Symposium on the Foundations of Software Engineering (2012)
4. Ciresan, D., Meier, U., Schmidhuber, J.: Multi-column deep neural networks for image classification. In: IEEE Conference on Computer Vision and Pattern Recognition (2012)
5. Collobert, R., Weston, J.: A unified architecture for natural language processing: deep neural networks with multitask learning. In: Proceedings of the 25th International Conference on Machine Learning (2008)

6. Collobert, R., Weston, J., Bottou, L., Karlen, M., Kavukcuoglu, K., Kuksa, P.: Natural language processing (almost) from scratch. The Journal of Machine Learning Research **12**, 2493–2537 (2011)
7. Dahl, G., Mohamed, A., Hinton, G.E.: Phone recognition with the mean-covariance restricted Boltzmann machine. In: Advances in Neural Information Processing Systems (2010)
8. Erhan, D., Manzagol, P., Bengio, Y., Bengio, S., Vincent, P.: The difficulty of training deep architectures and the effect of unsupervised pre-training. In: Proceedings of International Conference on Artificial Intelligence and Statistics (2009)
9. Feldman, R., Sanger, J.: The Text Mining Handbook: Advanced Approaches in Analyzing Unstructured Data. Cambridge University Press (2007)
10. Hindle, A., Barr, E., Su, Z., Gabel, M., Devanbu, P.: On the naturalness of software. In: Proceedings of 34th International Conference on Software Engineering (2012)
11. Hinton, G., Osindero, S., Teh, Y.: A fast learning algorithm for deep belief nets. Neural Computation **18**(7), 1527–1554 (2006)
12. Krizhevsky, A., Sutskever, I., Hinton, G.: ImageNet classification with deep convolutional neural networks. In: Advances in Neural Information Processing Systems (2012)
13. Lazar, F., Banias, O.: Clone detection algorithm based on the abstract syntax tree approach. In: Proceedings of 9th IEEE International Symposium on Applied Computational Intelligence and Informatic (2014)
14. Lu, H., Cukic, B., Culp, M.: Software defect prediction using semi-supervised learning with dimension reduction. In: Proceedings of the 27th IEEE/ACM International Conference on Automated Software Engineering (2012)
15. Mohamed, A., Dahl, G., Hinton, G.: Acoustic modeling using deep belief networks. IEEE Transactions on Audio, Speech, and Language Processing **20**(1), 14–22 (2012)
16. Mou, L., Peng, H., Li, G., Xu, Y., Zhang, L., Jin, Z.: Tree-based convolution: a new neural architecture for sentence modeling (2015). CoRR abs/1504.01106. http://arxiv.org/abs/1504.01106
17. Socher, R., Chen, D., Manning, C., Ng, A.: Reasoning with neural tensor networks for knowledge base completion. In: Advances in Neural Information Processing Systems (2013)
18. Socher, R., Le, Q., Manning, C., Ng, A.: Grounded compositional semantics for finding and describing images with sentences. In: NIPS Deep Learning Workshop (2013)
19. Socher, R., Perelygin, A., Wu, J., Chuang, J., Manning, C., Ng, A., Potts, C.: Recursive deep models for semantic compositionality over a sentiment treebank. In: Proceedings of Conference on Empirical Methods in Natural Language Processing (2013)
20. Sutskever, I., Martens, J., Hinton, G.: Generating text with recurrent neural networks. In: Proceedings of the 28th International Conference on Machine Learning (2011)
21. Yamaguchi, F., Lottmann, M., Rieck, K.: Generalized vulnerability extrapolation using abstract syntax trees. In: Proceedings of 28th Annual Computer Security Applications Conference (2012)

The Use of k-Means Algorithm to Improve Kernel Method via Instance Selection

Lulu Wang[(⊠)]

Department of Computer Science and Technology,
JiLin University, Changchun 130012, China
naruto7@icloud.com

Abstract. The kernel method is well known for its success in solving the curse of dimension of linearly inseparable problems. But as an instance-based learning algorithm it suffers from high memory requirement and low efficiency in that it needs to store all of the training instances. And when there are noisy instances classification accuracy can suffer. In this paper we present an approach to alleviate both of the problems mentioned above by using k-means algorithm to select only k representativeness instances of the training data. And we view the selected k instances as the new data set, where the choice of the value of k is influenced by the size and the character of the data set. It turn out that with a carefully selected k we can still get a good performance while the number of the instances stored are greatly decreased.

Keywords: k-means · Instance selection · Kernel method

1 Introduction

There are mainly two kinds of problems in supervised learning: regression problem and classification problem, and until now we have many successful algorithms to solve different kinds of problems [1]. These algorithms can be classified into two kinds, one of which is parameter-based learning algorithm and the other is instance-based learning algorithm.

For the parameter-based learning algorithm, we use the training instances to train our model, usually by applying some methods (such as gradient descent) to change the parameter of the model until reaching a local or global minima of the cost function, and then we get the target parameter of the model. After that we don not need the instance any more so the model is light and of lower cost in predicting the value or the class of a new instance. And by now, most of the supervised learning algorithm is parameter-based (such as logistic regression, decision tree and so on).

However, there are some algorithms that are instance-based which means that the algorithm need to store all of the training instances and use these instances to predict a new input. Unfortunately these algorithms are limited by its high requirement for memory and low speed in computation especially in large scale problem [5]. And the kernel method is one of the instance-based approach.

© Springer International Publishing Switzerland 2015
S. Zhang et al. (Eds.): KSEM 2015, LNAI 9403, pp. 554–559, 2015.
DOI: 10.1007/978-3-319-25159-2_50

The kernel method is successfully used in some learning algorithms such as SVM, however it also suffers from the problems mentioned above. Motivated by that we study how to improve the kernel method and in this paper we provide a simple way to achieve this goal. We use the k-means algorithm to select just a small part of the instances to train the model. We run the k-means algorithm on our training set and separate the training set into k parts, then we make a statistic on the label of the instances in every part individually and use the cluster centroid as a new instance and the most appeared label in that cluster as its label, then we get the new training set with only k instances. And since the new training set is much smaller, the algorithm do not need as much memory as before and can also run much faster. While running the k-means we have ignored the noisy instances in choosing the new label and the new instance thus this approach will also increase the robustness of the kernel method.

There is still a problem before we can run the k-means algorithm, that is the choice of k. Intuitively, the larger the k is the more accuracy the result is but the more memory and time the algorithm needs, because in running the k-means algorithm we will lose some information of the data set which will result in the decrease of the accuracy. So we need to get a compromise between the accuracy and the cost of the algorithm. In practice (just as how we choose a proper dimension when we use PCA to decrease the dimension of our data), we can choose a k that decrease the accuracy within our tolerance (for example 1% loss of the accuracy or even 5% loss of the accuracy).

2 Problem Formalism

In supervised learning problem, we are given a set of labeled training data of m instances $\{(x^{(i)}, y^{(i)}) | i = 1, 2, 3, ..., m\}$. Here each $x^{(i)} \in R^n$ is an n dimensional feature vector, for classification problem, $y^{(i)} \in \{1, 2, ..., C\}$ is the corresponding class label (for regression problem $y^{(i)} \in R$). In general kernel method algorithm we need all of the m instance, but here we will use the k-means algorithm to select only k new instances $\{(x_n^{(i)}, y_n^{(i)}) | i = 1, 2, 3, ..., k\}$ (the subscript n indicates that it is a instance from the new data set) to replace the m original set and here k should be smaller than m. Finally we use this new data set to train our model.

3 Algorithm

Kernel method can be used in many different models, such as SVM, logistic regression, etc.in this paper we describe just one example of how to use the algorithm. We will use the Gaussian kernel SVM as our training model to demonstrate our method.

3.1 Instance Selection

In this section, we will give the detail steps of how to get the labeled data set $\{(x_n^{(i)}, y_n^{(i)}) | i = 1, 2, 3, ..., k\}$ from the larger original data set $\{(x^{(i)}, y^{(i)}) | i = 1, 2, 3, ..., m\}$. We will apply k-means to finish this task, and we will use the

Euclidian distance to describe the similarity between two instances. Before we run the k-means algorithm we need to choose different value of k. And then we need to randomly choose k instances from the original data set $\{x^{(1)}, x^{(2)}, ..., x^{(m)}\}$ (here we temporally ignore the label of each $x^{(i)}$) as the initial value of the k centroids $\{x_n^{(1)}, x_n^{(2)}, ..., x_n^{(k)}\}$. After that we run the k-means algorithm until the partition of the data set dose not change. After that, we got k clusters of instances and k centroids $\{x_n^{(1)}, x_n^{(2)}, ..., x_n^{(k)}\}$. Then use the label appears most in a cluster as the label for the corresponding centroid, and view the k centroids and its label as the new training set of the problem.

3.2   Training the Model

Kernel SVM is a variation of SVM. SVM is well known for its good property: it can create a hyperplane with a maximum margin between different labeled data set. In some cases when the data set is linearly inseparable we need to project the input feature to a higher dimensional feature in Hilbert space. However as the dimension of the input feature increases the dimension of the projected feature will increase exponentially. Under this case, we can use the kernel SVM to solve this problem. Generally, kernel SVM is a linear combination of the kernel function $\sigma(x, x^{(i)})$ for each input $x^{(i)}$. It successfully solved the dimensional explosion, but there also exist some drawbacks as we have already mentioned. In our previous work we get a training set with much smaller number of instances than the original big one, and use it to train our kernel SVM. Now we will give the following algorithm to illustrate the whole process.

Algorithm: instance selection and model training

```
Input: The original data set x[1]...x[n], y[1]...y[n] and k.
1. Running the k-means algorithm to get k clusters from
   the original training set.
2. Label each cluster with the mostly appeared label
   in that cluster.
3. Construct a new instance set nx[1]...nx[k],
   ny[1]...ny[k], use the k clusters centroid and its label.
4. Use the new instance to train a kernel SVM.
Output: A improved kernel SVM.
```

3.3   Experiments

In our experiments we trained a SVM with Gaussion kernel:

$$K(x, z) = \exp(-\frac{\|x - z\|^2}{2\sigma^2})$$

Table 1. The description of the data set used for the experiment.

data set	attributes	training set size	test set size	classes
A small data set	2	2589	500	2
Skin Segmentation Data Set	3	24500	4500	2

Table 2. The result of the first experiment when $k = m, k = 0.2m, k = 0.1m$ and $k = 0.05m$.

the value of k	$k = m$	$k = 0.2 * m$	$k = 0.1 * m$	$k = 0.05 * m$
accuracy of test set	96.93%	95.92%	**95.85%**	93.93%
training time	37.82s	3.46s	**2.09s**	0.74s
memory requirements	60.68kb	12.14kb	**6.07kb**	3.05kb

and we set the standard SVM regularization parameter $C = 1$, and $\sigma = 0.1$. We apply the model to two learning tasks: A small data set [1] and The Skin Segmentation Data Set [2] which was shown in Table 1. We did the experiments in a computer with a 2.5GHz Intel Core i5 CPU, a 4GB 1600 MHz memory and the operation system is MacOS.

In the following two experiments we use the Gaussian kernel SVM as our classifier (the detail of the parameters are mentioned above), and to make the result more intuitionist, we choose the small data set as our first task which has only two attributes and two classes. We choose different k ($k = m$,$k = 0.2m$, $k = 0.1m$ and $k = 0.05m$) when we running the k-means algorithm to get our new instances, and we plotted the new data sets for different k as well as the original dataset in Fig.1. According to the result, we can find that the k-means algorithm works with good performance in generating the new data set, and intuitively we can find that the distribution of the new data set is almost the same with the original data set, thus we can assume that the new data set can also work well in training our model as the original data set. To prove this hypothesis we trained a Gaussian kernel SVM for each new data set as well as the original data set and the result was shown in Table 2. We can learning from the result that we can still get a accuracy of 95.85% with only 10 percent of the size of the original data set when we choose $k = 0.1m$.

In our second experiment we will use a larger data set: The Skin Segmentation Data Set, which contains much more instances than the previous one. In this experiment we will choose different k ($k = m$,$k = 0.1m$, $k = 0.01m$ and $k = 0.005m$) then we running the k-means algorithm to get our new instances individually. After that we got 4 different data sets and we use these data sets to train a Gaussian kernel SVM the same as the first experiment individually and use the test set to get the accuracy for each SVM. The experiment result was shown in Table 3. As the first experiment, the result is also acceptable. Here we

---

[1] This data set comes from the experiment of Andrew Ngs Machine learning class.
[2] This data set comes from: archive.ics.uci.edu/ml/datasets/Skin+Segmentation but we only use a part of it

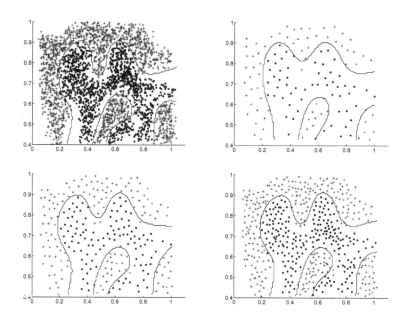

Fig. 1. The 2 pictures in the first row is the result of the first experiment where $k = m$ and $k = 0.2m$, and the 2 pictures in the second row is the result of the first experiment where $k = 0.1m$ and $k = 0.05m$.

Table 3. The result of the second experiment when $k = m, k = 0.1m, k = 0.01m$ and $k = 0.005m$.

the value of k	$k = m$	$k = 0.1 * m$	$k = 0.01 * m$	$k = 0.005 * m$
accuracy of test set	99.47%	**97.25%**	85.56%	82.11%
training time	1543.8s	**7.2s**	0.62s	0.27s
memory requirements	765.81kb	**76.59kb**	7.69kb	3.84kb

can also choose $k = 0.1 * m$ to get the accuracy of 97.25% which is only 2.22% lower than the result of the original data set.

3.4   Discussion

In this paper we provide a method that can alleviate the problem caused by the kernel method when the training instances are too many. We use k-means algorithm to divide the training set into k different clusters and label each cluster according to the instances of the cluster. We use kernel SVM to test our algorithm and the result turns to be fairly good. From the Fig.1 we can see that the instance selection process works and it generate a new data set that have a similar distribution with the original data set. In our experiments we choose different k to get different data set, and in both experiment we can get a good result if we choose $k = 0.1m$. Generally we can not say that for every data set

$k = 0.1*m$ will always get a good result, because k is influenced by the characters of the data set. Therefore we need to choose different k and use the test set to get the perfomance of the corresponding classifier, and as we can see from the result of the experiments, we will lose some of the accuracy if k is lower than m, and the smaller the k is the lower the accuracy is. That is easy to explain: during the instance selection we loss some of the information of data set. So one of the most important thing we need to think about when use this method in practice is to make a balance between the lose of accuracy and the size of the new data set.

However there are still two problems need to be solved: the high cost of the k-means and how to generate good clusters. For the first problem we can solve it by setting a max iteration times instead of repeating until converging. For the second problem we can repeat the k-means several times (for example 10 times), and each time select k random instances to initialize the centroids and use the Distortion function[3]:

$$D(x^{(1)}, x^{(2)}, ..., x^{(m)}) = \sum_{i=1}^{m} \left\| x^{(i)} - x_n^{(ci)} \right\|^2$$

to compute the total distance between each instance and its centroid, after that select the clusters with the minima value of the distortion function so that we can greatly reduce the possibility of bad clusters.

At last, to generalize our approach we may need to use different distance (in this paper we use Euclidian distance) to calculate the similarity in the k-means algorithm and different kernel function for different problem.

References

1. Wu, X.: Top 10 algorithms in data mining. Knowledge and Information Systems **14**(1), 1–37 (2008)
2. Shawe-Taylor, J., Cristianini, N.: Kernel Methods for Pattern Analysis. Cambridge University Press (2004)
3. Gretton, A., et al.: A kernel method for the two-sample-problem. In: Advances in Neural Information Processing Systems (2006)
4. Brighton, H., Mellish, C.: Advances in instance selection for instance-based learning algorithms. Data Mining and Knowledge Discovery **6**(2), 153–172 (2002)
5. Aha, D.W., Kibler, D., Albert, M.K.: Instance-based learning algorithms. Machine Learning **6**(1), 37–66 (1991)
6. Lange, T., Buhmann, J.M.: Fusion of similarity data in clustering. In: Proceeding of Advances in Neural Information Processing Systems (2005)
7. Zavrel, J., Daelemans, W.: Memory-based learning: using similarity for smoothing. In: Proceedings of the Eighth Conference on European Chapter of the Association for Computational Linguistics (1997)

---

[3] In the function $x_n^{(ci)}$ means the centroid for instance $x^{(i)}$.

Detection Methods and Analysis

An Effective Hybrid Fraud Detection Method

Chenfei Sun[1], Qingzhong Li[1]([✉]), Lizhen Cui[1], Zhongmin Yan[1], Hui Li[1],
and Wei Wei[2]

[1] School of Computer Science and Technology,
National Engineering Laboratory for Ecommerce, Shandong University,
Jinan, China
sun.chenfei@163.com, {lqz,clz,yzm,lih}@sdu.edu.cn
[2] Shandong Hoteam Software Co., Ltd., Jinan, China
ww@hoteamsoft.com

Abstract. The rapid growth of data makes it possible for us to study human behavior patterns. Knowing the patterns of human behavior is of great use to help us detect the unusual fraud human behavior. Existing fraud detection methods can be divided into two categories: pattern based and outlier detection based methods. However, because of the sparsity and complex granularity of big data, these methods have high false positive in fraud detection. In this paper, we propose an effective hybrid fraud detection method. We propose SSIsomap which improves isomap to cluster behaviors into behavior classes and propose SimLOF which improves LOF to conduct outlier detection, then we use Dempster-Shafer evidence Theory for combining behavior pattern evidence and outlier evidence, which yields a degree of belief of fraud to the new coming claim. The experiment result shows our method has significantly higher accuracy than exsiting methods in medical insurance fraud detection.

Keywords: Fraud detection · Dempster-Shafer evidence Theory

1 Introduction

Recent years we have witnessed the rapid growth of big data, which makes it possible for us to study human behavior patterns.Knowing the patterns of human behavior is of great use to help us detect the unusual fraud human behavior. Fraud detection methods available can be divided into two categories: behavior pattern based fraud detection and outlier detection[7]. The behavior pattern based fraud detection devotes to find unusual behavior according to the discovered patterns. The outlier detection based fraud detection aims to find unusual records according to statistical information. However, there are challenges which disrupt the accuracy of the existing fraud detection methods.

Supported by the National Natural Science Foundation of China under Grant No.61303005, the Science and Technology Development Plan Project of Shandong Province No. 2014GGX101019 and No. 2014GGX101047, the Fundamental Research Funds of Shandong University No.2014JC025, the National Key Technologies R&D Program No.2012BAH54F02 and No.2012BAH54F04.

S. Zhang et al. (Eds.): KSEM 2015, LNAI 9403, pp. 563–574, 2015.
DOI: 10.1007/978-3-319-25159-2_51

Complex granularity is the biggest challenge for behavior pattern recognition, which results in the curse of cardinality. Complex granularity means that behaviors can be described by a large number of symbols. The granularity of symbols is so fine that some behaviors represented by different symbols may belong to the same class in a more coarse-grained granularity. Due to the curse of cardinality, traditional pattern recognition methods can't find latent patterns that can be found at a more coarse-grained granularity of data and can't be found from the original granularity of data. In general, the support of a specific pattern decreases significantly with the growing cardinality. In other words, the higher the cardinality, the rarer the patterns are.

Example 1. Given three applicants' medical insurance claim records during a hospital stay:

$$A1:(a,d,f); \quad A2:(b,e,h); \quad A3:(c,g,i)$$

For the three sequences above, if we apply pattern mining on the original level of symbols, we can't find any frequent pattern.However, if we can group the symbols in the following way:

$$A=\{a,b,c\}; \quad B=\{d,e,g\}; \quad C=\{f,h,i\}$$

Recode the sequences with the group A,B,C,we can find that (A,B,C) is a frequent (class) pattern with support of 100%.

Data sparsity is the biggest challenge for outlier detection.The outlier detection methods cant work very well and have high false positive rate in big data. So we propose carrying out outlier detection by peer group comparison combined with self comparison for further analysis.

In this paper, we propose an effective hybrid fraud detection method. We combine behavior pattern evidence in a more coarse-grained granularity and outlier evidence in a finer granularity using Dempster-Shafer evidence Theory. The experiment shows that our method has significantly higher accuracy than exsiting fraud detection methods.

Rest of the paper is organized as follows. Section 2 reviews the related work in the problem of fraud detection. Section 3 presents a behavior pattern based fraud detection method. Section 4 introduces an outlier based fraud detection method. Section 5 combines the identified two evidences using Dempster-Shafer evidence Theory. Section 6 provides an empirical study of our algorithm with real medical insurance data. Section 7 concludes our work and discusses several interesting directions.

2   Related Work

Fraud and abuse has resulted in billions of dollars loss every year and posed a major threat to fund security and hampers the implementation of national policy in many countries. Therefore, fraud has become a social problem. Scholars also carried thorough research on fraud detection.

In recent years, numerous statistical methods and systems are proposed to detect fraud. The proposed statistical methods can be classified into two groups: supervised methods and unsupervised methods. Supervised methods require a training dataset in which all cases are labeled by domain experts. Several supervised methods have served to fraud detection, including neural networks (NNs), decision trees, fuzzy logic, and Bayesian networks. Unsupervised methods do not need labeled training set and aims to find outliers in all cases. LOF[14] is a representative density-based algorithm for outlier detection. However, the time complexity of LOF is too high. Supervised methods may be more accurate than unsupervised methods because additional information on dependent variable is employed in the training sample. But the major limitations of supervised methods are as follows: On one hand, it may be difficult or costly to obtain accurate labels for training sample, incorrect labels may lead to misclassification problem; On the other hand, the unbalanced data (fraudulent cases number is too few comparing with legitimate ones) is almost inevitable and requires specific treatment.

Fraud pattern recognition is an important part in fraud detection. Musal [8] proposed use of cluster analysis for geographical analysis of potential fraud. W.-S. Yang and S.-Y. Hwang[9] proposes a data-mining framework that utilizes the concept of clinical pathways to facilitate automatic and systematic construction of an adaptable and extensible detection model, the proposed approaches have been evaluated objectively by a real world data set gathered from the National Health Insurance (NHI) program in Taiwan. Nonetheless, due to the complexity of data, pattern recognition methods cannot find latent patterns which can be found in a more coarse-grained granularity. Manifold learning is proposed for clustering of high dimensional data. Nowadays, there are numerous advanced algorithms for manifold learning, in which many approaches rely on the similarity matrix eigenvalue decomposition to obtain the manifold embedding. For instance, Isomap[15] is a popular method that embed a graph into an Euclidean space. However, isomap is an unsupervised method so that it ignores some existing category information. As a consequence, its clustering effect is not ideal enough in most situations.

As mentioned above, existing fraud detection methods are not adaptive in big data. So we focus on overcoming the challenges of data sparsity and complex granularity in fraud detection of big data.

3   Behavior Pattern Based Fraud Detection

3.1   Problem Formalization

Definition 1 (Behavior) *the way a person acts or behaves at some point. Behavior can be represented as a triple b={subject, action, time}. subject is the person who conducts the behavior, action depicts the content of the behavior such as taking a drug or treatment, time represents the time when the behavior happened. Behavior set can be represented as $B=\{b_1, b_2, \ldots, b_n\}$, where $b_1, b_2, \ldots, b_n$ represent different behaviors.*

Definition 2 *(Behavior Sequence) a sequence of behaviors carried out by the same subject during a specific time period in accordance with the time ascending, which can be represent as bs= $(b_i, b_j, \ldots, b_m)$, $b_i, b_j, \ldots, b_m \in B$. Behavior Sequence set can be represented as BS=$\{bs_1, bs_2, \ldots, bs_n\}$.*

Definition 3 *(Behavior Sequence Graph) a weighted graph G(V,E,W) with vertex set V=B defined in Definition 1 and edges E, weight W. Node i corresponds to b_i and node j corresponds to b_j in behavior set B. The weight of edge between node i and j is defined as an $|B| \times |B|$ matrix W*

$$W_{ij} = \sum_{\substack{1 \leq i \leq N \\ b_i, b_j \in B}} \frac{1}{N} f(d(i,j)) \tag{1}$$

where N is the number of behavior sequences in behavior sequence set BS, b_i and b_j are behavior pairs co-occurrence in the same behavior sequence BS_n, n is the mark number of behavior sequence BS. And d(i,j) presents the distance between i and j in the behavior sequence BS_n.

$$d(i,j) = loc(j, BS_n) - loc(i, BS_n) \tag{2}$$

where $loc(j, BS_n)$ and $loc(i, BS_n)$ represent the corresponding location of j and i in behavior sequence BS_n.

$$f(d(i,j)) = \begin{cases} 0 & d(i,j) > r \\ 1 & d(i,j) \leq r \end{cases} \tag{3}$$

where r is a predefined integer parameter that controls the range that neighbors relevant.

However, the number of behavior symbols is too enormous to conduct effective behavior pattern recognition. In other word, two different behaviors in original granularity may belong to the same behavior class in a more coarse-grained granularity. Behavior class can be achieved by the clustering of behavior sequences according to the actions of behaviors. Behaviors in the same class have actions which have similarities as larger as possible, behaviors in different classes have actions which have similarities as smaller as possible.

Definition 4 *(Behavior Class) the cluster of action in behavior, which represents categories of actions in behaviors. It can be represented as C:($b_o, b_p, \ldots, b_t$), $b_o, b_p, \ldots, b_t \in B$. In behavior class, we pay attention to the action of behavior merely, so the behavior $b_o, b_p, \ldots, b_t$ here can be represented with corresponding actions.*

Definition 5 *(Behavior Pattern) the latent patterns can be found at a more coarse-grained granularity of data(recoding the original behavior sequences with behavior class) and cant be found from the original granularity of data. Behavior pattern can be represented as a sequence of behavior class bp = $C_1 \rightarrow C_2 \rightarrow \ldots \rightarrow C_n$, where $C_1, C_2, \ldots, C_n$ represent different behavior classes sorted in time ascending.*

3.2   Behavior Pattern Based Fraud Detection

Behavior pattern based fraud detection can be divided into three steps: Firstly, transform the data records to behavior sequences and cluster the behaviors using SSIsomap method to get behavior class; Secondly, recoding the original behavior sequences using behavior class and conduct behavior pattern mining; Thirdly, calculate the fraud probability of new claim according to discovered behavior patterns.

Algorithm 1. Behavior pattern based fraud detection

---

input: new claim $Claim$, history records R
output: fraud probability of each c in Claim
 1: Transform(R)and get B,BS
 2: **for all** $b_i, b_j \in B$ **do**
 3:     CaculateWeight(b_i, b_j)
 4:     **if** $LCS(b_i, b_j) < l$ **then**
 5:        label b_i, b_j) with same category label
 6:     **end if**
 7: **end for**
 8: Construct behavior sequence graph G
 9: D=Compute shortest path(G)
10: **if** $label(b_i) = label(b_j)$ **then**
11:     $\Delta = 0$
12: **else**
13:     $\Delta = 1$
14: **end if**
15: $D' = D - min(D)\Delta$
16: Cluster by KNN and obtain Behavior class C
17: Recoding(BS) and mining BP
18: cluster BP
19: **for all** $c \in Claim$ **do**
20:     $p(c) = 1 - COS(c, BP)$
21:     **return** p(c)
22: **end for**

3.2.1   Behavior Cluster.
Transform the given records to behavior set B and obtain behavior sequence set BS. Behavior set B contains unique behavior appeared in records. Each behavior sequence in BS represents behaviors of the same entity during a specified period sorting by time ascending. Construct behavior sequence graph G according to definition 3.

From Eq.(1),we know that the weight of edge represent the closeness of the nodes with each other. The larger the w_{ij} is, the more often b_i and b_j appear close to each other in the behavior sequences.

To cluster the behavior into behavior class, first of all, we need to embed the behavior in a lower dimension in which the behavior can be clustered using traditional clustering methods such as KNN (K Nearest Neighbor). Manifold learning is the process of estimating a low-dimensional structure which underlies a collection of high-dimensional data. To carry on the embedding, we take advantage of the manifold embedding of the graph. If two behavior b_i and b_j are temporally more related, their distance in embedded space will be small as well.

Isomap [15] is a popular method that embed a graph into an Euclidean space. However, isomap is an unsupervised method so that it ignores some existing category information. So we propose SSIsomap which improves isomap to semi-supervised method to cluster the behavior. Firstly, we label some points with their category information using LCS[13]–a classical algorithm for calculating the similarity between character strings. For each behavior pair b_i and b_j, if $LCS(b_i,b_j)$ is longer than the empirical threshold l, we label b_i and b_j with the same category label. Secondly, we calculate the distance between points in Euclidean space with the formulation:

$$D' = D - min(D)\Delta \qquad (4)$$

where D is the shortest path matrix of graph $G, \Delta = 1$ if two points belong to the same category, otherwise, $\Delta = 0$.

We find that it can provide spatially more unfolded embedding which can help us to cluster the behavior into behavior class. Meanwhile, we utilize domain language to adjust the adjacency parameter k. More specifically, we adjust k so that drugs or treatment in the same category in pharmacopeia can be clustered into the same class.

3.2.2 Behavior Pattern Mining.
Recoding the original behavior sequences using the obtained behavior class, and cluster the obtained behavior sequences which are composed of behavior class. For the original behavior sequences, it is hard to define distances between sequences or extract features. If we can represent the behavior sequences with behavior class, the difficulty will be tackled. More importantly, we re-summarizes the behavior in the form of behavior class, therefore we can obtain more repeated subsequences and more meaningful sequential features.

When the behavior sequences are represented by only a reasonably small number of behavior, we can extract some useful features, such as the counts of each behavior sequence composed of behavior class. It turns out that such a straightforward approach can effectively cluster the behavior sequences. Combine the discovered frequent behavior sequences with domain knowledge and we can cluster the behavior patterns.

3.2.3 Fraud Probability Evaluation.
According to the behavior patterns we obtain from the historical data, for a new coming medical insurance claim, we can measure its Cosine similarity compared with the behavior patterns and get the probability of fraud of the claim. The fraud probability p can be calculated as

$$p = 1 - Cos(\boldsymbol{c}, \boldsymbol{BP}) \qquad (5)$$

where c is the behavior sequence composed of behavior class corresponding the new coming medical claim, BP is the behavior pattern set we obtain from behavior pattern mining, $Cos(c, BP)$ represent the similarity between c and BP.

From Eq.(5)The larger the $Cos(c, BP)$ is, the less probability that the new coming claim exists fraud; the smaller the $Cos(c, BP)$ is , the more probability that the new coming claim exists fraud.

4   Outlier Detection Based Fraud Detection

Traditional outlier detection methods focus on self comparison.Howerver, the data of each individual applicant are so sparse that it is not sufficient enough to find the outliers. Therefore, we propose to first get distribution of many applicants. Then single applicant may exist fraud if its distance from group distribution is too far.

4.1   Feature Selection

To get the distribution of group applicants, we first need to divide the applicants into groups. Traditional group is divided by some coarse granularity such as the applicants can be divided into young people, middle aged people and elder people according to the age range. However, the group is too coarse-grained to do outliers detection effectively.We find features which have great influence to fraud detection and the group can be represented by a tuple gp= (feature$_1$, feature$_2$,..., feature$_n$), where feature$_1$, feature$_2$,..., feature$_n$ represent the features chosen to group the applicants. For given fraud factor(factors which can depict the probability of fraud), we compare the fraud factor distribution P(x) of total data and the fraud factor distribution Q(x) in subsets of data divided by feature$_i$. Then we calculate the Kullback-Leibler divergence between P(x) and Q(x).If $D_{KL}(P\|Q)$ of feature$_i$ is greater than the predefined threshold β(an empirical value), feature$_i$ will be chosen to group the applicants.

4.2   Group Distribution

For each group g$_p$, the distribution of this group can be represented by discontinuous variable distribution law:

$$p(X = x_k) = p_k, k = 1, 2, \ldots, n \qquad (6)$$

where X represents the fraud factor, x$_1$,x$_2$,...,x$_n$ represent the values of fraud factor which can depict fraud. p$_1$,p$_2$,...,p$_n$ represent the probability of x$_1$,x$_2$,...,x$_n$ respectively.

4.3   Outlier Detection

We propose SimLOF which reduces the number of objects and simplifies the density of object to conduct outlier detection. As a consequence, SimLOF reduces the time complexity of LOF. The density of object a refers to the probability of x_i which contain a.

$$p(a) = p(x = x_i), a \in x_i \tag{7}$$

$$density(c) = \frac{1}{K} \sum_{i=1}^{n} p(x_i) \tag{8}$$

The outlier based fraud probability p of a new coming claim c can be obtained by the density of x_i which contain c. $x_1, x_2, \ldots, x_k$ represents the k nearest neighbors of c.

$$p' = 1 - density(c) \tag{9}$$

where p' indicates the probability that c is an outlier. The larger the probability p' is, the more probability the claim existing fraud.

5   Dempster-Shafer Evidence Theory

We can obtain two kinds of evidences(behavior pattern based evidence and outlier detection based evidence) through the above process expounded in Section 3 and 4. For a new claim c, Behavior pattern based evidence and outlier based evidence can give a probability of fraud respectively. Simple vote rules are not adaptive when the two evidence give conflict conclusion. To combine the identified two evidences, we employ the Dempster-shafer evidence theory [12], which aims to combines evidences from different sources and obtains a degree of belief that takes all the available evidences into account. This indeed aligns well with our goal that is to determine the unusual fraudulent behavior by combining the two kinds of evidences. Dempster-shafer evidence theory combines behavior pattern evidence with outlier evidence and yields a more robust degree of belief of fraud to the new coming claim.

6   Experiment

In this section, we evaluate the performance of the proposed approach for fraud detection. The data set used in this experiment is collected from the medical insurance system in Zibo, Shandong province. The data set consists of more than 40 million records of medical insurance claims of 40000 applicants.

6.1   Behavior Pattern Based Fraud Detection

Here, we conduct fraud detection by our behavior pattern based fraud detection and our goal is to estimate the probability of existing fraud in each record.

The number of behavior is so enormous that we cant find any pattern using traditional pattern recognition methods. We embed the behavior into European space using SSIsomap and cluster the behaviors into behavior class. In choosing the embedding dimensions, we typically choose two or three dimensions. We investigate the residual variance in the SSIsomap with regard to the number of selected embedding dimensions. As shown in Figure 1, in real-world medical insurance data sets, the residual variance drops most significantly with the first few dimensions. Finally, we choose two dimensions. Figure 1(a) shows the behavior embedded in European space using isomap Figure 1(b) shows the behavior embedded in European space using our SSIsomap. As we can see, our method has a high clustering accuracy than the original isomap method. Table 1 shows example of the behavior class we achieve according to the embedded result. We recode the original behavior sequences with behavior class, we obtain new behavior sequences. Then we perform clustering on the transformed sequences using the frequent patterns detected to extract features as discussed in Section 3.2.2. We focus on a few dominant clusters in which the applicants have relatively longer

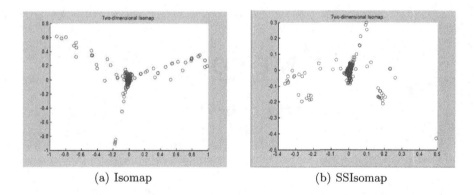

(a) Isomap   (b) SSIsomap

Fig. 1. Behavior embedded in European space using Isomap and SSIsomap

Table 1. Example of behavior class

behavior class	behavior class name	behavior	behavior size
C1	Heart related inspection	cardiac monitoring Holographic dynamic electrocardiogram (ecg) SAHRV,...	8
C2	purchase cardiovascular drugs	heartprotect musk pill, WSHX,...	32
C3	injection	disposable syringe, intravenous injection,...	17
C4	purchase cold medication	Compound ganmaoling granules, brown mixture,...	65
C5	purchase anti-inflammatory drugs	Chuanbei Pipa Gao (CPG), penicillin,...	98

behavior sequences. The behavior sequences corresponding to some dominant clusters covering 2089 applicants, by connecting each behavior of the sequence embedded in the two dimensional plane. Here, each cluster corresponds to one type of applicants with a unique admitting diagnosis. Combined with domain knowledge, we summarized some of the mined behavior patterns in Table 2. BP-Growth[3] examines typical optimizing strategies for association rule mining

Table 2. Example of behavior pattern

class	behavior pattern	size
coronary heart disease(CHD)	$C1 \rightarrow C2$	256
	$C1 \rightarrow C3 \rightarrow C4 \rightarrow C2$	689
upper respiratory infection (URI)	$C5 \rightarrow C3 \rightarrow C4$	541
	$C5 \rightarrow C4 \rightarrow C3 \rightarrow C2$	603

and study the feasibility of applying them to behavior pattern mining. However, because of the curse of cardinality, BP-Growth can hardly mine frequent itemsets which compose of more than two behaviors.

6.2   Outlier Detection Based Fraud Detection

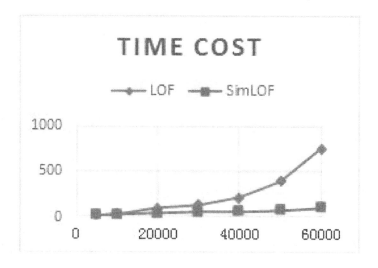

Fig. 2. Time cost of LOF and SimLOF

Given the fraud factor daily cost in hospital, we first choose features that have significant influence to fraud detection.According to statistical result,age and admitting diagnosis are the two features chosen to group applicants.

Then we group the applicants according to their age and admitting diagnosis. Group applicants in a finer granularity according to the features chosen can help us to find outlier more accurately. Figure 2 shows the time cost of our SimLOF compared with LOF. The result shows that SimLOF reduces the time complexity obviously than LOF.

6.3   Dempster-Shafer Evidence Theory

The experimental dataset is labeled with "normal" or "fraud" in medical insurance system. We sample N records in which 2% is labeled as fraud each time. N is set to 1000,10000,100000 and 1000000 respectively. Figure 3 shows that our method has significantly higher accuracy than baseline methods in medical insurance fraud detection.

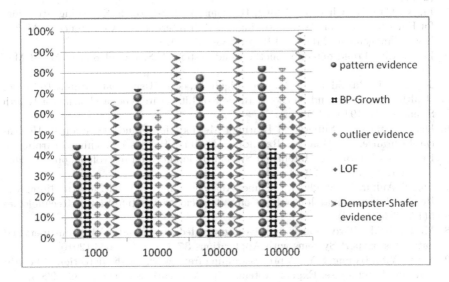

Fig. 3. Accuracy of methods in different sizes of dataset

7   Conclusion

In this paper, we propose an effective hybrid method for fraud detection. To obtain behavior pattern based evidence, we propose SSIsomap to cluster the behavior whose number is enormous into behavior classes which represent the behavior in a more coarse-grained. As a result, it can tackle the challenge of curse of cardinality. For better outlier detection performance, we propose SimLOF which reduces the time complexity of LOF to detect the outliers in a finer granularity.To obtain more robust evidences for fraud detection, we combine the two evidence using Dempster-shafer Evidence Theory.Finally, we conduct comprehensive experiments with real-world medical insurance claims data to demonstrate the effectiveness of our method. The experimental results show that the proposed approach could achieve higher accuracy than existing fraud detection methods.

References

1. Huang, Z., Dong, W., Ji, L., et al.: Discovery of clinical pathway patterns from event logs using probabilistic topic models. Journal of Biomedical Informatics **47**, 39–57 (2014)
2. Tsai, Y.H., Ko, C.H., Lin, K.C.: Using Common KADS Method to Build Prototype System in Medical Insurance Fraud Detection. Journal of Networks **9**(7), 1798–1802 (2014)
3. Li, X., Cao, H., Chen, E., Xiong, H., Tian, J.: BP-Growth: Searching Strategies for Efficient Behavior Pattern Mining. In: 13th International Conference on Mobile Data Management (MDM 2012), pp. 238–247 (2012)
4. Fano, A.E.: Fraud detection method and system: U.S. Patent 8,725,524, 13 May 2014
5. Joudaki, H., Rashidian, A., Minaei-Bidgoli, B., et al.: Using Data Mining to Detect Health Care Fraud and Abuse: A Review of Literature. Global Journal of Health Science **7**(1), 194 (2014)
6. Dua, P., Bais, S.: Supervised Learning Methods for Fraud Detection in HealthcareInsurance. In: Dua, S., Rajendra, U., Dua, P. (eds.) Machine Learning in Healthcare Informatics. Intelligent Systems Reference Library, vol. 56, pp. 261–285. Springer, Heidelberg (2014)
7. Yagnik Ankur, N., Singh, A.S.: Oulier Analysis Using Frequent Pattern Mining CA Review. International Journal of Computer Science and Information Technologies **5**(1), 47–50 (2014)
8. Musal, R.M.: Two models to investigate Medicare fraud within unsupervised databases. Expert Systems with Applications **37**(12), 8628–8633 (2010)
9. Yang, W.S., Hwang, S.Y.: A process-mining framework for the detection of healthcare fraud and abuse. Expert Systems with Applications **31**(1), 56–68 (2006)
10. An, W., Liang, M., Liu, H.: An improved one-class support vector machine classifier for outlier detection. Proceedings of the Institution of Mechanical Engineers, Part C: Journal of Mechanical Engineering Science **229**(3), 580–588 (2015)
11. Yang, W., Su, Q.: Process mining for clinical pathway: literature review and future directions. In: 2014 11th International Conference on Service Systems and Service Management (ICSSSM), pp. 1–5. IEEE (2014)
12. Shafer, G.: A Mathematical Theory of Evidence. Princeton University Press (1976)
13. Bergroth, L., Hakonen, H., Raita, T.: A Survey of longest common subsequence algorithms. In: Proceedings of Seventh International Symposium on String Processing and Information Retrieval, SPIRE 2000, pp. 39–48. IEEE (2000)
14. Breunig, M.M., Kriegel, H.P., Ng, R.T., et al.: LOF: identifying density-based local outliers. In: ACM Sigmod Record, vol. 29(2), pp. 93–104. ACM (2000)
15. Tenenbaum, J.B., De Silva, V., Langford, J.C.: A global geometric framework for nonlinear dimensionality reduction. Science **290**(5500), 2319–2323 (2000)

A Fuzzy Inspired Approach to Seismic Anomaly Detection

Vyron Christodoulou[1]([✉]), Yaxin Bi[1], and Guoze Zhao[2]

[1] School of Computing and Mathematics, Ulster University,
Jordanstown Newtownabbey, Co. Antrim BT37 0QB, UK
christodoulou-v@email.ulster.ac.uk, y.bi@ulster.ac.uk
[2] State Key Laboratory of Earthquake Dynamics, Institute of Geology, China
Earthquake Administration,Yard No.1, Hua Yan Li,
Chaoyang District, Beijing, China
zhaogz@ies.ac.cn

Abstract. In this work we investigate the use of a fuzzy inspired approach for anomaly detection in different electromagnetic sequential time series datasets. The method proposed consists of simple component methods that are aggregated in a serialized way to achieve anomaly detection. Each of the component methods adds an element towards anomaly detection, i.e. a smoothing filter removes any unwanted noise, an automated peak finding with Fast Fourier Transformation and correlation, reduces the dimensionality of the signal, a fuzzy inference system encodes the signal before the final comparison and its respective output. This method is evaluated on 6 benchmark datasets with promising results in terms of F-measure accuracy. The method is also evaluated over real datasets gathered from the SWARM satellites for the detection of possible anomalies in relation to seismic events. The preliminary experimental results also prove to be promising for the proposed method for the detection of anomalies in electromagnetic sequential time series datasets.

Keywords: Anomaly detection · Fuzzy inference system · Time series · Fast fourier transformation · Electromagnetic signal · Swarm satellites

1 Introduction

Today's rapid data accumulation growth is the stimulant behind the creation of novel approaches. Data abundance can provide new ways to understand, identify patterns and solve problems that were previously hard to consider due to the limited data available. Because of the amount of data available, the anomaly detection (AD) problem is especially relevant in sequential time series data. For that reason it has become an important field in data analysis. Some of the methods employed draw knowledge from statistics, data mining, artificial intelligence, machine learning and pattern recognition. Time series data are collected everyday for medical applications, financial market analytics, network traffic and can extend to a variety of different observable effects that need investigation such

© Springer International Publishing Switzerland 2015
S. Zhang et al. (Eds.): KSEM 2015, LNAI 9403, pp. 575–587, 2015.
DOI: 10.1007/978-3-319-25159-2_52

as the one that is investigated in the current work, the earth's magnetic field intensity (MFI).

Various approaches from different settings have been developed and applied into time series AD settings. For instance, a frequently used approach in a time series AD setting is the use of a sliding window method. The Ionospheric Total Electron Content (TEC) property was used in [11] and is one of the most studied. By defining anomaly boundaries by quartile and standard deviation statistics for the windows the authors indicate that they also detected anomalies prior to seismic events. There is no limit in the variety of methods evaluated under time series AD. Specifically in connection to this work, a number of studies have investigated the possible precursory connection between variations in the earth's indicators and seismic activities over a specific region. In [10] temperature data are investigated with the use of simple statistical methods. The methods were able to detect anomalous occurrences prior to the seismic events. A more intelligent statistical method, called Geometric Moving Average Martingale (GMAM) was used in [13] for detecting anomalies in long-wave radiation data. The proposed method can effectively identify anomalies which could be possibly related to seismic activities.

As seen, a range statistical methods has been used to address the AD problem. With the recent convergence of statistics in conjunction with machine learning, there has been a different direction to more intelligent, but more computationally expensive methods. An intelligent method in the form of One-Class Support Vector Machines (OCSVM) was used in [8]. The method proposed, incorporates kernels for detecting changes and classifying observations and had succesful results. HOT-SAX [9] is also a widely used method to detect anomalies and is widely used in a lot of applications because it only needs one parameter tuning, the length of the anomalous subsequence. It has shown very promising results in a range of different time series signals. The different machine learning methods for TEC variations are compared in [6] , with a Genetic Algorithm (GA) having the best results. A wavelet based method was used in [15] for the analysis of electromagnetic (EM) variations from earthquake regions. The analysis proved successful for detecting possible anomalous variations.

In this work we consider another intelligent approach, the use of a fuzzy inspired approach for AD. Fuzzy systems have been used for AD in terms of clustering and classifying normal and anomalous subsequences. A fuzzy-c-means clustering algorithm optimized by intelligent methods was used in [4], [5]. All these kind of approaches are evaluated in terms of clustering anomalies and the number of optimal clusters created. To date, a fuzzy approach for AD in time series satellite EM data has not been explored. In this work a Fuzzy Inference System (FIS) is proposed as the core of our approach to detect the anomalies in EM sequential time series data. A FIS is appropriate for use in an AD setting as there is not always a clear boundary between an anomalous and a normal subsequence. It is believed that a FIS will help in this kind of distinction. As mentioned earlier the FIS is used as a component of the whole system to process the dataset. In this work it acts as a means to encode the original EM signal.

A number of equally important processing components are also implemented to achieve the final form of the output and the AD.

The outline of this work is as follows: Section 2 includes the description of the methodology and the explanation of the proposed method, in Section 3 the experimental results on the benchmark and real datasets for the earthquakes are presented and analyzed. Furthermore, in Sections 4 and 5 the work is discussed and concluded respectively.

2   Methodology

2.1   Notation

Time Series: T of length n is a successive set of real numbers of length n that belong to the sequence $t_1, t_2...t_n$

Subsequence: Given a time series T of length n, a subsequence C of T is a subset of length $m \leq n$ that starts from an observation p so that $C = t_p, ..., t_{p+n-1}$ for $1 \leq p \leq m - n + 1$

Expanding Window: Given a time series T of length n, an expanding window, W is an automatically selected subsequence of variable length $m \leq n$ that is a subset of and slides accross a time series T of length n and can extract all possible subsequences C.

Minimum Distance Window: Given an expanding window, W of length m, the minimum distance window, denoted as t_i^+, is a window of length $l = m$ that is the result of the cross-correlation between the Fast Fourier Transformation (FFT) of the Time Series T and the FFT of the expanding window, W, calculated for each t_{n+m}.

Anomaly: An observation x_i at point i, of a subsequence C, is considered an anomaly when $x_i \geq h$, where h is the pre-defined defined threshold.

2.2   Data

The benchmark datasets were downloaded from the UCR Time Series Archive[1] and consist of electrocardiographs (ECG) and satellite datasets. The label vector used for the evaluation of the algorithm was created by the use of expert knowledge given in [9], indicating where the anomalies should be labelled in the dataset. For this purpose, the labels have a window length of 100 data points that are used for the evaluation of the algorithm.

The real datasets used consist of observations gathered by two identical satellites, SWARM A and SWARM B. Data from SWARM C satellite were not available because as of 5th November the Absolute Scalar Magnetometer (ASM) stopped responding and it is likely to not work again[2]. The datasets acquired

---

[1] http://www.cs.ucr.edu/~eamonn/discords/
[2] https://earth.esa.int/web/guest/missions/esa-operational-eo-missions/swarm/news/-/article/asm-anomaly-on-swarm-c-satellite

by the ESA website[3] are in the common data format (CDF) format. The data used are captured by the satellites' ASM over a time period of 72 days of the earth's MFI. More specifically, the data range from 21st November to 31st January. Therefore, the total data from the two satellites, consist of 2x86400x72 arrays. Figure 1 refers to the data extracted and their relation to the epicenter at [23.3°N, 100.3° E] of the two 6th December seismic events in the Yunnan region of China. Both events are located in the same middle cell. Data were also missing in the 21st and 22nd of December for both satellites, as well as, in the 11th January for SWARM A. The interpolated values were computed by MATLAB's *TriScatteredInterp* function.

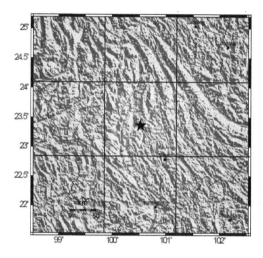

Fig. 1. Area and location of the epicenter of the Yunnan seismic events

2.3   Preprocessing

As previously mentioned, each day consists of a total of 22 parameter fields and 86400 records. We are interested in the area around the vicinity of the earthquakes. As such, we extract the data that cover the area from [13°N-33°N, 80°E-110°E] which includes the everyday observations near the epicenter from the satellites' swath. The parameter field extracted was the earth's MFI observations by the ASM instrument. The objective of the preprocessing is to reduce the dimensionality in a more manageable processing size and also achieve it with a minimal loss of meaningful information. For that reason, each segment was further segmented into 10 smaller segments and the mean value of each segment was computed. The final result is a 1-D vector of the 720 mean values from 21st November to 31st January. The process followed can be seen in Algorithm 1.

---

[3] https://earth.esa.int/web/guest/swarm/data-access

Input: Raw Swarm Dataset
Result: Reduced Output from Raw Swarm Dataset
begin
    Segment Data into ten equal segments, s
    foreach s **do**
        | compute mean value (s);
    end
end
Output: Reduced and Segmented Output from Raw Swarm Signal

Algorithm 1. Pseudocode for the Preprocessing step

2.4 The Anomaly Detection Process

In this section the whole AD process is presented step by step and explained thoroughly. Each component works as an input to the next and has its own distinct role. How the process works can be seen in Algorithm 2.

Input: RawData
Output: Array of Anomalous Data Points
foreach *User Selected* N, M **do**
    | SG Smoothing;
end
for $i \leftarrow MinPeakDistance$ **to** $MaxPeakDistance$ **do**
    | find peaks
end
foreach *PeakDistIteration* **do**
    compute FFT and xcorrelate with original signal;
    if *xcorr(Orig.,Reduced(i))*; ==*max(xcorr(Orig.,Reduced(i))* ;
    then
        | go to FIS;
    else
        | go back to the start of current method
    end
end
end
foreach *Peak* **do**
    | Compute the gradient
end
Compute Fuzzy Output
Encode Fuzzy Output
foreach *Encoded Subsequence* **do**
    Compute Euclidean Distance between subsequences
    if *IntensityBasedEuclid > ShapeBasedEuclid*;
    then
        | IntensityBasedEncoding
    else
        | ShapeBasedEncoding
    end
end
Compare Normal vs anomalous subsequences and identify anomalies
Return Output

Algorithm 2. Pseudocode of the Algorithm

Smoothing. An important step towards the AD process is the smoothing. Smoothing is pertinent to the AD problem as noise is an aspect that has always led to problems in carrying out an AD. A smoothing and denoising function allows the algorithm to perform better peak detection. A Savitzky-Golay (SG) smoothing filter is used in this work. It has been found that it is appropriate for specific types of signals [1] and has been also tested in satellite datasets. While it is known that it is not the best filter to remove noise, thanks to its attractive property to minimize signal distortion and preserve any vital information that are needed, the SG filter was selected. In every case the smoothing and the peak finding algorithms lead to loss of information. In order to keep it at a minimal level, there is an attempt to preserve the meaningful information of each dataset. An SG filter uses convolution to achieve smoothing. In short, it replaces the value of the signal with a new value which is obtained by a polynomial fit to $2N + 1$ polynomial points. The variable, N has to be greater or equal to the order of the polynomial, M . Therefore, the parameters to be selected are the order of the polynomial and the data points, N, to be fitted.

The general SG filter formula is given below for a set of N data points $t_p, p = 1, ..., N$

$$W_n = \sum_{j=-n_L}^{n_R} c_j t_{k+j} \qquad (1)$$

where n_L, n_R are the number of samples left and right of the center index k and $c_n = 1/(n_L + n_R + 1)$, is the coefficient vector. The process can also be regarded as the discrete version of the convolution between the coefficient, c_n and the function t_p.

Peak Finding. Peak detection efficiently reduces the amount of data gathered and makes AD faster and more effective. The aim in this component method is to preserve the important variations and the peaks within the data, thereby reducing the raw dataset's dimensions but without resulting in too much of a different output. This method has been proven to be useful in detecting anomalies in signals and seismic activities [2]. The problem faced here is the selection of what is the most appropriate minimum window length between peaks. Moreover, a starting point window length has to be set. The user does not need to choose this parameter. We try to keep the dimensionality reduction proportionate to all datasets. Therefore the algorithm works down on a reduction rate similar to all datasets. The algorithm uses the basic calculation of comparing a data point with its two neighboring points. The final minimum window distance between two peaks is decided by the algorithm implemented, using the FFT.

Fast Fourier Transformation (FFT). In this case the FFT is used a guidance of which minimum window length between two peaks is appropriate to select and does not result in a totally unrelated signal to the original. For this reason, a cross correlation between the original and the compressed signal by the peak finding algorithm is computed by the FFT. The algorithm iterates between the different peak window lengths and compares each time all the possible outputs from the peak finding method with the original. The maximum correlation is then used to find the most closely similar signal with the original. This ensures that the reduced signal keeps its similarity to the original, since it has to be used as an input to the fuzzy system. Overall, an automatic selection of the minimum window length between detected peaks is achieved and produces the most similar to the original dataset based on the cross correlation similarity measurement.

For the cross-correlation of the signals the inbuilt MATLAB function *xcorr2* was used. It simply works out the product of the two complex, after the FFT, vectors. A higher output means higher similarity.

The FFT is a faster discrete fourier transformation algorithm that reduces the computations needed by N points from $2N^2$ to $2Nlog_2N$ and is defined by the equation:

Let $y_0, ..., y_{N-1}$ be complex numbers

$$C_k = \sum_{n=0}^{N-1} y_n e^{-i2\pi k(n/N)} \tag{2}$$

where k is a real number and can take values between $[0, N-1]$

Fuzzy Inference System (FIS) and Encoding. The fuzzy system has two inputs. The first one is the amplitude of each peak. The second input is derived by computing the gradient of each peak with the consecutive one. Therefore, the output of the system is a function of both inputs. In Fig. 2 the output from the fuzzy system for SWARM A is shown and how the algorithm encodes the signal. A point worth mentioning is that loss of information is caused during the encoding. For example here, the angle of each shape is not taken into account. The notion of approximate similarity or self-similarity is employed here. At this point we are mostly concerned about describing the most important characteristics of the signal, something that is achieved. In this example the subsequence with the most occurrences is the subsequence 'BABABAD'.

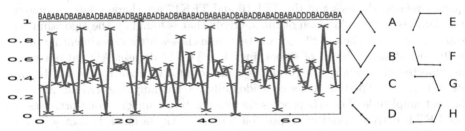

Fig. 2. SWARM A encoding (left) and how the encoding is decided (right)

The second kind of symbolic representation is based on intensity, shown in Fig. 3. The fuzzy output space is segmented in 5 equal segments with 'A' denoting the highest and 'E' the smallest possible case. The algorithm uses both representations at first. The final decision is made after the calculation of the euclidean distance between the normality measure of each encoding with each subsequence. As a normality measure the subsequence with the most occurrences in the encoded sequence is considered. Here it is the subsequence 'CCCD'.

The representation with the largest euclidean distance between the normal subsequence and the anomalous is finally selected. The length of the most similar subsequences is calculated by the algorithm. Finally, for identifying the location of the anomaly a simple logical operation between the normal and the anomalous subsequences is used.

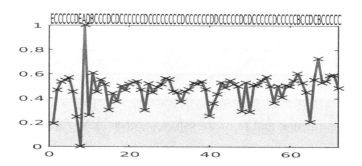

Fig. 3. Swarm B encoding process. A=[1, 0.8], B=(0.8, 0.6], C=(0.6, 0.4], D=(0.4, 0.2], E=(0.2, 0]

3 Performance Evaluation

3.1 Benchmark Datasets

The six benchmark datasets used were specifically chosen in order to evaluate the algorithm in different kinds of anomalies. Both chfdb275 and chf13 consist of small and high intensity cases respectively. The mitdb100 datasets consist of frequency related changes and the TEK16 and TEK17 are shape related. Some of the datasets and the location of the anomaly that is found by the algorithm are shown in Fig. 4. Different SG parameters were chosen after experimenting manually with different levels of smoothing. The TEK17 dataset AD did not work as expected and although it produces some results the algorithm is not basing its AD on the shape but rather coincidentally the anomaly detected has also the highest amplitude. The AD process therefore is based under wrong premises as the FFT is driven away from a possible similar to the original dataset solution. The fault originates from the peak finding component method. A different minimum distance between peaks selected could provide a solution. The minimum peak distance window length starting point for each FFT iteration was selected based on the period of each signal.

Table 1 shows that the algorithm can work very well on different types of anomalies. A user selected threshold, h, of ten equal segments is used to evaluate the algorithm. As seen the method can achieve very good results on all occasions. It is noted that the single most important step is the first step. The smoothing applied can change the original signal and it is very probable that in small anomalies it smooths the signal to the point of normality. This is alleviated by

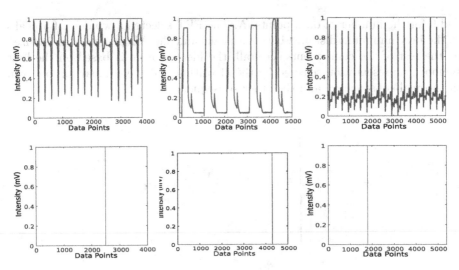

Fig. 4. Anomaly Detection, left to right: Chfdb275 feat2, TEK16, mitdb100 feat1

Table 1. The Performance of the Algorithm

Dataset	SG parameters	FFT	Best F-Score	Mean F-Score
mitdb100feat1	(2,61)	1	100	76.4
mitdb100 feat 2	(2,61)	1	100	77.2
TEK16	(3,9)	1	100	85
TEK17	(3,9)	21	100	66.4
chf13 feat 1	(2,61)	1	100	89.3
chf13 feat 2	(2,61)	1	100	87.4
chfdb275 feat 1	(2,61)	1	100	92.5
chfdb275 feat 2	(2,61)	1	100	93.1

the use of the SG filter but the problem always persists because of the loss of information due to smoothing.

3.2 SWARM satellites' datasets

The proposed method detects anomalous subsequences close to and after the date of the seismic events . Although it is difficult to associate the identified anomalies with the seismic events the results are interesting from a detection perspective. Fig. 5 shows the peak finding component and the anomalies detected by the algorithm from the data gathered from SWARM A. The date of the anomaly is shown by the vertical line. There are anomalous variations detected a week before until the date of the event. Anomalies are detected even after 15 days of the event. In Fig. 5, the SWARM B data show similar variations after the seismic event although the lack of anomalies before the date of the seismic event fails to provide more confidence to the results. The SG filter parameters selected for the smoothing were the same for both datasets: 3 for the order of the polynomial, M, and 9 for the number of data points, N. The FFT selected a window of 5 peaks as the best minimum distance between peaks and the AD process was finalized by the rest of the components. Overall, the identification is based on the best symbolic representation selected by the algorithm and the comparison between the normal subsequence and the other subsequences.

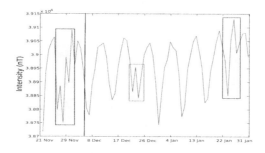

Fig. 5. Anomalous subsequences detected from SWARM A data

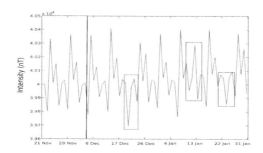

Fig. 6. Anomalous subsequences detected from SWARM B data

4 Discussion

The experimental results on the benchmark datasets show that the algorithm is capable of working in diverse settings with minimal prior knowledge. A worthy point is that the smoothing plays a major part in the outcome and should be tested beforehand. It can easily alter the properties of the original signal. Difficulties might also appear with the selection of the fuzzy membership functions (MF) which depend a lot on the form of the input signals. Even small changes produce very different results. Moreover, the minimum starting window length to be selected by the peak finding algorithm which is based on the FFT should be based proportionately on the total length of the signal, as done throughout this work. Overall all the components work in a straightforward manner without any other user input. As expected the smoothing factor plays a deal-breaker role, as in the case of TEK17 the input was smoothed too much and the algorithm was confused.

The SWARM satellite datasets proved to be ideal for the evaluation of the algorithm. The detection prior to the seismic events is useful as a possible earthquake precursor but the datasets proved to be especially challenging for the algorithm as they produced some conflicting results.

5   Conclusion

In this work we have proposed a fuzzy inspired algorithm that incorporates four simple component methods towards the final AD. Each component works towards the narrowing down of possible anomalous subsequences. Although each step on its own has a lot of parametrization, the algorithm itself works on a mostly automated fashion. The only parameters the user has to select are the order, M and length, N of the SG smoothing. Although the smoothing itself can be automated at this stage it is preferable to see the results beforehand. It is also shown that the FFT is able to work on the reduced version of the dataset based on its similarity with the original. A main issue of the algorithm is that if the parameters are not selected after careful consideration the loss of valuable information will become a certainty. The use of the algorithm then can be counter-productive.

The proposed algorithm showed it performs very well in the benchmark datasets used in a variety of anomalies. This alone is a promising result. Further work is needed in possibly a better selection method for the minimum window length between the peaks. Appropriate statistical metrics can also be incorporated into the system because as shown in TEK17 dataset the system might get confused. The fuzzy system offers an easy and appropriate method to model the fuzziness of the anomalies but it is also very dependent on the user selection of the MFs. An adaptive method can be used. In general, keeping MFs simple is helpful to avoid complex results that may lead to wrong interpretations. Overall, while a downside might be the many parameters of the system, they can be easily automated as proposed in this work. Further evaluation with real datasets and possible improvements in the selection of the best reduced signal is needed to produce results with higher accuracy.

Another important point that needs investigation is the method used for symbolic representation. Future work is needed to identify more appropriate representations without losing meaningful information. The concept of self-similarity is worthy of further work.

Regarding the real datasets the algorithm successfully detected anomalies in both datasets. It is difficult though to see if there is any possible connection between seismic events and anomalies in the MFI without any further work.

Another aspect left little explored is the similar patterns appearing due to seasonality in the same time period in different months. This is an aspect worth exploring that might help in the understanding of the anomalies and the patterns behind them.

Acknowledgments. This work is supported by the Dragon 3 program, a collaboration between the European Space Agency and the Ministry of Science and Technology of China. The authors would also like to acknowledge some additional support received from the project funded by the National Natural Science Foundation of China (Grant No. 41374077) and the European Space Agency for making SWARM data available for our research.

References

1. Pandia, K., Revindran, S., Cole, R., Kovacs, G., Giaovangrandi, L.: Motion artifact ncancellation to obtain heart sounds from a single chestworn accelerometer, In: Proc.ICASSP-2010, pp. 590–593 (2010)
2. Chang, G., Yu, B., Vetterli, M.: Adaptive Wavelet Thresholding for Image Denoising and Compression. IEEE T. Image Process **9**(9), 1532–546 (2000)
3. Montgomery, D. C.: Introduction to statistical quality control. John Wiley and Sons (2007)
4. Abraham, H., Snášel, A., Fuzzy, V.: Fuzzy clustering using hybrid fuzzy c-means and fuzzy particle swarm optimization. In: NaBIC 2009 World Congress on Nature and Biologically Inspired Computing, 2009, pp. 1690–1694. IEEE, December 2009
5. Ensafi, R., Dehghanzadeh, S., Mohammad, R., Akbarzadeh, T.: Optimizing fuzzy k-means for network anomaly detection using pso. In: IEEE/ACS International Conference on Computer Systems and Applications, 2008. AICCSA 2008, pp. 686–693. IEEE, March 2008
6. Akhoondzadeh, M.: Genetic algorithm for TEC seismo-ionospheric anomalies detection around the time of the Solomon (Mw = 8.0) earthquake of 06. Adv. Space Res. **52**(4), 59–581 (2013)
7. Solaimani, M., Iftekhar, M., Khan, L., Thuraisingham, B.: Statistical technique for online anomaly detection using spark over heterogeneous data from multi-source VMware performance data. In: 2014 IEEE International Conference on Big Data (Big Data), pp. 1086–1094. IEEE, October 2014
8. Aurino, F., Folla, M., Gargiulo, F., Moscato, V., Picariello, A., Sansone, C.: One-class SVM based approach for detecting anomalous audio events. In: 2014 International Conference on Intelligent Networking and Collaborative Systems (INCoS), pp. 145–151. IEEE, September 2014
9. Lin, J., Keogh, E., Wei, L., Lonardi, S.: Experiencing SAX: a novel symbolic representation of time series. Data Mining and knowledge discovery **15**(2), 107–144 (2007)
10. Saradjian, M.R., Akhoondzadeh, M.: Thermal anomalies detection before strong earthquakes (M > 6.0) using interquartile, wavelet and Kalman filter methods. Natural Hazards and Earth System Science **11**(4), 1099–1108 (2011)
11. Li, J., Meng, G., Wang, M., Liao, H., Shen, X.: Investigation of ionospheric TEC changes related to the 2008 Wenchuan earthquake based on statistic analysis and signal detection. Earthquake Science **22**(5), 545–553 (2009)

12. XiaoYang, Z., XiaoDong, R.E.N., FengBo, W.U., YuYang, C.H.E.N.: A New Method for Detection of Pre-Earthquake Ionospheric Anomalies. Chinese Journal of Geophysics **56**(2), 213–222 (2013)

13. Kong, X., Bi, Y., Glass, D.H.: Detecting Seismic Anomalies in Outgoing Long-Wave Radiation Data. IEEE Journal of Selected Topics in Applied Earth Observations and Remote Sensing **8**(2), 649–660 (2015)

14. Wang, Y.D., Pi, D.C., Zhang, X.M., Shen, X.H.: Seismo-ionospheric precursory anomalies detection from DEMETER satellite data based on data mining. Natural Hazards **76**(2), 823–837 (2015)

15. Xiong, P., Shen, X., Gu, X., Meng, Q., Bi, Y., Zhao, L., Dong, J.: Satellite detection of IR precursors using bi-angular advanced along-track scanning radiometer data: a case study of Yushu earthquake. Earthquake Science **28**(1), 25–36 (2015)

Two-Phased Event Causality Acquisition: Coupling the Boundary Identification and Argument Identification Approaches

Yanan Cao[1], Cungen Cao[2], Jingzun Zhang[1], and Wenjia Niu[1](✉)

[1] Institute of Information Engineering, Chinese Academy of Science, Beijing, China
{caoyanan,niuwenjia}@iie.ac.cn, xxtjingzun@buu.edu.cn
[2] Institute of Computing Techonology, Chinese Academy of Science, Beijing, China
cgcao@ict.ac.cn

Abstract. Event causality is indispensable for knowledge-driven intelligent systems. In this paper, we propose a supervised method of extracting event causalities such as *forest is cut down→forest is destroyed* from web text. While relation identification using lexico-syntactic patterns (LSPs) is not novel, it is still challenging to extract the event expressions with necessary arguments from identified causality mentions. To address this issue, our method divides event-pair extraction into two phases: event boundary identification and missing argument identification. In the first phase, we propose a Naive Baysian probability method to identify the boundary of causal events, and extract the corresponding text fragments as event expressions. Secondly, we learn a multi-class decision tree (LADTree) to identify the missing argument for each incomplete event. Experimental results showed the good effectiveness of our approach on a large-scale open corpus.

Keywords: Event causality · Causal relation · Boundary identification · Argument recognition

1 Introduction

Causality refers to the relation between two events when the occurrence of one event (the cause) leads to the occurrence of the other one (the effect). Recently, the growing interest in practical Natural Language Procession (NLP) applications places increasing demands on the processing of causal relations between textual fragments. For example, several researchers used causal knowledge to improve the performance of Question Answering (QA) systems in answering 'why' question [1–3]. In general NLP tasks, some reference must be resolved by recourse to causality knowledge. To meet the demands, a crucial issue is how to automatically acquire causal relations between events from a large-scale corpus.

Motivated by this issue, several research groups have made attempts at causality acquisition. They generally utilized lexico-syntactic co-occurrence patterns (LSPs) [1,3,4] or heuristic statitical scores based on distributional characteristics [5,8–10] to discover related events. In these works, the event expression

S. Zhang et al. (Eds.): KSEM 2015, LNAI 9403, pp. 588–599, 2015.
DOI: 10.1007/978-3-319-25159-2_53

is usually a word, typically noun or verb, rather than a phrase including event arguments; if so, event-argument analysis is based on the manual annotated corpus [4] or deep natural language process technology, such as dependency parsing and Semantic Role Labeling [5,6]. In [7], we proposed an unsupervised method to acquire causal events with arguments, and this work is based on well extracted event expressions which will be discussed below.

In this paper, we aim to extract the cause event e_1 and the corresponding effect event e_2 constituting a causal relation $e_1 \rightarrow e_2$ from the web text. First of all, we identify causality mentions from the web text using pairs of connective marker (such as "because...so", which is usually used in Chinese). And then, we extract related event expressions from the causality mentions, which involves two subtasks : event boundary identification and missing argument identification. During the first phase, we proposed a Naive Bayesian probability method to identify the boundary of effect event, and extract the corresponding text fragments as event expressions. The identified event boundaries partition a sentence into several chunks, which may induce missing argument problems. To address this issue, we provided a multi-class decision tree to identify the missing argument and judge its argument-value. Experimental results demonstrated that the precision of our approach achieved around 85%. Even though the corpus for experiments is Chinese, our method is applicable to many other languages since most of our ideas are language-independent.

2   Related Work

For event causality extraction, previous methods can roughly be categorized as lexico-syntactic pattern based [1,2,4] method and statistic based method [5,8–10,15]). Most of these works used specific words (such as noun, verb, etc.) as causality event, and focused on effective linguistic clues or distributional characteristics to mine the target relationship.

In the pioneering LSP based works, [1] automatically discovered the pattern $< NP_1\ Verb\ NP_2 >$, where the verb is a synonym of cause (such as "product") reflecting the causal relationship between events expressed by noun phrases. [2] also used the lexical NP pairs as LSPs, and exploited the probability distribution of NP_1 and NP_2 to quantify the co-occurrence preferences of both phrases in a large corpus. More researches focused on causal events triggered by verbs. Typically, [4] used explicit connective marker tame, such as "because", "since", "as the result", etc., to discover causal relation between verbs from two adjacent sentences. To ensure the accuracy of acquired knowledge, these works usually introduced a classifier to prune extracted relations and achieved around 60-80% accuracy. However, these supervised methods are weak in knowledge coverage and the applicability to new fields or new data sets.

Existing statistical methods for causality acquisition used one or more distribution characteristics of two events in the text. These major features are: (1) Co-Occurrence feature: the cause event and effect one may co-occur frequently; (2) Object-Sharing feature: the related two events may share a common participant; (3) Temporal feature: the cause event occur before (or simultaneously with) the effect event; (4) Distance feature: the two events may appear inside locally coherent text (in the same sentence particularly). Involving these features, previous unsupervised approaches [5,8–10] designed different models to determine whether or not two events are in a causal relationship, and they have achieved around 45-60% accuracy.

In recent years, causality event-argument analysis has proved significant in the future event predication [11,12] and the future scenario generation [6]. Although many attempts have been made to causality mining, just a few works paid attention to event-argument analysis; if so, they are based on the manual annotated corpus [3,4] or deep natural language process technology, such as dependency parser, SRL and Discourse analysis [6]. Motivated by this background, we proposed an unsupervised method to mine causality events with arguments [7]. In this previous work, event boundary is predefined by several separators, which brought boundary errors and missing argument problems, which are addressed in this paper.

3   Approach

Fig. 1 illustrates this process using a simple case. Our target language here is Chinese, which allows a pair of causal conjunctions to co-occur in a sentence. Examples in this section are translated to English for ease of explanation.

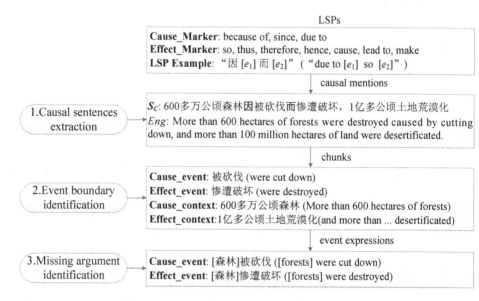

Fig. 1. Overall procedure of the proposed approach

3.1 Causal Mentions Extraction from the Web Text

To extract large-scale causality mentions, we follow the method in Cao et al.(2014), which instantiated causal grammatical patterns to retrieve source text from the web. Here, we use a pair of causality connectors including causal connectives, causal prepositions and causative verbs to construct more generic patterns formalized as *"Cause_Marker [event1] Effect_Marker [event2]"*. In this pattern, *Cause_Marker* and *Effect_Marker* are causality connectors, and the event expressions are generally short phrases or clauses. We extract causal sentences from the web pages hit by this pattern, and identify the related event pairs.

3.2 Probability-Based Event Boundary Identification

Analysis of Causality Expressions. A causality mention is generally a complex sentence which contains at least one clause, or a sentence with nested structure. According to the scope of each event predicate, we divided a causal sentence into four nonoverlapping segments. More formally:

Definition 1. *Given a causal sentence $S_c = w_1 w_2 \ldots w_{n-1} w_n$, where w_i is Cause_*
Marker and w_j is Effect_Marker $(1 \le i < j < n)$, there exists a word w_k which divides S_c into four chunks $(j < k \le n)$.

- *Cause Chunk: $C_{ca} = w_{i+1} w_{i+2} \ldots w_{j-1}$ denotes the cause event expression in S_c , while its left boundary is the Causal_Marker, and the right one is w_j;*
- *Effect Chunk: $C_{Ef} = w_{j+1} w_{j+2} \ldots w_{k-1}$ denotes the effect event expression in S_c, while its left boundary is the Effect_Marker, and w_k is the end marker;*
- *Cause Context: $C_{Ap} = w_1 \ldots w_{i-1}$ denotes the text above the cause expression, which begins from the first letter of S_c to the Causal_Marker. If $i = 1$, $C_{Ap} = \varepsilon$ is a null string.*
- *Effect Context: $C_{Lp} = w_k \ldots w_n$ denotes the text below the effect expression, which begins from w_k to the ending of S_c. If $k = n$, $C_{Lp} = \varepsilon$ is a null string.*

Because *Cause_Marker* and *Effect_Marker* are pre-defined, the boundaries of *Cause Chunk* and *Cause Context* are specific. That is, we can easily extract the cause event from the text. So, the key issue is to identify the effect boundary word w_k which determines the boundary of *Effect Chunk* and *Effect Context*. Due to the rich diversity of natural language, causal relation may be represented as a complete sentence or a sentence component.

1. When S_c is a causal sentence without nested structure, w_k is generally the first separator after *Effect_Marker*, such as comma, semicolon and other punctuations (*Example 1*).
2. When the causal relation is a component of S_c, w_k is also the boundary of this component. There are four main types of components which causal expressions can act as, including subject, object, attribute and prepositional phrase. In this case, the boundary word may be an adverb (*Example 2*), a verb (*Example 3*), an auxiliary word (*Example 4,5*), etc.

Example1 [在首盘休伊特以 5:4 领先时，比赛]$_{Ap}$ 因[下雨]$_{Ca}$ 而[被迫中止]$_{Ef}$[，只能择日重赛。]$_{Lp}$

Eng: *When Hewitt got 5:4 ahead at the first game, the game was forcefully terminated due to the rain, and was postponed to another day.*

Example2 [学生]$_{Ap}$ 因[老师批评]$_{Ca}$ 而[离家出走]$_{Ef}$[也是时有所闻。]$_{Lp}$

Eng: *That some students ran away from home due to their teachers' criticism is heard.*

Example3 [人最应该保护的是呼吸系统，以防止]$_{Ap}$ 因[寒冷]$_{Ca}$ 而[引起的疾病。]$_{Ef}$

Eng: *People should protect the respiratory system to prevent disease caused by cold.*

Example4 因[公开批评队友]$_{Ca}$ 而[丢了队长职务]$_{Ef}$[的加拉斯本场重回"枪手"阵营。]$_{Lp}$

Eng: *Callas who lost captain because of public criticism of his teammates had to return to the "Gunner" camp.*

Example5 [中国将对]$_{Ap}$ 因[服用奶粉]$_{Ca}$ 而[患结石病]$_{Ef}$[的患儿实行免费治疗。]$_{Lp}$

Eng: *China decided to implement free medical treatment on babies who suffer from lithiasis due to taking milk.*

Fig. 2. Examples for Causality Expressions

From the analysis above, we propose a hypothesis that the type of event boundary is mainly determined by the syntactic structure of S_C. So, we use syntax features in the boundary identification method. Bayesian theory and Maximum entropy worked fine in several similar tasks [3,13]), which are domain-specific (such as news and engineering). In this paper, we propose a Bayesian learning based method to identify the right boundary of the effect event automatically.

Naive Bayesian Learning. Given an arbitrary sentence S_c, there are multiple potential boundary words, denoted by $\widetilde{w}$. Let A denote the context features of the candidate boundary word $\widetilde{w}$, and let C denote the possible class $\widetilde{w}$ belongs to. Each $\widetilde{w}$ could be represented using a vector of attributes $\overrightarrow{a} = <a_1, a_2, ...a_m>$, $\overrightarrow{a} \in A$. Then, given an attribute vector $\overrightarrow{a}$, we can compute the conditional probability $\widetilde{w}$ belongs to different class, which is $P(c|\overrightarrow{a})$. Since $P(\overrightarrow{a})$ doesn't depend on the boundary type, it can be ignored when estimating the maximum posteriori probability.

$$arg\, max_{c \in C} P(c|\overrightarrow{a}) = arg\, max_{c \in C} P(c)P(\overrightarrow{a}|c) \qquad (1)$$

The Naive Bayesian probability estimates this posteriori probability from a training dataset based on the assumption that individual attributes are conditionally independent of each other given the boundary type. As such, the posteriori probability can be estimated as:

$$P(\overrightarrow{a}|c) = P(a_1, a_2, ...a_n|c) = \prod_{i=1}^{m} P(a_i|c) \tag{2}$$

In the above formulation, we use maximum likelihood estimation to compute the conditional probability $P(a_i|c)$:

$$P(a_i|c_j) = \frac{count(a_i \wedge c_j)}{count(c_j)}, \tag{3}$$

where $count(c_j)$ denotes the number of candidate words of boundary type c_j in the training set; $count(a_i \wedge c_j)$ denotes the number of times the attribute a_i occurs in all causality mentions of boundary type c_j.

To avoid the value of $P(a_i|c_j)$ equals to zero when the attribute a_i never occurs in the training samples, we use m-estimation as follows:

$$P(a_i|c_j) = \frac{count(a_i \wedge c_j) + 1}{count(c_j) + |A|}, \tag{4}$$

where $|A|$ denotes the total number of all distinct attributes for all classes. This measurement ensures the sum of conditional probability of each attribute value in one class, $P(a_i = *|c_j)$, is 1.

The prior probability of boundary type $P(c_j)$ can be easily estimated from the training samples:

$$P(c_j) = \frac{count(c_j)}{N}, \tag{5}$$

where N denotes the total number of candidate boundary words in all types.

Based on above formulations, given an attribute vector $\overrightarrow{a}$, we can judge the class label of its corresponding word $\widetilde{w}$. If $\widetilde{w}$ is the real boundary word, its class label is c_1; otherwise, c_2.

Features for Boundary Identification. We use three types of features in the boundary identification model, and Table 1 shows the main ones.

Syntactic Structure Feature. In Table 1, the first four features determine the structure of the causal sentence to some extent and constrain the Part-of-Speech (POS) of the boundary word. *Has_Verb* and *Has_Prep* indicate the major types of clauses containing causal relations. For example, sentences with link verb always have subject clause and sentences with preposition words always have pre-object clause.

POS Feature. *Cand_Pos* and *Eff_Seq* are POS features of the effect event. As mentioned above, the event boundary words are generally auxiliary words, conjunctions, punctuations and so on. And the POS sequence of the effect event reflects its linear grammar structure.

Table 1. Features for event boundary identification

Feature	Description
Eff_Mark	effect marker word
Has_Verb	whether there is a verb in the context
Has_Prep	whether there is a preposition word in the context
Eff_Verb	whether the first verb is a transitive word in the candidate effect event
Cand_Pos	POS of the candidate word
Eff_Seq	POS sequence of the *Effect Chunk*
Eff_Pre	POS sequence of the *R* left nearest words of the candidate word
Eff_Suf	POS sequence of the *R* right nearest words of the candidate word

Context Feature. *Eff_Pre* and *Eff_Suf* indicate the neighbor context features of the event boundary word. We use the POS sequence of R nearest neighbor words, where R is less than 5.

The above features are different from those used in Kim (2007). In order to gain better learning effectiveness, we use several binary functions as classification features instead of muti-valued ones.

3.3   Decision Tree Based Missing Argument Identification

According to the identified event boundary, we can extract event causalities from the causal mentions. As an example, we could obtain *"were cut down →
were destroyed"* from the sentence in Fig. 1. We find that, as an independent language segment, the cause and the effect missed their subject "forests" during the extraction process which leads to the incomplete event description. To ensure the integrity and availability of causal relations, we propose an approach to supplement extracted events with their missing arguments.

Missing Argument Analysis. In a causal sentence, event expression is usually a word or a phrase, which may lack some arguments. There are two main reasons for the missing argument problem. One is the co-reference phenomenon, and the other is the event chunking phase. In the former situation, the cause event and the effect event always share an argument, which may be mentioned only in one event expression. In the latter case, the missing argument is out of scope of the event predicate, while it appears in the event context. This phenomenon generally occurs in sentences with nested structures. Take Example 1 again: the missing argument "the game" appears in the *Cause Context*, rather than the *Effect Event*. In this paper, we don't make deep discussion on Co-reference Resolution which is still challenging in the field of Natural Language Process. We focus on the second situation in which the missing argument could be retrieved from the event context.

According to the analysis of the web corpus, we classified the missing argument into four classes:

(1) Subject of both the cause event and the effect event (see *Example 4*).

(2) Subject of the effect event (see *Example 1*).

(3) Object of the effect event (see *Example 3*).

(4) Object of the cause event, and Subject of the effect event (see *Example 2*).

According to the analysis above, the noun phrase (NP) which appears in the event context may be the missing argument, and it acts as the subject or object of the causal event pair. So, the key issue of missing argument identification is : to judge whether a noun phrase is an event-argument or not; if it is, to judge whether it is the subject or object of the target event.

Decision Tree Learning Method. We consider the missing argument identification as a classification problem. For a given NP, we try to construct a classifier which uses contextual features of the NP to judge its category label. Two methods are provided in this paper:

(1) Constructing two individual multi-class classifiers for the cause event and the effect event. The class labels are "N", "S" and "O" , which represent the NP "not the missing argument", "missing subject" and "missing object", respectively.

(2) Constructing a combined classifier for the cause event and the effect event. The class labels are "SS" , "OS" , "NS" , "NO" and "NN", where the first letter demonstrates the relationship between the NP and the cause event, and the second letter demonstrates the relationship between the NP and effect event. For instance, "OS" represents that the NP is the object of the cause event and the subject of the effect event.

Based on these classifiers, we desired to learn rules for missing argument identification, and applied it to new identification tasks. In this work, we employ LADTree [14] which is a multi-class classifier using LogitBoost strategy. This classifier combines decision trees with the predictive accuracy of boosting into a set of interpretable classification rules.

To ensure the accuracy of identified arguments, we only choose the NPs whose clause distance from the cause or the effect is less than 2 as candidate arguments. It is inspired by the hypothesis, that is: the closer the NP is to the event expression, the more likely it is to be the correlated argument.

Features for Argument Identification. Features used in the argument identification method are shown in Table 2, mainly including POS feature, context feature and location feature. To some degree, POS features about the boundary word and an event (cause or effect) reflect whether or not the event lacks a specific argument. From another level, context feature and location feature about a candidate NP reflect whether or not the NP is the missing one.

4 Experiments

4.1 Data Setting

For our experiments, we used 7 frequent causal conjunctions and 3 causative verbs in Cao et al. (2014), which compose 16 pairs of causality connectors

Table 2. Features for missing argument identification

Feature	Description
WK_Pos	POS of the boundary word w_k
Ca_Pos	POS sequence of the cause event
Eff_Pos	POS sequence of the effect event
Sen_Dis	the minimum clause distance between NP and two events
NP_Loc	whether NP is in the cause context or the effect context
NP_head	whether the head word of NP is a commonly used suffix
WK_Suf	whether NP is the right adjacency word of w_k
First_NP	whether NP is the first NP in a clause
Last_NP	whether NP is the last NP in a clause

in regular collocation. In order to get more focused relations, we employ a concrete verb as the cause event trigger. For this issue, we built a lexicon of over 10,00 common verbs with transitive labels, including 8,38 transitive verbs and 4,73 intransitive ones. Each verb was used to instantiate arbitrary wildcard between *Cause_Marker* and *Effect_Marker*. Then, we sent these pattern instances, as query items, to the Google Search Engine and downloaded relevant texts returned from the web. Causality mentions are extracted and filtered heuristically, and the final corpus contains 196,000 sentences.

In order to test our approach for event causality extraction, we randomly extracted 4000 sentences as the training dataset, and extracted another 4000 sentences as the testing one. These causal sentences were preprocessed, including segmentation and POS tagging, for the POS feature is both important in boundary identification and missing argument identification. For each causality mention in these datasets, we manually annotated the effect boundary word and the missing argument which are prepared for event boundary identification and missing argument identification.

4.2 Effectiveness of Event Boundary Identification

In this experiment, we took the methods proposed by Kim (2009) and Pechsiri (2010) as baselines, which are called *K-Bayesian* and *Max-Entropy* respectively. The basic algorithm used in Kim (2009) is also Naive Bayesian learning, while most of features were word sequences of potential events. Pechsiri (2010) employed maximum entropy learning to identify the effect boundary which outperformed Bayesian Network. Above methods were proved effective on domain datasets including plant disease news and engineering reports. Here, we implemented *K-Bayesian* and *Max-Entropy* on our common datasets.

From each causality mention in both the training data set and the testing one, we automatically extracted candidate boundary words and constructed their feature vectors. Then, we trained three classifiers respectively using our approach and the baseline ones, and evaluated their performances. The com-

Table 3. Comparison results for three approaches

Method	Precision	Recall	F-Score
C-Bayesian	86.3%	90.3%	88.3%
K-Bayesian	83.0%	58.0%	68.3%
Max-Entropy	80.7%	73.3%	76.8%

parison result is shown in Table 3. We can see that our boundary identification method outperform the baselines in both precision and recall.

For further analysis on the performance of *C-Bayesian*, we evaluated its dependent effects on different POS types of boundary words. We found that most boundary words are punctuations and auxiliary words, and both the precision and recall are relatively high. Most of errors occurred with the preposition or adverb boundary. In this situation, the causality sentences usually include the prepositional objective phrase or objective clause which lead to serious ambiguity. Besides, low precision is also induced when there are more than one auxiliary word in the set of candidate boundary word.

4.3   Effectiveness of Missing argument Identification

We evaluated the missing argument identification method basing on the same data sets used in causality boundary identification. For each causality sentence, we automatically identified noun phrases in the event context using the method in [16], and just utilized the NPs whose accuracy is higher than 98% as candidate missing arguments. Then, we trained a cause event classifier (CC), an effect event classifier (EC) and a combined classifier (BC) using LADTree algorithm implemented in Weka. The number of iterations was set to be 10 and ten-fold stratified cross-validations were ran to evaluate the performance of these classifiers. The final accuracy, recall and F-score of the identification task is respectively shown in Table 5.

Experimental results demonstrated that, the combined classifier, which introduced the dependencies between cause event and effect event, outperforms individual ones. Given a NP, we defined the relation between it and the cause event as $R1$, and that between it and effect event as $R2$. According to the analysis in Approach section, $R1$ and $R2$ are both three-valued. In theory, there should be 9 union classification results for $R1$ and $R2$, while there are 5 in actual. Our multi-class classifier is capable of discovering the implicit dependency between $R1$ and $R2$.

There are two reasons for the relatively low recall. Firstly, when an event expression (cause or effect) is just a verb, it's difficult to determine whether an missing argument is its subject or object. Secondly, many arguments have long distributional distance from the causality events, which brings much difficulty to argument identification just using syntactic features. To address these problems,

Table 4. Experimental results for missing argument identification

Classifier	Accuracy	Recall	F-Score
Cause Classifier	71.7%	53.8%	61.5%
Effect Classifier	80.9%	62.3%	70.4%
Combined Classifier	84.5%	65.7%	73.9%

we will involve more semantic features and statistical features in event-argument analysis.

5   Conclusion and the Future Work

In this paper, we proposed a supervised method to extract event causalities from the web text. Firstly, we identify causality mentions from the web text using pairs of connective marker. Then, we proposed a Naive Baysian probability method to identify the boundary of causality event, and extracted the corresponding text fragments as event expressions. In the last phase, we provided a multi-class decision tree to identify the missing argument and judge its argument-value of the target event. Experimental results demonstrated the good effectiveness of our approach. In the future work, we will introduce semantic features and statistical features to assist in event-argument analysis.

Acknowledgments. This work was supported by the National Natural Science Foundation of China grant (NO. 61403369), the Strategic Leading Science and Technology Projects of Chinese Academy of Sciences(No. XDA06030200), Beijing Key Lab of Intelligent Telecommunication Software and Multimedia (ITSM201502) and Guangxi Key Laboratory of Trusted Software (KX201418).

References

1. Girju, R.: Automatic detection of causal relations for question answering. In: Proceedings of the ACL 2003 Workshop on Multilingual Summarization and Question Answering, pp. 76–83 (2003)
2. Chang, D.-S., Choi, K.-S.: Causal relation extraction using cue phrase and lexical pair probabilities. In: Lee, J.-H., Tsujii, J., Su, K.-Y., Kwong, O.Y. (eds.) IJCNLP 2004. LNCS (LNAI), vol. 3248, pp. 61–70. Springer, Heidelberg (2005)
3. Pechsiri, C.H., Piriyakul, R.: Explanation Knowledge Graph Construction Through Causality Extraction from Texts. Journal of Computer Science and Technology, 1055–1070 (2010)
4. Inui, T., Inui, K., Matsumoto, Y.: Acquiring causal knowledge from text using the connective marker tame. ACM Transactions on Asian Language Information Processing (TALIP) 4(4), 435–474 (2005)

5. Do, Q.X., Chan, Y.S., Roth, D.: Minimally supervised event causality identification. In: Proceedings of the 2011 Conference on Empirical Methods in Natural Language Processing (EMNLP), pp. 294–303 (2011)
6. Hashimoto, C., Torisawa, K., et al.: Toward future scenario generation: extracting event causality exploiting semantic relation, context, and association features. In: Proceedings of the 52nd Annual Meeting of the Association for Computational Linguistics (ACL), pp. 987–997 (2014)
7. Cao, Y.N., Zhang, P., Guo, J., Guo, L.: Mining Large-scale Event Knowledge from Web Text. In: 14th International Conference on Computational Science (ICCS), pp. 478–487 (2014)
8. Torisawa, K.: An Unsupervised Learning Method for Commonsensical Inference Rules on Events. In: Proceedings of the Second CoLogNet-EIsNET Symposium (2003)
9. Beamer, B., Girju, R.: Using a bigram event model to predict causal potential. In: Gelbukh, A. (ed.) CICLing 2009. LNCS, vol. 5449, pp. 430–441. Springer, Heidelberg (2009)
10. Abe, S., Inui, K., Matsumoto, Y.: Two-phased event relation acquisition: Coupling the relation-oriented and argument-oriented approaches. In: Proceedings of the 22nd International Conference on Computational Linguistics (COLING), pp. 1–8 (2008)
11. Radinsky, K., Davidovich, S., Markovitch, S.H.: Learning causality for news events prediction. In: Proceedings of International World Wide Web Conference 2012 (WWW), pp. 909–918 (2012)
12. Radinsky, K., Horvitz, E.: Mining the web to predict future events. In: Proceedings of Sixth ACM International Conference on Web Search and Data Mining (WSDM), pp. 255–264 (2013)
13. Kim, S.H., Aurisicchio, M., Wallace, K.: Towards automatic causality boundary identification from root cause analysis reports. Journal of Intelligent Manufacturing 20(5), 581–591 (2009)
14. Holmes, G., Pfahringer, B., Kirkby, R., Frank, E., Hall, M.: Multiclass alternating decision trees. In: Proceeding of the ECML 13th European Conference on Machine Learning (ECML), pp. 161–172 (2002)
15. Riaz, M., Girju, R.: Another Look at Causality: Discovering Scenario-Specific Contingency Relationships with No Supervision. In: Proceedings of IEEE 4th International Conference on Semantic Computing (ICSC), pp. 361–368 (2010)
16. Wang, S., Cao, Y., Cao, X., Cao, C.G.: Learning concepts from text based on the inner-constructive model. In: Zhang, Z., Siekmann, J.H. (eds.) KSEM 2007. LNCS (LNAI), vol. 4798, pp. 255–266. Springer, Heidelberg (2007)

Change Detection Using L_0 Smoothing and Superpixel Techniques

Xiaoliang Shi, Yingying Xu, Guixu Zhang, and Chaomin Shen[✉]

Shanghai Key Laboratory of Multidimensional Information Processing,
East China Normal University, Shanghai 200241, China
cmshen@cs.ecnu.edu.cn

Abstract. We propose an unsupervised change detection method for satellite images using L_0 smoothing, superpixel techniques and k-means. First, we produce the difference image according to image types (synthetic aperture radar or optical images). Second, we use L_0 smoothing, an image editing method that can simultaneously sharpen major edges and smooth low-amplitude structures, to generate two difference images with distinct smooth levels. Third, k-means algorithm with $k = 2$ is applied on one smoothed difference image to cluster all pixels into changed or unchanged classes. Fourth, the Voronoi-Cells (VCells) algorithm is applied on the other difference image to obtain roughly uniform superpixels while preserving local image boundaries. Finally, we calculate the change degree for each superpixel, and the change detection map is produced by using k-means again. The novelties of this paper are that we use the L_0 smoothing to reduce noise and preserve edges, and utilize the spatial information with the help of superpixel. Experimental results on synthetic aperture radar and optical images show the effectiveness of our approach.

Keywords: Change detection $\cdot$ L_0 smoothing $\cdot$ Superpixel

1 Introduction

Change detection aims to identify differences in images acquired at the same place but at different times. Change detection techniques have been widely applied in a variety of areas such as medical diagnosis, video surveillance, and remote sensing [8][9].

In general, unsupervised and supervised approaches are two common techniques for change detection. The unsupervised approach has wider applications in real situations, since it does not need labeled samples which are hard to obtain. In this paper we focus on unsupervised bi-temporal change detection for remote sensing images and refer to this as change detection later throughout the paper if there is no doubt. This type of change detection has important applications in land-use analysis, damage assessment and other change measurements [12].

We hereby describe the general roadmap for change detection. Before conducting change detection, it is assumed that the bi-temporal images (i.e., image

© Springer International Publishing Switzerland 2015
S. Zhang et al. (Eds.): KSEM 2015, LNAI 9403, pp. 600–611, 2015.
DOI: 10.1007/978-3-319-25159-2_54

pair) have the same resolution and have been registered. The roadmap can be divided into two stages for most change detection algorithms. In the first stage, the "difference map", which describes certain differences derived from the image pair under some criteria, is produced. For example, a difference image can be made by subtracting or dividing two images pointwise. In the second stage, a change map is produced from the difference image. Every pixel is labeled as 1 if the point is deemed as changed or 0 if unchanged.

Different change detection algorithms mainly abide by this two-stage roadmap, while they use their respective difference and change maps based on different theories, and tackle other issues such as noise encountered in real cases. The performance is usually validated by visual inspection or some indices or both. For example, in [3], two Bayesian theory based techniques, i.e., the expectation maximization (EM) based thresholding and the Markov random fields (MRF) based thresholding, are proposed. In [1], the generalized Gaussian model is used for synthetic aperture radar (SAR) images. In [2], change detection is formulated as a segmentation issue, which uses the level set method to segment a difference image into changed and unchanged areas.

In particular, Celik [5] introduces an algorithm based on principal component analysis (PCA) and k-means, in which a difference image is divided into several $n \times n$ non-overlapped blocks. All grey values within a block form a vector as the block feature. PCA is then applied on those features. The features are clustered into two classes with k-means. Finally, the change mask is generated by deeming the class with larger mean value as the changed one. The PCA transform, however, relies on the linear dependency within data points. Therefore, if the linearity is destroyed by noise, false detection may occur.

To overcome the noise effect, the wavelet transform based method [4] is proposed. In this approach, S-level undecimated discrete wavelet transform (UDWT) decomposition is applied on the difference image. After being extracted from the decomposed image and the difference image, the multiscale features will be clustered with k-means. This algorithm is robust to noise but it may fail to detect accurate region boundaries, because it uses the subbands of the decomposition directly.

Recently, Zheng et al. propose a method called combined difference image and k-means clustering (CDI-K) to generate the change map [15]. They firstly apply the probabilistic-patch-based (PPB) algorithm on the image pair to suppress the noise, then use the mean filter on the difference image obtained by the substraction operation, and apply the median filter on the difference image obtained by the log-ratio. The former image can maintain the local consistency, while the latter one can preserve the edge information. The combined difference is the linear combination of these two images. This approach provides a new difference image representation, but it also fails to classify the boundary pixels accurately since the filters may blur the boundaries.

A close observation of aforementioned approaches reveals two key obstacles: the noise effect and the inaccurate classification of boundary pixels. In this paper, we propose a change detection algorithm using a two-stage detection based on the L_0 smoothing [14] and superpixel techniques [13], which can overcome the two obstacles.

Our algorithm consists of two stages, as shown in Fig. 1. In the first stage, we apply the L_0 smoothing on the difference image to enhance edges and reduce noise. The improved difference image will be more suitable for change detection. We apply the k-means clustering algorithm with $k = 2$ to conduct a first detection which reduces noise.

In the second stage, we convert the traditional pixel based detection into a superpixel based problem. Therefore, the changed area is usually composed of several superpixels with changed properties. We use the Voronoi-Cells (VCells) [13] here to generate superpixels for the difference image. VCells not only generates roughly uniform subregions but also preserves local image boundaries. We calculate the change degree for each superpixel. We then apply the k-means with $k = 2$ again to cluster the superpixels into two classes. Due to superpixels, the change detection boundaries will be more accurate.

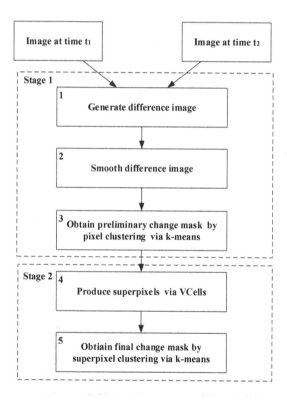

Fig. 1. The schematic diagram for the proposed method

2   Related Work

2.1 L_0 Smoothing Technique

L_0 smoothing is an edge-preserving smoothing method [14]. While traditional edge-preserving smoothing methods are achieved by local filtering, L_0 smoothing is based on the L_0-norm of gradients and is carried out in a global manner. It uses the object function:

$$\min_S \sum_p (S_p - I_p)^2 + \lambda \cdot C(S), \tag{1}$$

where I is the input image, S ranges through all smoothed images of I, p ranges through all positions in I, and $C(S)$ is the number of non-zero gradients given by

$$C(S) = \sharp\{p : |\partial_x S_p| + |\partial_y S_p| \neq 0\}.$$

Here $\partial_x S_p$ and $\partial_y S_p$ for the pixel p are the intensity differences between neighboring pixels along the x and y directions respectively, and λ is a balancing parameter.

In (1), the first term $\sum_p (S_p - I_p)^2$ is to control the similarity, while $C(S)$ in the second term is to constrain the image smoothness.

Because a discrete counting metric is involved, we introduce auxiliary variables to expand (1), i.e.,

$$\min_{S,h,v} \sum_p \{(S_p - I_p)^2 + \lambda \cdot C(h,v)p + \beta \cdot ((\partial_x S_p - h_p)^2 + (\partial_y S_p - v_p)^2)\}, \tag{2}$$

where $C(h,v) = \sharp\{p : |h_p| + |v_p| \neq 0\}$, h_p and v_p are auxiliary variables corresponding to $\partial_x S_p$ and $\partial_y S_p$, and β is an automatically adapting parameter to control the similarity between auxiliary variables and their corresponding gradients. (2) can be solved by minimizing h, v and S alternately. Here, S is initialized as I. The algorithm details can be found in [14].

2.2   Superpixel Technique

Superpixel technique can group pixels into several perceptually meaningful regions. Here we utilize VCells [13] to produce superpixels because it can efficiently generate rough subregions and preserve local boundaries.

We define a partition for image I as $\{P_k\}_{k=1}^n$, where n is the number of superpixels, and P_k is the set of pixels within the same superpixel. The centroid for the superpixel P_k is

$$g_k = \frac{1}{\sharp\{P_k\}} \sum_{p \in P_k} u(p),$$

where $\sharp\{P_i\}$ is the pixel number in P_i, and $u(p)$ is the gray value of pixel p. The edge-weighted distance between the pixel p and the centroid g_k is calculated as

$$\text{dist}\,(p, g_k) = \sqrt{|u(p) - g_k|^2 + 2 \cdot \rho \cdot \hat{n}_k(p)}, \tag{3}$$

where $\hat{n}_k = \sharp\{N_w(p) \setminus (P_k \cup p)\}$, and $N_w(p)$ is the set of pixels in the disk with radius ω and center p. The term $|u(p) - g_k|^2$ ensures the superpixel homogeneity. The term $2 \cdot \rho \cdot \hat{n}_k(p)$ is a compactness constraint ensuring the segmentation is less sensitive to noise, and ρ is a balancing parameter.

3   Proposed Change Detection Method

Let $\{I_{t_1}, I_{t_2}\}$ be an image pair obtained at times t_1 and t_2. Our goal is to represent the final change detection result by a binary change mask [9]:

$$CM(i, j) = \begin{cases} 1, & \text{if there is change in pixel } (i, j) \\ 0, & \text{otherwise,} \end{cases} \tag{4}$$

where (i, j) denote the image coordinates.

Our approach consists of five steps listed in Algorithm 1, where the first three steps form stage 1, and the next two steps form stage 2.

Algorithm 1. The proposed algorithm

Input: an image pair $\{I_{t_1}, I_{t_2}\}$
Output: the change mask CM_2

1 Generate the difference image D;
2 Preprocess D using L_0 smoothing with two different parameters to generate D_{s_1} and D_{s_2} respectively;
3 Generate CM_1 by clustering pixels in D_{s_1} using k-means with $k = 2$;
4 Generate the superpixel segmentation on D_{s_2} via VCells and calculate the change degree for each superpixel with CM_1;
5 Generate CM_2 by clustering the superpixels into two classes using k-means with $k = 2$.

In the first step, the difference image D is generated using the image pair $\{I_{t_1}, I_{t_2}\}$ according to input image types. For optical images, D can be calculated as the absolute-valued subtraction of the image pair $\{I_{t_1}, I_{t_2}\}$, i.e.,

$$D = |I_{t_1} - I_{t_2}|. \tag{5}$$

For SAR images, it is calculated as the absolute-valued log-ratio of the image pair $\{I_{t_1}, I_{t_2}\}$, i.e.,

$$D = \left|\log \frac{I_{t_1}}{I_{t_2}}\right|. \tag{6}$$

Unlike optical images, SAR images may suffer from multiplicative noise [10], thus the substraction operator cannot indicate the trend of change. On the other hand, the log-ratio operator can transform the multiplicative speckle noise into an additive noise [7], and it may reduce the noise effect to some extent.

After that, we normalize the difference image to zero-one scale, i.e.,

$$D = (D - \min D)/(\max D - \min D). \tag{7}$$

The difference image (7) can directly indicate the difference intensity of the image pair.

In the second step, we use L_0 smoothing to preprocess the difference image. As mentioned in Introduction, difference images always suffer from noise which causes difficulty to directly detect changes; meanwhile, how to make an accurate edge pixel classification is still a challenging problem. Therefore, we select the L_0 smoothing algorithm to improve the difference image here.

We apply the L_0 smoothing on the difference image to generate D_{s_1} and D_{s_2} which are used for the first stage detection and superpixel segmentation in the second stage respectively. This operation generates not only a more suitable difference image for k-means but also a better input for superpixel segmentation.

In the third step, we produce the first change mask CM_1 by clustering the pixels of D_{s_1} into two classes using k-means with $k = 2$. The class with higher average value is regarded as the changed class.

In this step, we produce the first change mask of a difference map without considering spatial information. According to Occam's Razor, we can avoid the error generated by a complex model to some extent and make CM_1 reliable for the further operation.

We take the next two steps as the second stage of the algorithm. In this stage, we convert the pixel classification into a superpixel classification, and generate the final change mask CM_2.

In the fourth step, we generate the superpixel segmentation on D_{s_2} via VCells.

We then calculate the change degree for each superpixel. The idea of the change degree comes from the concept of probabilistic superpixels [11] which is used to improve the foreground segmentation. Suppose that $\{P_i\}_{i=1}^n$ is the superpixel segmentation result of D_{s_2}, and p denote the image coordinates, the change degree for P_i can be calculated as

$$Q(P_i) = \min\left(1, \theta \cdot \frac{\sum_{p \in P_i} CM_1(p)}{\sharp\{P_i\}}\right).$$

The term $\sum_{p \in P_i} CM_1(p)$ is the number of the changed pixels within P_i according to (4), $\sharp\{P_i\}$ is the number of pixels within P_i, and θ is a balancing parameter.

In the final step, we cluster the superpixels into two classes by k-means with $k = 2$. We take the class with higher average change degree as the changed superpixel class, otherwise the unchanged superpixel class. We regard all pixels in the changed superpixels as the changed pixels, and all pixels in the unchanged ones as the unchanged pixels. Thus, the final change mask CM_2 is obtained.

We combine L_0 smoothing and VCells in our proposed method. Both of them are efficient. In L_0 smoothing method, 20-30 iterations are generally performed [14]. In the VCells algorithm, the main computational cost of each iteration is $O(\sqrt{n_c \cdot N})$, where n_c is the number of superpixels and N is the total number of pixels [13]. Overall, the proposed algorithm generally takes 8 seconds to detect a 512×512 image pair with 1500 superpixels on an Intel Core2 CPU@2.6G.

     (a)   (b)   (c)   (d)

Fig. 2. Mexico data set: (a) Image acquired in April, 2000; (b) Image acquired in May, 2002; (c) The corresponding difference image; and (d) The reference change mask.

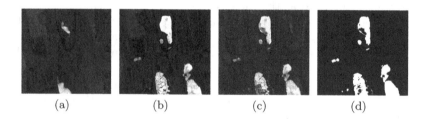

     (a)   (b)   (c)   (d)

Fig. 3. Alaska data set: (a) Image acquired on July 22, 1985; (b) Image acquired on July 13, 2005; (c) The corresponding difference image; and (d) The reference change mask.

4   Experimental Results

In this section, we introduce the data sets used in the experiments, give the quantitative measurements of the change detection algorithm, and present the results.

4.1   Description of Data Sets

We test our method on SAR and optical image data sets.

    The SAR data set is an image pair in Mexico. Fig. 2(a) and 2(b) show the image pair acquired in April 2000 and May 2002 with a section of 512×512 pixels.

Between the aforementioned dates, a fire burned a large portion of vegetation in this area [6]. Fig. 2(c) and 2(d) are the respective difference image and reference change mask.

The optical image data set consists of an image pair acquired by Landsat 5 TM in Alaska on July 22, 1985 and July 13, 2005, respectively. Between the two aforementioned dates, the ice layers melted due to the rise in average temperature. We select a section of 470×510 pixels with band 1 for the experiment. Fig. 3(a) and 3(b) show the experimental images. Fig. 3(c) shows the corresponding difference image generated by (5) and (7). Fig. 3(d) is the reference change mask.

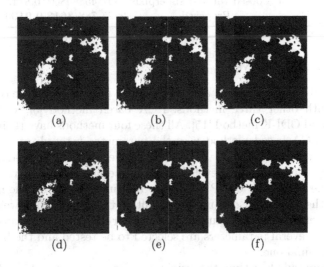

Fig. 4. Mexico data set: change mask provided by (a) PCA based method, (b) UDWT based method, (c) CDI-K without PPB, (d) Proposed method without superpixel, (e) Proposed method, and (f) The reference change mask.

4.2 Quantitative Measures

In order to conduct quantitative measures, we compare the algorithm results with the reference change masks made manually by visual analysis on image pairs. The performance is evaluated by indices of false alarm, missed alarm, overall error, and Kappa. False alarm is presented by the number of unchanged pixels misclassified into changed compared to the reference mask. Missed alarm is presented by the number of changed pixels misclassified into unchanged compared to the reference change mask. Overall error is presented by the total number of pixels misclassified, which is the sum of false and missed alarms.

Table 1. Comparison on Mexico and Alaska data set

Dataset	Method	FA	MA	OE	Kappa
	PCA based	2706	592	3298	0.9251
	UDWT based	4677	245	4922	0.8833
Mexico	CDI-K	3285	226	3511	0.9189
	Proposed without superpixel	5558	555	6113	0.8534
	Proposed	2054	450	**2504**	**0.9437**
	PCA based	4449	394	4843	0.8746
	UDWT based	4540	409	4949	0.8720
Alaska	CDI-K without PPB	4514	502	5016	0.8703
	Proposed without superpixel	4397	453	4850	0.8747
	Proposed	2825	788	**3613**	**0.9103**

4.3 Result and Analysis

To demonstrate the qualitative and quantitative performances, we compare our algorithm with other three methods: PCA based method [5], UDWT based method [4], and CDI-K method [15]. All these four methods have their respective parameters. PCA based method uses the parameter h to adjust the contribution of contextual information. UDWT based method uses the parameter S to adjust the wavelet transform level. In CDI-K method, PPB algorithm is used. Therefore, the parameter of PPB needs to be tuned to control the noise effect. Meanwhile, the parameter α is used to maintain the combination weight for two kinds of difference images. In our experiments, for each comparing algorithm and each data set, several parameters are selected to be tested and the best result is chosen as the final one.

In the proposed algorithm, the weight parameter ρ is set as 15 and the radius parameter ω is set as 3 for all data sets (ρ and ω are mentioned in (3)), while the smooth parameters λ_{s_1} and λ_{s_2}, the superpixel number N and the change degree parameter θ need to be tuned. We set λ_{s_1} and λ_{s_2} according to the noise level in the image pair. The larger parameter value, which brings larger smooth level, overcomes the noise effect consequently. We usually set these two parameters slightly different to meet different usages. We set the superpixel number N according to the distribution of the changed areas. For an image pair with more isolated small changed areas, a larger N needs to be set. The change degree parameter θ is used to meet different change detection demands, and the larger θ can detect more changes with small change level. In our experiment, θ is fixed as 3. The proposed algorithm is compared with the same algorithm without superpixel. It needs to be noted that all the parameters are set as same for the comparison.

Fig. 4 shows the visual results for the Mexico data set. Here we set the parameters as $\lambda_{s_1} = 0.001, \lambda_{s_2} = 0.005$ and $N = 1500$. As in Fig. 4(e), the result of the proposed algorithm performs better, because it results in fewer isolated unchanged pixels and takes the change area as a whole. There are a few isolated pixels in Fig. 4(d) which is the result of proposed method without superpixel. It turns out to be improved with the help of superpixel. Due to the fact that the superpixel is robust to noise, the noisy pixels are more likely to be corrected to cluster into the right class when the superpixel based k-means is applied. Table 1 shows that the proposed method is with the least false alarm, the least overall error and the highest Kappa index.

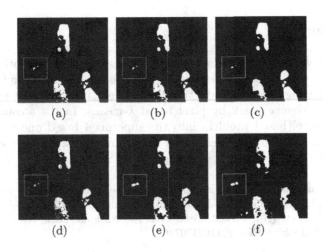

Fig. 5. Alaska data set: change mask provided by (a) PCA based method, (b) UDWT based method, (c) CDI-K without PPB, (d) Proposed method without superpixel, (e) Proposed method, and (f) The reference change mask.

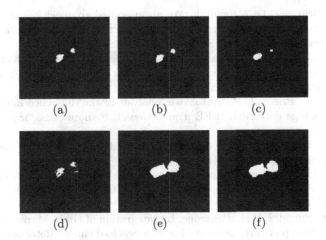

Fig. 6. Close-ups from the Fig. 5 (a) PCA based method, (b) UDWT based method, (c) CDI-K without PPB, (d) Proposed method without superpixel, (e) Proposed method, and (f) The reference change mask.

Fig. 5 shows the visual result for the Alaska data set. Here we set the parameters as $\lambda_{s_1} = 0, \lambda_{s_2} = 0.001$ and $N = 1000$. For CDI-K method, the PBB algorithm is not necessary since it is an optical image data set. Compared with other methods, the proposed method performs better. Especially in Fig. 6, close-ups show that the proposed algorithm detected the whole changed area while others failed. Table 1 shows that the proposed method is with the least false alarm, the least overall error and the highest Kappa index.

5   Conclusion

In this paper, we have proposed a two-stage change detection algorithm based on L_0 smoothing and superpixel techniques. We use the L_0 smoothing to improve the difference image for noise reduction and edge enhancement. In the first stage, we produce a change mask by pixel based k-means. In the second stage, we convert the pixel based problem into the superpixel based one to obtain the final change mask. With the help of L_0 smoothing and superpixel, our method can detect the boundary pixels of changed areas more accurately.

Acknowledgments. This work is supported by the National Science Foundation of China (No. 61273298), Science and Technology Commission of Shanghai Municipality under research grant (No. 14DZ2260800) and the National Basic Research Program (973 Program) of China (No. 2011CB707104).

References

1. Bazi, Y., Bruzzone, L., Melgani, F.: An unsupervised approach based on the generalized Gaussian model to automatic change detection in multitemporal sar images. IEEE Trans. Geosci. Remote Sens. **43**(4), 874–887 (2005)
2. Bazi, Y., Melgani, F., Al-Sharari, H.D.: Unsupervised change detection in multispectral remotely sensed imagery with level set methods. IEEE Trans. Geosci. Remote Sens. **48**(8), 3178–3187 (2010)
3. Bruzzone, L., Prieto, D.F.: Automatic analysis of the difference image for unsupervised change detection. IEEE Trans. Geosci. Remote Sens. **38**(3), 1171–1182 (2000)
4. Celik, T.: Multiscale change detection in multitemporal satellite images. IEEE Geosci. Remote Sens. Lett. **6**(4), 820–824 (2009)
5. Celik, T.: Unsupervised change detection in satellite images using principal component analysis and k-means clustering. IEEE Geosci. Remote Sens. Lett. **6**(4), 772–776 (2009)
6. Ghosh, A., Subudhi, B.N., Bruzzone, L.: Integration of Gibbs Markov random field and Hopfield-type neural networks for unsupervised change detection in remotely sensed multitemporal images. IEEE Trans. Image Process. **22**(8), 3087–3096 (2013)
7. Gong, M., Zhou, Z., Ma, J.: Change detection in synthetic aperture radar images based on image fusion and fuzzy clustering. IEEE Trans. Image Process. **21**(4), 2141–2151 (2012)

8. Lee, L., Romano, R., Stein, G.: Introduction to the special section on video surveillance. IEEE Trans. Pattern Anal. Mach. Intell. **22**(8), 740–745 (2000)
9. Radke, R.J., Andra, S., Al-Kofahi, O., Roysam, B.: Image change detection algorithms: a systematic survey. IEEE Trans. Image Process. **14**(3), 294–307 (2005)
10. Rignot, E.J., van Zyl, J.J.: Change detection techniques for ERS-1 SAR data. IEEE Trans. Geosci. Remote Sens. **31**(4), 896–906 (1993)
11. Schick, A., Bauml, M., Stiefelhagen, R.: Improving foreground segmentations with probabilistic superpixel Markov random fields. In: 2012 IEEE Computer Society Conference on Computer Vision and Pattern Recognition Workshops (CVPRW), pp. 27–31. IEEE (2012)
12. Singh, A.: Digital change detection techniques using remotely-sensed data. Int. J. Remote Sens. **10**(6), 989–1003 (1989)
13. Wang, J., Wang, X.: VCells: simple and efficient superpixels using edge-weighted centroidal voronoi tessellations. IEEE Trans. Pattern Anal. Mach. Intell. **34**(6), 1241–1247 (2012)
14. Xu, L., Lu, C., Xu, Y., Jia, J.: Image smoothing via l_0 gradient minimization. ACM Trans. Graph. **30**(6), 174 (2011)
15. Zheng, Y., Zhang, X., Hou, B., Liu, G.: Using combined difference image and k -means clustering for SAR image change detection. IEEE Geosci. Remote Sens. Lett. **11**(3), 691–695 (2014)

Rare Category Detection Forest

Haiqin Weng[1], Zhenguang Liu[1], Kevin Chiew[2], and Qinming He[1(✉)]

[1] College of Computer Science, Zhejiang University, Hangzhou, China
{hq_weng,zhenguangliu,hqm}@zju.edu.cn
[2] Handal Indah Sdn Bhd, Singapore Branch, Johor Bahru, Malaysia
kchiew@handalindah.com.my

Abstract. Rare category detecion (RCD) aims to discover rare categories in a massive unlabeled data set with the help of a labeling oracle. A challenging task in RCD is to discover rare categories which are concealed by numerous data examples from major categories. Only a few algorithms have been proposed for this issue, most of which are on quadratic or cubic time complexity. In this paper, we propose a novel tree-based algorithm known as RCD-Forest with $O(\varphi n \log(n/s))$ time complexity and high query efficiency where n is the size of the unlabeled data set. Experimental results on both synthetic and real data sets verify the effectiveness and efficiency of our method.

Keywords: Rare category detection · Relative density · Compact tree

1 Introduction

The aim of rare category detecion (RCD) is to find at least one representative data example from each rare category in a massive unlabeled data set with the help of a labeling oracle. In the further work rare category exploration (RCE) [2,8], these data examples are used as seeds to discover the remaining data examples in the same rare categories. One open challenge in RCD is to discover such rare categories that are hidden in data examples from major categories. However, there are only a few algorithms proposed for this issus, most of which pay little attention to the trade-off between time complexity and query efficiency, e.g. GRADE [4], FRED [9], CLOVER [5], RADAR [6], NNDM [3]. Motivated by Isolation Forest [7] and kd-tree, in this paper we develop a novel tree-based algorithm known as RCD-Forest, which has a comparatively low time complexity $O(\varphi n \log(n/s))$ and high query efficiency. In details, RCD-Forest contains three main stages, namely (1) Stage 1, it grows a series of resembling $cTrees$ (compact trees) to form a $cForest$ (compact forest), (2) Stage 2, it calculates average relative density $(\overline{Rd})$ for each data example and selects top m data examples to generate a coarse-grained candidate set, and (3) Stage 3, it refines the candidate set and discovers rare categories.

© Springer International Publishing Switzerland 2015
S. Zhang et al. (Eds.): KSEM 2015, LNAI 9403, pp. 612–618, 2015.
DOI: 10.1007/978-3-319-25159-2_55

2   An Illustration of RCD-Forest

2.1   Compact Tree

The idea of constructing $c\mathit{Trees}$ comes from the splitting process of kd-tree (k-dimensional tree), which has a space-partitioning data structure for orgnazing data examples in a k-dimensional space. Every non-leaf node of a kd-tree has a splitting item, which consists of a splitting dimension and value denoted as (i, v), and needs a *povit-choosing* to generate it; every leaf node contains only one data example. We observe that the rare category is continuesly splitted into a shrinking sub-space during the splitting process of a kd-tree, meaning that a high score of relative density (Rd) of data examples from a rare category.

Based on this dominant phenomenon, we come into the idea of constructing $c\mathit{Trees}$ with two improvements on kd-tree: (1) Split the data set by an optimal *pivot-choosing* rule. (2) Stop the splitting process when the data size belows a certain threshold. Fig. 1 shows the splitting process of a $c\mathit{Tree}$, from which we observe that: (1) Rare category is continuesly splitted into a shrinking sub-space. (2) the Rd of data examples from a major category are approximately to 1, data examples from anomalies less than 1 and data examples from a rare category greater than 1. Note that we construct a series of resembling $c\mathit{Trees}$ rather than one $c\mathit{Tree}$ in order to get an average Rd ($\overline{Rd}$ for convenience), which guarantees a coarse-grained candidate set with high proportion of data examples belonging to rare categories.

2.2   Pivot-Choosing Rule

Motivated by Ram $\mathit{el.}$ [10], we define our *pivot-choosing* rule due to the least integrated squared error (ISE), which is shown in the following.

Definition 1 (Pivot-Choosing Rule). Given the current non-leaf node N, choose a splitting dimension i randomly, and choose a splitting value $v =$
$\mathrm{argmin}_{v \in i} \left\{ -\dfrac{|N_l(i,v)|^2}{R(N_l(i,v))^d} - \dfrac{|N_r(i,v)|^2}{R(N_r(i,v))^d} \right\}$, where $N_l(\cdot)$, $N_r(\cdot)$ are the left

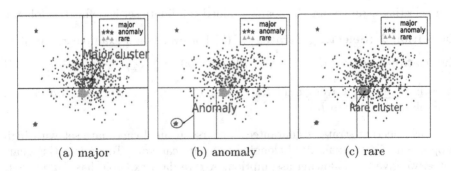

| (a) major | (b) anomaly | (c) rare |

Fig. 1. The splitting process of a $c\mathit{Tree}$

and right children node splitted by the splitting item (i, v) and $R(\cdot)$ is the radius of node.

We prove that a *cTree* with a small ISE is grown if following our *pivot-choosing* rule. First we give the definition of ISE in the following.

$$E = \min_{\hat{f}} \left\{ \int_X \left(\hat{f}(x) - f(x) \right)^2 dx \right\}. \tag{1}$$

In Eq. (1), $f(x)$ is the real data density and $\hat{f}(x) = \sum_{N \in \ell} \frac{|N|}{nV} I(x \in N)$, where ℓ is the set of leaf nodes, $|N|$ is the node size, n is data size, $I(x \in N)$ is the indicator function, $V = \alpha R(N)^d$ is the node volume, where α is a constant, d is the dimensionality, and $R(\cdot)$ is the radius.

Proof. By expanding the square item in Eq. (1), subsituting $\hat{f}(x)$ and using Monte-Carlo's solution $\int_X \hat{f}(x) f(x) dx = \frac{1}{n} \sum_i^n \hat{f}(x)$, we have

$$E = \min_{\ell} \int_X \left(\sum_{N \in \ell} \frac{|N|}{n\alpha R(N)^d} I(x \in N) \right)^2 dx - \frac{2}{N} \sum_i^n \sum_{N \in \ell} \frac{|N|}{n\alpha R(N)^d} I(x_i \in N)$$

Ignoring constants α, n and calculating E accroding data distribution in leaf node, we have

$$E = \min_{\ell} \left\{ -\sum_{N \in \ell} \frac{|N|^2}{R(N)^d} \right\}. \tag{2}$$

According to greedy policy, we solve the Eq. 2 by randomly choosing a splitting dimension i, which is for the purpose of less time cost, and a splitting value $v = \text{argmin}_{v \in i} \left\{ -\frac{|N_l(i,v)|^2}{R(N_l(i,v))^d} - \frac{|N_r(i,v)|^2}{R(N_r(i,v))^d} \right\}$ in every splitting process. Thus, we prove our *pivot-choosing* rule. ∎

2.3 Selecting Strategy

Our selecting strategy for the coarse-grained candidate set is defined as follows.

Definition 2 (Selecting Strategy). (1) For every data example x, calculate the relative density $Rd(x) = \frac{\hat{f}(x)}{\hat{f}_p(x)}$, where $\hat{f}_p(x) = \sum_{N \in \ell} \frac{|N_p|}{n\alpha R(N_p)^d} I(x \in N)$ in each *cTree*, then average all $Rd(x)$ to get $\overline{Rd}(x)$; (2) select the top m data examples according to $\overline{Rd}$.

This selecting strategy guarantees a coarse-grained candidate set with high proportion of data examples belonging to a rare category. To explain this guarantee, we give the following assumption. A rare data example has $Rd(x) \gg 1$, major data example $Rd(x) \approx 1$ and anomaly $Rd(x) \ll 1$.

Algorithm 1.   RCD-Forest algorithm

Input: $X = \{x_1, x_2, ..., x_n\}$-input dataset, p-proportion of the smallest category
Output: the data set Q of selected query data examples and L of their labels

1 Initialize $F = \varnothing, R = \varnothing, Q = \varnothing, L = \varnothing$
2 **for** $i = 1 : \varphi$ **do**
3      $\lfloor\ F = F \cup CompactTree(X, p \times n)$

4 **for** $i = 1 : n$ **do**
5      $\lfloor\ R = R \cup \overline{Rd}(x_i)$

6 Select top m data examples according to R to generate a candidate set C
7 $\forall c_j \in C, k_j = k\text{-distance}(c_j)$
8 **while** *not all the classes are discovered* **do**
9   Query $c_{min} = \text{argmin}_{c_i \in C} k_i$ for its label ℓ
10   **if** *l belongs a new class that has not been discovered* **then**
11          $\lfloor\ L = L \cup \ell$
12          $\forall c_j \in C$, s.t. $\|c_j - c_{min}\| \leqslant k_{min}$, set $k_j = \infty$
13      $\lfloor\ k_{min} = \infty, Q = Q \cup c_{min}$

2.4   RCD-Forest Algorithm

In Alogirthm 1, we present detailed steps of RCD-Forest. Given an unlabeled data set X with n data examples and proportion of the smallest rare category, RCD-Forest works as follows.

Stage 1. Construct a *cForest* containing a series of resembling *cTrees*. In line 3, we construct φ *cTrees* iteratively. After a lot of experiments, we choose the number in the range from 32 to 64 as the forest size.

Stage 2. Calculate $\overline{Rd}$ to generate a coarse-grained candidate set. In line 5, we calculate average relative density $\overline{Rd}$ interatively. In line 6, select top m data examples, where m is the size of all rare caregory data examples with prior information.

Stage 3. Refine the candidate set and discover rare categories. In line 7, calculate k-distance for every data example, where k is an adaptive paramater in the range from 5 to 10. Then, in the lines 8–13, we query an data example with minimal k-distance denoted as k_{min} repeatly until all categories have been discovered.

Time complexity of RCD-Forest consists of three parts. (1) RCD-Forest scan the data set once at every splitting process and stops when data size is below a threshold s, thus time complexity is $O(\varphi n \log (n/s))$. (2) calculateing $\overline{Rd}$ for every data example in φ *cTrees* takes $O(\varphi n)$. (3) The time consumption of refinement can be ignored. Therefore the overall time cost is $O(\varphi n \log (n/s))$.

3   Experimental Evaluation

In this section, we conduct experiments to verify the efficiency and effectiveness of RCD-Forest. All these algorithms are implemented in C++ and performed

Name	N	d	m	Largest class (%)	Smallest class (%)
Glass	214	9	6	35.1	4.21
Ecoli	332	7	6	43.07	1.51
PenDigit	1322	16	10	59.00	4.23
KDD99	3641	41	6	43.64	1.43
Satellite	4435	9	6	23.40	9.33
DSAA	58304	4	3	0.4	96.1

Table 1. Detailed information of data sets

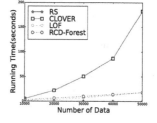

Fig. 2. Time Comparision

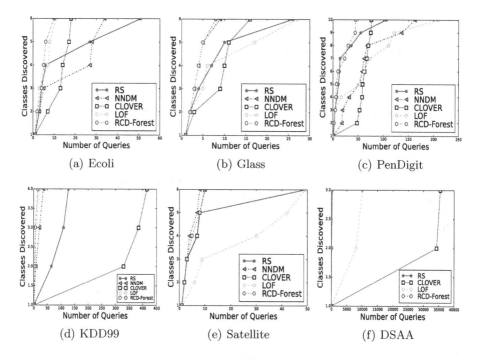

(a) Ecoli   (b) Glass   (c) PenDigit

(d) KDD99   (e) Satellite   (f) DSAA

Fig. 3. Performance Comparisions on Real Data Sets

on a desktop with 2.4GHz CPU and 8GB memeory. Table 1 lists some data sets used in our experiments, where n denotes the size of data examples, d the dimensionality, and m the size of total catetories.

3.1 Efficiency and Effectiveness

We verify the efficiency and effectiveness of RCD-Forest from two aspects, namely (1) time efficiency and (2) number of total queries from the labeling oracle. To test our algorithm, RCD-Forest is compared with NNDM, CLOVER, RS and LOF on both synthetic and real data sets (listed in Table 1) from UCI data repository [1] and MOOC [11], which is an online course platform. Among the six selected real data sets, five data sets namely Ecoli, Class, Pen Digit, Satellite and KDD99 are from UCI data reposity and the rest DSAA is from MOOC.

Fig. 3 illustrates the comparison of effectiveness on six real data sets. From the figure, we observe that RCD-Forest outperfroms RS, NNDM, CLOVER, LOF on five data sets namely Ecoli, Glass, Pen Digit, KDD, MOOC, means that RCD-Forest needs the least queries for the discovery of rare categories. More specificly, in Fig. 3(a), RCD-Forest needs 45 queries, RS 106, CLOVER 76, and NNDM 163.

Fig. 2 illustrates the comparision of time efficiency on synthetic set, where major categories follow uniform distribution and rare categories Gaussian distribution. The size of synthetic data sets varies from 10000 to 50000. It is shown from the figure that (1) RS, LOF and RCD-Forest consume less time than CLOVER; (2) time consumption of LOF and RCD-Forest is almost the same.

4   Conclusion

In this paper, we have proposed a novel tree-based method that uses average relative density to discover rare categories. For the next stage of study, a promising direction is to investigate a new partition selection criteria and use histogram to estimate the distribution rather than using priori information.

Acknowledgments. This work was supported by the NSFC Grant 61472359, and MOE-Google MOOC Research Found of China under Grant No.MOE-GOOGLE-MOOC14-01.

References

1. Asuncion, A., Newman, D.: UCI Machine Learning Repository (2007)
2. Hao, H., Kevin, C., Yunjun, G., Qinming, H., Qing, L.: Rare category exploration. Expert Syst. Appl. **41**(9), 4197–4210 (2014)
3. He, J., Carbonell, J.G.: Nearest-neighbor-based active learning for rare category detection. In: NIPS 2007, pp. 633–640 (2007)
4. He, J., Liu, Y., Lawrence, R.: Graph-based rare category detection. In: ICDE 2008, pp. 833–838 (2008)
5. Huang, H., He, Q., Chiew, K., Qian, F., Ma, L.: CLOVER: a faster prior-free approach to rare-category detection. Knowl. Inf. Syst. **35**(3), 713–736 (2013)
6. Huang, H., He, Q., He, J., Ma, L.: RADAR: rare category detection via computation of boundary degree. In: Huang, J.Z., Srivastava, J., Cao, L. (eds.) PAKDD 2011, Part II. LNCS, vol. 6635, pp. 258–269. Springer, Heidelberg (2011)
7. Liu, F.T., Ting, K.M., Zhou, Z.H.: Isolation forest. In: ICDM 2008, pp. 413–422 (2008)
8. Liu, Z., Huang, H., He, Q., Chiew, K., Gao, Y.: Rare category exploration on linear time complexity. In: Renz, M., Shahabi, C., Zhou, X., Chemma, M.A. (eds.) DASFAA 2015. LNCS, vol. 9050, pp. 37–54. Springer, Heidelberg (2015)

9. Liu, Z., Huang, H., He, Q., Chiew, K., Ma, L.: Rare category detection on $O(dN)$ time complexity. In: Ho, T.B., Zhou, Z.-H., Chen, A.L.P., Kao, H.-Y., Tseng, V.S. (eds.) PAKDD 2014, Part II. LNCS, vol. 8444, pp. 498–509. Springer, Heidelberg (2014)
10. Ram, P., Gray, A.G.: Density estimation trees. In: KDD 2011, pp. 627–635 (2011)
11. Weng, H.: Zhejiang University (2015). https://github.com/HaiQW/MOOC

Incremental Distributed Weighted Class Discriminant Analysis on Interval-Valued Emitter Parameters

Xin Xu[1], Wei Wang[2], Jiaheng Lu[3], and Jin Chen[4,5]($\boxtimes$)

[1] Science and Technology on Information System Engineering Laboratory,
NRIEE, Nanjing, China
[2] State Key Laboratory for Novel Software and Technology,
Nanjing University, Nanjing, China
[3] Key Laboratory of Data Engineering and Knowledge Engineering,
Renmin University, Beijing, China
[4] Department of Energy Plant Research Lab, Michigan State University,
East Lansing, USA
[5] Department of Computer Science and Engineering, Michigan State University,
East Lansing, USA
jinchen@msu.edu

Abstract. In the age of big data, the emitter parameter measurement data is generally characteristic of uncertainty in the form of normally-distributed intervals, enormous size and continuous growth. However, existing interval-valued data analysis methods generally assume a uniform distribution instead and are unable to adapt to the rapid growth of volume. To address the above problems, we have brought forward an incremental distributed weighted class discriminant analysis method on interval-valued emitter parameters. Extensive experiments indicate that our method is able to cope with these new characteristics effectively.

Keywords: Fuzzy pattern mining · Emitter identification · Class discriminant analysis · Incremental learning · Distributed computing · Signal processing

1 Introduction

It is widely recognized that emitter parameter analysis has played a crucial role in both military and civil applications. However, the emitter parameter measurement data is typically characteristic of uncertainty, enormous size and continuous growth. The parameter measurements typically fluctuate according to a certain normal distribution and an interval would be obtained with the minimum and maximum bounds. In addition the amount of parameter measurements are huge in size

This work was supported by National Natural Science Foundation of China (No. 61402426, 61373129) and Chemical Sciences, Geosciences and Biosciences Division, Office of Basic Energy Sciences, Office of Science, U.S. Department of Energy (No. DEFG02-91ER20021) and partially supported by Collaborative Innovation Center of Novel Software Technology and Industrialization.

S. Zhang et al. (Eds.): KSEM 2015, LNAI 9403, pp. 619–624, 2015.
DOI: 10.1007/978-3-319-25159-2_56

and being accumulated dynamically. The traditional methods generally assume that the data values are uniformly distributed in the interval and pay little attention to the dynamic growth of size and thus are inappropriate to be applied.

Inspired by the above problems, we bring forward an incremental distributed weighted class discriminant analysis method on interval-valued emitter parameters. It is not only adaptable for the normal distributed parameter measurements but also for incremental learning in a distributed environment.

The rest of the paper is organized as follows. We briefly review related work in interval-valued data analysis in Section 2. Our incremental distributed weighted class discriminant analysis method is formally proposed in Section 3. In Section 4, we present the experimental results. And we conclude in Section 5.

2   Related Work

A large amount of research work in interval-valued data analysis has been conducted. For instance, symbolic data analysis [6] has been proposed to extend the classical data models to take into account of the interval-valued information. The representative methods include point value replacement [3], p-box [4] and Hausdorff distance based ones [5]. However, they are generally based on the assumption of uniform distribution which is not true for emitter parameters. In addition, they are not adaptable for the dynamic growth of huge emitter parameter measurement data.

3   Method

In this section, we formally present our incremental distributed weighted class discriminant analysis method on interval-valued emitter parameters.

Suppose the interval-valued emitter data set E is composed of M observations, $\{o_m\}_{1 \leq m \leq M}$, and each observation o_m has N interval-valued measurements $\{I_{mn}\}_{1 \leq n \leq N}$ for parameters $p_1, p_2, ..., $ and p_N respectively. Each observation comes from one of the K different emitter types, $c_1, c_2, ..., $ and c_K. And assume for each measurement $I_{mn} = [L_{mn}, U_{mn}]$, w independent measurements $\{x_{mnr}\}_{1 \leq r \leq w}$ are provided which comply with the same *interval distribution* $\mathcal{N}(\mu_{mn}, \sigma_{mn}^2)$. The lower bound L_{mn} and upper bound U_{mn} correspond to the minimum and maximum value among the w measurements. In addition, for observations in the same emitter type, $\forall o_m \in \Omega_k$, the corresponding mean value μ_{mn} complies with the same *class distribution* $\mathcal{N}(\mu_{kn}, \sigma_{kn})$ as well. We also assume the variances σ_{mn}^2 and σ_{kn}^2 are approximately the same. The above assumptions are summarized in Equation 1.

$$\begin{cases} x_{mnr} \sim \mathcal{N}(\mu_{mn}, \sigma_{mn}^2) & 1 \leq r \leq w \\ \mu_{mn} \sim \mathcal{N}(\mu_{kn}, \sigma_{kn}^2) & \forall o_m \in \Omega_k \\ \sigma_{mn}^2 \approx \sigma_{kn}^2 \\ L_{mn} = min_{1 \leq r \leq w}\{x_{mnr}\} \\ U_{mn} = max_{1 \leq r \leq w}\{x_{mnr}\} \end{cases} \quad (1)$$

Our incremental distributed weighted class discriminant analysis method is consisted of the four major steps, interval distribution estimation, weighted class distribution inference, class discriminant analysis and incremental distributed learning.

3.1   Interval Distribution Estimation

Given an interval-valued measurement $I_{mn} = [L_{mn}, U_{mn}]$, since $L_{mn}, U_{mn} \sim \mathcal{N}(\mu_{mn}, \sigma_{kn}^2)$ and the w parameter measurements are independent with each other, the lower bound L_{mn} corresponds to the smallest order statistic while the upper bound U_{mn} corresponds to the largest order statistic.

The order statistics of standard normal random variables have been approximated [7]. One approximation for the rth highest order statistic out of w is given as $E(r, w) = -\Phi^{-1}(\frac{r-\alpha}{w-2\alpha+1})$, where $\Phi(x) = \int_{-\infty}^{x} \phi(z)dz$, $\phi(x) = 1/\sqrt{2\pi}exp(-\frac{1}{2}x^2)$ and it is recommended that $\alpha = 0.375$. Accordingly, we can infer the estimated $\widetilde{\mu_{mn}}$ and $\widetilde{\sigma_{mn}}$ as calculated below:

$$\begin{cases} \widetilde{\mu_{mn}} = \frac{L_{mn}+U_{mn}}{2} \\ \widetilde{\sigma_{mn}} = \frac{U_{mn}-L_{mn}}{\Phi^{-1}(\frac{1-\alpha}{w-2\alpha+1})-\Phi^{-1}(\frac{w-\alpha}{w-2\alpha+1})} \end{cases} \quad (2)$$

3.2   Weighted Class Distribution Inference

For each interval-valued measurement $I_{mn} = [L_{mn}, U_{mn}]$, the weights of the lower bound $W_{L_{mn}}$, the upper bound $W_{U_{mn}}$ and the middle point $W_{Mid_{mn}}$ would be calculated as the normalized probability of observing the corresponding measurements given the estimated normal distribution $\mathcal{N}(\mu_{mn}, \sigma_{mn}^2)$. Then, the normal class distribution $\mathcal{N}(\mu_{kn}, \sigma_{kn}^2)$ of parameter p_n for emitter type c_k could be further inferred by weighting all the lower bounds, upper bounds and middle points from observations in emitter type c_k, as below:

$$\begin{cases} W_x = \frac{prob(x|\mu_{mn},\sigma_{mn})}{\sum_{x \in \{L_{mn},U_{mn},Mid_{mn}\}} prob(x|\mu_{mn},\sigma_{mn})} \\ \widetilde{\mu_{kn}} = \frac{\sum_{om \in \Omega_k} \sum_{x \in \{L_{mn},U_{mn},Mid_{mn}\}} W_x x}{M_k} \\ \widetilde{\sigma_{kn}}^2 = \frac{\sum_{om \in \Omega_k} \sigma_{mn}^2}{M_k} \end{cases} \quad (3)$$

3.3   Class Discriminant Analysis

The discriminating power of parameter p_n for each emitter type pair $c_u - c_v$ could be evaluated by the welch t-test accordingly. A t-statistics t_{uvn} and the associate degree of freedom df_{uvn} are computed for each emitter type pair $c_u - c_v$ on each parameter p_n, where $1 \leq u, v \leq K$ and $1 \leq n \leq N$:

$$\begin{cases} t_{uvn} = \frac{\widetilde{\mu_{un}} - \widetilde{\mu_{vn}}}{\sqrt{\frac{\widetilde{\sigma_{un}}^2}{M_u} + \frac{\widetilde{\sigma_{vn}}^2}{M_v}}} \\ df_{uvn} = \frac{(\frac{\widetilde{\sigma_{un}}^2}{M_u} + \frac{\widetilde{\sigma_{vn}}^2}{M_v})^2}{\frac{\widetilde{\sigma_{un}}^4}{M_u^2(M_u-1)} + \frac{\widetilde{\sigma_{vn}}^4}{M_v^2(M_v-1)}} \end{cases} \quad (4)$$

In this way, a global ranking of all the interval-valued signal parameters could be obtained in ascending order of the average p-values over all the type pairs.

3.4   Incremental Distributed Learning

To facilitate the incremental distributed learning, we define the data description model consisted of a mean value matrix Σ_μ, a variation matrix Σ_{σ^2} and a data distribution vector V.

Definition 1 (mean value matrix Σ_μ). *We define each element of the two-dimensional mean value matrix $\Sigma_\mu(k, n)$ as the sum of weighted measurements of signal parameter p_n from all the observation o_s in type c_k, where $1 \leq n \leq N$ and $1 \leq k \leq K$. Mathematically speaking,*

$$\Sigma_\mu(k, n) = \sum_{o_m \in \Omega_k} \sum_{x \in \{L_{mn}, U_{mn}, Mid_{mn}\}} W_x x \tag{5}$$

Definition 2 (variation matrix Σ_{σ^2}). *We define each element of variation matrix $\Sigma_{\sigma^2}(k, n)$ as the sum of estimated variations of signal parameter p_n on all the observation o_m in emitter type c_k, where $1 \leq n \leq N$ and $1 \leq k \leq K$. Mathematically speaking,*

$$\Sigma_{\sigma^2}(k, n) = \sum_{o_m \in \Omega_k} \sigma_{mn}^2 \tag{6}$$

A *class distribution vector* V is defined as well, where $|V| = K$ and $V[k]$ denotes the number of observations for emitter type c_k.

The newly arrived observations would be distributed among a set of slave nodes. At each node, the interval distribution estimation would be conducted and the results would be stored in the local data description model. Then, a global merging of the data description models from the slave nodes would be implemented at the master node. After averaging the mean value matrix and variation matrix with the corresponding number of observations in each class and inferring the class mean and variation, a global class discriminant analysis would be updated at the master node incrementally.

4   Results

We evaluated the efficiency and effectiveness of our incremental distributed weighted class discriminant analysis method on a series of synthetic data sets. The synthetic data set was initialized as $50k$ ($M = 50k$) observations from five ($K = 5$) different emitter types, $10k$ ($NumPerCls = 10k$) observations for each type. And the original number of signal parameters was initialized as ten ($N = 10$).

The experiments were conducted on a Spark cluster composed of nine nodes, one master node and eight slave nodes. Each node was a PC running CentOS 6.6 with a Pentium quad-core CPU of 3.2GHz and a 8G RAM. The network bandwidth between two nodes was $100M$.

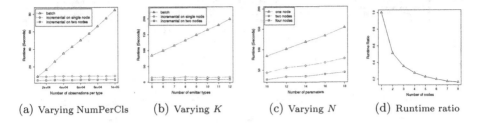

(a) Varying NumPerCls   (b) Varying K (c) Varying N (d) Runtime ratio

Fig. 1. Evaluation of efficiency

4.1 Evaluation of Efficiency

We compared the runtime of our weighted class discriminant analysis method under four different kinds of modes, batch learning on a single node ("batch"), batch learning on multiple nodes ("# nodes"), incremental learning one on a single node ("incremental on single node") and incremental learning on multiple nodes ("incremental on # nodes").

Firstly, we evaluated the efficiency of our method with varying number of observations of each emitter type $NumPerCls$ (Figure 1(a)). The runtime of batch learning increased approximately linearly with the increase of $NumPerCls$. Comparatively, the runtime of incremental learning was approximately fixed. The incremental learning on two nodes was much faster. Secondly, we varied the number of emitter types K from four to twelve while fixed the number of observations per emitter type as $100k$ and the number of signal parameters as ten. As shown in Figure 1(b), the two incremental modes have outperformed the batch mode significantly again. Thirdly, we varied the number of signal parameters N from nine to 18, while fixing the number of observations per emitter type as $100k$ and the number of emitter types as five (Figure 1(c)). Again, the runtime of the three batch modes was approximately linear with the increase in N. Finally, we report the average ratio of the runtime of the batch learning on multiple nodes to that of the batch learing on a single node in Figure 1(d).

4.2 Evaluation of Effectiveness

We evaluated the effectiveness of our method during incremental distributed learning when the number of observations per class ($NumPerCls$) was increased dynamically from 10 to $10k$. Figure 2 illustrates the inferred weighted class distributions for two different emitter types versus the interval mean distributions. The interval mean distribution curves were denoted in dotted and solid thin lines for the two types respectively while the weighted class distribution curves were highlighted in dash and dotted dash thick lines respectively. As can be observed, with the increase of the number of observations, the weighted class distributions converged fine towards the optimal one which shares the same mean value with the interval mean distribution but has a larger variance.

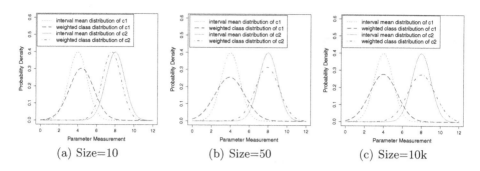

(a) Size=10   (b) Size=50   (c) Size=10k

Fig. 2. Evaluation of effectiveness when varying $NumPerCls$

5   Conclusion

In this work, we have brought forward an incremental distributed weighted class discriminant analysis method on interval-valued parameter measurement streams. Our method is robust to the uncertainty in interval-valued parameter measurements complying with normal distributions and adaptable for incremental learning in a distributed mode. Extensive experiments have validated its efficiency and effectiveness for practical application in emitter parameter analysis and identification.

References

1. Mballo, C., Diday, E.: Decision trees on interval valued variables. The Electronic Journal of Symbolic Data Analysis 3(1) (2005)
2. Caballero, A., Yen, K., Fang, Y., Abreu, J.L.: Method for classification in interval-valued information systems. In: Proceedings of the 12th WSEAS International Conference on Automatic Control, Modelling & Simulation (2010)
3. Lima Neto, E.A., de Carvalho, F.A.T.: Centre and range method to fitting a linear regression model on symbolic interval data. Computational Statistics and Data Analysis **52**, 1500–1515 (2008)
4. Utkin, L., Destercke, S.: Computing expectations with continuous p-boxes: Univariate case. International Journal of Approximate Reasoning **50**, 778–798 (2009)
5. De Carvalho, F., De Souza, R., Chavent, M., Lechevallier, Y.: Adaptive Hausdorff Distances and Dynamic Clustering of Symbolic Interval Data. Pattern Recognition Letters **27**(3), 167–179 (2006). Elsevier
6. Noirhomme-Fraiture, M., Brito, P.: Far beyond the classical data models: symbolic data analysis. Statistical Analysis and Data Mining **4**(2), 157–170 (2011)
7. Royston, J.P.: Expected Normal Order Statistics (Exact and Approximate). Journal of the Royal Statistical Society. Series C (Applied Statistics) **31**(2), 161–165 (1982)

Classification and Clustering

Privacy-Preserving Naive Bayes Classification

Mengdi Huai[1,2]($\boxtimes$), Liusheng Huang[1,2], Wei Yang[1,2], Lu Li[1,2],
and Mingyu Qi[1,2]

[1] School of Computer Science and Technology,
University of Science and Technology of China, Hefei 230026, China
mdhuai@mail.ustc.edu.cn
[2] Suzhou Institute for Advanced Study,
University of Science and Technology of China, Suzhou 215123, China

Abstract. In this paper, we propose differentially private protocols for Naive Bayes classification over distributed data. Compared with existing works, the privacy and security models in the proposed protocols are stronger: firstly, both the miner and parties can be arbitrarily malicious and can collude with each other to violate the remaining honest parties privacy; secondly, all communication channels between them can be assumed to be insecure. Specifically, we build a guarantee of differential privacy into the cryptographic construction so that the proposed protocols can tolerate collusions and resist eavesdropping attacks which are caused by insecure communication channels. Additionally, the proposed protocols can be implemented at lower computation and communication costs, and some extensions to our protocols (e.g. supporting parties dynamic joins or leaves) are also proposed in this paper. Both theoretical analysis and simulation results show that the proposed privacy-preserving protocols for Naive Bayes have strong security and better classification performance than the standard one.

Keywords: Distributed data mining · Naive Bayes · Differential privacy

1 Introduction

As a means of delivering valuable information, data mining has drawn more and more attention. The traditional data mining technology is based on the assumption that the miner can completely access to the data. But currently, it is common that data are distributed among various parties, who don't want to disclose their data due to privacy concerns. So the challenge here is how to accurately mine valuable knowledge from distributed data while effectively guaranteeing parties' privacy, especially when considering the miner or some parties are malicious.

In this paper, we focus on the distributed privacy-preserving of Naive Bayes (NB) learning, of which one of the most commonly used classifiers in the data-mining field. NB is based on statistic analysis and in distributed scenarios, the statistic queries over distributed parties are needed to obtain NB classifiers. However, the accurate query results always disclose private information of parties

© Springer International Publishing Switzerland 2015
S. Zhang et al. (Eds.): KSEM 2015, LNAI 9403, pp. 627–638, 2015.
DOI: 10.1007/978-3-319-25159-2_57

when deriving NB model parameters [1]. To protect the privacy of sensitive information, each party can add noises to their data so that the miner will derive noisy statistic results. Meanwhile, we should achieve two goals: providing useful results and preserving each party's privacy. Additionally, we can not ignore that some participating parties may be compromised and collude with the miner to infer others' sensitive information. Also, another point we need to note is insecure communication channels make their messages suffer from eavesdropping attacks.

To tackle the privacy concerns in distributed NB learning, various schemes have been proposed [4,6,10,12,14]. However, they either need to be implemented with high cost [4,6,10,14], or are easily subject to collusion attacks [4,12]. Also, the centralized private NB scheme [11] allows one party to add noises to data based on the standard differential privacy, achieving a good compromise between privacy and utility. However, their differential privacy mechanisms are not suitable for the distributed data-mining environment. This is because, too much accumulated error can be incurred from the distributed parties, and this will terribly affect the utility of NB classifiers learned from the distributed sceneries.

Given that, we propose the novel privacy-preserving NB protocols in this paper, and these protocols can deal with above situations with low computation and communication cost. In our protocols, we employ distributed differential privacy, a relaxation of differential privacy, which makes sense especially in distributed scenarios because it can provide rigorous privacy assurance and good utility. In our proposed protocols, distributed differential privacy not only lets the miner derive useful noisy results, but also guarantees the parties' data privacy even when some compromised parties collude with the untrusted miner by revealing their data and noises.

Although distributed differential privacy can preserve those honest parties' privacy, the magnitude of the noise generated by a specific party is not enough to ensure his data privacy since communication channels are insecure. So, we combine cryptography techniques with differential privacy to provide more secure guarantees, such that only negligible information of each party can be leaked even if the miner has arbitrary auxiliary information, which can be obtained in various ways (e.g. colluding with compromised parties). Specifically, each party firstly adds an appropriate noise to his data, and then encrypts the noisy data based on the encryption technology. At last, each party sends the encrypted noisy data to the miner who can decrypt the noisy results without learning anything else.

Additionally, parties' dynamic joins and leaves in distributed scenarios are well dealt with in our protocols. Another characteristic of our protocols is that they can support the incremental NB learning.

To sum up, our contributions in this paper are: firstly, we propose two distributed privacy-preserving NB protocols in the distributed environment where data is either horizontally or vertically partitioned, and the two protocols effectively resist both collusion and eavesdropping attacks; Secondly, compared with existing works, the proposed NB protocols can be implemented with lower computation and communication cost while ensuring only the miner having specific capability can get final NB classifiers. Thirdly, we extend them to make them more applicable in reality, such as supporting parties' dynamic joins or leaves.

2   Related Work

In the past, various privacy-preserving mechanisms for NB have been proposed. Using the rigorous privacy model of differential privacy, Vaidya et al. [11] construct a privacy-preserving NB classifier, in which the privacy model is that a data owner having centralized access to a dataset would like to release a NB classifier while preserving parties' data privacy. However, the centralized methods are not suitable to the distributed dataset.

Kantarcioglu et al. [4] in 2003 propose a private NB protocol for only horizontally partitioned data. One constrain in [4] is that they assume there are no collusion among all sites. Besides, their protocols transmit messages in a plain form, making those messages vulnerable to eavesdropping attacks. Yang et al. [14] in 2005 similarly propose a NB protocol over an horizontally distributed database, which is only suitable to a special scenario where each party just holds one instance. Using paillier cryptosystem, the authors in [12] also propose a horizontally private NB protocol, where the number of decryptions is at least $\min(\log_2 N_1, \log_2 N_2)/\log_2(n\mathcal{F})$ and there is no collusion between two parties.

The authors in [6] propose a private NB protocol over vertically distributed data streams using the secure multi-party computation, inevitably leading to high complexity. In [10], the authors present private NB protocols on both vertically and horizontally partitioned data, which cannot resist collusion attacks.

In 2005, Zhang et al. [13] combine data transform with data hiding to propose a new randomization method, to distort original data. Then, an effective NB classifier is presented to predict the class labels for unknown samples according to the distorted data. Yet, arbitrary randomization is not safe [5]. Compared with their methods, the differential privacy mechanisms used in our protocols can not only give rigorous mathematical proof but also provide good reconciliation between utility and privacy.

Motivated by those, we propose the novel privacy-preserving NB protocols. Firstly, the protocols need not any interaction among parties, which largely saves the system cost. Secondly, they can well deal with the scenarios where the miner colludes with parties and communication channels are insecure. Thirdly, they can be implemented with lower computation and communication cost.

3   System Model

3.1   System Setting

Here we consider the horizontally distributed scenarios, while leaving the vertically scenarios to section 5.4. We assume that there are a data miner, N samples and n parties and each party $\mathbf{P}_k$ ($k \in [n]$) has a local dataset.

Let $x = (a_1, ..., a_m)$ be a vector of observed random variables with no class label, where each feature a_i takes values from its domain A_i, i.e., $a_i \in A_i$. The set of all feature vectors is denoted as $\Omega = A_1 \times ... \times A_m$. The NB classifier will predict that x belongs to the class c_j (taken from $\{c_1, ..., c_r\}$) which has the highest posterior probability, conditioned on x. The NB classifier can be defined as follows: $NB(x) = argmax_{c_j} P(X = x|C = c_j)P(C = c_j) = argmax_{c_j} P(c_j) \prod_{i=1}^{m} P(a_i|c_j)$, where $P(c_j)$ represents the class prior probability and $P(a_i|c_j)$ represents the posterior probability.

By simply counting the frequency from the horizontally partitioned dataset, $p(a_i|c_j)$ is calculated as $p(a_i|c_j) = \frac{n_{ij}}{n_j} = \frac{\sum_{k=1}^{n} n_{ij}^k}{\sum_{k=1}^{n} n_j^k}$ and $p(c_j)$ is calculated as $p(c_j) = \frac{n_j}{N} = \frac{\sum_{k=1}^{n} n_j^k}{N}$, where n_j is the whole number of training samples whose class labels are c_j, and n_{ij} is the number of these training examples which also have a_i. And, n_j^k and n_{ij}^k denote the corresponding local counts. Get here, the goal we want to achieve here is how to let the miner get $\sum_{k=1}^{n} n_j^k$ and $\sum_{k=1}^{n} n_{ij}^k$ over n parties, while ensuring parties' privacy.

3.2   Attack Model

In our model, both parties and the miner can be arbitrarily malicious. We assume that the fraction of those uncompromised parties is γ, which can be estimated from priori knowledge, and the reminding compromised parties can collude with the miner to break honest parties' privacy. Besides, communication channels between them are assumed to be insecure, making parties' messages subject to eavesdropping attacks.

3.3   Designing Goals

1. **Utility and Privacy Guarantee.** In horizontally distributed environment, we should compute the sum statistic over n parties to get NB model parameters. Yet, accurate queries can violate parties' privacy [1]. So, each party can add an appropriate noise to his data to protect the data privacy. Meanwhile, two objectives should be compromised: preserving privacy and ensuring good utility, which can be achieved by differential privacy [1]. But, standard differential privacy let each party generate a noise to protect his privacy, making an $O(n)$ accumulated error (the difference with the accurate sum result). Instead, we resort to distributed differential privacy [9], allowing n parties collectively add only a geometric noise to each summation result.
   Also, the distributed differential privacy used in our protocols is collusion-tolerant, which means the privacy of trusted parties can be well protected even if the compromised parties collude with the miner.
2. **Security Guarantee.** Note that using distributed differential privacy, the accumulated error in the sum statistics is only an copy geometric noise, but the magnitude of the noise incorporated to each party' data is not large enough to protect the data privacy. So, the security of data can be violated if only based on the distributed differential privacy since communication channels make parties' data suffer from eavesdropping attacks. We can improve this by incorporating cryptographic techniques. Given this, we design a (ϵ, δ)-differential privacy mechanism combining with the cryptographic construction to provide both security and privacy guarantee. The

main security goal in our NB protocols is to ensure that the miner learns only the final summation results, and nothing else about parties' private data.

3. **Additional Guarantee.** The computation and communication cost should be low since parties' resources are usually limited in reality. Also, distributed parties' dynamic leaves and joins need also to be considered. And, some other situations, such as data pollution should also be considered.

4 Basic Protocol Blocks

4.1 Protocol Sketch

Here, we give a high level description of the proposed horizontally differential private NB protocol (HDPNB). As previously mentioned, two techniques, i.e., differential privacy and applied cryptography methods, are used in HDPNB to provide privacy and security guarantee.

Firstly, each party independently adds an appropriate noise to his data using the data perturbation scheme mentioned below, then encrypts his noisy data using the corresponding encryption scheme and at last sends the encrypted noisy data to the miner who can decrypt summation statistics queries ($\sum_{k=1}^{n} n_{ij}^k$ and $\sum_{k=1}^{n} n_j^k$), and then privately get NB model parameters. Note that all parties collectively add a geometric noise (required for differential privacy) to every summation query count, i.e., $\sum_{k=1}^{n} n_{ij}^k$ and $\sum_{k=1}^{n} n_j^k$. The data perturbation and encryption schemes are present below.

4.2 The Naive Data Perturbation Scheme

The standard differential privacy, which can provide information-theoretic privacy guarantees that hold against computationally unbounded adversaries and balance the tradeoff between privacy protection and utility loss, allows each distributed party in our HDPNB to incorporate a Laplace noise into their local data, coursing $O(n)$ accumulated error [1].

Definition 1. *Differential Privacy. A randomized function K gives ϵ-differential privacy (ϵ is the privacy parameter) if for all neighborhood dataset D_1 and D_2 differing in at most one record, and all $S \in Range(K)$,*

$$Pr[K(D_1) \in S] \leq exp(\epsilon) * Pr[K(D_2) \in S] \tag{1}$$

So, for HDPNB, to get strong privacy protection and good utility, we instead use the distributed differential privacy [9] to let the parties be responsible for ensuring the differential privacy of their own data, and this incurs only $O(1)$ accumulated error. Based on distributed differential privacy, Shi et al. [9] propose a data perturbation scheme, where each party $\mathbf{P}_k$ ($k \in [n]$) generates an additive noise r_k ($r_k \in \mathbb{Z}_p$) following β-diluted geometric distribution to his data x_k ($x_k \in \mathbb{Z}_p$). As a consequence, roughly one copy of geometric noise $Geom(\alpha)$ is added to the original summation $\sum_{k=1}^{n} x_k$, which is the minimum amount of noise required to ensure ε-differential privacy [2]. And, they in [9] present below theorem 1 to show that the naive data perturbation scheme is computationally differentially private [8].

Definition 2. *Geometric Distribution. Let $\alpha > 1$. $Geom(\alpha)$ denotes the symmetric geometric distribution with parameter α. Its probability mass function at k ($k = 0, \pm1, \pm2, ...$) is $\frac{\alpha-1}{\alpha+1} \cdot \alpha^{-|k|}$.*

Definition 3. *β-Diluted Geometric Distribution. Let $\alpha = exp(\frac{\varepsilon}{\Delta})$ ($\alpha > 1$) and $\beta = min(\frac{1}{\gamma n}log\frac{1}{\delta}, 1)$ ($0 < \beta \leq 1$). A random variable follows β-diluted Geometric distribution $Geom(\alpha)^{\beta}$ if it is sampled from $Geom(\alpha)$ with probability β, and is set to 0 with probability $(1 - \beta)$. ε and δ are privacy parameters, and Δ is sensitivity.*

Theorem 1. *Let $0 < \delta < 1$, $\varepsilon > 0$, $\alpha = exp(\frac{\varepsilon}{\Delta})$ and $\beta = min(\frac{1}{\gamma n}log\frac{1}{\delta}, 1)$, where γ is the fraction of honest parties. If each party adds a noise $Geom(\alpha)^{\beta}$, the above naive perturbation scheme achieves (ε, Δ)-distributed differential privacy.*

We here use this naive scheme to perturb both $\sum_{k=1}^{n} n_{ij}^k$ and $\sum_{k=1}^{n} n_j^k$ to protect parties' privacy, since accurate results always disclose privacy [1]. Yet, this naive scheme can not support parties' dynamic joins and leaves, which is solved next at only $O(1)$ error and low cost.

4.3   The Improved Data Perturbation Scheme

In the naive data perturbation scheme, each party utilizes the number of parties n to set parameter $\beta = min(\frac{1}{\gamma n}log\frac{1}{\delta}, 1)$ (parameters γ and δ are constant), such that all parties collectively add just one geometric noise to final results. But it requires large communication cost for each party join and leave since the exact value of n needs to be sent to the parties. Obviously, it conflicts with the lower communication cost goal.

Considering this, we give Alg.1, which relax the accuracy requirement on the value of n such that n does not have to be updated for every party' join and leave and only incurs low error and cost. Each party uses u rather than n to set parameter β. u is updated appropriately when some parties join or leave, but may not always reflect the real number of parties.

Theorem 2. *The average computation error of Alg.1 is roughly within twice of the geometric noise, required for differential privacy.*

Proof. Here, we first prove that $\forall k, u_k \in (\frac{n}{2}, n]$. Clearly, in the initial phase, we always have $\forall k, u_k \in (\frac{n}{2}, n]$. Suppose that all party's u_k initially are set as $\lfloor\frac{n}{2}\rfloor + 1, \lfloor\frac{n}{2}\rfloor + 1, \lfloor\frac{n}{2}\rfloor + 2, ..., n, n$, i.e., n is even. After a party's join, the pattern becomes $\lfloor\frac{n}{2}\rfloor + 1, \lfloor\frac{n}{2}\rfloor + 2, \lfloor\frac{n}{2}\rfloor + 2, ..., n + 1, n + 1$ and the number of parties now becomes $n + 1$ (odd), making that $\lfloor\frac{n}{2}\rfloor = \lfloor\frac{n+1}{2}\rfloor$. So, in this case, we have $\forall k, u_k \in (\frac{n}{2}, n]$. Similarly, when a party leaves, that $\forall k, u_k \in (\frac{n}{2}, n]$ also is

---

Algorithm 1. Procedures run by the trusted dealer to manage the values of u

---

Require: n : the real number of party
Require: u_k : the number of party that party $\mathbf{P}_k$ uses to set parameter β
 1: **Initialization:**
 2: **if** n is even **then**
 3:     $u_1, u_2, ..., u_n \leftarrow \lfloor \frac{n}{2} \rfloor + 1, \lfloor \frac{n}{2} \rfloor + 1, \lfloor \frac{n}{2} \rfloor + 2, \lfloor \frac{n}{2} \rfloor + 2, ..., n, n;$
 4: **else**
 5:     $u_1, u_2, ..., u_n \leftarrow \lfloor \frac{n}{2} \rfloor + 1, \lfloor \frac{n}{2} \rfloor + 2, \lfloor \frac{n}{2} \rfloor + 2, ..., n, n;$
 6: **end if**
 7:
 8: **Join:**
 9: **if** Party $\mathbf{P}_k$ joins **then**
10:     $n \leftarrow n + 1;$
11:     $u_k \leftarrow n;$
12:     Find a party j with $u_j = \min\{u_1, u_2, ..., u_n\};$
13:     $u_j \leftarrow n;$
14: **end if**
15:
16: **Leave:**
17: **if** Party $\mathbf{P}_k$ leaves **then**
18:     $n \leftarrow n - 1;$
19:     Find a party $\mathbf{P}_j$ with $u_j = \max\{u_1, u_2, ..., u_n\};$
20:     **if** There exists another party $\mathbf{P}_m$ with $u_m = u_j$ **then**
21:         $u_m \leftarrow u_k;$
22:         $u_j \leftarrow \lfloor \frac{n}{2} \rfloor + 1;$
23:     **end if**
24: **end if**

---

true. In other two situations where a parties leaves or joins when n is odd, that $\forall k, u_k \in (\frac{n}{2}, n]$ also holds, of which the analysis is leaved to the full paper. In all those four cases, the condition that $\forall k, u_k \in (\frac{n}{2}, n]$ always holds. When $u \leq n$, at least one copy of geometric noise is added to ensure differential privacy; when $u > \frac{n}{2}$, at most one more copy of geometric noise is added. Here, this theorem is proved.

4.4   The Improved Encryption Scheme

The authors in [9] propose an aggregation encryption scheme, which doesn't require parties' interactions, keeps parties' secret keys ($H(t)^{sk_i}$ and H denotes a hash function) fresh, and can achieve strong security guarantees.

Yet, this naive encryption scheme [9] leaves one open problem. To compute the aggregation value $X = \sum_{k=1}^{n} x_k$ (x_k denotes parties' private data), the miner has to compute the discrete log, making their cryptographic construction not support large plaintext spaces. At small plaintext spaces, decryption can be achieved through a brute-force search. Even using Pollard's lambda method, decryption time is roughly square root in the plaintext space. Additionally, this scheme is not failure-tolerant and can't support parties' dynamic joins and leaves, both of which are solved in our methods.

Instead, we propose a computational efficient method, allowing the miner to directly and efficiently get the final results. Specifically, we use the modular property $(1 + p)^m = 1 + mp \mod p^2$ to improve the encryption scheme in [9].

Based on the above equation, we get that $\prod_{k=1}^{n}(1+p)^{x_k} = \prod_{k=1}^{n}(1+p \cdot x_k) = (1 + p\sum_{k=1}^{n} x_k) \mod p^2$ $(x_k \in \mathbb{Z}_p)$. With the above property, the decryption time is only $O(1)$. The improved scheme, used in HDPNB, has three steps:

- **Setup(n,λ)**: This step, run by a trusted dealer, takes the number of parties n, and a security parameter λ as inputs. It outputs: $(params, sk_0, \{sk_k\}_{k \in [n]})$, where $params$ are system parameters. sk_0 is distributed to the miner and sk_k $(k \in [n])$ is a secret key distributed to the party $\mathbf{P}_k(k \in [n])$, such that $sk_0 + sk_1 + ... + sk_n = 0$. The parties will use their secret keys to encrypt their data, and the miner will use its sk_0 to decrypt the sum. The setup algorithm only need to be performed once during the whole learning procedure.
- **Encrypt(sk_k, x_k, t)**: At time t, each $\mathbf{P}_k$ first calculates $(1 + x_k \cdot p) \mod p^2$. Then the party multiplies it by secret parameter $H(t)^{sk_k}$ to get: $\mathbf{C}_k = (1 + x_k \cdot p) \cdot H(t)^{sk_k} \mod p^2$. Then, he uploads the ciphertext $\mathbf{C}_k$ to the miner.
- **Decrypt($sk_0, \{\mathbf{C}_k\}_{k \in [n]}, t$)**: After receiving $\{\mathbf{C}_k\}_{k \in [n]}$ from all parties, the miner calculates: $C = H(t)^{sk_0} \cdot \prod_{k=1}^{n} \mathbf{C}_k = H(t)^{sk_0} \cdot \prod_{k=1}^{n}(1+x_k \cdot p) \cdot H(t)^{sk_k} = (1 + p\sum_{k=1}^{n} x_k) \mod p^2$. Then, the miner only needs to calculate $(C - 1)/p \mod p = \sum_{i=1}^{n} x_k \mod p$ to decrypt the summation $\sum_{i=1}^{n} x_k$ $(x_k \in \mathbb{Z}_p)$. Two different modular operations used here don't affect the decryption [3].

The decryption time in our proposed method is only $O(1)$, while that in the naive encryption scheme [9] is at least $O(\sqrt{n\Delta})$, only when the plaintext space is small. For the large plaintext space, the decryption time will be inconceivable.

Updating Secrets. In the above encryption scheme, when a party joins or leaves, all parties' encryption keys need to be updated, resulting high communication cost in a large system. We address this by employing the interleaved grouping technique, behind which the key idea is to divide the parties into interleaved groups, where each group shares some parties with other groups. Owe to the space restriction, its detailed introduction is omitted here.

5   The Horizontally Differential-private NB Protocol

5.1   Computation of Sensitivity

Before presenting the proposed horizontally privacy-preserving NB protocol, we firstly analyze the sensitivity Δ. Note that, each party perturbs private data by adding a noise variable which follows β-diluted Geometric distribution $Geom(\alpha = exp(\frac{\varepsilon}{\Delta}))^{\beta}$ (parameters ε and β are usually predetermined), where Δ is the sensitivity of sum with respect to one party's change. In other words, if a single participants changes his data, the sum changes by at most Δ. Obviously, in our summation situation, the sensitivity is set as $\Delta = max(N_1, N_2, ..., N_n)$. Remarkably, $\Delta = max(N_1, N_2, ..., N_n)$ can be privately and efficiently computed using the approaches proposed in [3], where N_k denotes the size of the local dataset owned by the party $\mathbf{P}_k$ ($k \in [n]$), such that $N = \sum_{k=1}^{n} N_k$.

5.2 Protocol Description

HDPNB works as follows:

- **Setup.** Similar to the improved encryption scheme, each party $\mathbf{P}_k$ obtains the private key sk_k ($sk_k \in \mathbb{Z}_p$), and the miner obtains the capability sk_0.
- **CountQuery.** In this phase, each party $\mathbf{P}_k$ locally computes n_{ij}^k and n_j^k.
- **DataPert.** To ensure their differential privacy, each party $\mathbf{P}_k$ adds an appropriate noise which is produced based on the naive data perturbation scheme to the original data before encrypting them. We use the notation $\hat{n}_{ij}^k$ and $\hat{n}_j^k$ to denote the noisy plaintext of each party $\mathbf{P}_k$. Note that, honest participants will follow this protocol, but compromised participants may not add noise or even reveal their noise to the miner. The naive data perturbation scheme ensures that the accumulated noise to n_{ij} and n_j added by honest parties is large enough to protect their privacy. In the end, each party $\mathbf{P}_k$ will derive his randomized data $\hat{n}_{ij}^k$ and $\hat{n}_j^k$ by the above additive noise.
- **DataEnc.** Using the improved encryption scheme, each party $\mathbf{P}_k$ respectively encrypts the randomized data, i.e., $\hat{n}_{ij}^k$ and $\hat{n}_j^k$. Here, we use $\bar{n}_{ij}^k$ and $\bar{n}_j^k$ to represent the ciphertexts of $\hat{n}_{ij}^k$ and $\hat{n}_j^k$ respectively.
- **ResultDec.** As soon as receiving those encrypted ciphertexts $(\bar{n}_{ij}^1, \bar{n}_{ij}^2, ..., \bar{n}_{ij}^n)$ and $(\bar{n}_j^1, \bar{n}_j^2, ..., \bar{n}_j^n)$ from all parties, the miner then can obtain the summation plaintexts $(\hat{n}_{ij} = \sum_{k=1}^{n} \hat{n}_{ij}^k$ and $\hat{n}_j = \sum_{k=1}^{n} \hat{n}_j^k)$ by simply summing up these ciphertexts. That is to say, through the decryption algorithm in the improved encryption scheme, the miner can obtain the noisy statistic $\hat{n}_{ij} = \sum_{k=1}^{n} \hat{n}_{ij}^k =sum(\bar{n}_{ij}^1, \bar{n}_{ij}^2, ..., \bar{n}_{ij}^n)$ and $\hat{n}_j = \sum_{k=1}^{n} \hat{n}_j^k =sum(\bar{n}_j^1, \bar{n}_j^2, ..., \bar{n}_j^n)$. Finally, the miner calculates $\hat{p}_{ij} = \hat{n}_{ij}/\hat{n}_j$. The probability p_j can also be calculated as $\hat{p}_j = \hat{n}_j/N$.

Note that, n distributed parties collectively add one copy of geometric noise $Geom(\alpha)$ to $\sum_{k=1}^{n} \hat{n}_{ij}^k$, i.e., $\sum_{k=1}^{n} \hat{n}_{ij}^k = \sum_{k=1}^{n} n_{ij}^k + r$ (r is a geometric noise). The same is to $\sum_{k=1}^{n} \hat{n}_j^k$.

5.3 Protocol Privacy and Security Analysis

The theorem 2 indicates that even if the compromised parties collude with the miner, the noise added by honest parties is large enough to ensure their differential privacy, i.e., achieving (ε, Δ)-distributed differential privacy, which shows that HDPNB is collusion-tolerant. The security analysis in [9] shows that the encryption scheme are secure enough under insecure communication channels to resist polynomial-time adversaries. To sum up, HDPNB provides differential privacy guarantee to resist polynomial-time adversaries, as our encryption schemes is secure enough against polynomial-time adversaries.

5.4 Extension

Vertically Differential-Private NB. Here, we address vertically differential private NB classification (VDPNB). Since vertically partitioned data must have a key attribute at all parties, we assume that each record owned by each party includes its class attribute value. We suppose the party $\mathbf{P}_k$ ($k \in [n]$) just have the k-th attributes A_k. In this way, there are n attribute in total. A sample x with n possible attributes values $a_1, ..., a_n$ is classified as: $NB(x) = argmax_{c_j} \frac{n_j}{N} \prod_{i=1}^{n} \frac{n_{ij}}{n_j}$, where N is the number of training samples, n_j ($n_j, n_{ij} \in \mathbb{Z}_p$) is the total number of training examples whose class label is c_j and n_{ij} is the number of those training examples that also have a_i. And, N and n_j are publicly known. So, the goal is to privately obtain the product $\prod_{i=1}^{n} n_{ij}$ over those n parties, where n_{ij} just need to be estimated from one party's local data. To ensure differential privacy, each party can himself independently generate an additive Laplace noise [1] to his n_{ij} (the sensitivity Δ is set as 1). To give more strong security guarantee, we also allow parties to firstly perturb their data, then encrypt his noisy data and lastly send encrypted ciphertexts to the miner. The encryption scheme used here is an variant of the naive encryption scheme used in HDPNB, where each party sends the ciphertext $n_{ij} \cdot H(t)^{sk_i}$ rather than $(1 + n_{ij} \cdot p) \cdot H(t)^{sk_i}$ to the miner, which can directly decrypt the product $\prod_{i=1}^{n} n_{ij}$.

Dynamic Joins or Leaves. In distributed environment, some parties, who agree to perform the above NB protocols, may dynamically leave, and new parties may join, which we address both problems in the improved data perturbation scheme, i.e., Alg.1.

Others. In reality, some other challenges, including data pollution, fault tolerance, malicious modification and the incremental NB learning, also need to be considered, which we don't introduce due to the limited space.

6   Performance Analysis

6.1   Complexity Analysis

Here, we discuss the computation and communication complexities in our protocols. In the horizontal NB protocol, the communications just exist in steps **DataEnc** and **ResultDec**, where each party sends his encrypted ciphertext c to the miner. Therefore, the total number of bits transferred by each party will be $O(|c|)$, where $|c|$ represents the total bit length of c. The dominant computation cost in the step **CountQuery** is $O(l)$ (l is the number of samples owned by every party), while the computation cost in other steps is only $O(1)$.

Similarly, the computation and communication cost for each party is $O(l)$ and $O(|c|)$ respectively, where l is number of whole samples and $|c|$ is the bit length of transferred ciphertext c in each party side.

The communication cost in Alg.1 is very small: when a party leaves, at most two remaining parties with the maximum u are updated; when a party joins, the joining one and another one with the minimum u are updated.

6.2   Experimental Evaluations

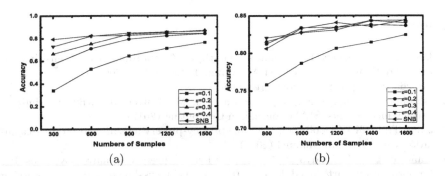

Fig. 1. Classification accuracy comparison

In this section, we respectively compare the classification performance between: standard NB (SNB for short) and HDPNB, SNB and VDPNB. Fig.1 shows simulation results on the dataset of Car Evaluation [7]. Fig.1 (a) gives the classification accuracy comparison between SNB and HDPNB, while Fig.1 (b) between SNB and VDPNB. For every subfigure in Fig.1, we vary the number of parties n, and compare their practical utility (i.e., classification accuracy) under fixed privacy parameters ($\epsilon = 0.1, 0.2, 0.3, 0.4$ respectively). For each n, we average and record the ten-fold cross-validation accuracy over 2000 runs, since it is a randomized algorithm. Specifically, for the proposed HDHNB, we assume that each party just has one sample, and γ is set to be 1 in Fig.1 (a) (assuming no compromised parties). The simulation results show that both HDPNB and VDPNB have comparable or even better classification performance when compared with SNB, especially when the number of samples increases. In addition, from Fig.1, we can clearly see that the larger ε is, the better classification performance the two proposed HDPNB and VDPNB have. Thus, the proposed privacy-preserving NB protocols are practical in reality.

7   Conclusion

This paper presents privacy-preserving protocols for learning NB classifiers over both horizontally and vertically distributed data. The proposed protocols guarantee the privacy of sensitive information even a subset of malicious parties collude with the untrusted miner, and still ensure the reminding honest parties' differential privacy while guaranteeing good NB classification performance, and they are also secure enough under insecure communication channels, while at low cost. Additionally, we also make some extension to it. The experimental results show that our protocols are effective to be applicable in practice.

Acknowledgments. This work is partially supported by the National Natural Science Foundation of China (Nos. U1301256, 61170058, 61202028, 61303206, 61202407).

References

1. Dwork, C., McSherry, F., Nissim, K., Smith, A.: Calibrating noise to sensitivity in private data analysis. In: Halevi, S., Rabin, T. (eds.) TCC 2006. LNCS, vol. 3876, pp. 265–284. Springer, Heidelberg (2006)
2. Ghosh, A., Roughgarden, T., Sundararajan, M.: Universally utility-maximizing privacy mechanisms. SIAM Journal on Computing (2012)
3. Jung, T., Li, X.-Y.: Collusion-tolerable privacy-preserving sum and product calculation without secure channel (2014)
4. Kantarcioglu, M., Vaidya, J., Clifton, C.: Privacy preserving naive bayes classifier for horizontally partitioned data. In: IEEE ICDM Workshop on Privacy Preserving Data Mining, pp. 3–9 (2003)
5. Kargupta, H., Datta, S., Wang, Q., Sivakumar, K.: On the privacy preserving properties of random data perturbation techniques. pp. 99–106. IEEE (2003)
6. Keshavamurthy, B.N., Toshniwal, D.: Privacy-preserving Naïve Bayes classification using trusted third party computation over vertically partitioned distributed progressive sequential data streams. In: Nagamalai, D., Kaushik, B.K., Meghanathan, N. (eds.) CCSIT 2011 Part II. CCIS, vol. 132, pp. 444–452. Springer, Heidelberg (2011)
7. Lichman, M.: UCI machine learning repository (2013)
8. Mironov, I., Pandey, O., Reingold, O., Vadhan, S.: Computational differential privacy. In: Halevi, S. (ed.) CRYPTO 2009. LNCS, vol. 5677, pp. 126–142. Springer, Heidelberg (2009)
9. Shi, E., Chan, T-.H.H., Rieffel, E.G., Chow, R., Song, D.: Privacy-preserving aggregation of time-series data. In: NDSS (2011)
10. Vaidya, J., Kantarciouglu, M., Clifton, C.: Privacy-preserving naive bayes classification. VLDB **17**(4), 879–898 (2008)
11. Vaidya, J., Shafiq, B., Basu, A., Hong, Y.: Differentially private naive bayes classification. In: IEEE/WIC/ACM on Web Intelligence (WI) and Intelligent Agent Technologies (IAT), vol. 1, pp. 571–576. IEEE (2013)
12. Yi, X., Zhang, Y.: Privacy-preserving naive bayes classification on distributed data via semi-trusted mixers. Information Systems **34**(3), 371–380 (2009)
13. Zhang, P., Tong, Y., Tang, S., Yang, D.: Privacy preserving naive bayes classification. In: Li, X., Wang, S., Dong, Z.Y. (eds.) ADMA 2005. LNCS (LNAI), vol. 3584, pp. 744–752. Springer, Heidelberg (2005)
14. Yang, Z., Zhong, S., Wright, R.N.: Privacy-preserving classification of customer data without loss of accuracy. In: SDM. SIAM (2005)

PSFK: A Student Performance Prediction Scheme for First-Encounter Knowledge in ITS

Yonghao Song[1,2(✉)], Yan Jin[1(✉)], Xiaohui Zheng[1,2], Haiyan Han[1,2],
Yunqin Zhong[1], and Xiaofang Zhao[1]

[1] Institute of Computing Technology, Chinese Academy of Sciences, Beijing, China
{songyonghao,zhengxiaohui,hanhaiyan,zhongyunqin,
zhaoxf}@ict.ac.cn, jinyan@ncic.ac.cn
[2] University of Chinese Academy of Sciences, Beijing, China

Abstract. As a user modeling method, Bayesian Knowledge Tracing (BKT) has been extensively used in the area of Intelligent Tutoring Systems (ITS). Thereafter the various schemes based on BKT are proposed to model student knowledge state and learning process. However, these schemes seldom consider the situation when a student first encounters a knowledge component (KC). That is, the existing models cannot be applied directly to predict student performance on a first-encounter KC. To solve this issue, combined user-based collaborative filtering and BKT model, a novel student performance prediction scheme PSFK is proposed in this paper. The PSFK scheme contains three major steps: first, building BKT models for each student and each KC he or she has encountered; then, finding the top-k similar students for a specified student S; finally, predicting S's response on first-encounter KC. We evaluate our scheme on a real-world data set (which contains 4883 students and 177 KCs). The experiments show that the student performance prediction results of the proposed PSFK are acceptable (the RMSE can be decreased to 0.403).

Keywords: Bayesian Knowledge Tracing (BKT) · Collaborative filtering · Predicting student performance (PSP) · Intelligent Tutoring Systems (ITS)

1 Introduction

As intelligent tutoring system (ITS), such as ASSISTments[1], ALEKS[2] and Carnegie Learning[3], is being widely used, the issues that how to obtain students' knowledge state and correspondingly how to improve students' learning performance have attracted much researchers' attention [1,2,3,4]. It is well known that the model which accurately predicts long-term future performance of a student can help the student find his shortcomings [5], help the teacher improve the design of the related lessons [6], and help the ITS recommends the appropriate questions [7]. Thus, based on

---

[1] https://www.assistments.org/
[2] http://www.aleks.com/
[3] http://www.carnegielearning.com/

© Springer International Publishing Switzerland 2015
S. Zhang et al. (Eds.): KSEM 2015, LNAI 9403, pp. 639–650, 2015.
DOI: 10.1007/978-3-319-25159-2_58

students' interaction records with ITS, predicting student performance (PSP) accurately is of practical important.

Many works have been proposed to solve the PSP issue. The well-known method, which is called Bayesian Knowledge Tracing (BKT) model, is popularized by Corbett and Anderson [1]. This model makes an effort to model students' changing knowledge state during skill acquisition, which can be used to predict the student performance and to determine whether the student has mastered a particular skill [7]. However, it does not allow for individual learning rates or individual student initial knowledge. Although some of its variants, such as [8] and [9] have considered this issue, they could not predict students' performance on a first-encounter knowledge component (KC). In addition, to solve PSP issue, prior researches using classification techniques are appropriate in general academic systems rather than ITS and need sufficient background knowledge of domain (e.g. the meta data about the student) [7], such as confidence, shyness, attitude and marital status, which is not practical for ITS scenario. Based on the classic rating problem in recommender system, other prior research works mapped PSP problem into rating prediction task, e.g. collaborative filtering approach [10], cannot fully utilize the special feature in field of education.

Motivated by the above observations, to better predict students' performance on a first-encounter KC, a PSFK scheme is proposed in this paper, which includes three major phases: firstly, building a BKT model for each student and each KC which he or she has encountered; secondly, given a student s and a new KC k, finding the top-k similar students for s who have encountered k; thirdly, calculating the probability that s responses k correctly. Our main contributions can be summarized as follows:

- We proposed a novel scheme that combines user-based collaborative filtering and BKT model to solve the PSP issue, which can solve the scenario when a student first encounter a KC (he or she has never encountered before).
- Extensive experiment on the real world data set [11] which contains 4883 students and 177 KCs are carried out. The experimental results in predicting real word data is acceptable.

2   Related Work

The problem of PSP has been well studied for years. According to the techniques have been used on PSP, the existing works can be grouped into three categories.

In the first category, the PSP problem is generalized into classification and regression problem. For example, Adhatraoet al. used ID3 and C4.5 classification techniques to predict the general and individual performance of freshly admitted students in future examinations [12]. Elbadrawyet al. proposed a class of collaborative multi-regression models which allow sharing information among students and generating personalized predictions [13]. Naser et al. developed an artificial neural network model to predict the performance of students who enroll in engineering majors [14]. However, these classification methods need sufficient background knowledge of the domain, which is not practical for ITS scenario.

In the second category, most of the state-of-art works on PSP problem focus on modeling students' learning process. For instance, Corbett et al. proposed the BKT model to describe students' learning process and evaluate students' knowledge state, which is the most famous method to predict student performance [1]. Basically, BKT is a Hidden Markov Model (HMM) with a hidden node (knowledge component) and an observed node (student performance). BKT model has four parameters: initial knowledge ($P(L)$), learning rate ($P(T)$), guessing rate ($P(G)$) and slipping rate ($P(S)$). However, for a specified KC every student has the same four parameters. That is, this model does not take individualization into account. Zachary et al. improved the original BKT proposed by [1] and proposed the prior per student model, which takes individual learning rates and individual initial knowledge into account [8]. However, when a student encounters a KC which he or she never meets before, these models are not applied directly for such situation.

In the third category, researchers map PSP problem into rating prediction task in recommender system, where the student, problem, and performance would be mapped to the user, item and rating, respectively [15]. Cetintas et al. proposed a temporal collaborative filtering approach, which automatically predicts the correctness of students' problem solving in an intelligent math tutoring system [10]. Nguyen et al. proposed a novel approach which uses tensor factorization for forecasting student performance [16]. However, these works rarely considered the special feature of education, especially, the learning process of students.

Thus, a particular merging scheme is proposed to predict student performance in ITS, which takes the above-mentioned deficiencies into account.

3   Preliminaries

3.1   Notations and Definitions

The mathematical denotation throughout the paper is listed in Table 1.

Table 1. Mathematical notations

Notation	Description
M	Number of students
N	Number of knowledge components
$S = \{s_1, s_2, \ldots, s_i, \ldots, s_M\}$	Set of students where s_i is the student i
$K = \{k_1, k_2, \ldots, k_j, \ldots k_N\}$	Set of KCs where k_j is the KC j
$K^i = \{k_1^i, k_2^i, \ldots, k_n^i\}$	Set of KCs which s_i has exercised
$S^j = \{s_1^j, s_2^j, \ldots, s_m^j\}$	Set of students who have exercised k_j
$r^{i,j}$	Response of s_i on k_j
$R^{i,j} = r_1^{i,j} r_2^{i,j} \ldots$	Response sequence, e.g. 01001011111
D^{train}	Training data set
$Sim(s_i, s_j)$	Similarity between s_i and s_j

Table 1. (*continued*)

$P_{i,j}(L_0)$	Probability that s_i masters KC k_j initially.
$P_{i,j}(T)$	Probability that s_i transforms k_j from unlearned state to learned state
$P_{i,j}(G)$	Probability that s_i guesses correctly on k_j
$P_{i,j}(S)$	Probability that s_i slips (make a mistake) on k_j
$s_i k_j$	BKT model of s_i for k_j, it's a four-tuple: $< P_{i,j}(L_0), P_{i,j}(T), P_{i,j}(G), P_{i,j}(S) >$
$SK_{M \times N}$	Matrix formed based on BKT models where $SK_{ij} = s_i k_j$
$Sim_i(k)$	Map set that keeps top-k similar students and their similarities with s_i

In Table 1, we define M is the number of students, each of whom has a set of KCs $K^i = \{k_1^i, k_2^i, \ldots, k_n^i\}$, which records the KCs that student i has exercised. N is the number of KCs and each KC has a set of students $S^j = \{s_1^j, s_2^j, \ldots, s_m^j\}$, which records the student who have exercised k_j. For each $k_j^i \in K^i$, there are response records which student s_i has completed on k_j ordered by interaction time. To be specific, we define $R^{i,j} = r_1^{i,j} r_2^{i,j} \ldots$ is the response sequence where $r^{i,j}$ is a response of s_i for k_j, which $r^{i,j} = 1$ represents s_i answered k_j correctly and $r^{i,j} = 0$ represents s_i answered k_j incorrectly.

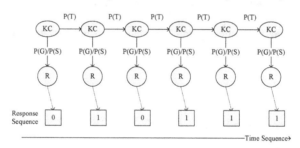

Fig. 1. The BKT model of Rachel on addition

As shown in Fig. 1, a student named Rachel has a response sequence [010111] for addition (+), and $R^{Rachel,+} = 010111$ represents Rachel answers addition incorrectly for the first time, which probably means Rachel does not master the addition when she first encounters (addition is in the unlearned state for Rachel). The second time when Rachel meets addition she answers correctly, which probably means Rachel guess correctly. The third time Rachel answers incorrectly, which she maybe makes a mistake or does not master this KC. Rachel answers correctly on the following three times, which means she probably has mastered the addition.

Definition 1 (Similarity between Two Students). Given student s_i and s_j, let $K^i = \{k_1^i, k_2^i, \ldots, k_n^i\}$ be a set of KCs which s_i has exercised and $K^j = \{k_1^j, k_2^j, \ldots, k_n^j\}$ be a set of KCs which s_j has exercised. Let $I_{i,j} = K^i \cap K^j$ and $k_k \in I_{i,j}$. The similarity between s_i and s_j is

$$Sim(s_i k_k, s_j k_k) = 1 - \frac{1}{2} \bullet$$

$$\sqrt{(P_{i,k}(L_0) - P_{j,k}(L_0))^2 + (P_{i,k}(T) - P_{j,k}(T))^2 + (P_{i,k}(G) - P_{j,k}(G))^2 + (P_{i,k}(S) - P_{j,k}(S))^2} \quad (1)$$

$$Sim(s_i, s_j) = \frac{1}{|I_{i,j}|} \sum_{k=1}^{|I_{i,j}|} Sim(s_i k_k, s_j k_k) \quad (2)$$

Based on definition 1, the definition of top-k similar students for a specified student can be defined as follows.

Definition 2 (Top-K similar students for a specified student). Given a student s_i, the top-k similar students is a set of students which are the most k similar students with s_i. Formally, let $Sim_{s_i} = \{s_1, s_2, \dots, s_k, s_{k+1}, \dots, s_{m_i}\}$ be a set of students who are similar with s_i, where $m_i < M$. $Sim_{s_i}(k) = \{s_1, s_2, \dots, s_k\}$ represents the top-k similar students of s_i on condition that for each student $s_j \in Sim_{s_i}(k)$ and each student $s'_j \in Sim_{s_i}$, where $Sim(s_i, s_j) \geq Sim(s_i, s'_j)$.

3.2   PSP Problem Formulation

Based on the notation and definition we have provided, the PSP problem to be solved in this paper is formulated as follow.

Problem. Given a set of students S, a set of KCs K, and $R \in \{0, 1\}$ be a student response for a particular KC. Let $D^{train} \subseteq (S \times K \times R)^*$ be a set of records which are observed student performances and $D^{test} \subseteq (S \times K \times R)^{\#}$ be a set of records which are unobserved student performances. Let $(s, k)^* \in D^{train}, (s, k)^{\#} \in D^{test}$ and $s \in S, k \in K$, where $(s, k)^* \neq (s, k)^{\#}$. Then the problem of student performance prediction is, give D^{train} and D^{test}, to find

$$\hat{R} = \hat{r}_1, \hat{r}_2, \dots, \hat{r}_{|D^{test}|} \text{ and } \hat{R} = \arg \min err(R, \hat{R})$$

where

$$err(R, \hat{R}) = \sqrt{\frac{1}{|D^{test}|} \sum_{l=1}^{|D^{test}|} (r_l - \hat{r}_l)^2} \quad (3)$$

4   PSFK Scheme

In this section, we present our scheme PSFK in detail. The design of our algorithm is inspired by a simple idea: for a student s and all the KCs which he or she has exercised, if the learning process of s is similar with other students (top-k similar students), then when s first encounters a KC k, we can use these similar students' performances on k to predict whether s is able to answer k correctly. Based on the

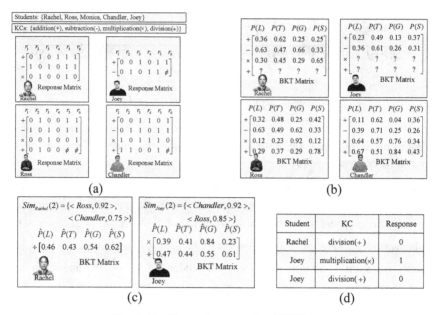

Fig. 2. The illustrative example of PSFK

Scheme PSFK (s_i, k_j, D^{train})

Description: Using user-based collaborative filtering for predicting student performance

Input: s_i : the student to be predicted; k_j : the KC s_i will response where $k_j \notin K^i$;

Output: $r^{i,j}$: the response of s_i for k_j .

Initial Step:
//initializing the variables will be used in the following steps.
Obtain the set of students S from D^{train} ;

Step 1:
//obtaining the value of $SK_{M \times N}$.
$SK_{M \times N} \leftarrow$ LBKT (S, D^{train}, d);   // d is the threshold of stopping learning

Step 2:
//finding the top-k similar students for student s_i .
$Sim_i(k) \leftarrow$ FTKSS ($s_i, k_j, SK_{M \times N}, D^{train}, k$);   // k is the number of students who are top-k
similar ones with s_i

Step 3:
//calculating the probability that s_i will response correctly on k_j .
$P_{i,j}(correctly) \leftarrow$ CPNK ($s_i, k_j, SK_{M \times N}, Sim_i(k)$);

Finalized step:
return $P_{i,j}(correctly)$

Fig. 3. The pseudo code of PSFK scheme

above idea, the PSFK scheme that combines user-based collaborative filtering and BKT model is proposed, which is composed of, the following three major steps (the pseudo code is shown in Fig. 3).

Step1: Modeling the learning process for students (algorithm LBKT is shown in Fig. 4);
Step2: Calculating the similarity between two students and finding the top-k similar students for a specified student (algorithm FTKSS is shown in Fig. 5);
Step3: For a given student s and KC k, calculating the probability that student s will answer k correctly (algorithm CPNK is shown in Fig. 6).

To understand the work mechanism of PSFK scheme, we give an illustrative example in Fig. 2, and each step of PSFK is introduced in the following subsections.

4.1 Learning BKT Models for Each Student

As illustrated in Fig. 1, the BKT model proposed by Corbett and Anderson [1] is a simple HMM with one hidden node and one observed node for tracking student knowledge in ITS. For each student and each KC that he or she has encountered, one BKT model which has four parameters need to be constructed and learnt. We use the classical Baum-Welch algorithm to find the unknown parameters of a HMM. The Baum-Welch algorithm uses the well-known EM algorithm to find the maximum likelihood estimate of the parameters of a HMM given a set of observed feature vectors. The algorithm of learning BKT models for each student is shown in Fig. 4.

Algorithm: LBKT (S, D^{train}, d)

Description: for each student, learning the four parameters of BKT model that he or she has learned each KC.
Input: S : the student set; D^{train} : the training data set; d: the threshold of stopping learning.
Output: $SK_{M \times N}$:the matrix formed based on BKT model where $SK_{ij} = s_i k_j$.

```
 1:  initBKT ← construct the initial BKT;
 2:  for each student s_i ∈ S do
 3:      Obtain the set of KCs K^i from D^train ;
 4:      for each KC k_j^i ∈ K^i do
 5:          Get the response sequence R^{i,j} from D^train ;
 6:          do
 7:              learntBKT ← learn the BKT model according to initBKT and R^{i,j} ;
 8:              distance ← calculate the distance between initBKT and learntBKT;
 9:          while (distance < d)
10:      end for
11:      Insert learntBKT into SK_{M×N}
12:  end for
13:  return SK_{M×N}
```

Fig. 4. The pseudo code of LBKT scheme

Fig. 2 (a) shows that student Rachel has a response sequence [010111] on KC addition. Based on the response sequence, we can utilize Algorithm LBKT to learn the four parameters for Rachel on addition. As showed in Fig. 2 (b), the probability that Rachel has mastered addition is 0.36, in addition, the learning rate, guessing rate and slipping rate are 0.62, 0.25 and 0.25, respectively.

4.2   Finding Top-K Similar Students

Based on Definition 1 and Definition 2, for a specified student/KC pair $^{(s_i, k_j)}$, we utilize Algorithm FTKSS to find top-k similar students for ^{s_i} who first encounters k_j. Fig. 2 (c) illustrates that the top-2 similar students of Rachel are Ross and Chandler with 0.92 similarity and 0.75 similarity, respectively.

Algorithm: FTKSS ($s_i, k_j, SK_{M \times N}, D^{train}, k$)

Description: finding the top-k similar students for student s_i.

Input: s_i : the student to be predicted; k_j : the KC s_i will response; $SK_{M \times N}$: the matrix formed based on BKT model for all the student in the training set where $SK_{ij} = s_i k_j$; D^{train} : the training data set; k: the number of students who are top-k similar ones with s_i.

Output: $Sim_i(k)$: a map set that keeps top-k similar students and their similarities with s_i.

```
 1:  Obtain the set of KCs K^i from D^train ;
 2:  Obtain the set of students S^j from D^train ;
 3:  for each student s_j ∈ S^j do
 4:      Sim(s_i, s_j) ← 0;
 5:          Obtain the set of KCs K^j from D^train ;
 6:          I_{i,j} = K^i ∩ K^j ;
 7:      if I_{i,j} is not null then
 8:          for each KC k_j ∈ I_{i,j} do
 9:              Calculate Sim(s_i k_j, s_j k_j) ;
10:              Sim(s_i, s_j) ← Sim(s_i, s_j) + Sim(s_i k_j, s_j k_j) ;
11:          end for
12:          Insert < s_j, Sim(s_i, s_j) > into  Sim_i(k) ;
13:      else
14:          Insert < s_j, 0 > into  Sim_i(k) ;
15:      end if
16:  end for
17:  Remove all entries from Sim_i(k) except for the topK entries;
18:  return Sim_i(k)
```

Fig. 5. The pseudo code of FTKSS scheme

4.3   Predicting Student Performances for New KCs

Given a specified student/KC pair (s_i, k_j), algorithm CPNK calculates the probability that s_i responses k_j correctly, which is based on the results from algorithm LBKT and algorithm FTKSS. As illustrated in Fig. 2 (c), the probability of Rachel has mastered division is 0.46, Rachel's learning rate on division is 0.43, her guessing rate is 0.54 and slipping rate is 0.62. The PSP result of Rachel is $P_{Rachel,division}(correctly) =$ 0.47 which is derived from Eq. (3) of Algorithm CPNK, therefore, when Rachel first encounters division she probably answers incorrectly.

Algorithm: CPNK ($s_i, k_j, SK_{M \times N}, Sim_i(k)$)

Description: calculate the probability that s_i will response correctly on k_j.

Input: s_i : the student to be predicted; k_j : the KC s_i will response; $SK_{M \times N}$: the matrix formed based on BKT model for all the student in the training set where $SK_{ij} = s_i k_j$; $Sim_i(k)$: a map set that keeps top-k similar student and their similarities with s_i.

Output: $P_{i,j}(correctly)$: the probability student s_i will response correctly for k_j.

1: **Normalize** the $Sim(s_i, s_j)$ in $Sim_i(k)$;

2: **for each** $s_k \in Sim_i(k)$ **do**

3: $\quad \hat{P}_{i,j}(L_0) = P_{k,j}(L_0) * Sim(s_i, s_k)$

4: $\quad \hat{P}_{i,j}(G) = P_{k,j}(G) * Sim(s_i, s_k)$

4: $\quad \hat{P}_{i,j}(S) = P_{k,j}(S) * Sim(s_i, s_k)$

5: **end for**

6: $\quad\quad P_{i,j}(correctly) = \hat{P}_{i,j}(L_0) * (1 - \hat{P}_{i,j}(S)) + (1 - \hat{P}_{i,j}(L_0)) * \hat{P}_{i,j}(G)$ (4)

7: **return** $P_{i,j}(correctly)$

Fig. 6. The pseudo code of CPNK scheme

5   Experiment

In this section, we evaluate the proposed PSFK scheme on the real-world data set assistments_2009_2010 [12,17], which is published by the ASSISTments Platform. Specifically, we discussed three factors which can affect the predicting results. These factors are the length of the student response sequence, the selection of the parameter k and the strategies for setting the initial parameters of BKT, respectively. We implemented our approaches in java, and all experiments were run on a laptop with 2.5GHz CPU and 4GB RAM.

5.1   Experimental Data

The ASSISTments data set contains 8519 students, 336 KCs, and 4 answer types which are choose_1, algebra, fill_in and open_response. Limited by computing resources, the experimental data set only contains choose_1 answer type, which contains 4883 students and 177 KCs. The training data set is the records, which one of fields, called skill (the meaning of skill and KC is equivalent), has the length of response sequence more than three. The testing data set is the records which student/KC pair only appears once.

5.2   Experimental Result

Due to the initial parameters has significant impact to the result of BKT models which were learned with EM, there are three ways to initial the parameters: setting initial individualized knowledge to Random values; setting initial individualized knowledge based on empiric values and based on global percent correct [8].

Impact of Parameter k
The prediction performance of the PSFK scheme is calculated in terms of root mean square error (RMSE) which is derived from Eq. (3).   In this group of experiments, we probe the impact of parameter k and the strategies initialing the parameters on prediction performance, where k is ranged from 1 to 6 and the strategies to initial the parameters are random, empiric and global. For the empiric strategies, the initial knowledge rate, learning rate, guessing rate and slipping rate are 0.5, 0.5, 0.3 and 0.7, respectively. Fig. 7 shows that with the increase of the value of k, the value of RMSE decreases. That means the accuracy of the prediction performance increases. The reason is that more similar students to be used to infer other one's learning process can improve the accuracy of the BKT model. In addition, Fig. 7 shows that setting initial individualized knowledge based on global percent correct is the appropriate strategy to initial the parameters of BKT model. It is due to the fact that more related information to be considered can enhance the accuracy of the prediction performance.

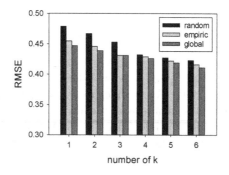

Fig. 7. Impact of k on PSFK

Impact of Response Sequence Length

In this group of experiments, k is set to 6 and the strategy to initial parameters is global. Fig. 8 shows that the length of response sequence has significant impact to the prediction performance. The reason is that, if a student completes more problems on one specified KC, the learning process represent by BKT model is more accurate.

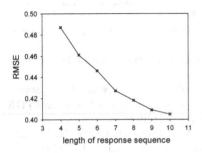

Fig. 8. Impact of response sequence length   **Fig. 9.** Impact of Training Data Set Size

Impact of Training Data Set Size

In this group of experiments, k is set to 5 and the strategy to initial parameter is global. We set up the training data set in three scales which are small, medium and large. The number of records in small, medium and large size is 503, 1506 and 2231, respectively. Fig. 9 shows that larger data set can decrease the value of RMSE. It is due to the fact that large data set can improve the degree of students' similarity which PSFK can find out. Finally, the RMSE can be decreased to 0.403.

6   Conclusion

This paper proposed a novel PSFK scheme to solve the PSP issue, which is based on the BKT model and user-based collaborative filtering. Specifically, we first defined the problem of PSP for a first-encounter KC, the similarity between students and the top-k similar students for a specified student. Then, based on the definitions and the mathematical notations, we introduced PSFK scheme which has three major steps: learning the four parameters of the BKT for each student and each KC, finding the top-k similar students for the student who needs to be predicted and calculating the probability of the student answer correctly for first-encounter KCs. Finally, we discussed the impact of the response sequence length and the selection of parameter k on predicting the student's performance.

There are several possibilities to extend the research in the future. First, forgetting rate (probability that students may forget KCs) can be taken into account in BKT model to characterize the learning process of students more completely. Second, to improve the results of experiment, more social properties, e.g. social relationship among students, can be taken into account in PSFK scheme, such as social relationship between students[18].

Acknowledgment. This work is supported by the National Natural Science Foundation of China (Grant No. 61202413).

References

1. Corbett, A.T., Anderson, J.R.: Knowledge Tracing: Modeling the Acquisition of Proce-dural Knowledge. UMUAI. **4**, 253–278 (1995)
2. Ma, Y., Liu, B., Wong, C.K., Yu, P.S., Lee, S.M.: Targeting the right students using data mining. In: SIGKDD, pp. 457–464 (2000)
3. Baker, R.S.J.d.: Modeling and understanding students' off-task behavior in intelligent tutoring system. In: CHI, pp. 1059–1068 (2007)
4. Sahebi, S., Huang, Y., Brusilovsky, P.: Predicting student performance in solving parameterized exercises. In: Trausan-Matu, S., Boyer, K.E., Crosby, M., Panourgia, K. (eds.) ITS 2014. LNCS, vol. 8474, pp. 496–503. Springer, Heidelberg (2014)
5. Piech, C., Huang, J., Nguyen, A., Phulsuksombati, M., Sahami, M., Guibas, L.: Learning program embeddings to propagate feedback on student code. In: ICML, vol. 37 (2015)
6. Romero, C., Ventura, S.: Educational Data Mining: A Review of the State of the Art. IEEE Transactions on Systems, Man, and Cybernetics **40**(6) (2010)
7. Thai-Nghe, N.: Predicting Student Performance in an Intelligent Tutoring System. PhD thesis, University of Hildesheim (2011)
8. Pardos, Z.A., Heffernan, N.T.: Modeling individualization in a bayesian networks implementation of knowledge tracing. In: Chin, D., Kobsa, A., De Bra, P. (eds.) UMAP 2010. LNCS, vol. 6075, pp. 255–266. Springer, Heidelberg (2010)
9. Pardos, Z.A., Heffernan, N.T.: Using HMMs and bagged decision trees to leverage rich features of user and skill from an intelligent tutoring system dataset. In: KDD cup 2010: Improving Cognitive Models with Educational Data Mining (2010)
10. Cetintas, S., Si, L., Xin, Y.P., Hord, C.: Predicting correctness of problem solving in its with a temporal collaborative filtering approach. In: Mostow, J., Kay, J., Aleven, V. (eds.) ITS 2010, Part I. LNCS, vol. 6094, pp. 15–24. Springer, Heidelberg (2010)
11. http://teacherwiki.assistments.org/index.php/Assistments_2009-2010_Full_Dataset
12. Adhatrao, K., GayKar, A., Dhawan, A., Jha, R., Honrao, V.: Predicting Students' Perfor-mance Using ID3 and C4.5 Classification Algorithm. IJDKP **3**(5) (2013)
13. Elbadrawy, A., Studham, R.S., Karypis, G.: Collaborative multi-regression models for predicting students' performance in course activities. In: LAK, pp. 16–20 (2015)
14. Naser, S.A., Zaqout, I., Ghosh, M.A., Atallah, R., Alajrami, E.: Predicting Student Performance Using Artificial Neural Network: in the Faculty of Engineering and Information Technology. IJHIT **8**(2), 221–228 (2015)
15. Thai-Nghe, N., Drumond, L., Krohn-Grimberghe, A., Schmidt-Thieme, L.: Recommender system for predicting student performance. In: RecSysTEL, vol. 01, pp. 1–9 (2010)
16. Thai-Nghe, N., Drumond, L., Horváth, T., Nanopoulos, A., Schmidt-Thieme, L.: Matrix and tensor factorization for predicting student performance. In: CSEDU, pp. 69–78 (2011)
17. Feng, M., Heffernan, N.T., Koedinger, K.R.: Addressing the assessment challenge in an Intelligent Tutoring System that tutors as it assesses. The Journal of User Modeling and User-Adapted Interaction. **19**, 243–266 (2009)
18. Vázquez, M.R., Romero, F.P., Vanoye, J.R., Olivas, J.A., Guerrero, J.S.: An extension of fuzzy deformable prototypes for predicting student performance on web-based tutoring systems. In: IFSA, pp. 556–563 (2015)

CSRA: An Efficient Resource Allocation Algorithm in MapReduce Considering Data Skewness

Ling Qi[1,2], Zhuo Tang[1](✉), Yunchuan Qin[1,2], and Yu Ye[1,2]

[1] College of Information Science and Engineering, Hunan University,
Changsha 410082, China
ztang@hnu.edu.cn, qilinghunan@163.com
[2] State Key Laboratory of Software Engineering, Wuhan University,
Wuhan 430072, China

Abstract. MapReduce offers a promising programming model for big data processing. One significant issue in practical applications is data skew, its an important reason for the emergence of stragglers which makes the data assigned to each reducer imbalance. This paper presents CSRA, an efficient resource allocation algorithm in MapReduce considering data skew. CSRA aims at reducing the running time and coefficient of variation by reordering the task list and splitting the big clusters. Through thinking over the actual status of tasks, this method largely squares up the resource utilization. After we implement CSRA in Hadoop, the experiments show that CSRA has negligible overhead and can speed up the execution time of some popular applications obviously.

Keywords: MapReduce · Data skew · Splitting

1 Introduction

Large-scale data processing has been gaining more and more attentions in this information society. As a parallel programming model, MapReduce [1] has become a popular tool for distributed data processing. It provides load balancing, data distributing, fault tolerance, resource allocating and job scheduling programming environment for many applications.

MapReduce is a distributed programming framework which allows programmers just to concentrate on the data processing algorithm. Since the parallel controlling works have already been done by the MapReduce system, programmers only need to overwrite map or reduce functions. Hadoop has developed into version 2.0 Yarn [2]. It provides resource management and scheduling service for a lot of applications. But the functions that the system provides are not efficient enough for some problems met by users, for example the problem of data skew.

In the input relations, some ⟨*key, value*⟩ pairs may appear much more often than others, this is called data skew problem. Data skew problem can lead to significantly longer job execution time and lower cluster throughput. What's more, this is invisible and imperceptible for programmers before running the system.

© Springer International Publishing Switzerland 2015
S. Zhang et al. (Eds.): KSEM 2015, LNAI 9403, pp. 651–662, 2015.
DOI: 10.1007/978-3-319-25159-2_59

In this paper, we address a new resource allocation method named Cluster Splitting based Resource Allocation algorithm (CSRA) which focuses on solving the problem of data skew. After studying the source code of Yarn, we know that resource requirements of a task can be described as a 5-tuple: $\langle priority, hostname, capability, containers, relax\_locality \rangle$, denote job priorities, host location of expectation resources, the amount of resources, the number of container and whether relaxation locality. To ranking the tasks properly, we evaluate the process speed considering resources the task consumed and the data finished by each node. By choosing an appropriate host name to allocate resources, the data skew can be avoid largely.

The contributions of this paper include the following:

We put forward an innovative schedule algorithm CSRA to reduce the data skew and improve the resource use efficiency. By considering the resources a task applied, the priority of the task can be calculated much more accurately. At the same time, CSRA implements an innovative approach to balance the workload among the reduce tasks by splitting reduce tasks associated with a single large cluster into multiple. We evaluate the performance of CSRA with some popular and widely used applications. The experimental results show that CSRA can improve the performance of system quite considerably.

The remainder of this paper is organized as follows:

We introduce the background and the causes of data skew in different aspects in Section 2. Section 3 describes task executing time model, task priority model and splitting method used in this paper. In Section 4, we present the implementation details of CSRA. The experimental results and analyses are presented in Section 5. Section 6 concludes the whole paper.

2   Background and Related Works

2.1   Yarn Workflow

Yarn is a new concept that bring up as an upgraded version of MapReduce. The two most important functions that Yarn provides are resource management and scheduling service for many type of applications. There is no more concept of Slots but Container replaced in Yarn. The most typical contribution of Container is that it encapsulates the resources (CPU and Memory two resource categories) on a node. And the node allocates resources based on the amount of resources the task applied.

After users submit an application on Yarn, Application Master will then start. It will run the application in two steps: apply resources for it and then monitor its operation until the entire application is completed.

There are two kinds of applications running on YARN: short application and long application. Short application means some applications which can complete operation and normal exit in a certain time, such as MapReduce task, Tez DAG task. Long application is a kind of never-ending application not surprisingly, usually are some services, such as Storm Service, HBase Service. And as a framework they provide programming interfaces for users.

2.2   Cause of Data Skew

In a Yarn application, data skew may exist in many phases, and the causes of those skews are quite different. Some are caused by the uneven distributed data sets, some are resulted by the node's low efficiency of data executing ability, some are just leaded by the error of the executing code, etc.. After summarizing the paper written by Kwon [3] and Dhawalia [4], we know that there are two typical kinds of data skew which can arise in a Yarn application. We divide them into two categories according to which phase the skew happens.

Sources of Map-side Skew. Users can run arbitrary code as long as it conforms to the MapReduce interface (map or reduce), and typically initialization and cleanup. Such flexibility enabled users to push the boundaries of what map and reduce phases have been designed to do: each map output can depend on a group of input records. Such map task is non-homomorphic. On the other hand, some records require more CPU and Memory to process than others. These expensive records may simply be larger than other records, or the runtime of map may depend on the value of records.

Sources of Reduce-side Skew. As in the case of expensive records processed by map, expensive $\langle key, value \rangle$ pairs can imbalance the runtime of reduce tasks. Since reduce phase operates key groups instead of individual record, the expensive input problem can be more pronounced.

Both kinds of data skew will lead to the inefficiency of system. In this paper, we introduce CSRA to solve the problems caused by data skew.

2.3   Related Works

Based on the advantages MapReduce provides, many data-intensive applications can be easily implemented. And scholars have studied many kinds of advancing methods to improve the performance of MapReduce, such as scheduling to meet deadlines [5], co-scheduling [6] and SkewedJoin in Pig [7]. However, in some papers, users still need to implement their own methods for their specific applications to tackle the data skew problem, such as CloudBurst [8].

Okcan et al. [9] proposes a skew optimization for the join by adding two pre-run sampling and counting jobs. Chen [10] provides a special method to split large clusters in the join and CloudBurst applications (e.g., weighted range partitioning in [3]). Guo [11] and Xu [12] suggest ways to avoid the creation of skew in tasks. The works of Kwon [13] and Guo [14] are based on detecting and mitigating skew dynamically.

All these methods have their advantages, but most of them just focused on one type of solutions. These algorithms can only be used in specific applications and bring non-negligible extra sampling cost. They cannot solve the data skew problem and improve the performance of system as efficiently as the applications need.

3   The Task Executing Time Model for Data Skew

3.1   Data Skewness Model

We know that data skew often comes from the physical properties of objects and hot spots on subsets of the entire domain (e.g., the word frequency appearing on the documents obeys a Zipfian distribution). By varying parameter σ of a data set which following Zipf distribution, we can control the degree of data skew. A common measurement for data skew is the coefficient of variation:

$$COV(\sim X) = \frac{stddev(\sim x)}{mean(\sim x)} \tag{1}$$

where $\sim x$ is a vector that contains the data size processed by each task. $stddev(\sim x)$ is the standard deviation of $\sim x$. Larger coefficient indicates heavier skew.

3.2   Resource Use Efficiency

Here we come up with a new method to divide the resource more efficient by taking the left resource of the node into consideration. The task scheduling algorithm bases on this method performs quite well in some special applications such as Grep, Join, etc..

In this paper, the priority of a task is calculated by executing time and resource use efficiency (RUE) of each node. RUE is decided by the execution time per resource unit (RU) costs when process a certain number of tasks and the efficiency of a node. To calculate RUE, we have to evaluate the process speed and the data finished by each node. Here we suppose RU as a constant value that refers to the sum of CPU and Memory a task applied from a node, defined as Eq. (2):

$$RU = (1 + \alpha \times CPU\_Quantity) \times [1 + (1 - \alpha) \times Mem\_Quantity] \tag{2}$$

where $CPU\_Quantity$ is the unit of CPU, $Mem\_Quantity$ is the unit of Memory. α reflects the tradeoff between CPU and Memory where the value is between 0 and 1. And the value is setted based on the job being tested.

Once a task is scheduled, the resource then is determined and unchangeable. We can get the size of resource (R_apply) and calculate the number of resource unit (N_RU) this task required using Eq. (3):

$$N\_RU = \frac{R\_apply}{RU} \tag{3}$$

As the RUE is a dynamic element, to calculate the value more accurately, we choose a model to predict it which is related to the past station. There are many prediction models in other papers, such as Exponentially Weighted Moving Average (EWMA) [15] and Markov Chain Monte-Carlo Particle Filter (MCMC

PF) [16]. In this paper, we choose the EWMA scheme which can be expressed as Eq. (4):

$$E\_RUE(t) = \beta \times RUE(t) + (1 - \beta) \times E\_RUE(t - \triangledown), 0 \leq \beta \leq 1 \qquad (4)$$

where $E\_RUE(t)$ stands for estimated resource use efficiency and $RUE(t)$ stands for observed resource use efficiency at time t. β reflects the tradeoff between stability and responsiveness. We set the value of β as 0.2 in this paper. By analyzing the definition and characteristic of RUE, the value of RUE at time t can be calculated as Eq. (5):

$$RUE(t) = \frac{Data\_finish}{(t - t_0) \times N\_RU} \qquad (5)$$

where $Data\_finish$ refers to the finished data from current time t to start time t_0. N_RU is the resources being occupied. As we can see, the more data the node output, the bigger will the value of RUE be.

To divide the resources, Hadoop monitors progress tasks need to select an appropriate task who has the highest priority. Here, we use the current executing time of a task represents its priority. As real time process speed of a node will cause calculating delay, we use the average process speed to estimate the executing time like Eq. (6):

$$exe\_time[i] = \frac{Data[i]}{R\_apply \times \overline{RUE}} \qquad (6)$$

where R_apply is the resource the task applied from the node. As we can see, the key point of $exe\_time[i]$ is to find a node with the highest $\overline{RUE}$.

3.3 Splitting Large Intermediate Cluster

If applications treat each intermediate cluster with the same $\langle key, value \rangle$ pairs independently in reduce phase, this can be quite improper. Enabling cluster splitting will then have a profound impact on data skew mitigation.

Considering the REU we have analyzed before, we provide an effective cluster splitting strategy and modify the partition decision include both the partition keys and the partition size. That is a partition decision record $(k; s)$. It means that one of the partition point is s of key k. Before reducer reads the partition, the monitor compares the partition size s with $\frac{data}{num\_r \times RUE}$. Eq. (7) shows the splitting data size level.

$$R\_data = \begin{cases} R\_data & ; s \leq \frac{data}{num\_r \times RUE} \\ \frac{data}{num\_r \times RUE} & ; s > \frac{data}{num\_r \times RUE} \end{cases} \qquad (7)$$

here num_r is the number of reducers. For a reducer, if there is data in the cluster to be read, it only read $\frac{data}{num\_r \times RUE}$ keys and the remaining keys left for other reducers to process. R_data' means the data that have not been executed calculated as Eq. (8):

$$R\_data' = R\_data - \frac{data}{num\_r \times RUE} \qquad (8)$$

4   Resource Allocation Algorithm

4.1   The Task Priority Based on Executing Time

We have introduced a method to estimate the executing time. Here we define a priority model for a task as $P < L, T >$, where L stands for level and T stands for exe_time. In this paper, we set $L = 1$ for failed task, which gets the highest priority, $L = 2$ for unscheduled tasks, which gets the average priority, $L = 3$ for speculative executed task, which gets the lowest priority. To improve the speculation performance in heterogeneous environment, we use Eq. (9) as a task's speculative execution priority determination method.

$$specPriority = (1 - progress)/progressRate \qquad (9)$$

If there is any node which has free Container to apply for tasks, the tasks waiting online obey the 2-tuples priority determination method $P < L, T >$. The specific process is given in the following Task_Priority algorithm.

Algorithm 1. Task_Priority algorithm

Input:
    N: the tasks collection;
    P: the processors collection.
Output:
    $P < L, T >$: the priority of tasks.
1: **for** each $i \in [1, n]$ **do**
2:    Calculate $exe\_time[i]$;
3:    Get the execution status task $N[i]$;
4:    **if** The $N[i]$ is judged to be failed task **then**
5:        Set $L[i] = 1$;
6:    **else if** $N[i]$ is judged to be unscheduled task **then**
7:        Set $L[i] = 2$;
8:    **else if** $N[i]$ is judged to be speculative task **then**
9:        Set $L[i] = 3$;
10:    **end if**
11:    Range $L[i]$ with increasing order;
12:    Rearrange the order with the same $L[i]$ in nondecreasing based on the $\overline{exe\_time[i]}$

13:    Update $P < L, T >$
14: **end for**
15: **return** $P < L, T >$.

Here the executing time of a task is not only determined by the data size and the process speed of node, but also determined by real-time resource utilization of the node which improves the performance of the system quite marked. For example, each node has its own real-time E_RUE. If E_RUE of a node is quite low while it has enough spare resource for other tasks to apply. Once it applies the tasks successfully, compared with other nodes whose E_RUE in real-time are much higher, it will lead to a long execution time. So we should judge if the apply should be accepted.

4.2   Resource Allocation Algorithm

Container Allocator (CA) is a responsible module for applications, and the allocation of resources. In Yarn, resource requirements of the job can be described as a 5-tuple. By resetting the priority and choosing a best fit node, we can schedule the tasks more effectively and avoid data skew.

Algorithm 2. CSRA algorithm

Input:
    N: the tasks collection;
    P: the processors collection;
    $P < L, T >$: the priority of tasks.

Output:
    Using CSRA to get a proper resource allocation method.

1: **while** $P < L, T >$ is not NULL **do**
2:    **if** $R\_data[i] > \frac{data}{num\_r \times RUE}$ **then**
3:      $R\_data[i] = \frac{data}{num\_r \times RUE}$; //split the big cluster;
4:      $R\_data[i]' = R\_data[i] - \frac{data}{num\_r \times RUE}$;//make the left data a new task;
5:      n++;
6:      $R\_data[n] = R\_data[i]'$;
7:      $s = n$;
8:    **end if**
9: **end while**
10: Get a new task list $L[i]$
11: **for** each $i \in [1, s]$ //i stands for task i **do**
12:    **for** each $j \in [1, n]$ //j stands for processor j **do**
13:      Calculate the E_RUE of each node ;
14:      Get a list ranks based on E_RUE in descending $P[i]$;
15:      Chose the first processor $P[t]$ with the highest E_RUE ;
16:      **if** $R\_apply[j] < R\_left[j]$ **then**
17:        Divide $L[i]$ to $P[t]$;
18:      **else**
19:        t++;
20:      **end if**
21:    **end for**
22: **end for**
23: **return** A proper resource allocation method.

CA divides all the tasks into three kinds. They are failed map task, map task and reduce task. The priorities that CA gives to them are 5, 10 and 20. That is to say, if these three kind of tasks apply resource simultaneously, CA will first assign resource to the failed map task. Similar with this resource allocation mechanism, we fine-tune the first element of this 5-tuples: priority by setting it variable instead of constant.

We know that the resource in a node is constant once a job is submitted. Here we can calculate the resource left in a node like Eq. (10):

$$R\_left(t) = R\_total - \sum_{i=0}^{n} R\_used(t_i) \times [u(t_i) - u(t_i - t_{i,0})], n = 0, 1, 2, \cdots$$

(10)

As we all know that the resource left at time t is equal to the total resource minus the used resource. In Eq. (10), $R\_left(t)$ stands for the resource left in time t, R_total means the total resource on the node and $R\_used(t_i)$ means the resource being divided to task i, $u(t_i) - u(t_i - t_{i,0})$ is a phase signal and $R\_used(t_i) \times [u(t_i) - u(t_i - t_{i,0})]$ means the resource being occupied by task i in $t_{i,0} < t_i < t$ and released on another time. n stands for the number of tasks who apply resources on the node.

According to all the analysis demonstrate above, we design CSRA to allocate resources. The whole specific processes are shown in algorithm 2.

5   Experiments and Result

In this section, we evaluate and compare the performance of CSRA with traditional scheduling algorithms, Hadoop hash and Hadoop range, following those three applications: Sort, Join and Grep. As Zipf distribution typically expresses the idea of data skew and it is quite common in the data coming from the real world, the data we used in the experiments follow its feature.

The comparisons of the experiments are based on the following two performance metrics:

Average Execution Time. The execution time of an algorithm is its running time for obtaining the output schedule of a given task graph. Among all the three algorithms, the one who gets the minimization average execution time is the one most practical implementation.

Coefficient of Variation. We compute the coefficient of variation in data size across reduce tasks to measure the effectiveness of skew mitigation. We compute the coefficient of variation in data size processed by different reducers. The smaller the coefficient is, the litter will data skew on reducer be.

5.1   Experimental Settings

The hardware configuration in our experiment is 15 servers and each server contains dual-Processors (2.4GHz Xeon E5620), 24GB of RAM and two 150GB disks. We set up our Hadoop 2.4.0 (Yarn) cluster on those severs which are connected by 1Gbps Ethernet (the nodes within a rack are connected through a single switch) and managed by CloudStack which is an open source cloud operating system. We use a virtualization software KVM to construct medium sized VMs with 2 virtual cores, 4GB RAM and 30GB of disk space.

We compare the performance of the three algorithms in various data skew degree, different sizes of data and different output percentage in Grep. The every following experiments conducted a detailed analysis of each group.

5.2 Estimate in Various Data Skew Degree

In the first set of experiments, to compare the performance of CSRA with the original hash and range algorithms in Hadoop, we randomly generated 10GB synthetic data following Zipf distribution. Without loss of generality, we take Join as the application. As Join is a reduce-input heavy application, choosing it can obviously highlight the superiority of splitting phase in CSRA. The results have been given in Fig. 1.

Fig. 1(a) depicts the average execution time in different data skew. When σ is relatively low, the execution time of CSRA and Hash is almost the same. But once σ further increased, their gap become obviously. As we can see, the execution time increased substantially when the degree of the skew reaches to a certain threshold 0.8. This phenomenon indicates that when the value of σ is small, it does not have many differences between Hash and CSRA. But when σ increased from 0.8 to 1.0, the growth rate for Hash is 38.6% and 22.0% for CSRA. While Range doesn't increase obviously.

Fig. 1(b) shows the impact does σ have on coefficient of variation. As shown in the picture, the increase of σ has the least impact on CSRA compared with the other two algorithms. Coefficient of variation increases substantially once the degree of skew reaches to a certain threshold. The reason that the two strategies in Hadoop performs worse than CSRA is that they do not detect or split large intermediate clusters.

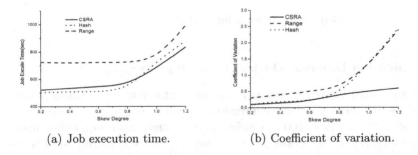

(a) Job execution time.   (b) Coefficient of variation.

Fig. 1. Performance in various data skew degree.

From this experiment, we can conclude that the overhead of CSRA is negligible even in the absence of skew ($\sigma = 0.2$).

5.3 Estimate in Different Data Size

For an efficient comparison, we estimate the effect of data scale. The size of data used in our experiments are varied from 4GB to 12GB, the value of data skew degree is $\sigma = 1.2$.

Fig. 2(a) shows the great superiority of CSRA considering execution time compared with the other two algorithms. This result becomes prominent when the data size is 12GB. The time CSRA saved is almost 23.5% compared with Range. When the data set is in a small size, the perform of CSRA shows litter superiority than Hash and Rang as the function of cluster splitting phase does not play an effective function, but task priority ranking method still play a light role.

As shown in Fig. 2(b), with the increasing of data size, the coefficient of variation here shows considerable gap among all of these three algorithms. The reason is that both Hash and Range allocate resources evenly without considering the actual feature of data. When data skew situation appeared non-negligible, both the execution time and the coefficient of variation performance are not good. For CSRA, cluster splitting phase makes the impact of data skew to the lowest level.

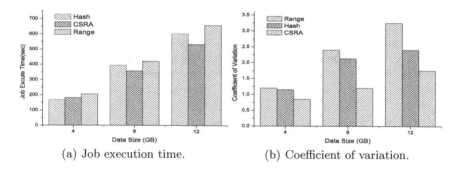

(a) Job execution time.   (b) Coefficient of variation.

Fig. 2. Estimate in different data size.

5.4 Estimate in Different Output Percentage in Grep

As we all know that Grep is a command-line utility for searching plain-text data sets for lines matching a regular expression. In order to make the output percentage varies from 10% to 100%, we change the search expression deliberately.

Fig. 3 shows the change of the job execution time and the coefficient of variation when the output percentage increase. To run this application, we randomly generated 10GB synthetic data following Zipf distribution ($\sigma = 1.0$) as usual.

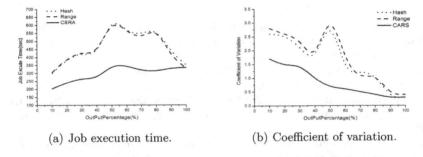

(a) Job execution time.   (b) Coefficient of variation.

Fig. 3. Evaluate in different output percentage.

Fig. 3(a) shows the big difference of those algorithms considering the execution time with increasing output percentage. We can see the disparity among those three algorithms. When the output percentage is 50%, they meet their biggest gap. CSRA saves about 78% execution time compared with Hash. It is own to the good performance of cluster splitting and a efficient task priority ranking method. The execution time shows less difference when the output percentage become bigger than 90%, as the application at this moment has very small data skew. The data divided to all the reducers almost evenly.

As we can see from the Fig. 3(b), CSRA performs significantly better when the output percentage is low. When searching unpopular words in the input files like generate results with heavy data skew, CSRA has a considerable advantage over the other two algorithms. When the output percentage is high, the resulting data become more evenly distributed and the performance difference becomes smaller.

6   Conclusion

Data skew alleviation is important in improving the performance of Yarn. This paper has presented CSRA, an algorithm that implements an innovative skew mitigation strategy to improve the performance of Yarn system. The unique features of CSRA are its task priority ranking and supports for cluster splitting. CSRA can handle data skew, but the system reliability should be considered in the future. Performance evaluation demonstrates that the performance improvement of CSRA is significant, and it can adapts to using in various parallel applications on heterogeneous environment.

Acknowledgments. This work is supported by the Key Program of National Natural Science Foundation of China (Grant No. 61133005, 61432005), National Natural Science Foundation of China (Grant Nos. 61370095, 61572176), and Open Foundation of State Key Laboratory of Software Engineering (SKLSE2012-09-18).

References

1. Dean, J., Ghemawat, S.: Mapreduce: simplified data processing on large clusters. In: Communications of the ACM - 50th anniversary issue, **51** (1), pp. 107–113. ACM, New York (2008)
2. Introduction for Yarn. http://en.wikipedia.org/wiki/Yarn
3. Kwon, Y., Balazinska, M., Howe, B., Rolia, J.: Skewtune: mitigating skew in mapreduce applications. In: SIGMOD 2012 Proceedings of the 2012 ACM SIGMOD International Conference on Management of Data, pp. 25–36. ACM, New York (2012)
4. Dhawalia, P., Kailasam, S., Janakiram, D.: Chisel: A resource savvy approach for handling skew in mapreduce applications. In: IEEE Sixth International Conference Cloud Computing (CLOUD), pp. 652–660. IEEE Press, Santa Clara (2013)
5. Kc, K., Anyanwu, K.: Scheduling hadoop jobs to meet deadlines. Cloud Computing Technology and Science (CloudCom). In: IEEE Second International Conference, pp. 388–392. IEEE Press, Indianapolis (2010)
6. Polo, J., Carrera, D., Becerra, Y., Torres, J., Ayguad, E., Steinder, M., and Whalley, I.: Performance-driven task co-scheduling for mapreduce environments. In: Network Operations and Management Symposium (NOMS), pp. 373–380. IEEE Press, Osaka (2010)
7. Gates, N., Chopra, S.: Building a high-level dataflow system on top of map-reduce: the pig experience. Proceedings of the VLDB Endowment, vol. 2, no. 2. (2009)
8. Schatz, M.: Cloudburst: highly sensitive read mapping with mapreduce. In: Proceedings of the VLDB Endowment on Bioinformatics, vol. 25, no. 11. pp. 1363–1369. ACM New York (2009)
9. Okcan, A., Riedewald, M.: Processing theta-joins using mapreduce. In: Proceedings of the 2011 ACM SIGMOD International Conference on Management of data, pp. 949–960. ACM. New York (2011)
10. Chen, Q., Yao, J., Xiao, Z.: Libra: Lightweight data skew mitigation in mapreduce. In: IEEE Transactions on Parallel and Distributed Systems, pp. 1–14 (2014)
11. Guo, Z., Fox, G.: Improving mapreduce performance in heterogeneous network environments and resource utilization. In: Proceedings of the 2012 12th IEEE/ACM International Symposium on Cluster. Cloud and Grid Computing (Ccgrid 2012), pp. 714–716. IEEE Press, Ottawa (2012)
12. Xu, Y., Kostamaa, P.: Efficient outer join data skew handling in parallel dbms. Proceedings of the VLDB Endowment **2**(2), 1390–1396 (2009)
13. Kwon, Y., Balazinska, M., Howe, B., Rolia, J.: Skew-resistant parallel processing of feature-extracting scientific user-defined functions. In: Proceedings of the 1st ACM symposium on Cloud computing, pp. 75–86. ACM. New York (2010)
14. Guo, Z., Pierce, M., Fox, G., Zhou, M.: Automatic task reorganization in mapreduce. In: 2011 IEEE International Conference Cluster Computing (CLUSTER), pp. 335–343. IEEE Press, Austin (2011)
15. Domangue, R., Patch, S.: Some omnibus exponentially weightedmoving average statistical process monitoring schemes. Technometrics **33**(3), 299–313 (1991)
16. Bardet, F., Chateau, T.: Mcmc particle filter for real-time visual tracking of vehicles. In: 11th International IEEE Conference Intelligent Transportation Systems (ITSC), pp. 539–544. IEEE Press, Beijing (2008)

Imbalanced Web Spam Classification Using Self-labeled Techniques and Multi-classifier Models

Xiaonan Fang[1,2], Yanyan Tan[1,2], Xiyuan Zheng[1,2],
Huaxiang Zhang[1,2(✉)], and Shuang Zhou[1,2]

[1] Department of Science and Engineering, Shandong Normal University,
Jinan 250014, China
[2] Shandong Provincial Key Laboratory for Novel Distributed Computer Software
Technology, Shandong Normal University, Jinan 250014, China
franknan@126.com, {yytan928,huaxzhang}@163.com,
{306732399,1282358834}@qq.com

Abstract. Web spam has become a critical problem in web search area. Unfortunately, highly imbalanced distribution and too many unlabeled instances always disturb the performance of classifiers. In this paper, we focus on solving the serious imbalance distribution of web spam under the semi-supervised learning frame. First, we introduce the self-labeled techniques and the multi-classifier mode. Second, the imbalance situation of web spam data sets and five combination methods are proposed. Particularly, we propose several improved self-labeled methods by using classic over-sampling technique SMOTE in pre-processing stage, and then balance the uneven labeled sets. Further, considering the serious imbalance situation of web spam, we introduce the AUC value into semi-supervised classification. Experiments under WEBSPAM UK2007 indicate that our methods can get better performance both on recall and AUC values.

Keywords: Imbalanced datasets · Web spam · Semi-supervised learning · Self-labeled techniques · Multi-classifier models · Ensemble learning

1 Introduction

Web spam is a method of manipulating search engines results by improving ranks of spam pages. It takes various forms and lacks a consistent definition [1,2]. In 2006, it was estimated that approximately one seventh of English Web pages were spam, and these spam pages became obstacles in users information acquisition process. Therefore, spam detection is regarded as a major challenge for web search service providers.

Since the number of spam pages is far less than normal pages, high imbalance of dataset often disturbs the effect of classification. As outlined in Table 1, there are serious imbalances in real-world data sets WEBSPAM-UK2007 [3]. The proportion of nonspam and spam samples is about 18:1, such serious imbalances

© Springer International Publishing Switzerland 2015
S. Zhang et al. (Eds.): KSEM 2015, LNAI 9403, pp. 663–668, 2015.
DOI: 10.1007/978-3-319-25159-2_60

make a classifier divide all data into the majority class frequently, resulting in decline in the performance of the classifier. Therefore, solving the serious imbalance of web spam data set is one of the key issues.

Table 1. Web spam data set

	labeled hosts	spam	nonspam
Training data set	3849	208	3641
Test data set	1948	113	1835
Total	5797	321	5476

Furthermore, there are a great number of unlabeled instances. As shown in Table 1, only 5797 instances are labeled, but the total number of all instances is 114,529, that is, there are about 95% instances are not labeled. Whether can these instances be used to enhance the effect of web spam recognition?

In recent years, self-labeled techniques [4] have become a promising topic in semi-supervised learning field. These techniques consider both labeled and unlabeled instances to improve the classification capability of traditional supervised classifiers. In this paper, we propose an improved web spam classification strategy under semi-supervised learning paradigm which can solve the above two problems. First, we introduce the self-labeled techniques and the multi-classifier mode. Second, the imbalance situation of web spam data sets is analyzed and five combination methods are proposed. Concretely, we insert SMOTE into the pre-processing stage of these methods, then the uneven labeled sets are balanced. At last, we introduce AUC, the most important evaluation criterion in imbalanced classification to measure the effects of semi-supervised methods. Experimental results on WEBSPAM UK2007 [3] indicate that our methods can effectively improve the classification performance of self-labeled and multi-classifier methods.

The rest of this paper is organized as follows. In section 2, we describe the self-labeled techniques and multi-classifier models we use. In section 3, we introduce the performance criteria facing imbalanced data and our combined methods. Experimental results and discussion can be found in section 4. Finally, we conclude our research and give future plan in section 5.

2   Self-labeled Techniques and Multi-classifier Models

The Semi-Supervised Learning (SSL) paradigm has attracted much attention in many different fields, where it is easier to obtain unlabeled than labeled data because it requires less effort, expertise and time consumption. Multi-classifier models [4] combine the learned hypotheses with several classifiers to predict the class of unlabeled instances. These methods are motivated, to some extent, by the empirical success of ensemble learning methods [4].

In this paper, we select four representative multi-classifier methods Tri-training [5], Co-forest [6], Adaptive co-forest editing [7] and Classification algorithm based on local clusters centers [8]. In addition, we include a classic single-classifier method standard self-training [9] in comparisons.

3   Facing Imbalance

3.1   Imbalanced Performance Criteria

In semi-supervised classification field, the typical performance criteria are accuracy or error rate. But when considering the highly imbalanced web spam data distribution, we choose an overall performance criterion widely used in imbalanced classification AUC, additionally, a single class criterion recall of spam (minority) class is adopted as the other criterion.

3.2   Combination of SMOTE and Self-labeled Methods

In this paper, we focus on the problem of web spam classification under highly imbalanced distribution. Considering there are a large amount of unlabeled instances in data sets, we combine classic under-sampling method SMOTE [10,11] and widely used self-labeled methods. Table 2 shows a list of combined methods we proposed. The complete name and abbreviation are provided for each one.

Table 2. Combination methods proposed in this paper

Complete name	Abbr.
SMOTE Standard self-training	SSelf
SMOTE Tri-training	STri
SMOTE Co-forest	SCoF
SMOTE Adaptive co-forest editing	SACoF
SMOTE Classification algorithm based on local clusters centers	SCLCC

In order to better understand, we select SMOTE Co-forest as example to introduce our strategy. L denotes labeled set, U denotes unlabeled set, L_{spam} denotes labeled set of spam labels, L_{non} denotes labeled set of non-spam labels, H_i denotes combination of ensemble classifiers which do not include classifier h_i, and L'_i denotes high confidence instances set got by ith classifier h_i. The main idea of SCoF is listed as follows:

Step 1 Build a random forest including N random trees.
Step 2 Over-sample L_{spam} by SMOTE algorithm, then an enlarged spam class set L'_{spam} is got.
Step 3 Combine L_{non} and L'_{spam} into a new training set L'.

Step 4 Train classifiers N times using L', then $h_i(i \in (1, ..., N))$ are built.

Step 5 For every random trees h_i, loop through every instance $\mathbf{x}$ in U, then H_i voted to $\mathbf{x}$ to decide whether it is be added into L'_i.

Step 6 Retrain h_i with $L' \cup L'_i$, then a high confidence classifier mode H' is got.

4   Experiments

4.1   Data Sets and Parameters

In this paper, we choose WEBSPAM-UK2007 [3] as an experimental data set. In order to study the influence of the amount of labeled data, we take different ratios when dividing the training set. In our experiments, four ratios are used: 10%, 20%, 30% and 40%. In summary, this experimental study involves a total of 4 web spam data sets. In experiments we also use 10-fold cross validation to obtain the results.

In this paper, the configuration parameters of all the methods are selected according to the recommendations of the corresponding authors of each algorithm [4], which are also the default parameter settings included in the KEEL software [12]. We select classic decision tree classifier C4.5, which is widely used in imbalanced classification and ensemble learning field.

4.2   Experimental Results Before and After SMOTE

Table 3 shows the experimental results before and after SMOTE, and the maximum values are set to bold. As shown in this table, before the data-sets are balanced, the recall values of all the five methods are very low. The best method Tri(C45) only gets 0.2002, and the average value of these methods is 0.1082, that is, only 10% spam instances are correctly classified. In particular, CLCC misclassifies all spam instances into nonspam class, which leads to zero on recall values. These indicate that CLCC is seriously affected by the highly imbalance distributions of web spam data sets.

After we combine SMOTE with self-labeled methods, the experimental results change obviously. Firstly, the recall values of STri(C45) and SSelf(C45) are higher than others, which indicates that these methods can find more spam instances after combining with SMOTE. Secondly, we can find SCof and SACoF performs well on AUC values on balanced datasets. These show that they can remain their overall accuracy when more spam class instances are classified. This is a good ability for classifiers facing imbalanced data sets.

4.3   Discussion

From the table above, the first conclusion is that the combination method we proposed can improve the recall value of spam class and AUC value. Before combination, the average recall value of all methods under four labeled rate is 0.1082, and after SMOTE is combined, this value is 0.2571, increasing 137%.

Table 3. Experimental results before and after SMOTE

	40%		30%		20%		10%	
	recall	AUC	recall	AUC	recall	AUC	recall	AUC
CoF	0.1402	0.5684	0.1184	0.5588	0.0935	0.5455	0.0560	0.5269
Self(C45)	0.1526	0.5693	0.1402	0.5604	**0.2430**	**0.6047**	**0.1866**	**0.5790**
Tri(C45)	**0.2493**	**0.6152**	**0.2054**	**0.5942**	0.1652	0.5749	0.1809	0.5732
ClCC	0.0000	0.5000	0.0000	0.5000	0.0000	0.5000	0.0000	0.5000
ACoF	0.0935	0.5463	0.0748	0.5372	0.0437	0.5216	0.0219	0.5106
SCoF	0.3520	0.6540	0.3054	0.6361	0.2303	0.5977	0.2026	**0.5924**
SSelf(C45)	0.3521	0.6388	0.3923	0.6318	**0.4111**	**0.6347**	**0.2897**	0.5711
STri(C45)	**0.4392**	0.6552	**0.4045**	**0.6448**	0.3650	0.6284	0.2741	0.5863
SClCC	0.0188	0.5068	0.0000	0.5000	0.0000	0.5000	0.0000	0.5000
SACoF	0.3705	**0.6619**	0.2805	0.6223	0.2835	0.6199	0.1712	0.5711

Before combination, the average AUC value is 0.5493, and after combination, this value is 0.5976, increasing 8%. These indicate that methods in this paper can find more spam instances under different labeled rates, and then effectively improve the overall classification effects of highly imbalanced web spam data sets. Secondly, we can find that most multi-classifier methods perform better than self-training on AUC values when datasets are balanced. Although self-training can find some spam instances and get high recall values, but it misclassifies more nonspam instances, so the overall AUC values are not satisfactory. At last, our combination methods perform worse under 10% label rate than under 40% label rate. These come from the defect of SMOTE technique. So there is a problem to solve the imbalanced situation when very few instances are labeled.

5   Conclusion and Further Work

In this paper, we propose the combination method of SMOTE and self-labeled and multi-classifier technique to solve the problem of highly imbalanced web spam data set classification. Experimental results prove that our methods can improve the recall value of spam class then enhance the overall AUC value. In future work, we will try to use unlabeled sample to balance the datasets and find more powerful multi-classifier algorithms to avoid misclassification.

Acknowledgments. The work is partially supported by the National Science Foundation of China (No.61170145, 61373081, 61402268, 61401260), the Technology and Development Project of Shandong (No.2013GGX10125), Shangdong Province Young and Middle-Aged Scientists Research Awards Fund (No.BS2014DX006, 2015BSB01090), and the Taishan Scholar Project of Shandong, China.

References

1. Gyongyi, Z., Garcia-Molina, H.: Web spam taxonomy. In: First International Workshop on Adversarial Information Retrieval on the Web (2005)
2. Luckner, M., Gad, M., Sobkowiak, P.: Stable Web Spam Detection Using Features Based on Lexical Items. Computers & Security **46**, 79–93 (2014)
3. Web Spam Collections. http://barcelona.research.yahoo.net/webspam/datasets/
4. Triguero, I., Garca, S., Herrera, F.: Self-labeled techniques for semi-supervised learn-ing: taxonomy, software and empirical study. Knowledge and Information Systems **42**(2), 245–284 (2013)
5. Zhou, Z.H., Li, M.: Tri-training: Exploiting unlabeled data using three classifiers. IEEE Transactions on Knowledge and Data Engineering **17**(11), 1529–1541 (2005)
6. Li, M., Zhou, Z.H.: Improve computer-aided diagnosis with machine learning tech-niques using undiagnosed samples. IEEE Transactions on Systems, Man and Cybernetics, Part A: Systems and Humans **37**(6), 1088–1098 (2007)
7. Deng, C., Zu Guo, M.: A new co-training-style random forest for computer aided diag-nosis. Journal of Intelligent Information Systems **36**(3), 253–281 (2011)
8. Huang, T., Yu, Y., Guo, G., Li, K.: A classification algorithm based on local cluster centers with a few labeled training examples. Knowledge-Based Systems **23**(6), 563–571 (2010)
9. Yarowsky D.: Unsupervised word sense disambiguation rivaling supervised methods. In: Proceedings of the 33rd Annual Meeting of the Association for Computational Linguistics, pp. 189–196 (1995)
10. Chawla, N.V., Bowyer, K.W., Hall, L.O., Kegelmeyer, W.P.: SMOTE: synthetic mi-nority over-sampling technique. Journal of Artificial Intelligence Research, 321–357 (2002)
11. Zhang, H., Li, M.: RWO-Sampling: A random walk over-sampling approach to imbal-anced data classification. Information Fusion **20**, 99–116 (2014)
12. Alcal-Fdez, J., Snchez, L., Garca, S., del Jesus, M.J., Ventura, S., Garrell, J.M., Otero, J., Romero, C., Bacardit, J., Rivas, V.M., Fernndez, J.C., Herrera, F.: KEEL: a software tool to assess evolutionary algorithms for data mining problems. Soft Comput **13**(3), 307–318 (2009)

Ensemble of SVM Classifiers with Different Representations for Societal Risk Classification

Jindong Chen and Xijin Tang[✉]

Institute of Systems Science, Academy of Mathematics and Systems Science,
Chinese Academy of Sciences, Beijing 100190, People's Republic of China
j.chen@amss.ac.cn, xjtang@iss.ac.cn

Abstract. Using the posts of Tianya Forum as the data source and adopting the societal risk indicators from socio psychology, we conduct document-level multiple societal risk classification of BBS posts. Two kinds of models are applied to generate the representations of posts respectively: Bag-of-Words focuses on extracting the occurrence information of words in posts, and a deep learning model as Post Vector is designed to capture the semantics and word order of posts. Based on the different post representations, two types of support vector machine (SVM) classifiers are developed and compared in the societal risk classification of the posts. Furthermore, as the complementary information contained in the two different post representations, several SVM ensemble methods at the decision score level of the two SVM classifiers are proposed to improve the performance of societal risk classification. The experimental results reveal that the SVM ensemble method achieves better results in document-level societal risk classification than SVM based on single representation.

Keywords: Societal risk classification · Tianya forum · Deep learning · Bag-of-Words · Support vector machine

1 Introduction

To monitor the daily risk classes and level of Tianya Zatan Broad of Tianya Forum timely, societal risk classification of BBS posts is the main task. Since the framework of societal risks includes 7 main categories and 1 risk free category, societal risk classification of BBS posts is document-level multiple classification [1, 2]. The document-level multiple societal risk classification is a quite difficult task, since i) the document-level classification brings more challenges, such as the big variance of the text length, the complicated syntax, the involvement of multiple topics in one document; ii) the multiple risk classes also increase the complexity of text classification.

For text classification, the primary step is to represent text as vectors. The traditional method is Bag-of-Words (BOW), disregarding semantic and word order but keeping multiplicity. To overcome the issues of BOW representation, the distributed representation using deep learning method was proposed [3]. In this method, the semantic and word order features are encoded in the distributed vectors through sliding-window training mode. Recently, many prominent deep learning algorithms have been proposed for word vector construction, such as: SENNA [4], Word2Vec [5] and GloVe [6]. Le et al.

© Springer International Publishing Switzerland 2015
S. Zhang et al. (Eds.): KSEM 2015, LNAI 9403, pp. 669–675, 2015.
DOI: 10.1007/978-3-319-25159-2_61

[7] proposed a more flexible deep learning method to realize the distributed representation of paragraph or document [5]. Combined with an additional paragraph vector, the method includes two models: PV-DM and PV-DBOW for paragraph representation, where the paragraph vector contributes to predict the next word in many contexts sampled from the paragraph [7]. To realize the distributed representation of Chinese online documents, a deep learning method as Post Vector (PV) model was proposed, the model showed its effectiveness for Chinese document representation [8].

The representative classifiers for text classification are K-Nearest Neighbor, naïve Bayes and support vector machine (SVM), etc. Due to the good performance of SVM for societal risk classification of Baidu hot word [9], SVM method is chosen. However, based on BOW representation, SVM method hardly achieved the expected performance in societal risk classification, even though the training set was increased and the feature word selection method was optimized. Therefore, with the deep learning method as PV model, we focus on realizing the distributed representation of BBS posts, and developing SVM classifier based on the distributed representations. Furthermore, as the complementary information contained in BOW representation and the distributed representation, we construct an ensemble model at decision score level of SVM classifiers, for performance improvement in societal risk classification of BBS posts.

2   Post Vector Model

The deep learning method as PV is mainly designed for the distributed representation of Chinese documents [8]. In PV framework (Figure 1), the Chinese documents of posts are segmented into words using segmentation tools. The post ID which is treated as another word is concatenated with the segmented words of the post, and combined with other words sampled from the post to predict the next word of the post. To enhance the performance of PV model, the words after the predictive word are also taken into consideration. Each post is represented by a unique vector, which is a column in post matrix D and every word of post is also represented by a unique vector, which is a column in word matrix W, where D and W are real matrix, the initial values are $[-0.5/l, 0.5/l]$, where l is the word vector size . For the random initialization of word matrix and post matrix, large corpus is preferred for training. After the training, the word matrix and post matrix can be obtained simultaneously.

Formally, PV model can be viewed as a three-layer network: input, hidden and output. Before the model training, set the word vector size as l and window size as k. For a given post, it can be viewed as a post ID and a sequence of words: w_{ID}, w_1, w_2, w_3,...w_T, T is the number of words in context. To predict the word w_t, t=1,2, ...,T, k words before or after w_t are taken into input.   The objective of the Post Vector model is to maximize the average log probability

$$\frac{1}{T}\sum_{t=k}^{T-k}\log p(w_t|w_{ID},w_{t-k},...,w_{t+k}) \tag{1}$$

In the training process, input features are of fixed-length and sampled from a sliding window over the document of the post. The document vector (the vector of w_{ID}) is updated across all contexts generated from the same post. Hence, the document vector acts as a memory that remembers what is missing from the current context or the topic of the post. The word vector matrix W is used by all posts. i.e., *vector*(拆迁, demolition) is the same for all posts. The training process of PV model can be regarded as the process of dimension reduction of document vector.

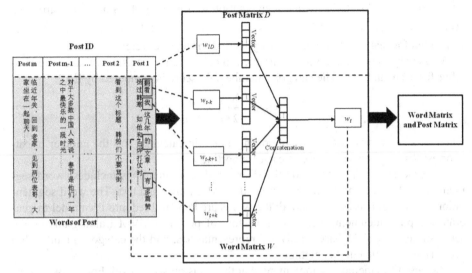

Fig. 1. A framework for learning word vectors and post vectors.

3   Data Sets, Experimental Procedure

3.1   Data Sets

To compare the effectiveness of different methods in societal risk classification, the labeled posts of Dec. 2011-Mar. 2012 are used. The amount of posts of these four months and the amount of posts in different societal risk categories of each month are presented in Table 1.

Table 1. The risk distribution of posts on Tianya Zatan board of different months

Risk Category \ Period	Dec.2011	Jan.2012	Feb.2012	Mar.2012
Total	12125	12032	20330	37946
Risk free	1278	2047	2645	14569
Government Management	3373	1809	3099	6879
Public Morality	3337	3730	8715	6065
Social Stability	954	1013	1746	2108
Daily Life	2641	3063	3142	6920
Resources & Environments	223	147	309	329
Economy & Finance	248	133	460	609
Nation's Security	71	90	214	467

3.2   Experimental Procedures

The process of SVM based on BOW representations for societal risk classification toward BBS posts includes: word segmentation, feature selection, feature weight and SVM training and test. The word segmentation tool is Ansj, the stop words are from HIT (Information Retrieval Laboratory, Harbin Institute of Technology), the χ^2-test is adopted for feature selection and *tf-idf* is used for feature weight.

A category membership score is applied to calculate the decision value of the classifier for each category. The category membership score is computed by Eq.2.

$$score = \frac{\sum S_i}{2*k} + \frac{k}{2*n} \tag{2}$$

where k is the number of voters supporting a certain category; n is the number of categories; S_i is the decision score of each supporting voter.

The process of SVM based on the distributed representations includes: word segmentation, Post Vector model training and SVM training and test. The word segmentation tool is same as before, and all the words are kept and fed into PV model to generate the post document vectors (the vectors of post ID). SVM training adopts the same strategy as SVM based on BOW representations, and the category membership score is also applied in this method.

The ensemble method is implemented at the decision score level. For a new post p_i, due to the One-Against-One training strategy, SVM classifier based on BOW representations or the distributed representations outputs 28 decision scores respectively. Based on the decision scores, the category membership scores of each SVM classifier are calculated. Using weighted or softmax regression method, the decision scores and category membership scores are combined to improve the performance of societal risk classification.

4   Experiment Results and Discussions

4.1   SVM Based on BOW Representations

For χ^2-test, the ratio is set as 0.4. The kernel function for SVM is chosen as RBF. After parameter optimization, the parameters of SVM are $C=1.4$ and $g=0.5$. 5-fold cross-validations are implemented on the data set. The classification results are presented in Table 2. The performance measures of classification results for each fold are computed as Ref. [10]. 8 classes of societal risks are taken into consideration.

Table 2. The *Macro_F* and *Micro_F* of SVM based on BOW representations

i^{th} fold	1	2	3	4	5	Mean
Macro_F	53.89%	54.85%	53.66%	53.45%	54.84%	54.14%
Micro_F	60.52%	60.91%	60.30%	60.60%	61.15%	60.69%

4.2 SVM Based on the Distributed Representations

For Post Vector model training, the training set is the posts during November of 2011 to March of 2013, 16-month new posts every day, more than 470 thousands posts. Through the unsupervised training of Post Vector model, the distributed representations of the posts in the data set are yielded. Based on the distributed representations, SVM method is applied for societal risk classification of posts.

The kernel function for SVM is chosen as RBF. Through parameter optimization, the parameters of PV are *window size*=3 and *vector size*=250, the parameters of SVM are C=2 and g=0.5. 5-fold cross-validations are implemented on the data set. The classification results are presented in Table 3.

Table 3. The *Macro_F* and *Micro_F* of SVM based on the distributed representations

ith fold	1	2	3	4	5	Mean
Macro_F	50.20%	51.01%	50.28%	50.73%	52.36%	50.91%
Micro_F	58.20%	58.99%	58.14%	58.51%	58.98%	58.56%

4.3 The SVM Classifiers Ensemble

To further improve the performance of risk classification, the SVM classifiers ensemble methods are proposed. According to the description of Section 3.2, at the decision scores level, the two SVM classifiers are combined. Three kinds of methods are developed and tested:

I) Softmax regression. The 8 category membership scores of the two SVMs are concatenated as the input of softmax regression. 2000 labeled posts from the training set are used to identify the parameters of softmax regression. After the training, the softmax regression model is used to predict the risk category of the testing samples.

II) Max_Voter. Based on the 56 decision scores, the supporting votes of each risk category can be counted. The risk category with the maximum votes will be the risk label of the testing post. If more than one risk category gets the maximum supporting votes, the risk category with a bigger sum of the category membership scores of the two SVM classifiers will be applied to label the testing post.

III) Max_Score. If two SVM classifiers classify the testing post into the same risk category, the risk category of the testing post is confirmed. Otherwise, the label of testing post is as same as the risk category with the highest category membership score of the two SVM classifiers.

All the results of the three ensemble methods are present in Table 4.

Table 4. The *Macro_F* and *Micro_F* of the SVM classifiers ensemble methods

Methods	ith fold	1	2	3	4	5	Mean
Softmax	Macro_F	50.77%	53.51%	51.25%	52.00%	52.86%	52.08%
Regression	Micro_F	59.43%	60.25%	59.43%	59.13%	60.28%	59.70%
Max_Voter	Macro_F	52.42%	53.47%	51.98%	53.05%	54.56%	53.09%
	Micro_F	61.05%	61.23%	60.57%	61.24%	61.39%	61.10%
Max_Score	Macro_F	53.53%	54.47%	52.64%	53.31%	54.37%	53.66%
	Micro_F	61.05%	61.60%	60.92%	61.28%	61.41%	61.25%

From the results of Table 4, although the logistic regression is the most popular stacking method, softmax regression method gets better performance than SVM based on the distributed representations, but worse than SVM based on BOW representations. Max_Voter method improves *Micro_F*, but with the larger decrease in *Macro_F*, then the whole performance is still worse than SVM based on BOW representations. Although the decrease of *Macro_F* is still found, the improvement of *Micro_F* is more obvious, the entire performance of the Max_Score method is better than SVM based on single representation: BOW or the distributed representation. Therefore, the ensemble method Max_Score achieves state-of-the-art performance in societal risk classification.

5　Conclusions

The contributions of the paper can be summarized as follows.
An effective deep learning method Post Vector for the distributed representation of Chinese BBS posts is applied in this study;

1) SVM based on the distributed representation method are tested in societal risk classification, through cross validation, SVM based on the distributed representation method do not show its improvement in societal risk classification;
2) Three ensemble methods of the two SVM classifiers are tested, and Max_Score method gets the state of the art performance in societal risk classification.

Acknowledgements. This research is supported by National Natural Science Foundation of China under Grant Nos.71171187, 71371107 and 61473284. The authors would like to thank other members of our team for their effort in data collection and post labeling.

References

1. Zheng, R., Shi, K., Li, S.: The influence factors and mechanism of societal risk perception. In: Zhou, J. (ed.) Complex 2009. LNICST, vol. 5, pp. 2266–2275. Springer, Heidelberg (2009)
2. Tang, X.J.: Exploring On-line Societal Risk Perception for Harmonious Society Measurement. Journal of Systems Science and Systems Engineering **22**(4), 469–486 (2013)
3. Bengio, Y., Ducharme, R., Vincent, P., Jauvin, C.: A neural probabilistic language model. Journal of Machine Learning Research **3**, 1137–1155 (2003)
4. Collobert, R., Weston, J., Bottou, L., Karlen, M., Kavukcuoglu, K., Kuksa, P.: Natural Language Processing (Almost) from Scratch. Journal of Machine Learning Research **12**, 2461–2505 (2011)
5. Mikolov, T., Chen, K., Corrado, G., Dean, J.: Efficient estimation of word representations in vector space. In: International Conference on Learning Representations (ICLR 2013), Scottsdale, pp. 1–12 (2013)
6. Jeffrey, P., Richard, S., Christopher, M.: Glove: Global vectors for word representation. In: Proceedings of the Empirical Methods in Natural Language Processing (EMNLP 2014), pp. 1532–1543. Association for Computational Linguistics, Stroudsburg (2014)

7. Le, Q., Mikolov, T.: Distributed representations of sentences and documents. In: Proceedings of the 31st International Conference on Machine Learning (ICML 2014). JMLR Workshop and Conference Proceedings, Beijing, pp. 1188–1196 (2014)

8. Chen, J.D., Tang, X.J.: Societal risk classification of post based on paragraph vector and KNN method. In: Wang, S.Y., Nakamori, Y., Huynh, V.N. (Eds.) Proceedings of the 15th International Symposium on Knowledge and Systems Sciences, Sapporo, November 1–2, pp. 117–123. JAIST Press (2014). ISBN: 978-4-903092-39-3

9. Hu, Y., Tang, X.: Using support vector machine for classification of baidu hot word. In: Wang, M. (ed.) KSEM 2013. LNCS, vol. 8041, pp. 580–590. Springer, Heidelberg (2013)

10. Wen, S.Y., Wan, X.J.: Emotion classification in microblog texts using class sequential rules. In: Proceedings of the Twenty-Eighth AAAI Conference on Artificial Intelligence, Québec, pp. 187–193 (2014)

Mobile Data Analytics and Knowledge Management

Discovering User's Background Information from Mobile Phone Data

Rong Xie[1(✉)], Yang Yue[2], and Yuchen Wang[1]

[1] International School of Software, Wuhan University, Wuhan 430079, China
xierong@whu.edu.cn
[2] Shenzhen Key Laboratory of Spatial Smart Sensing and Services,
Shenzhen University, Shenzhen 518060, China
yueyang@szu.edu.cn

Abstract. Data collected from mobile phone have potential knowledge to provide background information of a mobile phone user, such as work location, home location, job occupation, income, consumption and even lifestyle etc., which are quite valuable to many location-aware applications. In the existing research, there is relatively few commercial software or application systems to fully meet the requirements of effectively mining these personal behavioral characteristics. In the paper, we propose approaches to analyzing personal activity characteristics and mining behavioral regularity from mobile phone location information, automatically generating some semantic labels by integrating mobile phone log data with map data and web data, and location prediction for personalized advertising services. We use actual mobile phone data to perform the functions for discovering background information and demonstrate effectiveness of our approaches.

Keywords: Mobile phone log data · Region of Interest (ROI) · Point of Interest (POI) · User label · Location prediction

1 Introduction

Huge amount of data collected from mobile phone record trajectories in our everyday life in form of calling logs, having potential knowledge to provide background information of a mobile phone user, such as work location, home location, job occupation, income, consumption and even lifestyle etc. It is a rich information source for analyzing and discovering individual activity characteristics and regularity. Understanding and extracting these meaningful personal background information is valuable to many location-aware applications, like recommendation system, location-based advertisement (LBA), social network and urban analysis etc. For instance, if we summarize information of a user about his/her frequently visited places, consumption level, weekend traveling pattern etc., it would be quite helpful to provide the user with more intelligent and customized services, and benefit service providers as well.

Although increasing mobile phones are currently equipped with built-in GPS, mobile phone location data are recorded in terms of connected cell towers. Different from those continuous and fine-grained GPS-enabled data, mobile phone location data

S. Zhang et al. (Eds.): KSEM 2015, LNAI 9403, pp. 679–690, 2015.
DOI: 10.1007/978-3-319-25159-2_62

are discrete, sparse, less precise, and in certain extent uncompleted (Isaacman *et al.*, 2011), because they are generated only when a user makes a phone call or uses a data communication service, such as short message services (SMS) and website browsing based on cell tower locations, or makes any other forms of communication action. Therefore, mobile phone location data are coarse in space at granularity of cellular tower coverage radius, and sparse in time when a communication event happens (Licoppe *et al.*, 2008). Under most circumstances, accuracy ranges from 100-200m (urban area) to several square kilometers (Eagle *et al.*, 2009).

Previous studies have carried out to handle pattern discovery, semantic identification and call prediction by means of mobile phone data. However, several challenges are still needed to be addressed in the aspects of mobile phone-based data analysis and mining as follows. 1) It is difficult to directly access meaningful information about background of a user since all call logs are in low level data unit (Bayir *et al.*, 2009; 2011). To make mobile phone data more readily accessible to related applications, higher level of data abstraction is required. 2) Some classical algorithms in the traditional data mining, ignoring spatiotemporal characteristics, often lead to incomplete, even wrong knowledge, and cannot be fully used in discovering individual mobility patterns. 3) In the current research, there is relatively few commercial software or application systems to fully meet the requirements of effectively mining personal behavioral characteristics.

Privacy issue aside, the aim of our work is to overcome the limitations of mobile phone log data, and discover a user's background information. In the paper, we focus on approaches to analyzing personal activity characteristics and mining behavioral regularity from mobile phone location information, automatically generating some semantic labels by integrating mobile phone log data with map data and web data, and location prediction for personalized advertising service.

The rest of the paper is organized as follows. We present related work in Section 2. Our approaches are proposed to discover mobile phone user's background information in Section 3. Section 4 shows our visualization results of handling semantic label generation and location prediction. Conclusions and future work are finally presented in Section 5.

2   Related Work

To study pattern mining in human mobility, González *et al.* (2008) study trajectories of 100,000 anonymized mobile phone users during six-month period and find a high regularity degree in human trajectories contrasting with estimation by prevailing Lévy flight and random walk models. Eagle *et al.* (2006) introduce a system for sensing complex social systems with data collected from 100 mobile phone users over 9 months and demonstrate the ability to use standard bluetooth-enabled mobile telephones to measure information access and use in different contexts, recognize social patterns in daily user activity, infer relationships, identify socially significant locations, and model organizational rhythms. Bayir *et al.* (2009) present formal definitions to capture cellphone users' mobility patterns and profiles, and provide a complete framework–*Mobility Profiler*, for discovering mobile users' profiles from cell-based location log data. They use real-world cellphone log data to demonstrate their framework and experiments.

Isaacman *et al.* (2011) use ZIP codes to define ROI. But it is still very limited to understanding a user's characteristics for their studies on extracting personal features from important places, such as home and work location and other ROIs. Phithakkitnukoon and Dantu (2010) develop an *activity-aware map* that describes the most probable activity associated with a specific area of space based on POIs information from a large mobile phone data of nearly one million records of users in the central Metro-Boston area. They find a strong correlation in daily activity patterns within the group of people who share a common work area's profile.

To study call prediction, Phithakkitnukoon and Dantu (2007) propose a Call Predictor (CP) that computes probability of receiving calls and makes call prediction based on a caller's behavior and reciprocity. They also propose (2008) a concept of Call Predicted List (CPL) that provides a phone user with ability to predict future incoming calls as well as improvement over the "last received calls" functionality.

3   Approach to Discovering User's Background Information

Where a person lives, works and goes for leisure, to a great extent, reflects some activity characteristics and regularity of the person. We can start our work from analysis of some information about frequently visited places where a user stays, which is helpful to further estimate the user's work location, home location, job occupation, income and consumption.

Definition 1 (*Stop*): A *stop* is a position that a user stays within the range of a cell tower at some time stamps. Distribution of a user's stops is scattered on map. Since our interest is in the type of activities associated with the space, we thus make these stops in clusters, i.e., Region of Interests (ROI). Moreover, under the condition of base station-based positioning, only (latitude, longitude)-coordinate is available, without any business information, it is thus required to search for Point of Interest (POI). Here we introduce two concepts about POI and ROI as follows.

Definition 2 (*POI*): POI (Point of Interest) is defined as some entities with geographical significant locations within a localized region, such as hotels, schools, hospitals, shopping malls, stadiums etc. Each POI contains name, category, latitude and longitude coordinates etc., describing location and properties of these entities.

Definition 3 (*ROI*): ROI (Region of Interest) is defined as a region where a person visits frequently within a certain time period, represented as a polygon.

Definition 4 (*User Label*): User label is defined as some keywords attached to a user, that represent behavioral characteristics of the user, regarding work location, home location, job occupation, income, consumption and lifestyle etc.

We propose approaches to discovering background information of a mobile phone user. We identify frequent activity regions closely attached to a user, i.e., ROI, by spatially aggregating mobile phone location points. After clustering, we extract semantic meanings of these regions by integrating mobile phone log data with map and data collected from websites, including POI and real estate websites. Using comprehensive evaluation method, we can analyze the user's work location, home location, job occupation, income, consumption to generate the user's personal labels. Location prediction helps infer user's next possible location. This task is executed to push LBA services to the user on the basis of analysis of his/her level of consumption.

3.1   ROI Extraction

We use *ST-DBSCAN* clustering algorithm (Birant and Kut, 2007) to cluster mobile phone location data. The algorithm is a density based clustering algorithm, defining a cluster of a set of points which are density connected. Areas with high density are divided into a cluster. As a result, the cluster with arbitrary shape can be found in the spatial multi-dimensional data set. Effective radius and density threshold, ROI information are chosen to extract ROI information.

Two important parameters are required to determine in this algorithm, i.e., neighborhood radius (*Eps*) and density threshold (*MinPts*). After several tests, we choose the best combination with *Eps*=1000 and *MinPts*=10, representing *Eps* as 1 km and 10 minimum number of *MinPts*, respectively.

The steps of the algorithm are described as follows. 1) Input database of n objects, *Eps* and *MinPts*. 2) Read an unhandled point from the database. 3) If the point is a core point, find all objects which are reachable to the point satisfying the certain density and construct a cluster. 4) If the point is the edge point (i.e., non-core object), search for the next point. 5) Repeat until all points are processed. 6) Output all generated clusters, which satisfying with *Eps* and *MinPts*.

3.2   POIs Extraction

Similar to Koubei (http://bendi.koubei.com/list.htm), some reviewing portals of consumption and entertainment collects various reviewing information on merchants from consumers. We can extract POI information we need from these websites, including merchant information, as well as the corresponding geocoding.

Using firebug tool of browser, we can analyze structure of the target web page and crawl its merchant information, including name, address, business, number of reviewing persons, positive feedback and per capita consumption etc. Through regular expression, we can also extract the corresponding (*latitude*, *longitude*)-coordinate. In the paper, base station POI is extracted based on the Koubei website.

Source code of web pages of the target website can be analyzed. Use *BeautifulSoup*, a kind of html/xml parser of python, we can read source codes and generate a parse tree, and then extract the required POI merchant information. The steps are as follows.

Step 1: The following python scripts read web source code of the target website into *BeautifulSoup*. Here, *urllib2* package reads *url* source code and crawls the page through the *BeautifulSoup* processor.

content=urllib2.urlopen(url).read()

soup=BeautifulSoup(content,fromEncoding="utf-8")

Step 2: Using the following *find* method of *BeautifulSoup*, search for each layer of html one by one.

store_list=soup.find('ul',{'id':'store-list'})

store=store_list.find('li')

Step 3: Replace the *url* for the next page link, iteratively read and crawl.

The steps of coordinate extraction are as follows. 1) Use python *urllib2* package, read geographical address of source code in the target web page as a text. 2) Construct the regular expression: *pattern=re.compile('var Pos.*?=".*?"')*, parse the matched text, and extract (latitude, longitude)-coordinate. 3) Go to the next page for the continuing iteration until all pages are parsed. After a series of conversion, geographical codes are extracted. Similarly, from some real estate web site, like Taobao (http://house.taobao.com/?city=530100), some housing price information are also available, including housing address, real estate name, total price of house, price per square meter etc., as well as longitude coordinate, latitude coordinate.

3.3   User Label Generation

The process of generating a user's personal labels is described as follows. 1) Make clusters for all stops of a user to get ROIs. Analyze staying time when the user stays at each ROI. If time is in range of "11pm-8am", identify the ROI as the area of the user's home. If time is in range of "9am-7pm", identify ROI as the area of the user's workplace. Calculate number of stops, select the maximum to further determine the user's work location and home location and make user labels of "*workplace*" and "*home*". 2) Analyze ROI where user's work location is located. Determine type of ROI by POI, like office, downtown or school etc. Analyze the scope of activities of the user to determine whether the user is a white-collar worker or the others. 3) Analyze consumption level and housing price of ROI where the user's living place is located, and define the user's income label as "*low*" and "*high*" respectively. 4) Query all stops during time period outside daily working hours and on weekends. Combined with POI information, analyze level of consumption of the user within ROIs and define consumption label as "*high*", "*middle*" or "*low*". 5) Count all stops within 11pm-8am to determine label of lifestyle. For example, if number of stop locations is more than 5, and number of stop times is greater than 3, then the user is labeled as "*night life*". If number of stops is less, then the user label is defined as "*regular*".

3.4   Location Prediction

Some traditional methods are used to predict next location of a user according to his/her current location. We propose a spatio-temporal approach to location prediction based on current location, current time and prediction time. We can discover some frequent patterns from trajectory data of a user's call logs, and get mobility rules, and predict user's next location through rule matching strategies. Considering factor of time, our prediction patterns shall be more accurate than traditional approaches.

Definition 5 (*Support*): Support of sequence S in database is defined as ratio of number of tuples that database contains S to number of all tuples in database, denoted as *support(S)*. For convenience, support count is used for representation in the paper.

Definition 6 (*Frequent Pattern*): A frequent pattern is defined as a set of tuples that appear in a user's trajectory data set frequently, whose support is greater than or equal to the pre-specified support threshold *min_sup*, denoted as $TP=\{<(c_1, t_1), (c_2, t_2), \ldots, (c_k, t_k)> \mid support(c_i) \geq min\_sup\}$, where $k>1$, that is, the user is located at the base station c_1 at time t_1, at the base station c_2 at the next time t_2 and so on.

Get all available mobility rules as follows from the frequent patterns, defining the left-hand side of a rule as the antecedent, the right-hand side as the consequent.

$<(c_1, t_1), (c_2, t_2), \ldots,(c_{k-1}, t_{k-1})> \rightarrow <(c_k, t_k)>$

Definition 7 (*Confidence*): For a mobility rule r_i: $<(c_1, t_1), (c_2, t_2), \ldots,(c_i, t_i)> \rightarrow <(c_{i+1}, t_{i+1}), \ldots,(c_k, t_k)>$, *confidence* is defined as in formula (1),

$$confidence(r_i) = \frac{support <(c_1,t_1),(c_2,t_2),\ldots,(c_k,t_k)>}{support <(c_1,t_1),(c_2,t_2),\ldots,(c_i,t_i)>} \quad (1)$$

To generate all possible mobility rules from frequent patterns, we calculate *confidence* for each rule. If *confidence* is greater than or equal to pre-specified confidence threshold *min_conf*, then a set of mobility rules R are generated. Use the rule set to match user's current time and current position for location prediction. Suppose a user' trajectory is $Tr=\{<c_1, t_1>, <c_2, t_2>, \ldots, <c_i, t_i>\}$, that is, the current location of the user is c_i, the current time is t_i. Search for some rules in the set of mobility rules whose antecedent is contained in the Tr and the last base station of the antecedent is c_i, defined as the matching rules. Store the first base station of the consequent of all matched rules and its confidence into an array. Put the array in descending order by the degree of confidence. Select the base station with the maximum confidence from the array list, that is, the prediction location of the user. Give an example of a user's trajectory data shown in Table 1. Set the minimum support threshold *min_sup* as 0.25, to get all frequent patterns in Table 2. Set the minimum confidence threshold *min_conf* as 0.5, to produce mobility rules set which are greater than or equal to the confidence threshold, as shown in Table 3.

Table 1. An example of a user's trajectory data.

Tray_ID	Trajectory
1	$\{<0, t_9>, <0, t_{11}>, <2, t_{16}>\}$
2	$\{<0, t_9>, <0, t_{11}>, <3, t_{16}>, <5, t_{20}>\}$
3	$\{<4, t_9>, <0, t_{11}>, <3, t_{16}>, <1, t_{19}>, <5, t_{20}>\}$
4	$\{<4, t_9>, <0, t_{11}>, <3, t_{16}>, <1, t_{19}>\}$
5	$\{<0, t_9>, <0, t_{11}>, <3, t_{16}>, <5, t_{16}>\}$

Table 2. Frequent patterns (support≥0.25).

Pattern	Sup	Pattern	Sup
$\{<0, t_9>\}$	3	$\{<0, t_{11}>, <3, t_{16}>\}$	4
$\{<0, t_{11}>\}$	5	$\{<3, t_{16}>, <1, t_{19}>\}$	2
$\{<1, t_{19}>\}$	2	$\{<4, t_9>, <0, t_{11}>\}$	2
$\{<3, t_{16}>\}$	4	$\{<0, t_9>, <0, t_{11}>, <3, t_{16}>\}$	2
$\{<4, t_9>\}$	2	$\{<0, t_{11}>, <3, t_{16}>, <1, t_{19}>\}$	2

Table 3. The mobility rules for prediction (*confidence*≥0.5).

Rule	Conf	Rule	Conf
$\{<0, t_9>\} \rightarrow \{<0, t_{11}>\}$	100%	$\{<0, t_9>, <0, t_{11}>\} \rightarrow \{<3, t_{16}>\}$	67%
$\{<0, t_{11}>\} \rightarrow \{<3, t_{16}>\}$	80%	$\{<0, t_{11}>, <3, t_{16}>\} \rightarrow \{<1, t_{19}>\}$	50%
$\{<3, t_{16}>\} \rightarrow \{<1, t_{19}>\}$	50%	$\{<4, t_9>\} \rightarrow \{<0, t_{11}>, <3, t_{16}>\}$	100%
$\{<4, t_9>\} \rightarrow \{<0, t_{11}>\}$	100%	$\{<4, t_9>, <0, t_{11}>\} \rightarrow \{<3, t_{16}>\}$	100%

Assume that the user moves to the current base station 0 at time t_{11} along a path $P=\{<3, t_9>, <4, t_9>, <2, t_{10}>, <0, t_{11}>\}$, then some rules $\{<0, t_{11}>\} \rightarrow \{<3, t_{16}>\}$, $\{<0, t_9>, <0, t_{11}>\} \rightarrow \{<3, t_{16}>\}$, $\{<4, t_9>, <0, t_{11}>\} \rightarrow \{<3, t_{16}>\}$ can be mined as the matched rules. The arranged array list is $[(<3, t_{16}>, 100\%)]$. Therefore, the base station 3 can be the prediction location of the user with the possibility 100%.

Under the implementation of location prediction, we can have several next stop points with a certain extent of possibility. Combined with user's personal label, targeted advertising service can be pushed to the user. For example, for a user with label "*high expenditure*" and "*night life*", who frequently visits some regions at night, we can give this user LBA services about "KTV" or "pub" etc.

4   Case Study

In this section, we summarize some detailed results of our implementation of discovering a specific user's background information from his/her mobile phone log data. Visualization results are shown on Google Map. The dataset for our work is collected by the telecommunication service provider involving actual call logs of 14 mobile phone users for the duration of September, 2010 in the city of Kunming, China. Taking user ID 91861 as an example, we present how to handle user label generation and location prediction for this user as below.

4.1   ROI Extraction of User 91861

Using ST-DBSCAN clustering method as described in Section 3.1, all stops of the user 91861 during September, 2010 are clustered. Figure 1 shows spatial distribution of this user's mobile phone location data in blue points, and three ROIs (cluster 1, cluster 2 and cluster 3) in red. Although these stops spread over a very wide area, there are three important regions attached to the user to be observed.

Considering time stamp associated with each mobile phone log data in the three clusters, we can analyze the regions where the user works and where the user lives. Here, we assume that people usually works at daytime and goes home at night. Table 4 presents time distribution of the user 91861's location on weekdays, where n is the number of stops, p is the percentage. From Table 4, judged by time slices when calling events occur, it is observed that the user stays in cluster 3 at most of the time from 8:00pm to 8:00am; while in cluster 1 at most of the time from 8:00am till 8:00pm. It is not difficult to infer that the user lives in cluster 3 and works in cluster 1. And at most of the time, the user goes to work and goes back home very regularly.

Fig. 1. Overview of mobile phone location data and ROIs of user 91861.

Table 4. Time distribution of user 91861's location on weekdays.

Time Slices	Cluster 1		Cluster 2		Cluster 3	
	n	p	n	p	n	p
2am-5am	0	0%	0	0%	36	23%
5am-8am	0	0%	0	0%	33	21%
8am-11am	73	29%	0	0%	0	0%
11am-2pm	97	39%	1	4%	1	1%
2pm-5pm	51	20%	15	68%	2	1%

Further, we can determine the user's work location and home location as follows. We acquire the top 3 places in each ROI that the user visits most frequently, shown in Table 5. Based on spatio-temporal analysis of frequent patterns, base station 51333 is observed to nearly appear during the time period from morning to night, so it is inferred that the user's workplace is most likely located at the base station 51333. On the other hand, the base station 51336 mainly appears in the evening, and also at the night until the next early morning. This is the time when person goes home and goes for rest, so by that reckoning that the user's home is located at the base station 51336.

Table 5. Top 3 frequently visited base stations where the user 91861 stays in each cluster.

Region	Base Station/Geographical Coordinates	Number of Stops
cluster 1	51333(103.15107, 24.92659)	357
	52821(103.18345, 26.93875)	16
	52572(103.16392, 25.9389)	10
cluster 2	22722(103.10973, 24.88576)	15
	35072(103.1165, 24.0375)	12
	37072(103.1167, 24.8377)	9
cluster 3	51336(103.14122, 24.72657)	37
	49803(103.12825, 24.33176)	26
	49801(103.13824, 24.63175)	21

4.2   POI Extraction of User 91861

Using the approach as described in Section 3.2, base station POIs related to the user 91861's activity regions are available from the Koubei website. The user's consumption can be also analyzed through the housing price information from the Taobao housing website.

Table 6 lists the top three categories of POIs in the cluster 2 collected from the POI reviewing website. Table 7 gives the housing price collected from the real estate website, showing that housing price is high in this area, mainly including dinning, entertainment and the others. The cluster 2 can be judged to be a leisure place.

Table 6. Top 3 categories of POIs in cluster 2.

POI	Cluster 2	
	n	*p*
Restaurant	70	26%
Recreation	59	22%
Educational Service	28	10%

Table 7. Housing price in cluster 2.

Housing Price	Percentage
$<6000¥/m^2$	0%
$6000\sim8000¥/m^2$	31%
$8000\sim10000¥/m^2$	18%
$>10000¥/m^2$	51%

Similarly, combined with the clustering merchant information and real estate website, POI information and housing prices of the cluster 1 where the user works can be also obtained as follows. The level of consumption in this region is not high, mainly including entertainment, restaurants, beauty and other consumer merchants. The mean price of this region is $8000/m^2$.

4.3   Background Information Analysis of User 91861

Besides work and home location, some other background information, such as job occupation, income, consumption etc., can be also analyzed as follows. As shown in Figure 1, user 91861's workplace is located in the cluster 1. From the extracted POI information of the cluster 1, scope of the user's workplace is very wide, with mostly dinning merchants. In addition, number of callings during working time shows that the user works very long, and mobile phone is frequently used during working time, particularly during meal time, up to more than three hundred times in a month, therefore it is estimated that the user may be a restaurant takeaway staff.

Similarly, we estimate the housing price from the real estate website of the cluster 3 where the user lives. It can be observed that 75% of the housing price is between 6000-8000¥/m². This is the average price in the Kunming city, China. Associated with the income of the user is possibly middle.

Figure 2(a) shows the ROIs of the user 91861 on weekends. The user spends most of day time in the leisure region, and stays at home at night. Analyzing consumption both in entertainment area and during weekend, it can be found that the user's level of consumption is very popular, not too high or too low. We estimate that consumption of the user is in the middle level. In contrast, Figure 2(b) shows the ROIs of another

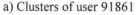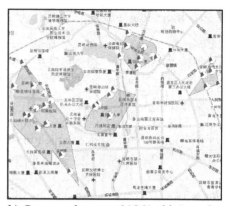

| a) Clusters of user 91861 | b) Compared to user 91861with "regular life", clusters of user 90865 with "night life" |

Fig. 2. Analysis of user's consumption level.

user who frequently visits four regions at night (6pm-11pm), extracted from the POI and web data, which are mostly restaurant, KTV, and pub etc.

4.4   User Label Definition of User 91861

Through the above analysis, the user may be an employee, the most probable a restaurant takeaway staff, with less time for rest, middle-income and mobile phone-related business. The place of work is located at the base station 51333, and the place of living at the base station 51336. User labels, shown in Figure 3, can be summarized as "*Workplace-51333; Home-51336; Job-Blue-collar; Income-middle; Consumption-middle; Lifestyle-regular*". Based on the generated user labels, some cheap tariff packages and sale information can be pushed to the user.

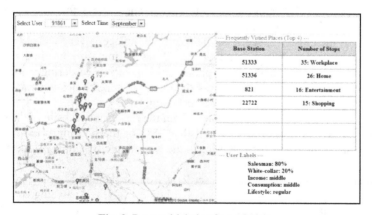

Fig. 3. Personal labels of user 91861.

4.5   Location Prediction of User 91861

Enter current time, base station ID and prediction time, the possible location and the possibility of the user 91861 are available using the approach to location prediction in Section 3.4. As shown in Figure 4, user's current location is presented in red bubble, prediction location in green bubble, and the possibility is 50%.

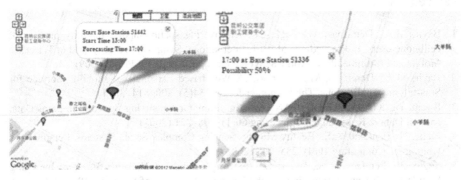

Fig. 4. Location prediction of user 91861.

5   Conclusion

In this paper, we propose approaches to mining personal background information from mobile phone log data and preliminarily implement some functions, including the aspects of ROI/POIs extraction, user label generation and location prediction. In particular, the contributions and novelties of this paper are listed as follows. 1) In most of the existing studies, personal characteristics are usually labeled manually. We propose an approach that can automatically generate user labels, identifying personally important places, not only home location and work location, but also other meaningful places (such as places for leisure etc.). Although these are coarse-level labels, they are valuable for high-end data mining and business services. 2) According to spatial and temporal correlation, we can predict location of a user that may arrive at the next moment. Combined with the generated user labels, a relative accurate LBA service can be pushed to the user. 3) We demonstrate our approaches by using actual mobile phone data. Visualization results are implemented to show functions of semantic label generation and location prediction. From these results over real data, we have shown that our approaches are capable of representing individual activities characteristics and discovering personal background information that can be used for wide applications.

As future work, we are going to work analyze correlations among different persons using mobile phone data for some new applications, such as social networking analysis and urban analysis etc.

Acknowledgement. This work is supported by National Nature Science Foundation of China under grant no. 41231171. The authors would like to thank Xiaoqing Zou at Kunming University of Science and Technology, Kunming, China for providing us with mobile phone data, and also thank Wei Feng and Jie Zhou at Wuhan University for their helpful algorithm development.

References

1. Bayir, M.A., Demirbas, M., Eagle, N.: Discovering spatiotemporal mobility profiles of cellphone users. In Proceedings of IEEE International Symposium on a World of Wireless, Mobile and Multimedia Networks & Workshops, pp. 1–9. IEEE Press (2009)
2. Bayir, M.A., Demirbas, M., Cosar, A.: A Web-based Personalized Mobility Service for Smartphone Applications. The Computer Journal **54**(5), 800–814 (2011)
3. Birant, D., Kut, A.: ST-DBSCAN: An Algorithm for Clustering Spatial-Temporal Data. Journal Data & Knowledge Engineering **60**(1), 208–221 (2007)
4. Eagle, N., Pentland, A.S.: Reality Mining: Sensing Complex Social Systems. Personal and Ubiquitous Computing **10**(4), 255–268 (2006)
5. Eagle, N., Pentland, A.S., Lazer, D.: Inferring Friendship Network Structure by Using Mobile Phone Data. Proceedings of the National Academy of Sciences (PNAS) **106**(36), 15274–15278 (2009)
6. González, M.C., Hidalgo, C.A., Barabási, A.L.: Understanding Individual Human Mobility Patterns. Nature **453**(5), 779–782 (2008)
7. Isaacman, S., Becker, R., Cáceres, R., Kobourov, S., Martonosi, M., Rowland, J., Varshavsky, A.: Identifying important places in people's lives from cellular network data. In: Lyons, K., Hightower, J., Huang, E.M. (eds.) Pervasive 2011. LNCS, vol. 6696, pp. 133–151. Springer, Heidelberg (2011)
8. Licoppe, C., Diminescu, D., Smoreda, Z., Ziemlicki, C.: Using Mobile Phone Geolocalisation for 'Socio-geographical' Analysis of Co-ordination, Urban Mobilities, and Social Integration Patterns. Journal of Economic & Social Geography (TESG) **99**(5), 584–601 (2008)
9. Phithakkitnukoon, S., Dantu, R.: Predicting calls – new service for an intelligent phone. In: Krishnaswamy, D., Pfeifer, T., Raz, D. (eds.) MMNS 2007. LNCS, vol. 4787, pp. 26–37. Springer, Heidelberg (2007)
10. Phithakkitnukoon, S., Dantu, R.: CPL: Enhancing mobile phone functionality by call predicted list. In: Meersman, R., Tari, Z., Herrero, P. (eds.) OTM-WS 2008. LNCS, vol. 5333, pp. 571–581. Springer, Heidelberg (2008)
11. Phithakkitnukoon, S., Dantu, R.: Mobile social closeness and similarity in calling patterns. In Proceedings of IEEE Conference on Consumer Communications & Networking Conference (CCNC 2010) Special Session on Social Networking (SocNets), pp. 1–5. IEEE Press (2010)
12. Phithakkitnukoon, S., Horanont, T., Di Lorenzo, G., Shibasaki, R., Ratti, C.: Activity-aware map: identifying human daily activity pattern using mobile phone data. In: Salah, A.A., Gevers, T., Sebe, N., Vinciarelli, A. (eds.) HBU 2010. LNCS, vol. 6219, pp. 14–25. Springer, Heidelberg (2010)

Unsupervised Race Walking Recognition Using Smartphone Accelerometers

Ye Wei[1], Li Liu[2][(✉)], Jun Zhong[1], Yonggang Lu[1][(✉)], and Letian Sun[1]

[1] School of Information Science and Engineering, Lanzhou University,
Lanzhou, Gansu, China
{weiy13,zhongj13,ylu,sunyt_13}@lzu.edu.cn
[2] School of Computing, National University of Singapore, Singapore, Singapore
liul@comp.nus.edu.sg

Abstract. In today's race walking competition, the determination of whether an athlete fouls is mainly affected by a referee's subjective judgment, leading to a high possibility of misjudgment. The purpose of this work is to determine whether race walking can be automatically recognized by accelerometers embedded in smartphones. In this work, acceleration data are collected by a smartphone app developed by ourselves. Nineteen features are extracted from the raw sensor data, and are used by an unsupervised classification method for activity recognition, named MCODE. We evaluate various data sampling rates and window lengths during feature extraction in the experiments. We also compare our method with other well-known methods on the metrics such as sensitivity, specificity and adjusted rank index. The results show that our method is viable to recognize race walking using smartphone accelerometers.

Keywords: Race walking · Activity recognition · Accelerometer · Smartphone

1 Introduction

Race walking began in 1932, and became a formal sport event of Olympic in 1992. The sport has two special technical requirements: an athlete should keep at least one foot contacting with ground, and the contacted leg (also called supporting leg) should not bend. In the competition, there must be someone witness the athlete. In current sport events, an athlete will be deprived of right for the event when he or she receives three or more fouls from different referees. The judgement is often subjective and may be fault.

Many researchers are trying to use the external equipment to detect whether an athlete fouls. Didik R. Santo *et al.* [1] used piezoelectric sensor to monitor the procedure of race walking. In their work the foul is only judged by the situation of whether both feet leaving the ground at the same time, but the supporting leg that is crooked or not is not concerned. Cui *et al.* [2] developed an intelligent wireless monitoring system for foul recognition. It uses pressure

© Springer International Publishing Switzerland 2015
S. Zhang et al. (Eds.): KSEM 2015, LNAI 9403, pp. 691–702, 2015.
DOI: 10.1007/978-3-319-25159-2_63

sensors installed among midsoles as the detector of vacating foul and strain transducer fixed in kneepads as the detector of knee-bent foul. However, wearing kneepads may affect the normal walking habits of an athlete. James B. Lee *et al.* [3] utilized the principle of statistics, inertial sensors and high speed camera to collect and analyze data. They demonstrated the feasibility of using inertial sensors in detecting the foul in race walking. They utilized an analytical system designed by Davey *et al.* [4] for human body movement recognition.

In recent year, devices embedded with accelerometers are widely used in activity recognition. Lester *et al.* [5] used multi-modal sensor board to collect and analyze the daily behavior data with a hidden Markov mixed model. Khan *et al.* [6] used an acceleration sensor placed in front of the chest to collect data of 15 movements, such as walking, running, *etc.* They achieved the average recognition rate of 97.5%. With the enormous development of mobile devices, smartphones are now equipped with high definition camera, accelerometer, gyroscope, *etc.* These sensors enable an alternative way to facilitate us in understanding our activities and improving the quality of our lives.

We intend to use accelerometers to recognize race walking. Particularly, we use smartphones to distinguish race walking from normal walking and running. We utilize Molecular Complex Detection method (MCODE for short) to recognize these sport activities using the features extracted from the raw acceleration data. MCODE is an unsupervised clustering method which is used for protein-protein interaction study originally. The MCODE method was successfully applied to recognize human daily living activities in our previous work [12]. The reason of using an unsupervised method rather than a supervised method such as SVM is that ground truth annotation is often an expensive task. It is tedious for an annotator to perform the annotation in real-time or scan through the raw sensor data to manually label all activities post-hoc [7]. To the best of our knowledge, it is the first time that the unsupervised classification method is used for race walking recognition.

The rest of paper is organized as follows. Section 2 discusses related work on activity recognition. Section 3 introduces the main methods used in this paper, including feature extraction and clustering method. Section 4 describes the results and discussion. Finally, Section 5 presents the conclusions.

2   Related Work

Many approaches have been proposed for human activity recognition, such as sensor-based and vision-based methods. Computer vision-based activity recognition has been at the forefront in this research field, where a large number of researchers investigated machine recognition of gestures and activities from still images and video in well-controlled environments or constrained settings [8]. Vision-based methods employ cameras to detect actions and gestures from video sequences. Although vision-based methods have contributed significantly to the research of human activity recognition, they require cameras that are fixed to predetermined points of interest; hence, these techniques provide very limited range, and are not very flexible in race walking recognition due to the requirement of deploying a large number of cameras.

Sensors can offer advanced human activity recognition capabilities to a variety of smartphone-based applications. The maturity of the miniaturized sensors and supporting technologies has pushed the research focuses of context-aware triggered activity recognition and inference for a number of real-world applications. Ravi *et al.* [10] designed a sensor-based classifier to distinguish eight movements and actions, namely, standing, walking, running, stairs up, stairs down, vacuuming, brushing, and situps. They compared seven supervised classification methods and their variants (Decision Tables, Decision Trees, kNN, SVM and Naïve Bayes) to classify these eight activities using the data collected from a single triaxial accelerometer. The average accuracy can achieve 95%. Kwapisz *et al.* [9] took six actions into consideration, which are walk, jog, up, down, sit and stand. Similarly, they use five supervised classification methods for comparison (Decision Trees, Regression, Neural Network and Straw-man) using phone-based accelerometers to recognize the six actions.

However, supervised methods require a large number of well-labelled dataset for training a classifier in order to improve the recognition accuracy. A huge challenge for sensor-based supervised human activity recognition task is the collection of annotated or labelled training data, especially for sport activity recognition where actions or movements are often instantaneous. In addition, motion data recorded from an accelerometer or gyroscope are often more difficult to interpret than data from cameras [8]. To this end, we employ an unsupervised method for recognizing race walking using smartphone sensors. Our method differs from these supervised methods as we provide a more general way of distinguishing race walking from normal walking and running without requiring a large number of training data. Our method is more practicable to detect the fouls for an athlete during race walking competition or for an amateur during race walking practice.

3   The Method

The whole process of our method consists of two parts. The first part is data collection at certain sampling rates using smartphones with a smartphone app developed by ourselves. The second part is feature extraction and classification. Fig. 1 shows the whole steps. After the data collection procedure we obtain the raw acceleration data. Nineteen features are extracted from the raw data within a predefined window. The Euclidean distance measurement between features are used to construct a complete undirected graph. Then the graph is processed by the MCODE clustering method to classify activities.

3.1   Data Collection

Four race walkers (two males and two females) with an average age of 25 volunteered for this study. One of them is a professional athlete, while the other

Fig. 1. The flow of our method.

three are amateurs. For each volunteer, we ask them to perform three activities including walking, race walking and running on a standard playground. Three amateurs (volunteer 1-3) performed each of the three activities for three times, while the professional athlete (volunteer 4) performed nine times for each. The data is recorded by a smartphone where one 3D accelerometer with three directions, i.e. x axis, y axis and z axis, is used by our app, as shown in Fig. 2(a). For each volunteer, each activity is continuously recorded in a 400 metre long athletic track for each time. Tab. 1 lists the time duration of each activity collected in our experiments.

Table 1. Data statistics of the three activities recorded in our experiments.

Activities	Duration(mins)					
	Volunteer 1	Volunteer 2	Volunteer 3	Volunteer 4	Average	Total
Walking	11.45	9.00	13.74	31.33	16.38	65.52
Race walking	7.34	5.38	10.26	41.91	16.22	64.89
Running	7.33	6.02	8.91	25.24	11.87	47.50
Total	26.12	20.40	32.91	98.48	44.47	177.91

The collection process can be started or stopped through a simple graphical user interface or an instructions sent from another smartphone. The smartphone is placed on the S1 vertebra of volunteers' sacrum, as shown in Fig. 2(b). The smartphone runs on Android OS 4.1.2. The acceleration data are collected at three different data sampling rates for each volunteer, i.e. 10Hz, 20Hz and 30Hz. Previous researches often use the fixed rate of 20Hz to collect data, such as Kwapisz et al. [13] and Weiss et al. [14]. In our previous work about daily living activity recognition, we also use the sensor data sampled at 20Hz. In this work we intend to study the effect of data sampling rates on recognition performance. Fig. 2(c) shows the acceleration data of a static smartphone as the baselines of the three axes. Fig. 3(a), Fig. 3(b) and Fig. 3(c) shows the examples of time series of acceleration data for the three activities sampled at 10Hz, 20Hz and 30Hz, respectively.

3.2   Feature Extraction

The raw data collected from the smartphone are first processed by a feature extraction method before using the MCODE method for recognition. The time series data are divided into several segments using a predefined window

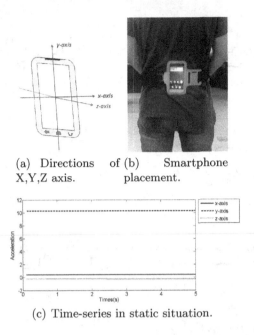

(a) Directions of X,Y,Z axis.   (b) Smartphone placement.

(c) Time-series in static situation.

Fig. 2. The directions and placement of smartphone.

length, where each segment represents an instance of an activity. We use 75%-overlapping sliding windows to produce instances. A total number of nineteen features, including means, standard deviations, variances, skewness, kurtosis, correlation and signal magnitude area, are extracted for each instance. Tab. 2 gives a description of these features.

Table 2. The features and descriptions.

Features	Descriptions
Mean	The average value of the acceleration data for each axis
Standard Deviation	Standard deviation
Variance	The square of the standard deviation
Skewness	The asymmetry of the probability distribution of each axis about its mean
Kurtosis	The "peakedness" of the probability distribution of each axis.
Correlation	Correlation between axis pair, XY, XZ, YZ
Signal magnitude area	The normalized integral of 3-axis

3.3 Recognizing Activities Using Clustering Method

After getting the features, we use the Molecular Complex Detection (MCODE) for recognition. The MCODE is an efficient clustering algorithm based on density.

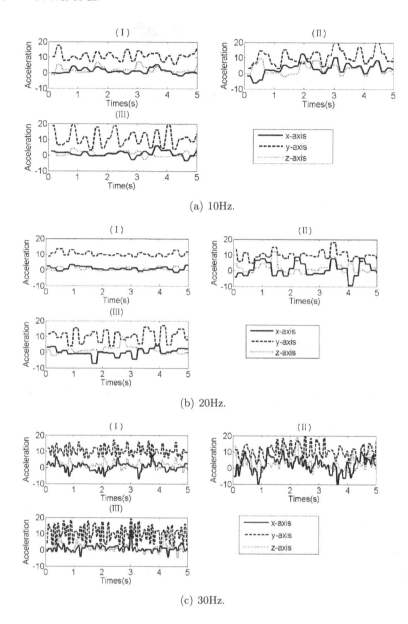

(a) 10Hz.

(b) 20Hz.

(c) 30Hz.

Fig. 3. The accelerometer time series of the three activities with different sampling rates. (I) walking, (II) race walking, and (III) running.

It is first applied to large protein-protein networks [15]. The input to MCODE is an undirected graph, denoted by G. The output are clusters. In activity recognition, each instance is regarded as a vertex in the graph. Every pair of nodes has an edge, leading to a complete graph. The set of all vertices and all edges in G are denoted as V and E, respectively. The weight on a link refers to the Euclidean distance between the two corresponding nodes of the link on the feature space.

MCODE is mainly divided into two steps. The first step is vertex weighting, and the second step is clustering. The density of G is defined as the number of E divided by the number of edges of a complete graph composed of V. For example, if a graph is a complete graph, its density is 1. K-core is defined as the minimal degree in a graph [16]. The precessing of vertex weighting iterates through all the vertices in G. For any vertex $v \in V$, within the subgraph N_v that are composed of v and its neighbors, the highest k-core subgraph called M is found. The weight of v is the product of M's k-core and M's density. In the second step, the vertex with the highest weight is set as seed vertex. We iterate all the neighbors of the seed vertex. If the weight of one of the neighbor vertices is larger than the product of the weight of the seed vertex and a parameter θ, the neighbor vertex and the seed vertex will be classified into the same class. Then the neighbor vertex will be set as the new seed. This procedure continues until all of the vertices in G are visited. The MCODE method is described by the following two pseudocodes: Algorithm 1 and Algorithm 2.

Algorithm 1.. MCODE

Require:
    $G = (V, E)$ - graph
    θ - the threshold
1: **for** all v in G **do**
2:    N_v = the graph composed by v and its neighbors;
3:    M = the subgraph of N_v which has highest K-core;
4:    k = k-core of M;
5:    $density$ = density of M;
6:    $\omega_v = k \times density$;
7: **end for**
8: **for** all v in G **do**
9:    **if** v is not null **then**
10:      v_{seed} = the vertex which has the largest weight in the graph G;
11:      **Call:** M_cluster(G,v_{seed},θ);
12:    **end if**
13: **end for**

---

4   Results and Discussion

We use Adjusted Rand Index (ARI) [17], Sensitivity and Specificity to evaluate our proposed method. The ARI is used to access the global congruence of two

---

Algorithm 2.. MCODE–M_cluster

Require:
    $G = (V, E)$ - graph
    v_{seed} - seed vertex
    θ - the threshold
1: **if** v_{seed} is already visited **then**
2:    return;
3: **end if**
4: **for all** $v_a \in N_{v_{seed}} - \{v_{seed}\}$ **do**
5:    **if** $\omega_{v_a} > \omega_{v_{seed}} \times (1 - \theta)$ **then**
6:       Add v_a to the cluster containing v_{seed};
7:       **Call:** M_cluster(G, v_a, θ);
8:    **end if**
9: **end for**

---

typing methods. It gives the overall concordance of two methods taking into account that the agreement between partitions could arise by chance alone.

$$ARI = \frac{a + d - n_c}{a + b + c + d - n_c}$$

where

$$n_c = \frac{n(n^2 + 1) - (n + 1)\sum n_{i\cdot}^2 - (n + 1)\sum n_{\cdot j}^2 + \sum\sum \frac{n_{ij}^2}{n}}{2(n - 1)}$$

$$\begin{cases} a = \frac{1}{2}\sum_{i=1}^{|X|}\sum_{j=1}^{|Y|} n_{ij}(n_{ij} - 1) \\[2mm] b = \frac{1}{2}\left[n^2 + \sum_{i=1}^{|X|}\sum_{j=1}^{|Y|} n_{ij}^2 - \left(\sum_{i=1}^{|X|} n_{i\cdot}^2 + \sum_{j=1}^{|Y|} n_{\cdot j}^2\right)\right] \\[2mm] c = \frac{1}{2}\left(\sum_{j=1}^{|Y|} n_{\cdot j}^2 - \sum_{i=1}^{|X|}\sum_{j=1}^{|Y|} n_{ij}^2\right) \\[2mm] d = \frac{1}{2}\left(\sum_{i=1}^{|X|} n_{i\cdot}^2 - \sum_{i=1}^{|X|}\sum_{j=1}^{|Y|} n_{ij}^2\right) \end{cases}$$

where

$$a + b + c + d = \binom{n}{2} = \frac{n(n - 1)}{2}$$

where n is the total number of vertices in the graph and $n_{i\cdot}$ is the number of vertices belonging to the cluster i of race walking, and $n_{\cdot j}$ is the number of vertices belonging to the cluster j of normal walking or running. The maximum value of the ARI is 1, which means that the two clustering results are exactly the same. When the two partitions are picked at random which corresponds to the null model, the ARI is 0. A larger value of ARI means a better result. Sensitivity and Specificity are statistical measures of the performance of a binary classification test. In our experiment, since we mainly intend to distinguish race walking form normal walking and running, we assume race walking as one class and normal walking and running as the other one. Sensitivity, also called the true positive rate, measures the proportion of positives which are correctly identified as such, i.e. Sensitivity$= \frac{TP}{TP+FN}$, where TP is the number of the instances of race walking that are successfully clustered, and FN is the number of the instances of race walking that are falsely clustered as normal walking and running. Specificity, also called the true negative rate, measures the proportion of negatives which are correctly identified as such, i.e. Specificity$= \frac{TN}{TN+PF}$, where TN is the number of the instances of normal walking and running that are successfully clustered, and PF is the number of the instances of normal walking and running that are falsely clustered as race walking.

We first conduct an experiment to evaluate the method's performance using various sampling rates and window sizes. Fig. 4(a) shows the results of the evaluation using ARI. It is found that the method with the sampling rate of 30Hz outperforms that with other sampling rates overall. Window size may also affect the recognition results with different sampling rates. Particularly, the method with sampling rate of 10Hz performs the best when the window size is 120, while it performs the best with the sampling rate of 20Hz when the window size is 180. When the sampling rate is 30Hz, our experiment shows that the method get likely performance under the settings of various window sizes. Similarly, Fig. 4(b) shows the results of the evaluation on Sensitivity. Similar to the results on ARI, it is found that the method with the sampling rate of 30Hz outperforms the others. We get the same conclusion on Sensitivity as that on ARI under different settings of sampling rate and window sizes. Fig. 4(c) shows evaluation results on Specificity. It seems that the method with the sampling rates of 10Hz and 30Hz performs better than that of 20Hz. In summary, the experimental results are best overall when the data are collected at the sampling rate of 30Hz with the window size of 180. The average ARI is 0.9513 when the window size of the feature extraction is 180. The average sensitivity and specificity for the four volunteers are 96.04% and 97.43%, respectively, as the acceleration data is sampled 30Hz and the window size for the feature extraction is 180.

The second experiment we conduct is to compare our method with other clustering method on activity recognition. All of the features are extracted at the sampling rate of 30Hz with the window length of 180. We compare our MCODE method with K-MEANS clustering method. The recognition results are evaluated on ARI, Sensitivity and Specificity. Fig. 5 shows the comparison results of the two clustering methods. It can be seen from the Fig. 5(a) that the MCODE clustering method outperforms K-MEANS on ARI for all of the four volunteers. The results produced by the MCODE and K-MEANS are very close on Sensitivity, as shown in Fig. 5(b). From the Fig. 5(c), the MCODE performs better than the K-MEANS. In summary, the MCODE performs much better than the K-MEANS for activity recognition on average.

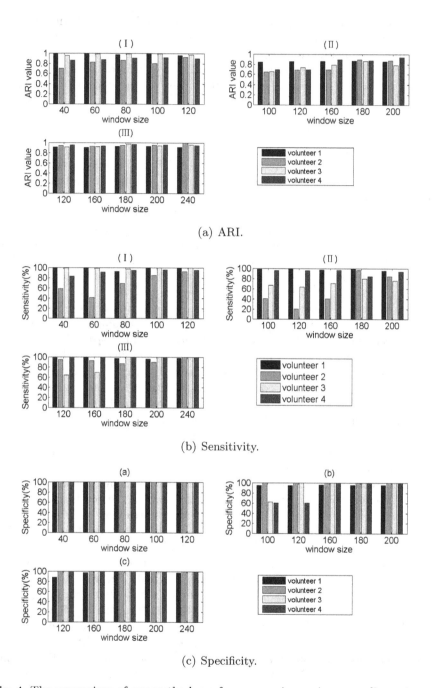

(a) ARI.

(b) Sensitivity.

(c) Specificity.

Fig. 4. The comparison of our methods performance using various sampling rates and window sizes. (I) 10Hz; (II) 20Hz; (III) 30Hz.

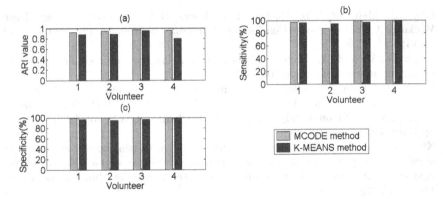

Fig. 5. The comparison results between the MCODE and the K-MEANS. (a) ARI, (b) Sensitivity, and (c) Specificity.

5 Conclusion

In this paper we propose an unsupervised method for race walking recognition using smartphone accelerometers. The experimental results show that our method is practicable to distinguish race walking from normal walking and running using smartphone accelerometers. Particularly, our MCODE method is more efficient than the K-MEANS method. We also investigate the effect of sampling rates and sliding windows for feature extraction on the final recognition results. Generally, the higher the sampling rates, the more accuracy on the race walking recognition. In our future work, we will collect more data about race walking from professional athletes and conduct more experiments for comparisons. In addition, we will also develop a smartphone app that can notify fouls for amateurs to help them correct their false race walking stances during training.

Acknowledgments. This work is supported by the National Science Foundation of China (Grants No. 61272213),Cuiying Grant of China Telecom, Gansu Branch(grant no. lzudxcy-2013-3), Science and Technology Planning Project of Chengguan District, Lanzhou grant no. 2013-3-1), and Scientific Research Foundation for the Returned Overseas Chinese Scholars, State Education Ministry (grant no. 44th). The authors want to thank the volunteers for their time and effort to help us collecting data.

References

1. Santoso, D.R., Setyanto, T.A.: Development of Precession Instrumentation System for Differentiate Walking from Running in Race Walking by Using Piezoelectric Sensor (2013)
2. Yan-Song, C.: Intelligent wireless monitoring system for foul play in a walking race based on UWB (2011)

3. Lee, J.B., Mellifont, R.B., Burkett, B.J., James, D.A.: Detection of Illegal Race Walking: A Tool to Assist Coaching and Judging. Sensors **13**(12), 16065–16074 (2013)
4. Davey, N., Wixted, A., Ohgi, Y., James, D.A.: A low cost self contained platform for human motion analysis (2008)
5. Lester, Jonathan, Choudhury, Tanzeem, Borriello, Gaetano: A practical approach to recognizing physical activities. In: Fishkin, Kenneth P., Schiele, Bernt, Quigley, Aaron, Nixon, Paddy (eds.) PERVASIVE 2006. LNCS, vol. 3968, pp. 1–16. Springer, Heidelberg (2006)
6. Khan, A.M., Lee, Y.-K., Lee, S.Y., Kim, T.-S.: A triaxial accelerometer-based physical-activity recognition via augmented-signal features and a hierarchical recognizer. IEEE Transactions on Information Technology in Biomedicine **14**(5), 1166–1172 (2010)
7. Bulling, A., Ward, J.A., Gellersen, H.: Multimodal recognition of reading activity in transit using body-worn sensors. ACM Transactions on Applied Perception (TAP) **9**(1), 2 (2012)
8. Bulling, A., Blanke, U., Schiele, B.: A tutorial on human activity recognition using body-worn inertial sensors. ACM Computing Surveys (CSUR) **46**(3), 33 (2014)
9. Kwapisz, J.R., Weiss, G.M., Moore, S.A.: Activity recognition using cell phone accelerometers. ACM SIGKDD Explorations Newsletter **12**(2), 74–82 (2011)
10. Ravi, N., Dandekar, N., Mysore, P., Littman, M.L.: Activity recognition from accelerometer data. In: Proceedings of the Conference on Innovative Applications of Artificial Intelligence 2005, pp. 1541–1546
11. Kwapisz, Jennifer R., Weiss, Gary M., Moore, Samuel A.: Activity recognition using cell phone accelerometers. ACM SigKDD Explorations Newsletter **12**(2), 74–82 (2011)
12. Zhong, J., Liu, L., Wei, Y., Luo, D., Sun, L., Lu, Y.: Personalized activity recognition using molecular complex detection clustering. In: 11th IEEE International Conference on Ubiquitous Intelligence and Computing (UIC 2014), 2014 IEEE UIC/ATC/ScalCom Multi-Conference (2014)
13. Kwapisz, J.R., Weiss, G.M., Moore, S.A.: Activity recognition using cell phone accelerometers. In: Proceedings of the Fourth International Workshop on Knowledge Discovery from Sensor Data, vol. 12, pp. 10–18 (2010)
14. Weiss, G.M., Lockhart, J.W.: The impact of personalization on smartphone-based activity recognition. In: Workshops at the Twenty-Sixth AAAI Conference on Artificial Intelligence (2012)
15. Bader, G.D., Hogue, C.W.V.: An automated method for finding molecular complexes in large protein interaction networks. BMC Bioinformatics **4**(1), 2 (2003)
16. Casale, P., Pujol, O., Radeva, P.: Personalization and user verification in wearable systems using biometric walking patterns. Personal & Ubiquitous Computing **16**(5), 563–580 (2012)
17. Hubert, Lawrence: and P. Comparing partitions. Journal of Classification **2**(1), 193–218 (1985)

Subspace Clustering on Mobile Data for Discovering Circle of Friends

Tao Wu[1,2], Yujie Fan[1,2], Zhiling Hong[3(✉)], and Lifei Chen[1,2]

[1] School of Mathematics and Computer Science, Fujian Normal University,
Fuzhou 350007, China
[2] Fujian Provincial Key Laboratory of Network Security and Cryptology,
Fujian Normal University, Fuzhou 350007, China
[3] Software School, Xiamen University, Xiamen 361005, China
hongzl@xmu.edu.cn

Abstract. The discovery of circle of friends has risen rapidly in recent years. Traditional methods are mainly based on social network analysis which relies heavily on self-report data, such that these methods have isolated successes with limited accuracy, breadth, and depth. In this paper, we propose a new method which combines clustering technique to automatically discover the circle of friends on mobile data. In our method, the circle of friends is modeled as non-overlapping subspace clusters on mobile data with a Vector Space Model (VSM) based representation, for which a new subspace clustering algorithm is proposed to mine the underlying friend-relationship. The experimental studies on real mobile data demonstrate the effectiveness of the new method, and the results show that our clustering algorithm achieves better performance than the existing clustering algorithms.

Keywords: Circle of friends · Mobile data · Non-overlapping subspaces · Subspace clustering

1 Introduction

Mining circle of friends has become a popular subject in recent years because of its multipurpose use. For individuals, the circle of friends helps them in finding friends of similar interests and sharing interests with each other. For e-shop, such as Amazon and Netflix, they exploit the friend relationship to find out what the users are interested in, in order to construct personalized recommender systems. Due to the benefit for different types of users, the automatic approaches in mining circle of friends are much needed.

Early work of mining circle of friends mainly based on social network analysis (SNA) [1–3], which is the study of mathematical models for relationships among entities such as people, organizations and groups in a social network [4]. From a statistical perspective, generally, a social network is modeled by a graph, in which the nodes and edge between pairs of nodes represent the entities and a direct relationship between two entities, respectively. Therefore, the problem

© Springer International Publishing Switzerland 2015
S. Zhang et al. (Eds.): KSEM 2015, LNAI 9403, pp. 703–711, 2015.
DOI: 10.1007/978-3-319-25159-2_64

of discovering circle of friends in SNA can be transformed into the problem of analyzing the structure in the graph. For instance, Kuan et al. [5] proposed a pre-processing algorithm based on n-clique extension for social networks to discover friend groups, while Java et al. [6] aimed at finding users' relationship based on the topological and geographical properties of Twitters social network.

Existing methods (including those discussed above) focus mainly on SNA, which relies heavily on self-report data involving both limited numbers of people and a limited number of time points, such that these methods have been constrained in accuracy, breadth, and depth [7]. Few attempts have been made to mine friend relationship on mobile data. As discussed in [7], data collected from mobile phones have the potential to provide insight into the underlying relational organizations, which can be regarded as the circle of friends. However, the method proposed in [7] aims at calculating the probability of being friend or nonfriend of two users; thus it cannot automatically identify the circle of friends on mobile data.

In this paper, a new method is proposed to automatically discover the circle of friends for Bluetooth data collected by mobile phone. The method is divided into two phases. In the first phase, Bluetooth data are represented in a Vector Space Model (VSM). Based on this representation, in the second phase, a new k-medoids type clustering method, named SC-CF (for Subspace Clustering of Circle of Friends), is proposed to mine the circle of friends, modeled as a set of projected clusters on the data. To the best of our knowledge, this is the first work of applying subspace clustering technique for discovering circle of friends on mobile data. The experimental results on real data demonstrate the effectiveness of our method.

The contributions of this paper can be summarized as follows: (1) We model the circle of friends on mobile data as a set of non-overlapping subspace clusters such that the problem of mining circle of friends can be easily transformed into a new problem of non-overlapping subspace clustering; (2) A new subspace clustering algorithm for mining circle of friends is proposed to solve the problem effectively.

The rest of the paper is organized as follows. In section 2, we describe the subspace clusters model and present our new method to discover the circle of friends on mobile data. Experimental results are presented in Section 3. Finally, conclusions are summarized in Section 4.

2   Subspace Clustering for Discovering Circle of Friends

2.1   Non-overlapping Subspace Clusters Model

In an era of information explosion, how to effectively dig out users' relationship from mobile data is of great importance. The mobile data often contains structured information on social network besides plain text, and the relationships on social network play a supporting role in miming circle of friends. On the other hand, the mobile data is plagued with issues such as bias, data sparsity, which would increase the difficulty of miming circle of friends.

The relationship between two individuals can be symmetric friend, asymmetric friend, or non-friend. Usually, the probability of proximity is much higher for friends than non-friends, and friends spend more time together in the same places at the same time [7]. This indicates that the circle of friends can be identified according to the location, time, and proximity. In addition, mobile electronic devices, e.g. smart phones, portable tablets, and wearable devices, can basically provide reliable data such as Bluetooth data, which satisfy the requirements above. We obtain the Bluetooth data from the Reality Mining dataset [7], and present its distribution in Fig. 1.

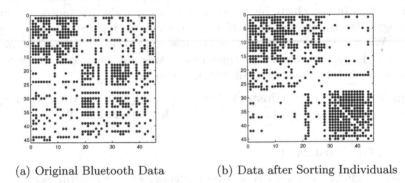

(a) Original Bluetooth Data   (b) Data after Sorting Individuals

Fig. 1. Non-overlapping Subspace Clusters of Bluetooth Data

As shown in Fig. 1, the Bluetooth data of each individual is represented by a row, and each column represents the Bluetooth address of individual. If a user's Bluetooth address is discovered by a periodic Bluetooth scan performed by another user, the corresponding position of user would be marked in a blue dot. The original Bluetooth data in Fig. 1 (a) shows the data distribution is sparsity and irregular, such that the circle of friends is not basically identified. However, after rearranging rows and columns of the data based on the real circle of friends, an interesting thing is that we can clearly identify two circles of friends corresponding to the dense region in Fig. 1 (b), and each circle of friends is closely related to some properties of column, respectively. We also see that the different circle of friends is associated with the different properties of column. From the subspace clustering perspective, the two block diagonals in Fig. 1(b) correspond to the two clusters. The clusters, which often exist only in specific subspaces of the original feature space, are generally called subspace clusters. Hence, the circle of friends can be modeled by non-overlapping subspace clusters. By exploiting the method of subspace clustering, we would be able to discover the circle of friends on mobile data.

Before giving a formal description of subspace clusters, we first introduce a few notations used throughout the paper. Let $DS = \{x_1, x_2, ..., x_N\}$ be a high-dimensional mobile data set of N data points, where $x_i \in R^D$ for $i = 1, 2, 3, ..., N$

is the ith data point represented by a D-dimensional vector. It is assumed that DS contains K clusters $C = \{c_1, c_2, ..., c_K\}$, and $v_k = <v_{k1}, v_{k2}, ..., v_{kD}>$ is the kth cluster c_k of cluster medoid vector, where $k = 1, 2, 3..., K$. The membership degree of x_i belonging to the kth cluster c_k is denoted as u_{ki}, satisfying

$$u_{ki} = \begin{cases} 1 & x_i \in c_k \quad k = 1, 2, 3 \dots, K; i = 1, 2, 3 \dots, N \\ 0 & otherwise \end{cases}$$

The cluster c_k is assigned an own weight vector $w_k = <w_{k1}, w_{k2}, ..., w_{kD}>$, and each weight w_{kj} indicates that what extent the jth dimension is relevant to the cluster c_k. The weight w_{kj} takes the value in $\{0,1\}$, where $j = 1, 2, 3, ..., D$ and $k = 1, 2, 3, ..., K$. Usually, different dimensions of clusters are assigned different weight values in the clustering process. The greater the relevance, the larger the weight. Hence, the subspace of a cluster can be represented by a weight vector. We can identify the subspace of the clusters from the weight matrix $W = \{w_{kj}\}_{K \times D}$ after subspace clustering. Using the notations we introduce above, we now define what we call subspace cluster.

Definition (Subspace Cluster). Let $SC_k = (u_k, w_k)$ be the kth subspace cluster of DS, where $u_k = \{u_{ki} | k = 1, 2, 3, ..., K; i = 1, 2, 3, ..., N\}$.

2.2   SC-CF Clustering

In order to cluster DS into K circle of friends, we need to project the data points into non-overlapping subspace. In other words, the weight vector for each cluster could be computed in the clustering process. The computational method is defined by the following expression [9].

$$w_{kj} = \begin{cases} 1 & z_{kj} \in T \quad k = 1, 2, 3, \dots, K; j = 1, 2, \dots, D \\ 0 & otheriwize \end{cases} \tag{1}$$

subject to

$$\begin{cases} D \geq 2 \\ Y_k = \frac{\sum_{j=1}^{D} X_{kj}}{D} \\ \sigma_k = \sqrt{\frac{\sum_{j=1}^{D} (X_{kj} - Y_k)^2}{D-1}} \\ z_{kj} = (X_{kj} - Y_k)/\sigma_k \\ Z = \{z_{kj}\}_{K \times D} \\ T \subset Z \end{cases}$$

Here, X_{kj} is defined to measure the average distance from the data points in *locality* L_i to the medoid v_k along with the jth dimension. According to Fig. 1, the number of relevant features in subspace is set to $2m/3$, where m is the number of original features on the mobile data set. T contains the $K \times (2m/3)$ numbers with the least values of Z. From Eq.(1), one can infer that a set of dimensions for each medoid are chosen whose average distances to the medoid is small compared to statistical expectation. Further details of this calculation are given in [10].

To find non-overlapping subspace clusters on mobile data, we propose a new non-overlapping subspace clustering algorithm, named SC-CF. Similar to k-medoids, SC-CF algorithm randomly selects the initialize medoids, and then iteratively improves the quality of clustering results. The procedure of SC-CF is described as follows.

Algorithm 1. SC-CF

Input:
   DS, K;
Output:
   $C = \{c_1, c_2, ..., c_K\}$, cluster medoid matrix $V = \{v_1, v_2, ..., v_K\}$
   and the associated weights W;
Initialization:
   Randomly Select K data points of DS as the medoids, denote V as $V^{(0)}$;
   Let p be the number of iterations, $p = 0$;
Repeat
1:   Compute the weight matrix $W^{(p)}$ by Eq.(1);
2:   For each medoid v_k and for each point x_i:
     Set $c_k = \{x_i | k = \arg\min_{l=1,2,3,...,K} dist(v_l, x_i)\}$,
     where $dist(v_l, x_i) = \sqrt{\sum_{j=1}^{D} w_{lj}(x_{ij} - v_{lj})^2}$;
3:   Update medoid matrix $V^{(p)}$ by following method:
     Set $v_k = \{x_i | i = \arg\min_{x_i \in c_k} T\cos t(x_i)\}$,
     where $T\cos t(x_i) = \sqrt{\sum_{l=1}^{N} \sum_{x_l \in c_k} \sum_{j=1}^{D} (x_{ij} - x_{lj})^2}$;
4:   $p = p + 1$;
   Until Convergence is achieved;

In SC-CF, the convergence condition is that all elements in cluster medoid matrix are not changed, or the number of iterations increases past 10. The SC-CF algorithm is an extension to the k-medoids clustering algorithm by adding one additional step to calculate the weights of each cluster in the iterative process. After the subspaces are identified, the very weighted Euclidean distance, which is commonly used in the existing algorithms [10–12], is used to assign data points to medoids, forming clusters.

3 Experimental Results

To show the performance of the proposed method, a set of experiments were conducted using the real mobile data. All experiments were conducted on a PC with Intel Core CPU of 3.2 GHz and 4 GB RAM.

3.1 Experiment Setup

In order to evaluate the performance of the proposed algorithm, five algorithms were chosen in our experiments, namely, PAM [13], PROCLUS [10], EWKM

[11], FSC [12], and MPC [13]. The reason why we chose PAM algorithm is that PAM is a classical k-medoids clustering algorithm, and can evaluate the performance of subspace clustering technique when comparing with SC-CF algorithm. PROCLUS is the benchmark projective clustering algorithm in the literature, and has similar feature weighting method with SC-CF. EWKM, FSC, and MPC are known as overlapping subspace clustering algorithms in the literature, and have similar algorithm structures to SC-CF. In addition, different parameters are used in these algorithms. In our experiments, we have used the most common setting, or author-recommended values, for these parameters. For example, we set $\alpha = 2.1$ for FSC, $\gamma = 0.5$ for EWKM. For fair comparison, the average dimensional number for PROCLUS was set to the same value as used in the SC-CF algorithm.

Since the external class labels are available for the experimental data set, we adopted three performance metric in this paper, namely, the normalized mutual information (NMI) [14], F-Score [15] and ARI [16]. Both NMI and F-Score take a value within the [0,1] interval. The higher value that an algorithm generates, the better the clustering quality is. The metric values above are equal to 1, when the clustering result and the original class label completely match [17].

3.2   Real Mobile Data

The performance of the proposed SC-CF algorithm was evaluated and compared with five existing clustering algorithms using the Bluetooth data. The Bluetooth data was obtained from the Reality Mining dataset provided by the MIT Media Laboratory. The Reality Mining dataset is a multi-view social network dataset, recording the user data about call logs, Bluetooth devices in proximity of approximately five meters, phone status, and so on. The dataset has been popularly used in related work, such as Eagle et al. [18] and Papalexakis [19].

The Bluetooth data can be divided into two circles of friends, one contains 27 device_macses, and the other contains 18 device_macses. Here, each individual is represented by a unique Bluetooth device MAC, and contains an own device_macs. The device_macs, which includes a list of Bluetooth scans over an extended period, cannot be applied for subspace clustering directly. This is because the device_macs data are unstructured. According to our analysis about the value of the device_macs, the device_macs data are represented in VSM, where device_macs of each individual is a vector in social network and each element of the vector indicates the frequency of the corresponding individual Bluetooth device in the device_macs. For the mobile data, we removed first incomplete and invalid user device_macs according to the real circle of friends provided by MIT, and used the preprocessing method described in [13] to compute the VSM. Then, the 45 Bluetooth devices were selected for the final data set. Due to that the mobile data remains quite challenging in terms of bias, data sparsity and noise [20], it is difficult to mine circle of friends on mobile data

3.3   Results and Analysis

Experiments were conducted with the real mobile data by running each algorithm 50 times with 50 randomly generated cluster centers at each setting so as to compute the mean and standard deviation of the NMI, F-Score and ARI values. Table 1 displays the average results of the SC-CF, PAM, PROCLUS, EWKM, FSC, and MPC. The average results are reported in the format $average \pm standard\ deviation$ in the table. The best clustering results are marked in bold typeface.

Table 1. Comparison of Clustering Results on the Mobile Data Set

Algorithm	NMI	F-Score	ARI
PROCLUS	0.5217 ± 0.0717	0.8437 ± 0.0147	0.5188 ± 0.0885
EWKM	0.4275 ± 0.0617	0.8102 ± 0.0197	0.4240 ± 0.1343
PAM	0.2509 ± 0.0633	0.7467 ± 0.0080	0.2268 ± 0.0654
FSC	0.4107 ± 0.0518	0.7933 ± 0.0121	0.3683 ± 0.0605
MPC	0.4338 ± 0.0370	0.8053 ± 0.0142	0.4032 ± 0.0788
SC-CF	$\mathbf{0.7063 \pm 0.0000}$	$\mathbf{0.9339 \pm 0.0000}$	$\mathbf{0.7455 \pm 0.0000}$

Table 1 illustrates that most algorithms are able to discover the circle of friends on the real mobile data. It is evident from Table 1 that among the six algorithms, SC-CF achieves outstanding performance in the clustering of the Bluetooth data. The performance of PROCLUS and EWKM is comparable or better than that of PAM, MPC and FSC. However, from the *standard deviation*, we also notice that these algorithms are sensitive to the initialization. By comparing PAM and the other algorithms, it is further noticed that PAM algorithm shows worst clustering performance. This indicates that subspace clustering technique is useful to discover circle of friends on the mobile data. These results suggest the SC-CF algorithm proposed in this paper is valid and promising.

Table 2. Average Runtime (in seconds) of Six Algorithms Performed on the Mobile Data Set

Algorithm	Runtime
PROCLUS	0.0050 ± 0.0004
EWKM	0.0022 ± 0.0000
PAM	0.0069 ± 0.0004
FSC	0.0041 ± 0.0000
MPC	$\mathbf{0.5286 \pm 0.0280}$
SC-CF	0.0346 ± 0.0006

The average runtime of the six algorithms performed on the real mobile data is measured and reported in Table 2. We can see that the execution time of the MPC algorithm was much longer than that of the other five clustering algorithms. Since the Newton-Raphson and bisection method, which is an iterative algorithm, is used for the MPC algorithm, it increases the running time of MPC in practice. We also observe that the SC-CF algorithm had higher runtime than that of PROCLUS, EWKM, PAM and FSC. This is due to the fact that the SC-CF algorithm is based on the k-medoids framework, and that it needs more time for computing the subspace and updating the medoids in each iteration.

4 Conclusion

In this paper, we proposed a new method which combines subspace clustering technique to mine circle of friends on mobile data. According to analyze the real distribution of mobile data, we modeled the circle of friends as a set of non-overlapping subspace clusters. Based on which, a new subspace clustering algorithm that discovers clusters with non-overlapping was proposed in this paper. The proposed algorithm can be seen as an extension to the k-medoids clustering algorithm by adding one additional step to calculate the weights of each cluster in the iterative process. The experimental results on the real-world mobile data show that the effectiveness of our proposed method. In our future work, we plan to extend our method from the following avenues: (1) Construct a system to identify circle of friends on mobile data using the proposed method; (2) Collect more mobile data and use it for better friend relationship mining.

Acknowledgments. This work was supported by the National Natural Science Foundation of China (No. 61175123), the Natural Science Foundation of China (No. 31200769) and the Fujian Normal University Innovative Research Team (IRTL1207).

References

1. Schwartz, M.F., Wood, D.: Discovering shared interests using graph analysis. Communications of the ACM **36**, 78–89 (1993)
2. Nakajima, S., Tatemura, J., Hino, Y., et al.: Discovering important bloggers based on analyzing blog threads. Annual Workshop on the Weblogging Ecosystem. Springer, Heidelberg (2005)
3. Domingos, P., Richardson, M.: Mining the network value of customers. In: Proceedings of the Seventh International Conference on Knowledge Discovery and Data Mining, pp. 57–66. ACM Press, New York (2001)
4. Shen, D., Sun, J.T., Yang, Q., et al.: Latent friend mining from blog data. In: International Conference on Data Mining, pp. 552–561. IEEE Press, Piscataway (2006)
5. Kuan, S.T., Wu, B.Y., Lee, W.J.: Finding friend groups in blogosphere. In: 22nd International Conference on Advanced Information Networking and Applications-Workshops, pp. 1046–1050. IEEE Press, Piscataway (2008)
6. Java, A., Song, X., Finin, T., et al.: Why we twitter: understanding microblogging usage and communities. In: Proceedings of the 9th WebKDD and 1st SNA-KDD Workshop on Web Mining and Social Network Analysis, pp. 56–65. ACM Press, New York (2007)

7. Eagle, N., Pentland, A.S., Lazer, D.: Inferring friendship network structure by using mobile phone data. Proceedings of the National Academy of Sciences. **106**, 15274–15278 (2009)
8. Park, H.S., Jun, C.H.: A simple and fast algorithm for K-medoids clustering. Expert Systems with Applications **36**, 3336–3341 (2009)
9. Aggarwal, C.C., Wolf, J.L., Yu, P.S., et al.: Fast algorithms for projected clustering. In: ACM SIGMOD Record, pp. 61–72. ACM Press, New York (1999)
10. Jing, L., Ng, M.K., Huang, J.Z.: An entropy weighting k-means algorithm for subspace clustering of high-dimensional sparse data. IEEE Transactions on Knowledge and Data Engineering. **19**, 1026–1041 (2007)
11. Gan, G., Wu, J., Yang, Z.-J.: A Fuzzy Subspace Algorithm for Clustering High Dimensional Data. In: Li, X., Zaïane, O.R., Li, Z. (eds.) ADMA 2006. LNCS (LNAI), vol. 4093, pp. 271–278. Springer, Heidelberg (2006)
12. Chen, L., Jiang, Q., Wang, S.: Model-based method for projective clustering. IEEE Transactions on Knowledge and Data Engineering **24**, 1291–1305 (2012)
13. Han, J., Kamber, M.: Data mining: concepts and techniques, 2nd edn. China Machine Press, Beijing (2007). Fan Ming, Meng Xiaofeng
14. Strehl, A., Ghosh, J.: Cluster ensembles-a knowledge reuse framework for combining multiple partitions. The Journal of Machine Learning Research **3**, 583–617 (2003)
15. Zhao, Y., Karypis, G.: Comparison of Agglomerative and Partitional Document Clustering Algorithms. Technical Report#02-014. University of Minnesota (2002)
16. Hubert, L., Arabie, P.: Comparing partitions. Journal of Classification **2**(1), 193–218 (1985)
17. Iam-On, N., Boongoen, T., Garrett, S., et al.: A Link-Based Approach to the Cluster Ensemble Problem. IEEE Transactions on Pattern Analysis & Machine Intelligence **33**, 2396–2409 (2011)
18. Eagle, N., De Montjoye, Y., Bettencourt, L.M.A.: Community computing: Comparisons between rural and urban societies using mobile phone data. In: International Conference on Computational Science and Engineering, pp. 144–150. IEEE, Piscataway (2009)
19. Papalexakis, E.E.: Automatic Unsupervised Tensor Mining with Quality Assessment (2015). arXiv:1503.0335
20. Farrahi, K., Gatica-Perez, D.: Daily routine classification from mobile phone data. Machine Learning for Multimodal Interaction. Springer, Heidelberg (2008)

Land Cover Classification Based on Adaptive Interval-Valued Type-2 Fuzzy Clustering Analysis

Hui He[1,2], Xianchuan Yu[1(✉)], and Dan Hu[1(✉)]

[1] College of Information Science and Technology, Beijing Normal University,
Beijing 100875, China
yuxianchuan@163.com, hd@bnu.edu.cn
[2] School of Information Technology, Beijing Normal University, Zhuhai 519085, China

Abstract. The classic methods, such as FCM, often fail to carry out accurate modeling for the high-level fuzzy uncertainty, and then cause the classification error that should not be ignored in the application. Fortunately, the type-2 fuzzy set is a tool to handle this type of uncertainty. An adaptive interval-valued type-2 fuzzy C-Means clustering algorithm (A-IT2FCM) is proposed, including:(1) a proper modeling method for interval-valued type-2 fuzzy set;(2) an effective type reduction approach by adaptively searching the equivalent type-1 fuzzy sets for the type-2. Three different type-2 fuzzy clustering algorithms are used: the algorithm based on Karnik-Mendel type reduction, a method based on simple type reduction, and A-IT2FCM presented in this article. The experimental data are two data windows of SPOT5 image from Zhuhai and Beijing, China. Results show that, A-IT2FCM outperforms the other algorithms compared. Especially when obvious density difference exists between objects in the data, A-IT2FCM can achieve more accurate class boundaries and higher classification accuracy.

Keywords: Type-2 fuzzy sets · Land cover classification · Adaptive fuzzy clustering · Remote sensing image · SPOT5

1 Introduction

Land cover classification is a classic study project. It has been widely applied and plays an important role in map update, target recognition, disaster monitoring, city planning etc. As they can achieve automatic classification, Un-supervised classification methods have obvious advantages in many remote sensing applications [1,2], such as disaster assessment, compared to supervised classification methods. Due to the uncertainties exist in the land cover classification [34], the ISODATA and K-Means, as the hard clustering methods, produce unsatisfying processing results, while the Fuzzy C-Means as a soft clustering method could often get better results [8]. However, When the pattern set has clusters of similar size and density with the hypersphere shape, the methods based on FCM are good. But if the clusters of the pattern set have significant different densities, the FCM will show quite different effects depending on the different fuzzifiers [9]. The reasons for the differences between the

© Springer International Publishing Switzerland 2015
S. Zhang et al. (Eds.): KSEM 2015, LNAI 9403, pp. 712–720, 2015.
DOI: 10.1007/978-3-319-25159-2_65

samples of the same class are physical ones, like shadows over some ground regions, different degrees of crop growth and sparsely vegetated arid areas. If those different samples were averaged together to build an ordinary fuzzy set, for example, the mean behavior of each class could be captured but the differences from the samples would be lost [10], therefore if we process the remote sensing images with great different densities and high order uncertainties by methods based on FCM, it is difficult to obtain satisfactory results. A type-2 fuzzy set is capable of capturing such differences, thus it is more appropriate to handle the uncertainties present at the characterization of each class than type-1 [11~12], and the interval type-2 fuzzy set, whose computation complexity gets significantly reduced , is used widely [11].

Type reduction is the characteristics and difficulty in the applications of the interval type-2 fuzzy set theory [11]. The most popular one is the centroid type-reduction strategy to carry out type reduction for type-2 fuzzy sets since Karnik and Mendel proposed an algorithm to compute the centroid of an interval type-2 fuzzy set efficiently [13], named the Karnik–Mendel(KM) algorithm. However, the initialization of the switch point in each application of the KM algorithm is not a good one so it is very computationally intensive. Many researchers extended the algorithm, such as a series of EKM [14], WM-UB [15], Nie-Tan [16], etc. So far, there is no literature on comprehensive comparison of performance between type reduction methods based KM and other type reduction methods. And which method is better is no consensus [17,18], and this indicates that in practice, the aforementioned various type reduction methods do not fundamentally break the limitations of KM algorithm. Different from the type reduction methods under the general fuzzy system frame [19], Wu and Tan [20] developed a more computationally efficient algorithm based on the concept known as equivalent type-1 sets (ET1Ss), a collection of type-1 sets that replicates the input-output map of a type-2 fuzzy logic system [20]. As for land cover classification, the accuracy of a type reducer is inversely correlated with the clustering error, the lower the clustering error, the higher the type reduction accuracy. So if introducing the clustering error at last iteration to the type reduction will make the classifier have better performance, such a referring model is presented in literature [20].

We proposed an adaptive interval-valued type-2 fuzzy C-means clustering (A-IT2FCM) for land cover classification, aims at minimizing the effects of uncertainties in the usual fuzzy rule-based classifiers. The main contribute is the automatic fuzzy classifier proposed based on interval type-2 fuzzy sets to be applied in land cover classification to capture the high-order fuzzy uncertainty. Also, we introduce an adaptive expansion factor for adjusting the interval width according to the clustering error at the last iteration, and develop an effective type reducer on ET1Ss.

2   A-IT2FCM

2.1   Adaptive Quick Type Reduction and Defuzzification

Firstly, the interval type-2 fuzzy sets are generated on the basis of image data, represented as $\mathbf{X} = \{\mathbf{x}_1, \mathbf{x}_2, \cdots, \mathbf{x}_n\}$, $\mathbf{x}_i = \{x_{i1}, x_{i2}, \cdots, x_{ip}\}, i = 1, 2, \cdots, n$. The definitions of the upper and lower bounds of the interval type-2 fuzzy sets are as follows:

Upper bound:
$$\bar{U} = [\bar{u}_j(\mathbf{x}_i)], \ \bar{u}_j(\mathbf{x}_i) = \frac{1}{\sum_{k=1}^{C} (\frac{d_{ji}}{d_{ki}})^{\frac{2}{m-1}}} \tag{1}$$

Lower bound:
$$\underline{U} = [\underline{u}_j(\mathbf{x}_i)], \ \underline{u}_j(\mathbf{x}_i) = \frac{1}{\sum_{k=1}^{C} (\frac{s_{ji}}{s_{ki}})^{\frac{2}{m-1}}} \tag{2}$$

Where $\bar{u}_j(\mathbf{x}_i)$ and $\underline{u}_j(\mathbf{x}_i)$ respectively denotes the upper and lower bounds of the membership degree of sample $\mathbf{x}_i$ to cluster j , then the interval $([\underline{u}_j(\mathbf{x}_i), \bar{u}_j(\mathbf{x}_i)])$ of membership degree is generated, d, s is the mean value and the maximum of the distance between $\mathbf{x}_i$ and cluster j respectively, $d_{ji} = mean(d_{ji}^L)$, $s_{ji} = \max(d_{ji}^L), L = 1, 2, \cdots, p$, d_{ji}^L is some distance metric, such as Euclidian distance, m is the fuzzy exponential.

Then an adaptive type reducer is generated on the concept of ET1Ss , clustering error, and expansion factor:

$$U(\mathbf{x}_i)_{eq}^{C_k} = \bar{U}(\mathbf{x}_i)^{C_k} - \beta(\bar{U}(\mathbf{x}_i)^{C_k} - \underline{U}(\mathbf{x}_i)^{C_k})$$

$$s.t \ \sum_{k=1}^{K} U(\mathbf{x}_i)_{eq}^{C_k} = 1, 0 \leq \sum_{i=1}^{n} U(\mathbf{x}_i)_{eq}^{C_k} \leq n \tag{3}$$

where K is the number of clusters, $U_{eq}^{C_k}$ is the membership degree of $\mathbf{x}_i$ belongs in cluster C_k after type reduction, $\bar{U}^{C_k}$ and $\underline{U}^{C_k}$ is the upper and lower bounds of the initial interval type-2 membership, see Eq.(1)and Eq. (2) for the definitions, $\beta(0 \leq \beta \leq 1)$ is the adaptive expansion factor and its general definition is showing in Eq.(4) and the justification and specific inference process, see literature [21]. When the normalized intra-class mean square error increases, β increases, means that the equiva-lent type-1 membership degree of $\mathbf{x}_i$ belongs in cluster C_k decreases and the width of the interval will enlarge, that is the possibility of $\mathbf{x}_i$ not belonging in C_k increases. When $\beta = 1$, $U(\mathbf{x}_i)_{eq}^{C_k} = \underline{U}(\mathbf{x}_i)^{C_k}$, the equivalent type-1 membership degree is the lower bound; Otherwise, when the normalized intra-class mean square error becomes zero, β will become zero and the equivalent type-1 membership degree is the upper bound, which means that the possibility of $\mathbf{x}_i$ belonging in C_k increases.

$$\beta = f(e) = 1 - \lambda \exp(-ke^2), \ \lambda \in (0,1), k > 0 \tag{4}$$

Where e is the normalized intra-class mean square error when $\mathbf{x}_i$ is classified into cluster C_k, see Eq. (5), the effects of the constants λ and k on β respectively are showing in Fig.1.

$$e = \frac{\sum\limits_{i \in C_k} u_{ik}^m \delta(\mathbf{x}_i, \mathbf{g}_k)}{n_k} \tag{5}$$

Where $\delta(\mathbf{x}_i, \mathbf{g}_k)$ is the dispersion from $\mathbf{x}_i$ to C_k, n_k is the number of samples in every dimension of C_k.

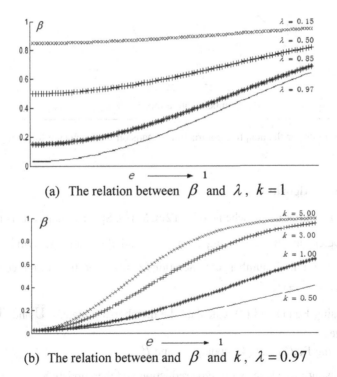

(a) The relation between β and λ, $k = 1$

(b) The relation between and β and k, $\lambda = 0.97$

Fig. 1. The constant parameters' effect on the adaptive expansion factor

From Fig.1 we can see that If λ is fixed ($\lambda = 0.97$), β correlates linearly with e when $k = 1$, which agrees with the requirement for controlling the interval's width according to the normalized intra-class mean square error. In the process of clustering, β may oscillate at the beginning stage of iterations, while the normalized intra-class mean square error becomes minimum, β will remain stable, that is $U_{eq}^{C_k}$ becoming stable and the type reduction process finishes, showing as Fig.2.

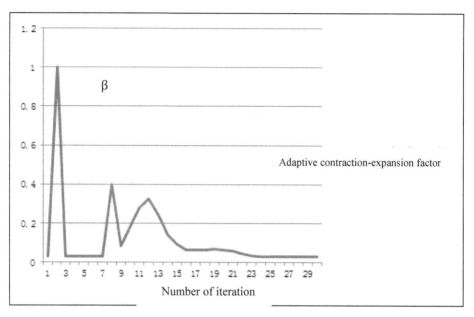

Fig. 2. An example for the adaptive contraction-expansion factor change following the clustering iteration

2.2 Steps of Algorithm

A-IT2FCM is similar to the scheme of IT2FCM [9]. Specific steps are as follows:

Step1: Determine the clustering number c and the parameters $m(1 < m < \infty)$, $\varepsilon = 10^{-5}$, the initial number of iterations $t = 0$, set the initial center matrix $V_i^t (1 \le i \le c), \beta = 0$;

Step2: Using Eq.(1) and (2), calculate the membership matrix $\overline{U}$ and $\underline{U}$ with V^t as the center;

Step3: Using Eq.(5) and (4), update e and β;

Step4: Using Eq.(3), carry out type reduction and then update V^t;

Step5: If $\left\| V^{t+1} - V^t \right\| < \varepsilon$, turn to the next step, otherwise set $t = t+1$, turn to Step2;

Step6: Get the final cluster centers and membership matrix, do hard partition by the principle of the closest to center.

The clustering result of A-IT2FCM can be obtained after the hard partition, and the final classification results are obtained after the clustering discriminant in the end.

3   Experimental Analysis

3.1   The Overall Scheme

The scheme of land cover classification based on A-IT2FCM is showing in Fig.3.

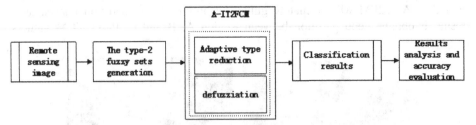

Fig. 3. The overall scheme of this study

Three different type-2 fuzzy clustering algorithms are used in our experiment: the algorithm based on Karnik-Mendel type reduction(KM-IT2FCM [13]), a method based on simple type reduction(Pa-IT2FCM [22]), and A-IT2FCM presented, with the same public parameters for the comparability.

3.2   Data Description

We select the SPOT5 multi-spectral data acquired in Hengqin Island, Zhuhai City(435x446 pixels), China. It is an 8-bit data with 10m spatial resolution. Features of the image are showing in Table 1. We extract (4, 3, 2) bands as the RGB channel to build the standard false color image for classification as shown in Fig. 5a. This kind of data is distributed within a relatively small hypersphere respectively. In this case, the classification results will evidently vary with the fuzzifier m. Thus it is difficult to get a satisfactory result with the model of type-1 fuzzy c-means, while the interval type-2 fuzzy c-means may lead to satisfactory results.

Table 1. Composition of the categories in the clustering resulting images

Data	Land cover class	Description
	grassland	Lawn, weeds, low bushes, etc.
	buildings	Towns, construction sites, settlements, highways, etc.
	water	Rivers, reservoirs, ponds, etc.
SPOT5 data from Zhuhai, China	woodland	Natural forests and plantations, etc.
	farmland	Orchards, vegetable plots, etc.
	tideland	Coastal beach

3.3   Results and Analysis

From Fig. 4(where (b) is the result of Pa-IT2FCM, (c) is the result of KM-IT2FCM and (d) is the result of A-IT2FM), we can see that, for land class with little difference between samples, as the green land and buildings shown in Fig.4, all the methods acquire good partition results and the boundaries between different class are substantially coherent and visible.

As for the spectrum aliasing serious regions, for example, regions A(tideland), B(water) and C (woodland) shown in Fig.4, there are obvious different partitions with different clustering methods , in the result of Pa-IT2FCM, the tideland is misclassified to woodland and in the result of KM-IT2FCM the tideland is misclassified to water. However, because by introducing the adaptive expansion factor and clustering validity index, A-IT2FM will ultimately guide the optimal fuzzy partition matrix, as a result, it obtains good partition between Region A, B and C. Pa-IT2FCM gathers

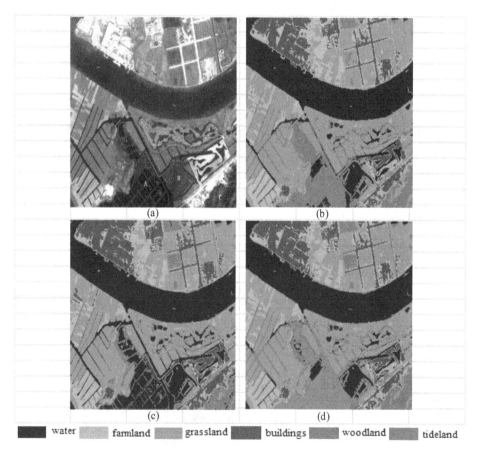

Fig. 4. Classification results for (a) the SPOT5 data from Zhuhai, China, using (b) Pa-IT2FCM, and (c) KM-IT2FCM, (d) A-IT2FCM

stronger relative to the other two algorithms, so it easily lead to "over-clustering" problem that is more likely to lead to the disappearance of small targets in the larger neighborhood category. All in all, from the visual interpretation of the resulting images, the A-IT2FCM significantly outperforms the other two algorithms.

In order to verify the results by objective evaluation, we selected 50 points randomly by GPS for ground validation. The classification accuracy and Kappa coefficient are shown in Table 2. According to objective evaluation results, clustering accuracy and Kappa coefficient of FCM are greatly affected by fuzzifier. The clustering accuracy and Kappa coefficient aren't monotonic relationship with the fuzzifier. The results indicate that our A-IT2FCM increases the classification accuracy and Kappa coefficient, and can obviously improve the clustering result. The objective result is also consistent with the visual interpretation.

Table 2. Comparison of the overall accuracy and Kappa for different algorithms mentioned in the experiments

Data	Method	Overall accuracy	Kappa
SPOT5 data from Zhuhai, China	Pa-IT2FCM	77%	0.695
	KM-IT2FCM($m_1 = 2, m_2 = 10$)	76%	0.677
	A-IT2FCM	91%	0.893

4   Conclusion

Fuzzy systems improve classification and decision support systems by allowing the use of overlapping class definitions and improve the interpretability of the results by providing more insight into the classifier structure and decision making process.Type-2 fuzzy sets are more appropriate to handle the high-order fuzzy uncertainties present in the land cover class. We proposed the A-IT2FCM, aims at finding an efficient type reducer and obtaining better classification result. On basis of the concept of ET1Ss and by introducing an adaptive interval control factor, our classification scheme based on A-IT2FCM significantly outperforms the classic IT2FCM algorithms, it is suitable for automatic land cover classification with high-resolution remote sensing data.

Acknowledgment. We wish to thank the Institute of Remote Sensing and Geographic Information Systems in Guangdong Province for providing the experimental data for this article.This work was sponsored by the National Natural Science Foundation of China [Grant Nos. 11001019, 41272359], the Specialized Research Fund for the Doctoral Program of Higher Education in China [Grant No. 20120003110032] and the PhD Start-up Fund of Natural Science Foundation of Guangdong Province, China [Grant No. 2014A030310415].

References

1. Li, B., Zhao, H., Lv, Z.H.: Parallel ISODATA clustering of remote sensing images based on Map Reduce. In: Proceedings of International Conference on Cyber-Enabled Distributed Computing and Knowledge Discovery, Huangshan, 2010, pp. 380–383 (2010)

2. Lv, Z., Hu, Y., Zhong, H., Wu, J., Li, B., Zhao, H.: Parallel K-means clustering of remote sensing images based on MapReduce. In: Lei, J., Wang, F.L., Luo, X., Gong, Z. (eds.) Web Information Systems and Mining. LNCS, vol. 6318, pp. 162–170. Springer, Heidelberg (2010)

3. Cheng, J.C., Guo, H.D., Shi, W.Z.: The Uncertainty of Remote Sensing Data. Science Press, Beijing (2004)

4. Rocchini, D., Foody, G.M., Nagendra, H., et al.: Uncertainty in ecosystem mapping by remote sensing. Computers & Geosciences **50**, 128–135 (2013)

5. Yu, X.C., An, W.J., He, H.: A Method of Auto Classification based on Object Oriented Unsupervised Classification. Progress in Geophysics **27**(2), 744–749 (2012)

6. Zhang, W.J., Kang, J.Y.: Segmentation of high resolution remote sensing image using modified FCM combined with optimization method. Journal of Information and Computational Science **9**(15), 4591–4598 (2012)

7. Huang, Q.R, Wu, G.M, Chen, J.M., et al.: Automated remote sensing image classification method based on FCM and SVM. In: Proceedings of Remote Sensing, Environment and Transportation Engineering, Nanjing, pp. 1–4 (2012)

8. Xie, J., Zhang, X.L.: Clustering of hyper spectral image based on improved fuzzy C means algorithm. Journal of Convergence Information Technology **7**(12), 320–327 (2012)

9. Hwang, C., Rhee, F.C.: Uncertain fuzzy clustering: Interval type-2 fuzzy approach to C-means. IEEE Transactions on Fuzzy Systems **15**(1), 107–120 (2007)

10. Lucas, L.A., Centeno, T.M., Delgado, M.R.: Land cover classification based on general type-2 fuzzy classifiers. International Journal of Fuzzy Systems **10**(3), 207–216 (2008)

11. Sheng, L.: Theory and Application of Type-2 Fuzzy System [Doctoral dissertation]. University of Electronic Science and Technology of China (2012)

12. Chen, W., Sun, Z.Q.: Research on of Type-2 Fuzzy Logic System and Its Application. Fuzzy Systems and Mathematics **19**(1), 126–135 (2005)

13. Karnik, N.N., Mendel, J.M.: Centroid of a type-2 fuzzy set. Information Sciences **132**(1–4), 195–220 (2001)

14. Wu, D., Mendel, J.M.: Enhanced karnik-mendel algorithms. IEEE Transactions on Fuzzy Systems **17**(4), 923–934 (2009)

15. Wu, H., Mendel, J.M.: Uncertainty bounds and their use in the design of interval type-2 fuzzy logic systems. IEEE Transactions on Fuzzy Systems **10**(5), 622–639 (2002)

16. Nie, M, Tan, W.W.: Towards an efficient type reduction method for interval type-2 fuzzy logic systems//Fuzzy Systems. In: IEEE International Conference on FUZZ-IEEE 2008 (IEEE World Congress on Computational Intelligence), pp. 1425–1432. IEEE (2008)

17. Mendel, J.M.: On KM Algorithms for Solving Type-2 Fuzzy Set Problems. IEEE Transactions on Fuzzy Systems **21**(3), 426–446 (2013)

18. Greenfield, S., Chiclana, F.: Accuracy and complexity evaluation of defuzzification strategies for the discretised interval type-2 fuzzy set. International Journal of Approximate Reasoning **54**(8), 1013–1033 (2013)

19. Mendel, J.M., John, R.I., Liu, F.: Interval type-2 fuzzy logic systems made simple. IEEE Transactions on Fuzzy Systems **14**(6), 808–821 (2006)

20. Wu, D, Tan, W.W.: Computationally efficient type reduction strategies for a type-2 fuzzy logic controller. In: Proceedings of 14th IEEE International Conference on Fuzzy Systems, Reno, NV, pp. 353–358 (2005)

21. Li, H.X., Miao, Z.H.: Variable Universe Stable Adaptive Fuzzy Control of a Nonlinear System. Computers & Mathematics with Applications **44**(5–6), 799–815 (2002)

22. Tizhoosh, H.R.: Image thresholding using type II fuzzy sets. Pattern Recognition **38**(12), 2363–2372 (2005)

GPS-Based Location Recommendation Using a Belief Network Model

Kunlei Zhu[1](✉), Jiajin Huang[1], and Ning Zhong[1,2]

[1] International WIC Institute, Beijing University of Technology,
Beijing 100024, China
{s201302176,hjj}@emails.bjut.edu.cn, zhong@maebashi-it.ac.jp
[2] Department of Life Science and Informatics, Maebashi Institute of Technology,
Maebashi 371-0816, Japan

Abstract. With the increasing popularity of location-based services, location recommendation is one of important applications. In this paper, according to a user's preference, we recommend locations to a user by extending an information retrieval model, namely, belief network model. We regard the user's preference as a query, a location as a document, categories as index terms. And then, we use the belief network model to recommend locations to a user by adding expert information. Experimental results on a real world data set show that recommendation effectiveness can be improved.

Keywords: Belief network · Location recommendation · Expert information

1 Introduction

Location-based service (LBS) can collect trajectories of users in a city based on GPS logs [1]. By using these data, we can analyze a user's behavior and preference, and then we can recommend the locations that a user may visit. The user-based collaborative filtering algorithm and item-based collaborative filtering algorithm are classical recommendation algorithms [2,3]. V.W. Zheng [4] used the user-based collaborative filtering to recommend locations combining the actives. Y. Takeuchi [5] used the item-based collaborative filtering approach to recommend the similar stores which the user visited. M.H. Park [6] used the user's preference and the location context to recommend restaurants to a user by using bayesian network algorithm.

One of location recommendation methods is to rank locations according to a user's preference in a descending order. And then top locations are selected to recommend to the user. The idea is similar to information retrieval which ranks documents based on the relevance with the submitted query. In the information retrieval techniques, text term weighting technique is the most common. A document can be represented by a weight vector of index term [7]. The vector space model of information retrieval use the similarity between a user query and documents to sort documents [8]. In addition, there are two typical bayesian network

© Springer International Publishing Switzerland 2015
S. Zhang et al. (Eds.): KSEM 2015, LNAI 9403, pp. 721–731, 2015.
DOI: 10.1007/978-3-319-25159-2_66

models in information retrieval, namely, the inference network model [9] and brief network model [10]. The belief network model is a variant of the inference network model. The belief network model defines a concept space to express the users and the documents. Belief network model can use the operator of query language to integrate additional evidence source. HITS can analyze the import of web page, and it always used in knowledge discover, such as finding expert [11].

There are strong relevance between recommender system and information retrieval, so some methods of information retrieval are applied to recommender systems. The method of item ranking in information retrieval is applied to collaborative filtering [12]. A model of information retrieval is integrated into collaborative filtering [13]. But few study considers expert information to give a user some advices. When a user goes to a unfamiliar place and wants to experience the unique local attractions, diet and culture, and then the user's travel experience is no enough. It needs to find experts who have rich travel experiences on this location [14].

In this paper, we use a belief network model of information retrieval to find a location. In order to use the model, we also employ categories to represent a user's preference and a theme of a location by the TF-IDF method. Furthermore, we use HITS [11] algorithm to find expert users, and we take use of the travel experience of experts to recommend locations to a user.

The rest of the paper is organized as follows. In section 2, we model the user vector and location vector. In section 3, we model the recommendation algorithm. In section 4, we present the experimental parameters and the experimental results. Finally, we conclude the paper in section 5.

2   Data Model

A user's trajectory consists of sequence of time-stamped GPS points. The user's stay point is a region consisting of a set of GPS points in his trajectory, where he stays longer than a time threshold, and the distance of these points is greater than the distance threshold. In order to avoid that different stay points represent the same region, the stay points need to be clustered in a location. we aim to recommend locations which the user may like. So we can use the feature of location to represent the user's preferences.

2.1   Multi-user Cooperative Location Mining

In order to provide a user with location recommendation based on theme, we extract location categories as theme information. A location is a set of stay point, and it has more than one category [15]. As mentioned in [16], location is the basic units of location recommendation. The category information reflects location theme [17]. Let $D = \{d_1, d_2, \cdots, d_{|D|}\}$ be the location set, $C = \{c_1, c_2, \cdots, c_{|C|}\}$ be category set, and $U = \{u_1, \cdots, u_{|U|}\}$ be user vector. As some location categories are more popular than others, so we use TF-IDF method to calculate the weighting value of a category in a location [16].

$$t_{ij} = \frac{|\{d_j.c = c_i\}|}{|d_j.C|} \times \log \frac{|D|}{|\{d_j : d_j.c = c_i\}|} \tag{1}$$

where $|\{d_j.c = c_i\}|$ is the number of stay points whose category is c_i in d_j, $|d_j.C|$ is the total number of stay points of all categories in d_j, $|D|$ is the total location number in D vector, $|\{d_j : d_j.c = c_i\}|$ is the number of the locations whose category are c_i. Based on the TF-IDF method, we define a region d_j as $\overrightarrow{d}_j = (t_{1j}, t_{2j}, \cdots, t_{ij}, \cdots, t_{|C|j})$, where t_{ij} is the weighting category of a location. In the whole recommender system, we regard the location as the most basic unit.

2.2 Personal Preference Discovery

According to location extraction method [18], we take the GPS trajectory of the single user for the input, and then we get a location set. If a user likes the location of one category, the user will frequently visit the location. We use the TF-IDF model to weight a user's preference. We use the categories to reflect a user preference. A category weight of a user can be calculated by follows [14]:

$$w_{ij} = \frac{|\{u_i.c = c_j\}|}{|u_i.C|} \times \log \frac{|U|}{|\{u_i : u_i.c = c_j\}|} \tag{2}$$

where $|\{u_i.c = c_j\}|$ is the number which user u_i visits category c_j, $|u_i.C|$ is the total number which u_i visits, $|U|$ is the size of the U vector, and $|\{u_i : u_i.c = c_j\}|$ counts the number of users who have visited category c_j.

By using weight values, we define a user u_i as $\overrightarrow{u}_i = (w_{i1}, w_{i2}, \cdots, w_{ij}, \cdots, w_{i|C|})$, where w_{ij} is the TF-IDF weighting value of category c_j of a user. User vector is regarded as recommendation model input.

3 Recommendation Model

In this paper, we regard the belief network of retrieval model as a recommendation algorithm, a user vector as a query term of retrieval model, and a location as a document. This section mainly discusses how to apply the belief network model [10] to location recommendations. As the belief network can be integrated evidence sources, so we can add expert information to the recommendation algorithm.

3.1 Expert Information Source Selections

If a user has visited a kind of locations many times, we can assume that the user has a wealth of travel experience on the location, and we call the user as a expert user. The expert user can provide good travel suggestions to a user.

HITS algorithm [11] can be used to find expert users. What a user visit a location simulates the link relationship of each web page [19]. When a user visits a location many times, we can consider the user has a rich knowledge of the location. And the location is visited by multiple users, and the region is considered that the location is a hot region. Each user's authority value is the sum of the hub value of the locations, and each location hub value is the sum of the authority value of the users. We use iteration method to continuously replace the user authority value and location hub value. The user whose value of the final authority is maximal is expert users.

$$A_c(u) = \sum_{d \in D | u \to d} H_c(d) \tag{3}$$

$$H_c(d) = \sum_{u \in U | u \to d} A_c(u) \tag{4}$$

where $A_c(u)$ is the normalized authority value of user u in category c, and $H_c(d)$ is the normalized hub value of location in category c.

After using HITS algorithm to calculate $A_c(u)$ of each category of a user, we can find expert users. The travel advice is provided by experts who are chosen for a user by recommender system. The travel advice not only meets user's preference, but also recommends locations to a user. We select three kinds of experts [14].

- Random expert ERU: Random experts are the experts who are randomly selected in the expert list. ERU does not require that the similarity of the user's preference between expert and the given user is high, but it may recommend locations whose popularity is not high and which are distinctive to the user.
- Senior expert EU: Senior experts have the highest similarity with the given user. EU recommends locations which meet the user's preference to the given user.
- Random senior expert REU: We selected two experts in the expert list, and we choose the one whose similarity value with a given user is more hight as the REU. The random senior expert is a expert whose similarity is higher of two experts who are randomly selected in the expert list. To a certain extent, the random senior can recommend locations which have the low popularity but be distinctive.

The recommendation system will assign weights of three kinds of experts as α , β , γ. After three kinds of experts are added to the belief network, we can get three ranking probabilities P_0, P_1, P_1. The final ranking probability can be $P = \alpha \times P_0 + \beta \times P_1 + \gamma \times P_2$, where $\alpha + \beta + \gamma = 1$. The ranking probability of locations will be calculated from the belief network.

3.2 Algorithm Models

Belief Network Model. In order to use the belief network [10], we define the category set C as the concept space of the belief network model. The user set and location set are described with a subset of C.

In the belief network model, we use $P(d_j|u)$ to measure the relevance between u and d_j. Let $\overrightarrow{k}$ be an $|C|$-dimensional vector, and we define $\overrightarrow{k} = \{k_1, k_2, \cdots, k_{|C|}\}$, where $k_1, k_2, \cdots, k_{|C|}$ are binary random variables. Let $k_i = \{0, 1\}$, we have

$$g(i, \overrightarrow{k}) = \begin{cases} 1 & k_i = 1 \\ 0 & \text{other} \end{cases} \tag{5}$$

So we have vector $\overrightarrow{k_i} = \overrightarrow{k} \mid g(i, \overrightarrow{k}) = 1 \bigwedge \forall_{i \neq j} g(j, \overrightarrow{k}) = 0$. Using bayes theorem and conditional probability formula [10], we have

$$P(d_j|u) \sim \sum_{\forall i} P(d_j|\overrightarrow{k_i}) \times P(u|\overrightarrow{k_i}) \times P(\overrightarrow{k_i}) \tag{6}$$

In the above section, we use the TF-IDF method to describe user and location. And then we have

$$P(u|\overrightarrow{k_i}) = \frac{w_{ij}}{\sqrt{\sum_{i=1}^{|C|} w_{ij}^2}} \tag{7}$$

$$P(d_j|\overrightarrow{k_i}) = \frac{t_{ij}}{\sqrt{\sum_{i=1}^{|C|} t_{ij}^2}} \tag{8}$$

Expert Belief Network Model. When a user is not familiar with a location, the user hopes to get a travel guidance given by experts. We need an approach to add the expert information to the belief network model to solve the above problem. The expert belief network model use the boolean query language of information retrieval to integrate additional expert information. The boolean query syntax consists of basic queries and boolean operators. The model uses the OR operator to integrate multiple information sources [10]. We regard an expert as u_1, which is taken for current user I with given user u, so $I = u \vee u_1$. If two user have at least one common category of user vector, we define the two user is relevant. I is relevant to u_1 and u. Let $C_+ = (c_{+1}, c_{+2}, \cdots, c_{+i}, \cdots c_{+|C|})$ model the context of expert evidence u_1 related to I. Let C_+ be the concept space. Similar to the belief network model in information retrieval, we do not consider the joint impact of two or more preferences of an expert in order to simplify the calculation. In the expert belief network model, we use $P(d_j|I)$ to sort the location d_j [10].

Let $\overrightarrow{m}$ be an $|C_+|$-dimensional vector, and we define $\overrightarrow{m} = \{m_1, m_2, \cdots, m_{|C_+|}\}$, where $m_1, m_2, \cdots, m_{|C_+|}$ is binary random variable. So we define $m_i = \{0, 1\}$. We define

$$g(i, \overrightarrow{m}) = \begin{cases} 1 & m_i = 1 \\ 0 & \text{other} \end{cases} \tag{9}$$

So we have vector $\overrightarrow{m_i} = \overrightarrow{m}|\ g(i,\overrightarrow{m}) = 1 \bigwedge \forall_{i \neq j}\ g(j,\overrightarrow{m}) = 0$. And then we have:

$$P(d_j|\overrightarrow{m_i}) = \frac{r(d_j, c_{+i})}{max\ r} \tag{10}$$

Where $r(d_j, c_{+i})$ is defined as the number which the expert visit the category c_{+i} of the location d_j, and $max\ r$ is defined as the maximum number of $r(d_j, c_{+i})$.

$$P(u_1|\overrightarrow{m_i}) = \frac{\overrightarrow{u} \cdot \overrightarrow{u_1}}{|\overrightarrow{u}| \times |\overrightarrow{u_1}|} \tag{11}$$

After we have the above probabilities, we have the $P(d_j|I)$ by the following method of combining evidential sources in the brief network proposed in [10].

$$P(d_j|I) = \frac{1}{P(I)} \times \sum_{\forall i} P(d_j|\overrightarrow{k_i}, \overrightarrow{m_i}) \times P(I|\overrightarrow{k_i}, \overrightarrow{m_i}) \times P(\overrightarrow{k_i}) \times P(\overrightarrow{m_i})$$

$$= \frac{1}{P(I)} \times \sum_{\forall \overrightarrow{k_i}, \overrightarrow{m_i}} [1 - (1 - P(d_j|\overrightarrow{k_i}) \times (1 - P(d_j|\overrightarrow{m_i})))] \times P(u|\overrightarrow{k_i}) \times$$

$$P(u_1|\overrightarrow{m_i}) \times P(\overrightarrow{k_i}) \times P(\overrightarrow{m_i}) \tag{12}$$

where $P(u|\overrightarrow{k_i})$ and $P(d_j|\overrightarrow{k_i})$ are obtained by Equ. (7) and Equ. (8), respectively. $P(I)$ is defined by $P(I) = \frac{1}{|U|}$.

4   Experiments

4.1   Experiment Settings

We use real travel data of 182 users in Beijing to test the model. It is collected the five-year data from April 2007 to August 2012. This data set contains 17,621 tracks, and its total distance is up to 1,292,951 km. The data set mainly comes from the GPS logs and GPS phones. This data set includes not only track which users go home and to work, but also recreation and outdoor sports, such as shopping, sightseeing, dining and so on [20]. The GPS track information of the data sets consist latitude, longitude, time, date, etc. The paper will get the category information of locations form baidu POI service. The data set is divided into training set and the testing set. The training set is used to train the model and determine the parameters of the model, and the testing set is used to predict the locations that the user likes. 80% data are regarded as the training test.

To evaluate the effectiveness of the recommender system, we use the recall and precision rate to measure the effect of the recommendation. Let $R(u)$ be the number of the recommended locations, $T(u)$ be the number of locations which user u visited in the test set. We have the recall and precision by follows:

$$recall = \frac{\sum_{u \in U} |R(u)| \cap |T(u)|}{\sum_{u \in U} |T(u)|}$$

$$precision = \frac{\sum_{u \in U} |R(u)| \cap |T(u)|}{\sum_{u \in U} |R(u)|} \tag{13}$$

4.2 Experimental Results

In our location recommendation, we follow the study [14] to identify the location. we firstly see the impact of location size and user number. And then we will test the impact of different experts. Finally, in order to verify that what the information retrieval model is used for location recommendation has good recommendation performance, we choose the basic inference network model (RNM), expert inference network combined with expert information source (ERNM), the basic belief network model (BNM), experts believe the belief network model combined with expert information source (EBNM), vector space model (VSM) to compare with user-based collaborative filtering algorithm (UCF), which is to test the recommendation effect of the retrieval model.

Impact of the User Number. In the recommender system, we use multi-user collaborative way to discover stay points of all users, and take use of grid clustering algorithm to divide the city into different locations. The change of the user number will impact the location size. The smaller the user number is, the sparser the number of stay points in a location is. There is less choice for the users to select the stay points of a location. We will vary the user number from 50 to 162. In order to avoid other uncertain parameters affecting the result, we define the region size $|r|=300$, $\alpha = 0.7$, $\beta = 0.1$, $\gamma = 0.2$. Then we will discuss the effect of the user number on location recommendation.

From Fig. 1, we can see when the number of users $|u|=162$, recommendation system has the best performance. The recommendation effect becomes better with the increase of the user number.

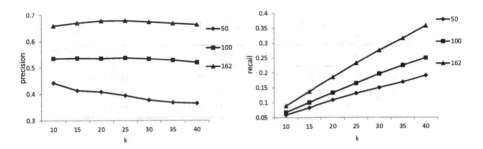

Fig. 1. Impact of the user number

Impact of the Location Size. In the location recommendation, we may prefer smaller location size so that the user can easily find what she wants in the recommended locations. We will vary the location size by varying the location width from 200 to 500. Before the experience, we define the user number is 162, $\alpha = 0.7, \beta = 0.1, \gamma = 0.2$. And then we will discuss the recommendation effect of impact of the location size.

From Fig. 2, we can see when the location width is 300, the recommendation effect is best. The smaller a location width is, the less the user can choose. So when the region width is 200, the recommendation effect is poor. Too large location size make the user difficult to find stay points in the location. So when the location width is 500, the precision rate and the recall rate is low.

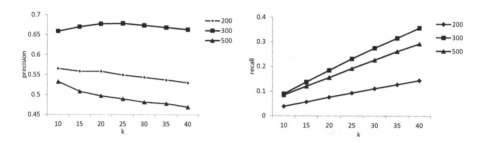

Fig. 2. Impact of the location size

Impact of Parameters α, β, γ. In order to make recommendation best, we design a experiment to determine the parameters of three kinds of experts α, β, γ. Before the experience, we define the user number $|u|$=162, the region size $|d|$=300. Table 1 and Table 2 shows different parameters in ERNM and EBNUM to recommend top-N (N=30) locations. From the two table, we can see the high precision and recall with $\alpha = 1, \beta = 0, \gamma = 0$ in ERNM, and $\alpha = 0.7, \beta = 0.1, \gamma = 0.2$ in EBNM.

Table 1. The result of ERNM

parameters	precision	recall
$\alpha = 0.6 \quad \beta = 0.3 \quad \gamma = 0.1$	0.519547	0.201795
$\alpha = 0.7 \quad \beta = 0.2 \quad \gamma = 0.1$	0.525514	0.202570
$\alpha = 1 \quad \beta = 0 \quad \gamma = 0$	0.530041	0.206208

Table 2. The result of EBNM

parameters	precision	recall
$\alpha = 0.7$ $\beta = 0.2$ $\gamma = 0.1$	0.67284	0.273934
$\alpha = 0.7$ $\beta = 0.1$ $\gamma = 0.2$	0.673663	0.274776
$\alpha = 1$ $\beta = 0$ $\gamma = 0$	0.663786	0.267561

Comparative Results of Different Models. The user vector in the training data set are regarded as the input of the model, and then the model will generate a recommendation list. We take the top-k region and calculate the precision rate and the recall rate of RNM, ERNM BNM EBNM, VSM, UCF to evaluation recommendation effect.

From Fig. 3, we can get EBNM is the best, so the EBNM is regarded as a recommendation algorithm. Information retrieval model RNM, ERNM, BNM, EBNM, VSM performance better than UCF. ERNM performances better than RNM , and EBNM performances better than BNM in the recommendation effect, which illustrate that the expert information source makes better recommendations. The performance of BNM is similar with VSM in the recommendation effect.

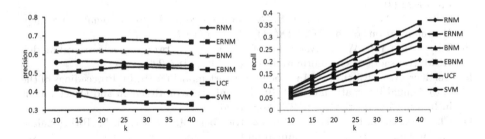

Fig. 3. Precision rate and recall rate of different models with different K value

5   Conclusions

This paper uses the brief network model in Information Retrieval to combine expert sources to make recommendations. The model takes categories as location themes and recommends the location whose theme match the user's preference to a user. Experimental results show the expert belief network model on location recommendation has better prediction. Although the model performance a good effect on location recommendation, there are many aspects to be improved. The model does not reflect the context. In the future work, we will take into account the user mood, time factor, the conditions of weather and traffic and so on to built relevant context model.

References

1. Zheng, Y., Li, Q., Chen, Y., Xie, X., Ma, W.Y.: Understanding mobility based on GPS data. In: Proceedings of ACM Conference on Ubiquitous Computing, pp. 312–321 (2008)
2. Breese, J., Heckerman, D., Kadie, C.: Empirical analysis of predictive algorithms for collaborative filtering. In: Proceedings of the Fourteenth Conference on Uncertainty in Artificial Intelligence, pp. 43–52 (1998)
3. Horozov, T., Narasimhan, N., Vasudevan, V.: Using location for personalized recommendations in mobile environments. In: Proceedings of the International Symposium on Applications on Internet, pp. 124–129 (2006)
4. Zheng, V.W., Zheng, Y., Xie, X., Yang, Q.: Towards mobile intelligence: learning from GPS history data for collaborative recommendation. Aritifical Intelligence **184–185**(2012), 17–37 (2012)
5. Takeuchi, Y., Sugimoto, M.: CityVoyager: an outdoor recommendation system based on user location history. In: Tsai, J.J.-P., Jin, H., Ma, J., Yang, L.T. (eds.) UIC 2006. LNCS, vol. 4159, pp. 625–636. Springer, Heidelberg (2006)
6. Park, M.-H., Hong, J.-H., Cho, S.-B.: Location-based recommendation system using Bayesian user's preference model in mobile devices. In: Ma, J., Ungerer, T., Yang, L.T., Indulska, J., Cao, J. (eds.) UIC 2007. LNCS, vol. 4611, pp. 1130–1139. Springer, Heidelberg (2007)
7. Yang, Y.: Expert network: effective and efficient learning from human decisions in text categorization and retrieval. In: Proceedings of 17th Annual International ACM SIGIR Conference on Research and Development in Information Retrieval, pp. 13–22 (1994)
8. Salton, G., Wong, A., Yang, C.S.: A vector space model for automatic fndexing. Communications of the ACM **18**(11), 613–620 (1975)
9. Turtle, H., Croft, W.B.: Evaluation of an inference network-based retrieval model. ACM Transactions on Information Systems **9**(3), 187–222 (1991)
10. Berthier, A.N., Ribeiro, R.M.: A belief network model for IR. In: Proceedings of the 19th Annual International ACM SIGIR Conference on Research and Development in Information Retrieval, pp. 253–260 (1996)
11. Chakrabarti, S., Dom, B., Gibson, D., Kleinberg, J., Raghavan, P., Rajagopalan, S.: Automatic resource list compilation by analyzing hyperlink structure and associated text. In: Proceedings of 7th International Conference on World Wide Web, pp. 65–74 (1998)
12. Wang, J., de Vries, A.P., Reinders, M.J.T.: A user-item relevance model for log-based collaborative filtering. In: Rüger, S.M., Tsikrika, T., Tombros, A., Yavlinsky, A., MacFarlane, A., Lalmas, M. (eds.) ECIR 2006. LNCS, vol. 3936, pp. 37–48. Springer, Heidelberg (2006)
13. Bellogn, A., Wang, J., Castells, P.: Bridging memory-based collaborative filtering and text retrieval. Information Retrieval **16**(6), 697–724 (2013)
14. Bao, J., Zheng, Y., Mokbel, M.F.: Location-based and preference-aware recommendation using sparse geo-social networking data. In: Proceedings of the 2012 International Conference on Advances in Geographic Information Systems, pp. 199–208 (2012)
15. Zheng, Y., Zhang, L., Xie, X., Ma, W.Y.: Mining interesting locations and travel seuuences from GPS trajectories. In: Proceedings of the 18th International Conference on World Wide Web, pp. 791–800 (2009)

16. Zheng, V.W., Zheng, Y., Xie, X., Yang, Q.: Collaborative location and activity recommendations with gps history data. In: Proceedings of the 19th International World Wide Web Conference, pp. 1029–1038 (2010)

17. Zheng, Y., Capra, L., Wolfson, O., Yang, H.: Urban computing: concepts, methodologies, and applications. ACM Transactions on Intelligent Systems and Technology $5(3)$, 38–55 (2014)

18. Zheng, Y., Xie, X.: Learning travel recommendations from user-generated gps traces. ACM Transactions on Intelligent Systems and Technology $2(1)$, 2 (2012)

19. Ying, J.C., Kuo, W.N., Tseng, V.S.: Mining user check-in behavior with a random walk for urban point-of-interest Recommendations. ACM Transactions on Intelligent Systems and Technology $5(1)$, 2 (2014)

20. Herlocker, J., Konstan, J., Borchers, A., Riedl, J.: An algorithmic framework for performing collaborative filtering. In: Proceedings of the 1999 Conference on Research and Development in Information Retrieval (1999)

A Partitioning Algorithm for Solving Capacitated Arc Routing Problem in Ways of Ranking First Cutting Second

Wei Zhang, Lining Xing[⊠], Ting Xi, Lei He, and Jinyuan Liu

College of Information System and Management,
National University of Defense Technology, Changsha 410073, China
{823760217,42242354,1243604953,603385430,382444526}@qq.com
http://www.springer.com/lncs

Abstract. Capacitated Arc Routing Problem (CARP) is one of the hot issues of logistics research. Specifically, Ranking First Cutting Second (RFCS) could be used. This research proposed a novel partitioning algorithm - the Multi-Label algorithm which obtained better TSP paths meeting the backpack limit on the basis of a complete TSP return. In addition, by experimental verification on questions in the standard question database, the experimental results showed that compared with general partitioning algorithms, for the same complete TSP return, many TSP paths with the shortest total length could be obtained by the Multi-Label algorithm.

Keywords: Partitioning algorithm · Capacitated arc routing problem · Ranking first cutting second

1 Introduction

The Capacity Arc Routing Problem (CARP) is one of the hot issues of logistics research, originating from the Seven Bridges Problem two and a half century ago[1,2]. The more general problem model referred to today is proposed by Golden and Wong in 1981 and they also proved that this problem is an NP-hard problem[3,4].

CARP can be solved by transforming it into CVRP (Capacity Vehicle Routing Problem) so as to make the arc of CARP equivalent with points of CVRP. Specifically, CFRS or RFCS (Rank First Cut Second) can be used to solve the problem[5]. In RFCS, each arc is regarded as points to carry out TSP ranking and then the partitioning algorithm is used to partition a complete TSP return into many TSP paths which meet the backpack limit for generating an optimization scheme.

The partitioning algorithm is a very important link in an arc routing problem[6,7]. Under different segmentation principles, different distance values of the same path may be obtained. For example, in the genetic algorithm, its fitness

© Springer International Publishing Switzerland 2015
S. Zhang et al. (Eds.): KSEM 2015, LNAI 9403, pp. 732–737, 2015.
DOI: 10.1007/978-3-319-25159-2_67

values are different, while in the ant colony algorithm, its optimal paths are different[8]. It has an important follow-up effect on the next iteration[9,10].

Partitioning algorithms in combination with optimization algorithms are also designed by researchers at home and abroad. Alain Hertz (2005) put forwards a partitioning algorithm of TSP paths that meet the upper bound of the number of vehicles[11]. C. PRINS*, N. LABADI and M. REGHIOUI(2008) proposed the Greedy randomized adaptive search procedure in the course of solving CVRP and CARP[12]. Yu Bin,Yang Zhong-Zhen and Yao Baozhen (2009) optimized the partitioning results in combination with the ACO algorithm[13]. Furthermore, Li Xiangyang (2004) pointed out that important warehouse points in the partitioning algorithm should be integrated into the genetic algorithm so as to solve CVRP[14].

It is discovered in this paper that the segmentation efficiency of adopting common segmentation principles is low and the realization of partitioning algorithms proposed in combination with intelligent optimization is complex[15,16]. Thus, a partitioning algorithm, the Multi-Label algorithm which is appropriate for solving CARP in the way of RFCS and partitioning a complete TSP path into several TSP paths meeting the backpack limit is proposed. The experimental results of comparing it with ordinary segmentation principles indicate that for the same complete TSP return, many TSP paths with the shortest total length can be obtained by the Multi-Label algorithm. The rest of this paper is organized as follow:Section 2 is Multi-Label partitioning algorithm,the algorithm cut the route considering the combination of the formal car and latter car ;Section 3 is Simulation experiment;Section 4 is the conclusion and some discussion.

2 Multi-label Partitioning Algorithm

Multi-Label algorithm is a partitioning algorithm similar to traversal algorithm. Nevertheless, compared with the division by traversing the full path, Multi-Label algorithm is simpler. By successively scanning every point (or side) of the full path, this algorithm inserts assumption based on the optimal partition scheme obtained in last point (or side) and then rejects the exceed cars capacity constraint of this point (or side). Figure 1 shows the information of the full path, in which the circle is the starting point and the box is the number of service point (or side) in algorithm model. Figure 2,3,4,5,6 is the route divisional example of several partitioning algorithms and Multi-Label algorithm. The numbers above the box are the service demand of this point (or side) while he numbers under the arrows are the distance of two points (or sides). It is assumed that the distance from the starting point to all points is 5 and the car capacity is 10.

In figure 2, the division is carried out by using the principle of assigning next car after previous car reaches capacity limit. The total driving distance of the two cars is $21 + 8 = 29$.

In figure 3, the division is implemented by using the principle of assigning next car after previous car reaches a certain percentage of capacity limit. Here, 80% is taken as the percentage. The total driving distance is $12 + 11 + 5 = 28$. In

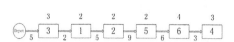

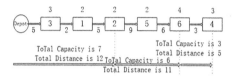

Fig. 1. The information of the full path

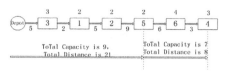

Fig. 2. Assigning next car after previous car reaches capacity limit

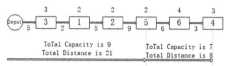

Fig. 3. Assigning next car after previous car reaches 80% of capacity limit

Fig. 4. Assigning next car after the ratio of the distance to nest service point (or side) and the demanded quality of this point (or side) is larger than 10

figure 4, the division is carried out by adopting the principle of assigning next car after the ratio of the distance to nest service point and the demanded quantity of this point is larger than a certain value. Here, the ratio is 10. The total driving distance is $21 + 8 = 29$. In figure 5, like the division in figure 4. Here, the ratio is 4. The total driving distance is $12 + 14 = 26$. In figure 6, Multi-Label algorithm is applied to the division. The total driving distance is $12 + 5 + 8 = 25$. Design procedure of Multi-Label algorithm: In figures, four numbers in every row of every task of Multi-Label algorithm respectively represent: Car Number, Car Carrying Capacity, Car Length, Total Distance of This Stage.

$Project_i$ means Project Number; $Capacity_i$ means Car Carrying Capacity $Length_i$ means Car Length; $TLength_i$ means Total Distance of This Stage

Step 1: Traverse each segmental arc (Arc_i) in the complete TSP path successively and generate a new project ($Project_i$) at the same time. Capacity of the car ($Capacity_i$) is the weight to be serviced at current segmental arc, length of the car ($Length_i$) is the distance between the initial point and the starting point of this segmental arc, and the shortest length of the path ($TLength_i$) is the sum ($TLength_i + Length_i$) of the shortest length of the last segmental arc and the length of this car.

Step 2: If the last residual capacity of the car in existing project can serve the segmental arc, change the capacity ($Capacity_i$) of the car in the project to be the sum ($Capacity_i + q(T_{i,j})$) of existing capacity and the service capacity of the segmental arc, change the length ($Length_i$) of the car in the project to be the sum ($Length_i + dc(T_{i,j})$) of existing length of the car and the distance between the last segmental arc and the new segmental arc, and change the shortest length of the path ($Tlength_i$) to be the sum ($TLength_i + dc(T_{i,j})$) of existing shortest path and the distance between the last segmental arc and new segmental arc.

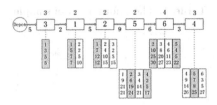

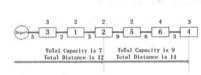

Fig. 5. Assigning next car after the ratio of the distance to nest service point and the demanded quality of this point (or side) is larger than 4

Fig. 6. Multi-label Algorithm

Step 3: Implement the above steps to the last segmental arc, use the project which has the shortest total path length ($Tlength_i$) among all projects as the complete TSP path segmentation project.

3   Simulation Experiment

To better verify the performance of Multi-Label algorithm in path partition some typical living samples are taken so as to compare algorithms in virtue of algorithm realization. The test data are chosen from standard CVRP living samples in http://www.uv.es/belengue/carp.html [17]. The whole compare of the algorithm result between Multi-Label algorithm and other algorithm can be seen in Table 1. And The whole compare of the algorithm cost between can be seen in Table 2.

The service side number of living example is taken as the number to randomly generate 1000 full paths. Car capacity constraint, service demand of service sides and distance between service sides should be subject to the living example. Every full path should be divided according to the five principles above. To improve the accounting efficiency, length of the arc itself is not taken into account in the accounting process, and finally the optimized value of each partitioning algorithm is found.

Optimization results of the partitioning algorithm obtained from the ascending order of an example scale are shown in Figure 7. As the example scale increases, differences among algorithms also increase. Compared with other algorithms, the Multi-Label algorithm has a significant advantage. On the premise of meeting the vehicle capacity constraint, the algorithm in which another vehicle will be arranged for service when the ratio of the distance from the current location of a vehicle to the next service point (or side) and the service demand of this point (or side) is better than the algorithms in which another vehicle will be arranged for service after one vehicle reaches the capacity constraint and another vehicle will be arranged for service after one vehicle reaches a certain percent of the capacity constraint.

Comparison results of time cost of various partitioning algorithms obtained from the ascending order of an example scale are displayed in Figure 8. An

Table 1. The information of sample

Name	Number of point	Number of arc	Capacity	Total Capacity
Gdb1	12	22	5	252
Gdb2	12	26	5	291
Gdb3	12	22	5	233
Gdb4	11	19	5	238
Gdb5	13	26	5	316
Gdb6	12	22	5	260
Gdb7	12	22	5	262
Gdb8	27	46	27	210
Gdb9	27	51	27	219
Gdb10	12	25	10	252
Val1A	24	39	200	220
Val2A	24	34	180	256
Val3A	24	35	80	89
Val4A	41	69	225	465
Val5A	34	65	220	510
Val6A	31	50	170	297
Val7A	40	66	200	352
Val8A	30	63	200	483
Val9A	50	92	235	405
Val10A	50	97	250	585

Table 2. Computational results of multi-label algorithm

Name	Multi-Label	Normal	80%percentage	Ratio10	Ratio4
Gdb1	129	180.4	177.5	141	138
t/s	1.129	1.379	1.634	1.519	2.027
Gdb2	155.6	213.3	215.4	170.7	174.7
t/s	1.366	1.488	1.437	1.614	1.555
Gdb3	121.7	189.6	190.6	132.9	139.8
t/s	1.04	1.239	1.804	1.252	1.199
Gdb4	108	180.6	181.7	127	127.7
t/s	1.112	1.233	1.101	1.589	1.234
Gdb5	181.8	248.5	260.7	195.8	202.8
t/s	1.278	2.15	1.694	1.883	1.659
Gdb6	131.8	179.9	174.4	139.7	149.1
t/s	1.448	2.773	1.484	1.659	1.644
Gdb7	131	220.5	188.8	133	153
t/s	1.073	1.807	1.922	2.105	1.542
Gdb8	283	435.5	433.4	408.2	382.4
t/s	2.384	2.192	1.891	1.45	1.279
Gdb9	258.8	359.4	343.3	317.4	308.6
t/s	2.783	2.035	2.621	1.939	1.466
Gdb10	101.3	173.7	194.5	150.8	108.3
t/s	1.432	1.184	1.902	2.001	2.389
Val1A	183.8	295.5	295.5	295.5	292.1
t/s	3.857	1.538	1.492	1.496	1.547
Val2A	306.4	377.2	369.2	377.2	342.3
t/s	3.388	1.308	1.335	1.143	1.304
Val3A	98.5	128.3	130.3	128.3	124.5
t/s	2.115	1.371	1.366	1.448	1.303
Val4A	646.4	811.2	849.4	792.4	735.4
t/s	4.111	1.486	1.629	1.733	1.662
Val5A	644.7	773.6	781.6	758.6	726.7
t/s	3.812	1.669	1.859	2.374	1.555
Val6A	285.4	438	441.4	438	428
t/s	2.803	1.525	1.665	1.479	1.479
Val7A	409.6	631.5	641.3	631.5	625.2
t/s	3.694	1.591	1.778	1.51	1.527
Val8A	543.8	703.5	710.6	703.5	685.5
t/s	3.419	1.689	1.659	1.473	1.466
Val9A	560.2	765.4	789.4	765.4	737.4
t/s	6.016	1.751	1.792	1.605	1.667
Val10A	723.4	850.4	852.4	850.4	817.1
t/s	6.751	1.584	1.414	1.574	1.86

uptrend is presented in the growth of time cost in different example scales. Due to features of example points and arcs, time cost does not increase strictly. When the example size is small, time cost of the Multi-Label algorithm is slightly less than that of other algorithms. With the increase of the example size, the increase of time cost of the Multi-Label algorithm is greater than that of other algorithms.

4　Conclusion

The partitioning algorithms used in solving CARP with the RFCS method are studied in this paper. For the same complete TSP return, final results of CARP might be different if different partitioning algorithms are used. A good partitioning algorithm can partition the shortest total path of CARP for a TSP return. In this paper, the Multi-Label partitioning algorithm is put forward and several common partitioning algorithms are provided at the same time. By contrast tests of questions in the standard question database, it is proved that compared with other partitioning algorithms, the Multi-Label algorithm boasts better efficiency of segmentation.

In addition, only segmentation of the same vehicle model is considered here. However, in actual life, many vehicle models can cooperate with each other for delivery. Therefore, it is necessary to carry out further research about how to expand the usage field of the Multi-Label algorithm.

References

1. Dantzig, G., Ramser, J.: The truck dispatching problem. Management Science **6**, 80–91 (1959)
2. Christofides, N.: The optimum traversal of a graph. Omega **1**(6), 719–732 (1973)
3. Gloden, B.L., Wong, R.T.: The truck dispatching problem. Networks **6**, 11 (1981)
4. Hirabayashi, R., Saruwatari, Y., Nishida, N.: Tour construction algorithm for the capacitated arc routing problem. Operations Research **1**(48), 129–135 (2000)
5. Liu, M., Singh, H.K., Ray, T.: Application specific instance generator and a memetic algorithm for capacitated arc routing problems. Transportation Research Part C **43**, 249–266 (2014)
6. Brandão, J., Eglese, R.: A deterministic tabu search algorithm for the capacitated arc routing problem. Computers & Operations Research **35**, 1112–1126 (2008)
7. Christofides, N.: Computational experiments with algorithms for a class of routing problems. Computers and Operations Research **1**(10), 47–59 (1983)
8. Santos, L., Coutinho-Rodrigues, J., Current, J.R.: An improved ant colony optimization based algorithm for the capacitated arc routing problem. Transportation Research Part B **44**, 246–266 (2010)
9. Chen, S., Golden, B., Wong, R., Zhong, H.: Arc-Routing Models for Small-Package Local Routing. Transportation Science **1**(43), 43–55 (2009)
10. Bode, C., Irnich, S.: Arc-routing Models For Small-package Local Routing. Operations Research **5**(60), 1167–1182 (2012)
11. Hertz, A.: Recent trends in arc routing. Graph Theory, Combinatorics and Algorithms: Interdisciplinary Applications **1**, 215–236 (2005)
12. Prins*, C., Labadi, N., Reghioui, M.: Tour splitting algorithms for vehicle routing problems. International Journal of Production Research **2**(47), 507–535 (2009)
13. Bin, Y., Zhong-Zhen, Y., Baozhen, Y.: An improved ant colony optimization for vehicle routing problem. International Journal of Production Research **196**, 171–176 (2009)
14. Xiang-yang, L.: Genetic algorithm for VRP. International Journal of Production Research **2**(25)
15. Polacek, M., Doerner, K.E., Hartl, R.F., Maniezzo, V.: A variable neighborhood search for the capacitated arc routing problem with intermediate facilities. Journal of Heuristics **14**(5), 405–423 (2008)
16. Laporte, G., Musmanno, R., Vocaturo, E.: An Adaptive Large Neighbourhood Search Heuristic for the Capacitated Arc-Routing Problem with Stochastic Demands. Transportafion Science **160**(1), 139–153 (2009)
17. Huang, S.-H., Lin, T.-H.: Using An t Colony Optimization to solve Periodic Arc Routing Problem with Refill Points. Journal of Industrial and Production Engineering **31**(7), 441–451 (2014)

UBS: A Novel News Recommendation System Based on User Behavior Sequence

Haoye Dong, Jia Zhu$^{(\boxtimes)}$, Yong Tang, Chuanhua Xu, Rui Ding,
and Lingxiao Chen

School of Computer, South China Normal University, Guangzhou, China
{dong,jzhu,ytang,chxu,ding,chenlingxiao}@m.scnu.edu.cn

Abstract. News recommendation recently has attracted wide spread research attention because of the fast propagation of information on the Internet. Due to the large volume of information, a recommendation system which can provide the most important and useful information is required. Most of existing researches focus on providing recommendation based on news contents and predict the category of news only, which is inefficient if the news pool is very large or contains a lot of noisy data. In this study, we propose a novel news recommendation system called UBS, which recommends personalized news based on User Behavior Sequence (UBS) with high efficiency. We formulate the mining problem of user behavior sequence for Internet news reading, which can significantly enhance the performance of recommendation. Experimental validation was conducted using real datasets that obtained from news website. The results show that UBS can provide reasonable news recommendation compared to content-based recommendation as well as collaborative filtering.

Keywords: Behavior sequence pattern · News recommendation · Similarity ranking · Personalization

1 Introduction

Recently, news reading has become an indispensable part of our life. For instance, Google News and CaiXin[1] news, have become increasingly prevalent due to provide abundant of news from various information sources. In the face of vast amount of information, recommending news quickly and precisely which is a key challenge of news websites to provide news that users are interested in [1,2]. At present, although most of the research has been devoted to solve those problems already, such as content based recommendation [1,13,15,18], collaborative filtering [3,14,16] and hybrid version of all above [7]. Those approaches improve the efficiency and accuracy of the news recommendation in specific areas. Besides, recall that [1–6,15,16] transformed the news recommendation into a problem of category assignment, which leads to an actual problem is that users cannot get

---

[1] http://www.caixin.com

© Springer International Publishing Switzerland 2015
S. Zhang et al. (Eds.): KSEM 2015, LNAI 9403, pp. 738–750, 2015.
DOI: 10.1007/978-3-319-25159-2_68

the information they want easily. Therefore, we found that the ultimate goal of news recommendation system is to provide news articles to users rather than the category of news articles. Users may be concerned about how interested the recommended news articles are. Hence, in this paper, we split the datasets into training datasets, with the testing datasets which are the users' last clicked time and the others are training datasets. And this news recommendation system's goal is to recommend the users' next clicked news article to individual users.

Furthermore, in some applications [1–11], they failed to consider users current situations, and thus ignored the different preferences of users in different contexts. For instance, when a user visits a website, the context is reflected in the sequence of user's behaviors, which the user has clicked in his/her current interaction. In order to avoid obtaining unreliable results, our aim is to build a scalable online news recommendation engine that could be used for making personalized news recommendations on a large web property. In this paper, we try to investigate the unsolved problem of mining behaviors sequence pattern. A key task for news recommendation in this paper is to devise an algorithm base on users' sequential behaviors to calculate the high-quality approximate result efficiently with low cost.

The rest of the paper is organized as follows. Section 2 reviews related work. Section 3 presents the proposed mining algorithm in detail. Section 4 shows experimental results on real datasets. Section 5 concludes the paper and discusses future directions.

2   Related Work

Recently, news recommendation has been extensively researched in the literature. Meanwhile, sequence pattern mining has been well studied in the literature in the context of deterministic data, but not for recommending news base on user behavior sequence. From the methodology perspective, recommendation methods can be categorized into three different groups: collaborative filtering [3, 14, 16], content-based methods [1, 13, 15, 18] and hybrid approaches [7].

Collaborative Filtering. Collaborative filtering does not consider the content of a news item, but uses the opinions of other similar users to generate recommendations. Collaboraive filtering [3, 14, 16] has been widely used as a personalized recommendation algorithm in news recommendation system. [3] recommends news to a user by considering others' ratings of news articles. [16] may be insufficient to simply represent users' profiles by a bag of words for capturing the reading preference of users. [3] is essentially a collaborative filtering method, using MinHash clustering, PLSI and visitation counts.

Content-Based Method. This method is the extend and development of collaborative filtering, which is mainly based on the results of information extract and filter, and they recommend items according to the content characters of recommended items. For this reason, [13] proposed a method based on two aspects: users' profile and the features associated with the products or services in the system. Those methods usually employ clutering algorithm to cluster items and recommend items to users which are in the same cluster. Such as the hierarchal clustering [16], word2vec clustering [18] and so on. [1] proposed a method to conduct analysis on the traces of a users' activities and then predicting users' interested news based on Bayesian framework. [15] tells us the only focus on the interested news article to users could be regressive, and uses the "submodularity" property to model news selection problem.

Hybrid Recommendation Approaches. For better results some recommendation systems combine different techniques of collaborative approaches and content based approaches [7]. To solve the inability of both content filtering and collaborative filtering, many researchers investigate the feasibility of combining these two types of methods, and propose hybrid solutions to news recommendation [16]. However, most hybrid filtering methods either focus on analyzing explicit ratings in the data, or assume that demographic and other auxiliary information of users are available and other auxiliary information of users are available. Although it is possible to incorporate user behaviors into these methods, they still suffer from the difficulty of comprehensively capsuling highorder relations within news reading community[26].

Others. In order to solve scalability and sparseness problem, [22] proposes recommendation algorithm based on item quality and user rating preferences. In some real-life scenarios, in order to activate users reading motivations, [23] provides approach on the evolution of user interests in real life, in which using absorbing random walk model to increase the diversity of the recommended news list. Furthermore, [25] introduces a algorithm of news recommendation systems based on context trees, which analyzes the present browsing behaviour anonymous visitors. [24] investigates the feasibility of integrating content-based methods, collaborative filtering and information diffusion models by employing probabilistic matrix factorization techniques. Moreover, [24] proposed news recommendation framework via implicit social experts, in which the opinions of potential influence on virtual social networks. [21] pointed out that traditional recommendation system failed to consider users' current situations and neglected the different preferences of users in different contexts. Besides, [21] put forward the concept of Sequential Topic Patterns (STPs) and formulate the mining problem of User-aware Rare STPs (URSTPs), which can be apply in many real-life scenarios, such as personalized context-aware recomendation. But the application in news recommendation has not been used in their research.

Yet, to the best of our knowledge, there is no work related to analysing the users' sequential behaviors in personalized news recommendation system. As the experiments section shown, the original and simple algorithms, which are not as effective and efficient as those in this paper.

3   Proposed Mining Algorithm

In this section, we will firstly define some major concepts, then we will present how we formalize our model for analysis in mathematical terms, and describe the architecture of personalized news recommendation system.

3.1   Definitions

As we discussed in the introduction, one of the goals of this paper is to effectively and efficiently select news which users are interested from a large volume of published news articles. In this paper, we define news article as follows:

Definition 1 (News Article). *Let* $N = \{(nid_1, t_1), (nid_2, t_2), \ldots, (nid_n, t_n)\}$ *be a news article set, where* nid_i *represents user* i *and* $t_i = \{term_1, term_2, \ldots\}$ *is a term set of news title. Then, Let* $T = \{t_1, t_2, \ldots, t_n\}$ *be a news title set.*

In order to represent users' behavior sequence, we define a terminology called news sequence:

Definition 2 (News Sequence). *Let* $NS = \{ns_1, ns_2, \ldots, ns_n\}$ *be a news sequence which is make of readers' history sequential clicked on news, where* $ns_i = \{nid_1, nid_2, \ldots, nid_k\}$ *is one among them.*

To avoid any unnecessary confusion, in this paper, we define user profile in news recommendation system as follows:

Definition 3 (User Profile). *Let* $U = \{u_1, u_2, \ldots, u_m\}$ *be a set of users, where* $u_i = (uid_i, nidList_i)$, *with* uid_i *is the user's id and* $nidList_i$ *is history news set.*

For the sake of presentation, we define recommended news set as follows:

Definition 4 (Recommended News Set). *At last, we generate a news id set recommended to each users. Define it as* $RS = \{(u_1, ns_1), (u_2, ns_2), \ldots, (u_n, ns_n)\}$.

In our experiments, we set up some rules to obtain optimum value for the algorithms. Therefore, we define them as follows:

Definition 5 (Set Contain Rule). *Suppose* S_1 *is a set of terms that belongs to news title* t_1 *and* S_2 *is another set of the terms that belongs to news title* t_2; *if* $S_1 \subseteq S_2$, *then t1 and t2 are very likely to refer to the same thing.*

Definition 6 (Set Similarity Rule). *Suppose* S_1 *is a set representation of the term* t_1, *and* S_2 *is a set representation of the term* t_2. *We use both Jaccard coefficient and longest common subsequence (LCS) to compute the similarity between two sets, because it considers not only the single longest common substring, but also the different patterns in different sequential terms there.*

In order to represent news articles which users are most interested in, we call them hot news queue and define them as follows:

Definition 7 (Hot News Queue). *Suppose Hot(nid) is a function represen-tation of how frequently the news be click is. click(nid) represents the news was clicked or not. Hot(nid) is define as followed Eq. (1).*

$$Hot\,(nid) = \sum_{i=1}^{n} click\,(nid) \tag{1}$$

Hence, let $HNQ = \{nid_1, nid_2, \ldots, nid_n\}$ be a hot news queue.

3.2 Mining Algorithm

Generally speaking, traditional recommendation systems have been extensively used based on content-based and users' history profiles. However,they failed to consider users' current situations and thus neglected the different profiles of users in different history contexts. Such as, the users' sequential behaviors of the click history, which represent the users' current situations, plays an important role in the recommendation system. For example, when a user visits a news website, the context is reflected by the sequence of news articles which the user has clicked in his/her current situation. Therefore, we apply our approach to integrate users' sequential click behaviors and use contain rules and compute similarity by using Jaccard. For the sake of presentation, we design the main process for sequential behaviors pattern is shown in Fig. 1.

Fig. 1. Users' Sequential Behaviors

Fig. 1 tells us that the two sequential click history records were very similar, due to set contain rule (Define. 5) and set similarity rule (Define. 6). According to them, the users in the picture have the common term (100958525) and longest common subsequence ($< 100658325, 100755832, 100658666, 100958525 >$), with computing the similarity by the Eq. (2). We conclude that the two sequen-tial click history set were similar. Hence, we can predict user2 will click the news(10095832) which is the last on in user1's sequential click history set.

$$Similarity(U_i, N_i) = \frac{\alpha * J(U_i, N_i) + \beta * L(U_i.nidList, N_i) + \gamma * Hot(N_i)}{\sqrt{\alpha^2 + \beta^2 + \gamma^2}} \tag{2}$$

$$J(A, B) = \frac{|A \cap B|}{|A \cup B|} \tag{3}$$

Eq. (3) computes the users' genuine interested news based on the click dis-tributions in current situation. Eq. (2) computes the similarity between user's most interested news and other news, with the parameter α, β, γ which can help Eq. (2) to get optimum value. The length of LCS can be computed by the Eq. (4).

$$L[i,j] = \begin{cases} 0 & \text{if } i = 0 \text{ } or \text{ } j = 0 \\ L[i-1,j-1]+1 & \text{if } i,j > 0 \text{ } and \text{ } x_i = y_j \\ max(L[i-1,j], L[i,j-1]) & \text{if } i,j > 0 \text{ } and \text{ } x_i \neq y_j \end{cases} \quad (4)$$

In this section, we propose the UBS Mining Model Architecture as shown in Fig. 2. Initially, we should update the users' news sequence set and history news of all users regularly. So that we can obtain latest datasets which can reflect the real current situation of users. Firstly, in order to get better useful information from the datasets with stopwords and illegal character, it is necessary to preprocess the datasets. Secondly, we should extract the sequence news from each user, we define it as NS. Then, we use the Jaccard coefficient and LCS to compute similarity between two users in U. When the sililarity computing is completed, we should set up the shrehold (θ_r) to limit the number of similar users and then group news into one set from similar users. By now, we have been generated similar news set ($simSet$) of each user from his/her similar users. Secondly, we extract user from U circularly and then select his/her most interested news as fave news set ($faveSet$). Thirdly, it is necessary to compute and generate frequent news queue ($hotNews$) by Eq. (1), due to guarantee the recommendation quality. Finally, there are following significant steps to take which include contain rule and similarity computing. If the term of $simSet$ is in $faveSet$, then extract it and compute similarity with $faveSet$, with grouping them into $mostFaveSet$. At last, it iterates over the $mostFaveSet$ that if $mostFaveSet$'s term in $hotNews$, then group it into recommended news set.

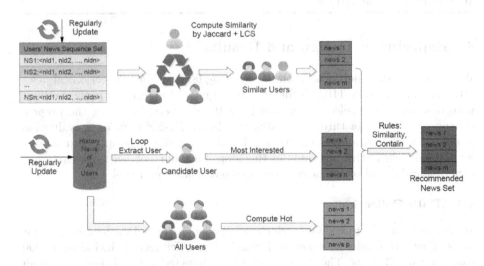

Fig. 2. Overview of UBS Architecture

According to the architecture of UBS (Fig. 2), we provide a comprehensive investigation of persionalized news recommendation and employing efficient processing algorithm which is shown in Algorithm 1.

In Algorithm 1, we need to set up a parameter θ_r in order to limit the maximum number of recommended news to each user. In addition, the value of θ_r has to be changed in different users because the similarity of two users are different under different rules, as we mentioned in the previous section. Quite obviously, the lower θ_r is, the more effective of recommendation obtain. In our proposed model, we set the value of θ_r is 1 by default. In most cases, parameters are tuned based on some empirical studies. The sensitivity of the parameters will be a major task as our future research work.

Algorithm 1. news recommendation base on UBS

Input: $NQ = \{< nid_1, nid_5, \ldots, nid_q >, \ldots, < nid_6, nid_2, \ldots, nid_r >\}$;
$\quad\quad U = \{(u_1, nidList_1), (u_2, nidList_2), \ldots, (u_m, nidList_m)\}$; and
$\quad\quad$ recommend set size threshold θ_r.
Output: $R = \{(u_1, nidList_1), (u_2, nidList_2), \ldots, (u_m, nidList_m)\}$
1 $recommendList \leftarrow \emptyset$
2 $hotNewsSet \leftarrow Hot(U, 50)$
3 $similarUserNewsMap \leftarrow ComputeSimilarity(NQ, U, 0.5)$
4 **for** $i \leftarrow 1$ **to** n **do**
5 $\quad faveNewsSet \leftarrow similarUserNewsMap.get(u_i)$
6 $\quad recomSet \leftarrow faveNewsSet \cap hotNewsSet$
7 $\quad$ **for** $j \leftarrow 1$ **to** θ_r **do**
8 $\quad\quad recomPair \leftarrow (u_i, recomSet)$
9 $\quad\quad recommendList.add(recomPair)$
10 **return** $recommendList$

---

4 Experiment Design and Results

We carry out our experimental studies by using large volume collections of news articles, which include 116,225 click records of individual users. Firstly, we start with describing and selecting futures from the datasets, including the preprocessing, combining features. Secondly, we choose F1-Measure as a evaluation of our recommendation system model. Thirdly, in order to support our model, we compare with other methods in this step. Last but not least, we carry out experimental detail of our news articles recommendation model.

4.1 Data Collection

We crawled data from CaiXin[2], which is considered the main source of data for news. Then, we randomly generate 116,225 users' click records including 10,000 users and 6,183 news. The datasets mainly conducted news clicked time from

---

[2] http://www.caixin.com

user_id	news_id	news_published_time	news_clicked_time	news_titile
1698962	100658325	1396018020	1396022782	中央巡视组要求广东复查茂名窝案
9106173	100650795	1394860263	1394871962	奥巴马重申不接受克里米亚全民公决

Fig. 3. Some Columns of Datasets

March 01, 2014 to March 31, 2014, while news published time ranges from June 05, 2000 to March 31, 2014. Fig. 3 summarizes some important details of our datasets.

In order to remove some unexpected noise and ensure the quality of the recommendation system experiment. We carried out some preprocessing steps on the crawled news texts:

1) Removing invalid records, such as the records which include empty column, the invalid news published time and clicked time.
2) Using ICTCLAS[3](Institute of Computing Technology, Chinese Lexical Analysis System) Chinese word segmentation tools to process the news title and extract representative words from each title.
3) Removing stopwords.
4) Removing the news have never been clicked.

After preprocessed, it turns out that there are 9,991 valid users and 101,225 news records are stored, with 5,653 news. We conducted analysis on the datasets based on the news article title, news article content, click history, news published time and news clicked time. We found out users' sequential behaviors play an important role in data futures. Therefore, base on this observation, we extract the users' sequential click records group by news id and users' id, as shown in set NS = $\{ns_1, ns_2, \ldots, ns_k\}$.

4.2 Model Evaluation

In this subsection, we evaluate the performance of our algorithms using real datasets. Since our work is innovative and focus on users' sequential behavior, we will show its effectiveness by the three standard measure, including Precision, Recall, F1-Score as the following Eq. (5) shown.

$$F1 = \frac{2PR}{P+R} \tag{5}$$

$$Precision = \frac{\sum_{i=1}^{N} hitNews(i)}{\sum_{i=1}^{N} preNews(i)} \tag{6}$$

$$Recall = \frac{\sum_{i=1}^{N} hitNews(i)}{\sum_{i=1}^{M} totalNews(i)} \tag{7}$$

---

[3] http://ictclas.nlpir.org

Where N is the number of users who take part in the recommendation. On one hand, value of the function $hitNews(i)$ is either 0 or 1, so that $\sum_{i=1}^{N} hitNews(i)$ is the number of news of user i being recommended correctly. On the other hand, function $preNews(i)$ represents the number news which was recommended to user i and $\sum_{i=1}^{N} preNews(i)$ is the total number of news articles which recommend to users. The function $totalNews(i)$ means the number of news which user i views really in testting datasets. Hence, this formula $\sum_{i=1}^{M} totalNews(i)$ represents the number of all news articles in testing datasets.

4.3   Comparison with Other Methods

We implement serveral baseline methods on recommendation system and conducted several experiments with different vector size and feature selection methods. In order to ensure the fair comparison, the parameters of these baseline methods are optimal in our experiment. The results are show in Fig. 4.

- HAC (hierarchal clustering [16]): This method uses word segmentation tools to process the news title and extract representative words from each title. Scanning the preprocessed title, We make a rule that states that two clusters can be merged if they have common phrase. Then compare news which users have been clicked, to generate the recommended news list.
- W2V (based-word2vec clustering [17,18]): In this approach, the clusters are generated by word2vec[4] tools which implement by deep learning network, then cluster of news id were contructed. Lastly, recommending the news in cluster which has never been click to the user.
- UBCF (user-based collaborative filtering [11,12]): This is a traditional approach to the personalized news recommendation system. It compute the similarity almong the users, then select similar users for candidate user, with generating recommended news article from the similar users.
- IBCF (item-based collaborative filtering [13]): The method is contrary to the UBCF, which is due to computing the similarity among the item not the user. It chooses user's last click news article as his/her most interested news category and generates recommended news from them.

In Fig. 4, we have the following observations that in traditional personalized news recommendation approaches, they handle this problem as a taxonomy problem, which goal is to findout the correct category of news article. However, generally and in reality, users want to find the news they are interested in, rather than news category. Meanwhile, Fig. 4 shows the result. As we expect, the more news article were recommended to users, the less percision and F1-Score it has. On the contray, the percentage of recall increase exponentially. In a word, Fig. 4 tells us that those methods are not suitable for recommending news in real life.

In order to verify the effectiveness of our proposed mining model, we show the experimental results in the following Fig. 5(a), Fig. 5(b) and Fig. 5(c). The horizontal axis of the all figures means the top ranked news articles being recommmended to users.

---

[4] http://code.google.com/p/word2vec

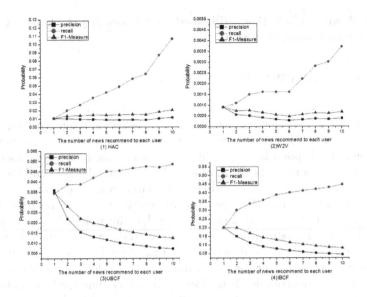

Fig. 4. Comparision with Baseline Algorithm.

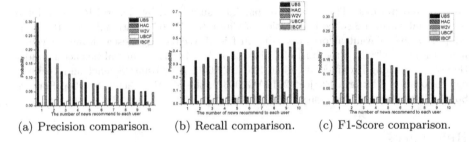

(a) Precision comparison.   (b) Recall comparison.   (c) F1-Score comparison.

Fig. 5. Performance Comparison of Different Methods.

Note that, in Fig. 5, the probabilities of W2V in all figures are almost close to zero, with HAC, IBCF and UBCF are obtaining low probabilities too, which tells us that the W2V, HAC, IBCF and UBCF aren't suitabe for recommending news in such condition. Fig. 5 tells us that they failed to consider users' current situations, and thus ignored the different preferences of users in different contexts.

Although the probabilities in Fig. 5 seems not very large, considering that we have set evaluation rule that predict the users' next news article being click. Yet, the other methods's goal are clustering the news articles in different category and then predict the news correct category. Frankly speaking, predicting user's next behavior is more significant than predicting news category in real life. Note that for most data points in the graph, all of the methods are outperformed when recommend one news article to each user respectively. From the findings we obtained, we conclude that UBS-based model does play a significant role in the news recommendation system.

5 Conclusions and Future Work

We propose a novel framework for personalized news recommendation system, which provides a new method based on user behavior sequence, due to the sequence of users' behaviors are reflecting the current situation of users in reality. Another remarkable point is the real-life evaluation of the recommendation models, which lets user's next clicked id of news be a testing dataset, and the others be the trianing dataset. Our experiments on large volume collections of news articles, which are from public news website and have provide positive results. The experiments based on real data sets show that the approach is very effective and efficient for personalized news recommendation system on the Internet.

In our future work, we will make a plan for studying the extension of our UBS's framework. Moreover, based on our mining model and experiments, we will try to define more complex behaviors, such as including the length of clicked time. What's more, we will apply our UBS model to practice and develop practical tools about our approach.

Acknowledgments. This research is partially supported by General Research Fund of National Natural Science Foundation of China (61272067), National High–It can be adopted some relevant algorithms using in friend Technology Research and Development Program ("863" Program) of China (2013AA01A212), Natural Science Foundation of Guangdong Province of China (S2012030006242), Foshan Science and Technology Innovation Platform Project(2013AG10032), the Youth Teacher Startup Fund of South China Normal University (No. 14KJ18).

References

1. Liu, J., Dolan, P., Pedersen, E.: Personalized news recommendation based on click behavior. In: Intelligent User Interfaces, pp. 31–40 (2010)
2. Li, L., Wang, D., Zhu, S., Li, T.: Personalized news recommendation: A review and an experimental investigation. Journal of Computer Science and Technology **26**(5), 754–766 (2011)
3. Das, A.S., Datar, M., Garg, A., et al.: Google news personalization: scalable online collaborative filtering. In: Proceedings of the 16th International Conference on World Wide Web (2007)
4. Marung, U., Theera-Umpon, N., Auephanwiriyakul, S.: Applying memetic algorithm-based clustering to recommender system with high sparsity problem. Journal of Central South University September **21**(9), 3541–3550 (2014)
5. Gao, H., Tang, J., Liu, H.: Addressing the cold-start problem in location recommendation using geo-social correlations. Data Mining and Knowledge Discovery (2014)
6. Kavitha Devi, M.K., Venkatesh, P.: Smoothing approach to alleviate the meager rating problem in collaborative recommender systems. Future Generation Computer Systems **29**, 262–270 (2013)

7. Wanaskar, U., Sheetal, R., Mukhopadhyay, D.: A Hybrid Web Recommendation System Based on the Improved Association Rule Mining Algorithm. Journal of Software Engineering and Applications, 396–404 (2013)

8. Li, D., Lv, Q., Xie, X., Li, S., et al.: Interest-based real-time content recommendation in online social communities. Knowledge-Based Systems **28**, 1–12 (2012)

9. Sergio, C., Juan, M., Juan, F.: Top-N news recommendations in digital newspapers. Knowledge-Based Systems **27**, 180–189 (2012)

10. Wen, H., Fang, L., Guan, L.: A hybrid approach for personalized recommendation of news on the Web. Expert Systems with Applications **39**, 5806–5814 (2012)

11. Garcin, F., Zhou, K., Faltings, B., Schickel, V.: Personalized news recommendation based on collaborative filtering. In: IEEE/WIC/ACM International Conferences on Web Intelligence and Intelligent Agent Technology (2012)

12. Wang, J., Vries, A.P., Reinders, M.J.T.: Unifying user-based item-based collaborative filtering approaches by similarity fusion. In: SIGIR 2006 Proceedings of the 29th annual international ACM SIGIR conference on Research and Development in Information Retrieval, pp. 501–508 (2006)

13. Pazzani, M.J., Billsus, D.: Content-based recommendation systems. In: Kobsa, A., Nejdl, W., Brusilovsky, P. (eds.) Adaptive Web 2007. LNCS, vol. 4321, pp. 325–341. Springer, Heidelberg (2007)

14. Sarwar, B., Karypis, G., Konstan, J., Riedl, J.: Item-based collaborative filtering recommendation algorithms. In: Proceedings of the 10th International Conference on World Wide Web, pp. 285–295 (2001)

15. Li, L., Wang, D., Li, T., Knox, D., Padmanabhan, B.: SCENE: a scalable two-stage personalized news recommendation system. In: Proceedings of the 34th International ACM SIGIR conference on Research and Development in Information Retrieval (SIGIR 2011), pp. 125–134 (2011)

16. Li, L., Li, T.: News recommendation via hypergraph learning: encapsulation of user behavior and news content. In: Proceedings of the Sixth ACM International Conference on Web Search and Data Mining (WSDM 2013), pp. 305–314 (2013)

17. Bai, X., Chen, F., Zhan, S.: A New Clustering Model Based on Word2vec Mining on Sina Weibo Users Tags. International Journal of Grid Distribution Computing **7**, 41–48 (2014)

18. Yuan, Y., He, L., Peng, L., Huang, Z.: A New Study Based on Word2vec and Cluster for Document Categorization. Journal of Computational Information Systems **10**, 9301–9308 (2014)

19. Xin, Z., Zhao, J., Gu, M., Sun, J.: Integrating collaborate and content-based filtering for personalized information recommendation. In: Hao, Y., Liu, J., Wang, Y., Cheung, Y., Yin, H., Jiao, L., Ma, J., Jiao, Y.-C. (eds.) CIS 2005. LNCS, vol. 3801, pp. 476–482. Springer, Berlin Heidelberg (2005)

20. Goto, M., Komatani, K., et al.: Hybrid collaborative and content-based music recommendation using probabilistic model with latent user preferences. In: Proceedings of the 7th International Conference on Music Information Retrieval, pp. 296–301 (2006)

21. Hu, Z., Wang, H., Zhu, J., Li, M., Qiao, Y., Deng, C.: Discovery of rare sequential topic patterns in document stream. In: Proc. Siam International Conference On Data Mining 2014, pp. 533–541 (2014)

22. Guan, Y., Cai, S., Shang, M.: Recommendation algorithm based on item quality and user rating preferences. Frontiers of Computer Science **8**(2), 289–297 (2014)

23. Li, L., Zheng, L., Yang, F., et al.: Modeling and broadening temporal user interest in personalized news recommendation. Expert Systems with Applications **41**(7), 3168–3177 (2014)
24. Lin, C., Xie, R., Guan, X., et al.: Personalized news recommendation via implicit social experts. Information Sciences **254**, 1–18 (2014)
25. Garcin F., Dimitrakakis C., Faltings B.: Personalized news recommendation with context trees. In: 7th ACM Recommender Systems Conference (Recsys 2013), pp. 105–112 (2013)
26. Lei, L., Tao, L.: News recommendation via hypergraph learning: encapsulation of user behavior and news content. In: WSDM 2013. ACM (2013)

A Shilling Attack Detection Method Based on SVM and Target Item Analysis in Collaborative Filtering Recommender Systems

Wei Zhou[1], Junhao Wen[2(✉)], Min Gao[2], Ling Liu[2], Haini Cai[2], and Xibin Wang[1]

[1] College of Computer Science, Chongqing University, Chongqing 400030, China
zhouwei@cqu.edu.cn
http://www.springer.com/lncs
[2] School of Software Engineering, Chongqing University, Chongqing 400030, China
{wjhcqu,gaomin,liuling,hainic}@cqu.edu.cn
http://www.springer.com/lncs

Abstract. The open nature of recommender systems makes them vulnerable to shilling attacks. Biased ratings are introduced in order to affect recommendations, have been shown to cause great harm to collaborative filtering algorithms. Most of previous research focuses on the differences between genuine profiles and attack profiles, ignoring the group characteristics in an attack. There exists class unbalance problems in SVM based detecting methods, that is, the detecting performance is not good when the amount of samples of attack profiles in training set is small. In this paper, we study the use of SVM based method and group characteristics in attack profiles to detect attack profiles. Based on this, a two phase detecting method SVM-TIA is proposed. In the first phase, Borderline-SMOTE method is used to alleviate the class unbalance problem in classification; a rough detecting result is obtained in this phase; the second phase is a fine-tuning phase whereby the target items in the potential attack profiles set are analysed. We conduct experiments on the MovieLens 100K Dataset and compare the performance of SVM-TIA with other shilling detecting methods to demonstrate the effectiveness of the proposed approach.

Keywords: Shilling attack detection · Unbalanced data · SVM · Target item analysis

1 Introduction

With the development of information technology, people come from era of lack of information into an information overload era. Collaborative filtering recommender system is an important tool to resolve this contradiction. But studies have shown that collaborative filtering technology itself has serious shortcomings

© Springer International Publishing Switzerland 2015
S. Zhang et al. (Eds.): KSEM 2015, LNAI 9403, pp. 751–763, 2015.
DOI: 10.1007/978-3-319-25159-2_69

and deficiencies. Collaborative filtering techniques rely on user preferences files to provide users with personalized recommendations, which make collaborative filtering algorithm can be attacked by injecting attack profiles. Due to the open nature of collaborative filtering recommender systems, they suffer vulnerabilities of being attacked by malicious users by injecting profiles consisting of biased ratings [1]. These attacks are carried out in order to influence the system's behavior, and have been termed "shilling" or "profile injection" attacks, and attackers as shillers or attackers [2]. To ensure the trustworthiness of recommender systems, attack profiles need to be detected and removed accurately. The word "shilling" was first proposed in [3]. There have been some recent research efforts aimed at detecting and reducing the effects of profile injection attacks [4–7]. These attacks consist of a set of attack profiles, each containing biased rating data associated with a fictitious user identity. Since "shilling" profiles look similar to genuine profiles, it is difficult to identify them. There are three categories of attack detection algorithms: supervised, unsupervised, and semi-supervised.

In the first category, attack detection techniques are modelled as a classification problem. A lot of research has been undertaken to employ supervised learning for shilling attack detection [8]. Three classification algorithms, kNN-based, C4.5-based and SVM-based, are used to improve the robustness of the recommender system [9]. These supervised algorithms need a large number of labeled users to enhance the accuracy [10]. However, these algorithms do not perform well when the attack profiles are obscured.

In the second category, unsupervised detection approaches address these issues by training on an unlabeled dataset. The benefit of this is that these techniques facilitate online learning and improve detection accuracy. There has been significant research interest focused on detecting attack profiles using the unsupervised approach. Some of the techniques use clustering, association rules methods and statistical approaches [11–13]. An unsupervised shilling attack detection algorithm using principal component analysis (PCA) was proposed in [14]. Unsupervised detection approaches need prior knowledge of recommender system before detection.

In the third category, semi-supervised detection approaches, such as [15,16], make use of both unlabelled and labelled user profiles for multi-class modelling. Cao et al. [15] proposes a new semi-supervised method called $Semi\text{-}SAD$ shilling attack detection algorithm using both types of data. HySAD introduces MC-Relief to select effective detection metrics, and semi-supervised Naive Bayes (SNBλ) to precisely separate random-filler model attackers and average-filler model attackers from normal users.

The limitation for SVM based detection methods is that class unbalance problem exists in SVM classifiers. Borderline-SMOTE method is used to alleviate the class unbalance problem, on the other side, target item analysis method is also used to reduce false positive rate of the detection result. The rest of the paper is organized as follows. In the next section, we examine previous work and background in the area of attack detection in recommender systems; in the

Section 3 we describe the details of our approaches. Our experimental results are presented in Section 4. We discuss and summarize our research in Section 5.

2 Related Work

In this section, background knowledge is introduced. Firstly, we describe several common attack models and their characteristics. Secondly, we introduce the main idea of target item analysis. Finally, we analysis class unbalance problem of SVM based detecting methods in shilling detection.

2.1 Attack Models

An attack consists of attack profiles that are introduced into the system in order to alter recommendation lists of a set of target items. Based on different assumptions about the attacker's knowledge and purpose, a number of attack models have been identified [1]. There are four popular attack models in recommender systems: random attack, average attack, bandwagon attack, and segment attack models. Ratings in an attack profile can be divided into three sets of items: a target item I_T; a selected item I_S, selected set is a set of widely popular items or items that have common features, which is usually used to perform group attacks; and a set of filler items usually randomly chosen I_F, filler items in a malicious profile are a set of items that make the profile look normal and makes a malicious profile harder to detect. Structure of the attack models is shown in Table 1.

Table 1. Structure of the attack models

Attack model	I_S(Selected Items)	I_F(Filler Items)	I_T(Target Items)
Random Attack	$\emptyset$	random ratings	r_{max}/r_{min}
Average Attack	$\emptyset$	mean of each item	r_{max}/r_{min}
Bandwagon Attack	r_{max}	random ratings	r_{max}/r_{min}
Segment Attack	r_{max}	random ratings	r_{max}/r_{min}

2.2 Data Unbalance and Target Item Analysis

Previous research apply SVM method to attack detection in recommender systems by extracting user profile features and building attack detection model. Comparing with other supervised learning methods such as decision trees, neural networks, SVM has a better overall performance than other methods [10,17,18]. Class unbalance problem exists in classification when using machine learning methods [19,20]. Classification performance of the traditional classifiers is always restricted when facing unbalance data [21]. For example, when the positive data in the data set is much less than the negative data, the classification result be more inclined to the negative data. No exception in shilling attack detection base on SVM based methods. The performance of attack detecting is not good when the attack size is small. In previous research [22,23], Borderline-SMOTE method is used to alleviate the class unbalance problem. In this paper, classification algorithms for unbalanced data is borrowed and applied in shilling attack detecting, thereby increasing the recall of detecting results. By using target item analysis method, reduce false positive rate of detecting results. The key idea of target item analysis is to find the target item(s) ID, and consider all profiles rate on that target item as attack profiles. We have introduced how target item analysis works in our previous research in [24,25], no repeat in this paper.

3   The Proposed Method

In this section, we first introduce the idea of target item analysis. Based on target item analysis, a detection method based on Borderline-SMOTE method is proposed. SVM-TIA consists of two stages: stage of classification and stage of target item analysis.

Single profile can not affect the recommendation list of an item in the recommender system [6]. Attack profiles reaches a certain quantities can alter the recommendation list of the target item. Based on this consideration, we can abstain a better overview of attack profiles when consider them as a whole. In this paper, we propose a shilling detecting framework, which contains two phases. In the first phase, a rough detection method is used to get a suspicious profile set contains attack profiles and genuine profiles. The second phase is a fine-tuning phase whereby the target items in the potential attack profiles set are analysed. Based on the analysis we can then remove genuine profiles from this set, which can reduce false positives in the final result. Figure 1 shows the two phase shilling detecting framework in recommender system.

SVM, which is based on the structural risk minimization principle, has a good generalization performance [26]. It can find a decision surface that optimally separates the instances into two classes. Therefore, we use SVM as the machine learning algorithm to detect profile injection attacks. Figure 2 is the flow of SVM-TIA shilling detecting method based Borderline-SMOTE.

4   Experiments and Analysis

In this section, we first show datasets we used. Then we describe the evaluation metrics of false positive rate, recall and precision. Finally, we make an analysis on the experimental results.

4.1   Experimental Data and Settings

The datasets used in the experiments are the widely used *MovieLens* 100k Dataset by the GroupLens Research Project in the University of Minnesota. There are 100,000 ratings (1-5) from 943 users on 1682 movies in MovileLens

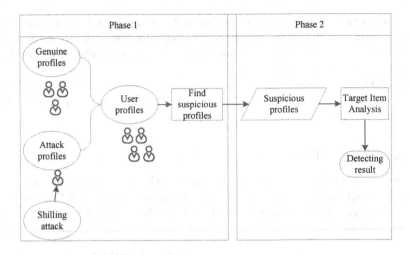

Fig. 1. Framework of two phase shilling detecting in recommender systems

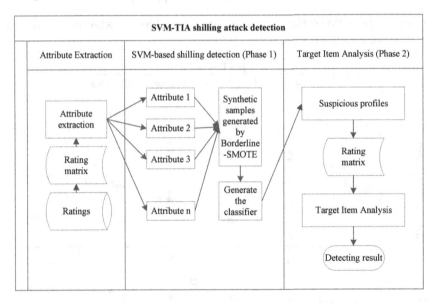

Fig. 2. Flow of SVM-TIA shilling detecting method based Borderline-SMOTE

100k Dataset. Each user has rated at least 20 movies. Each user can rate a movie from 1 to 5. Where 1 is the lowest and 5 is the highest.

Filler size is defined as the ratio between the number of items rated by a user and the number of entire items in the recommender system. Attack size is defined as the ratio between the number of attack profiles in an attack and the number of entire profiles in the recommender system. The distribution of filler size for genuine users in the Movielens 100K Dataset indicate that the majority of genuine users only rate a small number of items. In order to make the attack profiles hard to be detected, the attackers may use the same or similar filler sizes as genuine users do. In our experiments, the range of filler sizes for attack profiles is set between 1% and 20%.

The platform we implement all the experiments as flows: Hardware: CPU is Intel Core i7 processors, Windows 7, with 16G RAM. Software: All of our tests is on Matlab 2012b.

4.2 Evaluation Metrics

To evaluate the performance of our proposed method, detection rate, false positive rate, recall and precision are used in this paper, which is defined as flows. False positive rate is the ratio of the number of false positives with the number of attack profiles.

$$False\ Positive\ Rate = \frac{\#False\ Positives}{\#Genuines} \tag{1}$$

Recall is the ratio of the number of attack profiles in detecting result with the number of attack profiles.

$$Recall = \frac{\#True\ Positives}{\#True\ Positives + False\ Negatives} \tag{2}$$

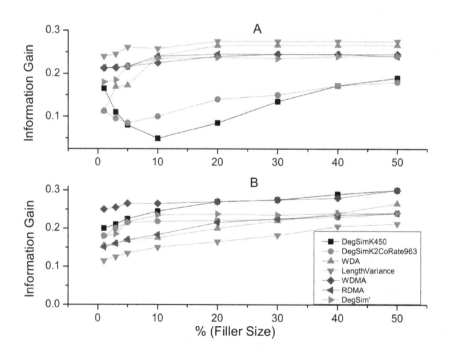

Fig. 3. Information gain of profile attributes in different attack models

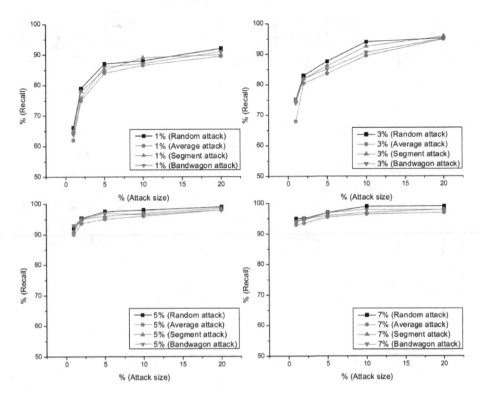

Fig. 4. Detection rate of different attack models when attack size and filler size vary in push attack

Precision is the ratio of the number of attack profiles in detecting result with the number of profiles of detecting result.

$$Precision = \frac{\#True\ Positives}{\#True\ Positives + False\ Positives} \tag{3}$$

4.3 Analysis of Information Gain

As one of the most widely used measures for evaluating how informative an attribute is, information gain evaluates the importance of an attribute to a classification system, where larger information gain denotes more importance of the attribute. Therefore, we first use information gain to evaluate the importance of the attributes in this paper. We also analysis information gain of the attribute we proposed in paper [24].

Clearly, greater information gain value of a feature indicates greater contribution to the classification, thus attributes of greater information gain value are chosen as eigenvectors. Profile attributes including RDMA, DegSim, WDMA, WDA, LengthVar, MeanVar, FillerMeanDiff and $DegSim'$, $DegSim'$ is a new profile attribute we proposed in [24]. Information gain is different when the filler

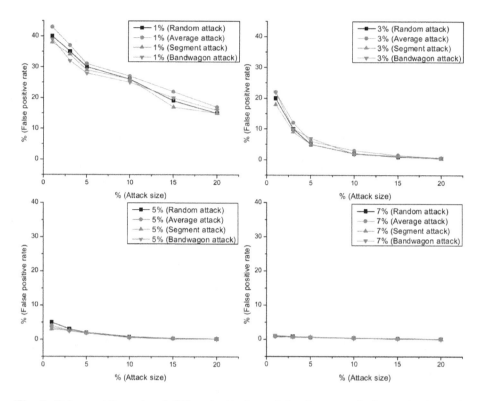

Fig. 5. False positive rate of different attack models when attack size varies in push attack

size and attack size are different. In the experiments below, we calculate the mean information gain when the attack size is 5%, and filler size varies from 1% to 50%. Information gain of profile attributes in different attack models is shown in Figure 3. Figure 3(A) is from push attack type while Figure 3(B) is from nuke attack type. Information gain is different when the attack type and filler size different.

4.4   Experimental Results and Analysis

In this section, detection results of the proposed shilling detecting method SVM-TIA is shown. In order to study performance of SVM-TIA when filler size and attack size varies, two experiments are designed. To evaluate the performance of our proposed method, detection rate, false positive rate, recall and precision are used in this paper.

To create the training set, we randomly select 200 genuine profiles from the Movielens 100K Dataset as samples of genuine profiles. Samples of attack profiles are generated by random, average, segment and bandwagon attacks with filler sizes varies from 1%, 3%, 5%, 7%. To balance the proportion between genuine

Table 2. Detection result of different methods when filler size is 3% and attack size varies in push attack

Attack size			1%	2%	5%	10%	20%
Random attack	Recall	SVM	0.512	0.685	0.724	0.86	0.91
		RSVM	0.987	0.992	0.993	0.995	0.996
		C4.5	0.98	0.985	0.99	0.994	0.997
		KNN	0.715	0.753	0.804	0.95	0.996
		SVM-TIA	0.642	0.856	0.92	0.93	0.92
	Precision	SVM	0.55	0.62	0.73	0.82	0.91
		RSVM	0.79	0.82	0.9	0.95	0.98
		C4.5	0.853	0.86	0.867	0.874	0.88
		KNN	0.972	0.973	0.972	0.97	0.978
		SVM-TIA	**0.98**	**0.991**	**0.992**	**0.994**	**0.995**
Average attack	Recall	SVM	0.489	0.55	0.698	0.82	0.9
		RSVM	0.987	0.992	0.993	0.995	0.996
		C4.5	0.98	0.985	0.99	0.994	0.997
		KNN	0.715	0.753	0.804	0.95	0.96
		SVM-TIA	0.586	0.814	0.915	0.92	0.91
	Precision	SVM	0.532	0.602	0.715	0.806	0.889
		RSVM	0.79	0.82	0.9	0.95	0.98
		C4.5	0.853	0.86	0.867	0.874	0.88
		KNN	0.972	0.973	0.972	0.97	0.978
		SVM-TIA	**0.974**	**0.982**	**0.986**	**0.992**	**0.993**
Bandwagon attack	Recall	SVM	0.523	0.69	0.75	0.852	0.9
		RSVM	0.984	0.991	0.992	0.992	0.995
		C4.5	0.95	0.955	0.989	0.994	0.995
		KNN	0.702	0.723	0.824	0.954	0.965
		SVM-TIA	0.684	0.884	0.93	0.92	0.91
	Precision	SVM	0.53	0.6	0.69	0.79	0.88
		RSVM	0.77	0.81	0.9	0.95	0.97
		C4.5	0.823	0.835	0.856	0.868	0.879
		KNN	0.984	0.981	0.972	0.977	0.987
		SVM-TIA	**0.985**	**0.986**	**0.991**	**0.993**	**0.995**

profiles and attack profiles in the training set, we construct attack profiles with attack size varies from 1%, 3%, 5%, 10%, 20% for each attack. For each detecting result, detecting is repeated 20 times and the average values of detection results are reported for the experiments.

In the tests, we use Libsvm 3.0 [26] to generate the classifier. Target items are chose randomly when generating each attack profile. Push attacks are introduced in this paper, however, the proposed method can be put into effect to detect the nuke attacks.

Figure 4 shows the recall of detecting different attack models when attack size and filler size vary in push attack. Four subfigures are the recall when detecting different attack models when the filler size is 1%, 3%, 5%, 7% respectively. In each subfigure, recall efficiency increase with the increasing of attack size.

Table 3. Detection result of different algorithms when filler size is 3% and attack size varies in nuke attack

Attack size			1%	2%	5%	10%	20%
Random attack	Recall	SVM	0.522	0.676	0.753	0.884	0.931
		RSVM	0.997	0.994	0.996	0.995	0.997
		C4.5	0.972	0.975	0.991	0.993	0.994
		KNN	0.725	0.756	0.818	0.953	0.997
		SVM-TIA	0.712	0.862	0.9	0.914	0.92
	Precision	SVM	0.56	0.64	0.74	0.83	0.92
		RSVM	0.79	0.83	0.92	0.96	0.99
		C4.5	0.823	0.865	0.857	0.874	0.882
		KNN	0.968	0.971	0.974	0.981	0.983
		SVM-TIA	**0.981**	**0.992**	**0.993**	**0.995**	**0.996**
Average attack	Recall	SVM	0.46	0.56	0.692	0.739	0.878
		RSVM	0.981	0.984	0.988	0.99	0.993
		C4.5	0.981	0.975	0.993	0.992	0.996
		KNN	0.725	0.733	0.824	0.942	0.996
		SVM-TIA	0.604	0.826	0.91	0.9	0.913
	Precision	SVM	0.51	0.62	0.72	0.81	0.91
		RSVM	0.78	0.81	0.87	0.93	0.95
		C4.5	0.833	0.839	0.847	0.846	0.858
		KNN	0.962	0.953	0.961	0.958	0.964
		SVM-TIA	**0.978**	**0.985**	**0.988**	**0.992**	**0.992**
Bandwagon attack	Recall	SVM	0.46	0.525	0.658	0.782	0.886
		RSVM	0.988	0.993	0.994	0.993	0.996
		C4.5	0.954	0.965	0.979	0.984	0.991
		KNN	0.732	0.742	0.814	0.924	0.947
		SVM-TIA	0.718	0.816	0.906	0.91	0.93
	Precision	SVM	0.54	0.695	0.78	0.825	0.93
		RSVM	0.79	0.82	0.91	0.95	0.98
		C4.5	0.825	0.815	0.844	0.868	0.88
		KNN	0.964	0.961	0.972	0.969	0.98
		SVM-TIA	**0.978**	**0.982**	**0.991**	**0.991**	**0.995**

While recall increases with the increasing of filler size when the attack size is the same.

While Figure 5 shows false positive rate of SVM-TIA. Figure 5 shows the false positive rate when detect different attack models when attack size and filler size vary in push attack. Four subfigures are the false positive rate when detecting different attack models when the filler size is 1%, 3%, 5%, 7% respectively. In each subfigure, false positive rate efficiency decrease with the increasing of attack size. While false positive rate decreases with the increasing of filler size when the attack size is the same. We can come to a conclusion that the false positive of detecting result using SVM-TIA is high when the quantity of attack profiles is small; the precision rate can be promoted by employing target item analysis method.

In order to test the effectiveness of our proposed method SVM-TIA when attack size varies, we also compare the detection result using different detecting method in the second experiment, including SVM, RSVM, C4.5, KNN shilling detecting method. In the experiments, we use the same profile attributes in SVM based detecting method and SVM-TIA based detecting method. In MovieLens 100K Dataset, the filler size is 3%, and the attack size varies from 1%, 2%, 5%, 10%, 20% respectively. Some attack models are used including random attack model, average attack model and bandwagon attack model. The detecting result is shown in Table 2 and Table 3.

Table 2 shows that the comprehensive result is best in all three attack types. The precision increases with the increasing of attack size. The precision reaches 100% when the attack size is over 10%.

From Table 2 and Table 3 we can see that, the recall of SVM based method and SVM-TIA method increase with the increase of attack size; and SVM-TIA has the higher recall than that of SVM method. The recall of SVM-TIA method is not as good as other methods. The precision of SVM-TIA is always high, which means the false positive in the detecting result is low. There is no big difference in the detecting result between push attack type and nuke attack type.

5 Conclusions and Future Work

In this paper, we propose a method to detect shilling attacks based on SVM and target item analysis method. Experiments on the MovieLens Dataset show the effectiveness of SVM-TIA in detecting shilling attacks. The limitation for SVM based detection method is that class unbalance problem exists in SVM classifier. Borderline-SMOTE method is used to alleviate the class unbalance problem, on the other side, target item analysis method is used to reduce false positive rate of the detection result. In our future work, we will enhance the function of target item analysis method to detect more complex attack models.

Acknowledgments. Research reported in this paper has been supported by NSFC under grant No.61379158, and the Ph.D. Programs Foundation of Ministry of Education under grant No. 20120191110028, 2014M560704 and the Fundamental Research Funds for the Central Universities under Grant 106112014CDJZR095502.

References

1. Burke, R., Mobasher, B., Williams, C., Bhaumik, R.: Classification features for attack detection in collaborative recommender systems. In: Proceedings of the 12th ACM SIGKDD International Conference on Knowledge Discovery and Data Mining, pp. 542–547. ACM (2006)
2. Lam, S.K., Riedl, J.: Shilling recommender systems for fun and profit. In: Proceedings of the 13th International Conference on World Wide Web, pp. 393–402. ACM (2004)

3. Cheng, Z., Hurley, N.: Effective diverse and obfuscated attacks on model-based recommender systems. In: Proceedings of the third ACM Conference on Recommender systems, pp. 141–148. ACM (2009)
4. Mehta, B., Hofmann, T., Nejdl, W.: Robust collaborative filtering. In: Proceedings of the 2007 ACM Conference on Recommender systems, pp. 49–56. ACM (2007)
5. Mehta, B., Nejdl, W.: Attack resistant collaborative filtering. In: Proceedings of the 31st Annual International ACM SIGIR Conference on Research and Development in Information Retrieval, pp. 75–82. ACM (2008)
6. Burke, R., Mobasher, B., Bhaumik, R., Williams, C.: Segment-based injection attacks against collaborative filtering recommender systems. In: Fifth IEEE International Conference on Data Mining, p. 4. IEEE (2005)
7. Carrer-Neto, W., Hernández-Alcaraz, M.L., Valencia-García, R., García-Sánchez, F.: Social knowledge-based recommender system. application to the movies domain. Expert Systems with Applications 39(12), 10990–11000 (2012)
8. Burke, R., Mobasher, B., Williams, C., Bhaumik, R.: Detecting profile injection attacks in collaborative recommender systems. In: The 8th IEEE International Conference on Enterprise Computing, E-Commerce, and E-Services, pp. 23–23. IEEE (2006)
9. Williams, C.A., Mobasher, B., Burke, R.: Defending recommender systems: detection of profile injection attacks. Service Oriented Computing and Applications 1(3), 157–170 (2007)
10. Zhang, F., Zhou, Q.: Hht-svm: An online method for detecting profile injection attacks in collaborative recommender systems. Knowledge-Based Systems 65, 96–105 (2014)
11. Hurley, N., Cheng, Z., Zhang, M.: Statistical attack detection. In: Proceedings of the Third ACM Conference on Recommender Systems, pp. 149–156. ACM (2009)
12. Fu, L., Goh, D.H.-L., Foo, S.S.-B., Na, J.-C.: Collaborative querying through a hybrid query clustering approach. In: Sembok, T.M.T., Zaman, H.B., Chen, H., Urs, S.R., Myaeng, S.-H. (eds.) ICADL 2003. LNCS, vol. 2911, pp. 111–122. Springer, Heidelberg (2003)
13. Zhang, S., Chakrabarti, A., Ford, J., Makedon, F.: Attack detection in time series for recommender systems. In: Proceedings of the 12th ACM SIGKDD International Conference on Knowledge Discovery and Data Mining, pp. 809–814. ACM (2006)
14. Mehta, B., Nejdl, W.: Unsupervised strategies for shilling detection and robust collaborative filtering. User Modeling and User-Adapted Interaction 19(1–2), 65–97 (2009)
15. Cao, J., Wu, Z., Mao, B., Zhang, Y.: Shilling attack detection utilizing semi-supervised learning method for collaborative recommender system. World Wide Web 16(5–6), 729–748 (2013)
16. Wu, Z., Wu, J., Cao, J., Tao, D.: Hysad: a semi-supervised hybrid shilling attack detector for trustworthy product recommendation. In: Proceedings of the 18th ACM SIGKDD International Conference on Knowledge Discovery and Data Mining, pp. 985–993. ACM (2012)
17. Horng, S.-J., Su, M.-Y., Chen, Y.-H., Kao, T.-W., Chen, R.-J., Lai, J.-L., Perkasa, C.D.: A novel intrusion detection system based on hierarchical clustering and support vector machines. Expert Systems with Applications 38(1), 306–313 (2011)
18. Ch, S., Sohani, S., Kumar, D., Malik, A., Chahar, B., Nema, A., Panigrahi, B.K., Dhiman, R.: A support vector machine-firefly algorithm based forecasting model to determine malaria transmission. Neurocomputing 129, 279–288 (2014)

19. Zhang, H., Berg, A.C., Maire, M., Malik, J.: Svm-knn: Discriminative nearest neighbor classification for visual category recognition. In: 2006 IEEE Computer Society Conference on Computer Vision and Pattern Recognition, vol. 2, pp. 2126–2136. IEEE (2006)
20. Zhang, F., Wang, B.: Approach of detecting user profile attacks based on svm and Rough set theory. Journal of Chinese Computer Systems 35(1), 108–113 (2014)
21. Lv, S., Wang, W.: A shilling attacks detection method of recommender systems based on hybrid strategies. Computer Engineering & Science 35(8), 174–179 (2013)
22. Chawla, N.V., Bowyer, K.W., Hall, L.O., Kegelmeyer, W.P.: Smote: synthetic minority over-sampling technique. Journal of Artificial Intelligence Research 16(1), 321–357 (2002)
23. Han, H., Wang, W.-Y., Mao, B.-H.: Borderline-SMOTE: a new over-sampling method in imbalanced data sets learning. In: Huang, D.-S., Huang, G.-B., Zhang, X.-P. (eds.) ICIC 2005. LNCS, vol. 3644, pp. 878–887. Springer, Heidelberg (2005)
24. Zhou, W., Koh, Y.S., Wen, J., Alam, S., Dobbie, G.: Detection of abnormal profiles on group attacks in recommender systems. In: Proceedings of the 37th International ACM SIGIR Conference on Research & Development in Information Retrieval, pp. 955–958. ACM (2014)
25. Zhou, W., Wen, J., Koh, Y.S., Alam, S., Dobbie, G.: Attack detection in recommender systems based on target item analysis. In: 2014 International Joint Conference on Neural Networks (IJCNN), pp. 332–339. IEEE (2014)
26. Chang, C.-C., Lin, C.-J.: Libsvm: a library for support vector machines. ACM Transactions on Intelligent Systems and Technology (TIST) 2(3), 27 (2011)

Robust Dynamic Background Model with Adaptive Region Based on T2FS and GMM

Yun Guo, Yi Ji[✉], Jutao Zhang, Shengrong Gong, and Chunping Liu

School of Computer Science & Technology, Soochow University,
No.1 Shizi Street, Suzhou, China
{guoyun,jiyi,jtzhang,srgong,cpliu}@suda.edu.cn
http://www.suda.edu.cn

Abstract. For many tracking and surveillance applications, Gaussian mixture model (GMM) provides an effective mean to segment the foreground from background. Though, because of insufficient and noisy data in complex dynamic scenes, the estimated parameters of the GMM, which are based on the assumption that the pixel process meets multi-modal Gaussian distribution, may not accurately reflect the underlying distribution of the observations. And the existing block-based GMM (BGMM) method may be able to segment only rough foreground objects with time-consuming calculations. To solve these difficulties, this paper proposes to use type-2 fuzzy sets (T2FSs) to handle GMM's uncertain parameters (T2GMM). Furthermore, this paper also introduces a novel representation of contextual spatial information including the color, edge and texture features for each block which is faster and almost lossless (T2BGMM). Experimental results demonstrate the efficiency of the proposed methods.

Keywords: Background modeling · Fuzzy set Theory · GMM

1 Introduction

In surveillance systems, the accurate detection of moving objects in real-time is an important step in the process of tracking and recognition [1,3]. To achieve desirable foreground detection under variant dynamic environments, a lot of methods have been proposed over the years, such as histogram-based method [2], kernel density estimation(KDE), GMM and code-book. Among these solutions, GMM has become the defacto standard.

Recently, Zeng et al. [7] advised that insufficient or noisy data may affect the uncertain parameters of GMM, and type-2 fuzzy sets (T2FSs)[8] can provide a theoretically well founded framework to handle the uncertainty. Braf and Vachon [9] put the T2FSs method on background model. But they don't explain why T2FSs can improve the results in theory base and only made experiments on infrared videos which are not representative enough. Similar method is also mentioned but not fully exploited in work of Yeo et al. [13].

© Springer International Publishing Switzerland 2015
S. Zhang et al. (Eds.): KSEM 2015, LNAI 9403, pp. 764–770, 2015.
DOI: 10.1007/978-3-319-25159-2_70

2   Proposed Algorithm

This paper will focus on improving the robustness of the GMM and ensuring the complete foreground objects in low contrast scenes. The proposed robust Region-T2FS-Based GMM (T2BGMM) algorithm, its main components are listed as following:

1. Provide the statistical experiments to test the pixels in dynamic scene background. This gives a better explanation of T2GMM's efficiency in real background model. Then, T2GMM is applied to handle some uncertainty to improve the GMM precision.

2. Divide the given frame into overlapping blocks and do a 2-dimension discrete cosine transform(DCT) for each block to get the low-level spatial features. After that, the most import 4 feature coefficients are used to replace the original pixel values. GMM then is used to model the new feature model.

3. Generate foreground mask based on the step 2 and 3 from a probability way which can minimize the number of false positives quite effectively.

2.1   GMM Based on T2FSs

GMM is not stationary enough for dynamic scenes because the pixels do not strictly meet the gaussian distribution. This paper did an experiment on I^2R dataset [6] to show a more clear pixel distribution pattern. The I^2R dataset contains 9 different dynamic indoor or outdoor scenes. In experiments, ten pure background pixels are chosen from dynamic areas in each scene. For each pixel, the experiments record its all pixel values in whole corresponding scene (see Fig. 1). It shows that the pixels almost meet the gaussian or mixture of Gaussian distributions. But the more complex backgrounds are, the more non-stationary the distributions become. It's hard to capture the pixel distribution with an accurate model. However, by integration of some mathematical models, it will be better response to the supposed distribution. Fig. 2 presents one distribution of a dynamic pixel. Though, in most cases, the pixel distribution area can be

Fig. 1. The distribution of selected pixels in dynamic scenes from I^2R dataset

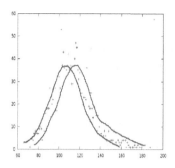
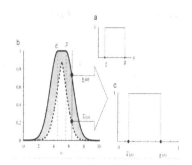

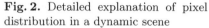

Fig. 2. Detailed explanation of pixel distribution in a dynamic scene

Fig. 3. Gaussian primary MF with uncertain mean

easily captured by two gauss curves though moving the left gauss curve to the right one's location. The usage of two curves is more robust than one pure Gaussian model.

Now the physical meaning of using T2FSs can be clearly described to handle the uncertainty of GMM. In Fig. 3, the shaded region is the footprint of uncertainty(FOU), and the thick solid and dashed lines denote the lower and upper membership functions (MFs). Comparing with the Fig. 2, the FOU is similar with the area made by uncertainty of pixel process.

In this paper, the algorithm uses factor k_m control the intervals in which the parameter vary as follows:

$$\underline{\mu} = \mu - k_m\sigma, \overline{\mu} = \mu + k_m\sigma, k_m \in [0,3] \tag{1}$$

The factor also controls the area of the FOU. The bigger k_m or the larger the FOU, which implies the greater uncertainty.

In foreground detection step, when a new frame incomes at times $t+1$, a match test is made for each block. For this, the length between two bounds of the log-likelihood interval is used as, $H(x) = |\ln(\underline{h}(x)) - \ln(\overline{h}(x))|$. In Fig. 3, the gaussian primary MF with uncertain mean has:

$$H(x) = \begin{cases} \frac{2k_m|x-\mu|}{\sigma} & if \ x < \underline{\mu} \ or \ x \geqslant \overline{\mu} \\ \frac{|x-\mu|}{2\sigma^2} + \frac{k_m|x-\mu|}{\sigma} + \frac{k_m^2}{2} & if \ \underline{\mu} < x < \overline{\mu} \end{cases} \tag{2}$$

So, a pixel is ascribed to a background if: $\sum_{i=1}^{3} H(x_i) < k * \sigma$.

2.2   Spatial Feature Extraction

Shen and Sethi [10] proved that the DCT coefficients of image are full of vision features such as intensity , horizontal and vertical edge feature and texture feature. Take a block for example, among its DCT coefficients, $F(0,0)$ is DC coefficient which reflects average intensity, $F(0,1)$ and $F(1,0)$ reflects the vertical and horizontal edge feature respectively, $F(1,1)$ represents the textual visual feature of the block. So, the four coefficients are the most important ones to represent the block's spatial information. According to Fig. 4, the algorithm chooses 8×8 block which overlap its neighbours by 6 pixels in both the horizontal and vertical directions, then replaces the four corresponding 4 pixels by the first 4 coefficients. The experiments shows that it's faster and almost no loss of accuracy comparing to Reddy's method [12] which can also ensure the completeness of foreground objects.

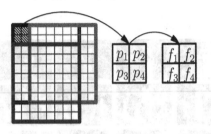

Fig. 4. Using block features to replace original pixels

After that, a feature 'matrix' is built to replace the original RGB image for the GMM model as in Zivkovic et al. [11] to make background model.

2.3   Foreground Mask Generation

To generate the final mask, a novel build method T2BGMM is proposed to consider the merits of both BGMM and T2GMM. The key of combining multiple classifiers is to evaluate their individual reliability. Here it is simple and convenient to use T2GMM and BGMM background masks. Considering a foreground region R_t generated by T2GMM and a foreground region R_b generated by BGMM, R_t is almost always the subset of R_b, as in Fig. 5. So to a pixel $x \in R_t - R_b$, the likelihood to be background in term of R_t is $m_t = max(\omega_t * f_t(x))$ and in term of R_b is $m_b = max(\omega_b * f_b(x))$, if $m_t * m_b > T_b$, then x is labeled as background and vice versa. Here T_b is an experimental constant value.

Fig. 5. T2BGMM: area combination of BGMM and T2GMM

3   Experimental Results

The proposed algorithm was compared to methods based on GMMs [11], feature histograms [2], and the method proposed by Reddy et al. [12]. All experiments are performed on I^2R dataset. Fig. 6 shows the qualitative results. Other algorithms either are sensitive to noise or rough to segmenting objects. The algorithm proposed in this paper makes use of multiple visual features and extracts the foreground objects accurately with smooth outlines in dynamic scenes.

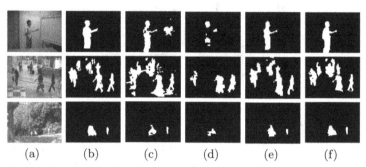

Fig. 6. Qualitative comparison results: (a)input; (b)Ground Truth; (c)GMM; (d)Histogram; (e)Block-Based; (f)Proposed Method

A surfing video with a very high wave is used to test the limitation of these approaches as in Fig. 7. In the video, the figure of surfer is rather small comparing to the big wave background and the waves are dynamic at all times, which will cause much difficulty in foreground/background segmentation. For traditional GMM, MRF or BGMM processes, the results are very poor in detecting any frontal objects and only some meaningless areas are located. In this special case, T2GMM and T2BGMM algorithms successfully find the surfer as foreground. Even though with some noisy on the lower right side, the results are much improved from previous work.

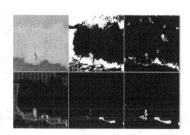

Fig. 7. Surfing in a very high wave. (from left to right respectively): Above: Original, GMM and MRF. Below: BGMM, T2GMM and T2BGMM.

4 Summary and Conclusions

This paper introduces an improved robust GMM model, which fused the T2FSs and block-based detection method. Firstly by analyzing the distribution characteristic of background pixels in the dynamic scenes, this paper explains the statistical significance of using T2FSs in background model. Then, a novel block spatial features extraction ensured the effectiveness of improved GMM in timeliness. Such the proposed algorithms T2GMM and T2BGMM achieved a good balance between complexity and performance. The experimental results show good robustness and detection performance in dynamic environments which are full of noise and unstable elements.

Acknowledgments. This work was supported by National Natural Science Foundation of China (61170124& 61272258& 61301299), and partially supported by Collaborative Innovation Center of Novel Software Technology and Industrialization.

References

1. Zhong, F., Qin, X., Peng, Q.: Transductive segmentation of live video with non-stationary background. In: CVPR 2010, pp. 2189–2196. IEEE Press, San Francisco (2010)
2. Kita, Y.: Background modeling by combining joint intensity histogram with time-sequential data. In: ICPR 2010, pp. 991–994. IEEE Press, Istanbul (2010)
3. Lim, C.H., Vats, E., Chan, C.S.: Fuzzy human motion analysis. Pattern Recogn. **48**(5), 1773–1796 (2015)
4. Zivkovic, Z., van der Heijden, F.: Recursive unsupervised learning of finite mixture models. PAMI **26**(5), 651–656 (2004)
5. Fang, X.H., Xiong, W., Hu, B.J., Wang, L.T.: A moving object detection algorithm based on color information. Journal of Physics: Conference Series **48**(1), 384–387 (2006)
6. Li, L., Huang, W., Gu, I.Y.H., Tian, Q.: Foreground object detection from videos containing complex background. In: Multimedia Proceedings of the Eleventh ACM International Conference on Multimedia, pp. 2–10. ACM, New York (2003)
7. Zeng, J., Xie, L., Liu, Z.Q.: Type-2 fuzzy Gaussian mixture models. Pattern Recognition **41**(12), 3636–3643 (2008)
8. Mendel, J.M.: Type-2 fuzzy sets and systems: an overview. Comp. Intell. Mag. **2**(1), 20–29 (2007)
9. Baf, F.E., Bouwmans, T., Vachon, B.: Fuzzy statistical modeling of dynamic backgrounds for moving object detection in infrared videos. In: OTCBVS, pp. 60–65. IEEE Press, Miami (2009)

10. Shen, B., Sethi, I.K.: Direct feature extraction from compressed images. In: SPIE: Storage and Retrieval for Image and Video Databases IV, vol. 2670, pp. 404–414 (1996)
11. Stauffer, C., Grimson, W.E.L.: Learning patterns of activity using real-time tracking. PAMI **22**(8), 747–757 (2000)
12. Reddy, V., Sanderson, C., Lovell, B.C.: Robust foreground object segmentation via adaptive region-based background modelling. In: ICPR, pp. 3939–3942. IEEE Press, Istanbul (2010)
13. Yeo, B.C., Lim, W.S., Lim, H.S.: Scalable-width temporal edge detection for recursive background recovery in adaptive background modeling. Appl. Soft Comput. **13**(4), 1583–1591 (2013)

Deriving an Effective Hypergraph Model for Point of Interest Recommendation

Meng Qi[1], Xin Li[1(✉)], Lejian Liao[1], Dandan Song[1], and William K. Cheung[2]

[1] Beijing Engineering Application Research Center of High Volume Language
Information Processing and Cloud Computing Applications,
School of Computer Science, Beijing Institute of Technology, Beijing 10081, China
{86856220,xinli,liaolj,sdd}@bit.edu.cn
[2] Department of Computer Science, Hong Kong Baptist University,
Kowloon Tong, Hong Kong
william@comp.hkbu.edu.hk

Abstract. Point of interest (POI) recommendation on Location Based
Social Networks (LBSN) is challenging as the data available for predicting the next point of interest is highly sparse. Addressing the sparsity
issue becomes one of the keys to achieve accurate POI recommendation.
A promising approach is to explore various types of relevant information
carried by the network, e.g, network structures, spatial-temporal information and relations. In this paper, we put forward a hypergraph model
to incorporate the higher-order relations of LBSNs for POI recommendation. Accordingly, we propose a hypergraph random walk (HRW) to
be applied to such a complex hypergraph. The steady state distribution
gives our derived recommendation on venues for each user. Experiments
based on a real data set collected from Foursquare have been conducted
to evaluate the efficiency and effectiveness of our proposed model with
promising results obtained.

Keywords: Hypergraph learning · POI recommendation

1 Introduction

Location-based social networks (LBSNs) have recently attracted much attention.
Such LBSN systems include, but not limited to Foursquare[1] and Loopt[2], where
users can share their geographic information and emotions anywhere and anytime. Therefore, personalized location recommendation (a.k.a. Point of Interest
Recommendation) is a significant task in LBSNs as it helps user find the very
place he could be interested in among thousands of possible locations. The conventional recommendation systems are notorious for their data sparsity and cold-
start problems. The situation for POI recommendation is even worse. According

---

X. Li—The work of Xin Li is partially supported by National Program on Key
Basic Research Project under Grant No. 2013CB329605 and NSFC under Grant No.
61300178.

[1] www.foursquare.com
[2] www.Loopt.com

© Springer International Publishing Switzerland 2015
S. Zhang et al. (Eds.): KSEM 2015, LNAI 9403, pp. 771–777, 2015.
DOI: 10.1007/978-3-319-25159-2_71

to the statistics of our collected data, it occurs that almost 87% of the venues have been visited only once. Due to the sparsity of data, the collaborative filtering based approaches which work well for the recommendation in domains like movies and books are no longer satisfactory for POI recommendation.

In this paper, we propose a unified hypergraph framework to model high-order relations in LBSNs to deal with the sparsity. Furthermore, we formulate POI recommendation as a graph-ranking problem and propose a generalized random walks for the specialized hypergraph of LBSN (Hypergraph Random Walk). Random walk on simple graphs has been extensively adopted for many applications like classification, ranking and link prediction. But there is few research working on random walk on hypergraphs. There are two main challenges to generalize random walk for hypergraphs. In simple graphs, transitions occur only among vertices of the same type and the transition probability is proportional to the weights of edges. However, for hypergraphs, how to make a reasonable transition among various types of vertices and edges is debatable. Secondly, when we calculate the transition probability among vertices, we need to consider the different types of vertices. In this paper, we first construct a specialized hypergraph to represent high-order relations as shown in Fig 1. And then, we propose a generalized random walk process for LBSN hypergraph to achieve the location ranking list.

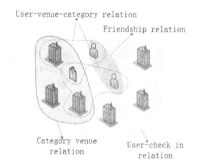

Fig. 1. Specialized Hypergraph for LBS which include three types of vertices(user, venue and category) and four types of hyperedges as labeled in the figure.

2   Related Work

Location recommendation is an important task in location based social networks. The most widely used recommendation approach is collaborative filtering[1] which leverages on the individuals' check-in data for the prediction. As the amount of data is ever increasing, low-dimensional matrix factoring methods[7,8] have been proposed for collaborative filtering(CF). In [5], Bellogin proposed a graph partitioning technique for neighbour selection in user-based collaborative. Among the algorithms tested in [10], the collaborative filtering (CF) approach has been found most effective for online recommendation, and the random walk based model was able to consistently achieve the best performance, where the social ties and the venue-visit patterns are inferred simultaneously. Many learning tasks performed over hypergraphs are based on random walks. Random walk on simple graph has achieved many accomplishments. The simplest random walk for hypergraph is proposed by Avin et al.[2], where the hypergraph surfer chooses vertices from hyperedges uniformly at random. Zhou et al. propose a learning algorithm for weighted hypergraph[3]. Jiajun Bu et al. proposed a manifold ranking algorithm leveraging the intrinsic geometrical structure of the hypergraph for music recommendation[6]. They proposed to optimize a cost function which is derived based on the idea that the ranking scores of vertices belonging to the same hyperedge should be close to each other.

3   LBSN Hypergraph Modelling

In this section, we provide the hypergraph basics and the proposed personalized hypergraph model for POI recommendation.

3.1   Unified Hypergraph for LBS

Let $G(V, E, \omega)$ denote a hypergraph where V is the set of vertices, E is the set of hyperedges and $\omega > 0$ is a weight value associated with each hyperedge e. Each hypergraph $e \in E$ is a subset of V. For a hyperedge $e \in E$, its degree is defined to be $\delta(e) = |e|$. For a vertex $v \in V$, its degree is defined to be $d(v) = \sum_{\{e \in E | v \in e\}} \omega(e)$. And we say a hyperedge e is incident with a vertex v when $v \in e$. A hypergraph is then represented by a $|V| \times |E|$ matrix H in which the value of entry $h(v, e)$ is 1 if $v \in e$ and 0 otherwise. So the degrees of hyperedge and vertex for a weighted hypergraph are defined as follows $d(v) = \sum_{e \in E} \omega(e) h(v, e)$ and $\delta(e) = \sum_{v \in V} h(v, e)$.

Our specialized LBSN hypergraph include three types of vertices with respect to user(U), venues(V) and categories(C) and four types of hyperedges: $E^{(1)}$: Hyperedges indicating pairwise friendships. $E^{(2)}$: Hyperedges each of which contains all the venue vertices belong to the same category. $E^{(3)}$: Hyperedges each of which contains a triplet of user, check-in venue and venue category vertices, the weight is defined as: $\omega(e) = \sum_{u,v \in E^{(3)}} \phi(u, v) h(u, v)$ where $\phi(u, v)$ is the sentiment intensity value of venue v from user u which is calculated by tips. We conduct the experiments to verify the effectiveness of the sentiment analysis incorporation. $E^{(4)}$: Hyperedges each of which contains all the venues one user has ever visited. And weights for hyperedges $E^{(1)}, E^{(2)}$ and $E^{(4)}$ are set to be 1.

3.2   Adapting Random Walk with Restart For LBSN Hypergraph

Note that our proposed HRWR method is not the same as the approaches proposed in [11] where the focus is more on a general mathematical approach instead of practical applications. In this paper, we focus on boosting the accuracy of POI recommendation via RWR in hypergraphs. In [11], the surfing happens among all the vertices, and the steady-state probability distribution is over all vertices.

As for our LBS recommendation, we propose a fair prediction by letting RWR only surf between venues vertices and the transition probability is achieved by utilizing the information carried in the whole hypergraph structure. In our LBS hypergraph model, there are four types of hyperedges, how to select a proper hyperedge as the transition edge is a vital problem. Based on the idea that if two users have visited many common venues, they should have the similar behavior patterns. Thus, we believe choosing the hyperedge $E^{(4)}$ as transition edge is a good choice.

In each step of HRWR, given the current vertex v_i, we first randomly choose a hyperedge $e^4 \in E^{(4)}$ with which the vertex v_i is incident, then we choose another destination venue vertex v_j in e^4, and u_j is the user vertex incident with e^4. To determine the transition probability $P(v_i, v_j)$ from vertex v_i to vertex v_j, we mainly consider three parts of the structure influence. Let $\Phi(v_i)$ denote the set of hyperedges $E^{(4)}$ each of which is incident with v_i. $\omega(v_j, u_j)$ denotes the weight of hyperedge $E^{(3)}$ that contains v_j and u_j. Then, all parts of the probability values are calculated as below:

- For each pairwise friendship relation,

$$P_1(v_i, v_j) = \sum_{e^1 \in E^{(1)}} \sum_{v_j \in e^1} \frac{h(\mu(v_i), u_j)w(e^1)}{\sqrt{d_{\mu(v_i)} d_{u_j}}} \tag{1}$$

where $\mu(v_i)$ denote the user node where $\mu(v_i)$ and v_i are incident with hyperedge e^4.

- For the category information,

$$P_2(v_i, v_j) = \sum_{e^2 \in E^{(2)}} \omega(e^2) \frac{h(v_i, e^2)}{d(v_i)} \frac{h(v_j, e^2)}{\delta(e^2)} \tag{2}$$

- For the venues and users,

$$P_3(v_i, v_j) = \frac{\omega(v_j, u_j)}{\sigma(e)} \tag{3}$$

where $\sigma(e) = \sum_{e^4 \in \Phi(v_i)} \frac{\sum_{v_j \in e} \omega(v_j, u_j)}{\delta(e)}$. In the other words, $\sigma(e)$ is sum of normalized weight of all the venues vertices in $\Phi(v_i)$. $\sigma(e)$ also can be written as $\sigma(e) = \sum_{e^4 \in E^{(4)}} \frac{h(e^4, v_i)}{\delta(e)} \sum_{e^4 \in E^{(4)}} h(e^4, v_j)\omega(v_j, u_j)$.

Finally, $\hat{P} = P_1 + P_2 + P_3$ is obtained. We adopt PageRank(PR) to guarantee irreducibility and aperiodicity. At step t, if the current node is v_i, PR will surfer to nodes which are incident with v_i at a certain probability and surfer to the source node with a small probability called damping factor α[3]. It also ensures the graph to be irreducible as random walk always has the probability of surfer

---

[3] In our experiments, the empirical value of α is 0.2.

to any other nodes. Here we illustrate the adaption of the random walk with restart process to our hypergraph model, given as:

$$p^{(t+1)} = (1 - \alpha)p^t P + \alpha q, \tag{4}$$

where $p^{(t)}, p^{(t+1)}$ and q are column vector. p^t expresses the probability distribution at each step t. The restart vector q is defined as follows:

$$\hat{q}(i) = \begin{cases} \omega(e_{u,v_i}^3), & \text{if u has visited venues } v_i; \\ 0, & \text{otherwise.} \end{cases} \tag{5}$$

$$q = \hat{q}./ \sum_i q(i) \tag{6}$$

4 Experimental Evaluation

The data we used in experiments is the check-in data from Foursquare[4]. Three competitive recommendation algorithms are utilized as baselines for the comparison, namely, Random walk with restart in simple graph, user-based collaborative filtering(CF)[9] and supervised random walk[3] in simple graph.

Fig. 2 and Fig. 3 show the prediction performances with respect to precision and recall achieved by our proposed methodology and the compared approaches. It's very obvious that our proposed methodology outperforms the competitive approaches. Note that CF works worst. This is because the user-venue matrix is extremely sparse, and it is quite hard to perceive the similarities of users and of venues through the matrix. Random walk outperforms CF but is beat by our proposed approach. This is because random walk over simple graph utilizes the multiple information extracted from the simple graph but overlooked the high order relations which the simple graph fails to present. We adapt the supervised

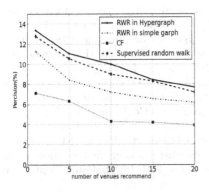

Fig. 2. Precision @N

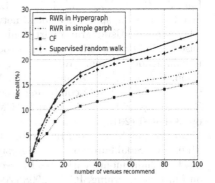

Fig. 3. Recall @N

random walk by partitioning the dataset into two categories: like and dislike, according to our sentiment analysis to the check-in tips and force the random walk to surf among those vertices labeled as like. The performance of supervised random walk is still slightly lower than that of our HRWR. Again, the observed outperformance of our approach is due to the incorporation of structured high order relations.

5   Conclusion

In this paper, we propose a unified hypergraph model for location recommendation. Our model focus on making most use of multiple types of information and high-order relations of the location-based social network. Accordingly, we also propose a personalized random walk with restart working on our proposed LBSN hypergraph(HRWR). The distance restriction is used to shorten the venue candidate list. Thus, we can heavily reduce the computation complexity. The sentiment analysis to the check-in posts are used to refine the hypergraph modeling and further boost the prediction performance. We have conducted extensive experiments on a real dataset and demonstrated the effectiveness of our model compared to several state-of-the-art methods. Our model can be also applied to other ranking problems that have complex relations by nature.

References

1. Adomavicius, G., Tuzhilin, A.: Toward the next generation of recommender systems: A survey of the state-of-the-art and possible extensions. IEEE Transactions on Knowledge and Data Engineering **17**(6), 734–749 (2005)
2. Avin, C., Lando, Y., Lotker, Z.: Radio cover time in hyper-graphs. In: Proceedings of the 6th International Workshop on Foundations of Mobile Computing, pp. 3–12. ACM (2010)
3. Backstrom, L., Leskovec, J.: Supervised random walks: predicting and recommending links in social networks. In: Proceedings of the fourth ACM International Conference on Web Search and Data Mining, pp. 635–644. ACM (2011)
4. Bao, J., Zheng, Y., Mokbel, M.F.: Location-based and preference-aware recommendation using sparse geo-social networking data. Gis, pp. 199–208 (2012)
5. Alejandro, B.: Using graph partitioning techniques for neighbour selection in user-based collaborative filtering. In: Proceedings of the Sixth ACM Conference on Recommender Systems, RecSys 2012, pp. 213–216. ACM (2012)
6. Chen, C., Wang, C., Zhang, L., He, X., Bu, J., Tan, S.: Music recommendation by unified hypergraph: combining social media information and music content. In: Proceedings of the 18th Annual ACM International Conference on Multimedia, pp. 391–400 (2010)
7. Mnih, A., Salakhutdinov, R.: Probabilistic matrix factorization. In: NIPS (2007)
8. Mnih, A., Salakhutdinov, R.: Bayesian probabilistic matrix factorization using markov chain monte carlo. In: Proceedings of the 25th International Conference on Machine Learning, ICML 2008 (2008)
9. Koren, C.V.Y., Bell, R.: Matrix factorization techniques for recommender systems. IEEE Computer **42**(8), 30–37 (2009)

10. Xie, X., Ma, W-Y., Zheng, Y., Zhang, L.: Mining interesting locations and travel sequences from GPS trajectories. In: Proc. of 2009 Int. World Wide Web Conf. (WWW 2009), pp. 791–800 (2009)
11. Zhou, D., Huang, J., Schölkopf, B.: Learning with hypergraphs: clustering, classification, and embedding. In: Advances in Neural Information Processing Systems, pp. 1601–1608 (2006)

ProbLog Program Based Ontology Matching

Yuanyuan Wang[✉]

Academy of Mathematics and System Science, Chinese Academy of Sciences,
No.55 Zhongguancun East Road, Beijing 100190, China
wyuanyuan16@gmail.com

Abstract. Ontology matching reconciles semantic heterogeneity between ontologies to find correspondence of entities, including classes, properties, and instances. We propose using ProbLog program to tackle this problem. It uses probabilistic facts to encode initial similarities (priors) of candidate matching pairs and exploits definite clauses and annotated disjunctions to respectively express certain and probabilistic influence of matching pairs. We experimentally evaluate our method on the datasets of conference track in Ontology Alignment Evaluation Initiative. Experimental results show: (1) recall is improved compared with priors; (2) our method is better in precision, recall and F_1-measure than the most related Markov logic networks.

1 Introduction

Ontology matching aims to dealing with semantic heterogeneity between ontologies to enhance their interoperation. It finds correspondence of related entities, including concepts, properties and instances. Since it is boring and time-consuming to manually get the matching entities pairs, there are many automatic or semi-automatic uncertain ways to tackle ontology matching. Besides, it is necessary to incorporate complex, relational structures in ontology. In this paper, we propose ProbLog program to automatically deal with ontology matching.

The first method of combining probability with logic applied to ontology matching is Markov logic networks (MLN) [1] in CODI [2] system. It treats ontology matching as MAP and exploits many strategies to compute the prior of two entities, formalizes the constraints into formulas of Markov logic networks, and finally uses integer linear programming to do inference after formulas transformed to grounded Markov networks.

Our method is different from that approach in several aspects. First, the rules are directed, not like MLN, making logical knowledge on the influence more interpretable and easy to understand. Secondly, as for the bidirectional influence, we construct two rules, each with different probability, thus describing influential matching pairs at varied degrees. Finally, experimental results show our method is better than MLN in precision, recall and F_1-measure.

© Springer International Publishing Switzerland 2015
S. Zhang et al. (Eds.): KSEM 2015, LNAI 9403, pp. 778–783, 2015.
DOI: 10.1007/978-3-319-25159-2_72

2   ProbLog Program

A ProbLog program is a probabilistic extension of Prolog [3]. It consists two parts: labeled facts (F), modeling the probabilistic data and rules (R), expressing the consequence of uncertain facts.

As for the probabilistic facts F, there are two forms: probabilistic facts and intentional probabilistic facts to model the uncertain data. The former form is $p_i :: f_i$, meaning the probability of grounded f_i representing random events with true assignment is p_i. While the later is $p::f(X_1, X_2, ..., X_n): -body$, with body a conjunction of non-probabilistic facts defining the domain of the variables X_1, X_2, ... and X_n (Fierens et al. 2013). It means a whole set of facts with the same probability p_i if the bodies are true.

For the rules R, there are two kinds: definite clauses (Prolog rules) and annotated disjunctions [4]. Prolog rules are certain to determine consequence of probabilistic facts [5]. Annotated disjunctions, which has the form : $p_1 :: h_1, p_2 :: h_2, ..., p_n :: h_n \leftarrow b_1, b_2, ..., b_m$, where p_i corresponds to the probability of head h_i, thus summing p_i is less than 1 (if the summation is strictly less than 1, it means that there are no cause leading the head to being true) (Shterionov et al. 2015) and b_i is the body. When doing inference, these annotated disjunctions will be converted to probabilistic facts and definite clause.

Its semantics is based on distribution semantics [6] to decide a distribution on possible worlds (Least models). A probabilistic fact $p_i :: f_i$ is called an atomic choice, specifying choosing f_i with or discarding it with $(1 - f_i)$ in a world. Let w be a possible world. A total choice, set of atomic choices, defines a probability distribution over random events as $P(w) = \prod_i p_i$, where p_i is the probability of individual atomic choice.

3   Matching Scheme

The matching operation determines an alignment, a set of correspondences, for a pair of ontologies $\mathcal{O}_1$ and $\mathcal{O}_2$ with parameters [7]. In this paper, we are interested in finding the equivalence relation of class and property, i.e. the relation is equivalent relation and entities are classes and properties. A widely adopted cardinality constraint for ontology matching is one-to-one. That means for each entity e_1 in $\mathcal{O}_1$, there is at most one and only one entity e_2 in $\mathcal{O}_2$ corresponded to it and vice versa. We also use this restriction here. However, we will show that our approach can be extended to other cardinality constraints such as many-to-many, many-to-one, one-to-many.

As for our methods, first, even there are many strategies mentioned in [8], we use some similarities metrics, such as, edit-distance, WordNet and TF-IDF, to calculate the similarity (prior) of two entities. Then we incorporate them to ProbLog program to compute the marginal probability of candidate matching entities e_1 and e_2 in $\mathcal{O}_1$ and $\mathcal{O}_2$. Finally, we exploit cardinality constraint and thresholds to filter matched pairs. In the following, we mainly introduce the rules and inference scenarios.

Rules and Their Meanings. We use the following rules to describe potential matching influence of two pairs. Here, Rules from R_1 to R_5 improve the recall, because they express the positive influence, while R_7 and R_8 are beneficial to improve the precision. R_6 is the influence of prior to experimental probability. The meanings of the predicate in rules are expressed in Table 1^1.

$R_1 : p : \mathtt{match}(Y, N) \leftarrow \mathtt{sub1}(X, Y), \mathtt{sub2}(M, N), \mathtt{match1}(X, M).$

$R_2 : p : \mathtt{match}(X, M) \leftarrow \mathtt{sub1}(X, Y), \mathtt{sub2}(M, N), \mathtt{match1}(Y, N).$

$R_3 : p : \mathtt{match}(Y, N) \leftarrow \mathtt{sib1}(X, Y), \mathtt{sib2}(M, N), \mathtt{match1}(X, M).$

$R_5 : p : \mathtt{match}(Y, N) \leftarrow \mathtt{hasdomain1}(X, Y), \mathtt{hasdomain2}(M, N), \mathtt{match1}(X, M).$

$R_5 : p : \mathtt{match}(Y, N) \leftarrow \mathtt{hasrange1}(X, Y), \mathtt{hasrange2}(M, N), \mathtt{match1}(X, M).$

$R_6 : \quad \mathtt{match}(X, Y) \leftarrow \mathtt{match1}(X, Y).$

$R_7 : \quad \mathtt{notamatch}(Y, N) \leftarrow \mathtt{sub1}(X, Y), \mathtt{disjoint2}(m, n), \mathtt{match}(X, M).$

$R_8 : \quad \mathtt{match}(Y, N) \leftarrow \mathtt{sub2}(X, Y), \mathtt{disjoint1}(M, N), \mathtt{match}(X, M).$

$R_9 : \quad \mathtt{match}(X, Y) \leftarrow \quad \backslash + \mathtt{notamatch}(X, Y).$

Table 1. Meaning of predicates in the rules

Notation	Meaning of predicates
$\mathtt{sub1}(X, Y)$	owl:Class X is subClassOf owl:Class Y
$\mathtt{dis1}(X, Y)$	owl:Class X is disjointWith owl:Class Y
$\mathtt{hasrange1}(X, Y)$	owl:ObjectProperty X has range owl:Class Y
$\mathtt{hasdomain1}(X, Y)$	owl:ObjectProperty X has domain owl:Class Y
$\mathtt{sib1}(X, Y)$	owl:Class X shares the same superclass owl:Class Y
$\mathtt{match1}(X, Y)$	the prior of candidate matching entities X and Y
$\mathtt{match}(X, Y)$	the marginal probability of matching entities X and Y

Inference Scenarios. Current, the way to do inference on definite clause and annotated disjunctions as we know is mentioned in [5] captured by ProbLog. This is called the **MARG** task [9]. Let Q be the interested query atoms and E be the observations. As in our cases, $E = \oslash$ then what we to calculate is P(Q|E), i.e., marginal probability of query atom.

When doing inference, there are four steps: 1) transforms the ProbLog program with annotated disjunctions to new program only contains probabilistic facts and definite clauses; 2) converts the new program to weighted Boolean formulas; 3) compiles these formulas to smooth d-DNNF [10]; 4) converts smooth d-DNNF into arithmetic circuits to get the marginal probability of query atoms. In the below, we introduce the detailed steps for the transformation.

Step 1. To translate this program into program only with probabilistic facts and definite clauses, surrogate probabilistic fact and one constraint are added to ensure the correctness of conversion (Shterionov et al. 2015). Surrogate probabilistic fact specifies an explicit choice while the constraint ensure it does not introduce undesired combinations of values [5].

---

[1] Considering the space, c notations are incomplete, for example, the sub-class relation of properties. For $\mathcal{O}_2$, the representation is similar, i.e., changing 1 to 2.

Step 2. After the ProbLog program contains only facts and definite clauses, it is converted to an equivalent Boolean formula. There are three kinds, i.e. probabilistic facts, derived facts and definite rules. To be more specific, 1) for probabilistic fact f_i, the probability of grounded fact is transformed to f_i with p_i and f_i with $1 - p_i$. 2) for derived fact, it is converted to f_i with 1 and f_i with 1. 3) for the rules, since the rules may be cyclic or acyclic, we introduce the transformation respectively. If the rules are cyclic, we use proof-based conversion [11] to change the rules to be acyclic. As for these acylic rules, we use Clark's completion [12] of the rules to convert them.

Step 3. We then transform the weighted formulas to smooth d-DNNF. This process is detailed in [10]. A d-DNNF is a rooted directed acyclic graph satisfies three conditions: 1) A literal labels each leaf node and conjunction or disjunction labels internal node; 2) No children has common atom for every conjunction; 3) All children represent logically inconsistent formulas for every disjunction. The reason for using d-DNNF is that inference task after transformation is tractable because it shifts the complexity to the compilation stage, even complexity of original inference is #P. A smooth d-DNNF also satisfies the conditions: all children use same set of atoms for every disjunction node.

Step 4. Then this smooth d-DNNF is compiled to Arithmetic Circuit. There are two steps (Darwiche 2009): 1)replace all conjunctions with multiplications and disjunctions with summations in the internal node, 2) replace every leaf node with a multiplication, which has two leaf children, i.e., one with an indicator for literal and another with its weight.

After above four steps, we can get the marginal probability of query atoms in the rooted node. Then we can filter the matched pairs using one-to-one constraint.

4   Experimental Evaluation

We use the data of conference track in 2014[2]. It contains 21 reference alignments for 7 of 16 ontologies from conference organization. To evaluate our methods, we compare experimental results in three aspects: 1) priors, 2) baselines, i.e., StringEqiv and enda, given by OAEI, 3) other systems. For evaluation, we use the standards: precision (P), recall (R) and F_1-measure (F_1), given by OAEI.

Compared with the Baselines Under Different Thresholds. We compare our results with the baselines under different thresholds t. Table 2 shows that our priors are better compared with the two baselines under all thresholds tested.

Comparison with the Priors. In order to evaluate the effect of ProbLog program, we also compare our results with thresholds 0.7 and 0.75 respectively.

---

[2] http://oaei.ontologymatching.org/2014/conference/index.html

Table 2. Comparison with the standards under different thresholds(t), String-Eqiv and enda are two baselines given by OAEI.

Measures	StringEqiv	enda	t=0.5	t=0.55	t=0.6	t=0.65	t=0.7	t=0.75
P	0.8	0.76	0.6661	0.6435	0.6158	0.7085	0.7745	0.8240
R	0.43	0.49	0.5874	0.6184	0.6665	0.5888	0.5843	0.5341
F_1	0.56	0.6	0.6030	0.6079	0.6202	0.6249	0.6504	0.6334

These two rank the top 2 compared with priors. Table 3 shows the comparison between the priors and using ProbLog program. It is obvious that recall is improved in Table 3. This is caused by the fact ProbLog program can improve the probability of matching pairs with rules.

Table 3. Comparison with priors. t_i is the initial result, while t_{ii} is the result using ProbLog program.

Measures	t_1=0.7	t_2=0.75	t_{11}=0.7	t_{22}=0.75
P	0.7745	0.8204	0.7653	0.8194
R	0.5843	0.5364	0.5964	0.5843
F_1	0.6504	0.6334	0.6591	0.6578

Table 4. Comparison with other system. CODI uses MLN; iMatch exploits Markov Network; LogMap is the second system in OAEI 2014

Measures	CODI	ProbLog	iMatch
P	0.74	0.82	0.6
R	0.57	0.58	0.45
F_1	0.64	0.66	0.52

Comparison with Other Systems. Here we compare our methods with the most related: CODI, iMatch [13]. iMatch uses Markov Network as a framework to tackle ontology matching. It utilizes edges to express the potential influence between matching pairs. From Table 4, it is obvious that our methods is better than CODI and iMatch in precision, recall and F_1-measure.

5   Conclusion

In this paper, we proposed using ProbLog program as a framework for ontology matching. Even we only focused on the correspondence of class and properties, experimental results show ProbLog program based approach can improve the recall even under different priors and gain higher results in precision, recall and F_1-measure compared with MLN based, thus showing it a promising method. As the method of learning the probability of annotated disjunctions in ProbLog program was not available and not fully studied, thus research on it is the future work. Besides, experimental results of conference track were promising, but more experiments are needed to test our approach in the future work.

Acknowledgments. This work was supported by the Natural Science Foundation of China (No. 61232015), the Knowledge Innovation Program of the Chinese Academy of Sciences (CAS), Key Lab of Management, Decision and Information Systems of

CAS, and Institute of Computing Technology of CAS. Besides, we own many thanks to Dimitar Shterionov and Wannes Meert helping us tame the tool, i.e., ProbLog and sharing the insights of probabilistic logic programs captured by this tool.

References

1. Domingos, P., Richardson, M.: 1 markov logic: A unifying framework for statistical relational learning. Statistical Relational Learning (2007) 339
2. Niepert, M., Meilicke, C., Stuckenschmidt, H.: A probabilistic-logical framework for ontology matching. In: AAAI. Citeseer (2010)
3. De Raedt, L., Kimmig, A., Toivonen, H.: Problog: A probabilistic prolog and its application in link discovery. In: IJCAI, vol. 7
4. Vennekens, J., Verbaeten, S., Bruynooghe, M.: Logic programs with annotated disjunctions. In: Lifschitz, V., Demoen, B. (eds.) ICLP 2004. LNCS, vol. 3132, pp. 431–445. Springer, Heidelberg (2004)
5. Shterionov, D., Renkens, J., Vlasselaer, J., Kimmig, A., Meert, W., Janssens, G.: The most probable explanation for probabilistic logic programs with annotated disjunctions. status: accepted (2015)
6. Sato, T.: A statistical learning method for logic programs with distribution semantics. In: Proceedings of the 12th International Conference on Logic Programming (ICLP95). Citeseer (1995)
7. Shvaiko, P., Euzenat, J.: Ontology matching: state of the art and future challenges. IEEE Transactions on Knowledge and Data Engineering **25**, 158–176 (2013)
8. Euzenat, J., Shvaiko, P., et al.: Ontology Matching, vol. 18. Springer, Heidelberg (2007)
9. Fierens, D., Van den Broeck, G., Renkens, J., Shterionov, D., Gutmann, B., Thon, I., Janssens, G., De Raedt, L.: Inference and learning in probabilistic logic programs using weighted boolean formulas. In: Theory and Practice of Logic Programming, pp. 1–44 (2013)
10. Darwiche, A.: New advances in compiling cnf to decomposable negation normal form. In: Proc. of ECAI, pp. 328–332. Citeseer (2004)
11. Mantadelis, T., Janssens, G.: Dedicated tabling for a probabilistic setting. In: Technical Communications of the 26th International Conference on Logic Programming, vol. 7, pp. 124–133 (2010)
12. Lloyd, J.W.: Foundations of logic programming. Springer Science & Business Media (2012)
13. Albagli, S., Ben-Eliyahu-Zohary, R., Shimony, S.E.: Markov network based ontology matching. Journal of Computer and System Sciences **78**, 105–118 (2012)

Bioinformatics and Computational Biology

Person Re-identification via Learning Visual Similarity on Corresponding Patch Pairs

Hao Sheng, Yan Huang[(⊠)], Yanwei Zheng, Jiahui Chen, and Zhang Xiong

State Key Laboratory of Software Development Environment, School of Computer
Science and Engineering, 100191 Beijing, People's Republic of China
{shenghao,yanhuang,zhengyw,chenjiahui1991,xiongz}@buaa.edu.cn

Abstract. Since humans concentrate more on differences between relatively small but salient body regions in matching person across disjoint
camera views, we propose these differences to be the most significant
character in person re-identification (Re-ID). Unlike existing methods
focusing on learning discriminative features to adapt viewpoint variation using global visual similarity, we propose a learning visual similarity algorithm via corresponding patch pairs (CPPs) for person Re-ID.
The novel CPPs method is introduced to represent the corresponding
body patches of the same person in different images with good robustness to body pose, viewpoint and illumination variations. The similarity
between two people is measured by an improved bi-directional weight
mechanism with a TF-IDF like patches weight. At last, a complementary similarity measure and a mutually-exclusive regulation are presented
to enhance the performance of Re-ID. With quantitative evaluation on
public datasets, the best rank-1 matching rate on the VIPeR dataset is
improved by 4.14%.

Keywords: Person re-identification · Corresponding patch pairs · Patch
weight · Visual similarity · Cross-camera

1 Introduction

Person re-identification (Re-ID), from a series of candidate images captured in
distributed locations or different times, is essential to several computer vision
problems such as image retrieval, person identification, re-acquisition and cross-
camera person tracking [1],[2],[3],[4],[5]. To associate the images of the same individual and discard irrelevant ones, person Re-ID mostly relies on pairwise data
to evaluate the similarity. Designing robust person descriptor is one of the key
technologies in person Re-ID, including the entire image descriptor [2],[6],[7],[8]
and the one without background [4],[9],[10],[11],[12]. However, despite years of
research, state-of-the-art algorithms are no match for human's abilities in person
Re-ID for the existence of the variations of viewpoint, illumination, pose, and
other factors.

To eliminate the effects caused by the variations, many discriminative features
are proposed for designing the person descriptors on the entire image. Gray et al. [2]

© Springer International Publishing Switzerland 2015
S. Zhang et al. (Eds.): KSEM 2015, LNAI 9403, pp. 787–798, 2015.
DOI: 10.1007/978-3-319-25159-2_73

Fig. 1. The CPPs sampled from the same person in different camera views.

introduce the ensemble of localized features via boosting algorithm. To absorb the illumination variation in different camera views, a descriptor that combines biologically inspired feature and covariance descriptor is given by Ma et al. [6],[7]. Prosser et al. [13] formulate person Re-ID as a ranking problem, and learn the feature weight based on RankSVM; Zheng et al. [8] propose a relative distance comparison model to maximize the pairwise likelihood in person Re-ID. Both of them use the entire image features, a mixture of color (RGB, YCbCr, HSV) and texture (Gabor [14] and Schmid [15]) histogram features, designed in [2].

To minimize the effect of background clutters, many effective body segmentation methods [10],[11],[12] have been put forward for person Re-ID. Considering that background region is far away from the body center, Farenzena et al. [4] downgrade the weights of patches which are more distant from the symmetry axis of body. Bak et al. [12] present the body appearance based on haar-like features and dominant color descriptors. A gaussian descriptor includes the mixing characteristics of color, texture and spatial structure of body is demonstrated in [16]. However, confined by the strongly inhomogeneous background and low-resolution image, existing body segmentation methods cannot accurately capture the body contour. Good body segmentation method can efficiently improve the person Re-ID matching rate, but it is not the emphasis in our research. In this work, we try to solve person Re-ID problem based on body region. Instead of developing a better body segmentation method, a complementary similarity measure is proposed to enhance the performance of person Re-ID.

In this paper, we discuss a novel corresponding patch pairs (CPPs) method to learn visual similarity for person Re-ID. On the present state of studies, patch-based person Re-ID methods have obtained good performance in several works. Cai et al. [17] collect signatures of patches along body contour. These patches are matched with corresponding patches that aid by dominant color representation and geometric constraints. Since salient regions can effectively distinguish the appearance of different persons and are general enough to identify person across different camera views. Zhao et al. [18] divide images into small patches and extract color and SIFT feature in each patch for salience matching. In order to automatically discover effective patches to learn mid-level filter for person Re-ID, patches are qualitatively measured and classified with their discriminative power in [19]. Different from previous works, CPPs is proposed to learn visual similarity which can effectively represent all the patch pairs variations in visual for the same person in different views (shown in Fig. 1).

To sample CPPs which are robust to illumination, background and pose variations, three processes are proposed including: visual pattern feature clustering, Hungarian adjacency constrained search and CPPs candidate quantification after image preprocessing. An improved bi-directional weight mechanism that respectively exploits a TF-IDF like method and the learned distance metric on CPPs to calculate the patch weight and patch pair similarity, is used to measure the similarity of individuals. Furthermore, a complementary similarity measure that can reduce the effect of background clutters caused by inaccurate body segmentation, is used to enhance our approach. At last, a mutually-exclusive regulation is proposed to achieve better rank-1 performance. We demonstrate the validity of our approach on the VIPeR [20] and CAVIAR4REID [5] datasets. The results show that our approach achieve very competitive results by quantitative evaluation.

2   Image Preprocessing

Considering the original person images easily change with the variations of background and illumination. In the first stage, the pedestrian parsing method is used to discard the background and the illumination equalization method is used to reduce the influence caused by the illumination.

As shown in Fig. 2, after normalizing the V channel in HSV color space for illumination equalization, the Deep Decompositional Network (DDN) [10] is used to remove background and parse person body into five parts, including hair, head, body, arms and legs. Then, the foreground mask and boundary between upper and lower body can be obtained by the parsing result. Due to the lack of differentiation, the head and foot parts are ignored. DDN is able to accurately estimate complex pose variation with good robustness to occlusions and background clutters, details can be found in [10]. In addition, erosion is used to erase the burrs in foreground region to get smooth body contour. At last, the upper and lower bodies are segmented respectively into grid of local patches. We set the size of patch is 8x8 and the grid step is 4. A 672-dimensional dColorSIFT feature which is robust to the variations of viewpoint and illumination is extracted from each patch. Many researches such as [18],[19] and [21] show great effect by using the dColorSIFT feature as patch descriptor.

3   Sampling Corresponding Patch Pairs

3.1   Visual Pattern Feature Clustering

Patches with different visual information are mixed together. Therefore, clustering is performed to group patches into subsets with coherent visual information. CPPs are sampled from the same cluster. Patches clustering, between probe image and gallery image, is the first step of sampling CPPs.

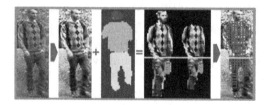

Fig. 2. Image preprocessing: The first column shows the original image. The second column shows the illumination equalization result. The third column shows the parsing result by DDN. The body contour and boundary given by the column 2 and 3 are shown in the fourth column. The last column shows the grid of patch partition.

In this task, the feature dimension of patch is high, and the distributions of data clusters are often in different densities and sizes. Therefore, graph degree linkage (GDL) algorithm [22] is employed for patch clustering since it can well cope with these problems. However, due to the difficulty to determine the appropriate cluster granularity, some patch clusters have mixed visual patterns [19]. It cannot accurately sample CPPs from these clusters. Thus two kinds of patch clustering trees (PCTs) are constructed for upper and lower bodies respectively. Given a probe image A and a a gallery image B, upper body patch set $P_u^{A,B} = P_u^A \cup P_u^B$ and lower body patch set $P_l^{A,B} = P_l^A \cup P_l^B$. Two PCTs are built with order O and depth D, e.g. each parent node in upper PCT has O_u children and there are D_u layers of nodes. Considering a certain degree of differences among upper and lower body, we set $O_u = 2, D_u = 3$ and $O_l = 3, D_l = 2$ in our experiment. The root nodes of upper and lower PCT contain all the patches in $P_u^{A,B}$ and $P_l^{A,B}$, respectively. Specially, the second-layer node of upper PCT would not be expanded in which the number of patches are less than τ_{min}. We set τ_{min} equals a quarter of the patches in $P_u^{A,B}$. The clustering results is denoted as c_i where i is the index of clusters. As shown in Figure 3, c_i is corresponding to the leaf nodes of PCT.

Fig. 3. Different colors of leaf nodes represent different clusters. Specially, upper body patches are clustered to 3 or 4 clusters under our pruning condition.

3.2 Hungarian Adjacency Constrained Search

Based on the clustering results, Hungarian adjacency constrained search is proposed to select CPPs candidates in relaxed adjacent vertical space. Specially, our experiments only use the upper body patches because of the good discriminative power they have. To go against multi-to-one patch matching, Hungarian algorithm is introduced to improve adjacency constrained search strategy [18]. The CPPs candidates between the probe image A and the corresponding gallery image A' should belong to the same cluster c_i, which is defined as $S^{A,A'}$:

$$S^{A,A'} = \{s_x^{A,A'} | x = 1...N_{row}\}, s_x^{A,A'} = H(M(P_x^{A,c_i}, \varepsilon(P_x^{A,c_i}))), \qquad (1)$$

where x is the row number and $P_x^{A,c_i} \in c_i$ denotes a patch set at the x-th row of image A, $\varepsilon(P_x^{A,c_i})$ is the corresponding patch set of P_x^{A,c_i} in image A', which is formulated as:

$$\varepsilon(P_x^{A,c_i}) = \{p_{k,y}^{A',c_i} | p_{k,y}^{A',c_i} \in c_i, y = 1...N_{col}, k = max(0, x-\delta)...min(N_{row}, x+\delta)\}, \qquad (2)$$

$p_{k,y}^{A',c_i}$ represents the patch at the k-th row and the y-th column in image A', δ is the height of vertical search space ($\delta = 2$ in our experiment, the setup is the same as in [18]). In Equ. 1, $H(\cdot)$ represents the Hungarian assignment algorithm and $M(\cdot)$ is cost matrix among patches between P_x^{A,c_i} and $\varepsilon(P_x^{A,c_i})$ sets. The Hungarian assignment algorithm is used for finding CPPs candidate with minimum total cost. Supposing there are M patches in P_x^{A,c_i}, and N patches in $\varepsilon(P_x^{A,c_i})$. M is formulated as:

$$M = [d_{m,n}(F_m^A, F_n^{A'})]_{M \times N}, m = 1...M, n = 1...N, \qquad (3)$$

where F is the feature of patch, d is Radial Basis function.

3.3 Quantitative Description on CPPs Candidates

Some incorrect CPPs which lead to erroneous estimations of visual similarity are sampled in CPPs condidate. Therefore, visual similarity score (VSS) is presented to quantify the visual similarity of each pair in CPPs candidates. The pairs, whose VSSs are higher than the mean value of all CPPs candidates' VSSs are selected as CPPs for visual similarity learning. Intuitively, a large number of similar patches in corresponding images (e.g. A and A') with small difference in visual pattern are most likely to be selected as CPPs. In another aspect, patches in non-corresponding images are similar with each other should be penalized. Thus, we define the VSS as follows:

$$VSS(p_j^{A,c_i}, p_j^{A',c_i}) = \frac{d(F_j^{A,c_i}, F_j^{A',c_i}) \cdot (\frac{N_{c_i}^A}{N^A} + \frac{N_{c_i}^{A'}}{N^{A'}})}{\sum_{id=1}^{N_{per}} (\frac{N_{c_{i'}}^A}{N^A} + \frac{N_{c_{i'}}^{G_{id}}}{N^{G_{id}}}) \cdot \zeta\{N_{c_{i'}}^{G_{id}} \neq 0\} - (\frac{N_{c_i}^A}{N^A} + \frac{N_{c_i}^{A'}}{N^{A'}})}, \qquad (4)$$

where j is the pair index of CPPs candidates, d is Radial Basis function, F_j^{A,c_i} and F_j^{A',c_i} are features of patches in p_j^{A,c_i} and p_j^{A',c_i}. N_α^β is the number of patches, where α and β represent the cluster and person image respectively. N^β denotes the number of patches in β (contains all clusters). N_{per} is the number of person in gallery set. If $N_{c_{i'}}^{G_{id}} \neq 0$ indicator function $\zeta\{\cdot\}$ equals 1 and 0 otherwise. Specially, when the patch p_j^{A,c_i} is clustered with patches in image G_{id}, c_i becomes $c_{i'}$ which represents a common cluster between A and G_{id}.

4   Matching Based on CPPs

4.1   Patch Weight Calculation

Patches with distinct features are discriminative in finding the same person in different views [18]. The frequency of patch clustering with different persons can effectively reflect the discriminative power of the patch. Patches with high weight have higher discriminative power than others. Based on that reason, a TF-IDF like function is proposed to calculate patch weight on upper and lower body, which is defined as:

$$\omega(p_{x,y}^{A,c_{i'}}) = exp(\frac{T(p_{x,y}^{A,c_{i'}})/I(p_{x,y}^{A,c_{i'}})}{2\sigma^2}), \tag{5}$$

where $p_{x,y}^{A,c_{i'}} \in c_{i'}$ is the patch at the x-th row and the y-th column in image A, and σ is bandwidth. $T(p_{x,y}^{A,c_{i'}})$, which is measured by the frequency of visual similar patches clustering in image A itself, is defined as:

$$T(p_{x,y}^{A,c_{i'}}) = \sum_{id=1}^{N_{per}} \frac{N_{c_{i'}}^A}{N^A} \cdot \zeta\{N_{c_{i'}}^{G_{id}} = 0\}. \tag{6}$$

If $N_{c_{i'}}^{G_{id}} = 0$ indicator function $\zeta\{\cdot\}$ equals 1 and 0 otherwise. $I(p_{x,y}^{A,c_{i'}})$, which measures whether the patch is common or rare according to the patch clustering frequency between persons in Equ. 5, is defined as:

$$I(p_{x,y}^{A,c_{i'}}) = ln(N_{per}/(1 + N_{per} - N_{per'})), \tag{7}$$

$N_{per'}$ is the number of persons who do not have any patches to cluster with $p_{x,y}^{A,c_{i'}}$.

4.2   Integrated Matching

In our experiment, Locally-Adaptive Decision Function (LADF) [23] is used to learn the similarity of CPPs. With the bi-directional weighting mechanism [18], a person matching model based on LADF training result and patch weight is defined as:

$$d_{CPPs}(A, B) = \sum_{k=1}^{N} \frac{\omega(p_k^A) \cdot s(p_k^A, p_k^B) \cdot \omega(p_k^B)}{1 + |\omega(p_k^A) - \omega(p_k^B)|}, \tag{8}$$

where $s(p_k^A, p_k^B)$ represents the distance between patch p_k^A and p_k^B which is measured with LADF training result, with k being the index of patch pair. For sampling patch pairs of unlabeled persons, visual pattern features clustering step is ignored for keeping enough patch pairs in similarity measure. Hungarian adjacency constrained search method is used directly in finding the patch pairs between A and B (testing set) without considering clusters. Supposing N is the number of patch pairs between A and B. For fair comparison, we use the first N_{pair} distances. N_{pair} is defined as:

$$N_{pair} = min(N_i), i = 1...N_{per}, \tag{9}$$

where N_i is the number of patch pairs between A and the i-th person in gallery set.

5   Enhancing Re-ID Performance

5.1   Complementary Similarity Measure

Integrating several types of features with complementary nature are presented in most Re-ID methods [4],[2],[24],[25],[26]. Therefore, a complementary similarity measure is designed to make up for the shortcomings (In general, body segmentation method cannot accurately find the body contour.) of the entire image (EI) and human body (HB) matching. The distance $d_{eCPPs}(*)$ between two images can be computed as:

$$d_{eCPPs}(A, B) = d_{CPPs}(A, B) + d_{EI}(F_{EI}^A, F_{EI}^B) + d_{HB}(F_{HB}^A, F_{HB}^B), \tag{10}$$

where $d(*)$ is distance measure between person A and B. d_{CPPs} is in Equ. 10. d_{EI} and F_{EI} correspond to the distance measure and feature in [23] and [27], respectively. d_{HB} and F_{HB} correspond to the distance measure and feature in [16].

5.2   Mutually-Exclusive Regulation

A mutually-exclusive regulation (MER) is proposed to find the best-matching person in Single versus Single (S vs. S), only one exemplar per individual is available both in probe and gallery sets. Two steps of MER are presented as follows. First, if d_{CPPs}, d_{EI} and d_{HB} between person A (in probe set) and B (in gallery set) are all minimum respectively, it means B is the most similar and the best matching with A. So B is removed from matching candidates and keep matching with A only. The result is verified by the three independence distance.

Second, if one (denoted as G_B) in gallery set is the best matching with multiple individuals (denoted as P) in probe set measured by d_{eCPPs}, then the best-matching person in P have a relative lower similarity probability compared with others in gallery set. After that, a rank swaps between G_B and the second most similar candidates of the rest in P achieve better rank-1 performance.

6   Results and Analysis

Dataset. We demonstrate the evaluation results on two public datasets: VIPeR [20] and CAVIAR4REID [5]. The CAVIAR4REID dataset contains 1220 images of 72 persons with different viewpoints, poses and resolutions, each image captured from cameras inside a shopping mall, as shown in Fig. 4(a). The CAVIAR4REID dataset is measured in Single versus Multiple(S vs. M), multiple exemplars per individual are available in the probe set and only the first exemplar per individual in the gallery set. For a fair comparison, we use the same training and testing protocol mentioned in [23] that randomly divide the 72 persons into two sets, 36 persons for training and the rest for testing on CAVIAR4REID dataset, . The VIPeR is another challenging benchmark dataset for person Re-ID. This dataset contains 1264 images of 632 persons, each person has two images in different views with complex background and illumination variations, as shown in Fig. 4(b). The same experiment setup mentioned in [4] is used on VIPeR dataset. Ten trials of evaluation are conducted on two datasets and the average result is reported. In addition, the result is shown using the cumulative matching characteristic (CMC) curve [20], where the horizontal coordinate exploits top ranking k and the vertical coordinate donates the correct matching rates.

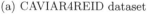

(a) CAVIAR4REID dataset   (b) VIPeR dataset

Fig. 4. A set of 16 randomly taken images pairs from the CAVIAR4REID and VIPeR dataset. The images in the same column belong to the same person.

6.1   Framework Verification

Tab. 1 illustrates several intermediate results and final results on two datasets. Because there are more than two images of each person, MER is ignored on CAVIAR4REID dataset. From the Re-ID results, the separate results of d_{EI}, d_{HB} and d_{CPPs} can generate the low matching rates. From the analysis of d_{CPPs} on two datasets, the good performance of CPPs is shown on CAVIAR4REID dataset, which is easy to achieve relatively perfect body segmentation since the background changes small with fewer clutter. Nonetheless, it is not relatively efficient on VIPeR dataset because the background changes considerably. The results of $d_{EI} + d_{HB}$, $d_{HB} + d_{CPPs}$ and $d_{EI} + d_{CPPs}$ manifest that the fusion of different features can make up for the shortcomings of any one. Compared with above results of the features fusion, $d_{EI} + d_{CPPs}$ achieves the best result since the result of d_{EI} is designed with the entire image features and d_{CPPs} pays more attention to the features of human body. Since both of d_{HB} and d_{CPPs} are based on the features of human body, the improvement of $d_{HB} + d_{CPPs}$ is not significant. Compared with results of $d_{HB} + d_{EI}$, the matching rate of d_{eCPPs} increases from 36.05% to 41.17% on CAVIAR4REID dataset. And it also has similar results on VIPeR dataset. In addition, the validity of mutually-exclusive regulation is shown by the increase of the matching rate from 44.56% to 47.53% on VIPeR dataset. The CMCs are shown in Fig. 5.

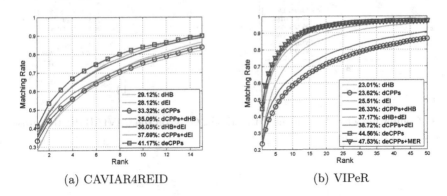

(a) CAVIAR4REID   (b) VIPeR

Fig. 5. Comparing with intermediate results. CMC on the CAVIAR4REID dataset (a) and the VIPeR dataset (b).

6.2   Quantitative Evaluation on Public Datasets

Fig. 6(a) shows that our approach achieves the best rank-1 accuracy 41.17% and outperforms other methods on CAVIAR4REID dataset in S vs. M scenario, including SDALF [4], PS [5], LMNN [28], ITML [29], GaLF [16] and LADF [23]. Comparison with PCCA [30], SDALF [4], LF [31], eSDC [18], LADF [23],

Table 1. Performance comparisons on CAVIAR4REID and VIPeR dataset

Method	CAVIAR4REID(%)(G=36)				VIPeR(%)(P=316,G=316)			
	r=1	r=3	r=5	r=7	r=1	r=5	r=10	r=15
d_{HB}	29.12	48.04	59.10	66.45	23.00	45.39	57.00	64.73
d_{EI}	28.12	49.06	60.97	68.87	25.50	59.57	74.73	82.34
d_{CPPs}	**33.31**	**50.88**	**60.32**	**67.54**	23.62	45.90	58.37	65.88
$d_{CPPs} + d_{HB}$	35.05	53.59	62.56	69.05	26.32	51.80	63.87	71.31
$d_{HB} + d_{EI}$	36.05	56.90	66.99	74.02	37.16	69.92	82.27	87.57
$d_{CPPs} + d_{EI}$	37.69	56.99	67.53	75.31	38.72	71.52	84.24	89.95
d_{eCPPs}	**41.17**	**60.84**	**71.14**	**77.57**	**44.56**	**75.11**	**86.75**	**91.72**
d_{eCPPs}+MER					**47.53**	**75.32**	**86.84**	**91.77**

SalMatch [21], kBiCov [7] and eMidF [19] on VIPeR dataset is shown in Fig. 6(b). The result shows our approach improves the best state-of-the-art rank-1 matching rate on the VIPeR dataset by 4.14%.

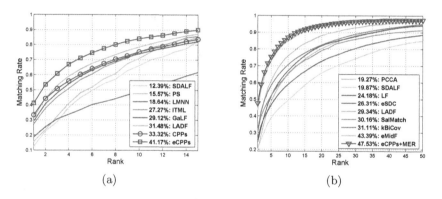

(a)   (b)

Fig. 6. Comparing with state-of-the-art methods. CMC on the CAVIAR4REID dataset (a) and the VIPeR dataset (b).

7   Conclusion

We have presented a learning visual similarity algorithm via CPPs for person Re-ID. Contrary to global visual similarity measure methods, a novel CPPs description method represent the corresponding body patch pairs of the same person with good robustness to body pose, viewpoint and illumination variations. After calculating the score of salience and matched patches with a TF-IDF like patches weight and a learning CPPs method, the similarity between two people is evaluated by an improved bi-directional weight mechanism. To further enhance Re-ID performance, a hierarchical descriptor makes our approach insensitive to background changes and a mutually-exclusive regulation improves the rank-1 performance. We demonstrate the validity of our approach on two public datasets, achieving very competitive results in terms of quantitative evaluation.

Acknowledgment. This study was partially supported by the National Natural Science Foundation of China (No. 61472019), the National High Technology Research and Development Program of China (No. 2013AA01A603) and the National Aerospace Science Foundation of China (No. 2013ZC51). Supported by the Programme of Introducing Talents of Discipline to Universities and the Open Fund of the State Key Laboratory of Software Development Environment under grant #SKLSDE-2015ZX-21.

References

1. Weiming, H., Min, H., Zhou, X., Tan, T., Lou, J., Maybank, S.J.: Principal axis-based correspondence between multiple cameras for people tracking. PAMI **28**, 663–671 (2006)
2. Tao, H., Tao, H., Gray, D., Gray, D.: Viewpoint invariant pedestrian recognition with an ensemble of localized features. In: Forsyth, D., Forsyth, D., Zisserman, A., Zisserman, A., Torr, P., Torr, P. (eds.) ECCV 2008, Part I. LNCS, vol. 5302, pp. 262–275. Springer, Heidelberg (2008)
3. Schwartz, W.R., Davis, L.S.: Learning discriminative appearance-based models using partial least squares. In: SIBGRAPI. IEEE, vol. XXII, pp. 322–329 (2009)
4. Farenzena, M., Bazzani, L., Perina, A., Murino, V., Cristani, M.: Person re-identification by symmetry-driven accumulation of local features. In: CVPR, pp. 2360–2367. IEEE (2010)
5. Cheng, D.S., Cristani, M., Stoppa, M., Bazzani, L., Murino, V.: Custom pictorial structures for re-identification. In: BMVC. BMVA, pp. 1–11 (2011)
6. Ma, B., Su, Y., Jurie, F.: Bicov: a novel image representation for person re-identification and face verification. In: BMVC. BMVA, pp. 1–11 (2012)
7. Bingpeng Ma, Y.S., Jurie, F.: Covariance descriptor based on bio-inspired features for person re-identification and face verification. Image Vision Computing **32**, 379–390 (2014)
8. Zheng, W., Gong, S., Xiang, T.: Reidentification by relative distance comparison. PAMI **35**, 653–668 (2013)
9. Bak, S., Suresh, S., Brmond, F., Thonnat, M.: Fusion of motion segmentation with online adaptive neural classifier for robust tracking. In: VISAPP, vol. II, pp. 410–416. INSTICC (2009)
10. Luo, P., Wang, X., Tang, X.: Pedestrian parsing via deep decompositional network. In: ICCV, pp. 2648–2655. IEEE (2013)
11. Jojic, N., Perina, A., Cristani, M., Murino, V., Frey, B.J.: Stel component analysis: modeling spatial correlations in image class structure. In: CVPR, pp. 2044–2051. IEEE (2009)
12. Bak, S., Corvee, E., Brmond, F., Thonnat, M.: Person re-identification using haar-based and dcd-based signature. In: AVSS, pp. 1–8. IEEE (2010)
13. Prosser, B., Zheng, W., Gong, S., Xiang, T.: Person re-identification by support vector ranking. In: BMVC. BMVA, vol. I, pp. 1–11 (2010)
14. Fogel, I., Sagi, D.: Gabor filters as texture discriminator. Biological Cybernetics **61**, 103–113 (1989)
15. Schmid, C.: Constructing models for content-based image retrieval. In: CVPR, pp. 39–45 (2001)

16. Ma, B., Ma, B., Li, Q., Li, Q., Chang, H., Chang, H.: Gaussian descriptor based on local features for person re-identification. In: Jawahar, C.V., Shan, S., Shan, S., Jawahar, C.V., Jawahar, C.V., Jawahar, C.V. (eds.) ACCV 2014 Workshops. LNCS, vol. 9010, pp. 505–518. Springer, Heidelberg (2015)

17. Cai, Y., Huang, K., Tan, T.: Human appearance matching across multiple non-overlapping cameras. In: ICPR, pp. 1–4. IEEE (2008)

18. Zhao, R., Ouyang, W., Wang, X.: Unsupervised salience learning for person re-identification. In: CVPR, pp. 3586–3593. IEEE (2013)

19. Zhao, R., Ouyang, W., Wang, X.: Learning mid-level filters for person re-identification. In: CVPR, pp. 144–151. IEEE (2014)

20. Gray, D., Brennan, S., Tao, H.: Evaluating appearance models for recognition, reacquisition, and tracking. In: IEEE International Workshop on Performance Evaluation of Tracking and Surveillance. Citeseer (2007)

21. Zhao, R., Ouyang, W., Wang, X.: Person re-identification by salience matching. In: ICCV, pp. 2528–2535. IEEE (2013)

22. Zhang, W., Zhang, W., Wang, X., Wang, X., Zhao, D., Zhao, D., Tang, X., Tang, X.: Graph degree linkage: agglomerative clustering on a directed graph. In: Fitzgibbon, A., Fitzgibbon, A., Lazebnik, S., Lazebnik, S., Perona, P., Perona, P., Sato, Y., Sato, Y., Schmid, C., Schmid, C. (eds.) ECCV 2012, Part I. LNCS, vol. 7572, pp. 428–441. Springer, Heidelberg (2012)

23. Li, Z., Chang, S., Liang, F., Huang, T.S., Cao, L., Smith, J.R.: Learning locally-adaptive decision functions for person verification. In: CVPR, pp. 3610–3617. IEEE (2013)

24. Bazzani, L., Cristani, M., Perina, A., Murino, V.: Multiple-shot person re-identification by chromatic and epitomic analyses. Pattern Recognition Letters 33(7), 898–903 (2012)

25. Wang, X., Doretto, G., Sebastian, T., Rittscher, J., Tu, P.: Shape and appearance context modeling. In: ICCV, pp. 1–8. IEEE (2007)

26. Loy, C.C., Liu, C., Gong, S.: Person re-identification by manifold ranking. In: ICIP, vol. 1, p. 5. Citeseer (2013)

27. Zhou, X., Cui, N., Li, Z., Liang, F., Huang, T.S.: Hierarchical gaussianization for image classification. In: ICCV, pp. 1971–1977. IEEE (2009)

28. Weinberger, K.Q., Blitzer, J., Saul, L.K.: Distance metric learning for large margin nearest neighbor classification. In: NIPS, pp. 1473–1480 (2005)

29. Davis, J.V., Kulis, B., Jain, P., Sra, S., Dhillon, I.S.: Information-theoretic metric learning. In: ICML, pp. 209–216. ACM (2007)

30. Mignon, A., Jurie, F.: Pcca: A new approach for distance learning from sparse pairwise constraints. In: CVPR, pp. 2666–2672. IEEE (2012)

31. Pedagadi, S., Orwell, J., Velastin, S.A., Boghossian, B.A.: Local fisher discriminant analysis for pedestrian re-identification. In: CVPR, pp. 3318–3325. IEEE (2013)

Person Re-identification by Unsupervised Color Spatial Pyramid Matching

Yan Huang[(✉)], Hao Sheng, Yang Liu, Yanwei Zheng, and Zhang Xiong

State Key Laboratory of Software Development Environment, School of Computer
Science and Engineering, Beijing 100191, People's Republic of China
{yanhuang,shenghao,liu.yang,zhengyw,xiongz}@buaa.edu.cn

Abstract. In this paper, we propose a novel unsupervised color spatial pyramid matching (UCSPM) approach for person re-identification. It is well motivated by our study on spatial pyramid to build effective structural object representation for person re-identification. Through the combination of illumination invariance color feature, UCSPM can well cope with the variations of viewpoint, illumination and pose. First, local superpixel regions are divided to accurately represent the color feature. Second, human body are divided into increasing fine vertical sub-regions to construct the spatial pyramid matching scheme. Third, the color feature and its spatial distribution information are used in a pyramid match kernel for calculating the similarity between person and person. The effectiveness of our approach is validated on the VIPeR dataset and CUHK campus dataset. Comparing with other approaches, our UCSPM improves the best unsupervised rank-1 matching rate on the VIPeR dataset by 3.08% with only one kind of feature—color.

Keywords: Person re-identification · Color spatial pyramid · Structural object representation · Unsupervised · Cross-camera

1 Introduction

The problem of person re-identification (Re-ID) requires the ability to re-identify an individual across multiple disjoint camera views, is becoming one of the most challenging tasks in computer vision [1],[2],[3],[4],[5]. It is also important in the field of video surveillance by searching a person from large amounts of video sequences as accurately as possible. In recent years, the methods of Re-ID are dominated by supervised learning that aim to learn an optimal metric or distance function [6],[7],[3]. These works usually require identity label of person that must be annotated manually for each pair of camera views, as training data. By employing supervised models, discriminative features are extracted to cope with the appearance variations of the same person under cross-view cameras. However, since video surveillance system can capture hundreds of pedestrians for a while, some of them may have a similar appearance. In addition, the same person observed in different camera views often under significant variations in viewpoint, illumination, pose, background, etc. Therefore, the training data should

© Springer International Publishing Switzerland 2015
S. Zhang et al. (Eds.): KSEM 2015, LNAI 9403, pp. 799–810, 2015.
DOI: 10.1007/978-3-319-25159-2_74

be as sufficient and as diverse as possible to enhance the generalization ability of training model that can implicitly discover the visual features of intra-class variations. To this end, it needs lots of manual annotation and sample selection. That is difficult to implement in a large scale video surveillance system.

Another widely used method in person Re-ID is unsupervised learning that aim to explore intuitive feature of human appearance and match directly by distance function (Euclidean distance, Mahalanobis distance, Gaussian distance, etc). The unsupervised methods are much better adaptability to different camera pair setting, although it may sacrifice matching accuracy. To seek more stable feature that can cope with the intra-class variations, various visual techniques are presented in previous works [1],[8],[9],[5]. Among these techniques, color features extraction of person image, a simple but efficient and important technique is used in person Re-ID, are commonly employed to construct human representation. Beyond that, the spatial layout information of features is also important to confine the feature distribution. Building effective structural object representation can effectively presents the spatial layout information, especially when the same person under disjoint camera views in the presence of large viewpoint or pose variations. Therefore, [10] introduces a kernel based recognition method that works by computing rough geometric correspondence on a global scale using an efficient approximation technique adapted from the spatial pyramid matching scheme of Grauman and Darrell [11]. In this method, the global non-invariant representation based on aggregating statistics of local features over fixed sub-regions significantly improves the recognize performance over methods based on detailed geometric correspondence.

Inspired from the pyramid matching scheme, this paper proposes a new approach based on unsupervised color spatial pyramid matching (UCSPM). Although we pursue spatial pyramid matching, this work is different from previous attempts. The similarity of local features is computed at increasingly fine vertical stripes of sub-region as shown in Fig.1. Spatial layout information aided by spatial pyramid is used to confine feature distribution and match between images. Beyond that, in order to control variations and misalignment between images, Hungarian algorithm and mean distance vector are used in the pyramid match kernel [10]. The color feature used in this work with the property of illumination invariance [12]. That is particularly applicable to camera views under outdoor areas. Furthermore, color features are usually extracted from the entire image, human body (without background) or local patches [13],[9],[5]. In general, these areas including a variety of colors can hardly represent the color property of human. Therefore, in this paper, superpixel-based segmentation technique is used to subdivide person images into local superpixel regions. In comparison with local patch method, superpixel method shows a significant improvement in our experiments.

The contributions of this paper can be summarized in two-folds. First, an unsupervised color spatial pyramid scheme is proposed to build effective structural object representation for person Re-ID. Second, superpixel-based color feature is presented with the combination of spatial pyramid framework that achieves competitive performance. Although we only use the color information in our pyramid framework, the comparative evaluations on two public datasets (VIPeR [14] and CUHK campus [15]) demonstrate that our method outperforms not only existing unsupervised learning methods, but also quite a bit of supervised learning methods.

2 Related Work

Many supervised learning methods have been put forward for person Re-ID [2],[6],[7],[3],[16],[17]. Prosser et al. [2] use ensemble RankSVMs to learn pairwise similarity that formulate person Re-ID as a ranking problem. A Mahalanobis distance learning method that is optimal for k-nearest neighbour classification using a maximum margin formulation is proposed by Dikmen et al. [6]. In [7], a relaxed pairwise metric learning is presented which takes advantages of the structure of the data with reduced computational cost, and achieves the state-of-the-art with simple feature descriptors. Another idea is trying to solve metric learning in a probabilistic manner used in person Re-ID. Zheng et al. [3] focuses on maximizing the probability that a true match pair has a smaller distance than a false matched pair. In addition to these metric learning, transfer learning based methods are also popular for person Re-ID. Zheng et al [16] reformulate person Re-ID problem as verification task and show that discriminant information can be learnt from unlabelled data. A transfer RankSVM to adapt a model trained on the source domain to target domain is proposed in [17].

For supervised learning method, their performance is limited by the fact that it is based on the subtraction of misaligned feature vectors, which can cause significant information loss. In the case of existing methods, the research on unsupervised learning methods are another important branch of person Re-ID. Many effective researches of features are proposed in unsupervised methods. Farenzena et al. [1] exploit the symmetry property in person image and propose the symmetry driven accumulation of local featrues. A combination of biologically inspired features and covariance descriptors that handle both background and illumination variations is proposed in [8]. Considering certain features play more important role than others, Liu et al. [4] employ a feature mining framework to optimise the weights of global features. Since color, shape and texture features can capture different aspects of information contained in image, Ma et al. [9] extract 7-d features of each pixel based on color, position and gradient and represent them by Gaussian models. Inspired by human eye that recognize person identities based on salient regions, Zhao et al. [5] proposed a patch based feature to learn salient regions in human appearance. In this paper, an unsupervised color spatial pyramid scheme is given to build effective structural object representation, it achieves competitive performance with only one kind of feature—color.

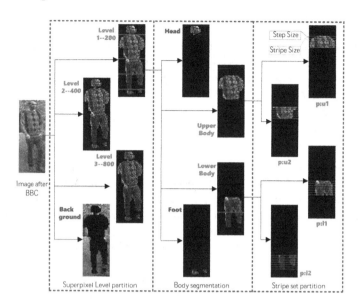

Fig. 1. Image in the leftmost column is processed by Bayesian Color Constancy method. After that, person image is divided into superpixel regions with increasing granularity from 200 to 800 (entire image, from coarse to fine). Aided by the Deep Decompositional Network, the background is discarded and the body is divided into four part. Considering the discriminative power, only upperbody and lowerbody are retained and divided into two vertical part (u1, u2, l1, l2) respectively. Stripes are divided in each part of vertical body regions.

3   Color Spatial Pyramid Matching

3.1   Data Pre-processing

In the first stage of UCSPM, color constancy and pedestrian parsing methods are used to depress the influence caused by the variation of illumination and discard background clusters, respectively.

Specifically, Bayesian Color Constancy (BCC) [18] method is used to depress the influence of illumination for each image. BCC can perceive surface color consistently, despite variations in ambient illumination. Compared to Grey World Color Constancy method, used in the pre-processing step in person Re-ID [9], the performance of BCC outperforms it that proven by [18]. After depressing the influence of illumination, Deep Decompositional Network (DDN) [19] is used to parse pedestrian into five regions, and discard background. DDN is able to accurately estimate contour of body and parse it into semantic regions such as hair, head, body, arms and legs, with robustness to occlusions and background clutters.

3.2 Spatial Pyramid Matching

Given two sets of feature vectors, spatial pyramid matching is proposed to find an approximate correspondence between them. It works by placing a sequence of increasingly coarser grids over the feature space and taking a weighted sum of the number of matches that occur at each level of resolution [10]. In previous attempts, two points match if they fall into the same cell of the grid at any fixed resolution and high weight is given in finer resolutions than coarser ones. For these reasons, spatial pyramid can effective confine the features distribution and keep the spatial layout information for matching. In our work, we construct a sequence of level $1, ..., L$, each level corresponding to different vertical stripe size and superpixel granularity as shown in Fig.1.

Let $F_l^{A,U_p} = \left\{ f_{l_{x,y}}^{A,U_p} \right\}$ denotes the feature set in one stripe, and $f_{l_{x,y}}^{A,U_p}$ represents a d-dimensional feature of superpixel (detial is shown in section 3.3) at l-th stripe in p-th part ($p = u1, u2, l1$ or $l2$, shown in Fig.1) of person U from camera A, x and y represent the centroid of superpixel that should satisfy $(x, y) \in l$. We simple use the City Block distance to measure the similarity between $f_{l_{x,y}}^{A,U_p}$ and its corresponding superpixel in person V from camera B:

$$D(f_{l_{x,y}}^{A,U_p}, f_{l'(k)_{x',y'}}^{B,V_p}) = \sum_{i=1}^{d} \left| f_{l_{x,y}}^{A,U_p}(i) - f_{l'(k)_{x',y'}}^{B,V_p}(i) \right|, \qquad (1)$$

where i is i-th element in feature vector, $l'(k)$ represents k-th adjacency constrained search stripe corresponding to l:

$$k = max(0, l - \delta), ..., min(N_{sripe}^p, l + \delta), \qquad (2)$$

N_{stripe}^p is the number of stripes in part p. If person in image do not exist vertical pose variation, $\delta = 0$. However, we set $\delta = 1$ in our experiment to tolerate the vertical spatial variation. In the following, we use a four-tuple e.g. (A, U, p, l) represents a stripe l in p-th part of person U from camera A.

Due to the pose variation between different images, matching superpixel directly can easily lead to that more than one regions are most similar to a single one between different images. Therefore, we specify matching in units of stripes instead of superpixel regions. In order to find the best matching stripes in adjacency search areas by Equ.2, the City Block distance (Equ.1) is calculated between any two superpixels from one stripe in (A, U, p, l) to another stripe in $(B, V, p, l'(k))$.

$$M^p = [D(F_l^{A,U_p}(m), F_{l'(k)}^{B,V_p}(n))]_{M \times N}, m = 1, ..., M, n = 1, ..., N, \qquad (3)$$

where m(n) represent m-th(n-th) superpixel in stripe $l(l'(k))$. The elements in M^p are the similarity between any two superpixels from l and $l'(k)$ measured by Equ.1. Hungarian algorithm is used in M^p to find the best superpixel assignment $D_H^p(i), i = 1, ..., min(m, n)$ (i represents the i-th matching pair in M^p, D is City Block distance) and cope with the case of multi-to-one matching between two stripes. Therefore, the similarity between two stripes can be quantized as a mean distance vector:

$$D^p_{l,l'(k)} = \sum_{i=1}^{\overline{min(m,n)}} (D^p_H(i)),   (4)$$

At last, the similarity between one stripe in image U and its adjacency stripe in image V is:

$$D^p_{l,l'} = min(D^p_{l,l'(k)}),   (5)$$

where k is given by Equ.2.

The similarity between two person images U and V can be obtained in different body parts by the stripe similarity. Considering the discriminative power of different body parts, more higher weight is given to upperbody parts u1 and u2 than lowerbody parts l1 and l2:

$$D(U,V) = \sum_{i=1}^{n1} D^{u1}_{l(i),l'} + \sum_{j=1}^{n2} D^{u2}_{l(j),l'} + 0.5 \cdot (\sum_{x=1}^{n3} D^{l1}_{l(x),l'} + \sum_{y=1}^{n4} D^{l2}_{l(y),l'}),   (6)$$

where $n1$, $n2$, $n3$ and $n4$ are the number of stripes in different body parts that have corresponding stripe in adjacency constrained search area by Equ.5. If one image U matching with multiple images V, there are uncertain number of $n1$, $n2$, $n3$ and $n4$ between one image U and different image V. For fair comparison, the minimum $n1$, $n2$, $n3$ and $n4$ between U and any one of V are selected for calculating the similarity between U and multiple V among different body part. Further, if any one of the $n1$, $n2$, $n3$ and $n4$ larger than the minimum value in its own body part when U is matching with one V, the first minimum $n1$, $n2$, $n3$ or $n4$ similarity distances will be selected for matching. In Equ.6, we simply consider that the discriminative power of upperbody is almost twice as lowerbody, so the weight is set to 0.5. The weight used in our experiment was somewhat haphazard, so it is likely that better weight may still be found by using a validation set.

For all the level $1, ..., L$, we want to penalize matches found in stripe with larger size and superpixel with coarser granularity, sine they involve increasingly dissimilar features. Putting all the level together, we get the following definition of a pyramid match kernel:

$$k^L(U,V) = \sum_{\iota=1}^{L} \frac{1}{2^{L-\iota+1}} D^\iota(U,V),   (7)$$

where $D^\iota(U,V)$ is defined in Equ.6.

3.3   Color Feature Extraction

The color feature is widely used in person Re-ID. However, due to the variation of illumination, it is hard to remain reliable and even vary significantly. As far as the present state of study, a wide range of color features have been proposed in [12],[20],[21]. Considering the illumination invariance property, two color features: hue histogram and opponent histogram from Van de Weijer and Schmid [12] are briefly reviewed in this paper. These two features are extracted for each superpixel and their performance will be given in section 4.

According to Van de Weijer and Schmid [12], the computation of hue with small value of saturation will bring uncertainties. Hence, it should be counted less in histogram. In the computation of hue histogram, hue is weighted by its saturation in [12]. Hue and saturation are computed as follows:

$$hue = \arctan(\frac{O_1}{O_2}) = \arctan(\frac{\sqrt{3}(R-G)}{R+G-2B}), \tag{8}$$

$$saturation = \sqrt{O_1^2 + O_2^2} = \sqrt{\frac{2}{3}(R^2 + G^2 + B^2 - RG - RB - GB)}, \tag{9}$$

where O_1 and O_2 are both from opponent color space:

$$O_1 = \frac{1}{\sqrt{2}}(R-G), O_2 = \frac{1}{\sqrt{6}}(R+G-2B), \tag{10}$$

In opponent color space, the opponent angle ang_x^O is supposed to be specular invariant in [12]. The ang_x^O is defined as:

$$ang_x^O = \arctan(\frac{O_{1x}}{O_{2x}}), \tag{11}$$

where O_{1x} and O_{2x} are the first order derivative of O_1 and O_2 respectively. Van de Weijer and Schmid [12] define ang_x^O as the weight for the opponent angle as an error analysis to the opponent angle:

$$\partial ang_x^O = \frac{1}{\sqrt{O_{1x}^2 + O_{2x}^2}}, \tag{12}$$

Finally, both of hue and opponent histograms are quantized to 36 bins.

A 72-dimensional color feature is extracted from each superpixel. The color features obtained in different body parts $(u1, u2, l1, l2)$ of all person are grouped together respectively to calculate the color dictionaries of local appearances by k-mean clustering. Four color dictionaries corresponding to $u1, u2, l1$ and $l2$ can be obtained, each dictionary includes the centers of cluster based on the number of clusters specified in advance. The feature used in Equ.1 is calculated by squared Euclidean distance between the 72-dimensional color histogram feature and its corresponding color dictionary in different body parts.

4   Experiments

We evaluate our unsupervised color spatial pyramid matching approach on two public datasets: the VIPeR dataset [14] and the CUHK campus dataset [15].

The VIPeR dataset is the most widely used person Re-ID dataset for evaluation. The CUHK campus dataset contains more images than VIPeR. Both datasets are very challenging since they under significant variations in viewpoint, illumination, pose, and background. The quantitative results are presented in standard Cumulated Matching Characteristics (CMC) curves [14]. The rank-k in CMC indicates the percentage of the correct matches found in the top k ranks from probe images to gallery images.

For fair comparison, the same experiment setup mentioned in [13] is used which divides the dataset into two parts, 50% for training and 50% for testing, without overlap on person identities. Images captured from camera A are as probe and camera B as gallery. Each probe image is matched with every gallery image. We conduct 10 trials of evaluation in experiment. Tab.1 gives settings for different pyramid levels. It is worth noting that the superpixel obtained from the entire image, but we only use the ones on body region. In our experiment, the superpixel regions are divided using the method in [22]. In addition, to validate the usefulness of superpixel based color spatial pyramid, we construct a set of contrast experiments based on patch. Fig.2 shows a comparison between superpixel and patch. The feature extracted from each patch and the comparison results are given on both datasets. Specifically, these patches are divided in each stripe. The patch size and step size in horizontal direction are the same as stripe size and its step size as shown in Tab.1. Notice that the experiment steps are the same as in the contrast experiment except for the regions of color feature extraction. For different levels, we denote the patch and superpixel based approaches by *patchLevel1-3* and *spLevel1-3* respectively. Using the spatial pyramid, the patch and superpixel based approaches are denoted by *patchPyramid* and *spPyramid(UCSPM)*, respectively.

VIPeR Dataset. The VIPeR dataset contains 632 person image pairs captured in different camera views. Most pairs show significant variations of viewpoint, illumination and pose as shown in Fig.3(a). In our experiment, all images are normalized to 512×192. Fig 4(a) shows the comparison between different levels and their combinations by spatial pyramid approach. Since superpixel can better locate color regions than patch, much more better performance is achieved in different levels. Using the spatial pyramid match kernel, the performance of

Table 1. Different pyramid level corresponding to different settings. The ι is used in Equ.7. Superpixel granularity, stripe size and stripe step can be found in Fig.1. The number of clusters is defined in section 3.3.

Pyramid Level (ι)	Superpixel Granularity (regions)	Stripe Size (pixels)	Stripe Step (pixels)	Number of Clusters
1	200	16	8	100
2	400	24	12	200
3	800	32	16	400

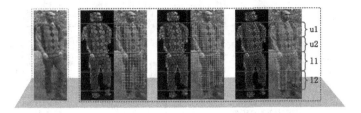

Fig. 2. Dividing person into superpixel regions and patches corresponding to different pyramid levels

(a) VIPeR dataset   (b) CUHK campus dataset

Fig. 3. Sets of 16 image pairs from the VIPeR and CUHK campus datasets

spPyramid is better than *patchPyramid*, which indicates superpixel is much effective than patch in color feature extraction in our color spatial pyramid matching approach.

We also compare *UCSPM* with several unsupervised approaches including CPS [23], SDALF [1], eBiCov [8], eSDC [5], PatMatch [24] and SalMatch [24], and five supervised learning approaches including ELF [13], PRDC [3], LMNN-R [6], PCCA [25] and MidF [26]. Our *UCSPM* achieves 33.24% at rank-1 and outperforms all these approaches. In addition, *UCSPM* outperforms the state-of-the-art unsupervised approach SalMatch [24] by 3.08%. What's more, our approach only use color and spatial information without the benefit of any salience information on human appearance proposed in [24].

CUHK Campus Dataset. The CUHK campus dataset is also a very challenging dataset. It contains 971 persons, each person has two images in each camera view. Specially, camera A captures the frontal or back view of person and camera B is the side view. Different from VIPeR dataset, most persons in CUHK dataset have their salience regions i.e. color bags, clothes or shoes etc (as shown in Fig.3(b)). All the images are normalized to 512×192 in our experiment.

Besides comparison between patch and superpixel-based pyramid approaches Fig.5(a). We also compare our approach with available results including L1-norm [24], L2-norm [24], LMNN [15], ITML [15], SDALF [1], GenericMetric [15], PatMatch [24] and SalMatch [24] as shown in Fig.5(b). Since SalMatch [24]

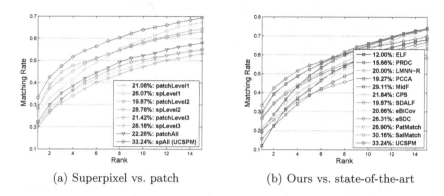

(a) Superpixel vs. patch

(b) Ours vs. state-of-the-art

Fig. 4. CMC on the VIPeR dataset. Rank-1 matching rate is marked before the name of each approach.

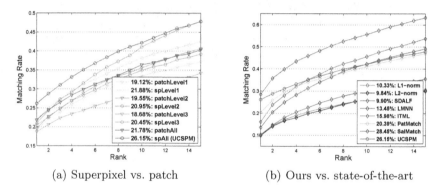

(a) Superpixel vs. patch

(b) Ours vs. state-of-the-art

Fig. 5. CMC on the CUHK campus dataset. Rank-1 matching rate is marked before the name of each approach.

focuses on unsupervised salience matching and the CUHK campus dataset are more suitable to show the effectiveness of salience matching. The accuracy of our approach is slightly lower than SalMatch [24] by 2.3%. However, comparison with other approaches, our method shows effectiveness on CUHK campus dataset.

5   Conclusions

In this paper, we propose a color spatial pyramid approach for person Re-ID. We explore spatial pyramid to build effective structural object color representation and cope with large viewpoint or pose variations. We compute the similarity of local features at increasingly fine vertical stripes and use pyramid match kernel for matching. To depress the variation of illumination, Bayesian Color Constancy method and illumination invariance color feature are used for stable color feature extraction. To accurately represent color features, we use superpixel-based segmentation technique to subdivide person into local regions. Experimental results show our color spatial pyramid approach improves the performance of unsupervised person re-identification.

Acknowledgments. This study was partially supported by the National Natural Science Foundation of China (No.61272350), the National High Technology Research and Development Program of China (No.2013AA01A603) and the National Aerospace Science Foundation of China (No.2013ZC51). Supported by the Programme of Introducing Talents of Discipline to Universities and the Open Fund of the State Key Laboratory of Software Development Environment under grant #SKLSDE-2015ZX-21.

References

1. Farenzena, M., Bazzani, L., Perina, A., Murino, V., Cristani, M.: Person re-identification by symmetry-driven accumulation of local features. In: Conference on Computer Vision and Pattern, pp. 2360–2367 (2010)
2. Prosser, B., Zheng, W.-S., Gong, S., Xiang, T.: Person re-identification by support vector ranking. In: British Machine Vision Conference, pp. 1–11 (2010)
3. Zheng, W.-S., Gong, S., Xiang, T.: Person re-identification by probabilistic relative distance comparison. In: Conference on Computer Vision and Pattern Recognition, pp. 649–656 (2011)
4. Liu, C., Gong, S., Loy, C.C.: On-the-fly feature importance mining for person re-identification. Pattern Recognition **47**(4), 1602–1615 (2014)
5. Zhao, R., Ouyang, W., Wang, X.: Unsupervised salience learning for person re-identification. In: Conference on Computer Vision and Pattern Recognition, pp. 3586–3593 (2013)
6. Dikmen, M., Akbas, E., Huang, T.S., Ahuja, N.: Pedestrian recognition with a learned metric. In: Asian Conference on Computer Vision, pp. 501–512 (2010)
7. Hirzer, M., Roth, P.M., Köstinger, M., Bischof, H.: Relaxed pairwise learned metric for person re-identification. In: European Conference on Computer Vision, pp. 780–793 (2012)
8. Ma, B., Su, Y., Jurie, F.: Bicov: a novel image representation for person re-identification and face verification. In: British Machine Vision Conference, pp. 1–11 (2012)
9. Ma, B., Li, Q., Chang, H.: Gaussian descriptor based on local features for person re-identification. In: Jawahar, C.V., Shan, S. (eds.) ACCV 2014 Workshops. LNCS, vol. 9010, pp. 505–518. Springer, Heidelberg (2015)
10. Lazebnik, S., Schmid, C., Ponce, J.: Beyond bags of features: spatial pyramid matching for recognizing natural scene categories. In: Conference on Computer Vision and Pattern Recognition, pp. 2169–2178 (2006)
11. Grauman, K., Darrell, T.: The pyramid match kernel: discriminative classification with sets of image features. In: Tenth IEEE International Conference on Computer Vision, 2005, ICCV 2005, vol. 2, pp. 1458–1465 (2005)
12. van de Weijer, J., Schmid, C.: Coloring local feature extraction. In: European Conference on Computer Vision, pp. 334–348 (2006)

13. Gray, D., Tao, H.: Viewpoint invariant pedestrian recognition with an ensemble of localized features. In: European Conference on Computer Vision, pp. 262–275 (2008)
14. Gray, D., Brennan, S., Tao, H.: Evaluating appearance models for recognition, reacquisition, and tracking. In: Proc. IEEE International Workshop on Performance Evaluation for Tracking and Surveillance (PETS), vol. 3 (2007)
15. Li, W., Zhao, R., Wang, X.: Human reidentification with transferred metric learning. In: Asian Conference on Computer Vision, pp. 31–44 (2012)
16. Zheng, W.-S., Gong, S., Xiang, T.: Transfer re-identification: from person to setbased verification. In: Computer Vision and Pattern Recognition, pp. 2650–2657 (2012)
17. Ma, A.J., Yuen, P.C., Li, J.: Domain transfer support vector ranking for person reidentification without target camera label information. In: International Conference on Computer Vision, pp. 3567–3574 (2013)
18. Gehler, P.V., Rother, C., Blake, A., Minka, T.P., Sharp, T.: Bayesian color constancy revisited. In: Conference on Computer Vision and Pattern (2008)
19. Li, W., Zhao, R., Xiao, T., Wang, X.: Deepreid: deep filter pairing neural network for person re-identification. In: Conference on Computer Vision and Pattern Recognition, pp. 152–159 (2014)
20. Koen, E.A., van de Sande, T.G., Snoek, C.G.M.: Evaluating color descriptors for object and scene recognition. IEEE Trans. Pattern Analysis and Machine Intelligence **32**(9), 1582–1596 (2010)
21. Burghouts, G.J., Geusebroek, J.-M.: Performance evaluation of local colour invariants. Computer Vision and Image Understanding **113**(1), 48–62 (2009)
22. Achanta, R., Shaji, A., Smith, K., Lucchi, A., Fua, P., Süsstrunk, S.: SLIC superpixels compared to state-of-the-art superpixel methods. IEEE Trans. Pattern Anal. Mach. Intell. **34**(11), 2274–2282 (2012)
23. Cheng, D.S., Cristani, M., Stoppa, M., Bazzani, L., Murino, V.: Custom pictorial structures for re-identification. In: British Machine Vision Conference, pp. 1–11 (2011)
24. Zhao, R., Ouyang, W., Wang, X.: Person re-identification by salience matching. In: International Conference on Computer Vision, pp. 2528–2535 (2013)
25. Mignon, A., Jurie, F.: PCCA: a new approach for distance learning from sparse pairwise constraints. In: Conference on Computer Vision and Pattern Recognition, pp. 2666–2672 (2012)
26. Zhao, R., Ouyang, W., Wang, X.: Learning mid-level filters for person re-identification. In: Conference on Computer Vision and Pattern Recognition, pp. 144–151 (2014)

Prediction of Single Nucleotide Mutation Patterns in Microsatellites

Jun Tan[1,2(✉)], Cheng Ouyang[2], and Jun Yu[2,3]

[1] College of Bio-information, Chongqing University of Posts
and Telecommunications, Chongqing 400065, China
tanjun@cqupt.edu.cn
[2] College of Computer Science and Technology,
Chongqing University of Posts and Telecommunications, Chongqing 400065, China
[3] Beijing Institute of Genomics, Chinese Academy of Sciences, Beijing 100101, China

Abstract. Single nucleotide mutations in the middle of a microsatellite fragment the microsatellite into two shorter ones. Respectively, 96.5% and 96.4% of human and mouse SNPs located in the middle of imperfect microsatellites come from single nucleotide mutations happened in perfect microsatellites. On chromosome 1, there are more transversions in mouse mononucleotide repeats (MNRs), but similar mutation patterns in human and mouse dinucleotide repeats (DNRs) and trinucleotide repeats (TNRs). Different single nucleotide mutation patterns in different microsatellites of human and mouse hint these mutations are under different natural selections. Our method can help to detect mutation patterns of different genomes without homogenous sequence alignments, and to observe the conserved mutations in microsatellites which cannot be found by traditional SNP methods.

Keywords: Single nucleotide mutation · SNP · Microsatellite · Transversion rate

1   Introduction

Microsatellites are tandem repetitive nucleotide sequences of short (1–6 bp) units, are ubiquitous in eukaryotic genomes and undergo rapid length changes due to insertion or deletion of one or multiple repeat units [1]. Microsatellite instability is not only implicated in cancer, but also responsible for over 40 neurological disorders [1,2]. The most commonly proposed mutation mechanism for microsatellites is replication slippage, the two DNA strands might realign incorrectly after dissociation, introducing a loop at one strand and leading to microsatellite expansion/contraction. Similar kinds of slippages also happen during recombination and mismatch repair which is the dominant type of repair for microsatellites [3,4]. Mechanisms other than slippage such as nucleotide mutation, insertion/deletion might contribute to microsatellite mutability mainly due to its disappearing [5]. Especially, single nucleotide mutation in the middle of a perfect microsatellite interrupts it into two fragments. More mutations at different positions can change the imperfect microsatellite into non-microsatellite genomic sequence finally (Fig. 1).

© Springer International Publishing Switzerland 2015
S. Zhang et al. (Eds.): KSEM 2015, LNAI 9403, pp. 811–818, 2015.
DOI: 10.1007/978-3-319-25159-2_75

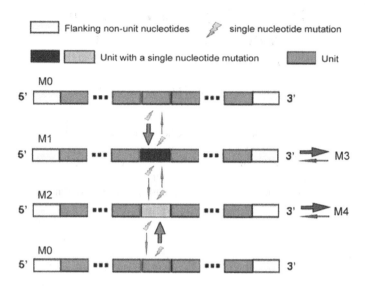

Fig. 1. Single nucleotide mutation interrupts a perfect microsatellite in the middle. M1 and M2 are different single nucleotide mutations on same position (red arrows) of a perfect microsatellite M0. M3 and M4 have the second single nucleotide mutations on the other positions (blue arrows) based on M1 and M2. In SNP data, there are M0/M1, M0/M2, and M1/M2 pairs. The former two (M0/M1 and M0/M2) come from single nucleotide mutations in perfect microsatellites predominately.

Mutations have pivotal functions in the onset of genetic diseases and are the fundamental substrate for evolution as the vast majority of mutations with observable effects are deleterious [6]. Mutation pattern of SNP (single nucleotide polymorphism) can be influenced by neighboring nucleotide composition [7]. Research found single nucleotide mutation rate increases close to insertions/deletions in eukaryotes [8]. Mutation accumulation (MA) method are useful for mutation rate and mutation pattern research (transitions and transversions with direction), but whole genome wide sequencing of MA strains is not experimental feasible [9]. For human and mouse, more than 14 million reference SNPs are in NCBI dbSNP database (build 128) respectively, and about half of them are validated. Because SNPs come from sequence alignment only, information about mutation direction cannot be obtained [10].

In this paper, human and mouse SNP data are used to demonstrate that the frequency of SNPs in perfect microsatellites is enough high to determine mutations with directions. Mutation patterns in microsatellites obtained by checking units in and surrounded are analyzed and discussed.

2   Result

2.1   Mutation Types of SNPs Surrounded Poly A and Poly T, and Predicted Mutation Types Based on Surrounded Poly A and Poly T on Human and Mouse Chromosome 1

In SNP data, 907,272 SNPs and 1,207,284 SNPs are found on human and mouse chromosome 1 respectively. Including them, 175,988 and 219,990 are neighbored by two A or T at both sides. The properties of their mutation types (2 kinds of transitions are more than 4 kinds of transversions) are similar with that of all SNPs. There are 2,465 and 554 SNPs surrounded by more than 5 poly A or poly T, the mutation types

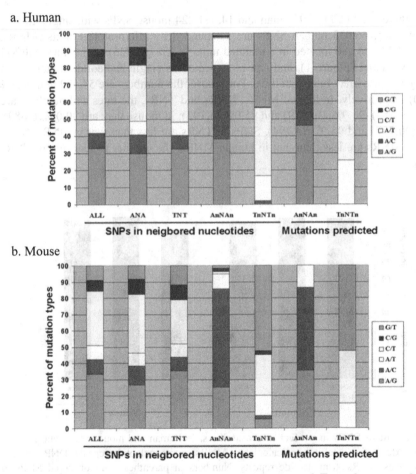

Fig. 2. Distribution of mutation types surrounded by As and Ts on human and mouse chromosome 1. ALL is all SNPs matched on chromosome 1. N means mutation type neighbored by As and Ts. Repeat number n is more than 5 (ploy A or poly T).

are different with the formers, only 3 kinds of types including A or T are predomi-
nated, more than 97% and 92% for human and mouse respectively. The frequency of
single nucleotide mutations in perfect poly A or poly T is higher, and mutation patterns can be predicted most correctly based on the non-mutated units surrounded.
Using human and mouse chromosome 1 reference sequences, 15,006 and 6,004 mutations in poly A or poly T are observed and their types are predicted out. For mouse,
the types are more similar with that in SNPs (Fig. 2).

2.2   More than 96% Human and Mouse SNPs Located in the Middle of Imperfect Microsatellites Come from Single Nucleotide Mutations in Perfect Microsatellites

In total, there are 11,271,559 human and 14,031,224 mouse SNPs with single nucleotide mutations. 66,023 human SNPs are surrounded by microsatellite units (MNRs,
DNRs and TNRs) and located in a mutated unit, 96.5% (63,725) of them are M0/M1
and M0/M2 pairs (Figure 1), and can be expected as single nucleotide mutations in
middle units of perfect microsatellites. For mouse, the numbers are 54,192 and 96.4%
(52,240) respectively. In human MNRs, DNRs and TNRs, the rates and numbers are
96.4% (29,353), 96.9% (30,179) and 95.0% (4,193); in mouse they are 90.0% (6,689),
97.6% (40,757) and 95.9% (4,794). SNPs in TNRs are less than that in DNRs. SNPs
in mouse MNRs are less than that in human MNRs, the number is near that in TNRs
(Fig. 3).

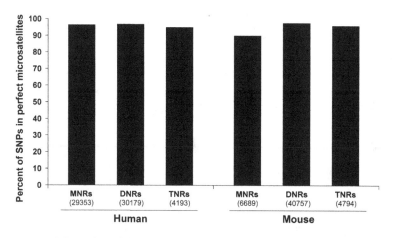

Fig. 3. Percent of SNPs in perfect microsatellites. In human and mouse SNP data, rates of
SNPs in perfect microsatellites are calculated. MNRs, mononucleotide repeats. DNRs, dinucleotide repeats. TNRs, trinucleotide repeats. Numbers in parentheses are observed SNPs in
microsatellites.

2.3   Predicted Single Nucleotide Mutation Patterns in Microsatellites on Human and Mouse Chromosome 1

On human and mouse chromosome 1, proportions of transversions in mouse MDRs are higher than that of human MDRs. In AT/TA DNRs, the numbers of mutations observed in mouse are less than that in human, and proportions of transversions are obviously lower.   But in AC/GT DNRs, numbers and proportions of transversions for mouse are more. Complex patterns of mutations in different microsatellites showed in Table 1 are informative for further research. In table 2 are mutation patterns observed by TNRs with A/T or G/C at either side of the mutations.

Table 1. Proportion of transversions (Tv%) in MNRs, DNRs and TNRs on human and mouse chromosome 1.

	LNR	In MNRs (Tv%)	In DNRs (Tv%)				In TNRs (Tv%)			
			A	T	C	G	A	T	C	G
Human	ANA	54.0 (4025)	–	46.3 (986)	50.5 (770)	46.8 (384)	–	41.4 (87)	56.8 (71)	27.6 (21)
	TNT	54.0 (4075)	39.9 (774)	–	43.7 (320)	48.4 (749)	43.1 (78)	–	41.7 (30)	46.3 (56)
	CNC	37.3 (216)	40.7 (234)	27.0 (82)	–	28.6 (2)	63.0 (17)	29.8 (28)	–	43.8 (7)
	GNG	40.3 (259)	35.8 (125)	44.7 (247)	50.0 (2)	–	47.2 (25)	78.2 (43)	43.5 (10)	–
Mouse	ANA	64.5 (3010)	–	17.2 (308)	45.7 (2583)	61.3 (1745)	–	47.8 (55)	47.7 (125)	27.4 (37)
	TNT	67.6 (2994)	18.4 (338)	–	58.5 (1731)	44.0 (2448)	52.2 (72)	–	30.5 (40)	53.9 (125)
	CNC	74.9 (511)	65.6 (986)	13.2 (148)	–	10.3 (3)	93.0 (40)	18.5 (32)	–	62.5 (10)
	GNG	73.1 (507)	19.3 (205)	66.8 (1061)	14.8 (4)	–	26.0 (39)	67.6 (23)	43.8 (7)	–

LNR, left and right neighbored nucleotides. Only nucleotides neighbored by As, Ts, Cs, Gs are showed in this table. MNRs, DNRs and TNRs are as same as in Fig. 2. Numbers in parentheses are observed transversion mutations.

Table 2. Proportion of transversions (Tv%) in TNRs on human and mouse chromosome 1.

LNR	Human (Tv%)				Mouse (Tv%)			
	A	T	C	G	A	T	C	G
ANT	39.1 (54)	41.1 (57)	38.5 (5)	25.0 (2)	35.2 (44)	27.2 (28)	38.5 (5)	28.0 (7)
TNA	47.6 (59)	40.4 (65)	39.5 (15)	29.1 (16)	37.8 (31)	36.6 (34)	29.5 (13)	31.6 (12)
ANC	18.0 (18)	23.9 (17)	18.4 (21)	45.9 (17)	19.6 (28)	16.7 (10)	17.9 (21)	8.9 (4)
GNT	14.3 (12)	24.5 (25)	25.0 (8)	21.7 (18)	20.0 (11)	25.8 (34)	34.8 (23)	18.4 (26)
ANG	18.6 (25)	52.2 (23)	100.0 (1)	17.9 (28)	15.5 (31)	56.7 (17)	–	9.5 (64)
CNT	56.4 (22)	16.7 (19)	18.2 (27)	100 (3)	31.8 (7)	21.9 (37)	7.0 (44)	12.5 (1)
CNA	51.2 (22)	66.7 (4)	28.6 (14)	–	67.9 (38)	33.3 (2)	17.7 (14)	33.3 (1)
TNG	25.0 (1)	35.0 (14)	–	21.7 (10)	42.9 (3)	70.2 (33)	0 (0)	32.4 (24)
TNC	41.7 (5)	37.1 (23)	35.0 (35)	66.7 (30)	46.2 (6)	20.0 (27)	29.2 (100)	66.7 (32)
GNA	26.7 (16)	0.0 (0)	71.4 (35)	27.8 (22)	13.8 (22)	44.4 (4)	56.1 (23)	35.0 (146)
CNG	81.1 (30)	69.2 (18)	55.6 (15)	40.7 (11)	54.5 (12)	55.5 (10)	35.3 (6)	46.2 (6)
GNC	–	–	18.2 (2)	50.0 (3)	–	–	20.0 (1)	0.0 (0)

Legend is same as in table 1.

3   Discussion

The main issue that we are addressing in this paper is whether single nucleotide mutations in and surrounded by microsatellite units can be used as a tool to predict mutation patterns. Furthermore, our interest is to ascertain the predicted mutation patterns, and to analyze their evolutional information initially.

3.1   Significances of Mutation Detection

Mutation patterns are variable in different genome regions according to function and evolution [11,12,13]. Genome-wide mutation pattern analysis becomes more and more a hotspot especially in cancer to provide information about its multi-step development [14,15]. Expect SNP method, other bioinformatic ways to mining more mutation information from genomic sequences are helpful to do mutation analysis.

In former work of our lab, we found substitutions and insertions are impetus for the born of new microsatellites with human gene mutation data [16]. In this paper, we demonstrated that mutation patterns in the dying microsatellites can be observed without alignment based on human and mouse SNP data. This method can be used to do whole genome wide mutation scan, then got mutation patterns in microsatellites of different genomic regions for evolution research compared with homologous genomes.

3.2   Single Nucleotide Mutation Patterns in Microsatellites

The single nucleotide mutation patterns observed in microsatellites are different with microsatllites and genomic regions. SNP data represent polymorphisms of different strains, there is no information for conserved sequences of different strains and mutation directions. For the SNP data we used in this paper, almost all of human SNPs are in genes, but almost all of the mouse SNPs are in genomic regions. So, the predicted mutation patterns are not so similar with that in SNPs. Single nucleotide mutations in microsatellites not only can check all SNPs in microsatellite out, but also get conserved mutations keeping units around. It can be used to research on evolutional selection compared to SNPs.

It was found that within the microstatllites with repeated units consisting of one, two or three nucleotides, point mutations occur approximately twice as frequently as one would expect on the basis of the 1.2% difference between the human and chimpanzee genomes [17]. Other mutation patterns such as continuous same mutation which induce microsatellite exchange between different motifs are founded in microsatellites (data not show).

Of course, frequencies are variable for single nucleotide mutations in different microsatellite motifs and different genome or genomic regions. In human and mouse genome, A/T rich microsatellites are more than other kinds of microsatellites, some of them are related with retrotransposons such as Alu [5]. Future works are how to normalize the bias, and to built a database of new and conserved single nucleotide mutations in microsatellites for different genomes, genomic regions etc.

4 Materials and Methods

4.1 Mutation Types of SNP Data and Mutation Prediction

Human (build 129) and mouse (build 128) SNP data are downloaded from NCBI dbSNPs. Single nucleotide mutations surrounded by microsatellite units and within mutated units are selected. For mononucleotide repeats, at least 6 units are at both ends of the mutated unit; for dinucleotide repeats, the number is 3; for trinucleotide repeats, it is 2. Based on the surrounded units, the mutation patterns are predicted out.

4.2 Single Nucleotide Mutation Patterns in Microsatellites

Human and mouse genomic chromosome 1 sequences are downloaded from NCBI. All single nucleotide mutations in microsatellites are predicted. Grouped by A + T content at adjacent sites, percent of transversion mutations are calculated. All programs used in this paper are written in perl script.

References

1. Hans, E.: Microsatellites: simple sequences with complex evolution. Nature Reviews Genetics **5**, 435–445 (2004)
2. Sergei, M.M.: Expandable DNA repeats and human disease. Nature **447**, 932–940 (2007)
3. Pearson, C.E., Edamura, N.K., Cleary, J.D.: Repeat instability: Mechanisms of dynamic mutations. Nat. Rev. Genet. **6**, 729–742 (2005)
4. Kelkar, Y.D., Tyekucheva, S., Chiaromonte, F., Makova, K.D.: The genome-wide determinants of human and chimpanzee microsatellite evolution. Genome Res. **18**, 30–38 (2008)
5. Danilo, P., Borut, O., Branko, B.: Replication slippage versus point mutation rates in short tandem repeats of the human genome. Mol. Genet. Genomics **279**, 53–61 (2008)
6. Charles, F.B., Michael, M.M., Dee, R.D.: Mutation rate variation in multicellular eukaryotes: causes and consequences. Nature Review Genetics **8**, 619–631 (2007)
7. Fengkai, Z., Zhongming, Z.: The influence of neighboring-nucleotide composition on single nucleotide polymorphisms (SNPs) in the mouse genome and its comparison with human SNPs. Genomics **84**, 785–795 (2004)
8. Dacheng, T., Qiang, W., Pengfei, Z., Hitoshi, A., Sihai, Y., Martin, K., Thomas, N., Richard, H., Joy, B., JianQun C.: Single-nucleotide mutation rate increases close to insertions/deletions in eukaryotes (2008) (published online)
9. Dee, R.D., Krystalynne, M., Michael, L., Thomas, W.K.: High mutation rate and predominance of insertions in the Caenorhabditis elegans nuclear genome. Nature **430**, 679–682 (2004)
10. Hans, E., Nick, G.C.S., Matthew, T.W.: Mutation rate variation in the mammalian genome. Current Opinion in Genetics & Development **13**, 562–568 (2003)
11. Ziheng, Y., Anne, D.Y.: Estimation of the Transition/Transversion Rate Bias and Species Sampling. J. Mol. Evol. **48**, 274–283 (1999)
12. Huiqi, Q., Steve, G.L., Fan, G., Jacek, M., Constantin, P.: Strand bias in complementary single-nucleotide polymorphisms of transcribed human sequences: evidence for functional effects of synonymous polymorphisms. BMC Genomics **7**, 213 (2006)

13. Irene, K., Douda, B., Richard, A.N.: Transition-transversion bias is not universal: a counter example from grasshopper Pseudogenes. PLoS Genetics **3**, 185–191 (2007)
14. Mullighan, C.G., Goorha, S., Radtke, I., Miller, C.B., Coustan-Smith, E., Dalton, J.D., Girtman, K., Mathew, S., Ma, J., Pounds, S.B., Su, X., Pui, C.H., Relling, M.V., Evans, W.E., Shurtleff, S.A., Downing, J.R.: Genome-wide analysis of genetic alterations in acute lymphoblastic leukaemia. Nature **446**, 758–764 (2007)
15. Wang, Y., Armstrong, S.A.: Genome-wide SNP analysis in cancer: leukemia shows the way. Cancer Cell **11**, 308–309 (2007)
16. Zhu, Y., Strassmann, J.E., Queller, D.C.: Insertions, substitutions, and the origin of microsatellites. Genetical Research **76**, 227–236 (2000)
17. Mikael, B., Hans, E.: Genome-wide analysis of microsatellite polymorphism in chicken circumventing the ascertainment bias. Genome Research **18**, 881–887 (2008)

Developing a Novel Method Based on Orthogonal Polynomial Equation to Approximate the Solution of Agent Based Model for the Immune System Simulation

Xuming Tong[1], Meijing Kong[1], Edwin Tawanda Mudzingwa[1], and Le Zhang[1,2(✉)]

[1] College of Computer and Information Science, Southwest University,
Chongqing 400715, People's Republic of China
{txm1111,a369,zhanglcq}@swu.edu.cn, edwin.mudzingwa@yahoo.com
[2] Department of Biostatistics and Computational Biology, Center for Biodefense Immune Modeling, University of Rochester, 601 Elmwood Avenue, Rochester, NY 14642, USA
zhanglcq@swu.edu.cn

Abstract. Since Agent based model (ABM) can describe the biological system in detail, it is broadly used for multi-scale immune system modeling. However, ABM requires such a high computing cost for the large scale biological modeling that prevents us employing it for the real time system simulation. For this reason, this study develops an orthogonal polynomial based model to approximate solution of ABM, which can obtain low computing cost and high approximating accuracy.

Keywords: Orthogonal polynomial equation · Agent based model · Cellular immune response

1 Introduction

Currently, mathematical model is employed as one of the most important methods to investigate the immune system. Agent based model (ABM)[1, 2] and differential equations model (DEM)[3, 4] are two widely used mathematical models in this field. Born with flexible features, ABM can be employed to reflect the real complex dynamic environment and is effectively used to describe a multi-scale system [5]. For example, Folcik et al.[6] built up the Basic Immune Simulator (BIS), one of ABM models, to study the interactions between cells of the innate and adaptive immune systems. Also, Ballet et al. [7] developed a multi-agent system (oRis) to model humoral immunity.

However, as a rule based model, ABM describes the system at the level of its constituent units but not at the top level, which directly results in the high computing cost for the simulation[8, 9]. For this reason, we are looking forward to developing such a model that can approximate the solution of ABM with low computing cost and high approximating accuracy. This study develop the orthogonal polynomial model (OPEABM) by using the output of ABM and the collocation method[4],[10]. We used experimental data from infection of mice with the H3N2 influenza virus A/X31 strain

© Springer International Publishing Switzerland 2015
S. Zhang et al. (Eds.): KSEM 2015, LNAI 9403, pp. 819–824, 2015.
DOI: 10.1007/978-3-319-25159-2_76

[11] to fit the model and the results turned out that OPEABM can quickly and accurately approximate the solution of ABM.

2   Materials and Methods

2.1   Summary of the Computational Approach

Fig. 1 shows the workflow of the OPEABM development. First, mapping function is employed to map Gauss nodes (**box1**) [12] from interval [a, b] to interval [0, 1]. Then, the mapped Gauss nodes (**box2**) are employed as the input of ABM (the mean of Gamma distribution) to generate the cell number (G_p^t) (**box4**) for each time point. Next, G_p^t is used as the input of the orthogonal polynomial (**box5**) to obtain the coefficients a_i^t (**box7**). Once the coefficients of orthogonal polynomial are determined, we can input any value Z (**box8**) (cell's division time) to obtain the cell number without computing ABM (**box9**).

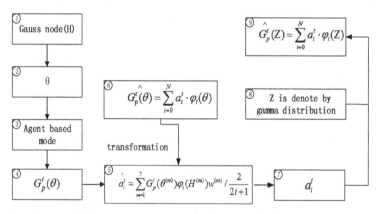

Fig. 1. The flow chart for the development of OPEABM

2.2   Using ABM to Simulate Immune System and Generate the Data for the OPEABM Development

There are nineteen types of cells in the model. Each type of cell is assigned an integer number (CT). Each type of cell has three phenotypes, which are quiescence, proliferation and dead phenotypes (CP). Moreover, the probability of the each type of cell's differentiation rate in different phenotypes is described by a transformation matrix (TM). The detail is illustrated by Table 1:

Table 1. Process of building agent based model

---

1) Read each cell information (CT, CP, TM) from the inputting file.

2) Every cell has at most 4 probabilities to change its state, such as differentiating to another cell type, keeping current phenotype, changing to one of the proliferation, quiescence or dead phenotypes. Especially, dead phenotype and proliferation phenotype should comply with a and b rules.

a. Goes to dead phenotype: the gamma distribution generator will produce the number of the runs for cell to die. The dead process cannot be interrupted.

b. Goes to proliferation phenotype: the gamma distribution generator will generate the number of the runs for cell to divide. It is noted that the cell can differentiate into another cell type or phenotype during the proliferation stage. The number of the runs will be reset to zero immediately once the proliferation process is done.

3) At each run, die function is employed to generate a random number between 0 and 1 for every cell and then, each cell will determine its next state by comparing this random number with its TM.

To simulate the process of cellular immunity, ABM is developed based on Table 1.

2.3   Using Orthogonal Polynomial Equation for the OPEABM Development

The key of the OPEABM is employing an orthogonal polynomial equation to approximate the solution of agent based model. Each state variable can be approximated by a set of orthogonal polynomials at any time step as Eq. 1.

$$\widehat{G_p^t}(Z) = \sum_{i=0}^{N} a_i^t \cdot \emptyset_i(Z) \tag{1}$$

Here, $\emptyset_i(Z)$ is the orthogonal polynomial basis, a_i^t is the constant coefficient of the ith orthogonal polynomial basis at time t, and $\widehat{G_p^t}(Z)$ is the approximated p^{th} state variable at time t. We assume that the time for the cell to divide or die follows a common gamma distribution $\Gamma(Z, v_a)$, where Z denotes the mean and v_a is the variance of the gamma distribute. Here, the value of v_a is 4.

$$\widehat{G_p^t}(Z) \approx \sum_{i=0}^{4} a_i^t \cdot \emptyset_i(Z) = a_0^t \cdot \emptyset_0(Z) + a_1^t \cdot \emptyset_1(Z) + a_2^t \cdot \emptyset_2(Z) + a_3^t \cdot \emptyset_3(Z) + a_4^t \emptyset_1(Z) \tag{2}$$

Since $\emptyset_i(Z)$ is a set of orthogonal polynomial, we compute the coefficient a_i^t as follows:

$$a_i^t = \int G_p^t(Z) \emptyset_i(Z) \omega_i(Z) dZ \tag{3}$$

To compute a_i^t, we integrate $\emptyset_i(Z)$ in [-1, 1] for both sides.

$$\int_{-1}^{1} G_p^t(Z) \emptyset_i(Z) \omega_i(Z) dZ = \int_{-1}^{1} a_i^t(Z) \emptyset_i(Z) \emptyset_i(Z) \omega_i(Z) dZ \tag{4}$$

Then,

$$a_i^t = \frac{\int_{-1}^{1} G_p^t(Z)\emptyset_i(Z)\omega_i(Z)dZ}{\int_{-1}^{1} \emptyset_i^2(Z)dZ} = \frac{\int_{-1}^{1} G_p^t(Z)\emptyset_i(Z)\omega_i(Z)dZ}{\frac{2}{2i+1}} \tag{5}$$

Eq.6 is the discrete form of Eq.5,

$$\widehat{a_i^t} \approx \frac{\sum_{m=1}^{Q} G_p^t(H^{(m)})\emptyset_i(H^{(m)})\omega_i(H^{(m)})\omega^{(m)}}{\frac{2}{2i+1}}, i = 0,1,2,3 \ldots \tag{6}$$

where $\omega_i(H)$ is the weight at the integration grids. Here Q is the number of Gauss nodes. $\widehat{a_i^t}$ is the approximated parameters of the orthogonal polynomial. $H^{(m)} = (H_1^{(m)}, \ldots, H_n^{(m)})$ is a set of nodes which belong to $[-1,1]$ and $\omega^{(m)}$ are the corresponding weights for Gauss nodes. The Legendre polynomial on $[-1,1]$ is described in [13]. Since the domain of the input parameter of ABM is between a and b, we employed transformation function to map variable H on interval [-1, 1] to variable θ, which can be considered as the mean of Gamma distribution between a and b

$$\theta = \frac{b-a}{2}H + \frac{b+a}{2} \tag{7}$$

Here $-1 \leq H \leq 1$ and $a \leq \theta \leq b$

The state variables of agent based model is described as Eq.8

$$G_p^t\left(\frac{b-a}{2}H + \frac{b+a}{2}\right) = G_p^t(\theta^{(m)}) \tag{8}$$

Eq. 9 is the Gauss integration form for Eq. 4 and the Gauss nodes and weights are in [12].

$$\widehat{a_i^t} = \frac{\sum_{m=1}^{7} G_p^t(\theta^{(m)})\emptyset_i(H^{(m)})\omega^{(m)}}{\frac{2}{2i+1}}, \quad i = 0,1,2,3 \tag{9}$$

After obtaining the values of parameters of Eq.6, we can approximate the solution of ABM by a set of polynomials.

3   Results

3.1   Simulated Results

We used experimental data from infection of mice with the H3N2 influenza virus A/X31 strain to fit the model and most of the parameter values of ABM come from the literatures[11],[14]. Limited to the pages, Fig. 2 only shows the two dynamics of cells' number at each time point (time=1, 2, 3..., 50). Here, the horizontal axis represents time and the vertical axis represents the number of cells. The black line and the line with circles represent the result of ABM and OPEABM, respectively.

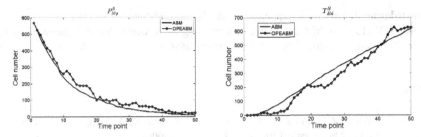

Fig. 2. Two cells number dynamics for ABM and OPEABM

3.2   Comparison of the Relative Error and Performance

We also compute the relative error between ABM and OPEABM by Eq. 10. In Fig. 3, the horizontal axis represents cell type or cell state in this study and the vertical axis represents the relative error. Fig.4 shows the computing time for ABM and OPEABM, respectively.

$$RE = \sum_{i=0}^{50} \left| G_{pOPEABM}^t(i) - G_{pABM}^t(i) \right| \tag{10}$$

Here, RE   and $G_{pOPEABM}^t(i)$ represent relative error and the cell number (G_p^t) at each time point i of OPEABM, respectively. $G_{pABM}^t(i)$ shows the cell number (G_p^t) for each time point i   of ABM.

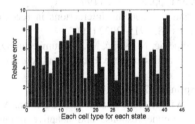

Fig. 3. The relative error between ABM and OPEABM

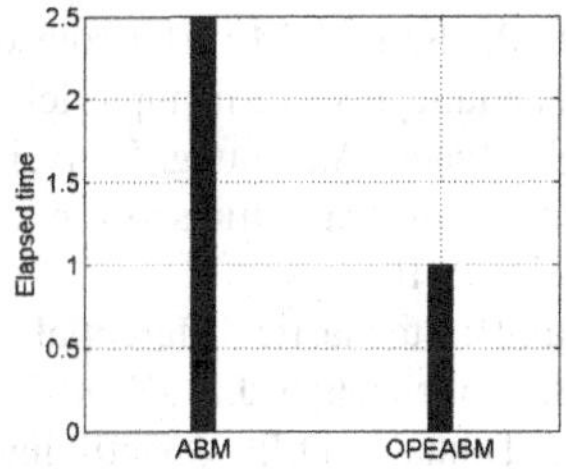

Fig. 4. Performance Comparison of the two models

4   Discussion

This research developed an OPEABM to approximate the solution of agent based model for the immune responses simulation. As we illustrated before, it is time-consuming for us to employ ABM to simulate immune system with different key parameter values. Thus, we developed the OPEABM model by employing the solution of ABM and collocation method [15]. With this novel OPEABM model, we can approximate the solution of ABM (Fig. 2) by inputting different key parameter values of ABM with low computing cost (Fig. 4) and high approximating accuracy (Fig. 3).

Acknowledgement. This work supported by the Natural Science Foundation of China under Grant No. 61372138 and the Chinese Recruitment Program of Global Youth Experts, as well as by USA NIH grants P30AI078498, HHSN272201000055C and U01 CA166886-01.

References

1. Zhang, L., Wang, Z., Sagotsky, J.A., Deisboeck, T.S.: Multiscale agent-based cancer modeling. Journal of Mathematical Biology **58**, 545–559 (2009)
2. Charles, M.M., Michael, J.: Tutorial on agent-based modeling and simulation part 2: how to model with agents. In: The 38th Conference on Winter Simulation, Monterey, California, pp. 73–83 (2006)
3. Ho, W.-H., Chan A.L.-F.: Hybrid taguchi-differential evolution algorithm for parameter estimation of differential equation models with application to HIV dynamics. Mathematical Problems in Engineering, **14** (2011)
4. Jones, D.S., Plank, M., Sleeman, B.D.: Differential equations and mathematical biology. CRC press (2011)
5. Wang, J., Zhang, L., Jing, C., Ye, G., Wu, H., Miao, H., Wu, Y., Zhou, X.: Multi-scale agent-based modeling on melanoma and its related angiogenesis analysis. Theoretical Biology and Medical Modelling **10**, 41 (2013)
6. Folcik, V.A., An, G.C., Orosz, C.G.: The Basic Immune Simulator: An agent-based model to study the interactions between innate and adaptive immunity. Theoretical Biology and Medical Modelling **4** (2007)
7. Ballet, P., Tisseau, J., Harrouet, F.: A multiagent system to model an human humoral response. In: 1997 IEEE International Conference on Systems, Man, and Cybernetics, 1997 Computational Cybernetics and Simulation, vol. 351, pp. 357–362 (1997)
8. Decuzzi, P., Ferrari, M.: The role of specific and non-specific interactions in receptor-mediated endocytosis of nanoparticles. Biomaterials **28**, 2915–2922 (2007)
9. Kojić, N., Huang, A., Chung, E., Ivanović, M., Filipović, N., Kojić, M., Tschumperlin, D.J.: A 3-D model of ligand transport in a deforming extracellular space. Biophysical Journal **99**, 3517–3525 (2010)
10. Øksendal, B: Stochastic differential equations. Springer (2003)
11. Miao, H., Hollenbaugh, J.A., Zand, M.S., Holden-Wiltse, J., Mosmann, T.R., Perelson, A.S., Wu, H., Topham, D.J.: Quantifying the early immune response and adaptive immune response kinetics in mice infected with influenza A virus. Journal of Virology **84**, 6687–6698 (2010)
12. Hale, N., Townsend, A.: Fast and accurate computation of Gauss-Legendre and Gauss-Jacobi quadrature nodes and weights. SIAM Journal on Scientific Computing **35**, A652–A674 (2013)
13. Agarwal, R.P., O'Regan, D.: Legendre Polynomials and Functions. Universitext, pp. 47–56 (2009)
14. Lee, H.Y., Topham, D.J., Park, S.Y., Hollenbaugh, J., Treanor, J., Mosmann, T.R., Jin, X., Ward, B.M., Miao, H., Holden-Wiltse, J.: Simulation and prediction of the adaptive immune response to influenza A virus infection. Journal of Virology **83**, 7151–7165 (2009)
15. Thorvaldsen, T.P., Huntington, G.T., Benson, D.A.: Direct Trajectory Optimization and Costate Estimation via an Orthogonal Collocation Method. Journal of Guidance Control & Dynamics **29**, 1435–1439 (2006)

fMRI Visual Image Reconstruction Using Sparse Logistic Regression with a Tunable Regularization Parameter

Hao Wu, Jiayi Wang, Badong Chen$^{(\boxtimes)}$, and Nanning Zheng

School of Electronic and Information Engineering,
Xi'an Jiaotong University, Xi'an 710049, China
{xuan.zhi,wangjiayiw}@stu.xjtu.edu.cn,
{chenbd,nnzheng}@mail.xjtu.edu.cn

Abstract. fMRI has been a popular way for encoding and decoding human visual cortex activity. A previous research reconstructed binary image using a sparse logistic regression (SLR) with fMRI activity patterns as its input. In this article, based on SLR, we propose a new sparse logistic regression with a tunable regularization parameter (SLR-T), which includes the SLR and maximum likelihood regression (MLR) as two special cases. By choosing a proper regularization parameter in SLR-T, it may yield a better performance than both SLR and MLR. An fMRI visual image reconstruction experiment is carried out to verify the performance of SLR-T.

Keywords:: fMRI · Visual image reconstruction · Sparse regression

1   Introduction

Functional magnetic resonance imaging (fMRI) is an effective means used by researchers to investigate brain activities to different kinds of tasks and stimuli noninvasively [1–8]. Many visual encoding and decoding experiments have been carried out. Kay showed that using the receptive field models, it's possible to identify images with fMRI signals [9]. Miyawaki reconstructed visual images directly using a sparse logistic regression (SLR) [10]. Each visual stimulus used in their experiment was made up of 10 by 10 square patches with each patch was either a gray patch or a flickering checkboard. SLR was applied to calculate the class label of voxel's fMRI signal patterns. The most significant feature of SLR is that it simultaneously performs feature (voxel) selection and training of the model parameters for classification [11], thus it may yield a very sparse classification model.

In this work, we propose a more general sparse logistic regression with a tunable regularization parameter (SLR-T). The SLR-T offers another point of view to explain the optimization equation derived from SLR, that is the optimization cost consists of a usual cost function and a regularization term. Thus, a more general regression model can be obtained by substituting a variable regularization coefficient for the constant value of

---

This work was supported by 973 Program (No. 2015CB351703).

S. Zhang et al. (Eds.): KSEM 2015, LNAI 9403, pp. 825–830, 2015.
DOI: 10.1007/978-3-319-25159-2_77

0.5 in SLR. By setting this coefficient to 0 and 0.5, SLR-T reduces to a maximum likelihood regression (MLR) and SLR respectively. By choosing a proper regularization coefficient, SLR-T can achieve a better performance than both SLR and MLR.

2   Materials and Methods

2.1   fMRI Experiment

Three subjects participated in this fMRI experiment. All of them are males, with an average age of 23, and have normal or corrected-to-normal visual acuity. Informed written consents were obtained from all subjects.

Two types of stimuli were used in the experiment. One is random shape stimuli and another is regular shape stimuli.

In random shape stimuli, totally 198 different random patterns were used. Each stimulus pattern consisted of 12×12 patches ($1.13° \times 1.13°$ each). There were two types of patch, a flickering checkboard and a neutral gray area. Each type of patch was randomly used with equal probability. Patterns, formed by different type of patches, were presented on a neutral gray background. A fixation spot was placed at the center of each stimulus to instruct subjects to fixate on it.

In regular shape stimuli, 10 kinds of stimulus patterns were used. Each kind of patterns consisted of specific shapes formed by the same types of patches as in random shape stimuli("B", "R", "A", "I", "N", "square", "arrow", "cross", "frame" and "X").

A 3.0-Tesla GE MR Scanner was used to collect functional MRI data at the First Affiliated Hospital of Xi'an Jiaotong University. A T1-Weighted, MP-RAGE sequence (TR: 2250ms; TE: 2.98ms; Tl: 900ms; Flip angle: 9°; FOV: 256 × 256mm; Voxel size: 1.0 × 1.0× 1.0mm), was firstly used to acquire high-resolution structure images. Then a T2*-weighted EPI sequence (TR: 4000ms; TE: 30ms; Flip angle: 80°; FOV: 192× 192mm; Voxel size: 1.875 × 1.875 × 3mm; Slice gap: 0mm; Number of slices: 48) was used to collect functional images covering the whole brain.

2.2   MRI Data Preprocessing

The first 3 volumes of each run were discarded in order to avoid the noise caused by MRI scanner's instability. SPM 12 was used to preprocess the MRI data.

The general linear model was used to model the BOLD signal and predict the amplitude of BOLD response of each voxel. For each voxel, we calculated the correlation between its BOLD time-series signal and stimuli time-series. Finally, we chose 998 voxels in V1 area that show high correlation.

2.3   Classification Algorithm

We first introduce the SLR algorithm proposed by Yamashita et al[11].

In a discriminant classification model, there is a discriminant function for each class:

$$f_c(x;\theta^{(c)}) = \sum_{d=1}^{D} \theta_d^{(c)} x_d + \theta_0^{(c)} \quad c = 1,\dots,C \tag{1}$$

where $x = (x_1,\dots,x_D)' \in \mathbb{R}^D$ is an input feature vector in D dimensional space (here it's a voxel response pattern vector) and $\theta^{(c)} = (\theta_0^{(c)},\theta_1^{(c)}\dots,\theta_D^{(c)})'$ is a weight vector including a bias term for x belonging to class c.

Then the probability of a new input x belonging to the class c can be calculated using the softmax function:

$$P(S_c \mid x) = \frac{\exp(f_c(x;\theta^{(c)}))}{\sum_{k=1}^{C}\exp(f_k(x;\theta^{(c)}))} \quad c = 1,\dots,C \tag{2}$$

One can estimate the free parameter θ by maximizing the following likelihood function,

$$P(y_1,\dots,y_N \mid x_1,\dots,x_N;\theta) = \prod_{n=1}^{N}\prod_{c=1}^{C} p_n^{(c)\,y_n^{(c)}} \tag{3}$$

SMLR assumes a prior Gaussian distribution for the parameters θ:

$$P(\theta_d \mid \alpha_d) = N(0,\alpha_d^{-1}) \quad d = 1,\dots,D \tag{4}$$

where α is a hyper-parameter representing the inverse of the variance of the weight value of the i'th feature and class d. Furthermore, a prior distribution is assumed for the hyper-parameter:

$$P(\alpha_d) = \alpha_d^{-1} \quad d = 1,\dots,D \tag{5}$$

With the above two prior distributions, SLR can obtain a sparse weight vector with most of the components being zeros.

Since it's difficult to calculate the posterior probability of θ directly, a variational Bayesian method is applied to get an approximation solution. After a few steps of derivations, the problem can be transformed into an optimization problem which aims to maximize the following cost function:

$$E(\theta) = \sum_{n=1}^{N}\left[\sum_{c=1}^{C} y_n^{(c)} x_n' \theta^{(c)} - \log\left\{\sum_{c=1}^{C}\exp\left(x_n'\theta^{(c)}\right)\right\}\right] - \frac{1}{2}\sum_{c=1}^{C}\theta^{(c)\mathrm{t}}\overline{A}^{(c)}\theta^{(c)} \tag{6}$$

where $\overline{A}^{(c)}$ is a diagonal matrix with each element on the diagonal being the expectation of $\alpha^{(c)}$. This optimization problem can be solved using Newton method.

Now we explain Eq. (6) from another point of view. The first term of Eq. (6) is a log function of Eq. (3), which is the log-likelihood function. It can be regarded as a usual cost function. The second term is a penalty term in that it is the sum of the L_2-norm of each weight value weighted by the inverse of their variances. Thus, we propose here to a free coefficient λ to the penalty term:

$$E(\theta) = \sum_{n=1}^{N} \left[\sum_{c=1}^{C} y_n^{(c)} x_n^t \theta^{(c)} - \log \left\{ \sum_{c=1}^{C} \exp\left(x_n^t \theta^{(c)}\right) \right\} \right] - \lambda \sum_{c=1}^{C} \theta^{(c)t} \overline{A}^{(c)} \theta^{(c)} \qquad (7)$$

By modifying the constant 0.5 in Eq. (6) to a variable λ, a trade-off between the fitness performance and the generalization capability can be obtained by adjusting λ. A small λ gives a high classification performance on the training data, but the generalization capability cannot be guaranteed. Meanwhile, the proposed model is a more general model, and it will reduce to MLR and SLR when λ is set to 0 and 0.5 respectively.

To reconstruct the center 8 by 8 patches (the outer patches are not concerned to eliminate the edge effects) of the stimuli, 64 local classifiers described above are used with each classifier classifying its corresponding patch's contrast (either 1 with flickering checkboard or 0 with a gray patch). All the local classifiers are trained on the training data separately, and λ is chosen from a predetermined set {1, 0.5, 0.5e-2, 0.5e-4, 0.5e-6, 0.5e-8, 0}.

3   Results

3.1   Performances of SLR-T

Classifiers trained with different λ values have different test performances. In Fig. 1, three patch classifiers' performances are shown. Each of them is trained with different λ chosen from the λ sets described in the above. Note that with λ set index being set to 2 and 7, SLR-T becomes SLR and MLR respectively. One can see that with a proper λ, a better test accuracy can be obtained by SLR-T.

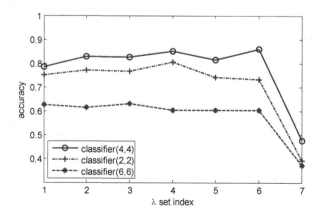

Fig. 1. Performances of 3 SLR-T classifiers trained with different λ

3.2   Image Reconstruction

Fig. 2 shows the accuracy of 30 classifiers trained using SLR-T method, SLR method and MLR method respectively. The mean accuracy of SLR and MLR is 0.6875 and 0.5005, while it is 0.7188 for SLR-T classifiers. The reconstructed results are shown in Fig. 3.

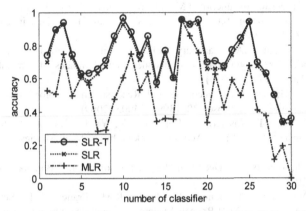

Fig. 2. Performance of 30 classifiers trained by SLR-T, SLR and MLR

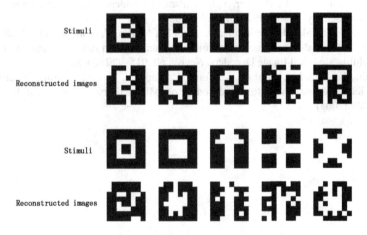

Fig. 3. Reconstructed images

4   Conclusion

A new sparse logistic regression model called SLR-T is proposed in this paper. The maximum likelihood regression and SLR are two special cases of SLR-T with the regularization coefficient being set to 0 and 0.5 respectively. An fMRI visual reconstruction experiment is carried out to verify the performance of SLR-T. The results show that, by choosing a proper regularization coefficient, the SLR-T may achieve a better performance than MLR and SLR on the test data set.

References

1. Vu, V.Q., Ravikumar, P., Naselaris, T., Kay, K.N., Gallant, J.L., Yu, B.: Encoding and decoding V1 fMRI responses to natural images with sparse nonparametric models. Ann. Appl. Stat. **5**, 1159–1182 (2011)
2. Engel, S.A., Glover, G.H., Wandell, B.A.: Retinotopic organization in human visual cortex and the spatial precision of functional MRI. Cereb. Cortex. **7**, 181–192 (1997)
3. Wandell, B.A., Dumoulin, S.O., Brewer, A.A.: Visual Field Maps in Human Cortex. Neuron **56**, 366–383 (2007)
4. Naselaris, T., Olman, C.A., Stansbury, D.E., Ugurbil, K., Gallant, J.L.: A voxel-wise encoding model for early visual areas decodes mental images of remembered scenes. NeuroImage **105**, 215–228 (2015)
5. Brouwer, G.J., Heeger, D.J.: Decoding and Reconstructing Color from Responses in Human Visual Cortex. J. Neurosci. **29**, 13992–14003 (2009)
6. Nishimoto, S., Vu, A.T., Naselaris, T., Benjamini, Y., Yu, B., Gallant, J.L.: Reconstructing Visual Experiences from Brain Activity Evoked by Natural Movies. Curr. Biol. **21**, 1641–1646 (2011)
7. Bannert, M.M., Bartels, A.: Decoding the Yellow of a Gray Banana. Curr. Biol. **23**, 2268–2272 (2013)
8. Goncalves, N.R., Ban, H., Sánchez-Panchuelo, R.M., Francis, S.T., Schluppeck, D., Welchman, A.E.: 7 Tesla fMRI Reveals Systematic Functional Organization for Binocular Disparity in Dorsal Visual Cortex. J. Neurosci. **35**, 3056–3072 (2015)
9. Kay, K.N., Naselaris, T., Prenger, R.J., Gallant, J.L.: Identifying natural images from human brain activity. Nature **452**, 352–355 (2008)
10. Miyawaki, Y., Uchida, H., Yamashita, O., Sato, M., Morito, Y., Tanabe, H.C., Sadato, N., Kamitani, Y.: Visual Image Reconstruction from Human Brain Activity using a Combination of Multiscale Local Image Decoders. Neuron **60**, 915–929 (2008)
11. Yamashita, O., Sato, M., Yoshioka, T., Tong, F., Kamitani, Y.: Sparse estimation automatically selects voxels relevant for the decoding of fMRI activity patterns. NeuroImage **42**, 1414–1429 (2008)

Evidence Theory and Its Application

A Temporal-Compress and Shorter SIFT Research on Web Videos

Yingying Zhu[1], Chuanhua Jiang[1], Xiaoyan Huang[2],
Zhijiao Xiao[1], and Shenghua Zhong[1(✉)]

[1] School of Computer Science & Software Engineering,
Shenzhen University, Shenzhen 518060, China
zhuyy@szu.edu.cn
[2] Oracle Research and Development Center Shenzhen Co., Ltd, Shenzhen 518057, China

Abstract. The large-scale video data on the web contain a lot of semantics, which are an important part of semantic web. Video descriptors can usually represent somewhat the semantics. Thus, they play a very important role in web multimedia content analysis, such as Scale-invariant feature transform (SIFT) feature. In this paper, we proposed a new video descriptor, called a temporal-compress and shorter SIFT(TC-S-SIFT) which can efficiently and effectively represent the semantics of web videos. By omitting the least discriminability orientation in three stages of standard SIFT on every representative frame, the dimensions of the shorter SIFT are reduced from 128-dimension to 96-dimension to save space storage. Then, the SIFT can be compressed by tracing SIFT features on video temporal domain, which highly compress the quantity of local features to reduce visual redundancy, and keep basically the robustness and discrimination. Experimental results show our method can yield comparable accuracy and compact storage size.

Keywords: Video semantics · Video descriptors · SIFT · Spatio-temporal features

1 Introduction

Following the rapid development and wide application of the Internet, Web has become a sharing information and effective tool for collaborative work, especially video data of Web. Researchers add meta data that can be understood by computer to documents on world wide web, so that the entire Internet can become a universal medium to exchange information. So, for the large scale of video data in Web, it is important to find the video descriptor that not only can be understood by computers but also can represent the video. To obtain video descriptor which can fully characterize the whole video, features can be obtained from each frame. Researchers have proposed a variety of means to detect local features on video frames, such as Scale-invariant feature transform(SIFT)[1,2] proposed by David Lowe, which is invariant to image translation, scaling, partially invariant to illumination changes and robust to local geometric distortion. Navneet Dalal and Bill Triggs described Histogram of

© Springer International Publishing Switzerland 2015
S. Zhang et al. (Eds.): KSEM 2015, LNAI 9403, pp. 833–843, 2015.
DOI: 10.1007/978-3-319-25159-2_78

Oriented Gradients(HOG)[3],and it performed well in human detection in videos. Herbert Bay presented Speeded Up Robust Feature(SURF)[4] that can be used for tasks such as object recognition or 3D reconstruction. Yan Ke proposed PCA_SIFT[5],which applied Principal Components Analysis (PCA) to the normalized gradient patch. Yi et al. developed another refinement method Conditional Random Field (CRF) based on both spatial and temporal relations [6]. Megrhi proposed a normalized ST descriptor which refines independent detection results of concepts by considering their correlations in video retrieval[7]. Coskun et al.[8]extracted the video features from both temporal and spatial domains. They considered the sequence of video frames as a 3-dimensional matrix, in which they extract the DCT and RBT as the global spatio-temporal feature. Mani et al.[9] extract the temporally informative representative images(TIRI) which is a weighted sum image of a sequence of frames, and then calculate the DCT as the spatio-temporal feature. Both [8] and [9] consider video features from the angle of spatio-temporal, but they extract several transform coefficients as the global feature which compressed too highly and not robust and distinctive enough to some video transformations.

As we know, all those features didn't solve the redundancy information in videos if we extracted those features on every frame. In this paper, we proposed a new video descriptor called a temporal-compress and shorter SIFT(TC-S-SIFT). By omitting the information in the least discriminability orientation in every stage of standard SIFT, TC-S-SIFT effectively reduced the space storage on video spatial domain. Then, tracing SIFT features on video temporal domain, we compressed the redundant features to save the   storage size of video. TC-S-SIFT not only effectively compressed the redundant features on video spatial and temporal domain but also kept the basic robustness.

The remainder of this paper is organized as follows. Section 2 discuss the proposed TC-S-SIFT in detail. Section 3 presents the experimental results. Conclusion is provided in Section 4.

2   A Temporal-Compress and Shorter SIFT

This section will outline the process of extracting the temporal-compress and shorter SIFT. Firstly, extracting video's key-frame. There are many video shot segmentation and key-frame extraction algorithms, but they all have some disadvantages: 1) Due to the huge amounts of videos, these methods cannot apply on all kinds of videos. 2) There isn't an exact and objective standard to define the key-frame. 3) The key-frame loses video temporal domain information. Instead of using these video shot segmentation and key-frame extraction algorithms, we extracted n video frames per second(n=15), these frames are on recorded as the representative frames. Compared with shot segmentation and key-frame extraction algorithms, this method was faster and kept the video temporal domain information. Secondly, extracting features on every representative frame, instead of using the standard SIFT features, we used a new feature, short SIFT is used to save video space storage. In this step, the two closed representative frames have many similar features and the quantity of these features are very large. Finally, by tracing the short SIFT on video temporal domain the similar features will be compressed, then the TC-S-SIFT descriptors are gotten.

2.1   A Shorter SIFT

We proposed a new algorithm to extract shorter SIFT feature on every representative frame based on the inhomogeneity of visual orientation in human visual system. The standard SIFT algorithm has three major steps: 1) keypoint detection and localization; 2) orientation assignment to keypoint; 3) keypoint descriptor. Differ from the standard SIFT, we ignore the information of oblique orientation in every stage. The first stage of keypoint detection is to detect locations that are invariant to scale change. One way is finding stable features across all possible scales. The scale space image of $I(x,y)$ can be defined as $L(x,y;s)$, which could be produced by the convolution of a variable-scale Gaussian $G(x,y;s)$ with $I(x,y)$, Where $G(x,y;s)$ is defined as Equations (2):

$$L(x, y; s) = G(x, y; s) * I(x, y) \tag{1}$$

$$G(x, y; s) = \frac{1}{2\pi s} e^{-(x^2+y^2)/2s} \tag{2}$$

The difference-of-Gaussians operator $DoG(x, y; s)$ computed from the difference of the two nearby scales:

$$\begin{aligned} DoG(x, y; s) &= L(x, y; s + \Delta s) - L(x, y; s) \\ &= (G(x, y; s + \Delta s) - G(x, y; s)) * I(x, y) \end{aligned} \tag{3}$$

Once DoG images have been obtained, keypoints are identified as local minima/maxima of the DoG images across scales. In the standard SIFT, this is done by comparing each pixel in the DoG images to its 26 neighbors pixel show in Fig.1(a). If the pixel value is the maximum or minimum among all compared pixels, it is selected as a keypoint. Different with standard SIFT in Fig. 1(a), our shorter SIFT only compares the 14 neighbors in cardinal orientation, as Fig.1 (b).

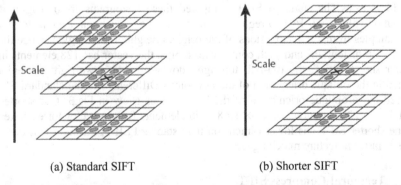

(a) Standard SIFT   (b) Shorter SIFT

Fig. 1. Maxima and minima are detected by comparing a pixel (marked with X) to its neighbors at the current & neighboring scales. (a) Standard SIFT comparing 26 neighbors. (b) Shorter SIFT comparing 14 neighbors.

In the second step of orientation assignment to keypoint, each keypoint is assigned one or more dominant orientations based on local image gradient directions. This is the key step in achieving invariance to rotation, as the keypoint descriptor can be represented relative to this orientation.

The scale space image $L(x,y;s)$ at the keypoint's scale s, the gradient magnitude $m(x,y;s)$ and $\theta(x,y;s)$ orientation   are precomputed using pixel differences:

$$m(x,y;s)=\sqrt{(L(x+1,y;s)-L(x-1,y;s))^2+(L(x,y+1;s)-L(x,y-1;s))^2} \quad (4)$$

$$\theta(x,y;s)=\tan^{-1}(\frac{L(x,y+1;s)-L(x,y-1;s)}{L(x+1,y;s)-L(x-1,y;s)}) \quad (5)$$

As computed in Equations (4) and (5), the magnitude and direction calculations for the gradient are calculated for every pixel around the keypoint. Then, the orientation histogram for every keypoint is formed. In the standard SIFT, the histogram has 36 bins,with 10 degrees per bin. In our shorter SIFT,by omitting the histogram in oblique orientation, the histogram only has 24 bins with 10 degrees per bin just as Fig. 2.

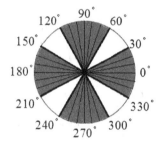
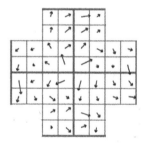

Fig. 2. Shorter SIFT orientation histogram with 24 bins and 10 degrees/bin.

Fig. 3. Subregions selection around keypoint of shorter SIFT.

In the third step of keypoint descriptor, the keypoint descriptor is a vector of orientation histograms.The standard SIFT computed these histograms from magnitude and orientation values in a 16×16 region around the keypoint such that each histogram contains samples from 4×4 subregions of the original neighborhood region. Since there are $4\times4=16$ histograms and each comes with 8 bins, the vector has 128 elements in total. To our shorter SIFT, the top-left, top-right, down-left and down-right subregions are located in the oblique orientation of the keypoints. Different with the standard SIFT, we ignored those oblique orientation of the keypoints as show in Fig.3. Our shorter SIFT used $3\times4=12$ subregions, and $3\times4\times8=96$ elements feature vector for each keypoint. So the shorter SIFT has lower dimension than standard SIFT, meaning that our shorter SIFT is faster in feature matching.

2.2   Temporal-Compress SIFT

Temporal-compress SIFT has two kinds of information, the temporal-compress and shorter SIFT descriptors and the video temporal domain information. The video temporal domain information is tracing the shorter SIFT features on every representative frame. Every video temporal domain track was composed of a series similar shorter SIFT on the representative frame in chronological order. The temporal-compress and shorter SIFT descriptors was the average value of the shorter SIFT on video temporal domain track. Tracing the shorter SIFT was a process of matching the shorter SIFT. If the ratio of the $dist(d,d_2)$ and the $dist(d,d_1)$ are bigger than δ, we called the d is matched with d_1.

$$\frac{dist(d,d_2)}{dist(d,d_1)} \geq \delta \ , \quad d \in D_{set_1}; d_1, d_2 \in D_{set_2}; d_1 \neq d_2 \tag{6}$$

where, d_1 was the shorter SIFT in D_{set_2} which is nearest to the shorter SIFT d, d_2 was the shorter SIFT in D_{set_2} which is the second nearest to the shorter SIFT d, the dist means Euclidean distance of the two shorter SIFT features. In the tracing process, because of the noise or the camera shake, the shorter SIFT may reappear after several representative frames, resulted to a video temporal domain track may split to several video temporal domain tracks. To this situation, those video temporal domain tracks should be connected, and avoid the video temporal domain track is too long because of the wrong matching. In this paper, we proposed a algorithms 2.2.1

Algorithm 2.2.1. Trace the short SIFT

Input: the shorter SIFT in every representative frame, the threshold θ_1 of the representative frame that the shorter SIFT reappeared, the threshold θ_2 of the video temporal domain trace's length.

Output: the video temporal domain track

1. From the first representative frame, tracing every shorter SIFT, we get the video temporal domain tracks. Suppose a video temporal domain track like that: $Track = \{d_{f_s},...,d_{f_i},...,d_{f_e}\}$, here, f_i means the representative frame that shorter SIFT appeared, d_{f_i} means the shorter SIFT.

2. Connect the video temporal domain track. For any two video temporal domain tracks $Track_i = \{d_{f_s},...,d_{f_e}\}$ and $Track_j = \{d_{f_b},...,d_{f_o}\}$, if the shorter SIFT d_{f_e} and d_{f_b} is matched, and $t = f_b - f_s < \theta_1$, then we connected the two video temporal domain tracks to one video temporal domain track $Track = \{d_{f_s},...,d_{f_e},d_{f_b},...,d_{f_o}\}$, where $\theta_1 = 3$ is a empirical value.

3. Split the video temporal domain track. To any $Track = \{d_{f_s},...,d_{f_i},...,d_{f_e}\}$, the distance of every near two shorter SIFT $Dist = \{d_1,d_2,...,d_i,...,d_{n-1}\}$, if the length of $Track$ $n > \theta_2$ and $\max(Dist) = d_i$, then we split the video temporal domain track to two video temporal domain tracks from f_i and f_{i+1}. We repeated this step until every video temporal domain track's length is small than θ_2, where, $\theta_2 = 15$ is an empirical value.

To extract TC-S-SIFT, there are three steps:

Step 1: Extract the shorter SIFT on every representative frame using the algorithm as above.

Step 2: Trace every shorter SIFT from the first representative frame using the algorithm 2.2.1, then we get the video temporal domain track, like Fig.4.

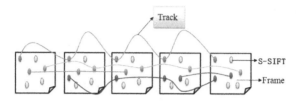

Fig. 4. Video temporal domain track

Step 3: Compute the temporal-compress and shorter SIFT descriptor, we compute the average value of the shorter SIFT on every video temporal domain track.

$$\text{TC-S-SIFT}_d = \hat{d} = n^{-1} \sum_{f=f_s}^{f_e} d_f \tag{7}$$

Where, d_f means the shorter SIFT that appeared in the number f representative frame, f_s means the video temporal domain track begin at the number f_s representative frame and f_e means the video temporal domain track end with the number f_e representative frame, n is the length of the video temporal domain track.

3   Experimental Results

In order to verify the validity of the proposed TC-S-SIFT, this section conducted three groups of experiments. The first group of experiments proved shorter SIFT not only has standard SIFT's robustness power but also reduce the redundancy information on video spatial domain. The second group verified whether TC-SIFT like SIFT has the robustness power and can be distinguished, and effectively reduced the number of features on video temporal domain. The third group verified TC-S-SIFT's compression performance compared with the standard SIFT.

In the stage of S-SIFT, we only consider the cardinal orientation as the dominant orientation, to prove this is effectively, we calculate the proportion of the dominant orientation of each keypoint in every image. The image is changed with optical zoom between $\times 1$ and $\times 10$ and with viewpoint angles θ between the camera axis and the normal to the painting varying from $0°$ (frontal view) to $80°$.

As listed in Table1, the oblique orientation has less possibility to become the dominant orientation, which proved that the lost information by ignored the oblique orientation of shorter SIFT is limited.

Table 1. Proportion of the dominant orientation

$\theta(°)$	Zoom×1		Zoom×10	
	Cardinal(%)	Oblique(%)	Cardinal(%)	Oblique(%)
+45	**75.78**	24.22	**72.97**	27.03
-45	**76.09**	23.91	**74.91**	25.09
+65	**75.37**	24.63	**76.01**	23.99
-65	**76.45**	23.55	**74.46**	25.54
+75	**73.67**	26.33	**79.13**	20.87
-75	**75.25**	24.75	**81.78**	18.22
+80	**74.02**	25.98	**82.31**	17.69
-80	**76.96**	23.04	**83.68**	16.32

 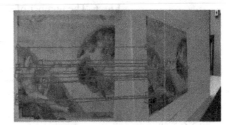

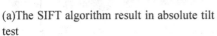

(a)The SIFT algorithm result in absolute tilt test

(b)The Shorter SIFT algorithm result in absolute tilt test

Fig. 5. Experimental results for feature detection and matching on absolute tilts test. (a) and (b) are the results in absolute tilt test. SIFT has 8 correct matches and shorter SIFT obtains 17 correct matches.

To prove S-SIFT robustness, exploring S-SIFT in image matching experiment. Fig.5 proved that S-SIFT has standard SIFT's robustness power.

We used the UCF50[21] dataset and divided the dataset into five groups, extract TC-SIFT and standard SIFT features. Then compared the number of TC-SIFT with standard SIFT features to prove TC-SIFT's better performance on compressing the visual content redundancy on video temporal domain. Fig. 6 showed the number of standard SIFT and TC-SIFT. Fig.7 showed the compression ration CR of TC-SIFT with different threshold δ which is defined by Equation (6).

$$CR = \frac{m}{n} \tag{8}$$

Where m is the number of TC-SIFT, n is the number of standard SIFT.

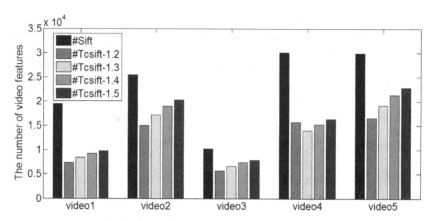

Fig. 6. The number of standard SIFT and TC-SIFT

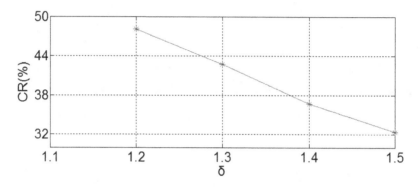

Fig. 7. The compression ratio of TC-SIFT with different threshold

As shown in Fig.7, compared with the standard SIFT, our TC-SIFT can compress many redundant features on video temporal domain. When tracing the shorter SIFT, the smaller the threshold δ, the compression ratio is bigger. When δ is 1.2, the compression can reduce the video features by over a half. It is very useful for video retrieval. But if the threshold δ is too small, it will result the video features lose the distinguished power. To balance the number and distinguished power, δ is a empirical value.

To prove the discrimination of TC-SIFT, the TC-SIFT on the comparison between source video with its video copy,such as inserting frames into a video. We used five videos as above to do a series of changes, then the source videos are matched with its video copies and some irrelevant videos. Formula (9) is to determine the similarity of two videos.

$$\eta = \frac{2 \times n_c}{n_s + n_p} \qquad (9)$$

Where, n_c is the TC-SIFT of source video matched with the TC-SIFT of video copy, n_s is the number of source video's TC-SIFT, n_p is the number of   video copy's TC-SIFT.

Table 2. The number of source video's TC-SIFT

Video	Video1	Video2	Video3	Video4	Video5
TC-SIFT	7398	14983	5620	15729	16547

Table 2 showed the number of source video's TC-SIFT. Table 3 showed the number of video copy's TC-SIFT and the matching TC-SIFT between the source video and its video copies. From Table 3, we can see that the   video copy matched a lot of features with the source video, but the irrelevant video almost not matched with the source video. Copy 2 has less matched numbers because we insert other frames into the video. So its matching number is less than other   video copies.

Table 3. The number of video copy 's TC-SIFT   and the matching TC-SIFT.

TC-SIFT / matching	Geometric Change (GC)	Picture in Picture (PP)	Add Frame (AF)	Forward or Rewind (FR)	Gamma Change (GC)	Grayscale Change (SC)	Irrelevant
SourceV1	5231	8064	7667	7398	7136	7174	14983
	2535	1799	2694	7380	3719	3774	360
Source V2	10609	17614	15046	11641	9279	14074	5620
	3601	2742	5963	3849	3446	5121	599
Source V3	5402	6404	5671	5620	5620	5682	15729
	1976	1039	1194	5592	5592	1750	797
Source V4	12636	12382	14771	13765	15913	15620	16547
	3327	2663	5738	5545	3550	5929	283
Source V5	12199	18058	15755	15952	16547	16027	7398
	3826	3148	5942	5185	16500	5843	240

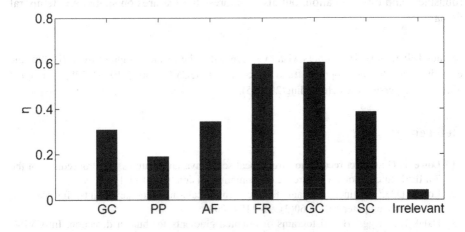

Fig. 8. The source video with the video copy and irrelevant video's matched rotation.

As shown in Fig.8, we can fund that TC-SIFT matched with its video copy, almost not matched with the irrelevant video. So TC-SIFT has better distinguished power.

Table 4. SIFT and TC-S-SIFT's storage size on five videos from UCF50 database

Video	SIFT	TC-S-SIFT	CR(%)
Video1	12.7MB	**6.38MB**	50.2
Video2	17.1MB	**7.72MB**	45.1
Video3	34.8MB	**24.1MB**	69.3
Video4	33.1MB	**23.4MB**	70.6
Video5	24.9MB	**12.3MB**	49.3

From the experiment results, we can fund that TC-S-SIFT reduced a large number of redundant information on video spatial and temporal domain and also kept the basically robustness and discrimination power.

4   Conclusion

With the high development of the Internet, video descriptor plays a very important role in semantic web. In this paper, we presented a new video descriptor, a temporal-compress and shorter SIFT. Without using video shot segmentation and representative frame extraction algorithms, we extracted video sequence every one second as the representative frames. Then extracting the shorter SIFT on every representative frame by omitting the information in the least discriminability orientation in three stage of the standard SIFT. The short SIFT reduced the dimension from 128-dimension to 96-dimension which saved the video space size. By tracing the shorter SIFT on video temporal domain, it can compress a larger number of redundant features and save video storage size.The experiments showed that TC-S-SIFT not only has the basically robustness and discrimination, but also compress the features on spatial and temporal domain.

Acknowledgements. The authors wish to acknowledge the financial support from: (i) Strategic emerging industry development fund of Shenzhen (JCYJ20130326105637578), and (ii) Shenzhen university research funding(201535).

References

1. Lowe, D.G.: Object recognition from local scale-invariant features. In: Proceedings of the 7th IEEE International Conference on Computer Vision, pp. 1150–1157 (1999)
2. Lowe, D.G.: Distinctive image features from scale-invariant key points. International Journal of Computer Vision **60**(2), 91–110 (2004)
3. Dalal, N., Triggs, B.: Histograms of oriented gradients for human detection. In: CVPR, pp. 886–893 (2005)

4. Bay, H., Ess, A., Tuytelaars, T., Gool, L.V.: SURF: Speeded up robust features. CVIU **110**(3), 346–359 (2008)
5. Ke, Y., Sukthankar, R.: PCA-SIFT: a more distinctive representation for local image descriptors. In: Proceedings of Computer Vision and Pattern Recognition, pp. 560–513 (2004)
6. Yi, J., Peng, Y., Xiao, J.: Exploiting semantic and visual context for effective video annotation. IEEE Trans. Multimed., 1400–1414 (2013)
7. Megrhi, S., Souidene, W., Beghdadi, A.: Spatio-temporal salient feature extraction for perceptual content based video retrieval. In: CVCS, pp. 1–7 (2013)
8. Coskun, B., Sankur, B., Memon, N.: Spatio-temporal transform based video hashing. IEEE Trans. on Multimedia, pp. 1190–1208 (2006)
9. Malekesmaeili, M., Fatourechi, M., Ward, R.K.: Video copy detection using temporally informative representative images. In: International Conference on Machine Learning and Applications, pp. 69–74 (2009)
10. Li, F.F., Fergus, R., Torralba, A.: Recognizing and learning object categories. In: Proceedings of the 12th IEEE International Conference on Computer Vision, Short course. The 2004 IEEE Computer Society Conference on Computer Vision and Pattern Recognition, pp. 506–513 (2009)
11. Brown, M., Lowe, D.G.: Automatic panoramic image stitching using invariant features. International Journal of Computer Vision, 59–73 (2007)
12. Qian, Y., Hui, R., Gao, X.H.: 3D CBIR with sparse coding for image-guided neurosurgery. Signal Processing **93**, 1673–1683 (2013)
13. Burghouts, G.J., Geusebroek. J.M.: Performance evaluation of local colour invariants. Computer Vision and Image Understanding, 48–62 (2009)
14. Saeedi, P.P., Lawrence, D., Lowe, D.G.: Vision-based 3-D trajectory tracking for unknown environments. IEEE Transaction on Robotics **22**(1), 119–136 (2006)
15. Zhong, S.H., Liu, Y., Wu, G.S.: S-SIFT: a shorter SIFT without least discriminability visual orientation. In: Proceedings of the 2012 IEEE/WIC/ACM International Conference on Web Intelligence, vol. 1, pp. 669–672 (2012)
16. Zhu, G.K., Wang, Q., Yuan, Y., Yan, P.K.: SIFT on manifold: An intrinsic description. Neurocomputing **113**, 227–233 (2013)
17. Laptev, I., Lindeberg, T.: Local descriptors for spatio-temporal recognition. In: MacLean, W. (ed.) SCVMA 2004. LNCS, vol. 3667, pp. 91–103. Springer, Heidelberg (2006)
18. Girshick, A.R., Landy, M.S., Simoncelli, E.P.: Cardinal rules: visual orientation perception reflects knowledge of environmental statistics. Nat. Neurosci. **14**, 926–932 (2011)
19. Reddy, K., Shah, M.: Recognizing 50 human action categories of web videos. In: Proc. Mach. Vision Applicat., pp. 1–11 (2012)

Belief Revision over Infinite Propositional Language

Hua Meng[1]([✉]), Yayan Yuan[2], Jielei Chu[1], and Hongjun Wang[1]

[1] Southwest Jiaotong University, Chengdu, China
{menghua,wanghongjun}@swjtu.edu.cn, jieleichu@home.swjtu.edu.cn
[2] Henan Normal University, Xinxiang, China
yayanyuan@hotmail.com

Abstract. There are different models to characterize AGM belief revision framework. When the background language is finite propositional language, Katsuno and Mendelzon (KM) proposed in 1991 a representation model using total preorder on worlds. This 'preorder' model is very influential and has been extended to characterize epistemic state in iterated belief revision. KM showed an approach how to construct the preorder via a belief set and an AGM belif revision operator, however, this approach does not work well when the language is infinite. In this paper, we argue when the language is infinite propositional language, how to construct a preorder on world to model AGM belief revision framework, and then we generalize the representation theorem of KM over an infinite language.

1 Introduction

Belief revision mainly characterizes how an agent changes her belief with new evidence. Logic based belief revision has been extensively studied in AI in the past three decades [1–4,7,8,11,13,19].

The AGM framework of belief revision represents the agent's belief as a set of sentences which is deductively closed (called a belief set), and represents the new evidence by a sentence [1]. The revision result is also a belief set. Alchourron et al. showed the basic rules of believe revision via revision operator (see Section 2). To semantically characterize AGM revision operators, researchers introduced several different models such as system of spheres [6], epistemic entrenchment [5] and total preorder on worlds [8]. In [8], Katsuno and Mendelzon argued belief revision over a finite proposition language. They showed an important representation theorem that for each belief set K and an AGM revision operator, there is a total preorder $\preceq$ on worlds such that for any proposition φ, $K \circ \varphi$ is totally decided by the minimal φ worlds. This representation theorem shows AGM revision operator can be totally characterized by total preorder. This total

This work was partially supported by NSFC (Grant No. 61100046) and the Fundamental Research Funds for the Central Universities of China (Grant No.2682014ZT28).

© Springer International Publishing Switzerland 2015
S. Zhang et al. (Eds.): KSEM 2015, LNAI 9403, pp. 844–854, 2015.
DOI: 10.1007/978-3-319-25159-2_79

preorder model is very influential and has been extended to characterize iterated belief revision [3]. However, when the language is infinite, KM's approach does not work well (see Section 3). A natural question is whether we can also use total preorder on worlds to characterize belief change under a infinite language, and how to generalize the representation theorem of KM in this situation. In this paper, we mainly argue this question.

The remainder of this paper is structured as follows: Section 2 introduces basic notions of belief revision. Section 3 introduces the motivation of this paper. In Section 4 we show the equvalience between system of spheres model and total preorder model over a finite propositional language. Section 5 then presents an approach how to construct a total preorder on worlds when the language is infinte. Section 6 and Section 7 are related work and conclusion.

2   Belief Revision and AGM Theory

2.1   Notation and Definitions

In this paper, we restrict our discussion to belief revision in a propositional language L. A theory K of L is a set of propositions which is deductively closed, i.e., $\varphi \in K$ iff $K \vdash \varphi$. We denote by T_L the set of all theories. We say a theory K is complete iff for all $\varphi \in L$ either $\varphi \in K$ or $\neg\varphi \in K$. Suppose W is the set of all consistent complete theories of L. Since L is sound and complete, for each $\omega \in W$, ω can be seen as an interpretation, such that $\omega \models \phi$ iff $\varphi \in \omega$. In this sense, ω is also called a world of φ. We will not distinguish consistent complete theories and worlds. Suppose $U \subseteq W$, we denote by $U \models \varphi$ if for each $\omega \in U$, then we have $\omega \models \varphi$. For each proposition φ, we denote by $[\varphi]$ the set of all worlds of φ. It is easy to see $\omega \in [\varphi]$ iff $\omega \models \varphi$. For each set of propositions Γ, we denote by $[\Gamma] = \{\omega \mid \text{for all } \varphi \in \Gamma, \omega \models \phi\}$ and $Cn(\Gamma) = \{\varphi \mid \Gamma \vdash \varphi\}$. For a theory K and a proposition ψ, we denote by $K + \psi = Cn(K \cup \{\psi\})$. For each $U \subseteq W$, we denote by U^c the complement set of U and $U \setminus V = U \cap V^c$.

A (partial) preorder $\preceq$ on a nonempty set A is a binary relation on A, which is reflexive and transitive. A preorder $\preceq$ is called *total* if any two elements in A are comparable. That is, for any $x, y \in A$, we have either $x \preceq y$ or $y \preceq x$. We write $x \sim y$ if $x \preceq y$ and $y \preceq x$, and $x \prec y$ if $x \preceq y$ but $y \npreceq x$. For each $B \subseteq A$, B is called an upper set if for any $x \in B$ and $x \preceq y$, then $y \in B$. We denote by $\uparrow x = \{y \mid x \preceq y\}$ and $\downarrow x = \{y \mid y \preceq x\}$. If $\preceq$ is a preorder on A, then it is easy to see $x \preceq y$ iff $\uparrow y \subseteq \uparrow x$.

2.2   AGM Theory

The most famous belief revision framework is AGM theory which contains eight postulates [1]. In AGM framework, an agent's belief is represented by a theory which is always called a belief set. A revision operator $\circ$ is a function mapping a belief set and a proposition to a new belief set. We call $\circ$ an AGM revision operator if $\circ$ satisfies the following AGM postulates.

$(K * 1)$ $K \circ \varphi$ is a theory of L.

$(K * 2)$ $\varphi \in K \circ \varphi$.

$(K * 3)$ $K \circ \varphi \subseteq Cn(K \cup \{\varphi\})$.

$(K * 4)$ If $K \cup \{\varphi\}$ is consistent then $Cn(K \cup \{\varphi\}) \subseteq K \circ \varphi$.

$(K * 5)$ If φ is consistent then $K \circ \varphi$ is consistent.

$(K * 6)$ If $\varphi \equiv \psi$ then $K \circ \varphi = K \circ \psi$.

$(K * 7)$ $K \circ (\varphi \wedge \psi) \subseteq (K \circ \varphi) + \psi$.

$(K * 8)$ If $(K \circ \varphi) + \psi$ is consistent then $(K \circ \varphi) + \psi \subseteq K \circ (\varphi \wedge \psi)$.

To improve readability, in this paper, we neglect the limiting cases when φ is inconsistent and assume that φ is always consistent. Note that if K is inconsistent, then we have $K = L$. In this case we shall have $K \circ \varphi = Cn(\varphi)$. In the following, we also assume that K is a consistent theory.

2.3 Representation Theorem Over Finite Propositional Language

Katsuno and Mendelzon (KM) rephrased AGM postulates under a finite propositional logic setting [8]. They showed a famous representation theorem by using total preorder on worlds. In KM's model, the belief set is represented by a single proposition which is the conjunction of all propositions in belief set. On the other hand, each consistent proposition ψ can also be seen as a belief set $K_\psi = \{\varphi \mid \psi \vdash \varphi\}$. So we do not distinguish between ψ and K_ψ over a finite language.

Definition 1. *[8] A function that maps each belief set K to a total preorder $\preceq_K$ on W is called a faithful assignment if and only if:*

(1) If $\omega_1, \omega_2 \models K$ then $\omega_1 \sim_K \omega_2$;

(2) If $\omega_1 \models K$ and $\omega_2 \not\models K$ then $\omega_1 \prec_K \omega_2$;

(3) If $K_1 \equiv K_2$ then $\preceq_{K_1} = \preceq_{K_2}$.

Theorem 1. *[8] A revision operator $\circ$ satisfies postulates $(K * 1)$-$(K * 8)$ precisely when there exists a faithful assignment that maps each belief set K into a total preorder $\preceq_K$ such that:*

$$(RT) \ [K \circ \varphi] = Min([\varphi], \preceq_K).$$

If L is finite, then for a subset $A \subseteq W$, we denote by FORM(A) a proposition whose worlds are exactly those in A. Clearly, we have FORM$([\psi]) \equiv \psi$ and $[(\text{FORM}(A))] = A$. In the proof of Theorem 1, Katsuno and Mendelzon showed that if an operator $\circ$ satisfies $(K * 1)$-$(K * 8)$, then for any two worlds ω_1, ω_2, the result of revising K by FORM$(\{\omega_1, \omega_2\})$ is exactly one of FORM$(\{\omega_1\})$, FORM$(\{\omega_2\})$ and FORM$(\{\omega_1, \omega_2\})$. From the revision result, $\preceq_K$ is characterized as follows [8]:

(PR1) $\omega_1 \prec_K \omega_2$ iff $K \circ \text{FORM}(\{\omega_1, \omega_2\}) = \text{FORM}(\{\omega_1\})$.

(PR2) $\omega_2 \prec_K \omega_1$ iff $K \circ \text{FORM}(\{\omega_1, \omega_2\}) = \text{FORM}(\{\omega_2\})$.

(PR3) $\omega_1 \sim_K \omega_2$ iff $K \circ \text{FORM}(\{\omega_1, \omega_2\}) = \text{FORM}(\{\omega_1, \omega_2\})$.

We conclude that for each belief set K and an AGM operator $\circ$, there is a total preoreder $\preceq_K$ following with $(PR1) - (PR3)$ such that $K \circ \varphi$ is totally decided by $\preceq_K$ via (RT). Conversely, for each total preoreder $\preceq$ on W, suppose K is the theory such that $[K] = Min(W, \preceq)$. Then $\preceq$ can also derive a revision operator on K via (RT), which satisfies $(K*1)$-$(K*8)$. KM's representation theorem is very important, especially in iterated belief revision [3].

3   Motivation

However, when the language L is infinite, it is easy to see (PR1)-(PR3) are not suitable in this case. On one hand, when L is infinite, for any $\omega_1, \omega_2 \in W$, there is not a proposition φ, such that $[\varphi] = \{\omega_1, \omega_2\}$. Moreover, when the atoms of L are infinite we have the following lemma.

Lemma 1. *If L is infinite, then W is infinite, furthermore, for each $\varphi \in L$, if φ is consistent then $[\varphi]$ is infinite.*

The above lemma shows that we can not establish a total preorder by the way of (PR1)-(PR3) over an infinite language. On the other hand, suppose U is a nonempty subset of W. Then there may not exist a theory K_U such that $[K_U] = U$. Furthermore, suppose $\preceq$ is a total preorder $\preceq$ on W. Then there may not exist a theory K such that $Min([\varphi], \preceq) = [K]$. Hence, a total preorder on W may not always derive an AGM operator via (RT). A natural question is how to generalize the KM's representation theorem over an infinite language? In this paper, we will show for each AGM operator there is a class of special total preorder on W, which can represent the AGM operator like "KM-style". We will also show a new approach how to induce a total preorder from an AGM revision operator and a belief set.

In the rest of the paper, we first introduce another semantic model of AGM revision operator, which is called system of spheres. We show when L is finite, the system of spheres model is equivalent to the total preorder model. However, when L is infinite, the system of spheres model also works well to characterize AGM revision operator (cf. [15,16]). Secondly, when L is infinite, we will show an approach to construct a special class of total preorders by the system of spheres.

4   Sphere-Based Revision

Grove in [6] proposed the system of spheres model to characterize belief revision. Suppose $A \subseteq W$ and $S \subseteq 2^W$. Then we say S is a system of spheres at A if S satisfies the following conditions:

(S1) If $U, V \in S$, then $U \subseteq V$ or $V \subseteq U$.
(S2) $A \in S$ and $A \subseteq U$ for any $U \in S$.
(S3) $W \in S$.
(S4) For every consistent φ in L (i.e., $[\varphi] \neq \varnothing$), there is a smallest set $V \in S$ such that $[\varphi] \cap V \neq \varnothing$. That is, if $V' \in S$ and $[\varphi] \cap V' \neq \varnothing$, then $V \subseteq V'$.

We denote by $C_S(\varphi)$ the smallest set in S intersecting $[\varphi]$. From (S1)-(S3), we can see that S is totally ordered by $\subseteq$. A is the bottom element of S and W is the top element.

Suppose K is a belief set. Then each AGM operator will induce a system of sphere centred at $[K]$. Conversely, every system of spheres centred at $[K]$ gives rise to an AGM operator. We have the following theorem.

Theorem 2. *([16]) Suppose K is a theory and $\circ$ is a function from $T_L \times L$ to T_L. Then $\circ$ satisfies $(K*1)$-$(K*8)$ iff there is a system of spheres S centred at $[K]$ satisfying (S^*).*

$$(S^*)\ K \circ \varphi = \bigcap\{\omega \mid \omega \in C_S(\varphi) \cap [\varphi]\}.$$

From Theorem 1 and 2, we know that for any belief set K and an AGM revision operator $\circ$, we can use either $\preceq_K$ or S_K to characterize $\circ$. Next, we show if L is finite, then there is a 1-1 correspondence between S_K and $\preceq_K$. Firstly, we show an equivalent characterisation of (S^*)

Lemma 2. *Suppose L is finite. Then for each nonempty $U \subseteq W$, we have $[\bigcap U] = U$. Moreover, (S^*) is equivalent to the following (S^e).*

$$(S^e)\ [K \circ \varphi] = C_S(\varphi) \cap [\varphi].$$

Proof. For each $\omega \in U$, ω is a complete consistent theory, we have $\bigcap U \subseteq \omega$. Then $\omega \models \bigcap U$. This means $U \subseteq [\bigcap U]$. Since L is finite, for each nonempty $U \subseteq W$ there is a proposition ψ such that $[\psi] = U$. For each $\omega \in U$, we have $\omega \models \psi$. Hence, $\psi \in \omega$. Then we have $\psi \in \bigcap U$. This means $[\bigcap U] \subseteq [\psi] = U$. So we get $[\bigcap U] = U$. Furthermore, $[K \circ \varphi] = [\bigcap\{\omega \mid \omega \in C_S(\varphi) \cap [\varphi]\}] = C_S(\varphi) \cap [\varphi]$. Then (S^*) is equivalent to (S^e). ∎

Definition 2. *Suppose S is a system of spheres at $[K]$. Then for each $\omega \in W$, we denote by $I_S(\omega) = \{U \in S \mid \omega \in U\}$. For every $\omega_1, \omega_2 \in W$, we define an order $\preceq_S$ on W as follow: $\omega_1 \preceq_S \omega_2$ if $I_S(\omega_2) \subseteq I_S(\omega_1)$.*

Theorem 3. *Suppose S is a system of spheres at $[K]$. Then $\preceq_S$ is a total pre-oreder, and for every $\varphi \in L$ we have*

$$[K \circ \varphi] = C_S(\varphi) \cap [\varphi] = Min([\varphi], \preceq_S).$$

Proof. For each $\omega \in W$, if $U \in I_S(\omega)$, then for all $V \in S$, $U \subseteq V$, we have $V \in I_S(\omega)$. This means $I_S(\omega)$ is a upper set of $(S, \subseteq)$. Since S is a chain, it is easy to verify for any two upper set $I_S(\omega_1)$ and $I_S(\omega_2)$, we have either $I_S(\omega)_1 \subseteq I_S(\omega)_2$ or $I_S(\omega)_2 \subseteq I_S(\omega_1)$. Hence, $\preceq_S$ is total. From Definition 2, we know $\omega_1 \preceq_S \omega_2$ iff for all $U \in S$ and $\omega_2 \in U$, we have $\omega_1 \in U$. It is not difficult to verify that $\preceq_S$ is reflexive and transitive. So we conclude that $\preceq_S$ is a total preorder.

Since L is finite, we have $[K \circ \varphi] = C_S(\varphi) \cap [\varphi]$. Next, we only need to show $C_S(\varphi) \cap [\varphi] = Min([\varphi], \preceq_S)$. Since $C_S(\varphi)$ is the smallest element in S intersecting $[\varphi]$, for each $\omega \in C_S(\varphi) \cap [\varphi]$, we have $I_S(\omega) = \{U \in S \mid C_S(\varphi) \subseteq U\}$. For each

$\omega' \in [\varphi] \setminus C_S(\varphi)$, we know $C_S(\varphi) \not\subseteq I_S(\omega')$. Hence we have $I_S(\omega') \subset I_S(\omega)$. This means $\omega \prec_S \omega'$. Hence $C_S(\varphi) \cap [\varphi]$ is exactly the minimum worlds of $[\varphi]$ under $\preceq_S$, i.e., $C_S(\varphi) \cap [\varphi] = Min([\varphi], \preceq_S)$.

On the other hand, we also can construct a system of spheres from a total preorder. For each total preorder $\preceq$ on W, if there is a theory K such that $Min(W, \preceq) = [K]$, then we say $\preceq$ is a *total preorder at* $[K]$.

Definition 3. *Suppose $\preceq$ is a total preorder at K, we define $S_{\preceq}$ a collection of nonempty subsets of W as follow,*

$$S_{\preceq} = \{\downarrow \omega \mid \omega \in W\} \cup \{W\}$$

Remark 1. Notice that, when W is finite, there is always a $\omega \in W$ such that $\downarrow \omega = W$. In this case, $S_{\preceq} = \{\downarrow \omega \mid \omega \in W\}$. But, when W is infinite, there may not be a $\omega \in W$ such that $\downarrow \omega = W$. In next section, we will discuss the case when W is infinite.

Theorem 4. *Suppose $\preceq$ is a total preorder at $[K]$. Then $S_{\preceq}$ is a system of spheres at $[K]$ such that*

$$[K \circ \varphi] = Min([\varphi], \preceq) = C_{S_{\preceq}}(\varphi) \cap [\varphi]$$

Proof. First, we need to show $S_{\preceq}$ satisfies (S1)-(S4). We take (S4) as an example, and others are similar or simpler. To show $S_{\preceq}$ satisfies (S4), we only need to show for each consistent $\varphi \in L$, there is a $\omega \in W$ such that $\downarrow \omega \cap [\varphi] \neq \varnothing$, and for all $\omega^* \prec \omega$, $\downarrow \omega^* \cap [\varphi] = \varnothing$. Since W is finite, $Min([\varphi], \preceq) \neq \varnothing$ for each consistent φ. Suppose $\omega \in Min([\varphi], \preceq)$, then $\downarrow \omega \cap [\varphi] \neq \varnothing$. For any other (if exit) $\omega' \in Min([\varphi], \preceq)$, we have $\omega \sim \omega'$. This means $\downarrow \omega = \downarrow \omega'$. Hence, we conclude that all the minimal elements are in $\downarrow \omega$. Furthermore, for any $\omega^* \prec \omega$, we have $[\varphi] \cap \downarrow \omega^* = \varnothing$, because ω is the minimal element of $[\varphi]$. This means $\downarrow \omega$ is the smallest element in $S_{\preceq}$ intersecting $[\varphi]$. Hence $S_{\preceq}$ is a system of spheres, and $C_{S_{\preceq}}(\varphi) = \downarrow \omega$.

Second, if $\omega_1 \in [\varphi]$ but $\omega_1 \notin Min([\varphi], \preceq)$, then $\omega \prec \omega_1$ and $\omega_1 \notin \downarrow \omega$. Hence, $Min([\varphi], \preceq) = [\varphi] \cap \downarrow \omega$. From Theorem 1, we have $[K \circ \varphi] = Min([\varphi], \preceq) = C_{S_{\preceq}}(\varphi) \cap [\varphi]$.

From Definition 2 and 3, it is easy to see if $S_1 \neq S_2$ then $\preceq_{S_1} \neq \preceq_{S_2}$, and if $\preceq_1 \neq \preceq_2$ then $S_{\preceq_1} \neq S_{\preceq_2}$. We conclude that there is a 1-1 corresponding between total preorder on worlds and system of spheres. They are equivalent to derive AGM operator via Theorem 3 and Theorem 4.

Example 1. *Suppose L has two propositional atoms a and b. Then all worlds of L can be represented as $W = \{\omega_1 = a \wedge b, \omega_2 = a \wedge \neg b, \omega_3 = \neg a \wedge b, \omega_4 = \neg a \wedge \neg b\}$. Suppose $\omega_1 \prec \omega_2 \sim \omega_3 \prec \omega_4$ is a total preorder on W. Then $S_{\preceq} = \{\{\omega_1\}, \{\omega_1, \omega_2, \omega_3\}, W\}$ by Definition 3. Conversely, given a system of sphere $S = \{\{\omega_2, \omega_4\}, \{\omega_2, \omega_3, \omega_4\}, W\}$, we have $\omega_2 \sim_S \omega_4 \preceq_S \omega_3 \preceq_S \omega_1$ is a total preorder by Definition 2.*

5   Representation Theorem Over Infinite Language

In this section, we discuss belief revision over an infinite propositional language. In this situation, both L and W are infinite. Recall that for each $\omega \in W$, there is no longer a proposition φ such that $[\varphi] = \{\omega\}$. Moreover, for a nonempty set $U \subseteq W$, there may be not a proposition ψ such that $[\psi] = U$. We show an example here. Suppose ψ is a consistent proposition and $\omega_1 \in [\psi]$, let $U = [\psi] \setminus \{\omega_1\}$, then we have the following property:

Property 1. If $U \models \varphi$, then $[\psi] \models \varphi$.

Proof. Suppose $[\psi] \not\models \varphi$, since $U = [\psi] \setminus \{\omega\}$ and $U \models \varphi$, we have $\omega_1 \not\models \varphi$. Hence $\omega_1 \models \neg\varphi$. Furthermore, $\omega_1 \models \neg\varphi \wedge \psi$. This means $\neg\varphi \wedge \psi$ is consistent. Hence $[\neg\varphi \wedge \psi]$ is infinite. There is a $\omega_2 \neq \omega_1$ such that $\omega_2 \models \neg\varphi \wedge \psi$. Since $\omega_2 \models \psi$, we have $\omega_2 \in U$. This means $\omega_2 \models \varphi$, which is in contradiction with $\omega_2 \models \neg\varphi \wedge \psi$. So $[\psi] \models \varphi$.

From above property, we know there is no proposition φ such that $[\varphi] = U$. We next show an example that for a total preorder on worlds, it may be not suitable to define an AGM revision operator via (RT) over an infinite language.

Example 2. *Let ψ be a consistent proposition such that $[\psi] \neq W$. Suppose $\omega_1 \in \neg\psi$. Then we define a total preorder as follows:*

(1) If $\omega, \omega' \in [\psi]$ or $\omega, \omega' \in [\neg\psi] \setminus \{\omega_1\}$, then $\omega \sim \omega'$.
(2) If $\omega \in [\psi]$ and $\omega' \in [\neg\psi] \setminus \{\omega_1\}$, then $\omega \prec \omega'$.
(3) If $\omega \in [\psi]$ or $\omega \in [\neg\psi] \setminus \{\omega_1\}$, then $\omega \prec \omega_1$.

It is easy to see $Min(W, \preceq) = [\psi]$. Let $K = \{\varphi \mid \psi \models \varphi\}$. Then $[K] = [\psi]$. Following with Theorem 1, we have $[K \circ \neg\psi] = Min([\neg\psi], \preceq) = [\neg\psi] \setminus \{\omega_1\}$. However, there is not a theory whose model set is $[\neg\psi] \setminus \{\omega_1\}$ by Property 1. This means, when W is infinite, not all the total preorders on worlds can derive an AGM revision operator via (RT).

Pappes in [15] introduced a notion of *elementary* set as follow.

Definition 4. *[15] Suppose $U \subseteq W$ is a nonempty set. We call U is elementary if $U = [\bigcap_{\omega \in U} \omega]$*

In fact, each elementary set is exactly the model of some theory. In [14], Meng et al. presented a topological characterization of elementary set. The following lemma is an immediate inference from [14].

Lemma 3. *Suppose U is a nonempty subset of W. Then*

(1) U is elementary iff $K_U = \{\psi \mid U \subseteq [\psi]\}$ is a theory such that $[K_U] = U$.
(2) Suppose $\{U_i \mid i \in I\}$ is a collection of elementary sets, if $\bigcap_{i \in I} U_i \neq \varnothing$ then $\bigcap_{i \in I} U_i$ is elementary.

Corollary 1. *If W is finite then every nonempty subset of W is elementary.*

Proof. From Lemma 2, $U = [\bigcap_{\omega \in U} \omega]$ always holds over a finite language. Hence, U is elementary.

Corollary 2. *Suppose L is infinite. Then for each consistent $\Gamma \subseteq L$, $[\Gamma]$ is elementary.*

Proof. If Γ is consistent, then $K_\Gamma = \{\varphi \mid \Gamma \vdash \varphi\}$ is a theory such that $[\Gamma] = [K_\Gamma]$. Hence, $[\Gamma]$ is elementary.

The above corollary shows the model set of each consistent Γ is elementary. For each nonempty $U \subseteq W$, $\bigcap_{\omega \in U} \omega$ is consistent. Hence, $[\bigcap_{\omega \in U} \omega]$ is elementary. It is easy to check $[\bigcap_{\omega \in U} \omega]$ is the smallest elementary set containing U.

Definition 5. *For each nonempty subset $U \subseteq W$, we denote by $\overline{U} = [\bigcap_{\omega \in U} \omega]$.*

From the definition, we know if U is elementary, then $\overline{U} = U$.

Definition 6. *Suppose S is a system of spheres. We denote by $\overline{S} = \{\overline{U} \mid U \in S\}$. We call S is an elementary system of spheres if $S = \overline{S}$.*

That is to say, S is an elementary system of spheres iff S is a system of spheres such that for each $U \in S$, U is elementary. For each system of spheres S, $\overline{S}$ is also a system of spheres, moreover, $\overline{S}$ and S derive the same AGM revision operator via (S^*). The following lemma was argued in [18] and [14].

Lemma 4. *If S is a system of spheres at K, then $\overline{S}$ is also a system of spheres at K. Furthermore, suppose $\circ$ is the corresponding revision operator of $\overline{S}$. Then $[K \circ \varphi] = \overline{C_S(\varphi)} \cap [\varphi] = C_{\overline{S}}(\varphi) \cap [\varphi]$.*

The following lemma shows AGM revision operator can be characterized by elementary system of spheres.

Lemma 5. *[14] For each theory K of L, $\circ$ is an AGM revision operator iff $S_{K,\circ} = \{\overline{\bigcup_{\psi \in Cn(\{\varphi\})}[K \circ \psi]} \mid \varphi \in L\}$ is an elementary system of spheres at $[K]$ such that $[K \circ \varphi] = C_{S_{K,\circ}}(\varphi) \cap [\varphi]$.*

Definition 7. *A total preorder $\preceq$ on W is called an elementary total preorder if for each consistent $\varphi \in L$, then $Min([\varphi], \preceq)$ is elementary.*

Theorem 5. *If S is an elementary system of spheres at $[K]$, then $\preceq_S$ is an elementary total preorder at $[K]$. Conversely, if $\preceq$ on W is an elementary total preorder at $[K]$, then $S_\preceq$ is an elementary system of spheres at $[K]$. Where, $\preceq_S$ ($S_\preceq$ respectively) are defined in Definition 2 (Definition 3 respectively).*

Proof. On one hand, suppose S is an elementary system of spheres at $[K]$. Then it is easy to verify $\preceq_S$ is a total preorder at $[K]$. We only need to show that for every $\varphi \in L$, $Min([\varphi], \preceq_S)$ is elementary. Since S is elementary, we know there is a $C_S(\varphi) \in S$ such that $C_S(\varphi) \cap [\varphi]$ is elementary. From the definition of $C_S(\varphi)$, we know that if $V \in S$ and $V \subset C_S(\varphi)$, then we have $V \cap [\varphi] = \varnothing$. Then for any $\omega_1 \in C_S(\varphi) \cap [\varphi]$ we have $I_S(\omega_1) = \{V \in S \mid C_S(\varphi) \subseteq V\}$. For each

$\omega_2 \in ([\varphi] \backslash C_{\mathcal{S}}(\varphi))$, we have $C_{\mathcal{S}}(\varphi) \not\subseteq I_{\mathcal{S}}(\omega_2)$. This means $I_{\mathcal{S}}(\omega_2) \subset I_{\mathcal{S}}(\omega_1)$. Hence, $\omega_2 \prec \omega_1$. We can conclude that $Min([\varphi], \preceq_{\mathcal{S}}) = C_{\mathcal{S}}(\varphi) \cap [\varphi]$, and $Min([\varphi], \preceq_{\mathcal{S}})$ is elementary.

On the other hand, suppose $\preceq$ is an elementary total preorder at $[K]$. Then, it is easy to verify $\mathcal{S}_{\preceq} = \{\downarrow \omega \mid \omega \in W\} \cup \{W\}$ satisfies (S1)-(S3). For each consistent $\varphi \in L$, $Min([\varphi], \preceq)$ is elementary. For any $\omega \in Min([\varphi], \preceq)$, we have $\downarrow \omega \in \mathcal{S}_{\preceq}$ and $\downarrow \omega \cap [\varphi] = Min([\varphi], \preceq)$. Furthermore, if $\omega' \prec \omega$, then $\downarrow \omega' \cap [\varphi] = \varnothing$. Hence $\downarrow \omega$ is the smallest element in $\mathcal{S}_{\preceq}$ intersecting $[\varphi]$. Moreover, $\downarrow \omega \cap [\varphi]$ is elementary. So $\mathcal{S}_{\preceq}$ is an elementary system of spheres at $[K]$.

From Theorem 5 and Lemma 5, we get the following theorem, which generalizes KM's representation theorem over an infinite language.

Theorem 6. *Suppose L is infinite. A revision operator $\circ$ satisfies postulates $(K*1)$-$(K*8)$ iff for any theory K, there exists an elementary total preorder $\preceq_K$ at $[K]$ such that (RT) is satisfied, i.e.,*

$$[K \circ \varphi] = Min([\varphi], \preceq_K)$$

Proof. On one hand, if there is an elementary total preorder $\preceq_K$ at $[K]$ such that $[K \circ \varphi] = Min([\varphi], \preceq_K)$, then there is an elementary system of spheres $\mathcal{S}_{\preceq_K}$ at $[K]$. It is easy to check that $Min([\varphi], \preceq_K) = C_{\mathcal{S}_{\preceq_K}}(\varphi) \cap [\varphi]$. Hence, $\circ$ satisfies postulates $(K*1)$-$(K*8)$. On the other hand, If $\circ$ satisfies postulates $(K*1)$-$(K*8)$ then for each theory K, $S_{K,\circ}$ is an elementary system of spheres at $[K]$. Moreover, $\preceq_{S_{K,\circ}}$ is an elementary total preorder. It is easy to check that $[K \circ \varphi] = C_{\mathcal{S}_{K,\circ}}(\varphi) \cap [\varphi] = Min([\varphi], \preceq_{S_{K,\circ}})$. Let $\preceq_K = \preceq_{S_{K,\circ}}$, then the theorem is hold.

From the above theorem, we conclude that when L is infinite, the elementary total preorder on worlds can be used to capture AGM revision operator.

Definition 8. *Suppose K is a belief set and $\circ$ is an AGM operator. For any $\omega_1, \omega_2 \in W$, we denote by $\omega_1 \preceq_{K,\circ} \omega_2$ if $I_{\mathcal{S}_{K,\circ}}(\omega_2) \subseteq I_{\mathcal{S}_{K,\circ}}(\omega_1)$.*

Corollary 3. *Suppose K is a belief set and $\circ$ is an AGM revision operator. Then $\preceq_{K,\circ}$ is an elementary total preorder such that for each consistent φ,*

$$[K \circ \varphi] = Min([\varphi], \preceq_{K,\circ})$$

Above corollary shows that the approach in Definition 8 constructs an elementary total preorder on W which can represent AGM operator via (RT). In the end of this section, recall that when L is finite, each total preorder on W will derive an AGM revision operator via (RT). But when L is infinite, not all total preorders on W can deriver an AGM revision operator. However, when the total preorder is elementary, it always can derive an AGM revision operator over an infinite language. In fact, when L is finite, each total preorder on W is elementary by Corollary 1.

6   Related Work

Total preorder on worlds is a influential model for characterizing AGM belief revision framework. Katsuno and Mendelzon first showed in [8] that when the backgroud language is finite propositional language, AGM belief revision can be totally decided by total preorders on worlds. KM showed a representation theorem that the models of $K \circ \varphi$ are exactly the minimal worlds of φ. Following with KM, Darwiche and Pearl (DP for short) used total preorder to characterized epistemic state which is used to replace belief set. In their model, belief revision can be seen as revising a total preorder by proposition. As a development, Benferhat et al. further used partial preorders, rather than total preorders, to represent epistemic states and belief revision [2]. Recently, Ma et al. also considered how to revise a total preorder by a partial preorder [12] and revise a partial preorder by another partial order [10, 11]. All these works represented belief revision over a finite propositional language. However, if the background language is infinite, KM's approach does not work well. In this paper, we mainly argue when the background language is infinite whether we can also use total preorder on worlds to capture belief revision. We show a new approach to construct an elementary total preorder on worlds to capture AGM belief revision. Following this approach, it is feasible to generalize the results a bout belief revision with finite propositional language to infinite propositional language, such as DP's postulates about iterated belief revision. We will discuss this problem in our future work.

When the background language is infinite, Peppas in [15, 17] used system of spheres model to characterize belief revision . Surendonk in [18] first introduced a topology on worlds to characterize belief revision. Meng and Li in [14] showed a characterization of belief revision over an infinite propositional language by using the same topology. They showed a set is elementary iff it is closed. This is why the intersection of elementary sets is also elementary. Moreover, over an infinite language, Lindstrom in [9] generalized AGM belief revision to multiple revision. Multiple revision can be seen as revising a theory by a set of propositions. In [20], Zhang et al. use an order structure on sentences (called nicely-ordered partition) to characterise multiple revision. A nicely-ordered partition is very similar to an epistemic entrenchment. Overall, our approach shows the elementary total preorder can be used to capture belief revision over infinite propositional language, and it is interesting to used total preorder model to capture multiple revision in future.

7   Conclusion

In this paper, we argue how to capture AGM style belief revision over an infinite propositional language. Since KM's approach is not suitable with infinite language, we show a new method how to construct a special total preorder (called elementary total preorder) on worlds by using the elementary system of spheres. We show the revision result is also decided by the minimal worlds of new evidence over an infinite language, which generalize KM's representation theorem.

Our approach is different with KM's approach. However, when the background language is finite, these two approaches are equivalent.

References

1. Alchourron, C.E., Gärdenfors, P., Makinson, D.: On the logic of theory change: Partial meet contraction and revision functions. J. Symb. Log. **50**(2), 510–530 (1985)
2. Benferhat, S., Lagrue, S., Papini, O., et al.: Revision of partially ordered information: axiomatization, semantics and iteration. In: IJCAI, pp. 376–381 (2005)
3. Darwiche, A., Pearl, J.: On the logic of iterated belief revision. Artificial Intelligence **89**(1), 1–29 (1997)
4. Delgrande, J.P.: Revising beliefs on the basis of evidence. International Journal of Approximate Reasoning **53**(3), 396–412 (2012)
5. Gärdenfors, P., Makinson, D.: Revisions of knowledge systems using epistemic entrenchment. In: Proceedings of the 2nd Conference on Theoretical Aspects of Reasoning About Knowledge, pp. 83–95. Morgan Kaufmann Publishers Inc. (1988)
6. Grove, A.: Two modellings for theory change. Journal of Philosophical Logic **17**(2), 157–170 (1988)
7. Jin, Y., Thielscher, M.: Iterated belief revision, revised. Artificial Intelligence **171**(1), 1–18 (2007)
8. Katsuno, H., Mendelzon, A.O.: Propositional knowledge base revision and minimal change. Artificial Intelligence **52**(3), 263–294 (1991)
9. Lindström, S.: A semantic approach to nonmonotonic reasoning: inference operations and choice. Uppsala Prints and Preprints in Philosophy, Department of Philosophy, University of Uppsala, vol. 6 (1991)
10. Ma, J., Benferhat, S., Liu, W.: Revision over partial pre-orders: a postulational study. In: Link, S., Fober, T., Seeger, B., Hüllermeier, E. (eds.) SUM 2012. LNCS, vol. 7520, pp. 219–232. Springer, Heidelberg (2012)
11. Ma, J., Benferhat, S., Liu, W., et al.: Revising partial pre-orders with partial pre-orders: a unit-based revision framework. In: KR (2012)
12. Ma, J., Liu, W., Benferhat, S., et al.: A belief revision framework for revising epistemic states with partial epistemic states. In: AAAI, pp. 333–338 (2010)
13. Meng, H., Kou, H., Li, S.: Belief revision with general epistemic states. In: Proceedings of the Twenty-Ninth AAAI Conference on Artificial Intelligence, January 25–30, 2015, Austin, Texas, USA, pp. 1553–1559 (2015)
14. Meng, H., Li, S.: A topological characterisation of belief revision over infinite propositional languages. In: Pham, D.-N., Park, S.-B. (eds.) PRICAI 2014. LNCS, vol. 8862, pp. 77–90. Springer, Heidelberg (2014)
15. Peppas, P.: The limit assumption and multiple revision. Journal of Logic and Computation **14**(3), 355–371 (2004)
16. Peppas, P.: Belief revision. Handbook of Knowledge Representation **3**, 317–359 (2008)
17. Peppas, P., Koutras, C.D., Williams, M.A.: Maps in multiple belief change. ACM Transactions on Computational Logic (TOCL) **13**(4), 30 (2012)
18. Surendonk, T.: Revising some basic proofs in belief revision (1997)
19. Falappa, M.A., García, A.J., Simari, G.R., Tamargo, L.H.: A change model for credibility partial order. In: Benferhat, S., Grant, J. (eds.) SUM 2011. LNCS, vol. 6929, pp. 317–330. Springer, Heidelberg (2011)
20. Zhang, D., Foo, N.: Infinitary belief revision. Journal of Philosophical Logic **30**(6), 525–570 (2001)

Retraction Note to: A Situation-Aware Method Based on Ontology Analysis of the Semantic Social Network

Wenbin Hu and Huan Wang

Retraction Note to:
Chapter "A Situation-Aware Method Based on Ontology
Analysis of the Semantic Social Network" in:
S. Zhang et al. (Eds.): *Knowledge Science, Engineering*
and Management, **LNAI 9403,**
https://doi.org/10.1007/978-3-319-25159-2_9

The authors have retracted this chapter [1] because the method described in the chapter is based on the wrong data set, which means that the experimental results cannot be reproduced. All authors agree with this retraction.

1. Hu, W., Wang, H.: A Situation-Aware Method Based on Ontology Analysis of the Semantic Social Network. In: Zhang, S., Wirsing, M., Zhang, Z. (eds.) KSEM 2015. LNAI, vol. 9403, pp. 102–114, Springer International Publishing Switzerland (2015). https://doi.org/10.1007/978-3-319-25159-2_9.

The retracted version of this chapter can be found at
https://doi.org/10.1007/978-3-319-25159-2_9

Author Index

Printed in the United States
by Baker & Taylor Publisher Services

Printed in the United States
by Baker & Taylor Publisher Services